4TH EDITION

Information Technology for Management

TRANSFORMING ORGANIZATIONS IN THE DIGITAL ECONOMY

EDITION

Information Technology for Management

TRANSFORMING ORGANIZATIONS IN THE DIGITAL ECONOMY

EFRAIM TURBAN, *City University of Hong Kong*

EPHRAIM MCLEAN, *Georgia State University*

JAMES WETHERBE, *Texas Tech University*

with contributions by:

DOROTHY LEIDNER, *Baylor University*

DENNIS VIEHLAND, *Massey University, New Zealand*

LINDA LAI, *City University of Hong Kong*

CHRISTY CHEUNG, *City University of Hong Kong*

DANIEL TSE, *City University of Hong Kong*

WILEY JOHN WILEY & SONS, INC.

ACQUISITIONS EDITOR	Beth Lang Golub
DEVELOPMENT EDITOR	Johnna Barto
MARKETING MANAGER	Gitti Lindner
ASSOCIATE EDITOR	Lorraina Raccuia
SENIOR PRODUCTION EDITOR	Norine M. Pigliucci
COVER DESIGNER	Madelyn Lesure
TEXT DESIGNER	Kenny Beck
ILLUSTRATION EDITOR	Anna Melhorn
PHOTO EDITOR	Lisa Gee
PRODUCTION MANAGEMENT SERVICES	Suzanne Ingrao
COVER PHOTO	©Steve Vidler/SuperStock

This book was set in 10/12 Meridien Roman by TechBooks and printed and bound by Von Hoffmann Press. The cover was printed by Von Hoffmann Press.

This book is printed on acid free paper. ∞

Library of Congress Cataloging-in-Publication Data

Turban, Efraim.
  Information technology for management: transforming organizations in the digital
  economy / Efraim Turban, Ephraim McLean, James Wetherbe; with contributions by
  Dorothy Leidner ... [et al.].
      p. cm.
  ISBN 0-471-22967-9 (cloth)
  1. Management information systems, I. McLean, Ephraim R. II. Wetherbe, James C.
III. Leidner, D. E. (Dorothy E.) IV. Title.

T58.6.T765 2003
658.4'038'011—dc22

2003063356

Printed in the United States of America

10 9 8 7 6 5 4 3 2 1

Preface

In the last few years we have been witnessing one of the most important events in human history thus far—the digital and Web revolution. The Web is not only changing the way that we work, study, play, and conduct our lives, but it is doing so much more quickly than any other revolution (such as the Industrial Revolution), with impacts that are more far-reaching. Furthermore, all we have seen is the tip of the iceberg. It is difficult to predict all the implications. The Web revolution is facilitated by ever-changing information technologies.

Computerized systems in general and Web-based systems in particular can be found today in even the smallest businesses. It is almost impossible to run a competitive business without a computerized information system. Indeed, global competitive pressures and continuous innovations are forcing many organizations to *rethink* how they do business. To do so requires the ability to successfully incorporate *electronic commerce, knowledge management, customer relationship management, enterprise resource planning, supply chain management,* and *mobile computing* into an organization, frequently under the umbrella of e-business. Furthermore, it must be done wisely, eliminating failures and unnecessary expense.

Information Technology for Management, 4th Edition, addresses the basic principles of MIS in light of these new developments. For example, one of the major changes occurring in IT is the ability to deliver systems over the Web, rather than build them. This option, which is delivered by application server providers, is a strategic option for the prudent managers of the digital economy. It is the beginning of the move toward utility computing, or "on-demand" computing, which may change the need for software and hardware. But does it fit all organizations? Such issues resulting from the Web revolution are discussed in this textbook. Its major objective is to prepare managers and staff in the modern enterprise to understand the role of information technology in the digital economy.

TRANSFORMING ORGANIZATIONS TO THE DIGITAL ECONOMY

This book is based on the fundamental premise that the major role of information technology is to provide organizations with *strategic advantage by facilitating problem solving, increasing productivity and quality, increasing speed, improving customer service, enhancing communication and collaboration,* and *enabling business process restructuring.* By taking a practical, managerial-oriented approach, the book demonstrates that IT can be provided not only by information systems department but also by end users and vendors as well. Managing information resources, new technologies, and communications networks is becoming a—or even *the*—critical success factor in the operations of many organizations, private and public, and will be essential to the survival of organizations in the digital economy.

Many introductory textbooks on information systems are geared toward yesterday's environment, where the important issues were the technology, the construction of information systems, and the support of traditional business functional applications. This book's approach is different. While recognizing the importance of the technology, system development, and functional transaction processing systems, we emphasize the *innovative* uses of information technology throughout the enterprise. The rapidly increased use of the Web, the Internet, intranets, extranets, e-business and e-commerce, and mobile computing changes the manner in which business is done in almost all organizations. This fact is reflected in our book: Every chapter and major topic points to the role of the Web in facilitating competitiveness, effectiveness, and profitability. Of special importance is the emergence of the second-generation e-commerce applications such as m-commerce, c-commerce, e-learning, and e-government. Also, the integration of ERP, CRM, and knowledge management with e-commerce is of great importance.

FEATURES OF THIS TEXT

In developing the fourth edition of *Information Technology for Management,* we have tried to craft a book that will serve the needs of tomorrow's managers. During the process of revising and reorganizing this edition, we have been guided by certain recurring themes that are important to succeed in business in the digital economy. This book reflects our vision of where information systems are going and the direction of IS education in business and e-business programs. This vision is represented by the following features that we have integrated throughout the book.

• *Digital Economy Focus.* This book was written with the recognition that organizations desire to transform themselves successfully to the digital economy. To do so companies need not only to use Web-based systems, but also to have an appropriate e-strategy and ability to plan click-and-mortar systems as well as new business models. Furthermore, they need to plan the transformation process, which is dependent on information technology and enabled by it.

• *Managerial Orientation.* Most IS textbooks identify themselves as either technology or socio-behavioral oriented. While we recognize the importance of both, our emphasis is on *managerial* orientation. To implement this orientation, we assembled all of the major technological topics in five Technology Guides, located on the book's Web site. Furthermore, we attempted not to duplicate detailed presentations of behavioral sciences topics, such as dealing with resistance to change or motivating employees. Instead, we concentrate on managerial decision making, cost-benefit justification, supply chain management, organizational restructuring, and CRM as they relate to information technology.

• *New Computing Environments.* Most textbooks ignore some of the major developments that will completely change both IT and its enabling role. Most notable are mobile and wireless computing, utility computing, pervasive computing, Web services, semantic Web, and grid computing. We introduce these topics as well as explain their impact on IT vendors, IS departments, and end users.

• *Functional Relevance.* Frequently, non–IS major students wonder why they must learn tech-nical details. In this text the relevance of information technology to the major functional areas is an important theme. We show, through the use of icons, the relevance of topics to accounting, finance, marketing, production/operations management, human resources management, and government. Finally, our examples also cover small service industries as well as the international setting.

• *E-Business, E-Commerce, and the Use of the Web.* We strongly believe that e-business, e-commerce, and the use of the Internet, intranets, and extranets are changing the world of business. Not only is an entire extended chapter (Chapter 5) dedicated to e-commerce, but we also demonstrate the significance of e-business in every chapter and major topic. The world of business is changing, and it is important that students understand these changes and their implications. For example, world-class companies such as General Electric, IBM, FedEx, Dell Computer and Wal-Mart are introducing extremely innovative supply chain and logistics systems supported by information technologies. This text tells you about all these innovations.

• *Real-World Orientation.* Extensive, vivid examples from large corporations, small businesses, government, and not-for-profit agencies make concepts come alive by showing students the capabilities of information technology, its cost and justification, and some of the innovative ways real corporations are using IT in their operations.

• *Failures and Lessons Learned.* Whereas most IT and MIS books introduce only the success of information systems, we acknowledge the fact that many systems do fail. Many chapters include discussion or examples of failures, and the lessons learned from them. For example, Chapter 8 cites some ERP failures, and Chapter 13 discusses economic aspects of failures and runaway projects.

• *Solid Theoretical Backing.* Throughout the book we present the theoretical foundation necessary for understanding information technology, ranging from Moore's law to Porter's competitiveness models, including his latest e-strategy adaptation. Furthermore, we provide extensive references and many exercises and Web resources to supplement the theoretical presentations.

• *Very Current.* The book presents the most current topics of information technology, as evidenced by the many new cases and examples throughout the book and by 2002 and 2003 citations. Every topic in the book has been researched to find the most up-to-date information and features.

- *Economic Justification.* Information technology is mature enough to stand the difficult test of economic justification, a topic ignored by most textbooks. It is our position that investment in information technology must be scrutinized like any other investment, despite the difficulties of measuring technology benefits. In addition to discussion throughout the text, we are unique in devoting a complete chapter (Chapter 13, "IT Economics") to this subject.

- *Integrated Systems.* In contrast to many books that highlight isolated functional information systems, we emphasize those systems that support enterprise resources planning (ERP) and supply chain management. Interorganizational systems are particularly highlighted, including the latest innovations in global e-exchanges. Also integration efforts by the major vendors such as Websphere from IBM, .Net from Microsoft, and 9i, from Oracle, are presented.

- *Global Perspective.* The importance of global competition, partnerships, and trading is rapidly increasing. IT facilitates export and import, management of multinational companies, and electronic trading around the globe. International examples are highlighted with a special globe icon, and the book's Web site includes several international cases.

- *Comprehensiveness and Ease of Reading.* All major topics of information technology are covered, many with more details than you will find elsewhere. Furthermore, the book is very user friendly, easy to understand and follow, and it is full of interesting real-world examples and "war stories" that keep readers' interest at a very high level.

- *Ethics.* The importance of ethics is growing rapidly in the digital economy. Therefore we introduce the essentials of ethics as an appendix to Chapter 1. Topics relating to ethics are introduced in every chapter, and are highlighted by icons in the margin. Finally, a primer on ethics is provided on the Web site; this resource poses 14 ethics scenarios and asks students to think about responses to these situations. The ethics primer also contains a detailed list of references for further reading and research.

WHAT'S NEW IN THIS EDITION?

In preparing the new, fourth edition we made the following large-scale changes:

- Added a new chapter, Chapter 6, on mobile and wireless computing, and m-commerce.
- Combined into one chapter, Chapter 12, the coverage on supporting management and decision making with the material on intelligent support systems.
- Created extensive Web resources for most of the chapters (over 100 online files). Specific pointers to the online files tie the text narrative to the online material; marginal icons highlight these cross-references.
- Changed the emphasis from e-commerce to the broader concept of e-business.
- Increased emphasis on trends toward utility computing and outsourcing.
- Increased coverage of information security.
- Emphasized information integration and the role of Web Services in such integration.
- Added a Virtual Company assignment near the end of each chapter (see description in the "Pedagogical Features" section, below).
- Completely revised most of the chapters, to introduce new research, current examples and case studies, and updated reference materials.
- Streamlined and smoothed the logical flow throughout the text.
- Added 14 specially crafted ethical scenarios (in the online Ethics Primer).

ORGANIZATION OF THE BOOK

The book is divided into five major parts, composed of 16 regular chapters supplemented by five Technology Guides. Parts and chapters break down as follows.

- *Part I: IT in the Organization.* Part I gives an overview of IT in the organization. The three chapters in Part I introduce the drivers of the use of information technology in the digital economy. It also presents the foundations of information systems and their strategic use. Special attention is given to the role information systems play in facilitating Web-based business models and strategic information systems.

• **Part II: The Web Revolution.** The three chapters in Part II introduce the Web-based technologies and applications, starting with telecommunications networks and the role of the Internet, intranets, and extranets in contributing to communication, collaboration, and information discovery (Chapter 4). Electronic commerce is presented in a comprehensive way (Chapter 5), followed by mobile and wireless computing in new Chapter 6.

• **Part III: Organizational Applications.** Part III begins with the basics: IT applications in transaction processing, functional applications, and customer relationship management (Chapter 7). We then cover supply chain management and Web-based enterprise systems (Chapter 8). Planning for technology and the necessary organizational restructuring is discussed next (Chapter 9).

• **Part IV: Managerial and Decision Support Systems.** Part IV discusses the many ways information systems can be used to support the day-to-day operations of a company, with a strong emphasis on the use of IT in managerial decision making. The three chapters in this part address some of the ways businesses are using information technology to solve specific problems and to build strategic, innovative systems that enhance quality and productivity. Special attention is given to innovative applications of knowledge management (Chapter 10), data analysis and data management (Chapter 11), and decision support and intelligent support systems (Chapter 12).

• **Part V: Implementing and Managing IT.** Part V explores several topics related to the implementation, evaluation, construction, and maintenance of information systems. We consider several issues ranging from the economics of information technology (Chapter 13) to building or outsourcing information systems (Chapter 14) to the management of IT resources and IT security (Chapter 15). Finally, Chapter 16, which is available online at the book's Web site, assess the impact of IT on individuals, organizations, and society.

The five **Technology Guides,** which are available online at the book's Web site, cover hardware, software, databases, telecommunications, and the essentials of the Internet. They contain condensed, up-to-date presentations of all the material necessary for the understanding of these technologies.

They can be used as a self-study refresher or as a basis for a class presentation. The Technology Guides are supplemented online by a glossary for the terms in the Tech Guides, questions for review and discussion, and case studies, all of which are available on our Web site (*www.wiley.com/college/turban*).

PEDAGOGICAL FEATURES

We developed a number of pedagogical features to aid student learning and tie together the themes of the book.

• **Chapter Outline.** The chapter outline provides a quick indication of the major topics covered in the chapter.

• **Learning Objectives.** Learning objectives listed at the beginning of each chapter help students focus their efforts and alert them to the important concepts that will be discussed.

• **Opening Cases.** Each chapter opens with a *real-world* example that illustrates the use of information technology in modern corporations. These cases have been carefully chosen to demonstrate the relevance, for business students, of the topics introduced in the chapter. They are presented in a standard format (problem or opportunity, IT solution, and results) that helps model a way to think about business problems. The Opening Case is followed by a brief section (called Lessons Learned from this Case) that ties the key points of the opening case to the topic of the chapter.

• **"A Closer Look" Boxes.** These boxes contain detailed, in-depth discussions of specific concepts or procedures, often using real-world examples. Some boxes enhance the in-text discussion by offering an alternative approach to information technology. Some of these boxes are included in the online materials.

• **"IT at Work" Boxes.** The IT at Work boxes spotlight some real-world innovations and new technologies that companies are using to solve organizational dilemmas or create new business opportunities. Each box concludes with "for further exploration" questions and issues. Some of these boxes are online.

• **Highlighted Icons.** As indicated earlier, icons appear throughout the text to relate the topics covered within each chapter to some major themes of the book. The icons alert students to the related functional areas, to IT failures, and to global and ethical issues. Icons also indicate where related enrichment resources can be found on the book's companion Web site. The following list summarizes these icons.

 Ethics-related topic

 Global organization

 Lessons to be learned from IT failures

 Accounting example

 Finance example

 Government example

 Human resources management example

 Marketing example

 Production/operations management example

 Service-company example

 Material at the book's Web site: *www.wiley/com/college.turban*

• **Managerial Issues.** The final text section of every chapter explores some of the special concerns managers face as they adapt to an increasingly tech-nological environment. The issues highlighted in this section can serve as a springboard for class discussion and challenge business students to consider some of the actions they might take if placed in similar circumstances.

• **Key Terms.** The key terms and concepts are typeset in boldface blue when first introduced in a chapter, and are listed at the end of the chapter. All key terms are defined in the end-of-book glossary.

• **Chapter Highlights.** All the important concepts covered in the chapter are listed at the end of the chapter and are linked by number to the learning objectives introduced at the beginning of each chapter, to reinforce the important ideas discussed.

• **End-of-Chapter Questions and Exercises.** Different types of questions measure student comprehension and their ability to apply knowledge. Questions for Review ask students to summarize the concepts introduced. Discussion Questions are intended to promote class discussion and develop critical thinking skills. Exercises are more challenging assignments that require students to apply what they have learned.

• **Group Assignments.** Comprehensive group assignments, including Internet research, oral presentations to the class, and debates are available in each chapter.

• **Internet Exercises.** Close to 200 hands-on exercises send the students to interesting Web sites to explore those sites, find resources, investigate an application, compare, analyze, and summarize information, or learn about the state of the art of a topic.

• **Minicases.** Two real-world cases at the end of each chapter highlight some of the problems encountered by corporations as they develop and implement information systems. Discussion questions and assignments are included. A number of additional minicases are available online at the book's Web site.

• **Virtual Company Assignment.** The Virtual Company Assignment centers around the ongoing situation at a simulated company, The Wireless Café (TWC), a technology-savvy 1950s–style diner. Students are "hired" by the diner as consultants and in each chapter are given assignments that require them to use the information presented in the chapter to develop solutions and produce deliverables to present to the owners of The Wireless Café. These assignments get the student into active, hands-on learning to complement the conceptual coverage of the text.

• *Additional Online Cases.* Longer real-world cases were chosen specifically for their ability to bring together many of the overriding concepts from each part of the text. These can be found on our Web site (*www.wiley.com/college/turban*). Also at the Web site are several cases from countries around the globe (including multinational corporations).

SUPPLEMENTARY MATERIALS

An extensive package of instructional materials is available to support this fourth edition.

• *Instructor's Manual.* The Instructor's Manual presents objectives from the text with additional information to make them more appropriate and useful for the instructor. Chapter overviews provide an explanation of how each chapter fits in with previous chapters and the entire course. The manual also includes practical applications of concepts, case study elaboration, answers to end-of-chapter questions, questions for review, questions for discussion, and Internet exercises.

• *Test Bank.* The test bank contains approximately 1,000 questions and problems (about 50 per chapter) consisting of multiple-choice, short answer, fill-ins, and critical thinking/essay questions.

• *Computerized Test Bank.* This electronic version of the test bank allows instructors to customize tests and quizzes for their students.

• *PowerPoint Presentation.* A series of slides designed around the content of the text incorporates key points from the text and illustrations where appropriate.

• *Video Series.* A collection of videos provides students and instructors with dynamic and interesting business examples directly related to the concepts introduced in the text. The video clips illustrate the ways in which computer information systems are utilized in various companies and industries.

• *Business Extra Select.* (*www.wiley.com/college/bxs*) Business Extra Select enables you to add copyright-cleared articles, cases, and readings from such leading business resources as *INSEAD, Ivey* and *Harvard Business School Cases, Fortune, The Economist, The Wall Street Journal,* and more. You can create your own custom CoursePack, combining these resources along with content from Wiley's Business Textbooks, your own content such as lecture notes, and any other third-party content. Or you can use a ready-made CoursePack for Turban's *IT for Management 4th edition.*

• *The Turban Web Site.* (*www.wiley.com/college/turban*) The book's Web site greatly extends the content and theme of the text to provide extensive support for instructors and students. Organized by chapter, it includes additional text, tables, figures, cases, questions, exercises, and downloadable PowerPoint slides, self-testing material for students, working students' experiences with using IT, links to resources on the Web, and links to many of the companies discussed in the text and to the "The Virtual Company" Web site.

ACKNOWLEDGMENTS

Several individuals helped us with the creation of the fourth edition: Dorothy Leidner (Baylor University) revised Chapter 9, Linda Lai (City University of Hong Kong) updated Chapter 14, Dennis Viehland (Massey University, New Zealand) revised Chapter 3, Christy Cheung (City University of Hong Kong), helped in revising Chapters 9 and 16, and Daniel Tse (City University of Hong Kong) revised the Technology Guides. Robert Davison (City University of Hong Kong) revised the ethics appendix and wrote the ethical scenarios. Thanks to all for their contributions.

Recognition also goes to those who contributed to the previous editions, especially to Ralph Westfall (California Polytech University Pomona), Jay Aronson (University of Georgia), Narsi Belloju (City University of Hong Kong), Joe Walls (University of Michigan), Wallace Wood (Bryant College), and Kelly Rainer (Auburn University). In addition, dozens of students participated in the class testing of the material, helped develop exercises and find illustrative applications, and contributed valuable suggestions and annotations for the text. It is not possible to name all of them, but they all certainly deserve recognition and thanks.

Faculty feedback was essential to the development of the book. Many individuals participated in focus groups and/or acted as reviewers. Several others created portions of chapters or cases, especially international cases, some of which are in the text and others on the Web site. Thanks, first, to

Carolyn Jacobson (Marymount University) who read through completed chapters and offered valuable insights. Thanks to the following reviewers: Samuel Abraham, Siena Heights University; Chandra Amaravadi, Western Illinois University; Bay Arinze, Drexel University; Mary Astone, Troy State University; Kakoli Bandyopadhyay, Lamar University; Cynthia Barnes, Lamar University; Rahul Basole, Georgia Institute of Technology; Robert Bonometti, Shenandoah University; Apiwan D. Born, University of Illinois at Springfield; Richard Bush, Lawrence Technological University; Sonny Butler, Georgia Southern University; Jose Castillo, Colorado State University-Pueblo; Qiyang Chen, Montclair State University; Jyoti Choudrie, Brunel University; Marlene V. Davidson, California State Polytechnic University; Ray Eldridge, Freed-Hardeman University; John Gudenas, Aurora University; James Hu, Fairfield University; Kim Hunter, College of Mt. St. Joseph; Sung-kwan Kim, University of Arkansas Little Rock; Jack Klag, Colorado Technical University; Hsiang-Jui Kung, Georgia Southern University; Kevin Lertwacharra, University of Connecticut; Susan Li, Adelphi University; Steve Loy, Eastern Kentucky University; Dana McCann, Central Michigan University; Ahmet Ozkul, Clemson University; Mahesh S. Raisinghani, University of Dallas; Eliot Rich, University at Albany; Paula Ruby, Arkansas State University; Dolly Samson, Hawaii Pacific University, SUNY; Marc Schniederjans, University of Nebraska-Lincoln; Richard Segall, Arkansas State University; Ray Tsai, St. Cloud State University; Barbara D. Turner, Gloucester County College; and Bruce White, Quinnipiac University.

We are grateful to the following faculty for their contributions to the *third edition:* Martin Bariff, Illinois Institute of Technology; Debabroto Chatterjee, Washington State University; Jason Chen, Gonzaga University. Marlene Davidson, California State Polytechnic University–Pomona; John C. Di Renzo, Jr., Cameron University; Dennis Galletta, University of Pittsburgh; Chittibabu Govindarajulu, Drexel University; Randy Guthrie, California State Polytechnic University–Pomona; Shohreh S. Hashemi, University of Houston–Downtown; Gregory R. Heim, Boston College; Bobbie Hyndman, West Texas A&M University; Joan B. Lumpkin, Wright State University; Jane Mackay, Texas Christian University; Ravi Nath, Creighton University; Roger Alan Pick, University of Missouri–Kansas City; Mahesh S.

Raisinghani, University of Dallas; Dolly Samson, Weber State University; Kenneth David Smith, Cameron University; Amita Suhrid, Keller Graduate School of Management; Peter Tarasewich, University of Maine; Stephen Thorpe, La Salle University; Thomas Triscari, Jr., Rensselaer Polytechnic Institute; Barbara D. Turner, Rowan University; Robert D. Wilson, California State University–San Bernardino; Wallace A. Wood, Bryant College; and Jigish Zaveri, Morgan State University.

The following individuals helped us with the *second edition:* Christine P. Andrews, SUNY at Fredonia; Marzi Astanti, Winona State University; V. Bose, Texas A&M University; Marek Ejsmont, Keyano College (Alberta, Canada); George Fettes, Camosun College; David R. Fordham, James Madison University; Lisa Friedrichsen, Keller Graduate School; David Hale, University of Alabama; Fred G. Harold, Florida Atlantic University; Jeff Harper, Athens State College; Myron Hatcher, California State University, Fresno; Chin-Yuan Ho, National Central University (Taiwan); Change T. Hsieh, University of Southern Mississippi; Grace Johnson, Marietta College; Dorothy Leidner, Baylor University; James Linderman, Bentley College; Munir Mandviwalla, Temple University; Ji-Ye Mao, University of Waterloo; Vicki McKinney, University of Texas, Arlington; Derrick Neufeld, University of Manitoba; E. F. Peter Newson, University of Western Ontario; Floyd D. Ploeger, Southwest Texas State University; Larisa Preiser-Houy, California State University–Pomona; Mary Ann Robbert, Bentley College; Dolly Samson, Weber State University; Vijay Sethi, Nanyang Technological University (Singapore); Kathy Stewart, Georgia State University; Ted Strickland, University of Louisville; Edward Tsang, University of Essex (United Kingdom); and Liang Chee Wee, Luther College.

The following individuals participated in focus groups and/or acted as reviewers of the *first edition:* Mary Anne Atkinson, University of Delaware; Benedict Arogyaswamy, University of South Dakota; James Carroll, Georgian Court College; Paul Cheney, University of South Florida; Candace Deans, Thunderbird School, AGIM; Bill DeLone, American University; Phillip Ein-Dor, Tel Aviv University (Israel); Michael Eirman, University of Wisconsin-Oshkosh; Paul Evans, George Mason University; Deb Ghosh, Louisiana State University; Oscar Gutierrez, University of Massachusetts-Boston; Rassule Hadidi,

Sangamon State University; Fred Harold, Florida Atlantic University; Jaak Jurison, Fordham University; Eugene Kaluzniacky, University of Winnipeg; Astrid Lipp, Clemson University; Jo Mae Maris, Northern Arizona University; E. F. Peter Newson, University of Western Ontario; Michael Palley, CUNY-Baruch College; Keri Pearlson, University of Texas; Bill Richmond, George Mason University; Larry Sanders, University of Buffalo; A. B. Schwarzkopf, University of Oklahoma; Henk Sol, Delft Institute of Technology (The Netherlands); Timothy Smith, DePaul University; Timothy Staley, DeVry Institute of Technology; Shannon Taylor, Montana State University; Robert Van Cleave, University of Minnesota; Kuang-Wei Wen, University of Connecticut; Anthony Wensley, University of Toronto (Canada); Jennifer Williams, University of Southern Indiana; G. W. Willis, Baylor University; Gayle Yaverbaum, Pennsylvania State University.

Also, we recognize those faculty who contributed cases to the first edition of the text: Kimberly Bechler, International Institute of Management Development (Switzerland); Christer Carlsson, Abo Akademi University (Finland); Guy Fitzgerald, University of London (United Kingdom); Young Moo Kang, Dong-A University (Korea); Ossi Kokkonen, Metsa-Serla Oy (Finland); Donald Marchand, International Institute of Management Development (Switzerland); David McDonald, Georgia State University; Boon-Siong Neo, Nanyang Technological University (Singapore); Nicolau Reinhard, University of Sao Paulo (Brazil); Chris Sauer, University of New South Wales (Australia); Scott Schneberger, Georgia State University; Pirkko Walden, Abo Akademi University (Finland); Leslie Willcocks, Templeton College, Oxford University (United Kingdom); and Ronaldo Zwicker, University of Sao Paulo (Brazil). University.

Many individuals helped us with the administrative work. Of special mention are Mavis Chan of City University of Hong Kong and Judy Lang of Eastern Illinois University, who devoted considerable time to typing and editing. Judy also contributed cases, conducted research, and assisted in many other aspects of the book. Several other individuals helped with typing, figure drawing, and more. Among those are Eric Leung, Tom Zhao, Dong Ming Xu, Kenny Xyz, and Daphne Turban. Hugh Watson of the University of Georgia, the Information Systems Advisor to Wiley, guided us through various stages of the project. Finally, we would like to thank the dedicated staff of John Wiley & Sons: Lorraina Raccuia, Jeanine Furino, and Norine Pigliucci. A special thank you to Johnna Barto, Beth Lang Golub, Ann Torbert, Suzanne Ingrao of Ingrao Associates, and Shelley Flannery, whose considerable energy, time, expertise, and devotion have contributed significantly to the success of this project.

Finally, we recognize the various organizations and corporations that provided us with material and permission to use it.

Efraim Turban
Ephraim McLean
James Wetherbe

About the Authors

DR. EFRAIM TURBAN

Dr. Efraim Turban obtained his MBA and Ph.D. degrees from the University of California, Berkeley. His industry experience includes eight years as an industrial engineer, three of which were spent at General Electric Transformers Plant in Oakland, California. He also has extensive consulting experience to small and large corporations as well as to governments. In his over thirty years of teaching, Professor Turban has served as Chaired Professor at Eastern Illinois University, and as Visiting Professor at Nanyang Technological University in Singapore, and University of Science and Technology in Hong Kong. He has also taught at UCLA; USC; Simon Fraser University; Lehigh University; California State University, Long Beach; and Florida International University.

Dr. Turban was a co-recipient of the 1984/85 National Management Science Award (Artificial Intelligence in Management). In 1997 he received the Distinguished Faculty Scholarly and Creative Achievement Award at California State University, Long Beach.

Dr. Turban has published articles in over 110 leading journals, including the following: *Management Science, MIS Quarterly, Operations Research, Journal of MIS, Communications of the ACM, International Journal of Electronic Commerce, Information Systems Frontiers, Decision Support Systems, International Journal of Information Management, Heuristics, Expert Systems with Applications, International Journal of Applied Expert Systems, Journal of Investing, Accounting, Management and Information Systems, Computers and Operations Research, Computers and Industrial Engineering, IEEE Transactions on Engineering Management, Omega, International Journal of Electronic Commerce, Organizational Computing and Electronic Commerce,* and *Electronic Markets.* He has also published 21 books, including best sellers such as *Neural Networks: Applications in Investment and Financial Services* (2nd edition) (co-editor with R. Trippi), Richard D. Irwin, 1996; *Decision Support Systems and Intelligent Systems* (Prentice Hall, 7th edition, 2004); *Expert Systems and Applied Artificial Intelligence,* (MacMillan Publishing Co., 1992), *Electronic Commerce: A Managerial Approach,* 3rd edition, (Prentice Hall, 2004), *Introduction to Information Technology 2nd edition* (Wiley, 2003), and *Introduction to Electronic Commerce* (Prentice Hall, 2003).

Professor Turban is currently on the faculty of City University of Hong Kong, Department of Information Systems, Faculty of Business Administration. Professor Turban's current major interest is electronic commerce, strategy, and implementation.

DR. EPHRAIM MCLEAN

Dr. Ephraim McLean obtained his Bachelor of Mechanical Engineering degree from Cornell University in 1958. After brief service in the U.S. Army Ordnance Corps, he worked for Procter & Gamble Co. for seven years, first in manufacturing management and later as a computer systems analyst. In 1965, he left P&G and entered the Sloan School of Management at the Massachusetts Institute of Technology, obtaining his master's degree in 1967 and his doctorate in 1970.

While at MIT, he began an interest in the application of computer technology to medicine, working on his dissertation at the Lahey Clinic in Boston. While there, he was instrumental in developing the Lahey Clinic Automated Medical History System.

During the same period, he served as an instructor at MIT and also assisted in the preparation of the books *The Impact of Computers on Management* (MIT Press, 1967); *The Impact of Computers on Collective Bargaining* (MIT Press, 1969); and *Computers in Knowledge-Based Fields* (MIT Press, 1970).

Dr. McLean left MIT and joined the faculty of the Anderson Graduate School of Management at the University of California, Los Angeles (UCLA) in the winter of 1970. He was the founding Director of the Information Systems Research Program and the first Chairman of the Information Systems area, both within the Anderson Graduate School of Management. In fall 1987, he was named to the George E. Smith Eminent Scholar's Chair at the

College of Business Administration at Georgia State University in Atlanta, Georgia.

Dr. McLean has published over 80 articles in such publications as the *Harvard Business Review; Sloan Management Review; California Management Review; Communications of the ACM; MIS Quarterly; Information Systems Research, Information & Management; Journal of MIS; Journal of Risk and Insurance; DATA BASE; InformationWEEK; Datamation; Computer-World;* and the *Journal of the American Hospital Association.* He is the co-author of *Strategic Planning for MIS* (Wiley Interscience, 1977) and co-editor of a book of programs entitled *APL Application in Management.* He was a founding Associate Editor for Research of the *MIS Quarterly* and is currently senior co-editor of the *DATA BASE for Advances in Information Systems.* He was twice on the national Executive Council of the Society for Information Management (SIM). In 1980, he helped organize the Interna-tional Conference on Information Systems (ICIS) and was Conference Cochairman in 1981 in Cambridge, Massachusetts; Conference Chairman in 1986 in San Diego, California; and Conference Cochairman in 1997 in Atlanta, Georgia. He is currently Vice President for Affiliated Organizations of the Association for Information Systems (AIS).

In addition to university work, he has served as a consultant to such firms as the IBM Corporation, General Electric Company, Atlantic Richfield Company, Digital Equipment Corporation, BellSouth Corporation, the National Science Foundation, American Hospital Supply Corporation, McCormick & Company, Security Pacific National Bank, Pennsylvania Financial Corporation (now Primerica), and Citibank, N.A. of New York. He has also made executive presentations and conducted management workshops in Asia, Australia, Europe, South Africa, and throughout North America.

DR. JAMES C. WETHERBE

Dr. James C. Wetherbe is Stevenson Chair of Information Technology at Texas Tech University as well as Professor of MIS at the University of Minnesota where he directed the MIS Research Center for 20 years. He is internationally known as a dynamic and entertaining speaker, author, and leading authority on the use of computers and information systems to improve organizational performance and competitiveness. He is particularly appreciated for his ability to explain complex technology in straightforward, practical terms that can be strategically applied by both executives and general management.

Dr. Wetherbe is the author of 18 highly regarded books and is quoted often in leading business and information systems journals. He has also authored over 200 articles, was ranked by *InformationWEEK* as one of the top dozen information technology consultants, and is the first recipient of the MIS Quarterly Distinguished Scholar Award. He has also served on the faculties of the University of Memphis, where he was FedEx Professor and Director of the Center for Cycle Time Research, and the University of Houston.

Dr. Wetherbe received his Ph.D. from Texas Tech University.

Brief Contents

PART I
IT in the Organization

1 Information Technology in the Digital Economy **1**
2 Information Technologies: Concepts and Management **47**
3 Strategic Information Systems for Competitive Advantage **89**

PART II
The Web Revolution

4 Network Computing: Discovery, Communication, and Collaboration **125**
5 E-Business and E-Commerce **175**
6 Mobile, Wireless, and Pervasive Computing Environments **236**

PART III
Organizational Applications

7 Transaction Processing, Functional Applications, CRM, and Integration **295**
8 Supply Chain Management and Enterprise Resource Planning **354**
9 IT Planning and Business Process Redesign **396**

PART IV
Managerial and Decision Support Systems

10 Knowledge Management **448**
11 Data Management: Warehousing, Analyzing, Mining, and Visualization **490**
12 Management Decision Support and Intelligent Systems **541**

PART V
Implementing and Managing IT

13 Information Technology Economics **588**
14 Building Information Systems **632**
15 Managing Information Resources and IT Security **679**
16 The Impacts of IT on Organizations, Individuals, and Society
   Online at www.wiley.com/college/turban

Glossary

Technology Guides Online at www.wiley.com/ college/turban

T1 Hardware
T2 Software
T3 Data and Databases
T4 Telecommunications
T5 The Internet and the Web

Contents

PART I
IT In the Organization

1 Information Technology in the Digital Economy 1
Siemens AG Is Transforming Itself into an E-Business 2
1.1 Doing Business in the Digital Economy 3
1.2 Business Pressures, Organizational Responses, and IT Support 11
1.3 Information Systems Definitions and Examples 18
1.4 Information Technology Developments and Trends 24
1.5 Why Should You Learn About Information Technology? 32
1.6 Plan of the Book 33
Minicases: (1) Dartmouth College Goes Wireless / (2) Voice-Based 511 Traveler Information Line 38

Chapter 1 Appendix Ethics in Information Technology Management 42

2 Information Technologies: Concepts and Management 47
Building an E-Business at FedEx Corporation 48
2.1 Information Systems: Concepts and Definitions 50
2.2 Classification and Evolution of Information Systems 52
2.3 Transaction Processing versus Functional Information Systems 57
2.4 How IT Supports Various Types of Organizational Activities 59
2.5 How IT Supports Supply Chain and CRM Operations 62
2.6 Information Systems Infrastructure and Architecture 65
2.7 Web-Based Systems 71
2.8 New Computing Environments 74
2.9 Managing Information Resources 76
Minicases: (1) Maybelline / (2) JCPenney 82

Appendix 2A Build-to-Order Production 87

3 Strategic Information Systems for Competitive Advantage 89
Rosenbluth International: Competing in the Digital Economy 90
3.1 Strategic Advantage and Information Technology 92
3.2 Porter's Competitive Forces Model and Strategies 98
3.3 Porter's Value Chain Model 107
3.4 Interorganizational Strategic Information Systems 110
3.5 A Framework for Global Competition 111
3.6 Strategic Information Systems: Examples and Analysis 112
3.7 Implementing and Sustaining SIS 116
Minicases: (1) Cisco Systems / (2) Aeronautica Civil 120

PART II
The Web Revolution

4 Network Computing: Discovery, Communication, and Collaboration 125
National Semiconductor Corporation 126
4.1 Network Computing—An Overview 128
4.2 Discovery 132
4.3 Communication 141
4.4 Collaboration 144
4.5 Collaboration-Enabling Tools: From Workflow to Groupware 150
4.6 E-Learning, Distance Learning, and Telecommuting 156
4.7 Some Ethical and Integration Issues 160
Minicases: (1) General Motors (2) Cisco Systems 169

5 E-Business and E-Commerce 175
Hi-Life Corporation 176
5.1 Overview of E-Business and E-Commerce 177
5.2 EC Mechanisms: Electronic Auctions and Bartering 183
5.3 Business-to-Consumer Applications 185

5.4 Market Research and Online Advertising **192**

5.5 B2B Applications **200**

5.6 Intrabusiness and Business-to-Employees **204**

5.7 E-Government and Consumer-to-Consumer EC **205**

5.8 E-Commerce Support Services **208**

5.9 Legal and Ethical Issues in E-Business **215**

5.10 Failures and Strategies for Success **219**
  Minicases: (1) Freemarkets.com / (2) Restaurants.com **226**

Appendix 5A EDI and Extranets **231**

6 Mobile, Wireless, and Pervasive Computing Environments 236
  NextBus **237**

6.1 Mobile Computing and Commerce: Overview, Benefits, and Drivers **238**

6.2 Mobile Computing Infrastructure **245**

6.3 Mobile Applications in Financial Services **253**

6.4 Mobile Shopping, Advertising, and Content-Providing **256**

6.5 Mobile Intrabusiness and Enterprise Applications **259**

6.6 Mobile B2B and Supply Chain Applications **265**

6.7 Mobile Consumer and Personal Service Applications **265**

6.8 Location-Based Commerce **269**

6.9 Pervasive Computing **273**

6.10 Inhibitors and Barriers of Mobile Computing **282**
  Minicases: (1) Hertz / (2) Washington Township Fire Department **290**

PART III
Organizational Applications

7 Transaction Processing, Functional Applications, CRM, and Integration 295
  Dartmouth-Hitchcock Medical Center **296**

7.1 Functional Information Systems **298**

7.2 Transaction Processing Information Systems **300**

7.3 Managing Production/Operations and Logistics **306**

7.4 Managing Marketing and Sales Systems **312**

7.5 Managing the Accounting and Finance Systems **322**

7.6 Managing Human Resources Systems **329**

7.7 Customer Relationship Management (CRM) **335**

7.8 Integrating Functional Information Systems **341**
  Minicases: (1) Dollar General / (2) QVC **349**

8 Supply Chain Management and Enterprise Resource Planning 354
  ChevronTexaco **354**

8.1 Essentials of the Supply and Value Chains **356**

8.2 Supply Chain Problems and Solutions **360**

8.3 Computerized Systems: MRP, MRPII, SCM, and E-Integration **365**

8.4 Enterprise Resource Planning (ERP) **369**

8.5 E-Commerce and Supply Chains **377**

8.6 Partner Relationship Management **385**

8.7 Global Supply Chains **386**
  Minicases: (1) Quantum Corporation / (2) Green Mountain Coffee Roasters **392**

9 IT Planning and Business Process Redesign 396
  TruServe **397**

9.1 IT Planning—A Critical Issue for Organizations **398**

9.2 Strategic IT Planning **401**

9.3 Information Requirements Analysis, Resource Allocation, Project Planning **408**

9.4 Planning IT Architectures **411**

9.5 Some Issues in IT Planning **415**

9.6 Planning for Web-based Systems and E-Commerce **417**

9.7 Business Process Redesign **420**

9.8 The Role of IT in Business Process Redesign **423**

9.9 Restructing Processes and Organizations **427**

9.10 Organization Transformation and Change Management **433**
  Minicases: (1) Oregon's GIS Plan / (2) National City Bank **442**

PART IV
Managerial and Decision Support Systems

10 Knowledge Management 448
  Siemens AG **449**

10.1 Introduction to Knowledge Management **451**

10.2 Knowledge Management Initiatives **456**

10.3 Approaches to Knowledge Management **458**

10.4 Information Technology in Knowledge Management **460**

10.5 Knowledge Management Systems Implementation **464**

10.6 Roles of People in Knowledge Management **471**

10.7 Ensuring Success of KM Efforts **474**
Minicases: (1) DaimlerChrysler / (2) Chevron **484**

11 **Data Management: Warehousing, Analyzing, Mining, and Visualization** **490**
Harrah's Entertainment **491**

11.1 Data Management: A Critical Success Factor **493**

11.2 Data Warehousing **500**

11.3 Information and Knowledge Discovery with Business Intelligence **505**

11.4 Data Mining Concepts and applications **510**

11.5 Data Visualization Technologies **514**

11.6 Marketing Databases in Action **523**

11.7 Web-Based Data Management Systems **526**
Minicases: (1) Sears / (2) Dallas Area Rapid Transit **534**

12 **Management Decision Support and Intelligent Systems** **541**
Singapore and Malaysia Airlines **542**

12.1 Managers and Decision Making **543**

12.2 Decision Support Systems **550**

12.3 Group Decision Support Systems **554**

12.4 Enterprise and Executive Decision Support Systems **555**

12.5 Intelligent Support Systems: The Basics **559**

12.6 Expert Systems **563**

12.7 Other Intelligent Systems **568**

12.8 Web-Based Management Support Systems **574**

12.9 Advanced and Special Decision Support Topics **576**
Minicases: (1) A DSS Reshapes the Railway in the Netherlands / (2) Gate Assignment Display Systems **584**

Appendix 12A **Intelligent Software Agents** (online)

PART V
Implementing and Managing IT

13 **Information Technology Economics** **588**
State of Iowa **589**

13.1 Financial and Economic Trends **590**

13.2 Evaluating IT Investment: Benefits, Costs, and Issues **597**

13.3 Methods for Evaluating and Justifying IT Investment **603**

13.4 IT Economic Strategies: Chargeback and Outsourcing **611**

13.5 Economics of Web-Based Systems and e-commerce **617**

13.6 Other Economic Aspects of Information Technology **618**
Minicases: (1) Intranets / (2) Kone Inc. **627**

14 **Building Information Systems** **632**
Utility Computing **633**

14.1 The Concept of a Systems Development Life Cycle **634**

14.2 Methods for Complex or Quickly Needed Systems **640**

14.3 Component-Based Development and Web Services **647**

14.4 Systems Developed Outside the IS Department **653**

14.5 Building E-Business Applications **661**

14.6 Some Important Systems Development Issues **665**
Minicases: (1) "Do or Die" / (2) University of Nebraska **675**

15 **Managing Information Resources and Security** **679**
Cybercrime in the New Millennium **680**

15.1 The IS Department and End Users **681**

15.2 The CIO in Managing the IS Department **686**

15.3 IS Vulnerability and Computer Crimes **687**

15.4 Protecting Information Resources: From National to Organizational Efforts **698**

15.5 Securing the Web, Intranets, and Wireless Networks **706**

15.6 Business Continuity and Disaster Recovery Planning **712**

15.7 Implementing Security: Auditing and Risk Analysis **716**
Minicases: (1) Home Depot / (2) Managing Security **727**

16 Impacts of IT on Organizations, Individuals, and Society
Online at *www.wiley.com/college/turban*
MP3.com, Napster, and Intellectual Property Rights

16.1 Does IT Have Only Positive Effects?

16.2 Impacts of IT on Organizations

16.3 Impacts of IT on Individuals at Work

16.4 Societal Impacts

16.5 Virtual Communities

16.6 Concluding Thoughts
Minicases: (1) Australian Fishing Community / (2) American Stock Exchange

Technology Guides Online at
www.wiley.com/college/turban

T1 Hardware

T1.1 What Is a Computer System?

T1.2 The Evolution of Computer Hardware

T1.3 Types of Computers

T1.4 The Microprocessor and Primary Storage

T1.5 Input/Output Devices

T2 Software

T2.1 Types of Software

T2.2 Application Software

T2.3 Systems Software

T2.4 Programming Languages

T2.5 Software Development and CASE Tools

T2.6 Software Issues and Trends

T3 Data and Databases

T3.1 File Management

T3.2 Databases and Database Management Systems

T3.3 Logical Data Organization

T3.4 Creating Databases

T3.5 Emerging Database Models

T3.6 Data Warehouses

T3.7 Physical Database Organization

T3.8 Database Management

T3.9 An Emerging Technology: IP-based Storage

T4 Telecommunications

T4.1 Telecommunications Concepts

T4.2 Communications Media (Channels)

T4.3 Network Systems: Protocols, Standards, Interfaces, and Topologies

T4.4 Network Architecture: Open Systems and Enterprise Networking

T4.5 Telecommunications Applications

T5 The Internet and the Web

T5.1 What Is the Internet?

T5.2 Basic Characteristics and Capabilities of the Internet

T5.3 Browsing and the World Wide Web

Glossary G-1

Photo Credits P-1

Name Index NI-1

Subject Index SI-1

4TH EDITION

Information Technology for Management

TRANSFORMING ORGANIZATIONS IN THE DIGITAL ECONOMY

PART I
IT in the Organization

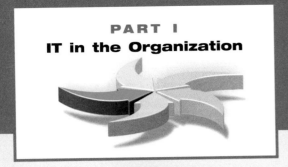

▶ 1. Information Technology in the Digital Economy
2. Information Technologies: Concepts and Management
3. Strategic Information Systems for Competitive Advantage

CHAPTER

Information Technology in the Digital Economy

1.1
Doing Business in the Digital Economy

1.2
Business Pressures, Organizational Responses, and IT Support

1.3
Information Systems: Definitions and Examples

1.4
Information Technology Developments and Trends

1.5
Why Should You Learn About Information Technology?

1.6
Plan of the Book

Minicases: (1) Dartmouth College / (2) Voice-Based 511 Traveler Information Line

Chapter 1 Appendix
Ethics in Information Technology Management

LEARNING OBJECTIVES

After studying this chapter, you will be able to:

1 Describe the characteristics of the digital economy and e-business.

2 Recognize the relationships between business pressures, organizational responses, and information systems.

3 Identify the major pressures in the business environment and describe the major organizational responses to them.

4 Define computer-based information systems and information technology.

5 Describe the role of information technology in supporting the functional areas, public services, and specific industries.

6 List the new technology developments in the areas of generic and networked computing and Web-based systems.

7 Understand the importance of learning about information technology.

SIEMENS AG IS TRANSFORMING ITSELF INTO AN E-BUSINESS

➡️ THE PROBLEM

Siemens AG (*siemens.com*) is a German-based 150-year-old diversified and global manufacturer. With 484,000 employees, Siemens does business in 190 countries and has 600 manufacturing and R & D (research and development) facilities in over 50 countries. Its product lines and services are extremely varied, including communication and information, automation and controls, power, transportation, medical equipment, and lighting. Besides its own 13 operating divisions, Siemens AG has interests in other companies like Bosch (household appliances), Framatome (in France's nuclear power industry), and Fujitsu computers.

Facing hundreds of competitors, most of which are in foreign countries, the company had difficulties expanding its business in a fast-changing business environment and was unable to enjoy the profit margin of some of its competitors. A major problem area was the coordination of the internal units of the company. Another one was the collaboration with so many suppliers and customers. In particular, its *supply chain*—the flow of materials from suppliers through manufacturing, distribution, and sales—is very complex. Finally, it was necessary to find ways to contain costs and to increase customer service.

➡️ THE SOLUTION

By the late 1990s the company decided to transform itself into a 100 percent "e-business" (a company that performs various business functions electronically), by introducing Web-based systems and electronic commerce applications in all of its operations. The reason for such an ambitious goal was the need to solve the problems caused by multilocation, multiple supply chain operations. Embarking on a four-year plan, the company started the transformation in 1999.

Siemens has decided on a dual approach: It will use its own in-house information systems capabilities where it makes sense to do so, but it will also go out-of-house to purchase some systems from major vendors. Siemens strategic goals are to:

- Improve its readiness for extended electronic commerce by standardizing hundreds of business processes across multiple divisions. (For example, the company went from over 300 different process applications to 29.)
- Redesign the information technology infrastructure to enable integration of "best-of-breed" software (software components that best fit the company's needs, each from a different vendor), integrated into an enterprisewide platform.

Besides being able to handle electronic transactions, Siemens also wants to create an easily accessible central corporate *knowledge base*—a companywide storehouse of proven methodologies (known as "best practices").

Using SAP R/3 systems (see Chapter 8), along with software from i2 Technology and IBM, the company is building functional systems that link the enterprise, ensure support functions, and connect with the company's supply

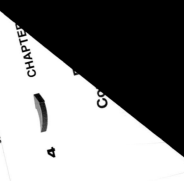

chain partners. Functions such as taking custome
materials and components that go into the manufac
with business partners in developing products, and
ucts are being integrated across the company, using th
sible. Also, the system is designed to provide better cus
business customers.

 THE RESULTS

In its 2000 fiscal year, the company saw its electronic commerce sales and its electronic procurement transactions reach 10 percent of its total sales and purchases, respectively. In 2002, online sales increased by 25 percent, and e-procurement grew 60 percent over its 2000 level.

By March 2003, 350,000 employees were networked throughout the company. They had direct access to the Internet, and a portal through which employees could access corporate information was in use. This portal offered various workplace aids, including search engines, forms, travel booking, and electronic expense account reporting.

The transformation to an e-business and the managing of change will cost Siemens around $1 billion (euro) by the time the transition is completed. President and CEO Heinrich von Pierer says, "This will make us faster and help us further cut costs. . . . All of this is aimed at meeting today's e-economy goals directly, with the promise of operational economies in return."

Sources: Compiled from Schultz (2002), *aberdeen.com* (accessed September 2002), and *siemens.com* (accessed March 2003).

 LESSONS LEARNED FROM THIS CASE

This brief section ties the key points of the opening case to the topics that will be covered in the chapter.

This case illustrates that fierce global competition drives even large corporations to find ways to reduce costs, increase productivity, and improve customer service. These efforts are best achieved by using Web-based systems, which are the major enablers in the transformation to an *e-business* or *e-company* in the digital economy.

In this chapter we present the characteristics and concepts of the digital economy and how it is changing business processes. In addition, we will describe the extremely competitive business environment in which companies operate today, the business pressures to which they are subject, and what companies are doing to counter these pressures. Futhermore, you will learn what makes information technology a necessity in supporting organizations, and what and why any manager in the twenty-first century should know about it.

1.1 DOING BUSINESS IN THE DIGITAL ECONOMY

Conducting business in the digital economy means using Web-based systems on the Internet and other electronic networks to do some form of electronic commerce. First we will consider the concepts of electronic commerce and networked computing and then look at the impact they have made on how companies do business.

Electronic Commerce and Networked Computing

As described in the opening case, Siemens AG was an established "old-economy" company that has seen the need to transform itself into an **e-business,** a company that performs most of its business functions electronically, in order to enhance its operations. Its use of Web-based systems to support buying, selling, and customer service exemplifies **electronic commerce** (**EC** or **e-commerce**). In e-commerce, business transactions are done electronically over the Internet and other computing networks. EC is becoming a very significant global economic element in the twenty-first century (see Evans and Wurster, 2000 and Drucker, 2002).

The infrastructure for EC is **networked computing** (also known as *distributed computing*), which connects computers and other electronic devices via telecommunication networks. Such connections allow users to access information stored in many places and to communicate and collaborate with others, all from their desktop (or even mobile) computers. While some people still use a standalone computer exclusively, or a network confined to one location, the vast majority of people use multiple-location networked computers. These may be connected to the *global networked environment,* known as the **Internet,** or to its counterpart within organizations, called an **intranet.** In addition, some companies link their intranets to those of their business partners over networks called **extranets.** The connection typically is done via wireline systems, but since 2000 more and more communication and collaboration is done via wireless systems.

Networked computing is helping some companies excel and is helping others simply to survive. Broadly, the collection of computing systems used by an organization is termed **information technology (IT),** which is the focus of this book. Almost all medium and large organizations in developed countries, and many small ones, private or public, in manufacturing, agriculture, or services, use information technologies, including electronic commerce, to support their operations.

Why is this so? The reason is simple: IT has become the major facilitator of business activities in the world today. (See for instance, Dickson and DeSanctis, 2001 and Tapscott et al., 2000.) Note that here and throughout the book, in using the term "business" we refer not only to for-profit organizations, but also to not-for-profit public organizations and government agencies, which need to be run like a business. IT is also a catalyst of fundamental changes in the structure, operations, and management of organizations (see Carr, 2001), due to the capabilities shown in Table 1.1. These capabilities, according to Wreden (1997), support the following five business objectives: (1) improving productivity (in 51% of corporations), (2) reducing costs (39%), (3) improving decision making (36%), (4) enhancing customer relationships (33%), and (5) developing new strategic applications (33%). Indeed, IT is creating a transformation in the way business is conducted, facilitating a transition to a digital economy.

What Is the Digital Economy?

The **digital economy** refers to an economy that is based on digital technologies, including digital communication networks (the Internet, intranets, and private *value-added networks* or VANs), computers, software, and other related information technologies. The digital economy is also sometimes called the *Internet economy,* the *new economy,* or the *Web economy* (see Brynolfsson and Kahin, 2001 and Slywotsky and Morrison, 2001).

TABLE 1.1 Major Capabilities of Information Systems

- Perform high-speed, high-volume, numerical computations.
- Provide fast, accurate, and inexpensive communication within and between organizations.
- Store huge amounts of information in an easy-to-access, yet small space.
- Allow quick and inexpensive access to vast amounts of information, worldwide.
- Enable communication and collaboration anywhere, any time.
- Increase the effectiveness and efficiency of people working in groups in one place or in several locations.
- Vividly present information that challenges the human mind.
- Facilitate work in hazardous environments.
- Automate both semiautomatic business processes and manually done tasks.
- Facilitate interpretation of vast amounts of data.
- Can be wireless, thus supporting unique applications anywhere.
- Accomplish all of the above much less expensively than when done manually.

In this new economy, digital networking and communication infrastructures provide a global platform over which people and organizations interact, communicate, collaborate, and search for information. This platform includes, for example, the following, according to Choi and Whinston (2000):

- A vast array of digitizable products—databases, news and information, books, magazines, TV and radio programming, movies, electronic games, musical CDs, and software—which are delivered over the digital infrastructure any time, anywhere in the world
- Consumers and firms conducting financial transactions digitally—through digital currencies or financial tokens carried via networked computers and mobile devices
- Physical goods such as home appliances and automobiles, which are embedded with microprocessors and networking capabilities

The following icon is used throughout the book to indicate that additional related resources are available at the book's Web site, *www.wiley.com/college/turban.*

The term *digital economy* also refers to the convergence of computing and communication technologies on the Internet and other networks, and the resulting flow of information and technology that is stimulating e-commerce and vast organizational change. This convergence enables all types of information (data, audio, video, etc.) to be stored, processed, and transmitted over networks to many destinations worldwide. The digital economy has helped create an economic revolution, which was evidenced by unprecedented economic performance and the longest period of uninterrupted economic expansion in history from 1991 until 2000 (see Online File W1.1).

OPPORTUNITIES FOR ENTREPRENEURS. The new digital economy is providing unparalleled opportunities for thousands of entrepreneurs, some of them in their teens, to apply EC business models to many business areas. As we will see throughout the book, many of these initiatives were started by one or two individuals. Others were started by large corporations. These startup companies not only sold products, but many also provided support services ranging from computer infrastructure to electronic payments. Known as *dot-coms*, these companies saw an opportunity to do global business electronically. An interesting

IT at Work 1.1
DIAMONDS FOREVER—ONLINE

The gems market is a global one with thousands of traders buying and selling about $40 billion worth of gems each year. This age-old business is very inefficient in terms of pricing: Several layers of intermediaries can jack up the price of a gem 1,000 percent between wholesale and final retail prices.

Chanthaburi, Thailand, is one of the world's leading centers for processing gems, and that is where Don Kogen landed, at the age of 15, to search for his fortune. And indeed, he found it there. After failing to become a gem cutter, Kogen moved into gem sorting, and soon he learned to speak Thai. After three years of observing how gem traders haggle over stones, he decided to try the business himself. Having only a small amount of "seed" money, Kogen started by purchasing low-grade gems from sellers who arrived early in the morning and selling them for a small profit to dealers from India and Pakistan who usually arrived late in the day. Using advertising, he reached the U.S. gem market and soon had 800 potential overseas customers. Using faxes, he shortened the order time, which resulted in decreasing the entire time from order to delivery. These various business methods enabled him to grow his mail-order business to $250,000 per year by 1997.

In 1998, Kogen decided to use the Internet. Within a month, he established a Web site *thaigem.com* and sold his first gem online. By 2001, the revenue reached $4.3 million, growing to $9.8 million in 2002. Online sales account for 85 percent of the company's revenue. The buyers are mostly jewelry dealers or retailers such as Wal-Mart or QVC. Kogen buys raw or refined gems from all over the world, some online, trying to cater to the demands of his customers.

Thaigem's competitive edge is low prices. The proximity to gem-processing factories and the low labor cost enable Kogen to offer prices significantly lower than his online competitors (such as Tiffany's at *tiffany.com*). Kogen makes only 20 to 25 percent profit, much less than other dealers make. To make the business even more competitive, Kogen caters even to small buyers. Payments are made safely, securely, and conveniently using either PayPal or Escrow.com. Delivery to any place is made via Federal Express, at $15 per shipment.

Dissatisfied customers can return merchandise within 30 days, no questions asked. No jewel is guaranteed, but Kogen's name is trusted by over 68,000 potential customers worldwide. Kogen enjoys a solid reputation on the Web. For example, he uses eBay to auction gems as an additional selling channel. Customers' comments on eBay are 99 percent positive versus 1 percent negative.

Sources: Compiled from *thaigem.com* (March 2003) and from Mevedoth (2002).

For Further Exploration: Go to *blackstartrading.com* and compare the two sites; which one do you think is better? What kinds of business and revenue models were used? Were they effective?

"IT at Work" boxes spotlight innovations and technologies used by real organizations to solve business problems.

example is entrepreneur Don Kogen and his Thaigem.com business, described in *IT at Work 1.1.*

The New vs. the Old: Illustrative Examples

The changes brought by the digital economy are indeed significant. Computer-based information systems of all kinds have been enhancing business competitiveness and creating strategic advantage on their own or in conjunction with e-commerce applications (see Carr, 2001 and Galliers et al., 1999). In a study conducted by Lederer et al. (1998), companies ranked the number-one benefit of Web-based systems as "enhancing competitiveness or creating strategic advantage." Let's look at a few examples that illustrate differences between doing business in the new economy and the old one.

EXAMPLE #1: PHOTOGRAPHY.   We begin with an activity that millions of people like to do—taking photos.

Old Economy.   You buy film at the store, insert it into your camera, and take pictures. Once you complete the film, sometimes weeks or months after you began the roll, you take it to the store (or mail it) for processing. You get back the photos and examine them, to see which ones you like. You go back to the store and pay for enlargements and duplications. You go home, put some of the photos in envelopes, and mail them to your family and friends. Of course, if you want to take moving pictures, you need a different camera.

New Economy.   In first-generation digital photography, you used the old-economy process up to the point of getting the pictures back from the photo lab. Then, you could scan the ones you liked, and then make reprints, enlarge them, or send them to your family and friends via e-mail.

In the second generation of digital photography, you use a *digital camera* that can also take videos. No film is needed, and no processing is required. You can see the results immediately, and you can enlarge photos and position and print them quickly. In minutes, you can send the pictures to your family and friends (see Online File W1.2 at the book's Web site). They can view the pictures on their personal computer, personal digital assistant (PDA), or cell phone. You can print pictures, or use them in a multimedia presentation.

In the third generation of digital photography, your digital camera can be small enough to be installed in your cell phone, a palmtop computer, or a pair of binoculars. You are traveling, and you see interesting scenery or an athletic event. You take pictures with your tiny digital camera, and within a few seconds they are sent to any destination on the Internet for viewing or reprints. Cameras of this type are already in use.

EXAMPLE #2: CROSSING INTERNATIONAL BORDERS.   Assume you are traveling to another country, say Australia. Your plane lands after a long flight, but before you can make your way to your lodgings, you must first go through immigration.

Old Economy.   You wait in line to be processed by the immigration officers. The inspectors are slow, and some are new and need help from time to time. Processing certain people takes several minutes. You are tired, upset, and stressed. You may wait 10 minutes, 20 minutes, or close to an hour.

New Economy.   You submit your passport and it is scanned. At the same time, a photo of your face is taken. A computer compares that picture with the picture in the passport and with one in a database. In 10 seconds you are through immigration and on your way out of the airport. The world's first system of this kind was initiated in Australia in 2003. In some countries (e.g., Israel), an image of your fingerprints is taken and compared to a stored image. Again, in seconds you are on your way. These systems use a technology called *biometrics* (see Chapter 15) that not only expedites processing but also increases security by eliminating the entry of people with false passports.

EXAMPLE #3: SUPPLYING COMMERCIAL PHOTOS.   Thousands of companies around the globe provide photos of their products to retailers who advertise products in newspapers, in paper catalogs, or online. The new economy has changed the process by which these photos are supplied.

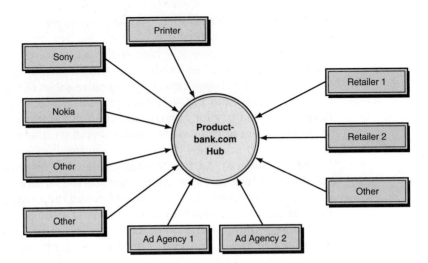

FIGURE 1.1 Changing a linear supply chain to a hub.

Old Economy. In the old economy, the retailer sends the manufacturer a request for a picture of the item to be advertised, say a Sony TV set. Sony then sends to a designated ad agency, by courier, alternative pictures that the agency can use. The agency selects a picture, designs the ad, gets an approval from the retailer and sends the picture by courier to the printer. There it is rephotographed and entered into production for the catalog. (An improvement introduced several years ago allows the ad agency to send the picture to a scanning house. There, a digital image is made, and that image is moved to the printer.) Both the retailer and the ad agency may be involved in a quality check at various times, slowing the process. The cycle time per picture can be four to six weeks. The total processing cost per picture is about $80.

New Economy. Orbis Inc., a very small Australian company, changed the old-economy linear supply chain to a hub-like supply chain, as shown in Figure 1.1. In the new process, the manufacturer (e.g., Sony) sends many digitized pictures to Orbis (at *productbank.com.au*), and Orbis organizes the pictures in a database. When a retailer needs a picture, it enters the database and selects a picture, or several alternatives. The ID number of the chosen picture is e-mailed to the ad agency. The agency enters the database, views the digitized pictures, and works on them. Then, either the final digitized pictures are e-mailed to the printer, or the printer is told to pick them up from the database. The entire process takes less than a week at a cost of about $50 per picture.

EXAMPLE #4: PAYING FOR TRANSPORTATION IN NEW YORK CITY. Millions of people all over the world take public transportation. Metal tokens were the preferred solution in some major cities for generations.

Old Economy. For over 50 years, New Yorkers have used tokens to pay for transportation on buses and subways. The tokens save time and are liked by travelers. However, it costs $6 million a year to manufacture replacement tokens and to collect the tokens out of turnstiles and fare boxes ("NYC Transit Tokens. . . ," 2003). New York City needs this money badly for other services.

New Economy. The new-economy solution has been to switch to Metro-Cards. By 2002, only 9 percent of all commuters were still using tokens. Despite the fact that they have to occasionally swipe the MetroCard through the card reader several times, travelers generally like the new cards. (A new generation of contactless cards does not have this problem.) MetroCards are offered at discounts, which riders like. Other cities have made the transition to electronic cards as well. Chicago's transit moved to cards in 1999, replacing the century-old tokens. Washington, D.C., Paris, and London also use transit cards. In Hong Kong, millions use a contactless card not only for transportation but also to pay for telephone, Internet access, food in vending machines, and much more.

EXAMPLE #5: SHOPPING FROM HOME. As time passes people are getting busier and busier. There is more to do, learn, and enjoy. Shopping in physical stores is a time-consuming activity. Although shopping *is* recreation for some people, for others it is an unenjoyable, disliked task.

Old Economy. You have a choice of selecting a store and shopping there when it is open. You have to get there and carry your goods back home. In a few stores you can place phone orders, but this option is generally unavailable. Unless you are willing to spend the time and energy to go from place to place to compare prices, you pay what vendors ask you to pay.

New Economy #1. You still go to stores, but you expedite the process. For example, at Kmart and other stores, you can check yourself out. This saves the time of standing in line to pay. Also, in Wal-Mart and other stores you do not have to write a check anymore. Just present a blank check, and your account will be automatically debited. You still have to carry the goods home, of course.

New Economy #2. There is no need to go to stores anymore. Shopping online, you have many thousands of stores to choose from and many thousands of products. You can compare prices and get opinions about reliability of the stores. In some cases you may join a group of shoppers and get a quantity discount. Everything you buy will be shipped to your home or workplace.

In each of the examples above, we can see the advantage of the new economy over the old one in terms of at least one of the following: cost, quality, speed, and customer service. What is amazing is the *magnitude* of this advantage. In the past, business improvements were in the magnitude of 10 to 25 percent. Today, improvements can be hundreds or even thousands of times faster or cheaper. For example, it is about 250 times faster to get through immigration now, and there are fewer mistakes (Walker, 2003). The new economy brings not only digitization but also the opportunity to use new business models, such as Don Kogen uses at Thaigem.com—selling from the Internet.

Business Models in the Digital Economy

The Internet is challenging the economic, societal, and technological foundations of the old economy. In essence a revolution has been underway. And like all successful revolutions, when it ends, the landscape will look significantly different. Entrepreneurs are developing new models for business, the economy, and government.

A **business model** is a method of doing business by which a company can generate revenue to sustain itself. The model spells out how the company adds value that consumers are willing to pay for, in terms of the goods and/or services the company produces in the course of its operations. Some models are very simple. For example, Nokia makes and sells cell phones and generates profit from these sales. On the other hand, a TV station provides free broadcasting. Its survival depends on a complex model involving factors such as advertisers and content providers. Internet portals, such as Yahoo, also use a complex business model.

Some examples of new business models brought about by the digital revolution are listed in *A Closer Look 1.1*. Further discussion of these models will be found throughout the book (especially in Chapter 5), and also in Afuah and Tucci (2003), Applegate (2001), Weill and Vitale (2001), and Turban et al. (2004), and at *digitalenterprise.org*. In part, these new business models have sprung up in response or reaction to business pressures, which is the topic we turn to next.

"A Closer Look" boxes contain detailed, in-depth discussion of specific concepts, procedures, or approaches.

A CLOSER LOOK
1.1 FIVE REPRESENTATIVE BUSINESS MODELS OF THE DIGITAL AGE

NAME-YOUR-OWN-PRICE. Pioneered by Priceline.com, this model allows the buyer to state a price he or she is willing to pay for a specific product or service. Using information in its database, Priceline will try to match the buyer's request with a supplier willing to sell on these terms. Customers may have to submit several bids before they find a price match for the product they want. Priceline's major area of operation is travel (airline tickets, hotels).

TENDERING VIA REVERSE AUCTIONS. If you are a big buyer, private or public, you are probably using a *tendering* (bidding) system to make your major purchases. In what is called a request for quote (RFQ), the buyer indicates a desire to receive bids on a particular item, and would-be sellers bid on the job. The lowest bid wins (if price is the only consideration), hence the name *reverse auction*. Now tendering can be done online, saving time and money. Pioneered by General Electric Corp. (*gxs.com*), tendering systems are gaining popularity. Indeed, several government entities are mandating electronic tendering as the only way to sell to them. Electronic reverse auctions are fast, they reduce administrative costs by as much as 85 percent, and products' prices can be 5 to 20 percent lower.

AFFILIATE MARKETING. *Affiliate marketing* is an arrangement in which marketing partners place a banner ad for a company, such as Amazon.com, on their Web site. Every time a customer clicks on the banner, moves to the advertiser's Web site, and makes a purchase there, the advertiser pays a 3 to 15 percent commission to the host site. In this way, businesses can turn other businesses into their *virtual commissioned sales force*. Pioneered by CDNow (see Hoffman and Novak, 2000), the concept is now employed by thousands of retailers or direct sellers. For details see Chapter 5 and Helmstetter and Metiviers (2000).

GROUP PURCHASING. It is customary to pay less per unit when buying more units. Discounts are usually available for such quantity purchases. Using e-commerce and the concept of *group purchasing*, in which purchase orders of many buyers are aggregated, a small business or even an individual can get a discount. EC brings in the concept of *electronic aggregation* for group purchasing, in which a third party finds the individuals or SMEs (small/medium enterprises) that want to buy the same product, aggregates their small orders, and then negotiates (or conducts a tender) for the best deal. The more that join the group, the larger the aggregated quantity, and the lower the price paid. Some leading aggregators can be found at *etrana.com* and *usa-llc.com*.

E-MARKETPLACES AND EXCHANGES. Electronic marketplaces have existed in isolated applications for decades. An example is the stock exchanges, some of which have been fully computerized since the 1980s. But, since 1999, thousands of electronic marketplaces of different varieties have sprung up. E-marketplaces introduce operating efficiencies to trading, and if well organized and managed, they can provide benefits to both buyers and sellers. Of special interest are *vertical marketplaces*, which concentrate on one industry (e.g., chemconnect.com in the chemical industry). (Chapter 5 will explore e-marketplaces and exchanges in more detail.)

1.2   BUSINESS PRESSURES, ORGANIZATIONAL RESPONSES, AND IT SUPPORT

Environmental, organizational, and technological factors are creating a highly competitive business environment in which customers are the focal point. Furthermore, these factors can change quickly, sometimes in an unpredictable manner (see Tapscott et al., 2000). Therefore, companies need to react frequently and quickly to both the *problems* and the *opportunities* resulting from this new business environment (see Freeman and Louca, 2001 and Drucker, 2001). Because the pace of change and the degree of uncertainty in tomorrow's competitive environment are expected to accelerate, organizations are going to operate under increasing pressures to produce more, using fewer resources.

Boyett and Boyett (1995) emphasize this dramatic change and describe it with a set of what they call **business pressures,** or *drivers*. These business pressures are forces in the organization's environment that create pressures on (that is, that "drive") the organization's operations.

Boyett and Boyett maintain that in order to succeed (or even merely to survive) in this dynamic world, companies must not only take traditional actions such as lowering costs, but also undertake innovative activities such as changing structure or processes. We refer to these reactions, some of which are interrelated, as **critical response activities.** These activities can be performed in some or all of the processes of the organization, from the daily routines of preparing payroll and order entry, to strategic activities such as the acquisition of a company. A response can be a reaction to a pressure already in existence, an initiative intended to defend an organization against future pressures, or an activity that exploits an opportunity created by changing conditions. Most response activities can be greatly facilitated by information technology. In some cases IT is the only solution to these business pressures (see Dickson and DeSanctis, 2001 and Freeman and Louca, 2001).

The relationships among business pressures, organizational responses, and IT are shown in Figure 1.2. This figure illustrates a model of the new world of business. The business environment contains pressures on organizations, and organizations respond with activities supported by IT (hence the bidirectional nature of the arrows in the figure).

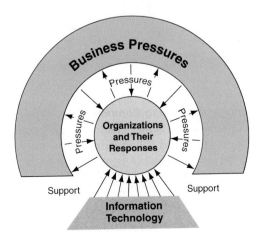

FIGURE 1.2 IT support for organizational responses.

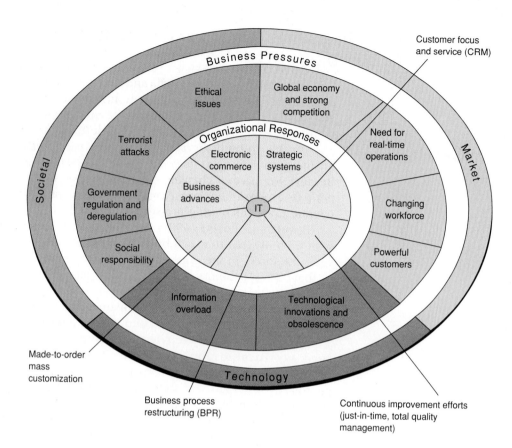

FIGURE 1.3 Business pressures, organizational responses, and IT support.

In the remainder of this section, we will examine two components of the model—business pressures and organizational responses—in more detail.

Business Pressures

The business environment consists of a variety of factors—social, technological, legal, economic, physical, and political. Significant changes in any of these factors are likely to create business pressures on organizations. In this book, we will focus on the following business pressures: market pressures, technology pressures, and societal pressures. Figure 1.3 (the inner circle) presents a schematic view of these major pressures, which may interrelate and affect each other. These pressures are described next.

MARKET PRESSURES. The market pressures that organizations feel come from a global economy and strong competition, the changing nature of the workforce, and powerful customers.

Global Economy and Strong Competition. Within the last 20 or so years, the foundation necessary for a global economy has taken shape. This move to globalization has been facilitated by advanced telecommunication networks and especially by the Internet. Regional agreements such as the North American Free Trade Agreement (United States, Canada, and Mexico) and the creation of a unified European market with a single currency, the euro, have contributed to increased world trade. Further, reduction of trade barriers has allowed products and services to flow more freely around the globe.

One particular pressure that exists for businesses in a global market is the cost of labor. Labor costs differ widely from one country to another. While the hourly industrial wage rate (excluding benefits) is over $15 in some developed countries, it can be less than $1 in many developing countries, including those in Asia, South America, Eastern Europe, and Africa. In addition, companies in developed countries usually pay high fringe benefits to employees, which makes their costs of doing business even higher. Therefore, many companies in labor-intensive industries have found it necessary to move their manufacturing facilities to countries with low labor costs. Such a global strategy requires extensive communication and collaboration, frequently in several languages and under several cultural, ethical, and legal conditions. This can be greatly facilitated with IT (Chapter 4).

Using IT in a multicountry/multicultural environment may create ethical issues, such as invasion of privacy of individuals whose private data are taken across borders (see Appendix 1A at the end of this chapter). *Global competition* is especially intensified when governments become involved through the use of subsidies, tax policies, import/export regulations, and other incentives. Rapid and inexpensive communication and transportation modes increase the magnitude of international trade even further. Competition is now becoming truly global.

Need for Real-Time Operations. The world is moving faster and faster. Decisions need to be made very quickly, and speed is needed to remain competitive (Gates, 1999; Davis, 2001; and Wetherbe, 1996). Led by Cisco Systems, some companies are even attempting to close their accounting books in a day—a process that used to take as many as 10 days (McCleanahen, 2002).

Changing Nature of the Workforce. The workforce, particularly in developed countries, is changing rapidly. It is becoming more diversified, as increasing numbers of women, single parents, minorities, and persons with disabilities work in all types of positions. In addition, more employees than ever prefer to defer retirement. Finally, more and more workers are becoming knowledge workers (Drucker, 2002). Information technology is easing the integration of this wide variety of employees into the traditional workforce, and it enables homebound people to work from home (telecommute). (For more, see the discussions of telecommuting in Chapter 4, and of support for the disabled in online Chapter 16.)

Powerful Customers. Consumer sophistication and expectations increase as customers become more knowledgeable about the availability and quality of products and services. On the Web, consumers can now easily find detailed information about products and services, compare prices, and buy at electronic auctions. As we mentioned earlier, in some cases buyers can even name the price they are willing to pay. Therefore, consumers have considerable power (Pitt et al., 2002). Companies need to be able to deliver information quickly to satisfy these customers.

Customers today also want *customized products and services,* with high quality and low prices. Vendors must respond, or lose business. For example, a large department store in Japan offers refrigerators in 24 different colors with a delivery time of just a few days. Dell Computer will take an order over the Internet for a computer, made to specifications of your choice, and will deliver that computer to your home within 72 hours. And Nike will let you design your own sneakers online and will make and ship them to arrive at your home in two weeks (*nike.com*). Finally, automakers are selling build-to-order cars whose configuration is done on the Internet (see *jaguar.com*). The old saying, "The customer is king," has never before been so true. (For further discussion of how IT enhances customization, see Chapters 5 and 7.)

The importance of customers has created "competition over customers." This competition forces organizations to increase efforts to acquire and retain customers. An enterprisewide effort to do just that is called **customer relationship management (CRM)** (see Greenberg, 2002). This topic will be addressed in detail in Chapter 7.

TECHNOLOGY PRESSURES.   The second category of business pressures consists of those related to technology. Two major pressures in this category are technological innovation and information overload.

Technological Innovation and Obsolescence.   Technology is playing an increased role in both manufacturing and services. New and improved technologies create or support substitutes for products, alternative service options, and superb quality. In addition, some of today's state-of-the-art products may be obsolete tomorrow. Thus, technology accelerates the competitive forces. Many technologies affect business in areas ranging from genetic engineering to food processing. However, probably the technology with the greatest impact is Web-based information technology (see Evans and Wurster, 1999 and Carr, 2001).

An example of technological obsolesence is illustrated in Minicase 1 (Maybelline) at the end of Chapter 2. The technology of interactive voice response (IVR), which is still new for many companies, is being replaced by mobile devices, which are being replaced by wireless devices.

Information Overload.   The Internet and other telecommunication networks increase the amount of information available to organizations and individuals. Furthermore, the amount of information available on the Internet more than doubles every year, and most of it is free! The information and knowledge generated and stored inside organizations is also increasing exponentially. The world is facing a flood of information. Thus, the accessibility, navigation, and management of data, information, and knowledge, which are necessary for managerial decision making, become critical. The only effective solutions are provided by information technology (e.g., search engines, intelligent databases).

SOCIETAL PRESSURES.   The third category of business pressures consists of those related to society. The "next society," as Drucker (2001, 2002) calls it, will be a knowledge society, and also a society of aging populations. Both of these have important societal implications related to education and health care (e.g., see the case of Elite-Care in Chapter 6), and treatment of such issues likely will involve various information technologies. Other important societal issues include social responsibility, government regulation/deregulation, spending for social programs, and ethics.

Social Responsibility.   The interfaces between organizations and society are both increasing and changing rapidly. Social issues that affect business range from the state of the physical environment to companies' contributions to education (e.g., by allowing interns to work in the companies). Corporations are becoming more aware of these and other social issues, and some are willing to spend time and/or money on solving various social problems. Such activity is known as organizational *social responsibility*. Online File W1.3 at the book's Web site lists some major areas of social responsibility related to business.

Government Regulations and Deregulation. Several social responsibility issues are related to government regulations regarding health, safety, environmental control, and equal opportunity. For example, U.S. companies that spray products with paint must use paper to absorb the overspray. The paper must then be disposed of by a licensed company, usually at a high cost. Such regulations cost money and make it more difficult to compete with countries that lack such regulations. They also may create the need for changes in organizational structure and processes. Government regulations are usually viewed as expensive constraints on all who are affected. Government deregulation, on the other hand, can be a blessing to one company but a curse to another that had been protected by the regulation. In general, deregulation intensifies competition.

Terrorist Attacks and Protection. Since September 11, 2001, organizations have been under increased pressure to protect themselves against terrorist attacks. In addition, employees in the military reserves may be called up for active duty, creating personnel problems. Information technology and especially intelligent systems may make a valuable contribution in the area of protection, by providing security systems and possibly identifying patterns of behavior that will help to prevent terrorist attacks and cyberattacks against organizations.

Use of this icon highlights IT-related ethics discussions.

Ethical Issues. **Ethics** relates to standards of right and wrong, and *information ethics* relates to standards of right and wrong in information processing practices. Organizations must deal with ethical issues relating to their employees, customers, and suppliers. Ethical issues are very important since they have the power to damage the image of an organization and to destroy the morale of the employees. Ethics is a difficult area because ethical issues are not cut-and-dried. What is considered ethical by one person may seem unethical to another. Likewise, what is considered ethical in one country may be seen as unethical in another.

The use of information technology raises many ethical issues. These range from the monitoring of electronic mail to the potential invasion of privacy of millions of customers whose data are stored in private and public databases. We consider ethical issues so significant that we have appended to this chapter a general framework of ethics in business and society (Appendix 1A). Specific ethical issues are discussed in all chapters of the book (and are highlighted by an icon in the margin). Also, an Ethics Primer is available online.

The environments that surrounded organizations are becoming more complex and turbulent. Advances in communications, transportation, and technology create many changes. Other changes are the result of political or economic activities. Thus, the pressures on organizations are mounting, and organizations must be ready to take responsive actions if they are to succeed. In addition, organizations may see opportunities in these pressures. For a *Framework for Change Analysis* see Online File W1.4 at the book's Web site. Organizational responses to the increasing business pressures are described next.

Organizational Responses

Traditional organizational responses may not be effective with new types of pressures. Therefore many old solutions need to be modified, supplemented, or eliminated. Organizations can also take *proactive* measures, to create a change in the marketplace. Such activities also include exploiting opportunities created by the external pressures.

Organizations' major responses are divided here into seven categories: strategic systems, customer focus, continuous improvement, restructuring, make-to-order and mass customization, business alliances, and e-business. These responses can be interrelated, so the categories sometimes overlap.

STRATEGIC SYSTEMS.   Strategic systems provide organizations with strategic advantages that enable them to increase their market share and/or profit, to better negotiate with suppliers, or to prevent competitors from entering their territory (Callon, 1996). There are a variety of IT-supported strategic systems, as we will show in Chapter 3. According to Moss-Kanter (2001), the Internet is transforming companies and their strategies, changing the competitive landscape and requiring commitment to change. In particular these days, Web-based systems are providing considerable strategic advantage to companies (Lederer et al., 2001 and Amit and Zott, 2001).

A prime example of strategic systems is Federal Express's overnight delivery system, which can track the status of every individual package, anywhere in the delivery chain. The Federal Express (FedEx) system is heavily supported by IT. A major challenge with this kind of strategic system is the difficulty of sustaining competitive advantage. Most of FedEx's competitors duplicated the system. So FedEx moved the system to the Internet. However, the competitors quickly followed, and FedEx is now continuously introducing new innovations to keep or expand market share. For example, in an application called "My Account," FedEx will provide you comprehensive account management, including an on-line address checker (for shipping destinations) and an online wireless portal. An increasing number of mobile-computing-based strategic systems are appearing (e.g., see the Expedia case in *IT at Work 3.3*).

CUSTOMER FOCUS.   Organizational attempts to provide super customer service sometimes make the difference between attracting and keeping customers, or losing them to other organizations. With a slew of IT tools, sophisticated mechanisms and innovations are designed to make customers happy (see Chapter 7).

CONTINUOUS IMPROVEMENT.   :Many companies continuously conduct programs that attempt to improve their productivity and quality (see Brue, 2002), and they frequently do so with the facilitation of IT. Examples of such programs include total quality management (TQM) and Six Sigma, knowledge management, productivity and creativity improvements, just-in-time (JIT) processing, improvements in decision-making processes, change management, and customer service improvements. The underlying purpose of IT support in continuous improvement is (1) to monitor and analyze performance and productivity and (2) to gather, share, and better use organizational knowledge. (See Online File W1.5 at the book's Web site for more details.) We will provide examples throughout the book of how IT is contributing to continuous improvement.

RESTRUCTURING BUSINESS PROCESSES.   Organizations may discover that continuous improvement efforts have limited effectiveness in an environment full of strong business pressures. Therefore, a relatively new approach may be needed. This approach, initially called **business process reengineering (BPR),**

refers to a situation in which an organization fundamentally and radically re-designs its business process to achieve dramatic improvements (Hammer and Champy, 1993). Such redesign effects a major innovation in an organization's structure and the way it conducts its business. If done on a smaller scale than corporatewide, the redesign process may be referred to as a *restructuring* (see El-Sawy, 2001). Technological, human, and organizational dimensions of a firm may all be changed in restructuring and BPR (see Chapter 8). Information tech-nology plays a major role in restructuring. It provides automation; it allows busi-ness to be conducted in different locations; it provides flexibility in manufactur-ing; it permits quicker delivery to customers; it creates or facilitates new business models; and it supports rapid and paperless transactions among suppliers, man-ufacturers, and retailers. The major areas in which IT supports restructuring are described in Chapter 9.

MAKE-TO-ORDER AND MASS CUSTOMIZATION.   A major response area is the trend to produce customized products and services. This strategy is referred to as **build-to-order.** As today's customers demand customized products and services, the business problem is how to provide customization and do it efficiently. This can be done, in part, by changing manufacturing processes from mass produc-tion to mass customization (Anderson, 2002 and Pine and Gilmore, 1999; see also Appendix 2A in this book). In mass production, a company produces a large quantity of identical items. In **mass customization,** items are produced in a large quantity but are customized to fit the desires of each customer. IT and EC are ideal facilitators of mass customization, for example, by enabling interactive communication between buyers and designers so that customers can quickly and correctly configure the products they want. Also, electronic ordering reaches the production facility in minutes. For more on the relationship between IT and mass customization, see Appendix 2A.

BUSINESS ALLIANCES.   Many companies realize that alliances with other com-panies, even competitors, can be very beneficial. For example, General Motors and Ford created a joint venture to explore electronic-commerce applications, and the major airlines in Southeast Asia created a joint portal in 2003 that pro-motes travel to the region. There are several types of alliances: sharing re-sources, doing procurement jointly, establishing a permanent supplier-company relationship, and creating joint research efforts. Any of these might be undertaken in response to business pressures and usually is supported by IT.

One of the most interesting types of business alliance is the **virtual corpo-ration,** which operates through telecommunications networks, usually without a permanent headquarters. (The term is used by some to describe a purely on-line business that does not have physical stores.) Virtual corporations may be temporary or permanent. A *temporary* virtual corporation is typically a joint ven-ture in which companies form a special company for a specific, limited-time mission. A *permanent* virtual corporation is designed to create or assemble productive resources rapidly or frequently, on an ongoing basis. The virtual corporation form of organization could become common in the future. More details of virtual corporations are provided in Chapter 9.

A more permanent type of business alliance that links manufacturers, sup-pliers, and finance corporations is known as *keiretsu* (a Japanese term). *Keiretsu*-style collaboration refers to agreements in which the partners learn each other's needs and trust each other, usually signing long-term partnership contracts. This and other types of business alliances can be heavily supported by information technologies ranging from collaborative portals to electronic transmission of drawings.

ELECTRONIC BUSINESS AND E-COMMERCE. As seen in the opening case, companies are transforming themselves into e-businesses. Doing business electronically is the newest and perhaps most promising strategy that many companies can pursue (see Turban et al., 2004). Several of the business models introduced earlier (in *A Closer Look 1.1*) are in fact e-commerce. Chapter 5 will focus extensively on this topic, and e-commerce applications are introduced throughout the book.

To illustrate the importance of e-commerce, let's look at what a management guru, Peter Drucker, has to say about EC.

> The truly revolutionary impact of the Internet Revolution is just beginning to be felt. But it is not "information" that fuels this impact. It is not "artificial intelligence." It is not the effect of computers and data processing on decision-making, policy-making, or strategy. It is something that practically no one foresaw or, indeed even talked about ten or fifteen years ago: e-commerce—that is, the explosive emergence of the Internet as a major, perhaps eventually *the* major, worldwide distribution channel for goods, for services, and, surprisingly, for managerial and professional jobs. This is profoundly changing economics, markets and industry structure, products and services and their flow; consumer segmentation, consumer values and consumer behavior, jobs and labor markets. But the impact may be even greater on societies and politics, and above all, on the way we see the world and ourselves in it. (Drucker, 2002, pp. 3–4)

E-business not only is revolutionizing business but, according to Earl and Khan (2001), is changing the face of IT by pushing companies to redefine technology's role in new business models. For example, many EC systems need to be built quickly and inexpensively since they are used only for a short time, due to rapid technological and market changes. Some companies are introducing dozens of EC projects that enable them to compete globally. For example, see Minicase W1.1 about Qantas Airlines at the book's Web site.

While some critical response activities can be executed manually, the vast majority require the support of information systems. Before we provide more examples on the role of information systems and IT, let us briefly explore the terms themselves.

1.3 INFORMATION SYSTEMS: DEFINITIONS AND EXAMPLES

What Is an Information System?

An **information system (IS)** collects, processes, stores, analyzes, and disseminates information for a specific purpose. Like any other system, an information system includes *inputs* (data, instructions) and *outputs* (reports, calculations). It *processes* the inputs by using technology such as PCs and produces outputs that are sent to users or to other systems via electronic networks. A *feedback* mechanism that controls the operation may be included (see Figure 1.4). Like any other system, an information system also includes people, procedures, and physical facilities, and it operates within an *environment*. An information system is not necessarily computerized, although most of them are. (For more on systems, see Online File W1.6 at the book's Web site.)

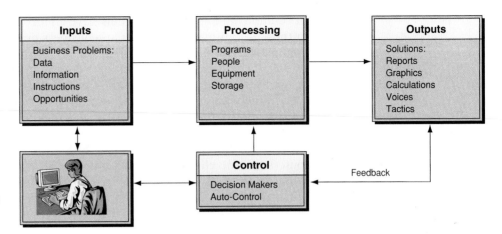

FIGURE 1.4 A schematic view of an information system.

FORMAL AND INFORMAL INFORMATION SYSTEMS.   An information system can be formal or informal. *Formal* systems include agreed-upon procedures, standard inputs and outputs, and fixed definitions. A company's accounting system, for example, would be a formal information system that processes financial transactions.

Informal systems take many shapes, ranging from an office gossip network to a group of friends exchanging letters electronically. It is important for management to understand that informal systems exist. These systems may consume information resources and may sometimes interface with the formal systems. They may also play an important role in employees' resistance to change. On the other hand, some of them may be used to influence people and processes or even to encourage change.

WHAT IS A COMPUTER-BASED INFORMATION SYSTEM?   A **computer-based information system (CBIS)** is an information system that uses computer technology to perform some or all of its intended tasks. Such a system can include as little as a personal computer and software. Or it may include several thousand computers of various sizes with hundreds of printers, plotters, and other devices, as well as communication networks (wireline and wireless) and databases. In most cases an information system also includes people. The basic components of information systems are listed below. Note that not every system includes all these components.

- *Hardware* is a set of devices such as processor, monitor, keyboard, and printer. Together, they accept data and information, process them, and display them.
- *Software* is a set of programs that enable the hardware to process data.
- A *database* is a collection of related files, tables, relations, and so on, that stores data and the associations among them.
- A *network* is a connecting system that permits the sharing of resources by different computers. It can be wireless.
- *Procedures* are the set of instructions about how to combine the above components in order to process information and generate the desired output.
- *People* are those individuals who work with the system, interface with it, or use its output.

In addition, all information systems have a *purpose* and a *social context*. A typical purpose is to provide a solution to a business problem. In the Siemens case, for example, the purpose of the system was to coordinate internal units, to collaborate with the many suppliers and customers, and to improve costs and customer service. The social context of the system consists of the values and beliefs that determine what is admissible and possible within the culture of the people and groups involved.

THE DIFFERENCE BETWEEN COMPUTERS AND INFORMATION SYSTEMS. Computers provide effective and efficient ways of processing data, and they are a necessary part of an information system. An IS, however, involves much more than just computers. The successful application of an IS requires an understanding of the business and its environment that is supported by the IS. For example, to build an IS that supports transactions executed on the New York Stock Exchange, it is necessary to understand the procedures related to buying and selling stocks, bonds, options, and so on, including irregular demands made on the system, as well as all related government regulations.

In learning about information systems, it is therefore not sufficient just to learn about computers. Computers are only one part of a complex system that must be designed, operated, and maintained. A public transportation system in a city provides an analogy. Buses are a necessary ingredient of the system, but more is needed. Designing the bus routes, bus stops, different schedules, and so on requires considerable understanding of customer demand, traffic patterns, city regulations, safety requirements, and the like. Computers, like buses, are only one component in a complex system.

WHAT IS INFORMATION TECHNOLOGY?   Earlier in the chapter we broadly defined *information technology* as the collection of computer systems used by an organization. Information technology, in its narrow definition, refers to the technological side of an information system. It includes the hardware, software, databases, networks, and other electronic devices. It can be viewed as a subsystem of an information system. Sometimes, though, the term information technology is also used interchangeably with *information system*. In this book, we use the term *IT* in its broadest sense—to describe an organization's collection of information systems, their users, and the management that oversees them. The purpose of this book is to acquaint you with all aspects of information systems/information technology.

Now that the basic terms have been defined, we present some examples of IS applications worldwide.

Examples of Information Systems

Millions of different information systems are in use throughout the world. The following examples are intended to show the diversity of applications and the benefits provided. At the end of each example, we list the *critical response activities* supported by the system. (More examples are shown in Online File W1.7 at the book's Web site.)

As the examples in this section show, information systems are being used successfully in all functional areas of business. We provide here five examples, one for each of the major functional areas: accounting, production/operations management, marketing, human resource management, and finance. Beginning here, and continuing throughout this book, icons positioned in the margins will call out the functional areas to which our real-world examples apply. In addition we will point to IT applications in government and in other public services such as health care and education by using icons. Finally, you've already seen that other icons will identify global examples—IT used by non-U.S.-based companies or by any company with significant business outside the United States. For a key that identifies the icons, see the marginal note at left and the preface.

Managing Accounting Information Across Asia. Le Saunda Holding Company (Hong Kong) manages 32 subsidiaries in four Asian countries, mostly in the manufacture, import, and sale of shoes (*lesaunda.com.hk*). Managing the financing and cash flow is a complex process. All accounting information flows to headquarters electronically. Also, sales data are electronically collected at point-of-sale (POS) terminals. The sales data, together with inventory data (which are updated automatically when a sale occurs), are transferred to headquarters. Other relevant data, such as advertising and sales promotions, merchants, and cash flow, are also transmitted electronically and collected in a centralized database for storage and processing.

To cope with the rapid growth of the company, a sophisticated accounting software package was installed. The result was radical improvements in accounting procedures. For example, it now takes less than 10 minutes, rather than a day, to produce an ad-hoc complex report. The company's accountants can generate reports as they are needed, helping functional managers make quicker and better decisions. The system is also much more reliable, and internal and external auditing is easier. Headquarters knows what is going on almost as soon as it occurs. All these improvements have led to a substantial growth in revenue and profits for the firm. (*Source: lesaunda.com.hk*, press releases.)

Critical response activities supported: decision making, managing large amounts of information, improving quality, reduced cycle time.

Seattle Mariners Using Technology for Profitable Operation of a Stadium. Since July 1999, the Seattle Mariners baseball team has been playing in a modern stadium, a stadium that uses advanced information technologies to increase profitability. The stadium is wired with an integrated voice and data communication system. One of its major applications is to provide real-time inventory counts—so that hungry fans will never be without a hot dog or beer. All the cash registers are networked, and the concession vendors are equipped with wireless communication devices. All sales are monitored in real time, and replenishment is done according to these real-time sales records, so shortages and lost revenues are eliminated.

In addition to controlling inventories, the enterprise network is used to provide Internet access from certain "smart" seats, so you can find out what's going on outside the stadium at any time; to enable fans to purchase tickets for future games from kiosks that are scattered throughout the stadium; to produce a revenue report within hours after a game, rather than days; and to manage frequent-attendance promotions, in which visitors can swipe smart cards through readers and get points for attending games.

The only downside of the new system is that if a main data center fails, the company may lose 50 percent of the concession revenues that day. (*Source: seattle.mariners.mlb.com.*)

Critical response activities supported: decision making, increased sales, dissemination of information, electronic purchasing, improved supply chain.

"Integrating IT" icons highlight examples of IT applications in major functional areas of business, in government, and in public services. The codes used in these turquoise-colored icons are:
ACC—accounting
POM—production/operations management
MKT—marketing
HRM—human resources management
FIN—finance
GOV—government
and **SVC**—other public services

The Success Story of Campusfood.com. Campusfood.com's recipe for success was a simple one: Provide interactive menus to college students, using the power of the Internet to enhance traditional telephone ordering of meals. Launched at the University of Pennsylvania, the company has taken thousands of orders for local restaurants, bringing pizza, hoagies, and wings to the Penn community.

Founder Michael Saunders began developing the site in 1997, while he was a junior at Penn, and with the help of some classmates, launched the site in 1998. After graduation, Saunders began building the company's customer base. This involved registering other schools, attracting students, and generating a list of local restaurants from which students could order food to be delivered. Currently, this activity is outsourced to a marketing firm, and schools nationwide are being added to the list. By 2003 there were more than 200 participating schools and more than 1,000 participating restaurants.

Financed through private investors, friends, and family members, the site was built on an investment of less than $1 million. (For comparison, another company, with services also reaching the college-student market, has investments of $100 million.) Campusfood.com's revenue is generated through transaction fees; the site takes a 5 percent commission on each order.

When you visit *Campusfood.com,* you can do the following: Search a list of local restaurants, their hours of operation, addresses, phone numbers, and other information. Browse an interactive menu, which shows each participating restaurant's standard print menus, including the latest prices and a listing of every topping, every special, and every drink offered. Bypass busy-signals and place an order without being placed on hold, and avoid miscommunications. Get access to more specials, including discounts and meal deals available online exclusively to Campusfood.com customers. Have access to electronic payment capabilities and your own account record ("My Account"). (*Source:* Prince, 2002 and *campusfood.com.*)

Critical response activities supported: customer service, improved cycle time, and innovative marketing method.

State-of-the-Art Human Resources Management in China. International Information Products Company LTD (IIPC) produces IBM personal computers (PCs) in Shenzhen, China. The company is one of China's top-10 exporters and one of the world's most efficient manufacturers of IBM PCs. The company's success is attributed, in part, to its world-class Human Resources Information System (powered by PeopleSoft's HRMS). In operation since October 2001, the system includes these basic elements: employee record management, recruitment, variable pay analysis, performance appraisal, payroll, and management of fringe benefits and absence records. In addition, employees can self-manage their personal data and report leaves and absences on the intranet. Using e-kiosks placed in several locations within the plant (e.g., the cafeteria), employees who do not have Internet access at work or home can use the system as well.

China's employee tax and benefit systems (e.g., health care and social insurance) are very complex, requiring many computations. Using HRMS and its Global Payroll component, IIPC was able to reduce the payroll cycle from 11 days to 4 days, and to reduce the run time from 6 hours to 2 hours, while eliminating errors. The system automates labor-intensive HR processes such as workforce administration, enabling HR staff to concentrate on staffing, training, career planning, rewards and promotions, and other nonclerical HR services. Furthermore, the data collected in the system are used by top management for strategic decisions. (*Source:* Smith, 2002.)

Critical response activities supported: improved cycle time, improved dissemination of information, automated clerical tasks, use by employees for self-service.

Mobile Banking at Handelsbanken of Sweden. Handelsbanken of Sweden is the largest bank in Scandinavia, where more than 70 percent of the population over 15 years old carry mobile phones. Operating in a very competitive banking environment, the bank is trying to meet customers' expectations of using their mobile phones to organize their personal and working lives while on the move. Mobile banking services, including stock trading, was an opportunity for the bank to gain a competitive edge, and so the bank become the world's first to have mobile banking applications.

An interactive service allows customers to access up-to-the-minute banking information, including the latest stock market and interest rate data, whenever and wherever they like. Handelsbanken's e-banking has become so popular that it is used by tens of thousands of customers. It opens up critical business and personal information to safe and easy access from mobile devices. Both the bank's financial advisors and its customers can access general and personalized stock market and account information, transfer money, request loans, buy and sell stocks and bonds, and pay bills. This move into mobile banking is a key first step in a strategy to exploit the potential of e-business, while also extending the bank's brand reach. (*Sources:* Compiled from IBM's case study: Handelsbanken at *www-3.ibm.com/e-business/doc/content/casestudy/35433.html,* accessed March, 1, 2003, and from press releases at *handelsbanken.com.*)

Critical response activities supported: improved customer service, innovative marketing methods.

In addition to functional areas, we can classify applications by the industry in which they are used. For example, retailing, financial services, education, health care, social services, and government are heavy users. An example of a government service is provided in Minicase 2 at the end of this chapter. An example from the health care field is included in Online File W1.8 at the book's Web site.

Information Systems Failures

Use of this icon indicates a discussion of an IT failure, and the lessons that can be learned from it.

So far we have introduced you to many success stories. You may wonder, though, is IT always successful? The answer is, "Absolutely not." There are many failures. We will show you some of these (marked with a "lessons from failures" icon) in this book, and in some cases we present them on our Web site. (See, for example, the 2000 U.S. Presidential Election Case in Online File W1.8 at the Web site.) We can learn from failures as much as we can learn from successes, as illustrated in *IT at Work 1.2* (page 24).

As mentioned earlier, one area of failure is that of the dot-coms. As will be seen in Chapter 5, hundreds of dot-coms folded in 2000 and 2001. It was a shakeout that resulted from a rush to capitalize on e-commerce (see Kaplan, 2002). In addition there were many failures of Internet projects in established companies. (For example, the Go.com project of Walt Disney Company was supposed to manage all the Web sites owned by Disney and generate money from advertisers at the sites. Unfortunately, the income generated from advertising was not sufficient to keep the site going.) Like the gold rush and the rush to create companies when the automobile was invented, only a

IT at Work 1.2
HOW NIKE'S $400 MILLION SUPPLY CHAIN MANAGEMENT SOFTWARE SYSTEM FAILED

In certain retail stores, fans of Nike's Air Terra Humara 2 running shoe have hit the jackpot. Once selling for over $100 US, they were selling for less than $50 in fall 2001. The cheaper shoes were the aftermath of the breakdown in Nike's supply chain, a breakdown attributed to a software problem.

Nike had installed a $400 million supply chain system in early 2001. The system was supposed to forecast sales demand and plan supplies of raw materials and finished products accordingly. However, the newly deployed demand and supply planning application apparently overestimated the demand for certain shoes in some locations and underestimated demand in others. As a result, some raw materials were overpurchased, while inventory levels of other materials were insufficient. Some shoes were overmanufactured, while the most-demanded ones were undermanufactured. To speed the right shoes to market, Nike had to spend around $5 a pair in air freight cost, compared to the usual cost of 75 cents by ocean shipping. In all, Nike attributed some $100 million in lost sales in the third quarter of 2001 alone to this problem.

What went wrong? The system was developed with software from i2, a major software producer. However, Nike insisted on modifying the i2 standard software, customizing it to its needs. Specifically, Nike wanted a forecast by style level (several hundred kinds), by color, and by size. This resulted in a need to make thousands of forecasts, very rapidly, to quickly respond to changing market conditions and consumer preferences. To meet Nike's need it was necessary to customize the standard software, and to do so quickly because Nike wanted the system fast. The reprogramming was apparently done *too* fast. The software had bugs in it when it was deployed. Almost any new software contains bugs that need to be fixed; appropriate testing is critical, and it is a time-consuming task (see Murphy, 2003). Nike and i2 failed to recognize what was achievable.

Customizing standard software requires a step-by-step systematic process (see Chapter 14). It should be done only when it is absolutely necessary, and it must be planned for properly. Furthermore, Nike could have discovered the problem early enough if they had used appropriate deployment procedures (see Chapter 14).

To avoid disasters such as the one Nike experienced, companies must fully understand what they are trying to achieve and why. They must use performance-level indicators to properly measure the system during testing. Incidentally, Nike fixed the problem after spending an undisclosed amount of time and money in 2002.

Sources: Compiled from Sterlicchi and Wales, 2001 and from *nike.com* press releases, 2002.

For Further Exploration: Why did Nike need the detailed forecasting? How can a company determine if it really needs to customize software? Whose responsibility is it to test and deploy the software: the software vendor's or the user's?

relatively few made it. The rest failed. According to Barva et al. (2001), the reason for EC failures is that many of the models used were too narrow. In place of these models, they offer an e-business value model, which we describe in Chapter 5.

Another reason for failure is that it is hard to predict the future. It is especially hard to predict the future in the field of information technology, which is evolving and continuously changing, as shown next.

1.4 INFORMATION TECHNOLOGY DEVELOPMENTS AND TRENDS

In the previous sections, we described the role of IT in supporting business activities. We also pointed out (in Table 1.1) some of the capabilities that enable IT to play a support role. Next we will describe some of IT's developments and trends (see Chandra et al., 2000), and especially the move toward Web-based computing, wireless applications, and intelligent systems.

First imagine this scenario: It's a Monday morning in the year 2006. Executive Joanne Smith gets into her car, and her voice activates a wireless telecommunications-access workstation. She requests that all voice and mail messages open and pending, as well as her schedule for the day, be transmitted to her car. The office workstation consolidates these items from home and office databases. The message-ordering "knowbot" (knowledge robot), which is an enhanced e-mail messaging system, delivers the accumulated messages (in the order she prefers) to the voice and data wireless device in Joanne's car. By the time Joanne gets to the office, she has heard the necessary messages, sent some replies, revised her day's schedule, and completed a to-do list for the week, all of which have been filed in her virtual database by her personal organizer knowbot. She has also accessed the Internet by voice and checked the traffic conditions, stock prices, and top news stories.

The virtual organizer and the company intranet have made Joanne's use of IT much easier. No longer does she have to be concerned about the physical location of data. She is working on a large proposal for the Acme Corporation today; and although segments of the Acme file physically exist on several databases, she can access the data from her *wireless workstation* wherever she happens to be. To help manage this information resource, Joanne uses an *information visualizer* that enables her to create and manage dynamic relationships among data collections. This information visualizer has extended the graphical user interface to a three-dimensional graphic structure.

Joanne could do even more work if her car were able to drive itself and if it were able to find an empty parking space on its own. Although this kind of car is still in an experimental stage, it will probably be in commercial use before 2015 due to developments in pervasive computing (see Chapter 6).

It may be possible for parts of this year-2006 scenario to become a reality even sooner, owing to important trends in information technology. For example, voice access to the Internet is already becoming popular (e.g., see *tellme.com* and *i3mobile.com*). These trends, which are listed in Table 1.2 (page 26), fall into two categories: general and networked computing. Here we describe only *selected* items from Table 1.2. The rest are described in the Technology Guides on the book's Web site.

Five Technology Guides at the book's Web site provide up-to-date presentations on hardware, software, databases, telecommunications, and the Internet.

General Technological Trends

General trends are relevant to any computing system. Two representative examples are discussed below. Additional trends are presented in Chapter 2 and in the online Technology Guides.

COST-PERFORMANCE RATIO OF CHIPS: IMPROVEMENT BY A FACTOR OF AT LEAST 100. In about 10 years, a computer will cost the same as it costs today but will be about 50 times more powerful (in terms of processing speed, memory, and so on). At the same time labor costs could double, so the cost-performance ratio of computers versus manual work will improve by a factor of 100. This means that computers will have increasingly greater comparative advantage over people in performing certain types of work. This phenomenon is based on a prediction made in 1965 by Gordon Moore, the co-founder of Intel. Popularly called **Moore's Law,** this prediction was that the processing power of silicon chips would double every 18 months. And so it has, resulting in enormous increases in computer processing capacity and a sharp decline in cost (see Chapter 13).

TABLE 1.2 Major Technological Developments and Trends

General Developments and Trends
- The cost-performance advantage of computers over manual labor will increase.
- Graphical and other user-friendly interfaces will dominate PCs.
- Storage capacity will increase dramatically.
- Data warehouses will store ever-increasing amounts of information.
- Multimedia use, including virtual reality, will increase significantly.
- Intelligent systems, especially artificial neural computing and expert systems, will increase in importance and be embedded in other systems.
- The use of intelligent agents will make computers "smarter."
- There is a push for open architecture (e.g., the use of Web services).
- Object-oriented programming and document management will be widely accepted.
- Artificial intelligence systems are moving to learning-management systems.
- Computers will be increasingly compact, and more portable.
- There is proliferation of embedded technologies (especially intelligent ones).
- The use of plug-and-play software will increase.

Networked Computing Developments and Trends
- Optical computing will increase network capacity and speed, facilitating the use of the Internet.
- Storage networks will become popular.
- Mobile and wireless applications will become a major component of IT.
- Home computing will be integrated with the telephone, television, and other electronic services to create smart appliances.
- The use of the Internet will grow, and it will change the way we live, work, and learn.
- Corporate portals will connect companies with their employees, business partners, and the public.
- Intranets will be the dominating network systems in most organizations.
- E-commerce over the Internet will grow rapidly, changing the manner in which business is conducted.
- Intelligent software agents will roam through databases and networks, conducting time-consuming tasks for their masters.
- Interpersonal transmission will grow (one-to-one, one-to-many, many-to-many).
- More transactions among organizations will be conducted electronically, in what is called business-to-business (B2B) commerce.

Moore's Law applies to electronic chips. An extension of Moore's Law, according to McGarvey (2000) and *tenornetworks.com*, states that the performance of optical communication networks (see Technology Guide 4) is growing by a factor of 10 every three years. For example, according to Donofrio (2001), IBM is working on a supercomputer that will run at a petaflop (10^{15}) operations per second—which is 500 times faster than the fastest supercomputer of 2002. Such a computer will tackle brain-related diseases (such as Alzheimer's and stroke). It is expected to reach a speed of 20 to 30 petaflops in 2010.

STORAGE. Whereas Moore's Law expresses computing speed, improvements in storage contribute to the cost-performance ratio in a similar way. Large storage capabilities are essential for advanced applications. There are several new devices and methods to increase storage (see Technology Guide 3). Of special interest are memory sticks that in 2003 were capable of storing 150 gigabytes in a device the size of a credit card.

OBJECT-ORIENTED ENVIRONMENT, COMPONENTS, AND WEB SERVICES. An *object-oriented environment* is an innovative way of programming and using computers that is significantly reducing the costs of building and maintaining information systems. **Object technology** enables the development of self-contained units of software that can be shared, purchased, and/or reused. These information assets can be used for various purposes within a single organization's information systems, or they can be used in a worldwide network of interorganizational information systems. This technology enables developers to assemble information systems rather than building them from scratch. This is a faster and cheaper process. This environment includes object-oriented programming, databases, and operating systems (Chandra et al., 2000). Object technology applications include component-based development and Web services, both of which are based in part on object-oriented technology (described in Chapter 14).

SELF-HEALING COMPUTERS. IBM Corp. is developing computers, called *self-healing computers,* that can take care of themselves. The first such computer (named eLiza), a supercomputer at the National Center for Atmosphere Research, was installed at Blue Sky. With 2 trillion calculations per second, this computer (which, incidentally, is the world's most powerful) has the ability to repair itself and keep running without human intervention. For details see Van (2003).

QUANTUM COMPUTING. Researchers are looking into using the basic quantum states of matter as a fundamental unit of computing. If successful, quantum computers will be hundreds of times faster than today's fastest supercomputers.

NANOTECHNOLOGY. Sometime in the future there will be superfast molecular computers. Built on a crystalline structure, these still-experimental computers will be very tiny so they could be woven into our clothing. They will require very little power, yet they will have huge storage capacities and be immune to computer viruses, crashes, and other glitches.

Networked and Distributed Computing

The technology of networked and distributed computing is emerging rapidly. This technology enables users to reach other users and to access databases anywhere in the organization and in any other place, using intranets and the Internet. The networks' power stems from what is called **Metcalfe's Law.** Robert Metcalfe, a pioneer of computer networks, claimed that the value of a network grows roughly in line with the square of the number of its users (or nodes). Thus, if you increase the number of users, say from 2 to 10, the network's value will change from 2^2 (4) to 10^2 (100), or 25 times more. With 350 million Internet users, the value is (350 million)^2, an astronomical number.

Kelly (1999), in what is called *kelly's Extension* of Metcalfe's Law, claims that the value of the Internet is actually much larger. The reason is that Metcalfe's Law of n^2 is based on the idea of the telephone network, where the connections are point-to-point. On the Internet we can make multiple simultaneous connections between groups of people. So, claims Kelly, the potential value of the Internet is n^n, which is obviously a much larger number.

Network-based technologies are some of the most exciting IT developments, which we will discuss throughout the text. Here we provide an overview of some representative network-based technologies.

THE INTERNET AND THE WEB. From about 50 million Internet users in 1997, there could be as many as 750 million by 2007 (*forrester.com,* 2002). The wireless devices that access the Internet and the integration of television and computers will allow the Internet to reach every home, business, school, and other organization. Then the **information superhighway** will be complete. This is a national fiber-optic-based network and wireless infrastructure that will connect all Internet users in a country, and will change the manner in which we live, learn, and work. Singapore is likely to be the first country to have such a national information superhighway completely installed. Maui, Hawaii, is the first community to have a wireless Internet all over the island.

INTRANETS AND EXTRANETS. Just as use of the Internet is becoming common, so too is the use of *intranets* ("internal networks") that connect the members within individual organizations. As the intranet concept spreads and the supporting hardware and software are standardized, it is logical to assume that most organizations will use an intranet for internal communication. In addition, combining an intranet with the Internet, in what is called an *extranet,* creates powerful interorganizational systems for communication and collaboration.

MOBILE COMPUTING AND M-COMMERCE. **M-commerce (mobile commerce)** refers to the conduct of e-commerce via wireless devices. It is the commercial application of **mobile computing,** which is computing using *mobile devices* and done primarily by *wireless networks* (see Chapter 6). There is a strong interest in the topic of mobile commerce because according to industry research firms the number of mobile devices, including cell phones, is expected to top 1.4 billion by 2004 (*cellular.co.za/stats/stat_main.htm*). Furthermore, these devices can be connected to the Internet, enabling transactions to be made from anywhere and enabling many applications (see Sadeh, 2002 and *A Closer Look 1.2*). For example, m-commerce can offer customers the location information of anything they want to purchase. This is a useful feature for customers, but it is even more important for merchants because it enables customers to act instantly on any shopping impulse. This wireless application is referred to as *location-based commerce,* or **l-commerce.** (For details, see Chapter 6.)

PERVASIVE COMPUTING. Strongly associated with m-commerce and wireless networks is **pervasive computing,** in which computation becomes part of the environment. The computer devices (personal computer, personal digital assistant, game player) through which we now relate to computation will occupy only a small niche in this new computational world. Our relationship to pervasive computing will differ radically from our current relationship with computers. In pervasive computing, computation will be embodied in many things, not in what we now know as computers (see Chapter 6).

Physical space rarely matters in current human-computer interaction; but as computational devices become part of furniture, walls, and clothing, physical space becomes a necessary consideration. Relentless progress in semiconductor technology, low-power design, and wireless technology will make embedded computation less and less obtrusive. Computation is ready to disappear into the environment.

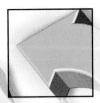

A CLOSER LOOK
1.2 MOBILE AND WIRELESS APPLICATIONS

Mobile computing supports existing and entirely new kinds of applications. For example:

● *Mobile personal communications capabilities*, such as personal digital assistants (PDAs) and cell phones for networked communications and applications.

● *Online transaction processing.* For example, a salesperson in a retail environment can enter an order for goods and also charge a customer's credit card to complete the transaction.

● *Remote database queries.* For example, a salesperson can use a mobile network connection to check an item's availability or the status of an order, directly from the customer's site.

● *Dispatching*, like air traffic control, rental car pickup and return, delivery vehicles, trains, taxis, cars, and trucks.

● *Front-line IT applications.* Instead of the same data being entered multiple times as they go through the value chain (the series of business activities that add value to a company's product or service), they are entered only once and transmitted electronically thereafter.

● *M-commerce.* Users of wireless devices can access the Internet, conduct information searches, collaborate with others and make decisions jointly, and buy and sell from anywhere.

Wireless communications support both mobile computing applications and low-cost substitutions for communication cables. For example:

● Temporary offices can be set up quickly and inexpensively by using wireless network connections.

● Wireless connections to permanent office locations are often practical in difficult or hazardous wiring environments.

● Installing a wireless connection can replace leased lines that are used to connect local area networks

(LANs), thus eliminating the costs of monthly line leases.

There are mobile and wireless application opportunities in many industries, such as:

● *Retail.* Retail applications have been very successful to date, particularly in department stores where there are frequent changes of layout. Also, retail sales personnel can conduct inventory inquiries or even sales transactions on the retail floor with wireless access from their PCs or cell phones.

● *Wholesale/distribution.* Wireless networking is used for inventory picking in warehouses with PCs mounted on forklifts, and for delivery and order status updates with PCs inside distribution trucks.

● *Field service/sales.* Mobile computing can be used for dispatching, online diagnostic support from customer sites, and parts-ordering/inventory queries in all types of service and sales functions.

● *Factories/manufacturing.* Environments and applications include mobile shop-floor quality control systems or wireless applications that give added flexibility for temporary setups.

● *Health care/hospitals.* Health care personnel can access and send data to patient records, or consult comparative diagnosis databases, wherever the patient or the health care worker may be located.

● *Education.* Pilot applications equip students with PCs in lecture halls, linked by a wireless network, for interactive quizzes, additional data and graphics lecture support, and online handout materials. (See Minicase 1 at the end of the chapter.)

● *Banking/finance.* Mobile transactional capabilities can assist in purchasing, selling, inquiry, brokerage, and other dealings, using the Internet or private networks.

We can already put computation almost anywhere. Embedded computation controls braking and acceleration in our cars, defines the capability of medical instruments, and runs virtually all machinery. Hand-held devices (especially cell phones and pagers) are commonplace; serious computational wristwatches and other wearables are becoming practical; computational furniture, clothes, and rooms are in the demonstration stage. Soon, **smart appliances,** which are home appliances that are connected to the Internet and among themselves for increased capabilities, will be integrated and managed in one unit. (See Chapter 6 for further discussion.)

At present, most large-scale applications of pervasive computing, such as intelligent cities, hospitals, or factories, are still under development. However, smaller-scale applications, such as the "intelligent restaurant" described in *IT at Work 1.3*, are already in place.

CORPORATE PORTALS.   A **corporate portal** refers to a company's Web site that is used as a *gateway* to the corporate data, information, and knowledge. Corporate portals may be used both by employees and by outsiders, such as customers or suppliers. (Employees have a password that allows them to access data through the portal that are not available to the public.) A variety of corporate portals provide a wide range of functionalities (see Chapter 4 for details).

THE NETWORKED ENTERPRISE.   The various components and technologies just described can be integrated together into an *enterprisewide network* that is a seamless system, extending the corporate contacts to all entities a company does business with. The networked enterprise provides two primary benefits: First, by creating new types of services, businesses can engage customers in a direct interactive relationship that results in customers getting precisely what they want when they want it, resulting in stronger customer relationships and better relationships with suppliers and other business partners. Second, by taking the entire product design process online—drawing partners and customers into the process and removing the traditional communication barriers that prevent rapid product design and creation—companies can bring products and services to market far more quickly.

The networked enterprise is shown schematically in Online File W1.9 at the book's Web site. As a result of the technology pressures discussed earlier, companies that implement standards-based intranets can quickly create or join extranets, as we discuss in Chapter 5.

THE NETWORK COMPUTER.   In 1997, the *network computer* was introduced. This computer does not have a hard drive. Instead, it is served by a central computing station. At a "dumb" (passive) terminal, it temporarily receives and can use applications and data stored elsewhere on the network. Also called "thin clients," network computers are designed to provide the benefits of desktop computing without the high cost of PCs. Prices of network computers are getting close to $200. A variation of the thin client is the **Simputer** or "simple computer" (see *simputer.org*).

OPTICAL NETWORKS.   A major revolution in network technology is *optical networks*. These are high-capacity telecommunication networks that convert signals in the network to colors of light and transmit these over fiber-optic filaments. Optical networks are useful in Internet, video, multimedia interaction, and advanced digital services. (For more, see Technology Guide 4.)

STORAGE NETWORKS.   **Network storage devices** are attached to the corporate network (usually intranets) and can be accessed from network applications throughout the enterprise. Their benefits are optimal data sharing, simplicity, scalability (ability to adapt to increased demands), and manageability.

IT at Work 1.3
PERVASIVE COMPUTING AT ROYAL MILE PUB

All of us are familiar with the service at restaurants, and most of us have encountered inconvenient scenarios such as long waits, cold food, or even service of a wrong order. These inconveniences are the result of a conventional process that works like this: A server takes your drink order and then walks to the bar to place the order. She or he knows that after approximately five minutes your drink will be ready, so in the meantime the server takes an order from someone else and then heads back to the bar. If your order is not ready, the server comes to your table, apologizes for the delay, and takes your food order. That order is written on a piece of paper, which the server carries to the kitchen and places on a revolving wheel, which the chef rotates into view when he or she is ready to begin preparing the next order. After 10 or 15 minutes, the server may find that the kitchen is out of this selection, so he or she comes to your table and asks you to reorder. Sometimes, the server makes a mistake in writing your order (or the chef reads the handwritten order incorrectly). In such a case, after a long wait, the customer is very frustrated at getting the wrong food. In the end, no one is happy.

But the situation is different at Royal Mile Pub (Silver Spring, Maryland), thanks to pervasive computing. The Royal Mile is a medium-size restaurant (about 20 tables), with a great bar, specializing in a wide selection of beverages. But what is really different about the Royal Mile is that the little green order pads have been replaced with iPaq PDAs connected to the kitchen using wireless networking.

The new system works as follows: The server uses a special PDA to take the orders. Most menu items are embedded in the device, which also has handwriting capabilities for writing in special instructions. It takes experienced servers about 15 minutes to be trained on how to use the devices. To take drink or food orders requires only one or two keystrokes. The server glances at the screen to verify that the correct item has appeared. Thanks to the Wi-Fi (wireless fidelity) system, which is a local area network that transmits the orders within the range of the restaurant (described further in Chapter 6), the orders appear immediately on screens in the kitchen and bar. After transmitting an order, the server can move to the next table rather than hurrying off to hand the orders to the cooks or bartenders. Servers now can spend more time on the floor with the customers, providing more selling opportunities.

The system is liked by all. Servers can spend more time with each customer and handle more tables because they make half as many trips out of the serving area, which enables pleasant customer relationships and higher tip income. The PDA interface tells servers which menu items are unavailable; getting that information immediately to the customers reduces servers' trips to the kitchen, thus eliminating another source of customer and server dissatisfaction. Because the kitchen becomes aware of orders immediately, the food arrives more quickly. The system also totals each bill, eliminating arithmetic errors.

The owner is very positive about the system's effects on his business. The order system costs about $30,000 to install. Its benefits include fewer errors, better inventory control, and smaller payrolls. As orders transmit, they are processed against the inventory database, allowing kitchen managers to track raw material purchases against the food orders and identify waste or other delivery and processing problems. Integration with the enterprise database and inventory control systems is fundamental to realizing cost reductions, improved workflow, and inventory and personnel management. The pervasive order system has reduced the error rate from several wrong meals per night to about one every two nights. Improvements occur not only in wasted (and replacement) meals, but also in customer satisfaction. In addition, now only three food servers are needed, meaning lasting cost reductions and lower overhead. Also, three data-entry stations on the serving floor for processing credit card charges were reduced to one, freeing up space on the serving floor.

Sources: Compiled from Stanford (2003), and *royalmilepub.com* (accessed March 2003).

For Further Exploration: Why would customers appreciate this pervasive computing system? If such a system is beneficial to all, why have not all restaurants adopted it? Why it is classified as pervasive computing?

Rather than handling their own server computers, many corporations are relying on outside outfits to manage their technology at remote data centers, which pipe data to their premises via the Web. According to Hamm (2001), this *piping technology* arrangement can cut a company's computing cost by 15 to 20 percent. Data centers are operated by a third party, such as application service providers (ASPs) (see Chapters 13 and 14). Major software vendors including IBM and SAP are in this business. For details on storage networks, see Technology Guide 3.

WEB SERVICES. By using universal prefabricated business process software, called **Web services,** computer users will soon be able to integrate applications, business processes, databases, and more into all kinds of applications, and do so rapidly and inexpensively. By using agreed-upon protocols and standards for the Web services, developers can create a truly open computing environment independent of any vendor or product. Web services will impact e-business application development, application integration, and application access. See Chapters 2, 4, 5, and 14 for details. Also see Clark et al. (2002).

All of these developments and prospects will increase the importance of IT both at home and at work. Therefore, it is obvious that to function effectively in the digital era, it makes sense to learn about IT.

1.5 WHY SHOULD YOU LEARN ABOUT INFORMATION TECHNOLOGY?

We have demonstrated in this chapter that we live in the digital economy, and that the ways we live and do business are changing dramatically. The field of IT is growing rapidly, especially with the introduction of the Internet and e-commerce, so the organizational impacts keep increasing. We are becoming more and more dependent on information systems. For example, on March 1, 2003, a computer glitch disturbed hundreds of flights in Japan.

In this part of the chapter we describe some specific benefits you can derive from studying IT.

Benefits from Studying IT

A major role of IT is being a *facilitator* of organizational activities and processes. That role will become more important as time passes. Therefore, it is necessary that every manager and professional staff member learn about IT not only in his or her specialized field, but also in the entire organization and in interorganizational settings as well.

Obviously, you will be more effective in your chosen career if you understand how successful information systems are built, used, and managed. You also will be more effective if you know how to recognize and avoid unsuccessful systems and failures. Also, in many ways, having a comfort level with information technology will enable you, off the job and in your private life, to take advantage of new IT products and systems as they are developed. (Wouldn't you rather be the one explaining to friends how some new product works, than the one asking about it? For help in that role, by the way, see *howthingswork.com.*) Finally, you should learn about IT because being knowledgeable about information technology can also increase employment opportunities. Even though computerization eliminates some jobs, it also creates many more.

The demand for traditional information technology staff—such as programmers, systems analysts, and designers—is substantial. In addition, many well-paid opportunities are appearing in emerging areas such as the Internet and e-commerce, m-commerce, network security, object-oriented programming, telecommunications, multimedia design, and document management. (See Online File W1.10 at the book's Web site for a listing of jobs in e-commerce.) The U.S. Department of Labor reported that among the 12 fastest-growing employment areas, four are IT-related. These four accounted in 2000 for about 50 percent of all additional jobs in the 12 areas. (In 2002, this declined to 35 percent, due to a technology slowdown related to the slow economy.) At about $60,000 per year, workers in the software and information services industries were the highest-paid U.S. wage earners in 2000, about twice that of the average worker in the private sector. Furthermore, earnings of IT employees were growing twice as fast as those in the entire private sector. Thus, salaries for IT employees are very high (see Online File W1.11).

To exploit the high-paying opportunities in IT, a college degree in any of the following fields, or combination of them, is advisable: computer science, computer information systems (CIS), management information systems (MIS), electronic commerce, and e-business. Within the last few years, many universities have started e-commerce or e-business degrees (e.g., see *is.cityu.edu.hk* and *cgu.edu*). Many schools offer graduate degrees with specialization in information technology.

Majoring in an IT-related field can be very rewarding. For example, students graduating with baccalaureate degrees in MIS usually earn the highest starting salaries of all undergraduate business majors (more than $45,000 per year). MBAs with experience in Web technologies and e-commerce are getting starting salaries of over $100,000/year, plus bonuses. Many students prefer a double major, one of which is MIS. Similarly, MBAs with an undergraduate degree in computer science have little difficulty getting well-paying jobs, even during recessionary times. Many MBA students select IS as a major, a second major, or an area of specialization. Finally, nondegree programs are also available on hundreds of topics. For details about careers in IT, see *techjourney.com* and also "Career resources" and "Technology careers" at *wageweb.com*.

Finally, another benefit from studying IT is that it may contribute to future organizational leadership. In the past, most CEOs came from the areas of finance and marketing. Lately, however, we see a trend to appoint CEOs who have strong IT knowledge and who emerge from the technology area. Because of the impact that IT is having on business, this trend is likely to continue. Therefore, IT education is necessary for anyone who aspires to lead a firm in the future.

1.6 PLAN OF THE BOOK

A major objective of this book is to demonstrate how IT in general and Web systems in particular support different organizational activities. In addition, we will illustrate the role that networked computing plays in our society today and will play tomorrow. Furthermore, we describe how information systems should be developed, maintained, and managed.

The book is divided into six parts. Figure 1.5 (page 34) shows how the chapters are positioned in each part and how the parts are connected. Notice that in the center of the figure are the five Technology Guides. These guides can be found on the book's Web site (*wiley.com/college/turban*).

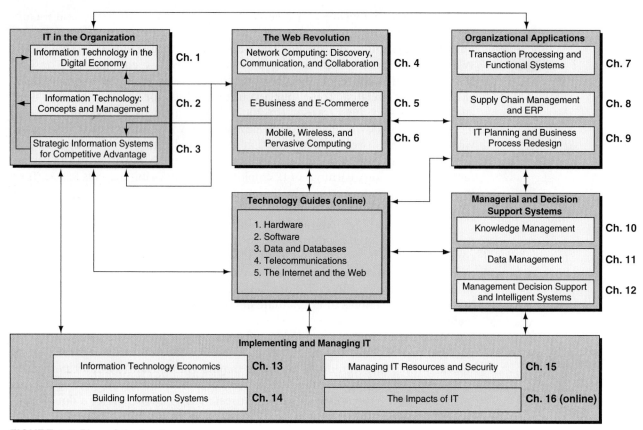

FIGURE 1.5 Plan of the book.

 ## MANAGERIAL ISSUES

At the end of every chapter, you will find a list of some of the special concerns managers face as they adapt technology to their organization's needs.

1. *Recognizing opportunities for using IT and Web-based systems.* These opportunities are highlighted and discussed in most chapters of the book, but especially in Chapters 3, 4, 5, 6, 7, 8, and 13.

2. *Who will build, operate, and maintain the information systems?* This is a critical issue because management wants to minimize the cost of IT while maximizing its benefits. Some alternatives are to outsource portions, or even all, of the IT activities, and to divide the remaining work between the IS department and the end users. Details are provided in Chapters 13 through 15.

3. *How much IT?* This is a critical issue related to IT planning. IT does not come free, but *not* having it may be much costlier. Chapters 9 and 13 deal with this issue.

4. *How important is IT?* In some cases, IT is the only approach that can help organizations. As time passes, the *comparative advantage* of IT increases.

5. *Is the situation going to change?* Yes, the pressures will be stronger as time passes. Therefore, the IT role will be even more important.

6. *Globalization.* Global competition will have an impact on many companies. However, globalization opens many opportunities, ranging from selling and buying products and services online in foreign markets, to conducting joint

ventures or investing in them. IT supports communications, collaboration, and discovery of information regarding all the above.

7. *Ethics and social issues.* The implementation of IT involves many ethical and social issues that are constantly changing due to new developments in technologies and environments. These topics should be examined any time an IT project is undertaken. Appendix 1A at the end of this chapter presents an introduction to ethics. Ethical issues are highlighted in most chapters throughout the book.

8. *Transforming the organization to the digital economy.* The transformation can be done on several fronts, as Siemens AG did. Management should study the opportunities, consider alternatives, and prioritize them. A prime area to start with is e-procurement (Chapters 5 and 8).

ON THE WEB SITE... Additional resources, including quizzes; online files of additional text, tables, figures, and cases; and frequently updated Web links to current articles and information can be found on the book's Web site (*wiley.com/college/turban*).

KEY TERMS

Build-to-order *17*

Business model *9*

Business pressures *11*

Business process reengineering (BPR) *16*

Computer-based information system (CBIS) *19*

Corporate portal *30*

Critical response activities *11*

Customer relationship management (CRM) *14*

Digital economy *4*

E-business *4*

Electronic commerce (EC) *4*

Ethics *15*

Extranet *4*

Information superhighway *28*

Information system (IS) *18*

Information technology (IT) *4*

Internet *4*

Intranet *4*

L-commerce *28*

Mass customization *17*

Metcalfe's Law *27*

M-commerce *28*

Mobile computing *28*

Moore's Law *25*

Network storage device *30*

Networked computing *4*

Object technology *27*

Pervasive computing *28*

Simputer *30*

Smart appliances *29*

Virtual corporation *17*

Web services *32*

CHAPTER HIGHLIGHTS (Numbers Refer to Learning Objectives)

1 The world is moving to a digital economy, which can be viewed as a major economic, societal, and organizational revolution. This revolution automates business processes by using the Internet, intranets, and extranets to connect organizations and people.

1 The digital economy is characterized by extensive use of information technology in general and the Internet in particular. These drive new business models that dramatically reduce cost and increase quality, customer service, and speed.

1 Companies are trying to transform themselves to e-businesses by converting their information systems to Web-based and by automating as many business processes as possible.

2 Many market, technology, and societal pressures surround the modern organization, which is responding with critical response activities supported by information technology.

3 An accelerated rate of technological change, complexity, and turbulence and a move toward a global economy today characterize the business environment. In addition, the competition faced by businesses is ever increasing.

③ Organizational responses include strategic information systems, continuous improvements, restructuring and business process reengineering, electronic commerce, and business alliances. IT plays a major role in all of these.

③ Organizations are adopting a customer-focused approach in order to succeed.

③ Organizations are changing their mode of operation by using IT-supported innovative approaches such as e-commerce, mass customization, CRM, and business alliances.

④ An information system collects, processes, stores, and disseminates information for a specific purpose. A computer-based information system uses computers to perform some or all of these activities.

④ Information technology refers to the network of all information systems in an organization.

⑤ Information technology is a major agent of change, supporting critical response activities in all functional areas, in all industries, and in both the private and the public sectors.

⑥ The major generic technological developments in IT are: increasing cost/performance, proliferation of object technology, and introduction of component-based development.

⑥ The major networked-computing developments are: increasing use of the Internet and intranets, mobile commerce, portals, optical networks, storage networks, and Web services.

⑦ Learning about IT is essential because the role of IT is rapidly increasing in the support of organizations. We are getting more dependent on IT as time passes. Also, more IT-related jobs with high salaries are available.

QUESTIONS FOR REVIEW

1. Define an information system and list its major components.
2. Define digital economy and list its major characteristics.
3. Define a business model by giving an example of one.
4. What are the major pressures in the business environment?
5. List the major critical response activities used by organizations.
6. Define information technology.
7. What is a virtual corporation?
8. Define mobile computing and m-commerce.
9. Define corporate portals.
10. Describe mass customization.
11. What are Moore's Law and Metcalfe's Law?
12. What is cycle-time reduction? Why is it so important?
13. Define Web services.
14. List the major capabilities of IT.
15. Define optical networks and network storage.
16. Describe a Simputer (simple computer).
17. Define the Internet, an intranet, and an extranet.
18. Define networked computing and networked organizations.

QUESTIONS FOR DISCUSSION

1. Discuss the motivation for becoming an e-business.
2. Review the examples of the new versus the old economy cases. In what way did IT make the difference?
3. Explain why IT is a business pressure and also an enabler of response activities that counter business pressures.
4. Why is m-commerce perceived as being able to increase EC applications?
5. Explain why the cost-performance ratio of IT will improve by a factor of 100, while performance is expected to improve only by a factor of 50.
6. Is IT a strategic weapon or a survival tool? Discuss.
7. It is said that networked computing changes the way we live, work, and study. Why?
8. Relate cycle-time reduction to improved financial and business performance.
9. Distinguish between network computers and networked computing.
10. Why is the Internet said to be the creator of new business models?
11. Explain why mass customization is desirable.
12. Discuss why some information systems fail.

EXERCISES

1. Review the examples of IT applications in Section 1.3, and identify the business pressures in each example.

2. The market for optical copiers is shrinking rapidly. It is expected that by 2005 as much as 85 percent of all duplicated documents will be done on computer printers. Can a company such as Xerox Corporation survive?
   a. Read about the problems and solution of Xerox in 2000–2003 at *fortune.com, findarticles.com,* and *google.com.*
   b. Identify all the business pressures on Xerox.
   c. Find some of Xerox's response strategies (see *xerox.com, fortune.com,* and *forbes.com*).
   d. Identify the role of IT as a contributor to the business technology pressures.
   e. Identify the role of IT as a facilitator of the critical response activities.

3. Reread the Siemans case at the start of the chapter and prepare a presentation to the CEO of a competing company. Stress both the benefits and the cost and limitations of such a transformation.

GROUP ASSIGNMENTS

1. Review the *Wall Street Journal, Fortune, Business Week,* and local newspapers of the last three months to find stories about the use of Web-based technologies in organizations. Each group will prepare a report describing five applications. The reports should emphasize the role of the Web and its benefit to the organizations. Cover issues discussed in this chapter, such as productivity, quality, cycle time, and globalization. One of the groups should concentrate on m-commerce and another on electronic marketplaces. Present and discuss your work.

2. Identify Web-related new business models in the areas of the group's interests. Identify radical changes in the operation of the functional areas (accounting, finance, marketing, etc.), and tell the others about them.

3. Enter *ecommerce.ncsu.edu/topics;* go to Net-centrism and read the latest "hungry minds" items there. Prepare a report regarding the latest in the digital age.

INTERNET EXERCISES

1. Enter the Web site of UPS (*ups.com*).
   a. Find out what information is available to customers before they send a package.
   b. Find out about the "package tracking" system; be specific.
   c. Compute the cost of delivering a 10" × 20" × 15" box, weighing 40 pounds, from your hometown to Long Beach, California. Compare the fastest delivery against the least cost.

2. Surf the Internet (use *google.com, brint.com,* or a similar engine) to find information about:
   a. International virtual corporations (at least two examples).
   b. Virtual corporations in general.

3. Enter *digitalenterprise.org.* Prepare a report regarding the latest EC developments in the digital age.

4. Visit some Web sites that offer employment opportunities in IT (such as *execunet.com* and *monster.com*). Compare the IT salaries to salaries offered to accountants. For other information on IT salaries, check *Computerworld's* annual salary survey and *techjourney.com.*

5. Prepare a short report on the role of information technology in government. Start with *whitehouse.gov/omb/egov/ 2003egov-strat.pdf, ctg.albany.edu, e-government.govt.nz,* and *worldbank.org/publicsector/egov.* Find e-government plans in Hong Kong and in Singapore (*cca.gov.sg;* check action plan).

6. Enter *x-home.com* and find information about the easy life of the future.

7. Enter *tellme.com* and *i3mobile.com.* Observe the demos. Write a report on the benefits of such technologies.

8. Experience customization by designing your own shoes at *nike.com,* your car at *jaguar.com,* your CD at *musicmaker.com,* and your business card at *iprint.com.* Summarize your experiences.

9. Enter *dell.com* and configure the computer of your dreams. (You do not have to buy it.) What are the advantages of such configuration?

Minicase 1
Dartmouth College Goes Wireless

Dartmouth College, one of the oldest in the United States (founded in 1769), was one of the first to embrace the wireless revolution. Operating and maintaining a campuswide information system with wires is very difficult, since there are 161 buildings with more than 1,000 rooms on campus. In 2000, the college introduced a campuswide wireless network that includes more than 500 Wi-Fi (wireless fidelity; see Chapter 6) systems. By the end of 2002, the entire campus became a fully wireless, always-connected community—a microcosm that provides a peek at what neighborhood and organizational life may look like for the general population in just a few years.

To transform a wired campus to a wireless one requires lots of money. A computer science professor who initiated the idea at Dartmouth in 1999 decided to solicit the help of alumni working at Cisco Systems. These alumni arranged for a donation of the initial system, and Cisco then provided more equipment at a discount. (Cisco and other companies now make similar donations to many colleges and universities, writing off the difference between the retail and the discount prices for an income tax benefit.)

As a pioneer in campuswide wireless, Dartmouth has made many innovative usages of the system, some of which are the following:

- Students are developing new applications for the Wi-Fi. For example, one student has applied for a patent on a personal-security device that pinpoints the location of campus emergency services to one's mobile device.
- Students no longer have to remember campus phone numbers, as their mobile devices have all the numbers and can be accessed anywhere on campus.
- Students primarily use laptop computers on the network. However, an increasing number of Internet-enabled PDAs and cell phones are used as well. The use of regular cell phones is on the decline on campus.
- An extensive messaging system is used by the students, who send SMSs (Short Message Services) to each other. Messages reach the recipients in a split second, any time, anywhere, as long as they are sent and received within the network's coverage area.
- Usage of the Wi-Fi system is not confined just to messages. Students can submit their classwork by using the network, as well as watch streaming video and listen to Internet radio.

- An analysis of wireless traffic on campus showed how the new network is changing and shaping campus behavior patterns. For example, students log on in short bursts, about 16 minutes at a time, probably checking their messages. They tend to plant themselves in a few favorite spots (dorms, TV room, student center, and on a shaded bench on the green) where they use their computers, and they rarely connect beyond those places.
- The students invented special complex wireless games that they play online.
- One student has written some code that calculates how far away a networked PDA user is from his or her next appointment, and then automatically adjusts the PDA's reminder alarm schedule accordingly.
- Professors are using wireless-based teaching methods. For example, students armed with Handspring Visor PDAs, equipped with Internet access cards, can evaluate material presented in class and can vote on a multiple-choice questionnaire relating to the presented material. Tabulated results are shown in seconds, promoting discussions. According to faculty, the system "makes students want to give answers," thus significantly increasing participation.
- Faculty and students developed a special voice-over-IP application for PDAs and iPAQs that uses live two-way voice-over-IP chat.

Sources: Compiled from McHugh (2002) and from *dartmouth.edu* (March 2003).

Questions for Minicase 1

1. In what ways is the Wi-Fi technology changing the life of Dartmouth students?
2. Some say that the wireless system will become part of the background of everybody's life—that the mobile devices are just an afterthought. Explain.
3. Is the system contributing to improved learning, or just adding entertainment that may reduce the time available for studying? Debate your point of view with students who hold a different opinion.
4. What are the major benefits of the wireless system over the previous wireline one? Do you think wireline systems will disappear from campuses one day? (Do some research on the topic.)

Minicase 2
Voice-Based 511 Traveler Information Line

Tellme Networks, Inc. (*tellme.com*) developed the first voice-activated 511 traveler information line in Utah, setting a national example for future 511 services to be launched by Department of Transportation (DOT) agencies on a state-by-state basis in the United States. The 511 application is a special case of voice portals (see Chapters 4 and 6), in which one can access the Web from any telephone by voice.

In July 2000, the U.S. Federal Communications Commission officially allocated 511 as the single nationwide number for traveler information, in the same way callers can dial 411 for directory assistance and 911 for emergency services. Previously, state governments and local transportation agencies used more than 300 local telephone numbers nationwide to provide traffic and traveler information. This marked the first time one number had been accessible for people to access travel information from anywhere, at any time.

The 511 service debuted on December 18, 2001. Simply by using their voices, callers on regular or cell phones within the state of Utah were able to request and get real-time information on traffic, road conditions, public transportation, etc. The answers are generated from the Internet and participating databases. The Utah 511 travel information line is provided as a free service by the Utah DOT.

During February 2002 Olympic Winter Games, callers were able to request event schedules, driving directions, up-to-the-minute news and announcements, and tips for avoiding traffic congestion. Martin Knopp, Director of Intelligent Transportation Systems, Utah DOT, said, "As the national 511 working group has stipulated, voice recognition is the way for callers to access information on 511, and it was important for us to be the first state to provide this capability. In addition, there was no up-front capital cost, and we were able to leverage the same information and investment we had made in our regular Web infrastructure" (quoted at *tellme.com*, accessed May 2002).

Tellme Networks is revolutionizing how people and businesses use the telephone by fundamentally improving the caller experience with Internet and voice technologies. Tellme enables businesses and governments to delight and empower their callers while slashing costs and complexity. "The phone is the ideal medium to make government services available and accessible to the general public," said Greg O'Connell, Director of Public Sector Operations at Tellme. "511 is a new wave in public information access" (quoted at *tellme.com*).

Source: Condensed from *tellme.com* (accessed May 5, 2002).

Questions for Minicase 2

1. Enter *tellme.com* and find more information about this case. Summarize the benefits to the users.
2. What is the role of *tellme.com*? What Internet technology is used?
3. Can this application be classified as m-commerce? As l-commerce? Why or why not?

Virtual Company Assignment
Starting Your Internship

Your diligence, coupled with your major advisor's connections, have landed you a summer internship with The Wireless Café (TWC). Your initial interview with Barbara Hopkins, co-owner of The Wireless Café, has piqued your interest in restaurant operations, and you are now on your way to meet Barbara's husband and co-owner Jeremy Hopkins, the office manager and accountant with whom you will be working closely.

Jeremy has created a Web site for The Wireless Café with information on the restaurant, its cuisine, and its operations. It can be accessed at *http://www.wiley.com/college/turban*.

Instructions

1. To better prepare yourself for your initial meeting with Barbara and Jeremy, visit the Web site and answer the following questions:
   a. What kind of restaurant is The Wireless Café?
   b. What types of special events does The Wireless Café feature?
   c. What is the organizational structure of The Wireless Café?
   d. Who are the cooks?
   e. Has The Wireless Café won any culinary awards?
   f. Are there currently any job openings at The Wireless Café?
   g. To what professional organizations does The Wireless Café belong? What are the benefits of belonging to these organizations?
   h. How would you contact The Wireless Café?
   i. What kind of intranet does The Wireless Café provide its employees?

2. What technology pressures does the The Wireless Café face?

3. What market and societal pressures are unique to the hospitality industry in general and to The Wireless Café in particular?

REFERENCES

Aberdeen.com, "Siemens' Private Marketplace Turns Procurement into Profit Center," Aberdeen Group Report, *aberdeen.com/2001/research/04012501.asp*. Boston, April 2001 (accessed September 18, 2002).

Afuah, A., and C. L. Tucci, *Internet Business Models and Strategies*, 2nd ed. New York: McGraw Hill, 2003.

Amit, R., and C. Zott, "Value Creation in E-Business," *Strategic Management Journal*, 22(6), 2001.

Anderson, D., *Build-to-Order and Mass Customization*. Los Angeles, CA: CIM Press, 2002.

Applegate, L. M., "E-Business Models: Making Sense of the Internet Business Landscape," in G. W. Dickson and G. DeSanctis, *Information Technology and the Future Enterprise: New Models for Managers*. Upper Saddle River, NJ: Prentice-Hall, 2001.

Barva A., et al., "Driving Business Excellence," *MIT Sloan Management Review*, Fall 2001.

Boyett, J. H., and J. T. Boyett, *Beyond Workplace 2000: Essential Strategies for the New American Corporation*. New York: Dutton, 1995.

Brue, G., *Six Sigma for Managers*. New York: McGraw-Hill, 2002.

Brynolfsson, E., and B. Kahin (eds.), *Understanding Digital Economy*. Cambridge: MIT Press, 2001.

Callon, J. D., *Competitive Advantage Through Information Technology*. New York: McGraw-Hill, 1996.

Campusfood.com (accessed January 2003).

Carr, N. G. (ed.), *The Digital Enterprise*. Boston: Harvard Business School Press, 2001.

Chandra, J., et al., "Information Systems Frontiers," *Communications of the ACM*, January 2000.

Choi, S. Y., and A. B. Whinston, *The Internet Economy: Technology and Practice*. Austin, TX: Smartecon.com pub, 2000.

Clark M., et al., *Web Services: Business Strategies and Architectures*. South Bend, IN: Expert Press, 2002.

Dartmouth.edu (accessed March 2003).

Davis, B., *Speed Is Life*. New York: Doubleday, 2001.

Dickson, G. W., and G. DeSanctis, *Information Technology and the Future Enterprise: New Models for Managers*. Upper Saddle River, NJ: Prentice-Hall, 2001.

Donofrio, N., "Technology Innovation for a New Era," *Computing & Control Engineering Journal*, June 2001.

Drucker, D. F., "The Next Society," *The Economist*, November 3, 2001.

Drucker, P., *Managing in the Next Society*. New York: Truman Talley Books, 2002.

Earl M., and B. Khan, "E-Commerce Is Changing the Face of IT," *MIT Sloan Management Review*, Fall, 2001.

El-Sawy, O., *Redesigning Enterprise Processes for E-Business*. New York: McGraw-Hill, 2001.

Evans, P. B., and T. S. Wurster, *Blown to Bits: How the New Economics of Information Transforms Strategy*. Boston: Harvard Business School Press, 2000.

Freeman, C., and F. Louca, *As Time Goes By: From Industrial Revolution to Information Revolution*. Oxford: Oxford University Press, 2001.

Galliers, D. E., et al., *Strategic Information Management*. Oxford, U. K.: Butterworth-Heinemann, 1999.

Gates, H. B., *Business @ the Speed of Thought*. New York: Penguin Books, 1999.

Greenberg, P., *CRM at the Speed of Light: Capturing and Keeping Customers in Internet Real Time*, 2nd ed. New York: McGraw-Hill, 2002.

Hammer, M., and J. Champy, *Reengineering the Corporation*. New York: Harper Business, 1993.

"Handelsbanken," IBM Case Study, *www-3.ibm.com/e-business/doc/content/casestudy/35433.html*. Accessed March 10, 2002.

Handelsbanken.com (accessed March 2002).

Helmstetter, G., and P. Metivier, *Affiliate Selling: Building Revenue on the Web*. New York: Wiley, 2000.

Hoffman, D. L., and T. P. Novak, "How to Acquire Customers on the Web," *Harvard Business Review*, May–June 2000.

Kaplan, P. J., *F'D Companies: Spectacular Dot.com Flameouts*. New York: Simon & Schuster, 2002.

Lederer, A. D., et al., "The Search for Strategic Advantage from the World Wide Web," *International Journal of Electronic Commerce*, 5(4), Summer 2001.

Lederer. A. L., et al., "Using Web-based Information Systems to Enhance Competitiveness," *Communications of the ACM*, July 1998.

LeSaunda.com (accessed January 2003).

McCleanahen, J., "The Book on the One-Day Close," *industryweek. com*, April 2002, pp. 31–33.

McGarvey, J., "Net Gear Breaks Moore's Law," *Interactive Week*, April 17, 2000.

Mevedoth, R., "From Rocks to Riches," *Forbes Global*, September 2, 2002.

Moss-Kanter, R., "You Are Here," *INC.*, February 2001.

Murphy, V., "The Exterminator," *Forbes Global*, May 26, 2003.

"New York City Transit Tokens May Take a Hike," Associated Press, January 27, 2003.

Nike.com (accessed January 2003).

Pine, J., II, and J. H. Gilmore, *The Experience Economy*. Boston: Harvard Business School Press, 1999.

Pitt, L. F., et al., "The Internet and the Birth of Real Consumer Power," *Business Horizons*, July–August, 2002.

Prince, M., "Easy Doesn't Do It," *Wall Street Journal*, July 17, 2002.

Sadeh, N., *Mobile Commerce: New Technologies, Services and Business Models*. New York: Wiley, April 2002.

Schultz, G., "Siemens: 100% e-Business," *APICS*, April 2002, pp. 32–25.

Seattle.mariners.mlb.com (accessed January 2003).

Slywotzky, A. J., and D. J. Morrison, *How Digital Is Your Business?* London: Nicholas Brealy, 2001.

Smith K., "IIPC: Vision to See, Faith to Believe, Courage to Do," *People Talk*, September–December, 2002.

Stanford V., "Pervasive Computing Puts Food on the Table," *Pervasive Computing*, January 2003.

Sterlicchi, J., and E.Wales, "Custom Chaos: How Nike Just Did It Wrong," *Business Online* (BolWeb.com), June 2001.

Tapscott, D., et al., *Digital Capital*. Boston: Harvard Business School Press, 2000.

Thaigem.com (accessed March 2003).

Tellme.com (accessed May 2002).

Turban, E., et al., *Electronic Commerce 2004*. Upper Saddle River, NJ: Prentice Hall, 2004.

Van, J., "Self-Healing Computers Seen as Better Fix," *Chicago Tribune*, March 24, 2003.

Walker, C., "World-First Technology Launched at Sydney International Airport," Western Australia E-Commerce Centre, February 4, 2003.

Weill, P., and M. R. Vitale, *Place to Space: Migrating to eBusiness Models*. Boston: Harvard Business School Press, 2001.

Wetherbe, J. C., *The World on Time*. Santa Monica, CA: Knowledge Exchange, 1996.

Wreden, N., "Business-Boosting Technologies," *Beyond Computing*, November–December 1997.

CHAPTER 1 APPENDIX

ETHICS IN INFORMATION TECHNOLOGY MANAGEMENT*

 Ethics is a branch of philosophy that deals with the analysis of decisions and actions with respect to their appropriateness in a given social context. Historical antecedents include the Bible's Ten Commandments, as well as elements of the philosophy of Confucius and Aristotle. As a discipline of study and practice, ethics applies to many different issues in information technology and information systems—and correspondingly, to many different people in industry and academia (managers, teachers, and students), in both the private and public sectors.

Ethics has been defined as involving the systematic application of moral rules, standards, and principles to concrete problems (Lewis, 1985). Some people believe that an ethical dilemma emerges whenever a decision or an action has the potential to impair or enhance the well-being of an individual or a group of people. Such dilemmas occur frequently, with many conflicts of interest present in the information society. A variety of sets of ethical guidelines have been devised. But we must emphasize: What is unethical may not necessarily be illegal, and what is legal may not necessarily be ethical. Furthermore, whether an action or decision is considered ethical will depend on many contributing factors, including those of the social and cultural environment in which the decision is made and the action is implemented.

Some General Ethical Principles

Many different ethical principles have been developed throughout human history. Each of us needs to make an individual choice about which principles to follow. Nevertheless, it is useful to consider a selection of some well-known and widely accepted ethical principles here.

- *The Golden Rule.* A widely applied general ethical principle, which has versions in the Bible as well as in Confucian philosophy, is known as the *Golden Rule*. It generally reads like this: "In everything that you do, treat other people in the same way that you would like them to treat

you." If you put yourself in the shoes of other people, and consider how you would feel if you were the object of a particular decision, then you should develop a good understanding of whether a decision is a good or fair one.

- *The Categorical Imperative.* "If an action is not suitable for everyone to take, then it is not suitable for anyone." This is Immanuel Kant's *categorical imperative.* If everyone undertook some action, what would be the consequence? Could society survive?

- *The Slippery Slope Rule.* "If an action can be repeated over and over again with no negative consequences, then no problem. But if such a repeated action would lead to disastrous consequences, then the action should not be undertaken even once." This is the *slippery slope rule.* Once you start down a slippery slope, you may not be able to stop before it is too late.

- *The Utilitarian Rule.* "The best action is the one that provides the most good for the most people." This is a form of *utilitarian rule.* It assumes that you are able to rank the various competing actions. Another version of the utilitarian rule can read as follows: "The best action is the one that leads to the least harm or costs the least." For example, this rule might be used to answer the question, Should one build an airport in the middle of a crowded neighborhood—or away from people?

- *No Free Lunch.* Every object (tangible or intangible) has an owner. If you want to use it, you should compensate the owner for doing so. This is akin to the idea that there is *no free lunch*—everything has a price.

These ethical principles are very general in nature. In putting ethics into practice, there are always exceptions and conflicts, so-called "ethical dilemmas."

Ethical Dilemmas

To illustrate the nature of an ethical dilemma, consider the following questions that relate to the copying/selling/distribution of software:

- Is it acceptable to buy a software product, and then to install it twice?

---

*This appendix was contributed by Robert Davison, Dept. of Information Systems, City University of Hong Kong.

- How about if you install it, then give it to a friend for personal use?
- Alternatively, what if you install it and use a CD writer to create 100 copies—and sell them for profit to anyone who wishes to buy?
- What about making the software available on a Web site for others to download?
- What about trading software on the Web (consumer to consumer)?

You may be surprised to discover that there are no "correct" answers to these questions. Legally, it depends on the jurisdiction where you live and work. Ethically, it depends on the specific cultural and social circumstances of the environment in which you live and work.

The wide application of IT and the pervasive nature of the Internet have created many opportunities for activities that some people may judge to be unethical. Here are some more sample dilemmas from a selection of application areas:

1. Does a company have the *right* to read its employees' e-mail?
2. Does a company have the *right* to monitor the Web sites that its employees visit from company computers?
3. Does an employee have the *duty* to the owners (stockholders) to use company resources only for company purposes/business?
4. Does an employee have the *duty* to report the misuse of company resources?
5. Does an individual have the *right* to data privacy?
6. Does an individual have the *duty* to ensure that personal data held about him or her is at all times accurate and up-to-date?
7. Does a software developer have the *right* to use disclaimers to minimize or eliminate responsibility for software failures?
8. Does an end-user have the *duty* to respect the intellectual property vested in a product—by not decompiling and modifying it, even if the purpose is to improve the product?
9. Does a data subject (e.g., member of the public) have the *right* to access and to correct data records held by government agencies and departments (e.g., police, anticorruption agencies, taxing agencies)?

10. Does a data user (e.g., the government) have the *duty* to ensure that it responds promptly to data subjects' requests for access to that data?

From this selection of questions, two key issues emerge:

1. The fact that rights must be balanced by duties.
2. The lack of concrete "correct" answers, due to legal and ethical differences in different societies.

The appropriate relationship between rights and duties is clearly critical. Any understanding of this relationship will be informed by social and cultural circumstances. For example, the concept of individual privacy is more developed in Europe and in North America than in Southeast Asia, where current cultural (and political) systems favor the benefits to society rather than the individual. Similarly, privacy laws are far more developed in some jurisdictions (Canada, Sweden, the United Kingdom, Hong Kong) than in others (China, Mexico).

IT Ethical Issues

Issues that are generally considered to fall under the umbrella of information technology ethics are the following:

- Codes of ethics
- Intellectual property rights (primarily digital property, such as software, films and music, but also trademarks, patents, blueprints, and books)
- Accountability (for actions or nonactions)
- Personal and data privacy (including "dataveillance," electronic monitoring, and data accuracy and accessibility)
- Freedom of speech versus censorship
- Ownership of information

We'll explore some of these issues in the sections that follow in this appendix, and throughout the book. For further information about ethical issues relating to information systems and IT, see the list of Web sites in Table 1A.1 (page 44).

Codes of Ethics

Codes of ethics involve the formalizing of some rules and expected actions. Violation of a code of ethics may lead to suspension of membership or termination of employment. In some professions such as law and medicine, membership in a professional society is a precondition of the right to practice, though this

TABLE 1A.1 URLs of Relevance to the IS/IT Ethics Debate

Organization/Ethical Concern	Address of Related Web Site
Centre for Professional and Applied Ethics	*valdosta.edu/cpae/*
Questions and answers on professional ethics	*members.aol.com/InternetEthics/*
Ethical principles in university teaching	*umanitoba.ca/academic_support/uts/stlhe/Ethical.html*
Ethical issues in the preparation and submission of research papers	*anu.edu.au/people/Roger.Clarke/SOS/ResPubEth.html*
Is IT Ethical? 1998 Ethicomp survey of professional practice	*ccsr.cms.dmu.ac.uk/resources/general/ethical/Ecv9no1.html*
European Group on Ethics in Science and New Technologies	*europa.eu.int/comm/secretariat_general/sgc/ethics/en/index.htm*
Centre for Computing and Social Responsibility	*ccsr.cms.dmu.ac.uk/*
Electronic Privacy Information Centre	*epic.org/*
The World Intellectual Property Association	*wipo.org/*
Software Piracy in Hong Kong and China—a study	*info.gov.hk/ipd/piracy.html*

is generally not the case with information systems. Codes of ethics are valuable for raising awareness of ethical issues and clarifying what is acceptable behavior in a variety of circumstances.

Codes of ethics have limitations, however, because of their natural tendency to generalize acceptable behavior—despite the variations in social and ethical values that exist in different communities. Certainly it would be arrogant to impose on people in Brazil the ethical standards developed in and appropriate for Norway, or indeed to do the reverse. Such impositions are unfortunately commonplace, and they tend to lead to outright rejection (rather than to higher ethical standards, which may be the intent).

Nevertheless, a comparison of codes of ethics for the computing profession will reveal a perhaps remarkable degree of similarity. For a list of various computing organizations and the Web sites where their codes of ethics can be found, see Table 1A.2.

Intellectual Property Rights

Intellectual property is the intangible property created by individuals or organizations. To varying degrees in different countries, intellectual property is protected under laws relating to copyright, patents, trademarks, and trade secrets. The copying of software is generally seen to be of greatest concern—at least to the software developers.

Why is the topic of *intellectual property rights (IPR)* so important? One critical reason relates to the fundamental right to private property—especially property that represents the fruit of one's endeavors (see Locke, 1964). IPR protects the way in which the ideas are expressed, but not the ideas themselves. IPR may be seen

as a mechanism for protecting the creative works of individual people and organizations. Yet this is problematic in societies that place less value on individual freedom and more on social order. In many developing countries, "individual claims on intellectual property are subordinated to more fundamental claims of social well-being" (Steidlmeier, 1993). In these countries, the welfare of society is considered to be more important than that of any individual.

Much of the discussion about IPR relates to the debate about rights and duties. Software developers demand the right of stringent legal protection for the fruits of their endeavors and compensation for resources expended in software development. Consumers are then deemed to have a duty to pay for

TABLE 1A.2 Representative Computing Organizations Worldwide and Their Web Sites

Organization	Address of Web Site
Association for Computing Machinery	*acm.org/*
Australian Computer Society	*acs.org.au/*
British Computer Society	*bcs.org.uk/*
Canadian Information Processing Society	*cips.ca/*
Computer Society of South Africa	*cssa.org.za/*
Hong Kong Computer Society	*hkcs.org.hk/*
Institute of Electrical and Electronics Engineers	*ieee.org/*
Singapore Computer Society	*scs.org.sg/*

that software and to respect the intellectual property, by not stealing (copying) it. Nevertheless, consumers may equally claim that the product they purchase should be free of defects (bugs), thus imposing a duty of quality (and professionalism) on software developers to ensure that a product is indeed bug-free and thus "fit for use."

Accountability

Accountability is an issue closely tied to many codes of conduct. In general, *accountability* refers to the acknowledgment that a person (or group of people) takes responsibility for a decision or action, is prepared to justify that decision/action, and if necessary to give compensation to affected parties if the decision/action causes negative effects, whether intended or otherwise. As the British Computer Society (2000) code states, "Members shall accept professional responsibility for their work."

Accountability is important "because it shows that high-quality work is valued, encourages people to be diligent in their work, and provides foundations for punishment/compensation when, for example, software does not perform according to expectations or professional advice turns out to be unreliable" (Davison, 2000). It is important that we identify who should be accountable for a decision or action because computers and information systems are widely used in our society, and so the potential for disasters caused by poor-quality work is always present.

Although accountability is a valuable concept, its value may be diminished in a number of ways. It is common, for example, for computers to be made scapegoats for human failings. If you call your travel agent and ask to book an airplane ticket, and the travel agent says, "Sorry, the computer is down," then the computer is being blamed. Perhaps the computer really is down, or perhaps the agent is too busy or can't be bothered to serve you. And if the computer is down, why is it down? Has a human action caused it to be down? Is it a design flaw, a software bug, a problem of installation or of maintenance? Of course, we never know the answers to these questions. But this means that it is all too easy to blame the computer, perhaps apologize, and then claim that nothing can be done. All of these actions tend to help people to avoid being accountable for their actions and work.

It is also common, unfortunately, for software developers to deny responsibility for the consequences of software use—even when this use has been in accordance with the purpose for which the software was designed. Software developers assert that they are selling the right to use a software product, not ownership of the product itself. In parallel, developers employ legal disclaimers to reduce as far as they possibly can any liability arising out of a customer's use of the software. At the same time, customers may use the software only in a manner defined by the tight restrictions of a software usage license. In this way, the rights of the user are severely eroded, whereas those of the developers are maximized. If the software has design flaws (bugs) that cause negative consequences for users, users are not permitted to fix those bugs themselves. Nor, it appears, are developers bound by any duty to fix them, let alone compensate users for the inconvenience suffered or damage caused by those bugs.

Data and Information Privacy

In general, *privacy* can be defined as the right to be left alone (Warren and Brandeis, 1890). The notion of privacy has become one of the most contentious issues of the information age, due to the capability of computers to perform actions previously impossible or impractical. Agranoff (1993) defines *information (data) privacy* as the "claim of individuals, groups, or institutions to determine for themselves when, and to what extent, information about them is communicated to others."

Nevertheless, the right to privacy is not absolute. It varies considerably in different cultures, as it has to be balanced by society's right to know. After 9/11/2001, for example, there was a major change in the United States in people's attitude toward privacy. The majority of people who previously objected to government surveillance of private citizens agreed that it should be done as part of the war on terrorism.

One of the most detailed sets of data-privacy principles to emerge in the last few years has come from the Privacy Commissioner's Office (PCO) in Hong Kong. These principles, and the legislative measures that underwrite them, were created in the mid-1990s and officially promulgated in December 1996. A summary of the six data-protection principles appears in *A Closer Look 1A.1*. These principles are designed to enshrine the reasonable rights and duties of both the data subject (the person described by the data) and data users (those who possess data).

A CLOSER LOOK
1A.1 SIX PRINCIPLES OF THE DATA PRIVACY ORDINANCE (HONG KONG)

1. *Purpose and manner of collection.* Data should be collected in a fair and lawful manner. Data users should explain to data subjects what data is being collected and how it will be used.

2. *Accuracy and duration of retention.* Personal data that has been collected should be kept accurate, up-to-date, and for no longer than is necessary.

3. *Use.* Data must be used only for the specific or directly related purpose for which it was collected. Any other use is conditional on consent of the data subject.

4. *Security.* Suitable security measures should be applied to personal data.

5. *Information availability.* Data users should be open about the kind of data that they store and what they use it for.

6. *Access.* Data subjects have the right to access their personal data, to verify its accuracy, and to request correction.

Source: Privacy Commissioner's Office (PCO), Hong Kong. More detailed information can be obtained at the Web site of the PCO: *pco.org.hk.*

References for Chapter 1 Appendix

Agranoff, M. H., "Controlling the Threat to Personal Privacy," *Journal of Information Systems Management,* Summer 1993.

British Computer Society, "British Computer Society Code of Conduct," *bcs.org.uk/aboutbcs/coc.htm,* 2000. Accessed November 2, 2000.

Davison, R. M., "Professional Ethics in Information Systems: A Personal View," *Communications of the AIS,* 3(8), 2000.

Lewis, P. V., "Defining Business Ethics: Like Nailing Jello to the Wall," *Journal of Business Ethics,* 4(5), 1985, pp. 377–383.

Locke, J., *Second Treatise of Civil Government.* New York: Bobbs-Merrill, 1964.

Steidlmeier, P., "The Moral Legitimacy of Intellectual Property Claims: American Business and Developing Country Perspectives," *Journal of Business Ethics,* 12(2), 1993, pp. 157–164.

Warren, S. D., and L. D. Brandeis, "The Right to Privacy," *Harvard Law Review,* 193, 1890, pp. 193–220.

PART I
IT in the Organization

1. Information Technology in the Digital Economy
▶ 2. Information Technologies: Concepts and Management
3. Strategic Information Systems for Competitive Advantage

CHAPTER

2

Information Technologies: Concepts and Management

2.1
Concepts and Definitions

2.2
Classification and Evolution of Information Systems

2.3
Transaction Processing versus Functional IS

2.4
How IT Supports Organizational Activities

2.5
How IT Supports Supply Chain and CRM Operations

2.6
IS, Infrastructure, and Architecture

2.7
Web-Based Systems

2.8
New Computing Environments

2.9
Managing Information Resources

Chapter 2A Appendix
Build-To-Order Production

LEARNING OBJECTIVES

After studying this chapter, you will be able to:

❶ Describe various information systems and their evolution, and categorize specific systems you observe.

❷ Describe and contrast transaction processing and functional information systems.

❸ Identify the major internal support systems and relate them to managerial functions.

❹ Describe the support IT provides along the supply chain, including CRM.

❺ Discuss information infrastructure and architecture.

❻ Compare client/server architecture, mainframe-based legacy systems, and P2P architecture and comment on their differences.

❼ Describe the major types of Web-based information systems and understand their functionalities.

❽ Describe new computing environments.

❾ Describe how information resources are managed and what are the roles of the ISD and end users.

BUILDING AN E-BUSINESS AT FEDEX CORPORATION

FedEx Corporation was founded in 1973 by entrepreneur Fred Smith. Today, with a fully integrated physical and virtual infrastructure, FedEx's business model supports 24–48-hour delivery to anywhere in the world. FedEx operates one of the world's busiest data-processing centers, handling over 100 million information requests per day from more than 3,000 databases and more than 500,000 archive files. It operates one of the largest real-time, online client/server networks in the world. The core competencies of FedEx are now in express transportation and in e-solutions.

  THE PROBLEM/OPPORTUNITY

Initially, FedEx grew out of pressures from mounting inflation and global competition. These pressures gave rise to greater demands on businesses to expedite deliveries at a low cost and to improve customer services. FedEx didn't have a business problem per se but, rather, has endeavored to stay ahead of the competition by looking ahead at every stage for opportunities to meet customers' needs for fast, reliable, and affordable overnight deliveries. Lately, the Internet has provided an inexpensive and accessible platform upon which FedEx has seen further opportunities to expand its business scope, both geographically and in terms of service offerings. FedEx is attempting to fulfill two of its major goals simultaneously: 100 percent customer service and 0 percent downtime.

THE IT SOLUTION/PROJECT

A prime software application used by FedEx is e-Shipping Tools, a Web-based shipping application that allows customers to check the status of shipments through the company's Web page. FedEx is also providing integrated solutions to address the entire selling and supply chain needs of its customers. Its e-Commerce Solutions provides a full suite of services that allow businesses to integrate FedEx's transportation and information systems seamlessly into their own operations. These solutions have taken FedEx well beyond a shipping company.

FedEx markets several e-commerce hardware/software solutions: FedEx PowerShipMC (a multicarrier hardware/software system), FedEx Ship Manager Server (a hardware/software system providing high-speed transactions and superior reliability, allowing an average of eight transactions per second), FedEx ShipAPI™ (an Internet-based application that allows customization, eliminating redundant programming), and FedEx Net-Return® (a Web-based item-return management system). This infrastructure is now known as FedEx Direct Link. It enables business-to-business electronic commerce through combinations of global virtual private network (VPN) connectivity, Internet connectivity, leased-line connectivity, and VAN (value-added network) connectivity.

Figure 2.1 provides an example of one of FedEx's e-commerce solutions. It shows how FedEx customers can tap into a network of systems through the Internet. When a customer places an online order, the order is sent to a FedEx Web server. Information about the order and the customer is then sent to the merchant's PC, and a message is sent to the customer to confirm receipt of the order. After the order is received and acknowledged, the FedEx Web server sends

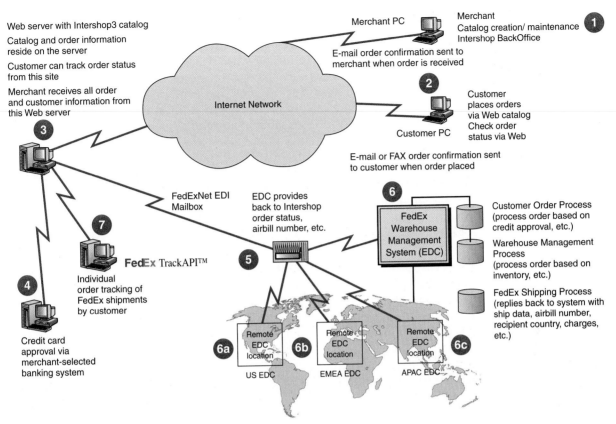

Web server with Intershop3 catalog

Catalog and order information reside on the server

Customer can track order status from this site

Merchant receives all order and customer information from this Web server

Merchant PC

Merchant
Catalog creation/ maintenance
Intershop BackOffice　**1**

E-mail order confirmation sent to merchant when order is received

2

Customer
places orders
via Web catalog
Check order
status via Web

Customer PC

E-mail or FAX order confirmation sent to customer when order placed

Internet Network

3

FedExNet EDI
Mailbox

EDC provides
back to Intershop
order status,
airbill number, etc.

6

FedEx
Warehouse
Management
System (EDC)

Customer Order Process
(process order based on
credit approval, etc.)

Warehouse Management
Process
(process order based on
inventory, etc.)

FedEx Shipping Process
(replies back to system with
ship data, airbill number,
recipient country, charges,
etc.)

7

FedEx TrackAPI™

5

Individual
order tracking of
FedEx shipments
by customer

4

Credit card
approval via
merchant-selected
banking system

Remote
EDC
location

6a

US EDC

Remote
EDC
location

6b

EMEA EDC

Remote
EDC
location

6c

APAC EDC

FIGURE 2.1 An example of a FedEx e-commerce solution. (*Source:* Based on a SIM 2000 award-winning paper written by William L. Conley, Ali F. Farhoomand, and Pauline S.P. Ng, at simnet.org/library/doc/2ndplace.doc. Courtesy of William Conley.)

a message to the merchant's bank to obtain credit approval. At the same time, the order is sent via electronic data interchange (EDI) to a FedEx mainframe that activates the *warehouse management system*. The order is processed (goods are picked and packed), the warehouse inventory system is updated, and the shipping process is activated. Information regarding the processing of the order is accessible at the three remote electronic data centers (EDCs) located in the United States, the Europe/Mediterranean (EMEA) region, and the Asia Pacific (APAC) region. During the entire process the customer, the merchant, and FedEx employees may track at any time the status of the order and its fulfillment via the Web.

➡ THE RESULTS

The new e-commerce-based FedEx business model creates value for its customers in a number of ways: It facilitates better communication and collaboration between the various parties along the selling and supply chains. It promotes efficiency gains by reducing costs and speeding up the order cycle. It encourages customers not only to use FedEx as a shipper but also to outsource to FedEx all their logistics activities. It also provides FedEx a competitive edge and increased revenue and profits. Thus, FedEx has changed from an old-economy shipping company to an e-business logistics enterprise.

Sources: Based on a SIM 2000 award-winning paper written by William L. Conley, Ali F. Farhoomand, and Pauline S.P. Ng, *simnet.org/library/doc/2ndplace.doc.* Courtesy of William Conley. Updated with information from *fedex.com,* accessed February 2003.

LESSONS LEARNED FROM THIS CASE

In the digital economy, how well companies transform themselves from traditional modes of operation to e-business will depend on how well they can adapt their structure and processes to take advantage of emerging technologies and what architecture and infrastructure they use. FedEx has transformed itself into an e-business by integrating physical and virtual infrastructures across information systems, business processes, and organizational bounds. FedEx's experience in building an e-business shows how a company can successfully apply its information technology expertise in order to pioneer "customercentric" innovations with sweeping structural and strategic impacts. It also shows the role of outsourcing, which frees companies to concentrate on their core business. In this chapter we describe how information systems of different kinds are structured, organized, and managed so that they can support businesses in the twenty-first century.

2.1 INFORMATION SYSTEMS: CONCEPTS AND DEFINITIONS

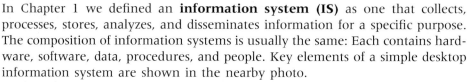

In Chapter 1 we defined an **information system (IS)** as one that collects, processes, stores, analyzes, and disseminates information for a specific purpose. The composition of information systems is usually the same: Each contains hardware, software, data, procedures, and people. Key elements of a simple desktop information system are shown in the nearby photo.

Another possible component of an information system is one or more smaller information systems. Information systems that contain smaller systems are typical of large companies. For example, FedEx's corporate information system contains hundreds of smaller information systems, which are referred to as "applications." An **application program** is a computer program designed to support a specific task or a business process (such as execute the payroll) or, in some cases, another application program.

There are dozens of applications in each functional area. For instance, in managing human resources, it is possible to find one application for screening job applicants and another for monitoring employee turnover. Some of the applications might be completely independent of each other, whereas others are interrelated. The collection of application programs in a single department is usually considered a *departmental information system,* even though it is made up of many applications. For example, the collection of application programs in the human resources area is called the *human resources information system (HRIS).*

Information systems are usually connected by means of *electronic networks.* The connecting networks can be *wireline* and/or *wireless.* Information systems can connect an entire organization, or even multiple organizations. If the entire company is networked and people can communicate with each other and access information throughout the organization, then the arrangement is known as an *enterprisewide information system.* An *interorganizational information system,* such as FedExNet, involves information flow among two or more organizations, and is used primarily in e-business applications.

The organization and management of information systems is emerging as a theoretical discipline, rather than simply as an applied field of study (O'Donovan and Roode, 2002). Before we focus on the details of IT and its management, it is necessary to describe the major concepts of information systems and organize the systems in some logical manner. That is the major purpose of this chapter.

Data, Information, and Knowledge

Information systems are built to attain several goals. One of the primary goals is to economically process data into information or knowledge. Let us define these concepts:

Data items refer to an elementary description of things, events, activities, and transactions that are recorded, classified, and stored, but not organized to convey any specific meeting. Data items can be numeric, alphanumeric, figures, sounds, or images. A student grade in a class is a data item, and so is the number of hours an employee worked in a certain week. A **database** consists of stored data items organized for retrieval.

Information is data that have been organized so that they have meaning and value to the recipient. For example, a student's grade point average is information. The recipient interprets the meaning and draws conclusions and implications from the data. Data items typically are processed into information by means of an application. Such processing represents a more specific use and a higher added value than simple retrieval and summarization from a database. The application might be a Web-based inventory management system, a university online registration system, or an Internet-based buying and selling system.

Finally, **knowledge** consists of data and/or information that have been organized and processed to convey understanding, experience, accumulated learning, and expertise as they apply to a current problem or activity. Data that are processed to extract critical implications and to reflect past experiences and expertise provide the recipient with *organizational knowledge,* which has a very high potential value. Currently, *knowledge management* is one of the hottest topics in the IT field (see Chapter 10).

Data, information, and knowledge can be *inputs* to an information system, and they can also be *outputs*. For example, data about employees, their wages, and time worked are processed as inputs in order to produce an organization's payroll information (output). The payroll information itself can later be used as an input to another system that prepares a budget or advises management on salary scales.

Information Systems Configurations

Information systems are made out of components that can be assembled in many different configurations, resulting in a variety of information systems and applications, much as construction materials can be assembled to build different homes. The size and cost of a home depend on the purpose of the building, the availability of money, and constraints such as ecological and environmental legal requirements. Just as there are many different types of houses, so there are many different types of information systems. We classify houses as single-family homes, apartments (or flats), townhouses, and cottages. Similarly, it is useful to classify information systems into groups that share similar characteristics. Such a classification may help in identifying systems, analyzing them, planning new systems, planning integration of systems, and making decisions such as the possible outsourcing of systems. This classification can be done in several alternative ways, as shown next.

2.2 CLASSIFICATION AND EVOLUTION OF INFORMATION SYSTEMS

Information systems are classified in this section by organizational levels and by the type of support provided. The section also looks at the evolution of support systems.

Classification by Organizational Levels

Organizations are made up of components such as divisions, departments, and work units, organized in hierarchical levels. For example, most organizations have functional departments, such as production and accounting, which report to plant management, which report to a division head. The divisions report to the corporate headquarters. Although some organizations have restructured themselves in innovative ways, such as those based on cross-functional teams, today the vast majority of organizations still have a traditional hierarchical structure. Thus, we can find information systems built for headquarters, for divisions, for the functional departments, for operating units, and even for individual employees. Such systems can stand alone, but usually they are interconnected.

Typical information systems that follow the organizational structure are *functional (departmental), enterprisewide,* and *interorganizational.* These systems are organized in a hierarchy in which each higher-level system consists of several (even many) systems from the level below it, as shown in Figure 2.2. As can be seen in the figure, a departmental system supports the functional areas in each company. At a higher level, the enterprisewide system supports the entire company, and interorganizational systems connect different companies.

FUNCTIONAL (DEPARTMENTAL) INFORMATION SYSTEMS. The major functional information systems are organized around the traditional departments—

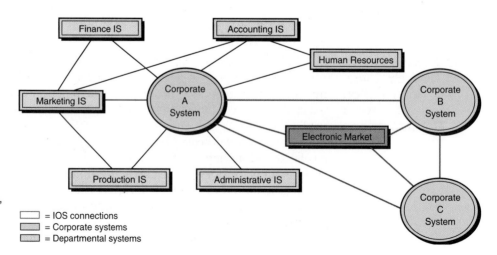

FIGURE 2.2 Departmental, corporate, and interorganizational information systems.

functions—in a company: manufacturing (operations/production), accounting, finance, marketing, and human resources.

ENTERPRISE INFORMATION SYSTEMS. While a departmental information system is usually related to a functional area, other information systems serve several departments or the entire enterprise. These information systems together with the departmental applications comprise the **enterprisewide information system (EIS).** One of the most popular enterprise applications is *enterprise resources planning (ERP),* which enables companies to plan and manage the resources of an entire enterprise. ERP systems present a relatively new model of enterprisewide computing (see Chapter 8).

A special enterprise system that crosses several departments is the *transaction processing system (TPS).* The TPS automates routine and repetitive tasks that are critical to the operation of the organization, such as preparing a payroll or billing customers. Transaction processing systems are described in Section 2.3 and in Chapter 7.

INTERORGANIZATIONAL SYSTEMS. Some information systems connect two or more organizations. They are referred to as **interorganizational information systems (IOSs).** For example, the worldwide airline reservation system is composed of several systems belonging to different airlines. Of these, American Airlines' SABRE system is the largest; thousands of travel agents and hundreds of airlines are connected to it. Such systems are common among business partners. Those that support international or global operations may be especially complex (see Mol and Koppius, 2002). Interorganizational information systems play a major role in e-commerce, as well as in supply chain management support.

Classification by the Type of Support Provided

Another way to classify information systems is according to the type of support they provide, regardless of the functional area. For example, an information system can support office workers in almost any functional area. Likewise, managers working from various geographical locations can be supported by a computerized decision-making system. The main types of support systems are listed and described in Table 2.1 (page 54) together with the types of employees they support. The evolution of these systems and a brief description of each follow. For more detail, see Online File W2.1.

The Evolution of Support Systems

The first business applications of computers did repetitive, large-volume, transactions-computing tasks. The computers "crunched numbers," summarizing and organizing transactions and data in the accounting, finance, and human resources areas. Such systems are called, generally, *transaction processing systems.*

As the cost of computing decreased and computers' capabilities increased, a new breed of information system, called *management information systems (MISs),* started to develop. These systems accessed, organized, summarized, and displayed information for supporting routine decision making in the functional areas. *Office automation systems (OASs)* such as word processing systems and airline reservation systems were developed to support office workers. Computers also were introduced in the manufacturing environment,

TABLE 2.1 Main Types of IT Support Systems

System	Employees Supported	Description	Detailed Description In:
Transaction processing system (TPS)	All employees	Processes an organization's basic business transactions (e.g., purchasing, billing, payroll).	Chapter 7
Management information system (MIS)	All employees	Provides routine information for planning, organizing, and controlling operations in functional areas.	Chapter 7
Office automation system (OAS)	Office workers	Increases productivity of office workers; includes word processing.	Chapters 4, 7
Word processing system	Office workers	Helps create, edit, format, distribute, and print documents.	Chapter 4
CAD/CAM	Engineers, draftspeople	Allows engineers to design and test prototypes; transfers specifications to manufacturing facilities.	Chapter 7
Communication and collaboration systems (e.g., e-mail, voice mail, call centers, others)	All employees	Enable employees and customers to interact and work together more efficiently.	Chapter 4
Desktop publishing system	Office workers	Combines text, photos, graphics to produce professional-quality documents.	Chapter 4
Document management system (DMS)	Office workers	Automates flow of electronic documents.	Chapter 11
Decision support system (DSS)	Decision makers, managers	Combines models and data to solve semistructured problems with extensive user involvement.	Chapter 12
Executive support system (ESS)	Executives, senior managers	Supports decisions of top managers.	Chapter 12
Group support system (GSS)	People working in groups	Supports working processes of groups of people (including those in different locations).	Chapter 12
Expert system (ES)	Knowledge workers, nonexperts	Provides stored knowledge of experts to nonexperts and decision recommendations based on built-in expertise.	Chapters 10, 11
Knowledge work system (KWS)	Managers, knowledge workers	Supports the gathering, organizing, and use of an organization's knowledge.	Chapters 10, 11, 12
Neural networks, case-based reasoning	Knowledge workers, professionals	Learn from historical cases, even with vague or incomplete information.	Chapters 10, 11
Data warehouse	Managers, knowledge workers	Stores huge amounts of data that can be easily accessed and manipulated for decision support.	Chapter 11
Business intelligence	Decision makers, managers	Gathers and uses large amounts of data for analysis by DSS, ESS, and intelligent systems.	Chapter 11
Mobile computing systems	Mobile employees	Support employees who work with customers or business partners outside the physical boundaries of the organization.	Chapter 6

with applications ranging from robotics to computer-aided design and manufacturing (CAD/CAM).

Additional increasing computing capabilities and reduced costs justified computerized support for a growing number of nonroutine applications, and *decision support systems* were developed to provide computerized support for complex, nonroutine decisions. The microcomputer revolution, which started around 1980, began the era of **end-user computing,** in which analysts, managers, and many other professionals can build and use systems on their own desktop computers. Decision support expanded in two directions: first, toward executives and then managers (*executive support systems* and *enterprisewide information systems*), and second, to people working in groups (*group support systems*).

Eventually, interest in programming computers to perform intelligent problem solving led to commercial applications known as *intelligent support systems (ISSs).* These include *expert systems,* which provide the stored knowledge of experts to nonexperts, and a new breed of intelligent systems with *machine-learning* capabilities (such as artificial neural networks and case-based reasoning) that can learn from historical cases.

As our economy has become more focused on knowledge work, *knowledge work systems* have been developed specifically to support the creating, gathering, organizing, integrating, and disseminating of an organization's knowledge. Included in this category are software for word processing, document management, and desktop publishing.

A major innovation in the evolution of support systems has been the development of *data warehousing.* A data warehouse is a database designed to support DSS, ESS, and other analytical and end-user activities. The use of data warehouses is a part of *business intelligence,* the gathering and use of large amounts of data for query or analysis by DSS, ESS, and intelligent systems.

The latest support system in organizations is **mobile computing.** Mobile computing supports mobile employees, those who are working with customers or business partners, outside the physical boundaries of their companies. The mobile employees carry portable devices, ranging from PDAs to cell phones and digital cameras, that can access the Internet. These devices enable communication with organizations and other individuals via wireline or wireless networks.

The information systems described so far were designed mostly to support the activities inside organizations. However, companies discovered that their *external* activities also can be improved with IT. The first type of IT system that was developed in the 1980s to improve communications with business partners was **electronic data interchange (EDI),** which involved computer-to-computer direct communication of standard business documents (such as orders and order confirmations) between business partners. These systems became the basis for *electronic markets,* which later developed into *electronic commerce.* These expanded later to improved *collaboration* of planning and other business activities among business partners, and some of the enterprisewide systems expanded to include more formalized business partner relationships. Later on came a wave of systems intended to support customers; these were grouped under the umbrella term *customer relationship management (CRM),* and they include services such as *call centers* (Chapter 7). Some of these external support systems are described further in Section 2.5.

FIGURE 2.3 Interrelated support systems. The TPS collects information that is used to build the DSS and ESS. The information in the data warehouse and DSS can be used as an input to the ESS.

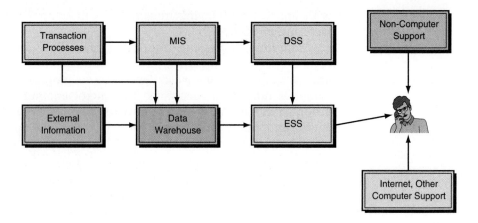

Major advances in external support are attributed to Web-based and mobile systems. *Web-based systems* started to be developed in the mid-1990s and picked up momentum in 2000. As their name implies, these systems deliver business applications via the Internet. As shown in the Siemens case in Chapter 1 and the FedEx case here, organizations are using Web-based systems to transform themselves into e-businesses. As will be shown *throughout the text,* today many—and probably most—of the innovative and strategic systems in medium and large organizations are Web-based. Using their browsers, people in these organizations communicate, collaborate, access vast amounts of information, and run most of the organization's tasks and processes by means of Web-based systems. (For more, see Section 2.7.)

In summary, the relationship among the different types of support systems can be described as follows: Each support system has sufficiently unique characteristics that it can be classified as a special entity. Yet there is information flow among these entities and systems. For example, an MIS extracts information from a TPS, and an ESS receives information from data warehouses and MIS (see Figure 2.3). In many cases, two or more support systems can be integrated to form a hybrid system, as is the case in business intelligence or mobile computing. Finally, as the technologies change, the interrelationships and coordination among the different types of systems continue to evolve. Ten years from now, the relationships shown in Figure 2.3 will probably look different from the way they look today.

INTEGRATED SUPPORT SYSTEMS. From the time of their inception, support systems were used both as standalone systems and as integrated systems composed of two or more of the support systems. Notable were systems that include some intelligent components (e.g., a DSS-ES combination). Such integration provides extended functionalities, making these systems more useful. As will be discussed in Section 2.7 and in Chapter 8, there is an increasing trend to integrate the various support systems as well as to integrate support systems with other systems. Integrated support systems can provide solutions to complex problems, as shown in *A Closer Look 2.1.*

Now that we have completed an overview of the different types of support systems and their evolution, we will look at some of the key systems in more detail.

A CLOSER LOOK
2.1 INTELLIGENT PRICE SETTING IN RETAILING

Pricing several thousands of items at Longs Drug Stores (a U.S. chain of about 400 drug stores) is decentralized. Each store is empowered to price each of the items it carries in the store, in order to better compete locally. Pricing traditionally was done manually by modifying the manufacturer's suggested retail price. Similar practices existed in most other retail chains, including supermarkets. Furthermore, when a price war occurred, or when a seasonal sales time arrived, prices were slashed across the board, without paying attention to demand forecast, profitability, pricing strategy, or price consistency across stores.

Now price setting is undergoing a radical change, largely as a result of improved IT support systems. Following what airlines and car leasing companies were doing for years, the retail industry, including Longs Drug Stores and about half of all other U.S. retailers, is introducing *price-optimization* programs. How do these programs work? Price-optimization programs (offered by Demand-Tech Inc., and others) combine support systems such as DSS, intelligent systems, data warehouses, and more to form a system that recommends a price for each item in each store. The input data used are seasonal sales figures, actual sales at each store (in real time), each product's price-demand curve, competitors' prices, profitability metrics, and more. The process is illustrated in Online File W2.2 at the book's Web site. Using the program, retailers can identify the most price-sensitive products, and they can test what impact a price change would have on profit margin (or other desired goal, such as sales volume) within seconds. Using each store's priorities, strategies can be developed and tested.

The models used are similar to *yield-management* models pioneered by the airline industry in the 1980s and since adopted by the car-leasing, financial services, consumer electronics, transportation, and other industries. Even casinos are introducing similar programs to determine the optimal payout for slot machines.

Initial results at Longs Drugs and at other retail stores that have used similar programs show volume, revenue, and profit increases of between 2 and 10 percent. The software is still fairly expensive, so only large retailers can use it now. As more competitors produce similar software, it will become cheaper in the future, and consumers will be the ultimate beneficiaries.

Source: Condensed from Cortese, 2002.

2.3 TRANSACTION PROCESSING VERSUS FUNCTIONAL INFORMATION SYSTEMS

Any organization that performs periodic financial, accounting, and other routine business activities faces repetitive tasks. For example, employees are paid at regular intervals, customers place purchase orders and are billed, and expenses are monitored and compared to the budget. Table 2.2 (page 58) presents a list of representative routine, repetitive business transactions in a manufacturing organization. The information system that supports such processes is called the *transaction processing system.*

Transaction Processing Systems

A **transaction processing system (TPS)** supports the monitoring, collection, storage, processing, and dissemination of the organization's basic business transactions. It also provides the input data for many applications involving support systems such as DSS. Sometimes several TPSs exist in one company. The transaction processing systems are considered critical to the success of any organization since they support core operations, such as purchasing of materials, billing customers, preparing a payroll, and shipping goods to customers.

TABLE 2.2 Routine Business Transactions in a Manufacturing Company

Payroll	*Sales*
Employee time cards	Sales records
Employee pay and deductions	Invoices and billings
Payroll checks	Accounts receivable
	Sales returns
Purchasing	Shipping
Purchase orders	
Deliveries	*Production*
Payments (accounts payable)	Production reports
	Quality-control reports
Finance and accounting	*Inventory management*
Financial statements	Material usage
Tax records	Inventory levels
Expense accounts	

The TPS collects data continuously, frequently on a daily basis, or even in *real time* (i.e., as soon as they are generated). Most of these data are stored in the corporate databases and are available for processing.

EXAMPLES OF TPS.   In retail stores, data flow from POS (point-of-sale) terminals to a database where they are aggregated. Sales reduce the level of inventory on hand, and the collected revenue from sales increases the company's cash position. TPS data may be analyzed by data-mining tools to find emerging patterns in what people buy. Such transactions occur all the time.

In banking, TPSs cover the area of deposits and withdrawals (which are similar to inventory levels). They also cover money transfers between accounts in the bank and among banks. Generating monthly statements for customers and setting fees charged for bank services are also typical transaction-processing activities for a bank.

Payroll is another area covered by TPSs for a business. Further details on TPS are provided in Chapter 7.

Functional Management Information Systems   The transaction-processing system covers the core activities of an organization. The *functional areas,* however, perform many other activities; some of these are repetitive, while others are only occasional. For example, the human resources department hires, advises, and trains people. Each of these tasks can be divided into subtasks. Training may involve selecting topics to teach, selecting people to participate in the training, scheduling classes, finding teachers, and preparing class materials. These tasks and subtasks are frequently supported by information systems specifically designed to support functional activities. Such systems are referred to as **functional management information systems,** or just **MIS.***

Functional management information systems are put in place to ensure that business strategies come to fruition in an efficient manner. Typically, a

---

*The term MIS here refers to a specific *application in* a functional area. The term MIS is also used in another context to describe the area of *management of* information systems.

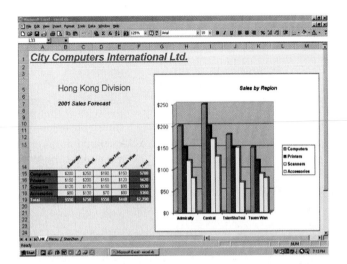

FIGURE 2.4 Sales forecast by region generated by marketing MIS.

functional MIS provides periodic information about such topics as operational efficiency, effectiveness, and productivity by extracting information from databases and processing it according to the needs of the user.

Management information systems are also used for planning, monitoring, and control. For example, a sales forecast by region is shown in Figure 2.4. Such a report can help the marketing manager make better decisions regarding advertising and pricing of products. Another example is that of a human resources information system (HRIS), which provides a manager with a daily report of the percentage of people who were on vacation or called in sick, as compared to forecasted figures.

So far we described what the support systems are. Now let's see *how* they support employees in organizations.

2.4 HOW IT SUPPORTS VARIOUS TYPES OF ORGANIZATIONAL ACTIVITIES

Another important way to classify information systems is by the nature of activities they support. Such support can be for operational, managerial, or strategic activities, as well as for knowledge workers in an organization.

Operational Activities

Operational activities deal with the day-to-day operations of an organization, such as assigning employees to tasks and recording the number of hours they work, or placing a purchase order. Operational activities are short-term in nature. The information systems that support them are mainly TPSs, MISs, and mobile systems. Operational systems are used by supervisors (first-line managers), operators, and clerical employees.

Managerial Activities

Managerial activities, also called tactical activities or decisions, deal in general with middle-management activities such as short-term planning, organizing, and control. Computerized managerial systems are frequently *equated with MISs,* because MISs are designed to summarize data and prepare reports. Middle managers also can get quick answers to queries from such systems as the need for answers arises.

TABLE 2.3 Support Provided by MISs for Managerial Activities

Task	MIS Support
Statistical summaries	Summaries of new data (e.g., daily production by item, monthly electricity usage).
Exception reports	Comparison of actual performances to standards (or target). Highlight only deviations from a threshold (e.g., above or below 5%).
Periodic reports	Generated at predetermined intervals.
Ad-hoc reports	Generated as needed, on demand. These can be routine reports or special ones.
Comparative analysis and early detection of problems	Comparison of performance to metrics or standards. Includes analysis such as trends and early detection of changes.
Projections	Projection of future sales, cash flows, market share, etc.
Automation of routine decisions	Standard modeling techniques applied to routine decisions such as when and how much to order or how to schedule work.
Connection and collaboration	Internal and external Web-based messaging systems, e-mail, voice mail, and groupware (see Chapter 4).

Managerial information systems are broader in scope than operational information systems, but like operational systems, they use mainly internal sources of data. They provide the types of support shown in Table 2.3.

Strategic Activities

Strategic activities are basically decisions that deal with situations that may significantly change the manner in which business is done. Traditionally, strategic decisions involved only long-range planning. Introducing a new product line, expanding the business by acquiring supporting businesses, and moving operations to a foreign country, are prime examples of long-range activities. A long-range planning document traditionally outlines strategies and plans for the next five or even 10 years. From this plan, companies derive their shorter-range planning, budgeting, and resource allocation. In the digital economy, the planning period has been dramatically reduced to one to two years, or even months. Strategic activities help organizations in two other ways.

First, *strategic response* activities can react quickly to a major competitor's action or to any other significant change in the enterprise's environment. Although they can sometimes be planned for as a set of contingencies, strategic responses are frequently not included in the long-range plan because the situations they respond to are unpredictable. IT is often used to support the response or to provide the response itself. For instance, when Kodak Corporation learned that a Japanese company was developing a disposable camera, Kodak decided to develop one too. However, Kodak faced a time problem because the Japanese were already in the middle of the development process. By using computer-aided design and other information technologies, Kodak was able to cut its design time by half and beat the Japanese in the race to be the first to have the cameras in retail outlets.

Second, instead of waiting for a competitor to introduce a major change or innovation, an organization can be the *initiator of change*. Such innovative strategic activities are frequently supported by IT, as shown by FedEx in the opening case and by many startup companies that exploit opportunities by using IT (e.g., see the Amazon.com story, in Chapter 5).

E-BUSINESS STRATEGIC SYSTEMS. As we saw in Chapter 1, e-commerce and e-business have become a new way of conducting business in the last decade or so. In this new approach, business transactions take place via telecommunications networks, primarily the Internet. E-commerce refers not only to buying and selling electronically, but also involves e-collaboration and e-learning. It aims at increasing productivity, reaching new customers, and sharing knowledge across institutions for competitive advantage. EC-supported strategic systems are changing how business is done. We will provide e-business strategic examples throughout the book.

Who Performs What Activities in Organizations?

So far in this section, we have looked at operational, managerial, and strategic activities, and at how IT supports them. Here, we take a different look at these activities by looking at the people who typically perform them in an organization. For example, line managers and operators usually make operational decisions, and middle managers make most of the managerial decisions. Strategic decisions are made almost entirely by an organization's top managers. The relationships between the people supported and the decision type are shown in Figure 2.5. The triangular shape of the figure also illustrates the quantity of employees involved in the various types of activities and the decisions relating to those activities. Top managers are few, and they sit at the top of the triangle.

KNOWLEDGE WORKERS, CLERICAL STAFF, AND DATA WORKERS. As you can see in Figure 2.5, an additional level of *staff support* is introduced between top and middle management. These are professional people, such as financial and marketing analysts. They act as advisors and assistants to both top and middle management. Many of these professional workers are classified as **knowledge workers,** people who create information and knowledge as part of their work and integrate it into the business. Knowledge workers are engineers, financial and marketing analysts, production planners, lawyers, and accountants, to mention just a few. They are responsible for finding or developing new knowledge for the organization and integrating it with existing knowledge. Therefore they must keep abreast of all

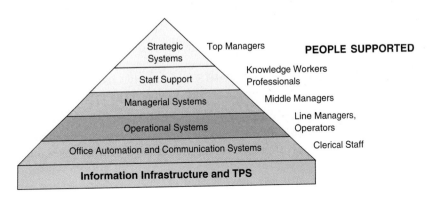

FIGURE 2.5 The information systems support of people in organizations.

developments and events related to their profession. They also act as change agents by introducing new procedures, technologies, or processes. In many developed countries, 60 to 80 percent of all workers are knowledge workers.

Information systems that support knowledge workers range from Internet search engines (which help knowledge workers find information) and expert systems (which support information interpretation), to Web-based computer-aided design (which shape and speed the design process) and sophisticated data management systems (which help increase productivity and quality of work). Knowledge workers are the major users of the Internet for business purposes.

Another large class of employees is *clerical workers,* who support managers at all levels. Among clerical workers, those who use, manipulate, or disseminate information are referred to as **data workers**. These include bookkeepers, secretaries who work with word processors, electronic file clerks, and insurance claim processors. Data workers are supported by office automation and communication systems including document management, workflow, e-mail, and coordination software.

INFRASTRUCTURE FOR THE SUPPORT SYSTEMS.   All of the systems in the support triangle are built on *information infrastructure.* Consequently, all of the employees who are supported work with infrastructure technologies such as the Internet, intranets, corporate portals, and corporate databases. Therefore, the information infrastructure is shown as the *foundation* of the triangle in Figure 2.5; it is described in more detail in Section 2.6.

2.5 HOW IT SUPPORTS SUPPLY CHAIN AND CRM OPERATIONS

As indicated in Chapter 1, organizations work with business partners in several areas, frequently along the supply chain.

The Basics of Supply Chains and Their Management

A **supply chain** is a concept describing the flow of materials, information, money, and services from raw material suppliers through factories and warehouses to the end customers. A supply chain also includes the *organizations* and *processes* that create and deliver these products, information, and services to the end customers. The term *supply chain* comes from a picture of how the partnering organizations are linked together. As shown in Figure 2.6, a simple linear supply chain links a company that processes milk (middle of the chain) with its suppliers (on the bottom) and its distributors and customers (on the top). The supply chain shown in Figure 2.6 is fairly simple. As will be shown in Chapter 8, supply chains can be much more complex. Note that the supply chain shows both physical flows and the flow of information. Not shown is the flow of money, which goes in the direction opposite to the flow of the physical materials.

SUPPLY CHAIN PARTS.   A supply chain can be broken into three major parts: upstream, internal, and downstream as shown in Figure 2.6.

- *The upstream supply chain.* The *upstream* part of the supply chain includes the activities of a manufacturing company with its first-tier suppliers (which can be manufacturers and/or assemblers) and their connection to their second-tier suppliers. The supplier relationship can be extended to the left in several tiers, all the way to the origin of the material (e.g.,

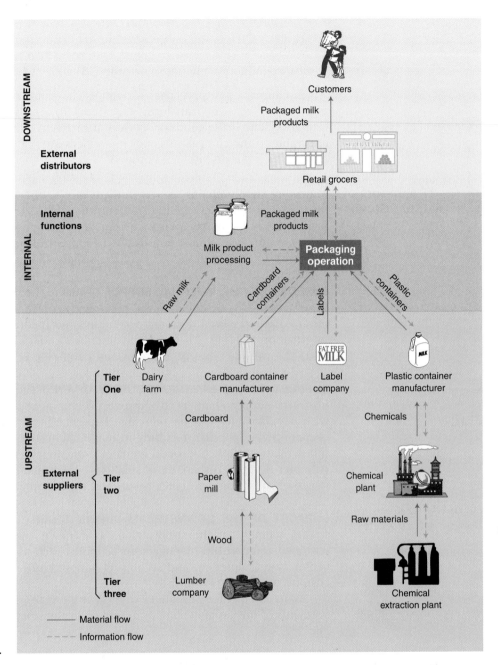

FIGURE 2.6 A simple supply chain for a manufacturer. Reid (2002).

mining ores, growing crops). In the upstream supply chain, the major activity is *procurement*.

● *The internal supply chain.* The *internal* part of the supply chain includes all of the *in-house* processes used in transforming the inputs received from the suppliers into the organization's outputs. It extends from the time the inputs enter an organization to the time that the products go to distribution outside of the organization. The internal supply chain is mainly concerned with production management, manufacturing, and inventory control.

● ***The downstream supply chain.*** The *downstream* part of the supply chain includes all the activities involved in delivering the products to the final customers. The downstream supply chain is directed at distribution, warehousing, transportation, and after-sale services.

A company's supply chain involves an array of business processes that not only effectively transform raw items to finished goods or services but that also make those goods or services attractive to customers. The activities that add value to the company's goods or services are part of what is called the *value chain,* which we discuss in Chapter 3.

IT Support of Supply Chains

Managing supply chains can be difficult due to the need to coordinate several business partners, several internal corporate departments, numerous business processes, and possibly many customers. Managing medium to large supply chains manually is almost impossible. IT support of supply chains can be divided according to the three segments of the supply chain.

SUPPORT OF THE INTERNAL SUPPLY CHAIN. The IT support of the internal supply chain was described in the previous two sections. It involves the TPS and other corporatewide information systems, and it includes all of the functional information systems. (These will be described in detail in Chapter 7.) It also supports the various types of activities and people described in Section 2.4.

SUPPORT OF THE UPSTREAM SUPPLY CHAIN. The major IT support of the upstream supply chain is to improve procurement activities and relationships with suppliers. As will be seen in Chapters 5 and 7, using e-procurement is becoming very popular, resulting in major savings and improvements in buyer-seller relationships. E-procurement is done in private and public exchanges (Chapter 5 and Turban et al., 2004). Relationship with suppliers can be improved by using a supplier portal and other supplier-relationship IT tools.

SUPPORT OF THE DOWNSTREAM SUPPLY CHAIN. IT support of the downstream segment of the supply chain is done in two areas. First, IT supports customer relationship management activities such as providing a customer call center (see Chapter 7), and second, IT supports order taking and shipments to customers (Chapters 5 and 8)

Many companies provide IT support to both the upstream and downstream segments of the supply chain, as described in the story about Best Buy in Online File W2.3.

MANAGING SUPPLY CHAINS. IT provides two major types of software solutions for managing—planning, organizing, coordinating, and controlling—supply chain activities. First is *enterprise resource planning (ERP)* software, which helps in managing both the internal and the external relationships with the business partners. Second is *supply chain management (SCM)* software, which helps in decision making related both to internal segments and to their relationships with external segments. Both types of software are described in Chapter 8.

Finally, the concept of build-to-order production that comes and of e-commerce has put a new spin on supply chain management; see Appendix 2A at the end of this chapter.

2.6 INFORMATION SYSTEMS INFRASTRUCTURE AND ARCHITECTURE

Infrastructure
An **information infrastructure** consists of the physical facilities, services, and management that support all shared computing resources in an organization. There are five major components of the infrastructure: (1) computer hardware, (2) software, (3) networks and communication facilities (including the Internet and intranets), (4) databases, and (5) information management personnel. Infrastructures include these resources as well as their integration, operation, documentation, maintenance, and management. If you go back and examine Figure 2.1 (which describes the architecture of the FedExNet), and introduce specific names instead of general ones (e.g., instead of "Merchant PC," say "Dell server"), you will get a picture of the system's infrastructure. Infrastructures are further discussed in Chapter 9, and in Broadbent and Weill (1997) and Weill and Vitale (2001). IT infrastructure is derived from the IT architecture.

The IT Architecture
Information technology architecture is a high-level map or plan of the information assets in an organization including the physical design of the building that holds the hardware.* On the Web, IT architecture includes the content and organization of the site and the interface to support browsing and search capabilities. The IT architecture of an e-business (a travel agency) is shown in Figure 2.7. It is a guide for current operations and a blueprint for future directions. It assures managers that the organization's IT structure will meet its strategic business needs. (See the *Journal of Information Architecture* for examples, tutorials, news, products, etc.)

Creating the IT architecture is a cyclical process, which is driven by the business architecture. **Business architecture** describes organizational plans, visions, objectives and problems, and the information required to support them. The potential users of IT must play a critical role in the creation of business

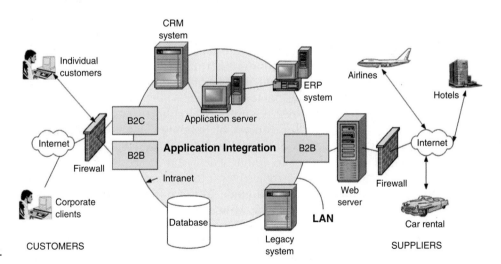

FIGURE 2.7 Architecture of an online travel agency.

Information technology architecture needs to be distinguished from *computer architecture* (see Technology Guide 1). For example, the architecture for a computer may involve several processors, or it may have special features to increase speed such as reduced instruction set computing (RISC). Our interest here is in information architecture only.

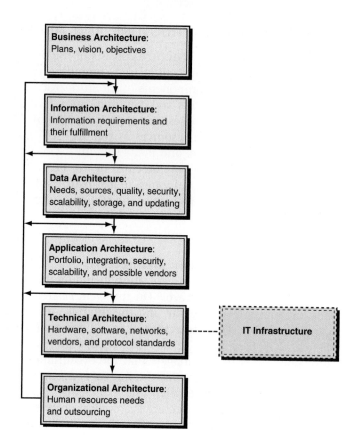

FIGURE 2.8 The steps in constructing IT architecture.

architecture, in order to have both a business architecture *and* an IT architecture that meets the organization's long-term needs. We can use the architecture of a house as an analogy. When preparing a conceptual high-level drawing of a house, the architect needs to know the requirements of the dwellers and the building constraints (time, money, materials, etc.). In preparing IT architecture, the designer needs similar information. This initial information is contained in the business architecture.

Once the business architecture is finished, the system developer can start a five-step process of building the IT architecture, as shown in Figure 2.8. The details and definitions of those steps are provided by Koontz (2000) and are shown in Online File W2.4 at the book's Web site. Notice that translating the business objectives into IT architecture can be a very complex undertaking. For a translation guide in the e-business environment, see Whipple (2001).

Let's look now at various basic elements of IT architecture.

Information Architecture According to Computing Paradigms (Environments)

A common way to classify information architecture is by computing paradigms, which are the core of the architecture. The major computing paradigms are: the mainframe environment, the PC environment, distributed computing, client/server architecture, and legacy systems.

MAINFRAME ENVIRONMENT. In the mainframe environment, processing is done by one or more mainframe computers. The users work with passive (or "dumb") terminals, which are used to enter or change data and access information from the mainframe and are controlled by it. This was the dominant architecture until the mid-1980s. Very few organizations use this type of architecture exclusively today due to its inflexibility and poor price-to-performance ratio (Ahmad, 2000).

An extension of this paradigm is an architecture that combines a mainframe with a number of PCs that are used as smart terminals. A **smart terminal** (also called *intelligent terminal*) contains a keyboard and screen (as does a "dumb terminal"), but it also comes with a disk drive that enables it to perform limited processing tasks when not communicating directly with the central computer. Yet the core of the system is the mainframe with its powerful storage and computational capabilities. The network computers (NCs) that were introduced in 1997 (see the discussion of client/server architecture, below) redefined the role of the centralized mainframe computing environment (for details see Amato-McCoy, 2002, and Ahmad, 2000).

PC ENVIRONMENT. In the PC configuration, *only* PCs (no mainframes) provide the computing power in the information system. Initially there was only one PC in each information system. Later it became possible to network several together.

PC-LANs. When PCs are connected via local area networks (LANs), a more flexible PC system is created. New functionalities can be added, including e-mail, Internet access, and the sharing of devices such as printers. This paradigm offers scalability (the ability to handle an increased load) and effectiveness, but it generally lacks the high security and integrity of a mainframe system, as well as efficient device coordination capability.

DISTRIBUTED COMPUTING. **Distributed processing** (*distributed computing*) divides the processing work between two or more computers, using a network for connection. The participating computers can be all mainframes, all PCs, or as in most cases, a combination of the two types. They can be in one location or in several. **Cooperative processing** is a type of distributed processing in which two or more geographically dispersed computers are teamed together to execute a specific task.

Thanks to communication networks and especially the Internet and intranets, distributed computing has become the dominant architecture of most organizations. This architecture permits intra- and interorganizational cooperation in computing; accessibility to vast amounts of data, information, and knowledge; and high efficiency in the use of computing resources. The concept of distributed computing drives today's new architectures, including those that are Web-based. An example is provided in *IT at Work 2.1* (page 68).

The Impact of Distributed Computing on IT. Traditional applications such as word processing were modeled as standalone applications: They offered users the capabilities to perform tasks using data stored on the system. Most new software programs, in contrast, are based on the *distributed computing* model, where applications collaborate to provide services and expose functionality to each other. As a result, the primary role of many new software programs is to support information exchange (through Web servers and browsers), collaboration (through e-mail and instant messaging), and individual expression (through

IT at Work 2.1
FLEXIBLE IT ARCHITECTURE AT CHASE MANHATTAN BANK

Chase Manhattan Bank and Chemical Bank merged in 1996, creating the then-largest bank in the United States. (It has since merged with J.P. Morgan, and now is J.P. Morgan Chase Company, *jpmorganchase.com.*) The unified Chase Manhattan Bank had to process 16 million checks daily across 700 locations in 58 countries. It also had to serve 25 million retail customers and thousands more institutional customers, with the customer base expected to grow by 6 to 10 percent a year. The problem was how to merge the different information systems of the two banks and create an IT architecture that would support the new bank's activities, including its future growth and additional planned acquisitions.

Previous mergers and acquisitions involving both Chase and Chemical had resulted in many problems in developing the IT architecture. "We needed to blueprint an architectural platform that provided operational excellence and customer privacy," says Dennis O'Leary, CEO and executive vice president of the new bank. "The platform also had to be functional and have the ability to integrate business at the retail, national, and global enterprise levels." One problem was the worldwide connectivity among more than 60,000 desktop computers, 14 large mainframes, 300 minicomputers, 1,100 T1 telecommunication lines, and more than 1,500 core applications.

The new architecture was constructed incorporating the Internet and intranets. (Specifically, the new architecture was based on the TCP/IP model, as described in Technology Guide 5.) An innovative three-layer system was designed. First was a global infrastructure; second were distribution networks that routed traffic among business units; and third were numerous access networks. This flexible structure allowed the addition of networks whenever needed. The global infrastructure was a network built on wide area networks (WANs), satellites, and related technologies. The architectural plan included several security devices called *firewalls,* mainly in the distribution network layer. The access networks were the internal networks of the different business units, now reformulated as intranets. The system also had many client/server applications as well as mainframes. All the desktops were managed on Windows NT.

In 1998/99 Chase Manhattan embarked on a major e-banking initiative, based on improved architecture. By 2003 the bank offered a wide range of online services such as Chase Online Plus for managing multiple accounts, extensive online shopping, online deep-discount investment services, an online service for small businesses, and a special online payroll system (called Powerpay). In addition the bank offered services to large businesses and partners. Mobile banking was on the planning board for 2004. All of these initiatives are easily scalable, so accommodating more acquisitions and mergers, like the one with J.P. Morgan, creates no problems.

All of this massive networking has one goal: giving customers extensive real-time access to accounts and a view of their assets.

Sources: Condensed from Girishankar (1997) and from miscellaneous Chase Manhattan and J.P. Morgan Chase press releases in 2002 and 2003 (e.g., see 1/13/2003).

For Further Exploration: Why are banks dependent on networks? Why is a three-layer system preferable to a single layer? What are the advantages of moving to e-business?

Weblogs, and e-zines). Essentially, this software provides services rather than discrete functionality.

The most important configuration of distributed processing is the *client/server architecture,* where several computers share resources and are able to communicate with many other computers via networks. The Internet, intranets, and extranets are based on the client/server model of distributed computing.

Client/Server Architecture. **Client/server architecture** divides distributed computing units into two major categories, *clients* and *servers,* all of which are connected by a network of some sort. A **client** is a computer such as a PC attached to a network, which is used to access shared network resources. A **server** is a machine that is attached to this same network and provides clients with some services. Examples of servers are a *database server* that provides a large storage capacity, or a *communication server* that provides connection to another network, to commercial databases, or to a powerful processor. In some client/server systems there are additional computing units, referred to as *middleware* (see Technology Guide 2).

There are several models of client/server architecture. In the most traditional model, the mainframe acts as a database server, providing data for analysis done by the PC clients using spreadsheets, database management systems, and application software. For other models and more details see Technology Guide 2.

The Benefits of Client/Server Architecture. The purpose of client/server architecture is to maximize the use of computer resources. Client/server architecture provides a way for different computing devices to work together, each doing the job for which it is best suited. For example, large storage and heavy computation power is more cost-effective on a mainframe than on a PC. Common office computing, such as word processing, is more conveniently handled by a PC. The role of each machine need not be fixed. A PC, for example, can be a client in one task and a server in another. Another important element is *sharing*. The clients, which are usually inexpensive PCs, share more expensive devices, the servers.

Client/server architecture gives a company as many access points to data as there are PCs on the network. It also lets a company use more tools to process data and information. Client/server architecture has changed the way people work in organizations. For example, people are empowered to access databases at will.

Enterprisewide Computing. Client/server computing can be implemented in a small work area or in one department, where its main benefit would be the sharing of resources within that department. However, many users frequently need access to data, applications, services, electronic mail, and real-time flows of data from different departments or in different databases. The solution is to deploy **enterprisewide computing,** a client/server architecture that connects data within an entire organization. This combination of client/servers and broad access to data forms a cohesive, flexible, and powerful computing environment. An example of such an architecture is provided in the FedExNet opening case. This architecture is the core of Web-based systems.

An enterprisewide client/server architecture provides total integration of departmental and corporate IS resources. It thereby allows for an additional class of applications that span the enterprise and benefit both corporate central management (providing controls) and end-user systems (providing empowerment). It also provides better control and security over data in a distributed environment. By implementing client/server computing as the architecture for enterprisewide information systems, organizations can maximize the value of information by increasing its availability.

Many new IT developments are based on the client/server concept. These include enterprise group support technologies such as Lotus Notes/Domino, Microsoft Exchange, Netscape Communicator, and Microsoft Outlook (see Chapter 4) as well as Web-based systems and the Internet, intranets, and extranets. Client/server architecture is quickly becoming a part of, or is being replaced by, Web-based systems.

We need to discuss a couple more topics related to information archi-tecture—legacy systems and peer-to-peer architecture—before we close this section.

LEGACY SYSTEMS. Legacy systems are older, usually mature, information systems. Although legacy systems are normally less desirable than and less compatible with modern equivalents, they are still, in some cases, part of the backbone of the overall IT infrastructure within an organization. They are usually part of a pure mainframe system or a distributed system in which the mainframe plays the major role. Newer legacy systems may include one or more LANs and even early client/server implementations.

Legacy systems were developed from the late 1950s through the 1980s for general-purpose business use in medium- to large-size companies. They were the primary mechanism for high-volume processing applications. Legacy systems typically are housed in a secured and costly computer center, operated by IS professional staff rather than by end users. Much of their work is repetitive, mainly in transaction processing. Some legacy systems are very large, including hundreds or even thousands of remote terminals networked to the mainframe processor.

Because companies invested lots of money and expertise in building legacy systems, many companies try to reengineer these systems rather than to replace them (see Chapter 14 and Martin, 2002). Erlikh (2002) provides some guide-lines on how to leverage legacy systems with Web-based architecture. An emerging way to integrate legacy systems with Web-based systems is by using Web services (described in Chapter 14).

PEER-TO-PEER ARCHITECTURE. In a client/server architecture some comput-ers or devices serve others. Peer-to-peer architecture is a special client/server architecture that provides some additional new and useful functionalities.

Peer-to-peer (P2P) architecture is a type of network in which each client computer shares files or computer resources (like processing power) *directly* with others *but not through a central server*. This is in contrast with the traditional client/sever architecture in which some computers serve other computers via a central server. P2P sharing typically had been done over private networks, but recently it moved to the Internet. P2P architecture is really two different things—the direct sharing of digital files, and the sharing of different comput-ers' processing power.

The main benefit of P2P is that it can expand enormously the universe of information accessible from a personal computer or a mobile device. Additionally, some proponents claim that a well-designed P2P architecture, especially when done on the Web, can offer better security, reliability, and availability of content than the client/server model, on which the Web is cur-rently based (e.g., see Agre, 2003, and Kini, 2002). Other advantages over client/server are that there is no need for a network administrator, the network is fast and inexpensive to set up and maintain, and each PC can make a backup copy of its data to other PCs for improved security. The technology is more productive than client/server because it enables direct connections between computers, so there is no need to incur the cost of setting up and maintaining servers.

P2P architecture is the basis of *file sharing* over the Web and the basis on which companies such as Napster, Kazaa, and Gnutella operate (see Chapters 4 and 16).

2.7 WEB-BASED SYSTEMS

The concept of client/server architecture has dominated IT architecture for several decades. But the specially structured client/server applications that were considered revolutionary in the mid-1990s may soon become obsolete due to the rapid development of Web-based systems, as well as the introduction of new concepts such as utility computing and software services (presented in Section 2.8). Although all of these new technologies are based on the client/server concept, their implementation is considerably less expensive than that of many specially structured client/server systems. Furthermore, the conversion of existing systems to Web-based ones can be easy and fast, and the functionalities of the Web-based can be larger than those available in non-Web-based client/server systems. Therefore, as is shown throughout the book and especially in Chapters 4 and 5, the Internet, intranets, and sometimes extranets are becoming an indispensable part of most IT architectures. New Web-based architectures may replace old architectures, or may integrate legacy systems into their structure (see Erlikh, 2002).

Technically, the term **Web-based systems** refers to those applications or services that are resident on a server that is accessible using a Web browser and is therefore accessible from anywhere in the world via the Web. The only client-side software needed to access and execute Web-based applications is a Web browser environment, and of course the applications must conform to the Internet protocols. An example of such an application would be an online store. Additionally, two other very important features of Web-based functionalities are (1) that the generated content/data are updated in real time, and (2) that Web-based systems are universally accessible via the Web to users (dependent on defined user-access rights). The major communication networks of the Web environments are the Internet, intranets, and extranets.

The Internet   Sometimes called simply "the Net," the *Internet* is a worldwide system of computer networks—a network of networks, in which users at any one computer can get information from any other computer (and sometimes talk directly to users at other computers). Today, the Internet is a public, cooperative, and self-sustaining facility accessible to hundreds of millions of people worldwide.

Physically, the Internet uses a portion of the total resources of the currently existing public telecommunication networks. Technically, what distinguishes the Internet is its use of a set of protocols called TCP/IP (for Transmission Control Protocol/Internet Protocol). The Internet applications and technology are discussed in more detail in Technology Guide 5. Two adaptations of Internet technology, intranets and extranets, also make use of the TCP/IP protocol.

Intranets   The concept of an intranet is a natural progression in the marriage of the enterprise and the Internet. An **intranet** is the use of Web technologies to create a private network, usually within one enterprise. Although an intranet may be a single local area network (LAN) segment that uses the TCP/IP protocol, it is typically a complete LAN, or several intraconnected LANs. A security gateway such as a firewall is used to segregate the intranet from the Internet and to selectively allow access from outside the intranet. (See Online Minicase W2.1 for an example in academia.)

Intranets have a variety of uses, as we show throughout the book and especially in Chapters 4 and 5. They allow for the secure online distribution of many forms of internal company information. Intranets are used for workgroup activities and the distributed sharing of projects within the enterprise. Other uses include controlled access to company financial documents, use of knowledge management, research materials, online training, and other information that requires distribution within the enterprise. Intranets are usually combined with and accessed via a corporate portal.

CORPORATE PORTALS. **Corporate portals** are Web sites that provide the gateway to corporate information from a single point of access. They aggregate information from many files and present it to the user. The function of corporate portals is often described as "corecasting," since they support decisions central to particular goals of the enterprise. Corporate portals also help to personalize information for individual customers and for employees. For further discussion of corporate portals, see Chapter 4.

Extranets

Extranets connect several intranets via the Internet, by adding to the Internet a security mechanism and possibly some functionalities. They form a larger virtual network that allows remote users (such as business partners or mobile employees) to securely connect over the Internet to the enterprise's main intranet. Typically, remote access software is used to authenticate and encrypt the data that pass between the remote user and the intranet. Extranets allow two or more enterprises to share information in a controlled fashion, and therefore they play a major role in the development of business-to-business electronic commerce (see Chapter 5 for details).

Web-Based E-Commerce Systems

Most e-commerce applications run on the Internet, intranet and extranets, using Web-based features. Therefore, Web-based systems are the engines of e-commerce. They enable business transactions to be conducted seamlessly 24 hours a day, seven days a week. A central property of the Web and e-commerce is that you can instantly reach millions of people, anywhere, any time. The major components of Web-based EC are electronic storefronts, electronic markets, mobile commerce, and the Enterprise Web.

ELECTRONIC STOREFRONTS. An **electronic storefront** is the Web-equivalent of a showroom or a physical store. Through the electronic storefront, an e-business can display and/or sell its products. The storefront may include electronic catalogs that contain descriptions, graphics, and possibly product reviews. Most electronic storefronts have the following common features and functions: an e-catalog, a shopping cart, a checkout mechanism (for shipments), payment processing, and an order-fulfillment system (see Chapter 5 and Turban et al., 2004).

ELECTRONIC MARKETS. Web-accessed electronic markets (see Chapter 5) are rapidly emerging as a vehicle for conducting e-commerce. An **electronic market** is a network of interactions and relationships over which information, products, services, and payments are exchanged. When the marketplace is electronic, the business center is not a physical building but a Web-based location where business interactions occur. In electronic markets, the principal participants—transaction handlers, buyers, brokers, and sellers—not only are at different locations but seldom even know one another. The means of interconnection vary among parties and can change from event to event, even between the same parties. Electronic markets can reside in one company, where there is either one seller and many buyers, or one buyer and many sellers. These are referred to as *private marketplaces*. (See Online Minicase W2.2 for an example of a Web-based private marketplace.) Alternatively, electronic markets can have many buyers and many sellers. Then they are known as *public marketplaces* or *exchanges*.

Electronic Exchanges. A form of electronic markets is **electronic exchanges,** which are Web-based public marketplaces where many buyers and many sellers interact dynamically. They were originally set as trading places for commodities. Since then a variety of exchanges have emerged for all kinds of products and services (see Chapter 5).

MOBILE COMPUTING AND MOBILE COMMERCE. *Mobile computing* is a computing paradigm designed for mobile employees and others who wish to have a real-time connection between a mobile device and other computing environment. **Mobile commerce** or **m-commerce** (see Chapter 6) is commerce (buying and selling of goods and services) in a wireless environment, such as through wireless devices like cellular telephones and PDAs. Also called "next-generation e-commerce," m-commerce enables users to access the Internet without needing to find a place to plug in. So-called *smart phones* offer Internet access, fax, e-mail, and phone capabilities all in one, paving the way for m-commerce to be accepted by an increasingly mobile workforce as well as millions of consumers. As **wireless computing**—content delivery over wireless devices—becomes faster, more secure, and scalable, there is wide speculation that m-commerce will surpass wireline e-commerce as the method of choice for digital commerce transactions (see *IT at Work 2.2,* page 74).

ENTERPRISE WEB. The **Enterprise Web** is an open environment for managing and delivering Web applications. The Enterprise Web combines services from different vendors in a technology layer that spans rival platforms and business systems, creating a foundation for building applications at lower cost. This foundation consists of the services most commonly used by Web applications, including business integration, collaboration, content management, identity management, and search, which work together via integrating technologies such as middleware (see Technology Guide 2), component-based development (Chapter 14), and Web services (Chapter 14).

The result is an environment that spans the entire enterprise, is open to all platforms for which adapters are available (or completely open with Web services), and is available to all audiences. Providing a common foundation for Web applications built on any platform lowers infrastructure and development costs; integrating resources from different systems into Web applications increases the return on those systems; and creating a common user experience for audiences across the enterprise to work together drives enterprise productivity and increases profits. Enterprise Web environments are available from all major software vendors (e.g., Microsoft, IBM, SAP, Oracle, BEA, PeopleSoft, and more). For more on the Enterprise Web, see Online File W2.5 at the book's Web site.

IT at Work 2.2
WIRELESS PEPSI INCREASES PRODUCTIVITY

Pepsi Bottling Group (PBG), the largest manufacturer, seller, and distributor of Pepsi-Cola, has a mountainous job stocking and maintaining their Pepsi vending machines—including a huge amount of paperwork and frustrating searches for parts and equipment necessary to fix the machines. Any time a machine is out of stock or not functioning, the company loses revenue and profits. There are tens of thousands of machines to serve.

In 2002, the company began to equip its service technicians with hand-held devices, hooked into a wireless wide area network (WWAN). A mobile database application allows wireless communications around the country in real time. The database includes the repair parts inventory that is available on each service truck, so dispatchers know where and who to send for maintenance at any given moment. It also has a back-office system that maintains the overall inventory. In the near future the company will also be able to locate the whereabouts of each truck in real

time, using global positioning systems (GPSs). The aim is to make scheduling and dispatching more effective.

In the summer of 2002 only about 700 technicians used the wireless system, but already the company was saving $7 million per year. Each technician has been able to handle one more service call each day than previously. PBG provided the wireless capability to about 300 more technicians in 20 more locations in late 2002, and many more technicians will be similarly equipped later on.

Sources: Compiled from Rhey (2002) and from *pepsi.com* (March 2003).

For Further Exploration: What are the capabilities of the hand-held devices? Relate the hand-held devices to the mobile database. The case deals with the maintenance issue. In what ways, if any, can wireless help with stocking issues?

2.8 NEW COMPUTING ENVIRONMENTS

During the last decade several new computing environments have emerged, some of which are based on Web technology. These systems are in the early stages of usage, and some are still under development, but they may reshape the IT field. In this section we provide several examples of these new initiatives. For a discussion of the issues that new networked computing systems need to address, see Online File W2.6. The following are representative initiatives of emerging computing environments.

Utility Computing

According to Bill Gates, **utility computing** is computing that is as available, reliable, and secure as electricity, water services, and telephony (Gates, public speech, January 2003). The vision behind utility computing is to have computing resources flow like electricity on demand from virtual utilities around the globe—always on and highly available, secure, efficiently metered, priced on a pay-as-you-use basis, dynamically scaled, self-healing, and easy to manage. In this setting, enterprises would plug in, turn on the computer, and (it is hoped) save lots of money. IBM (*On-Demand* Project), HP, Microsoft, Oracle, Sun Microsystems, SAP and other major software companies are backing the idea (see Cone, 2001).

If (or when) it becomes successful, utility computing will change the way software is sold, delivered, and used in the world. Some experts believe that all software will become a service and be sold as a utility one day (Cone, 2001). Preparing for this day, IBM is moving aggressively into the application services provider (ASP) area. The ASPs will operate the supply channels of utility computing (see Chapters 13 and 14).

Despite the bright promises and the efforts of the major vendors, progress is slow. According to Margulius (2002), key pieces of the technology are still missing. For example, utility computing is hard to do in heterogeneous data centers. Also, the utility concept works better for some applications than for others. Furthermore, utility computing needs extra security when traveling online. Finally, distribution of software differs from distribution of utilities (see Wainewright, 2002). These differences need to be overcome by vendors in order to offer utility computing in a way that appeals to customers. However, it looks like utility computing will start inside companies, where the IT department can offer utility-style services to business units for internal use, and from there may eventually spread to the computing public (see Margulius, 2002).

SUBSCRIPTION COMPUTING. Subscription computing, a variety of utility computing, puts the pieces of a computing platform together as services, rather than as a collection of separately purchased components (Bantz et al., 2002). Users can get programs, information, or storage over the Internet (usually protected by virtual private networks; see Technology Guide 4). The services provided by subscription computing and their value to users are summarized in Online File W2.7.

Grid Computing

Conventional networks, including the Internet, are designed to provide communication among devices. The same networks can be used to support the concept of **grid computing,** in which the unused processing cycles of all computers in a given network can be harnessed to create powerful computing capabilities. Grid computing is already in limited use, and most of the current grid applications are in areas that formerly would have required supercomputers. The grid does the computing at a much lower cost.

A well-known grid-computing project is the SETI (Search for Extraterrestrial Intelligence) @Home project. In this project, PC users worldwide donate unused processor cycle times to help the search for signs of extraterrestrial life by analyzing signals coming from outer space. The project relies on individual volunteers to allow the project to harness the unused processing power of the users' computers. This method saves the project both money and resources.

A major commercial application of grid computing in the consumer market is Sony's attempt to link online thousands of Sony video-game consoles. For details see Lohr (2003).

Pervasive Computing

As discussed in Chapter 1, with *pervasive computing* we envision a future in which computation becomes part of the environment. Computation will be embedded in *things*, not in computers. Relentless progress in semiconductor technology, low-power design, and wireless technology will make embedded computation less and less obtrusive. Pervasive computing is closely related with IT support systems, especially intelligent systems and DSS. For more details about pervasive computing, see Chapter 6.

Web Services

Web services are self-contained, self-describing business and consumer modular applications, delivered over the Internet, that users can select and combine through almost any device, ranging from personal computers to mobile phones. By using a set of shared protocols and standards, these applications permit disparate systems to "talk" with one another—that is, to share data and services—without requiring human beings to translate the conversation. The result promises to be on-the-fly and in-real-time links among the online processes of different systems and companies. These links could shrink corporate IT departments, foster new interactions among businesses, and create a more user-friendly Web for consumers. Web services provide for inexpensive and rapid solutions for application integration, access to information, and application development. See Chapters 4, 5, and 14.

Commercial Efforts in New Computing Environments

Three software companies currently are developing major products in the emerging computer environments. All will incorporate utility computing, pervasive computing, and Web services sometime in the future. Microsoft is launching a major research effort, known as *Microsoft.Net* (*www.microsoft.com/net/default.asp*). IBM is developing its WebSphere platform (*ibm.com/software/websphere*). And Sun Microsystems is building a new system architecture in its N1 Project. For more about these commercial ventures, see Online File W2.8.

Whether an organization uses mainframe-based legacy systems or cutting-edge Web-based ones, its information resources are extremely important organizational assets that need to be protected and managed. This topic is presented in Section 2.9.

2.9 MANAGING INFORMATION RESOURCES

A modern organization possesses many information resources. In addition to the infrastructures, numerous applications exist, and new ones are continuously being developed. Applications have enormous strategic value. Firms rely on them so heavily that, in some cases, when they are not working even for a short time, an organization cannot function. Furthermore, the acquisition, operation, security, and maintenance of these systems may cost a considerable amount of money. Therefore, it is essential to manage these information systems properly. The planning, organizing, implementing, operating, and controlling of the infrastructures and the organization's portfolio of applications must be done with great skill.

Which IT Resources Are Managed and By Whom

The responsibility for the management of information resources is divided between two organizational entities: the *information systems department (ISD)*, which is a corporate entity, and the *end users*, who are scattered throughout the organization. This division of responsibility raises important questions such as: Which resources are managed by whom? What is the role of the ISD, its structure, and its place in the organization? What are the relationships between the ISD and the end users? Brief answers to these questions are provided in this section.

There are many types of information systems resources, and their components may be from multiple vendors and of different brands. The major categories are *hardware* (all types of computers, servers, and other devices), *software* (development tools, languages, and applications), *databases, networks* (local, wide, Internet, intranets and extranets, and supporting devices), *procedures, security facilities,* and *physical buildings*. The resources are scattered throughout the organization, and some of them change frequently. Therefore, it may be rather difficult to manage IS resources.

There is no standard menu for the division of responsibility for the development and maintenance of IS resources between the ISD and end users. In some organizations, the ISD manages most of these resources, regardless of where they are located and how they are used. In others, the ISD manages only a few. The division depends on many things: the size and nature of the organization, the amount and type of IT resources, the organization's attitudes toward computing, the attitudes of top management toward computing, the maturity level of the technology, the amount and nature of outsourced IT work, and even the country in which the company operates.

Generally speaking, the ISD is responsible for corporate-level and *shared resources,* while the end users are responsible for departmental resources. Sometimes the division between the ISD and the end users is based on other approaches. For example, the ISD may acquire or build systems and the end users operate and maintain them.

Because of interdependencies of information resources, it is important that the ISD and the end users work closely together and cooperate regardless of who is doing what. We discuss this below and also in Chapter 15.

The Role of the IS Department

As Table 2.4 shows, the role of the ISD is changing from purely technical to more managerial and strategic. As a result of this changing role, the position of the ISD within the organization is tending to be elevated from a unit reporting to a functional department (such as accounting) to a unit reporting to a senior vice president of administration or even to the CEO. In this new role, the ISD must be able to work closely with external organizations such as vendors, business partners, consultants, research institutions, and universities. In addition, the ISD and the end-user units must be close partners. The mechanisms that build the required cooperation are described in Chapter 15.

The role of the director of the ISD is also changing, from a technical manager to a senior executive, sometimes referred to as the **chief information officer (CIO),** or the *chief technology officer (CTO).* Details are provided by Ball (2002) and in Chapter 15.

IT ISSUES. In early 2003, the major issues in IT management were how to cope with declining budgets, how to move an organization's IT systems to fit the digital age, how to integrate applications, how to secure information systems, how much to outsource, how to measure the return on IT investment, and how to deal with emerging technologies such as Web services. All of these issues are covered in many places throughout this book.

TABLE 2.4 The Changing Role of the Information Systems Department

Traditional Major IS Functions
Managing systems development and systems project management
Managing computer operations, including the computer center
Staffing, training, and developing IS skills
Providing technical services

New (Additional) Major IS Functions
Initiating and designing specific strategic information systems
Infrastructure planning, development, and control
Incorporating the Internet and electronic commerce into the business
Managing system integration including the Internet, intranets, and extranets
Educating the non-IS managers about IT
Educating the IS staff about the business
Supporting end-user computing
Partnering with the executive level that runs the business
Managing outsourcing
Proactively using business and technical knowledge to "seed" innovative ideas about IT
Creating business alliances with vendors and IS departments in other organizations

➡ MANAGERIAL ISSUES

1. **The transition to e-business.** Converting an organization to a networked-computing-based e-business may be a complicated process. The e-business requires a client/server architecture, an intranet, an Internet connection, and e-commerce policy and strategy, all in the face of many unknowns and risks. However, in many organizations this potentially painful conversion may be the only way to succeed or even to survive. When to do it, how to do it, what will be the role of the enabling information technologies, and what will be the impacts of such a conversion are major issues for organizations to consider.

2. **From legacy systems to client/server to intranets, corporate portals, and Web-based systems.** A related major issue is whether and when and how to move from the legacy systems to a Web-based client/server enterprisewide architecture. While the general trend is toward Web-based client/server, there have been several unsuccessful transformations, and many unresolved issues regarding the implementation of these systems. The introduction of intranets seems to be much easier than that of other client/server applications. Yet, moving to any new architecture requires new infrastructure and a decision about what to do with the legacy systems, which may have a considerable impact on people, quality of work, and budget. A major aspect is the introduction of wireless infrastructure. These important issues are discussed in detail in Chapters 13 and 14.

   It should be noted that many companies need high-speed computing of high-volume data. Here the client/server concept may not be effective. In such cases, management should consider transformation of the legacy systems to new types of mainframes that use innovations that make the systems smaller and cheaper.

3. **How to deal with the outsourcing and utility computing trends.** As opportunities for outsourcing (e.g., ASPs) are becoming cheaper, available, and viable, the concept becomes more attractive. In the not-so-distant future, we will see outsourcing in the form of utility computing. How much to outsource is a major managerial issue (see Chapters 13 and 14).

4. **How much infrastructure?** Justifying information system applications is not an easy job due to the intangible benefits and the rapid changes in technologies that often make systems obsolete. Justifying infrastructure is even more difficult since many users and applications share the infrastructure that will be used for several years in the future. This makes it almost impossible to quantify the benefits. Basic architecture is a necessity, but there are some options. Various justification methodologies are discussed in Chapter 13.

5. **The roles of the ISD and end users.** The role of the ISD can be extremely important, yet top management frequently mistreats it. By constraining the ISD to technical duties, top management may jeopardize an organization's entire future. However, it is not economically feasible for the ISD to develop and manage all IT applications in an organization. End users play an important role in IT development and management. The end users know best what their information needs are and to what degree they are fulfilled. Properly managed end-user computing is essential for the betterment of all organizations (see Chapters 9 and 14).

6. *Ethical issues.* Systems developed by the ISD and maintained by end users may introduce some ethical issues. The ISD's major objective should be to build efficient and effective systems. But, such systems may invade the privacy of the users or create advantages for certain individuals at the expense of others. See Ethics in IT Management (Appendix 1A in Chapter 1), the Ethics Primer (Chapter 1 online), and Chapter 16 (online) for details.

ON THE WEB SITE... Additional resources, including quizzes; online files of additional text, tables, figures, and cases; and frequently updated Web links to current articles and information can be found on the book's Web site (*wiley.com/college/turban*).

KEY TERMS

Application program *50*
Business architecture *65*
Chief information officer (CIO) *77*
Client *68*
Client/server architecture *68*
Cooperative processing *67*
Corporate portals *72*
Data item *51*
Data workers *62*
Database *51*
Distributed processing *67*
Electronic data interchange (EDI) *55*
Electronic exchanges *73*
Electronic markets *72*
Electronic storefront *72*

End-user computing *55*
Enterprise Web *73*
Enterprisewide computing *69*
Enterprisewide information system (EIS) *53*
Extranets *72*
Functional MIS *58*
Grid computing *75*
Information *51*
Information infrastructure *65*
Information system (IS) *50*
Information technology architecture *65*
Interorganizational information system (IOS) *53*
Intranet *71*
Knowledge *51*

Knowledge workers *61*
Legacy system *70*
Mobile commerce (m-commerce) *73*
Mobile computing *55*
Peer-to-peer (P2P) architecture *70*
Server *68*
Smart terminal *67*
Subscription computing *75*
Supply chain *62*
Transaction processing system (TPS) *57*
Utility computing *74*
Web-based systems *71*
Web services *75*
Wireless computing *73*

CHAPTER HIGHLIGHTS (Numbers Refer to Learning Objectives)

❶ Information systems can be organized according to organizational hierarchy (e.g., departmental, enterprisewide, and interorganizational) or by the nature of supported task (e.g., operational, managerial, and strategic).

❶ Interorganizational information systems (IOSs) connect two or more organizations and play a major role in e-business.

❷ The transaction processing system (TPS) covers the core repetitive organizational transactions such as purchasing, billing, or payroll.

❷ The data collected in a TPS are used to build other systems.

❷ The major functional information systems in an organization are accounting, finance, manufacturing (operations), human resources, and marketing.

②, ❸ The term *management information system* refers to the department that manages information systems in organizations. (The acronym MIS is also used more generally to describe the field of IT.)

❸ The main general support systems are office automation systems, decision support systems, executive support systems, group support systems, knowledge management systems, enterprise information systems, expert systems, and artificial neural networks.

❸ Managerial activities and decisions can be classified as operational, managerial (tactical), and strategic.

❹ Two of the major IT-supported managerial activities are improving supply chain operations and the introduction of a variety of customer relationship management (CRM) activities. IT is a major enabler of both.

❺ Information architecture provides the conceptual foundation for building the information infrastructure and specific applications. It maps the information requirements as they relate to information resources.

❺ There are three major configurations of information architecture: the mainframe environment, the PC environment, and the distributed (networked) environment. An emerging architecture is peer-to-peer.

❺ The information infrastructure refers to the shared information resources (such as a corporate database) and their linkages, operation, maintenance, and management.

❻ In client/server architecture, several PCs (the clients) are networked among themselves and are connected to databases, telecommunications, and other devices (the servers) that provide services.

❻ An enterprisewide information system is a system that provides communication among all the organization's employees. It also provides accessibility to any data or information needed by any employee at any location.

❻ Legacy systems are older systems in which the mainframe is at the core of the system.

❼ Web-based systems refer to those applications or services that reside on a server that is accessible using a Web browser. Examples are the Internet, intranets, extranets, e-commerce and storefronts, corporate portals, electronic markets and exchanges, and mobile commerce.

❽ There is a trend for renting application software as needed rather buying it. This way, there is no need to build systems or own software. This approach, called *utility computing*, is similar to buying water or electricity when needed.

❽ Wireless is becoming the network of choice for many applications.

❾ Information resources are extremely important, and they must be managed properly by both the ISD and end users. In general, the ISD manages shared enterprise information resources such as networks, while end users are responsible for departmental information resources, such as PCs.

❾ The role of the ISD is becoming more managerial, and its importance is rapidly increasing.

QUESTIONS FOR REVIEW

1. Define data, information, and knowledge.
2. Describe a TPS.
3. What is an MIS?
4. Explain the role of the DSS.
5. How does a KMS work?
6. Describe operational, managerial, and strategic activities.
7. What information systems support the work of groups?
8. What is an enterprisewide system?
9. What is information architecture?
10. Define information infrastructure.
11. Describe the evolution of support systems over time.
12. What is a Web-based system?
13. Define the Internet, intranet, and extranet.
14. What is mobile commerce?
15. List the information resources that are usually managed by end users.
16. Distinguish between a mainframe and a distributed environment.
17. Define a legacy system.
18. What is a client/server system?
19. Define utility computing.
20. What/who are knowledge workers?
21. Define peer-to-peer architecture.
22. Define grid computing.

QUESTIONS FOR DISCUSSION

1. Discuss the logic of building information systems in accordance with the organizational hierarchical structure.
2. Distinguish between interorganizational information systems (IOS) and electronic markets.
3. Describe how business architecture, IT architecture, and information infrastructure are interrelated.
4. Explain how operational, managerial, and strategic activities are related to various IT support systems.
5. Relate the following concepts: client/server, distributed processing, and enterprisewide computing.
6. Discuss the capabilities of P2P architecture.
7. Web-based applications such as e-commerce and e-government exemplify the platform shift from client/server computing to Web-based computing.

Discuss the advantages of a Web-based operating environment.

8. Is the Internet an infrastructure, architecture, or application program? Why? If none of the above, then what is it?
9. There is wide speculation that m-commerce will surpass wireline e-commerce (e-commerce that takes place over wired networks) as the method of choice for digital commerce transactions. What industries or application areas will be most affected by m-commerce?
10. Some speculate that utility computing will be the dominating option of the future. Do you agree? Discuss why or why not.

EXERCISES

1. Classify each of the following systems as one (or more) of the IT support systems:
   a. A student registration system in a university.
   b. A system that advises farmers about which fertilizers to use.
   c. A hospital patient-admission system.
   d. A system that provides a marketing manager with demand reports regarding the sales volume of specific products.
   e. A robotic system that paints cars in a factory.
2. Select two companies you are familiar with and find their mission statement and current goals (plans). Explain how these goals are related to operational, managerial, and strategic activities on a one-to-one basis. Then explain how information systems (by type) can support the activities (be specific).

3. Review the list of key IT management issues (see the subsection titled, "The Role of the IS Department," page 77).
   a. Present these issues to IT managers in a company you can access. (You may want to develop a questionnaire.)
   b. Have the managers vote on the importance of these items. Also ask them to add any items that are important to them but don't appear on the list. Report the results.
4. Review the following systems in this chapter and identify the support provided by IT:
   ● Chase Manhattan Bank
   ● Maybelline (Minicase 1)
   ● JCPenney (Minicase 2)
   ● Bomb detection by the FAA (see Online File W2.1)
   ● Best Buy online (see Online File W2.3)

GROUP ASSIGNMENTS

1. Observe a checkout counter in a supermarket that uses a scanner. Find some material that describes how the scanned code is translated into the price that the customers pay.
   a. Identify the following components of the system: inputs, processes, and outputs.
   b. What kind of a system is the scanner (TPS, DSS, ESS, ES, etc.)? Why did you classify it as you did?
   c. Having the information electronically in the system may provide opportunities for additional managerial uses of that information. Identify such uses.

   d. Checkout systems are now being replaced by self-service checkout kiosks and scanners. Compare the two.
2. Divide the class into teams. Each team will select a small business to start (a restaurant, dry cleaning business, small travel agency, etc.). Assume the business wants to become an e-business. Each team will plan the architecture for the business's information systems, possibly in consultation with Microsoft or another vendor. Make a class presentation.

INTERNET EXERCISES

1. Enter the site of Federal Express (*fedex.com*) and find the current information systems used by the company or offered to FedEx's customers. Explain how the systems' innovations contribute to the success of FedEx.

2. Surf the Internet for information about airport security regarding bomb- and weapon-detecting devices. Examine the available products, and comment on the IT techniques used.

3. Enter the Web site of Hershey Foods (*hersheys.com*). Examine the information about the company and its products and markets. Explain how an intranet can help such a company compete in the global market.

4. Investigate the status of utility computing by visiting *infoworld.com/forums/utility, aspnews.com* (discussion forum), *google.com, ibm.com, oracle.com,* and *cio.com.*

Prepare a report that will highlight the progress today and the current inhibitors.

5. Enter *argus-acia.com* and learn about new developments in the field of information architecture. Also, view the tutorials at *hotwired.com/webmonkey* on this topic. Summarize major new trends.

6. Investigate the status of pervasive computing by looking at *ibm.com/software/pervasive, computer.org/pervasive,* and *percom.org.* Prepare a report.

7. Enter *cio.com* and find recent information on the changing role of the CIO and the ISD. Prepare a report.

8. Enter *oracle.com* and *mysap.com* and identify material related to supply chain and enterprisewide systems. Prepare a report.

Minicase 1
E-Commerce Supports Field Employees at Maybelline

The Business Problem

Maybelline is a leader in color cosmetics products (eye shadow, mascara, etc.), selling them in more than 70 countries worldwide (*maybelline.com*). The company uses hundreds of salespeople (field merchandising representatives, or "reps"), who visit drugstores, discount stores, supermarkets, and cosmetics specialty stores, in an attempt to close deals. This method of selling has proved to be fairly effective, and it is used by hundreds of other manufacturers such as Kodak, Nabisco, and Procter & Gamble. Sales managers from any company need to know, as quickly as possible, when a deal is closed or if there is any problem with the customer.

Information technology has been used extensively to support sales reps and their managers. Until 2000, Maybelline, as well as many other large consumer product manufacturers, equipped reps with an interactive voice response (IVR) system, by means of which they were to enter, every evening, information about their daily activities. This solution required that the reps collect data with paper-based surveys completed for every store they visited each day. For example, the reps noted how each product was displayed, how much stock was available, how items were promoted, etc. In addition to the company's products the reps surveyed the competitors' products as well. In the evening, the reps translated the data collected into answers to the voice response system, which asked them routine questions. The reps answered by pressing the appropriate telephone keys.

The IVR system was not the perfect way to transmit sales data. For one thing, the IVR system consolidated information, delivering it to top management as a hard copy. Also, unfortunately, these reports sometimes reached top management days or weeks too late, missing important changes in trends and the opportunities to act on them in time. Frequently, the reps themselves were late in reporting, thus further delaying the needed information.

Even if the reps did report on time, information was inflexible, since all reports were menu-driven. With the voice system the reps answered only the specific questions that applied to a situation. To do so, they had to wade through over 50 questions, skipping the irrelevant ones. This was a waste of time. In addition, some of the material that needed to be reported had no matching menu questions. Considered a success in the 1990s, the system was unable to meet the needs of the twenty-first century. It was cumbersome to set up and operate and was also prone to input errors.

The E-Business Solution

Maybelline replaced the IVR system by equipping its reps with a mobile system, called Merchandising Sales Portfolio (MSP), from Thinque Corp. (*thinque.com*). It runs on hand-held, pen-based PDAs (personal digital assistants), which have handwriting recognition capability (from NEC), powered by Microsoft's CE operating system. The system enables reps to enter their information by hand-writing their reports directly at the clients' sites. From the hand-held device, data can be uploaded to a Microsoft SQL Server database at headquarters every evening. A secured Internet connection links the PDA to the corporate intranet (a synchronization process). The new system also enables district managers to electronically send daily schedules and other important information to each rep.

The system also replaced some of the functions of the EDI (electronic data interchange) system, the pride of the 1990s. For example, the reps' reports include inventory-scanned data from retail stores. These are processed quickly by an *order management system*, and passed whenever needed to the shipping department for inventory replenishment.

In addition to routine information, the new system is used for decision support. It is not enough to speed information along the supply chain; managers need to know the *reasons why* certain products are selling well, or not so well, in every location. They need to know what the conditions are at retail stores affecting the sales of each product, and they need to know it in a timely manner. The new system offers those capabilities.

The Results

The system provided managers at Maybelline headquarters with an interactive link with the mobile field force. Corporate planners and decision makers can now respond much more quickly to situations that need attention. The solution is helping the company forge stronger ties with its retailers, and it considerably reduces the amount of after-hours time that the reps spend on data transfer to headquarters (from 30–50 minutes per day to seconds).

The new system also performs market analysis that enables managers to optimize merchandising and customer service efforts. It also enables Maybelline to use a more sophisticated interactive voice response unit—to capture data for special situations. Moreover, it provides browser-based reporting tools that enable managers, regardless of where they are, to view retail information within hours of its capture. Using the error-checking and validation feature in the MSP system, reps make significantly fewer data entry errors.

Finally, the quality of life of Maybelline reps has been greatly improved. Not only do they save 30 to 40 minutes per day, but also their stress level has been significantly reduced. As a result, employee turnover has declined appreciably, saving money for the company.

Source: Compiled from "Industry Solutions—Maybelline," at *thinque.com* (accessed May 15, 2002).

Questions for Minicase 1

1. IVR systems are still popular. What advantages do they have over even older systems in which the reps mailed or faxed reports?

2. Summarize the advantages of the new system over the IVR one.

3. Explain why Maybelline's new reporting system is an e-commerce application.

4. The existing technology enables transmission of data any time an employee can access the Internet with a wireline. Technically, the system can be enhanced so that the data can be sent *wirelessly* from any location as soon as they are entered. Would you recommend a wireless system to Maybelline? Why or why not?

Minicase 2
Two Faces of JCPenney

In 2000, Dallas retailer JCPenney (*JCPenney.com*) enhanced its e-retail position in time for the holiday rush by adding homegrown site features that let customers more quickly locate and pay for merchandise. With *JCPenney.com*, the company unveiled express checkout services that let customers zip through a purchase in as few as two clicks. It also inaugurated electronic gift certificates that can be redeemed online, plus improved order tracking to give customers more accurate delivery estimates. These features followed the early November 2000 launch of Mercado Search, a search engine that lets shoppers prowl JCPenney's site by product category and receive results ranked according to relevance. In 2001, the company rolled out specialized sites dedicated to name-brand merchandise, making it easier for customers to find certain products. All these steps were designed to boost the company's online strategy.

The success of JCPenney.com, in large measure, is a result of a customer service and logistics infrastructure built to support a multibillion-dollar catalog business that has been extended online. JCPenney.com broadened its appeal by launching specialty sites to promote high-margin brands, including Sony, Levi Strauss, Nike, and Kitchen Aid (appliances). The idea is to drive purchases of name-brand merchandise by providing more detailed information on those products, as well as direct links to the manufacturers. JCPenney is also conducting auctions on its Web site.

The company boasts strong integration between its Web site and its offline infrastructure that helps the site reach its aggressive sales targets. Anything purchased online can be picked up or returned at any JCPenney or Eckerd store. JCPenney has 14 customer-service centers nationwide that handle catalog and phone inquiries, and employees have been cross-trained in e-mail. United Parcel Service (UPS) delivers most merchandise ordered online within 24 to 72 hours.

JCPenney serves customers via three sales channels—stores, catalogs, and the Web site. Integrating these three channels will eventually pay off, according to Forrester Research analyst Seema Williams. "As the number of online shoppers grows, the impact from multiple channels will be felt much more on JCPenney's bottom line," Williams said.

Despite the strong Web performance, e-commerce alone most likely cannot turn around a company of JCPenney's size. "The Web is such a small part of their business; there's no way it's going to turn around the company," said an expert. "The Web is icing on the cake, but the biggest part of the company, by far, is struggling."

Sources: Compiled from "The Two Faces of J.C. Penney," *www.internetweek.com/lead/lead_112400.htm* (November 2000) and from *jcpenney.com*, press releases Jan.–Feb. 2003.

Questions for Minicase 2

1. How does a search engine help JCPenney to do a better job in customer service?

2. Does its existing legacy system help JCPenney.com accomplish its goal in promoting its online business? Can any of the emerging technologies be used to further improve the situation?

3. What kind of information technologies can be used to help JCPenney to promote its business? To accomplish its business strategies?

4. Visit *JCPenney.com* to see how the company uses its storefront to provide customer services.

5. Visit *sears.com* and *marksandspencer.com*, and find out these companies' e-commerce strategies. Compare the functionalities offered there with those of JCPenney.

Virtual Company Assignment
TWC Information Architecture

You've enjoyed a few meals at The Wireless Café, and you're starting to learn your way around the restaurant's back office. Now, you need to get to work on a preliminary study of the restaurant's information architecture.

In addition to managing the restaurant operations, Jeremy has implemented most of the information technologies at The Wireless Café, though he has not had the time to document what he has done. To better understand where the restaurant's IT is headed, you need to understand where it is now. Jeremy has also asked you to help him document the existing infrastructure.

Instructions

1. Identify three people you want to interview at The Wireless Café to help you understand the current information architecture.
   a. For each person, prepare three questions you'll ask them to elicit information about their perspective on information needs.
   b. To better prepare yourself for the interviews, go online and do some research on the software and hardware available for the restaurant industry.
2. What kinds of information does The Wireless Café collect at the transaction level?
3. What kind of management and decision support information do Barbara and Jeremy need?
4. What competitive opportunities do you see for IT at The Wireless Café?

REFERENCES

Agre, P. E., "P2P and the Promise of Internet Equality," *Communications of the ACM*, 46(2), February 2003.

Ahmad, I., "Network Computers: The Changing Face of Computing," *IEEE Concurrency*, 8(4), October–December 2000.

Amato-McCoy, D. M., "Thin-Client Technology Trims IT Maintenance Costs, Adds Flexibility and Growth," *Stores*, November 2002.

Ball, L. D., "CIO on Center Stage: 9/11 Changes Everything," *Journal of Information Systems Management*, Spring 2002.

Bantz, D. F. et al., "The Emerging Model of Subscription Computing," *IT Pro*, 4(4), July–August 2002.

Best Buy, "Making the Best Buying Decisions," e-business case study, *http://www-3.ibm.com/e-business/doc/content/casestudy/43886.html* (accessed March 18, 2003).

Borland, J., "Fingerprinting P2P Pirates," *News.com*, February 20, 2003.

Broadbent, M., and P. Weill, "Management by Maxim: How Business IT Managers Can Create IT Infrastructures," *Sloan Management Review*, Spring 1997.

Conley, W. L. et al., "Building an E-Business at FedEx Corporation," *Society for Information Management Annual Awards Paper Competition*, 2000, *simnet.org/library/doc/2ndplace.doc*.

Cone, E., "New World Order: Software Giants Vie to Control the Supernet," *Interactive Week*, June 25, 2001.

Cortese, A., "The Power of Optimal Pricing," *Business 2.0*, September 2002.

Erlikh, L., "Leveraging Legacy Systems in Modern Architecture," *Journal of Information Technology Cases and Applications*, July–September 2002.

Friar, B., "Fast Data Relief," *Information Week*, December 2, 1996.

Girishankar, S., "Modular Net Eases Merger," *techweb.com/se/directlink.cgi, CWK19970421S0005*, April 1997.

Greenberg, P., *CRM at the Speed of Light: Capturing and Keeping Customers in Internet Real Time*, 2nd ed., New York: McGraw-Hill, 2002.

Hapgood, F., "Embedded Logic," *CIO Magazine*, May 1, 2000, *http://www.cio.com/archive/050100_revisit.html*.

"Industry Solutions—Maybelline," *Thinque.com*, May 15, 2002.

Khalidi, Y., "N1: Revolutionary IT Architecture for Business," 2002, *sun.com/software/solutions/n1/essays/khalidi.html*.

Kini, R. B., "Peer-to-Peer Technology: A Technology Reborn," *Information Systems Management*, Summer 2002.

Koontz, C., "Develop a Solid Architecture," *e-Business Advisor*, January 2000.

Kuo, J., "Network Computing: Evolution, Trends, and Challenges," *Computer Science and Information Systems Seminar*, October 31, 2000, University of Hong Kong.

Lipson, S., "Integration Building Blocks," *Oracle*, November–December 2001.

Lohr, S., "Sony to Supercharge Online Gaming," *International Herald Tribune*, February 28, 2003.

Margulius, D., "The Realities of Utility Computing," *Infoworld.com*, April 15, 2002.

Martin, C. F., "Legacy Value Engineering," *Information Technology: The Executive's Journal*, 2002.

Mol, M. J., and Koppius O. R., "Information Technology and the Internationalization of the Firm," *Journal of Global Information Management*, October–December 2002.

O'Donovan, B., and D. Roode, "A Framework for Understanding the Emerging Discipline of Information Systems," *Information Technology and People*, 15(1), 2002.

Parihor, M. et al., *ASP.Net Bible*. New York: Hungry Mind, 2002.

Reid, D., and N. Sanders, *Operations Management*. New York: John Wiley and Sons, 2002.

Rhey, E., "Pepsi Refreshes, Wirelessly," *PC*, September 17, 2002, pp. 4–5.

Santosus, M., "Wire Education," *CIO Web Business*, October 1998.

Schonfeld, E., "Computing to the Nth degree," *Business 2.0*, September 2002.

Stanford, V., "Using Pervasive Computing to Deliver Elder Care," *Pervasive Computing*, January–March, 2002.

"Success Story: Best Buy," *Microstrategy.com, http://www.microstrategy.com/Customers/Successes/bestbuy.asp*, 2003.

Tabor, R., *Microsoft.Net XML Web Services*. Indianapolis, IN: SAMS, 2002.

"The Two Faces of J.C. Penney," *http://www.internetweek.com/lead/lead_112400.htm*, November 2000.

Turban, E. et al., *Electronic Commerce: A Managerial Perspective*, 3rd ed. Upper Saddle River, NJ: Prentice Hall, 2004.

Wainewright, P., "The Power of Utility Computing," *ASPnews.com*, September 30, 2002.

Weill, P., and M. R. Vitale, *Place to Space: Migrating to eBusiness Models*. Boston: Harvard Business Press, 2001.

Whipple, L. C., "Master the Art of Translation," *e-Business Advisor*, March 2001.

APPENDIX 2A

BUILD-TO-ORDER PRODUCTION

The concept of build-to-order means that you start to make a product (service) only *after* an order for it is placed. This concept is as old as commerce itself, and was the only method of production until the Industrial Revolution began. According to this concept, if you need a pair of shoes, you go to a shoemaker who takes the measurement. You negotiate quality, design, and price, and you make a down payment. The shoemaker buys the materials and makes a customized product for you. Customized products were expensive, and it took a long time to finish them. This changed with the coming of the Industrial Revolution.

The Industrial Revolution started with the concept of dividing work into small parts. Such *division of labor* makes the work simpler, requiring less training for employees. It also allows for *specialization*. Different employees become experts in executing certain tasks. Because the work segments are simpler, it is easier to *automate* them. All this reduces the prices to consumers, and demand increases. So the concept of *build-to-market* developed. To build to market, it was necessary to design standard products, produce them, store them, and then sell them. The creation of standard products by automation drove prices down still further and demand accelerated. To meet the ever-increasing demand, the solution of mass production was created.

According to the concept of *mass production,* a manufacturer produces large amounts of standard products at a very low cost, and then "pushes" (markets) them to consumers. With increased competition and the desire to sell in remote markets, it was necessary to create special marketing organizations to do the sales. This new model also required the creation of large factories, and finance, accounting, personnel, and other departments to keep track of the many new and specialized business activities. In mass production, the workers do not know who the customers are, and frequently do not care about customers' needs or product quality. But the products are inexpensive, and their price fueled demand, so the concept became a dominant one. Mass production also required inventory systems at various places in the supply chain, which were based on forecasted demand. If the forecasted demand was wrong, the inventories were incorrect: Either the inventories were insufficient to meet demand, or there was too much inventory at hand.

As society became more affluent, the demand for customized products, especially cars, increased. To make sales, manufacturers had to meet this kind of demand. As long as the demand for customized product was small, there was no problem of meeting it. In purchasing a new car, for example, customers were asked to pay a premium and wait for a long time, and they were willing to do so. Slowly, the demand for customized products and services increased. In the 1970s, Burger King introduced the concept of "having it your way," and manufacturers began looking for solutions for providing customized products in large quantities. This idea is the essence of *mass customization.* Such solutions were usually enhanced by some kind of information technologies (Pine and Gilmore, 1999). Later, Dell Computer introduced the idea of customized PCs. This customization strategy was so successful that many other industries also wanted to try mass customization. However, they found that it is not so easy to do so (Zipkin, 2001; Agrawal et al., 2001).

Using e-commerce can facilitate the use of customization and even the use of mass customization (Holweg and Pil, 2001). To understand this strategy, let's look first at a comparison of mass production, also known as a *push system,* with mass customization, also known as a *pull system,* as shown in Figure 2A.1.

One important area in the supply chain is ordering. Using EC a customer can self-configure the desired product online. The order is received in seconds, and once it is verified and payment arranged, the order is sent electronically to the production floor. This saves processing time and money. For complex products, customers may collaborate in real time with the manufacturer's designers, as is done at Cisco Systems. Again, time and money are saved, and errors are reduced due to better communication and collaboration.

Other contributions of EC to mass customization are the following: The customers' needs are

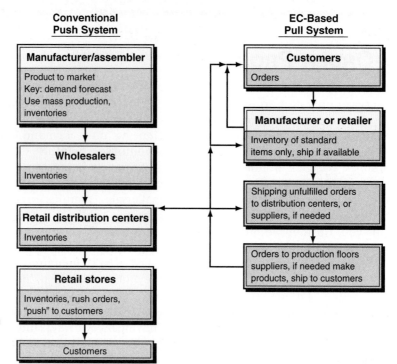

FIGURE 2A.1 Comparison of a push-based supply chain and a pull-based supply chain.

visible to all partners in the order-fulfillment chain (fewer delays, faster response time); inventories are reduced due to rapid communication; and digitizable products and services can be delivered electronically, at almost no additional cost.

Another key area in mass customization is understanding what the customers want, and EC is also very helpful here (see Chapter 4 and Holweg and Pil, 2001). E-commerce can help in expediting the production changeover from one item to another. Also, since most mass production is based on assembly of standard components, EC can help make the production configuration in minutes, including the identification of the needed components and their

location. Furthermore, a production schedule can be automatically generated, detailing deployment of all needed resources, including money. This is why many industries, and particularly the auto manufacturers, are planning to move to build-to-order using EC. As a result of this change in production methods, they are expecting huge cost reductions, shorter order-to-delivery time, and lower inventory costs. (See Exhibit 1 in Agrawal et al., 2001, and Holweg and Pil, 2001.)

Mass customization on a large scale is not easy to attain (Zipkin, 2001 and Agrawal et al., 2001), but if properly performed, it may become the dominant model in many industries.

References for Appendix 2A

Agrawal, M. T. V. et al., "The False Promise of Mass Customization," *McKinsey Quarterly,* No. 3, 2001.

Holweg, M., and F. Pil, "Successful Build-to-Order Strategies Start with the Customer," *MIT Sloan Management Journal,* 43(1), Fall 2001, pp. 74–83.

Pine, B. J., and J. Gilmore, "The Four Faces of Mass Customization," *Harvard Business Review,* January–February 1997.

Zipkin, P., "The Limits of Mass Customization," *MIT Sloan Management Review,* Spring 2001.

PART I
IT in the Organization

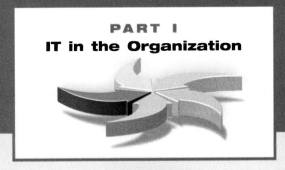

1. Information Technology in the Digital Economy
2. Information Technologies: Concepts and Management
▶ 3. Strategic Information Systems for Competitive Advantage

CHAPTER

3

Strategic Information Systems for Competitive Advantage

3.1
Strategic Advantage and Information Technology

3.2
Porter's Competitive Forces Model and Strategies

3.3
Porter's Value Chain Model

3.4
Interorganizational Strategic Information Systems

3.5
A Framework for Global Competition

3.6
Strategic Information Systems: Examples and Analysis

3.7
Implementing and Sustaining SIS

LEARNING OBJECTIVES

After studying this chapter, you will be able to:

❶ Describe strategic information systems (SISs) and explain their advantages.

❷ Describe Porter's competitive forces model and how information technology helps companies improve their competitive positions.

❸ Describe 12 strategies companies can use to achieve competitive advantage in their industry.

❹ Describe Porter's value chain model and its relationship to information technology.

❺ Describe how linking information systems across organizations helps companies achieve competitive advantage.

❻ Describe global competition and global business drivers.

❼ Describe representative SISs and the advantage they provide to organizations.

❽ Discuss the challenges associated with sustaining competitive advantage.

ROSENBLUTH INTERNATIONAL: COMPETING IN THE DIGITAL ECONOMY

 THE PROBLEM

Rosenbluth International (*rosenbluth.com*) is a major global player in the extremely competitive travel agent industry. Rosenbluth's mission is "to be the quality leader in the development and distribution of global travel services and information." The digital revolution has introduced various threats and business pressures to Rosenbluth and other agencies in the industry:

1. Airlines, hotels, and other service providers are attempting to displace travel agents by moving aggressively to electronic distribution systems (e.g., airlines are issuing electronic tickets and groups of airlines are sponsoring selling portals for direct sale of tickets and packages).

2. Some travel service providers have reduced commissions caps and have cut the commission percentage for travel agents from 10 percent to 8 and then to 5 percent.

3. A number of new online companies such as *expedia.com* are providing diversified travel services as well as bargain prices, mostly to attract individual travelers. These services are penetrating to the corporate travel area, which has been the "bread and butter" of the travel agents' business.

4. The competition among the major players is rebate-based. The travel agencies basically give back to their customers part of the commission they get from travel service providers.

5. Innovative business models that were introduced by e-commerce, such as auctions and reverse auctions, were embraced by the providers in the industry, adding to competitive pressures on travel agencies (see Turban et al., 2004).

All of these business pressures threatened the welfare of Rosenbluth.

 THE SOLUTION

The company responded with two strategies. First, it decided to get out of the leisure travel business, instead becoming a purely corporate travel agency. Second, it decided to rebate customers with the *entire* commission the agency receives and instead bill customers by service provided. Rosenbluth charges fees, for example, for consultation on how to lower costs, for development of in-house travel policies, for negotiating for their clients with travel providers, and for calls answered by the company staff. To implement this second strategy, which completely changed the company's business model, it was necessary to use several innovative information systems.

Rosenbluth uses a comprehensive Web-based business travel management solution that integrates Web-based travel planning technology, policy and profile management tools, proprietary travel management applications, and seamless front-line service/support. This browser-based service allows corporate travelers to book reservations any time, anywhere—within corporate travel policy—in minutes. Three of the customer-facing tools that comprise this system are:

- ***DACODA (Discount Analysis Containing Optimal Decision Algorithms).*** This is a patented yield-management system that enables travel managers to decipher complex airline pricing and identify the most favorable airline contracts. Use of this system optimizes a client corporation's travel savings.
- ***Global Distribution Network.*** This network electronically links the corporate locations and enables instant access to any traveler's itinerary, personal travel preferences, or corporate travel policy.
- ***iVISION.*** This proprietary back-office application provides Rosenbluth's clients with consolidated, global data to enable them to negotiate better prices with airlines, hotels, car rental companies, and other travel providers.

 THE RESULTS

Using its IT innovations, Rosenbluth grew from sales of $40 million in 1979 to over $5 billion in 2002. Today, the company has physical offices in 57 countries and employs over 4,700 associates. The company not only survived the threats of elimination but has become the third-largest travel management company in the world and a leader in customer service, travel technology, and integrated information management.

Sources: Compiled from Clemons and Hann (1999) and from information at *rosenbluth.com.*

 LESSONS LEARNED FROM THIS CASE

This opening case is a vivid example of a company that has achieved competitive advantage in the digital era by using IT. Rosenbluth's experience illustrates the following points:

- It is sometimes necessary to completely change business models and strategies to succeed in the digital economy.
- Web-based IT enables companies to gain competitive advantage and to survive in the face of serious corporate threat.
- Global competition is not just about price and quality; it is about service as well.
- IT may require a large investment over a long period of time.
- Extensive networked computing infrastructure is necessary to support a large global system.
- Web-based applications can be used to provide superb customer service.
- It is necessary to patent innovative systems to assure competitive advantage. Otherwise, competitors will copy the systems, and the advantage will disappear.

The most important lesson learned from this case is the double-sided potential of the Internet: It can become a threat to an entire industry, yet it can also be an extremely important tool for gaining strategic advantage for an innovative company. As a matter of fact, many executives who until 1998 were cynical about the strategic advantages of IT have completely reversed their attitudes. They are seeing the potential of Web-based systems to provide competitive advantage to organizations, and Web-based opportunities and risks are now attracting universal attention in executive boardrooms.

As a matter of fact, computer-based information systems of all kinds have been enhancing competitiveness and creating strategic advantage for several decades (e.g., see Griffiths et al., 1998, Galliers et al., 1999, and Ward and Peppard, 2002). Through numerous examples, this chapter demonstrates how different kinds of strategic information systems work. We also present some classic models upon which strategic information systems have been built and utilized from the 1970s to this very day.

3.1 STRATEGIC ADVANTAGE AND INFORMATION TECHNOLOGY

Strategic Information Systems

Strategic information systems (SISs), like the ones developed at Rosenbluth International, are systems that *support* or *shape* a business unit's competitive strategy (Callon, 1996, and Neumann, 1994). An SIS is characterized by its ability to *significantly* change the manner in which business is conducted, in order to give the firm strategic advantage. An SIS cannot be classified by organizational structure, functional area, or support system as described in the previous chapter. Any information system—EIS, OIS, TPS, KMS—that changes the goals, processes, products, or environmental relationships to help an organization gain a competitive advantage or reduce a competitive disadvantage is a strategic information system.

A *competitive strategy* is a broad-based formula for how a business is going to compete, what its goals should be, and what plans and policies will be required to carry out those goals (Porter, 1985). Through its competitive strategy an organization seeks a **competitive advantage** in an industry—an advantage over competitors in some measure such as cost, quality, or speed. Competitive advantage is at the core of a firm's success or failure (Porter and Millar, 1985, and Porter, 1996); such advantage seeks to lead to control of the market and to larger-than-average profits. A strategic information system helps an organization gain a competitive advantage through its contribution to the strategic goals of an organization and/or its ability to significantly increase performance and productivity. An SIS enables companies to gain competitive advantage and to benefit greatly at the expense of those that are subject to competitive disadvantage.

Competitive advantage in the digital economy is even more important than in the old economy, as will be demonstrated throughout this chapter. For some businesses the impact of the digital economy is revolutionary. Frequent changes in technologies and markets and the appearance of new business models can introduce radical changes in industry structure (Deise et al., 2000) and the nature of competition can shift rapidly (Afuah and Tucci, 2003, and Choi and Whinston, 2000).

At the same time, the digital economy has not changed the *core business* of most firms. For most businesses, Internet technologies simply offer the tools, sometimes very powerful tools, that can increase their success through their traditional sources of competitive advantage—be that low cost, excellent customer service, or superior supply chain management. For the overwhelming majority of businesses, the first step to competitive advantage in the digital economy is to ask and answer the question, "Where, given my industry and position, does my competitive advantage come from?" Then the follow-up question, "How can

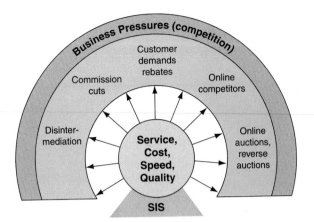

FIGURE 3.1 Strategic information systems at Rosenbluth—defending against business pressures and competition.

information technology, especially the Internet, help my business?" will be easier to answer (Bithos, 2001).

Let's examine Rosenbluth's competitive situation in light of the business pressures and organizational responses described in Chapter 1. As Figure 3.1 shows, there were five business pressures on the company. Rosenbluth's strategic response was (1) to eliminate the retailing activities, which were most likely to be impacted by the pressures, and (2) to change the revenue model from commission-based to fee-for-service-based. Such strategy required extensive IT support.

Originally, strategic information systems were considered to be *outwardly focused*—that is, aimed at increasing direct competition in an industry and visible to all. For example, strategic systems have been used to provide new services to customers and/or suppliers, to increase customer switching costs, and to lock in suppliers, all with the specific objective of achieving better results than one's competitors. But since the late 1980s, strategic systems have also been viewed *inwardly:* They are focused on enhancing the competitive position of the firm by increasing employees' productivity, streamlining business processes, and making better decisions. These approaches may not be visible to the competitors (and therefore are not as easily copied). An example of an inward-focused SIS is RadioShack Online, as described in *IT at Work 3.1* (page 94).

In order to better understand strategic information systems, next we will examine the role information technology plays in strategic management.

The Role of IT in Strategic Management

Strategic management is the way an organization maps the strategy of its future operations. The term *strategic* points to the long-term nature of this mapping exercise and to the large magnitude of advantage the exercise is expected to give an organization. Information technology contributes to strategic management in many ways (see Kemerer, 1997, and Callon, 1996). Consider these eight:

1. *Innovative applications.* IT creates innovative applications that provide direct strategic advantage to organizations. For example, Federal Express was the first company in its industry to use IT for tracking the location of every package in its system. Next, FedEx was the first company to make this database accessible to its customers over the Internet. FedEx has gone on to provide

IT at Work 3.1
RADIOSHACK ONLINE PROVIDES ALL THE ANSWERS

RadioShack's advertising tagline, "You've got questions. We've got answers" reflects a change from a geek-oriented business model to a for-everyone model that is intended to attract and keep customers who are not so technically literate and not so interested in "do-it-yourself" electronics. A key component of this new strategy is RadioShack Online (*radioshack.com*), an intranet that educates in-store associates about business processes and product information, making them better equipped to address customer questions and needs.

Applications supported by RadioShack Online include:

- *Customer ticket look-up.* Returns can be verified from any store, on any sale, for any date, with or without a receipt.

- *Parts look-up.* Each store is able to maintain catalogs featuring 100,000 items not ordinarily kept on-hand. Items can be ordered in the store and shipped directly to customers' homes.

- *Service contracts.* When a customer returns a defective product under a service contract, associates can go on-line to instantly verify that there is a contract and to get approval for fixing the merchandise.

- *Product availability.* When a desired item is out of stock, employees can search for it through the entire stock file for all stores in all regions.

- *Testing.* Tests that are part of RadioShack's employee-certification program can now be taken online in a store, with immediate feedback.

- *Electronic memos and manuals.* Paper manuals have now been put online for easier access and updating.

- *Online credit card applications.* Associates can type credit card applications directly into the online network and receive an approval or rejection within 60 seconds.

- *Sales reports.* These reports can illustrate performance by associate, store, and region.

Customers never see, touch, or use this internal network, but they benefit from its existence. Bob Gellman, Vice President for Online Strategies at RadioShack, says that thanks to RadioShack Online, shoppers view associates as "friendly, knowledgeable people who are very adept at de-mystifying technology." RadioShack benefits too by retaining happy customers.

Source: Fox (2002).

For Further Exploration: How does RadioShack Online fit into RadioShack's new business model? In addition to the benefits for customers and for RadioShack that were highlighted in the case, how do in-store associates benefit? Why would RadioShack Online qualify as a strategic information system?

---

e-fulfillment solutions based on IT and is even writing software for this purpose (Bhise et al., 2000).

2. *Competitive weapons.* Information systems themselves have long been recognized as a competitive weapon (Ives and Learmouth, 1984, and Callon, 1996). Amazon.com's one-click shopping system is considered so significant and important to the company's reputation for superior customer service that it has patented the system. Michael Dell, founder of Dell Computer, puts it bluntly: "The Internet is like a weapon sitting on the table, ready to be picked up by either you or your competitors" (Dell, 1999).

3. *Changes in processes.* IT supports changes in business processes that translate to strategic advantage (Davenport, 1993). For example, Berri is Australia's largest manufacturer and distributor of fruit juice products. The principal goal of its enterprise resource planning system implementation was "to turn its branch-based business into a national organization with a single set of unified business processes in order to achieve millions of dollars in cost-savings" (J.D. Edwards, 2002a). Other ways in which IT can change business processes

include better control over remote stores or offices by providing speedy communication tools, streamlined product design time with computer-aided engineering tools, and better decision-making processes by providing managers with timely information reports.

4. *Links with business partners.* IT links a company with its business partners effectively and efficiently. For example, Rosenbluth's Global Distribution Network allows it to connect agents, customers, and travel service providers around the globe, an innovation that allowed it to broaden its marketing range (Clemons and Hann, 1999). Other examples of interorganizational stategic information systems are presented later in this chapter.

5. *Cost reductions.* IT enables companies to reduce costs. For example, a Booz-Allen & Hamilton study found that: a traditional bank transaction costs $1.07, whereas the same transaction over the Web costs about 1 cent; a traditional airline ticket costs $8 to process, an e-ticket costs $1 (*ibm.com/partnerworld/pwhome.nsf/vAssetsLookup/ad2.pdf/$file/ad2.pdf*). In the customer service area, a customer call handled by a live agent costs $33, but an intelligent agent can handle the same request for less than $2 (Schwartz, 2000).

6. *Relationships with suppliers and customers.* IT can be used to lock in suppliers and customers, or to build in switching costs (making it more difficult for suppliers or customers to switch to competitors). For example, Master Builders sells chemical additives that improve the performance characteristics of concrete. The company offers customers MasterTrac, a tank-monitoring system that automatically notifies Master Builders when additive inventories fall below an agreed-on level. Master Builders then resupplies the tanks on a just-in-time basis. The customer benefits from an assured supply of product, less capital tied up in inventory, and reduced inventory management time and processing. Master Builders benefits because competitors face a more difficult task to convince concrete companies to switch to them (Vandenbosch and Dawar, 2002).

7. *New products.* A firm can leverage its investment in IT to create new products that are in demand in the marketplace. Federal Express's package-tracking software is one example. In Australia, ICI Explosives no longer views its business model as just selling explosives; it now also writes contracts for broken rock. ICI engineers developed computer models that specify drilling procedures and explosives use for different types of rockfaces to produce rock in the sizes that the customer needs. According to Vandenbosch and Dawar (2002), "The redefinition of ICI's role not only generated much higher margins for the business, it also gave ICI a much more defensible competitive position" (p. 38).

8. *Competitive intelligence.* IT provides competitive (business) intelligence by collecting and analyzing information about products, markets, competitors, and environmental changes (see Guimaraes and Armstrong, 1997). For example, if a company knows something important before its competitors, or if it can make the correct interpretation of information before its competitors, then it can act first, gaining strategic advantage through *first-mover advantage* (the competitive advantage gained by being the first to offer a particular product or service that customers deem to be of value). Because competitive intelligence is such an important aspect of gaining competitive advantage, we look at it in some detail next.

Competitive Intelligence

As in war, information about one's competitors can mean the difference between winning and losing a battle in business. Many companies continuously monitor the activities of their competitors to acquire **competitive intelligence.** Such information-gathering drives business performance by increasing market knowledge, improving knowledge management, and raising the quality of strategic planning. For example, consider the following uses of competitive intelligence, cited by Comcowich (2002):

- A sporting goods company found an activist group planning a demonstration and boycott months in advance, enabling the company to implement a counter strategy.
- Within days of launch, a software firm found dissatisfaction with specific product features, enabling the technicians to write a "patch" that fixed the problem within days instead of the months normally required to obtain customer feedback and implement software fixes.
- A packaging company was able to determine the location, size, and production capacity for a new plant being built by a competitor. The otherwise well-protected information was found by an automated monitoring service in building permit documents within the Web site of the town where the new plant was being built.
- A telecommunications company uncovered a competitor's legislative strategy, enabling the company to gain an upper hand in a state-by-state lobbying battle. (Remarkably, the strategy was posted on the competitor's own Web site.)
- The creative team embarking on development of a new video game used the Internet to identify cutting-edge product attributes that game-players prefer. The intensive research uncovered three key "gotta haves" that were not identified in focus groups and had not been included in the original design specification.

Competitive intelligence can be done with technologies such as optical character recognition, intelligent agents (Desouza, 2001), and especially the Internet.

The Internet is a company's most important tool to support competitive intelligence (see Teo, 2000, Bell and Harari, 2000, and Buchwitz, 2002). The visibility of information that a competitor places on the Internet and the power of Web-based tools to interrogate Web sites for information about prices, products, services, and marketing approaches have generated increased corporate interest in these intelligence-gathering activities. For example, online niche bookseller Fatbrain.com (now part of *barnesandnoble.com*) uses "e-spionage" firm Rivalwatch.com to keep track of competitors in Fatbrain's specialist professional and educational book market. By tracking prices at rival firms such as Amazon.com, Fatbrain can offer competitive prices without giving away profit margins when it does not need to (Cross, 2000).

Pawar and Sharda (1997) proposed a framework in which the Internet capabilities are shown to provide information for strategic decisions. According to the framework, shown in Figure 3.2, the external information required (upper left) and the methods of acquiring information (upper right) can be supported by Internet tools for communication, searching, browsing and information retrieval. Pawar and Sharda emphasize the search capability of the various tools of the Internet. Using these tools an organization can implement specific search strategies, as illustrated in *A Closer Look 3.1* (page 98).

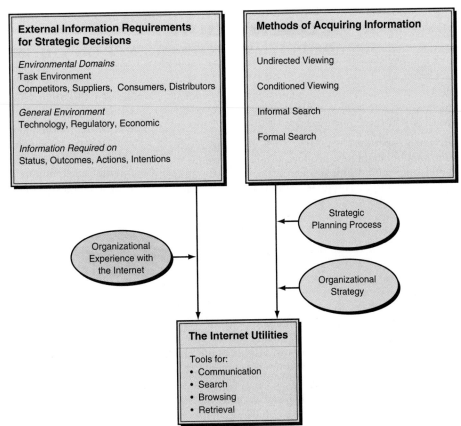

FIGURE 3.2 A framework for the Internet as a source of information for strategic decision making. *(Source:* Reprinted from *Long Range Planning,* 30, B. S. Pawar and R. Sharda, "Obtaining Business Intelligence on the Internet," 1997. With permission from Excerpta Media Inc.)

However, it's not enough just to gather information on a competitor. Analyzing and interpreting the information is as important as collecting it. For these tasks, one can use IT tools ranging from *intelligent agents* (software tools that allow the automation of tasks that require intelligence; see Chapter 11) to *data mining* (searching in large databases for relationships among bits of data, using specialized logic tools, see Chapter 11). For example, J.P. Morgan Chase (New York) uses data mining to track several sources of information. Chase's goal is to determine the possible impact of the information on the bank, the customers, and the industry.

Another, more sinister, aspect of competitive intelligence is *industrial espionage.* Corporate spies, which actually do exist in some industries, look for confidential marketing plans, cost analyses, proposed products/services, and strategic plans. Industrial espionage is considered to be unethical and usually illegal. One type of industrial espionage is the theft of portable computers at airports, hotels, and conferences. Many of the thieves are interested in the information stored in the computers, not the computers themselves. Protecting against such activities is an important part of maintaining competitive advantage. This topic is discussed in Chapter 15, and in McGonagle and Vella (1998).

This section has shown that IT can contribute to a firm's competitive advantage, and profitability, in many ways. In order to understand how and why this is so we next examine two classical strategic models.

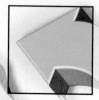

A CLOSER LOOK
3.1 COMPETITIVE INTELLIGENCE ON THE INTERNET

The Internet can be used to help a company conduct competitive intelligence easily, quickly, and relatively inexpensively in the following ways.

1. ***Review competitor's Web sites.*** Such visits can reveal information about new products or projects, trends in budgeting, advertising strategies, financial strength, and much more. Potential customers and business partners can be found by use of the Link:URL command in search engines to reveal what companies link to competitors' Web sites.

2. ***Analyze related electronic discussion groups.*** Internet newsgroups and Web site discussion boards can help you find out what people think about a company and its products. For example, newsgroup participants state what they like or dislike about products provided by you and your competitors. (For example, see *obo.co.nz* for a discussion board about field hockey equipment.) You can also examine potential customers' reactions to a new idea by posting a question.

3. ***Examine publicly available financial documents.*** This can be accomplished by entering a number of databases. Most charge nominal fees. The most notable database of financial documents is the Securities and Exchange Commission EDGAR database (*sec.gov/edgar.shtml*).

4. ***Do market research at your own Web site.*** You can conduct surveys or pose questions to visitors at your site. You can even give prizes to those visitors who best

describe the strengths and weaknesses of competitors' products.

5. ***Use an information delivery service to gather news on competitors.*** Information delivery services (such as Info Wizard, My Yahoo) find what is published on the Internet, including newsgroup correspondence about your competitors and their products, and send it to you. Known as *push technologies*, these services provide any desired information including news, some in real time, for free or for a nominal fee.

6. ***Use corporate research companies.*** Corporate research and ratings companies such as Dun & Bradstreet (*dnb.com*) and Standard & Poor's (*standardandpoors.com*) provide, for a fee, information ranging from risk analysis to stock market analysts' reports about your competitors.

7. ***Dig up the dirt on your competitors.*** Individual and business background checks are available from *knowx.com*. Credit report services such as the Red Book Credit Service (*thepacker.com*) can provide a credit history of competitors. "Actionable intelligence" on competitors is available from *rivalwatch.com*.

8. ***Find out what are the "going rates" for employee pay.*** Try *wageweb.com* for a free analysis of compensation rates.

9. ***Find corporation credit history.*** Dun & Bradstreet (*dnb.com*) offers credit histories for some companies. Other places to look would be court records, banks, annual reports, and credit bureaus.

3.2 PORTER'S COMPETITIVE FORCES MODEL AND STRATEGIES

The Impact of the Internet on Competition

The most well-known framework for analyzing competitiveness is Michael Porter's **competitive forces model** (Porter, 1985). It has been used to develop strategies for companies to increase their competitive edge. It also demonstrates how IT can enhance the competitiveness of corporations.

The model recognizes five major forces that could endanger a company's position in a given industry. (Other forces, such as those cited in Chapter 1, including the impact of government, affect all companies in the industry and therefore may have less impact on the relative success of a company within its industry.) Although the details of the model differ from one industry to another, its general structure is universal. The five major forces can be generalized as follows.

1. The threat of entry of new competitors
2. The bargaining power of suppliers

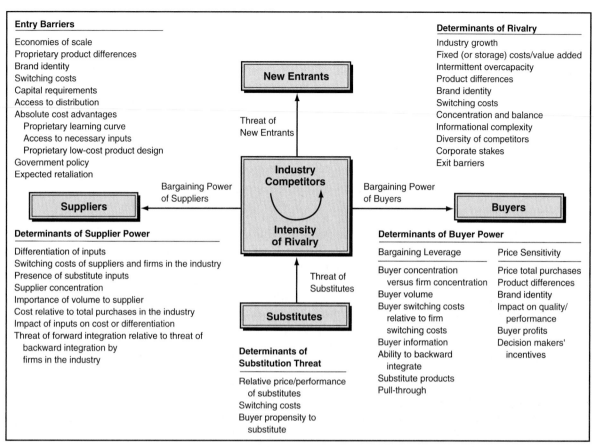

Entry Barriers

Economies of scale
Proprietary product differences
Brand identity
Switching costs
Capital requirements
Access to distribution
Absolute cost advantages
   Proprietary learning curve
   Access to necessary inputs
   Proprietary low-cost product design
Government policy
Expected retaliation

Determinants of Rivalry

Industry growth
Fixed (or storage) costs/value added
Intermittent overcapacity
Product differences
Brand identity
Switching costs
Concentration and balance
Informational complexity
Diversity of competitors
Corporate stakes
Exit barriers

New Entrants

Threat of New Entrants

Industry Competitors

Intensity of Rivalry

Bargaining Power of Suppliers

Bargaining Power of Buyers

Suppliers

Buyers

Determinants of Supplier Power

Differentiation of inputs
Switching costs of suppliers and firms in the industry
Presence of substitute inputs
Supplier concentration
Importance of volume to supplier
Cost relative to total purchases in the industry
Impact of inputs on cost or differentiation
Threat of forward integration relative to threat of
   backward integration by
   firms in the industry

Threat of Substitutes

Substitutes

Determinants of Substitution Threat

Relative price/performance
   of substitutes
Switching costs
Buyer propensity to
   substitute

Determinants of Buyer Power

Bargaining Leverage	Price Sensitivity
Buyer concentration versus firm concentration	Price total purchases
Buyer volume	Product differences
Buyer switching costs relative to firm switching costs	Brand identity
	Impact on quality/ performance
Buyer information	Buyer profits
Ability to backward integrate	Decision makers' incentives
Substitute products	
Pull-through	

FIGURE 3.3 Porter's five forces model, including the major determinant of each force. (*Source:* Adapted with permission of the Free Press, a division of Simon & Schuster, Inc., from Michael Porter, *Competitive Advantage: Creating and Sustaining Superior Performance*, p. 6. © 1985, 1998 by Michael Porter.)

3. The bargaining power of customers (buyers)
4. The threat of substitute products or services
5. The rivalry among existing firms in the industry

The strength of each force is determined by factors related to the industry's structure, as shown in Figure 3.3.

Just as the Internet has changed the nature of doing business, it has also changed the nature of competition. Some have suggested semiradical changes in Porter's model. For example, Harmon et al. (2001) propose adding a sixth force—bargaining power of employees—to the original five. Porter himself argues that the Internet doesn't change the model, but that it is only another tool to be used in seeking competitive advantage. In his words, "The Internet per se will rarely be a competitive advantage. Many of the companies that succeed will be the ones that use the Internet as a complement to traditional ways of competing, not those that set their Internet initiatives apart from their established operations" (Porter, 2001, p. 64).

Porter (2001) and Harmon et al. (2001) suggest some ways the Internet influences competition in the five factors:

1. *The threat of new entrants.* For most firms, the Internet *increases* the threat of new competitors. First, the Internet sharply reduces traditional barriers to entry, such as the need for a sales force or a physical storefront to sell goods and services. All a competitor needs to do is set up a Web site. This threat is especially acute in industries that perform an intermediation role as well as industries in which the primary product or service is digital. Second, the geographical reach of the Internet enables distant competitors to bring competition into the local market, or even an indirect competitor to compete more directly with an existing firm.

2. *The bargaining power of suppliers.* The Internet's impact on suppliers is mixed. On the one hand, buyers can find alternative suppliers and compare prices more easily, reducing the supplier's bargaining power. On the other hand, as companies use the Internet to integrate their supply chain and join digital exchanges, participating suppliers will prosper by locking in customers and increasing switching costs.

3. *The bargaining power of customers (buyers).* The Web greatly increases a buyer's access to information about products and suppliers, Internet technologies can reduce customer switching costs, and buyers can more easily buy from downstream suppliers. These factors mean that the Internet greatly increases customers' bargaining power.

4. *The threat of substitute products or services.* Information-based industries are in the greatest danger here. Any industry in which digitalized information can replace material goods (e.g., music, books, software) must view the Internet as a threat.

5. *The rivalry among existing firms in the industry.* The visibility of Internet applications on the Web makes proprietary systems more difficult to keep secret, reducing differences among competitors. In most industries, the tendency for the Internet to lower variable costs relative to fixed costs encourages price discounting at the same time that competition migrates to price. Both are forces that encourage destructive price competition in an industry.

Porter concludes that the *overall* impact of the Internet is to increase competition, which negatively impacts profitability. According to Porter, "The great paradox of the Internet is that its very benefits—making information widely available; reducing the difficulty of purchasing, marketing, and distribution; allowing buyers and sellers to find and transact business with one another more easily—also make it more difficult for companies to capture those benefits as profits" (2001, p. 66).

In many other ways Web-based systems are changing the nature of competition and even industry structure. Consider the following.

● Bookseller Barnes & Noble, hardware sales giant The Home Depot, and other companies have created independent online divisions, which are competing against the parent companies. Such companies are termed "click-and-mortar" companies, because they combine both "brick-and-mortar" and e-commerce operations.

● Any company that sells direct to consumers is becoming a distributor (wholesaler or retailer), competing against its own traditional distributors.

IT at Work 3.2
TECHNOLOGY INTRODUCES NEW COMPETITION FOR BRITANNICA

For generations *Encyclopaedia Britannica* was known for its world's-best content and brand name. However, in 1997 the company lost so much money that it was liquidated and sold for a fraction of its book value. What happened?

Microsoft started to sell a much-less-known encyclopedia, *Funk & Wagnalls*, on CD-ROMs for $50, under the name *Encarta*. Later on, the CD-ROMs were given away free with Microsoft PCs. In contrast, *Britannica*'s price was about $2,000. Furthermore, Encarta was media-rich. It included video clips, voices, and many pictures.

Britannica's sales declined rapidly. To compete, the company created a media-rich CD-ROM version, which was given free with the printed version. Without the print version, the CD-ROM was sold for $1,000. But very few people were willing to pay $1,000 when a competing product was available essentially for free.

Source: Venkatraman (2000).

For Further Exploration: What were the critical events that led to the demise of *Britannica*? What was the role of the Internet and Web in the demise of *Britannica*? Consult *britannica.com* to find out in what form *Britannica* has survived.

- The variable cost of a digital product is close to zero. Therefore, if large quantities are sold, the product's price can be so low that it might be given away, for free. For example, some predict that commissions for online stock trading will go to zero for this reason.

- Competitors are getting together and becoming more willing to share information. Examples are the vertical exchanges owned by industry leaders. The "Big Three" auto manufacturers, for example, operate the auto exchange *covisint.com*. Similar exchanges exist in the paper, chemical, and many other industries. (See Turban et al., 2004.)

In some cases it is not a specific strategic information system that changes the nature of competition, but it is the Web technology itself that renders obsolete traditional business processes, brand names, and even superior products. One example is provided in *IT at Work 3.2*.

Strategies for Competitive Advantage

Porter's model identifies the forces that influence competitive advantage in the marketplace. Of greater interest to most managers is the development of a *strategy* aimed at establishing a profitable and sustainable position against these five forces. To establish such a position, a company needs to develop a strategy of performing activities differently from a competitor.

Porter (1985) proposed cost leadership, differentiation, and niche strategies. Additional strategies have been proposed by other strategic-management authors (e.g., Neumann, 1994, Wiseman, 1988, Frenzel, 1996). We cite 12 strategies for competitive advantage here.

1. **Cost leadership strategy:** Produce products and/or services at the lowest cost in the industry. A firm achieves cost leadership in its industry by thrifty buying practices, efficient business processes, forcing up the prices paid by competitors, and helping customers or suppliers reduce their costs. A cost leadership example is the Wal-Mart automatic inventory replenishment system. This system enables Wal-Mart to reduce storage requirements so that Wal-Mart stores have one of the highest ratios of sales floor space in the

industry. Essentially Wal-Mart is using floor space to sell products, not store them, and it does not have to tie up capital in inventory. Savings from this system and others allows Wal-Mart to provide low-priced products to its customers and still earn high profits.

2. **Differentiation strategy:** Offer different products, services, or product features. By offering different, "better" products companies can charge higher prices, sell more products, or both. Southwest Airlines has differentiated itself as a low-cost, short-haul, express airline, and that has proven to be a winning strategy for competing in the highly competitive airline industry. Dell has differentiated itself in the personal computer market through its mass-customization strategy.

3. **Niche strategy:** Select a narrow-scope segment (niche market) and be the best in quality, speed, or cost in that market. For example, several computer-chip manufacturers make customized chips for specific industries or companies. Some of the best-selling products on the Internet are niche products. For example, *dogtoys.com* and *cattoys.com* offer a large variety of pet toys that no other pet toy retailer offers.

4. **Growth strategy:** Increase market share, acquire more customers, or sell more products. Such a strategy strengthens a company and increases profitability in the long run. Web-based selling can facilitate growth by creating new marketing channels, such as electronic auctions. An example is Dell Computer (*dellauction.com*), which auctions both new and used computers mainly to individuals and small businesses.

5. **Alliance strategy:** Work with business partners in partnerships, alliances, joint ventures, or virtual companies. This strategy creates synergy, allows companies to concentrate on their core business, and provides opportunities for growth. Alliances are particularly popular in electronic commerce ventures. For example, in August 2000 Amazon.com and Toysrus.com launched a co-branded Web site to sell toys, capitalizing on each others' strengths. In spring 2001 they created a similar baby-products venture. Of special interest are alliances with suppliers, some of whom monitor inventory levels electronically and replenish inventory when it falls below a certain level (e.g., Wal-Mart, Master Builders). Alliances can also be made among competitors in a strategy known as "co-opetition" (cooperation + competition). For example, airlines in global alliances such as OneWorld and the Star Alliance compete for ticket sales on some routes, but once the ticket is sold they may cooperate by flying passengers on competitor's planes to avoid half-full planes. Additional examples of alliances are provided in Chapters 5 through 8.

6. **Innovation strategy:** Introduce new products and services, put new features in existing products and services, or develop new ways to produce them. Innovation is similar to differentiation except that the impact is much more dramatic. Differentiation "tweaks" existing products and services to offer the customer something special and different. Innovation implies something so new and different that it changes the nature of the industry. A classic example is the introduction of automated teller machines (ATMs) by Citibank. The convenience and cost-cutting features of this innovation gave Citibank a huge advantage over its competitors. Like many innovative products, the ATM changed the nature of competition in the banking industry so that now an ATM network is a competitive necessity for any bank. Eight

TABLE 3.1 Areas of IT Related to Technological Innovations

Innovation	Advantage
New business models	Being the first to establish a new model puts one way ahead of possible competitors. The Web enables many innovative new business models, such as Priceline's "name-your-own-price" and Auto-by-Tel's infomediary model. Creating and applying these models can provide strategic advantage.
New markets, global reach	Finding new customers in new markets. Using the Web, Amazon.com is selling books in over 200 countries, all by direct mail. Rosenbluth International, backed by its communication systems, expanded to 57 countries.
New products	Constantly innovating with new competitive products and services. Electronic Art Inc. was first to introduce CD-ROM-based video games. MP3 Inc. enabled downloading of music from its Web site.
Extended products	Leveraging old products with new competitive extensions. When a Korean company was the first to introduce "fuzzy logic" in its washing machines, sales went up 50 percent in a few months.
Differentiated products	Gaining advantage through unique products or added value. Compaq Computers at one time became the leading PC seller after providing self-diagnostic disks with its computers. Dell Computer pioneered the concept of home delivery of customized computers.
Supersystems	Erecting competitive barriers through major system developments that cannot be easily duplicated. American Airlines' reservation system, SABRE, became so comprehensive that it took years to duplicate; a supersystem always stays ahead of the competition. Caterpillar's multibillion-dollar equipment maintenance system is difficult to duplicate.
Interorganizational systems	Linking two organizational information systems together can lock out the competition. In the 1980s, American Hospital Supply installed supply-reordering systems in hospitals, to its competitive advantage.
Computer-aided sales	Offering systems that provide computer support to marketing and sales. For example, a company might equip salespeople with wireless hand-held computers that allow them to provide price quotations at the customer's location.

ways that IT can introduce technological innovation for competitive advantage are shown in Table 3.1, and others will be provided in Chapter 11.

In the late 1990s innovation became almost synonymous with electronic commerce. The Internet, especially, enabled dot-com entrepreneurs to create innovative Web-based business models, such as Priceline's name-your-own-price model, Auto-by-Tel's infomediary model, and Amazon.com's affiliate program.

A key consideration in introducing innovation is the need to continually innovate. When one company introduces a successful innovation, other companies in the industry need to respond to the threat by attempting to duplicate or better that innovation. Especially in electronic commerce, the visibility of technologies on the Web makes keeping innovations secret more difficult.

7. **Operational effectiveness strategy:** Improve the manner in which internal business processes are executed so that a firm performs similar activities better than rivals (Porter, 1996). Such improvements increase employee and customer satisfaction, quality, and productivity while decreasing time to market. Improved decision making and management activities also contribute to improved efficiency. Web-based systems can improve the administrative efficiency of procurement, for example, by 20- to 30-fold.

8. **Customer-orientation strategy:** Concentrate on making customers happy, as is the case with RadioShack Online. Strong competition and the realization that the customer is king (queen) is the basis of this strategy. Web-based systems that support customer relationship management are especially effective in this area because they can provide a personalized, one-to-one relationship with each customer.

9. **Time strategy:** Treat time as a resource, then manage it and use it to the firm's advantage. "Time is money," "Internet time" (i.e., three months on the Internet is like a year in real time), first-mover advantage, just-in-time delivery or manufacturing, competing in time (Keen, 1988), and other time-based competitive concepts emphasize the importance of time as an asset and a source of competitive advantage. One of the driving forces behind time as a competitive strategy is the need for firms to be immediately responsive to customers, markets, and changing market conditions. A second factor is the time-to-market race. As Louis Gerstner, former CEO of IBM, has said, "A disproportionate amount of the economic value occurs in the early stages of a product's life. That's when the margins are most significant. So there is real value to speed, to being first" (quoted in Frenzel, 1996, p. 56).

10. **Entry-barriers strategy:** Create barriers to entry. By introducing innovative products or using IT to provide exceptional service, companies can create barriers to entry from new entrants. For example, Priceline.com has received U.S. patent 5,794,207 on its name-your-own-price business model (Lipton, 1998). Cisco's Dynamic Configuration Tool (*cisco.com/appcontent/apollo/configureHomeGuest.html*) allows prospective buyers to complete an online configuration of a Cisco product and receive intelligent feedback about compatibility and ordering. Service levels such as this make it difficult for new entrants to compete against Cisco.

11. **Lock in customers or suppliers strategy:** Encourage customers or suppliers to stay with you rather than going to competitors. Locking in customers has the effect of reducing their bargaining power. A classic example is frequent-flyer and similar buyer-loyalty programs in the airline, hospitality, and retail industries. Companies that have such programs have more customers who are "locked in" by the incentives the loyalty programs offer. A business-to-business example in the car industry is e-procurement system Covisint, which locks in car manufacturers as customers and parts manufacturers as suppliers.

12. **Increase switching costs strategy:** Discourage customers or suppliers from going to competitors for economic reasons. For example, Master Builders builds in switching costs with its concrete additive tank-monitoring system, as described earlier. Interorganizational information systems (discussed below) increase buyer and seller dependencies, making it difficult or more expensive for buyers to turn to competitors. E-procurement systems that record sales in a buyer's purchasing system can be difficult to set up, but offer a great deal of reliability and convenience for the buyer. Once set up, the buyers face switching costs to add or change suppliers.

These strategies may be interrelated. For example: Some innovations are achieved through alliances that reduce cost and increase growth; cost leadership improves customer satisfaction and may lead to growth; and alliances are key to

IT at Work 3.3
HOW EXPEDIA IS USING WEB SERVICES

Expedia.com is a leading online travel service in the United States, with localized versions in the United Kingdom, Canada, and Germany. Expedia operates in a very competitive marketplace with competition from similar services such as Travelocity and Orbitz, ticket discounters such as Priceline.com and Lastminute.com, traditional travel agencies such as Rosenbluth, and, increasingly, airlines and hotels themselves. Expedia harnesses the power of Web services to distinguish itself in this market.

Expedia's competitive strategy is driven by nearly every traveler's need to receive up-to-the-second, diverse information at any time and any place. Expedia actively supplies travelers with dynamic and real-time personalized information, such as flight status. This information is *pushed to* travelers (sent to them from Expedia) as well as *pulled from* the company's portal (accessed by the travelers through specific inquiries). Travelers use desktop computers, cell phones, and other Web-enabled devices to receive or access the information. This multichannel provision of timely travel information is the key for attracting new customers and for keeping existing customers.

To make this happen Expedia needs to connect to many service providers (airlines, hotels, car rental companies) as well as airports, news services, map services, and more. By using Web services the company solves the integration problem as well as creating device-independent information delivery. This way Expedia can write information only once and then deliver it via whichever method the customer wants—eliminating the need to rewrite the information for each delivery method. Expedia also can tie information into the users' existing "buddy lists" and calendars. This way customers do not have to reconstruct their contact lists and schedules within Expedia.

The solution is based on Microsoft's .NET Passport. A single sign-in for customers provides authentication and eliminates redundant log-on procedures. Using Passport's notification service, a user can choose to receive alerts to any device, including wireless ones. Furthermore, customers can, for example, automatically send notifications of flight plans to people on their contact lists. The users can also enter their itinerary schedule to their computer calendars in a second, moving it from .NET calendar.

The architecture of the system, shown in Online File W3.1, is flexible enough to work with non-Internet devices. For example, many people with PDAs do not have wireless capabilities. So they can receive information from Expedia via a synchronized solution (the users can synchronize the information from a PC to their PDAs and vice versa). By using a system development vendor (Microsoft), Expedia did not have to build its own services such as authentication, message notification, and calendaring. This enabled the company to be a first mover in getting these services to market. Using this XML-based service, Expedia adds value for its customers, which provides Expedia with an edge over its competitors.

Source: Compiled and condensed from Microsoft (2001) (*microsoft.com/servers/evaluation/casestudies/Expedia.doc*).

For Further Exploration: How many of the competitive strategies described in this section are exemplified in this case study? What is the advantage of being the first mover in this case? How can small travel agencies that cannot build such a system (at least for several years, until technology will be affordable) respond?

locking in customers and increasing switching costs. The Expedia case study in *IT at Work 3.3* illustrates several of the competitive strategies described above.

Porter's model is industry-related, assessing the position of a company in its industry. Companies can use the model for competitive analysis, to suggest specific actions. In most cases such actions involve the use of IT. With Porter's five forces model and various competitive strategies in mind, let us see an example of how the generic model works in practice. We will use Wal-Mart as an example (see Figure 3.4, page 106) to demonstrate the four steps involved in using Porter's model.

Step 1. List the players in each competitive force. An illustration of a competitive threat is online shopping, which may be offered by *e-tailers* (electronic retailers). In 2002, for example, Amazon.com started to sell clothes

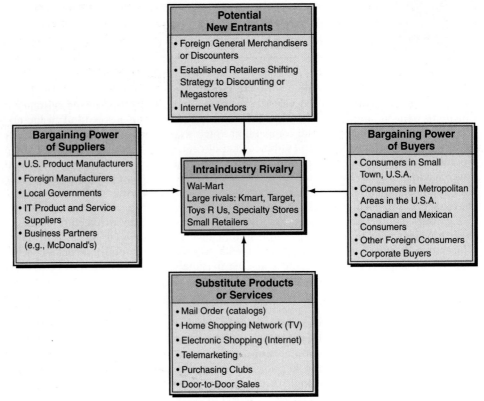

FIGURE 3.4 Porter's model for Wal-Mart. (*Source:* Adapted by Callon, 1996, and reprinted by permission of *Harvard Business Review*. From Michael Porter, "How Competitive Forces Shape Strategy," March–April 1979. © 1979 by Harvard Business School Publishing Corporation; all rights reserved.)

online, competing directly with Wal-Mart in one of Wal-Mart's largest product lines.

Step 2. Relate the major determinants of each competitive force (shown in Figure 3.3, p. 99) to each player in the market. For example, for Wal-Mart, with respect to online shopping, we can check the switching cost for the buyers, the buyers' propensity to substitute, and the convenience advantage of online shopping.

Step 3. Devise a strategy with which Wal-Mart can defend itself against the competitive forces, based on the specific players and the determinants. For example, to counter online shopping, Wal-Mart can provide playgrounds for children, hand out free samples of products, and recognize frequent shoppers personally. Wal-Mart can also respond by imitating the competition. In fact, the company did just that by introducing Wal-Mart Online.

Step 4. Look for supportive information technologies. An illustration of this step for online shopping is a technology for managing frequent shoppers. Wal-Mart uses a gigantic database, data-mining techniques, smart cards, and decision support capabilities to analyze shoppers' activities accurately and to act competitively in response. Wal-Mart uses IT extensively both to defend itself against the competition and to create innovative services and cost reduction, especially along its supply chain. (We'll provide more specific examples in Chapter 8.)

Almost 25 years after it was first published, Porter's competitive forces model remains the dominant framework for analyzing competitive advantage within an industry. A different way to analyze competition and the role of IT is provided in Porter's value chain model, which is the subject we turn to next.

3.3 PORTER'S VALUE CHAIN MODEL

The Model   According to the **value chain model** (Porter, 1985), the activities conducted in any manufacturing organization can be divided into two parts: *primary activities* and *support activities*. The five **primary activities** are those activities in which materials are purchased, processed into products, and delivered to customers. They are:

1. Inbound logistics (inputs)
2. Operations (manufacturing and testing)
3. Outbound logistics (storage and distribution)
4. Marketing and sales
5. Service

The primary activities usually take place in a sequence from 1 to 5. (An exception to this sequencing is Dell Computer's build-to-order strategy, as described in *IT at Work 3.4*, page 108.) As work progresses according to the sequence, *value* is added to the product or service in each activity. To be more specific, the incoming materials (1) are processed (in receiving, storage, etc.), and in this processing, value is added to them in activities called *inbound logistics*. Next, the materials are used in *operations* (2), where significant value is added by the process of turning raw materials into products. The products need to be prepared for delivery (packaging, storing, and shipping) in the *outbound logistics* activities (3), and so more value is added in those activities. Then *marketing and sales* (4) attempt to sell the products to customers, increasing product value by creating demand for the company's products. (The value of a sold item is much larger than that of an unsold one.) Finally, *after-sales service* (5) such as warranty service or upgrade notification is performed for the customer, further adding value. All of these value-adding, primary activities result (it is hoped) in profit.

Primary activities are supported by the following **support activities:**

1. The firm's infrastructure (accounting, finance, management)
2. Human resources management
3. Technology development (R&D)
4. Procurement

Each support activity can support any or all of the primary activities, and the support activities may also support each other.

A firm's value chain is part of a larger stream of activities, which Porter calls a value system. A **value system** includes the suppliers that provide the inputs necessary to the firm and their value chains. Once the firm creates products, they pass through the value chains of distributors (which also have their own value chains), all the way to the buyers (customers). All parts of these chains are included in the value system. Gaining and sustaining a competitive advantage, and supporting that advantage by means of IT, requires an understanding of this entire value system.

IT at Work 3.4
HOW DELL COMPUTER "BTOs" ITS VALUE CHAIN

Dell Computer is well-known for its ability to mass-produce computers that are customized to a customer's order, a production and operations process known as *mass-customization* or, in a value-chain context, a *build-to-order (BTO) strategy*. The ability to build to order depends on how well a company can efficiently meet customer demands at each stage of the value chain. At Dell, this ability depends on computer systems that link customer order information to production, assembly, and delivery operations.

At Dell the BTO process begins with receipt of the customer order from the Internet, fax, or telephone. It takes approximately one day to process the order and for production control to ensure that the necessary parts are in stock. Assembly and shipment takes another day, and delivery to the customer's home or office takes a final 1 to 5 days.

The value chain in place at most firms assumes a *make-to-forecast strategy*. That is, standard products are produced from long-term forecasts of customer demand. Thus the primary activities of the value chain move from inbound logistics to operations to outbound logistics and then marketing and sales, all based on projections of what customers will be buying and in what quantities. A make-to-forecast strategy offers efficiencies in production, but if the forecasts are inaccurate, as they frequently are, the results are lost sales (inadequate supply) or heavy discounting to move excess product (oversupply). Then the bottom line is, literally, less profit. Another major disadvantage of the make-to-forecast stategy is the inability of the firm to track ongoing changes in customer demand.

Dell's value chain moves the marketing and sales activity forward to the front of the value chain. In its build-to-order strategy, Dell assembles the product only after the customer has placed the order, so marketing and sales comes first. The primary disadvantage of the BTO strategy is system sensitivity to short-term changes in customer demand. For example, if a particular computer component suddenly becomes wildly popular or temporarily unavailable, the standard two-week supply in inventory may diminish fast and customer orders will not be completed on time.

A successful build-to-order strategy offers companies like Dell numerous benefits in process, product, and volume flexibility. For example, customer requirements are linked directly to production. As a result production decisions are based on up-to-the-minute customer demand, not long-range forecasts, which can be wildly inaccurate. This increases management's knowledge about trends in the marketplace and decreases inventory holding costs. BTO also offers partners in Dell's value system increased visibility to the demand and flow of goods. As noted in the text, understanding this entire value system can give additional insight and opportunities for competitive advantage. In addition, the support structures for BTO are naturally more flexibile, creating a higher sense of responsiveness within the firm and a more flexible and agile company. One outcome of such flexibility is that adjustable price and sales incentives can be used to manage demand levels, rather than reactively discounting excess stock. Finally, because the customer gets exactly what he or she wants, first-time customers are likely to become repeat customers and recommend Dell to friends and colleagues.

Executing a build-to-order strategy isn't easy, as many companies have found out. Not only must interconnected information systems be built, but BTO frequently requires a change in organizational culture, managerial thinking, and supplier interactions and support. Inevitably the process begins by acquiring a better understanding of customer demand; then improvements in information flow will produce the ability to increase responsiveness in all areas of the value chain.

Source: Holweg and Pil (2001).

For Further Exploration: Use the Internet, if necessary, to find other companies that use a BTO strategy. How would a BTO strategy work in another industry, for example, automobiles or toys? What are the implications of BTO for the value chains of suppliers of Dell components?

The value chain and value system concepts can be diagrammed for both products and services and for any organization, private or public. The initial purpose of the value chain model was to analyze the internal operations of a corporation, in order to increase its efficiency, effectiveness, and competitiveness. The model has since then been used as a basis for explaining the support IT can provide. It is also the basis for the *supply chain management* concept, which we will present in Chapter 8.

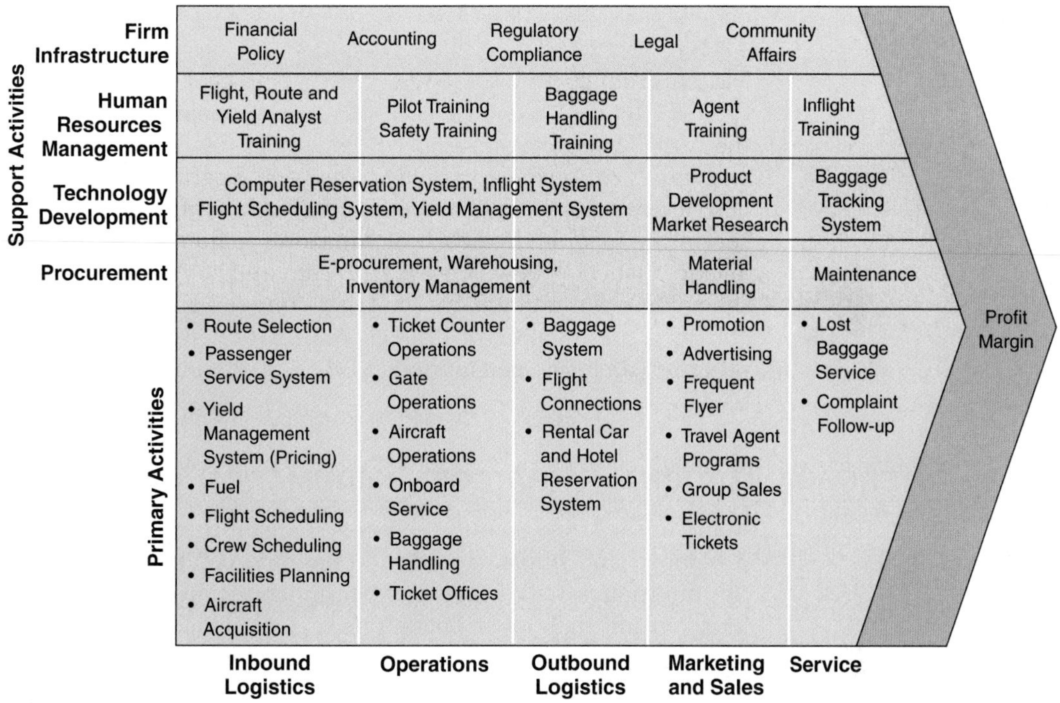

Firm Infrastructure	Financial Policy	Accounting	Regulatory Compliance	Legal	Community Affairs
Human Resources Management	Flight, Route and Yield Analyst Training	Pilot Training Safety Training	Baggage Handling Training	Agent Training	Inflight Training
Technology Development	Computer Reservation System, Inflight System Flight Scheduling System, Yield Management System			Product Development Market Research	Baggage Tracking System
Procurement	E-procurement, Warehousing, Inventory Management			Material Handling	Maintenance
	• Route Selection • Passenger Service System • Yield Management System (Pricing) • Fuel • Flight Scheduling • Crew Scheduling • Facilities Planning • Aircraft Acquisition	• Ticket Counter Operations • Gate Operations • Aircraft Operations • Onboard Service • Baggage Handling • Ticket Offices	• Baggage System • Flight Connections • Rental Car and Hotel Reservation System	• Promotion • Advertising • Frequent Flyer • Travel Agent Programs • Group Sales • Electronic Tickets	• Lost Baggage Service • Complaint Follow-up
	Inbound Logistics	**Operations**	**Outbound Logistics**	**Marketing and Sales**	**Service**

Support Activities / *Primary Activities* / *Profit Margin*

FIGURE 3.5 The airline industry value chain superimposed on Porter's value chain. (*Source:* Adapted by Callon, 1996, and reprinted by permission of *Harvard Business Review*. From Michael Porter, "How Competitive Forces Shape Strategy," March–April 1979. © 1979 by Harvard Business School Publishing Corporation; all rights reserved.)

The value chain model can be used in different ways. First, we can use it to do company analysis, by systematically evaluating a company's key processes and core competencies. To do so, we first determine strengths and weaknesses of performing the activities and the values added by each activity. The activities that add more value are those that might provide strategic advantage. Then we investigate whether by adding IT the company can get even greater added value and where in the chain its use is most appropriate. For example, Caterpillar uses EDI to add value to its inbound and outbound activities; it uses its intranet to boost customer service. In Chapters 5 through 12, we include many examples of how IT supports the various activities of the value chain for individual firms.

A second use for the value chain model is to do an industry analysis, as shown for the airline industry in Figure 3.5. As in the company analysis, once the various activities have been identified, then it is possible to search for specific information systems to facilitate these activities. For example, in "Marketing and Sales," agent training can be conducted on the corporate portal. Similarly, technology now allows preticketed customers to self-check their baggage at some airports.

Finally, the value chain model can be used either for an individual company or for an industry by superimposing different types of information systems that may help special activities. For example, EDI can help inbound and outbound logistics; virtual reality can help both advertising and product development.

Porter's Models in the Digital Age

The application of Porter's models is still valid today. But some adjustments may be needed to take into account the realities of business in the digital economy. Consider a company such as Amazon.com. Who are Amazon's competitors? It depends. In books they compete mainly against Barnes & Noble Online, in toys against Wal-Mart, Target, and Sears, and in music against CDNOW.com. Amazon.com could also be seen to compete against television, video games, and the Internet itself, because each of these compete for customers' leisure time. In that view, Amazon.com is not necessarily in the book-selling business, but in the entertainment business. Could we use one diagram such as Figure 3.3 (p. 99) to describe Amazon.com's competitive environment? Probably not. We might need several figures, one for each of Amazon's major products. Furthermore, due to alliances (such as between Amazon.com and Toysrus.com), the competition and the value chain analysis can be fairly complex and frequently in flux.

For a presentation of strategic information systems frameworks proposed by other researchers, see Online File W3.2 at the book's Web site.

3.4 INTERORGANIZATIONAL STRATEGIC INFORMATION SYSTEMS

Many of the strategic information systems of the 1970s through the 1990s were developed and implemented by individual companies. With the emergence of the Internet as a tool that could easily connect businesses, companies began to look outside their own operations to form alliances and business partnerships based on Internet connectivity. As discussed in Chapter 2, such systems are called *interorganizational information systems (IOSs)*, and they are considered a part of electronic commerce.

Several of the electronic markets (or exchanges) that emerged in the 1990s used private lines and/or EDI. (For more detail on how EDI works, see Appendix 5A.) An example is Citus Belgium (*citus.be*). Citus acts as a hub between customers and suppliers, hosting suppliers' catalogs electronically. Using a pioneering technology, the company gained incredible competitive advantage by significant cost reduction and the building of a loyal customer community (see Timmers, 1999).

However, traditional EDI was difficult and expensive to implement. "Old EDI" required the use of complex standards (e.g., ANSI or EDIFACT), expensive value-added networks (VANs), complex application-to-application software, and across-the-board buy-in (agreement) within the industry. Today, new interorganizational SISs use *Internet-based EDI*. In this "new EDI" the proprietary standards have been replaced by extensible markup language (XML), the VAN has been replaced by the Internet, and system-to-system connectivity gives organizations much greater flexibility in terms of internal implementation. The strategic benefits of Internet-based EDI—a faster business cycle, automation of business procedures, and reduced costs—have spurred the growth of interorganizational information systems and have provided many organizations greater advantage in a fierce competitive environment.

Another way in which groups of companies are using IT and the Internet to create interorganizational information systems to create or sustain competitive advantage includes establishing *consortia*—electronic exchanges for suppliers and buyers. Consortia can be considered either vertical or horizontal. *Vertical (industry) consortia* are organized, operated, and controlled by the major players in an industry (e.g., steel, paper, insurance, oil, cars, mining). These exchanges are used primarily for purchasing and are designed to reduce the bargaining power of suppliers. *Horizontal consortia* are organized by large companies from different industries for the purpose of purchasing maintenance, replacement, and operations (MRO) items. In Australia, all the largest corporations are organized in an e-purchasing exchange (see *corprocure.com*).

In a connected world, no organization can stand alone. Instead, competitive advantage is enhanced when businesses use the Internet and private networks to exchange information and conduct business as partners. Competitive strategies such as alliance and value systems imply organizations working together to achieve common goals, and all participants benefiting from the use of IT for executing competitive strategies.

3.5 A FRAMEWORK FOR GLOBAL COMPETITION

Many companies are operating in a global environment. First, there are the fully global or multinational corporations. Second, there are the companies that export or import. Third, a large number of companies face competition from products created in countries where labor and other costs are low, or where there is an abundance of natural resources. Other companies have low-cost production facilities in these same countries. Finally, electronic commerce facilitates global trading by enabling even small companies to buy from or sell to business partners in other countries. Thus, globalization is rapidly increasing.

Doing business in a global environment is becoming more and more challenging as the political environment improves and as telecommunications and the Internet open the door to a large number of buyers, sellers, and competitors worldwide. The increased competition forces companies to look for better ways to do global business. Porter and Youngman (1995), for example, propose an approach that focuses on employment policies and government regulations. Similarly, Ghemawat (2001) proposes a framework in which companies are urged to consider *cultural, administrative, geographical,* and *economic* dimensions to assess their ability to compete in global markets. Ghemawat calls this a "CAGE distance" framework, an acronym for the four dimensions to be considered by businesses that are selling products outside their local area, especially internationally.

A comprehensive framework that connects IT and global business was suggested by Ives et al. (1993). According to this *global business driver framework,* the success of companies doing business in a competitive global environment depends on the alignment of a company's information system and its global business strategy. This connection is demonstrated by Rosenbluth International, whose strategy enables it to compete with local travel agencies in 57 countries, and by Caterpillar Corporation, which employs a business strategy of strong support to dealers and customers worldwide by means of its effective global information system. The success of multinational firms and companies engaged in global activities, in a highly competitive global market, thus strongly depends on the link between their information systems and their business strategy. Information managers must be innovative in identifying the IT systems that a firm needs in order to be competitive worldwide and must tie them to the strategic business imperatives.

The global business driver framework provides a tool for identifying business entities, such as customers, suppliers, projects, and orders, that will benefit most from an integrated global IT management system. The basic idea is to apply IT through a firm's **global business drivers.** These are business factors that benefit from global economies of scale or scope and thus add value to a global business strategy. Typical global business drivers are risk reduction, availability of a skilled and/or inexpensive workforce, quality products/services, location of materials, supply and suppliers, location of customers, and a country's infrastructure. The idea of the global business drivers framework is to look at the drivers in terms of current and future information needs and to focus on worldwide implementation.

Advances in Internet availability and electronic commerce are of special interest to global traders. First, many of the business drivers can be facilitated by the Internet, which is much cheaper and more accessible than private communication networks. Second, the Internet and e-commerce are answers to several of the analysis questions related to global business drivers.

3.6 STRATEGIC INFORMATION SYSTEMS: EXAMPLES AND ANALYSIS

The models, strategies, and frameworks presented in the previous sections suggest opportunities that companies can pursue to gain strategic advantage. Several SISs developed in the 1970s and 1980s are considered classic illustrations of the power of IT to provide companies with strategic advantage (see Online File W3.3 at the book's Web site). In this section, we provide several contemporary examples of how IT has successfully supported the various strategies that companies use to gain competitive advantage.

Wiring the "Customer Supply Chain" at 1-800-Flowers. 1-800-Flowers sits in the middle of a complex and critical "customer supply chain." On one side of this supply chain are the customers who call the 1-800 number or visit the Web site (*800flowers.com*) to order flowers or gifts. On the other side are the 1,400 floral affiliates who actually create and deliver the product. Maintaining satisfactory customer relationships on both sides of this supply chain is critical to 1-800-Flowers's success, and the key to those relationships is the wired communication system the company has built.

When 1-800-Flowers opened for business in 1986 it was one of the first businesses to promote the 1-800 toll-free number system on a nationwide basis. The initial 1-800-Flowers system included a complex but effective system for directing incoming calls to agents in various call centers across the nation.

It was only natural that an intermediary that based its business on connecting customers and suppliers by a telephone network would be one of the first companies to see the potential of the Web. In 1995, 1-800-Flowers was one of the first three beta testers of the Netscape platform and launched its Web site later that year. Web-sourced orders, which amounted to approximately half of all orders in 2001, were woven into the existing telephone-based business through data networking services. Customer purchases, customer profiles, and internal information created an efficient, wired customer supply chain that helped 1-800-Flowers maintain a competitive advantage.

The next step was to wire-up the connection to the florists. In 1997, 1-800-Flowers initiated BloomLink, an extranet that sends orders out to affiliates and tracks progress in getting the shipments to customers. Additionally, BloomLink offers training programs and access to wholesale flower supply networks. This network helps lock in the suppliers and create switching costs. The significance of BloomLink is its ability to support both the business goal of order fulfillment and the competitive-advantage goal of supplier relationship management.

Like many companies in numerous industries, establishing and maintaining excellent relationships with customers and suppliers is critical to the success of

1-800-Flowers. By wiring up customers and suppliers on both sides of its supply chain, 1-800-Flowers has achieved its goals. (*Sources:* Reda, 2002; Kemp, 2001; *800flowers.com.*)

Increasing Tax Collection Efforts at the Wisconsin Department of Revenue. How does an organization in a noncompetitive industry measure competitiveness? Without the usual measures of market share or profitability, how does a charity, an association, a nongovernmental agency such as the Red Cross, or a governmental agency strive for competitive advantage?

One approach is to compete against yourself. Each year's goals are set higher than last year's performance, and "competitive strategies" are put into place to achieve those goals. Essentially, an organization is competing against its former performance. This was the approach adopted by the State of Wisconsin Department of Revenue for the collection of deliquent taxes.

The Department is responsible for processing and auditing various state taxes as well as for recovering deliquent taxes, to ensure that the state maximizes the income from its largest source of revenue. To realize its goals in the collection area, the Department implemented the Delinquent Tax System (DTS) "for case management and coordinating the actions involved in collections, including hearings, installment agreements, wage certifications, levies, bankruptcy, and warrant filing." The DTS was built in an object-oriented environment using IBM's DB2 database.

Some of the benefits from the DTS implementation have been increased productivity, ease of access to case information in geographically remote offices, reduction of overhead costs, and more standard treatment of cases. Competitively, it has achieved its greatest benefit in the results it has produced. Vicki Siekert, Director of Compliance for the Department, says, "In the last couple years, we've been much more successful at meeting our collection goals; I can say that the Deliquent Tax System has certainly helped our efforts." (*Source:* "Customer Case Study: State of Wisconsin Department of Revenue," no date.)

Time-Based Competitive Advantage at Cannondale. Companies in the motorsports bike industry are in a constant race to introduce new, innovative products. So when Cannondale introduced the FX400, its first-ever all-terrain vehicle, it wasn't surprised to learn that Suzuki and market leader Honda were not far behind. Challenged to put constant innovation into its design, test, and production processes to stay ahead, Cannondale turned to a relatively new kind of application—product life-cycle management (PLM) software.

The promise of PLM software is to share information associated with all phases of a product's life-cycle with everyone in an organization—engineering, purchasing, manufacturing, marketing, sales, aftermarket support—as well as with key suppliers and customers. Most PLM packages contain elements of project management, workflow, and collaboration software.

What have been the results for Cannondale? Paul Hammerstrom, head of R&D for Cannondale's Motorsport Division, says the PLM software has given his company the ability to react quickly in the rapidly changing marketplace. "They [Suzuki] will make 25,000 units in one factory run, and they'll be stuck with them. Thanks to this software we can constantly improve features even in the middle of a production run" (Raskin, 2002). The software "gives the 50-plus people involved in upgrading the bikes for 2003 near-instant access to constantly moving requests for design changes, product specifications, and work orders." He cites this example: "If five dealers walked in today and said 'This seat is way too hard,' I could have new ones in production in a couple of days. Speed is our friend" (Raskin, 2002).

As discussed earlier in this chapter, time is one of the major strategies for achieving competitive advantage. Just as speed enables its motorsport customers to win races, having speed as a friend helps Cannondale beat competitors in the marketplace. (*Source:* Raskin, 2002, and Stackpole, 2003.)

Southwest Airlines Flies High with SWIFT. Southwest Airlines is an outstanding success story in an industry in which many of the major carriers—American, United, and Canada Air, for example—are in or near bankruptcy. Southwest's success can be attributed to its well-known innovations—no-frills flights, no seating assignments, and an aircraft fleet of efficient 737 airplanes. Each of Southwest's 2,600 daily flights requires data about the flight route, fuel requirements, and in-route weather. If these data aren't in the right place at the right time, flights can be delayed or canceled. Efficient dispatching of a growing volume of flight information can be as critical a success factor as moving baggage or customers.

To handle Southwest's requirements for efficient delivery of flight information, Southwest created SWIFT—the Southwest Integrated Flight Tracking System. SWIFT is a set of applications for managing the aircraft fleet and dispatching flights. "SWIFT was developed using a multi-threaded, open server architecture. Clients are connected to the system database and a replication server that captures completed transactions. All clients are X-Motif applications executed on UNIX stations." One innovative piece of software in SWIFT is SmartSockets from Talarian, Inc. "SmartSockets functions as the transport mechanism for distributing real-time updates for Southwest's fleet management and operations and enables processes to communicate reliably and securely." This messaging software replaced a remote procedure call solution. The result has been elimination of system outages and a more stable SWIFT.

Innovations like SWIFT allow Southwest to fly higher than its competition in system sophistication, integration, and ease-of-use. These factors keep Southwest in the skies, flying ahead of its competitors in airline efficiency and profitability. (*Source:* Talarian, 2000.)

Using ERP to Meet Strategic Challenges at Turner Industries. Turner Industries is a Forbes 500 company that provides a variety of construction, maintenance, cleaning, and environmental services to its customers in refining, petrochemical, power generation, and other industries. It does so through 25,000 employees, a $100 million fleet of construction equipment, and advanced software applications designed to meet strategic challenges in time, cost, and customer satisfaction.

Two of the challenges Turner Industries faces is completing projects on time and within budget. A strategic solution to this challenge is Interplan. At the heart of Interplan is a J.D. Edwards ERP system with bolt-on applications that include scheduling software and project control and estimating systems. Interplan contributes to the goal of meeting or exceeding customer expectations by enabling the company to complete projects on time and without cost overruns. This keeps customers happy and wins Turner Industries repeat business and an increasing list of customers. Interplan is so effective that the company typically receives an increased profit margin on projects that use Interplan and is even able to pass on some of these cost savings to its customers.

An even larger contributor to meeting the customer-satisfaction challenge is Turner-Direct.com. Recognizing the need to help customers help themselves, in

1996 Turner Industries began to give customers Internet access to real-time manufacturing and shipping information. Lowell Vice, CIO of Turner Industries, attributes a dramatic rise in sales from the pipe-fabrication facility—from $20 million to $120 million in just a few years—to Turner-Direct.com.

These systems have not gone unnoticed by industry peers. Interplan was the winner of *Constructech*'s 2000 Vision award for software innovation in the heavy construction industry. That same year, Turner-Direct.com received *CIO Magazine*'s CIO-100 award for customer service and customer relationship management.

None of this success has caused Turner Industries to sit on its laurels. The company is building a business intelligence system that will collect up-to-the-minute data about the cost and revenue margins of any project and provide that data to the customer so that inefficiencies and glitches in projects can be identified early and fixed immediately. (*Source:* J.D. Edwards, 2002b).

The Port of Singapore Exports Its Intelligent Systems Over Its Enterprise Portal. The Port of Singapore is the world's busiest and largest container port in the world. Over 250 shipping companies use the port to ship goods to 600 ports in 123 countries. However, the port is experiencing strong competition from neighboring ports in Malaysia, Indonesia, and the Philippines. In these neighboring countries, labor, space, utilities, and services are significantly cheaper.

What has been the response? PSA, the company that operates the Port of Singapore, uses its Computer Integrated Terminal Operations System (CITOS) to automate many of its port services and reduce costs. Additionally, the port's intelligent systems reduce the cycle time of unloading and loading vessels. This cycle time is very important to ships, since their fixed cost is very high; the longer they stay in port, the higher the cost. An intelligent system is used to expedite trucks' entry into and exit from the port. As a result of using neural computing, the time is down to 30 seconds per truck instead of 3 to 5 minutes in other countries. Expert systems plan vessel loading, unloading, and container configuration, so cycle time can be as little as 4 hours (versus 16 to 20 hours in a neighboring port).

PSA's newest innovation is the export of its port operations expertise to other ports. Portnet.com, a fully owned subsidiary of PSA, has joint venture, franchise, or licensing agreements with 14 different ports in 9 different countries in all parts of the world. Essentially PSA is selling its e-business systems and expertise to its competitors. (*Sources:* Field, 2002; Tung and Turban, 1996; corporate sources in Singapore, July 2000; *portnet.com*.)

SUMMARY. The relationships between the competitiveness strategies presented earlier in the chapter and some of the company examples are summarized in Table 3.2.

TABLE 3.2 Company Examples and Competitiveness Strategies							
Company	Cost Leadership	Differentiation	Alliance	Innovation	Time	Customer Orientation	Lock in Suppliers or Customers
Rosenbluth	X	X		X		X	X
RadioShack		X				X	
Expedia	X	X	X		X	X	X
Cannondale					X		X
1–800Flowers		X	X		X		X

3.7 IMPLEMENTING AND SUSTAINING SIS

SIS Implementation

Implementing strategic information systems may be a complex undertaking due to the magnitude and the complex nature of the systems. In this section we will briefly look at several related issues: (1) SIS implementation, (2) SIS risks and failures, (3) finding appropriate SISs, and (4) sustaining SIS and strategic advantage.

Most SISs are large-scale systems whose construction may take months or even years. In later chapters we will discuss at more length various important issues relating to SIS implementation: Chapter 9 covers the development process of such systems, which starts with generic IS planning. Chapter 13 addresses the methodologies of how to justify strategic information systems, whose sometimes-intangible benefits may be difficult to value. Finally, Chapter 14 discusses in detail the general topic of systems development and implementation.

The magnitude and complexity of the continuous changes occurring both in technology and in the business environment may result in partial or even complete SIS failures. When SISs succeed, they may result in huge benefits and profits. When they fail, the cost can be extremely high. In some cases, SIS failure can be so high that a company may even go bankrupt as a result. For example, FoxMeyer, a large distributor of drugs in the United States, filed for bankruptcy in 1996 after failing to implement a SIS that cost several times its projected cost and processed far fewer orders per hour than its predessor (McHugh, 2000). The failure occurred despite the use of a major IT consulting firm and the leading enterprise resource planning (ERP) software.

Identifying appropriate strategic information systems is not a simple task. Two major approaches exist: One approach is to start with known problems or areas where improvements can provide strategic advantage, decide on a strategy, and then build the appropriate IT support. This is a *reactive approach*. It is basically what Rosenbluth International did. The second approach is to start with available IT technologies, such as Web-based EDI or e-procurement, and try to match the technologies with the organization's current or proposed business models. This is a *proactive approach*. In either case a SWOT (strengths, weaknesses, opportunities, threats) analysis or an application portfolio analysis tool such as an Internet portfolio map (Tjan, 2001) can be used to decide what systems to implement and in what order.

Sustaining SIS and Strategic Advantage

Strategic information systems are designed to establish a profitable and sustainable position against the forces that determine industry competition. A **sustainable strategic advantage** is a strategic advantage that can be maintained for some length of time. During the period from 1970 through the late 1990s, businesses implemented numerous successful IT-based strategic systems that lasted many years. These SISs enabled the companies that owned them to enjoy a competitive advantage for several years before competitors imitated their systems. For example, Federal Express's package-tracking system gave FedEx a competitive advantage for three to five years before it was copied by UPS, DHL, and others.

However, in the first decade of the twenty-first century, it has become increasingly difficult to *sustain* an advantage for an extended period. Due to advances in systems development, outward systems can now be quickly duplicated, sometimes in months rather than years. Also, innovations in technology may make even new systems obsolete rather quickly.

Therefore, the major problem that companies now face is how to sustain their competitive advantage. Ross et al. (1996) suggest the three IT assets—people, technology, and "shared" risk and responsibility—as a way to develop sustainable competitiveness. Porter (1996) expanded his classic competitive forces model to include strategies such as growth and internal efficiency that facilitate sustainability. Here we present some ways to accomplish competitive sustainability with the help of IT.

One popular approach is to use *inward systems* that are not visible to competitors. Companies such as General Motors and American Airlines, for example, use intelligent systems to gain strategic advantage, but the details of those systems are secret because they are in inward systems. It is known that several companies (such as John Deere Corp.) are using neural computing for investment decisions, but again the details are not known. The strategic advantage from use of such inward systems is sustainable as long as the systems remain a secret, or as long as competitors do not develop similar or better systems.

If a company uses outward systems to sustain competitive advantage, one way to protect those systems is to patent them, as Rosenbluth, Amazon.com, and Priceline did. Another approach to sustaining competitive advantage is to develop a comprehensive, innovative, and expensive system that is very difficult to duplicate. This is basically what Rosenbluth did, as did Caterpillar Corporation.

Finally, experience indicates that information systems, by themselves, can rarely provide a sustainable competitive advantage. Therefore, a modified approach that combines SISs with structural changes in the business may be likely to provide a sustainable strategic advantage. For example, Barnes & Noble not only started to sell on the Web but also created a completely independent organization to do so (*bn.com*). This strategy can work very well if the online and offline parts of a company can work in synergy. Barnes & Noble made a strategic move to regain market share lost to Amazon.com. Frequently this approach is implemented through business process reengineering and organizational transformation, which are described in Chapter 9.

➡ MANAGERIAL ISSUES

1. *Risk in implementing strategic information systems.* The investment involved in implementing an SIS is high. Frequently these systems represent a major step forward and utilize new technology. Considering the contending business forces, the probability of success, and the cost of investment, a company considering a new strategic information system should undertake a formal risk analysis.

2. *Planning.* Planning for an SIS is a major concern of organizations (Earl, 1993). Exploiting IT for competitive advantage can be viewed as one of four major activities of SIS planning. The other three (which will be discussed later in the book) are aligning investment in IS with business goals (Chapter 9), directing efficient and effective management of IS resources (Chapters 13 and 15), and developing technology policies and architecture (Chapter 9).

3. *Sustaining competitive advantage.* As companies become larger and more sophisticated, they develop sufficient resources to quickly duplicate the successful systems of their competitors. For example, Alamo Rent-a-Car now offers a frequent-renter card similar to the one offered by National car rental.

Sustaining strategic systems is becoming more difficult and is related to the issue of being a risk-taking leader versus a follower in developing innovative systems.

4. *Ethical issues.* Gaining competitive advantage through the use of IT may involve actions that are unethical, illegal, or both. Companies use IT to monitor the activities of other companies, which may invade the privacy of individuals working there. In using business intelligence (e.g., spying on competitors), companies may engage in tactics such as pressuring competitors' employees to reveal information or using software that is the intellectual property of other companies without the knowledge of these other companies. Companies may post questions and place remarks about their competitors with Internet newsgroups. Many such actions are technically not illegal, due to the fact that the Internet is new and its legal environment is not well developed as yet, but many people would certainly find them unethical.

ON THE WEB SITE... Additional resources, including quizzes; online files of additional text, tables, figures, and cases; and frequently updated Web links to current articles and information can be found on the book's Web site (*wiley.com/college/turban*).

KEY TERMS

Alliance strategy *102*

Competitive advantage *92*

Competitive forces model *98*

Competitive intelligence *96*

Cost leadership strategy *101*

Customer-orientation
strategy *104*

Differentiation strategy *102*

Entry-barriers strategy *104*

Global business drivers *111*

Growth strategy *102*

Increase switching costs
strategy *104*

Innovation strategy *102*

Lock in customers or suppliers
strategy *104*

Niche strategy *102*

Operational effectiveness
strategy *103*

Primary activities *107*

Strategic information
system (SIS) *92*

Strategic management *93*

Support activities *107*

Sustainable strategic
advantage *116*

Time strategy *104*

Value chain model *107*

Value system *107*

CHAPTER HIGHLIGHTS (Numbers Refer to Learning Objectives)

❶ Strategic information systems (SISs) support or shape competitive strategies.

❶ SIS can be outward (customer) oriented or inward (organization) oriented.

❶ Information technology can be used to support a variety of strategic objectives, including creation of innovative applications, changes in business processes, links with business partners, reduction of costs, acquiring competitive intelligence, and others.

❷ The Internet has changed the nature of competition, altering the traditional relationships between customers, suppliers, and firms within an industry.

❸ Cost leadership, differentiation, and niche were Porter's first strategies for gaining a competitive advantage, but today many other strategies exist. All of the competitive strategies can be supported by IT.

❹ Porter's value chain model can be used to identify areas in which IT can provide strategic advantage.

❺ Interorganizational information systems offer businesses opportunities to work together in partnerships to achieve strategic objectives.

❻ Multinational corporations and international traders need a special IT approach to support their business strategies.

6 Strategic information systems can be found in all types of organizations around the globe.

7 Some SISs are expensive and difficult to justify, and others turn out to be unsuccessful. Therefore, careful planning and implementation are essential.

8 Acquiring competitive advantage is hard, and sustaining it can be just as difficult because of the innovative nature of technology advances.

QUESTIONS FOR REVIEW

1. What is an SIS?
2. What is a competitive strategy and how is it related to competitive advantage?
3. What has been the impact of the digital economy on competition?
4. List eight ways IT can support the objectives of strategic management.
5. List the five forces in Porter's competitive forces model.
6. What has been the impact of the Internet on Porter's competitive forces model?
7. List 12 strategies for competitive advantage.
8. List the primary and support activities of Porter's value chain model.
9. What are the potential uses of Porter's value chain model in analyzing competitive advantage?
10. What are vertical consortia? What are horizontal consortia?
11. Compare the value chain to the value system.
12. Describe the global business drivers model.
13. Describe two approaches for identifying appropriate SISs for implementation.
14. List two reasons why it is difficult for businesses to sustain a competitive advantage.

QUESTIONS FOR DISCUSSION

1. A major objective of the Rosenbluth strategy was to create a very close relationship with the customer. Relate this objective to Porter's two models.
2. What is the importance of competitive intelligence in SIS? What role does the Internet play in intelligence gathering?
3. Discuss the relationship between the critical organizational responses of Chapter 1 and a *differentiation* strategy.
4. Give two examples that show how IT can help a defending company *reduce* the impact of the five forces in Porter's model.
5. Give two examples of how attacking companies can use IT to *increase* the impact of the five forces in Porter's model.
6. Why might it be difficult to justify an SIS?
7. Explain what unique aspects are provided by the global business drivers model.
8. Discuss the idea that an information system by itself can rarely provide a sustainable competitive advantage.

EXERCISES

1. Review the applications in Section 3.6 and relate them to Porter's five forces.
2. One area of intensive competition is selling cars online (see Slater, 1999). Examine the strategy of the players cited in the paper (available at *cio.com*). Identify the related new business models and relate them to the strategies promoted in this chapter.
3. Study the Web sites of Amazon.com and Barnes & Noble online (*bn.com*). Also, find some information about the competition between the two. Analyze Barnes & Noble's defense strategy using Porter's model. Prepare a report.
4. Identify the major competitors of Rosenbluth International. Visit three other travel agent Web sites, and compare their strategies and offerings to those of Rosenbluth.

GROUP ASSIGNMENTS

1. Assign group members to each of the major car rental companies. Find out their latest strategies regarding customer service. Visit their Web sites, and compare the findings. Have each group prepare a presentation on why its company should get the title of "best customer service provider." Also, each group should use Porter's forces model to convince the class that its company is the best competitor in the car rental industry.

2. The competition in retailing online is growing rapidly as evidenced in goods such as books, toys, and CDs. Assign groups to study online competition in the above industries and more. Identify successes and failures. Compare the various industries. What generalizations can you make?

3. Assign group members to each of the major airlines. Read Callon's (1996) chapter on competition in the

airline industry. Visit the Web sites of the major airlines. Explain how they deal with "buyers." What information technologies are used in the airlines' strategy implementation? Have each group make a presentation explaining why its airline has the best strategy.

4. Assign each group member to a company to which he or she has access, and have each member prepare a value-chain chart. The objective is to discover how specific IT applications are used to facilitate the various activities. Compare these charts across companies in different industries.

5. Assign members to UPS, FedEx, DHL, and the U.S. Postal Service. Have each group study the e-commerce strategies of one company. Then have members present the company, explaining why it is the best.

INTERNET EXERCISES

1. McKesson Drugs is the largest wholesale drug distributor in the world. Visit the company Web site (*mckesson.com*). What can you learn about its strategy toward retailers? What is its strategy toward its customers? What e-commerce initiatives are evidenced?

2. Enter the Web site of Dell Computer (*dell.com*) and document the various services available to customers. Then enter IBM's site (*ibm.com*). Compare the services provided to PC buyers at each company. Discuss the differences.

3. Research the online toys competition. Visit the sites of *toysrus.com, lego.com, KBKids.com,* and also check toy sales online by *sears.com, amazon.com,* and *walmart.com.* Finally, examine *dogtoys.com.* Prepare a report with your findings.

4. Enter some EDGAR-related Web sites (*edgar-online.com, hottools.com, edgar.stern. nyu.edu*). Prepare a list of the documents that are available, and discuss the benefits one can derive in using this database for conducting a competitive intelligence (see Kambil and Ginsburg, 1998).

Minicase 1
Net Readiness at Cisco Systems

Cisco Systems (*cisco.com*) richly deserves its self-designated title of "the worldwide leader in networking for the Internet." Virtually all of the data packets that swirl through the Internet pass through a Cisco-manufactured router on their way to their destination. However, Cisco doesn't see itself as a computer hardware company. Instead, Cisco considers its main product to be networking solutions. Through initiatives such as its Internet Business Solutions Group, Cisco provides businesses with the software, support, service, training, and, yes, hardware, they need

to create an information infrastructure to become e-businesses. In 2003, Cisco sells its products in over 100 countries and employs 34,500 employees. In fiscal year 2002, Cisco Systems had almost $19 billion of revenue and ranked 95 on the Fortune 500.

How does Cisco fulfill its vision to be a complete network solution provider? Three key strategic information systems that embody many of the principles discussed in this chapter enable Cisco to reach up and down its value system. Cisco has built a network linking its customers, prospects, business partners, suppliers, and employees in a seamless value chain (Hartman and Sifonis, 2000, p. 239). The SISs that support that seamless value chain include the three described below.

Cisco Connection Online (CCO) is its customer-facing SIS. The Cisco Web site (*cisco.com*) is the gateway for customers to price and configure orders, place orders, and check order status. CCO also offers customers the opportunity to help themselves to the information they need to do business with Cisco. And they do access it: CCO is accessed over 1.5 million times each month by its 150,000 active registered users. Customers use CCO to get answers to questions, diagnose network problems, and collaborate with other customers and Cisco staff. Currently Cisco is working with its major customers to integrate their enterprise applications directly into Cisco's back-end systems. The goals of this project are to provide better and speedier customer service, lock in customers, and generate operating expense savings of $350 million per year.

Manufacturing Connection Online (MCO) is an extranet application that links Cisco's partners up and down its supply chain. Its purpose is to provide real-time manufacturing information to Cisco's suppliers and employees in support of the manufacturing, supply, and logistics functions. MCO delivers forecast data, real-time inventory data, purchase orders, and related information through a secure connection and a graphical user interface. One of the most successful aspects of MCO is direct fulfillment. The old process had all products coming to Cisco for storage and then shipment to the customer. MCO's connections to Cisco's suppliers allows Cisco to forward a customer's order to a third-party supplier, who ships it directly to the customer. By pushing information down the supply chain instead of product up the supply chain, Cisco is able to reduce shipping time, save money, and make customers happy.

Cisco Employee Connection (CEC) is Cisco's inward-looking SIS, an intranet that addresses the unique needs of every Cisco employee. CEC offers ubiquitous communications (e.g., distribution of marketing materials, major corporate announcements), streamlined business processes (e.g., travel expense reimbursement), and integrated business systems (e.g., scheduling meetings, a problem-reporting system).

One application that illustrates CEC's benefits to both Cisco and its employees is Metro, a travel-expense reporting system. Assume an employee uses a corporate credit card to charge an expense. Metro displays all expenses on a current credit card statement, and the employee can then move all relevant charges to an expense report. In pre-Metro days, a travel reimbursement took four to five weeks; Metro reimburses the employee in two to three days.

Cisco has benefited richly from these strategic information systems. For example:

- Eighty percent of technical support requests are filled electronically, reducing help desk labor costs and almost always with a customer satisfaction rate that exceeds that of human intervention.
- Providing technical support to customers over the Internet has enabled Cisco to save more than $200 million annually, more money than what some of its competitors spend on research and development.
- CCO metrics show 98 percent accurate, on-time repair shipments, and customer satisfaction increased by 25 percent between 1995 and 2000.
- By outsourcing 70 percent of its production means, Cisco has quadrupled output without the time and investment required to build new plants.
- MCO has allowed Cisco to lower business costs in processing orders (from $125 per order to less than $5), improved employee productivity, and reduced order cycle times.
- Metro not only reimburses employees faster, it increases employee productivity and saves Cisco auditing costs. Today Cisco employs only two auditors to audit expenses for 15,000 Metro users per month.
- Cisco estimates total annual savings from CEC at $58 million, including $25 million in employee training savings and $16 million in employee communication.

A recent Cisco advertising campaign featured children and adults from all over the world asking the viewer, "Are you ready?" for the Internet. Cisco not only promotes Net readiness through its advertising, but also lives Net readiness by applying network connectivity throughout the company to maintain its competitiveness in network technology.

Sources: Hartman and Sifonis (2000); *newsroom.cisco.com.*

Questions for Minicase 1

1. How does each of Porter's five forces apply to Cisco?
2. The case emphasizes benefits to Cisco. How do suppliers benefit? How do customers benefit?
3. Are the initiatives in place at Cisco available only to such a high-tech company? Specifically, what difficulties would a more traditional company face in becoming Net ready?
4. How can Cisco use the knowledge it has acquired from internal implementation of these systems to fulfill its goal to be a network solution provider to its customers?

Minicase 2
Aeronautica Civil: Achieving Competitive Advantage in a Noncompetitive Industry

As noted in the chapter, competitiveness in government agencies can sometimes be expressed as "competing against yourself." Essentially, an organization sets goals that are significantly higher than current performance and puts processes and systems in place to meet those goals, thus effectively competing against its former performance.

Aeronautica Civil (*aerocivil.gov.co*) is Colombia's air-control agency. A divison of the Colombian Ministry of Transportation, Aeronautica Civil is responsible for over-seeing and developing Colombia's air transportation system, including 73 airports and 3,000 officers. The agency is responsible for efficiently managing the movement of more than 10 million passengers and 957,000 aircraft take-offs and landings each year.

In its review of computer systems for the Y2K problem, Aeronautica Civil became aware of significant deficiencies in the control of its financial operations. Billing was consistently in a three-month backlog, processing a customer statement took three days, bank accounts were being reconciled manually, and closing the monthly balance sheet was taking three months. Something needed to change, and the business drivers behind that change were:

- Increase the company's revenues and improve accounts receivable turnover.
- Prevent economic losses from bad debts plus generate and control revenue from other sources.
- Minimize resources wasted in responding to claims.
- Allow for procurement controls and control of fixed assets.

After a three-month evaluation process of ERP vendors, Aeronautica Civil selected consultant J.D. Edwards to develop and implement a system that could address the problems in the agency's financial operations and improve its performance. The system was successfully implemented in only nine months. Key factors in that implementation success were the full commitment of Aeronautica Civil's executives toward the initiative and an implementation team that included some of the best professionals in each of the agency's financial and administrative areas.

Success was defined as meeting many of the goals defined for the project. In comparison, and in competition, with its former self, now billing is up-to-date, customer statements are processed in two minutes, bank accounts are reconciled automatically every day, and the balance sheet is closed by the twentieth of the following month. More generally, these are the results: Management of accounts receivable and collections has been significantly improved. Managers have access to timely and reliable information for decision making. Decision-making and immediate response capabilities are more efficient, a critical factor in an air transport agency. Costs and execution times have been reduced. And operations and corruption control have been automated.

Today the new, more competitive Aeronautica Civil projects "an image of continuous modernization, better service, efficiency, control, and transparency among its customers and other governmental entities. Aeronautica Civil has become a model government-owned company, and a prototpe of systematization for aeronautics companies in other countries" (J.D. Edwards, 2002c, p. 2). Aeronautica Civil is one of many examples of not-for-profit or government agencies who have implemented a strategic information system to become more competitive in an industry in which the normal rules of competition do not apply.

Source: J.D. Edwards (2002c).

Questions for Minicase 2

1. Who is Aeronautica Civil competing against? What other approaches to measuring competitiveness can not-for-profit and government agencies use in measuring competitiveness?

2. Can profit-making organizations use the approach adopted by Aeronautica Civil? Why or why not?

3. What were some of the keys to success for Aeronautica Civil?

4. How did Aeronautica Civil measure competitive success? Specifically, compare "before" and "after" on the performance measures identified in this case.

5. Use the Internet to find another, similar organization that is competing against itself to achieve competitive advantage.

Virtual Company Assignment
IT Supports Competitiveness in Restaurant Industry

In your continuing quest for knowledge on restaurant management, you visited a Burger King restaurant last weekend and noticed that the manager was walking through the kitchen, tapping information on a PDA. At another restaurant, you were given a pager to wander the mall while awaiting your seat. Once you were seated, you noticed that the waitperson used a PDA to take your order. There are obviously many opportunities on the customer side for creative IT implementations. Your assignment this week is to identify some opportunities for The Wireless Café.

Instructions

1. What information weaknesses do you perceive at The Wireless Café?

2. What information is time critical? Can IT improve the quality of this information?

3. Two restaurant metrics are "guest count" and "per person amount." What do they measure and how would you obtain this data for the manager?

4. Barbara has used the terms "front of the house" and "back of the house." What do these terms mean in the restaurant context, and what innovative "front of the house" and "back of the house" IT applications can you recommend to her?

5. Apply Porter's competitive forces model to The Wireless Café. What are some competitive forces that could threaten The Wireless Café? Choose one force and identify several response strategies appropriate to The Wireless Café.

REFERENCES

800flowers.com. (Accessed April 22, 2003.)

Afuah, A., and C. L. Tucci, *Internet Business Models and Strategies*, 2nd ed. Boston: McGraw-Hill, 2003.

Bell, C. R., and O. Harari, *Deep! Deep! Competing in the Age of the Road Runner.* New York: Warner Books, 2000.

Bhise, H., et al., "The Duel for Doorstep," *McKinsey Quarterly*, No. 2, 2000.

Bithos, P., "Back to B2B Basics," *BusinessOnline*, June 2001, pp. 66–69.

Buchwitz, L., "Using the Internet for Competitive Intelligence." *members.attcanada.ca/~lillyb/CI/page1.html, 2002.*

Callon, J. D., *Competitive Advantage Through Information Technology.* New York: McGraw Hill, 1996.

Choi, S. Y., and A. B. Whinston, *The Internet Economy: Technology and Practice.* Austin, TX: SmartEcon Pub., 2000.

Clemons, E. K., and I. H. Hann, "Rosenbluth International: Strategic Transformation," *Journal of MIS*, Fall 1999.

Comcowich, W. J., "Integrated Internet Monitoring Solutions for CI," *SCIP Online*, 1(18), *scip.org/news/v1i18article1.asp.* October 23, 2002.

Cross, K., "Corporate E-spionage," *Business2.com*, November 28, 2000, p. 70.

"Customer Case Study: State of Wisconsin Department of Revenue" (no date). Retrieved from *cincom.com/industries/government/detail.asp?id=6&view=detail* on May 5, 2003.

Davenport, T. H., *Process Innovation: Reengineering Work Through Information Technology.* Boston: Harvard Business School Press, 1993.

Dell, M., *Keynote Address at the DirectConnect Conference*, Austin, Tx, August 25, 1999.

Deise, M. V., C. Nowikow, P. King, and A. Wright, *Executive's Guide to E-Business: From Tactics to Strategy.* New York: Wiley, 2000.

Desouza, K. C., "Intelligent Agents for Competitive Intelligence: Survey of Applications," *Competitive Intelligence Review*, 12(4), pp. 57–63, 4th quarter 2001.

Earl, M. J., "Experiences in Strategic Information Systems Planning," *MIS Quarterly*, March 1993.

Field, T., "The Port's Challenge: Keeping the Competitive Edge," *CIO Online*, *cio.com/online/022802_singapore.html*, February 28, 2002.

Fox, B., "Front-End System Reflects RadioShack's New Market Strategy," *Stores*, May 2002, pp. 24–26.

Frenzel, C. W., *Management of Information Technology*, 2nd ed. Cambridge, MA: Course Technology, 1996.

Galliers, R. et al. (eds.), *Strategic Information Systems: Challenges and Strategies in Managing Information Systems*, 2nd ed. Woburn, MA: Butterworth-Heinemann, 1999.

Gates, B., "Memo from Bill Gates to Developer & IT Professionals: Microsoft.NET Today," June 14, 2001, *microsoft.com/net/downloads/net_today.pdf.* Accessed May 6, 2003.

Ghemawat, P., "Distance Still Matters: The Hard Reality of Global Expansion," *Harvard Business Review*, September 2001, pp. 137–147.

Griffiths, P. M. et al. (eds.), *Information Management in Competitive Success.* New York: Pergamon Press, 1998.

Guimaraes, T., and C. Armstrong, "Exploring the Relationships Between Competitive Intelligence, IS Support, and Business Change," *Competitive Intelligence Review*, 9(3), 1997.

Harmon, P., M. Rosen, and M. Guttman, *Developing E-Business Systems and Architectures: A Manager's Guide.* San Francisco: Morgan Kaufmann Publishers, 2001.

Hartman, A., and J. Sifonis, *Net Ready: Strategies for Success in the E-conomy.* New York: McGraw-Hill, 2000.

Holweg, M., and F. K. Pil, "Successful Build-to-Order Strategies: Start with the Customer," *Sloan Management Review*, Fall 2001, pp. 74–83.

Ives B., and G. P. Learmouth, "The Information System as a Competitive Weapon," *Communications of the ACM*, December 1984.

Ives, B. et al., "Global Business Drivers: Aligning IT to Global Business Strategy," *IBM Systems Journal*, 32(1), 1993.

ibm.com/partnerworld/pwhome.nsf/ vAssetsLookup/ad2.pdf/$file/ad2.pdf (accessed May 2003).

J.D. Edwards, "Customer Profile: Berri," July 2002a. Retrieved from *jdedwards.com/content/enUS/Customer-Customers/Berri Limited Australia.pdf* on May 4, 2003.

J.D. Edwards, "Turner Industries Leverages J.D. Edwards to Achieve Leadership," August 2002b. Retrieved from *jdedwards.com/content/ enUS/Customer-Customers/TurnerIndustries.pdf* on May 4, 2003.

J.D. Edwards, "Aeronautica Civil: Flying Safely with J.D. Edwards," December 2002c. Retrieved from *jdedwards.com/content/ enUS/Customer-Customers/AeronauticaCivilLTR.pdf* on May 4, 2003.

Kambil, A., and M. Ginsburg, "Public Access Web Information Systems: Lessons from the Internet EDGAR Project," *Communications of the ACM*, July 1998.

Keen, P., *Competing in Time: Using Telecommunications for Competitive Advantage*. Ballinger Publishing, 1988.

Kemerer, C. (ed.), *Information Technology and Industrial Competitiveness: How IT Shapes Competition*. Boston: Kluwer Academic, 1997.

Kemp, T., "Online Retailers Smell the Roses," InternetWeek.com, September 17, 2001. Retrieved from *internetweek.com/customers/customers091701.htm* on May 20, 2003.

Lipton, B., "Start-up Wins e-Commerce Patent," CNET News.com, August 10, 1998. Retrieved from *news.com/News/Item/ 0,4,25111,00.html* on April 30, 2003.

McGonagle, J. J., and C. M. Vella, *Protecting Your Company Against Competitive Intelligence*. Westport, CT: Quorum Books, 1998.

McHugh, J., "Binge and Purge: Now We Know How ERP Software's Promise Died—and Who Killed It," *Business 2.0*, June 2000.

Microsoft, "XML Web Services Provide Travelers with Unprecedented Advantages," May 1, 2001. Retrieved from *microsoft.com/ servers/evaluation/casestudies/Expedia.doc* on May 20, 2003.

Neumann, S., *Strategic Information Systems—Competition Through Information Technologies*. New York: Macmillan, 1994.

Pawar, B. S., and R. Sharda, "Obtaining Business Intelligence on the Internet," *Long Range Planning*, April 1997.

Porter, M. E., *Competitive Advantage: Creating and Sustaining Superior Performance*. New York: Free Press, 1985.

Porter, M. E., "What Is a Strategy?" *Harvard Business Review*, November–December 1996.

Porter, M. E., "Strategy and the Internet," *Harvard Business Review*, March 2001.

Porter, M. E., and V. E. Millar, "How Information Gives You Competitive Advantage," *Harvard Business Review*, July–August 1985.

Porter, M. E., and J. A. Youngman, *Keeping America Competitive: Employment Policy for the Twenty-first Century*. Lakewood, CO: Glenbridge Publishing, 1995.

Raskin, A., "A Faster Ride to Market," *Business 2.0*, October 2002. Retrieved from *business2.com/articles/mag/0,1640,43543,00.html* on May 8, 2003.

Reda, S., "1-800-Flowers.com and AT&T Cultivate Relationship Rooted in Common Business Objectives," *Stores*, October 2002, pp. 54–58.

Ross, J. W. et al., "Develop Long-Term Competitiveness Through IT Assets," *Sloan Management Review*, Fall 1996.

Schwartz, E., "Web Bots Enhance Self-Serve Experience," *InfoWorld*, February 2000, p. 7.

Slater, D., "Car Wars," *CIO Magazine*, September 15, 1999.

Stackpole, B., "There's a New App in Town," *CIO Magazine*, May 15, 2003.

Talarian, Inc., "Airline Industy Maverick Leverages Real-Time Messaging to Deliver Flight Efficiency," 2000. Retrieved from *www.talarian.com/customers/casestudies/swair.shtml* on May 2, 2003.

Teo, T. S. H., "Using the Internet for Competitive Intelligence in Singapore," *Competitive Intelligence Review*, 2nd quarter, 2000.

Timmers, P., *Electronic Commerce: Strategies and Models for Business-to-Business Trading*. Chichester, UK: Wiley, 1999.

Tjan, A. K., "Finally, a Way to Put Your Internet Portfolio in Order," *Harvard Business Review*, February 2001, pp. 76–85.

Tung, L. L., and E. Turban, "Expert Systems Support Container Operations in the Port of Singapore," *New Review of Applied Expert Systems*, March 1996.

Turban, E. et al., *Electronic Commerce: A Managerial Perspective*, 3rd ed. Upper Saddle River, NJ: Prentice-Hall, 2004.

Vandenbosch, M., and N. Dawar, "Beyond Better Products: Capturing Value in Customer Interactions," *Sloan Management Review*, Summer 2002, pp. 35–42.

Venkatraman, N., "Five Steps to a Dot-Com Strategy: How to Find Your Footing on the Web," *Sloan Management Review*, Spring 2000.

Ward, J., and P. Griffiths, *Strategic Planning for Information Systems*, 2nd ed. Chichester: Wiley, 1997.

Ward, J., and J. Peppard, *Strategic Planning for Information Systems*, 3rd ed. New York: Wiley, 2002.

Wiseman, C., *Strategic Information Systems*. Burr Ridge, IL: Richard D. Irwin, 1988.

PART II
The Web Revolution

▶ 4. Network Computing: Discovery, Communication, and Collaboration
5. E-Business and E-Commerce
6. Mobile, Wireless, and Pervasive Computing

CHAPTER

4

Network Computing: Discovery, Communication, and Collaboration

4.1
Network Computing—
An Overview

4.2
Discovery

4.3
Communication

4.4
Collaboration

4.5
Collaboration-Enabling Tools:
From Workflow to Groupware

4.6
E-Learning, Distance
Learning, and Telecommuting

4.7
Some Ethical and Integration
Issues

LEARNING OBJECTIVES

After studying this chapter, you will be able to:

1 Understand the concepts of the Internet and the Web, their importance, and their capabilities.

2 Understand the role of intranets, extranets, and corporate portals for organizations.

3 Identify the various ways in which communication is executed over the Internet.

4 Demonstrate how people collaborate over the Internet, intranets, and extranets using various supporting tools, including voice technology and teleconferencing.

5 Describe groupware capabilities.

6 Describe and analyze the role of e-learning and distance learning.

7 Analyze telecommuting (teleworking) as a technosocial phenomenon.

8 Consider ethical and integration issues related to the use of network computing.

NATIONAL SEMICONDUCTOR CORPORATION

→ THE PROBLEM

The semiconductor (or chip) industry is one of the most competitive global industries. The rivalry among Japan, Korea, Taiwan, and the United States is fierce, and prices are continuously being driven down. When the economy is weak, demand for computers weakens, resulting in price cuts and losses to the chip manufacturers.

One way to survive is to customize products. National Semiconductor Corporation (NSC) (*national.com*) has over 10,000 products. However, this creates a problem for customers: When they need a chip, customers provide specifications to several chip manufacturers, collect catalogs and samples from the manufacturers, and then contact them for prices and technical details. This takes a considerable amount of time and effort.

Connectivity problems due to different hardware, software, and communication standards had forced NSC to resort to the telephone, fax, and regular mail to communicate and collaborate with its customers. The communication channels that were available prior to the Internet were either regular telephone lines or private communication lines, both of which were expensive. Electronic data interchange (EDI) was in use, but it was limited to transaction processing and was carried on an expensive value-added network (VAN), so many customers refused to use it. Transmission of pictures, charts, and diagrams, a major part of the NSC product catalog, was a very difficult task. NSC found it just too expensive and cumbersome to handle communication and collaboration with customers over its old system.

→ THE SOLUTION

NSC introduced an innovative solution. The company posts detailed descriptions of its 10,000 products on its *corporate portal** (*national.com*). The portal allows NSC's customers to access product information 24 hours a day. *Browsing* through the information, customers are able to download the documents they need. The Web site is also used by the company's employees to search out information quickly and accurately, and to receive more direct feedback from customers.

NSC's Web site visitors use a *search engine* that helps them find a matching product, based on product specifications in the online "Knowledge Base." It also uses custom software that can extract information from existing databases and automatically format it in the *HTML* programming language. (HTML helps in preparing documents that appear on the Internet; see Technology Guide 5.) Since 2002, National's customers also use a sophisticated *open system* customer interface based on WebMethods integrated platform and B2B standards introduced by RosettaNet. This enables fast search by customers for parts and components.

NSC customers can also build personalized Web sites (titled "My Bill of Materials"). These personalized sites can host information related to customer

---

*The Internet terms italicized in this case are defined later in this chapter, or in Technology Guide 5, or in Chapter 5. Another, generic source for Internet terms that you do not know is the Web site *whatis.com*.

projects and their requirements, and any other pertinent information. Customers can select the information to be made accessible to NSC. Through the personalized Web sites, NSC delivers the latest product information of interest to individual customers. This application is part of the corporate *extranet* system. The arrangement also allows NSC to watch the inventory level of chips at customers' facilities, and automatically ship products to them when the inventories are low. For example, the Internet links enabled Tektronix Inc. (a major customer) to discontinue paper files of past and current inventory parts. Product specifications and availability are automatically updated and linked to Tektronix's system. This in turn has enabled NSC to reengineer its distribution system.

The search process is supported by an *electronic form* that is easily filled in by customers, and by a menu of *hyperlinks* to related products and services. The system is used both by customers and by NSC engineers. Its benefits are the following: reducing the sample-ordering process by days or weeks; expediting the design of new products; increasing the exposure of NSC products by a factor of 10 (customers now download 10 times as many documents as they did using just e-mail); providing more information to customers; providing direct and expeditious feedback from customers; increasing quality and productivity; improving the company's relations with its business partners; and increasing profitability and competitiveness.

The NSC Web site offers design assistants and simulators to guide customers in designing their products. Using this facility, customers can input their system specifications, find the devices that fit the specifications, validate design by simulation, and order the required parts. NSC also provides behavioral models and software to support the design process. NSC's design-assistant tool kit was estimated to save National's design customers $50 million in the first year.

A visit to the site in April 2003 revealed many new features. For example, the *analog university* provides many online seminars, and there are an online technical journal, an online biweekly newsletter, online research tools, a locator to find the nearest distributors, a list of job openings, and much more. Information is available in several languages.

THE RESULTS

The Internet solution enables NSC to use *electronic catalogs* instead of paper ones, thus saving the company typesetting, printing, and mailing expenses. The electronic catalog also can be kept much more current than paper catalogs could. In addition, customers can view catalogs and download detailed documents in order to analyze products more closely. Large customers get customized catalogs. The e-mail capabilities allow rapid communication between NSC engineers and customers. The site also offers a configuration that helps customers to configure the chips they need. Added software and hardware, such as videoconferencing and screen sharing, let NSC engineers collaborate with customers electronically, allowing them to work simultaneously on the same documents from different locations. All this is done at a relatively low cost.

NSC's sales and profitability increased significantly immediately after the introduction of the Web-based applications and Internet solution. In 1998, NSC earned the best extranet application award from *Internet Week* and *Network Computing.* The system also has enabled the company to minimize the damage caused by the slowdown of sales of new technology by 20 to 40 percent in recent years.

Sources: Compiled from *Internet Week,* March 9, 1998; National Semiconductor press release, October 16, 2000, *WebMethods.com* (National Semiconductor Success Story, accessed May 5, 2003); and visit at *national.com* (April 19, 2003).

 LESSONS LEARNED FROM THIS CASE

The NSC opening case demonstrates the increasing role that the Internet, intranets, extranets, and corporate portals play in organizations, as well as their potential benefits. Using various Web-based applications, NSC enabled its employees to collaborate with its customers, to speed up design, and to cut costs. NSC made full use of Web technologies for both internal and external applications. Customers use the Web to discover information, to communicate with NSC's employees, and to collaborate with the technical staff.

In this chapter we learn about the major capabilities of network computing to support discovery of information, communication, and collaboration activities in organizations. We also learn how organizations are exploiting network computing for e-learning and telecommuting.

4.1 NETWORK COMPUTING—AN OVERVIEW

An Overview of the Internet and the Web

Many aspects of the way we work and live in the twenty-first century will be determined by the vast web of electronic networks, which was referred to generally as the **information superhighway** but now is usually called the Internet. As you know from Chapter 1, the **Internet** is a *global network of computer networks*. It links the computing resources of businesses, government, and educational institutions using a common computer communication protocol, TCP/IP (described in Technology Guide 5). Because of its capabilities, the Internet (frequently referred to as "the Net") is rapidly becoming one of the most important information technologies today. It is clearly the most widely discussed IT topic of the new century.

Future versions of the Internet will allow even larger volume and a more rapid flow of information. Eventually we may see several information superhighways. It is probable that the original concept of a scientific-educational system will be separated from the commercial one. For example, in order to support advanced network applications and technologies, over 180 U.S. universities, working in partnership with industry and government, are working on a project named **Internet2** (*internet2.edu*). On Internet2, advanced next-generation applications such as remote diagnosis, digital libraries, distance education, online simulation, and virtual laboratories will enable people to collaborate and access information in ways not possible using today's Internet (Choi and Whinston, 2000). Another vision is that there will be several types of interrelated Internets, one for e-commerce, one for education, and so forth.

THE WORLD WIDE WEB. The **World Wide Web—the Web**—is the most widely used application on the Internet. Are the Internet and the World Wide Web the same thing? Many people believe that the Web is synonymous with the Internet, but that is not the case. The Internet functions as the *transport mechanism,* and the Web (WWW, or W3) is an *application* that *uses* those transport functions. Other applications also run on the Internet, with e-mail being the most widely used.

The Web is a system with universally accepted standards for storing, retrieving, formatting, and displaying information via client/server architecture. The Web handles all types of digital information, including text, hypermedia, graphics, and sound. It uses graphical user interfaces, so it is very easy to use. See Technology Guide 5 for details.

THE EVOLUTION OF COMMERCIAL APPLICATIONS ON THE INTERNET. With the commercialization of the Internet in the early 1990s, we have seen an explosion of commercial applications. These applications evolve through four major phases: *presence, e-commerce, collaboration,* and *integration.* The major characteristics of each phase as they evolved over time are illustrated in Figure 4.1.

Specific applications in each phase are demonstrated in Chapter 5 and throughout this book. Another way to look at the applications of the Internet is via the generic categories that they support, as presented next.

INTERNET APPLICATION CATEGORIES. The Internet supports applications in the following major categories:

- *Discovery.* Discovery involves browsing and information retrieval. As shown in the opening case, it provides customers the ability to view information

TIME →

	Presence	E-Commerce	Collaboration and Interaction	Integration and Services
Emphasis	Eyeballs (human review)	Revenue, expansion	Profit	Capabilities, services
Type of transaction	No transaction	B2C, C2C, C2B, G2C, e-CRM	B2B, B2E, supply chain, c-commerce, G2B	Portals, e-learning, m-commerce, l-commerce
Nature	Publish information	Process transaction	Collaborate	Integrate, provide services
Target	Pages	Process transaction	Digital systems	Digital environments
Concentrate on	Web sites	Web-enabled existing systems, dot-coms	Business transformation consolidation	Internal and external integration
	1993-1994	1995-1999	2000-2001	2001-2005

FIGURE 4.1 The evolution of the Internet over time.

in databases, download it, and/or process it. Discovery is facilitated by software agents since the amount of information on the Internet and intranets is growing rapidly. Discovery methods and issues are described in Section 4.2.

● *Communication.* The Internet provides fast and inexpensive communication channels that range from messages posted on online bulletin boards to complex information exchanges among many organizations. It also includes information transfer (among computers and via wireline and wireless) and information processing. E-mail, chat groups, and newsgroups (Internet chat groups focused on specific categories of interest) are examples of major communication media presented in Section 4.3 and in Technology Guide 5.

● *Collaboration.* Due to improved communication, electronic collaboration between individuals and/or groups and collaboration between organizations are increasing rapidly. Several tools can be used, ranging from screen sharing and teleconferencing to group support systems, as we will illustrate in Section 4.4. Collaboration also includes resource-sharing services, which provide access to printers and specialized servers. Several collaboration software products, called groupware and workflow, can be used on the Internet and on other networks.

The Net is also used for education, entertainment, and work. People can access the content of newspapers, magazines, and books. They can download documents, and they can do research. They can correspond with friends and family, play games, listen to music, view movies and other cultural events, and even visit many major museums and galleries worldwide.

The Network Computing Infrastructure: Intranets and Extranets

In addition to the Internet and the Web there are two other major infrastructures of network computing: the intranet and the extranet.

INTRANETS. As discussed in Chapter 2, an **intranet** is a network designed to serve the internal informational needs of a company, using Internet concepts and tools. It is a network confined to an organization for its internal use. It provides easy and inexpensive browsing and search capabilities.

Intranets also support communication and collaboration. They are frequently connected to the Internet, enabling a company to conduct e-commerce activities. (Such activities are facilitated by *extranets,* as described later in this chapter and in Chapter 5.) Using screen sharing and other groupware tools, intranets can be used to facilitate the work of groups. Companies also publish newsletters and deliver news to their employers via their intranets. For extensive information about intranets, see *intranetjournal.com.*

Intranets have the power to change organizational structures and procedures and to help reengineer corporations. Intranets can be implemented using different types of local area network (LAN) technologies including wireless LANs (see Technology Guide 4). *IT at Work 4.1* illustrates how a hospital intranet can be used effectively with a wireless LAN.

Intranets are used in all types of organizations, from businesses to health care providers to government agencies, to educational institutions. Examples

IT at Work 4.1
WIRELESS LANs SPEED HOSPITAL INSURANCE PAYMENTS

The Bridgeton, a holding company that operates four hospitals in New Jersey, uses wireless LANs to process insurance paperwork. The goal is to reduce the number of claims being denied by insurers.

The network environment broadcasts data over a distance of about 120 feet from nursing workstations. Nurses log on to the hospital's intranet using notebook computers and can move with their notebooks from the nursing workstation into patient rooms while maintaining a network connection. When a nurse takes a notebook computer from one nursing station to another, the radio card in the notebook computer goes into a roaming mode similar to a cellular phone. In the course of their work, whether at the nurses' station or in patient rooms, the nurses collect and record information needed for insurance claims (such as patient treatments and drugs administered).

The company is getting a good return on investment, savings in six-figure dollar amounts each year, for a moderate cost of setting up the network (about $200 for each notebook computer radio card and $750 for each of 28 wireless access points).

Source: Compiled from Cope (2000).

For Further Exploration: What are the disadvantages of using a wireless LAN?

of several intranet applications are available in Online File W4.1 at the book's Web site.

EXTRANETS. An intranet's infrastructure is confined to an organization's boundaries, but not necessarily geographical ones; intranets can also be used to connect offices of the same company in different locations. As discussed in Chapter 2, another type of infrastructure that connects the intranets of *different organizations* is an **extranet.** An extranet is an infrastructure that allows *secure communications* among *business partners* over the Internet (using VPN; see Technology Guide 4). It offers limited accessibility to the intranets of the participating companies, as well as the necessary interorganizational communications, using Internet tools.

The use of extranets is rapidly increasing due to the large savings in communication costs that can materialize. Extranets enable innovative applications of business-to-business (B2B) e-commerce (see Chapter 5). The National Semiconductor Corporation case study at the beginning of this chapter illustrates how NSC's customers could save time and effort in design by using design assistance offered through extranets. Finally, extranets are closely related to improved communications along the supply chain (for details see Technology Guide 4 and in Ling and Yen, 2001).

The Internet, intranets, and extranets can be used in various ways in a corporate environment in order to gain competitive advantage. Examples are provided throughout the book and in Online File W4.2. An example of how a hypothetical company, Toys Inc., might use all network computing infrastructures is shown in Figure 4.2 (page 132).

The *discovery, communication,* and *collaboration* capabilities available at low cost on the Internet, intranets, and extranets provide for a large number of useful applications. In the next four sections of this chapter, we discuss these capabilities. Many other applications are presented in Chapter 5 and throughout the book.

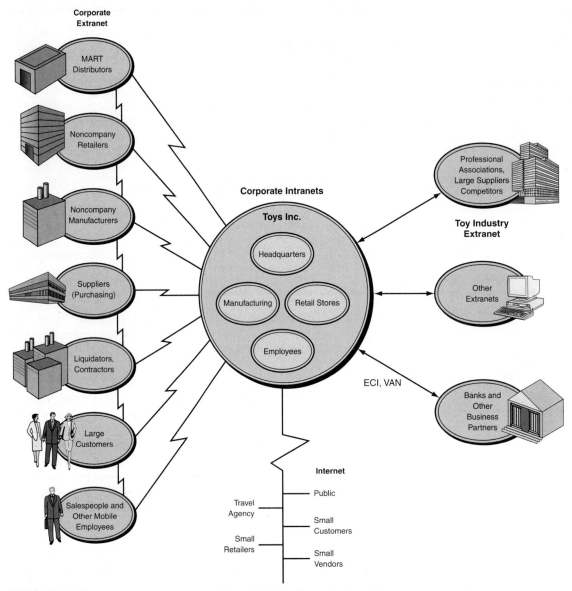

FIGURE 4.2 How a company uses the Internet, intranet, and extranets.

4.2. DISCOVERY

The Internet permits users to access information located in databases all over the world. Although only a small portion of organizational data may be accessible to Internet users, even that limited amount is enormous. Many fascinating resources are accessible. The discovery capability can facilitate education, government services, entertainment, and commerce. Discovery is done by *browsing* and *searching* data sources on the Web. Information can be either *static,* meaning staying basically unchanged, or *dynamic.* Dynamic information, such as stock prices or news, is changing constantly. The major problem of discovery is the huge amount of information available. The solution is to use different types of search and other software agents.

The Role of Internet Software Agents

A large number of Internet software agents can be used to automate and expedite discovery. **Software agents** are computer programs that carry out a set of routine computer tasks on behalf of the user and in so doing employ some sort of knowledge of the user's goals. We examine some of these agents in this section.

SEARCH ENGINES, DIRECTORIES, SOFTWARE, AND INTELLIGENT AGENTS. The amount of information on the Web is at least doubling every year. This makes navigating through the Web and gaining access to necessary information more and more difficult. *Search engines* and *directories* are two fundamentally different types of search facilities available on the Web. A **search engine** (e.g., Altavista, Google) maintains an index of hundreds of millions of Web pages and uses that index to find pages that match a set of user-specified keywords. Such indexes are created and updated by software robots called **softbots.** A **directory** (e.g., Yahoo, About.com), on the other hand, is a hierarchically organized collection of links to Web pages. Directories are compiled manually, unlike indexes, which are generated by computers.

Search engines and directories often present users with links to thousands or even millions of pages. It is quite difficult to find information of interest from such a large number of links. Therefore we can use additional tools to refine the search. For example, *meta searchers* search several engines at once (e.g., Metacrawler.com). Most of these helpers use software agents, some of which exhibit intelligent behavior and learning and are called **intelligent agents** (Weiss, 1999; Murch and Johnson, 1999). The topic of intelligent agents is discussed more fully in Chapter 12. Here we present only a few examples of Internet-based software agents, which appear under names such as *wizards, softbots,* and *knowbots.* Three major types of agents available for help in browsing and searching are Web-browsing-assisting agents, FAQ agents, and indexing agents.

Web-Browsing-Assisting Agents. Some agents can facilitate browsing by offering the user a tour of the Internet. Known as *tour guides,* they work while the user browses. For example, WebWatcher is a personal agent, developed at Carnegie Mellon University, that helps find pages related to the current page, adding hyperlinks to meet the user's search goal and giving advice on the basis of the user's preference.

NetCaptor (*netcaptor.com*) is a custom browser application with a simple-to-navigate Windows interface that makes browsing (only with Internet Explorer) more pleasurable and productive. NetCaptor opens a separate tabbed space for each Web site visited by the user. Users can easily switch between different tabbed spaces. The CaptorGroup feature creates a group of links that are stored together so the user can get single-click access to multiple Web sites. The PopupCaptor feature automatically closes pop-up windows (see Chapter 5) displayed during browsing. NetCaptor also includes a utility, called Flyswat, to turn certain words and phrases into hyperlinks. Clicking on these links opens a window with links to Web sites with relevant information.

For more details on Web-browsing assistants see Tan and Kumar (2002), *botspot.com,* and Lieberman et al. (1999).

Frequently Asked Questions (FAQ) Agents. *FAQ agents* guide people to the answers to frequently asked questions. When searching for information, people tend to ask the same or similar questions. In response, newsgroups, support staffs, vendors, and others have developed files of those FAQs and an appropriate answer to each. But there is a problem: People use natural language, asking the same questions in several different ways. The FAQ agent (such as FAQFinder developed at the University of Chicago) addresses this problem by indexing a large number of FAQ files. Using the text of a question submitted in natural language, the software agent can locate the appropriate answer. GTE Laboratories developed an FAQ agent that accepts natural-language questions from users of Usenet News Groups and answers them by matching question-answer pairs. A solution to natural language may be provided by a semantic Web. (See Chapter 12 and Berners-Lee et al., 2001.)

AskJeeves (*askjeeves.com*), another popular FAQ assistant, makes it easy to find answers on the Internet to questions asked in plain English. The system responds with one or more closely related questions to which the answers are available. Parts of such questions may contain drop-down menus for selecting from different options. After the user selects the question that is closest to the original question, the system presents a reply page containing different sources that can provide answers. Due to the limited number of FAQs and the semistructured nature of the questions, the reliability of FAQ agents is very high.

Search and Indexing Agents. Another type of discovery agent on the Internet traverses the Web and performs tasks such as information retrieval and discovery, validating links, and generating statistics. Such search agents are called *Web robots, spiders,* and *wanderers.*

Indexing agents can carry out a massive autonomous search of the Web on behalf of a user or, more commonly, of a search engine like Google, HotBot, or Altavista. First, they scan millions of documents and store an index of words found in document titles, key words, and texts. The user can then query the search engine to find documents containing certain key words.

Special indexing agents are being developed for knowledge sharing and knowledge acquisition in large databases and documents. **Metasearch engines** integrate the findings of the various search engines to answer queries posted by the users. (Examples include *MetaFind, QueryServer, surfwax, Metacrawler, Profusion, Sherlockhound, Search, ixquick, All-in-One, Dogpile, Copernic,* and *Web Compass.* See *suite101.com* for details.)

IT at Work 4.2 provides an insight into a specific application of search and indexing technology in education.

Internet-Based Web Mining

The term *data mining* refers to sophisticated analysis techniques for sifting through large amounts of information. Data mining permits new patterns and relationships to be discovered through the use of software that can do much of the mining process (see Chapter 11). Software agents are key tools in discovering previously unknown relationships, especially in complex data structures. *Query-and-reporting tools,* on the other hand, demand a predefined database structure and are most valuable when asking specific questions to confirm hypotheses. For more on Web mining and its varieties, see Chapter 11.

IT at Work 4.2
CATCHING CASES OF PLAGIARISM AT SCHOOLS

The Internet provides abundant information to students who may be tempted to download material and submit it as their own work. Some companies are offering Internet-based antiplagiarism technology to identify cases of plagiarism (e.g., *turnitin* from *plagiarism.org*).

Here's how the process used to find cases of plagiarism works: Instructors register their classes at *turnitin.com*, and request their students to upload term papers or manuscripts into databases designed for specific courses. Each manuscript is converted into an abstract representation using a proprietary technology, and it is then checked against a database of other manuscripts collected from different universities and classes and from all over the Internet. The cases of gross plagiarism are flagged, and an originality report, accessible only to the instructor, is generated for each paper.

To try to stay ahead of desperate students, the manuscript collection databases are constantly updated through a series of automated Web robots that scout the Internet for rogue term-paper mills.

Sources: Compiled from *plagiarism.org,* and *turnitin.com,* site accessed April 17, 2003.

For Further Exploration: Do you support using antiplagiarism technology to catch cases of cheating at school? Elaborate on your reasons. Can you think of any other means of finding cases of plagiarism?

Other Discovery Aids

Hundreds of other search engines and discovery aids are available (e.g., see Carroll, 2003). Here are some useful ones:

- *Webopedia.com.* This is a directory of technology-related terms, which are arranged alphabetically. If you know the term for which you want a definition, you can go to it directly. In addition to a definition you will find relevant Internet resources with links. If you do not know the exact term you are looking for, you can use some key word to find it.
- *What Is?* (*whatis.com*). This knowledge exploration tool provides information about IT, especially about the Internet and computers. It contains over 4,000 individual encyclopedic definitions/topics and a number of "Fast Reference" pages. The topics contain about 12,000 hyperlinked cross-references between definitions/topics and to other sites for further information.
- *eBizSearch* (*gunther.smeal.psu.edu*). This engine searches the Web as well as academic and commercial articles for various aspects of e-business.
- *Elibrary* (*ask.library.com*). This site searches for books, articles, maps, pictures, and so on that you can have for a seven-day free trial. After that, you must pay for the files. Abstracts are free.
- *Howstuffworks.com.* You can learn about thousands of products, things, concepts, etc. at this educational and entertaining site. It combines a search engine and a menu system.
- *Findarticles.com.* This search engine specializes in finding articles, usually from trade magazines, on topics of your choice. Like library search engines, it is limited to certain magazines.

Toolbars

To get the most out of search engines, you may use add-on toolbars and special software. Some are attached to the popular search engines, others are independent. Most are free. Examples are: Google Toolbar (*toolbar.google.com*), Copernic Agent Basic (*copernic.com*), KartOO (*kartoo.com*), Yahoo Companion (*companion.yahoo.com*), and Grokker (*groxis.com*).

A CLOSER LOOK
4.1 AUTOMATIC TRANSLATION OF WEB PAGES

Automatic translation of Web pages is an application offered by many vendors. Not all automatic translations are equally good, so some evaluation of these products is needed. According to Sullivan (2001), the best way to assess machine translation is to use the following three criteria: (1) intelligibility—how well a reader can get the gist of a translated document, (2) accuracy—how many errors occur during a translation, and (3) speed—how many words per second are translated. Because the quality of automatic translation has not always been as good as human translation, many experts advocate use of the computer as a pro-

ductivity booster, with human translation as a double-check. However, as time passes, automatic translation is becoming better (see Sullivan, 2001).

Some major translation products are: WorldPoint Passport (*worldpoint.com*), Babel Fish Translation (*world. altavista.com*), *AutoTranslate* (offered in Netscape browser), "BETA" (*google.com/language-tools*), and products and services available at *trados.com* and *translationzone.com*. For details on these and other translators, see Online File W4.3 at the book's Web site.

Discovery of Material in Foreign Languages

There is a huge amount of information on the Internet in languages that you may not know. Some of this is vendors' information intended for global reach. Asking human translators for help is expensive and slow. A more useful tool is *automatic translation* of Web pages. Such translation is available to and from all major languages, and its quality is improving with time. We distinguish between real-time translation, which is offered by browsers (e.g., Netscape), and delayed translation, which is offered by many others. For details and examples of both types, see *A Closer Look 4.1*.

Information and Corporate Portals

With the growing use of intranets and the Internet, many organizations encounter information overload at a number of different levels. Information is scattered across numerous documents, e-mail messages, and databases at different locations and systems. Finding relevant and accurate information is often time-consuming and may require access to multiple systems.

As a consequence, organizations lose a lot of productive employee time. One solution to this problem is to use portals. A **portal** is a Web-based personalized gateway to information and knowledge in network computing. It attempts to address information overload through an intranet-based environment to search and access relevant information from disparate IT systems and the Internet, using advanced search and indexing techniques. A portal is the one screen from which we do all our work on the Web. In general, portals are referred to as information portals.

INFORMATION PORTALS. An **information portal** is a single point of access through a Web browser to critical business information located inside and outside of an organization, and it can be personalized for each user. One way to distinguish among portals is to look at their content, which can vary from narrow to broad, and their community or audience, which can also vary. We distinguish seven types of portals, described below.

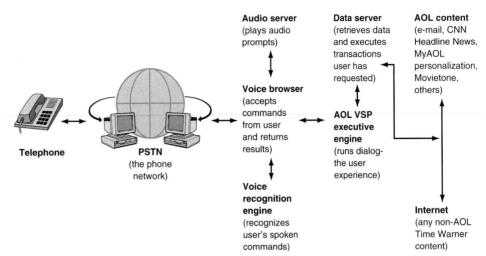

FIGURE 4.3 AOLbyphone.
[*Source:* DeYoung (2001), p. 10.]

1. **Commercial (public) portals** offer content for diverse communities and are the most popular portals on the Internet. Although they offer customization of the user interface, they are still intended for broad audiences and offer fairly routine content, some in real time (e.g., a stock ticker and news on a few preselected items). Examples are *yahoo.com, lycos.com,* and *msn.com.*

2. **Publishing portals** are intended for communities with specific interests. These portals involve relatively little customization of content, but they provide extensive online search and some interactive capabilities. Examples are *techweb.com* and *zdnet.com.*

3. **Personal portals** target specific filtered information for individuals. They offer relatively narrow content but are typically much more personalized, effectively having an audience of one.

4. **Affinity portals** support communities such as hobby groups or a political party (Tedeschi, 2000). They offer a single point of entry to an entire community of affiliated interests.

5. **Mobile portals** are portals accessible from mobile devices. Although most of the other portals mentioned here are PC-based, increasing numbers of portals are accessible via mobile devices. One example is i-mode from DoCoMo in Japan.

6. **Voice portals** are Web portals with audio interfaces, which enables them to be accessed by a standard or cell phone. AOLbyPhone is an example of a service that allows you to retrieve e-mail, news, and other content by voice. (See Figure 4.3.) Companies such as *tellme.com* and *i3mobile.com* offer the software for such services. Voice portals use both speech recognition and text-to-speech technologies. The 511 system described in Chapter 1 is an example of an e-government voice portal.

7. **Corporate portals** coordinate rich content within relatively narrow corporate and partners' communities. Kounadis (2000) defines a corporate portal as a personalized, single point of access through a Web browser to critical business information located inside and outside of an organization. They are also known as *enterprise portals* or *enterprise information portals.*

CORPORATE PORTALS.   In contrast with publishing and commercial portals such as Yahoo, which are gateways to general information on the Internet, corporate portals provide single-point access to *specific* enterprise information and applications available on the Internet, intranets, and extranets.

Corporate portals offer employees, business partners, and customers an organized focal point for their interactions with the firm any time and from anywhere. Through the portal, these people can have structured and personalized access to information across large, multiple, and disparate enterprise information systems, as well as the Internet. Many large organizations have already implemented corporate portals to cut costs, free up time for busy executives and managers, and improve profitability. (See ROI white papers and reports at *plumtree.com*.) In addition, corporate portals offer customers and employees self-service opportunities (see CRM in Chapter 7), which reduces a company's cost. (See discussion and examples at *Peoplesoft.com*.) *A Closer Look 4.2* describes several types of corporate portals.

Online File W4.4 takes a look at the corporate portals of some well-known companies. Also, look at Online Minicase W4.3, which tells about a business intelligence portal at Amway.

Figure 4.4 depicts a corporate portal framework based on Aneja et al. (2000) and Kounadis (2000). This framework illustrates the features and capabilities required to support various organizational activities using internal and external information sources.

A CLOSER LOOK
4.2 TYPES OF CORPORATE PORTALS

The following types of portals can be found in organizations.

A PORTAL FOR SUPPLIERS. Using corporate portals, suppliers can manage their own inventories online. They can view what they sold to the portal owner and for how much. They can see the inventory levels of products at the portal owner's organization, and they can send material and supplies when they see that a reorder level is reached. Suppliers can also collaborate with corporate buyers and other staff via the portal.

A PORTAL FOR CUSTOMERS. Customers can use a *customer-facing portal* for viewing products and services and placing orders, which they can later self-track. They can view their own accounts and see what is going on there in almost real time. Thus, customers personalize their views of the corporate portal. They can configure products (services), place orders, and pay for and arrange delivery and warranty. They can see their outstanding invoices as well.

A PORTAL FOR EMPLOYEES. Such portals are used for training, dissemination of news and information, and workplace discussion groups. They also are used for self-service activities, mainly in the human resources area (e.g., change your address, fill in an expense report, register for classes, get reimbursed for tuition). Employees' portals are sometimes bundled with supervisors' portals (see next item).

SUPERVISORS' PORTALS. These portals, sometimes called *workforce portals,* enable managers and supervisors to control the entire workforce management process—from budgeting to scheduling workforce.

OTHER TYPES. Several other types of corporate portals also exist: *business intelligence portals* (Imhoff, 2001, Ferguson, 2001, and Online Minicase W4.3), *intranet portals* (Ferguson, 2001), and *knowledge portals* (Kesner, 2003).

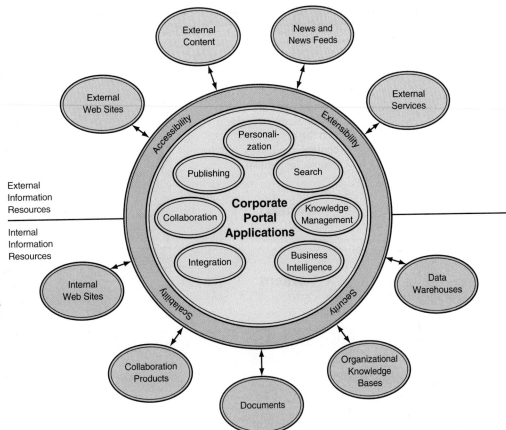

FIGURE 4.4 A corporate portal framework. (*Sources:* Compiled from A. Aneja et al., "Corporate Portal Framework for Transforming Content Chaos on Intranets," *Intel Technology Journal,* Q1, 2000, and from T. Kounadis, "How to Pick the Best Portal," *e-Business Advisor,* August 2000.)

APPLICATIONS OF CORPORATE PORTALS. According to a survey by the Delphi Group, over 55 percent of its 800 respondents had begun corporate portal projects, with about 42 percent of them conducting the projects at the enterprisewide level (cited in Stackpole, 1999). The number of corporate portals can only have increased since that study was conducted. The top portal applications cited in the study, in decreasing order of importance, were: knowledge bases and learning tools; business process support; customer-facing sales, marketing, and service; collaboration and project support; access to data from disparate corporate systems; internal company information, policies, and procedures; best practices and lessons learned; human resources and benefits; directories and bulletin boards; identification of subject matter experts; and news and Internet access.

The Delphi Group also found that poor organization of information and lack of navigation and retrieval tools contributed to over 50 percent of the problems for corporate portal users. (For further details see *delphigroup.com/pubs/corporate-portal-excerpt.htm.*) For this reason it is advisable for organizations to develop a corporate portal strategy, as discussed in Online File W4.5.

INTEGRATION OF PORTALS. Many organizations are creating several corporate portals. While in some cases these portals are completely independent of each other, in other cases they are interrelated. For example, they may share content, and they may draw from the same applications and databases.

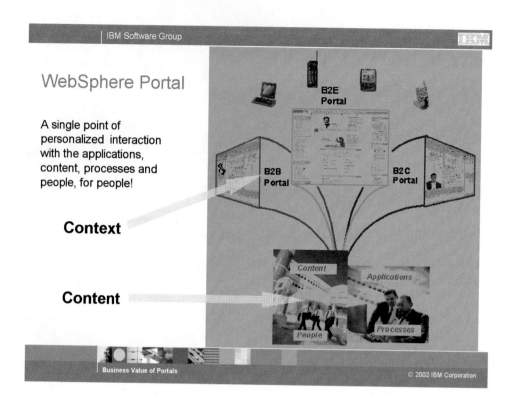

FIGURE 4.5 Websphere portal. (*Source:* ibm.com.)

Tool-building software, such as WebSphere Portal (from IBM), allows companies to create multiple portals as one unit. Figure 4.5 shows three different portals used by a single company—a portal for business partners (B2B), a portal for employees (B2E), and a portal for customers (B2C). If portals are built one at a time over a long period, and possibly with different tools, it is wise to keep in mind that it may be beneficial to integrate them (Ojala, 2002).

INDUSTRYWIDE COMMUNICATION NETWORKS (PORTALS). In addition to single-company portals, there are also portals for entire industries. Thanks to the Internet, entire industries can now create communication networks (portals). An example is *chaindrugstore.net,* which links retailers and product manufacturers, and provides product and industry news and recall and promotional information. The site was created in 2001 by the National Association of Chain Drug Stores. The objective is to facilitate the rapid exchange of needed information. The site has an offshoot for independent pharmacies (called CommunityDrugStore.net). The service, according to Brookman (2003), reaches more than 130 retailers representing 32,000 stores. The service is free to the retailers; suppliers pay annual fees, in exchange for being able to use the portal to communicate information to retailers (e.g., to advertise special deals, to notify retailers about price changes). The portal also provides industry news, and it can be personalized for individual retailers. Retailers also use it as a productivity tool. For example, the site has "Call Me" and "Send Me" buttons, so retailers can click and receive product information in seconds. Although some people fear that the site will reduce the effectiveness of face-to-face meetings, the participants are more than happy with the communication and collaboration support. The membership renewal rate has been 100 percent, and additional members have joined. For details see Brookman (2003).

4.3 COMMUNICATION

Communication is an interpersonal process of sending and receiving symbols with messages attached to them. Through communication, people exchange and share information as well as understand and influence each other. Most managers spend as much as 90 percent of their time communicating. Managers serve as "nerve centers" in the information-processing networks called organizations, where they collect, distribute, and process information continuously. Since poor communication can mean poor management, managers must communicate effectively among themselves and with others, both inside and outside of organizations. Information technologies have come to play a major role in providing communication support for organizations.

Factors Determining the Uses of Information Technologies for Communication

Several factors determine the IT technologies that could be used to provide communication support to a specific organization or group of users. The major ones are the following:

- *Participants.* The number of people sending and receiving information can range from two to many thousands.
- *Nature of sources and destinations.* Sources and destinations of information can include people, databases, sensors, and so on.
- *Media.* Communication can involve one or several IT-supported media, such as text, voice, graphics, radio, pictures, and animation. Using different media for communicating can increase the effectiveness of a message, expedite learning, and enhance problem solving. Working with multiple media may, however, reduce the efficiency and effectiveness of the system (its speed, capacity, quality) and may significantly increase its cost.
- *Place (location).* The sender(s) and receiver(s) can be in the same room, in different rooms at the same location, or at different locations.
- *Time.* Messages can be sent at a certain time and received almost simultaneously. Such **synchronous (real-time) communication** is provided by telephones, instant messaging online, teleconferencing, and face-to-face meetings. **Asynchronous communication,** on the other hand, refers to communication in which the receiver gets an answer sometime after a request was sent. E-mail and electronic bulletin boards are examples.

A TIME/PLACE FRAMEWORK. The last two factors in the preceding list—place and time—were used by DeSanctis and Gallupe (1987) to create a framework for classifying IT communication and collaboration support technologies. According to this framework, IT communication is divided into four cells, as shown in

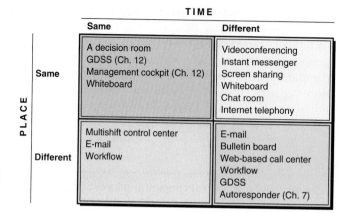

FIGURE 4.6 A framework for IT communication support.

Figure 4.6, with a representative technology in each cell. The time/place cells are as follows:

1. **Same-time/same-place.** In this setting, participants meet face-to-face in one place and at the same time. An example is communication in a meeting room, which can be electronically supported by group systems (see *group systems.com* and Chapter 12).

2. **Same-time/different-place.** This setting refers to a meeting whose participants are in different places but communicate at the same time. A telephone conference call, desktop videoconferencing, chat rooms, and instant messaging are examples of such situations.

3. **Different-time/same-place.** This setting can materialize when people work in shifts. The first shift leaves electronic or voice messages for the second shift.

4. **Different-time/different-place.** In this setting, participants are in different places, and they send and/or receive messages at different times.

Businesses require that messages be transmitted as fast as they are needed, that the intended receiver properly interprets them, and that the cost of doing this be reasonable. Communication systems that meet these conditions have several characteristics. They allow two-way communication: Messages flow in different directions, sometimes almost simultaneously, and messages reach people regardless of where they are located. Efficient systems also allow people to access various sources of information (such as databases). IT helps to meet these requirements through the electronic transfer of information using tools such as e-mail.

The Internet has become a major supporter of interactive communications. People are using a variety of Internet technologies—Internet phones, smart cell phones, Internet videoconferencing, Internet radio, whiteboards, chat rooms, and more—for communication. In Section 4.5 we will discuss some of the IT tools cited in connection with Figure 4.5 (page 140). E-mail, including instant and universal messaging services, is discussed in Online File W4.6 at the book's Web site. Other Internet-based communication tools and technologies are described in Technology Guide 4.

Web-Based Call Centers
Effective personalized customer contact is becoming an important aspect of customer support through the Web. Such service is provided through *Web-based call centers* (also known as *customer care centers*). Enabling Web collaboration and

simultaneous voice/Web contact can differentiate a company from its competitors. There are at least four categories of capabilities employed by Web-based call centers—e-mail, interactive text chat, callbacks, and simultaneous voice and Web sessions. (For discussion of how companies might decide among the possible choices for Web-based call centers, see Drury, 1999.) WebsiteAlive (*websitealive.com*), a Web-based call center support product, delivers live customer-service capabilities for any online company. Further details and examples are provided in Chapter 7.

Electronic Chat Rooms

Electronic chat refers to an arrangement whereby participants exchange messages in real time. The software industry estimates that millions of chat rooms exist on the Internet. A **chat room** is a virtual meeting place where groups of regulars come to gab. Chat programs allow you to send messages to people who are connected to the same channel of communication *at the same time*. It is like a global conference call system. Anyone can join in the online conversation. Messages are displayed on your screen as they arrive, even if you are in the middle of typing a message.

The chat rooms can be used to build a community, to promote a commercial, political, or environmental cause, to support people with medical problems, or to let hobbyists share their interest. And since many customer-supplier relationships have to be sustained without face-to-face meetings, online communities are increasingly being used to serve business interests, including advertising (see *Parachat.com* and Technology Guide 5). Chat capabilities can be added to a business site for free by letting software chat vendors host your session on their site. You simply put a chat link on your site and the chat vendor does the rest, including the advertising that pays for the session.

Two major types of chat programs exist: (1) Web-based chat programs, which allow you to send messages to Net users using a Web browser and visiting a Webchat site (e.g., *chat.yahoo.com*), and (2) an e-mail-based (text only) program called *Internet Relay Chat (IRC)*. A business can use IRC to interact with customers, provide online experts' answers to questions, and so on.

Voice Communication

The most natural mode of communication is voice. When people need to communicate with each other from a distance, they use the telephone more frequently than any other communication device. Voice communication can now be done on the Internet using a microphone and a sound card (see *protocols. com/VOIP*). You can even talk long distance on the Internet without paying the normal long distance telephone charges. This is known as **Internet telephony (voice-over IP),** and it is described in Technology Guide 5. Voice communication enables workers, from forklift drivers to disabled employees to military pilots, to have portable, safe, and effective access to computer technology from their work areas. In addition, voice communication is faster than typing (about two and half times faster), and fewer errors in voice data entry are made compared to keyboard data entry.

Your can get freeware (free software) for Internet telephony from *roispeed.com*. Also, some browsers provide you with Internet telephony capability. To connect from computers to regular telephones try, for example, *dialpad.com*, which offers low-cost long-distance calls through the Internet to regular telephones in U.S. cities from anywhere in the world. For more information see *tellenet.com/it*.

Voice and data can work together to create useful applications. **Voice mail,** a well-known computerized system for storing, forwarding, and routing telephone messages, is one such application. For some other applications of voice technologies, see Online File W4.7 at the book's Web site. More advanced applications of voice technology such as natural language speech recognition and voice synthesis are described in Chapter 12.

Weblogging (Blogging)

The Internet offers an opportunity for individuals to do personal publishing using a technology known as **Weblogging,** or **blogging.** A **blog** is a personal Web site, open to the public, in which the owner expresses his or her feelings or opinions. People can write stories, tell news, and provide links to other articles and Web sites. At some blogs you can reach fascinating items that you might otherwise have overlooked. At others, you can rapidly get up to speed on an issue of special interest. Blogs are growing rapidly, estimated by BBC News (February 2003) to be close to 500,000.

Blogs became very popular after the terrorist attacks of September 11, 2001, and during the 2003 Iraqi war. People were looking for as many sources of information as possible and for personal connections. Blogs are comforting for people in times of stress. They are a place at which people feel their ideas get noticed, and they can result in two-way communication and collaboration and group discussion.

Building blogs is becoming easier and easier. Programs downloadable from *blogger.com, pitas.com,* and others are very user friendly. "Bloggers" (the people who create and maintain blogs) are handed a fresh space on their Web site to write in each day. They can easily edit, add entries, and broadcast whatever they want by simply clicking on the send key.

Blogs are criticized for their tendency to coalesce into self-referential cliques. Bloggers are blamed for their mutual backslapping, endlessly praising and linking to one another's sites. However, bloggers are creating their own communities and have developed a rich terminology. (For a bloggers dictionary, see *marketingterms.com/dictionary/blog* and *samizdata.net/blog/glossary.*) Blogs have just begun to be used for commercial purposes. For example, Weidlich (2003) reports that some company executives use blogs for informal talk to customers. For further discussion on blogs, see Phillips (2002).

4.4 COLLABORATION

One of the abiding features of a modern organization is that people collaborate to perform work. **Collaboration** refers to mutual efforts by two or more individuals who perform activities in order to accomplish certain tasks. The individuals may represent themselves or organizations, or they may be members of a team or a group. Group members work together on tasks ranging from designing products and documents, to teaching each other, to executing complementary subtasks. Also, people work with customers, suppliers, and other business partners in an effort to improve productivity and competitiveness. Finally, group members participate in decision making. In all of the above cases they need to collaborate. Collaboration can be supported electronically by several technologies as described later in this chapter.

The Nature of Group Work

Group work is increasing in importance. Indeed, it is a cornerstone in some business process restructuring (BPR) projects and in e-commerce. Also, group work is needed in virtual corporations as well as in multinational organizations. The use of group work is also increasing due to the support provided by IT, especially the support provided to groups whose members are in different locations.

The term **workgroup** refers to two or more individuals who act together to perform some task. The group can be permanent or temporary. It can be in one location (face-to-face meetings) or in several. If group members are in different locations we say we have a **virtual group (team),** and they conduct *virtual meetings* (they "meet" electronically). Members can meet concurrently or at different times. The group can be a committee, a review panel, a task force, an executive board, a team, or a department. Groups conduct their work by using different approaches or processes.

CONVENTIONAL APPROACH TO GROUP WORK. For years, people have recognized the benefits of collaborative work. Typical benefits that relate to decision making in groups are listed in Table 4.1. But despite the many benefits of group interaction, groups are not always successful. The reason is that the process of collaborative work is frequently plagued by dysfunctions, as listed in Table 4.2.

To reconcile these differences, researchers have worked for many years to improve the work of groups. If the causes of group dysfunctions could be lessened or eliminated, the benefits of group work would be greatly enhanced. Several approaches have been developed to attempt to solve the problems inherent in group work. Two representative methods are the *nominal group technique* and the *Delphi method* (see Online File W4.8 for explanations of those two methods).

The limited success of the above approaches to group work and the availability of IT tools and the Internet has created an opportunity for supporting groups electronically, which is part of virtual collaboration. We describe the general support in this section. The support that is intended to facilitate decision making is described in Chapter 12.

TABLE 4.1 Benefits of Working in a Group
● Groups are better than individuals at understanding problems.
● People are accountable for decisions in which they participate.
● Groups are better than individuals at catching errors.
● A group has more information (knowledge) than any one member and, as a result, more alternatives are generated for problem solving.
● Synergy can be produced, so the effectiveness and/or quality of group work can be greater than the sum of what is produced by independent individuals.
● Working in a group may stimulate the participants and the process.
● Group members have their egos embedded in the decision they make, so they will be committed to its implementation.

TABLE 4.2 Dysfunctions of Group Process
● Social pressures to conform ("groupthink") may eliminate superior ideas.
● Group process can be time-consuming, slow, and costly.
● Work done in a group may lack appropriate coordination.
● Some members may dominate the agenda.
● Some group members ("free riders") may rely on others to do most of their work.
● The group may compromise on solutions of poor quality.
● The group may be unable to complete a task.
● Unproductive time is spent socializing, getting ready, waiting for people, or repeating what has already been said.
● Members may be afraid to speak up.

Virtual Collaboration

Virtual collaboration (or *e-collaboration*) refers to the use of digital technologies that enable organizations or individuals to collaboratively plan, design, develop, manage, and research products, services, and innovative IT and EC applications. Although e-collaboration can involve noncommerce applications, the term usually refers to **collaborative commerce**—collaboration among business partners. An example would be a company that it is collaborating electronically with a vendor that designs a product or a part for the company (see Minicase 1, about General Motors). Collaborative commerce implies communication, information sharing, and collaborative planning done electronically through tools such as groupware and specially designed EC collaboration tools. For details see Turban (2004) and Poirier (2001).

Numerous studies (e.g., *line56.com,* 2002) suggest that collaboration is a set of relationships with significant improvements in organizations' performance. Major benefits cited are cost reduction, increased revenue, and improved customer retention. These benefits are the results of fewer stockouts, less exception-processing, reduced inventory throughout the supply chain, lower material costs, increased sales volume, and increased competitive advantage. According to a survey conducted by Deloitte Consulting and reported in *Manageradvisor.com* (2002), 70 percent of the companies conducting collaborative commerce are showing higher profitability than those who do not. Of those companies surveyed, 75 percent consider online collaboration, especially linking business processes, to be a top executive priority. These figures, gathered in 2002, are more than 20 percent higher than responses from 2000. Finally, 85 percent of all companies plan to have advanced collaborative commerce initiatives by 2005. Some of the major strategic benefits reported are an increase in process flexibility, faster delivery speed, and improved customer service.

C-commerce activities are usually conducted between and among supply chain partners. For example, Webcor Builders is using a communication hub to facilitate collaboration, as described in *IT at Work 4.3.*

The Webcor case shows how one company becomes a *nucleus firm,* or a hub, for collaboration. Such arrangement can be expanded to include all business partners, as shown in Figure 4.7. This concept is the basis for many-to-many e-marketplaces (see Chapter 5), in which a third-party company is the nucleus firm, creating a place not only for collaboration but also for trade.

There are several other varieties of virtual collaboration, ranging from joint design efforts to forecasting. Collaboration can be done both between and within organizations. The following are some types and examples of virtual collaboration.

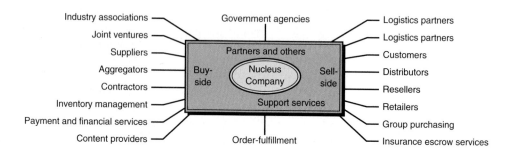

FIGURE 4.7
E-collaboration for commerce.

IT at Work 4.3
WEBCOR GOES ONLINE WITH ITS PARTNERS

Webcor Builders (*webcor.com*) builds apartment buildings, hotels, and office parks, with revenues of about $500 million a year. For years the company suffered from poor communication with its partners (architects, designers, building owners, subcontractors) and struggled with too much paperwork. Reams of documents were sent back and forth via "snail mail." In a very competitive industry, inefficiencies can be costly. So, Webcor decided to introduce c-commerce into its operations. Webcor's goal was to turn its computer-aided design (CAD) drawings, memos, and other information into shared digital information. The nearby figure shows the connections among Webcor's partners via its extranet.

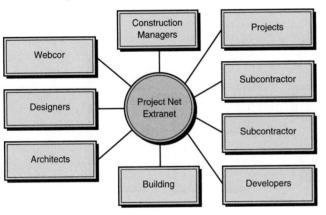

Webcor Builders goes online.

To enable online collaboration, Webcor is using an application service provider (ASP) that hosts Webcor's projects using ProjectNet software on a secured extranet. The software is complex, so there was a problem getting everyone to accept ProjectNet, and some user training was necessary. However, Webcor found itself in a strong enough position to be able to say that in the near future, it would not partner with anyone who would not use ProjectNet.

With everyone on the ProjectNet system, Webcor's business partners can post, send, or edit complex CAD drawings, digital photos, memos, status reports, and project histories. ProjectNet provides a central meeting place where users can both download and transmit information to all parties, all with a PC. Everyone involved in a project is more accountable, because there is a digital trail, and partners now get instant access to new building drawings.

One of the major benefits of ProjectNet is that employees now spend more time managing their work and less time on administrative paperwork. Several clerical workers were laid off, and the saved cost of their salaries is covering the software rental fees.

Sources: Compiled from Webcor.com press releases at *webcor.com* (2000–2002), and from DiCarlo (1999).

For Further Exploration: What are the benefits of this c-commerce project to Webcor? What are the benefits of this project to Webcor's partners? To it clients?

COLLABORATIVE NETWORKS. Traditionally, collaboration took place among supply chain members, frequently those that were close to each other (e.g., a manufacturer and its distributor, or a distributor and a retailer). Even if more partners are involved, the focus has been on the optimization of information and product flow between existing nodes in the traditional supply chain.

The traditional collaboration resulted in a vertically integrated supply chain. However, as discussed in earlier chapters, IT and Web technologies can *fundamentally change* the shape of the supply chain, as well as the number of players within it and their individual roles and collaboration patterns. The new supply chain can be a hub, as in the Webcor case, or even a network. A comparison between the traditional supply chain collaboration and the collaborative network is shown in Figure 4.8 (page 148). Notice that the traditional chain (part a, for the food industry) is basically linear. The collaborative network (part b) shows that partners at any point in the network can interact with each other, bypassing traditional partners. Interaction may occur among several manufacturers

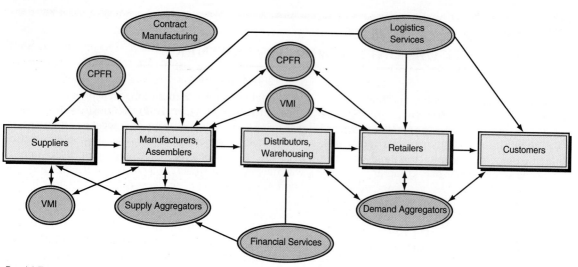

Part (a) Traditional collaboration, including CPFR. Collaboration agents and efforts are shown as ovals.

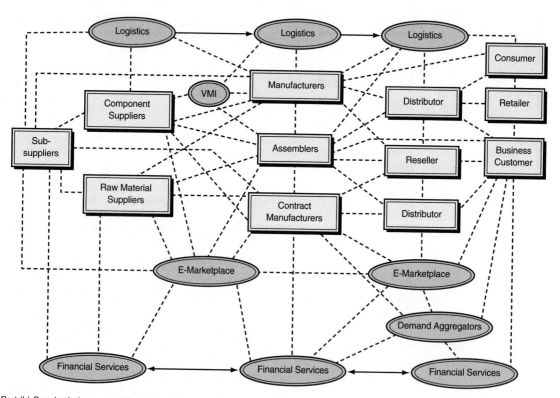

Part (b) Supply chains are evolving into collaborative networks. Ovals designate agents and services.

FIGURE 4.8 Comparing traditional supply chain collaboration and collaborative networks. (*Sources:* Part (a) based on Walton and Princi, 2000, p. 193, Fig. 1.8. Part (b) based on Poirier, 2001, p. 9-8, Fig. 1.)

and/or distributors, as well as with new players such as software agents that act as aggregators, B2B e-marketplaces, or logistics providers.

The collaborative network can take different shapes depending on the industry, the product (or service), the volume of flow, and more. Examples of collaborative networks are provided by Poirier (2001) and by Walton and Princi (2000).

REPRESENTATIVE EXAMPLES OF VIRTUAL COLLABORATION. Leading businesses are moving quickly to realize the benefits of e-collaboration. For example, the real estate franchiser RE/MAX uses an e-collaboration platform to improve communications and collaboration among its nationwide network of independently owned real estate franchises, sales associates, and suppliers. Similarly, Marriott International, the world's largest hospitality company, started with an online brochure and then developed a c-commerce system that links corporations, franchisees, partners, and suppliers, as well as customers, around the world. In addition, as described in Online File W4.9, Nygard of Canada has developed a collaborative system along its entire supply chain.

There are many examples of e-collaboration. Here we present some additional representative ones. For more see Schram (2001), and Davison and de Vreede (2001).

Information Sharing Between Retailers and Their Suppliers: P&G and Wal-Mart. One of the most notable examples of information sharing is between Procter & Gamble (P&G) and Wal-Mart. Wal-Mart provides P&G access to sales information on every item Wal-Mart buys from P&G. The information is collected by P&G on a daily basis from every Wal-Mart store, and P&G uses the information to manage the inventory replenishment for Wal-Mart. By monitoring the inventory level of each P&G item in every Wal-Mart store, P&G knows when the inventories fall below the threshold that triggers a shipment. All this is done electronically. The benefit for P&G is that they can sell to a good customer, and the benefit to Wal-Mart is adequate inventory on its shelves. P&G has similar agreements with other major retailers.

Retailer–Supplier Collaboration: Target Corporation. Target Corporation (*targetcorp.com*) is a large retail conglomerate (owner of Target Stores, Marshall Field, Mervyn's, and Target.direct.com). It needs to conduct EC activities with about 20,000 suppliers. In 1998, then operating under the name Dayton-Hudson Corporation, the company established an extranet-based system for those suppliers that were not connected to its VAN-based EDI. The extranet enabled the company not only to reach many more partners, but also to use many applications not available on the traditional EDI. The system enabled the company to streamline its communications and collaboration with suppliers. It also allowed the company's business customers to create personalized Web pages that were accessible via either the Internet or the company's private VAN.

Reduction of Product Development Time: Caterpillar, Inc. Caterpillar, Inc. (*caterpillar.com*) is a multinational heavy-machinery manufacturer. In the traditional mode of operation, cycle time along the supply chain was long because the process involved paper-document transfers among managers, salespeople, and technical staff. To solve the problem, Caterpillar connected its engineering and manufacturing divisions with its active suppliers, distributors, overseas factories, and customers through an extranet-based global collaboration system. By means of the collaboration system, a request for a customized tractor component, for example, can be transmitted from a customer to a Caterpillar dealer and on to designers and suppliers, all in a very short time. Customers also can use the extranet to retrieve and modify detailed order information while the vehicle is still on the assembly line. Remote collaboration capabilities between the customer and product developers have decreased cycle time delays caused by rework time. Suppliers are also connected to the system, so they can deliver materials or parts directly to Caterpillar's repair shops or directly to the customer if appropriate. The system also is used for expediting maintenance and repairs.

For comprehensive coverage of collaborative virtual design environments, see Ragusa and Bochenek (2001). See also Minicase 1 at the end of this chapter.

Barriers to E-Collaboration and C-Commerce

Despite the many potential benefits, e-collaboration and c-commerce are moving ahead fairly slowly. Reasons cited in various studies include technical reasons involving integration, standards, and networks; security and privacy concerns over who has access to and control of information stored in a partner's database; internal resistance to information sharing and to new approaches; and lack of internal skills to conduct collaborative commerce (Schram, 2001). A big stumbling block to the adoption of c-commerce is the lack of defined and universally agreed-on standards. New approaches such as the use of XML and its variants and the use of Web services could lessen significantly the problem of standards. (See Bradley, 2002, and *cpfr.com* for discussion of the CPFR—collaboration, planning, forecasting, and replenishing—initiative.)

Sometimes collaboration is an organizational culture shock—people simply resist sharing. One reason is the lack of trust, especially in ad-hoc relationships. According to Gibson-Paul (2003), companies such as Boeing and Spalding are grappling with the trust factor. Some techniques she suggested include starting small (e.g., synchronizing one type of sales data), picking up projects that are likely to provide a quick return on investment for both sides, meeting face-to-face at the beginning of a collaboration; and showing the benefits to all parties. Despite initial lack of trust, if potential collaborators judge the benefits of collaboration to be sufficient, and about equal among collaborators, they will be more eager to join in.

Finally, global collaboration involves all of these potential barriers, and more. For further discussion, see Davison and de Vreede (2001) and Carmel (1999).

4.5 COLLABORATION-ENABLING TOOLS: FROM WORKFLOW TO GROUPWARE

As mentioned earlier, corporate portals facilitate e-collaboration. Also available for this purpose are a large number of tools and methodologies, whose types and features are listed in Online File W4.10. In this section we present workflow technologies, groupware, and other collaboration-enabling tools.

Workflow Technologies

Workflow is the movement of information as it flows through the sequence of steps that make up an organization's work procedures. **Workflow management** is the automation of workflows, so that documents, information, or tasks are passed from one participant to another in a way that is governed by the organization's rules or procedures. Workflow management involves all of the steps in a business process from start to finish, including all exception conditions.

The key to workflow management is the tracking of process-related information and the status of each activity of the business process, which is done by workflow systems (see van der Aalst, 2002). **Workflow systems** are business process automation tools that place system controls in the hands of user departments. They employ a set of software programs that automate almost any information-processing task. The major workflow activities to be managed are job routing and monitoring, document imaging, document management, supply chain optimization, and control of work. These activities are done by workflow applications.

TYPES OF WORKFLOW APPLICATIONS. Workflow applications fall into three major categories—collaborative, production, and administrative workflow.

- *Collaborative workflow.* *Collaborative workflow* products address project-oriented and collaborative types of processes. They are administered centrally, yet they are capable of being accessed and used by workers from different departments and even from different physical locations. The goal of collaborative workflow tools is to empower knowledge workers. Some leading vendors of collaborative workflow applications are Lotus, JetForm, FileNet, and Action Technologies.

- *Production workflow.* *Production workflow* tools address mission-critical, transaction-oriented, high-volume processes. They are often deployed only in a single department or to a certain set of users within a department. Often, these applications include document imaging, and storage and retrieval capabilities. They also can include the use of intelligent forms, database access, and ad-hoc capabilities. The leading vendors of production workflow systems are FileNet, Staffware, IBM(MQ3), and Eastman WorkFlow. An example of production workflow that is mixed with collaboration workflow is presented in *IT at Work 4.4* (page 152).

- *Administrative workflow.* *Administrative workflow* can be considered a cross between the previous two types of workflow. The flow is predefined (such as the steps required to approve an expense report), but can be changed, if needed. The goal of administrative workflow applications is to reduce clerical costs in systems with a low volume of complex transactions. The major vendors are Staffware, InTempo, and Metro.

There are multiple benefits of workflow management systems. For example, they improve control of business processes, with far less management intervention, and far less chance for delays or misplaced work than other systems. They also improve the quality of services, by quicker response, with the best person available. They lower costs, both of staff training (since the work can be guided through complex procedures) and of management in general, because managers can have a far wider span of control while also being able to concentrate on nurturing the employees and handling special cases rather than routine reporting and distribution issues. Finally, workflow management systems also improve user satisfaction. Users typically have greater confidence that they are doing the best they can and the satisfaction of completing that work with fewer conflicting requirements. For more information on workflow management, see Fischer, 2002, and Basu and Kumar, 2002. Also, visit *wfmc.com, aim.org, waria.com,* and *omg.org.*

Since workflow management systems support more than one individual, they are considered by some to be a subset of groupware, our next topic.

Groupware   **Groupware** refers to software products that support groups of people who share a common task or goal and who collaborate on its accomplishment. These products provide a way for groups to share resources and opinions. Groupware

IT at Work 4.4

USING A WORKFLOW SYSTEM TO MANAGE CURRENCY FLOWS AT A GERMAN BANK

Dresdner Bank, in Germany, has automated the way it handles the trading of currency orders. Whether they originate from within a single operation or across its trading rooms worldwide, the bank routes these orders using a workflow system called Limit Order Application (LORA). This workflow system, built on top of Microsoft Exchange, replaced previous telephone and fax-based processes.

One of the main problems that Dresdner Bank sought to solve with the system was the allocation and uptake of orders between different trading rooms around the world. Being able to route orders would allow more efficient trading across the different time-zones—for instance, making it easier for traders to execute a Frankfurt order in New York after close of business in Germany.

Three types of bank staff—traders, controllers, and administrators—use this system, which works as follows: First, when an order is received, it is placed into an electronic folder by the controller. All order folders are held in a "public" file and can be viewed by the relevant staff. Next, when a trader accepts an order, he or she is responsible for that order from that moment on. Although the order can still be canceled or reversed at this stage, the details of price and order quantity cannot be changed. The status of the order is displayed, and any order is locked when accessed, to prevent anyone from altering it. (Even small changes in the details of an order could result in huge profits or losses for the bank or its clients.) Finally, when the order is executed, or if it is canceled or reversed or it expires, then it is sent to a subfolder to be archived.

The bank dropped an initial plan of implementing global common folders that could be accessed by any of its 1,000 traders, in any location. It did so because of resistance from the traders, who did not like the idea of relinquishing local control and allowing other traders to process or execute their orders. Instead, the bank has implemented a system of local folders that reside within the branch of origin; these can be read by, but cannot be processed by, traders elsewhere.

With LORA, users can respond more quickly and accurately to customer queries, because they are able to access and view on the computer screen the precise status of orders. There is also improved control, with responsibility for any order always assigned to a specific staff member. The user interface was carefully designed to meet stringent requirements with respect to efficiency and ease of use.

LORA was built mainly using Visual Basic, with provisions to extend the system to allow reuse of existing components. The system was implemented in about six months, first to support the bank's 500 dealers in Frankfurt. By 2003 it was implemented in all of the bank's other branches.

Sources: Compiled from *microsoft.com/resources/casestudies/CaseStudy. asp?CaseStudyID=13324* (accessed January 4, 2003), and from *Dresdner-bank.com* (accessed March 2003).

For Further Exploration: Identify the parties in this case that need to collaborate with each other. How does the system facilitate collaboration? How does the workflow system differ from typical transaction-oriented application systems in this bank?

implies the use of networks to connect people, even if the people are in the same room. Many groupware products are available on the Internet or an intranet, enhancing the collaboration of a large number of people worldwide. There are many different approaches and technologies for the support of groups on the Internet.

Groupware products come either as a standalone product supporting one task (such as e-mail), or as an integrated kit that includes several tools. In general, groupware technology products are fairly inexpensive and can be easily incorporated into existing information systems. The Internet, intranets, extranets, and private communication lines provide the infrastructure needed for the hardware and software of groupware. The software products are mostly Web-based, which is the trend today. In this section we will describe some of the most common groupware products.

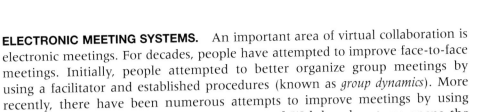

ELECTRONIC MEETING SYSTEMS.   An important area of virtual collaboration is electronic meetings. For decades, people have attempted to improve face-to-face meetings. Initially, people attempted to better organize group meetings by using a facilitator and established procedures (known as *group dynamics*). More recently, there have been numerous attempts to improve meetings by using information technologies. The advancement of Web-based systems opens the door for electronically supported **virtual meetings,** those whose members are in different locations, frequently in different countries.

The events of September 11, 2001 and the economic slowdown of 2001–2003 made virtual meetings more popular, as corporate travel waned. It is also hard for companies to ignore reported cost savings, such as the $4 million a month that IBM reported it saved just from cutting travel expenses to meetings (Callaghan, 2002). In addition, improvements in supporting technology, reductions in the price of technology, and the acceptance of virtual meetings as a respected way of doing business are fueling their growth (see Vinas, 2002).

Virtual meetings can be supported by a variety of tools, as will be shown in the remainder of this section. The support provided to decision making is presented in Chapter 12.

ELECTRONIC TELECONFERENCING.   **Teleconferencing** is the use of electronic communication that allows two or more people at different locations to have a simultaneous conference. There are several types of teleconferencing. The oldest and simplest is a telephone conference call, where several people talk to each other from three or more locations. The biggest disadvantage is that it does not allow for face-to-face communication. Also, participants in one location cannot see graphs, charts, and pictures at other locations. One solution is *video teleconferencing*, in which participants can see each other as well as the documents.

Video Teleconferencing.   In a **video teleconference** (or *videoconference*), participants in one location can see participants at other locations. Dynamic pictures of the participants can appear on a large screen or on a desktop computer. Originally, video teleconferencing was the transmission of live, compressed TV sessions between two or more points. Video teleconferencing today, however, is a digital technology capable of linking various types of computers across networks. Once conferences are digitized and transmitted over networks, they become a computer application.

With videoconferencing, participants can share data, voice, pictures, graphics, and animation. Data can also be sent along with voice and video. Such **data conferencing** makes it possible to work on documents together and to exchange computer files during videoconferences. This allows several geographically dispersed groups to work on the same project and to communicate by video simultaneously.

Video teleconferencing offers various benefits. We've already mentioned three of them—providing the opportunity for face-to-face communication for individuals in different locations, supporting several types of media during conferencing, and lower travel time and costs. Other benefits of video teleconferencing are shown in Online File W4.11 at the book's Web site.

Web Conferencing.   **Web conferencing** is conducted on the Internet for as few as two and as many as thousands of people. Web conferencing is done *solely* on the Web. (Videoconferencing is usually done on regular telephone lines, although it may also be done on the Web.) Like video teleconferencing, Web conferencing allows users to simultaneously view something, such as a sales presentation in Microsoft PowerPoint or a product drawing, on their computer screens; interaction takes place via messaging or a simultaneous phone teleconference. However, Web conferencing is much cheaper than videoconferencing because it runs on the Internet.

The latest technological innovations permit both business-to-business and business-to-consumer applications of Web conferencing. For example, banks in Alaska use *video kiosks* in sparsely populated areas instead of building branches that will be underutilized. The video kiosks operate on the banks' intranet and provide videoconferencing equipment for eye-to-eye interactions. Some examples of other uses are: to educate staff members about a new product line or technology; to amplify a meeting with investors; or to walk a prospective client though an introductory presentation.

Web conferencing is becoming very popular. Almost all Web conferencing products provide whiteboarding (see discussion below) and polling features, and allow you to give presentations and demos and to share applications. Popular Web conferencing products are: Centra EMeeting, Genesys Meeting Center, PlaceWare, and WebEx Meeting Center.

RTC TOOLS. The Internet, intranets, and extranets offer tremendous potential for real-time and synchronous interaction of people working in groups. *Real-time collaboration (RTC)* tools help companies bridge time and space to make decisions and to collaborate on projects. RTC tools support synchronous communication of graphical and text-based information. These tools are being used in distance training, product demonstrations, customer support, and sales applications. RTC tools can be either purchased as standalone tools or used on a subscription basis. Some examples follow:

Interactive Whiteboards. Computer-based **whiteboards** work like the "physical world" whiteboards with markers and erasers, except with one big difference: Instead of one person standing in front of a meeting room drawing on the whiteboard, all participants can join in. Throughout a meeting, each user can view and draw on a single document "pasted" onto the electronic whiteboard on a computer screen. Digital whiteboarding sessions can also be saved for later reference or other use. Some whiteboarding products let users insert graphics files that can be annotated by the group.

Take, for example, an advertisement that needs to be cleared by a senior manager. The proposed ad would be scanned into a PC, and both parties would see it on their screens. If the senior manager does not like something, he or she can highlight what needs to be changed, using a stylus pen. The two parties can also share applications. For example, if party A works with Excel, party B does not have to have Excel in order to work with it in the whiteboarding tool.

Besides being used for supporting people working on the same task, whiteboards are also used for training and learning. See Online File W4.12 for discussion of two whiteboarding products that can be used for training and learning.

Screen Sharing. In collaborative work, members are frequently in different locations. Using **screen sharing** software, group members can work on the same document, which is shown on the PC screen of each participant. For example, two authors can work on a single manuscript. One may suggest a correction and execute it so the other author can see the change. Collaborators can work together on the same spreadsheet or on the resulting graphics. Changes can be done by using the keyboard or by touching the screen. This capability can expedite the design of products, the preparation of reports and bids, and the resolution of conflicts. A special screen sharing capability is offered by Groove Inc. (*groove.net*). Its product synchronizes people, computers, and information to enable the joint creation and/or editing of documents on your PC.

Instant Video. With the spread of **instant messaging** and Internet telephony has come the idea to link people via both voice and audio. Called *instant video,* the idea is for a kind of video chat room. It allows you to chat in real time, seeing the person you are communicating with. A simple way to do it is to add video cameras to the participants' computers. A more sophisticated approach that produces pictures of better quality is to integrate existing online videoconferencing service with instant messaging software, creating a service that offers the online equivalent of a videophone.

INTEGRATION AND GROUPWARE SUITES. Because groupware technologies are computer-based, it makes sense to integrate them with other computer-based or computer-controlled technologies. A *software suite* is created when several products are integrated into one system. Integrating several technologies can save time and money for users. For example, PictureTel Corporation (*picturetel.com*), in an alliance with software developer Lotus, developed an integrated desktop video teleconferencing product that uses Lotus Notes. Using this integrated system, publisher Reader's Digest has built several applications combined with videoconferencing capabilities. A seamless integration is provided in groupware suites. Lotus Notes/Domino is one example of popular *groupware suites*. For discussion of others, see Online File W4.13.

Lotus Notes/Domino. The **Lotus Notes/Domino** suite includes a document management system, a distributed client/server database, and a basis for intranet and e-commerce systems, as well as a communication support tool. It enhances real-time communications with asynchronous electronic connections (e.g., electronic mail and other forms of messaging).

Thanks to electronic networks, e-mail, and the ability to exchange or update data at any time and from any place, group members using Lotus Notes/Domino might store all their official memos, formal reports, and informal conversations related to particular projects in a shared, online database. Then, as individual members need to check on the contents, they can access the shared database to find the information they need.

Lotus Notes provides online collaboration capabilities, workgroup e-mail, distributed databases, bulletin whiteboards, text editing, (electronic) document management, workflow capabilities, instant virtual meetings, application sharing, instant messaging, consensus building, voting, ranking, and various application development tools. All these capabilities are integrated into one environment with a graphic menu-based user interface. By the end of 2002, there were over 60 million Notes users worldwide (*lotus.com*, 2002). For even more capabilities of Lotus Notes/Domino, see Internet Exercise 3 at the end of the chapter.

Implementation Issues of Virtual Collaboration

Throughout this chapter we have discussed issues of online collaboration of one sort or another. Here we mention a few implementation issues that must be addressed when planning online collaboration. First, to connect you and your business partners, you need an effective collaborative environment. Such an environment is provided by groupware suites such as Lotus Notes/Domino. Another issue is the need to connect collaborative tools with file management products on the intranet. Two such products are e/pop servers and clients (*wiredred.com*) and eRoom's server (*documentum.com*).

In addition, throughout the book, we have documented the general trend toward moving e-commerce applications onto the Web. To change the read-only Web to a truly collaborative environment, one needs *protocols,* rules that determine how two computers communicate with one another over a network. The protocols make possible the integration of different applications and standardize communication. One such protocol, which is relatively new, is WebDAV (Web Distributed Authoring and Versioning protocol). For details see *webdav.org.*

Finally, we should point out that online collaboration is not a panacea for all occasions or in all situations. Many times, a face-to-face meeting is a must. Human workers do sometimes need the facial cues and the physical closeness that no computer system can currently provide. (A technology called *pervasive computing* attempts to remove some of these limitations, e.g., by interpreting facial cues. For more, see Chapter 6.)

4.6 E-LEARNING, DISTANCE LEARNING, AND TELECOMMUTING

Web-based systems enable many applications related to discovery, communication, and collaboration. Several important applications are presented in this section—e-learning, distance learning, and telecommuting.

E-Learning versus Distance Learning

There can be some confusion between e-learning and distance learning since they overlap each other. Therefore we begin with brief definitions.

E-learning refers to learning supported by the Web. It can be done inside classrooms, as was demonstrated in the Dartmouth College case in Chapter 1. It can be done as a support to conventional teaching, such as when students work on the Web at home or in the classroom. It also can be done in *virtual classrooms,* in which the entire coursework is done online and classes do not meet face-to-face, and then it is a part of distance learning.

Distance learning (DL) refers to situations where teachers and students do not meet face-to-face. It can be done in different ways. The oldest mode was correspondence, where all communication was done by mail. As early as the 1920s the radio was added to support DL. Then came voice cassettes, videotapes, and TV for delivering lectures. Students communicated with professors by "snail mail," telephone, and faxes. A breakthrough occurred when the CD-ROM was introduced, since they are media rich and enabled self-testing and feedback. Finally the Web provided a multimedia interactive environment for self-study. (For an overview of DL see Matthews, 1999, and Bunker, 1999.)

Therefore, e-learning is only one channel of distance learning. At the same time, some parts of e-learning are done in the face-to-face mode, and not from a distance. What is common to the two is some of the delivery tools as well as some pedagogical issues. In both cases, Web-enabled systems make knowledge accessible to those who need it, when they need it, any time, anywhere. E-learning and DL can be useful both as an environment for facilitating learning at schools and as an environment for efficient and effective corporate training.

Liaw and Huang (2002) describe how Web technologies can facilitate learning. For an overview and research issues related to e-learning, see Piccoli et al. (2001); this resource also provides a comparison of e-learning with traditional classroom teaching. Our discussion here concentrates on e-learning, which in its broader scope is known as *e-education* (see Albalooshi, 2003).

The Benefits of E-Learning

In theory, there are many benefits to e-learning: Self-paced and self-initiated learning has been shown to increase content retention (Urdan and Weggen, 2002). Online materials offer the opportunity to deliver very current content, of high quality (created by content experts), and consistent (presented the same way every time). Students in e-learning situations have the flexibility of learning from any place, at any time, and at their own pace. Finally, some learners in both educational and corporate settings appreciate what they perceive as the risk-free environment offered by e-learning, in which they feel more free to express themselves than in a face-to-face learning setting. In corporate training centers, learning time generally is shorter, and more people can be trained due to the faster training time. As a result, training costs can be reduced by 50 to 70 percent (Urdan and Weggen, 2002), and savings can be made on facility space as well.

E-learning provides a new set of tools that can add value to traditional learning modes. It does not usually replace the classroom setting, but enhances it, taking advantage of new content and delivery technologies. The better the match of content and delivery vehicle to an individual's learning style, the greater the content retention, and the better the learning results. Advanced e-learning support environments, such as Blackboard and WebCT, add value to traditional learning in higher education. See *A Closer Look 4.3* for descriptions of these e-learning tools, with which you may already be familiar from personal experience. Several other e-learning courseware tools are discussed in Online File W4.14.

A CLOSER LOOK
4.3 BLACKBOARD AND WEBCT

There is a good chance that you will use the Blackboard Inc. or WebCT frameworks when taking a class or using this text. These competing products provide the Internet infrastructure software for e-learning in schools, serving one of the fastest-growing industry segments in the world. Eduventures.com, a leading independent e-learning industry analyst, projected that the higher-education e-learning market will grow from $4 billion in 2001 to $11 billion by 2005 (*eduventures.com*, 2001).

The publisher places a book's content, teaching notes, quizzes, etc. on Blackboard or WebCT in a standardized format. Instructors can access modules and transfer them into their own specific Blackboard or WebCT sites, which can be accessed by their students.

Blackboard Inc. offers a complete suite of enterprise software products and services that power a total "e-education infrastructure" for schools, colleges, universities, and other education providers. Of special interest are the discussion rooms that can be for everyone or for a restricted group.

WebCT provides a similar set of tools, but with a different vision and strategy. It uses advanced pedagogical tools to help institutions of higher education make distance-learning courses possible. Such courses enable schools to expand campus boundaries, attract and retain students and faculty, and continually improve course and degree program quality.

Textbook publishers are embracing these tools by making their major textbooks Blackboard and/or WebCT enabled. Thus, your professor can easily incorporate this book's content into the software that is used by thousands of universities worldwide.

Sources: Compiled from *webct.com* and *blackboard.com* (spring 2003).

Some drawbacks do exist that offset the benefits of e-learning. Issues cited as possible drawbacks of e-learning are discussed in Online File W4.15 at the book's Web site. Suggestions on how to overcome such drawbacks and prevent e-learning failures are provided by Weaver (2002) and by Hricko (2003).

Virtual Universities

The concept of **virtual universities**—online universities from which students take classes from home or an off-site location, via the Internet—is expanding rapidly. Hundreds of thousands of students in dozens of countries, from Great Britain to Israel to Thailand, are studying via such institutions. A large number of existing universities, including Stanford University and other top-tier institutions, offer online education of some form. Some universities, such as University of Phoenix (*phoenix.com*), California Virtual Campus (*cvc.edu*), and the University of Maryland (*umuc.edu/distance*), offer thousands of courses and dozens of degrees to students worldwide, all online. Other universities offer limited online courses and degrees and also use innovative teaching methods and multimedia support in the traditional classroom.

The virtual university concept allows universities to offer classes worldwide. Moreover, we may soon see integrated degrees, where students can customize a degree that will best fit their needs by taking courses at different universities. Several all-virtual schools include *eschool-world.com*, *walden.com*, and *trainingzone.co.uk*.

For information about specific e-learning programs, see *Petersons.com*, *ECollege.com*, *icdl.open.ac.uk*, and *usdla.org*. For experiences in moving courses and partial courses to e-learning environments, see Berger (1999), Boisvert (2000), Dollar (2000), and Schell (2000). Hofmann (2002) describes the role of the Internet in distance learning in higher education, surveying implementation issues in terms of technology, course content, and pedagogy.

Online Corporate Training

Like educational institutions, a large number of business organizations are using e-learning on a large scale (e.g., see Kapp, 2002). Web-based learning technologies allow organizations to keep their employees up-to-date, and training via the Web can run 24 hours per day, every day ("24/7"). Online corporate training also offers striking cost advantages: Conventional classroom training costs (in 2000) were about $75 an hour, with full-week programs costing $3,000 to $5,000 (ENTmag.com, 2000). Computer-based training costs about half that amount, without travel costs or class-size restrictions. IBM estimates a savings of $500,000 for every 1,000 hours of training not done in the traditional classroom (Reeder, 2002).

Corporate training is often done via the intranet and corporate portals. However, in large corporations with multiple sites, and for studies from home, the Internet is used to access the online material. Some companies, like Barclays Bank, COX Industries, and Qantas Airways, offer online training in learning centers that they call "universities." For discussion of strategies for implementing corporate e-learning, see Delahoussaye and Zemke (2001). Vendors of online training and educational materials can be found at *digitalthink.com*, *ftfinance.com*, *click2learn.com*, *deitel.com*, and *smartplanet.com*.

E-learning is radically changing education and corporate training, and the socioeconomic and technological changes should be examined as the learning behaviors and expectations of learners change. There is a sharply growing demand for flexible and adaptive learning environments that are independent of time and geography (Meso and Liegle, 2000). For an overview of and guidelines for e-learning, see Piskurich (2003), Hartley (2002), and Cone and Robinson (2001).

Virtual Work and Telecommuting

Virtual (distributed) work environments refer to geographically distributed work teams, global project teams, interorganizational teams, and nontraditional work environments such as virtual organizations, satellite work centers, and telecommuting. The use of such distributed work environments in organizations is increasing rapidly. Many of the participants in such environments are mobile workers. The popularity of these environments is growing in direct relationship to the IT support for them. Wireless and wearable devices are one example, and the groupware tools described earlier are another.

Due to the large number of people participating in virtual work, organizations are faced with problems of how to implement virtual work environments and how to use the IT support (see Belanger et al., 2002). In Chapter 12 we will deal with one aspect of virtual work, the support to group decision making. The topic of supporting mobile employees is covered throughout the book. Here we deal with one such virtual work environment—telecommuting.

TELECOMMUTING. **Telecommuting,** or **teleworking,** refers to an arrangement whereby employees can work at home, at the customer's premises, in special work places, or while traveling, usually using a computer linked to their place of employment. Regular and overnight mail, special messengers, and fax typically have been used to support telecommuting, but they are relatively slow and expensive, and the Internet is gradually replacing them. Almost all groupware technologies can be used to support telecommuting.

The first telecommuters were typists and bookkeepers who simply used their homes as an office. Today, a growing number of professionals do a significant portion of their work at home or on the road (Hartley, 2001). (See Online File W4.16.) Telecommuting, which is used by many corporations in large cities, is also appealing to small entrepreneurs. Many people work at home for their own businesses, using the Internet as a supportive tool (e.g., see Cobe and Parlapiano, 2001).

Telecommuting can be used on a temporary basis. For example, during the 1996 Summer Olympics, Atlanta employers anticipated that the 750,000 additional cars of spectators would create a traffic nightmare. So, many Atlanta companies set up temporary data transmission network lines and told employees to work at home. Vendors cooperated: Symantec and U.S. Robotics offered companies free software to provide remote access to corporate networks. The Olympics offered many employees and companies their first taste of telecommuting.

Impact on Individuals and Organizations. Telecommuting has a number of potential advantages for employees, employers, and society. For example, the opportunity to work at home helps single parents with young children or other homebound people assume more responsible managerial positions in organizations. For more advantages of telecommuting, see Online File W4.17 at the book's Web site.

However, telecommuting also has some potential disadvantages. The major disadvantages for the *employees* are increased feelings of isolation, loss of fringe benefits, lower pay (in some cases), no workplace visibility, with in turn the potential of slower promotions, and lack of socialization. The major disadvantages to *employers* are difficulties in supervising work (for how to overcome it, see Fisher and Fisher, 2000), potential data security problems, training costs, and the high cost of equipping and maintaining telecommuters' homes.

Companies and employees evidently have decided that the advantages of telecommuting outweigh the disadvantages: The use of telecommuting is on the increase. Some experts predict that in 10 to 15 years, 50 percent of all work will be done at home, on the road, or at the customer's site. For a detailed list of advantages and disadvantages of telecommuting, see Nilles (1998). Major reasons for failure of telecommuting programs and possible preventive measures are presented in Online File W4.18 at the book's Web site. For a complete discussion of the impacts of telecommuting see Pinsonneault and Boisvert (in Johnson, 2001).

One important advantage of telecommuting—perhaps its key impact—is productivity.

Telecommuting and Productivity. Why would productivity go up if people work at home? Strangely enough, reduced absenteeism has been cited by many organizations as a reason for increased productivity. Paul Ruper, Associate Director of New Ways to Work, claims absenteeism can be reduced by telecommuting because telecommuting eliminates "sort-of" illnesses. He refers to those mornings when an employee wakes up and feels just "sort of blah." The trip to work and a whole day at the office are not likely to make the worker feel any better, so he or she stays home. A telecommuter in the same situation is likely to try to get some work done, though perhaps in a bathrobe.

Telecommuting also forces managers to manage by results instead of by overseeing. Telecommuting forces both employees and managers to ask some serious questions about the real purpose of a job. For more on teleworking, see Shin et al. (2000).

Even though many employees are attracted to telecommuting, it is not for everybody and should not be mandatory. Some employees need to work with others, and for those employees telecommuting may not be an option. Also, not all jobs can be done while telecommuting, and not all managers can participate. The American Telecommuting Association (ATA) provides information, developments, ideas, and lists of equipment required for supporting teleworkers (*knowledgetree.com/ata.html*). Khalifa and Davison (2000), based on a survey of over 100 telecommuters in North America, identify key factors that contribute to the decision to telecommute. (For more studies of telecommuting outcomes, see Guimaraes and Dallow, 1999; Higa et al., 2000; and Watad and DiSanzo, 2000. For a comprehensive analysis, see Belanger et al., 2001.)

4.7 SOME ETHICAL AND INTEGRATION ISSUES

Of the many issues involved in implementing network computing environments, ethics and integration issues are discussed here.

Ethics on the Net

Several ethical, legal, and security issues have been raised as a result of the use of electronic networks in general and the Internet in particular. For example:

● Does an employer have the right to look at your e-mail without your permission?

- Is someone's desire to download pornographic images from a newsgroup protected by freedom of speech and privacy laws?
- Should someone post critical comments about a product, service, or person to a newsgroup?
- Should an Internet access provider be held liable for the content of the traffic on the network?

Whenever there are no specific answers to such questions and their legal dimensions are vague, ethics become an important factor. Here we discuss some representative ethical issues.

PRIVACY AND ETHICS IN E-MAIL. The increased use of e-mail raises the question of privacy. While letters are sealed, e-mail material is open (unless encrypted). Many organizations are monitoring e-mail, which they have the *legal* right to do in most states; this raises questions of invasion of privacy (see discussion in Chapter 16). Other issues include the use of e-mail at work for personal purposes and for sending and receiving material that is not related to work. (For privacy protection tips surrounding e-mail, see *PC World*, February 1997.)

RIGHT TO FREE SPEECH. The dissemination of information such as pornographic and racist material via e-mail, newsgroups, electronic bulletin boards, and public networks may offend some people. But dissemination of such information in the United States is believed to be a right protected by the U.S. Constitution. At the time of this writing, the degree of freedom in the online world, and who should be liable for transmissions that are illegal, is still very much in debate. Legislation has been proposed that would require providers to create filters allowing adults to keep children from accessing inappropriate material. In fact, the commercial online providers have largely done so. The Internet, however, remains entirely accessible for anyone with a direct connection.

COPYRIGHT. The material you access on the Internet may be marked as being in the public domain; in that case it can be used by anyone for any purpose. Some material is marked as "copyrighted," which indicates that you need permission for anything other than a "fair use." *Fair use* refers to use for educational and not-for-profit activities. If you make a profit from use of copyrighted material, you should pay the copyright owner some fee or royalties.

Much of the material on the Internet is not marked as either in the public domain or copyrighted. Therefore, at least from an ethical point of view, it should be considered copyrighted. This includes software: You cannot legally copy any licensed software. However, *freeware* on the Internet can be downloaded and distributed. *Shareware* can be downloaded for review, but you are expected to pay for it if you decide you want to use it.

THE PRIVACY OF PATIENTS' INFORMATION. In the United States, several specialized online healthcare networks exist, such as Telemed, a network that tracks tuberculosis patients in order to prescribe the most suitable drugs. These systems could be abused. How do patients know they are getting qualified advice? What if personal medical records fall into the wrong hands? The growth of computerized networks makes medical confidentiality harder to preserve. The problem is how to strike a balance between the benefits of health information systems and their potential ethical problems.

INTERNET MANNERS. It is easy to offend people or tread on their toes when you cannot see their faces or you do not know who they are. Two well-known behaviors on the Internet are spamming and flaming. **Spamming** refers to indiscriminate distribution of messages, without consideration for their appropriateness. Spamming is a major problem online. Spamming is frequently answered by **flaming,** which refers to sending angry messages. The Internet can become a war zone between spammers and flamers. Both sides may be equally guilty of ruining newsgroups. Flamers are known for their attacks on inexperienced visitors to newsgroups as well as on those who make spelling errors. A *spam shield* can stop spamming (for examples see *siegesoft.com, spamcop.com,* and *stopspam.org*). For more discussion of spamming, see online Chapter 16.

There are certain general "rules," called *netiquette* (network etiquette), governing Internet manners. One of these "rules," for example, is to think carefully before sending a message; keep in mind that you are making your reputation internationally through the messages you send out. Another useful rule of Internet manners is to apply the Golden Rule: Do unto others in cyberspace as you would do unto them face to face, which is, of course, as you would want them to do unto you. A list of various netiquette rules is shown in Online File W4.19 at the book's Web site.

Likewise, it is far easier to take offense online because online interaction excludes the nuances of body language, rhythm, mood, and context. E-mail users developed an expressive language that can be used to overcome this problem. A sample is shown in Online File W4.20.

UNSOLICITED ADVERTISING. An extension of spamming is the use of junk mail which may clog providers' systems and which frequently annoys people. Similarly, the use of pop-ups (see Chapter 5) irritates many people.

MONITORING EMPLOYEES' USE OF THE INTERNET. Some companies use special software that monitors time spent on the Internet by each employee (and by site address). The objective is to eliminate abuse of access during working hours and the accessing of "indecent" sites. Other companies simply disconnect sites they do not want their employees to visit. Some people believe that such monitoring is either unethical or an infringement of their freedom of speech. Is freedom of speech an absolute right, or does it also involve associated responsibilities?

MONITORING STUDENTS' USE OF THE INTERNET. In Chapter 1 we introduced the issue of using a university's network for nonstudy use (e.g., for P2P file sharing). This usage may result in insufficient bandwidth in many universities. Some universities monitor students' activities on the Internet. Some students question whether it is ethical for universities to do so.

Integration Issues   When people discover, communicate, and collaborate by just using the Internet or other open systems, there are no problems of doing so. But in many cases, network computing involves other types of networks, such as value-added networks (VANs), as well as legacy and other specialized systems, such as computer-aided-design (CAD) or wireless systems. In such a case, users may encounter problems in connecting such systems, a problem known as *integration*. The problem of integration was ranked by a group of chief information officers (CIOs) surveyed in 2001, 2002, and 2003 as their number-one technology problem.

On the Web we distinguish three communication modes:

- *People-to-people.* This was the earliest mode of network communication, when people used e-mail and newsgroups. They also discovered information on bulletin boards and communicated there.
- *People-to-machine.* This was the next step, when people conducted discovery on the Web, searching and finding information.
- *People and machine-to-machine.* This mode occurs when applications need to "talk" to applications, either in complete automation or in automation but including people. An example is buying online with a credit card. When you provide your credit card number to a merchant (say to Amazon.com), the authorization process is done automatically, by several applications residing on several servers, all in a few seconds.

The integration issue can be complicated since information systems involve not only networks, applications, and people, but also hardware, software, and support services of multiple organizations. We discussed the integration problem briefly in Chapter 2 and here. Many possible solutions to the integration problem have been developed over the years. They will be discussed in Chapters 5, 7, 8, and 14. One of the newest and most promising approaches to this problem is Web services, as discussed in Chapter 2 and again in more detail in Chapters 7, 8, and 14. An example of how Expedia is using Web services was provided in Chapter 3.

➡ MANAGERIAL ISSUES

1. *Security of communication.* Communication via networks raises the issue of the integrity, confidentiality, and security of the data being transferred. The protection of data in networks across the globe is not simple (see Chapter 15).

2. *Installing digital dashboards.* Many companies are installing "digital dashboards," which are a sort of one-way portal that is continuously updated with online displays. The dashboard is available to employees in visible places around the company and is also accessible from PCs, PDAs, etc. Large companies, such as General Electric, believe that the cost of the dashboards can be justified by the better discovery and communication they promote within the company.

3. *Control of employee time and activities.* To control the time that employees might waste "surfing the Net" during working hours, some companies limit the information that employees have access to or use special monitoring software. Providing guidelines for employee use of the Internet is a simple but fairly effective approach.

4. *How many portals?* A major issue for some companies is how many portals to have. Should there be separate portals for customers, suppliers, employees, for example? Regardless of the answer, it is a good idea to integrate the separate portals. If you build a separate portal, make sure it can be easily connected to the others (see the tips at "Experts offer key tips. . . ," 2002).

5. *Organizational impacts.* Technology-supported communication may have major organizational impacts. For example, intranets and groupware force people to cooperate and share information. Therefore, their use can lead to significant changes in both organizational culture and the execution of business process reengineering. Further impacts may be felt in corporate structure and the redistribution of organizational power.

6. *Telecommuting.* Telecommuting is a compelling venture, but management needs to be careful. Not all jobs are suitable for telecommuting, and allowing only some employees to telecommute may create jealousy. Likewise, not all employees are suitable telecommuters; some need the energy and social contact found in an office setting.

7. *Cost-benefit justification.* The technologies described in this chapter do not come free, and many of the benefits are intangible. However, the price of many networking technologies is decreasing.

8. *Controlling access to and managing the content of the material on an intranet.* This is becoming a major problem due to the ease of placing material on an intranet and the huge volume of information. Flohr (1997) suggests tools and procedures to manage the situation.

 ON THE WEB SITE... Additional resources, including quizzes; online files of additional text, tables, figures, and cases; and frequently updated Web links to current articles and information can be found on the book's Web site (*wiley.com/college/turban*).

KEY TERMS

Affinity portals *137*

Asynchronous communication *141*

Blog *144*

Blogging (Web logging) *144*

Chat room *143*

Collaborative commerce *146*

Collaboration *144*

Commercial (public) portals *137*

Corporate portals *137*

Data conferencing *153*

Directories *133*

Distance learning (DL) *156*

E-learning *156*

Extranet *131*

Flaming *162*

Groupware *151*

Information portal *136*

Information superhighway *128*

Instant messaging *155*

Intelligent agents *133*

Internet *128*

Internet2 *128*

Internet telephony (voice-over IP) *143*

Intranet *130*

Lotus Notes/Domino *155*

Metasearch engines *134*

Mobile portals *137*

Personal portals *137*

Portal *136*

Publishing portals *137*

Screen sharing *154*

Search engine *133*

Softbot *133*

Software agents *133*

Spamming *162*

Synchronous (real-time) communication *141*

Telecommuting (teleworking) *159*

Teleconferencing *153*

Video teleconference *153*

Virtual collaboration *146*

Virtual group (team) *145*

Virtual meetings *153*

Virtual universities *158*

Virtual work (distributed work) *159*

Voice mail *144*

Voice portals *137*

Web conferencing *153*   Workflow *150*   Workflow systems *150*
Whiteboard (electronic) *154*   Workflow management *150*   Workgroup *145*
World Wide Web (the Web) *129*

CHAPTER HIGHLIGHTS (Numbers Refer to Learning Objectives)

① The Internet and the Web will enable us to integrate voice, text, and other interactive media and bring them into every home, school, and business.

① The Internet is a network of many networks.

② Intranets are an implementation and deployment of Web-based network services within a company.

② Intranets and extranets have the power to change organizational structures and procedures.

③ There are four ways of supporting communication in meetings: same-time/same-place, same-time/different-place, different-time/same-place, and different-time/different-place.

③ Electronic mail allows quick communication across the globe at minimal cost.

④ Electronic meeting systems, computer-supported cooperative work, groupware, and other names designate various types of computer support to groups.

④ Video teleconferencing utilizes several technologies that allow people to communicate and view each other as well as view and transfer documents.

④ Voice technologies can be used to increase productivity and usability of communication.

⑤ Lotus Notes/Domino is a major integrated software that supports the work of dispersed individuals and groups.

⑥ Software agents help to carry out mundane tasks on the Internet such as searching, browsing, and sorting e-mail.

⑦ Distance learning and telecommuting are supported by network computing.

⑧ Ethical behavior on the Internet is critical in order to conduct business in a professional way. You need to know what is right and wrong.

QUESTIONS FOR REVIEW

1. List the major advantages of the Internet.
2. Define an intranet.
3. Define discovery, communication, and collaboration.
4. Describe corporate portals and their benefits.
5. Distinguish corporate portals from information (Internet) portals.
6. What are some major benefits and limitations of working in groups?
7. Describe the time/place framework.
8. Define software agents applications and list their Internet applications.
9. Describe differences and relationships between intranets and extranets.
10. Define groupware.
11. Describe the major capabilities of real-time collaboration tools.
12. List the major capabilities of teleconferencing.
13. Define workflow systems.
14. Describe software agents.
15. List the major Internet-based agents.
16. Define Internet and Internet2.
17. Define voice technology and list its major business uses.
18. Describe and distinguish between DL and e-learning.
19. Define telecommuting and describe its benefits.
20. Define flaming and contrast it with spamming.
21. Define netiquette.

QUESTIONS FOR DISCUSSION

1. Identify some commercial tools that allow users to conduct browsing, communication, and collaboration simultaneously.
2. Describe how agents can help people find specific information quickly.

3. Explain the advantages of electronic mail over regular mail.

4. Explain the advantages of using Web-based e-mail over server-based e-mail.

5. Discuss the role of Web-based call centers and their contribution to competitive advantage.

6. Explain why the topic of group work and its support is getting increased attention.

7. It is said that collaboration tools can change organizational culture. Explain how.

8. How can computers support a team whose members work at different times?

9. Based on what you know about Lotus Notes, can it support different-time/different-place work situations?

10. Relate telecommuting to networks.

11. Distinguish between flaming and spamming. How are they related? How is flaming related to netiquette?

EXERCISES

1. From your own experience or from the vendor's information, list the major capabilities of Lotus Notes/Domino. Do the same for Microsoft Exchange. Compare and contrast the products. Explain how the products can be used to support knowledge workers and managers.

2. Visit *picturetel.com* and sites of other companies that manufacture conferencing products for the Internet. Prepare a report. Why are conferencing products considered part of video commerce?

3. Marketel is a fast-growing (hypothetical) telemarketing company whose headquarters are in Colorado, but the majority of its business is in California. The company has eight divisions, including one in Chicago. (The company has just started penetrating the Midwest market.) Recently the company was approached by two large telephone companies, one in Los Angeles and one in Denver, for discussions regarding a potential merger.

   Nancy Miranda, the corporate CEO who was involved in the preliminary discussions, notified all division managers on the progress of the discussions. Both she and John Miner, the chief financial officer, felt that an immediate merger would be extremely beneficial. However, the vice presidents for marketing and operations thought the company should continue to be independent for at least two to three years. "We can get a much better deal if we first increase our market share," commented Sharon Gonzales, the vice president for marketing.

   Nancy called each of the division managers and found that five of them were for the merger proposal and three objected to it. Furthermore, she found that the division managers from the West Coast strongly opposed discussions with the Colorado company, and the other managers were strongly against discussions with the Los Angeles company. Memos, telephone calls, and meetings of two or three people at a time resulted in frustration. It became apparent that a meeting of all concerned individuals was needed. Nancy wanted to have the meeting as soon as possible in spite of the busy travel schedules of most division managers. She also wanted the meeting to be as short as possible. Nancy called Bob Kraut, the chief information officer, and asked for suggestions about how to conduct a conference electronically. The options he outlined are as follows.

   (1) Use the corporate intranet. Collect opinions from all division managers and vice presidents, then disseminate them to all parties, get feedback, and repeat the process until a solution is achieved.

   (2) Fly all division managers to corporate headquarters and have face-to-face meetings there until a solution is achieved.

   (3) Use the Web for a meeting.

   (4) Fly all division managers to corporate headquarters. Rent a decision room (a facility designed for electronic meetings) and a facilitator from the local university for $2,000 per day, and conduct the meetings there.

   (5) Conduct a videoconference. Unfortunately, appropriate facilities exist only at the headquarters and in two divisions. The other division managers can be flown to the nearest division that has equipment. Alternatively, videoconferencing facilities can be rented in all cities.

   (6) Use a telephone conference call.

   Answer the following questions:

   a. Which of these options would you recommend to management and why?

   b. Is there a technology not listed that might do a better job?

   c. Is it possible to use more than one alternative in this case? If yes, which technologies would you combine, and how would you use them?

GROUP ASSIGNMENTS

1. You are a member of a team working for a multinational finance corporation. Your team's project is to prepare a complex financing proposal for a client within one week. Two of the team members are in Singapore, one is in Seoul, South Korea, one is in London, and one is in Los Angeles. You cannot get the team members together in one place. Your team does not have all the required expertise, but other corporate employees may have it. There are 8,000 employees worldwide; many of them travel. You do not know exactly who are the experts in your company.

   Your company has never prepared such a proposal, but you know that certain parts of the proposal can be adapted from previous proposals. These proposals are filed electronically in various corporate databases, but you are not sure exactly where. (The company has over 80 databases, worldwide.) Finally, you will need a lot of external information, and you will need to communicate with your client in China, with investment groups in Japan and New York, and with your corporate headquarters in London.

   If the client accepts your proposal, your company will make more than $5 million in profit. If the contract goes to a competitor, you may lose your job.

   Your company has all the latest information and communication technologies.

   a. Prepare a list of tasks and activities that your team will need to go through in order to accomplish the mission.
   b. Describe what information technologies you would use to support the above tasks. Be specific, explaining how each technology can facilitate the execution of each task.

2. The world of the Internet is growing very fast, and it keeps changing. The task for the group is to report on the latest developments on the Internet's uses. Members of the group will prepare a report to include the following:
   a. New business applications on the Internet.
   b. New books about the Internet.
   c. Information about new software products related to the Internet.
   d. New managerial and technological issues related to the Internet.
   e. Also, send an e-mail message about a topic of concern to you to the White House and include the reply in your report.

3. Assign each group member to an integrated group support tool kit (Lotus Notes, Exceloncorp.com, GroupWise, etc.). Have each member visit the Web site of the commercial developer and obtain information about this product. As a group, prepare a comparative table of the major similarities and differences among the kits.

4. Assign each team to a college collaborative tool such as Blackboard, WebCT, etc. Establish common evaluative criteria. Have each team evaluate the capabilities and limitations of its tool, and convince each team that its product is superior.

5. Have each team download a free copy of Groove from *groove.net*. Install the software on the members' PCs and arrange collaborative sessions. What can the free software do for you? What are its limitations?

INTERNET EXERCISES

1. Your friend wishes to pursue graduate studies in accounting in the United States. She is especially interested in two universities: the University of Illinois and the University of Southern California. Use the Internet to find information that will help her choose between the two universities. Such information should include, *but not be limited to,* the following:
   a. The types of degree programs in accounting offered by the two universities.
   b. The admission procedures and school calendar.
   c. Coursework and dissertation requirements of the programs under consideration.
   d. The costs of tuition and other expenses associated with the programs.

2. You plan to take a three-week vacation in Hawaii this December, visiting the big island of Hawaii. Using the Internet, find information that will help you plan the trip. Such information includes, *but is not limited to,* the following:
   a. Geographical location and weather conditions in December.
   b. Major tourist attractions and recreational facilities.
   c. Travel arrangements (airlines, approximate fares).
   d. Car rental; local tours.
   e. Alternatives for accommodation (within a moderate budget) and food.
   f. Estimated cost of the vacation (travel, lodging, food, recreation, shopping, etc.).
   g. State regulations regarding the entrance of your dog that you plan to take with you.
   h. Shopping (try to find an electronic mall).

3. Enter *lotus.com* and identify the various tools it provides for collaboration. Mark the capabilities that are not cited in this chapter.

4. Visit *cdt.org*. Find what technologies are available to track users' activities on the Internet.

5. You are assigned the task of buying desktop teleconferencing equipment for your company. Using the Internet:
   a. Identify three major vendors.
   b. Visit their Web sites and find information about their products and capabilities.
   c. Compare the least expensive products of two vendors.
   d. Find a newsgroup that has an interest in video teleconferencing. Post new questions regarding the products selected. (For example, what are the users' experiences with the products?)
   e. Prepare a report of your findings.

6. Both Microsoft Explorer and Netscape Navigator have the capability for Internet telephony; all you need is a sound card, microphone, and speakers on your PC. (If you do not have these browsers, access the VocalTec Web site at *vocaltec.com/*, and download and install its fully functional Internet long-distance telephone software.) Get a friend in another city to do the same. Contact each other via the Internet using your computer as a telephone. What are the advantages and disadvantages of using the Internet for telephone service? Compare your experience to that of making a standard telephone call.

7. Visit *albion.com/netiquette/netiquiz.html* and take the online quiz about netiquette.

8. Visit *talarian.com* and examine its Smartsockets product. Read the Southwest Airlines case at that site and prepare a list of the advantages of the system.

9. Visit *microsoft.com* and *slipstick.com* and find information about their digital dashboards. Examine their capabilities and compare them to information portals.

10. Enter *intranets.com*. Is this site a portal or an advertising company? Why are the services provided of interest to real estate companies?

11. Enter *hpe-learning.com*. Find what programs they have and how they conduct training. Write a report.

12. Enter *setiathome.ssl.Berkeley.edu* and download the free software. Join the efforts to analyze radiotelescope data. Comment about this collaborative effort. Explain why it uses P2P technology.

13. Enter *PCSVision.com*. Describe its services.

Minicase 1
How General Motors Is Collaborating Online

The Problem

Designing a car is a complex and lengthy task. Take, for example, General Motors (GM). Each model created needs to go through a frontal crash test. So the company builds prototypes that cost about one million dollars for each car and tests how they react to a frontal crash. GM crashes these cars, makes improvements, then makes new prototypes and crashes them again. There are other tests and more crashes. Even as late as the 1990s, GM crashed as many as 70 cars for each new model.

The information regarding a new design and its various tests, collected in these crashes and other tests, has to be shared among close to 20,000 designers and engineers in hundreds of divisions and departments at 14 GM design labs, some of which are located in different countries. In addition, communication and collaboration is needed with design engineers of the more than 1,000 key suppliers. All of these necessary communications slowed the design process and increased its cost. It took over four years to get a new model to the market.

The Solution

GM, like its competitors, has been transforming itself into an e-business. This gradual transformation has been going on since the mid-1990s, when Internet bandwidth increased sufficiently to allow Web collaboration. The first task was to examine over 7,000 existing legacy IT systems, reducing them to about 3,000, and making them Web-enabled. The EC system is centered on a computer-aided design (CAD) program from EDS (a large IT company, subsidiary of GM). This system, known as Unigraphics, allows 3-D design documents to be *shared online* by both the internal and external designers and engineers, all of whom are hooked up with the EDS software. In addition, collaborative and Web-conferencing software tools, including Microsoft's NetMeeting and EDS's eVis, were added to enhance teamwork. These tools have radically changed the vehicle-review process.

To see how GM now collaborates with a supplier, take as an example a needed cost reduction of a new seat frame made by Johnson Control. GM electronically sends its specifications for the seat to the vendor's product data system. Johnson Control's collaboration systems (eMatrix) is integrated with EDS's Unigraphics. This integration allows joint searching, designing, tooling, and testing of the seat frame in real time, expediting the process and cutting costs by more than 10 percent.

Another area of collaboration is that of crashing cars. Here designers need close collaboration with the test engineers. Using simulation, mathematical modeling, and a Web-based review process, GM is able now to electronically "crash" cars rather than to do it physically.

The Results

Now it takes less than 18 months to bring a new car to market, compared to 4 or more years before, and at a much lower design cost. For example, 60 cars are now "crashed" electronically, and only 10 are crashed physically. The shorter cycle time enables more new car models, providing GM with a competitive edge. All this has translated into profit. Despite the economic slowdown, GM's revenues increased more than 6 percent in 2002, while its earnings in the second quarter of 2002 doubled that of 2001.

Sources: Compiled from Sullivan (2002), press releases at *gm.com,* and from *amrresearch.com* as reported by Sullivan (October 2002).

Questions for Minicase 1

1. Why did it take GM over four years to design a new car?
2. Who collaborated with whom to reduce the time-to-market?
3. How has IT helped to cut the time-to-market?

Minicase 2
Cisco Systems Pioneers E-Learning

The Problem

Cisco Systems is one of the fastest-growing high-tech companies in the world, selling devices that connect computers and networks to the Internet and other networks. Cisco's products are continuously being upgraded or replaced; so extensive training of employees and customers is needed. Cisco has recognized that its employees, business partners, and independent students seeking professional certification all require training on a continuous basis. Traditional classroom training was flawed by its inability to scale rapidly enough. Cisco offered in-house classes for each course, 6 to 10 times a year, in many locations, but the rapid growth in the number of students, coupled with the fast pace of technological change, made the training both expensive and ineffective.

The Solution

Cisco believes that *e-learning* is a revolutionary way to empower its workforce and partners with the skills and knowledge needed to turn technological change to an advantage. Therefore, Cisco implemented e-learning programs that allow students to learn new software, hardware, and procedures. Cisco believes that once people experience e-learning, they will recognize that it is the fastest, easiest way to get the information they need to be successful. The company created the Delta Force—made up of the CEO, the IT unit, and the Internet Learning Solution Group—to implement e-learning. The first project was to build two learning portals, one for 40 partner companies that sell Cisco products, and one for 4,000 systems engineers who implement the products after the sale.

To encourage its employees to use e-learning, Cisco:

- Makes e-learning "nonthreatening" by using an anonymous testing and scoring process that focuses on helping people improve rather than penalizing those who fail
- Gives those who fail the tests precision learning targets (remedial work, modules, exercises, or written materials) to help them pass and remove the fear associated with testing
- Enables managers to track, manage, and ensure employee development, competency change, and, ultimately, performance change
- Offers additional incentives and rewards such as stock grants, promotions, and bonuses to employees who pursue specialization and certification through e-learning

- Adds e-learning as a strategic top-down metric for Cisco executives, who are measured on their deployment of IT in their departments
- Makes e-learning a mandatory part of employees' jobs
- Offers easy access to e-learning tools via the Web

Cisco also wants to serve as a model of e-learning for its customers, hoping to convince them to use e-learning programs.

Cisco operates E-Learning Centers for Excellence that offer training at Cisco's centers as well as at customers' sites via intranets and the Internet. Some of the training requires the use of partnering vendors. Cisco offers a variety of training programs supported by e-learning. For example, in 2001, Cisco converted a popular 4 1/2-day, instructor-led training (ILT) course on Cisco's signature IOS (interorganizational information system) technologies into an e-learning program that blends both live and self-paced components. The goal was to teach seasoned systems engineers how to sell, install, configure, and maintain those key IOS technologies, and to do so in a way that would train more people than the 25 employees the ILT course could hold.

The Results

On the IOS course alone, Cisco calculated its return on investment as follows:

- It cost $12,400 in labor to develop the blended course.
- The course saved each system engineer one productivity day and 20 percent of the travel and lodging cost of a one-week training course in San Jose. Estimating $750 for travel and lodging and $450 for the productivity day, the savings totaled $1,200 per engineer.
- Seventeen system engineers attended the course the first time it was offered, for a total savings of $20,400. Cisco therefore recovered the development costs in the first offering—and saved $8,000 over and above the development costs. Since March 2001, the IOS Learning Services team has presented two classes of 40 engineers per month. At that rate, Cisco saves $1,152,000 net for just this one course every 12 months.

In 2003, there were over 10,000 corporate salespeople, 150,000 employees of business partners, and 200,000 independent students, all taking courses at Cisco learning centers, many using the e-learning courses. By 2003, Cisco had developed over 100 e-learning courses and was planning to develop many more soon. According to Galagan (2002), e-learning became a major force in Cisco's economic recovery, which started in 2002.

Sources: Compiled from miscellaneous news items at *Cisco.com* (2001–2003), Galagan (2002), and Delahoussaye and Zemke (2001).

Questions for Minicase 2

1. What were the drivers of e-learning at Cisco?
2. How can e-learning empower employees and partners?
3. What, in your opinion, made this project a success?
4. Can a small company use such e-training? Why or why not?

Virtual Company Assignment
Network Computing in The Wireless Café

With 24/7 operations, The Wireless Café has three shifts of workers. This adds complexity to both the physical operation of the restaurant (there's no downtime for cleaning and maintenance) as well as communications across the shifts. (How would you hold a staff meeting with everybody in attendance?) Barbara and Jeremy have noticed some missed communications and misunderstandings among the three shift managers, and so they are looking for ways to improve round-the-clock information flows. Your task is to identify ways network computing can facilitate better staff communications.

Instructions

1. Based on your experiences in restaurants, and by looking at The Wireless Café's organizational chart, consider the different kinds of interpersonal and transactional communications that occur during and across shifts.

   a. List three business-related transactions and the kind of communication they require.

   b. For each of these transactions, identify data items that should be captured.

   c. What kinds of networked solutions discussed in the chapter might be useful in facilitating communications?

2. The Wireless Café has created a rudimentary employee portal at *wiley.com/college/turban/The Wireless Cafe*. Review what is there now, and describe other kinds of information you think would be useful for the employees of The Wireless Café.

3. Jeremy is concerned that the implementation of new networked communications applications will cost more than the benefits provided. Identify some tangible and intangible costs and benefits that would help Jeremy evaluate the financial impact of implementing new networked communications applications. Use these costs and benefits to give Jeremy a set of criteria to evaluate various discovery, communication, and collaboration applications.

REFERENCES

"2000 Buyer's Guide of Tools for Conferences, Meetings, and Distance Learning," *Presentations*, 13(12), December 1999.

Abbott, C., "At Amway, BI Portal Speeds Product R&D," *DM Review*, October 2000.

Albalooshi, F., *Virtual Education: Cases in Learning and Teaching Technologies*. Hershey, PA: The Idea Group, 2003.

Aneja, A. et al., "Corporate Portal Framework for Transforming Content Chaos on Intranets," *Intel Technology Journal*, Q1, 2000.

Athens, G., "Supercomputer Tops 1 Teraflop," *Computerworld*, January 2, 1997.

Basu, A., and A. Kumar, "Research Commentary: Workflow Management Issues in e-Business," *Information System Research*, March 2002.

BBC, "Blogging Goes Mobile," *BBC News*, February 23, 2003, *news.bbc.co.uk/1/hi/technology/2783951.stm*. (Accessed May 13, 2003.)

Belanger, F. et al., "Aligning IS Research and Practice: A Research Agenda for Virtual Work," *Information Resources Management Journal*, July–September 2002.

Belanger, F. et al., "Technology Requirements and Work Group Communication for Telecommuters," *Information Systems Research*, June 2001.

Berger, N. S., "Pioneering Experiences in Distance Learning: Lessons Learned," *Journal of Management Education*, 23(6), December 1999.

Berners-Lee, T. J. et al., "The Semantic Web," *Scientific American*, May 2001, *scientificamerican.com/article.cfm?articleID=00048144-10D2-1C70-84A9809EC588EF21&catID=2*. (Accessed May 2003.)

blackboard.com. (Accessed spring 2003.)

Boisvert, L., "Web-Based Learning: The Anytime Anywhere Classroom," *Information Systems Management*, 17(1), Winter 2000.

Bradley, P., "CPFR Gaining Converts," *Logistics*, April 2002.

Brookman, F., "ChainDrugStore.Net Facilitates Rapid Exchange of Needed Information," *Stores*, January 2003.

Bunker, E., "History of Distance Education," Center for Excellence in Distance Learning (CEDL), Lucent Technologies, *lucent.com/cedl/*, 1999.

Cadinfo.NET, "Collaborative Workflow Streamlines Engineering Process Change," *cadinfo.net/editorial/dct.htm*. (Accessed January 3, 2003.)

Callaghan, D., "IBM: E-Meetings Save $4 Million a Month," *eWeek*, June 26, 2002.

Carmel, E., *Global Software Teams: Collaboration Across Borders and Time Zones*. Upper Saddle River, NJ: Prentice Hall, 1999.

Carroll, S., "How to Find Anything Online," *PC Magazine*, May 27, 2003, *pcmag.com/article2/0,4149,1047718,00.asp*. (Accessed May 30, 2003.)

Chaffee, D., *Groupware, Workflow and Intranets: Reengineering the Enterprise with Collaborative Software*. Boston: Digital Press, 1998.

Choi, S. Y., and A. B. Whinston, *The Internet Economy: Technology and Practice*. Austin, TX: SmartEcon Publishing, 2000.

Cobe, P., and E. H. Parlapiano, *Mompreneurs Online: Using the Internet to Build Work-at-Home Success*. Scarsdale, NY: Perigee, 2001.

Cone, J. W., and D. G. Robinson, "The Power of E-Performance," *Training and Development*, August 2001.

Cope, J., "Wireless LANs Speed Hospital Insurance Payments, *Computerworld*, April 10, 2000, *computerworld.com/industrytopics/manufacturing/story/0,10801,44377,00.html*. (Accessed May 12, 2003.)

Davison, R., and G. de Vreede, "The Global Application of Collaborative Technologies," *Communications of the ACM*, 44(12), 2001.

Delahoussaye, M., and R. Zemke, "About Learning Online," *Training*, September 2001.

DeSanctis, G., and B. Gallupe, "A Foundation for the Study of Group Decision Support Systems," *Management Science*, 33(5), 1987.

DeYoung, J., "Through the Voice Portal," *PC Magazine*, August 2001, p. 10.

DiCarlo, L., "Case Study: Webcor Builders," *PC Computing*, December 1999.

Dollar, G., "Web-Based Course Delivery: An Empirical Assessment of Student Learning Outcomes," *Proceedings of the Americas Conference of the Association for Information Systems*, Milwaukee, WI, August 2000.

Drury, J., "Realistic Choices for Web-Based Call Centers," *Business Communications Review*, June 1999.

Eduventures.com, "Eduventures Releases Study of Higher Education E-Learning Market, A Subset of E-Education; Forecasts E-Education Market Growth from $4.5 Billion in 2001 to $11 Billion in 2005," *Eduventures.com*, December 18, 2001, *eduventures.com/about/press_room/12_18_01.cfm*. (Accessed May 2003.)

ENTmag.com, "Lessons in Technical Training," ENTmag.com, June 2000, *entmag.com/archives/article.asp?EditorialsID=5273*. (Accessed May 2003.)

"Experts Offer Key Tips on Building, Integrating Portal Marts," *I/S Analyzer*, September 2002.

Ferguson, M., "Corporate and E-Business Portals," *myITAdvisor*, April 2001.

Fischer, L., *Workflow Handbook 2002*. Lighthouse Point, FL: Future Strategies, Inc., 2002.

Fisher, K., and M. D. Fisher, *The Distance Manager*. New York, McGraw-Hill, 2000.

Flohr, U., "Intelligent Intranets: Intranets Can Be Anarchy Until You Manage Who Can Do What Where," *Byte*, August 1997.

Galagan, P. A., "Delta Force at Cisco," *Training and Development*, July 2002.

Gaskin, J. E., "Software Helps Manage E-Mail Flood," *Interactive Week*, January 25, 1999.

Ghaoui, C., *Usability Evaluation of Online Learning Programs*. Hershey PA: The Idea Group, 2003.

Gibson-Paul, L., "Suspicious Minds," *CIO Magazine*, January 15, 2003.

Gotcher, R., "AFI Turns E-Mail Deluge into a Profitable Sales Resource," *Infoworld*, December 8, 1997.

Gray, S., "Collaboration Tools," *Syllabus*, January 1999.

Guimaraes, T., and P. Dallow, "Empirically Testing the Benefits, Problems, and Success Factors for Telecommuting Programs," *European Journal of Information Systems*, Vol. 8, 1999.

Hartley, D. E., "Observations of a Telecommuter," *Training and Development*, July 2001.

Hartley, D. E., "All Aboard the E-Learning Train," *Productivity Digest*, December 2002.

Higa, K. et al., "Understanding Relationships Among Teleworkers' E-Mail Usage, E-Mail Richness Perceptions, and E-Mail Productivity Perceptions Under a Software Engineering Environment," *IEEE Transactions on Engineering Management*, May 2000.

Hofmann, D. W., "Internet-Based Learning in Higher Education," *Techdirections*, August 2002, *computerworld.com/managementtopics/management/helpdesk/story/0,10801,61019,00.html*. (Accessed April 28, 2002.)

Hricko, M. F., *Design and Implementation of Web-enabled Teaching Tools*. Hershey PA: The Idea Group, 2003.

Imhoff, C., "Power Up Your Enterprise Portal," *e-Business Advisor,* May 2001.

Interactive Week, January 12, 1998.

Internet Week, March 9, 1998.

"Intranet Corner: How Big 5 Consulting Firms Use Intranets to Manage Their Employees', and Industry Experts' Knowledge and What They Can Teach Us," *Intranet Journal,* July 2000, *intranetjournal. com/articles/200007/ic_07_26_00e.html.* (Accessed May 2003.)

Kapp, K., "Anytime E-Learning Takes Off in Manufacturing," *APICS,* June 2002.

Kesner, R. M., "Building a Knowledge Portal: A Case Study in Web-Enabled Collaboration," *Information Strategy: The Executive Journal,* 2003.

Khalifa, M., and R. Davison, "Exploring the Telecommuting Paradox," *Communications of the ACM,* 43(3), March 2000.

Konicki, S., "The New Desktop: Powerful Portals," *Information Week,* May 1, 2000, *informationweek.com/784/portal.htm.* (Accessed May 2003.)

Kounadis, T., "How to Pick the Best Portal," *e-Business Advisor,* August 2000.

Liaw, S., and H. Huang, "How Web Technology Can Facilitate Learning," *Information Systems Management,* Winter 2002.

Lieberman, H., et al., "Let's Browse: A Collaborative Browsing Agent," *Knowledge-Based Systems,* Vol. 12, December 1999.

Lindstone, H., and H. Turroff, *The Delphi Method: Technology and Applications.* Reading, MA: Addison-Wesley, 1975.

line56.com, "Transportation and Warehousing Improving the Value of Your Supply Chain Through Integrated Logistics," May 1, 2002, *elibrary.line56.com/data/detail?id=1043954015_280&type=RES&x=1033897490.* (Accessed August 17, 2002.)

Ling, R. R., and D. C. Yen, "Extranet: A New Wave of the Internet," *SAM Advanced Management Journal,* Spring 2001.

Lotus.com, "Integration of TRADOS Software to Increase Functionality of Lotus Notes, September 25, 2002, *lotus.com, lotus.com/products/dmlt.nsf/0/90ff6c4f8a851a1485256966007084e6?OpenDocument.* (Accessed May 2003.)

Lotus Solutions, Winter 1998, pp. 10–11.

Manageradvisor.com, "Collaborative Commerce, the Way to Go?," *Manageradvisor.com, manageradvisor.com/doc/11546.* (Accessed May 12, 2003.)

Markel, M., "Distance Education and the Myth of the New Pedagogy," *Journal of Business and Technical Communication,* 13(2), April 1999.

Matthews, D., "The Origins of Distance Education and its Use in the United States," *T.H.E. Journal,* 27(2), September 1999.

Meso, P. N., and J. O. Liegle, "The Future of Web-Based Instruction Systems," *Proceedings of the Americas Conference of the Association for Information Systems,* Milwaukee, WI, August 2000.

Microsoft, "Case Studies: Dresdner Bank," *Microsoft.com/resources/casestudies/CaseStudy.asp?CaseStudyID=13324.* (Accessed January 4, 2003.)

Mochari, I., "Bold Storage," *Inc. Magazine,* March 15, 2000, *inc.com/articles/ops/office_management/telecommute/17883.html.* (Accessed May 12, 2003.)

Mottl, J. N., "Learn at a Distance," *Information Week,* No. 767, January 3, 2000.

Murch, R., and T. Johnson, *Intelligent Software Agents.* Upper Saddle River, NJ: Prentice-Hall, 1999.

National Semiconductor, "National Semiconductor's Webench 2.0 Delivers Breakthrough Design Cycles with Wireless, Power and Thermal Simulators," *National Semiconductor press release,* October

16, 2000, *national.com/news/item/0,1735,563,00.html.* (Accessed May 12, 2003.)

Nilles, J. M., "Managing Telework: Strategies for Managing the Virtual Work Force," *New Wiley,* 1998.

Ojala, M., "Drowning in a Sea of Information," *Econtent Magazine,* June 2002, *econtentmag.com/Articles/ArticleReader.aspx?ArticleID=977.* (Accessed May 12, 2003.)

Parsa, I., "Web Mining Crucial to e-Commerce," *DM News,* December 7, 1999.

PC World, February 1997.

Phillips, S., "'Blogs' Has Moved into the Big Time," *Financial Times,* June 19, 2002.

Piccoli, G. et al., "Web-Based Virtual Learning Environments," *MIS Quarterly,* December 2001.

Pinsonneault, A., and M. Boisvert, "The Impact of Telecommuting on Organizations and Individuals," in N. Johnson (ed.), *Telecommuting and Virtual Offices: Issues and Opportunities.* Hershey, PA: The Idea Group, 2001.

Piskurich, G. M., *Preparing Learners for E-Learning.* New York: Wiley, 2003.

Pitcher, N. et al., "Video Conferencing in Higher Education," *Innovations in Education and Training International,* August 2000.

plagiarism.org. (Accessed April 17, 2003.)

Poirier, C. C., "Collaborative Commerce: Wave Two of the Cyber Revolutions," *Computer Science Corporation Perspectives,* 2001.

Ragusa, J. M., and G. M. Bochenek, "Collaborative Virtual Design Environments," *Communications of the ACM,* 44(12), 2001.

Reeder, J., "E-Learning: Not Your Father's Correspondence Course," *Sireview.com,* 2002, *sireview.com/articles/elearning.html.* (Accessed May 2003.)

Reid, K. A., "Impact of Technology on Learning Effectiveness," Center for Excellence in Distance Learning (CEDL), Lucent Technologies, *lucent.com/cedl,* 1999.

Schell, G. P., "The 'Introduction to Management Information' Course Goes Online," *Proceedings of the Americas Conference of the Association for Information Systems,* Milwaukee, WI, August 2000.

Schram, P., *Collaborative Commerce: Going Private to Get Results.* New York: Deloitte Consulting, *dc.com.* (Accessed June 8, 2001.)

Shin, B., et al., "Telework: Existing Research and Future Directions," *Journal of Organizational Computing and Electronic Commerce,* 10(2), 2000.

Stackpole, B., "Rent an App and Relax," *Datamation,* July 1999.

Stephenson, W., "Nygard Goes Electronic," *Winnipeg Sun,* June 3, 1999.

Sullivan, D., "Machine Translation: It Can't Match the Human Touch," *E-Business Advisor,* June 2001.

Sullivan, J. R., and K. A. Walstrom, "Consumer Perspectives on Service Quality of Electronic Commerce Web Sites," *Journal of Computer Information Systems,* 2001.

Sullivan, M., "GM Moves into the Passing Lane," *Forbes (Best of the Web* supplement), October 7, 2002.

Tan, P. N., and V. Kumar, "Discovery of Web Robots Sessions Based on Their Navigational Patterns," *Data Mining and Knowledge Discovery,* 6(9), 2002.

Tedeschi, B., "A Fresh Spin on 'Affinity Portals' to the Internet," *New York Times,* April 17, 2000.

Turban, E. et al., *Electronic Commerce,* 3rd ed. Upper Saddle River, NJ: Prentice Hall, 2004.

turnitin.com. (Accessed April 17, 2003.)

Urdan, T., and C. Weggen, "Corporate E-Learning: Exploring a New Frontier," W.R. Hambrecht & Co., March 2000, *http://www.*

e-learning.nl/publicaties/marktonderzoek/New_Frontier.pdf. (Accessed May 13, 2003.)

van der Aalst, W. M. P., *Workflow Management: Models, Methods and Systems.* Boston: MIT Press, 2002.

Vinas, T., "Meeting Makeover," *Industryweek,* February 2002.

Walton B., and M. Princi, "From Supply Chain to Collaborative Network," white paper, Gordon Andersen Consulting, 2000 (see *Walton.ASCET.com*).

Watad, M. M., and F. J., DiSanzo, "Case Study: The Synergism of Telecommuting and Office Automation," *Sloan Management Review,* 41(2), Winter 2000.

Weaver, P., "Preventing E-Learning Failure," *Training and Development,* 56(8), August 2002.

Webcor.com, "Webcor Builders Pushes its IT Edge: Pilots On-Line Project Management," *webcor.com.* (Accessed May 2003.)

Webcor.com, "Wired at Webcor," *webcor.com,* November 20, 2000. (Accessed May 2003.)

webct.com. (Accessed Spring 2003.)

Webmethods.com, "Success Story: National Semi Conductor," *Webmethods.com, webmethods.com/PDF/National_Semi_ss.pdf.* (Accessed May 5, 2003.)

Weidlich, T., "The Corporate Blog Is Catching On," *New York Times,* June 22, 2003.

Weiss, G., *Multiagent Systems: A Modern Approach to Distributed AI.* Cambridge, MA: MIT Press, 1999.

PART II
The Web Revolution

4. Network Computing: Discovery, Communication, and Collaboration
▶ 5. E-Business and E-Commerce
6. Mobile, Wireless, and Pervasive Computing

CHAPTER

5

E-Business and E-Commerce

5.1
Overview of E-Business and E-Commerce

5.2
Electronic Auctions and Bartering

5.3
Business-to-Consumer Applications

5.4
Market Research and Online Advertising

5.5
B2B Applications

5.6
Intrabusiness and B2E

5.7
E-Government and Consumer-to-Consumer EC

5.8
E-Commerce Support Services

5.9
Legal and Ethical Issues

5.10
Failures and Strategies for Success

Appendix 5A EDI and Extranets

LEARNING OBJECTIVES

After studying this chapter, you will be able to:

1. Describe electronic commerce, its scope, benefits, limitations, and types.

2. Understand auctions and bartering.

3. Describe the major applications of business-to-consumer commerce, including service industries.

4. Discuss the importance and activities of B2C market research and online advertising.

5. Describe business-to-business applications.

6. Describe emerging EC applications such as intra-business and B2E commerce.

7. Describe e-government activities and consumer-to-consumer e-commerce.

8. Describe the e-commerce support services, specifically payments and logistics.

9. Discuss some ethical and legal EC issues.

10. Describe EC failures and strategies for success.

E-COMMERCE PROVIDES DECISION SUPPORT TO HI-LIFE CORPORATION

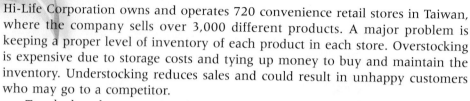

➡ THE PROBLEM

Hi-Life Corporation owns and operates 720 convenience retail stores in Taiwan, where the company sells over 3,000 different products. A major problem is keeping a proper level of inventory of each product in each store. Overstocking is expensive due to storage costs and tying up money to buy and maintain the inventory. Understocking reduces sales and could result in unhappy customers who may go to a competitor.

To calculate the appropriate level of inventory, it is necessary to know exactly how many units of each product are in stock at specific times. This is known as *stock count*. Periodic stock count is needed since the actual amount in stock frequently differs from the theoretical amount (inventory = previous inventory − sales + arrivals). The difference is due to "shrinkage" (e.g., theft, misplaced items, spoilage, etc.). Until 2002, stock count at Hi-Life was done manually. Using data collection sheets, where the products' names were preprinted, employees counted the quantity of each product and recorded it on the data collection sheets. Then, the data were painstakingly keyed into each store's PC. The process took over 21 person-hours, in each store, each week. This process was expensive and frequently was delayed, causing problems along the entire supply chain due to delays in count and errors. Suppliers, employees, and customers were unhappy.

➡ THE SOLUTION

The first phase of improvement was introduced in spring 2002. Management introduced a pocket PC (a hand-held device) from Hewlett-Packard that runs on Microft Windows (Chinese version). The pocket PC, called Jornada, enables employees to enter the inventory tallies directly on the forms on the screen by hand, using Chinese characters for additional notes. Jornada has a syncronized cradle called Activesync. Once the pocket PC is placed in its cradle, inventory information can be relayed instantly to Hi-Life's headquarters.

In the second phase of improvement, in 2003, a compact bar code scanner was added on in the pocket PC's expansion slot. Employees now can scan the products' bar codes and then enter the quantity found on the shelf. This new feature expedites data entry and minimizes errors in product identification. The up-to-the second information enables headquarters to compute appropriate inventory levels, shipment schedules, and purchasing strategies, using decision support system formulas, all in minutes. The stores use the Internet (with a secured VPN) to upload data to the intranet at headquarters.

➡ THE RESULTS

The results have been astonishing. Inventory taking has been reduced to less than four hours per store. Errors are down by more than 90 percent, order placing is simple and quick, and administrative paperwork has been eliminated. Furthermore, quicker and more precise inventory counts have resulted in lower inventory levels and in shorter response times for changes in demand. Actually, the entire product-management process became more efficient, including purchasing, stocking, selling, shelf-price audit and price checks, reticketing, discontinuance, and customer inquiries.

The employees like the new electronic commerce-based system too. It is very user friendly, both to learn and to operate, and the battery provides at least 24 hours of power, so charging can be done after-hours. Finally, Hi-Life's employees now have more time to plan, manage, and chat with customers. More important, faster and better decisions are enabled at headquarters, contributing to greater competitiveness and profitability for Hi-Life.

Sources: Compiled from *hp.com/jornada jornada,* and from *microsoft.com/asia/mobile* (May 2002).

 LESSONS LEARNED FROM THIS CASE

The output of an information system is only as good as the inputted data. When data are inaccurate and/or delayed, the decisions that use the data are not the best, as in Hi-Life's old system, which resulted in high inventories and low customer satisfaction. The solution described in this case was provided by an electronic-commerce system that expedited and improved the flow of information to the corporate headquarters. Electronic commerce (EC), which is the subject of this chapter, describes the process of buying, selling, transmitting, or exchanging products, services, and information via computerized networks, primarily by the Internet (see Turban et al., 2004). This case illustrates an intrabusiness application, involving employees, and it is referred to as business-to-employees (B2E) e-commerce. There are several other types of EC, and they all are the subject of this chapter. We also provide here an overview of the EC field and comment on its relationship to other information systems.

5.1 OVERVIEW OF E-BUSINESS AND E-COMMERCE

Definitions and Concepts

Electronic commerce (EC, or e-commerce) describes the process of buying, selling, transferring, or exchanging products, services, and/or information via computer networks, including the Internet. Some people view the term *commerce* as describing only transactions conducted between business partners. When this definition of commerce is used, some people find the term electronic commerce to be fairly narrow. Thus, many use the term e-business instead. **E-business** refers to a broader definition of EC, not just the buying and selling of goods and services, but also servicing customers, collaborating with business partners, conducting **e-learning,** and conducting electronic transactions within an organization. Others view e-business as the "other than buying and selling" activities on the Internet, such as collaboration and intrabusiness activities.

In this book we use the broadest meaning of electronic commerce, which is basically equivalent to e-business. The two terms will be used *interchangeably* throughout the chapter and the remainder of the text.

PURE VERSUS PARTIAL EC. Electronic commerce can take several forms depending on the *degree of digitization* (the transformation from physical to digital) involved. The degree of digitization can relate to: (1) the *product* (service) sold, (2) the *process,* or (3) the *delivery agent* (or intermediary). Choi et al.

(1997) created a framework that explains the possible configurations of these three dimensions. A product can be physical or digital, the process can be physical or digital, and the delivery agent can be physical or digital. In traditional commerce all three dimensions are physical, and in *pure EC* all dimensions are digital. All other combinations include a mix of digital and physical dimensions. If there is at least one digital dimension, we consider the situation electronic commerce but only *partial EC*. For example, buying a shirt at Wal-Mart Online, or a book from Amazon.com is partial EC, because the merchandise is physically delivered by FedEx. However, buying an e-book from Amazon.com or a software product from Buy.com is *pure EC*, because the product, its delivery, payment, and transfer agent are all done online.

EC ORGANIZATIONS. Pure physical organizations (corporations) are referred to as **brick-and-mortar** (or old-economy) **organizations,** whereas companies that are engaged *only* in EC are considered **virtual** (or pure-play) **organizations. Click-and-mortar** (or click-and-brick) **organizations** are those that conduct some e-commerce activities, yet their primary business is done in the physical world. Gradually, many brick-and-mortar companies are changing to click-and-mortar ones (e.g., Wal-Mart Online).

INTERNET VERSUS NON-INTERNET EC. Most e-commerce is done over the Internet. But EC can also be conducted on private networks, such as *value-added networks* (VANs, networks that add communication services to existing common carriers), on local area networks (LANs), or even on a single computerized machine. For example, buying food from a vending machine and paying with a smart card or a cell phone can be viewed as EC activity.

Types of E-Commerce Transactions

E-commerce transactions can be done between various other parties, as follows:

- **Business-to-business (B2B):** In B2B transactions, both the sellers and the buyers are business organizations. The vast majority of EC volume is of this type.

- **Collaborative commerce (c-commerce):** In c-commerce, business partners collaborate electronically. Such collaboration frequently occurs between and among business partners along the supply chain (see Chapters 4 and 8).

- **Business-to-consumer (B2C):** In B2C, the sellers are organizations, and the buyers are individuals.

- **Consumer-to-business (C2B):** In C2B, consumers make known a particular need for a product or service, and suppliers compete to provide the product or service to consumers. An example is Priceline.com, where the customer names a product and the desired price, and Priceline tries to find a supplier to fulfill the stated need.

- **Consumer-to-consumer (C2C):** In C2C, an individual sells products or services to other individuals. (You also will see the term C2C used as "customer-to-customer." The terms are interchangeable, and both will be used in this book to describe individuals selling products and services to each other.)

- **Intrabusiness (intraorganizational) commerce:** In this case an organization uses EC internally to improve its operations. A special case of this is known as **B2E (business to its employees) EC,** which was illustrated in the opening case.

- **Government-to-citizens (G2C) and to others:** In this case the government provides services to its citizens via EC technologies. Governments can do business with other governments as well as with businesses (G2B).
- **Mobile commerce (m-commerce):** When e-commerce is done in a wireless environment, such as using cell phones to access the Internet, we call it m-commerce.

EC Business Models

Each of the above types of EC is executed in one or more **business models,** the method by which a company generates revenue to sustain itself. For example, in B2B one can sell from catalogs, or in auctions. The major business models of EC are summarized in Table 5.1. (Note that this is an expanded version

TABLE 5.1 E-Commerce Business Models

EC Model	Description
Online direct marketing	Manufacturers or retailers sell directly to customers. Very efficient for digital products and services. Can allow for customization.
Electronic tendering systems	Businesses conduct online tendering, requesting quotes from suppliers. Use B2B *reverse auctions* mechanism.
Name-your-own-price	Customers decide how much they are willing to pay. An intermediary (e.g., Priceline.com) tries to match a provider.
Find-the-best-price	Customers specify a need. An intermediary (e.g., Hotwire.com) compares providers and shows the lowest price. Customer must accept the offer in a short time or may lose the deal.
Affiliate marketing	Vendors ask partners to place logos (or banners) on partner's site. If customers click, come to vendors, and buy, vendors pay commision to partners.
Viral marketing	Spread your brand on the Net by word-of-mouth. Receivers will send your information to their friends. (Be on the watch for viruses.)
Group purchasing (e-co-ops)	Aggregating the demands of small buyers to get a large volume. Then conduct tendering, or negotiate a low price.
Online auctions	Placing auctions of various types on the Internet. Very popular in C2C, but gaining ground in other types of EC.
Product customization	Using the Internet to self-configure products or services, price them, and then fulfill them quickly (build-to-order).
Electronic marketplaces and exchanges	Create virtual marketplaces (private or public) where transactions can be conducted in an efficient way (more information to buyers and sellers, less transaction cost).
Value-chain integrators	Aggregate information and package it for customers, vendors, or others in the supply chain.
Value-chain service providers	Provide specialized services in supply-chain operations such as providing logistics or payment services.
Information brokers	Provide services related to EC information such as trust, content, matching buyers and sellers, evaluating vendors and products.
Bartering online	Exchanging surplus products and/or services with the process administered completely online by an intermediary. Company receives "points" for its contribution, and the points can be used to purchase other needed items.
Deep discounters	Gain market share via deep discounts (e.g., Half.com). For customers who consider only price in their purchasing decisions.
Membership	Only members can use the services provided, including access to certain information, conducting trades, etc. (e.g., Egreetings.com).
Supply-chain improvers	Restructure supply chains to hubs, or other configuration. Increase collaboration, reduce delays, and smooth supply-chain flows.

of the list of five representative models introduced in *A Closer Look 1.1*, page 10.) For details see Turban et al. (2004).

Brief History and Scope of EC

E-commerce applications began in the early 1970s with such innovations as electronic transfer of funds. However, the applications were limited to large corporations and a few daring small businesses. Then came electronic data interchange (EDI), which automated routine transaction processing and extended EC to all industries. (See Appendix 5A.)

Since the commercialization of the Internet and the introduction of the Web in the early 1990s, EC applications have expanded rapidly. By 2000 there was a major shakeout in EC activities when hundreds of dot-com companies went out of business. The shakeout lasted about three years. Since 2003, EC continues its steady progress. Today, most medium and large organizations and many small ones are practicing some EC.

THE SCOPE OF EC. The field of e-commerce is broad, and we use Figure 5.1 to describe it. As can be seen in the figure, there are many EC applications (top of the figure), some of which were illustrated in the opening case about Hi-Life Corp; others will be shown throughout the book. (Also see Huff et al., 2001, and Farhoomand and Lovelock, 2001.)

To execute these applications, companies need the right information, infrastructure, and support services. Figure 5.1 shows that the EC applications are supported by infrastructure and by five support areas (shown as supporting pillars):

- *People:* Sellers, buyers, intermediaries, information systems specialists and other employees, and any other participants.
- *Public policy:* Legal and other policy and regulating issues, such as privacy protection and taxation, that are determined by the government.
- *Marketing and advertising:* Like any other business, EC usually requires the support of marketing and advertising. This is especially important in B2C online transactions where the buyers and sellers usually do not know each other.
- *Support services:* Many services are needed to support EC. These range from payments to order delivery and content creation.
- *Business partnerships:* Joint ventures, e-marketplaces, and business partnerships of various sorts are common in EC. These occur frequently throughout the supply chain (i.e., the interactions between a company and its suppliers, customers, and other partners).

The supporting infrastructure includes hardware, software, and networks, ranging from browsers to multimedia.

All of these EC components require good management practices. This means that companies need to plan, organize, motivate, devise strategy, and reengineer processes as needed.

Benefits and Limitations/Failures of E-Commerce

Few innovations in human history encompass as many benefits to organizations, individuals, and society as does e-commerce. These benefits have just begun to materialize, but they will increase significantly as EC expands. The major benefits are summarized in Table 5.2 (page 182).

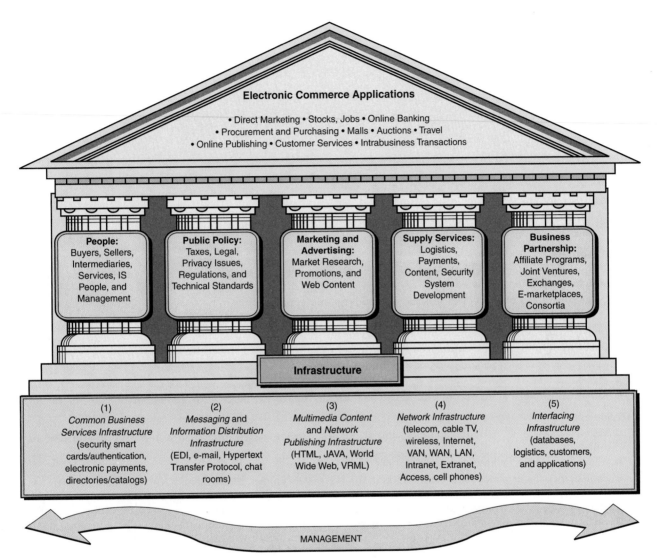

FIGURE 5.1 A framework for e-commerce.

Counterbalancing its many benefits, EC has some limitations, both technological and nontechnological, which have slowed its growth and acceptance. Those limitations and inhibitors are listed in Table 5.3. Some have been contributing factors in the failures of many EC projects and dot-com companies in recent years. As time passes, the limitations, especially the technological ones, will lessen or be overcome. In addition, appropriate planning can minimize the negative impact of some of them.

Despite its limitations and failures, e-commerce has made very rapid progress. Also, various B2B activities, e-auctions, e-government, e-learning, and some B2C activities are ballooning. As experience accumulates and technology improves, the ratio of EC benefits to cost will increase, resulting in an even greater rate of EC adoption.

TABLE 5.2 Benefits of E-Commerce

To Organizations

- Expands a company's marketplace to national and international markets. With minimal capital outlay, a company can quickly locate more customers, the best suppliers, and the most suitable business partners worldwide.
- Enables companies to procure material and services from other companies, rapidly and at less cost.
- Shortens or even eliminates marketing distribution channels, making products cheaper and vendors' profits higher.
- Decreases (by as much as 90 percent) the cost of creating, processing, distributing, storing, and retrieving information by digitizing the process.
- Allows lower inventories by facilitating "pull"-type supply chain management (see Appendix 2A). This allows product customization and reduces inventory costs.
- Lowers telecommunications costs because the Internet is much cheaper than value-added networks (VANs).
- Helps some small businesses compete against large companies.
- Enables a very specialized niche market.

To Customers

- Frequently provides less expensive products and services by allowing consumers to conduct quick online searches and comparisons.
- Gives consumers more choices in selecting products and vendors.
- Enables customers to shop or make other transactions 24 hours a day, from almost any location.
- Delivers relevant and detailed information in seconds.
- Enables consumers to get customized products, from PCs to cars, at competitive prices.
- Makes it possible for people to work and study at home.
- Makes possible electronic auctions that benefit buyers and sellers (see Section 5.9).
- Allows consumers to interact in electronic communities and to exchange ideas and compare experiences.

To Society

- Enables individuals to work at home and to do less traveling, resulting in less road traffic and less air pollution.
- Allows some merchandise to be sold at lower prices, thereby increasing people's standard of living.
- Enables people in developing countries and rural areas to enjoy products and services that otherwise are not available. This includes opportunities to learn professions and earn college degrees, or to receive better medical care.
- Facilitates delivery of public services, such as government entitlements, reducing the cost of distribution and chance of fraud, and increasing the quality of social services, police work, health care, and education.

TABLE 5.3 Limitations of E-Commerce

Technological Limitations	Nontechnological Limitations
• Lack of universally accepted standards for quality, security, and reliability.	• Unresolved legal issues (see Section 5.9).
• Insufficient telecommunications bandwidth.	• Lack of national and international government regulations and industry standards.
• Still-evolving software development tools.	• Lack of mature methodologies for measuring benefits of and justifying EC.
• Difficulties in integrating the Internet and EC applications and software with some existing (especially legacy) applications and databases.	• Many sellers and buyers waiting for EC to stabilize before they take part.
• Need for special Web servers in addition to the network servers.	• Customer resistance to changing from a real to a virtual store. People do not yet sufficiently trust paperless, faceless transactions.
• Expensive and/or inconvenient Internet accessibility for many would-be users.	• Perception that EC is expensive and unsecured.
	• An insufficient number (critical mass) of sellers and buyers exists for profitable EC operations.

5.2 E-COMMERCE MECHANISMS: AUCTIONS AND BARTERING

The major mechanism for buying and selling on the Internet is the electronic catalog. However, in order to better understand how e-commerce works, let's first look at two common mechanisms used in its implementation: **electronic auctions** and bartering online.

Electronic Auctions (E-Auctions)

An *auction* is a market mechanism by which sellers place offers and buyers make sequential bids. The primary characteristic of auctions, whether offline or online, is that prices are determined dynamically by competitive bidding. Auctions have been an established method of commerce for generations, and they are well-suited to deal with products and services for which conventional marketing channels are ineffective or inefficient. Auctions can expedite the disposal of items that need liquidation or a quick sale (for an example, see Minicase 1).

The Internet provides an efficient infrastructure for executing **electronic auctions**—auctions conducted online—at lower administrative cost and with many more involved sellers and buyers (see Kambil and Van-Heck, 2002). Individual consumers and corporations alike can participate in this rapidly growing form of e-commerce. There are several types of auctions, each with its motives and procedures. Auctions are divided here into two major types: *forward* auctions and *reverse* auctions.

FORWARD AUCTIONS. **Forward auctions** are auctions that *sellers* use as a selling channel to many potential buyers. Usually, items are placed at sites for auction, and buyers will bid continuously for the items. The highest bidder wins the items. Sellers and buyers can be individuals or businesses. The popular auction site eBay.com is a forward auction. According to Gallaugher (2002) there are two types of forward e-auctions. One is for *liquidations,* the other one is to *increase marketing efficiency,* as defined and shown in Figure 5.2.

Liquidation Auctions:

Seek first to maximize existing channels and reduce inventory before using auction

Seek lowest price on widely available goods and services

Disincentives to use auction shrink supply over time

Market Efficiency Auctions:

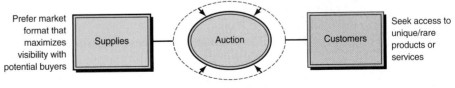

Prefer market format that maximizes visibility with potential buyers

Seek access to unique/rare products or services

Incentives to use auction increase supply over time

FIGURE 5.2 Types of forward auctions. (*Source:* Gallaugher, 2002, Fig. 3, p. 91.)

IT at Work 5.1
eBAY—THE WORLD'S LARGEST AUCTION SITE

eBay (ebay.com) is the world's largest auction site, and one of the most profitable e-businesses. The successful online auction house has its roots in a 50-year-old novelty item—Pez candy dispensers. Pamela Kerr, an avid collector of Pez dispensers, came up with the idea of trading them over the Internet. When she expressed this idea to her boyfriend (now her husband), Pierre Omidyar, he was instantly struck with the soon-to-be-famous e-business auction concept.

In 1995, the Omidyars created a company called AuctionWeb. Later renamed eBay, the company has since become the premier online auction house, with millions of unique auctions in progress and over 500,000 new items added each day. eBay is now much more than an auction house, as we will see. But its initial success was in electronic auctions. The business model of eBay was to provide an electronic infrastructure for conducting mostly C2C auctions, although it caters to small businesses as well. Technology replaces the traditional auctioneer as the intermediary between buyers and sellers.

On eBay, people can buy and sell just about anything. The company collects a submission fee upfront, plus a commission as a percentage of the sale amount. The submission fee is based on the amount of exposure you want your item to receive. For example, a higher fee is required if you would like to be among the "featured auctions" in your specific product category, and an even higher fee if you want your item to be listed on the eBay home page under Featured Items.

The auction process begins when the seller fills in the registration information and posts a description of the item for sale. The seller must specify a minimum opening bid. Sellers might set the opening bid lower than the *reserve price*, a minimum acceptable bid price, to generate bidding activity. If a successful bid is made, the seller and the buyer negotiate the payment method, shipping details, warranty, and other particulars. eBay serves as a liaison between the parties; it is the interface through which sellers and buyers can conduct business. eBay does not maintain a costly physical inventory or deal with shipping, handling, or other services that businesses such as Amazon and other retailers must provide.

After a few years of successful operations and tens of millions of loyal users, eBay started to do e-tailing, mostly in fixed prices. By 2003, eBay operated several specialty sites, such as eBay Motors, and made wireless trading possible. eBay also operates a business exchange in which small- and medium-sized enterprises can buy and sell new and used merchandise, in B2B or B2C modes. In addition, *half.com*, the famous discount e-tailer, is now part of eBay and so is PayPal.com, the P2P payment company.

eBay operates globally, permitting international trades to take place. Country-specific sites are located in over 25 countries. Buyers from more than 160 other countries also participate. Finally, eBay operates locally: It has over 60 local sites in the United States that enable users to easily find items located near them, to browse through items of local interest, and to meet face-to-face to conclude transactions. As of fall 2002, eBay had close to 50 million registered users, and according to company financial statements, eBay transacted over $14.87 billion in sales in 2002.

The impact of eBay on e-business has been profound. Its founders took a limited-access off-line business model—auctions—and, by using the Internet, brought it to the desktops of consumers worldwide. This business model consistently generates a profit and promotes a sense of community—a near addiction that keeps traders coming back. As a matter of fact, the only place where people are doing more online business than offline business (and considerably more, at that) is auctions. For comparison, e-tailing is less than 2 percent of the total retailing.

Sources: Compiled from press releases at *eBay.com* (2001–2003), and from Cohen (2001) and Deitel et al. (2001).

For Further Exploration: Is bigger always better in auctions? Does eBay's 2003 change of business model, from auctions to e-tailing, make sense? Why are wireless auctions promoted?

REVERSE AUCTIONS. In **reverse auctions,** there is one buyer, usually an organization, that wants to buy a product or a service. Suppliers are invited to submit bids. Online bidding is much faster than conventional bidding, and it usually attracts many more bidders. The reverse auction is the most common auction model for large purchases (in terms of either quantities or price). Governments and large corporations frequently mandate this approach, which may provide considerable savings.

Auctions are used in B2C, B2B, C2B, e-government, and C2C commerce, and they are becoming popular in many countries. Their benefits for sellers, buyers, and auctioneers are listed in Online File W5.1 at the book's Web site. Electronic auctions started in the 1980s on private networks, but their use was limited. The Internet opens many new opportunities for e-auctions.

As we have discussed, auctions can be conducted from the seller's site, the buyer's site, or from a third-party site. For example, as described in *IT at Work 5.1*, eBay, the best-known third-party site, offers hundreds of thousands of different items in several types of auctions. Over 300 other major companies, including Amazon.com and Dellauction.com, offer online auctions as well.

Bartering
Related to auctions is **electronic bartering,** the exchange of goods or services *without a monetary transaction.* In addition to the individual-to-individual bartering ads that appear in some newsgroups, bulletin boards, and chat rooms, there are several intermediaries that arrange for corporate e-bartering (e.g., *barterbrokers. com*). These intermediaries try to match online partners to a barter.

5.3 BUSINESS-TO-CONSUMER APPLICATIONS

Forrester Research Institute, the Gartner Group, and others predict that online B2C will be in the range of $300 to $800 billion in the year 2004, up from $515 million in 1996 (see *cyberatlas.com* and *emarketer.com*). For 2004 the total of B2C and B2B is estimated to be in the range of $3.5 billion to $8 billion (depending on the estimator and their definitions of what they measure). Here we will look at some of the major categories of B2C applications.

Electronic Retailing: Storefronts and Malls
For generations home shopping from catalogs has flourished, and television shopping channels have been attracting millions of shoppers for more than two decades. However, these methods have drawbacks: Both methods can be expensive; paper catalogs are sometimes not up-to-date; many people are troubled by the waste of paper used in catalogs that just get tossed out; and television shopping is limited to what is shown on the screen at any given time. Shopping online offers an alternative to catalog and television shopping that appeals to many consumers.

Like any mail-order shopping experience, e-commerce enables you to buy from home, and to do so 24 hours a day, 7 days a week. However, EC overcomes some of the limitations of the other forms of home shopping. It offers a wide variety of products and services, including the most unique items, often at lower prices. Furthermore, within seconds, shoppers can get very detailed information on products, and can easily search for and compare competitors' products and prices. Finally, using the Internet, buyers can find hundreds of thousands of sellers. **Electronic retailing** (*e-tailing*) is the direct sale of products through electronic storefronts or electronic malls, usually designed around an electronic catalog format and/or auctions.

Both goods and services are sold online. Goods that are bought most often online are computers and computer-related items, office supplies, books and magazines, CDs, cassettes, movies and videos, clothing and shoes, toys, and food. Services that are bought most often online include entertainment, travel services, stocks and bonds trading, electronic banking, insurance, and job matching. (Services will be presented as a separate topic later in this section.) Directories and hyperlinks from other Web sites and intelligent search agents help buyers find the best stores and products to match their needs. Two shopping locations online are electronic storefronts and electronic malls.

ELECTRONIC STOREFRONTS. Hundreds of thousands of solo storefronts can be found on the Internet, each with its own Internet name and EC portal. Called **electronic storefronts,** they may be an *extension* of physical stores such as Home Depot, The Sharper Image, or Wal-Mart. Or, they may be new businesses started by entrepreneurs who saw a niche on the Web, such as Amazon.com, CDNow, Uvine.com, Restaurant.com (see Minicase 2), and Alloy.com. Besides being used by retailers, such as Officedepot.com, storefronts also are used by manufacturers, such as Dell.com. Retailers' and manufacturers' storefronts may sell to individuals and/or to organizations. There are two types of storefronts, general and specialized. The *specialized* store sells one or a few products (e.g., flowers, wines, or dog toys). The *general* storefronts sell many products.

ELECTRONIC MALLS. An **electronic mall,** also known as a cybermall or e-mall, is a collection of individual shops under one Internet address. The basic idea of an electronic mall is the same as that of a regular shopping mall—to provide a one-stop shopping place that offers many products and services. Representative cybermalls are Downtown Anywhere (*da.awa.com*), Cactus Hill HandCrafters Mall (*cactushill.com*), America's Choice Mall (*mall.choicemall.com*), and Shopping 2000 (*shopping2000.com*). A unique e-mall is *2bsure.com,* which specializes in services (financial, legal, etc.) but also sells computers and other electronic products, as well as providing price comparisons.

Two types of malls exist. First, there are *referral malls,* such as *hawaii.com.* You cannot buy in such a mall, but instead you are transferred to a participating storefront. In the second, more traditional type of mall, such as *store.yahoo.com,* you can actually make a purchase. At this type of mall, you might shop from a variety of stores, but are able to make only one purchase transaction at the end; an electronic shopping cart enables you to gather items from various vendors and pay for them all together in one transaction. (The mall organizer, such as Yahoo, takes a commission from the sellers for this service.)

Each cybermall may include thousands of vendors. For example, *shopping.yahoo.com* and *eshop.msn.com* include tens of thousands of products from thousands of vendors.

As is true for vendors that locate in a physical shopping mall, a vendor that locates in an e-mall gives up a certain amount of independence. Its success depends on the popularity of the mall, as well as on its own marketing efforts. On the other hand, malls generate streams of prospective customers who otherwise might never have stopped by the store.

E-Tailing: The Essentials

The concept of retailing and e-tailing implies sales of goods and/or services to individual customers. However, the distinction between B2C and B2B e-commerce is not always clear cut. For example, Amazon.com sells books mostly to individuals

(B2C), but it also sells to corporations (B2B). Amazon.com's rival, Barnes & Noble Online (*bn.com*), has a special division that caters only to business customers. Walmart.com sells to both individuals and businesses (via Sam's Club). Dell.com sells its computers to both consumers and businesses, as does Staples.com, and some insurance sites sell both to individuals and corporations.

There are several models of B2C (see Turban et al., 2004). One of the most interesting properties of these models is the ability to offer customized products at a reasonable price and fairly fast (as done by Dell Computer). Many sites (e.g., *nike.com* and *lego.com*) offer product self-configuration from their B2C portals. (For more on build-to-order and its impact on e-commerce, see Appendix 2A.) The most well known B2C site is Amazon.com, whose story is presented in IT At Work 5.2.

Issues in E-Tailing The following are the major issues faced by e-tailers that may be handled and supported by IT tools:

- *Resolving channel conflict.* If a seller is a click-and-mortar company, such as Levi's or GM, it may face a conflict with its regular distributors when it sells directly online. Known as **channel conflict,** this situation can alienate the regular distributors. Channel conflict has forced some companies (e.g., Lego.com) to limit their B2C efforts; others (e.g., some automotive companies) have decided not to sell direct online. An alternative approach is to try to collaborate in some way with the existing distributors whose services may be restructured. For example, an auto company could allow customers to configure a car online, but require that the car be picked up from a dealer, where customers would arrange financing, warranties, and service. IT tools can facilitate resolution of channel conflict, for example, by using a group DSS (Chapter 12).

- *Resolving conflicts within click-and-mortar organizations.* When an established company decides to sell direct online, on a large scale, it may create a conflict within its existing operations. Conflicts may arise in areas such as pricing of products and services, allocation of resources (e.g., advertising budget), and logistics services provided by the offline activities to the online activities (e.g., handling of returns of items bought online). As a result of these conflicts, some companies have completely separated the "clicks" (the online portion of the organization) from the "mortar" or "bricks" (the traditional brick-and-mortar part of the organization). Such separation may increase expenses and reduce the synergy between the two. The decisions about how to organize the online and offline operations and whether or not to separate them can be facilitated by IT tools. In addition, group DSS can be used to resolve conflicts.

- *Organizing order fulfillment and logistics.* E-tailers face a difficult problem of how to ship very small quantities to a large number of buyers. This can be a difficult undertaking, especially when returned items need to be handled. IT-supported decision models can help with scheduling, routing, shipments, inventory management, and other logistics-related decisions.

- *Determining viability and risk of online e-tailers.* Many pure online e-tailers folded in 2000–2002 (see Kaplan, 2002), the result of problems with customer acquisition, order fulfillment, and demand forecasting. Online competition, especially in commodity-type products such as CDs, toys, books, or groceries, became very fierce, due to the ease of entry to the marketplace. So a problem most young e-tailers face is to determine how long to operate while

IT at Work 5.2
AMAZON.COM: THE KING OF E-TAILING

Entrepreneur Jeff Bezos, envisioning the huge potential for retail sales over the Internet, selected books as the most logical product for e-tailing. In July 1995, Bezos started Amazon.com, an e-tailing pioneer, offering books via an electronic catalog from its Web site. Key features offered by the Amazon.com "superstore" were broad selection, low prices, easy searching and ordering, useful product information and personalization, secure payment systems, and efficient order fulfillment. Early on, recognizing the importance of order fulfillment, Amazon.com invested hundreds of millions of dollars in building physical warehouses designed for shipping small packages to hundreds of thousands of customers.

Over the years since its founding, Amazon.com has continually enhanced its business models and electronic store by expanding product selection, improving the customer's experience, and adding services and alliances. For example, the company now offers specialty stores, such as its professional and technical store. It has expanded its editorial content through partnerships with experts in certain fields. It has increased product selection with the addition of millions of used and out-of-print titles. It also is expanding its offerings beyond books. For example, in June 2002 it became an authorized dealer of Sony Corp. for selling Sony products online.

In 1997, Amazon started an extensive affiliates program. By 2002, the company had more than 500,000 partners that refer customers to Amazon.com. Amazon pays a 3 to 5 percent commission on any resulting sale. Amazon.com has undertaken alliances with major "trusted partners" that provide knowledgeable entry into new markets, such as cars, health and beauty aids, toys, and even wireless phone service providers. In yet another extension of its services, in September 2001 Amazon signed an agreement with Borders Group Inc., providing Amazon's users with the option of picking up books, CDs, etc. at Borders' physical bookstores. Amazon.com also is becoming a Web fulfillment contractor for national chains such as Target and Circuit City.

Amazon.com is recognized as an online leader in creating sales through customer intimacy and customer relationship management (CRM), which are cultivated by informative marketing front-ends and one-to-one advertising. In addition, sales are supported by highly automated, efficient back-end systems. When a customer makes a return visit to Amazon.com, a cookie file identifies the user and says, for example, "Welcome back, Sarah

Shopper," and then proceeds to recommend new books from the same genre of previous customer purchases. The company tracks customer purchase histories and sends purchase recommendations via e-mail to cultivate repeat buyers. These efforts usually result in satisfactory shopping experiences and encourage customers to return. The site has an efficient search engine and other shopping aids.

Customers can personalize their accounts and manage orders online with the patented "One-Click" order feature. This personalized service includes an *electronic wallet,* which enables shoppers to place an order in a secure manner without the need to enter their address, credit card number, and so on, each time they shop. One-Click also allows customers to view their order status and make changes on orders that have not yet entered the shipping process.

Annual sales for Amazon.com have trended upward, from $15.7 million in 1996 to $600 million in 1998 to about $4 billion by 2002. With over 17 million book, music, and DVD/video titles (including over 1 million Japanese-language titles), Amazon.com has sold products to some 20 million customers. According to Retail Forward's study, *Top E-Retail 2001* (*emarketer.com,* August 1, 2002), Amazon was the number-one e-tailer in 2001, generating $3.12 billion. This level of sales represented 22 percent of the total online sales for all 50 companies in the study. According to Bayers (2002), Amazon is becoming very successful in reducing its costs and increasing its profitability.

In January 2002, Amazon.com declared its first-ever profit—for the 2001 fourth quarter—and followed that by a profitable first quarter of 2002. Yet its financial success is by no means assured: The company sustained operating losses in the second and third quarters of 2002, though they were smaller than losses in the same quarters in preceding years. In the fourth quarter of 2002, the company again made a profit; 2003 will be the first year with profit in each quarter. Like all businesses, and especially all e-tailing businesses, Amazon.com will continue to walk the fine line of profitability for the forseeable future.

Sources: Compiled from Bayers (2002), Daisey (2002), and *New York Times* (2002).

For Further Exploration: What are the critical success factors of Amazon? What advantages does it have over other e-tailers (e.g., Wal-Mart online or *toysrus.com*)? What disadvantages? What is the purpose of the alliances Amazon.com has made?

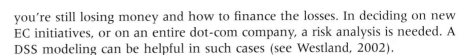

you're still losing money and how to finance the losses. In deciding on new EC initiatives, or on an entire dot-com company, a risk analysis is needed. A DSS modeling can be helpful in such cases (see Westland, 2002).

- *Identifying appropriate revenue models.* Many dot-com companies were selling goods at or below cost, with the objective of attracting many customers and advertisers to their sites. One early dot-com model was to generate enough revenue from advertising to keep the business afloat until the customer base reached critical mass. This model did not work. Too many dot-com companies were competing for too few advertising dollars, which went mainly to a small number of well-known sites such as AOL and Yahoo. In addition, there was a "chicken-and-egg" problem: Sites could not get advertisers to come if they did not have enough visitors. To succeed in EC, it is necessary to identify appropriate revenue models. For further discussion of revenue models, see Turban et al. (2004).

Service Industries Online

Selling books, toys, computers, and most other products on the Internet may reduce vendors' selling costs by 20 to 40 percent. Further reduction is difficult to achieve because the products must be delivered physically. Only a few products (such as software or music) can be digitized to be delivered online for additional savings. On the other hand, delivery of *services,* such as buying an airline ticket or buying stocks or insurance online, can be done 100 percent electronically, with considerable cost reduction potential. Therefore, delivery of services online is growing very rapidly, with millions of new customers added annually. Indeed, in many ways e-commerce is now simply a part of traditional commerce. Like the addition of credit card payment capabilities a generation ago, many people expect companies to offer some form of e-commerce.

We will take a quick look here at the leading online service industries: banking, trading of securities (stocks, bonds), job matching, travel services, and real estate.

CYBERBANKING. **Electronic banking,** also known as **cyberbanking** and *online banking,* includes various banking activities conducted from home, from a business site, or on the road instead of at a physical bank location. Electronic banking has capabilities ranging from paying bills to applying for a loan. It saves time and is convenient for customers. For banks, it offers an inexpensive alternative to branch banking (for example, about 1 cent cost per transaction versus $1.07 at a physical branch) and a chance to enlist remote customers. Many banks now offer online banking, and some use EC as a major competitive strategy (see Athitakis, 2003).

Electronic banking offers several of the benefits of EC listed in Section 5.1, such as expanding the customer base and saving the cost of paper transactions. In addition to regular banks with added online services, we are seeing the emergence of **virtual banks,** dedicated solely to Internet transactions, such as *netbank.com.*

International and Multiple-Currency Banking. International banking and the ability to handle trading in multiple currencies are critical for international trade. Although some international retail purchasing can be done by giving a credit card number, other transactions may require cross-border banking support. For example, Hong Kong and Shanghai Bank (*hsbc.com.hk*) has developed a special system (called Hexagon) to provide electronic banking in 60 countries. Using this system, the bank has leveraged its reputation and infrastructure in the developing economies of Asia, to rapidly become a major international bank without developing an extensive new branch network (Peffers and Tunnainen, 1998). Transfers of electronic funds and electronic letters of credit are other important services in international banking. An example of support for EC global trade is provided by TradeCard (*tradecard.com*), which is done in conjuction with Master-Card. Banks and companies such as Oanda also provide currency conversion of over 160 currencies. International foreign-currency traders can be assisted by many other online services (see *financialsupermarket.com* and *foreign-trade.com*).

ONLINE SECURITIES TRADING. It is estimated that by 2004, about 35 million people in the United States will be using computers to trade stocks, bonds, and other financial instruments (eMarketer, 2003). In Korea, more than half of stock traders are using the Internet for that purpose. Why? Because it makes a lot of dollars and "sense": An online trade typically costs the trader between $3 and $15, compared to an average fee of $100 from a full-service broker and $25 from a discount broker. There is no waiting on busy telephone lines. Furthermore, the chance of making mistakes is small because online trading does away with oral communication with a securities broker in a frequently very noisy physical environment. Orders can be placed from anywhere, any time, even from your cell phone. Investors can find on the Web a considerable amount of information regarding investing in a specific company or in a mutual fund (e.g., *money.cnn.com, bloomberg.com*).

How does online trading work? Let's say you have an account with Charles Schwab. You access Schwab's Web site (*schwab.com*) from your PC or your Internet-enabled mobile device, enter your account number and password to access your personalized Web page, and then click on "stock trading." Using a menu, you enter the details of your order (buy or sell, margin or cash, price limit, market order, etc.). The computer tells you the current "ask" and "bid" prices, much as a broker would do on the telephone, and you can approve or reject the transaction. Some well-known companies that offer only online trading are E*Trade, Ameritrade, and Suretrade.

However, both online banking and securities trading require tight security. Otherwise, your money may be at risk. Here is what happened in Korea on August 23, 2002: According to news items (*Korean Times,* August 24, 2002), an unknown criminal managed to get an account number and a password of a large investor in Korea (Hyundai Investment). Sitting in an Internet café, the criminal placed an order with the company that managed the investment, Daewoo Securities, to buy five million shares of Delta Information Communication. Within 90 seconds 2.7 million shares were sold by 100 sellers, at a much higher than normal price. When the fake order was discovered and the news broke, the price of the shares spiraled down. Daewoo Securities ended with 2.7 million unwanted shares. Some analysts have suggested that one or more sellers hired the hacker so they could sell at a high price. Whatever the motive, Daewoo lost a huge amount of money. Most online bank stock traders use only ID numbers and passwords. Yet this may not be secure enough. See Chapter 15 on how to improve online security.

THE ONLINE JOB MARKET. The Internet offers a perfect environment for job seekers and for companies searching for hard-to-find employees. The online job market is especially effective for technology-oriented jobs. However, there are thousands of companies and government agencies that advertise available positions of all types of jobs, accept resumes, and take applications via the Internet. The online job market is used by:

- *Job seekers.* Job seekers can reply to employment ads online. Or they can take the initiative and place resumes on their own home pages or on others' Web sites, send messages to members of newsgroups asking for referrals, and use recruiting firms such as Career Mosaic (*careermosaic.com*), Job Center (*jobcenter.com*), and Monster Board (*monster.com*). For entry-level jobs and internships for newly minted graduates, job seekers can use *jobdirect.com*. Need help writing your resume? Try *resume-link.com* or *jobweb.com*. Finally, if you want to know if you are underpaid or how much you can get if you relocate to another city, consult *wageweb.com*.

- *Job offerers.* Many organizations advertise openings on their Web site. Others use sites ranging from Yahoo to bulletin boards of recruiting firms. In many countries governments must advertise openings on the Internet.

- *Recruiting firms.* Hundreds of job-placement brokers and related services are active on the Web. They use their own Web pages to post available job descriptions and advertise their services in electronic malls and on others' Web sites. Recruiters use newsgroups, online forums, bulletin boards, and chat rooms. Job-finding brokers help candidates write their resumes and get the most exposure. Matching of candidates and jobs is done by companies such as Peopleclick.com.

Due to the large number of job market resources available on the Internet, it is too expensive and time-consuming to evaluate them manually. Resumix (*resumix.com*) can help (see Chapter 7 for details).

TRAVEL SERVICES. The Internet is an ideal place to plan, explore, and economically arrange almost any trip. Potential savings are available through special sales, comparisons, use of auctions, and the elimination of travel agents. Examples of comprehensive travel online services are Expedia.com, Travelocity.com, and Orbitz.com. Services are also provided online by all major airline vacation services, large conventional travel agencies, car rental agencies, hotels (e.g., *hotels.com*), and tour companies. Online travel services allow you to purchase airline tickets, reserve hotel rooms, and rent cars. Most sites also support an itinerary-based interface, including a fare-tracker feature that sends you e-mail messages about low-cost flights to your favorite destinations or from your home city. Finally, Priceline.com allows you to set a price you are willing to pay for an airline ticket or hotel accommodations and Priceline then attempts to find a vendor that will match your price. A similar service offered by Hotwire.com tries to find the lowest available price for you.

REAL ESTATE. Real estate transactions are an ideal area for e-commerce, for the following reasons. First, you can view many properties on the screen, saving time for you and the broker. Second, you can sort and organize properties according to your preferences and decision criteria, and can preview the exterior and interior designs of the properties, shortening the search process. Finally, you can find detailed information about the properties and frequently get even more detail than brokers will provide.

In some locations brokers allow the use of real estate databases only from their offices, but considerable information is now available on the Internet. For example, Realtor.com allows you to search a database of over 1.2 million homes across the United States. The database is composed of local "multiple listings" of all available properties and properties just sold, in hundreds of locations. Those who are looking for an apartment can try Apartments.com.

In another real estate application, homebuilders use three-dimensional floor plans for potential home buyers on their Web sites. They use "virtual models" that enable buyers to "walk through" mockups of homes.

5.4 MARKET RESEARCH AND ONLINE ADVERTISING

We now turn our attention in another direction—market research and online advertising. To successfully conduct electronic commerce, especially B2C, it is important to find out who are the actual and potential customers and what motivates them to buy. Several research institutions collect Internet-usage statistics (e.g., *acnielsen.com, emarketer.com*), and they also look at factors that inhibit shopping. Merchants can then prepare their marketing and advertising strategies based on this information.

Finding out what specific groups of consumers (such as teenagers or residents of certain geographical zones) want is done via **segmentation**, dividing customers into specific segments, like age or gender. However, even if we know what groups of consumers in general want, each individual consumer is very likely to want something different. Some like classical music while others like jazz. Some like brand names, while price is more important to many others. Learning about customers is extremely important for any successful business, especially in cyberspace. Such learning is facilitated by *market research.*

A MODEL OF CONSUMER BEHAVIOR ONLINE. For decades, market researchers have tried to understand consumer behavior, and they have summarized their findings in various models of consumer behavior. The purpose of a consumer behavior model is to help vendors understand how a consumer makes a purchasing decision. If the process is understood, a vendor may try to influence the buyer's decision, for example, by advertising or special promotions.

Figure 5.3 shows the basics of these consumer behavior models, adjusted to fit the EC environment. The EC model is composed of the following parts:

- *Independent (or uncontrollable) variables,* which are shown at the top of Figure 5.3. They can be categorized as personal characteristics and environmental characteristics.
- *Vendor-controlled variables* (intervening or moderating variables), which are divided into market stimuli (on the left) and EC systems (at the bottom).
- The *decision-making process,* shown in the center of the figure, is influenced by the independent and intervening variable. This process ends with the buyers' decisions (shown on the right), resulting from the decision-making process.
- The *dependent variables* that describe the decisions made.

Figure 5.3 identifies some of the variables in each category. In this chapter, we deal briefly with only some of the variables. Discussions of other variables can be found in Internet-marketing books, such as Strauss et al. (2003) and Sterne (2001, 2002) and in Online File W5.2.

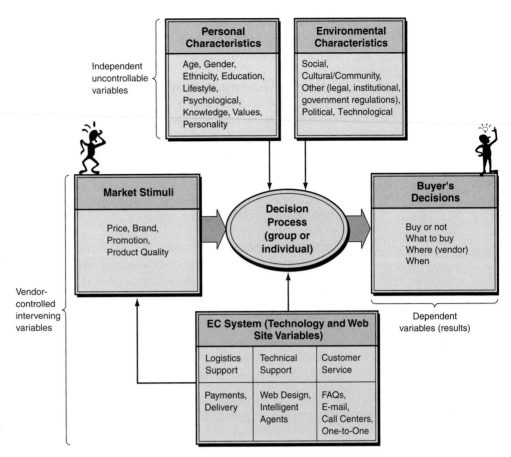

FIGURE 5.3
E-commerce consumer behavior model.

Before we discuss some of the model's variables, let's examine who the EC consumers are. Online consumers can be divided into two types: *individual consumers,* who get much of the media attention, and *organizational buyers,* who do most of the actual shopping in cyberspace. Organizational buyers include governments, private corporations, resellers, and public organizations. Purchases by organizational buyers are generally used to create products (services) by adding value to raw material or components. Also, organizational buyers such as retailers and resellers may purchase products for resale without any further modifications.

The above model is simplified. In reality it can be more complicated, especially when new products or procedures need to be purchased. For example, for online buying, a customer may go through the following five adoption stages: awareness, interest, evaluation, trial, and adoption. (For details see McDaniel and Gates, 2001, and Solomon, 2002.) Understanding the structure of the model in Figure 5.3, or any more complicated one, is necessary, but in order to really make use of such models, we need to learn about the decision-making process itself, as discussed next.

The Consumer Decision-Making Process

Let's return to the central part of Figure 5.3, where consumers are shown making purchasing decisions. Several models have been developed in an effort to describe the details of the decision-making process that leads up to and culminates in a purchase. These models provide a framework for learning about the process in order to predict, improve, or influence consumer decisions. Here we introduce two relevant purchasing-decision models.

A GENERIC PURCHASING-DECISION MODEL. A general purchasing-decision model consists of five major phases. In each phase we can distinguish several activities and, in some of them, one or more decisions. The five phases are: (1) need identification, (2) information search, (3) evaluation of alternatives, (4) purchase and delivery, and (5) after-purchase evaluation. Although these phases offer a general guide to the consumer decision-making process, do not assume that all consumers' decision making will necessarily proceed in this order. In fact, some consumers may proceed to a point and then revert back to a previous phase, or skip a phase. For details, see Strauss et al. (2003).

A CUSTOMER DECISION MODEL IN WEB PURCHASING. The above purchasing-decision model was used by O'Keefe and McEachern (1998) to build a framework for a Web-purchasing model, called the *Consumer Decision Support System (CDSS)*. According to their framework, shown in Table 5.4, each of the phases of the purchasing model can be supported by both CDSS facilities and Internet/Web facilities. The CDSS facilities support the specific decisions in the process. Generic EC technologies provide the necessary mechanisms, and they enhance communication and collaboration. Specific implementation of this framework is demonstrated throughout the text.

TABLE 5.4 Purchase Decision-Making Process and Support System

Decision Process	Consumer Decision Support System Facilities	Generic Internet and Web Support Facilities
Need recognition ↓	Agents and event notification	Banner advertising on order Web sites URL on physical materials Discussions in newsgroups
Information search (what, from whom?) ↓	Virtual catalogs Structured interaction and question/answer sessions Links to (and guidance on) external sources	Web directories and classifiers Internal search on Web site External search engines Focused directories and information brokers
Evaluation, negotiation, selection ↓	FAQs and other summaries Samples and trials Provisions of evaluative models Pointers to (and information about) existing customers	Discussion in newsgroups Cross-site comparisons Generic models
Purchase, payment, and delivery ↓	Product or service ordering Arrangement of delivery	Electronic cash and virtual banking Logistics providers and package tracking
After-purchase service and evaluation	Customer support via e-mail and newsgroups E-mail communication	Discussion in newsgroups

Source: Modified from O'Keefe, R. M., and T. McEachern, "Web-Based Customer Decision Support System." *Communications of the ACM,* March 1998, ACM, Inc. Used with permission.

How Market Research Finds What Customers Want

There are basically two ways to find out what customers want. The first is to ask them, and the second is to infer what they want by observing what they do in cyberspace.

ASKING CUSTOMERS WHAT THEY WANT. The Internet provides easy, fast, and relatively inexpensive ways for vendors to find out what customers want by interacting directly with them. The simplest way is to ask potential customers to fill in electronic questionnaires. To do so, vendors may need to provide some inducements. For example, in order to play a free electronic game or participate in a sweepstakes, you are asked to fill in an online form and answer some questions about yourself (e.g., see *bizrate.com*). Marketers not only learn what you want from the direct answers, but also try to infer from your preferences of music, for example, what type of books, clothes, or movies you may be likely to prefer.

In some cases, asking customers what they want may not be feasible. Also, customers may refuse to answer questionnaires, or they may provide false information (as is done in about 40 percent of the cases, according to studies done at Georgia Tech University). Also, questionnaires can be lengthy and costly to administer. Therefore, a different approach may be needed—observing what customers do in cyberspace.

TRACKING CUSTOMER ACTIVITIES ON THE WEB. Today it is possible to learn about customers by observing their *behavior* on the Internet. Many companies offer site-tracking services, based on cookies, Web bugs, or spyware programs. For example, Nettracker (from *sane.com*) collects data from client/server logs and provides periodic reports that include demographic data such as where customers come from or how many customers have gone straight from the home page to ordering.

The Web is an incredibly rich source of business intelligence, and many enterprises are scrambling to build data warehouses that capture the knowledge contained in the *clickstream data* (data recovered from customers' "clicks" as they move around online) obtained from their Web sites. By analyzing the user behavior patterns contained in these clickstream data warehouses (see Sweiger et al., 2002), savvy businesses can expand their markets, improve customer relationships, reduce costs, streamline operations, strengthen their Web sites, and plot their business strategies.

Using Software Agents to Enhance B2C and Market Research

As discussed in Chapter 12, *software agents* are computer programs that conduct routine tasks, search and retrieve information, support decision making, and act as domain experts. These agents sense the environment and act autonomously without human intervention. This results in a significant savings of users' time. There are various types of agents that can be used in EC, ranging from software agents, which are those with no intelligence, to learning agents that exhibit some intelligent behavior.

Agents are used to support many tasks in EC. But first, it will be beneficial to distinguish between search engines and the more intelligent type of agents. As discussed in Chapter 4, a *search engine* is a computer program that can automatically contact other network resources on the Internet, search for specific information or key words, and report the results. Unlike search engines, an **intelligent agent** uses expert, or knowledge-based, capabilities to do more than just "search and match." For example, it can monitor movements on a Web site to check whether a customer seems lost or ventures into areas that may not fit his or her profile, and the agent can then notify the customer and even provide corrective assistance. Depending on their level of intelligence, agents can do many other things. In this section we will concentrate on intelligent agents for assisting shoppers (see Yuan, 2003). (For other uses of intelligent agents, see Chapter 12.)

BRAND- AND VENDOR-FINDING AGENTS AND PRICE COMPARISONS. Once the consumer has decided what to buy, a type of intelligent agent called a *comparison agent* will help in doing comparisons, usually of prices, from different vendors. A pioneering price-comparison agent was Bargainfinder from Andersen Consulting. This agent was used only in online shopping for CDs. It queried the price of a specific CD from a number of online vendors and returned the list of vendors and prices. Today much more sophisticated agents, such as Mysimon.com, Pricescan.com and Dealtime.com, make comparisons. Some of these look at multiple criteria, not just price, and even let you prioritize the criteria. Then, the agent makes a recommendation based on your stated preferences.

SEARCH AGENTS. Search agents, another type of intelligent agent, can help customers determine what to buy to satisfy a specific need (e.g., Likemind.com, Gifts.com). This is achieved by looking for specific product information and critically evaluating it. The search agent helps consumers decide what product best fits their profile and requirements (e.g., see *salesmountain.com*).

COLLABORATIVE FILTERING AGENTS. Once a company knows a consumer's preferences (e.g., what music they like), it would be useful if the company could predict, without asking, what other products or services this consumer might enjoy. One way to do this is through use of **collaborative filtering agents,** which use customer data to *infer* customer interest in other products or services. There are several methods and formulas, all using software agents, to execute collaborative filtering. Some collaborative filtering agents base predictions on statistical formulas derived from behavioral sciences (see *sins.berkeley.edu/resources.collab/* for details). Some base their predictions on what is known about other customers with similar profiles. (For details of the different methods and formulas, see Ridell et al., 2002.) One of the pioneering filtering agents was Firefly (now embedded in Microsoft's Passport System).

OTHER AGENTS. Many other software agents can aid buyers and sellers in e-commerce. Examples are: *UPS.com* for optimizing deliveries, *e-Falcon.com* for fraud detection, and *webassured.com* for increasing trust levels. Other agents are described throughout the book.

   The information collected by market research is used for customer relationship management (CRM), described in Chapter 7, and for advertising, the topic we discuss next.

Advertising Online   Advertising is an attempt to disseminate information in order to influence a buyer–seller transaction. Traditional advertising on TV or in newspapers is impersonal, one-way mass communication. Direct-response marketing (telemarketing) contacts individuals by means of direct mail or by telephone calls and requires them to respond in order to make a purchase. The direct-response approach personalizes advertising and marketing, but it can be expensive, slow, and ineffective (and from the consumer's point of view, annoying).

Internet advertising redefines the advertising process, making it media-rich, dynamic, and interactive. It improves on traditional forms of advertising in a number of ways: Internet ads can be updated any time at minimal cost, and therefore can always be timely. Internet ads can reach very large number of potential buyers all over the world and they are sometimes cheaper in comparison to print (newspaper and magazine), radio, or television ads. Ads in these other media are expensive because they are determined by space occupied (for print ads), by how many days (times) they are run, and on the number of local and national stations and print media that run them. Internet ads can be interactive and targeted to specific interest groups and/or to individuals. Finally, the use of the Internet itself is growing very rapidly, and it makes sense to move advertising to the Internet, where the number of viewers is growing.

Nevertheless, the Internet as an advertising medium does have some shortcomings, most of which relate to the difficulty in measuring the effectiveness and justifying the ads. For example, it is difficult to measure the actual results of placing a banner ad or sending a marketing e-mail, and the audience is still relatively small (compared to television, for example). For a comparison of advertising media, see Online File W5.3.

ADVERTISING METHODS. The most common advertising methods online are banners, pop-ups, and e-mails. The essentials of these and some other methods are briefly presented next.

Banners. **Banners** are, simply, electronic billboards; banner advertising is the most commonly used form of advertising on the Internet. Typically, a banner contains a short text or graphical message to promote a product or a vendor. It may even contain video clips and sound. When customers click on a banner, they are transferred to the advertiser's home page. Advertisers go to great lengths to design banners that catch consumers' attention.

There are two types of banners: **Keyword banners** appear when a predetermined word is queried from a search engine. It is effective for companies who want to narrow their target to consumers interested in particular topics. **Random banners** appear randomly and might be used to introduce new products to the widest possible audience, or for brand recognition.

A major advantage of using banners is the ability to customize them to the target audience. Keyword banners can be customized to a market segment or even to an individual user. If the computer system knows who you are or what your profile is, you may be sent a banner that is supposed to match your interests. However, one of the major drawbacks of using banners is that limited information is allowed due to its small size. Hence advertisers need to think of creative but short messages to attract viewers. Another drawback is that banners, which were a novelty in late 1990s and so were noticed by viewers, are ignored by many viewers today. A new generation of banner-like ads are the pop-ups.

Pop-Up, Pop-Under, and Similar Ads. One of the most annoying phenomena in Web surfing is the increased use of pop-up, pop-under, and similar ads. These ads are contained in a new browser window that is automatically launched when one enters or exits a site, or by other triggers such as a delay during Internet surfing. A **pop-up ad** appears in front of the current browser window. A **pop-under ad** appears underneath the active window; when users close the active window, they see the ad. Pop-ups and pop-unders are sometime difficult to close. These methods are controversial: Many users strongly object to these ads, which they consider intrusive. For further discussion, see Martin and Ryan, 2002, and Online File W5.4.

E-Mail Advertising. E-mail is emerging as an Internet advertising and marketing channel that affords cost-effective implementation and a better and quicker response rate than other advertising channels (such as print ads). Marketers develop or purchase a list of e-mail addresses, place them in a customer database, and then send advertisements via e-mail. A list of e-mail addresses can be a very powerful tool because the marketer can target a group of people, or even individuals. For example, Restaurants.com (see Minicase 2) uses e-mail to send restaurant coupons to millions of customers. However, as with pop ups, there is a potential for misuse of e-mail advertising, and some consumers are receiving a flood of unsolicited mail (see the section on unsolicited advertising, below).

Electronic Catalogs and Brochures. Printed catalogs have been an advertising medium for a long time. Recently electronic catalogs have been gaining popularity. The merchant's objective in using online catalogs is to advertise and promote products and services. From the customer's perspective, online catalogs offer a source of information that can be searched quickly with the help of special search engines. Also, comparisons involving catalog products can be made very effectively.

Sometimes merchants find it useful to provide a *customized catalog* to a regular customer. Such a catalog is assembled specifically for the particular buyer, usually a company but sometimes even an individual who buys frequently or in large quantities.

Other Forms of Internet Advertising. Online advertising can be done in several other forms, including posting advertising in chat rooms (newsgroups) and in classified ads (see *classifieds 2000.com*). Advertising on Internet radio is just beginning, and soon advertising on Internet television will commence. Of special interest is advertising to members of Internet communities. Community sites (such as *geocities.com*) are gathering places for people of similar interests and are therefore a logical place to promote products related to those interests. Another interesting method is wireless ads, which we will describe in Chapter 6.

SOME ADVERTISING ISSUES AND APPROACHES. There are many issues related to the implementation of Internet advertising: how to design ads for the Internet, where and when to advertise, and how to integrate online and off-line ads. Most of such decisions require the input of marketing and advertising experts. Here, we present the following illustrative issues.

Unsolicited Advertising: Spamming and More. A major issue related to pop ups and e-mail advertising is *spamming*, the practice of indiscriminate distribution of electronic ads without permission of the receiver. E-mail spamming, also known as *unsolicited commercial e-mail* or *UCE*, has been part of the Internet for years. Unfortunately, the situation is getting worse with time. The drivers of spamming and some of potential solutions are described in Online File W5.5.

Permission Marketing. Permission marketing is one answer to e-mail spamming. **Permission marketing** asks consumers to give their permission to voluntarily accept advertising and e-mail. Typically, consumers are asked to complete a form that asks what they are interested in and requests permission to send related marketing information. Sometimes consumers are offered incentives to receive advertising; at the least, marketers try to send information in an entertaining, educational, or other interesting manner.

Permission marketing is the basis of many Internet marketing strategies. For example, millions of users receive e-mails periodically from airlines such as American and Southwest. Users of this marketing service can ask for notification of low fares from their home town to their favorite destinations. Users can easily unsubscribe at any time. Permission marketing is also extremely important for market research (e.g., see *mediametrix.com*).

In one particularly interesting form of permission marketing, companies such as Clickdough.com, Getpaid4.com, and CashSurfers.com built customer lists of millions of people who are happy to receive advertising messages whenever they are on the Web. These customers are paid $0.25 to $0.50 an hour to view messages while they do their normal surfing. They may also be paid $0.10 an hour for the surfing time of any friends they refer to the above sites.

Viral Marketing. **Viral marketing** refers to online word-of-mouth marketing. The main idea in viral marketing is to have people forward messages to friends, asking them, for example, to "check this out." A marketer can distribute a small game program, for example, which comes embedded with a sponsor's e-mail, that is easy to forward. By releasing a few thousand copies, vendors hope to reach many more thousands. Word-of-mouth marketing has been used for generations, but its speed and reach are multiplied manyfold by the Internet. Viral marketing is one of the new models being used to build brand awareness at a minimal cost (e.g., see *alladvantage.com*). It has long been a favorite strategy of online advertisers pushing youth-oriented products.

Unfortunately, though, several e-mail hoaxes have spread via viral marketing. Also, a more serious danger of viral marketing is that a destructive computer virus can be added to an innocent advertisement, game, or message. However, when used properly, viral marketing can be both effective and efficient.

Interactive Advertising and Marketing. Conventional advertising is passive, targeted to mass audiences, and for that reason it may be ineffective. Therefore, all advertisers, whether online or not, attempt to customize their ads to special groups and, if possible, even to individuals. A good salesperson is trained to interact with sales prospects, asking questions about the features they are looking for and handling possible objections as they come up. Online advertising comes closer to supporting this one-to-one selling process than more traditional advertising media possibly can.

Ideally, in interactive marketing, advertisers present customized, one-on-one ads. The term *interactive* points to the ability to address an individual, to gather and remember that person's responses, and to serve that customer based on his or her previous, unique responses. When the Internet is combined with database marketing, interactive marketing becomes a very effective and affordable competitive strategy.

Online Promotions: Attracting Visitors to a Site. A Web site without visitors has little value. The following are two examples of ways to attract visitors to a Web site.

- *Making the top list of a search engine.* Web sites submit their URLs to search engines. The search engine's intelligent program (called a *spider*) crawls through the submitted site, indexing all related content and links. Some lists generated by search engines include hundreds or thousands of items. Users that view the results submitted by a search engine typically start by clicking on the first 10 or so items, and soon get tired. So, for best exposure, advertisers like to make the top 10 of the list. How to do it? If a company understands how a search engine's program ranks its findings, it can get to the top of a search engine's list merely by adding, removing, or changing a few sentences on its Web pages. However, this is not easy, as everyone wants to do it, so there are sometimes several thousand entries competing to be in the top 10. It is easier to pay the search engine to put a banner at the top of the lists (e.g., usually on the right-hand side of the screen at *google.com*'s results).

● *Online events, promotions, and attractions.* People generally like the idea of something funny or something free, or both. Contests, quizzes, coupons, and free samples are an integral part of e-commerce as much as, or even more than, they are in off-line commerce. Running promotions on the Internet is similar to running off-line promotions. These mechanisms are designed to attract visitors and to keep their attention. For innovative ideas for promotions and attractions used by companies online, see Sterne (2001) and Strauss et al. (2003).

5.5 B2B APPLICATIONS

In *business to business (B2B) applications,* the buyers, sellers, and transactions involve only organizations. Business-to-business comprises about 85 percent of EC volume. It covers a broad spectrum of applications that enable an enterprise to form electronic relationships with its distributors, resellers, suppliers, customers, and other partners. By using B2B, organizations can restructure their supply chains and partner relationship (e.g., see Warkentin, 2001).

There are several business models for B2B applications. The major ones are sell-side marketplaces, buy-side marketplaces, and electronic exchanges.

Sell-Side Marketplaces

In the **sell-side marketplace** model, organizations attempt to sell their products or services to other organizations electronically, from their own private e-marketplace and/or from a third-party site. This model is similar to the B2C model in which the buyer is expected to come to the seller's site, view catalogs, and place an order. In the B2B sell-side marketplace, however, the buyer is an organization.

The key mechanisms in the sell-side model are: (1) electronic catalogs that can be customized for each large buyer and (2) forward auctions. Sellers such as Dell Computer (*dellauction.com*) use auctions extensively. In addition to auctions from their Web sites, organizations can use third-party auction sites, such as eBay, to liquidate items. Companies such as Freemarkets.com are helping organizations to auction obsolete and old assets and inventories (see Minicase 1).

The sell-side model is used by thousands of companies and is especially powerful for companies with superb reputations. Examples are major computer companies such as Cisco, IBM, and Intel. The seller in this model can be either a manufacturer, a distributor (e.g., *bigboxx.com* and *avnet.com*), or a retailer. In this model, EC is used to increase sales, reduce selling and advertising expenditures, increase delivery speed, and reduce administrative costs. This model is especially suitable to customization. For example, customers can configure their orders online at *cisco.com, dell.com,* and others. This results in fewer misunderstandings about what customers want and in much faster order fulfillment.

Buy-Side Marketplaces

The **buy-side marketplace** is a model in which organizations attempt to buy needed products or services from other organizations electronically, usually from their own private e-marketplace. A major method of buying goods and services in the buy-side model is a reverse auction. Here, a company that wants to buy items places a *request for quotation (RFQ)* on its Web site, or in a third-party bidding marketplace. Once RFQs are posted, sellers (usually preapproved suppliers) submit bids electronically. Such auctions attract large pools of willing sellers, who can be either a manufacturer, a distributor, or a retailer. The bids are routed via the buyer's intranet to the engineering and finance departments for evaluation. Clarifications are made via e-mail, and the winner is notified electronically.

The buy-side model uses EC technology to streamline the purchasing process in order to reduce the cost of items purchased, the administrative cost of procurement, and the purchasing cycle time. General Electric, for example, has calculated that it saves 10 to 15 percent on the cost of the items placed for bid and up to 85 percent on the administrative cost of procurement (Turban et al., 2004); in addition, cycle time is reduced by about 50 percent. Procurements using a third-party buy-side marketplace model are especially popular for medium and small organizations.

E-PROCUREMENT.   Purchasing by using electronic support is referred to as **e-procurement.** In addition to *reverse auctions* just discussed, e-procurement uses other mechanisms. Two popular ones are group purchasing and desktop purchasing.

Group purchasing.   In **group purchasing,** the requirements of many buyers are aggregated so that they total to a large volume, and may merit more seller attention. Once buyers' orders are aggregated, they can be placed on a reverse auction, and a volume discount can be negotiated. The orders of small buyers usually are aggregated by a third-party vendor, such as Consarta.com and Shop2gether.com. Group purchasing is especially popular in the health care industry (see *all-health.com*).

Desktop purchasing.   In this variation of e-procurement, known as **desktop purchasing,** suppliers' catalogs are aggregated into an internal master catalog on the buyer's server, so that the company's purchasing agents (or even end users) can shop more conveniently. Desktop purchasing is most suitable for *maintenance, replacement, and operations (MRO) indirect items,* such as office supplies. (The term *indirect* refers to the fact that these items are not inputs to manufacturing.) In the desktop purchasing model, a company has many suppliers, but the quantities purchased from each are relatively small. This model is most appropriate for large companies (such as Schlumberger, as described in *IT at Work 5.3*) and for government entities.

Electronic Exchanges

E-marketplaces in which there are many sellers and many buyers are called **public exchanges (Electronic exchanges).** They are open to all, and frequently are owned and operated by a third party. According to Kaplan and Sawhney, 2000, there are basically four types of exchanges:

1. *Vertical distributors for direct materials.* These are B2B marketplaces where *direct materials* (materials that are inputs to manufacturing) are traded in an environment of long-term relationships, known as *systematic sourcing.*

IT at Work 5.3
E-PROCUREMENT AT SCHLUMBERGER

Schlumberger is an $8.5 billion company with 60,000 employees in 100 countries. That makes it the world's largest oil-service company. In 2000 the company installed a Web-based automated procurement system in Oilfield Services, its largest division. With this system, employees can buy office supplies and equipment as well as computers direct from their desktops.

The system replaced a number of older systems, including automated and paper-based ones. The single desktop system streamlined and sped up the purchasing operation, reducing costs as well as the number of people involved in the process. The system also enables the company to consolidate purchases for volume discounts from vendors.

The system has two parts:

1. The internal portion uses CommerceOne's BuySite procurement software and runs on the company's intranet. Using it is like shopping at an online store: Once the employee selects the item, the system generates the requisition, routes it electronically to the proper people for approval, and turns it into a purchase order.

2. CommerceOne's MarketSite transmits the purchase orders to the suppliers. This B2B Internet marketplace connects Schlumberger with hundreds of suppliers with a single, low-cost, many-to-many system.

Negotiation of prices is accomplished with individual vendors. For example, Office Depot's entire catalog is posted on the MarketSite, but the Schlumberger employees see only the subset of previously negotiated products and prices. (In the future, the company plans to negotiate prices in real time through auctions and other bidding systems.)

The benefits of the system are evident in both cost and processes. The cost of goods has been reduced, as have the transaction costs. Employees spend much less time in the ordering process, giving them more time for their true work. The system is also much more cost efficient for the suppliers, who can then pass along savings to customers. By using one system worldwide, Schlumberger saves time for employees who are transferred—they don't spend time learning a new system wherever they go. Procurement effectiveness can be increased because tracing the overall procurement activity is now possible.

Getting the system up and running was implemented in stages and ran at the same time as existing systems. There were no implementation issues for employees (once the system was in place, the old system was disabled), and there were no complaints in regard to the old system being shut down (no one was using the old system anymore).

Sources: Compiled from Ovans (2000) and *commerceone.com* (1999 and 2003).

For Further Exploration: What are the benefits of the e-procurement system to Schlumberger? How does it empower the buyers? Why would real-time price negotiations be beneficial?

Examples are Plasticsnet.com and Papersite.com. Both fixed and negotiated prices are common in this type of exchange

2. *Vertical exchanges for indirect materials.* Here indirect materials in one industry are purchased on an "as-needed" basis (called *spot sourcing*). Buyers and sellers may not even know each other. ChemConnect.com and Isteelasia.com are examples. In such vertical exchanges, prices are continually changing, based on the matching of supply and demand. Auctions are typically used in this kind of B2B marketplace, sometimes done in private trading rooms, that are available in exchanges like ChemConnect.com (see *IT at Work 5.4*).

3. *Horizontal distributors.* These are "many-to-many" e-marketplaces for indirect (MRO) materials, such as office supplies, used by any industry. Prices are fixed or negotiated in this systematic sourcing-type exchange. Examples are EcEurope.com, Globalsources.com, and Alibaba.com.

4. *Functional exchanges.* Here, needed services such as temporary help or extra space are traded on an "as-needed" basis (spot sourcing). For example,

IT at Work 5.4
CHEMICAL COMPANIES "BOND" AT CHEMCONNECT

Buyers and sellers of chemicals and plastics today can meet electronically in a large vertical exchange called ChemConnect (*chemconnect.com*). Using this exchange, *global* industry leaders such as British Petroleum, Dow Chemical, BASF, Hyundai, Sumitomo, and many more can reduce trading cycle time and cost and can find new markets and trading partners around the globe.

ChemConnect provides a public trading marketplace and an information portal to more than 9,000 members in 150 countries. In 2003, over 60,000 products were traded in this public, third-party-managed e-marketplace.

Chemconnect provides three marketplaces (as of April 21, 2003): a commodity markets platform, a marketplace for sellers, and a marketplace for buyers.

1. The commodity markets platform is a place where pre-qualified producers, customers, consumers, distributers, and others come together in real time to sell and buy chemical-related commodities like natural gas liquids, oxygenates, olefins, and polymers. They can even simultaneously execute multiple deals. Transactions are done through regional trading hubs.

2. The marketplace for sellers has many tools ranging from electronic catalogs to forward auctions. It enables companies to find buyers all over the world. ChemConnect provides all the necessary tools to expedite selling and achieve the best prices. It also allows for negotiations.

3. The marketplace for buyers is a place where thousands of buyers shop for chemical-related indirect materials (and a few direct materials). The market provides for automated *request for proposal* (RFP) tools as well as a complete online reverse auction. The sellers' market is connected to the buyers' market, so that sellers can connect to the RFPs posted on the marketplace for buyers. (Note that RFP and RFQ are interchangeable terms; RFP is used more in government bidding.)

For the three marketplaces, ChemConnect provides logistics and payment options as well as connectivity solutions (such as integration connection with ERPs). Also, market information is provided as well as a network of industry experts and contact with third-party service providers and other business partners.

In all of its trading mechanisms, up-to-the-minute market information is available and can be translated into 30 different languages. Members pay transaction fees only for successfully completed transactions. Business partners provide several support services, such as financial services for the market members. The marketplaces work with certain rules and guidelines that ensure an unbiased approach to the trades. There is full disclosure of all legal requirements, payments, trading rules, etc. (Click on "Legal info and privacy issues" at the ChemConnect Web site.) ChemConnect is growing rapidly, adding members and trading volume.

Source: Compiled from *chemconnect.com* (accessed April 11, 2003).

For Further Exploration: What are the advantages of the ChemConnect exchange? Why there are there three trading places? Why does the exchange provide information portal services?

Employease.com can find temporary labor using employers in its Employease Network. Prices are dynamic, and they vary depending on supply and demand.

All four types of exchanges offer diversified support services, ranging from payments to logistics. Vertical exchanges are frequently owned and managed by a group of big players in an industry (referred to as a *consortium*). For example, Marriott and Hyatt own a procurement consortium for the hotel industry, and ChevronTexaco owns an energy e-marketplace. The vertical e-marketplaces offer services exactly suited to the particular e-community they serve.

Since B2B activities involve many companies, specialized network infrastructure is needed. Such infrastructure works either as an Internet/EDI or as extranets (see Apendix 5A to this chapter). A related EC activity, usually done between and among organizations, is collaborative commerce (see Chapters 4 and 8).

5.6 INTRABUSINESS AND BUSINESS-TO-EMPLOYEES

E-commerce can be done not only between business partners, but also within organizations. Such activity is referred to as *intrabusiness* EC or in short, *intrabusiness*. Intrabusiness can be done between a business and its employees (B2E); among units within the business (usually done as c-commerce); and among employees in the same business.

Business-to-Its-Employees (B2E) Commerce

Companies are finding many ways to do business electronically with their own employees. They disseminate information to employees over the intranet, for example. They also allow employees to manage their fringe benefits and take training classes electronically. In addition, employees can buy discounted insurance, travel packages, and tickets to events on the corporate intranet, and they can electronically order supplies and material needed for their work. Also, many companies have electronic corporate stores that sell a company's products to its employees, usually at a discount. Of the many types of employees that benefit from B2E we have chosen to focus on sales people in the field. Note that in the literature on B2E commerce, B2E includes all things employees need for work, not just for communication, compensation, and benefits; so productivity software, such as sales force automation, is considered part of B2E.

SALES FORCE AUTOMATION. *Sales force automation (SFA)* is a technique of using software to automate the business tasks of sales, including order processing, contact management, information sharing, inventory monitoring and control, order tracking, customer management, sales forecast analysis, and employee performance evaluation. Of special interest in the context of B2E e-commerce is the support provided to employees when they are in the field. Recently, SFA become interrelated with CRM, since the salespeople constitute the contact point with customers. IT can empower salespeople and other customer-facing employees to make quick decisions, when they are in the customer's office. Advancement in wireless technologies is creating opportunities for providing salespeople with new capabilities, such as shown in the case of PAVECA Corp. in *IT at Work 5.5*. Many other companies, ranging from Maybelline (see Minicase in Chapter 2) to Kodak, have equipped their sales forces with similar mobile devices.

E-Commerce Between and Among Units Within the Business

Large corporations frequently consist of independent units, or *strategic business units (SBUs)*, which "sell" or "buy" materials, products, and services from each other. Transactions of this type can be easily automated and performed over an intranet. An SBU can be considered as either a seller or a buyer. An example would be company-owned dealerships, which buy goods from the main company. This type of EC helps in improving the internal supply chain operations.

E-Commerce Between and Among Corporate Employees

Many large organizations allow employees to post classified ads on the company intranet, through which employees can buy and sell products and services from each other. This service is especially popular in universities, where it has been conducted since even before the commercialization of the Internet. The Internet is used for other collaboration as well.

IT at Work 5.5
PAVECA OF VENEZUELA USES WIRELESS IN SALES FORCE AUTOMATION

PAVECA, Venezuela's largest paper goods manufacturer and exporter manufactures toilet paper, paper towels, tissues, and other paper products. The company enjoys a significant amount of market share, and seeking to maintain that, it chose to use some e-commerce technologies to cut operational costs and improve customer service at the same time.

PAVECA implemented a wireless system that allows its sales reps to use their wireless PDAs to connect to the Internet while they are in the field. Via the Internet connection, the salespeople can log directly into the company intranet to get all the information they need in real time. Orders can then be entered into the system in real time.

The system revolves around two pieces of software from iWork Software (*iworksoftware.com*): an automatic data collection system, and a workflow integration solution. The combination allows salespeople to automatically register sales transactions into the ERP system (Chapter 8) as they occur. Each salesperson has a PDA that connects them directly to the company's ERP system in real time. When an order is entered into the PDA, it goes into the ERP system and follows a predefined automated workflow. The savings produced by the new system as compared to the ERP/manual system were dramatic. For example, order processing time was reduced by 90 percent, order approval time by 86 percent, shipment time by 50 percent, and the time between orders taken and order posting was reduced from three days to 20 seconds. The faster order processing time not only led to faster order approval but also increased the number of daily shipments out of their warehouse.

While the main goal was to improve workflow, there's another potential benefit here: better customer service. Because of the direct links and integration, customers can get their orders faster, and there's less chance of errors occurring. Customers are happier and more loyal, and so indirectly, the company's profit increases because customers are more likely to place additional orders in the future. Finally, the transmitted data enter directly into the corporate DSS models, enabling quick decisions in reponse to the field reports filed by the salespeople.

Sources: Compiled from Paperloop Inc. (2002).

For Further Exploration: What are the benefits of PAVECA's new system? What segments of the supply chain are supported? What are the advantages of using wireless systems?

5.7 E-GOVERNMENT AND CONSUMER-TO-CONSUMER EC

E-Government

As e-commerce matures and its tools and applications improve, greater attention is being given to its use to improve the business of public institutions and governments (country, state, county, city, etc). **E-government** is the use of Internet technology in general and e-commerce in particular to deliver information and public services to citizens, business partners and suppliers, and those working in the public sector. It is also an efficient way of conducting business transactions with citizens and businesses and within the governments themselves.

E-government offers a number of potential benefits: It improves the efficiency and effectiveness of the functions of government, including the delivery of public services. It enables governments to be more transparent to citizens and businesses by giving access to more of the information generated by government. E-government also offers greater opportunities for citizens to provide feedback to government agencies and to participate in democratic institutions and processes. As a result, e-government may facilitate fundamental changes in the relationships between citizens and governments.

E-government applications can be divided into three major categories: *government-to-citizens (G2C)*, *government-to-business (G2B)*, and *government-to-government (G2G)*. In the first category, government agencies are increasingly using the

IT at Work 5.6
E-GOVERNMENT IN WESTERN AUSTRALIA

The focus of the Western Australian (WA) government agency Contract and Management Services (CAMS) is to develop online contract management solutions for the public sector. CAMS Online allows government agencies to search existing contracts to discover how to access the contracts that are in common use by different government agencies (for example, lightbulbs or paper towels bought by various government units). It also enables suppliers wanting to sell to the government to view the current tenders (bids) on the Western Australia Government Contracting Information Bulletin Board, and to download tender documents from that site.

CAMS Online also provides government departments and agencies with unbiased expert advice on e-commerce, Internet, and communication services, and how-to's on building a bridge between the technological needs of the public sector and the expertise of the private sector. The center also offers various types of support for government procurement activities.

WA's e-commerce activities include electronic markets for government buying. The *WA Government Electronic Market* provides online supplier catalogs, electronic purchase orders, and electronic invoicing, EFT, and check and credit card payments. The Victoria government and the New South

Wales government in Western Australia spent over $500 million (U.S.) on e-procurement systems under the Government Electronic Market System (*ecc.online.wa.gov.au/news.19*, September 2002).

Government-to-government e-commerce functions include *DataLink*, which enables the transfer of data using a secure and controlled environment. *DataLink* is an ideal solution for government agencies needing to exchange large volumes of operational information. Another G2G function is a videoconferencing service that offers two-way video and audio links, enabling government employees to meet together electronically from up to eight sites at any one time.

In addition to G2B functions, the G2G Web site also offers online training to citizens. A service called *Westlink* delivers adult training and educational programs to remote areas and schools, including rural and regional communities.

Source: business.wa.gov.au (February, 2001), *ecc.online.wa.gov.au/news* (June–November 2002).

For Further Exploration: How is contract management facilitated by e-commerce tools? Describe the WA online training program. Why would government want to take on a role in promoting e-learning?

Internet to provide various services to citizens. An example is **electronic benefits transfer (EBT),** in which governments (usually state or national) transfer benefits, such as Social Security and pension benefits, directly to recipients' bank accounts or to smart cards. Governments also are using the Internet to sell to or buy from businesses. For example, electronic tendering systems using reverse auctions are becoming mandatory, in order to ensure the best price for government procurement of goods and services. Chen (2003) presents several specific e-government initiatives. For an example of one initiative in Australia, see *IT at Work 5.6.*

IMPLEMENTING E-GOVERNMENT. Like any other organization, government entities want to move into the digital era, becoming click-and-mortar organizations. However, the transition from traditional delivery of government services to full implementation of online government services may be a lengthy process. The business consulting firm Deloitte and Touche conducted a study (see Wong, 2000) that identified six stages in the transition to e-government:

Stage 1: Information publishing/dissemination

Stage 2: "Official" two-way transactions, with one department at a time

Stage 3: Multipurpose portals

Stage 4: Portal personalization

Stage 5: Clustering of common services

Stage 6: Full integration and enterprise transformation

The speed at which a government moves from stage 1 to stage 6 varies, but usually the transition is very slow. Deloitte and Touche found that in 2000, most governments were still in stage 1 (Wong, 2000). The implementation issues that are involved in the transition to e-government depend on which of the six stages of development a government is in, on the plan for moving to higher stages, and on the available funding. In addition, governments are concerned about maintaining the security and privacy of citizens' data, so time and effort must be spent to ensure that security. According to *emarketer.com* (October 2, 2002), the number of U.S. government Web sites with *security policies* increased from 5 percent in 2000 to 34 percent in 2002; the percentage of those with *privacy policies* increased from 7 percent in 2000 to 43 percent in 2002.

In general, implementation of G2B is easier than implementation of G2C. In some countries, such as Hong Kong, G2B implementation is outsourced to a private company that pays all of the startup expenses in exchange for collecting future transaction fees. As G2B services have the potential for rapid cost savings, they can be a good way to begin an e-government EC initiative.

Consumer-to-Consumer E-Commerce

Consumer-to-consumer (C2C) (also sometimes called *customer-to-customer*) e-commerce refers to e-commerce in which both the buyer and the seller are individuals (not businesses). C2C is conducted in several ways on the Internet, where the best-known C2C activities are auctions.

C2C AUCTIONS. In dozens of countries, selling and buying on auction sites is exploding. Most auctions are conducted by intermediaries, like eBay.com. Consumers can select general sites such as *eBay.com* or *auctionanything.com*, and they can use specialized sites such as *buyit.com* or *bid2bid.com*. In addition, many individuals are conducting their own auctions. For example, *greatshop.com* provides software to create C2C reverse auction communities online.

CLASSIFIED ADS. People sell to other people every day through classified ads in newspapers and magazines. Internet-based classified ads have one big advantage over these more traditional types of classified ads: They offer a national, rather than a local, audience. This wider audience greatly increases the supply of goods and services available and the number of potential buyers. For example, *infospace.com/info.cls2k* contains a list of 3 million job openings and about 500,000 cars, compared with the much smaller numbers you might find locally. Another example is *recycler.com*. Often, placing an ad on one Web site brings it automatically into the classified sections of numerous partners. This increases ad exposure, at no cost. In addition, Internet-based classifieds often can be edited or changed easily, and in many cases they display photos of the product offered for sale.

Like their counterparts in printed media, classified ad Web sites accept no responsibility for the content of any advertisement. Advertisers are identified by e-mail address. A password is used to authenticate the advertiser for future changes in an ad. Most classified ads are provided for free.

The major categories of online classified ads are similar to those found in newspapers: vehicles, real estate, employment, general merchandise, collectibles, computers, pets, tickets, and travel. Classified ads are available through most Internet service providers (AOL, MSN, etc.), at some portals (Yahoo, etc.), and from Internet directories, online newspapers, and more. To help narrow the search for a particular item on several sites, shoppers can use search engines. Once users find an ad and get the details, they can e-mail or call the other party for additional information or to make a purchase. Classified sites generate revenue from affiliated sites.

PERSONAL SERVICES.   Numerous personal services are available on the Internet (lawyers, handy helpers, tax preparers, investment clubs, dating services). Some are in the classified ads, but others are listed in specialized Web sites and directories. Some are for free, some for a fee. *Be very careful before you purchase any personal services.* Fraud or crime could be involved. For example, a lawyer online may not be an expert in the area they profess, or may not deliver the service at all.

SUPPORT SERVICES TO C2C.   When individuals buy products or services from individuals, they usually buy from strangers. The issues of ensuring quality, receiving payments, and preventing fraud are critical to the success of C2C. One service that helps C2C is payments by companies such as Paypal.com (see Section 5.8). Another one is *escrow services,* intermediaries that take the buyer's money and the purchased goods, and only after making sure that the seller delivers what was agreed upon, deliver the goods to the buyer and the money to the seller (for a fee).

5.8   E-COMMERCE SUPPORT SERVICES

The implementation of EC may require several support services. B2B and B2C applications require payments and order fulfillment. Portals require content, and so on. Figure 5.4 portrays the collection of the major EC services. They include: e-infrastructure (mostly technology consultants, system developers and integrators, hosting, security, and networks), e-process (mainly payments and logistics), e-markets (mostly marketing and advertising), e-communities (different audiences and business partners), e-services (CRM, PRM, and directory services), and e-content (supplied by content providers). All of these services support the EC applications in the center of the figure, and all of the services need to be managed.

Here we will discuss only two of the above topics—payments and order fulfillment. For details on the other services, see Turban et al. (2004).

Electronic Payments   Payments are an integral part of doing business, whether in the traditional way or online. Unfortunately, in most cases traditional payment systems are not effective for EC, especially for B2B.

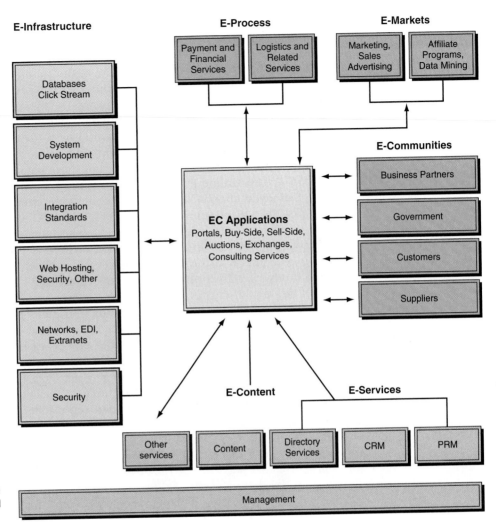

FIGURE 5.4 E-commerce services. (*Sources:* Modified from Choi, 1997, p. 18.)

LIMITATIONS OF TRADITIONAL PAYMENT INSTRUMENTS. Nonelectronic payment methods such as using cash, writing a check, sending a money order, or giving your credit card number over the telephone have several limitations in EC. First, cash cannot be used because there is no face-to-face contact. Second, if payment is sent by mail, it takes time for it to be received. Even if a credit card number is provided by phone or fax, it takes time to process it. Nor is it convenient to have to switch from the computer to the phone to complete a transaction, especially if the same telephone line is used. Also, not everyone accepts credit cards or checks, and some buyers do not have credit cards or checking accounts. Finally, contrary to what many people believe, it may be less secure for the buyer to use the telephone or mail to arrange or send payment, especially from another country, than to complete a secured transaction on a computer.

Another issue is that many EC transactions are valued at only a few dollars or even cents. The cost of processing such **micropayments** needs to be very low; you would not want to pay $5 to process a purchase valued at only a few dollars. The cost of making micropayments offline is just too high.

For all of these reasons, a better way is needed to pay for goods and services in cyberspace. This better way is *electronic payment systems*.

ELECTRONIC PAYMENT SYSTEMS. As in the traditional marketplace, so too in cyberspace, diversity of payment methods allows customers to choose how they wish to pay. The following instruments are acceptable means of electronic payment: electronic checks, electronic credit cards, purchasing cards, electronic cash, stored-value cards, smart cards, and person-to-person payments. In addition we discuss electronic bill presentment and/or payment, both online and from ATMs. Here we will look at each of these payment mechanisms. In Chapter 15 and in Online File W5.6 we consider how to make them secure.

Electronic checks. **Electronic checks (e-checks)** are similar to regular checks. They are used mostly in B2B (see Reda, 2002). Here is how they work: First, the customer establishes a checking account with a bank. Next, the customer contacts a seller, buys a product or a service, and e-mails an encrypted electronic check to the seller. The seller deposits the check in a bank account, and funds are transferred from the buyer's account and into the seller's account.

Like regular checks, e-checks carry a signature (in digital form) that can be verified (see *echeck.net*). Properly signed and endorsed e-checks are exchanged between financial institutions through electronic clearinghouses (see Eccho, 2002, and *eccho.org* for details). For the process of how e-checks work as done by eCheck Secure (*echecksecure.com*), see Figure 5.5.

Electronic credit cards. *Electronic credit cards* make it possible to charge online payments to one's credit card account. It is easy and simple for a buyer to e-mail his or her credit card number to the seller. The risk here is that if the

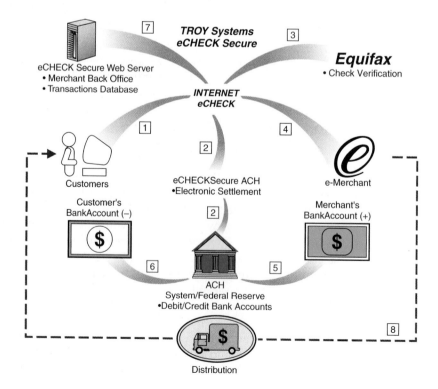

FIGURE 5.5 eSecure check.

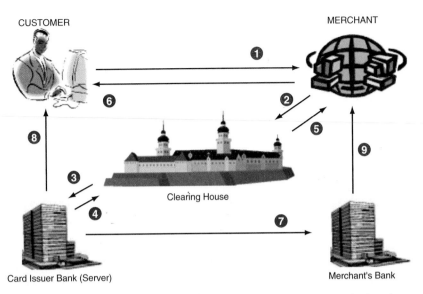

CUSTOMER

MERCHANT

Clearing House

Card Issuer Bank (Server)

Merchant's Bank

1 Customer places order (encrypting credit card number). **2** Merchant's server contacts clearing house's server for authorization. **3** Clearing house checks balance with card issuer; card issuer debits customer and **4** sends an answer to clearing house. **5** Merchant gets credit notice. **6** Customer is notified (yes or no). **7** Money is transferred to merchant's bank. **8** Customer gets debit notice in monthly statement. **9** Merchant gets a credit in monthly statement.

FIGURE 5.6 How e-credit cards work.

card number is not encrypted, then hackers will be able to read it and may use it illegally. Sender authentication is also difficult. (New technologies will solve this problem in 2 to 3 years, however.) Therefore, for security, only encrypted credit cards should be used. (Credit card details can be encrypted by using the SSL protocol in the buyer's computer, which is available in standard browsers. This process is described in Online File W5.6.)

Here is how electronic credit cards works: When you buy a book from Amazon, your credit card information and purchase amount are encrypted in your browser. So the information is safe while "travelling" on the Internet. Furthermore, when this information arrives at Amazon, it is not opened but is transferred automatically (in encrypted form) to a clearinghouse, where the information is decrypted for verification and for money transfer from the payer's account to the payee's bank account. The process is illustrated in Figure 5.6. Electronic credit cards are used mainly in B2C and in shopping by SMEs (small to medium enterprises).

Purchasing Cards. The B2B equivalent of electronic credit cards is *purchasing cards*. In some countries companies pay other companies primarily by means of purchasing cards, rather than by traditional checks. Unlike credit cards, where credit is provided for 30 to 60 days (for free) before payment is made to the merchant, payments made with purchasing cards are settled within a week.

Purchasing cards typically are used for unplanned B2B purchases, and corporations generally limit the amount per purchase (usually $1,000 to $2,000). Purchasing cards can be used on the Internet much like regular credit cards. They expedite the process of unplanned purchases, usually as part of *desktop purchasing* described earlier. (For details see Segev and Gebauer, 2001.)

Electronic Cash. Cash is the most prevalent consumer payment instrument. Traditional brick-and-mortar merchants prefer cash since they do not have to pay commissions to credit card companies, and they can put the money to use as soon as it is received. Also, some buyers pay with cash because they do not have checks or credit cards, or because they want to preserve their anonymity. It is logical, therefore, that EC sellers and some buyers may prefer electronic cash. **Electronic cash (e-cash)** appears in three major forms: stored-value cards, smart cards, and person-to-person payments.

Stored-Value Money Cards. A typical e-payment card is known as a **stored-value money card.** It is the one that you use to pay for photocopies in your library, for transportation, or for telephone calls. It allows a fixed amount of prepaid money to be stored on it. Each time you use the card, the amount is reduced. One successful example is used by the New York Metropolitan Transportation Authority (MTA), described in Chapter 1. Similar cards are used in many cities around the world. Some of these cards are reloadable, and some are discarded when the money is depleted. The transportation card Octopus in Hong Kong is used in trains, buses, and shopping in stores and from vending machines (for details see Poon and Chan, 2001).

Cards with stored-value money can be also purchased for Internet use. To use such cards, you enter a third-party Web site and provide an ID number and a password, much as you do when you use a prepaid phone card. The money can be used only in participating stores online.

Smart Cards. Although some people refer to stored-value money cards as smart cards, they are not really the same. True **smart cards** contain a microprocessor (chip), which enables them to store a considerable amount of information (more than 100 times that of a stored-value card) and conduct processing. Such cards are frequently *multipurpose;* they can be used as a credit card, debit card, or stored-value card. In addition, when used in department store chains (as a *loyalty card*), they may contain the purchasing information of shoppers.

Advanced smart cards have the ability to transfer funds, pay bills, buy from vending machines, or pay for services such as those offered on television or PCs (see Shelter and Procaccino, 2002). Money values can be loaded onto advanced smart cards at ATMs, kiosks, or from your PC. For example, the VISA Cash Card allows you to buy goods or services at participating gas stations, fast-food outlets, pay phones, discount stores, post offices, convenience stores, coffee shops, and even movie theaters. Smart cards are ideal for micropayments.

Smart cards can also be used to transfer benefits from companies to their employees, as when retirees get their pension payments, and from governments that pay citizens various entitlements. The money is transferred electronically to a smart card at an ATM, kiosk, or PC.

Person-to-Person Payments. **Person-to-person payments** are one of the newest and fastest-growing payment schemes. They enable the transfer of funds between two individuals, or between an individual and a business, for a variety of purposes like repaying money borrowed from a friend, sending money to students at college, paying for an item purchased at an online auction, or sending a gift to a family member.

One of the first companies to offer this service was PayPal (*paypal.com*). PayPal (now an eBay company) claimed (on its Web site, accessed January 6, 2003) to have had about 20 million customer accounts in 2003, handling more than 35 percent of all transactions of eBay and funneling $8.5 billion in payments through its servers annually. Other companies offer similar services;

Citibank c2it (*c2it.com*), AOL QuickCash, One's Bank eMoneyMail, Yahoo Pay-Direct, and WebCertificate (*webcertificate.com*) are all PayPal competitors.

Virtually all of these person-to-person payment services work in a similar way. Assume you want to send money to someone over the Internet. First, you select a service and open up an account. Basically, this entails creating a user name, selecting a password, giving your e-mail address, and providing the service with a credit card or bank account number. Next, you add funds from your credit card or bank account to your account. Once the account has been funded you're ready to send money. You access PayPal (for example) with your user name and password. Now you specify the e-mail address of the person to receive the money, along with the dollar amount that you want to send. An e-mail is sent to the payee's e-mail address. The e-mail will contain a link back to the service's Web site. When the recipient clicks on the link, he or she will be taken to the service. The recipient will be asked to set up an account to which the money that was sent will be credited. The recipient can then credit the money from this account to his or her credit card or bank account. The payer pays a small amount (around $1) per transaction.

Electronic Bill Presentment and Payments. An increasing number of people prefer to pay online their recurring monthly bills, such as telephone, utilities, credit cards, and cable TV. The recipients of such payments are even more enthusiastic about such service than the payers, since online payments enable them to reduce processing costs significantly. The following are the major existing payment systems in common use: automatic payment of mortgages; automatic transfer of funds to pay monthly utility bills; paying bills from an online banking account; merchant-to-customer direct billing; and use of an intermediary to aggregate bills into one payable Web site.

Paying Bills at ATMs. In some countries (e.g., Hong Kong, Singapore) customers can pay bills at regular ATMs. The bills are sent by regular mail or can be viewed online. When you receive the bills, you go to an ATM, slide in your bank card, enter a password and go to "bill payments" on the menu. All you need to do is insert the account number of the biller and the amount you want to pay; that amount will be charged to your bank card and sent to the biller. You get a printed receipt on the spot. In addition to utilities you can pay for purchases of products and services (e.g., for airline tickets). Merchants love it and many give a discount to those who use the service, since they do not have to pay 3 percent to Visa or MasterCard.

SECURITY IN ELECTRONIC PAYMENTS. Two main issues need to be considered under the topic of payment security: what is required in order to make EC payments safe, and the methods that can be used to do so.

Security Requirements. Security requirements for conducting EC are the following:

1. ***Authentication.*** The buyer, the seller, and the paying institutions must be assured of the identity of the parties with whom they are dealing.
2. ***Integrity.*** It is necessary to ensure that data and information transmitted in EC, such as orders, reply to queries, and payment authorization, are not accidentally or maliciously altered or destroyed during transmission.

3. *Nonrepudiation.* Merchants need protection against the customer's unjustified denial of placing an order. On the other hand, customers need protection against merchants' unjustified denial of payments made. Such denials, of both types, are called *repudiation*.

4. *Privacy.* Many customers want their identity to be secured. They want to make sure others do not know what they buy. Some prefer complete anonymity, as is possible with cash payments.

5. *Safety.* Customers want to be sure that it is safe to provide a credit card number on the Internet. They also want protection against fraud by sellers or by criminals posing as sellers.

Security Protection. Several methods and mechanisms can be used to fulfill the above requirements. One of the primary mechanisms is encryption, which is often part of the most useful security schemes. For a coverage of security protection see Online File W5.6 and Chapter 15. Other representative methods are discussed below.

E-Wallets. **E-wallets** (or **digital wallets**) are mechanisms that provide security measures to EC purchasing. The wallet stores the financial information of the buyer, including credit card number, shipping information, and more. Thus, sensitive information does not need to travel on the Net, and the buyer and seller save time. E-wallets can contain digital certificates (see Online File W5.6), e-loyalty information, and so on. As soon as you place an order, say at Amazon.com, your e-wallet at Amazon is opened, and Amazon can process your order.

The problem is that you need an e-wallet with each merchant. One solution is to have a wallet installed on your computer (e.g., MasterCard Wallet). In that case, though, you cannot make a purchase from another computer, nor is it a totally secured system. Another solution is a *universal* e-wallet such as Microsoft's Passport (Rosenbaum, 2002) and the Liberty Alliance (Costa, 2002). Universal systems are becoming popular since they provide a *digital identity* as well. For a description of how Microsoft's Passport works, see Rosenbaum (2002). At our Web site, in Online File W5.7, you can see how Liberty Alliance works.

Virtual Credit Cards. *Virtual credit cards* are a service that allow you to shop with an ID number and a password instead of with a credit card number. They are used primarily by people who do not trust browser encryption sufficiently to use their credit card numbers on the Internet. The virtual credit card gives an extra layer of security. The bank that supports your traditional credit card, for example, can provide you with a transaction number valid for use online for a short period. For example, if you want to make a $200 purchase, you would contact your credit card company to charge that amount to your regular credit card account, and would be given a transaction number that is good for charges up to $200. This transaction number is encrypted for security, but even in the worst possible case (where some unauthorized entity obtained the transaction number), your loss would be limited, in this case to $200. For another example of virtual credit cards, see *americanexpress.com*.

Payment Using Fingerprints. An increasing number of supermarkets allow their regular customers to pay by merely using their fingerprint for identification. A computer template of your fingerprint is kept in the store's computer system. Each time you shop, your fingerprint is matched with the template at the payment counter. You approve the amount, which is then charged either to your credit card or bank account. See Alga (2000) for details.

Order Fulfillment

We now turn our attention to another important EC support service—**order fulfillment.** Any time a company sells direct to customers it is involved in various order fulfillment activities. It must: quickly find the products to be shipped, and pack them; arrange for the packages to be delivered speedily to the customer's door; collect the money from every customer, either in advance, by COD, or by individual bill; and handle the return of unwanted or defective products.

It is very difficult to accomplish these activities both effectively and efficiently in B2C, since a company may need to ship small packages to many customers, and do it quickly. For this reason, both online companies and click-and-mortar companies have difficulties in their B2C supply chain. Here, we provide only a brief overview; a more detailed discussion is provided in Turban et al. (2004) and in Bayles (2001).

Order fulfillment includes not only providing customers with what they ordered and doing it on time, but also providing all related customer service. For example, the customer must receive assembly and operation instructions to a new appliance. (A nice example is available at *livemanuals.com*.) In addition, if the customer is not happy with a product, an exchange or return must be arranged. (See *fedex.com* for how returns are handled via FedEx.) Order fulfillment is basically a part of a company's back-office operations.

During the last few years, e-tailers have faced continuous problems in order fulfillment, especially during the holiday season. The problems resulted in inability to deliver on time, delivery of wrong items, high delivery costs, and the need to heavily compensate unhappy customers. Several factors can be responsible for delays in deliveries. They range from inability to forecast demand accurately to ineffective supply chains. Some such problems exist also in offline businesses. One factor that is typical of EC, though, is that it is based on the concept of "pull" operations, which begin with an order, frequently a customized one. This is in contrast with traditional retailing that begins with a production to inventory, which is then "pushed" to customers (see Appendix 2A on build-to-order). In the pull case it is more difficult to forecast demand, due to unique demands of customized orders and lack of sufficient years of experience.

For many e-tailers, taking orders over the Internet could well be the easy part of B2C e-commerce. Fulfillment to customers' doors is the sticky part. Fulfillment is less complicated in B2B where several effective methods are in use (see Bayles, 2001). For more on order fulfillment and IT-supported solutions, see Chapter 8.

5.9 LEGAL AND ETHICAL ISSUES IN E-BUSINESS

Ethical standards and their incorporation into law frequently trail technological innovation. E-commerce is taking new forms and enabling new business practices that may bring numerous risks—particularly for individual consumers—along with their advantages. Before we present some specific issues, we discuss the topic of market practices and consumer/seller protections.

Market Practices and Consumer and Seller Protection

When buyers and sellers do not know each other and cannot even see each other (they may even be in different countries), there is a chance that dishonest people will commit fraud and other crimes over the Internet. During the first few years of EC, the public witnessed many of these, ranging from the creation of a virtual bank that disappeared along with the investors' deposits, to manipulation of stock prices on the Internet. Unfortunately, fraudulent activities on the Internet are increasing.

FRAUD ON THE INTERNET. Internet fraud and its sophistication have grown as much as, and even faster than, the Internet itself. In most of these stock-fraud cases, stock promoters falsely spread positive rumors about the prospects of the companies they touted, to boost the price. In other cases the information provided might have been true, but the promoters did not disclose that they were paid to talk up the companies. Stock promoters specifically target small investors who are lured by the promise of fast profits.

Stocks are only one of many areas where swindlers are active. Auctions are especially conducive to fraud, by both sellers and buyers. Other areas of potential fraud include selling bogus investments and phantom business opportunities. Financial criminals now have access to far more people, mainly due to the availability of electronic mail. The U.S. Federal Trade Commission (*ftc.gov*) regularly publishes examples of 12 scams most likely to arrive via e-mail or be found on the Web.

There are several ways buyers can be protected against EC fraud. Representative methods are described next.

BUYER PROTECTION. Buyer protection is critical to the success of any commerce where buyers do not see the sellers, and this is especially true for e-commerce. Some tips for safe electronic shopping are shown in Table 5.5. In short, do not forget that you have shopper's rights. Consult your local or state consumer protection agency for general information on your consumer rights.

TABLE 5.5 Tips for Safe Electronic Shopping

- Look for reliable brand names at sites like Wal-Mart Online, Disney Online, and Amazon.com. Before purchasing, make sure that the site is authentic by entering the site directly and not from an unverified link.
- Search any unfamiliar selling site for the company's address and phone and fax numbers. Call up and quiz the employees about the sellers.
- Check out the vendor with the local Chamber of Commerce or Better Business Bureau (*bbbonline.org*). Look for seals of authenticity such as TRUSTe.
- Investigate how secure the seller's site is by examining the security procedures and by reading the posted privacy notice.
- Examine the money-back guarantees, warranties, and service agreements.
- Compare prices to those in regular stores. Too-low prices are too good to be true, and some "catch" is probably involved.
- Ask friends what they know. Find testimonials and endorsements in community sites and well-known bulletin boards.
- Find out what your rights are in case of a dispute.
- Consult the National Fraud Information Center (*fraud.org*).
- Check *consumerworld.org* for a listing of useful resources.

SELLER PROTECTION. Sellers, too, may need protections. They must be protected against consumers who refuse to pay or who pay with bad checks, and from buyers' claims that the merchandise did not arrive. They also have the right to protect against the use of their name by others, as well as to protect the use of their unique words and phrases, slogans, and Web address (trademark protection). Another seller protection applies particularly to electronic media: Sellers have legal recourse against customers who download without permission copyrighted software and/or knowledge and use it or sell it to others.

Ethical Issues

Many of the ethical and global issues related to IT apply also to e-commerce. These are discussed in Appendix 1A, in Chapter 16 online, and in the Ethics Primer at our Web site. Here we touch on issues particularly related to e-commerce.

PRIVACY. Most electronic payment systems know who the buyers are; therefore, it may be necessary to protect the buyers' identities. Another privacy issue may involve tracking of Internet user activities by intelligent agents and "cookies" (a string of characters stored on the user's hard drive to record the history of the user's visits to particular Web sites). A privacy issue related to employees also involves tracking: Many companies monitor employees' e-mail and have installed software that performs in-house monitoring of Web activities. Yet many employees don't want to feel like they are under the watchful eye of "Big Brother," even while at work.

WEB TRACKING. By using tracking software, companies can track individuals' movements on the Internet. Programs such as "cookies" raise a batch of privacy concerns. The tracking history is stored on your PC's hard drive, and any time you revisit a certain Web site, the computer knows it (see NetTracker at *sane.com*). Programs such as Cookie Cutter, Cookie Crusher, and Spam Butcher are designed to allow users to have some control over cookies. (For further discussion see Chapter 16 and Alwang, 2001).

DISINTERMEDIATION. The use of EC may result in the elimination of some of a company's employees as well as brokers and agents. This result is called *disintermediation*—that is, eliminating the intermediary. The manner in which these unneeded workers, especially employees, are treated may raise ethical issues, such as how to handle the displacement.

Legal Issues Specific to E-Commerce

Many legal issues are related to e-commerce (Cheeseman, 2001, Doll et al., 2003, and Isenberg, 2002). Representative examples are discussed below.

DOMAIN NAMES. Internet addresses are known as **domain names.** Domain names appear in levels. A top-level name is *wiley.com* or *stanford.edu*. A second-level name will be *wiley.com/turban* or *ibm.com.hk* (for IBM in Hong Kong). Top-level domain names are assigned by central nonprofit organizations that check for conflicts and possible infringement of trademarks. Obviously, companies who sell goods and services over the Internet want customers to be able to find them easily, so it is best when the URL matches the company's name.

Problems arise when several companies that have similar names compete over a domain name. For example, if you want to book reservations at a Holiday Inn hotel and you go to *holidayinn.com*, you get the Web site for a hotel at Niagara

Falls, New York. In order to get to the hotel chain's Web site, you have to go to *holiday-inn.com*. Several cases of disputed names are already in court. An international arbitration organization is available as an alternative to the courts. The problem of domain names was alleviated somewhat in 2001 after several upper-level names were added to "com" (such as "info" and "coop").

Cybersquatting. **Cybersquatting** refers to the practice of registering domain names in order to sell them later at a higher price. For example, the original owner of *tom.com* received about $8 million for the name. The case of *tom.com* was ethical and legal. But in other cases, cybersquatting can be illegal or at least unethical (e.g., see Stead and Gilbert, 2001). Companies such as Christian Dior, Nike, Deutsche Bank, and even Microsoft have had to fight or pay to get the domain name that corresponds to their company's name. The Anticybersquatting Consumer Protection Act (1999) lets trademark owners in the United States sue for statutory damages.

DISINTERMEDIATION AND REINTERMEDIATION. One of the most interesting EC issues is that of *intermediation*. Intermediaries provide two types of services: (1) matching and providing information and (2) value-added services such as consulting. As seen in the Rosenbluth case (at the beginning of Chapter 3), the first type of services (matching and providing information) can be fully automated, and therefore, these services are likely to be assumed by e-marketplaces and portals that provide free services. The second type of services (value-added services) requires expertise, and these can be only partially automated. Rosenbluth decided to charge only for the second type of service. Intermediaries who provide only (or mainly) the first type of service may be eliminated, a phenomenon called **disintermediation.** On the other hand, brokers who provide the second type of service or who manage electronic intermediation, also known as *infomediation,* are not only surviving, but may actually prosper, as Rosenbluth did. This phenomenon is called **reintermediation.**

The Web offers new opportunities for reintermediation. First, brokers are especially valuable when the number of participants is enormous, as with the stock market or when complex information products are exchanged. Second, many brokering services require information processing; electronic versions of these services can offer more sophisticated features at a lower cost than is possible with human labor. Finally, for delicate negotiations, a computer mediator may be more predictable, and hence more trustworthy, than a human. For example, suppose a mediator's role is to inform a buyer and a seller whether a deal can be made, without revealing either side's initial price to the other, since such a revelation would influence subsequent price negotiations. An independent auditor can verify that a software-based mediator will reveal only the information it is supposed to; a human mediator's fairness is less easily verified. The subject of reintermediation and intermediation is further discussed in Chapters 7 and 16.

TAXES AND OTHER FEES. Federal, state, and local authorities are scrambling to figure out how to get a piece of the revenue created electronically. The problem is particularly complex for interstate and international commerce. For example, some claim that even the state in which a *server* is located deserves to receive some sales tax from an e-commerce transaction. Others say that the state in which the *seller* is located deserves the entire sales tax (or value-added tax, VAT, in some countries).

In addition to sales tax, there is a question about where (and in some cases, whether) electronic sellers should pay business license tax, franchise fees, gross-receipts tax, excise tax, privilege tax, and utility tax. Furthermore, how should tax collection be controlled? Legislative efforts to impose taxes on e-commerce are opposed by an organization named the Internet Freedom Fighters. Their efforts have been successful so far: At the time this edition was written, there was a ban on taxing business done on the Internet in the United States and many other countries (sales tax only), which could remain valid until fall 2006.

COPYRIGHT. Intellectual property, in its various forms, is protected by copyright laws and cannot be used freely. Copyright issues and protection of intellectual property are discussed in Chapter 16.

5.10 FAILURES AND STRATEGIES FOR SUCCESS

In the concluding section of this chapter we pay attention to EC failures and successes.

E-Commerce Failures

In this and other chapters of the book we presented dozens of examples that illustrate the success of the new economy and EC. Yet, failures of EC initiatives are fairly common. Furthermore, during 2000–2002, large numbers of dot-com companies failed. In this section we will look at some examples of failures and their causes. We will also look into some success factors that can be used to prevent failure.

PRE-INTERNET FAILURES. Failures of e-commerce systems should not seem surprising, since we have known about failures of EDI systems for more than 10 years. A typical example involved the attempt of the U.S. Food and Drug Administration (FDA) to install an online collaboration system to reduce drug-review time (Williams et al., 1997). It was basically an electronic submission system and then an intranet-based internal distribution and review system. The system failed for various reasons. We present them in list form below; many of these reasons are typical of the reasons for EC failures in general, so we have highlighted the key words, for your future reference.

- *No standards* were established for submitted documents.
- There was *resistance to change* to the new system, and the FDA did not force reviewers to work electronically.
- The system was merely an electronic version of existing documents. *No business process reengineering (BPR)* was undertaken in planning (or improving) the new sysetm.
- The FDA *lacked technical expertise* in interorganizational information sysetms and in collaborative commerce.
- *No training* or even information was provided to the FDA's end users.
- There were *learning curve difficulites,* and no time was allotted to learn different document systems.
- Clients (the pharmaceutical companies) *were not encouraged* to make electronic submissions.
- There was *no IS planning*. The FDA knew that a business process design study was needed, but did not do it.

However, the FDA learned from its mistakes. An improved EDI-based system was installed in 1998/1999—after a BPR was done, training was completed, and standards were provided. The system became a full success in 1999.

INTERNET-RELATED EC FAILURES. Failures of e-commerce initiatives started as early as 1996. Early on, pioneering organizations saw the potential for EC, but expertise and EC business models were just developing. However, the major wave of failures started in 2000, as secondary funding that was needed by Internet-based EC began to dry up. Here are some examples (again, with key words highlighted).

- PointCast, a pioneer in personalized Web-casting, folded in 1998 due to an *incorrect business model.* Similarly, Dr. Koop, a medical portal, was unable to raise the needed advertising money, so the company folded. The diagnosis: death due to *incorrect business model.*

- An Internet mall, operated by Open Market, was closed in 1996 due to *an insufficient number of buyers.*

- Several toy companies—Red Rocket (a Viacom Company), eparties.com, and babybucks.com—failed due to *too much competition, low prices,* and lack of cash. Even E-toys, a virtual toy retailer that affected the entire toy industry, folded in 2001 due to its inability to generate profits and the need for additional funding for expanding its logistics infrastructure. It was sold to kbkids.com.

- Garden.com closed its doors in December 2000 due to *lack of cash.* Suppliers of venture capital were unwilling to give the company any more money to "burn."

- Living.com, the online furniture store, closed in 2000. The *customer acquisition cost* was too high.

- PaperX.com, an online paper exchange in the U.K., folded due to *lack of second-round funding* (funding subsequent to a firm's original funding but before it goes to the stock market with a stock offering).

- Webvan, an online grocery and same-day delivery company, invested over $1 billion in infrastructure of warehouses and logistics. But its *income was insufficient* to convince investors to fund it further. It collapsed in 2002. Kozmo, another same-day delivery company in New York, Boston, and other large cities was unable to show sufficient profit and collapsed in 2001.

- In late 2000 Chemdex.com, the "granddaddy" of the third-party exchanges, closed down. Ventro.com, its parent company, said that the *revenue growth* was too slow and that a *new business model* was needed. Because of the difficulty in obtaining enough buyers and sellers fast enough (before the cash disappears), some predicted that as many as 90 percent of all 1998–2001 exchanges would collapse (Ulph, Favier, and O'Connell, 2001). And indeed, during 2001–2003 large numbers of exchanges folded or changed their business models.

Even Amazon.com, considered by many as one of the most successful e-commerce sites, did not reach profitability until the end of 2001.

The major lessons of the Internet-based EC failures were summarized by Useem (2000) in his "12 truths" and by Agrawal et al. (2001). The major reasons for failure are incorrect revenue model, lack of strategy and contingency planning, inability to attract enough customers, lack of funding, channel conflict with distributors, too much online competition in standard (commodity) products (e.g., CDs, toys), poor order fulfillment infrastructure, and lack of qualified management.

To learn more about EC failures, visit *whytheyfailed.com* and *techdirt.com*. Also, see Kaplan (2002).

FAILED EC INITIATIVES. Whereas failing companies, especially publicly listed ones, are well advertised, failing EC initiatives within companies, especially within private companies, are less known. However, news about some failed EC initiatives has reached the media and been well advertised. For example, Levi Strauss stopped online direct sales of its apparel (jeans and its popular Dockers brand) on its Web site (*levistrauss.com*) after its major distributors and retailers put pressure on the company not to compete with their brick-and-mortar outlets (*channel conflict*). Another EC initiative that failed was a joint venture between Intel and SAP, two world-class companies, which was designed to develop low-cost solutions for SMEs. It collapsed in August 2000. Large companies such as Citicorp, Disney, and Merril Lynch also closed EC initiatives after losing millions of dollars in them.

Success Stories and Lessons Learned

There are hundreds of EC success stories, primarily in specialty and niche markets (see Athitakis, 2003). One example is Puritan.com, a successful vitamin and natural health care product store. Another one is Campusfood.com, which serves takeout food to college students. Monster.com is doing very well, and so is Southwest Airlines Online (*iflyswa.com*). Alloy.com is a successful shopping and entertainment portal for young adults.

Here are some of the reasons for EC success and some suggestions from EC experts on how to succeed:

- Thousands of brick-and mortar companies are slowly adding online channels with great success. Examples are Uniglobe.com, Staples.com, Homedepot.com, Clearcommerce.com, 1-800-FLOWERS (*800flowers.com*), and Southwest Airlines (*iflyswa.com*).

- As of late 2000, more companies were pursuing mergers and acquisitions (e.g., Ivillage.com with Women.com, though each maintains its separate Web site). Mergers seem to be a growing trend (see Bodow, 2000).

- Peter Drucker, the management guru, provides the following advice: "Analyze the opportunities, go out to look, keep it focused, start small (one thing at a time), and aim at market leadership" (quoted in Daly, 2000).

- A group of Asian CEOs recommend the following factors that are critical for success: select robust business models, understand the dot-com future, foster e-innovation, carefully evaluate a spinoff strategy, co-brand, employ ex-dot-com staffers, and focus on the e-generation as your market (e.g., *alloy.com* and *bolt.com*) (Phillips, 2000).

- Consultant PricewaterhouseCoopers (*pwcglobal.com*) suggests avoiding technology malfunctions (e.g., inability to handle a surge of orders quickly enough), which erode consumer trust.

- Many experts (e.g., The National Institute for Standards and Technology, NIST) recommend contingency planning and preparing for disasters (as reported by Buchholz, 2002).

- Agrawal et al. (2001) suggest that companies should match a value proposition with customer segmentation, control extensions of product lines and business models, and avoid expensive technology.

● Huff et al. (1999) suggest the following critical success factors for e-commerce: add value, focus on a niche and then extend that niche, maintain flexibility, get the technology right, manage critical perceptions, provide excellent customer service, create effective connectedness, and understand Internet culture.

Conclusion Analyzing successful companies, researchers have suggested that if they do careful planning to reach profitability quickly, many click-and-mortar companies are likely to succeed. Joint ventures and partnerships are very valuable, and planning for satisfactory infrastructure and logistics to meet high demand is needed. In short, do not forget that e-business has a "business" side!

Finally, let's not forget that history repeats itself. When the automobile was invented, there were 240 startup companies between 1904 and 1908. In 1910 there was a shakeout, and today there are only three U.S. automakers. However, the auto industry has grown by hundredfolds. The same is happening in EC: Despite the 2000–2003 failures, the total volume of EC activities continued to grow exponentially. For example, *emarketer.com* reported on May 19, 2003 that B2C revenues in 2002 reached $76 billion, a 48 percent increase over 2001. The estimate for 2003 is $96 billion—more than a 30 percent increase over 2002 (reported by Biz Report, 2003).

➡ MANAGERIAL ISSUES

1. *Managing resistance to change.* Electronic commerce can result in a fundamental change in how business is done, and resistance to change from employees, vendors, and customers may develop. Education, training, and publicity over an extended time period offer possible solutions to the problem.

2. *Integration of e-commerce into the business environment.* E-commerce needs to be integrated with the rest of the business. Integration issues involve planning, competition for corporate resources with other projects, and interfacing EC with databases, existing IT applications, and infrastructure.

3. *Lack of qualified personnel and outsourcing.* Very few people have expertise in e-commerce. There are many implementation issues that require expertise, such as when to offer special promotions on the Internet, how to integrate an e-market with the information systems of buyers and sellers, and what kind of customer incentives are appropriate under what circumstances. For this reason, it may be worthwhile to outsource some e-commerce activities. Yet, as shown in Chapter 13, outsourcing decisions are not simple.

4. *Alliances.* It is not a bad idea to join an alliance or consortium of companies to explore e-commerce. Alliances can be created at any time. Some EC companies (e.g., Amazon.com) have thousands of alliances. The problem is which alliance to join, or what kind of alliance to form and with whom.

5. *Implementation plan.* Because of the complexity and multifaceted nature of EC, it makes sense to prepare an implementation plan. Such a plan should include goals, budgets, timetables, and contingency plans. It should address the many legal, financial, technological, organizational, and ethical issues that can surface during implementation.

6. *Choosing the company's strategy toward e-commerce.* Generally speaking there are three major options: (1) *Lead:* Conduct large-scale innovative e-commerce activities. (2) *Watch and wait:* Do nothing, but carefully watch

what is going on in the field in order to determine when EC is mature enough to enter it. (3) *Experiment:* Start some e-commerce experimental projects (learn by doing). Each of these options has its advantages and risks.

7. *Privacy.* In electronic payment systems, it may be necessary to protect the identity of buyers. Other privacy issues may involve tracking of Internet user activities by intelligent agents and cookies, and in-house monitoring of employees' Web activities.

8. *Justifying e-commerce by conducting a cost-benefit analysis is very difficult.* Many intangible benefits and lack of experience may produce grossly inaccurate estimates of costs and benefits. Nevertheless, a feasibility study must be done, and estimates of costs and benefits must be made. For example, see the proposal for assessing EDI investment presented by Hoogewelgen and Wagenaar (1996).

9. *Order fulfillment.* Taking orders in EC may be easier than fulfilling them. To learn about the problems and solutions related to order fulfillment, see Chapter 8.

10. *Managing the impacts.* The impacts of e-commerce on organizational structure, people, marketing procedures, and profitability may be dramatic. Therefore, establishing a committee or organizational unit to develop strategy and to manage e-commerce is necessary.

ON THE WEB SITE... Additional resources, including quizzes; online files of additional text, tables, figures, and cases; and frequently updated Web links to current articles and information can be found on the book's Web site (*wiley.com/college/turban*).

KEY TERMS

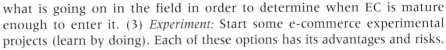

Auction *183*

Banners *197*

Brick-and-mortar organizations *178*

Business models *179*

Business-to-business (B2B) *178*

Business-to-consumer (B2C) *178*

Business-to-employees (B2E) *178*

Buy-side marketplace *201*

Channel conflict *187*

Click-and-mortar organizations *178*

Collaborative commerce (c-commerce) *178*

Collaborative filtering agents *196*

Consumer-to-business (C2B) *178*

Consumer-to-consumer (C2C) *178*

Cybersquatting *218*

Desktop purchasing *201*

Disintermediation *217*

Domain names *217*

E-business *177*

E-government *205*

E-procurement *201*

E-wallets (digital wallets) *214*

Electronic auctions *183*

Electronic banking (cyberbanking) *189*

Electronic bartering *184*

Electronic benefits transfer (EBT) *206*

Electronic cash (e-cash) *212*

Electronic checks (e-checks) *210*

Electronic commerce (EC) *177*

Electronic mall *186*

Electronic retailing (e-tailing) *185*

Electronic storefronts *186*

Forward auction *183*

Government-to-citizens (G2C) *179*

Group purchasing *201*

Intelligent (software) agents *195*

Intrabusiness EC *178*

Keyword banner *197*

Micropayments *209*

Mobile commerce *179*

Order fulfillment *215*

Permission marketing *198*

Person-to-person payments *212*

Pop-under ad *197*

Pop-up ad *197*

Public exchange (exchange) *201*

Random banner *197*

Reintermediation *218*

Reverse auction *184*

Segmentation *192*

Sell-side marketplace *200*

Smart cards *212*

Stored-value money
  cards *212*

Viral marketing *199*
Virtual banks *189*

Virtual organization *178*

CHAPTER HIGHLIGHTS (Numbers Refer to Learning Objectives)

1 E-commerce can be conducted on the Web, by e-mail, and on other networks. It is divided into the following major types: business-to-consumer, consumer-to-consumer, business-to-business, e-government, collaborative commerce, and intrabusiness. In each type you can find several business models.

1 E-commerce offers many benefits to organizations, consumers, and society, but it also has limitations (technological and nontechnological). The current technological limitations are expected to lessen with time.

2 A major mechanism in EC is auctions. The Internet provides an infrastructure for executing auctions at lower cost, and with many more involved sellers and buyers, including both individual consumers and corporations. Two major types exist: one for selling, which is the traditional process of selling to the highest bidder (forward auctions), and one is for buying, using a tendering system of buying at the lowest bid (reverse auctions).

2 A minor mechanism is online bartering, in which companies arrange for *exchange* of physical items and/or services.

3 The major application areas of B2C commerce are in direct retailing, banking, securities trading, job markets, travel, and real estate. Several issues slow the growth of B2C, notably channel conflict, order fulfillment, and customer acquisition. B2C e-tailing can be pure (such as Amazon.com), or part of a click-and-mortar organization.

3 Direct marketing is done via solo storefronts or in malls. It can be done via electronic catalogs, or by using electronic auctions.

3 Understanding consumer behavior is critical to e-commerce. Finding out what customers want can be determined by asking them, in questionnaires, or by observing what they do online. Other forms of market research can be conducted on the Internet by using intelligent agents.

4 Like any commerce, EC requires advertising support, much of which can be done online by methods such as banner ads, pop-ups, and customized ads. Permission marketing, interactive and viral marketing, electronic catalogs, making it to the top of search-engine listings, and online promotions offer ways for vendors to reach more customers.

5 The major B2B applications are selling from catalogs and by forward auctions, buying in reverse auctions and in group and desktop purchasing, and trading in exchanges.

5 Most organizations employ B2B collaborative commerce, usually along the supply chain.

6 EC activities can be conducted inside organizations. Three types are recognized: between a business and its employees, between units of the business, and among emloyees of the same organizations. Many methods and tools exist in conducting the above.

7 E-government commerce can take place between government and citizens, between businesses and governments, or among government units. EC makes government operations more effective and efficient.

7 EC can also be done between consumers (C2C), but should be undertaken with caution. Auction is the most popular C2C mechanism.

8 Traditional, nonelectronic payment systems are insufficient or inferior for doing business on the Internet. Therefore, electronic payment systems are used. Electronic payments can be made by e-checks, e-credit cards, e-cash, stored-value and smart cards, electronic bill presentment and payment, and e-wallets.

8 Order fulfillment is especially difficult in B2C, making B2C expensive at times (solutions are provided in Chapter 8).

9 Protection of customers, sellers, and intellectual property is a major concern, but so are the value of contracts, domain names, and how to handle legal issues in a multicountry environment.

9 There is increasing fraud and unethical behavior on the Internet, including invasion of privacy by sellers and misuse of domain names. Both sellers and buyers need to be protected.

10 Periods of innovations produce both many successes and many failures. There have been many of both in e-commerce.

10 Major reasons for EC failure are insufficient cash flow, too much competition, conflicts with existing systems, wrong revenue models, and lack of planning. Despite the failures, overall EC volume is growing exponentially.

QUESTIONS FOR REVIEW

1. Define e-commerce and distinguish it from e-business.
2. List the major types of EC (by transaction).
3. Distinguish between business-to-consumer, business-to-business, and intrabusiness EC.
4. List major technological and nontechnological limitations of EC (three each).
5. Describe electronic storefronts and malls.
6. List the benefits of cyberbanking.
7. Describe electronic securities trading.
8. Describe the online job market.
9. Explain how electronic auctions work.
10. Describe the EC consumer behavior model.
11. Describe EC market research and its tools.
12. Describe the major support areas of intelligent agents in EC.
13. Describe online advertising, its methods, and benefits.
14. Describe pop-up ads and the issues surrounding them.
15. Briefly describe the sell-side marketplace.
16. Describe the various methods of e-procurement.
17. Describe how forward and reverse auctions are used in B2B commerce.
18. Describe the role of exchanges in B2B.
19. Describe c-commerce and its benefits.
20. Describe e-government and its benefits.
21. Describe e-bartering.
22. Describe some C2C activities.
23. Describe intrabusiness and B2E commerce.
24. List the various electronic payment mechanisms.
25. List the security requirements for EC.
26. Describe the issues in EC order fulfillment.
27. Describe some areas of potential fraud on the Internet.
28. Describe buyer protection in EC.
29. List some ethical issues in EC.
30. List the major legal issues of EC.
31. List five reasons for EC failures.
32. List five suggestions for EC success.

DISCUSSION QUESTIONS

1. Discuss the major limitations of e-commerce. Which of them are likely to disappear? Why?
2. Why is the electronic job market popular, especially among the high-tech professions?
3. Distinguish between business-to-business forward auctions and buyers' bids for RFQs.
4. Discuss the benefits to sellers and buyers of a B2B exchange.
5. What are the major benefits of e-government?
6. Why are online auctions popular?
7. Discuss the reasons for EC failures.
8. Discuss the various ways to pay online in B2C. Which one(s) do you prefer and why?
9. Why is order fulfillment in B2C considered difficult?
10. Distinguish between smart cards and value-added cards. Discuss the advantages of each.
11. Discuss the online consumer behavior model and explain why it is needed.
12. Discuss the reasons for having multiple EC business models.

EXERCISES

1. Assume you're interested in buying a car. You can find information about cars at *autos.msn.com*. Go to *autoweb.com* or *autobytel.com* for information about financing and insurance. Decide what car you want to buy. Configure your car by going to the car manufacturer's Web site. Finally, try to find the car from *autobytel.com*. What information is most supportive of your decision-making process? Write a report about your experience.
2. Consider the opening case about Hi-Life.
   a. How was the corporate decision making improved?
   b. Summarize the benefits to the customers, suppliers, store management, and employees.
   c. The data collected at Activesys can be uploaded to a PC and transmitted to the corporate intranet via the Internet. It is suggested that transmision be done using a wireless system. Comment on the proposal.
3. Compare the various electronic payment methods. Specifically, collect information from the vendor cited in the chapter, and find more with *google.com*. Be sure you pay attention to security level, speed, cost, and convenience.

GROUP ASSIGNMENTS

1. Have each team study a major bank with extensive EC strategy. For example, Wells Fargo Bank is well on its way to being a cyberbank. Hundreds of brick-and-mortar branch offices are being closed. In Spring 2003 the bank served more than a 1.2 million cyberaccounts (see *wellsfargo.com*). Other banks to look at are Citicorp, Netbank, and HSBC (Hong Kong). Each team should attempt to convince the class that its e-bank is the best.

2. Assign each team to one industry. Each team will find five real-world applications of the major business-to-business models listed in the chapter. (Try success stories of vendors and EC-related magazines.) Examine the problems they solve or the opportunities they exploit.

3. Have teams investigate how B2B payments are made in global trade. Consider instruments such as electronic letters of credit and e-checks. Visit *tradecard.com* and examine their services to SMEs. Also, investigate what Visa and MasterCard are offering. Finally, check Citicorp and some German and Japanese banks.

INTERNET EXERCISES

1. Access *etrade.com* and register for the Internet stock simulation game. You will be bankrolled with $100,000 in a trading account every month. Play the game and relate your experiences to IT.

2. Use the Internet to plan a trip to Paris.
   a. Find the lowest airfare.
   b. Examine a few hotels by class.
   c. Get suggestions of what to see.
   d. Find out about local currency, and convert $1,000 to that currency with an online currency converter.
   e. Compile travel tips.
   f. Prepare a report.

3. Access *realtor.com*. Prepare a list of services available on this site. Then prepare a list of advantages derived by the users and advantages to realtors. Are there any disadvantages? To whom?

4. Enter *alibaba.com*. Identify the site capabilities. Look at the site's private trading room. Write a report. How can such a site help a person who is making a purchase?

5. Try to find a unique gift on the Internet for a friend. Several sites can help you do it. (You might try *shopping.com* and *amazon.com*, for example.) Describe your experience with such a site.

6. Enter *campusfood.com*. Explore the site. Why is the site so successful? Could you start a competing one? Why or why not?

7. Enter *dell.com*, go to "desktops" and configure a system. Register to "my cart" (no obligation). What calculators are used there? What are the advantages of this process as compared to buying a computer in a physical store? What are the disadvantages?

8. Enter *bizrate.com* and complete one of the questionnaires that entitles you to participate in their rewards and receive information. What data do they collect? Why?

9. Enter *nike.com* and configure a pair of shoes; then go to *jaguar.com* and configure a car; and finally go to Lands' End (*landsend.com*) and configure some clothing for yourself. Summarize your experiences.

10. Enter *checkfree.com* and find their services. Prepare a report.

11. Enter *authorizenet.com* and find *echeck.net*; view the payment diagram. Compare this process to the one described in Figure 5.6. Comment on the relationships.

Minicase 1
FreeMarkets.com

FreeMarkets (*freemarkets.com*) is a leader in creating B2B online auctions for buyers of industrial parts, raw materials, commodities, and services around the globe. The company has created auctions for goods and services in hundreds of industrial product categories. FreeMarkets auctions more than $5 billion worth of purchase orders a year and saves buyers an estimated 2 to 25 percent of total expenses (administrative and items).

FreeMarkets operates two types of marketplaces. First, the company helps customers purchase goods and services through its B2B global marketplace where reverse auctions usually take place. Second, FreeMarkets helps companies improve their asset-recovery results by getting timely market prices for surplus assets through the FreeMarkets Asset Exchange, employing a *forward auction* process, as well as other selling models.

FreeMarkets Onsite Auctions include (1) asset disposal recovery and (2) sourcing (e-procurement) functions. These functions provide the following:

- **Asset disposal analysis.** Market makers work with sellers to determine the best strategy to meet asset-recovery goals.
- **Detailed sales offering.** The company collects and consolidates asset information into a printed or online sales offering for buyers.
- **Targeted market outreach.** FreeMarkets conducts targeted advertising to a global database of 500,000 buyers and suppliers.
- **Event coordination.** The company prepares the site, provides qualified personnel, and enforces auction rules.
- **Sales implementation.** FreeMarkets summarizes auction results and assists in closing sales.

Asset-Recovery Success Stories

FreeMarkets helped the following companies make asset recoveries.:

New Line Cinema (*newline.com*) had unique memorabilia that they had stored for years. In 2001 they decided to auction these via Freemarket's auction marketplace (AssetExchange). The release of a movie sequel titled *Austin Powers: The Spy Who Shagged Me* provided an opportunity for New Line to experiment with the asset-recovery auction. Items from the original production were put up for auction; these items included a 1965 Corvette driven by Felicity Shagwell (sold in the auction for $121,000) and one of Austin's suits (sold for $7,500). In addition to freeing storage space and generating income, the auction provided publicity for the sequel through the newspaper and television coverage it received. An additional benefit was that the auction was linked to the company's online store. If you were unable to afford the 1965 Corvette, you instead could have purchased a new T-shirt or a poster of the new movie. Finally, the auction created a dedicated community of users. The auction was a great success, and since then New Line Cinema has conducted similar auctions on a regular basis.

Another success story for FreeMarkets' auctions was American Power Conversion Corp. (*apcc.com*), which needed a channel for end-of-life (old models) and refurbished power-protection products. These were difficult to sell in the regular distribution channels. Before using auctions, the company used special liquidation sales, which were not very successful. FreeMarkets deployed the auction site (using its standard technology, but customizing the applications). It also helped the company determine the auction strategies (such as starting-bid price and auction running length), which were facilitated by DSS modeling. The site became an immediate success. The company is considering selling regular products there, but only merchandise for which there would be no conflict with the company's regular distributors.

E-Procurement (Sourcing) Success Story

Besides providing companies with successful efforts in asset recovery, FreeMarkets has also helped companies conduct reverse auctions either from their own sites (with necessary expertise provided by FreeMarkets) or from FreeMarkets' site. Singapore Technologies Engineering (STE), a large integrated global engineering group specializing in the fields of aerospace, electronics, land systems, and marine had the following goals when it decided to use e-procurement (sourcing) with the help of FreeMarkets: to minimize the cost of products they need to buy, such as board parts; to identify a new global supply base for their multisourcing strategy; to ensure maximized efficiency in the procurement process; to find new, quality suppliers for reliability and support; and to consolidate existing suppliers. These are typical goals of business purchasers.

FreeMarkets started by training STE's corporate buyers and other staff. Then it designed an improved process that replicated the traditional negotiations with suppliers. Finally, it took a test item and prepared an RFQ, placing it for bid in the FreeMarkets Web site. FreeMarkets uses a five-step tendering process that starts with the RFQ and ends with supplier management (which includes suppliers' verification and training). STE saved 35 percent on the cost of printed circuit board assemblies.

Sources: Compiled from *freemarkets.com*, see success stories (site accessed December 15, 2002 and March 28, 2003).

Questions for Minicase 1

1. What makes FreeMarkets different from eBay?
2. Why do you think FreeMarkets concentrates on asset recovery and on e-procurement?
3. Why is the RFQ mechanism popular?
4. In 2003 the company shifted attention to global supply management. What does the company mean by that?

Minicase 2
Marketing Dining Certificates Online

Restaurants.com was founded in 1999 as an all-purpose dining portal with menus, online video tours, and a reservation feature. Like other dot-coms, the company was losing money. Not too many restaurants were willing to pay the fees in order to put their Web page on the *restaurants.com* site. The company was ready to pull the plug when its owner learned that CitySpree, which was selling dining certificates (coupons) online, was for sale in a bankruptcy auction. Realizing that Restaurants.com might have a better model for selling dining certificates online than did CitySpree, the owner purchased CitySpree. This enabled him to change the company from "just another dining portal" to a gift-certificate seller.

Here is how the new business model works: Restaurants are invited to place, for free, dining certificates at *restaurants.com*, together with information about the restaurant, menu, parking availability, and more. The dining certificates traditionally had been found in newspapers or newspaper inserts. Placing them online is free to the restaurants' owners; some use the online coupons to replace the paper coupons, and others supplement the paper coupons with the online version. Restaurants.com *sells* these certificates online, and collects all the fees for itself. The restaurants get broad visibility, since Restaurants.com advertises on Orbitz, Yahoo, and MSN; it even auctions certificates at eBay.

The certificates offer 30–50 percent off the menu price, so they are appealing to buyers. By using a search engine, you can find a restaurant with a cuisine of your choice, and you can look for certificates when you need them. Although you pay $5–$15 to purchase a certificate, you get usually a better discount than is offered in the newspapers. You pay with your credit card, print the certificate, and are ready to dine. Customers are encouraged to register as members, free of charge. Then they can get e-mails with promotions, news, and so on. In their personalized account, customers can view past purchases as well. Customers also

can purchase gift certificates to be given to others. And bargains can be found: For example, a $50-off-regular-price certificate to New York City's Manhattan Grille was auctioned for only $16.

The business model worked. By going to eBay, the world's largest virtual mall, Restaurants.com found an audience of millions of online shoppers. By e-mailing coupons to customers it saves the single largest cost of most conventional coupon marketers—printing and postage. Finally, the model works best in difficult economic times, when price-conscious consumers are looking for great deals.

The financial results are striking: Revenues doubled during the first five months of operation (late 2001). The company has been profitable since the third quarter of 2002. And by June 2003, the company was selling over 80,000 certificates a month, grossing over $5 million in 2002, and expecting about $10 million in 2003.

Sources: Compiled from Athitakis (2003) and *restaurants.com* (June 1, 2003).

Questions for Minicase 2

1. Visit *restaurants.com*. Find an Italian restaurant in your neighborhood and examine the information provided. Assuming you like Italian food, is the gift certificate a good deal?
2. Review the "lessons from failures" described in Section 5.10 and relate them to this case.
3. Why was it necessary to purchase CitySpree? (Speculate.)
4. What motivates restaurants to participate in the new business model when they refused to do so in the old one?
5. Given that anyone can start a competing business, how can Restaurants.com protect its position? What are some of its competitive advantages?

Virtual Company Assignment
E-Commerce in the Diner

As the head hostess for The Wireless Café, Barbara has noticed more customers using wireless devices at their tables, sending e-mails and messages, looking up information during business lunches, as well as talking on the phone. She has shared this observation with you and asked you to identify ways The Wireless Café can attract more customers through e-commerce. After reading Chapter 5, you are now aware that e-commerce is more than just business-to-customer relationships, so you ask her if you can broaden the scope of your analysis. Barbara agrees.

1. Identify the category, participants, and benefits of e-commerce for the following activities:
   a. Ordering food supplies
   b. Financial reporting (city, state, federal)
   c. Employee benefits management
   d. Customer reservations and communication
   e. Job postings and applications
2. Inventory management is more than just ordering food supplies. It includes table-setting items (dishes, glassware, cutlery, napkins), and cleaning and office supplies in addition to ingredients for the daily menu offerings. How would Internet-based EDI benefit The Wireless Café in managing these inventories? Can you find any products and services on the Internet that would help The Wireless Café do this?
3. Identify for Barbara some lessons learned in implementing successful e-commerce projects and how they can help ensure The Wireless Café's success.

REFERENCES

Agrawal, M., et al. "E-Performance: The Path to Rational Exuberance," *The McKinsey Quarterly*, Vol. 1 (2001).

Alga, N., "Increasing Security Levels," *Information Systems Control Journal*, March–April 2002.

Athitakis, M., "How to Make Money on the Net," *Business 2.0*, May 2003.

Alwang, G., "Cookie Managers," *PC Magazine*, January 16, 2001.

Bayers, C., "The Last Laugh (of Amazon's CEO)," *Business 2.0*, September 2002.

Bayles, D. L., *E-Commerce Logistics and Fulfillment*, Upper Saddle River, NJ: Prentice Hall, 2001.

Business.wa.gov.au, February 2001.

Biz Report, "Making Sense of U.S. B2C E-Commerce Findings," *BizReport.com*, bizreport.com/article.php?art_id=4410&PHPSESSID=5cf146ce4ed3554cf3906c3c9e842ddd. (Accessed June 2003.)

Bodow, S., "Getting Hitched," *Business 2.0*, November 28, 2000.

Braiker, B., and E. Christenson, "Bidding War," *MSNBC News*, April 12, 2003, msnbc.com/news/899433.asp. (Accessed June 2003.)

Buchholz, G. A., "The Worst Disaster Is Not Planning for One," *Primavera*, 1(2), 2002, primavera.com/files/magazine/Primavera Magazine_062002.pdf. (Accessed June 2003.)

Cheeseman, H. R., *Business Law*, 4th ed. Upper Saddle River, NJ: Prentice Hall, 2001.

Chemconnect.com. (Accessed April 11, 2003.)

Chen, H., "Digital Government: Technologies and Practices," *Decision Support Systems* (special issue), February 2003.

Choi, S. Y., et al., *The Economics of Electronic Commerce*. Indianapolis, IN: Macmillan Technical Publications, 1997.

CIO Magazine, October 1, 1999.

Cohen, M., et al., "Decision Support with Web-Enabled Software," *Interfaces*, March–April 2001.

CommerceOne.com, "Schlumberger Oilfield Services Selects Commerce One Solution to Fully Automate its Worldwide Procurement Process," February 1, 1999, commerceone.com/news/releases/schlumberger.html. (Accessed July 2003.)

CommerceOne.com, "Customer Snapshot: Schlumberger," 2003, commerceone.com/customers/profiles/schlumberger.pdf. (Accessed July 2003.)

Costa, D., "Identity Crisis (Digital IDs)," *PC Magazine*, October 18, 2002.

Daisey, M., *21 Dog Years: Doing Time @ Amazon.com*. New York: Free Press, 2002.

Daly, J., "Sage Advice," *Business 2.0*, August 22, 2000.

Deitel, H. M. et al., *e-Business and e-Commerce for Managers*. Upper Saddle River, NJ: Prentice Hall, 2001.

Dell.com, dell.com/us/en/gen/services/service_servicesportfolio.htm, 2002.

Doll, M. W. et al., *Defending the Digital Frontier*. New York: John Wiley & Sons, eBay.com (2001–2003).

ECCHO: Electronic Check Clearing House Organization, "Managing Value in the Transition to Electronic Payments: Executive Summary," eccho.org, April 11, 2002.

ecc.online.wa.gov.au/news, June–November 2002.

Emarketer.com, "Most 2001 Top 10 E-Retailers are Multi-Channel," *Emarketer.com*, August 1, 2002, emarketer.com/products/database.php?f_search_type=Basic&f_arg_0=Top+E-Retail+2001+. (Accessed June 2003.)

Emarketer.com, "U.S. Government Web Sites Concentrate on Security, Privacy," *Emarketer.com*, October 2, 2002, emarketer.com/products/database.php?PHPSESSID=2515ad2c217044be3b62d2b36dbe7a4de&f_search_type=Basic&f_arg_0=e-gov+security+policies. (Accessed June 2003.)

Emarketer, "Popular Online Activities among Internet Users in the U.S. 2002," April 11, 2003, *emarketer.com/products/database.php? f_arg_0=US+online+stock+trading+2003&f_arg_0_b=US+online+ stock+trading+2003&f_num_args_changed=1&f_num_articles_found =1&f_num_charts_found=0&f_num_reports_found=0&f_reports_found =&f_request=&f_search_type=Basic&Image81.x=56&Image81.y=17.* (Accessed July 2003.)

Farhoomand, A., and P. Lovelock, *Global E-Commerce.* Singapore: Prentice Hall, 2001.

FreeMarkets.com, see Success Stories. (Accessed December 15, 2002 and March 28, 2003.)

Gallaugher, J. M., "E-Commerce and the Undulating Distribution Channel," *Comunications of the ACM,* July 2002.

hp.com/jornada jornada. (Accessed May 3, 2002.)

Huff, S. L. et al., *Cases in Electronic Commerce.* New York: McGraw-Hill, 2001.

Huff, S. et al., "Critical Success Factors for Electronic Commerce," in *Cases in Electronic Commerce,* Irwin/McGraw-Hill, 1999.

Isenberg, D., *The Gigalaw: Guide to Internet Law.* New York: Random House, 2002.

Kambil, A., and E. van-Heck, *Making Markets.* Boston: Harvard Business School, 2002.

Kaplan, P. J., *F'D Companies: Spectacular Dot.com Flameouts,* New York: Simon & Schuster, 2002.

Kaplan, S., and M. Sawhney, "E-Hubs: The New B2B Marketplaces," *Harvard Business Review,* May 1, 2000.

Korean Times, August 24, 2002.

Martin, D., and M. Ryan, "Pop-ups Abound but Most Advertisers Remain Inline," *NetRatings,* 2002, *adrelevance.com/intelligence/intel_ snapshot.jsp?pr=020829.* (Accessed June 6, 2002.)

McDaniel, C., and R. H. Gates, *Marketing Research: The Impact of the Internet.* Cincinnati, OH: South-Western Publishing, 2001.

microsoft.com/asia/mobile. (May 2002.)

New York Times online (news item), June 5, 2002.

O'Keefe, R. M., and T. McEachern, "Web-Based Customer Decision Support System," *Communications of the ACM,* March 1998.

Ovans, A., "E-Procurement at Schlumberger," *Harvard Business Review,* May–June 2000.

Paperloop, Inc., "The Profits of Going Wireless," *Paperloop Magazines,* Paper and Pulp International, Inc., August 2002.

Paypal.com. (Accessed January 6, 2003.)

Peffers, K., and V. K. Tunnainen, "Expectations and Impacts of Global Information System: The Case of a Global Bank in Hong Kong," *Global Information Technology Management,* 1(4), 1998.

Phillips, M., "Seven Steps to Your New E-Business," *Business Online,* August 2000.

Poon, S., and P. Y. K. Chan, "Octopus: The Growing e-Payment System in Hong Kong," *Electronic Markets,* 11(2), 2001.

Press-Telegram, "Can't Find Saddam? Look for Him on eBay," *Press Telegram,* April 12, 2003, p. A10.

Reda, S., "Online Check Service Expands Internet Payment Options," *Stores,* February 2002.

Restaurants.com. (Accessed on May 29 and June 1, 2003.)

Ridell, J. et al., *Word of Mouse: The Marketing Power of Collaborative Filtering,* New York: Warner Books, 2002.

Rosenbaum, D., "Passport Purchasing," *PC Magazine,* January 29, 2002.

schlumberger.com press releases, 2002.

Segev, A., and J. Gebauer, "B2B Procurement and Marketplace Transformation," *Information Technology and Management,* July 2001.

Solomon, M. R., *Consumer Behavior.* Upper Saddle River, NJ: Prentice Hall, 2002.

Stead, B. A., and J. Gilbert, "Ethical Issues in Electronic Commerce," *Journal of Business Ethics,* No. 34, 2001.

Sterne, J., *Web Metrics.* New York: John Wiley & Sons, 2002.

Sterne, J., *World Wide Web Marketing,* 3rd ed. New York: John Wiley & Sons, 2001.

Strauss, J., et al., *E-Marketing,* 3rd ed. Upper Saddle River, NJ: Prentice Hall, 2003.

Shelter, K. M, and J. D. Procaccino, "Smart Card Evaluation," *Communications of the ACM,* July 2002.

Sweiger, M. et al., *Clickstream Data Warehousing.* New York: John Wiley & Sons, 2002.

Turban, E. et al., *Electronic Commerce 2004.* Upper Saddle River, NJ: Prentice Hall, 2004.

Ulph, R., J. Favier, and P. O'Connell, "Integrated Marketing Needs Hubs," *Tech Strategy Report, forrester.com/ER/Research/Report/Summary/ 0,1338,13712,00.html,* December 2001.

Useem, J., "Dot-Coms: What Have We Learned?" *Fortune,* October 2000.

Warkentin, M., ed., *B2B Electronic Commerce: Challenges and Solutions.* Hershey, PA: The Idea Group, 2001.

Westland, J. C., "Transaction Risk in Electronic Commerce," *Decision Support Systems,* May 2002.

Williams, J., et al., "IT Lessons Learned from FDA," *Failures and Lessons Learned in IT Management,* 1(1), 1997.

Wong, W. Y., *At the Dawn of E-Government.* New York: Deloitte Research, Deloitte & Touche, 2000.

Xelus.com, "Dell's Case Study," *xelus.com, Xelus.com/casestudies/ cs_dell.asp, 1999.* (Accessed June 2000.)

Yuan, S. T., "A Personalized and Integrative Comparison-Shopping Engine and Its Applications," *Decision Support Systems,* January 2003.

APPENDIX 5A

EDI AND EXTRANETS

E-commerce transactions must be executable world-wide without any delays or mistakes. Infrastructure may be of many types (see *Online File W5.8* and Technology Guides 4 and 5). But, their detailed description is outside the scope of this book. Here we deal with only two infra-structures: EDI and extranets.

Electronic Data Interchange (EDI)

As discussed briefly in Chapter 2, **EDI** is the electronic movement of specially formatted standard business documents, such as orders, bills, and confirmations sent between business partners. Figure 5A.1 shows the order-delivery cycle with and without EDI. Many companies use EDI to foster relationships with their

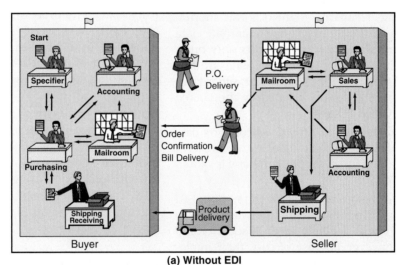

(a) Without EDI

(b) With EDI

FIGURE 5A.1 Order delivery cycle with and without EDI.

suppliers and/or customers. The major advantages of EDI are summarized in On-line File W5.9 at the book's Web site.

Like e-mail, EDI allows sending and receiving of messages between computers connected by a communication link. However, EDI has the following special characteristics:

- **Business transactions messages.** EDI is used primarily to electronically transfer *repetitive* business transactions. These include various transactions essential in EC: purchase orders, invoices, approvals of credit, shipping notices, confirmations, and so on.

- **Data formatting standards.** Since EDI messages are repetitive, it is sensible to use some format-ting (coding) standards. Standards can shorten the length of the messages and eliminate data entry errors, since data entry occurs only once. In the United States and Canada, data are for-matted according to the ANSI X.12 standard. An international standard developed by the United Nations is called EDIFACT.

- **EDI translators.** An *EDI translator* converts data into standard EDI format code. An example of such formatting for a shipping company is shown in Figure 5A.2.

- **Private lines versus the Internet.** In the past, EDI ran on expensive value-added networks. These networks provided a high level of security and capacity. However, because of cost, their imple-mentation was confined mainly to large trading partners. There were also some problems of compatibility. As a result, large companies doing business with thousands of other companies

were unable to place most of them on the EDI. For example, Boeing Commercial Airplane Group, which sells aircraft parts, was using EDI with only 30 out of 500 customers. With the emergence of Internet-based EDI (EDI/Internet). this situation is rapidly changing, as shown in a story about Hewlett-Packard in Online File W5.10 at our Web site.

Note that Internet-based EDI does not have the same capabilities as VAN-based EDI. Therefore, at least in the short run, it is viewed as supplementary to the VAN, permitting more companies to use EDI. Also, Internet EDI may be cheaper, but it still re-quires coordination and integration with the com-pany's back-end processing systems. In cases of high use of EDI, such as in financial services, the tradi-tional EDI must be used. But in many cases where low volume of transactions is involved, EDI/Internet is becoming the chosen solution.

HOW DOES EDI WORK? *A Closer Look 5A.1* illustrates how EDI works. Information flows from the hospi-tal's information systems into an EDI station that includes a PC and an EDI translator. From there the information moves, using a modem if necessary, to a VAN. The VAN transfers the formatted information to a vendor(s) where an EDI translator converts it to a desired format.

INTERNET-BASED EDI. There are a number of rea-sons for firms to create EDI ability over the Internet: The Internet is a publicly accessible network with few geographical constraints. The Internet's global

FIGURE 5A.2 Translating data to EDI code.

	Sample Invoice	Formatted Into X12 Standard
Ship To:	The Corner Store 601 First Street Crossroads, MI 48106	N1∗ST∗THE CORNER STOREN/L N3∗601 FIRST STREETN/L N4∗CROSSROADS∗MI∗48106N/L
Charge To:	Acme Distributing Company P.O. Box 33327 Anytown, NJ 44509	N1∗BT∗ACME DISTRIBUTING CON/L N3∗P.O. BOX 33327N/L N4∗ANYTOWN∗NJ∗44509N/L
Terms of Sale:	2% 10 days from invoice date	ITD∗01∗3∗2∗∗10N/L

A CLOSER LOOK
5A.1 HOW EDI CUTS COSTS OF ORDERING SUPPLIES

An average hospital generates about 15,000 purchase orders each year, at a processing cost of about $70 per order. The Health Industry Business Communication Council esimates that EDI can reduce this cost to $4 per order—potential yearly savings of $840,000 per hospital. The required investment ranges between $8,000 and $15,000, which includes purchase of a PC with an EDI translator, a modem, and a link to the mainframe-

based information system. The hospital can have two or three ordering points. These are connected to a value-added network (VAN), which connects the hospital to its suppliers (see figure below). The system also can connect to other hopsitals, or to centralized joint purchasing agencies.

Source: Based on G. Nussbaum (1992).

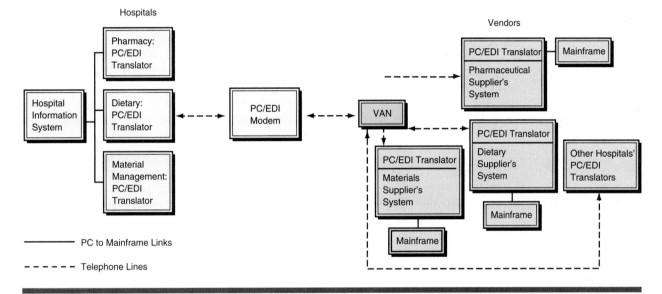

network connections offer the potential to reach the widest possible number of trading partners of any viable alternative currently available. In addition, the Internet's largest attribute—large-scale connectivity (without the need to have any special networking architecture)—is a seedbed for growth of a vast range of business applications. Internet-based EDI can complement or replace current EDI applications. Internet tools such as browsers and search engines are very user-friendly; most users today know how to use them, so new training is minimized. Using the Internet to exchange EDI transactions is consistent with the growing interest of businesses in delivering an ever-increasing variety of products and services electronically, particularly through the Web. Finally, a "bottom-line" reason to move to Internet-based

EDI is cost: Using the Internet can cut EDI communication costs by over 50 percent. For implementation of EDI in Singapore (Tradenet) see Online File W5.11 at our Web site.

Extranets

The major network structure used in e-marketplaces and exchanges is an extranet, or "extended intranet." As discussed in Chapter 2, an **extranet** is a network that links business partners to one another over the Internet by tying together their corporate intranets. It connects with both the Internet and individual companies' intranets. An extranet adds value to the Internet by increasing its security and expanding the available bandwidth.

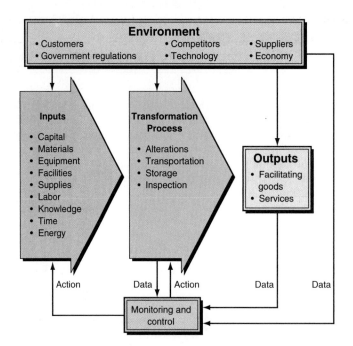

FIGURE 5A.3 The extranet framework.

The use of an extranet as a B2B infrastructure is growing rapidly. In contrast with electronic data interchange (EDI), which mostly supports *transaction processing* between two business partners, an extranet can be used for collaboration, discovery of information, trading support, and other activities. Also, EDI is mostly used to support company-centric transactions (where relationships are fairly permanent), whereas extranets are used also in exchanges (where relationships may be of a "one-deal-only" nature).

The main goal of extranets is to foster collaboration between organizations. Extranets may be used, for example, to allow inventory databases to be searched by business partners, or to transmit information on the status of an order. An extranet typically is open to selected suppliers, customers, and other business partners, who access it on a private wide-area network, or usually over the Internet with a virtual private network (VPN) for increased security and functionality.

Extranets allow the use of capabilities of both the Internet and intranets among business partners. External partners and telecommuting employees can use the extranet to place orders, access data, check status of shipments, and send e-mail. The Internet-based extranet is far more economical than the creation and maintenance of proprietary networks. Extranets support all types of the B2B models described earlier, but

especially many-to-many exchanges. Buy-side and sell-side e-marketplaces are supported frequently by EDI/Internet. Extranets are especially useful in supporting *collaborative commerce (c-commerce).*

An extranet uses the TCP/IP protocol to link intranets in different locations (as shown in Figure 5A.3). Extranet transmissions are usually conducted over the Internet, which offers little privacy or transmission security. Therefore, it is necessary to add security features. This is done by creating tunnels of secured data flows, using cryptography and authorization algorithms, to provide secure transport of private communications. An Internet with tunneling technology is known as a **virtual private network (VPN)** (see Technology Guide 4 for details).

Extranets provide secured connectivity between a corporation's intranets and the intranets of its business partners, materials suppliers, financial services, government, and customers. Access to an extranet is usually limited by agreements of the collaborating parties, is strictly controlled, and is available only to authorized personnel. The protected environment of an extranet allows partners to collaborate and share information and to perform these activities securely.

Because an extranet allows connectivity between businesses through the Internet, it is an open and flexible platform suitable for supply chain activities. To further increase security, many companies replicate the portions of their databases that they are willing to share with their business partners and separate them physically from their regular intranets.

According to Szuprowicz (1998), the benefits of extranets fall into five categories:

1. *Enhanced communications.* The extranet enables improved internal communications; improved business partnership channels; effective marketing, sales, and customer support; and facilitated collaborative activities support.

2. *Productivity enhancements.* The extranet enables just-in-time information delivery, reduction of information overload, productive collaboration between workgroups, and training on demand.

3. *Business enhancements.* The extranet enables faster time to market, potential for simultaneous engineering and collaboration, lower design and production costs, improved client relationships, and creation of new business opportunities.

4. *Cost reduction.* The extranet results in fewer errors, improved comparison shopping, reduced travel and meeting time and cost, reduced administrative and operational costs, and elimination of paper-publishing costs.

5. *Information delivery.* The extranet enables low-cost publishing, leveraging of legacy systems, standard delivery systems, ease of maintenance and implementation, and elimination of paper-based publishing and mailing costs.

Rihao-Ling and Yen (2001) reported additional advantages of extranets, such as ready access to information, ease of use, freedom of choice, moderate setup cost, simplified workflow, lower training cost, and better group dynamics. They also listed a few disadvantages, such as difficulty in justifying the investment (measuring benefits and costs), high user expectations, and drain on resources.

While the extranet provides the communication line between intranets, it is still necessary to connect applications. For example, Brunswick Corp. connects all of its boat-brand manufacturing with an extranet called Compass, using IBM's WebSphere and Web services to provide the connectivity (see Chen, 2003, for details).

KEY TERMS

Electronic data interchange (EDI) *231*

Extranet *233*

Virtual private network (VPN) *234*

REFERENCES

Chen, A., "Boating Extranet Sets Sail," *eweek,* April 28, 2003.

Rihao-Ling, R., and D. C. Yen, "Extranet: A New Wave of Internet," *SAM Advanced Management Journal,* Spring 2001.

Szuprowicz, B., *Extranet and Intranet: E-Commerce Business Strategies for the Future.* Charleston, SC: Computer Technology Research Corp., 1998.

PART II
The Web Revolution

4. Network Computing: Discovery, Communication, and Collaboration
5. E-Business and E-Commerce
▶ 6. Mobile, Wireless, and Pervasive Computing

CHAPTER

6

Mobile, Wireless, and Pervasive Computing

6.1
Mobile Computing and Commerce: Overview, Benefits, and Drivers

6.2
Mobile Computing Infrastructure

6.3
Mobile Applications in Financial Services

6.4
Mobile Shopping, Advertising, and Content-Providing

6.5
Mobile Intrabusiness and Enterprise Applications

6.6
Mobile B2B and Supply Chain Applications

6.7
Mobile Consumer and Personal Service Applications

6.8
Location-Based Commerce

6.9
Pervasive Computing

6.10
Inhibitors and Barriers of Mobile Computing

LEARNING OBJECTIVES

After studying this chapter, you will be able to:

1. Discuss the characteristics and attributes of mobile computing and m-commerce.
2. Describe the drivers of mobile computing.
3. Understand the technologies that support mobile computing.
4. Describe wireless standards and transmission networks.
5. Discuss m-commerce applications in financial and other services, advertising, and providing of content.
6. Describe the applications of m-commerce within organizations.
7. Understand B2B and supply chain applications of m-commerce.
8. Describe consumer and personal applications of m-commerce.
9. Describe some non-Internet m-commerce applications.
10. Describe location-based commerce (l-commerce).
11. Discuss the key characteristics and current uses of pervasive computing.
12. Describe the major inhibitors and barriers of mobile computing and m-commerce.

NEXTBUS: A SUPERB CUSTOMER SERVICE

▶ THE PROBLEM

Buses in certain parts of San Francisco have difficulty keeping up with the posted schedule, especially in rush hours. Generally, buses are scheduled to arrive every 20 minutes, but at times, passengers may have to wait 30 to 40 minutes. The schedules become meaningless, and passengers are unhappy because they waste time.

▶ THE SOLUTION

San Francisco bus riders carrying an Internet-enabled wireless device, such as a cell phone or PDA, can quickly find out when a bus is likely to arrive at a particular bus stop. The system tracks public transportation buses in *real time.* Knowing where each bus is and factoring in traffic patterns and weather reports, NextBus (*nextbus.com*) dynamically calculates the estimated arrival time of the bus to each bus stop on the route. The arrival times are also displayed on the Internet and on a public screen at each bus stop.

The NextBus system has been used successfully in several other cities around the United States, in Finland, and in several other countries. Figure 6.1 shows how the NextBus system works. The core of the NextBus system is a GPS satellite that

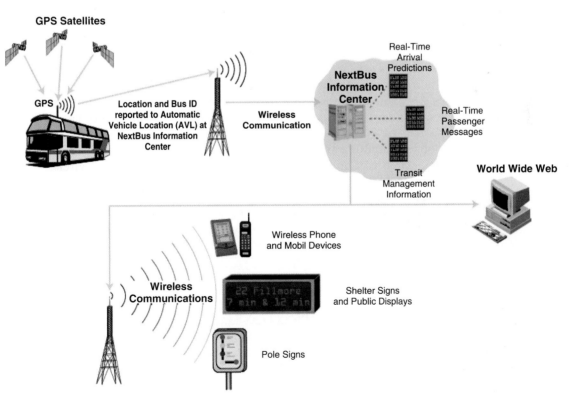

FIGURE 6.1 NextBus operational model. *(Source: NextBus.com/corporate/works/index.htm, 2002. Used with permission of NextBus Information Systems.)*

can tell the NextBus information center where a bus is at any given time. Based on a bus's location, the scheduled arrival time at each stop can be calculated in real time. Users can access the information from their cell phones or PCs, any time, anywhere. NextBus schedules are also posted in real time on passenger's shelters at bus stops and public displays.

Currently, NextBus is an ad-free customer service, but in the near future advertising may be added. As the system knows exactly where you are when you request information and how much time you have until your next bus, it could send you to the nearest Starbucks for a cup of coffee, giving you an electronic discount coupon for a cup of coffee as you wait.

 THE RESULTS

Passengers in San Francisco are happy with the NextBus system; worries about missing the bus are diminished. A similar system is used in rural areas in Finland, where buses are infrequent and winters are very cold; passengers can stay in a warm coffeehouse not far from the bus stop rather than waiting in the cold for a bus that may be an hour late. Also, using the system, a bus company can do better scheduling, arrange for extra buses when needed, and improve its operations.

Sources: Compiled from ITS America 2001; Murphy, 1999; and *nextbus.com*, accessed 2003.

 LESSONS LEARNED FROM THIS CASE

This opening vignette is an example of location-based e-commerce, which is an application of *mobile commerce*, in which EC services are provided to customers wherever they are located at the time they need them. This capability, which is not available in regular EC, may change many things in our lives. The vignette also exemplifies *pervasive computing*, in which services are seamlessly blended into the environment without the user being aware of the technology behind the scenes. This application is also a part of *mobile computing*, a computing paradigm designed for workers who travel outside the boundaries of their organizations or for travelers of any kind.

Mobile computing and commerce are spreading rapidly, replacing or supplementing wired computing. Mobile computing involves mostly wireless infrastructure. Mobile computing may reshape the entire IT field (see Intel, 2002; Sadeh, 2002; and Mennecke and Strader, 2003). The technologies, applications, and limitations of mobile computing and mobile commerce are the main focus of this chapter. Later in the chapter, we will look briefly at futuristic applications of *pervasive computing*.

6.1 MOBILE COMPUTING AND COMMERCE: OVERVIEW, BENEFITS, AND DRIVERS

The Mobile Computing Landscape

In the traditional computing environment it was necessary to come to the computer to do some work on it. All computers were connected to each other, to networks, servers, etc. via wires. This situation limited the use of computers and created hardship for people and workers on the move. In particular, salespeople, repair people, service employees, law enforcement agents, and utility workers can be more effective if they can use information technology while at their jobs

in the field or in transit. There are also mobile vacationers, people on holiday who wish to be connected with home or office.

The first solution was to make computers small enough so they can be easily carried about. First, the laptop computer was invented, and later on smaller and smaller computers, such as the PDAs and other handhelds, appeared. These carriable computers are called **mobile devices.** They have become lighter with time and more powerful as far as processing speed and storage. At the end of the day, mobile workers could download (or upload) information from or to a regular desktop computer in a process known as *synchronization*. To speed up the "sync," special connecting cradles (docking stations) were created (see Minicase 2 at the end of this chapter and the Maybelline Minicase in Chapter 2).

These devices provided the first application of **mobile computing,** a computing paradigm designed for workers who travel outside the boundaries of their organizations or for any other people traveling outside their homes. Salespeople were able to make proposals at customers' offices; a traveler could read and answer all of the day's e-mails while on a plane. One could work with the mobile device as long as the battery was working.

For example, Millstone Coffee equipped its 300 drivers with handheld devices and mobile applications for use while they are on the road selling roasted coffee beans to 13,000 stores in the United States. Using the devices the drivers can track inventory, generate invoices, and capture detailed sales and marketing data at each store. The system does not use wireless; instead, the drivers synchronize ("sync") their handhelds with the company's main system at the end of the day, a process that takes only 2 minutes. This strategy has proven to be cheaper for Millstone than going wireless, at least with the 2002 technology (see Cohen, 2002).

The second solution to the need for mobile computing was to replace wires with *wireless communication media.* Wireless systems have been in use in radio, TV, and telephones for a long time, so it was natural to adapt them to the computing environment (for more, see *Wired*, 2003).

The third solution was a combination of the first two, namely to use mobile devices in a wireless environment. Referred to as **wireless mobile computing,** this combination enables a real-time connection between a mobile device and other computing environments, such as the Internet or an intranet. This innovation is creating a revolution in the manner in which people use computers. It is spreading at work and at home. It is also used in education, health care, entertainment, and much more. The new computing model is basically leading to *ubiquity*—meaning that computing is available anywhere, at any time. (Note: Since many mobile applications now go wireless, the term *mobile computing* today is often used generally to describe wireless mobile computing.)

Due to some current technical limitations, we cannot (yet) do with mobile computing all the things that we do with regular computing. However, as time passes we can do more and more. On the other hand, we can do things in mobile computing that we cannot do in the regular computing environment. A major boost to mobile computing was provided in 2003 by Intel with its Centrino chip. This chip, which will be a standard feature in most laptops by 2005 (Estrada, 2002), includes three important capabilities: (1) a connection device to a wireless local area network, (2) low usage of electricity, enabling users to do more work on a single battery charge, and (3) a high level of security. The Centrino is expected to make mobile computing the common computing environment.

A second driving development of mobile computing is the introduction of the third- and fourth-generation wireless environments known as 3G and 4G. We will describe these later on.

Mobile Commerce

While the impact of mobile computing on our lives will be very significant, a similar impact is already occurring in the way we conduct business. This impact is described as **mobile commerce** (also known as *m-commerce* and *m-business*), which is basically any e-commerce or e-business done in a wireless environment, especially via the Internet. Like regular EC applications, m-commerce can be done via the Internet, private communication lines, smart cards, or other infrastructures (e.g., see Sadeh, 2002; Mennecke and Strader, 2003; and Kalakota and Robinson, 2001).

M-commerce is not merely a variation on existing Internet services; it is a natural extension of e-business. Mobile devices create an opportunity to deliver new services to existing customers and to attract new ones. Varshney and Vetter (2001) classified the applications of m-commerce into 12 categories, as shown in Table 6.1. (A classification by industry is provided at *mobile.commerce.net*. Also see *mobiforum.org*.)

Many of these applications, as well as some additional ones, will be discussed in this chapter. According to Sarshar (2003), as much as $1.8 trillion in consumer transactions could be made from mobile devices by the year 2005. The Yankee Group forecasted that mobile transactions will exceed $15 billion in the U.S. alone (TechLive, 2001).

Mobile Computing Basic Terminology

Let's build a foundation for further discussion by defining some common mobile computing terms:

- *Global positioning system (GPS).* A satellite-based tracking system that enables the determination of a GPS device's location. (See Section 6.8 for more on GPS.)

TABLE 6.1 Classes of M-Commerce Applications

Class of Applications	Examples
1. Mobile financial applications (B2C, B2B)	Banking, brokerage, and payments by mobile users
2. Mobile advertising (B2C)	Sending user-specific and location-sensitive advertising to users
3. Mobile inventory management (B2C, B2B)	Location tracking of goods, boxes, troops, and people
4. Proactive service management (B2C, B2B)	Transmitting to vendors information related to distributing components
5. Product locating and shopping (B2C, B2B)	Locating/ordering certain items from a mobile device
6. Wireless reengineering (B2C, B2B)	Improvement of business services
7. Mobile auction or reverse auction (B2C)	Services for customers to buy or sell certain items
8. Mobile entertainment services (B2C)	Video-on-demand and other services to a mobile user
9. Mobile office (B2C)	Working from traffic jams, airports, and conferences
10. Mobile distance education (B2C)	Taking a class using streaming audio and video
11. Wireless data center (B2C, B2B)	Downloading information by mobile users/vendors
12. Mobile music/music-on-demand (B2C)	Downloading and playing music using a mobile device

Source: Varshney and Vetter (2000), pp. 107–109.

- **Personal digital assistant (PDA).** A small portable computer, such as the family of Palm handhelds and the Pocket PC devices from companies like HP.
- **Short Messaging Service (SMS).** A technology, in existence since 1991, that allows for the sending of short text messages (up to 160 characters in 2003) on certain cell phones. Data are borne by the radio resources reserved in cellular networks for locating mobile devices and connecting calls. SMS messages can be sent or received concurrently, even during a voice or data call. Used by hundreds of millions of users, SMS is known as the e-mail of m-commerce.
- **Enhanced Messaging Service (EMS).** An extension of SMS that is capable of simple animation, tiny pictures, and short melodies.
- **Multimedia Messaging Service (MMS).** The next generation of wireless messaging, this technology will be able to deliver rich media.
- **Bluetooth.** A chip technology wireless standard designed for temporary, short-range connection (data and voice) among mobile devices and/or other devices (see *bluetooth.com*).
- **Wireless Application Protocol (WAP).** A technology that offers Internet browsing from wireless devices (see Section 6.2).
- **Smartphones.** Internet-enabled cell phones that can support mobile applications. These "phones with a brain" are becoming standard devices. They include WAP microprocessors for Internet access and the capabilities of PDAs as well.
- *Wi-Fi (short for Wireless Fidelity).* Refers to a standard 802.11b on which most of the wireless local area networks (WLANs) run.
- *WLAN (Wireless Local Area Network).* A broad term for all 802.11 standards. Basically, it is a wireless version of the Ethernet networking standard. (For discussion of the Ethernet standard, see Technology Guide 4.)

With these terms in mind, we can now look more deeply at the attributes and drivers of mobile computing.

Attributes and Drivers of Mobile Computing

Generally speaking, many of the EC applications described in Chapter 5 can be done in m-commerce. For example, e-shopping, e-banking, and e-stock trading are gaining popularity in wireless B2C. Auctioning is just beginning to take place on cell phones, and wireless collaborative commerce in B2B is emerging. However, there are several *new* applications that are possible only in the mobile environment. To understand why this is so, let's examine the major attributes of mobile computing and m-commerce.

SPECIFIC ATTRIBUTES OF MOBILE COMPUTING AND M-COMMERCE. Mobile computing has two major characteristics that differentiate it from other forms of computing: *mobility* and *broad reach*.

- *Mobility.* Mobile computing and m-commerce are based on the fact that users carry a mobile device everywhere they go. Mobility implies portability. Therefore, users can initiate a *real-time* contact with other systems from wherever they happen to be if they can connect to a wireless network.
- *Broad reach.* In mobile computing, people can be reached at any time. Of course, users can block certain hours or certain messages, but when users carry an open mobile device, they can be reached instantly.

These two characteristics break the barriers of geography and time. They create the following five value-added attributes that drive the development of m-commerce: ubiquity, convenience, instant connectivity, personalization, and localization of products and services.

Ubiquity. *Ubiquity* refers to the attribute of being available at *any location* at *any given time*. A mobile terminal in the form of a smartphone or a PDA offers ubiquity—that is, it can fulfill the need both for real-time information and for communication, independent of the user's location.

Convenience. It is very convenient for users to operate in the wireless environment. All they need is an Internet-enabled mobile device such as a smartphone. By using GPRS (General Packet Radio Service, a cell phone standard), it is easier and faster to access the Web without booting up a PC or placing a call via a modem. Also, more and more places are equipped with Wi-Fi, enabling users to get online from portable laptops any time (as was shown in the Dartmouth College case in Chapter 1). You can even watch an entire movie on a PDA (see *pocketpcfilms.com*).

Instant Connectivity. Mobile devices enable users to connect easily and quickly to the Internet, intranets, other mobile devices, and databases. Thus, wireless devices could become the preferred way to access information.

Personalization. *Personalization* refers to the preparation of customized information for individual consumers. For example, a user who is identified as someone who likes to travel might be sent travel-related information and advertising. Product personalization is still limited on mobile devices. However, the emerging need for conducting transactions electronically, combined with availability of personalized information and transaction feasibility via mobile portals, will move personalization to new levels, leading ultimately to the mobile device becoming a major EC tool. The process of personalization is illustrated in Figure 6.2 and is described by Dogac and Tumer (2002).

Localization of Products and Services. Knowing where the user is physically located at any particular moment is key to offering relevant products and services. E-commerce applications based on localization of products and services are known as *location-based e-commerce* or *l-commerce*. Precise location information is known when a GPS is attached to a user's wireless device. For example, you might use your mobile device to find the nearest ATM or FedEx drop box. In addition, the GPS will tell others where you are. Localization can be general, such as to anyone in a certain location (e.g., all shoppers at a shopping mall). Or, even better, it can be targeted so that users get messages that depend both on where they are and what their preferences are, thus combining localization and personalization. For instance, if it is known that you like Italian food and you are strolling in a mall that has an Italian restaurant, you might receive a SMS that tells you that restaurant's "special of the day" and gives you a 10 percent discount. GPS may be a standard feature in many mobile devices by 2005.

Vendors and telecommunication carriers can *differentiate* themselves in the competitive marketplace by offering new, exciting, and useful services based on these attributes. Such services will help vendors attract and keep customers and increase their revenues.

DRIVERS OF MOBILE COMPUTING AND M-COMMERCE. In addition to the value-added attributes just discussed, the development of mobile computing and m-commerce is driven by the following factors.

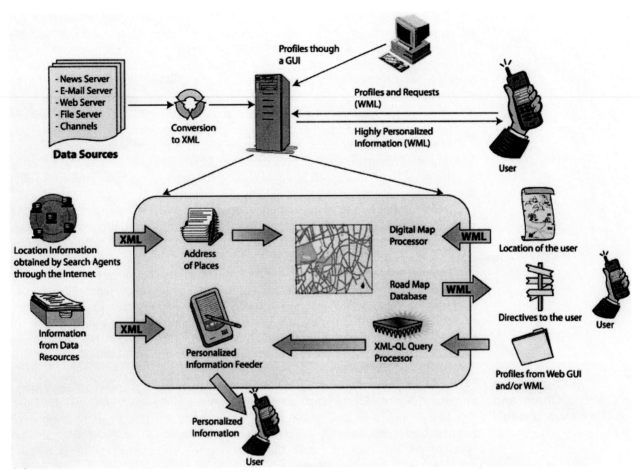

FIGURE 6.2 How a wireless system provides personalized information. (*Source:* Dogac and Tumer (2002), p. 40.)

Widespread Availability of Mobile Devices. The number of cell phones throughout the world exceeds 1.3 billion (*cellular.co.za/stats/stats-main.htm*). It is estimated that within a few years, about 70 percent of cell phones will have Internet access. Thus, a potential mass market is available for conducting discovery, communication, collaboration, and m-commerce. Cell phones are spreading quickly in developing countries. In 2002, for example, the number of cell phones in China exceeded 200 million, virtually equaling the number of fixed line phones in that country (CellularOnline, 2002). This growth enables developing countries to leap-frog to m-commerce.

No Need for a PC. Because the Internet can be accessed via smartphone or other Internet-enabled wireless device, there is no need for a PC to access the Internet. Even though the cost of a PC that is used primarily for Internet access, such as the Simputer (a "simple computer"), can be as low as $300 (or even less), that amount is still a major expense for the vast majority of people in the world. Furthermore, one needs to learn how to operate a PC, service it, and replace it every few years to keep it up-to-date. Smartphones and other wireless devices obviate the need for a PC.

The Handset Culture. Another driver of m-commerce is the widespread use of cell phones, which is becoming a social phenomenon, especially among the 15-to-25-year-old age group. These users will constitute a major force of online buyers once they begin to make and spend larger amounts of money. The use of SMS has been spreading like wildfire in several European and Asian countries. In the Philippines, for example, SMS is a national phenomenon in the youth market. As another example, Japanese send many more messages through mobile phones than do Americans, who prefer the desktop for e-mail.

Vendors' Push. Vendors also are pushing m-commerce. Both mobile communication network operators and manufacturers of mobile devices are advertising the many potential applications of mobile computing and m-commerce so that they can sell new technologies, products, and services to buyers.

Declining Prices and Increased Functionalities. With the passage of time, the price of wireless devices is declining, and the per-minute pricing of mobile services is expected to decline by 50 to 80 percent before 2005. At the same time, functionalities are increasing.

Improvement of Bandwidth. To properly conduct m-commerce, it is necessary to have sufficient bandwidth for transmitting text; however, bandwidth is also required for voice, video, and multimedia. The 3G (third-generation) technology (described in Section 6.2) provides the necessary bandwidth, at a data rate of up to 2 Mbps. This enables information to move 35 times faster than when 56K modems are used. Wi-Fi moves information even faster, at 11 Mbps.

M-Commerce Value Chain and Revenue Models

Like EC, m-commerce is a complex process involving a number of operations and a number of players (customers, merchants, mobile operators, and the like). The key elements in the m-commerce value chain (for delivering m-commerce content and applications to end users) are summarized in Table 6.2. Several types of vendors provide value-added services to m-commerce. These include:

TABLE 6.2 M-Commerce Value Chain

Link	Function	Provider
Transport	Maintenance and operation of the infrastructure supporting data communication between mobile users and application providers	Technology platform vendors
Enabling services	Server hosting, data backup, and system integration	Infrastructure equipment vendors
Transaction support	Mechanisms for assisting with transactions, security, and billing	Application platform vendor
Presentation services	Conversion of content of Internet-based applications to applications suitable for mobile devices	Application developer
Personalization support	Gathering of users' preferences, information, and devices in order to provide individualized applications	Content developer
User applications	General and specialized applications for mobile users	Mobile service provider
Content aggregators	Design and operation of portals that offer categorized information and search facilities	Mobile portal provider

Source: Compiled from Siau et al. (2001).

mobile portals, advertisers, software vendors, content providers, mobile portal, mobile network operator and more (See Sadeh 2002, p. 34.)

The revenue models of m-commerce are the following: access fees, subscription fees, pay-per-use, advertising, transaction fees, hosting, payment clearing, and point-of-traffic (Coursaris and Hassanein, 2002).

6.2 MOBILE COMPUTING INFRASTRUCTURE

Mobile computing requires hardware, software, and networks. The major infrastructure components of mobile computing are described in this section.

Mobile Computing Hardware

To conduct m-commerce, one needs devices for data entry and access to the Internet, applications, and other equipment. Several mobile computing devices are used in m-commerce. The major ones are:

- *Cellular (mobile) phones.* All major cell phone manufacturers are making (or plan to make) Internet-enabled phones, also known as *smartphones.* These cell phones are improving with time, adding more features, larger screens, keyboards, and more. Over 35 percent of the new cell phones have color screens (Pilato, 2002), for example. An example of an Internet-enabled cell phone is the Nokia 3510i, which includes Internet access, multimedia messaging (MMS), support for small Java applications (like games), a calculator, scheduler, address book, and more. Note that even phones without screen displays (regular or cellular phones) can be used to retrieve voice information from the Web (see *tellme.com* and the discussion of voice portals later in this Section).

- *Attachable keyboard.* Transactions can be executed with the regular handset entry keys, but it is fairly time-consuming to do so. An alternative is to use a larger cell phone such as the Nokia 9290 that contains a small-scale keyboard. Yet another solution is to plug an attachable keyboard into the cell phone. (Attachable keyboards are also available for other wireless devices, such as PDAs.)

- *PDAs.* Personal digital assistants (PDAs) with Internet access are now available from several vendors, and their capabilities are increasing. Using special software, users can connect these PDAs to the Internet via a wireless modem. PDAs for *corporate users* include additional capabilities, such as e-mail synchronization and exchange of data and backup files with corporate servers. (Examples of PDAs for corporate users are Jornada from HP, IPAQ from Compaq, Sony NX70V, and MobilePro from NEC.)

- *Interactive pagers.* Some two-way pagers can be used to conduct limited mobile computing and m-commerce activities on the Internet (mainly sending and receiving text messages, such as stock market orders).

- *Screenphones.* A telephone equipped with a color screen, possibly a keyboard, e-mail, and Internet capabilities, is referred to as a **screenphone.** Initially, these were *wire-lined*; that is, they were regular phones connected by wires to a network. As of 2000, wireless screenphones became available.

- *E-mail handhelds.* To enhance wireless e-mail capabilities, one can use devices such as the BlackBerry Handheld (*blackberry.net*). This device, which includes a keypad, is an integrated package, so there is no need to dial into an Internet provider for access. A variety of services for data communication enable users to receive and send messages from anywhere. For example, the law firm of Paul, Hastins, Janofsky, & Walker (with offices in major U.S. cities) has deployed Blackberry handhelds to its 900 lawyers, who can now receive their e-mail in real time and can enter billing information while on the road. Furthermore, they can be alerted whenever they have a voice mail or fax waiting. A third of the company's lawyers have returned their laptops, and the company has saved $260,000 each year. New applications are coming with each new version of the handhelds (for details, see Cohen, 2002). A product demo is available at *blackberry.net.*

● *Other devices.* Many other wireless support devices are on the market. For example, the Seiko SmartPad (*siibusinessproducts.com*) allows you to handwrite from a notepad instantly to a cell phone or PDA screen, overcoming the small screen size of these devices. Some new cell phones have built-in cameras; you can take a picture and e-mail it immediately from your mobile location. Finally there is a wireless mouse, which works up to 15 feet, so it can be used for presentations. For an overview of devices see Kridel (2003).

There is a significant trend toward the *convergence* of PDAs and cell phones. On the one hand, the PDA manufacturers are providing PDAs with cellular or wireless capabilities. On the other hand, the cellular phone manufacturers and systems providers are offering phones with PDA capabilities.

In addition to the hardware described above, m-commerce also requires the following infrastructure hardware, most of which the user does not see or know about, but which is essential for wireless connectivity.

● A suitably configured wireline or wireless *WAN modem, wireless LAN adapter,* or *wireless MAN* (metro-area network) adapter.

● A *Web server* with wireless support, a WAP gateway, a communications server, and/or a mobile communications server switch (MCSS). Such a Web server provides communications functionality that enables the handheld device to communicate with the Internet or intranet infrastructure (see *mobileinfo.com*).

● An *application* or *database server* with application logic and a business application database.

● A large *enterprise application server.*

● A *GPS locator* that is used to determine the location of the person carrying the mobile computing device. This is the basis for location-based applications, as described in Section 6.8.

Mobile Computing Software

Developing software for wireless devices is challenging because, as of 2002, there is no widely accepted standard for wireless applications. Therefore, software applications need to be customized for each type of device with which the application may communicate. The major software products required for mobile computing are presented in Table 6.3.

Wireless Wide Area Networks (WWANs)

At the core of most mobile computing applications are *mobile networks.* These are of two general types: the *wide area* and the *local area.* The wide area networks for mobile computing are known as **wireless wide area networks (WWAN).** The breadth of coverage of WWANs directly affects the availability of services (see Intel, 2002). Breadth of coverage depends on the transmission media and the generation of wireless.

TABLE 6.3 Software for Mobile Computing

Software	Description
Microbrowser	A browser with limited bandwidth and memory requirements. Provides wireless access to the Internet.
Operating system (OS) for mobile client	An OS for mobile devices. Examples: Palmos, Windows 2001NT, Win CE. Specialized OSs: Blackberry and Web browser.
Bluetooth (named for a Viking king)	Chip technology for short-range (30 meters in 2003) communication among wireless devices. Uses digital two-way radio frequency (RF). It is an almost universal standard for wireless Personal Area Network (WPAN) for data and voice. See *bluetooth.com*.
User interface	Application logic for handheld devices. It is often controlled by the microbrowser.
Legacy application software	Residing on the mainframe, it is a major source of data to wireless systems.
Application middleware	Provides connection among applications, databases, and Web-based servers.
Wireless middleware	Links wireless networks to application servers.
Wireless Application Protocol (WAP)	A set of communication protocols that enables wireless devices to "talk" to a server on a mobile network, so users can access the Internet. Specially designed for small screen. A competing standard is the J2ME platform that offers better security and graphics (see *wapforum.org*).
Wireless Markup Language (WML)	An XML-based scripting language for creating content for wireless systems.
Voice XML	An extension of XML designed to accommodate voice.

The global communications and cellular phone companies operate most of the wireless wide area networks. A very simple mobile system is shown in Figure 6.3. At the edge of the system are the mobile handsets. A **mobile handset** consists of two parts—terminal equipment that hosts the applications (e.g., a PDA) and a mobile terminal (e.g., a cell phone) that connects to the mobile network.

TRANSMISSION MEDIA. Several transmission media can be used for wireless transmission. These media differ in both capabilities and cost. The major ones are shown in Online File W6.1.

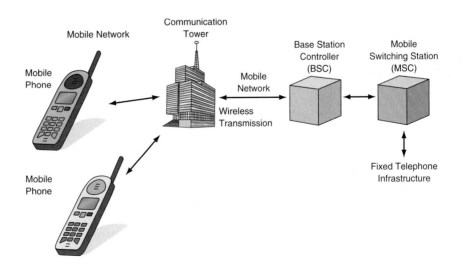

FIGURE 6.3 Mobile system architecture.

COMMUNICATION GENERATIONS OF WIRELESS WIDE AREA NETWORKS. The success of mobile computing depends on the capabilities of the WWAN communication systems. Four generations of communications technology are distinguished:

- **1G.** The first generation of wireless technology. It was an analog-based technology, in effect from 1979 to 1992.
- **2G.** The second generation of digital wireless technology. In existence today, 2G is based on digital radio technology and mainly accommodates text.
- **2.5G.** An interim technology based on GPRS (General Packet Radio Services) and EDGE (Enhanced Data Rates for Global Evaluation) that can accommodate limited graphics.
- **3G.** The third generation of digital wireless technology, which supports rich media such as video clips. It started in 2001 in Japan, and reached Europe in 2002 and the United States in 2003. As of 2003, the number of 3G cell phones in operation was around 150 million (a small percentage of the total number of cell phones in use today) (Dunne, 2001).
- **4G.** The expected next generation after 3G. The arrival of 4G, which will provide faster display of multimedia, is expected between 2006 and 2010. Experimental HGs were used in Japan as early as 2003.

For details on transmission media, see Sadeh (2002) and Mennecke and Strader (2003).

SOME NETWORK COMPONENTS. Some mobile handsets, especially in Europe, contain a **subscriber identification module (SIM) card.** This is an extractable storage card that is used not only for identification but also for providing customer location information, transaction processing, secure communications, and the like. A SIM card makes it possible for a handset to work with multiple phone numbers.

The mobile handset communicates with a *base-transceiver station.* There are thousands of these throughout the world. A base-transceiver station is connected to a *base-station controller* that handles the handoff from one transceiver to the next as the customer or user travels from one place to another. The various base-station controllers are connected to *mobile switching centers* that connect the mobile network with the public wired phone network.

COMMUNICATION PROTOCOLS IN WWAN. One of the major problems facing the mobile communication system providers is how to service extremely large numbers of users given limited communication bandwidth. This can be done through multiplexing protocols (see Technology Guide 4). In today's mobile world (2003), there are three main protocols:

- **Frequency Division Multiple Access (FDMA).** Used by 1G systems, this protocol gives each user a different frequency to communicate on.
- **Time Division Multiple Access (TDMA).** Used with some of the more popular 2G systems, this protocol assigns different users different time slots on a given communications channel (e.g., every 1/8 time slot).
- **Code Division Multiple Access (CDMA).** Used with most 2.5G and 3G systems, this protocol separates different users by assigning different codes to the segments of each user's communications.

In today's mobile world most of the networks rely on either TDMA or CDMA. The relationships between these two multiplexing methods and the major network standards are detailed in Online File W6.2 along with the evolution of these standards from today's 2G world to tomorrow's 3G and 4G world.

Wireless Local Area Networks and Wi-Fi

For the past few years, much of the discussion about mobile computing and m-commerce has revolved around WWANs with cellular technologies, especially the 3G one. Slowly but surely, another technology (one that has been around for at least a decade)—wireless local area networks—has been making its way to the forefront as the market factors impeding its growth are being addressed. As the name implies, a **wireless LAN (WLAN)** is like a wired LAN but without the cables. WLANs transmit and receive data over the airwaves.

In a typical configuration, a transmitter with an antenna, called a **wireless access point,** connects to a wired LAN from a fixed location or to satellite dishes that provide an Internet connection. A wireless access point provides service to a number of users within a small geographical perimeter (up to a couple hundred feet), known as a "hot spot" zone, or **hotspot.** Several wireless access points are needed to support larger numbers of users across a larger geographical area. End users can access a WLAN with their laptops, desktops, or PDAs by adding a wireless network card. As of 2004 most PC and laptop manufacturers incorporate these cards directly in their PCs (as an option). For how to connect your PC quickly and securely with no wires, see Stafford and Brandt (2002).

WLANs provide fast and easy Internet or intranet broadband access from public hotspots like airports, hotels, Internet cafes, and conference centers. WLANs are also being used in universities (recall the Dartmouth case in Chapter 1), offices, and homes, in place of the traditional wired LANs. In this way users are free to roam across the campus, office, or throughout their homes (see *weca.net*).

Most of today's WLANs run on a standard known as **802.11b** that was developed by the IEEE (Institute of Electrical and Electronics Engineers). That standard is also called **Wi-Fi (wireless fidelity).** WLANs employing this standard have communication speeds of 11 mbps. While most wired networks run at 100 mbps, 11 mbps is actually sufficient for many applications. Two other new standards, 802.11a and 802.11g, support data transmissions at 54 mbps. The 802.11g standard is beginning to show up in commercial products because it is compatible with the 802.11b standard. While PCs can take advantage of 54 mbps, today's (2004) PDAs cannot, because their expansion (network) cards are limited to the 11 mbps speed. As of 2004 there is even hardware and software that supports voice over Wi-Fi (*telephony*).

The major benefits of Wi-Fi are its lower cost and its ability to provide simple Internet access. As a matter of fact it is the greatest facilitator of the *wireless Internet* (see Anderson, 2003). The Wi-Fi market got a boost at the end of 2002 when AT&T, Intel, and IBM, along with two global investment firms, joined forces to create Cometa Networks, Inc. Cometa (*cometa.com*) works with major retail chains, hotels, universities, and real estate firms to deploy Wi-Fi hotspots throughout the top 50 U.S. metropolitan areas.

WIRELESS PERSONAL AREA NETWORKS (WPANs). A *wireless personal area network (WPAN)* is a kind of WLAN that people have at their home offices. With such a network, one can connect PCs, PDAs, mobile phones, and digital music players that detect each other and can interact. Also, one can add a digital payment system and personal security technologies. The network maintains constant connectivity among devices, which is useful for users in office settings, including those who use wearable devices.

ILLUSTRATIVE APPLICATIONS OF WI-FI. The year 2004 may be a breakthrough year for wireless networking in offices, airports, hotels, and campuses around the United States. Each month brings new examples of businesses that have added Wi-Fi services for their employees or customers. Several examples are presented below. Many more examples of Wi-Fi are included in this chapter and throughout the book.

- Like a number of airports in the United States, the Minneapolis–St. Paul International airport is served by Wi-Fi. The Northstar Crossing concession area, the Northwest Airlines' World Club lounge, the United Airlines' Red Carpet Club, and many of the main terminal concourses provide wireless Internet access to anyone with a laptop or handheld device and a Wi-Fi network card. iPass is hosting the Internet service. The fee is $7.95 for unlimited daily access.

- Lufthansa offers in-flight Wi-Fi service on its long-haul fleet. The hotspots on the aircrafts are connected to the Internet via satellites. While a news channel is free, there is a charge of $25 for use during the flight (Bloomberg News, 2003).

- In 2002, T-Mobile installed Wi-Fi networks in approximately 2,000 Starbucks stores in the United States. Starbucks has plans to add Wi-Fi to 70 percent of its 6,000 locations worldwide over the next few years. T-Mobile is also installing Wi-Fi in hundreds of Borders Books & Music Stores. T-Mobile is charging $30 a month for unlimited access, with walk-in customers paying $2.99 for the first 15 minutes and 25 cents a minute thereafter.

- McDonald's piloted a program in April 2003 in which it initially offered Wi-Fi wireless access in 10 restaurants in New York City (*mcdwireless.com*). The company has an access point (hotspot) in each of these restaurants. If you buy a "value meal" you get one hour of free access. Alternatively, you can pay $3 an hour (which is significantly cheaper than the $12 an hour charged by Kinko's and many others for using regular desktop computers). McDonald's will eventually offer the program in thousands of its restaurants (watch for the window sign on the restaurants, that will combine McDonald's arches with a Wi-Fi symbol). With tens of thousands of McDonald's restaurants worldwide, this service can greatly help travelers accessing the Internet. Furthermore, if you have an Internet access via AOL or other ISPs, you will get the services free, even without buying the value meal.

- Similarly, Panera Bread Company has added hotspots in many of its restaurants in St. Louis, Missouri, where Panera is headquartered. The addition of hotspots is a marketing tactic aimed at attracting customers.

- Using a wireless ticketing system, Universal Studios in Hollywood is shortening the waiting lines for tickets at its front gate. The ticket sellers, armed with Wi-Fi–enabled devices and belt-mounted printers, not only sell tickets but also provide information. For details, see Scanlon (2003).

● CVS Corp., the largest retail pharmacy in the United States, uses Wi-Fi–based devices throughout its 4,100 stores. The hand-held computers support a variety of in-store applications, including direct store delivery, price management, inventory control, and receiving. Benefits include faster transfer rates, increasing productivity and performance, reduced cost, and improved customer service. For details see *symbol.com* (1998).

BARRIERS TO COMMERCIAL WI-FI GROWTH. Two factors are standing in the way of Wi-Fi market growth: cost and security. First, some analysts question why anyone would pay $30 a month, $7.95 a day, or any other fee for Wi-Fi access when it is readily available in many locations for free. Because it's relatively inexpensive to set up a wireless access point that is connected to the Internet, a number of businesses offer their customers Wi-Fi access without charging them for the service. In fact, there is an organization, Freenetworks.org, aimed at supporting the creation of free community wireless network projects around the globe. In areas like San Francisco, where there is a solid core of high-tech professionals, many "gear heads" have set up their own wireless hotspots that give passersby free Internet connections. This is a part of a new culture known as *war chalking* and *war driving* (see *A Closer Look 6.1*).

One of the primary aims of people engaged in war driving is to highlight the lax security of Wi-Fi hotspots. This is the second barrier to widespread acceptance of Wi-Fi. Using radio waves, Wi-Fi can be interrupted by walls (resulting in poor quality at times), and it is difficult to protect. Wi-Fi does have a built-in security system, known as *Wireless Encryption Protocol* (*WEP*), which encrypts the communications between a client machine (laptop or PDA) and a wireless access point. However, WEP provides weak encryption, meaning that it is secured against casual hacking as long as the person setting up the network remembers

A CLOSER LOOK
6.1 WAR CHALKING AND WAR DRIVING

Free Wi-Fi Internet hubs are marked in some places by symbols on sidewalks and walls to indicate nearby wireless access. This practice is called *war chalking*. It was inspired by the practice of hobos during the Great Depression who used chalkmarks to indicate which homes were friendly.

A number of people have also made a hobby or sport out of war driving. *War driving* is the act of locating wireless local area networks while driving around a city or elsewhere (see *wardriving.com*). To war drive, you need a vehicle, a computer or PDA, a wireless card, and some kind of an antenna that can be mounted on top of or positioned inside the car. Because a WLAN may have a range

that extends beyond the building in which it is located, an outside user may be able to intrude into the network, obtain a free Internet connection, and possibly gain access to important data and other resources. The term war driving was coined by computer security consultant Peter Shipley and derives from the term *war dialing*, a technique in which a hacker programs his or her system to call hundreds of phone numbers in search of poorly protected computer dial-ups. The term war dialing in turn came from the movie *WarGames*, which features Matthew Broderick performing the technique.

Source: Compiled from Kellner (2003).

to turn on the encryption. Unfortunately, many small business owners and homeowners with wireless LANs fail to do just that. For more on WEP, see Online File W6.3.

Mobile Computing and M-Commerce Security Issues

In 2001 a hacker sent an e-mail message to 13 million users of the i-mode wireless data service in Japan. The message had the potential to take over the recipient's phone, causing it to dial Japan's emergency hotline (1-1-0). NTT Docomo, which provides the i-mode service, rapidly fixed the problem so no damage was done. At the beginning of 2002, researchers in Holland discovered a bug in the operating system used by many Nokia phones that would enable a hacker to exploit the system by sending a malformed SMS message capable of crashing the system. Again, no real damage was done.

Today, most of the Internet-enabled cell phones in operation are incapable of storing applications and, in turn, incapable of propagating a virus, worm, or other rogue program from one phone to another. Most of these cell phones also have their operating systems and other functionalities "burned" right into the hardware. This makes it difficult for a rogue program to permanently alter the operation of a cell phone. However, as the capabilities of cellular phones increase and the functionality of PDAs and cell phones converge, the threat of attack from malicious code will certainly increase.

Just because a mobile device is less susceptible to attack by malicious code does not mean that m-commerce is more secure than e-commerce in the wired world. By their very nature mobile devices and mobile transactions produce some unique security challenges. See Raina and Harsh (2002), and Online File W6.4.

Because m-commerce transactions eventually end up on a wired Internet, many of the processes, procedures, and technologies used to secure e-commerce transactions can also be applied in mobile environments. Of particular importance is the *public key infrastructure* (see Chapter 5 Online Files). The security approaches that apply directly to mobile devices and networks are presented in Online File W6.5.

Voice Systems for M-Commerce

The most natural mode of human communication is voice. When people need to communicate with each other from a distance, they use the telephone more frequently than any other communication device. Voice communication can now also be done on the computer using a microphone and a sound card. As computers are getting better at recognizing and understanding the human voice, voice systems are improving, and the number and types of voice technology applications are growing. (For further discussion of voice recognition, see Kumagai, 2002, and Chapter 12 of this book.)

Voice technologies have various advantages: The most obvious one is portability; users do not have to go to a stationary computer. The hands- and eyes-free operations of voice technologies increase the productivity, safety, and effectiveness of mobile computer users, ranging from forklift drivers to military pilots. Also, for those users in dirty or moving environments, voice terminals operate better than keyboards because they are more rugged. Voice technologies also enable disabled people to tell a computer to perform various tasks. Another advantage is speed; people can communicate about two-and-a-half times faster talking than typing. In most circumstances, speaking also results in fewer data entry errors than does keyboard data entry, assuming a reliable voice recognition system is used.

Voice and data can work together to create useful applications. For example, operators of PBXs (private branch exchanges, which are basically the command center of intracompany phone systems) are letting callers give simple computer commands using interactive voice response (e.g., spelling the last name of the person one is calling).

VOICE PORTALS. A **voice portal** is a Web site with an audio interface. Voice portals are not really Web sites in the normal sense because they are accessed through a standard or a cell telephone. A certain phone number connects you to a participating Web site where you can request information verbally. The system finds the information, translates it into a computer-generated voice reply, and tells you what you want to know. (See the demo at *3iobile.com*.) Several of these new sites are in operation. An example of this application is the voice-activated 511 traveler information line developed by Tellme.com (see Chapter 1). *Tellme.com* and *bevocal.com* allow callers to request information about weather, local restaurants, current traffic, and other handy information (see Kumagai, 2002).

In addition to retrieving information, some sites provide true interaction. *iPing.com* is a reminder and notification service that allows users to enter information via the Web and receive reminder calls. In addition, iPing.com can call a group of people to notify them of a meeting or conference call.

The real value for Internet marketers is that these voice portals can help businesses find new customers. Several of these sites are supported by ads; thus, the customer profile data they have available can deliver targeted advertising very precisely. For instance, a department-store chain with an existing brand image can use short audio commercials on these sites to deliver a message related to the topic of the call.

With the development of technical standards and continuing growth of wireless technologies, the number of m-commerce applications is growing rapidly. Applications are derived from providing wireless access to existing B2C, intrabusiness, and CRM applications and from creating new location-based and SMS-based applications. In Sections 6.3 through 6.8 of this chapter, we will study m-commerce applications in a number of diverse categories.

6.3 MOBILE APPLICATIONS IN FINANCIAL SERVICES

Mobile financial applications include banking, wireless payments and micropayments, wireless wallets, bill payment services, brokerage services, and money transfers. While many of these services are simply a subset of their wire-line counterparts, they have the potential to turn a mobile device into a business tool, replacing banks, ATMs, and credit cards by letting a user conduct financial transactions with a mobile device, any time and from anywhere. In this section we will look at some of the most popular mobile applications in financial services.

Mobile Banking   Throughout Europe, the United States, and Asia, an increasing percentage of banks offer mobile access to financial and account information. For instance, Merita Bank in Sweden pioneered many services (Sadeh, 2002), and Citibank in the U.S. has a diversified mobile banking service. Consumers in such banks can use their mobile handsets to access account balances, pay bills, and transfer funds using SMS. The Royal Bank of Scotland uses a new mobile payment service (Lipset, 2002), and Banamex, one of Mexico's largest banks, is a strong provider of wireless services to customers. Many banks in Japan allow for all banking transactions to be done via cell phone. A study of banks in Germany, Switzerland, and Austria found that over 60 percent offered some form of mobile financial services (Hornberger and Kehlenbeck, 2002).

To date, though, the uptake of mobile banking has been minimal. Yet surveys indicate there is strong latent demand for these offerings; customers seem to be waiting for the technology and transmission speeds to improve. The same picture holds true for other mobile financial applications like mobile brokering, insurance, and stock market trades.

Wireless Electronic Payment Systems

Wireless payment systems transform mobile phones into secure, self-contained purchasing tools capable of instantly authorizing payments over the cellular network. In Italy, for example, DPS-Promatic has designed and installed the first parking meter payable by mobile telephone (DPS-Promatic, 2002). In the United States, Cellbucks offers a mobile payment service to participating sports stadiums that enables fan to purchase food, beverages, and merchandise by cell phone and have it delivered to their seats. Any fan who is a member of the Cellbucks Network can dial a toll-free number provided on a menu of choices, enter his or her pass code and seat location, then select numbered items that correspond to desired menu selections. Once authorized, the purchase is passed on to stadium personnel and is in turn delivered to the fan's seat. An e-mail detailing the transaction is sent to the fan as further confirmation of the order. In Europe and Japan buying tickets to movies and other events are popular (Sadeh, 2002).

Micropayments

If you were in Frankfurt, Germany, and took a taxi ride, you could pay the taxi driver using your cell phone. As discussed in Chapter 5, electronic payments for small-purchase amounts (generally less than $10) are called *micropayments*. The demand for wireless micropayments systems is fairly high. An A.T. Kearney study (CyberAtlas, 2002) found that more than 40 percent of mobile phone users surveyed would like to use their mobile phone for small cash transactions such as transit fares or vending machines. The desire for such service was highest in Japan (50 percent) and lowest in the United States (38 percent). The percentage of mobile phone users who had actually used their phones for this purpose was only 2 percent, reflecting the fact that very few vendors participate in micropayments systems.

An Israeli firm, TeleVend, Inc. (*televend.com*), has pioneered a secure platform that allows subscribers to make payments using mobile phones of any type on any cellular infrastructure. A customer places a mobile phone call to a number stipulated by the merchant, to authorize a vending device to dispense the service. Connecting to a TeleVend server, the user selects the appropriate transaction option to authorize payment. Billing can be made to the customer's bank or credit card account or to the mobile phone bill.

Micropayment technology has wide-ranging applications, such as making payments to parking garages, restaurants, grocery stores, and public transportation. The success of micropayment applications, however, ultimately depends on the costs of the transactions. Transaction costs will be small only if there is a large volume of transactions.

Mobile (Wireless) Wallets

An *e-wallet* (see Chapter 5) is a piece of software that stores an online shopper's credit card numbers and other personal information so that the shopper does not have to reenter that information for every online purchase. In the recent past, companies like SNAZ offered **mobile wallet** (**m-wallet,** also known as wireless wallet) technologies that enabled cardholders to make purchases with a single click from their mobile devices. While most of these companies are now defunct, some cell phone providers have incorporated m-wallets in their offerings. A good example is the Nokia wallet. This application provides users with a secure storage space in their phones for information (such as credit card numbers) to be used in mobile payments. The information can also be used to authenticate transactions by signing them digitally. Microsoft is about to offer its e-wallet, Passport, in a wireless environment.

Wireless Bill Payments

In addition to paying bills through wireline banking or from ATMs (see Chapter 5), a number of companies are now providing their customers with the option of paying their bills directly from a cell phone (Lipset, 2003). HDFC Bank of India (*hdfcbank.com*), for example, allows customers to pay their utility bills through SMS. An example of how bill payments can be made using a mobile device is shown in Figure 6.4. This service is offered by Nordea, a pioneering provider of wireless banking services in Scandinavia.

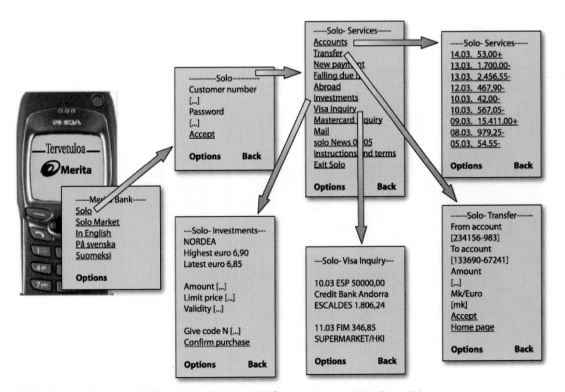

FIGURE 6.4 Nordea's WAP solo banking portal. (*Source:* Sadeh (2002, Fig. 1.4).)

6.4   MOBILE SHOPPING, ADVERTISING, AND CONTENT-PROVIDING

Like EC, m-commerce B2C applications are concentrated in three major areas—retail shopping, advertising, and providing content for a fee (see Rupp and Smith, 2002).

Shopping from Wireless Devices

An increasing number of online vendors allow customers to shop from wireless devices. For example, customers who use Internet-ready cell phones can shop at certain sites such as *mobile.yahoo.com* or *amazon.com*. Shopping from wireless devices enables customers to perform quick searches, compare prices, use a shopping cart, order, and view the status of their order using their cell phones or wireless PDAs. Wireless shoppers are supported by services similar to those available for wire-line shoppers.

An example of restaurant food shopping from wireless devices is that of a joint venture between Motorola and Food.com. The companies offer restaurant chains an infrastructure that enables consumers to place an order for pickup or delivery virtually any time, anywhere. Donatos Pizzeria was the first chain to implement the system in 2002.

Cell phone users can also participate in online auctions. For example, eBay offers "anywhere wireless" services. Account holders at eBay can access their accounts, browse, search, bid, and rebid on items from any Internet-enabled phone or PDA. The same is true for participants in Amazon.com Auctions.

An example of purchasing movie tickets by wireless device is illustrated in Figure 6.5. Notice that the reservation is made directly with the merchant. Then money is transferred from the customer's account to the merchant's account.

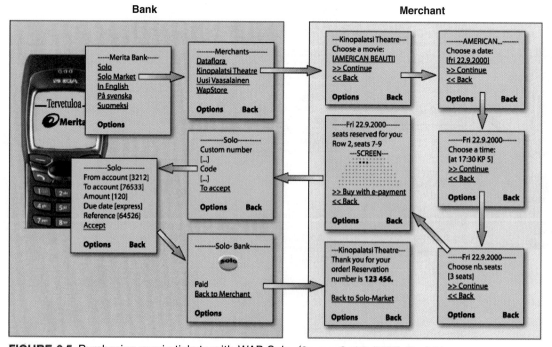

FIGURE 6.5 Purchasing movie tickets with WAP Solo. (*Source:* Sadeh (2002), Fig 1.5.)

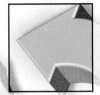

A CLOSER LOOK
6.2 WIRELESS ADVERTISING IN ACTION

The following are a few examples of wireless advertising in action.

Vindigo.com (*vindigo.com*) has a large database of customers (over 600,000 in early 2003) willing to accept promotional materials on their wireless devices. This is known as *permission marketing.* The users download special software on their PDAs that allows Vindigo.com to deliver timely, accurate information about places to go and things to do in their area. Along with every listing, the company can deliver a customized message to the users at a time and place where it is of most interest to them and they are most likely to act on it.

The company targets ads by city (New York, San Francisco, Los Angeles, etc.) and channel (Eat, Shop, or Play). Vindigo.com tracks which ads a user sees and selects, and even allows a user to request information from an advertiser via e-mail. Vindigo.com determines a user's location through GPS or by asking which neighborhoods they want to be matched with. For example, if you own an Italian restaurant chain, you can use Vindigo.com to send a message to anyone looking for Italian food within a few blocks of one of your locations. You can give them directions to that restaurant and even offer them the list of specials on the menu and discounts.

MyAvantGo.Com (*avantgo.com*) has over 2,500 content channels and over 7 million registered users (AvantGo, 2002). The content is delivered to PDAs and handsets running Palm or PocketPC operating systems. MyAvantgo offers an m-business channel and direct promotions to deliver advertising from some of the world's top brands including American Airlines, Chevy Trucks, the Golf Channel, CNN, the *New York Times,* and Yahoo. For details see Stanford (2002).

Hoping to become the king of location-based Web domains, Go2Online (*go2online.com*) helps mobile travelers find everything from lodging (choose *go2hotels*) to Jiffy Lube stations (choose *go2oilchanges*). Partnering with Sprint, NexTel, Verizon, and BellSouth, Go2 makes its services available on every Web-enabled phone, Palm i705, and BlackBerry RIM pager in America. Entering "JiffyLube" or hundreds of other brand names into the Go2 system will bring up the nearest location where a shopper can find that product or service.

Sources: Compiled from the Web sites of Vindigo.com, AvantGo.com, and GO2Online.com.

Targeted Advertising   Knowing the current location of mobile users (using GPS) and their preferences or surfing habits, marketers can send user-specific advertising messages to wireless devices. Advertising can also be location-sensitive, informing a user about shops, malls, and restaurants close to where a potential buyer is. SMS messages and short paging messages can be used to deliver this type of advertising to cell phones and pagers, respectively. Many companies are capitalizing on targeted advertising, as shown in *A Closer Look 6.2.*

As more wireless bandwidth becomes available, content-rich advertising involving audio, pictures, and video clips will be generated for individual users with specific needs, interests, and inclinations. Also, depending on the interests and personality types of individual mobile users, the network provider may consider using "push" or "pull" methods of mobile advertising on a per user basis or to a class of users (market segmentation). The number of ads pushed to an individual customer should be limited, to avoid overwhelming a user with too much information and also to avoid the possibility of congestion over the wireless networks. Wireless network managers may consider ad traffic to be of a lower priority compared with ordering or customer interaction. Finally, since ad pushers need to know a user's current location, a third-party vendor may be used to provide location services. This will require a sharing of revenues with a location service provider. A futuristic area of advertisement, which is based on GPS tracking, is described in Section 6.8.

GETTING PAID TO LISTEN TO ADVERTISING.　Would you be willing to listen to a 10-second ad when you dial your cell phone if you were paid 2 minutes of free long-distance time? As in the wire-line world, some consumers are willing to be paid for exposure to advertising. It depends on which country you are in. In most places where it was offered in the United States, this service was a flop and was discontinued.

In Singapore, though, getting paid to listen to advertising works very well. Within a few months of offering the ads, more than 100,000 people subscribed to the free minutes in exchange for listening to the ads offered by SingTel Mobile (Eklund, 2001). Subscribers to SingTel's service fill out a personal questionnaire when they sign up. This information is fed into the Spotcast database and encrypted to shield subscribers' identities—Spotcast cannot match phone numbers to names, for example. To collect their free minutes—one minute per call, up to 100 minutes a month—subscribers dial a four-digit code, then the phone number of the person they want to talk to. The code prompts SingTel to forward the call to Spotcast and, in an instant, Spotcast's software finds the best ad to send to the subscriber based on the subscriber's profile.

THE FUTURE OF WIRELESS ADVERTISING.　In 2002, the Yankee Group concluded that the U.S. wireless advertising market would be worth only $10 million by 2004, substantially below earlier estimates that pegged the market at $130 million by that year (Yankee Group, 2002). By 2003 almost all wireless advertising initiatives have been merely trials. As the Yankee Group noted, the most promising avenues of success for wireless advertising will incorporate it with other advertising media (e.g., hardcopy advertising that directs consumers to wireless or mobile ads offering incentives) or wireless ads directing users to Web sites or physical locations. According to the Yankee Group, many wireless advertising firms are betting their futures on the wide-scale acceptance of SMS, even in the United States where its usage currently is small.

Mobile Portals　A **mobile portal** is a customer channel, optimized for mobility, that aggregates and provides content and services for mobile users (see Bughin et al., 2001; Sadeh 2002; and Chapter 4 for additional discussion of portals). Examples of best "pure" mobile portals (those whose only business is to be a mobile portal) are Room 33 (*room33.com*) in Europe and *zed.com* from Sonera in Finland. Nordea's Solo banking portal was illustrated in Figure 6.4. The world's best-known mobile portal, with over 40 million members, mostly in Japan, is i-mode from DoCoMo.

The services provided by mobile portals include news, sports, e-mail, entertainment and travel information; restaurants and event information; leisure-related services (e.g., games, TV and movie listings); community services; and stock trading. A sizeable percentage of the portals also provide downloads and messaging, music-related services, and health, dating, and job information. Mobile portals frequently charge for their services. For example, you may be asked to pay 50 cents to get a weather report over your mobile phone. Alternatively, you may pay a monthly fee for the portal service and get the report free any time you want it. In Japan, for example, i-mode generates revenue mainly from subscription fees.

Increasingly, the field of mobile portals is being dominated by a few big companies (Global Mobile Suppliers Association, 2002). The big players in Europe, for instance, are companies like Vodafone, Orange, O2, and T-Mobile; in the United States the big players are Cingular, Verizon, and Sprint PCS. Also, mobile-device manufactures offer their own portals (e.g., Club Nokia portal, My Palm portal). And, finally, the traditional portals (such as Yahoo, AOL, and MSN) have mobile portals as well.

6.5 MOBILE INTRABUSINESS AND ENTERPRISE APPLICATIONS

Although B2C m-commerce is getting considerable publicity, most of today's applications are used within organizations. According to Estrada (2002), employees connected to Wi-Fi increase their productivity by up to 22 percent due to better and faster connectivity. This section looks at how mobile devices and technologies can be used *within* organizations.

Support of Mobile Workers

Mobile workers are those working outside the corporate premises. Examples of mobile workers are salespeople in the field, traveling executives, telecommuters, people working in corporate yards and warehouses, and repair or installation employees who work at customers' sites or on utility lines. These mobile workers need the same corporate data available to employees working inside the company's offices. Yet, using wire-line devices, even portable ones, may be inconvenient or impossible when employees are away from their offices.

The solution is myriad smaller, simple wireless devices—the smartphones and handheld companions carried by mobile workers and the in-vehicle information systems installed in cars. Many of these wireless devices are wearable.

WEARABLE DEVICES. Employees who work on buildings, electrical poles, or other difficult-to-climb places may be equipped with a special form of mobile wireless computing devices called **wearable devices.** Examples of wearable devices include:

- *Screen.* A computer screen is mounted on a safety hat, in front of the wearer's eyes, displaying information to the worker. (See item 1 in the photo on page 260.)
- *Camera.* A camera is mounted on a safety hat. (See item 2 in photo.) Workers can take digital photos and videos and transmit them instantly to a portable computer nearby. Photo transmission to a wearable device or computer is made possible via Bluetooth technology.
- *Touch-panel display.* In addition to the wrist-mounted keyboard, mobile employees can use a flat-panel screen, attached to the hand, which responds to the tap of a finger or stylus. (See item 3 in photo.)
- *Keyboard.* A wrist-mounted keyboard enables typing by the other hand. (See item 4 in photo.) (Wearable keyboards are an alternative to voice recognition systems, which are also wireless).
- *Speech translator.* For those mobile employees who do not have their hands free to use a keyboard, a wearable speech translator is handy (see Smailagic et al., 2001).

For an example of wearable devices used to support mobile employees, see *IT at Work 6.1* (page 260) and *wearable.com.au.*

IT at Work 6.1
WEARABLE DEVICES FOR BELL CANADA WORKERS

For years mobile employees, especially those who had to climb trees, electric poles, or tall buildings, were unable to enjoy the new technologies designed to make employees work or feel better. Thus, their productivity and comfort were inferior, especially where computers were involved. That is all beginning to change.

On a cold, damp November day in Toronto, Chris Holm-Laursen, a field technician with Bell Canada (*bell.ca*), is

out and about as usual, but this time with a difference: A small but powerful computer sits in a pocket of his vest, a keyboard is attached to the vest's upper-left side, and a flat-panel display screen hangs by his waist. A video camera attached to his safety hat enables him to take pictures without using his hands and send them immediately to the office. A cell phone is attached as well, connected to the computer. A battery pack to keep everything going sits against his back. (See nearby photo.)

Holm-Laursen and 18 other technicians on this pilot project were equipped like this for 10 weeks during fall 2000. By summer 2003 an increasing number of Bell

Canada's employees have been equipped with similar devices. The wearable devices enabled the workers to access work orders and repair manuals wherever they were. These workers are not typical of the group usually most wired up, that is, white-collar workers. The hands-free aspect and the ability to communicate any time, from anywhere, represent major steps forward for these utility workers. A wide variety of employees—technicians, medical practitioners, aircraft mechanics, and contractors—are using or testing such devices.

So far, only a few companies make and sell wearables for mobile workers. Bell Canada's system was developed by Xybernaut, a U.S. company that in 2002 had more than a thousand of its units in use around the world, some in operation and others in pilot programs (see *xybernaut.com*, 2003). Minneapolis-based ViA is another supplier, most of whose systems are belt-worn (*bell.ca*). Meanwhile, Bell Canada was impressed with the initial results, and is equipping most of its technicians with wearable devices.

Of course, a practical problem of wearable devices in many countries is the weather: What happens when the temperature is minus 50 degrees or the humidity is 99 percent? Other potential problems also exist: If you are wearing thick gloves, how can you use a keyboard? If it is pouring rain, will the battery short circuit? Various solutions are being developed, such as voice input, tapping on a screen instead of typing, and rainproof electrical systems.

Sources: Compiled from XyberFlash, 2000, and *xybernaut.com*, 2003.

For Further Exploration: What are some other industrial applications of similar wearable devices? How do you think wearable devices could be used in entertainment?

JOB DISPATCH. Mobile devices are becoming an increasingly integral part of groupware and workflow applications. For example, non-voice mobile services can be used to assist in dispatch functions—to assign jobs to mobile employees, along with detailed information about the task. The target areas for mobile delivery and dispatch services include the following: transportation (delivery of food, oil, newspapers, cargo, courier services, tow trucks, and taxis); utilities (gas, electricity, phone, water); field service (computer, office equipment, home repair); health care (visiting nurses, doctors, social services); and security (patrols, alarm installation).

A dispatching application for wireless devices allows improved response with reduced resources, real-time tracking of work orders, increased dispatcher

IT at Work 6.2
U.S. FLEET SERVICES AND WIRELESS NETWORKING

Started in 1997, U.S. Fleet Services URL (*usfleet.com*) has grown to be the leading provider of mobile, onsite fueling in the United States with customers such as FedEx, Home Depot, Coca-Cola, Nabisco, and Office Max. Using trucks that resemble home fuel-delivery vehicles, U.S. Fleet travels to its customers, refueling the customers' vehicles onsite, usually during off-hours. In 1999 U.S. Fleet considered building a wireless network for its drivers, but decided against it. Managers considered the project too hard and too expensive given the expected return on investment. However, toward the end of 2001, they changed their minds.

While a mobile wireless solution was the end goal, the first step in the project actually involved the implementation of an ERP system. This was followed by a Web-based application built on top of the ERP that provided customers with information about their fuel consumption and local gas taxes, enabling them to do better fleet management. Finally, U.S. Fleet equipped its drivers with handheld devices that could communicate with the company's intranet using Wi-Fi.

The handheld device U.S. Fleet selected was the Intermec 710 (*intermec.com*). Besides having a built-in barcode scanner, this device also runs Microsoft's Pocket PC operating system, supports Visual Basic programs, handles CompactFlash cards, and has an integrated wireless radio for short range Wi-Fi communications. The device is fairly lightweight with a drop-resistant case that is sealed to protect against harsh weather conditions.

The way the system works is this: Branch managers enter a delivery route and schedule for each driver into a centralized database via the company's intranet. Each driver starts his or her shift by downloading the route and schedule over the company's Wi-Fi network into a handheld. When the driver reaches a customer stop, the handheld is used to scan a barcode attached to the customer's truck. This provides the driver with the type of fuel required by the truck. After the truck is fueled, a meter on the delivery truck sends a wireless signal to the handheld. The handheld then syncs with the meter, capturing the type and quantity of fuel delivered. The data are stored on the handheld's CompactFlash memory card. When the driver returns to the home base, the data are unloaded over the Wi-Fi network to the central database. At this point, the data are available for U.S. Fleet and its customers to analyze using business intelligence tools.

Before the handhelds were deployed, drivers would record the data manually. The data were then faxed from the branch offices to headquarters and entered by hand into the system. Not only were there delays but the data were also subject to entry errors at both ends of the line. Now, the company and its customers have accurate data in a timely fashion, which provides the company with faster invoicing and cash flow. On average, the new system has also enabled drivers to service six to seven more stops per shift.

Sources: Compiled from Ludorf, 2002, *intermec.com* 2001, and *usfleet.com* 2003.

For Further Exploration: What systems did U.S. Fleet put in place before implementing its wireless solution? Why did U.S. Fleet select the device? How does the Intermec 710 handheld device communicate with the company's intranet? What are the major benefits that U.S. Fleet has realized by combining handheld devices with Wi-Fi?

efficiency, and a reduction in administrative work. AirIQ (*edispatch.com*), for example, offers an interesting solution. AirIQ's OnLine system combines Internet, wireless, GPS, digital mapping, and intelligent information technologies. The system tracks vital information about a vehicle's direction, speed, and location which is provided by a device housed in each of the vehicles being tracked. Managers can view and access information about the fleet on digital maps, monitor vehicles on the Internet, and maintain top operating condition of their fleet. AirIQ promises savings of about 30 percent in communication costs and increases in workforce efficiency of about 25 percent (*edispatch.com*).

IT at Work 6.2 provides a detailed description of a job-dispatching system being used by U.S. Fleet to benefit both itself and its customers.

SUPPORTING OTHER TYPES OF WORK. Wireless devices may support a wide variety of mobile workers. The applications will surely grow as the technology matures and as workers think up new ways to apply the functions of wireless devices to their jobs. Here are three examples.

1. Tractors equipped with sensors, onboard computers, and a GPS help farmers save time, effort, and money. GPS determines the precise location of the tractor and can direct its automatic steering. Because the rows of planting resulting from GPS-guiding are more exact, the farmers save both on seeds and on fertilizers, due to minimized overlapping and spillage. Farmers can also work longer hours with the satellite-controlled steering, taking advantage of good weather, for example. Another saving is due to instant notification to the service department of any machine that breaks down. For details see Scanlon (2003).

2. Taco Bell provided its mystery shoppers (shoppers who visit restaurants to conduct a survey unknown to the owners) with handheld computers so that they can communicate more quickly with the company's headquarters. The visitors must answer 35 questions, ranging from the speed of service to food quality. Before the devices, information was provided by filling out paper forms that were mailed overnight. This information was scanned into computers for processing. The information flow using the handhelds is both faster and more accurate.

3. Like e-mail, MSM can be used to bolster collaboration; because of its reach it has special applications. According to Kontzer (2003), the following are 10 applications of SMS for mobile workers: (1) alerting mobile technicians to system errors, (2) alerting mobile execs to urgent voice messages, (3) confirming with mobile sales personnel that a faxed order was received, (4) informing travelers of delays and changes, (5) enabling contract workers to receive and accept project offers, (6) keeping stock traders up to date on urgent stock activity, (7) reminding data services subscribers about daily updates, (8) alerting doctors to urgent patient situations, (9) enabling mobile sales teams to input daily sales figures into corporate database, and (10) sending mobile sales reps reminders of appointments and other schedule details.

Customer Support and CRM

Supporting customers is the essence of customer relationship management (CRM) systems. Mobile access extends the reach of CRM—both inside and outside the company—to both employees and business partners on a 24/7 basis, to any place where recipients are located. According to Eklund (2002), 12 percent of companies in the United States provided corporate users with mobile access to their CRM systems.

In the large software suites like Siebel's CRM, the two CRM functions that have attracted the most interest are sales force automation and field service. For instance, a sales person might be on a sales call and need to know recent billing history for a particular customer. Or, a field service representative on a service call might need to know current availability of various parts in order to fix a piece of machinery. It is these sorts of situations where mobile access to customer and partner data is invaluable. Two of the more recent offerings in this arena are Salesforce.com's Airforce Wireless Edition and Upshot's Alerts (*upshot.com*) (see Hill, 2002). See *A Closer Look 6.3* for descriptions of the use of mobile applications for customer support.

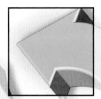

A CLOSER LOOK
6.3 MOBILE WORKPLACE APPLICATIONS FOR CUSTOMER SUPPORT

The following are two scenarios of wireless applications for mobile employees.

SALES SUPPORT. Linda is a member of the field sales team at Theru Tools (a fictitious company). Each day she drives out to her customers in a van stocked with products. For each sale, she has to note the customer name, the number and type of products sold, and any special discounts made. This record-keeping used to be done manually, and many errors were made, leading to customer complaints and lost sales.

Theru implemented a system using low-cost but powerful handheld wireless devices. Using Mobile Sales (an application for handhelds), accessed via the *mysap.com* Mobile Workplace, Linda and her coworkers in the field now have information at their fingertips, including updates on new products and special promotions. Linda can place orders without delay and get immediate feedback on product availability and delivery times. What's more, the system can prompt Linda as she enters orders, and it also can make plausibility checks on the orders, eliminating many of the errors associated with the manual process. It also checks to see if she is giving the right discounts to the right customer, and immediately triggers the invoicing process or prints out a receipt on the spot.

CUSTOMER SERVICE SUPPORT. Michael works for Euroblast, Inc. (another fictitious company) as a service engineer. It is his job to provide time-critical maintenance and support for the company's customers' electromechanical control systems. To do so, he needs to know immediately when a customer's system is faltering, what is malfunctioning, and what type of service contract is in effect.

Michael does not need to carry all of this information in his head, but instead has it in the palm of his hand. With only a few taps of a stylus, Michael accesses the *mysap.com* Mobile Workplace for all the data he requires, including the name and address of the next customer he should visit, equipment specifications, parts inventory data, and so forth.

Once he has completed the job, he can report back on the time and materials he used, and these data can be employed for timely billing and service quality analysis. In addition, his company is able to keep track of his progress and monitor any major fluctuations in activities. As a result, both Michael and his supervisors are better informed and better able to serve their customers.

Source: Compiled from SAP AG Corp. (2000) (advertisement).

Voice portal technology can also be used to provide enhanced customer service or to improve access to data for employees. For example, customers who are away from the office could use a vendor's voice portal to check on the status of deliveries to a job site. Sales people could check on inventory status during a meeting to help close a sale. There are a wide variety of CRM applications for voice portal technology. The challenge is in learning how to create the navigation and other aspects of interaction that makes customers feel comfortable with voice-access technology.

Wireless Intrabusiness Applications

Wireless applications in the non-Internet environment have been around since the early 1990s. Examples include such applications as: wireless networking, used to pick items out of storage in warehouses via PCs mounted on forklifts; delivery-status updates, entered on PCs inside distribution trucks; and collection of data such as competitors' inventories in stores and customer orders, using a handheld (but not networked) device, from which data were transferred to company headquarters each evening. (See the Maybelline minicase in Chapter 2, and the Hi-Life example in Chapter 5.)

Since then, a large number of Internet-based wireless applications have been implemented inside enterprises. Two examples of such intrabusiness applications are described below. For other examples, see Online File W6.6 at the book's Web site.

1. Employees at companies such as Telecom Italia Mobile (Republica IT, 2001) get their monthly pay slips as SMS messages sent to their mobile phone. The money itself is transferred electronically to a designated bank account. The method is much cheaper for the company and results in less paperwork than the old method of mailing monthly pay slips.

2. Kemper Insurance Company has piloted an application that lets property adjusters report from the scene of an accident. Kemper attached a wireless digital imaging system to a camera that lets property adjusters take pictures in the field and transmit them to a processing center (Henning, 2002; Nelson, 2000). The cameras are linked to Motorola's StarTac data-enabled cellular phone service, which sends the information to a database. These applications eliminate delays in obtaining information and in film processing that exist with conventional methods.

As just these two examples indicate, a variety of intrabusiness workflow applications are possible. Table 6.4 shows typical intrabusiness workflow applications before and after the introduction of wireless services. Some of these can be delivered on a wireless intranet; some are offered on the Internet. (For details on intrabusiness applications, see *mdsi-advantex.com* and *symbol.com.* The advantages offered by intrabusiness wireless solutions can be seen through an examination of workflow applications at *mdsi-advantex.com.*)

Mobile intrabusiness applications are very popular and are typically easier to implement than interbusiness applications, such as B2B and supply chain, discussed next.

TABLE 6.4 Intrabusiness Workflow Applications	
Before Wireless	**With Wireless**
Work orders are manually assigned by multiple supervisors and dispatchers.	Work orders are automatically assigned and routed within minutes for maximum efficiency.
Field service technicians commute to dispatch center to pick up paper work orders.	Home-based field service technicians receive first work order via mobile terminal and proceed directly to first assignment.
Manual record keeping of time, work completed, and billing information.	Automated productivity tracking, record keeping, and billing updates.
Field service technicians call in for new assignments and often wait because of radio traffic or unavailable dispatcher.	Electronic transmittal of additional work orders with no waiting time.
Complete work orders dropped off at dispatch center at the end of the day for manual entry into the billing or tracking system. Uncompleted orders are manually distributed to available technicians. Overtime charges often result.	Technicians close completed work orders from the mobile terminals as they are completed. At the end of the shift, the technicians sign off and go home.

Source: From the publicly distributed brochure "RALI Mobile" from Smith Advanced Technology, Inc. (2001).

6.6 MOBILE B2B AND SUPPLY CHAIN APPLICATIONS

Mobile computing solutions are also being applied to B2B and supply chain relationships. Such solutions enable organizations to respond faster to supply chain disruptions by proactively adjusting plans or by shifting resources related to critical supply chain events as they occur. With the increased interest in collaborative commerce comes the opportunity to use wireless communication to collaborate along the supply chain. For this to take place, integration is needed.

An integrated messaging system is at the center of B2B communications. By integrating the mobile terminal into the supply chain, it is possible to make mobile reservations of goods, check availability of a particular item in the warehouse, order a particular product from the manufacturing department, or provide security access to obtain confidential financial data from a management information system.

One example of an integrated messaging system is wireless *telemetry*, which combines wireless communications, vehicle monitoring systems, and vehicle location devices. (Telemetry is described further in Section 6.8.) This technology makes possible large-scale automation of data capture, improved billing timeliness and accuracy, less overhead than with the manual alternative, and increased customer satisfaction through service responsiveness. For example, vending machines can be kept replenished and in reliable operation by wirelessly polling inventory and service status continually to avert costly machine downtime.

Mobile devices can also facilitate collaboration among members of the supply chain. There is no longer any need to call a partner company and ask someone to find certain employees who work with your company. Instead, you can contact these employees directly, on their mobile devices.

By enabling sales force employees to type orders straight into the ERP while at a client's site, companies can reduce clerical mistakes and improve supply chain operations. By allowing them to check production schedules and inventory levels, and to access product configuration and *available-to-promise/capacity-to-promise* (ATP/CTP) functionality to obtain real-time delivery quotes, they empower their sales force to make more competitive and realistic offers to customers. Today's ERP systems tie into broader supply chain management solutions that extend visibility across multiple tiers in the supply chain. Mobile supply chain management (mSCM) empowers the workforce to leverage these broader systems through inventory management and ATP/CTP functionality that extend across multiple supply chain partners and take into account logistics considerations.

6.7 MOBILE CONSUMER AND PERSONAL SERVICE APPLICATIONS

A large number of applications exist that support consumers and provide personal services (see Coursaris and Hassanein, 2002, and Sadeh, 2002). As an example, consider the situation of a person going to an international airport. Tasks such as finding the right check-in desk, checking for delayed flights, waiting for lost luggage, and even finding a place to eat or the nearest washroom can be assisted by mobile devices. Online File W6.7 at the book's Web site lists

12 problem areas at airports that can be solved using mobile devices. The capabilities shown in the table in Online File W6.7 are now possible in some places and are expected to be more widely available by 2005.

Other consumer and personal service areas in which wireless devices can be used are described in the following sections. (See also *attws.com*.)

Mobile Games

In the handheld segment of the gaming market, Nintendo has been the long-time leader. In contrast, Nintendo has shown minimal interest in online or mobile games. Here, Sega has capitalized on the popularity of games such as Sonic the Hedgehog to garner 2.5 million Japanese subscribers for its mobile games and entertainment services (Becker, 2002). In Japan, where millions of commuters kill time during long train rides, cell phone games have become a cultural phenomenon.

With more than one billion cell phones in use today (CellularOnline, 2003), the potential audience for mobile games is substantially larger than the market for other platforms, Playstation and Gameboy included. Because of the market potential, Nokia has decided to enter the mobile gaming world, producing not only the phone/console but also the games that will be delivered on memory cards. It seeks to develop and market near-distance multiplayer gaming (over Bluetooth) and wide area gaming (using cellular networks) (Nokia, 2002).

In July of 2001 Ericsson, Motorola, Nokia, and Siemens established the Mobile Games Interoperability Forum (MGIF) (*mgif.org*) to define a range of technical standards that will make it possible to deploy mobile games across multigame servers, wireless networks, and over different mobile devices. Microsoft is moving into this field as well.

A topic related to games is *mobile entertainment,* discussed in Online File W6.8. Mobile gambling, another related topic, is extremely popular in some countries (e.g., horse racing in Hong Kong and racing and other events in Australia). (For more on mobile gambling, see *sportodds.com.au*.)

Hotel Services Go Wireless

A number of hotels now offer their guests in-room, high-speed Internet connection. Some of these same hotels are beginning to offer Wi-Fi Internet access in public areas and meeting rooms. One of these is Marriott, which manages 2,500 hotels worldwide. After a seven-month test, Marriott has partnered with STSN (*stsn.com*), an Internet service provider specializing in hotels, to provide Wi-Fi services in the 400 Marriott hotels that already have in-room broadband Internet access (Reuters, 2002). In the same vein, AT&T has partnered with Wayport Inc. to offer Wi-Fi in 475 hotels throughout the United States. In India the Taj Group is offering Wi-Fi access in its hotels (Taj Hotel, 2002), and Megabeam (a wireless provider in England) is starting to offer the same service in select Holiday Inn and Crowne Plaza hotels in London.

While Wi-Fi provides guests with Internet access, to date it has had minimal impact on other sorts of hotel services (e.g., check-in). However, a small number of hotels are testing use of the Bluetooth technology. Guests are provided with Bluetooth-enabled phones that can communicate with access points located throughout the hotel. This technology can be used for check-in and check-out, for making purchases from hotel vending machines and stores, for tracking loyalty points (see *tesalocks.com*), and for opening room doors in place of keys (Mayor, 2001). In 2001, Classwave signed a deal with Starwood Hotels

& Resorts worldwide to enable Bluetooth solutions within Starwood's hotels (Houck, 2001).

For a comparison of traditional and m-commerce hotel services, see Online File W6.9. These capabilities are now available only in some locations, but are expected to be widely available by 2006.

Wireless Telemedicine

Today there are two different kinds of technology used for *telemedicine* applications: (1) storage of data and transferring of digital images from one location to another, and (2) videoconferencing used for "real-time" consultation between a patient in one location and a medical specialist in another. In most of the real-time consultations, the patient is in a rural area and the specialist is in an urban location.

There are a number of impediments to telemedicine. Some states do not allow physicians to provide medical advice across state lines. The threat of malpractice suits is another issue since there is no "hands-on" interaction between the physician and patient. In addition, from a technical standpoint, many telemedicine projects are hindered by poor telecommunications support. However, those who are looking ahead to the needs of the aging population are seeing opportunities to meet some of those needs in emerging technologies. The new wireless and mobile technologies, especially the forthcoming generation, not only offer the possibility of overcoming the hurdles imposed by remote locations but also open a number of new and novel application opportunities. Examples include the following.

- Typically, physicians write a prescription and you take it to the pharmacy where you wait 15–30 minutes for it to be filled. Instead, some new mobile systems allow physicians to enter the patient prescription onto a palm-size device. That information goes by cellular modem (or Wi-Fi) to Med-i-net's (or similar companies') services. There, the information is checked for insurance eligibility and conformity to insurance company regulations. If all checks out, the prescription is transferred electronically to the appropriate pharmacy. For patients who need refills, the system tracks and notifies physicians when it is time to reorder, and the doctor can reissue a prescription with a few clicks.

- At the first warning signs of a heart attack, people are advised to contact emergency facilities as soon as possible. Manufacturers are working on wearable heart monitors linked to cell phones that can automatically contact doctors or family members at the first sign of trouble.

- The Swiss Federal Institute of Technology is designing portable devices that transmit the vital signs of avalanche victims up to 80 meters away (Baard, 2002). Not only does the device provide location information but it also provides information about body orientation that helps reduce injuries as rescuers dig for the victims.

- In-flight medical emergencies occur more frequently than one might think. Alaska Airlines, for example, deals with about 10 medical emergencies per day (Conrad, 2002). Mobile communications are already being used to attend to medical emergencies occurring on planes. MedLink, a service of MedAire in Phoenix, provides around-the-clock access to board-certified emergency physicians. These mobile services can also remotely control medical equipment, like defibrillators, located on board the plane.

● The military is involved in developing mobile telesurgery applications that enable surgeons in one location to remotely control robotic arms for surgery in another location. The technology was proven to be particularly useful in battlefield situations during the 2003 Iraq War.

Other Mobile-Computing Services for Consumers

Many other mobile computer services exist for consumers, in a variety of service categories. Examples include services providing news, weather, and sports reports; online language translations; information about tourist attractions (hours, prices); and emergency services. For more examples, see the case studies at *mobileinfo.com*.

Non-Internet Mobile-Computing Applications for Consumers

Non-Internet mobile applications for consumers, mainly those using smart cards, have existed since the early 1990s. Active use of the cards is reported in transportation, where millions of "contactless" cards (also called *proximity cards*) are used to pay bus and subway fares and road tolls. Amplified remote-sensing cards that have an RF (radio frequency) of up to 30 meters are used in several countries for toll collection. *IT at Work 6.3* describes one use of proximity cards for toll collection.

IT at Work 6.3
THE HIGHWAY 91 PROJECT

Route 91 is a major eight-lane, east-west highway near Los Angeles. Traffic is especially heavy during rush hours. California Private Transportation Company (CPT) built six express toll lanes along a 10-mile stretch in the median of the existing Highway 91. The express lane system has only one entrance and one exit, and it is totally operated with EC technologies. The system works as follows.

Only prepaid subscribers can drive on the road. Subscribers receive an automatic vehicle identification (AVI) device that is placed on the rearview mirror of the car. The device, about the size of a thick credit card, includes a microchip, an antenna, and a battery. A large sign over the tollway tells drivers the current fee for cruising the express lanes. In a recent year it varied from $0.50 in slow traffic hours to $3.25 during rush hours.

Sensors in the pavement let the tollway computer know that a car has entered; the car does not need to slow or stop. The AVI makes radio contact with a transceiver installed above the lane. The transceiver relays the car's identity through fiber-optic lines to the control center, where a computer calculates the fee for that day's trip. The system accesses the driver's account and the fare is auto-

matically deducted from the driver's prepaid account. A monthly statement is sent to the subscriber's home.

Surveillance cameras record the license numbers of cars without AVIs. These cars can be stopped by police at the exit or fined by mail. Video cameras along the tollway also enable managers to keep tabs on traffic, for example, sending a tow truck to help a stranded car. Also, through knowledge of the traffic volume, pricing decisions can be made. Raising the price as traffic increases ensures that the tollway will not be jammed.

The system saves commuters between 40 and 90 minutes each day, so it is in high demand. An interesting extension of the system is the use of the same AVIs for other purposes. For example, they can be used in paid parking lots. Someday you may be even recognized when you enter the drive-through lane of McDonald's and a voice asks you, "Mr. Smart, do you want your usual meal today?"

Source: 91expresslanes.com, 2002.

For Further Exploration: What is the role of the wireless component of this system? What are the advantages of the system to commuters?

6.8 LOCATION-BASED COMMERCE

As discussed in Section 6.1, **location-based commerce (l-commerce)** refers to the localization of products and services. Location-based services are attractive to both consumers and businesses alike. From a consumer's or business user's viewpoint, l-commerce offers safety (you can connect to an emergency service with a mobile device and have the service pinpoint your exact location), convenience (you can locate what is near you without having to consult a directory, pay phone, or map), and productivity (you can optimize your travel and time by determining points of interest within close proximity). From a business supplier's point of view, l-commerce offers an opportunity to provide services that meet customers' needs.

The basic l-commerce services revolve around five key areas:

- *Location:* determining the basic position of a person or a thing (e.g., car or boat).
- *Navigation:* plotting a route from one location to another.
- *Tracking:* monitoring the movement of a person or a thing (e.g., a package or vehicle).
- *Mapping:* creating maps of specific geographical locations.
- *Timing:* determining the precise time at a specific location.

L-Commerce Technologies

Providing location-based services requires the following location-based and network technologies:

- *Position Determining Equipment (PDE).* This equipment identifies the location of the mobile device (either through GPS or by locating the nearest base station). The position information is sent to the mobile positioning center.
- *Mobile Positioning Center (MPC).* The MPC is a server that manages the location information sent from the PDE.
- *Location-based technology.* This technology consists of groups of servers that combine the position information with geographic- and location-specific content to provide an l-commerce service. For instance, location-based technology could present a list of addresses of nearby restaurants based on the position of the caller, local street maps, and a directory of businesses.
- *Geographic content.* Geographic content consists of streets, road maps, addresses, routes, landmarks, land usage, Zip codes, and the like. This information must be delivered in compressed form for fast distribution over wireless networks.
- *Location-specific content.* Location-specific content is used in conjunction with the geographic content to provide the location of particular services. Yellow page directories showing the location of specific business and services exemplify this type of content.

Figure 6.6 (page 270) shows how these technologies are used in conjunction with one another to deliver location-based services. Underlying these technologies are global positioning and geographical information systems.

GLOBAL POSITIONING SYSTEM (GPS). As indicated at the start of the chapter, a **global positioning system (GPS)** is a wireless system that uses satellites to

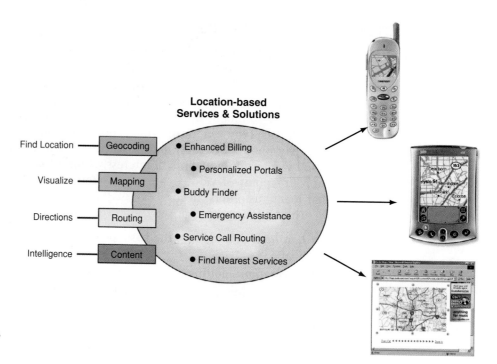

FIGURE 6.6 Location-based services involving maps. (*Source: Mapinfo.com, 2001.*)

enable users to determine their position anywhere on the earth. GPS equipment has been used extensively for navigation by commercial airlines and ships and for locating trucks and buses (as in the opening case study).

GPS is supported by 24 U.S. government satellites that are shared worldwide. Each satellite orbits the earth once every 12 hours on a precise path, at an altitude of 10,900 miles. At any point in time, the exact position of each satellite is known, because the satellite broadcasts its position and a time signal from its onboard atomic clock, which is accurate to one-billionth of a second. Receivers also have accurate clocks that are synchronized with those of the satellites.

GPS handsets can be stand-alone units or can be plugged into or embedded in a mobile device. They calculate the position (location) of the handsets (or send the information to be calculated centrally). Knowing the speed of the satellite signals (186,272 miles per second), engineers can find the location of any receiving station (latitude and longitude) to within 50 feet by *triangulation,* using the distance from a GPS to *three* satellites to make the computation. GPS software then computes the latitude and longitude of the receiver. For an online tutorial on GPS, see *trimble.com/gps.*

GEOGRAPHICAL INFORMATION SYSTEM (GIS). The location provided by GPS is expressed in terms of latitude and longitude. To make that information useful to businesses and consumers it is necessary in many cases to relate those measures to a certain place or address. This is done by inserting the latitude and longitude onto an electronic map, which is known as a **geographical information system (GIS).** The GIS data visualization technology integrates GSP data onto digitized map displays. (See Steede-Terry, 2000, for an explanation of how this is done.) Companies such as *mapinfo.com* provide the GIS core spatial

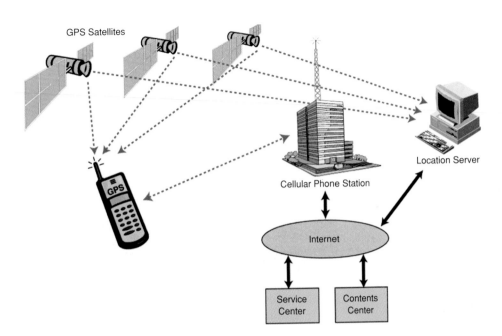

FIGURE 6.7 A smart-phone with GPS system in L-commerce.

technology, maps, and other data content needed in order to power location-based GIS/GPS services (see Figure 6.7).

An interesting application of GPS/GIS is now available from several car manufacturers (e.g., Toyota, Cadillac) and car rental companies (e.g., Hertz, Avis). Some cars have a navigation system that indicates how far away the driver is from gas stations, restaurants, and other locations of interest. The GPS knows where the car is at any time, so the application can map the route for the driver to a particular destination. Any GPS application can be classified as *telemetry,* a topic discussed further later on.

LOCATION-BASED ADVERTISING. Imagine that you are walking near a Starbucks store, but you do not even know that one is there. Suddenly your cell phone beeps with a message: "Come inside and get a 15 percent discount." Your wireless device was detected, and similar to the pop-up ads on your PC, advertising was directed your way (Needleman, 2002). You could use permission marketing to shield yourself from location-based advertising; if the system knows that you do not drink coffee, for example, you would not be sent a message from Starbucks.

Another use of wireless devices for advertising is described by Raskin (2003). In this case, a dynamic billboard ad could be personalized specifically for you when your car approaches a certain billboard and the system knows what your likes and preferences are. Your car will be tracked by a GPS, every 20 seconds. A computer scans the areas in which billboards are visible, and by cross-referencing information about your location and your likes, a personalized ad could be placed on the billboard so you would see it as you pass.

Yet another method of location-based advertising involves putting ads on the top of taxicabs. The ad will be changed based on the taxi location. For example, a taxi cruising in the theater district in New York City might show an ad for a play or a restaurant in that area; when the cab goes to another neighborhood, the ad might be for a restaurant or a business in the other area of the city.

E-911 Emergency Cell Phone Calls

If someone dials 911 from a regular wired phone, it is easy for the emergency 911 service to pinpoint the location of the phone. But, what happens if someone places a 911 call from a mobile phone? How can the emergency service locate the caller? A few years ago, the U.S. Federal Communication Commission (FCC) issued a directive to wireless carriers, requiring that they establish services to handle **wireless 911 (e-911)** calls. To give you an idea of the magnitude of this requirement, more than 156,000 wireless 911 calls are made every day, representing more than half the 911 calls made daily in the United States (Sarkar, 2003).

The e-911 directive is to take effect in two phases, although the specifics of the phases vary from one wireless carrier (e.g., AT&T, Cingular, Sprint, etc.) to another. Phase I requires carriers, upon appropriate request by a local *Public Safety Answering Point (PSAP)*, to report the telephone number of a wireless 911 caller and the location of the cellular antenna that received the call. Phase II, which is being rolled out over a four-year period from October 2002 to December 2005, requires wireless carriers to provide information that will enable the PSAP to locate a caller within 50 meters 67 percent of the time and within 150 meters 95 percent of the time. By the end of Phase II, 100 percent of the new cell phones and 95 percent of all cell phones will have these location capabilities. It is expected that many other countries will follow the example of the United States in providing e-911 service.

Some expect that in the future cars will have a device for **automatic crash notification (ACN).** This still-experimental device will automatically notify the police of an accident involving an ACN-equipped car and its location. Also, following a school bus hijacking in Pennsylvania, the state legislature is considering a bill to mandate satellite tracking in all school buses.

Telematics and Telemetry Applications

Telematics refers to the integration of computers and wireless communications in order to improve information flow (see Chatterjee et al., 2002, and Zhao, 2002). It uses the principles of *telemetry*, the science that measures physical remoteness by means of wireless transmission from a remote source (such as a vehicle) to a receiving station. MobileAria (*mobilearia.com*) is a proposed standards-based telematics platform designed to bring multimedia services and m-commerce to automobiles.

Using *mobile telemetry,* technicians can diagnose maintenance problems in equipment. Car manufacturers use the technology for remote vehicle diagnosis and preventive maintenance. Finally, doctors can monitor patients and control medical equipment from a distance.

General Motors Corporation popularized automotive telematics with its OnStar system. Nokia has set up a business unit, called Smart Traffic Products, that is focusing solely on telematics. Nokia believes that every vehicle will be equipped with at least one Internet Protocol (IP) address by the year 2010. Smart cars and traffic products are discussed in more detail in Section 6.9.

Barriers to L-Commerce

What is holding back the widespread use of location-based commerce? Several factors come into play:

● *Accuracy.* Some of the location technologies are not as accurate as people expect them to be. However, a good GPS provides a location that is accurate up to 15 meters. Less expensive, but less accurate, technologies can be used instead to find an approximate location (within about 500 meters).

- ***The cost-benefit justification.*** For many potential users, the benefits of l-commerce don't justify the cost of the hardware or the inconvenience and time required to utilize the service (e.g., Hamblen, 2001). After all, they seem to feel, they can just as easily obtain information the "old-fashioned" way.

- ***The bandwidth of GSM networks.*** GSM bandwidth is currently limited; it will be improved as 3G technology spreads. As bandwidth improves, applications will improve, which will attract more customers.

- ***Invasion of privacy.*** When "always-on" cell phones are a reality, a number of people will be hesitant to have their whereabouts and movements tracked throughout the day, even if they have nothing to hide. This issue will be heightened when our cars, homes, appliances, and all sorts of other consumer goods are connected to the Internet, as discussed in the next section.

6.9 PERVASIVE COMPUTING

Steven Spielberg's sci-fi thriller *Minority Report* depicts the world of 2054. Based on a 1956 short story by Philip K. Dick, the film immerses the viewer in the consumer-driven world of pervasive computing 50 years from now. Spielberg put together a three-day think tank, headed by Peter Schwartz, president of Global Business Network (*gbn.com*), to produce a realistic view of the future (Mathieson, 2002). The think tank projected out from today's marketing and media technologies—Web cookies, GPS, Bluetooth, personal video recorders, barcode scanners, and the like—to create a society where billboards beckon you by name, newspapers are delivered instantly over broadband wireless networks, holographic hosts greet you at retail stores, and cereal boxes broadcast live commercials. While the technologies in the film were beyond the leading edge, none was beyond the realm of the plausible.

A world in which virtually every object has processing power with wireless or wired connections to a global network is the world of **pervasive computing.** (The term pervasive computing also goes by the names *ubiquitous computing, embedded computing,* or *augmented computing.*) The idea of pervasive computing has been around for years. However, the current version was articulated by Mark Weiser in 1988 at the computer science lab of Xerox PARC. From Weiser's perspective, pervasive computing was the opposite of virtual reality. In virtual reality, the user is immersed in a computer-generated environment. In contrast, pervasive computing is invisible "everywhere computing" that is embedded in the objects around us—the floor, the lights, our cars, the washing machine, our cell phones, our clothes, and so on (Weiser, 1991, 2002).

Invisible Computing Everywhere

By "invisible," Weiser did not mean to imply that pervasive computing devices would not be seen. He meant, rather, that unlike a desktop computer, these embedded computers would not intrude on our consciousness. Think of a pair of eyeglasses. The wearer doesn't have to think about using them. He or she simply puts them on and they augment the wearer's ability to see. This is Weiser's vision for pervasive computing. The user doesn't have to think about how to use the processing power in the object; rather, the processing power automatically helps the user perform a task.

Invisible is how you would describe some of the new embedded technology already in use at Prada's "epicenter" stores in New York, San Francisco, and Los Angeles (Duan, 2002). Prada is a high-end fashion retailer. In the company's epicenters, the items for sale have an **RFID (radio frequency identification)** tag attached. The tag contains a processor and an antenna. If a customer wants to know about a particular item, she or he can move with the item toward one of the many displays around the store. The display automatically detects the item and provides sketches, video clips of models wearing the item, and information about the item (color, cut, fabric, materials, and availability). If a customer takes a garment into one of the dressing rooms, the tags are automatically scanned and detected via an antenna embedded in the dressing room. Information about the item will be automatically displayed on an interactive touch screen in the dressing room. The dressing rooms also have a video-based "Magic Mirror." When the customer tries on the garment and turns around in front of the mirror, the images will be captured and played back in slow motion. (See Section 6.10 for a related privacy issue.)

Invisible is also a term that characterizes a device manufactured and sold by Fitsense Technology (*fitsense.com*), a Massachusetts developer of Internet sports and fitness monitors. With this 1-ounce device that is clipped to a shoelace, runners are able to capture their speed and the distance they have run. The device transmits the data via a radio signal to a wrist device that can capture and transmit the data wirelessly to a desktop computer for analysis. Along the same lines, Champion Chip (*championchip.com*), headquartered in the Netherlands, has developed a system that keeps track of the tens of thousands of participants in very popular long-distance races. The tracking system includes miniature transponders attached to the runners' shoelaces or ankle bracelets and antenna mats at the finish line that use radio frequencies to capture start times, splits, and finish times as the runners cross them.

Active badges can be worn as ID cards by employees who wish to stay in touch at all times while moving around the corporate premises. The clip-on badge contains a microprocessor that transmits its (and its wearer's) location to the building's sensors, which send it to a computer. When someone wants to contact the badge wearer, the phone closest to the person is identified automatically. When badge wearers enter their offices, their badge identifies them and logs them on to their personal computers.

Similarly, *memory buttons* are nickel-sized devices that store a small database relating to whatever it is attached to. These devices are analogous to a bar code, but with far greater informational content and a content that is subject to change. For example, the U.S. Postal Service is placing memory buttons in residential mailboxes to track and improve collection and delivery schedules.

For a short list of the technical foundation of pervasive computing, see Online File W6.11 at the book's Web site.

Contextual Computing and Context Awareness

Location can be a significant differentiator when it comes to advertising services. However, knowing that the user is at the corner of the street will not tell you what he or she is looking for. For this, we might need to know the time of day, or access our user's calendar or other relevant *contextual attributes*. **Context awareness** refers to capturing a broad range of contextual attributes to better understand what the consumer needs, and what products or services he or she might possibly be interested in.

Context awareness is part of **contextual computing,** which refers to the enhancement of a user's interactions by understanding the user, the context, and the applications and information being used, typically across a wide set of user goals (see Pitkow et al., 2002 for details). Contextual computing is about actively adapting the computational environment for each user, at each point of computing.

Contextual computing and context awareness are viewed by many as the Holy Grail of m-commerce. They feel that contextual computing ultimately offers the prospect of applications that could anticipate our every wish and provide us with the exact information and services we are looking for—and also help us filter all those annoying promotional messages that we really do not care for. Such applications are futuristic at the present time, but as shown in *IT at Work 6.4* (page 276) they already exist in a research university.

Applications of Pervasive Computing

According to Estrin et al. (2000), 98 percent of all processors on the planet are not in traditional desktop computer systems, nor even in laptops. They are in household appliances, vehicles, and machines. Such existing and future applications of pervasive computing are illustrated in Figure 6.8 (page 277). Notice that all 15 devices can be connected to the Internet. Several of these applications are described in the remainder of this section. We will look at four applications in particular: smart homes, smart appliances, smart cars, and smart things.

Smart Homes

In a *smart home,* your home computer, television, lighting and heating controls, home security system, and many appliances within the home can "talk" to each other via the Internet or a home intranet. These linked systems can be controlled through various devices.

In the United States, tens of thousands of homes are already equipped with home-automation devices, and there are signs that Europe—which has much lower home Internet penetration levels—is also warming to the idea. For instance, a 2001 study by the UK's Consumers' Association found that almost half those surveyed were interested in having the functions a "smart home" could offer, if they were affordable (Edgington, 2001).

Some of the tasks supported today by home automation systems are:

- *Lighting.* You can program your lights to go on, off, or dim to match your moods and needs for comfort and security.
- *Energy management.* A home's HVAC (heat, ventilation, and air conditioning) system can be programmed for maximum energy efficiency, controlled with a touch panel, and can be accessed via your telephone or PDA.
- *Water control.* Watercop (*watercop.com*) is a device that relies on a series of strategically placed moisture-detection sensors. When the moisture level rises in one of these sensors, it sends a wireless signal to the Watercop control unit, which turns off the main water supply.
- *Home security and communications.* The window blinds, garage doors, front door, smoke detectors, and home security systems can all be automated from a network control panel. These can all be programmed to respond to scheduled events (e.g., when you go on vacation).
- *Home theater.* You can create a multi-source audio and video center around your house that you can control with a touch pad or remote. For example, if you have a DVD player in your bedroom but want to see the same movie in your child's room, you can just click a remote to switch rooms.

IT at Work 6.4

CONTEXT-AWARE ENVIRONMENT AT CARNEGIE MELLON UNIVERSITY

Carnegie Mellon University (CMU) is known for its advanced science projects including robotics and artificial intelligence. Students participate in a context-awareness experiment in the following manner: Each participating student is equipped with a PDA from which he or she can access Internet services via the campus Wi-Fi network. The students operate in a context-aware environment whose architecture is shown in the attached figure.

messages, and determine what to show to the students, and when. For example, while attending classes the student may block all messages, except from her boyfriend. That is, certain messages will be shown only if the student is in a certain place and/or time; others will not be shown at all.

A user's context information can be accessed by a collection of *personal agents,* each in charge of assisting with different tasks, while locating and invoking relevant Internet services identified through services registries (see the figure).

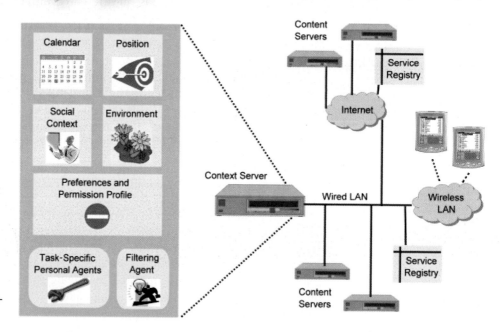

Carnegie Mellon's context-awareness system

A user's context (left of figure) includes his or her:

- Calendar information.
- Current location (position), which is regularly updated using location-tracking technology.
- Weather information, indicating whether it is sunny, raining, or snowing, and the current outside temperature (environment).
- Social context information, including the student's friends and his or her teachers, classmates, and so forth.

The preferences of each student are solicited and entered into system, as is a personal profile. This is shown as the "preferences and permissions" in the figure. All of the above information helps the system to filter incoming

An example of a simple agent is a *restaurant concierge* that gives suggestions to students about places to have lunch, depending on their food preferences, the time they have available before their next class, their location on campus, and the weather. For example, when it is raining, the agent attempts to find a place that does not require going outside of the building where the student is located. The recommendation (usually several choices) appears on the PDA, with an overall rating and a "click for details" possibility.

Source: Compiled from Sadeh (2002).

For Further Exploration: Does the usefulness of such a service justify the need to disclose private preferences? Can such a system be developed for consumers who are not members of a defined community such as a university?

FIGURE 6.8 Embedded computing devices everywhere. (*Source:* Estrin et al., 2000, pp. 38–39.)

1. Smart building materials:
   - Sense vibrations, temperature, moisture
   - Monitor premises for intruders
   - Cancel street noise
2. Bridge deck erected with smart building materials:
   - Senses, reports traffic, wind loads
   - Monitors structural integrity
3. Autonomous robo-sweeper
4. Wireless communication, including links to GPS satellites, Net access
5. Smart sensor pills:
   - Programmable delivery vehicles for pharmaceuticals
   - Internal sensing applications
6. Embedded automobile devices:
   - Antilock brakes
   - Air bags
   - Evaluate performance
   - Provide Net access
7. Fire hydrant measures water flow, senses heat, offers security mechanisms.
8. Autonomous robo-mailbot performing nominally manual labor.
9. Street light senses foot and motor traffic, polices area.
10. Banking/business:
    - ATM machines, cash registers, bar-code readers, credit card devices
    - Security devices offer personal Ids, but also sense vibrations and (body) heat and motion and monitors premises for intruders.
11. Home networks:
    - Most electrical appliances, including dishwashers, toasters, cable TV set-top boxes, toys, phones, thermostats, PCs
12. Smart building materials:
    - Smart paint
    - smart concrete
    - Smart gels
13. Smart cement detects earthquake activity.
14. Collar on dog for wireless location via GPS link. Clothes on man (personal cybernetics) offer similar abilities. As well as networking and heat sensors.

Analysts generally agree that the market opportunities for smart homes will take shape over the next three to five years. These opportunities are being driven by the increasing adoption of broadband (cable and DSL) services and the proliferation of wireless local area networks (Wi-Fi) within the home and by the trend to integrate currently independent devices. Online File W6.12 shows a wireless connected house.

Smart Appliances

One of the key elements of a smart home is the *smart appliance,* an Internet-ready appliance that can be controlled by a small handheld device or desktop computer via a home intranet (wire or wireless) or the public Internet.

One organization that is focused on smart appliances is the Internet Home Alliance (*internethomealliance.com*). The alliance is made up of a number of appliance manufacturers (e.g., Whirlpool and Sunbeam), computer hardware companies (e.g., IBM and Cisco), retailers (e.g., Best Buy), and vendors specializing in home automation (e.g., Lutron Electronics). The mission of the alliance is to accelerate the process of researching, developing, and testing new home products and services that require a broadband or persistent connection to the Internet. Online File W16.13 exemplifies some the types of smart appliances being developed by members of the alliance; in this case, however, the appliances are being used for commercial purposes, not in the home.

The appliance manufacturers are interested not only in the sale of appliances but also in service. In most cases, when an appliance is purchased and taken home, the manufacturer loses touch with the appliance unless the customer registers the product for warranty purposes. Potentially, a networked appliance could provide a manufacturer, as well as the owner of the appliance, with information that could be used to capture or report on the operation, performance, and usage of a device. In addition, the networked appliance could provide information for diagnostic purposes—for monitoring, troubleshooting, repairing, or maintaining the device (Pinto, 2002).

To date, however, consumers have shown little interest in smart appliances. As a result, the manufacturers of these appliances are focusing on improving people's lives by eliminating repetitive, non-quality tasks. One example is Sunbeam's corded HLT (Home Linking Technology) products that communicate with one another using an embedded technology called PLC (Power Line Communication). For instance, an HTL alarm clock can coordinate an entire morning's routine: The heating system, the coffee maker, and the lights in the kids' rooms go on, and the electric blanket goes off.

Whether offerings of this sort will prove successful is an open question. In the near term, one of the biggest technical barriers to widespread adoption of smart appliances will continue to be the fact that most homes lack broadband connection to the Internet. However, this situation is rapidly changing.

Smart Cars

Every car today has at least one computer on board to operate the engine, regulate fuel consumption, and control exhaust emissions. The average automobile on the road today has 20 or more microprocessors, which are truly invisible. They are under the hood, behind the dash, in the door panels, and on the undercarriage. Microprocessors control the radio, decide when your transmission should shift gears, remember your seat position, and adjust the temperature in the passenger cabin. They can make the suspension work better, help you see in the dark, and warn when a tire is low. In the shop, the onboard microprocessors are used to diagnose problems. Car computers often operate independently, but some swap data among themselves—a growing trend. The microprocessors in a car require little maintenance, continuing to operate through extreme temperature, vibration, and humidity.

In 1998, the U.S. Department of Transportation (DOT) identified eight areas where microprocessors and intelligent systems could improve or impact auto safety (*www.its.dot.gov/ivi/ivi.htm*). The list included four kinds of collision avoidance (see Jones, 2001), computer "vision" for cars, vehicle stability, and two kinds of driver monitoring. The automotive industry is in the process of testing a variety of experimental systems addressing the areas identified by the DOT. For example, GM in partnership with Delphi Automotive Systems has developed an Automotive Collision Avoidance System that employs radar, video cameras, special sensors, and GPS to monitor traffic and driver actions in an effort to reduce collisions with other vehicles and pedestrians (Sharke, 2003).

There is also a growing trend to connect car microprocessors to mobile networks and to the Internet (see Moore, 2000). Emergency assistance, driving directions, and e-mail are some of the services these connections can support. To increase safety, drivers can use voice-activated controls, even to access the Web (Bretz, 2001) GM's OnStar system (*onstar.com*) already supports many of these services (see Online File W6.13).

OnStar is the forerunner of smart cars of the future. The next generation of smart cars is likely to provide even more automated services, especially in emergency situations. For instance, although OnStar will automatically signal the service center when the air bags are deployed and will immediately contact emergency services if the driver and passengers are incapacitated, what OnStar cannot provide is detailed information about a crash. Newer systems are under development that will automatically determine the speed upon impact, whether the car has rolled over, and whether the driver and passengers were wearing seat belts. Information of this sort might be used by emergency personnel to determine the severity of the accident and what types of services will be needed.

Ideally smart cars eventually will be able to drive themselves. Known as "autonomous land vechicles" (ALVs), these cars follow GIS maps and use sensors in a wireless environment to identify obstacles. These vehicles are already on the roads in California, Pennsylvania, and Germany (on an experimental basis, of course).

Smart "Things" Several other devices and instruments can be made to be "smart." Some examples are discussed below.

BARCODES. A typical barcode, known as the *Universal Product Code (UPC),* is made up of 12 digits, in various groups. The first two show the country where it was issued, the next four represent the manufacturer, and the remaining six are the product code assigned by the manufacturer. On a package the code is represented by a series of bars and spaces of varying widths.

Barcodes are used at various points in the supply chain to track inventory and shipments and to identify items at the point of sale. A barcode scanner is required to support these tasks. It consists of a scanning device for reading the code and translating it into an electrical output, a decoder for converting the electrical output to data that a computer or terminal can recognize, and a cable that connects the decoder to a computer or terminal.

Barcodes have worked pretty well over the past 25 years. But, they have their limitations. First, they require line-of-sight of the scanning device. This is fine in a store but can pose substantial problems in a manufacturing plant, a warehouse, or on a shipping/receiving dock. Second, they are printed on paper, meaning that they can be ripped, soiled, or lost. Third, the barcode identifies the manufacturer and product, not the item. For example, every carton of milk of a given producer has the same barcode, regardless of when it was produced. This makes a barcode useless in determining things like the expiration date. There is an alternative identification method, called Auto-ID, that overcomes the limitations of barcodes.

AUTO-ID.   This method has been promoted over the past couple of years by the **Auto Identification (Auto-ID) Center** (*autoidcenter.org*), a joint partnership among more than 87 global companies and three of the world's leading research universities—MIT in the United States, the University of Cambridge in the U.K., and the University of Adelaide in Australia. The companies include manufacturers (e.g., Coca-Cola, Gillette, and Canon), retailers (e.g., Wal-Mart, Tesco in the U.K.), shippers (e.g., UPS and the U.S. Postal Service), standards bodies (e.g., Uniform Code Council), and government agencies (e.g., the U.S. Department of Defense).

The mission of the Auto-ID Center goes well beyond replacing one code with another. Its stated aim is to create an **Internet of "things,"** a network that connects computers to objects—boxes of laundry detergent, pairs of jeans, airplane engines. This Internet of things will provide the ability to track individual items as they move from factories to store shelves to recycling facilities. This will make possible near-perfect supply chain visibility.

The key technical elements of the Auto-ID system and the explanation of how it will work are provided in Online File W6.15.

RFID: CAPABILITIES AND COST.   RFID has been around awhile. During World War II, RFIDs were used to identify friendly aircraft. Today, they are used in wireless tollbooth systems, such as E-Z Pass. In Singapore they are used in a system called Electronic Road Pricing, which charges different prices to drive on different roads at different times, encouraging drivers to stay off busy roads at busy times. Every car has an RFID tag that communicates with card readers on the major roads (similar to the story of Highway 91 in *IT at Work 6.3*, page 268).

Until now the problem with RFID has been the expense. Tags have cost at least 50 cents, which makes them unusable for low-priced items. A California company called Alien Technology (*alientechnology.com*) has invented a way to mass-produce RFID tags for less than 10 cents apiece for large production runs. In January 2003, Gillette placed an order with Alien Technology for 500 million RFID tags (*RFID Journal*, 2002). Gillette is using the tags in a number of trial programs. In one of the early trials, Gillette attached the tags to the Mach 3 razors they ship to Wal-Mart, whose store shelves are equipped with special RFID readers. The overall success of RFID tags in the market place will depend on the outcome of trials such as this.

Large-Scale Pervasive Systems

Smart appliances, cars, and barcodes can certainly make our lives more comfortable, but pervasive computing can make an even larger contribution when large numbers of computing devices are put together, creating massive intelligent systems. These systems include factories, airports, schools, and even entire cities. At the moment most of them are experimental and on a relatively small scale. Let's look at some examples.

SMART SCHOOLS. The University of California at Los Angeles is experimenting with a smart kindergarten (Chen et al., 2002). Exploring communication between students, teachers, and the environment, the project aims to create a smart learning environment.

INTELLIGENT ELDER-CARE. The increased age of the population in many countries brings a problem of caring for more elderly for longer times. Long-term care facilities, where different patients require different levels of care, bring the problem of how to provide such care efficiently and effectively. The experimental project titled Elite-care has demonstrated the benefits of using pervasive computing in such settings, as described in *IT at Work 6.5* (page 282).

SMART OFFICES. The original work of Weiser (1991) centered around an intelligent office. And indeed several projects are experimenting with such an environment which can interact with users through voice, gesture, or movements and can anticipate their activities. By monitoring office employees, the SmartOffice (Le Gal et al., 2001) even anticipates user intentions and augments the environment to communicate useful information.

DIGITAL CITIES. According to Ishida (2002a) the concept of **digital cities** is to build an area in which people in regional communities can interact and share knowledge, experiences, and mutual interests. Digital cities integrate urban information (both real time and stored) and create public spaces for people living in or visiting the cities. Digital cities are being developed all over the world (see Ishida, 2002a, 2002b). In Europe alone there are over 100 projects (e.g., Amsterdam, Helsinki).

In the city of Kyoto, Japan, for example, the digital city complements and corresponds to the physical city (Ishida, 2002a). Three layers are constructed: The first is an information layer, where Web archives and real-time sensory data are integrated to provide information anywhere, any time. The second layer is 2D and 3D interfaces, which provide views of cars, buses, and pictures that illustrate city services (for attractive and natural presentation). Finally, there is an interactive layer. Extensive use of GIS supports the project. One area of emphasis is a digital tour guide for visitors. Also, the system uses avatars (animated computer characters) that appear on a handheld device and "walk" with visitors around the city in real time.

Another digital-city experiment is the city of Lancaster (U.K.), where wireless devices are being used to improve services to both visitors and residents (Davies et al., 2002). The experimental Lancaster City Guide is based on a network of Wi-Fi context-sensitive and location-aware applications. One area that was developed first is services to tourists. By knowing where the tourist is (using a GPS) and his (her) preferences, the system can recommend tourist sites in the same general area. (This application is similar to the Carnegie Mellon application described in *IT at Work 6.4*, page 276.)

For other digital-city experiments, see Raskin (2003), Mankins (2002), and Fleck et al. (2002). For information onother large-scale pervasive computing projects, see Weise (2002), and Standford (2002b).

IT at Work 6.5
USING PERVASIVE COMPUTING TO DELIVER ELDER CARE

Delivering health services to the elderly is becoming a major societal problem in many countries, especially in countries where there are relatively fewer and fewer young people to take care of more and more elderly. The problem is already acute in Japan, and it is expected to be very serious in 10 to 15 years in several European countries and in China. Managing and delivering health care involves large numbers of diversified decisions, ranging from allocation of resources to determining what treatment to provide to each patient at each given time.

Elderly residents in assisted-living facilities require differing levels of care. Some residents need minimal assistance, others have short-term memory problems, and yet others have more severe problems like Alzheimer's disease so they require more supervision and help. At Elite Care's Estates Cluster Residential Care Facility in Milwaukie, Oregon, pervasive computing is being used to increase the autonomy and care level of all of its residents, regardless of their individual needs.

Elite Care, a family-owned business (*elite-care.com*), has been built from the ground up to provide "high-tech, high-touch" programs. Its advisory committee, which includes, among others, representatives from the Mayo Clinic, Harvard University, the University of Michigan, the University of Wisconsin, and Sandia National Laboratory, has contributed a number of ideas that have been put into practice.

The entire facility is wired with a 30-mile network (wireline and wireless) of unobtrusive sensors and other devices including: biosensors (e.g., weight sensors) attached to each resident's bed; movement sensors embedded in badges worn by the residents and staff; panic buttons used to call for help; Internet access via touch screens in each room; video conferencing using Webcams; and climate control, lights, and other regulated appliances.

These devices and others allow the staff to monitor various patient activity. For example, staff can determine the location of any patient, to tell whether he or she is in an expected area of the facility. Devices that monitor length of absence from bed might alert personnel that the patient has fallen or is incapacitated in other ways. Medical personnel can watch for weight loss (possibly indicating conditions like impending congestive heart failure), restlessness at night (indicating conditions like insufficient pain medication), and frequency of trips to the bathroom (indicating medical problems like infection). Also, close monitoring of conditions enables staff to give medicine and/or other treatments as needed, rather than at predetermined periods. All of these capabilities enable true one-to-one care, which is both more effective and less expensive.

One of the initial concerns with these monitors is that the privacy of the residents would be unnecessarily invaded. To alleviate these concerns, residents and their families are given the choice of participating or not. Most choose to participate because the families believe that these monitors provide better tracking and care. The monitors also increase the autonomy of all the patients because their use reduces the need for staff to constantly monitor residents in person, especially those with more acute care needs.

All of these sensors and systems are connected through a high-speed Ethernet (see Tech Guide 4). The data produced by the sensors and systems are stored in a database and can be used to alert the staff in real time if necessary. These data are used for analytical purposes and for developing individualized care programs. The same database is also used for administrative purposes such as monitoring staff performance in timely delivery.

A similar concept is used in Swan Village of Care in Bentley, Australia. At the present time such projects are experimental and expensive, but some day they will be affordable to many.

Sources: Compiled from Stanford, 2002, *elite-care.com*, and *ECC. online.wa.gov.au/news* (January 14, 2003).

For Further Exploration: What types of data do these devices provide? How can pervasive computing increase the quality of elder care? What about the privacy issue?

6.10 INHIBITORS AND BARRIERS OF MOBILE COMPUTING

Several limitations are either slowing down the spread of mobile computing or are leaving many m-commerce customers disappointed or dissatisfied (e.g., see Islam and Fayad, 2003). Representative inhibitors and barriers of mobile computing are covered in the following discussion.

The Usability Problem

When mobile Internet users visit mobile Internet sites, the *usability* of the site is critical to attract attention and retain "user stickiness" (the degree to which users stay at a site). There are three dimensions to usability, namely *effectiveness, efficiency,* and *satisfaction.* However, users often find current mobile devices to be ineffective, particularly with respect to restricted keyboards and pocket-size screens, limiting their usability. In addition, because of the limited storage capacity and information access speed of most smartphones and PDAs, it is often difficult or impossible to download large files to these devices.

Mobile visitors to a Web site are typically paying premium fees for connections and are focused on a specific goal (e.g., conducting a stock trade). Therefore, if customers want to find exactly what they are looking for, easily and quickly, they need more than text-only devices with small screens. In 2003, many WAP applications were still text-based, and had only simple black-and-white graphics. This made tasks such as mobile shopping difficult. Because all the transactions were essentially text-based, mobile users could not "browse" an online picture-based catalog. However, more and faster multimedia are becoming available as 3G spreads.

The major technical and other limitations that have slowed the spread of m-commerce are summarized in Table 6.5.

Ethical and Legal Issues

Several ethical and legal issues are unique to mobile computing. For example, fashion retailer Benetton Group SpA was considering attaching RFID "smart

TABLE 6.5 Technical and Other Limitations of Mobile Computing

Limitation	Description
Insufficient bandwidth	Sufficient bandwidth is necessary for widespread use and it must be inexpensive. It will take a few years until 3G is in many places. Wi-Fi solves some of the problem.
Security standards	Universal standards were not available in 2003. It may take 3 or more years to have them.
Power consumption	Batteries with long life are needed for mobile computing. Color screens and Wi-Fi consume more electricity, but new chips are solving some of the power-consumption problems.
Transmission interferences	Weather and terrain problems as well as distance-limited connection exist with some technologies. Reception in tunnels and some buildings is poor.
GPS accuracy	GPS may be inaccurate in a city with tall buildings.
WAP limitations	According to *mofileinfo.com,* in 2002 there were only about 50,000 WAP sites (compared to millions of Web sites). WAP still is a cumbersome process to work with.
Potential health hazards	Potential health damage from cellular radio frequency emission is not known yet. However, more car accidents are related to drivers who were talking (some places bar the use of cell phones while you drive). Also, cell phones may interfere with sensitive medical devices.
Legal issues	Potential legal issues against manufacturers of cell phones and against service providers exist, due to the potential health problems (Borland, 2000).
Human interface with device	Screens and keyboards are too small and uncomfortable and tedious for many people to use.
Complexity	Too many optional addons are available (e.g., battery chargers, external keyboards, headset, microphones, cradles). Storing and using the optional add-ons is a problem to some.

tags" to its Sisley line of clothing to help track shipping, inventory, and sales in the company's 5,000 stores worldwide. (Also, the tags could help prevent shoplifting.) The idea was to integrate the RFID tag into the clothing labels. Using the tags, the store would know where each piece of clothing is, at any given time. However, privacy groups expressed concern that the tags could also be used to track buyers, and some groups even urged that the company's clothing be boycotted. As a result, Benetton backed away from the plan, at least until an impact study is done (Rosencrance, 2003).

According to Hunter (2002) privacy is in great danger in the world of ubiquitous computing because of the proliferation of networked devices used by individual, businesses, and government. The Elite-Care project described in *IT at Work 6.5* (page 282), for example, raised the issue of protecting information collected by sensors. Also, privacy is difficult to control in other types of context-aware systems (e.g., see Jiang and Landay, 2002). As indicated earlier, security is especially difficult in Wi-Fi systems.

Challenges in Deploying Ubiquitous Systems

For pervasive (ubiquitous) systems to be widely deployed, it is necessary to overcome both the technical and ethical/legal barriers associated with wireless computing, plus overcoming other barriers unique to pervasive computing. Davies and Gellersen (2002) provide a comprehensive list of technical challenges, social and legal issues, and economic concerns (including finding appropriate business models) in deploying ubiquitous systems. They also cite research challenges such as component interaction, adaptation and contextual sensitivity, user interface interaction, and appropriate management mechanisms.

Failures in Mobile Computing and M-Commerce

As with any other technology, especially a new one, there have been many failures of applications as well as entire companies in mobile computing and m-commerce. It is important to anticipate and plan for possible failures as well as to learn from them.

The case of Northeast Utilities provides some important insights. According to Hamblen (2001), Northeast Utilities (located in Berlin, Connecticut), which supplies energy products and services to 1.2 million customers from Maine to Maryland, embarked on a wireless project in 1995 in which its field inspectors used wireless devices to track spills of hazardous material and report them to headquarters in real time. After spending a year and a half and $1 million, the project failed. Some of the lessons learned were:

- Do not start without appropriate infrastructure.
- Do not start a full-scale implementation; use a small pilot for experimentation.
- Pick up an appropriate architecture. Some users don't need to be persistently connected, for example.
- Talk with a range of users, some experienced and some not, about usability issues.
- Users must be involved; hold bi-weekly meetings if possible.
- Use wireless experts if you are not one.
- Wireless is a different medium from other forms of communication. Remember that people are not used to the wireless paradigm.

Having learned from the failure, Northeast made its next wireless endeavor a success. Today, 15 field inspectors carry rugged wireless laptops that are connected to the enterprise intranet and databases. The wireless laptops are used to conduct measurements related to electricity transformers, for example. Then the laptops transmit the results, in real time, to chemists and people who prepare government reports about hazardous materials spills. In addition, time is saved, because all the information is entered directly into proper fields of electronic forms without having to be transcribed. The new system is so successful that it has given IT workers the confidence to launch other applications such as sending power-outage report to executives via smart phones and wireless information to crews repairing street lights.

MANAGERIAL ISSUES

1. *Comparing wireless to synchronized mobile devices.* In many cases, transmitting data in the evening, using a docking device, is sufficient. In others, real-time communication is needed, justifying a wireless system.

2. *Timetable.* Although there has been much hype about m-commerce in the last few years, only a small number of large-scale mobile computing applications have been deployed to date. The most numerous applications are in e-banking, stock trading, emergency services, and some B2B tasks. Companies still have time to carefully craft an m-commerce strategy. This will reduce the number of failed initiatives and bankrupted companies. For calculating the total cost of wireless computing ownership and how to justify it, see Intel (2002).

3. *Setting applications priorities.* Finding and prioritizing applications is a part of an organization's e-strategy. Although location-based advertising is logically attractive, its effectiveness may not be known for several years. Therefore, companies should be very careful in committing resources to m-commerce. For the near term, applications that enhance the efficiency and effectiveness of mobile workers are likely to have the highest payoff.

4. *Just a buzzword?* In the short run, mobile computing, m-commerce, and especially l-commerce, may be just buzzwords due to the many limitations they now face. However, in the long run, the concepts will be increasingly popular. Management should monitor the technological developments and make plans accordingly.

5. *Choosing a system.* The multiplicity of standards, devices, and supporting hardware and software can confuse a company planning to implement mobile computing. An unbiased consultant can be of great help. Checking the vendors and products carefully, as well as who is using them, is also critical. This issue is related to the issue of whether or not to use an application service provider (ASP) for m-commerce.

ON THE WEB SITE... Additional resources, including quizzes; online files of additional text, tables, figures, and cases; and frequently updated Web links to current articles and information can be found on the book's Web site (*wiley.com/college/turban*).

KEY TERMS

1G *248*

2G *248*

2.5G *248*

3G *248*

4G *248*

802.11b *249*

Auto Identification (Auto-ID)
Center *280*

Automatic crash notification
(ACN) *272*

Bluetooth *241*

Code Division Multiple Access
(CDMA) *248*

Context awareness *274*

Contextual computing *275*

Digital cities *281*

Enhanced messaging service
(EMS) *241*

Frequency Division Multiple Access
(FDMA) *248*

Geographical information system
(GIS) *270*

Global positioning system
(GPS) *269*

Hotspot *249*

Internet of things *280*

Location-based commerce
(l-commerce) *269*

M-wallet (mobile wallet) *255*

Mobile commerce (m-commerce,
m-business) *240*

Mobile computing *239*

Mobile devices *239*

Mobile handset *247*

Mobile portals *258*

Multimedia messaging service
(MMS) *241*

Personal digital assistant
(PDA) *241*

Pervasive computing *273*

Radio frequency identification
(RFID) *274*

Screenphones (wireless) *245*

Short messaging service (SMS) *241*

Smartphone *241*

Subscriber identification module
card (SIM) *248*

Telematics *272*

Time Division Multiple Access
(TDMA) *248*

Voice portal *253*

Wearable devices *259*

Wireless 911 (e-911) *272*

Wireless access point
(for Wi-Fi) *249*

Wireless Application Protocol
(WAP) *241*

Wireless fidelity (Wi-Fi) *249*

Wireless local area network
(WLAN) *249*

Wireless mobile
computing *239*

Wireless wide area networks
(WWAN) *246*

CHAPTER HIGHLIGHTS (Numbers Refer to Learning Objectives)

❶ Mobile computing is based on mobility and reach. These characteristics provide ubiquity, convenience, instant connectivity, personalization, and product and service localization.

❷ The major drivers of mobile computing are: large numbers of users of mobile devices, especially cell phones; no need for a PC; a developing "cell phone culture" in some areas; vendor marketing; declining prices; increasing bandwidth; and the explosion of EC in general.

❸ Mobile computing and m-commerce require mobile devices (e.g., PDAs, cell phones) and other hardware, software, and wireless technologies. Commercial services and applications are still emerging. These technologies allow users to access the Internet any time, anywhere.

❸ For l-commerce, a GPS receiver is also needed.

❹ Standards are being developed by several organizations in different countries, resulting in competing systems. It is expected that with time some of these will converge.

❺ Many EC applications in the service industries (e.g., banking, travel, and stocks) can be conducted with wireless devices. Also, shopping can be done from mobile devices.

❺ Location-based advertising and advertising via SMSs on a very large scale is expected.

❺ Mobile portals provide content (e.g., news) to millions.

❻ Large numbers of intrabusiness applications, including inventory management, sales force automation, wireless voice, job dispatching, wireless office, and more are already evident inside organizations.

❼ Emerging mobile B2B applications are being integrated with the supply chain and are facilitating cooperation between business partners.

❽ M-commerce is being used to provide applications in travel, gaming, entertainment, and delivery of medical services. Many other applications for individual consumers are planned for, especially targeted advertising.

❾ Most non-Internet applications involve various types of smart cards. They are used mainly in transportation, security, and shopping from vending machines and gas pumps.

⑩ Location-based commerce, or l-commerce, is emerging in applications such as calculating arrival time of buses (using GPS) and emergency services (wireless 911). In the future, it will be used to target advertising to individuals based on their location. Other innovative applications also are expected.

⑪ In the world of invisible computing virtually every object has an embedded microprocessor that is connected in a wired and/or wireless fashion to the Internet. This Internet of Things—homes, appliances, cars, and any manufactured items—will provide a number of life-enhancing, consumer-centric, and B2B applications.

⑪ In context-aware computing, the computer captures the contextual variables of the user and the environment and then provides, in real time, various services to users.

⑫ The major limitations of mobile computing are: small screens on mobile devices, limited bandwidth, high cost, lack of (or small) keyboards, transmission interferences, unproven security, and possible health hazards. Many of these limitations are expected to diminish over time. The primary legal/ethical limitations of m-commerce relate to privacy issues.

REVIEW QUESTIONS

1. Define mobile computing and m-commerce.
2. Define the following terms: PDA, WAP, SMS, GPS, Wi-Fi, and smartphone.
3. List the value-added attributes of mobile computing.
4. List at least five major drivers of mobile computing.
5. Describe the major hardware devices used for mobile computing.
6. List the major software items used for mobile computing.
7. Describe the major components of a mobile network.
8. Define the terms FDMA, TDMA, and CDMA.
9. List the major standards used by mobile phone systems (e.g., GSM).
10. Describe the major components of a WLAN.
11. Define 1G, 2G, 2.5G, 3G, and 4G.
12. List some of the key security issues in an m-commerce transaction.
13. List some of the uses of voice portals.
14. Discuss mobile micropayments.
15. Describe the m-wallet and wireless bill payments.
16. Describe how mobile devices can be used to shop.
17. Explain targeted advertising in the wireless environment and in pervasive computing.
18. Describe mobile portals and what kind of information they provide.
19. Describe wireless job dispatch.
20. Discuss how wireless applications can be used to provide customer support.
21. List some of the major intrabusiness wireless applications.
22. Describe wireless support along the supply chain.
23. How can telemetry improve supply chain operations?
24. Describe the application of wireless and mobile technologies to games and entertainment.
25. Discuss some of the potential applications of Wi-Fi and Bluetooth technologies in hotels.
26. Describe some potential uses of mobile and wireless technologies in providing medical care.
27. Describe some of the potential uses of l-commerce.
28. Discuss the technologies used in providing l-commerce services.
29. Describe GPS and GIS.
30. Discuss telematics.
31. List some of the barriers to l-commerce.
32. Define pervasive computing.
33. List some of the major properties of pervasive computing.
34. Discuss some of the ways that pervasive computing can be used in the home.
35. Describe a smart car.
36. Describe some of the ways that microprocessors are being used to enhance the intelligence of appliances.
37. What is contextual computing?
38. Discuss the role that usability plays in the adoption of m-commerce.
39. List the technical limitations of m-commerce.

DISCUSSION QUESTIONS

1. Discuss how mobile computing can solve some of the problems of the *digital divide* (the gap within a country or between countries with respect to people's ability to access the Internet). (See International Communications Union 1999 and Chapter 16 online).

2. Discuss how m-commerce can expand the reach of e-business.

3. Explain the role of protocols in mobile computing.

4. Discuss the impact of wireless computing on emergency medical services.

5. How do smartphones and screenphones differ? What characteristics do they share?

6. How are GIS and GPS related?

7. List three to four major advantages of wireless commerce to consumers, presented in this chapter, and explain what benefits they provide to consumers.

8. You can use location-based tools to help you find your car or the closest gas station. However, some people see location-based tools as an invasion of privacy. Discuss the pros and cons of location-based tools.

9. Discuss how wireless devices can help people with disabilities.

10. Discuss the benefits of telemetry-based systems.

11. Discuss the ways in which Wi-Fi is being used to support mobile computing and m-commerce. Describe the ways in which Wi-Fi is affecting the use of cellular phones for m-commerce.

12. Which of the applications of pervasive computing—smart cars, homes, appliances, and things—do you think are likely to gain the greatest market acceptance of the next few years? Why?

13. Which of the current mobile computing and m-commerce limitations do you think will be minimized within 5 years? Which ones will not?

14. Describe some m-commerce B2B applications along the supply chain.

15. It is said that Wi-Fi is winning a battle against 3G. In what sense this is true? In what sense this is false?

EXERCISES

1. Investigate the status of commercial applications of voice portals. Visit at least five vendors (e.g., *tellme.com, bevocal .com,* etc.). View the demos and lists of products at the sites.

   a. Prepare a list of capabilities offered by the different vendors.

   b. Prepare a list of actual applications.

   c. Comment on the value of such applications to users. How can the benefits be assessed?

2. Conduct a study on wearable computers. Find five vendors. Start with *nexttag.com, mobileinfo.com,* and *eg3.com/ wearable.htm,* and look for others as well.

   a. Identify 5 to 10 consumer-oriented wearable devices. What are the capabilities of these products? What advantages do they offer users?

   b. Identify 5 to 10 industry-oriented wearable devices. What are the capabilities of these products? What advantages do they offer users?

   c. See if you can find "What's cooking" in the research labs. For example, visit MIT's wearable computing lab.

3. Investigate commercial uses of GPS. Start with *gpshome .ssc.nasa.gov;* then go to *gpsstore.com.* Can some of the consumer-oriented products be used in industry? Prepare a report on your finding.

GROUP ASSIGNMENTS

1. Each team should examine a major vendor of mobile devices (Nokia, Kyocera, Motorola, Palm, BlackBerry, etc.). Each team will research the capabilities and prices of the devices offered by each company and then make a class presentation, the objective of which is to convince the rest of the class why one should buy that company's products.

2. Each team should explore the commercial applications of m-commerce in one of the following areas: financial services, including banking, stocks, and insurance; marketing and advertising; manufacturing; travel and transportation; human resources management; public services; and health care. Each team will present a report to the class based on their findings. (Start at *mobiforum.org.*)

3. Each team will investigate a global organization involved in m-commerce, such as *gmcforum.com* and *openmobilealliance.com.* The teams will investigate the membership and the current projects the organization is working on and then present a report to the class based on their findings.

4. Each team will investigate a standards-setting organization and report on its procedures and progress in developing wireless standards. Start with the following: *atis.org, etsi.org,* and *tiaonline.org.*

5. Each team should take one of the following areas—homes, cars, appliances, or other consumer goods like clothing—and investigate how embedded microprocessors are currently being used and will be used in the future to support consumer-centric services. Each team will present a report to the class based on their findings.

INTERNET EXERCISES

1. Learn about PDAs by visiting vendors' sites such as Palm, SONY, Hewlett-Packard, IBM, Phillips, NEC, Hitachi, Compaq, Casio, Brother, Texas Instruments, and others. List some m-commerce devices manufactured by these companies.

2. Access *progressive.com,* an insurance company, from your cell phone (use the "Go to..." feature). If you have a Sprint PCS wireless phone, do it via the Finance menu. Then try to visit *mobileprogressive.com* from a wireless PDA. If you have a Palm i705, you can download the Web-clipping application from Progressive. Report on these capabilities.

3. Research the status of 3G and the future of 4G by visiting *itu.int, 4g.newstrove.com,* and *3gnewsroom.com.* Prepare a report on the status of 3G and 4G based on your findings.

4. Explore *nokia.com.* Prepare a summary of the types of mobile services and applications Nokia currently supports and plans to support in the future.

5. Enter *kyocera-wireless.com.* Take the smart tour and view the demos. What is a smartphone? What are its capabilities? How does it differ from a regular cell phone?

6. Enter *www.i3mobile.com.* Run the Pronto demo. What types of services are provided by Pronto? What types of users would be more likely to use Pronto rather than a smart phone?

7. Enter *ibm.com.* Search for *wireless e-business.* Research the resulting stories to determine the types of wireless capabilities and applications IBM's software and hardware supports. Describe some of the ways these applications have helped specific businesses and industries.

8. Using a search engine, try to determine whether there are any commercial Wi-Fi hotspots in your area. Enter *wardriving.com.* Based on information provided at this site, what sorts of equipment and procedures could you use to locate hotspots in your area?

9. Enter *mapinfo.com* and look for the location-based services demos. Try all the demos. Find all of the wireless services. Summarize your findings.

10. Visit *ordersup.com, astrology.com,* and similar sites that capitalize on l-commerce. What features do these sites share?

11. Enter *packetvideo.com* and *microsoft.com/mobile/pocketpc.* Examine their demos and products and list their capabilities.

12. Enter *internethomealliance.com* and review their whitepapers. Based on these papers, what are the major appliances that are currently in most U.S. homes? Which of these appliances would most homeowners be likely to connect to a centrally controlled network?

13. Enter *onstar.com.* What types of *fleet* services does OnStar provide? Are these any different from the services OnStar provides to individual car owners?

14. Enter *autoidcenter.org.* Read about the Internet of Things. What is it? What types of technologies are needed to support it? Why is it important?

15. Enter *mdsi-advantex.com* and review the wireless products for the enterprise. Summarize the advantages of the different products.

16. Enter *attwireless.com/mlife* and prepare a list of the services available there.

17. Enter *wirelesscar.com.* Examine all the services provided and relate them to telemetry.

18. Enter the site of a wireless e-mail provider (BlackBerry, T-mobile, Handspring); collect information about the capabilities of the products and compare them.

19. Enter *zilog.com/about/partners/011600.html* and find information about smart appliances.

20. Enter *hel.fi/infocities* and write a report on the digitization of the city of Helsinki.

21. Enter *med-i-nets.com* and find information about Pharm-i-net. Trace the supply chain and the support of wireless. Make a diagram of the supply chain.

Minicase 1
Hertz Goes Wireless

The car rental industry is very competitive, and Hertz (*hertz.com*), the world's largest car rental company, competes against hundreds of companies in thousands of locations. The competition focuses on customer acquisition and loyalty. In the last few years, competition has intensified, and profits in the industry have been drifting downward. Hertz has been a "first mover" to information technologies since the 1970s, so it has naturally looked for new technologies to improve its competitive position. In addition to data warehousing and mining, a superb executive information system, and e-commerce, Hertz has pioneered some mobile commerce applications:

- *Quick rentals.* Upon arrival at the airport, Hertz's curbside attendant greets you and transmits your name wirelessly to the renting booth. The renting-booth employee advises the curbside attendant about the location of your car. All you need to do is go to the slot where the car is parked and drive away. This system, which once operated over a WLAN, is now part of a national wireless network that can check credit cards, examine your rental history, determine which airline to credit your loyalty mileage to, and more.

- *Instant returns.* Pioneered by Hertz in 1987, a handheld device connected to a database via a wireless system expedites the car return transaction. Right in the parking lot, the lot attendant uses a handheld device to calculate the cost of the rental and print a receipt for the renter. You check out in less than a minute, and you do not have to enter the renting booth at all.

- *In-car cellular phones.* Starting in 1988, Hertz began renting cell phones with its cars. Today, of course, this is not as "big a deal" as it was in 1988, when it was a major innovation.

- *NeverLost Onboard.* Some cars come equipped with an onboard GPS system, which provides route guidance in the form of turn-by-turn directions to many destinations. The information is displayed on a screen with computer-generated voice prompts. An electronic mapping system (GIS) is combined with the GPS, enabling you to see on the map where you are and where you are going. Also, consumer information about the locations of the nearest hospitals, gas stations, restaurants, and tourist areas is provided.

- *Additional customer services.* Hertz's customers can download city guides, Hertz's location guide, emergency telephone numbers, city maps, shopping guides, and even reviews of restaurants, hotels, and entertainment into their PDAs and other wireless devices. Of course, driving directions are provided.

- *Car locations.* Hertz is experimenting with a GPS-based car-locating system. This will enable the company to know where a rental car is at any given time, and even how fast it is being driven. Although the company promises to provide discounts based on your usage pattern, this capability is seen by many as an invasion of privacy. On the other hand, some may feel safer knowing that Hertz knows where they are at all times.

Hertz has been the top car rental company and still maintains that position. It is also a very profitable company that is expanding and growing continuously. Its success is attributed to being customer-centric, as facilitated by its use of wireless technologies and EC.

Source: hertz.com (2003) and Martin (2003).

Questions for Minicase 1

1. Which of these applications are intrabusiness in nature?
2. Identify any finance- and marketing-oriented applications.
3. What are the benefits to Hertz of knowing exactly where each of its cars is? As a renter, how do you feel about this capability?

Minicase 2
Washington Township Fire Department Goes Wireless

The Washington Township Fire Department (WTFD) is located just north of Columbus, Ohio. WTFD responds to more than 4,500 emergency medical services (EMS) calls every year. Time is critical when WTFD is responding to emergencies, which range from heart attacks to fire injuries to highway accidents. The service is run by emergency medical technicians (EMTs).

Rushing victims to the hospital is only one part of the service offered by these dedicated technicians. Providing first aid at the accidents' scene and while transporting the injured in the ambulances is the other part. When a patient is transferred to the hospital, the EMTs must also provide information on what treatments and medications were administered, and what health-related signs they observed in the patient. Such patient care reports are critical to the continuance of the treatment in the hospital, and they become a permanent part of the medical record. The information is also used to keep EMS records for planning, budgeting, training, and reporting to the state of Ohio.

In the past, the department had problems using 8" × 14," multipart, multicopy paper forms. According to Jack McCoy, using paper forms caused several problems. First, not everyone's handwriting is legible, so it was often difficult for hospital personnel as well as the WTFD office people to decipher the information. Second, on many occasions, the information was incomplete, or even inaccurate. To restore the information took considerable valuable time. Office employees at WTFD had to spend close to 1,800 hours a year processing information after the completion of the patient care report. In fact, 85 percent of one full-time office employee's time was required just to re-enter data that were already entered on the paper reports. But the major problem was the time spent by EMTs filling out forms, since this prevented them from returning quickly to the station, to respond to other emergency calls.

A solution to the paperwork problems was a mobile data collection device (MobilEMS of Clayton I.D.S. Corp. powered by SQL Anywhere Studio from Sybase Corp.). The device allows EMTs to collect patient information quickly, easily, and accurately at the scene and to deliver that information to the hospital in a print-out. This is done by using a series of data entry screens with drop-down menus containing vital information such as diagnoses, treatment rendered, drug administered, and even street names. It also includes a signature-capture feature that allows EMTs to document a patient's refusal of treatment as well as transfer of care to the hospital.

Once the incident data are entered into the system's embedded SQL database, printing reports is simple. The technician beams the information from MobilEMS to the hospital printer's infrared port and a clear document is produced. Back at the station, the EMTs synchronize the data in their handhelds with the department computer systems by placing MobilEMS in a docking station.

According to McCoy, it takes about 15 seconds to move the data into the system. This is a significant improvement over manual re-keying; using MobilEMS has reduced costs by more than 90 percent. Also by eliminating handwriting and mandating the completion of required data fields that previously could have been skipped, the accuracy increased significantly.

Finally, the system is customizable. Fields can be added and additional information can be stored. Thus, additional applications are leading to a completely paperless environment.

Source: Compiled from Sybase.com (2003).

Question for Minicase 2

1. The system uses a mobile device with a docking station for data synchronization, but no wireless is used. Would you recommend adding wireless? What for? Why or why not?
2. What are the potential legal issues in this case?
3. The system is based on electronic forms with checkmarks. Why not use a similar set of paper forms?
4. What are the benefits of the mobile system to the patient, to the hospital, and to the employees?
5. What are the benefits to WTFD?

Virtual Company Assignment
Mobility and The Wireless Café

While you were sitting at The Wireless Café's counter having a soda and thinking about data flows, you noticed that the wait-staff made a lot of trips to the kitchen counter to place orders and to check up on order readiness. You remembered seeing an ad for a product called Wireless Waitress (*http://wirelesswaitress.com/*) when you were browsing through some industry publications in Jeremy's office and decided to do some research on the genre of wireless products for wait-staff to present to the three shift managers.

Instructions

1. How would the Wireless Waitress be used in The Wireless Café? Describe some of the changes that this application would bring about in the way wait-staff do their job.

2. Are any of the location-based commerce applications or mobile commerce applications useful in the restaurant business? Pick an application described in the chapter and apply it to The Wireless Café.

3. It is clear that restaurants and The Wireless Café are headed in the direction of wireless applications. Prepare a memo to Barbara and Jeremy with your advice on how they should strategically position The Wireless Café vis-à-vis wireless applications.

REFERENCES

91expresslanes.com (accessed May 2002).

Amor, D., *Internet Future Strategies: How Pervasive Computing Services Will Change the World.* Upper Saddle River, NJ: Prentice-Hall, 2001.

Anderson, C., "Wi-Fi Revolution," special Wired report, May 2003, *wired.com/wired/archive/11.05/unwired/wifirevolution.html* (accessed June 2003).

AvantGo, "My AvantGo Hits 7 Million Registered Users." *Press Release,* November 12, 2002, *avantgo.com/news/press/press_archive/2002/release11_12_02.html* (accessed June 2003).

Baard, M., "After the Fall: Help for Climbers," *Wired News.* December 24, 2002, *wired.com/news/technology/0,1282,56146,00.html* (accessed June 2003).

Becker, D., "Sega Forms Mobile Games Division," *CNET News.com,* April, 2002, *news.zdnet.co.uk/story/0,t269-s2108679,00.html* (accessed June 2003).

Bennett, A., "Cutting-Edge Care for Village Retirees," *Western Australia E-Commerce Centre,* January 14, 2003, *ecommercecentre.oline.wa.gov.au/news/getarticle.asp?articleID=2827* (accessed June 2003).

Bloomberg News, "Lufthansa to Launch In-Flight Wi-Fi Service," May 28, 2003, *seattletimes.nwsource.com/html/boeingaerospace/134830929_boeingnet28.html* (accessed June 2003).

Borland, J., "Technology Tussle Underlines Wireless Web," *CNET News.com,* April 19, 2000, *news.com.com/2100-1033-239482.html?legacy=cnet* (accessed June 2003).

Bretz, E., "The Car, Just a Web Browser with Tires," *IEEE Spectrum,* January 2001.

Bughin, J., et al., "Mobile Portals Mobilize for Scale," *The McKinsey Quarterly,* April–June, 2001.

CellularOnline, "China Now Has More Than 200 Million Mobile Phone Users," November 2002, *cellular.co.za/news_2003/011003-china_now_has_more_than_200_mill.htm,* (accessed June 2003).

CellularOnline, "Latest Global, Handset, Base Station, & Regional Cellular Statistics Cellular." *co.za/stats/stats-main.htm* (accessed February 2003).

Chatterjee, A., et al., "A Road Map for Telematics," *McKinsey Quarterly,* April–June, 2002.

Chen, A., et al.,"A Support Infrastructure for Smart Kindergarten," *Pervasive Computing,* April–June, 2002, available at *ee.ucla.edu/faculty/papers/mbs_PervComp_apr-jun02.pdf* (accessed June 2003).

Cohen, A., "Off-Site, Online," *PC Magazine,* Sept, 17, 2002, *pcmag.com/article2/0,4149,481823,00.asp* (accessed June 2003).

Conrad, D., "Medlink to the Rescue," March 11, 2002, *alaskasworld.com/news/2002/03/11_MedLink.asp* (accessed June 2003).

Coursaris, C., and H., Hassanein, "Understanding M-Commerce: A Consumer-Centric Model," *Quarterly Journal of Electronic Commerce,* July–September 2002.

CyberAtlas, Mobile Users Yearning for Micropayments, March 12, 2002, *cyberatlas.internet.com/markets/wireless/article/0,1323,10094_995801,00.html,* (accessed June 2003).

Davies, N., and H. W., Gellersen, "Beyond Prototyping: Challenges in Deploying Ubiquitous Systems," *Pervasive Computing,* January–March 2002 available at *ee.oulu.fi/~skidi/teaching/mobile_and_ubiquitous_multimedia_2002/beyond_prototypes_challenges.pdf* (accessed June 2003).

Davies, N., et al., "Future Wireless Applications for a Networked City," *IEEE Wireless Communications,* February 2002.

Dogac, A., and A., Tumer, "Issues in Mobile Electronic Commerce," *Journal of Database Management,* January–February 2002.

DPS-Promatic, "Innovative Pay-by-GSM Meter." 2002, *dpspro.com/tcs_news_park.html,* (accessed June 2003).

Duan, M. "Enhancing the Shopping Experience, One $2,000 Suit at a Time," *Mpulse Magazine,* November 2002, *cooltown.hp.com/mpulse/1102-prada.asp* (accessed June 2003).

Dunne, D., "What Is 3G Technology?" *Darwin Magazine,* October 18, 2001, *darwinmag.com/learn/curve/column.html?ArticleID=182* (accessed July 2003).

Edgington, C., "How Internet Gateways and Smart Appliances Will Transform Our Homes," *TNTY Futures.* Vol. 1, no. 6, 2001, *tnty.com/newsletter/futures/technology.html* (accessed June 2003).

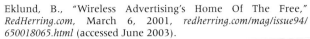

Eklund, B., "Wireless Advertising's Home Of The Free," *RedHerring.com*, March 6, 2001, *redherring.com/mag/issue94/650018065.html* (accessed June 2003).

Eklund, R., "Mobile CRM Comes of Age," *CRM Magazine*. July 15, 2002, *destinationcrm.com/articles/default.asp?ArticleID=2352* (accessed June 2003).

elite-care.com (accessed June 2003).

Estrada, M., "Bridging the Wireless Gap," *Knowledgestorm: The Upshot*, October 2002, *knowledgestorm.com/info/user_newsletter/092402/wireless.jsp* (accessed June 2003).

Estrin, D., et al., "Embedding the Internet," *Communications of the ACM*, May 2000.

Evers, J., "Dutch Police Fight Cell Phone Theft with SMS Bombs," *IDG News Service*, March 27, 2001, *idg.net/idgns/2001/03/27/DutchPoliceFightsCellPhoneTheft.shtml* (accessed June 2003).

Fikes, B., "Unguarded Wireless Networks a Snap for 'Stumbling'," *Californian North County Times*. January 12, 2003, *nctimes.net/news/2003/20030112/53511.html* (accessed June 2003).

Fleck, M., et al., "From Informing to Remembering: Ubiquitous Systems in Interactive Museums," *Pervasive Computing*, April–June 2002, *computer.org/pervasive/pc2002/b2013abs.htm* (accessed June 2003).

Global Mobile Suppliers Association (GSA), "Survey of Mobile Portal Services," Quarter 4, 2002, *gsacom.com/downloads/MPSQ4_2002.pdf* (accessed June 2003).

Hamblen, M., "Get Payback on Wireless," *Computer World*, January 1, 2001, *computerworld.com/mobiletopics/mobile/story/0,10801,54798,00.html* (accessed June 2003).

hertz.com (accessed May 2003).

Henning, T., "Wireless Imaging," *The Future Image Report*. 2002.

Hill, K., "Mobile CRM Software: The Race Is On. Wireless," *NewsFactor Network*, December 3, 2002, *crmbuyer.com/perl/story/20135.html* (accessed June 2003).

Hornberger, M., and C. Kehlenbeck, "Mobile Financial Services On The Rise In Europe," September 19, 2002, *banktech.com/story/wireless/BNK20020919S0005* (accessed June 2003).

Houck, J., "For Hotel Check-in, Press 1 Now," *Wireless News Factor*, February 15, 2001.

Hunter, R., *World without Secrets: Business, Crime, and Privacy in the Age of Ubiquitous Computing*. New York Wiley, 2002.

Intel, "Building the Foundation for Anytime Anywhere Computing," white paper 25 1290–002 Intel Corporation, June 13, 2002, *intel.com/eBusiness/it/management/pp022402_sum.htm* (accessed June 2003).

Intermec.com, "U.S. Fleet Services Refuels America's Commercial Fleets Using Intermec 710 Mobile Computer," December 18, 2001, *intermec.com/eprise/main/Intermec/Content/About/NewsPages/pressRelease?section=about&pressID=339* (accessed June 2003).

International Telecommunications Union, "Challenges to the Network: Internet for Development," October 1999, *itu.int/ITU-D/ict/publications/inet/1999/chal_exsum.pdf* (accessed June 2003).

Ishida, T., "Digital City Kyoto," *Communications of the ACM*, July 2002a.

Ishida, T., (ed.), *Understanding Digital Cities: Cross Cultural Perspective*. Cambridge MA: MIT Press, 2002b.

Islam, N., and M. Fayad, "Toward Ubiquitous Acceptance of Ubiquitous Computing," *Communications of the ACM*, February 2003.

ITS America, "NextBus Expands Real-Time Transit Information in the Bay Area with AC Transit," August 9, 2001, *itsa.org/ITSNEWS.NSF/0/34c13fd8352c4c3f85256aa400497aad?OpenDocument* (accessed June 2003).

Jiang, X., and J. A. Landay, "Modeling Privacy Control in Context-Aware Systems," *Pervasive Computing*, July–Sept. 2002.

Jones, W. D., "Keeping Cars," *IEEE Spectrum*, September 2001.

Kalakota, R., and M. Robinson, *E-Businesses: Roadmap for Success*. Reading, MA: Addison Wesley, 2001.

Kellner, M., "Is This the Year for Wireless Gear?" GCN, January 27, 2003, *gcn.com/22_2/buyers_guide/20950–1.html* (accessed June 2003).

Kontzer, T., "Top Ten Uses for SMS," *Information Week*, June 11, 2003, *informationweek.com/techcenters/networking/wireless* (accessed June 2003).

Kridel, T., "30 Mobile Miracles for Today and Tomorrow," *Laptop*, April 24, 2003, available at *bluetooth.com/news/news.asp?A=2&PID=689* (accessed June 2003).

Kumagai, J., "Talk to the Machine," *IEEE Spectrum*, September 2002, *ddl.co.uk/newsevents/press/articles/200209(talktothemachine).pdf* (accessed June 2003).

Le Gal, C., et al., "Smart Office: Design of an Intelligent Environment," *IEEE Intelligent Systems*, July–August, 2001.

Lipset, V., "Bluefish and Zaryba Enable Mobile Bill Payment," *MCommerce Times*, January 21, 2003, *mcommercetimes.com/Solutions/309* (accessed June 2003).

Lipset, V., "Magex Launches Mobile Payments Using SMS," *MCommerce Times*, December 3, 2002, *mcommercetimes.com/Solutions/299* (accessed June 2003).

Ludorf, C., "U.S. Fleet Services and Wireless Networking," *Transportation and Technology Today*, August 2002.

Mankins, M., "The Digital Sign in the Wired City," *IEEE Wireless Communication*, February 2002.

Martin, J. A., "Mobile Computing: Hertz In-Car GPS," *PC World*, March 13, 2003, *pcworld.com/howto/article/0,aid,109560,00.asp* (accessed June 2003).

Mathieson, R., "The Future According to Spielberg: Minority Report and the World of Ubiquitous Computing," *MPulse*. August, 2002, *cooltown.hp.com/mpulse/0802-minorityreport.asp* (accessed June 2003).

Mayor, M., "Bluetooth App Slams Door on Hotel Room Keys," *Wireless NewsFactor*, April 4, 2001, *wirelessnewsfactor.com/perl/story/8704.html* (accessed June 2003).

McDougall, P., "Wireless Handhelds Speed Inventory," *Information Week*, November 8, 1999.

Mennecke, B. E., and T. J. Strader, *Mobile Commerce: Technology, Theory and Applications*, Hershey, PA.: Idea Group Publishing, 2003.

Moore, J. F., "The Race to Put the Web into Cars," *Business 2.0*, Dec. 6, 2000, *business2.com/articles/web/0,1653,16117,FF.html* (accessed June 2003).

Mobileinfo.com, 2002. "Wireless Application Protocol–WAP: Future Outlook for WAP," *mobileinfo.com/WAP/future_outlook.htm*, 2001 (accessed June 2003).

Murphy, P., "Running Late? Take the NextBus," *Environmental News Network*, September 7, 1999, *enn.com/enn-features-archive/1999/09/090799/nextbus_4692.asp* (accessed June 2003).

Needleman, R., "Targeted Wi-Fi," *Business 2.0*, December 2002, *business2.com/articles/mag/print/0,1643,45451,00.html* (accessed June 2003).

Nelson, M., "Kemper Insurance Uses Wireless Digital Imaging to Lower Costs, Streamline Process," *InformationWeek*, September 25, 2000, *informationweek.com/805/photo.htm* (accessed June 2003).

nextbus.com (accessed June 2003).

Nokia, "Nokia Brings Mobility to the Games Industry by Making Rich Games Mobile.," November 4, 2002 *nokia-asia.com/apc/about_nokia/press/0,5854,36_2_71,00.html* (accessed June 2003).

Palm Computing, "United Center Scores with Mobile Point-Of-Sale System." *palm.com/enterprise/studies/study15.html* (accessed June 2003).

Picard, R. W., and J. Klein, "Toward Computers that Recognize and Respond to User Emotion," *Interacting with Computers*, February 2002.

Pilato, F., "World's Mobile Phone Production Expands 6.5 Percent-Short of 400 Million." Mobilemag.com, September 4, 2002, *mobilemag.com/content/100/101* 2002 (accessed June 2003).

Pinto, J., "The Pervasive Internet & Its Effect on Industrial Automation," *AutomationTechies.com*, November 2002, *jimpinto.com/writings/pervasive.html* (accessed June 2003).

Pitkow, J., et al., "Personalized Search," *Communications of the ACM*, September 2002.

Raina, K., and A. Harsh, *MCommerce Security.* New York: Osborne, 2002.

Raskin, A.,"Your Ad Could Be Here! (And Now We Can Tell You Who Will See It)," *Business 2.0*, May 2003, *business2.com/articles/mag/0,,48949,00.html* (accessed June 2003).

Republica IT, "Busta Paga en Pensione Lo Stipendio Arriva Via Sms," March 20, 2001, *repubblica.it/online/tecnologie_internet/tim/tim/tim.html* (accessed June 2003).

Reuters, "Marriott Hotels to Offer Wi-Fi Access," News.com, December 18, 2002, *news.com.com/2100-1033-978411.html* (accessed June 2003).

RFID Journal, "Gillette to Buy 500 Million EPC Tags," November 15, 2002, *216.121.131.129/article/articleprint/115/-1/1/* (accessed June 2003).

Rosencrance, L., "Update: Benetton Backs away from 'Smart Tags' in Clothing Line," *Computer World*, April 4, 2003, *computerworld.com/industrytopics/retail/story/0,10801,80061,00.html* (accessed June 2003).

Rupp, W. T., and A. D. Smith, "Mobile Commerce: New Revenue Machine, or a Black Hole?" *Business Horizons*, July–August, 2002.

Sadeh, N., *M-Commerce.* New York: Wiley, 2002.

SAP AG Corp., "CRM and the mySAP.com Mobile Workplace," (a publicly available brochure), 2000.

Sarkar, D., "Lawmakers Form 911 Caucus," *Federal Computer Week*, February 25, 2003, *fcw.com/fcw/articles/2003/0224/web-caucus-02-25-03.asp* (accessed July 2003).

Sarshar, A., "How Do 'Dot-Net,' Mobile Computing and PDAs Contribute to Your Bottom Line?" *Knowledgestorm: The Upshot*, February 2003, *knowledgestorm.com/info/user_newsletter/022003/geneva.jsp* (accessed June 2003).

Scanlon, J., "The Way We Work," special Wired Report, *Wired*, May, 2003, *wired.com/wired/archive/11.05/unwired* (accessed June 2003).

Sharke, P., "Smart Cars," Mechanical Engineering, May 2003, *memagazine.org/contents/current/features/smartcar/smartcar.html* (accessed June 2003).

Siau, K., et al., "Mobile Commerce: Promises, Challenges, and Research Agenda," *Journal of Database Management*, July–September 2001.

Smailagic, A., et al., "CMU Wearable Computers for Real-Time Speech Translation," *IEEE Personal Communications*, Vol. 8, No. 2, April 2001.

Stafford, A., and A. Brandt, "The No-Hassle Networking Guide," *PC World* (accessed May, 2002).

Standford, J., "Using Technology to Empower Assisted Living Patients," *Healthcare Review*, July 2, 2000a.

Standford, J., "Pervasive Computing goes to Work: Interfacing to the Enterprise," *Pervasive Computing*, July–Sept. 2000b.

Stanford, V., "Pervasive Computing Goes to Work: Interfacing to the Enterprise," *Pervasive Computing*, July–September 2002, available at *ee.oulu.fi/~skidi/teaching/mobile_and_ubiquitous_multimedia_2002/pervasive_computing_goes_to_work.pdf* (accessed June 2003).

Steede-Terry, K., *Integrating GIS and the Global Positioning System.* Redlands, CA: Environmental Systems Research Institute, 2000.

Sybase.com, "Clayton I.D.S and Washington/Norwich Township Fire Departments," Sybase Inc., *sybase.com/detail/1,6904,1023367,00.html* (accessed June 2003).

Symbol.com, "CVS Selects Symbol's Wireless Network System, Hand-Held Computers, June 3, 1998, *symbol.com/news/pressreleases/cvs.html* (accessed June 2003).

Taj Hotel, "Taj Hotels Introduce WiFi Facilities," *The Hindu*. July 31, 2002, *thehindu.com/2002/07/31/stories/2002073102321600.htm* (accessed June 2003).

Tech Live Staff, "Future of Mobile Commerce Murky," techtv.com, November 2, 2001, *techtv.com/news/internet/story/0,24195,3357949,00.html* (accessed July 2003).

Tennehouse, D. "Proactive Computing," *Communications of the ACM*, May 2000. *usfleet.com* (accessed June 2003).

Turban, E., and D. King, Introduction to E-commerce. Upper Saddle River, NJ: Prentice Hall, 2003.

Varshney, U., and R. Vetter, "Recent Advances in Wireless Networking," *IEEE Computer*, June 2000, pp. 107–109.

Weise, E., "Laundry Spins on the High Tech Cycle," *USA Today*, September 3, 2002, *usatoday.com/tech/techreviews/products/2002-09-02-wired-washers_x.htm* (accessed June 2003).

Weiser, M., "The Computer for the Twenty-First Century," *Scientific American*, September 1991. Reprinted in *Pervasive Computing*, January–March, 2002, available at *ubiq.com/hypertext/weiser/SciAmDraft3.html* (accessed June 2003).

Weiss, G., "Welcome to the (Almost) Digital Hospital," *IEEE Spectrum*, March 2002, *spectrum.ieee.org/WEBONLY/publicfeature/mar02/dighsb1.html* (accessed June 2003).

Wired, "Get Wireless," Special Wired Report. Supplement to *Wired*, May 2003 (11 articles), *wired.com/wired/current.html* (accessed June 2003).

WirelessDevNet Daily News, "PacketVideo Demonstrates Mobile-media on Nokia Series 60 Devices." November 19, 2002, *wirelessdevnet.com/news/newsitem.phtml?newsitemid=5231&channel=pda* (accessed June 2003).

XyberFlash, "Wearable Computers for the Working Class," *New York Times*, December 14, 2000.

Xybernaut.com, "Xybernaut Mobile Assistant: Productivity Gains in the Telecommunication Field," *xybernaut.com/case_studies/PDFs/Telecommunication_CS.pdf* (accessed June 2003).

Yankee Group, "Wireless Advertising: Still Waiting for Takeoff." October 30, 2002. *yankeegroup.com/public/products/research_note.jsp?ID=8907* (accessed June 2003).

Zhao, Y., "Telematics: Safe and Fun Driving," *IEEE Intelligent Systems*, January/February 2002, *ce.unipr.it/people/broggi/publications/si-its-01-2002.pdf* (accessed June 2003).

PART III
Organizational Applications

▶ 7. Transaction Processing, Functional Applications, CRM, and Integration
8. Supply Chain Management and Enterprise Resource Planning
9. IT Planning and Business Process Redesign

CHAPTER

7

Transaction Processing, Functional Applications, CRM, and Integration

7.1
Functional Information Systems

7.2
Transaction Processing Information Systems

7.3
Managing Production/Operations and Logistics

7.4
Managing Marketing and Sales Systems

7.5
Managing the Accounting and Finance Systems

7.6
Managing Human Resources Systems

7.7
Customer Relationship Management (CRM)

7.8
Integrating Functional Information Systems

LEARNING OBJECTIVES

After studying this chapter, you will be able to:

❶ Relate functional areas and business processes to the value chain model.

❷ Identify functional management information systems.

❸ Describe the transaction processing system and demonstrate how it is supported by IT.

❹ Describe the support provided by IT and the Web to production/operations management, including logistics.

❺ Describe the support provided by IT and the Web to marketing and sales.

❻ Describe the support provided by IT and the Web to accounting and finance.

❼ Describe the support provided by IT and the Web to human resources management.

❽ Describe the role of IT in facilitating CRM.

❾ Describe the benefits and issues of integrating functional information systems.

WIRELESS INVENTORY MANAGEMENT SYSTEM AT DARTMOUTH-HITCHCOCK MEDICAL CENTER

THE PROBLEM

Dartmouth-Hitchcock Medical Center (DHMC) is a large medical complex in New Hampshire with hospitals, a medical school, and over 600 practicing physicians in its many clinics. DHMC is growing rapidly and is encountering a major problem in the distribution of medical supplies. These supplies used to be ordered by nurses. But nurses are usually in short supply, so having them spending valuable time ordering supplies left them less time for their core competency—nursing. Furthermore, having nurses handling supply orders led to inventory management problems: Busy nurses tended to over-order in an effort to spend less time managing inventory. On the other hand, they frequently waited until the last minute to order supplies, which led to costly rush orders.

One solution would have been to transfer the task of inventory ordering and management to other staff, but doing so would have required hiring additional personnel and the DHMC was short on budget. Also, the coordination with the nurses to find what is needed and when, as well as maintaining the stock, would have been cumbersome.

What the medical center needed was a solution that would reduce the burden on the nurses, but also reduce the inventory levels and the last-minute, expensive ordering. Given the size of the medical center, and the fact that there are over 27,000 different inventory items, this was not a simple task.

THE SOLUTION

DHMC realized that their problem related to the supply chain, and so it looked to IT for solutions. The idea the DHMC chose was to connect wireless handheld devices with a purchasing and inventory management information system. Here is how the new system works (as of the summer of 2002): The medical center has a wireless LAN (Wi-Fi) into which handhelds are connected. Information about supplies then can be uploaded and downloaded from the devices to the network from anywhere within the range of the Wi-Fi. In remote clinics without Wi-Fi, the handhelds are docked into wireline network PCs.

For each item in stock a "par level" (the level at which supplies must be reordered) was established, based on actual usage reports and in collaboration between the nurses and the materials management staff. Nurses simply scan an item when it is consumed, and the software automatically adjusts the recorded inventory level. When a par level is reached for any inventory item, an order to the supplier is generated automatically. Similarly, when the inventory level at each nursing station dips below the station's par level, a shipment is arranged from the central supply room to that nursing station. The system also allows for nurses to make restocking requests, which can be triggered by scanning an item or scanning the supply cart (where items are stocked at each nursing station). The system works for the supplies of all non-nursing departments as well (e.g., human resources or accounting). Overall, the Wi-Fi system includes over 27,000 line items.

The system is integrated with other applications from the same vendor (PeopleSoft Inc.). One such application is Express PO, which enables purchasing managers to review standing purchase orders, e-procurement, and contract management.

 THE RESULTS

Inventory levels were reduced by 50 percent, paying for the system in just a few months. Materials purchasing and management now are consistent across the enterprise, the time spent by nurses on tracking materials has been drastically reduced, and access to current information has been improved. All of this contributed to reduced cost and improved patient care.

Sources: Compiled from Grimes (2003), and *peoplesoft.com* (site visited March 31, 2003).

 LESSONS LEARNED FROM THIS CASE

The DHMC case provides some interesting observations about implementing IT: First, IT can support the routine processes of inventory management, enabling greater efficiency, more focus on core competencies, and greater satisfaction for employees and management. The new system also helped to modernize and re-design some of the center's business processes (e.g. distribution, procurement), and was able to support several business processes (e.g., operations, finance, and accounting), not just one. Although the system's major application is in inventory management, the same software vendor provided ready-made modules, which were *integrated* with the inventory module and with each other (for example, with purchasing and contract management). The integration also included connection to suppliers, using the Internet. This IT solution has proven useful for an organization whose business processes cross the traditional functional departmental lines. In this case nursing is considered operations/production; inventory control, purchasing, and contract management are in the finance/accounting area.

To offer service in the digital economy, companies must continuously upgrade their functional information systems by using state-of-the-art technology. Furthermore, the functional processes must be improved as needed. Finally, as we will show in Chapter 8, supply chain software is needed in some segments of the supply chain. These segments may include functional information systems.

Functional information systems get much of their data from the systems that process routine transactions (*transaction processing systems, TPSs*). Also, many applications in business intelligence, e-commerce, CRM, and other areas use data and information from two or more functional information systems. Therefore, there is a need to integrate the functional systems applications among themselves, with the TPS, and with other applications. These relationships are shown in Figure 7.1 (page 298), which provides a pictorial view of the topics discussed in this chapter. (Not shown in the figure are applications discussed in other chapters, such as e-commerce and knowledge management.)

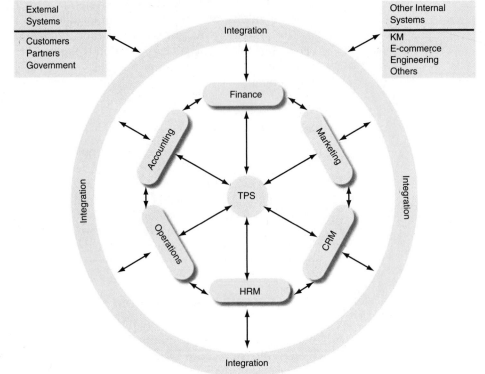

FIGURE 7.1 The functional areas, TPS, CRM, and integration connection. Note the flow of information from the TPS to the functional systems. Flow of information between and among functional systems is done via the integration component. (Not shown in the figure are applications discussed in other chapters, such as e-commerce and knowledge management.)

7.1 FUNCTIONAL INFORMATION SYSTEMS

The major functional areas in many companies are the production/operations, marketing, human resources, accounting and finance departments. Traditionally, information systems were designed within each functional area, to support the area by increasing its internal effectiveness and efficiency. However, as we will discuss in Chapter 9, the traditional functional hierarchical structure may not be the best structure for some organizations, because certain business processes involve activities that are performed in several functional areas. Suppose a customer wants to buy a particular product. When the customer's order arrives at the marketing department, the customer's credit needs to be approved by finance. Someone checks to find if the product is in the warehouse (usually in the production/operations area). If it is there, then someone needs to pack the product and forward it to the shipping department, which arranges for delivery. Accounting prepares a bill for the customer, and finance may arrange for shipping insurance. The flow of work and information between the different departments may not work well, creating delays or poor customer service.

One possible solution is to restructure the organization. For example, the company can create cross-functional teams, each responsible for performing a complete business process. Then, it is necessary to create appropriate information systems applications for the restructured processes. As we will discuss in Chapter 9, this arrangement can be a difficult-to-implement solution. In other cases, the company can use IT to create minor changes in the business processes

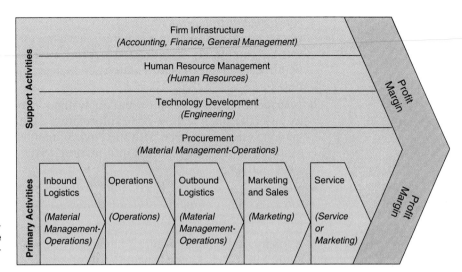

FIGURE 7.2 Typical functional areas mapped on the value chain of a manufacturing company.

and organizational structure, but this solution may not solve problems such as lack of coordination or an ineffective supply chain. One other remedy may be an *integrated approach* that keeps the functional departments as they are, but creates an integrated supportive information system to help communication, coordination, and control. The integrated approach is discussed in Section 7.8.

But even if the company were to restructure its organization, as suggested in Chapter 9, the functional areas might not disappear completely since they contain the expertise needed to run the business. Therefore, it is necessary to drastically improve operations in the functional areas, increasing productivity, quality, speed, and customer service, as we will see in this chapter.

Before we demonstrate how IT facilitates the work of the functional areas, and makes possible their integration, we need to see how they are organized and how they relate to the corporate value chain and the supply chain.

Porter's Value Chain Model and the Supply Chain

The *value chain* model, introduced in Chapter 3, views activities in organizations as either primary (reflecting the flow of goods and services) or secondary (supporting the primary activities). The organizational structure of firms is intended to support both of these types of activities. Figure 7.2 maps the major *functional departments* onto the value chain structure.

As described in Chapter 2, the *supply chain* is a business process that links all the procurement from suppliers, the transformation activities inside a firm, and the distribution of goods or services to customers via wholesalers and retailers. In this chapter we present innovative applications that increase mainly internal functional efficiency, and we provide examples of improved communication and collaboration with customers and business partners as a result of these applications. First, let us examine the characteristics of functional information systems.

Major Characteristics of Functional Information Systems

Functional information systems share the following characteristics:

- *Composed of smaller systems.* A functional information system consists of several smaller information systems that support specific activities performed in the functional area.

- *Integrated or independent.* The specific IS applications in any functional area can be integrated to form a coherent departmental functional system, or they can be completely independent. Alternatively, some of the applications within each area can be integrated across departmental lines to match a business process.

- *Interfacing.* Functional information systems may interface with each other to form the organization-wide information system. Some functional information systems interface with the environment outside the organization. For example, a human resources information system can collect data about the labor market.

- *Supportive of different levels.* Information systems applications support the three levels of an organization's activities: *operational, managerial,* and *strategic* (see Chapter 2).

A model of the IS applications in the production/operations area is provided in Online File W7.1. Other functional information systems have a similar basic structure.

In this chapter we describe IT applications in some of the key primary and support areas of the value chain. However, since information systems applications receive much of the data that they process from the corporate *transaction processing system,* we deal with this system first.

7.2 TRANSACTION PROCESSING INFORMATION SYSTEMS

The core operations of organizations are enabled by transaction processing systems.

Computerization of Routine Transaction Processes

In every organization there are business transactions that provide its mission-critical activities. Such transactions occur when a company produces a product or provides a service. For example, to produce toys, a manufacturer needs to buy materials and parts, pay for labor and electricity, build the toys, ship them to customers, bill customers, and collect money. A bank that maintains the toy company's checking account must keep the account balance up-to-date, disperse funds to back up the checks written, accept deposits, and mail a monthly statement.

Every transaction may generate additional transactions. For example, purchasing materials will change the inventory level, and paying an employee reduces the corporate cash on hand. Because the computations involved in most transactions are simple and the transaction volume is large and repetitive, such transactions are fairly easy to computerize.

As defined in Chapter 2, the information system that supports these *transactions* is the **transaction processing system (TPS).** The transaction processing system monitors, collects, stores, processes, and disseminates information for all routine core business transactions. These data are input to functional information systems applications, as well as to decision support systems (DSSs), customer relationship management (CRM), and knowledge management (KM). The TPS also provides critical data to e-commerce, especially data on customers and their purchasing history.

Transaction processing occurs in all functional areas. Some TPSs occur within one area, others cross several areas (such as payroll). Online File W7.2 provides a list of TPS activities mapped on the major functional areas. The

---

TABLE 7.1 The Major Characteristics of a TPS

- Typically, *large amounts of data* are processed.
- The *sources of data are mostly internal,* and the output is intended mainly for an *internal audience.* This characteristic is changing somewhat, since trading partners may contribute data and may be permitted to use TPS output directly.
- The TPS processes information on a *regular basis:* daily, weekly, biweekly, and so on.
- *Large storage (database) capacity* is required.
- *High processing speed* is needed due to the high volume.
- The TPS basically *monitors and collects past data.*
- Input and output *data are structured.* Since the processed data are fairly stable, they are formatted in a standard fashion.
- A *high level of detail* (raw data, not summarized) is usually observable, especially in input data but often in output as well.
- *Low computation complexity* (simple mathematical and statistical operations) is usually evident in a TPS.
- A high level of *accuracy, data integrity, and security* is needed. Sensitive issues such as privacy of personal data are strongly related to TPSs.
- *High reliability* is required. The TPS can be viewed as the lifeblood of the organization. Interruptions in the flow of TPS data can be fatal to the organization.
- *Inquiry processing* is a must. The TPS enables users to query files and databases (even online and in real time).

---

information systems that automate transaction processing can be part of the departmental systems, and/or part of the enterprisewide information systems. For a comprehensive coverage of TPSs, see Subrahmanyam (2002) and Bernstein and Newcomer (1997).

Objectives of TPS

The primary goal of a TPS is to provide all the information needed by law and/or by organizational policies to keep the business running properly and efficiently. Specifically, a TPS has to efficiently handle high volume, avoid errors due to concurrent operations, be able to handle large variations in volume (e.g., during peak times), avoid downtime, never lose results, and maintain privacy and security (see Bernstein and Newcomer, 1997). To meet these goals, a TPS is usually automated and is constructed with the major characteristics listed in Table 7.1

Specific objectives of a TPS may include one or more of the following: to allow for efficient and effective operation of the organization, to provide timely documents and reports, to increase the competitive advantage of the corporation, to provide the necessary data for tactical and strategic systems such as Web-based applications, to ensure accuracy and integrity of data and information, and to safeguard assets and security of information. It also is important to remember that TPSs must closely interface with many IT initiatives, especially with e-payment, e-procurement, and e-marketing.

It should be emphasized that TPSs are the most likely candidates for restructuring and usually yield the most tangible benefits of IT investments. They were the first to be computerized so they have had more improvement opportunities. Also, their information volume is high, so even a small improvement may result in a high payoff.

Activities and Methods of TPS

Regardless of the specific data processed by a TPS, a fairly standard process occurs, whether in a manufacturer, in a service firm, or in a government organization. First, data are collected by people or sensors and entered into the computer via any input device. Generally speaking, organizations try to automate the TPS data entry as much as possible because of the large volume involved.

Next, the system processes data in one of two basic ways: *batch* or *online processing.* In **batch processing,** the firm collects data from transactions as they occur, placing them in groups or batches. The system then prepares and processes the batches periodically (say, every night). Batch processing is particularly useful for operations that require processing for an extended period of time. Once a batch job begins, it continues until it is completed or until an error occurs. In **online processing,** data are processed as soon as a transaction occurs.

To implement online transaction processing, *master files* containing key information about important business entities are placed on hard drives, where they are directly accessible. The *transaction files* containing information about activities concerning these business entities, such as orders placed by customers, are also held in online files until they are no longer needed for everyday transaction processing activity. This ensures that the transaction data are available to all applications, and that all data are kept up-to-the-minute. These data can also be processed and stored in a data warehouse (Chapter 11). The entire process is managed by a *transaction manager* (see Subrahmanyam 2002, for details).

The flow of information in a typical TPS is shown in Figure 7.3. An event, such as a customer purchase, is recorded by the TPS program. The processed information can be either a report or an activity in the database. In addition to a scheduled report, users can query the TPS for nonscheduled information (such as, "What was the impact of our price cut on sales during the first five days, by day?"). The system will provide the appropriate answer by accessing a database containing transaction data.

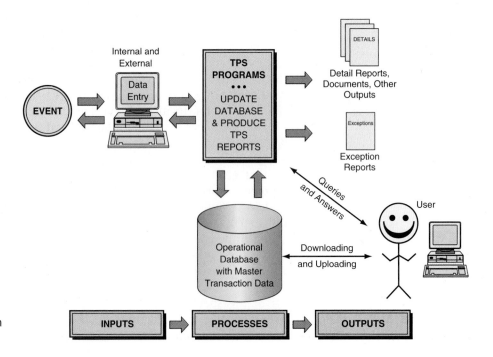

FIGURE 7.3 The flow of information in transaction processing.

Web-Based and Online Transaction Processing Systems

Transaction processing systems may be fairly complex, involving customers, vendors, telecommunications, and different types of hardware and software. Traditional TPSs are centralized and run on a mainframe. However, innovations such as online transaction processing require a client/server architecture. In **online transaction processing (OLTP),** transactions are processed as soon as they occur. For example, when you pay for an item at a POS at a store, the system records the effects of the sale by reducing the inventory on hand by a unit, increasing the store's cash position by the amount you paid, and increasing sales figures for the item by one unit. A relatively new form of Web-based transaction processing is *object-oriented transaction processing,* which is described in Online File W7.3.

With OLTP and Web technologies such as an extranet, suppliers can look at the firm's inventory level or production schedule in real time. The suppliers themselves, in partnership with their customers, can then assume responsibility for inventory management and ordering. Such Web-based systems would be especially useful in processing orders involving several medium-to-large business partners. Customers too can enter data into the TPS to track orders and even query it directly, as described in *IT at Work 7.1.*

WEB-BASED INTERACTIVE TRANSACTION PROCESSING. Rather than isolated exchanges of simple text and data over private networks, such as traditional EDI and EFT, transactions are increasingly conducted over the Internet and intranets

---

IT at Work 7.1
MODERNIZING THE TPS CUTS DELIVERY TIME AND SAVES MONEY

Here are some examples of how modernizing transaction processing systems has saved time and/or money:

Each time you make a copy at Kinko's, a copying transaction and a payment transaction occur. In the past you received a device (a card, the size of a credit card) and inserted it into a control device attached to the copy machine, and it recorded the number of copies that you made. Then you stood in line to pay: The cashier placed the device in a reader to see how many copies were made. Your bill was computed, with tax added. Kinko's cost was high in this system, and some customers were unhappy about standing in line to pay for only a few copies. Today, using Kinko's new system, you insert your credit card (or a stored-value card purchased from a machine) into a control device, make the copies, print a receipt, and go home. You no longer need to see a Kinko's employee to complete your purchase.

Grossman's Bargain Centers, a retailer in Braintree, Massachusetts, replaced all its point-of-sale terminals with a network of PCs. The network rings up sales, updates inventory, and keeps customers' histories at 125 stores. The PCs automatically record stock from a remote database and

trace out-of-stock items available at other stores. This way, customers can get locally unavailable items within hours or a day. Employees no longer have to count inventory or order merchandise. The $3 million investment paid for itself in less than two years.

Seconds after you enter an address and a Zip code into a terminal at UPS delivery outlets at a UPS Store, a shipping label and a receipt are generated. Your shipping record stays in the database, so if you send another package to the same person, you do not need to repeat the address again.

Using an object-oriented approach, Sprint Inc. has improved its order processing for new telephones. In the past it took a few days for a customer to get a new telephone line; with its new system, Sprint can process an order in only a few hours. The order application itself takes less than 10 minutes, experiences fewer errors, and can be executed on electronic forms on a salesperson's desktop or laptop computer.

For Further Exploration: Why is the back-ordering cycle usually reduced with a networked TPS? Could Kinko's operate without employees at their outlets? Why is there an attempt to save time, and whose time is being saved?

in a more complex manner. As a result, OLTP has broadened to become *interactive Internet TPS*. Internet transaction processing software and servers allow multimedia data transfer, fast response time, and storage of large amount of graphics and video—all in real time and at low cost. The interactivity feature allows for easy and fast response to queries. OLTP also offers flexibility to accommodate unpredictable growth in processing demand (scalability) and timely search and analysis of large databases. Companies that accept and process large number of orders, such as Dell Computer, tend to have a sophisticated Web-based ordering system.

Typical Tasks in Transaction Processing

Transaction processing exists in all functional areas. In later sections (7.3 through 7.6) we will describe the key TPS activities in major functional areas. Here we describe in some detail one application that crosses several functional areas—order processing.

ORDER PROCESSING.   Orders for goods and/or services may flow from customers to a company by phone, on paper, or electronically. Fast and effective order processing is recognized as a key to customer satisfaction. Orders can also be internal—from one department to another. Once orders arrive, an order processing system needs to receive, document, route, summarize, and store the orders. A computerized system can also track sales by product, by zone, or by salesperson, providing sales or marketing information that may be useful to the organization. As described in Chapter 6, more and more companies are providing systems for their salespeople that enable them to enter orders from a business customer's site using wireless notebook computers, PDAs, or Web-enabled cell phones. Some companies spend millions of dollars reengineering their order processing as part of their transformation to e-business (e.g., see Siemens case, Chapter 1). IBM, for example, restructured its procurement system so its own purchasing orders are generated quickly and inexpensively in its e-procurement system.

Orders can be for services as well as for products. Otis Elevator Company, for example, tracks orders for elevator repair. The processing of repair orders is done via wireless devices that allow effective communication between repair crews and Otis physical facilities. Orders also can be processed by using innovative IT technologies such as global positioning systems, as shown in *IT at Work 7.2*.

OTHER TPS ACTIVITIES.   Other typical TPS activities are summarized in Table 7.2 (page 306). Most of these routine tasks are computerized.

Transaction Processing Software

There are dozens of commercial TPS software products on the market. Many are designed to support Internet transactions. (See a sampler of TPS software products and vendors in Online File W7.4.)

The problem, then, is how to evaluate so many software packages. In Chapter 14, there is a discussion on software selection that applies to TPS as well. But the selection of a TPS software product has some unique features. Therefore, one organization, the Transaction Processing Performance Council (*tpc.org*), has been trying to assist in this task. This organization is conducting *benchmarking* for TPS. It checks hardware vendors, database vendors, middleware vendors, and so forth. Recently it started to evaluate e-commerce transactions (*tpc.org/tpcw*; there, see "transactional Web e-commerce benchmark"). Also, the organization has several decision support benchmarks (e.g., TPC-H, and TPC-R).

IT at Work 7.2
AUTOMATIC VEHICLE LOCATION AND DISPATCH SYSTEM IN SINGAPORE

Taxis in Singapore are tracked by a *global positioning system (GPS)*, which is based on the 24 satellites originally set up by the U.S. government. The GPS allows its users to get an instant fix on the geographical position of each taxi (see figure below).

Here's how the system works: Customer orders are usually received via cell phone, regular telephone, fax, or e-mail. Customers can also dispatch taxis from special kiosks (called CabLink) located in shopping centers and hotels. Other booking options include portable taxi-order terminals placed in exhibition halls. Frequent users enter orders from their offices or homes by keying in a PIN number over the telephone. That number identifies the user automatically, together with his or her pickup point. Infrequent customers use an operator-assisted system.

The computerized ordering system is connected to the GPS. Once an order has been received, the GPS finds a vacant cab nearest the caller, and a display panel in the taxi alerts the driver to the pickup address. The driver has 10 seconds to push a button to accept the order. If he does not, the system automatically searches out the next-nearest taxi for the job.

The system completely reengineered taxi order processing. First, the transaction time for processing an order for a frequent user is much shorter, even during peak demand, since they are immediately identified. Second, taxi drivers are not able to pick and choose which trips they want to take, since the system will not provide the commuter's destination. This reduces the customer's average waiting time significantly, while minimizing the travel distance of empty taxis. The system increases the capacity for taking incoming calls by 1,000 percent, providing a competitive edge to those cab companies that use the system. It also reduces misunderstanding between drivers and dispatchers, and driver productivity increased since they utilize their time more efficiently. Finally, customers who use terminals do not have to wait a long time just to get a telephone operator (a situation that exists during rush hours, rain, or any other time of high demand for taxis). Three major taxi companies with about 50,000 taxis are connected to the system.

Source: Complied from Liao (2003) and author's experience.

For Further Exploration: What tasks do computers execute in this order processing system? What kinds of priorities can be offered to frequent taxi customers?

Location tracking of taxicabs in Singapore.

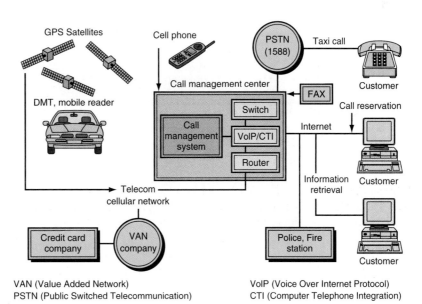

TABLE 7.2 Typical TPS Activities	
Activities	**Description**
The ledger	The entire group of an organization's financial accounts. Contains all of the assets, liabilities, and owner's (stockholders') equity accounts.
Accounts payable and receivable	Records of all accounts to be paid and those owed by customers. Automated system can send reminder notes about overdue accounts.
Receiving and shipping records	Transaction records of all items sent or received, including returns.
Inventory-on-hand records	Records of inventory levels as required for inventory control and taxation. Use of barcodes improves ability to count inventory periodically.
Fixed-assets management	Records of the value of an organization's fixed assets (e.g., buildings, cars, machines), including depreciation rate and major improvements made in assets, for taxation purposes.
Payroll	All raw and summary payroll records.
Personnel files and skills inventory	Files of employees' history, evaluations, and record of training and performance.
Reports to government	Reports on compliance with government regulations, taxes, etc.
Other periodic reports and statements	Financial, tax, production, sales, and other routine reports.

7.3 MANAGING PRODUCTION/OPERATIONS AND LOGISTICS

The *production and operations management (POM)* function in an organization is responsible for the processes that transform inputs into useful outputs (see Figure 7.4). In comparison to the other functional areas, the POM area is very diversified and so are its supporting information systems. It also differs considerably among organizations. For example, manufacturing companies use completely

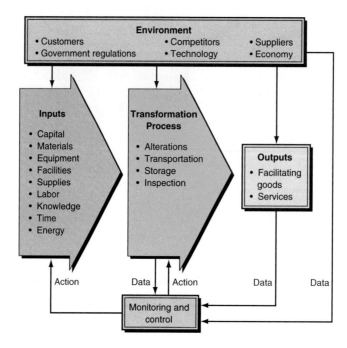

FIGURE 7.4 The productions/operations management functions transform inputs into useful outputs. (*Source:* J. R. Meredith and S. M. Shafer, *Operations Management.* New York: Wiley, 2002. Reprinted by permission of John Wiley & Sons, Inc.)

esses than do service organizations, and a hospital operates much differently from a university. (Look again at Online File W7.1 for an example of the complexity of the POM field. Note that the internal interfaces are on the left and the external ones on the right.)

Because of the breadth and variety of POM functions, here we present four IT-supported POM topics: in-house logistics and materials management, planning production/operations, computer-integrated manufacturing (CIM), and product lifecycle management (PLM). A fifth topic, automating design work and manufacturing, is presented in Online File W7.5.

In-House Logistics and Materials Management

Logistics management deals with ordering, purchasing, inbound logistics (receiving), and outbound logistics (shipping) activities. In-house logistics activities are a good example of processes that cross several primary and support activities in the value chain. Both conventional purchasing and e-procurement result in incoming materials and parts. The materials received are inspected for quality and then stored. While the materials are in storage, they need to be maintained until distributed to those who need them. Some materials are disposed of when they become obsolete or their quality becomes unacceptable.

All of these activities can be supported by information systems. For example, many companies today are moving to some type of e-procurement (Chapter 5). Scanners and voice technologies, including wireless ones, can support inspection, and robots can perform distribution and materials handling. Large warehouses use robots to bring materials and parts from storage, whenever needed. The parts are stored in bins, and the bins are stacked one above the other (similar to the way safe deposit boxes are organized in banks). Whenever a part is needed, the storekeeper keys in the part number. The mobile robot travels to the part's "address," takes the bin out of its location (e.g., using magnetic force), and brings the bin to the storekeeper. Once a part is taken out of the bin, the robot is instructed to return the bin to its permanent location. In intelligent buildings in Japan, robots bring files to employees and return them for storage. In some hospitals, robots even dispense medicines.

INVENTORY MANAGEMENT. *Inventory management* determines how much inventory to keep. Overstocking can be expensive; so is keeping insufficient inventory. Three types of costs play important roles in inventory decisions: the cost of maintaining inventories, the cost of ordering (a fixed cost per order), and the cost of not having inventory when needed (the shortage or opportunity cost). The objective is to minimize the total of these costs.

Two basic decisions are made by operations: when to order, and how much to order. Inventory models, such as the economic order quantity (EOQ) model, support these decisions. Dozens of models exist, because inventory scenarios can be diverse and complex. A large number of commercial inventory software packages to automate the application of these models are available at low cost. For example, using DSS models in a Web-based system, more and more companies are improving their inventory management and replenishment, better meeting customers' demand (Amato-McCoy, 2002c).

Once management has made decisions about how much to order and when, an information system can track the level of inventory for each item that management wants to control. (Not every item needs such control. For example, items whose consumption is basically fixed, such as toilet paper or pencils, may not be closely controlled.) When the inventory falls to a certain level, called the *reorder point,* the computer automatically generates a purchase order. The order is transferred electronically either to a vendor or, if the item is manufactured in-house, to the manufacturing department.

Many large companies (such as Wal-Mart) allow their suppliers to monitor the inventory level and ship when needed, eliminating the need for sending purchasing orders. Such a strategy, in which the supplier monitors inventory levels and replenishes when needed, is called **vendor-managed inventory (VMI).** The monitoring can be done by using mobile agents over the Internet. It also can be done by using Web services, as Dell Computer is doing.

In Chapter 8 we demonstrate how IT and EC help in reducing inventories.

QUALITY CONTROL. Manufacturing quality-control systems can be standalone systems or can be part of an enterprise-wide total quality management (TQM) effort. They provide information about the quality of incoming materials and parts, as well as the quality of in-process semifinished and finished products. Such systems record the results of all inspections. They also compare actual results to metrics.

Quality-control data may be collected by Web-based sensors and interpreted in real time, or they can be stored in a database for future analysis. Periodic reports are generated (such as percentage of defects, percentage of rework needed), and management can compare performance among departments on a regular basis or as needed.

Web-based quality control information systems are available from several vendors (e.g., HP and IBM) for executing standard computations such as preparing quality control charts. First, manufacturing data are collected for quality-control purposes by sensors and other instruments. After the data have been recorded, it is possible to use Web-based expert systems to make interpretations and recommend actions (e.g., to replace equipment).

Planning Production/ Operations

The POM planning in many firms is supported by IT. Some major areas of planning and their computerized support are described here.

MATERIAL REQUIREMENTS PLANNING (MRP). Inventory systems that use an EOQ approach are designed for those individual items for which demand is completely independent (for example, the number of chairs a furniture manufacturer will sell). However, in manufacturing systems, the demand for some items can be interdependent. For example, a company may make three types of chairs that all use the same legs, screws, and bolts. Thus, the demand for legs, screws, and bolts depends on the total demand for all three types of chairs and their shipment schedule.

The software that facilitates the plan for acquiring (or producing) parts, subassemblies, or materials in the case of interdependent items is called **material requirements planning (MRP).** MRP is computerized because of the complex interrelationship among many products and their components, and the need to change the plan each time that a delivery date or the order quantity is changed. Several MRP packages are commercially available.

MRP deals only with production scheduling and inventories. A more complex process will also involve allocation of related resources. In such a case, more complex, integrated software is available—MRP II.

MANUFACTURING RESOURCE PLANNING (MRP II). A POM system called **manufacturing resource planning (MRP II)** adds functionalities to a regular MRP. For example, in addition to the output similar to that of MRP, MRP II determines the costs of parts and the cash flow needed to pay for parts. It also estimates costs of labor, tools, equipment repair, and energy. Finally, it provides a detailed, computerized budget for the parts involved. Several MRP II software packages are commercially available. MRP II evolved to ERP, which is described in Chapter 8.

JUST-IN-TIME SYSTEMS. In mass customization and build-to-order production, the just-in-time concept is frequently used. **Just-in-time (JIT)** is an approach that attempts to minimize waste of all kinds (of space, labor, materials, energy, and so on) and to continuously improve processes and systems. For example, if materials and parts arrive at a workstation *exactly when needed,* there is no need for inventory, there are no delays in production, and there are no idle production facilities or underutilized workers. Many JIT systems are supported by software from vendors such as HP, IBM, CA, and Cincom Systems.

JIT systems have resulted in significant benefits. At Toyota, for example, benefits included reducing production cycle time from 15 days to 1 day, reducing cost by 30 to 50 percent, and achieving these cost savings while increasing quality. JIT is especially useful in supporting Web-based mass customization, as in the case of Dell Computer's model of assembling computers only after orders are received. To ship computers quickly, components and parts are provided just in time. As of 2001, car manufacturers were rapidly adopting a make-to-order process. To deliver customized cars quickly and with cost efficiency, manufacturers need a JIT system.

PROJECT MANAGEMENT. A *project* is usually a one-time effort composed of many interrelated activities, costing a substantial amount of money, and lasting for weeks or years. The management of a project is complicated by the following characteristics.

- Most projects are unique undertakings, and participants have little prior experience in the area.
- Uncertainty exists due to the generally long completion times.
- There can be significant participation of outsiders, which is difficult to control.
- Extensive interaction may occur among participants.
- The many interrelated activities make changes in planning and scheduling difficult.
- Projects often carry high risk but also high profit potential.

The management of projects is enhanced by project management tools such as the *program evaluation and review technique (PERT)* and the *critical path method (CPM)*. The essence of these tools is to break complex projects or operations into a sequence of events, to examine the relationships among these events, and to schedule these events to minimize the time needed to complete the project. These tools are easily computerized, and indeed there are dozens of commercial packages on the market. For example, developing Web applications is a major project, and several IT tools are available to support and help manage these activities (see *citadon.com*). Merrill-Lynch uses such computerized tools to plan and manage its main projects (Bielski, 2002), significantly improving resource allocation and decision making. For project cost estimation using special software, see Vijayakumar (2002).

WORK MANAGEMENT SYSTEMS. **Work management systems (WMSs)** automatically manage the prioritization and distribution of work. These systems deal with resource allocation, an activity that is missing from *workflow systems* (see Chapter 4). For example, if an operator is unavailable, a WMS recalculates the process and reallocates human resources to meet the business need. For details and a case study from the U.K., see Collins (1999).

TROUBLESHOOTING. Finding what's wrong in the factory's internal operations can be a lengthy and expensive process. Intelligent systems can come to the rescue. Bizworks, from InterBiz Solutions, is an example of a successful software product that tackles thorny POM problems, such as interpretation of data gathered by factory sensors. The product is useful for quality control, maintenance management, and more. Similar products cut diagnosis time from hours to seconds. Many detecting systems are Web-based (see *gensym.com*).

OTHER AREAS. Many other areas of planning production and operations are improved by IT. For example, Lee and Chen (2002) developed a Web-based production planning optimization tool. Factory layout planning and design also have been greatly improved due to IT tools (Benjaafar et al., 2002).

Computer-Integrated Manufacturing

Computer-integrated manufacturing (CIM) is a concept or philosophy that promotes the integration of various computerized factory systems. CIM has three basic goals: (1) the *simplification* of all manufacturing technologies and techniques, (2) *automation* of as many of the manufacturing processes as possible, and (3) *integration and coordination* of all aspects of design, manufacturing, and related functions via computer hardware and software. Typical technologies to be integrated are flexible-manufacturing systems (FMSs), JIT, MRP, CAD, CAE, and group technology (GT).

THE CIM MODEL. All of the hardware and software in the world will not make a computer-integrated manufacturing system work if it does not have the support of the people designing, implementing, and using it. According to Kenneth Van Winkle, manager of manufacturing systems at Kimball International, a furniture manufacturer, "Computer technology is only 20 percent of CIM. The other 80 percent is the *business processes* and *people*." In order to bring people together and formulate a workable business process, CIM must start with a plan. This plan comes from the CIM model, which describes the CIM vision and architecture. The basic CIM model is shown in Figure 7.5.

The CIM model is derived from the CIM *enterprise wheel* developed by the Technical Council of the Society of Manufacturing Engineers. Its outer circle represents general business management. The inner circles represent four major "families" of processes that make up CIM: (1) product and process definition, (2) manufacturing planning and control, (3) factory automation, and (4) information resource management. Each of these five dimensions is a composite of more specific manufacturing processes, and each dimension is interrelated with the others. Thus, when planning a CIM system, no dimension can be ignored.

The hub of the wheel (the solid gold circle and the lighter gold circle around it) represents the IT resources and technologies necessary for the integration of

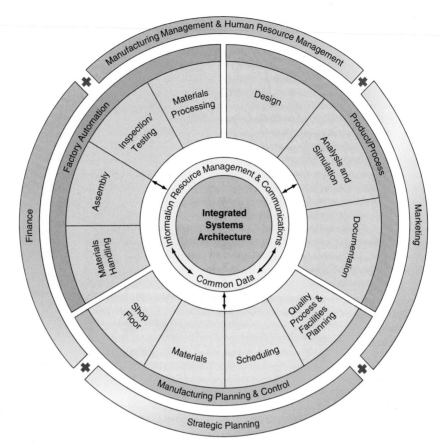

FIGURE 7.5 The CIM model: Integration of all manufacturing activities under unified management. (*Source:* Reprinted from the CASA/SME Manufacturing Enterprise Wheel, with permission from the Society of Manufacturing Engineers, Dearborn, Michigan, 1999, 3d ed.)

CIM. Without an integrated plan, trying to implement CIM would be next to impossible. There must be communication, data sharing, and cooperation among the different levels of management and functional personnel.

The major advantages of CIM are its comprehensiveness and flexibility. These are especially important in business processes that are being completely restructured or eliminated. Without CIM, it may be necessary to invest large amounts of money to change existing information systems to fit the new processes. For an example of how a furniture company uses CIM, see *kimball.com* (click on Electronic Manufacturing Services). For more on a unified framework for integrated manufacturing, using intelligent systems and PLM, see Zaremba and Morel (2003).

Product Lifecycle Management (PLM)

Product lifecycle management (PLM) is a business strategy that enables manufacturers to control and share product-related data as part of product design and development efforts and in support of supply chain operations (see Day, 2002). In PLM, Web-based and other new technologies are applied to *product development* to automate its *collaborative aspects,* which even within a given organization can prove tedious and time-consuming. By overlapping formerly disparate functions, such as a manufacturing process and the logistics that support it, a dynamic collaboration takes place among the functions, essentially forming a single large product team from the product's inception.

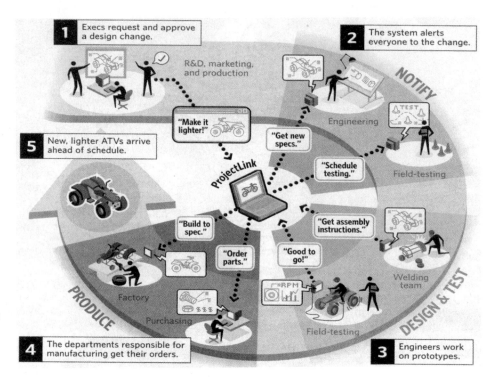

FIGURE 7.6 How product life cycle management works. (*Source:* Raskin, 2002, p. 50.)

An example of a Web-based PLM product (from PTC Corp.) for designing popular ATV bikes is provided in Figure 7.6. The collaboration is achieved via "ProjectLink" (at the center of the figure). Using this PLM, bike-maker Cannondale Corp. was able to design its 2003 model significantly faster.

PLM can have a significant beneficial impact in engineering change, cycle time, design reuse, and engineering productivity. Studies have shown that electronic-based collaboration can reduce product cost and travel expenses, as well as significantly reduce costs associated with product-change management. Moreover, an explosion of new products that have short life cycles, as well as increasing complexity in supply chain management, are driving the need for PLM.

PLM is a big step for an organization, requiring it to integrate a number of different processes and systems. Ultimately, its overall goal from the organization's point of view is to move information through an organization as quickly as possible in order to reduce the time it takes to get a product to market and to increase profitability. PLM tools are offered by SAP (MYSAP PLM), Matrix One, EDS, PTC, Dassault Systems, and IBM (IBM PLM).

7.4 MANAGING MARKETING AND SALES SYSTEMS

In Chapters 1 through 6 we emphasized the increasing importance of a customer-focused approach and the trend toward customization and consumer-based organizations. How can IT help? First we need to understand how products reach customers, which takes place through a series of marketing entities known as *channels*.

Channel systems are all the systems involved in the process of getting a product or service to customers and dealing with all customers' needs. The complexity of channel systems can be observed in Figure 7.7 (page 314), where seven major systems are interrelated.

Channel systems can link and transform marketing, sales, procurement, logistics and delivery, and other activities. Added market power comes from the integration of channel systems with the corporate functional areas. The problem is that a change in any of the channels may affect the other channels. Therefore, the supporting information systems must be coordinated or even integrated.

We describe only a few of the many channel-system activities here, organizing them into three groups: customer relations, distribution channels and in-store innovations, and marketing management. A fourth topic, telemarketing, is presented in Online File W7.6 on the book's Web site.

"The Customer Is King/Queen"

It is essential for companies today to know who their customers are and to treat them like royalty. New and innovative products and services, successful promotions, customization, and superb customer service are becoming a necessity for many organizations. In this section we will briefly describe a few activities related to *customer-centric* organizations. More are described in Section 7.7, where customer relationship management (CRM) is presented.

CUSTOMER PROFILES AND PREFERENCE ANALYSIS. Information about existing and potential customers is critical for success. Sophisticated information systems are being developed to collect data on customers, their demographics (age, gender, income level), and preferences.

Consumer behavior online can be tracked by cookies (small data files placed on a user's hard drive by a Web server). Then (as explained in Chapter 5), the consumer's online behavior can be analyzed and used for marketing purposes. By checking the demographics of its millions of customers and their locations, America Online (AOL), for example, can match appropriate ads of advertisers with specific customers. The effectiveness of such ads is very high. Even more powerful is the combination of offline and online data (e.g., see *doubleclick.com*). For approaches to targeted marketing and/or advertising, see Chapter 5 and Strauss et al. (2003).

PROSPECTIVE CUSTOMER LISTS AND MARKETING DATABASES. All firms need to know who their customers are, and IT can help create customer databases of both existing and potential customers. It is possible today to purchase computerized lists from several sources and then merge them electronically. These prospective-customer lists then can be analyzed and sorted by any desired classification for direct mailing, e-mailing, or telemarketing. Customer data can be stored in a corporate database or in special marketing databases for future analysis and use. For how Sears uses a marketing database, see Amato-McCoy (2002b). (We discuss database marketing further in Chapter 11.)

Several U.S. retailers ask customers to tell them only the Zip (postal) code in which they live. With this limited piece of information, the retailers do not get involved in privacy issues, yet they are able to gather valuable locational data. For example, they can match the geographical information with the items purchased in order to do sales analysis and make various marketing decisions. With

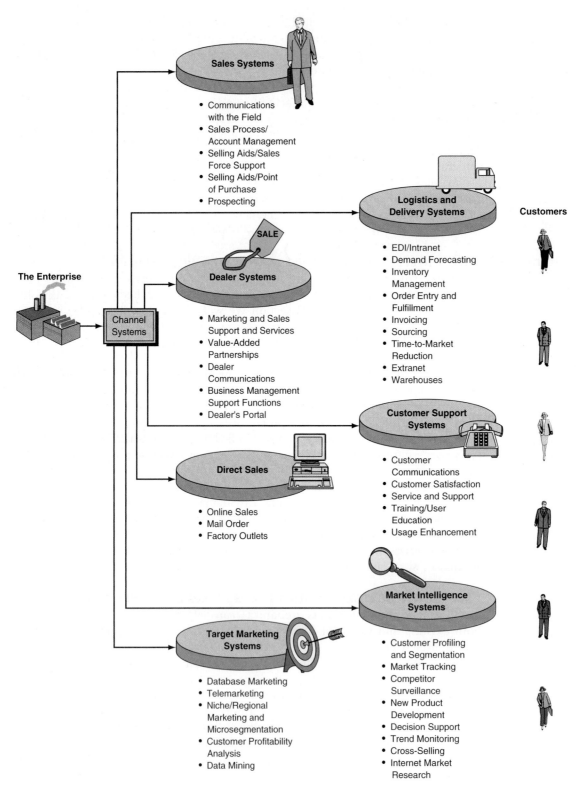

FIGURE 7.7 Marketing channel systems.

TABLE 7.3 The Changing Face of Marketing

	Old Model Mass and Segmented Marketing	New Model Customization
Relationships with customers	Customer is a passive participant in the exchange	Customer is an active co-producer
Customer needs	Articulated	Articulated and unarticulated
Segmentation	Mass market and target segments	Segments looking for customized solutions and "segments one" (a segment of only one person)
Product and service offerings	Line extensions and modification	Customized products, services, and marketing
New-product development	Marketing and R&D drive new-product development	R&D focuses on developing the platforms that allow consumers to customize
Pricing	Fixed prices and discounting	Customer-determined pricing (e.g., Priceline.com; auctions); value-based pricing models
Communication	Advertising and public relations	Integrated, interactive, and customized marketing communication, education, and entertainment
Distribution	Traditional retailing and direct marketing	Direct (online) distribution and rise of third-party logistics services
Branding	Traditional branding and co-branding	Use of the customer's name as the brand (e.g., My brand or Brand 4 ME)
Basis of competitive advantage	Marketing power	Marketing finesse and "capturing" the customer as "partner" while integrating marketing, operations, R&D, and information

Source: Wind (2001), p. 41.

this geographical information system (GIS) software, retailers can learn a lot about the company's customers and the location of competitors and can experiment with potential strategies, such as decisions about where to open new branches and outlets. (See Chapter 11 for more on use of GIS in decision making.)

MASS CUSTOMIZATION. Increasingly, today's customers want customized products. Some manufacturers offer different product configurations, and in some products dozens of options are available. The result is *mass customization,* as practiced successfully by Dell Computer and many other companies (see Appendix 2A). Customization is possible both in manufactured goods and in services.

Wind (2001) analyzed the impact of customization on marketing and the resultant changes (see Table 7.3). As shown throughout this book, these changes are being supported by IT. For example, the Web can be used to expedite the ordering and fulfillment of customized products, as demonstrated in *IT at Work 7.3* (page 316), about building a Jaguar.

Mass customization is not for everyone, and it does have several limitations (Zipkin, 2001). The major limitations are that it requires a highly flexible production technology, an elaborate system for eliciting customers' wants and needs, and strong direct-to-customer logistics system. Another limitation is

IT at Work 7.3
BUILD YOUR JAGUAR ONLINE

Prospective Jaguar car buyers can build, see, and price the car of their dreams online. As of October 2000, you can configure the car at *jaguar.com* in real time. Cars have been configured online since 1997, but Jaguar was an industry first to offer comprehensive services, delivered in many languages.

Using a virtual car, users can view more than 1,250 possible exterior combinations, rotating the car through 360 degrees, by moving directional arrows. As you select the model, color, trim, wheels, and accessories, both image and price information automatically update. The design choices are limited to current models. Up to 10 personalized car selections per customer can be stored in a "virtual garage." Customers can "test" virtual cars and conduct comparisons of different models. Once the buyer makes a decision, the order is forwarded to a dealer of his or her choice.

Like most other car manufacturers, Jaguar will not let you consummate the purchase online. To negotiate price, customers can go to a Jaguar dealer or use Auto By Tel (*autobytel.com*), which connects nearby dealers to the customer. However, Jaguar's system helps get customers to the point of purchase. It helps them *research* the purchase and explore, price, and visualize options. Customers thus

familiarize themselves with the Jaguar before even visiting a showroom. The ability to see a 3-D photo of the car is an extremely important customer service. Finally, the order for the customer-configured car can be transmitted electronically to the production floor, reducing the time-to-delivery cycle.

The IT support for this innovation includes a powerful configuration database integrated with Jaguar's production system (developed by Ford Motor Company and Trilogy Corp.) and the "virtual car" (developed by Global Beach Corp.).

As of mid-2000, most car manufacturers had introduced Web-based make-to-order systems. In order to avoid channel conflicts, these systems typically involve the dealers in the actual purchase. All major car manufacturers are attempting to move car ordering to the Web.

Sources: Compiled from *jaguar.com* press releases (October–November 2000); *ford.com* (2000) (go to Services); and *autobytel.com* (2002).

For Further Exploration: Why would manufacturers be interested in the Web if the actual purchase is done at the dealers' site?

cost: some people are unable or unwilling to pay even the slightly higher prices that customization often entails. Holweg and Pil (2001) provide some guidelines for how to overcome these limitations.

PERSONALIZATION. Using cameras, retailers can find what people are doing while they visit physical stores. Similarly, tracking software can find what people are doing in a virtual store. This technology provides information for real-time marketing and is also used in m-commerce (see Chapter 6 and also Sadeh, 2002). Personalized product offers then are made, based on where the customer spent the most time and on what what he or she purchased. A similar approach is used in Web-based *cross-selling* (or *up-selling*) efforts, in which advertising of related products is provided. For example, if you are buying a car, car insurance is automatically offered (see Strauss et al., 2003).

ADVERTISING AND PROMOTIONS. The Internet opens the door to a new advertising medium. As was shown in Chapter 5, online advertising, mainly via e-mail and banners, is growing rapidly. Innovative methods such as viral marketing (Reda, 2002) are possible only on the Internet. Wireless and pervasive computing applications also are changing the face of advertising (Chapter 6). For example, in order to measure attention to advertising, a mobile-computing device called Arbitron is carried by customers (see Gentile, 2002). Whoever is wearing the device automatically logs advertising seen or heard any time, anywhere in their daily travels.

Distribution Channels and In-Store Innovations

Organizations can distribute their products and services through several available delivery channels. For instance, a company may use its own outlets or distributors. Digitizable products can be distributed online, or can be delivered on CD ROMs. Other products can be delivered by trucks or trains, with the movement of goods monitored by IT applications. The Web is revolutionizing distribution channels (Chaudhury et al., 2001). Here we look at some representative topics relating to distribution channels.

NEW IT-SUPPORTED DISTRIBUTION CHANNELS. In addition to the Internet, IT enables other new or improved channels through which to distribute goods or services. For example, by connecting mapping technology with databases of local employers, retailers and fast-food marketers are providing goods and services to employees during their lunch breaks. Using the Internet, retailers offer special incentives (e.g., coupons) to lunchtime shoppers. According to Seidman (2002), fast food, paint, and tires top the list of items sold in this new channel. A leading vendor in this area is SBS Technologies (*sbs.com*); it works with Mapinfo.com, which provides electronic maps showing a marketer who is working where, so they can design promotions accordingly.

Another new distribution channel is self-service convenience stores, which are popular at railway stations, highway rest areas, airports, and gasoline stations. While some of these have an employee or two, most are without employees. They are used by manufacturers (e.g., Mattel) as well as by retailers to offer their products to the public. What is new about this distribution channel is that payment can be made by inserting a credit card into a card reader or by using a smart card, even for a small purchase amount.

IMPROVING SHOPPING AND CHECKOUT AT RETAIL STORES. The modern shopper is often pressed for time, and most are unhappy about waiting in long lines. Using information technology, it is possible to reengineer the shopping and the checkout process. For example:

- Several companies use handheld wireless devices that scan the bar code UPC of the product you want to buy, giving you all product information, including options such as maintenance agreements. The desired purchase is matched with your smart card (or credit card), and an order to send the product(s) to the cashier is issued. By the time you arrive at the cashier, the bill and the merchandise are ready.

- An alternative to the handheld computer is the information kiosk. The kiosks enable customers to view catalogs in stores, conduct product searches, and even compare prices with those of competitors. Kiosks at some stores (e.g., 7-Eleven stores in some countries) can be used to place orders on the Internet. (For details about use of in-store kiosks, see Online File W7.7 and Sweeney, 2001.)

- Video-based systems count the number of shoppers and track where they go in physical stores. These are not security systems per se; rather, their purpose is to gather information about shopping patterns. The collected data are analyzed and used for computer-based decisions regarding displays, store design, and in-store marketing messages and promotions. The information is also used to determine when shopping traffic is heaviest, in order to schedule employees (see Kroll, 2002, for details).

● Some stores that have many customers who pay by check (e.g., large grocery stores, Wal-Mart stores) have installed check-writers. All you have to do is submit the blank check to the cashier, who runs it through a machine attached to the cash register. The machine prints the name of the store as the payee and the amount, you sign the check, and in seconds the check is validated, your bank account is debited, and you are out of the store with your merchandise.

● Computerization of various activities in retail stores can save time and money and provide better customer service. Cash Register Express offers many products, such as Video Express and portable data collectors. For details about computerized cash register services, see *pcamerica.com.*

● An increasing number of retailers are installing self-check machines. For example, Home Depot just added self-checks in their stores. Not only does the retailer save the cost of employees' salaries, but customers are happier for saving time. (And some enjoy "playing cashier" briefly.) A major device is U-Scan, which is used in many supermarkets (see photo).

DISTRIBUTION CHANNELS MANAGEMENT. Once products are in the distribution channels, firms need to monitor and track them, since only fast and accurate delivery times guarantee high customer satisfaction and repeat business. FedEx, UPS, HDL, and other large shipping companies provide customers with sophisticated tracking systems. These shippers track the location of their trucks and airplanes using GPSs; they also scan the packages so they know their whereabouts. Shipping companies also offer customers the ability to self-track

U-Scan kiosk.

packages using Web-based systems, thus reducing the need for customer service employees.

Marketing Management

Many marketing management decision applications are supported by computerized information systems. (Online File W7.8 shows the marketing management decision framework.) Here are some representative examples of how this is being done.

PRICING OF PRODUCTS OR SERVICES. Sales volumes are largely determined by the prices of products or services. Price is also a major determinant of profit. Pricing is a difficult decision, and prices may need to be changed frequently. For example, in response to price changes made by competitors, a company may need to adjust its prices or take other actions.

Pricing decisions are supported by a number of computerized systems: Three pricing models for retailers with thousands of items to price were developed by Sung and Lee (2000). Many companies are using online analytical processing (OLAP) to support pricing and other marketing decisions (see Chapter 10). In Chapter 1 we discussed the optimization models used to support prices at Longs Drug Stores and others (see *A Closer Look 2.2*). Web-based comparison engines enable customers to select a vendor at the price they want, and they also enable vendors to see how their prices compare with others. For an overview on pricing and the Internet, including quick price testing, see Baker et al. (2001).

SALESPERSON PRODUCTIVITY. Salespeople differ from each other; some excel in selling certain products, while others excel in selling to a certain type of customer or in a certain geographical zone. This information, which is usually collected in the sales and marketing TPS, can be analyzed, using a comparative performance system, in which sales data by salesperson, product, region, and even the time of day are evaluated. Actual current sales can be compared to historical data and to standards. Multidimensional spreadsheet software facilitates this type of analysis. Assignment of salespeople to regions and/or products and the calculation of bonuses can also be supported by this system.

In addition, sales productivity can be boosted by Web-based systems. For example, in a Web-based call center, when a customer calls a sales rep, the rep can look at the customer's history of purchases, demographics, services available where the customer lives, and more. This information enables reps to work faster, while providing better customer service. Customers' information can be provided by marketing customer information file technology (MCIF) (see Totty, 2000).

Sales Force Automation. The productivity of salespeople in the field also can be greatly increased by what is known as **sales-force automation**—providing salespeople with mobile devices, access to databases, and so on. It empowers the field sales force to close deals at the customer's office and to configure marketing strategies at home. (Recall the Maybelline case, Chapter 2; for additional details, see Schafer, 1997). For other uses of the Web by the sales force, see Varney (1996) and the case of PAVECA (Chapter 5).

Sales force automation can be boosted in many ways by using Web-based tools. For example, Netgain (from *netgainservices.com*) lets a multimedia company's design and sales teams collaborate over the Web, passing off sales leads, bringing in new sales reps to clinch different parts of a deal, and tracking reports on sales progress.

Productivity Software. **Sales automation software** is especially helpful to small businesses, enabling them to rapidly increase sales and growth. Such Web-based software can manage the flow of messages and assist in writing contracts, scheduling, and making appointments. Of course it provides word processing and e-mail, and it helps with mailings and follow-up letters. Electronic stamps (e.g., *stamp.com*) can assist with mass mailings.

PROFITABILITY ANALYSIS. In deciding on advertising and other marketing efforts, managers often need to know the profit contribution of certain products and services. Profitability information for products and services can be derived from the cost-accounting system. For example, profit performance analysis software available from Comshare (*comshare.com*) is designed to help managers assess and improve the profit performance of their line of business, products, distribution channels, sales regions, and other dimensions critical to managing the enterprise. Northwest Airlines, for example, uses expert systems and DSS to set prices based on profitability. They also use a similar system to audit tickets and for calculating commissions to travel agents.

In addition, identification of profitable customers and the frequency with which they interact with the organization can be derived from special promotional programs, such as hotels' frequent-stayer programs. This information can be used for loyalty and other programs.

SALES ANALYSIS AND TRENDS. The marketing TPS collects sales figures that can be segregated along several dimensions for early detection of problems and opportunities, by searching for trends and relationships. For example, if sales of a certain product show a continuous decline in certain regions but not in other regions, management can investigate the declining region. Similarly, an increasing sales volume of a new product calls attention to an opportunity if it is found to be statistically significant. This application demonstrates the reliance of decision making on the TPS. Also, data mining can be used to find relationships and patterns in large databases (see Chapter 11).

NEW PRODUCTS, SERVICES, AND MARKET PLANNING. The introduction of new or improved products and services can be expensive and risky. An important question to ask about a new product or service is, "Will it sell?" An appropriate answer calls for careful analysis, planning, and forecasting. These can best be executed with the aid of IT because of the large number of determining factors and the uncertainties that may be involved. Market research also can be conducted on the Internet, as described in Chapter 5. A related issue is the speed with which products are brought to market. An example of how Procter & Gamble expedites the time-to-market by using the Internet is provided in *IT at Work 7.4.*

WEB-BASED SYSTEMS IN MARKETING. The use of Web-based systems in support of marketing and sales has grown rapidly, as demonstrated by the Procter & Gamble case. A summary of some Web-based impacts is provided in Figure 7.8.

Marketing activities conclude the primary activities of the value chain. Next we look at the functional systems that are secondary (support) activities in the value chain: accounting/finance and human resources management.

IT at Work 7.4

INTERNET MARKET RESEARCH EXPEDITES TIME-TO-MARKET AT PROCTER & GAMBLE

For decades, Procter & Gamble (P&G) and Colgate-Palmolive have been competitors in the market for personal care products. Developing a major new product, from concept to market launch, used to take over 5 years. First, a concept test was done; the companies sent product photos and descriptions to potential customers, asking whether they might buy it. If the feedback was negative, they tried to improve the product concept and then repeated the concept testing. Once positive response was achieved, sample products were mailed out, and customers were asked to fill out detailed questionnaires. When customers' responses met the companies' internal hurdles, the company would start with mass advertising on television and in magazines.

However, thanks to the Internet, it took P&G only three-and-a-half years to get Whitestrips, the teeth-brightening product, onto the market and to a sales level of $200 million a year—considerably quicker than other oral care products. In September 2000, P&G threw out the old marketing test model and instead introduced Whitestrips on the Internet, offering the product for sale on P&G's Web site. The company spent several months studying who was coming to the site and buying the product; it collected responses to online questionnaires, which was much faster than the old mail-outs.

The online research, which was facilitated by data mining conducted on P&G's huge historical data (stored in a data warehouse) and the new Internet data, revealed the most enthusiastic groups. These included teenage girls, brides-to-be, and young Hispanic Americans. Immediately, the company started to target these segments with appropriate advertising. The Internet created a product awareness of 35 percent, even before any shipments were made to stores. This "buzz" created a huge demand for the product by the time it hit the shelves.

From this experience, P&G learned important lessons about flexible and creative ways to approach product innovation and marketing. The whole process of studying the product concept, segmenting the market, and expediting product development has been revolutionized.

Sources: Compiled from Buckley (2002), and from *pg.com* (February–December 2002).

For Further Exploration: How did the Internet decrease time-to-market in this situation? What is the role of data mining? Why is so much testing needed?

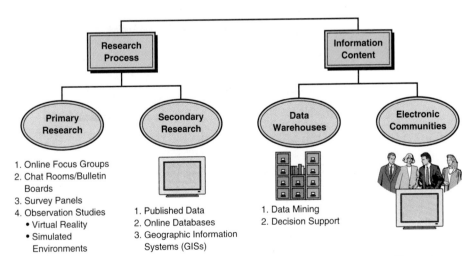

FIGURE 7.8 The impact of the Web on marketing information services. Channel-driven advantages are (1) transaction speed (real-time response) because of the interactive nature of the process, (2) global reach, (3) reduced costs, (4) multimedia content, and (5) reliability. (*Source:* P. K. Kannan et al., "Marketing Information on the I-Way," *Communications of the ACM*, 1999, p. 36. (Association for Computing Machinery, Inc. Reprinted by permission.)

7.5 MANAGING THE ACCOUNTING AND FINANCE SYSTEMS

A primary mission of the accounting/finance functional area is to manage money flows into, within, and out of organizations. This is a very broad mission since money is involved in all functions of an organization. Some repetitive accounting/financing activities such as payroll, billing, and cash management were computerized as early as the 1950s. Today, accounting/finance information systems are very diverse and comprehensive.

The general structure of an accounting/finance system is presented in Figure 7.9. It is divided into three levels: strategic, tactical, and operational. Information technology can support almost all the activities listed, as well as the communication and collaboration of accounting/finance with internal and external environments. We describe some selected activities in the rest of this section. For others, see Reed et al. (2001).

Financial Planning and Budgeting

Appropriate management of financial assets is a major task in financial planning and budgeting. Managers must plan for both the acquisition of financial

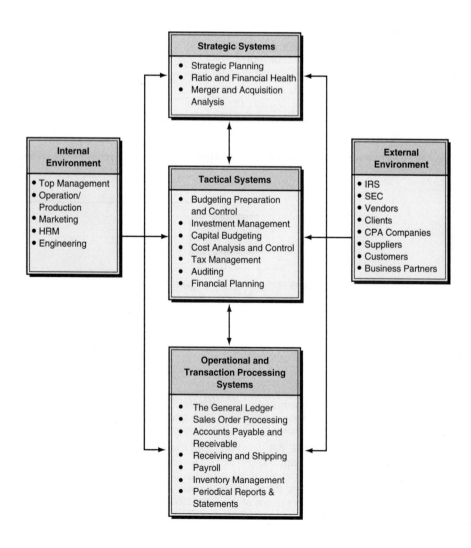

FIGURE 7.9 Major activities of the accounting/finance system.

resources and their use. Financial planning, like any other functional planning, is tied to the overall organizational planning and to other functional areas. It is divided into short-, medium-, and long-term horizons, much like activities planning. Financial analysts use Web resources and computerized spreadsheets to accomplish the organization's financial planning and budgeting activities.

FINANCIAL AND ECONOMIC FORECASTING. Knowledge about the availability and cost of money is a key ingredient for successful financial planning. Especially important is the projection of cash flow, which tells organizations what funds they need and when, and how they will acquire them. This function is important for all firms, but is especially so for small companies, which tend to have little financial cushion. Inaccurate cash flow projection is the number one reason why many small businesses go bankrupt. Availability and cost of money depend on corporate financial health and the willingness of lenders and investors to infuse money into the company (see Banks, 2001).

Financial and economic analysis is facilitated by intelligent systems such as neural computing (Chapter 12). Many software packages are available for conducting economic and financial forecasting. Economic and financial forecasts are also available for a fee, frequently over the Internet.

PLANNING FOR INCOMING FUNDS. Funds for running organizations come from several sources, including stockholders' investments, sale of bonds, loans from banks, sales of products and services, and income from investments. Using the information generated by financial and economic forecasts, the organization can build a decision support model for planning incoming funds. For example, if the forecast indicates that interest rates will be high, the company can defer borrowing until the interest rates drop. Decisions about when and how much to refinance can be supported by expert systems.

BUDGETING. The best-known part of financial planning is the annual budget, which allocates the financial resources of an organization among participants and activities. The budget is the financial expression of the organization's plans. It allows management to allocate resources in the way that best supports the organization's mission and goals. IT enables the introduction of financial intelligence into the budgeting process.

Software Support. Several software packages, many of which are Web-based, are available to support budget preparation and control (e.g., Budget 2000 from EPS Consultants and Profix Budgeting, from Profix.com) and to facilitate communication among all participants in the budget preparation.

Since budget preparation may involve both top-down and bottom-up processes, modeling capabilities in some packages allow the budget coordinator to take the top-down numbers, compare them with the bottom-up data from the users, and reconcile the two.

Software also makes it easier to build complex budgets that involve multiple sites, including foreign countries. Budgeting software also allows various internal and external comparisons. One of the latest trends is industry-specific packages such as for hospitals, banks, or retailing. Budgeting software is frequently bundled with financial analysis and reporting functions. For example, Comshare's MPC integrates budgeting with planning, financial analysis, forecasting, and production reporting (see *comshare.com/mpc/index.cfm*).

The major benefits of using budgeting software, according to Freeman (1997), are that it can: reduce the time and effort involved in the budget process, explore and analyze the implications of organizational and environmental changes, facilitate the integration of the corporate strategic objectives with operational plans, make planning an ongoing, continuous process, and automatically monitor exceptions for patterns and trends.

CAPITAL BUDGETING. *Capital budgeting* is the financing of asset acquisitions, including the disposal of major organizational assets. It usually includes a comparison of options, such as keep the asset, replace it with an identical new asset, replace it with a different one, or discard it. The capital budgeting process also evaluates buy-versus-lease options.

Capital budgeting analysis uses standard financial models, such as net present value (NPV), internal rate of return (IRR), and payback period, to evaluate alternative investment decisions. Most spreadsheet packages include built-in functions of these models.

Managing Financial Transactions

An accounting/finance information system is also responsible for gathering the raw data necessary for the accounting/finance TPS, transforming the data into information, and making the information available to users, whether aggregate information about payroll, the organization's internal managers, or external reports to stockholders or government agencies.

Many packages exist to execute routine accounting transaction processing activities. Several are available free on the Internet (try *tucows.com*). Many software packages are integrated. In these integrated systems, the accounting/finance activities are combined with other TPSs such as those of marketing and production and operations management. The data collected and managed for the accounting/finance transaction processing system are also inputs for the various functional information systems.

One such integrated system is MAS 90 and MAS 200 (from *bestsoftwareinc.com/mass90/index*). It is a collection of standard accounting modules, as shown in Figure 7.10 (the "wheel" in the diagram). Communication and inquiry modules (right side) support the accounting modules. The user can integrate as many of the modules as needed for the business. On the left side is a list of other business processes and functional applications that can interface with accounting applications. Note that the software includes an e-commerce module, which provides dynamic Web access to MAS 90. This module includes account and order inquiry capabilities as well as a shopping cart for order entry. The 2003 version of MAS 90 includes modules for business intelligence, e-commerce, CRM, sales force automation (SFA), and financial reporting.

Another integrated accounting software package is *peachtree.com* (from Best Software), which offers a sales ledger, purchase ledger, cash book, sales order processing, invoicing, stock control, job casting, fixed-assets register, and more. Other software vendors are Great Plains and Solomon (see Business Solutions at Microsoft.com); see their demos. Other accounting packages can be found at *2020software.com* and *findaccountingsoftware.com*.

The accounting/finance TPS also provides a complete, reliable audit trail of all transactions transmitted through the network. This feature is vital to accountants and auditors. (For more, see the "Control and Auditing" section below.)

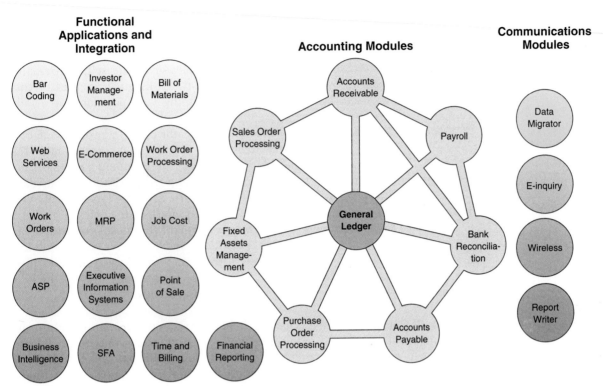

FIGURE 7.10 Integrated accounting/business software.

E-COMMERCE APPLICATIONS OF FINANCIAL TRANSACTIONS. Companies doing e-commerce need to access financial data of customers (e.g., credit line), inventory levels, and manufacturing databases (to see available capacity, to place orders, etc.). Great Plains (*bestsoftware.com*) offers 50 modules to choose from, to meet the most common financial, project, distribution, manufacturing, and e-business needs.

Diversified financial transactions also lend themselves to e-commerce applications, especially Web-based ones. In Chapter 5, we described e-banking, electronic transactions of stock markets, e-financial services, and more. Many of these can be done in a wireless environment (Chapter 6, and the Handlesbanken case in Chapter 1). Here we provide a few other examples.

Global Stock Exchanges. According to Maxemchuk and Shur (2001), financial markets are moving toward global, 24-hour, distributed electronic stock exchanges that will use the Internet for both the transactions and multicasting of real-time stock prices.

Handling Multiple Currencies. Global trade involves financial transactions in different currencies. Conversion ratios of many of them change every minute. Zakaria (2002) reports on a Web-based system (from SAP AG) that takes financial data from seven Asian countries and converts the currencies to dollars in seconds. Reports based on these data, which used to take weeks to generate, now take minutes. The system handles the multiplicity of languages as well.

E-Bonds. The World Bank is now using e-bonds, a system for marketing, distributing, and trading bonds over the Internet. The system expanded in 2003 to include electronic applications to currency and derivatives trading. For details see *gs.com* (2001).

Factoring Online. *Factors* are financial institutions that buy accounts receivable, usually at a discount. Factoring of receivables gives the selling company an immediate cash inflow. The factor takes on the risks and expenses of collecting the debts. Factoring on the Web is becoming very popular. For details see Salodof-MacNeil (2002).

Electronic Re-presentment of Checks. Companies face a problem of bad checks (insufficient funds). Paper checks that do not clear are usually re-presented (manually or electronically). Electronic re-presentment can be organized as part of cash management information systems. Such systems consolidate checks from different banks and conduct a return analysis (analysis of why checks are not honored, who is likely to pass bad checks, etc.).

Electronic Bill Presentment and Payments. One of the most successful areas of e-commerce is that of electronic presentment and payments. In its simplest form it is an electronic payment of bills. However, third-party companies provide a service in which they calculate, print, and electronically present the bills to customers (see Chapter 5 and Boucher-Ferguson, 2002).

VIRTUAL CLOSE. Companies close their books (accounting records) quarterly, mainly to meet regulatory requirements. Some companies want to be able to close their books any time, on short notice. Called a **virtual close,** the ability to close the books quickly may give almost real-time information on the financial health of a company (see McClenahen, 2002). With an advanced IT program developed by Cisco (see Online File W7.9) it will soon be possible, even for a large multinational corporation, to close the books in a matter of hours.

INTEGRATION OF FINANCIAL TRANSACTIONS WITH E-COMMERCE APPLICATIONS. ACCPAC International (*accpaconline.com*) integrated its financial accounting software with e-business solutions (software, system building, consulting, and integration) to help global traders. The e-commerce module (eTransact) is tightly integrated with ACCPAC for Windows, offering a single, unifying financial and business management system.

EXPENSE MANAGEMENT AUTOMATION. Expense management automation **(EMA)** refers to systems that automate data entry and processing of travel and entertainment expenses. These expenses can account for 20 percent of the operating expenses of large corporations (Degnan, 2003). EMA systems (by companies such as Captura, Concur, Extensity, and Necho) are Web-based applications that replace the paper forms and rudimentary spreadsheet. These systems let companies quickly and consistently collect expense information, enforce company policies and contracts, and reduce unplanned purchases of airline and hotel services. The software forces travelers to be organized before a trip starts. In addition to benefits to the companies, employees also benefited from quick reimbursement (since expense approvals are not held up by sloppy or incomplete documentation). (For details, see "What EMA systems now offer...," 2002.)

Investment Management

Organizations invest large amounts of money in stocks, bonds, real estate, and other assets. Some of these investments are short-term in nature; others are long-term. If you examine the financial records of publicly traded corporations, you will see that some of them have billions of dollars of assets. Furthermore, organizations need to pay pensions to their employees, so they need to manage the pension funds as an asset.

Investment management is a difficult task. For one thing, there are thousands of investment alternatives. On the New York Stock Exchange alone, there are more than 2,000 stocks, and millions of possible combinations for creating portfolios. Investment decisions are based on economic and financial forecasts and on various multiple and conflicting objectives (such as high yield, safety, and liquidity). The investment environment also includes opportunities in other countries. Another factor that contributes to the complexity of investment management is that investments made by many organizations are subject to complex regulations and tax laws. Finally, investment decisions need to be made quickly and frequently. Decision makers can be in different locations, and they need to cooperate and collaborate. Therefore, computerization is especially popular in financial institutions that are involved in investments, as illustrated in *IT at Work 7.5*.

 In addition, data-mining tools and neural networks (Chapter 12) are used by many institutional investment managers to analyze historical databases, so they can make better predictions. For a data-mining tool, see *wizsoft.com*. Some typical financial applications of neural computing are provided in Online File W7.10.

IT at Work 7.5
MATLAB MANAGES EQUITY
PORTFOLIOS AT DAIWA SECURITIES

Daiwa Securities of Japan (*daiwa.co.jp*) is one of the world's largest and most profitable multinational securities firms. Many of the company's traders are engineers and mathematicians who use computers to constantly buy and sell securities for the company's own portfolio. Daiwa believes that identifying mispricings in the stock markets holds great profit potential. Toward this end the company uses leading-edge computerized quantitative analysis methods to look for securities that are underpriced by the market. The software compares stock price performance of individual companies to that of other companies in the same market sector. In an attempt to minimize risk, the model then suggests a buy, sell, or sell-short solution for each investigated security.

The company is using an *arbitrage* approach, which looks for the opportunity to make profits with very little risk. It may keep undervalued stocks, but it sells short overvalued stocks and futures. The buy-sell recommendations are generated by a system (coded in MATLAB, from Mathworks.com) that is based on modern portfolio theory. The system uses two models: one for the short term (3 to 10 days) and one for the longer term (3 to 6 weeks). It

follows over 1,200 stocks and includes many variables, some of which are very volatile. Changes in the MATLAB model can be made quickly on the Excel spreadsheet it uses. Complex statistical tools are used for the computations. The system attempts to minimize the risk of the portfolio yet maximize its profit. Since these two goals usually contradict each other, trade-offs must be considered.

The system is based on neural networks and fuzzy logic. The advantage of neural networks is that they can closely approximate the underlying processes that may be moving the financial markets in a particular direction.

To motivate the traders to use the system, as well as to quickly build modifications using Excel, the company pays generous bonuses for successful trades. As a matter of fact, some young MBA and Ph.D. traders have commanded bonuses of hundreds of thousands of dollars each year.

Sources: Compiled from Pittaras (1996), and *daiwa.co.jp* (press releases 2000).

For Further Exploration: What is the logic of the arbitrage strategy? Why would bonuses be used to motivate employees to use the system?

The following are the major areas of support that IT can provide to investment management.

ACCESS TO FINANCIAL AND ECONOMIC REPORTS. Investment decisions require managers to evaluate financial and economic reports and news provided by federal and state agencies, universities, research institutions, financial services, and corporations. There are hundreds of Web sources, many of which are free; a sampling is listed in Online File W7.11. Most of these services are useful both for professional investment managers and for individual investors.

To cope with the large amount of online financial data, investors use three supporting tools: (1) Internet search engines for finding financial data, (2) Internet directories and yellow pages, and (3) software for monitoring, interpreting, and analyzing financial data and for alerting management.

FINANCIAL ANALYSIS. Financial analysis can be executed with a spreadsheet program, or with commercially available ready-made decision support software (e.g., see *tradeportal.com/tradematrix.asp*). Or it can be more sophisticated, involving intelligent systems. Other information technologies can be used as well. For example, Morgan Stanley and Company uses virtual reality on its intranet to display the results of risk analysis in three dimensions. Seeing data in 3-D makes it easier to make comparisons and intuitive connections than would seeing a two-dimensional chart.

One area of analysis that is becoming popular is referred to as **financial value chain management (FVCM).** According to this approach, financial analysis is combined with operations analysis. All financial functions are analyzed (including international trades). Combining financial and operations analysis provides better financial control. For example, if the organization runs its operations at a lower-than-planned level, it is likely to need less money; if it exceeds the operational plan, it may well be all right to exceed the budgeted amounts for that plan. For details see Aberdeen.com (2002).

Control and Auditing

The major reason organizations go out of business is their inability to forecast and/or secure sufficient *cash flow.* Underestimated expenses, overspending, financial mismanagement, and fraud can lead to disaster. Good planning is necessary, but not sufficient, and must be supplemented by skillful control. Control activities in organizations take many forms, including control and auditing of the information systems themselves (see Chapter 15). Information systems play an extremely important role in supporting organizational control, as we show throughout the text. Specific forms of financial control are presented next.

BUDGETARY CONTROL. Once the annual budget has been decided upon, it is divided into monthly allocations. Managers at various levels then monitor departmental expenditures and compare them against the budget and operational progress of the corporate plans. Simple reporting systems summarize the expenditures and provide *exception reports* by flagging any expenditure that exceeds the budget by a certain percent or that falls significantly below the budget. More sophisticated software attempts to tie expenditures to program accomplishment. Numerous software programs can be used to support budgetary control; most of them are combined with budget preparation packages such as Comshare BudgetPlus (*budgetplus.com*), Sumco ERP (*symcosof.com*), and Homepages.nildram.co.uk.

AUDITING. The major purpose of auditing is to ensure the accuracy and condition of the financial health of an organization. Internal auditing is done by the organization's accounting/finance personnel, who also prepare for external auditing by CPA companies. There are several types of auditing, including financial, operational, and concurrent. In *financial auditing* the accuracy of the organization's records are verified. The *operational audit* attempts to validate the effectiveness of the procedures of collecting and processing the information, for example, the adequacy of controls and compliance with company policies. When the operational audit is ongoing (all the time) it is called a *concurrent audit.*

IT can facilitate auditing. For example, intelligent systems can uncover fraud by finding financial transactions that significantly deviate from previous payment profiles. Also, IT provides real-time data whenever needed (see *peoplesoft.com/go/ pt_financials*).

FINANCIAL RATIO ANALYSIS. A major task of the accounting/finance department is to watch the financial health of the company by monitoring and assessing a set of financial ratios. These ratios are mostly the same as those used by external parties when they are deciding whether to invest in an organization, loan money to it, or buy it. But internal parties have access to much more detailed data for use in calculating financial ratios.

The collection of data for ratio analysis is done by the transaction processing system, and computation of the ratios is done by financial analysis models. The *interpretation* of the ratios, and especially the prediction of their future behavior, requires expertise and is sometimes supported by expert systems.

PROFITABILITY ANALYSIS AND COST CONTROL. Many companies are concerned with the profitability of individual products or services as well as with the financial health of the entire organization. Profitability analysis DSS software (see Chapter 12) allows accurate computation of profitability. It also allows allocation of overheads. One way to control cost is by properly estimating it. This is done by special software; see Vijayakumar (2002).

PRODUCT PRICING. The pricing of products is an important corporate decision since it determines competitiveness and profitability. The marketing department may wish to reduce prices in order to increase market share, but the accounting/finance system must check the relevant cost in order to provide guidelines for such price reductions. Decision support models can facilitate product pricing. Accounting, finance, and marketing, supported by integrated software and intranets, can team up to jointly set appropriate product prices.

Several more applications in the financial/accounting area are described in Online File W7.12. Many more can be found at Reed (2001).

7.6 MANAGING HUMAN RESOURCES SYSTEMS

Developments in Web-based systems increased the popularity of human resources information systems (HRISs) as of the late 1990s. Initial HRIS applications were mainly related to transaction processing systems. (For examples, see Thomas and Ray, 2000; and Bussler and Davis, 2001–2002.) In recent years, as systems generally have been moved to intranets and the Web, so have HRIS applications, many of which can be delivered via an HR portal (see Online File W7.13). Many organizations use their Web portals to advertise job openings and conduct online hiring and training. Ensher et al. (2002) describe the impact of the Internet on acquiring, rewarding, developing, protecting, and retaining human resources. Their findings are summarized in Table 7.4. Perhaps the biggest benefit to companies of human relations IT services is the release of HR staff from intermediary roles, so they can focus on strategic planning and human resources organization and development. In the following sections we describe in more detail how IT facilitates the management of human resources (HRM).

Recruitment

Recruitment is finding employees, testing them, and deciding which ones to hire. Some companies are flooded with viable applicants, while others have difficulty finding the right people. Information systems can be helpful in both cases. Here are some examples.

USING THE WEB FOR RECRUITMENT. With millions of resumes available online, it is not surprising that companies are trying to find appropriate candidates on the Web, usually with the help of specialized search engines. Also, hundreds of thousands of jobs are advertised on the Web (see Thomas and Ray, 2000, and Jandt and Nemnich, 1999). Many matching services exist (see Internet Exercise 3). Online recruiting is able to "cast a wide net" to reach more candidates, which may bring in better applicants. In addition, the costs of online recruitment are lower. Other benefits of online recruitment for employers, plus some disadvantages, are shown in Online File W7.14.

Recruitment online is beneficial for candidates as well. They are exposed to a larger number of job offerings, can get details of the positions quickly, and can begin to evaluate the prospective employer. To check the competitiveness of salary offerings, or to see how much one can make elsewhere in several countries, job candidates can go to *monster.com.*

Online recruitment may be facilitated by intelligent systems such as Resumix, described in *IT at Work 7.6* (page 332).

For a complete analysis of and guidelines for e-recruitment, see Thomas and Ray (2000) and Borck (2000).

POSITION INVENTORY. Large organizations frequently need to fill vacant positions. To do so, they maintain a file that lists all open positions by job title, geographical area, task content, and skills required. Like any other inventory, this position inventory is updated each time a position is added, modified, and so on. In some cases, position inventories are used to improve national employment conditions. The government of the Philippines, for example, provides a list of available positions in that country, and that list is accessible via the Internet. For those people without Internet access, the government provides access via computers in kiosks in public places and government facilities.

An advanced intranet-based position inventory system keeps the position inventory list current, matches openings with available personnel, and allows data to be viewed by an employee over the corporate portal from any location at any time. Outsiders can view openings from the Internet. In addition, it is possible to match openings to available personnel.

TABLE 7.4 Comparison of Traditional Human Resources to E-Human Resources

Key HR Process	Traditional HR	E-HR
Acquiring Human Resources		
Recruitment and selection	● Paper resumes and paper postings ● Positions filled in months ● Limited by geographical barriers	● Electronic resumes and Internet postings ● Positions filled in weeks or days ● Unlimited access to global applicants
Selection	● Costs directed at attracting candidates ● Manual review of resumes ● Face-to-face (FTF) interviewing process	● Costs directed at selecting candidates ● Electronic review of resumes (scanning) ● Some distance interviewing (mostly still FTF)
Rewarding Human Resources		
Performance evaluation	● Supervisor evaluation ● Face-to-face evaluation	● 360-degree evaluation ● Appraisal software (online and hard copy)
Compensation and benefits	● Time spent on paperwork (benefits changes) ● Emphasis on salary and bonuses ● Naïve employees ● Emphasis on internal equity ● Changes made by HR	● Time spent on assessing market salaries ● Emphasis on ownership and quality of work-life ● Knowledgeable employees ● Emphasis on external equity ● Changes made by employees online
Developing Human Resources		
Training and development	● Standardized classroom training ● Development process is HR-driven	● Flexible online training ● Development process is employee-driven
Career management	● HR lays out career paths for employees ● Reactive decisions ● Personal networking (local area only)	● Employees manage their careers in concert with HR ● Proactive planning with technology ● Electronic and personal networking
Protecting Human Resources		
Health and safety	● Building and equipment safety ● Physical fatigue ● Mostly reactive programs ● Limited to job-related stressors ● Focus on employee-management relations	● Ergonomic considerations ● Mental fatigue and wellness ● Proactive programs to reduce stress ● Personal and job-related stressors ● Focus on employee-employee relations
Employee relations/legal	● Stronger union presence ● Sexual harassment/discrimination ● Task performance monitoring	● Weaker union presence ● Equal employment opportunity ● Use of technology monitoring/big brother ● Intellectual property/data security ● Inappropriate uses of technology
Retaining Human Resources		
Retention strategies	● Not a major focal point	● Currently the critical HR activity ● Online employee opinion surveys ● Cultivating an effective company culture ● Mundane tasks done by technology, freeing time for more interesting work
Work-family balance	● Not a major focal point	● Development and monitoring of programs ● Providing childcare and eldercare ● Erosion of work-home boundaries

Source: Ensher et al. (2002), p. 240, Table 1.

IT at Work 7.6
RESUMIX

From the time a position becomes available or a resume is received, Resumix (*resumix.com,* now a subsidiary of Yahoo Enterprise Solutions) gives the recruiter the control while dispersing the work of processing job applications. Hiring managers can view job applications; operators can scan resumes; and a recruiter can search for a candidate or identify existing employees for training programs, redeployment opportunities, or new initiatives.

The core of this powerful system is Resumix's Knowledge Base. As a computerized intelligent system, it goes beyond simply matching words. The Knowledge Base interprets a candidate's resume, determining skills based on context and matching those skills to the position criteria. For example,

you might be looking for a product manager. Being a member of the AMA (American Marketing Association) might be one of the desirable properties for the job. However, with a basic keyword search, you might get candidates who have listed with AMA, but are really members of the American Medical Association or American Meatpackers Association. Those are not relevant to your search. Resumix Knowledge Base would select only the candidates with relevant skills.

Source: resumix.com (accessed May 3, 2003).

For Further Exploration: Can Resumix eliminate human resume evaluators? Is a machine probing into your resume an invasion of privacy?

By analyzing the position inventory and its changes over time, human resources personnel can find other useful information, such as those jobs with high turnover. Such information can support decisions about promotions, salary administration, and training plans.

HRM PORTALS AND SALARY SURVEYS. One advantage of the Web is the large amount of information related to job matching (see Chapter 5). There are also many private and public HR-related portals. The portal is a search engine, an index of jobs, posted on corporate-member sites. For example, several large companies (e.g., IBM, Xerox, GE) created jointly a career portal called DirectEmployers.com. Commercial, public online recruiters, such as Monster.com, help corporate recruiters find candidates for difficult-to-fill positions. For details see Harrington (2002).

Another area for HR portals is salary surveys. Salary surveys help companies determine how much to pay their employees. Companies used to pay consultants up to $10,000 for a one-time survey (Bussler and Davis, 2001–2002). Now they can conduct such surveys themselves by utilizing free data from vendors such as Salary.com.

EMPLOYEE SELECTION. The human resources department is responsible for screening job applicants, evaluating, testing, and selecting them in compliance with state and federal regulations. The process of employee selection can be very complex since it may involve many external and internal candidates and multiple criteria. To expedite the testing and evaluation process and ensure consistency in selection, companies use information technologies such as Web-based expert systems. Figure 7.11 shows the multiple criteria involved in employee selection and illustrates the role of an expert system in this process and in related tasks such as performance appraisal.

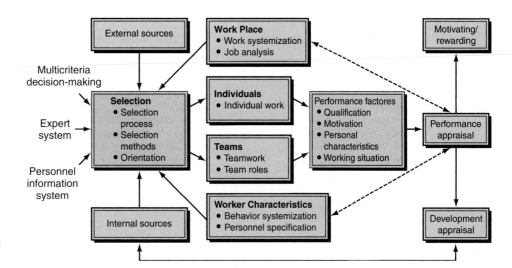

FIGURE 7.11 Intelligent personnel selection model. (*Source:* Jareb and Rajkoric, 2001.)

Human Resources Maintenance and Development

Once recruited, employees become part of the corporate human resources pool, which needs to be maintained and developed. Some activities supported by IT are the following.

PERFORMANCE EVALUATION. Most employees are periodically evaluated by their immediate supervisors. Peers or subordinates may also evaluate others. Evaluations are usually recorded on paper or electronic forms. Using such information manually is a tedious and error-prone job. Once digitized, evaluations can be used to support many decisions, ranging from rewards to transfers to layoffs. For example, many universities evaluate professors online. The evaluation form appears on the screen, and the students fill it in. Results can be tabulated in minutes. Corporate managers can analyze employees' performances with the help of expert systems, which provide an unbiased and systematic interpretation of performance over time.

Wage review is related to performance evaluation. For example, Hewlett-Packard's Atlanta-based U.S. Field Services Operations Group (USFO) has developed a paperless wage review (PWR) system. The Web-based system uses intelligent agents to deal with quarterly reviews of HP's 15,000 employees. The agent software lets USFO managers and personnel access employee data from both the personnel and functional databases. The PWR system tracks employee review dates and automatically initiates the wage review process. It sends wage review forms to first-level managers by e-mail every quarter.

TRAINING AND HUMAN RESOURCES DEVELOPMENT. Employee training and retraining is an important activity of the human resources department. Major issues are planning of classes and tailoring specific training programs to meet the needs of the organization and employees. Sophisticated human resources departments build a career development plan for each employee. IT can support the planning, monitoring, and control of these activities by using workflow applications.

IT also plays an important role in training (see discussion on e-learning, Chapter 4). Some of the most innovative developments are in the areas of *intelligent computer-aided instruction (ICAI)* and application of multimedia support for instructional activities. Instruction is provided online at 38 percent of all Fortune 1,000 corporations, according to OmniTech Consulting ("Web Breathes Life," 1988). Training salespeople is an expensive and lengthy proposition. To save money on training costs, companies are providing sales-skills training over the Internet or intranet. Online File W7.15 provides examples of the variety of employee training available on the Internet and intranets.

Training can be improved using Web-based video clips. For example, using a digital video-editing system, Dairy Queen's in-house video production department produced a higher-quality training video at 50 percent lower cost than outsourcing. The affordability of the videos encourages more Dairy Queen franchisees to participate in the training program. This improves customer service as well as employee skill.

Finally, training can be enhanced by virtual reality. Intel, Motorola, Samsung Electronic, and IBM are using virtual reality (Chapter 11) to simulate different scenarios and configurations. The training is especially effective in complex environments where mistakes can be very costly (see Boisvert, 2000).

Human Resources Planning and Management

Managing human resources in large organizations requires extensive planning and detailed strategy (Bussler and Davis, 2001–2002). In some industries, labor negotiation is a particularly important aspect of human resources planning. For most companies, administering employee benefits is also a significant part of the human resources function. Here are some examples of how IT can help.

PERSONNEL PLANNING. The human resources department forecasts requirements for people and skills. In some geographical areas and for overseas assignments it may be difficult to find particular types of employees. Then the HR department plans how to find (or develop from within) sufficient human resources.

Large companies develop qualitative and quantitative workforce planning models. Such models can be enhanced if IT is used to collect, update, and process the information.

LABOR–MANAGEMENT NEGOTIATIONS. Labor–management negotiations can take several months, during which time employees may present management with a large number of demands. Both sides need to make concessions and trade-offs. Large companies (like USX, formerly U.S. Steel, in Pittsburgh, Pennsylvania) have developed computerized DSS models that support such negotiations. The models can simulate financial and other impacts of fulfilling any demand made by employees, and they can provide answers to queries of the negotiators in a matter of seconds.

Another information technology that has been successfully used in labor–management negotiations is group decision support systems (see Chapter 12), which have helped improve the negotiation climate and considerably reduced the time needed to reach an agreement.

PAYROLL AND EMPLOYEES' RECORDS. The HR department is responsible for payroll preparation, which can be executed in-house or may be outsourced. It is usually done with the help of computers that print the payroll checks or transfer the money electronically to the employees' bank accounts (Bussler and Davis,

2001–2002). The HR department is also responsible for all personnel record keeping and its privacy and security. In most companies this is done electronically.

BENEFITS ADMINISTRATION. Employees' contributions to their organizations are rewarded by salary/wage, bonuses, and other benefits. Benefits include those for health and dental care as well as contributions for pensions. Managing the benefits system can be a complex task, due to its many components and the tendency of organizations to allow employees to choose and trade off benefits ("cafeteria style"). In large companies, using computers for benefits selection can save a tremendous amount of labor and time for HR staff.

Providing flexibility in selecting benefits is viewed as a competitive advantage in large organizations. It can be successfully implemented when supported by computers. Some companies have automated benefits enrollments. Employees can self-register for specific benefits using the corporate portal or voice technology. Employees self-select desired benefits from a menu. The system specifies the value of each benefit and the available benefits balance of each employee. Some companies use intelligent agents to assist the employees and monitor their actions. Expert systems can answer employees' questions and offer advice online. Simpler systems allow for self-updating of personal information such as changes in address, family status, etc. When employees enroll in benefits programs by themselves, change addresses and other demographic data, and conduct other HR record-keeping tasks electronically, there are very few data-entry errors.

For a comprehensive resource of HRM on the Web, see *shrm.org/hrlinks.*

EMPLOYEE RELATIONSHIP MANAGEMENT. In their effort to better manage employees, companies are developing *human capital management (HCM),* facilitated by the Web, to streamline the HR process. These Web applications are more commonly referred to as **employee relationship management (ERM).** For example, self-services such as tracking personal information and online training are very popular in ERM (and in CRM). Improved relationships with employees results in better retention and higher productivity. For an example of how ERM is done in a global grocery chain, see Buss, 2002. ERM technologies and applications are very similar to those of CRM, which we discuss next.

7.7 CUSTOMER RELATIONSHIP MANAGEMENT (CRM)

Customer relationship management (CRM) recognizes that customers are the core of a business and that a company's success depends on effectively managing relationships with them (see Greenberg, 2002). CRM focuses on building long-term and sustainable customer relationships that add value both for the customer and the company (Romano and Fjermestad, 2001–2002, and Kalakota and Robinson, 2000). (See also *crm-forum.com* and *crmassist.com.*)

What Is CRM?   Greenberg (2002) provides more than 10 definitions of CRM, several made by CEOs of CRM providers or users. The Patricia Seybold Group (2002) provides several additional definitions, as do Tan et al. (2002). Why are there so many definitions? The reason is that CRM is new and still evolving. Also, it is an interdisciplinary field, so each discipline (e.g., marketing, management) defines CRM differently. We will provide a well-known definition here: "CRM is a business strategy to select and manage customers to optimize long-term value. CRM requires a customer-centric business philosophy and culture to support effective marketing, sales and services processes" (Thompson, 2003).

Types of CRM   We distinguish among three major types of CRM activities: operational, analytical, and collaborative. *Operational CRM* is related to typical business functions involving customer services, order management, invoice/billing, and sales/marketing automation and management. *Analytical CRM* involves activities that capture, store, extract, process, interpret, and report customer data to a user, who then analyzes them as needed. *Collaborative CRM* deals with all the necessary communication, coordination, and collaboration between vendors and customers.

Other classifications of CRM have been devised by the types of programs (e.g., loyalty programs; see Tan, 2002) or by the service or product they offer (e.g., self-configuration, account tracking, call centers).

THE EVALUATION OF CRM.   In general, CRM is an approach that recognizes that customers are the core of the business and that the company's success depends on effectively managing relationships with them. (See Brown, 2000.) It overlaps somewhat with the concept of relationship marketing, but not everything that could be called relationship marketing is in fact CRM. Customer relationship marketing is even broader, in that it includes a *one-to-one* relationship of customer and seller. To be a genuine one-to-one marketer, a company must be able and willing to change its behavior toward a specific customer, based on what it knows about that customer. So, CRM is basically a simple idea: *Treat different customers differently.* It is based on the fact that no two customers are exactly the same.

Therefore, CRM involves much more than just sales and marketing, because a firm must be able to change how its products are configured or its service is delivered, based on the needs of individual customers. Smart companies have always encouraged the active participation of customers in the development of products, services, and solutions. For the most part, however, being customer-oriented has traditionally meant being oriented to the needs of the *typical* customer in the market—the average customer. In order to build enduring one-to-one relationships, a company must continuously interact with customers, *individually.* One reason so many firms are beginning to focus on CRM is that this kind of marketing can create high customer loyalty and, as a part of the process, help the firm's profitability.

eCRM.   CRM has been practiced manually by corporations for generations. However, since the mid-1990s, CRM has been enhanced by various types of information technologies. CRM technology is an evolutionary response to environmental changes, making use of new IT devices and tools. The term **eCRM** (electronic CRM) was coined in the mid-1990s, when customers started using Web browsers, the Internet, and other electronic touch points (e-mail, POS terminals, call centers, and direct sales). The use of these technologies made customer service, as well as service to partners (see PRM in Chapter 8), much more effective and efficient than it was before the Internet.

Through Internet technologies, data generated about customers can be easily fed into marketing, sales, and customer service applications and analysis. eCRM also includes online process applications such as segmentation and personalization. The success or failure of these efforts can now be measured and modified in real time, further elevating customer expectations. In a world connected by the Internet, eCRM has become a requirement for survival, not just a competitive advantage. eCRM covers a broad range of topics, tools, and methods, ranging from the proper design of digital products and services to pricing and loyalty programs (e.g., see *e-sj.org, Journal of Service Research,* and *ecrmguide.com*).

According to Voss (2000), there are three levels of eCRM: (1) *Foundational services* include the *minimum necessary* services such as Web site responsiveness (e.g., how quickly and accurately the service is provided), site effectiveness, and order fulfillment. (2) *Customer-centered services* include order tracking, configuration and customization, and security/trust. These are the services that *matter the most* to customers. (3) *Value-added services* are *extra services* such as dynamic brokering, online auctions, and online training and education.

Supporting Operational and Analytical CRMs

In order to better understand the contribution of IT to CRM, let's look at the areas in which IT supports CRM activities, which are shown in Figure 7.12. The applications in the figure are divided into two main categories: operational CRM

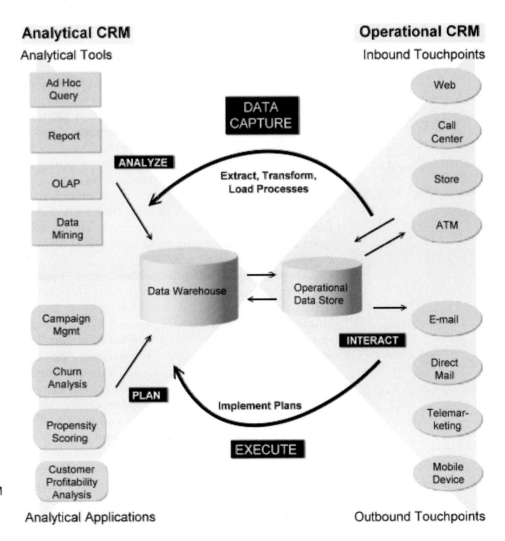

FIGURE 7.12
Classification of the CRM field. (*Source:* Goodhue et al., 2002.)

and analytical CRM. The major supported activities in each are listed in the figure. Many organizations are using the Web to facilitate their CRM activities.

Typical CRM activities and their IT support are listed in Online File W7.16. For other examples, see Brown (2000), Peppers and Rogers (1999), Petersen (1999), and Gilmore and Pine (2000).

CUSTOMER SERVICE ON THE WEB.   Customer service on the Web can take many forms, such as answering customer inquiries, providing search and comparison capabilities, providing technical information to customers, allowing customers to track order status, and of course allowing customers to place an online order. We describe these different kinds of Web-based customer services below. (For fuller details, see Greenberg, 2002.)

Providing Search and Comparison Capabilities.   One of the major wishes of consumers is to find what they want. With the hundreds of thousands of online stores, it is difficult for a customer to find what he or she wants, even inside a single electronic mall. Search and comparison capabilities are provided internally in large malls (e.g., *amazon.com*), or by independent comparison sites (*mysimon.com, compare.com*). For many other EC shopping aids, see Turban et al. (2004).

Providing Free Products and Services.   One approach companies use to differentiate themselves is to give something away free. Compubank.com, for example, once offered free bill payments and ATM services. Companies can offer free samples over the Internet, as well as free entertainment, customer education, and more. For further discussion, see Keen (2001), and Strauss et al. (2003).

Providing Technical and Other Information and Service.   Interactive experiences can be personalized to induce the consumer to commit to a purchase and remain loyal. For example, General Electric's Web site provides detailed technical and maintenance information and sells replacement parts for discontinued models for those who need to fix outdated home appliances. Such information and parts are quite difficult to find offline. Another example is Goodyear, which provides information about tires and their use at *goodyear.com.* The ability to download manuals and problem solutions at any time is another innovation of electronic customer service.

Allowing Customers to Order Customized Products and Services Online.   Dell Computer has revolutionized purchasing of computers by letting customers design computers and then delivering them to customers' home. This mass customization process has been moved to the Internet, and now is used by hundreds of vendors for products ranging from cars (see the Jaguar case) to shoes (Nike). Consumers are shown prepackaged "specials" and are given the option to "custom-build" systems using software configurators.

Other companies have found ways that are unique to their industries to offer customized products and services online. Web sites such as *gap.com* allow you to "mix and match" your entire wardrobe. Personal sizes, color and style preferences, dates for gift shipment, and so on, can be mixed and matched by customers, any way they like. This increases sales and the repeat business. Web sites such as *hitsquad.com, musicalgreetings.com,* or *surprise.com* allow consumers to handpick individual titles from a library and customize a CD, a feature that is not offered in traditional music stores. Instant delivery of any digitized entertainment is a major advantage of EC.

Letting Customers Track Accounts or Order Status. Customers can view their account balances at a financial institution and check their merchandise shipping status, at any time and from their computers or cell phones. For example, customers can easily find the status of their stock portfolio, loan application, and so on. FedEx and other shippers allow customers to track their packages. If you ordered books from Amazon or others, you can find the anticipated arrival date. Amazon even goes one step further; it notifies you by e-mail of the acceptance of your order, the anticipated delivery date, and later, the actual delivery date. Many companies follow the Amazon model and provide similar services.

All of these examples of customer service on the Web demonstrate an important aspect of CRM: a focus on the individual customer.

TOOLS FOR CUSTOMER SERVICE. There are many innovative Web-related tools to enhance customer service and CRM. Here are the major ones:

Personalized Web Pages. Many companies allow customers to create their own individual Web pages. These pages can be used to record purchases and preferences, as well as problems and requests. For example, using intelligent agent techniques, American Airlines generates personalized Web pages for each of about 800,000 registered travel-planning customers.

Also, customized information (such as product and warranty information) can be efficiently delivered when the customer logs on to the vendor's Web site. Not only can the customer pull information as needed or desired, but also the vendor can push information to the customer. Information that formerly may have been provided to the customer one to three months after a transaction was consummated is now provided in real or almost real time. Transaction information is stored in the vendor's database, and then accessed and processed to support marketing of more products and to match valuable information about product performance and consumer behavior.

FAQs. Frequently asked questions (FAQs) (see Chapter 4) are the simplest and least expensive tool to deal with repetitive customer questions. Customers use this tool by themselves, which makes the delivery cost minimal. However, any nonstandard question requires an e-mail. Also, FAQs are usually not customized. Therefore, FAQs produce no personalized feeling nor do they contribute much to CRM. They may do so one day, when the system will know the customer's profile and be able to present customized FAQs and answers.

Chat Rooms. Another tool that provides customer service, attracts new customers, and increases customers' loyalty is a chat room (see Chapter 4). For example, retailer QVC (see Minicase 2) offers a chat room where customers can discuss their experiences shopping with QVC.

E-Mail and Automated Response. The most popular tool of customer service is e-mail. Inexpensive and fast, e-mail is used to disseminate information (e.g., confirmations), to send product information, and to conduct correspondence regarding any topic, but mostly to answer inquiries from customers. For details, see Chapter 4.

Call Centers. One of the most important tools of customer service is the *call center*, also known as *customer care center*, etc. As defined in Chapter 4, a *call center* is a comprehensive customer service entity in which companies take care of their customer service issues, communicated through various contact channels. Call centers are typically the "face" of the organization to its customers.

For example, investment company Charles Schwab's call center effectively handles over 1 million calls from investment customers every day.

New products are extending the functionality of the conventional call center to e-mail and to Web interaction. For example, *epicor.com* combines Web channels, such as automated e-mail reply, Web knowledge bases, and portal-like self-service, with call center agents or field service personnel. Such centers are sometimes called *telewebs*. Examples and details were provided in Chapter 4.

Troubleshooting Tools. Large amounts of time can be saved by the customers if they can solve problems by themselves. Many vendors provide Web-based troubleshooting software to assist customers in this task. The vendors of course dramatically reduce their expenses for customer support when customers are able to solve problems without further intervention of customer service specialists.

Wireless CRM. Many of the CRM tools and applications are going wireless. As shown earlier, mobile sales force automation is becoming popular. In addition, use of wireless devices by mobile service employees is enabling these employees to provide communication with headquarters and better customers service from the customer's site. Also, using SMS and e-mail from handheld devices is becoming popular as a means of improving CRM. In Chapter 3, we presented the case of Expedia and its wireless customer service. Overall, we will see most of CRM services going wireless fairly soon.

CRM Failures

A large percentage of failures have been reported in CRM. For example, according to *Zdnetindia.com/news* (2000), the founder and CEO of Customer.com estimated that 42 percent of the top 125 CRM sites experienced failures. Numerous failures are also reported by *thinkanalytics.com, cio.com, CRM-forum.com,* and many more. However, according to *itgreycells.com,* CRM failures are declining, from a failure rate of up to 80 percent in 1998 to about 50 percent in 2000.

Some of the major issues relating to CRM failures are the following:

- Difficulty measuring and valuing intangible benefits. There are few tangible benefits to CRM.
- Failure to identify and focus on specific business problems.
- Lack of active senior management (non-IT) sponsorship.
- Poor user acceptance, which can occur for a variety of reasons such as unclear benefits (i.e., CRM is a tool for management, but doesn't help a rep sell more effectively) and usability issues.
- Trying to automate a poorly defined process.

Strategies to deal with these and other problems are offered by many. (For example, see *CIO.com* for CRM implementation. Also see *conspectus.com* for "10 steps for CRM success.")

CRM failures could create substantial problems. Some companies are falling behind in their ability to handle the volume of site visitors and the volume of buyers. DeFazio (2000) provides the following suggestions for implementing CRM and avoiding CRM failure:

- Conduct a survey to determine how the organization responds to customers.
- Carefully consider the four components of CRM: sales, service, marketing, and channel/partner management.

- Survey how CRM accomplishments are measured; use defined metrics. Make sure quality, not just quantity, is addressed. (For discussion of CRM metrics, see Online File W7.17.)
- Consider how CRM software can help vis-à-vis the organization's objectives.
- Decide on a strategy: refining existing CRM processes, or reengineering the CRM.
- Evaluate all levels in the organization, but particularly frontline agents, field service, and salespeople.
- Prioritize the organization's requirements as: must, desired, and not important.
- Select an appropriate CRM software. There are more than 60 vendors. Some (like Siebel) provide comprehensive packages, others provide only certain functions. Decide whether to use the best-of-breed approach or to go with one vendor. ERP vendors, such as PeopleSoft and SAP, also offer CRM products.

For more resources, see Ebner et al. (2001).

7.8 INTEGRATING FUNCTIONAL INFORMATION SYSTEMS

Functional information systems can be built in-house, they can be purchased from large vendors (such as Computer Associates, Best Software Inc., Microsoft, Oracle, IBM, or PeopleSoft), or they can be leased from application service providers (ASPs). In any of these cases, there is a need for their integration.

Reasons for Integration

For many years most IT applications were developed in the functional areas, independent of each other. Many companies developed their own customized systems that dealt with standard procedures to execute transaction processing/operational activities. These procedures are fairly similar, regardless of what company is performing them. Therefore, the trend today is to buy commercial, off-the-shelf functional applications or to lease them from ASPs. The smaller the organization, the more attractive such options are. Indeed, several hundred commercial products are available to support each of the major functional areas.

Development tools are also available to build custom-made applications in a specific functional area. For example, there are software packages for building financial applications, a hospital pharmacy management system, and a university student registration system. Some software vendors specialize in one or a few areas. For example, Lawson Software concentrates on retailing (see Minicase 1, and PeopleSoft's strength is in HRM).

However, to build information systems along business processes (which cross functional lines) requires a different approach. Matching business processes with a combination of several functional off-the-shelf packages may be a solution in some areas. For example, it may be possible to integrate manufacturing, sales, and accounting software if they all come from the same software vendor (as shown in the opening case). However, combining existing packages from several vendors may not be practical or effective. To build applications that will easily cross functional lines and reach separate databases often requires new approaches such as Web services and integrated suites, such as Oracle 9i (Chapter 2).

Information systems integration tears down barriers between and among departments and corporate headquarters and reduces duplication of effort. For example, Palaniswamy and Frank (2000) studied five ERP systems and found in all cases that better cross-functional integration was a critical success factor. A framework for an integrated information system was developed by Yakhou and Rahali (1992) and is shown in Online File W7.18. In their integrated framework, there is data sharing as well as joint execution of business processes across functional areas, allowing individuals in one area to quickly and easily provide input to another area. Various functional managers are linked together in an enterprisewide system.

As described in Chapter 2, 4, 8, and 14, one of the key factors for integration, especially with business partners, is agreement on appropriate standards (see *openapplications.org*).

Integrated information systems can be built easily in a small company. In large organizations, and even in multinational corporations, integration may require more effort, as shown in *IT at Work 7.7*.

IT at Work 7.7
WEB-BASED INTEGRATED EMPLOYEES
AND CUSTOMER PORTALS AT EUROPCAR

Europcar Internet *(europcar.com)*, the largest European-based car rental agency, changed the structure of its entire organization, in addition to changing everyday work processes and methods. To support these changes, the company combined 55 different mainframe and minicomputer systems into a single client/server center known as Greenway. Located at corporate headquarters near Paris, the $400 million system initially combined data from nine different countries within Europe, and today it has expanded to a global system.

The 55 original independent systems used various data types, many of which were incompatible and needed to be integrated. Europcar was interested in integrating the business processes, customer preferences, and related data into a single system. To complicate matters, the company had to simultaneously develop a uniform set of business practices (corporate standards) to support the new single business entity. Furthermore, Europcar had to consider the variety of languages spoken in the nine countries involved, as well as different cultures and currencies (before the Euro was adopted).

Key business processes—including reservations, billing, fleet management, cost control, and corporate finance—were all integrated into Greenway. The system serves employees via an employee portal and customers

via a customer portal. As Europcar has expanded to 100 countries worldwide (as of 2003), its information system has expanded considerably as well. Reservations can be made on the corporate portal, and a smart card is available to enable customers to check in and out rapidly. Other customer-related benefits include: (1) fast service to calling customers since clerks no longer have to manually verify credit cards or calculate bills, (2) reservation desks linked to airline reservation systems like SABRE or Amadeus, (3) online reservations accessed via the customers' portal, and (4) corporate customers managed from one location.

Europcar originally grew through the acquisition of geographically and culturally disparate entities. Through reengineering, IT helps support these business alliances to present more of a multicountry team-based organization. By 2003, several thousand Europcar employees at about 1,000 offices worldwide were using Greenway.

Sources: Based on *europcar.com/English* (press releases 2000–2003).

For Further Exploration: What are some of the difficulties of integrating 55 systems from nine countries speaking different languages? What functional areas can you identify in the integrated system? What is the role of the different portals?

Another approach to integration of information systems is to use enterprise resources planning software. However, ERP requires a company to fit its business processes to the software. As an alternative to ERP, companies can choose the best-of-breed systems on the market, or use their own home-grown systems and integrate them. The latter approach may not be simple, but it may be more effective.

By whatever method it is accomplished, integrating information systems helps to reduce cost, increase employees' productivity, and facilitate information sharing and collaboration, which are necessary for improving customer service.

Integration of Front-Office with Back-Office Operations

In Chapters 2 and 5 we discussed the need to integrate front-office with back-office operations. This is a difficult task. It is easier to integrate the front-office operations among themselves and the back-office operations among themselves (which is basically what systems such as MAS 90 are doing).

Software from various vendors offers some front-office and back-office integration solutions. Oracle Corp., for example, is continuously expanding its front-office software, which offers a capability of connecting back-office operations with it. To do so, the software uses new integration approaches, such as process-centric integration. **Process-centric integration** refers to integration solutions designed, developed, and managed from a business-process perspective, instead of from a technical or middleware perspective. Oracle's 9i product offers not only internal integration of the back office and front office, but also integration with business partners (see MCullough, 2002). Among its capabilities are:

- *Field sales online:* a Web-based customer management application.
- *Service contracts:* contract management and service options (with ERP).
- *Mobile sales and marketing:* wireless groupware for connecting different management groups.
- *Call center and telephony suite:* a Web-based call center.
- *Internet commerce:* an order-taking and payment unit interconnected with ERP back-office applications. It is also tightly connected to the call center for order taking.
- *Business intelligence:* identification of most-valuable customers, analysis of why customers leave, and evaluation of sales forecast accuracy.

Another integration software product is IBM's WebSphere architecture, which includes front office (WebSphere Portal), back office, and supportive infrastructure. (See Figure 4.5, page 140.)

Many other vendors offer complete enterprise packages. For example, Synco Software (*syncosoft.com*) offers ERP services, which include accounting, finance, marketing, production, and executive information system modules. SAP-AG, in its ERP R/3 product, offers more than 70 integrated modules, as will be shown in our next chapter.

➥ **MANAGERIAL ISSUES**

1. *Integration of functional information systems.* Integration of existing stand-alone functional information systems is a major problem for many organizations. Although client/server architecture (Chapter 2 and Technology

Guide 4) is more amenable to integration than legacy systems, there are still problems of integrating different types of data and procedures used by functional areas. Also, there is an issue of willingness to share information, which may challenge existing practices and cultures.

2. ***Priority of transaction processing.*** Transaction processing may not be an exotic application, but it deals with the core processes of organizations. It must receive top priority in resource allocation, balanced against innovative applications needed to sustain competitive advantage and profitability, because the TPS collects the information needed for most other applications.

3. ***The customer is king/queen.*** In implementing IT applications, management must remember the importance of the customer/end-user, whether external or internal. Some innovative applications intended to increase customers' satisfaction are difficult to justify in a traditional cost-benefit analysis. Empowering customers to enter into a corporate database can make customers happy since they can conduct self-service activities such as configuration and tracking and get quick answers to their queries. Self-services can save money for a company as well, but it may raise security and privacy concerns. Corporate culture is important here, too. Everyone in the organization must be concerned about customers. Management should consider installing a formal CRM program for this purpose.

4. ***Finding innovative applications.*** Tools such as Lotus Notes, corporate portals, and Web-based business intelligence enable the construction of many applications that can increase productivity and quality. Finding opportunities for such applications can best be accomplished cooperatively by end users and the IS department.

5. ***Using the Web.*** Web-based systems should be considered in all functional areas. They are effective, cost relatively little, and are user friendly. In addition to new applications, companies should consider conversion of existing applications to Web-based ones.

6. ***System integration.*** Although functional systems are necessary, they may not be sufficient if they work independently. It is difficult to integrate functional information systems, but there are several approaches to doing so. In the future, Web services could solve many integration problems, including connecting to a legacy system.

7. ***Ethical issues.*** Many ethical issues are associated with the various topics of this chapter. Professional organizations, relating to the functional areas (e.g., marketing associations) or in topical areas such as CRM, have their own codes of ethics. These codes should be taken into account in developing functional systems. Likewise, organizations must consider privacy policies. Several organizations provide comparisons of privacy policies and other ethics-related topics. For an example, see *socap.org*.

   In practicing CRM, companies may give priority to more valuable customers (e.g., frequent buyers). This may lead to perceived discrimination. For example, in one case, when a male customer found that Victoria's Secret charged him more than it did female buyers, he sued. In court it was shown that he was buying less frequently than the specific female he cited; the company was found not guilty of discrimination. Companies need to be very careful with CRM policies.

   HRM applications are especially prone to ethical and legal considerations. For example, training activities that are part of HRM may involve ethical issues in recruiting and selecting employees and in evaluating performance. Likewise, TPS data processing and storage deal with private information about people, their performance, etc. Care should be taken to protect this information and the privacy of employees and customers.

For more on business ethics as it applies to CRM and other topics in this chapter, see *ethics.ubc.ca/resources/business.*

ON THE WEB SITE... Additional resources, including quizzes; online files of additional text, tables, figures, and cases; and frequently updated Web links to current articles and information can be found on the book's Web site (*wiley.com/college/turban*).

KEY TERMS

Batch processing *302*

Channel systems *313*

Computer-integrated manufacturing (CIM) *310*

Customer relationship management (CRM) *335*

eCRM *336*

Employee relationship management (ERM) *335*

Expense management automation (EMA) *326*

Financial value chain management (FVCM) *328*

Just-in-time (JIT) *309*

Manufacturing resource planning (MRP II) *309*

Material requirements planning (MRP) *308*

Online processing *302*

Online transaction processing (OLTP) *303*

Process-centric integration *343*

Product lifecycle management (PLM) *311*

Sales automation software *320*

Sales-force automation *319*

Transaction processing systems (TPS) *300*

Vendor-managed inventory (VMI) *308*

Virtual close *326*

Work management systems (WMS) *310*

CHAPTER HIGHLIGHTS (Numbers Refer to Learning Objectives)

1 Information systems applications can support many functional activities. Considerable software is readily available on the market for much of this support (for lease or to buy).

2 The major business functional areas are production/operations management, marketing, accounting/finance, and human resources management.

3 The backbone of most information systems applications is the transaction processing system (TPS), which keeps track of the routine, mission-central operations of the organization.

4 The major area of IT support to production/operations management is in logistics and inventory management: MRP, MRP II, JIT, mass customization, PLM, and CIM.

5 Channel systems deal with all activities related to customer orders, sales, advertising and promotion,

market research, customer service, and product and service pricing. Using IT can increase sales, customers' satisfaction, and profitability.

6 Financial information systems deal with topics such as investment management, financing operations, raising capital, risk analysis, and credit approval.

6 Accounting information systems also cover many non-TPS applications in areas such as cost control, taxation, and auditing.

7 All tasks related to human resources development can be supported by human resources information systems. These tasks include employee recruitment and selection, hiring, performance evaluation, salary and benefits administration, training and development, labor negotiations, and work planning.

7 Web-based HR systems are extremely useful for recruiting and training.

⑧ CRM is a corporate-wide program that is composed of many activities aiming at fostering better relationships with customers. A Web-based call center is an example.

⑨ Integrated functional information systems are necessary to ensure effective and efficient execution of activities that cross functional lines or that require functional cooperation.

⑨ Integrating applications is difficult; it can be done in different ways, such as buying off-the-shelf applications or building custom systems. A promising new approach is that of Web services.

QUESTIONS FOR REVIEW

1. What is a functional information system?
2. List the major characteristics of a functional information system.
3. What are the objectives of a TPS?
4. List the major characteristics of a TPS.
5. Distinguish between batch and online TPS.
6. Explain how the Web enables mass customization.
7. Describe MRP.
8. Describe MRP II.
9. Describe VMI.
10. Define CIM, and list its major benefits.
11. Describe PLM, and list its benefits.
12. Define channel systems.
13. Define JIT, and list some of its benefits.
14. Define sales force automation.
15. What is product/customer profitability?
16. Describe some tactical and strategic accounting/finance applications.
17. List some budgeting-related activities.
18. List some EC activities in finance.
19. List IT-supported recruitment activities.
20. How can training go online?
21. Explain human resources information systems.
22. Define CRM and eCRM.
23. Describe a Web-based call center.
24. Describe the need for application integration.

QUESTIONS FOR DISCUSSION

1. Why is it logical to organize IT applications by functional areas?
2. Describe the role of a TPS in a service organization.
3. Why are transaction processing systems a major target for restructuring?
4. Which functional areas are related to payroll, and how does the relevant information flow?
5. Discuss the benefits of Web-based TPS.
6. It is said that in order to be used successfully, MRP must be computerized. Why?
7. The Japanese implemented JIT for many years without computers. Discuss some elements of JIT, and comment on the potential benefits of computerization.
8. Describe the role of computers in CIM.
9. Explain how Web applications can make the customer king/queen.
10. Why are information systems critical to sales-order processing?
11. Describe how IT can enhance mass customization.
12. Marketing databases play a major role in channel systems. Why?
13. Geographical information systems are playing an important role in supporting marketing and sales. Provide some examples not discussed in the text.
14. What is the role of software in PLM? Can PLM be done manually?
15. Discuss how IT facilitates the budgeting process.
16. Why is risk management important, and how can it be enhanced by IT?
17. Compare bill presentment to check re-presentment. How are they facilitated by IT?
18. How can the Internet support investment decisions?
19. Describe the benefits of an accounting integrated software such as MAS 90; compare it to MAS 2000.
20. Discuss the role IT plays in support of auditing.
21. Investigate the role of the Web in human resources management.
22. Discuss the benefits of self-service online by employees and customers. How can these activities be facilitated by IT?
23. Geographical information systems are playing an important role in supporting marketing and sales.

Provide some examples not discussed in the text. (See Chapter 11.)

24. Discuss the justification issues of CRM. What are metrics for? (See Minicase 2 and Online File W7.17.)

25. Discuss why Web-based call centers are critical for a successful CRM.

26. Discuss the need for application integration and the difficulty of doing it.

27. Discuss the approaches and reasons for integrating front-office with back-office operations.

EXERCISES

1. Compare the way Dartmouth-Hitchcock Medical center integrates its applications with integration via ERP software such as SAP R/3. Why might the latter not be appropriate for a medical center?

2. The chart shown in Figure 7.4 portrays the flow of routine activities in a typical manufacturing organization. Explain in what areas IT can be most valuable.

3. Argot International (a fictitious name) is a medium-sized company in Peoria, Illinois, with about 2,000 employees. The company manufactures special machines for farms and food-processing plants, buying materials and components from about 150 vendors in six different countries. It also buys special machines and tools from Japan. Products are sold either to wholesalers (about 70) or directly to clients (from a mailing list of about 2,000). The business is very competitive.

  The company has the following information systems in place: financial/accounting, marketing (primarily information about sales), engineering, research and development, and inventory management. These systems are independent of each other although they are all connected to the corporate intranet.

  Argot is having profitability problems. Cash is in high demand and short supply, due to strong business competition from Germany and Japan. The company wants to investigate the possibility of using information technology to improve the situation. However, the vice president of finance objects to the idea, claiming that most of the tangible benefits of information technology are already being realized.

  You are hired as a consultant to the president. Respond to the following:

  a. Prepare a list of 10 potential applications of information technologies that you think could help the company.

  b. From the description of the case, would you recommend any portals? Be very specific. Remember, the company is in financial trouble.

  c. How can Web services help Argot?

4. Enter *resumix.com*. Take the demo. Prepare a list of all the product's capabilities.

GROUP ASSIGNMENTS

1. Each group should visit (or investigate) a large company in a different industry and identify its channel systems. Prepare a diagram that shows the seven components in Figure 7.7. Then find how IT supports each of those components. Finally, suggest improvements in the existing channel system that can be supported by IT technologies and that are not in use by the company today. Each group presents its findings.

2. The class is divided into groups of four. Each group member represents a major functional area: production/operations management, sales/marketing, accounting/finance, and human resources. Find and describe several examples of processes that require the integration of functional information systems in a company of your choice. Each group will also show the interfaces to the other functional areas.

3. Each group investigates an HRM software vendor (Oracle, Peoplesoft, SAP, Lawson Software). The group prepares a list of all HRM functionalities supported by the software. Then the groups make a presentation to convince the class that its vendor is the best.

4. Create groups to investigate the major CRM software vendors, their products, and the capabilities of those products in the following categories (each group represents a topical area or several companies):

   ● Sales force automation (Oracle, Onyx, Siebel, Saleslogix, Pivotal)

   ● Call centers (Clarify, LivePerson, NetEffect, Inference, Peoplesoft)

   ● Marketing automation (Annuncio, Exchange Applications, MarketFirst, Nestor)

- Customer service (Brightware, Broadvision, Primus, Silknet)

- Sales configuration (Exactium, Newtonian)

Start with *searchcrm.com* and *crmguru.com* (to ask questions about CRM solutions). Each group must present arguments to the class to convince class members to use the product(s) they investigated.

INTERNET EXERCISES

1. Surf the Net and find free accounting software (try *shareware.cnet.com, clarisys.ca/free, rkom.com.free, tucows.com, passtheshareware.com,* and *freeware-guide.com*). Download the software and try it. Write a report on your findings.

2. Enter the site of Federal Express (*fedex.com*) and learn how to ship a package, track the status of a package, and calculate its cost. Comment on your experience.

3. Finding a job on the Internet is challenging; there are almost too many places to look. Visit the following sites: *headhunter.net, careermag.com, hotjobs.com, jobcenter.com,* and *monster.com.* What do these sites provide you as a job seeker?

4. Enter the Web sites *tps.com* and *nonstop.compaq.com,* and find information about software products available from those sites. Identify the software that allows Internet transaction processing. Prepare a report about the benefits of the products identified.

5. Enter the Web site *peoplesoft.com* and identify products and services in the area of integrated software. E-mail PeopleSoft to find out whether its product can fit the organization where you work or one with which you are familiar.

6. Examine the capabilities of the following financial software packages: Comshare MPC (from Comshare), Financial Analyzer (from Oracle), and CFO Vision (from SAS Institute). Prepare a report comparing the capabilities of the software packages.

7. Surf the Internet and find information from three vendors on sales-force automation (try *sybase.com* first). Prepare a report on the state of the art.

8. Enter *teknowledge.com* and review the products that help with online training. What are the most attractive features of these products?

9. Enter *salesforce.com* and take the quick tour. Review some of their products that support sales people in the field. What do they offer for CRM? Write a report.

10. Enter *siebel.com.* View the demo on e-business. Identify all e-business–related initiatives. Why is the company considered as the leader of CRM software?

11. Enter *anntaylor.com* and identify the customer services activities.

12. Enter *microsoft.com/businessSolutions/Solomon/default.mspx.* View three of the demos in different functional areas of your choice. Prepare a report on the capabilities.

13. Enter *sage.com/solutions/solutions.htm.* Identify functional software, CRM software, and e-business software products. Are these standalone or integrated? Explain.

Minicase 1
Dollar General Uses Integrated Software

Dollar General (*dollargeneral.com*) operates more than 6,000 general stores in the United States, fiercely competing with Wal-Mart, Target, and thousands of other stores in the sale of food, apparel, home-cleaning products, health and beauty aids, and more. The chain doubled in size between 1996 and 2002 and has had some problems in addition to the stiff competition, due to its rapid expansion. For example, moving into new states means different sales taxes, and these need to be closely monitored for changes. Personnel management also became more difficult with the organization's growth. An increased number of purchasing orders exacerbated problems in the accounts payable department, which was using manual matching of purchasing orders, invoices, and what was actually received in the "receiving" department before bills were paid.

The IT department was flooded with requests to generate long reports on topics ranging from asset management to general ledgers. It became clear that a better information system was needed. Dollar General started by evaluating information requirements that would be able to solve the above and other problems that cut into the company's profit.

A major factor in deciding which software to buy was the integration requirement among the existing information systems of the various functional areas, especially the financial applications. This led to the selection of the Financials suite (from Lawson Software). The company started to implement applications one at a time. Before 1998, the company installed the suite's asset management, payroll, and some HR applications which allow the tens of thousands of employees to monitor and self-update their benefits, 401k contributions, and personal data (resulting in big savings to the HR department). After 1998, the accounts payable and general ledger modules of Lawson Software were activated. The accounting modules allow employees to route, extract, and analyze data in the accounting/finance area with little reliance on IT personnel. During 2001–2003, Dollar General moved into the sales and procurement areas, thus adding the marketing and operation activities to the integrated system.

Here are a few examples of how various parts of the new system work: All sales data from the point-of-sale scanners of some 6,000 stores are pulled each night, together with financial data, discounts, etc., into the business intelligence application for financial and marketing analysis. Employee payroll data, from each store, are pulled once a week. This provides synergy with the sales audit system (from STS Software). All sales data are processed nightly by the STS System, broken into hourly journal entries, processed and summarized, and then entered into the Lawson's general ledger module.

The original infrastructure was mainframe based (IBM AS 400). By 2002, the 800 largest suppliers of Dollar General were submitting their bills on the EDI. This allowed instantaneous processing in the accounts payable module. By 2003, service providers, such as utilities, were added to the system. To do all this the systems was migrated in 2001 from the old legacy system to the Unix operating system, and then to a Web-based infrastructure, mainly in order to add Web-based functionalities and tools.

A development tool embedded in Lawson's Financials allowed users to customize applications without touching the computer programming code. This included applications that are not contained in the Lawson system. For example, an employee-bonus application was not available at Lawson, but was added to Financial's payroll module to accommodate Dollar General's bonus system. A customized application that allowed additions and changes in dozens of geographical areas also solved the organization's state sales-tax collection and reporting problem.

The system is very scalable, so there is no problem to add stores, vendors, applications, or functionalities. In 2003, the system was completely converted to Web-based, enabling authorized vendors, for example, to log on the Internet and view the status of their invoices by themselves. Also, the Internet/EDI enables small vendors to use the system. (An EDI is too expensive for small vendors, but the EDI/Internet is affordable.) Also, the employees can update personal data from any Web-enabled desktop in the store or at home. Future plans call for adding an e-purchasing (procurement) module using a desktop purchasing model (see Chapter 5).

Sources: Compiled from Amato-McCoy (2002a) and *lawson.com* (site accessed May 17, 2003).

Questions for Minicase 1

1. Explain why the old, nonintegrated functional system created problems for the company. Be specific.

2. The new system cost several million dollars. Why, in your opinion, was it necessary to install it?

3. Does it make sense to add a CRM module, or to keep CRM applications in a separate system?

4. Lawson Software Smart Notification Software (*lawson. com*) is being considered by Dollar General. Find information about the software and write an opinion for adoption or rejection.

5. Another new product of Lawson is Services Automation. Would you recommend it to Dollar General? Why or why not?

Minicase 2
QVC Moving CRM from TV to the Web

QVC (*qvc.com*) is known for its TV shopping channels. As a leading TV-based mail-order service, QVC is selling on the Web too. In 2000, QVC served more than 6 million customers, answered 125 million phone calls, shipped about 80 million packages, and handled more than a billion page views on its Web site. QVC's business strategy is to provide superb customer service in order to keep its customers loyal. QVC also appointed a senior vice president for customer service.

QVC's customer service strategy works very well for the TV business and is expected to work as well for the Web. For example, in December 1999, due to unexpected high demand, the company was unable to fulfill orders for gold NFL rings by Christmas Eve. When QVC learned about the potential delay, it sent an expensive NFL jacket, for free, and made sure the jacket would arrive before the holiday. This is only one example of the company's CRM activities.

To manage its huge business (about $4 billion a year), QVC must use the latest IT support. For example, QVC operates four state-of-the-art call centers, one for overseas operations. Other state-of-the-art technologies are used as well. However, before using technology to boost loyalty and sales, QVC had to develop a strategy to put the customers at the core of the corporate decision making. "Exceeding the expectations of every customer" is a sign you can see all over QVC's premises. As a matter of fact, the acronym QVC stands for Quality, Value, and Convenience—all from the customers' perspective. QVC created a superb service organization. Among other things, QVC provides education (demonstrating product features and functions), entertainment, and companionship. Viewers build a social relationship with show hosts, upon which the commercial relationship is built. Now QVC is attempting to build a social relationship with its customers on the Web (see *qvc.com*).

QVC knows that building trust on the TV screen is necessary, but not sufficient. So everyone in the company is helping. QVC's president checks customers' letters. All problems are fixed quickly. Everything is geared toward the long run. In addition, to make CRM work, QVC properly aligns senior executives, IT executives, and functional managers. They must collaborate, work toward the same goals, have plans that do not interfere with others' plans, and so forth. Also the company adopts the latest IT applications and offers training to its customer service reps in the new applications and in CRM continuously.

It is interesting to note that QVC is using metrics to measure customer service. (See Online File W7.17.) These metrics used to be calls per hour, sales per minute, and profitability per customer. Now, the metrics are:

- Friendliness of the call center reps
- How knowledgeable the reps are about the products
- Clarity of the instructions and invoices
- Number of people a customer has to speak with to get a satisfactory answer
- How often a customer has to call a second time to get a problem resolved

Data on customer service are collected in several ways, including tracking of telephone calls and Web-site movements. Cross-functional teams staff the call center, so complete knowledge is available in one place. Corrective actions are taken quickly, with attempts to prevent repeat problems in the future.

To get the most out of the call center's employees, QVC strives to keep them very satisfied. They must enjoy the work in order to provide excellent customer service. The employees are called "customer advocates," and they are handsomely rewarded for innovative ideas.

In addition to call centers, QVC uses computer-telephony integration technology (CTI), which identifies the caller's phone number and matches it to customer information in the database. This information pops up on the rep's screen when a customer calls. The rep can greet the customer by saying: "Nice to have you at QVC again, David. I see that you have been with us twice this year, and we want you to know that you are important to us. Have you enjoyed the jacket you purchased last June?"

To know all about the customer history, QVC maintains a large data warehouse. Customers' buying history is correlated by Zip code with psychodemographics data from Experian, a company that analyzes consumer information. This way, QVC can instantly know, for example, whether a new product is a hit with wealthy retirees or with young adults. The information is used for e-procurement, advertising strategy, and more. QVC also uses *viral marketing,* meaning the word-of-mouth of its loyal customers. In order not to bother its customers, QVC does not send any mail advertisements.

QVC is an extremely profitable business, growing at an annual double-digit rate since its start in 1986.

Sources: Compiled from *Darwin Magazine* (2000), and from *qvc.com* (accessed April 27, 2003).

Questions for Minicase 2

1. Enter *qvc.com* and identify actions that the company does to increase trust in its e-business. Also, look at all customer-service activities. List as many as you can find.

2. Visit the CRM learning center at *darwinmag.com/learn/ crm,* and identify some CRM activities not cited in this case that QVC may consider to further increase customer loyalty. Are any of the activities cited in this chapter applicable?

3. What is the advantage of having customers chat live online?

4. List the advantages of buying online vs. buying over the phone after watching QVC. What are the disadvantages?

5. Enter the chat room and the bulletin board. What is the general mood of the participants? Are they happy with QVC? Why or why not?

6. QVC said that the key to its success is customer trust. Explain why.

7. Examine the metrics that QVC uses to measure customer service. Can the company be successful by ignoring the productivity measures used before?

Virtual Company Assignment
Transaction Processing at the Wireless Café

Your restaurant vocabulary is increasing. You've learned that a "cover" is a guest, the cover count is something that Jeremy keeps a very close watch on, and the per-person amount is critical to TWC's success. Running a diner is more than cooking and serving hamburgers, and you've been able to identify activities and transactions at TWC that fit most of the categories discussed in this chapter. In fact, it seems to you that there are a lot more activities at the back of the house (kitchen and office) than at the front of the house (dining room).

Instructions

1. Describe TWC's value chain. What are some transactions that take place along this value chain?

2. Describe in detail the information used in one back-of-the-house transaction.

3. The host/hostess is the first point of contact customers have upon coming to TWC. In addition to welcoming the customers, he/she manages the table assignments, making sure that there is adequate waitstaff coverage as well as efficient table turnover. The host/hostess is a key figure in efficient dining room logistics. What automated tools might help the host/hostess in the job?

4. Barbara is interested in the potential of CRM to better understand customers' needs and serve repeat customers. You are unsure of the privacy and security issues and wonder if they outweigh the potential for personalization. Discuss the pros and cons of using CRM to better know TWC's customers.

REFERENCES

Aberdeen.com, "Best Practices in Streamlining the Financial Value Chain: Top Seven FVCM Implementations," *Aberdeen Group*, 2002, *aberdeen.com/ab_company/hottopics/fvcm2002/default.htm*. Accessed June 2003.

Amato-McCoy, D. M., "Dollar General Rings Up Back-Office Efficiencies with Financial Suite," *Stores*, October 2002a.

Amato-McCoy, D. M., "Sears Combines Retail Reporting and Customer Databases on a Single Platform," *Stores*, November 2002b.

Amato-McCoy, D. M., "Linens 'n Things Protects Inventory Investment with Supply Planning Suite," *Stores*, November 2002c.

Asian Wall Street Journal, February 2000.

autobytel.com, 2002.

Baker, W. et al., "Price Smarter on the Net," *Harvard Business Review*, February 2001.

Banks, E., *E-Finance: The Electronic Revolution*. London: John Wiley and Sons, Ltd., 2001.

Benjaafar, S. et al., "Next Generation Factory Layouts," *Interfaces*, Nov.–Dec. 2002.

Bernstein, P. A., and Newcomer, *The Principles of Transaction Processing*. San Francisco: Morgan Kaufmann, 1997.

Bielski, L., "Cutting Cost, Retaining Project Detail," *ABA Banking Journal*, May 2002.

Boisvert, L., "Web-based Learning," *Information Systems Management*, Winter 2000.

Borck, J. R., "Recruiting Systems Control Resume Chaos," *Infoworld*, July 24, 2000.

Boucher-Ferguson, R., "A New Shipping Rout (Web-EDI)," *eWeek*, September 23, 2002.

Brown, S. A., *Customer Relationship Management: Linking People, Process, and Technology*. New York: Wiley, 2000.

Buckley, N., "E-Route to Whiter Smile," *Financial Times*, August 26, 2002.

Buss, D., "Extended POS Initiative Aims to Connect Store and Consumer to the Entire Enterprise," *Store*, October 2002.

Bussler, L., and Davis, "Information Systems: The Quiet Revolution in Human Resource Management," *Journal of Computer Information Systems*, Winter 2001–2002.

Chaudhury, A. et al., "Web Channels in E-Commerce," *Communications of the ACM*, January 2001.

Collins, P., "Harnessing IT for Sustainable Excellence," *Management Services*, March 1999.

cscresearchservices.com, "The Long-Standing Gulf between Objects and Transactions Is Being Bridged," 1997, *cscresearchservices.com/foundation/library/104/RP19.asp*. Accessed July 2003.

daiwa.co.jp, 2000.

Darwin Magazine, "Nice Guys Finish First—Customer Relationship Management," *Darwin*, October 2000.

Day, M., "What is PLM?," *Cadserver*, April 15, 2002, *tenlinks.com/NEWS/ARTICLES/cadserver/plm.htm*. Accessed June 2003.

DeFazio, D., "The Right CRM for the Job," Technologydecisions.com, November 2000.

Degnan, C., "Best Practices in Expense Management Automation," Special Report. Boston: Aberdeen Group, January 2003, *aberdeen.com/ab_company/hottopics/emabp/default.htm*. Accessed June 2003.

Ensher, E. A. et al., "Tales from the Hiring Line," *Organizational Dynamics*, October–December 2002.

europcar.com/English, 2001.

Freeman, J., "Turn Your Budgeting Operations into a Profit Center," *Datamation*, 1997.

ford.com, 2000.

Galagan, P. A., "The Delta Force at Cisco," *Training and Development*, July 2002.

Gentile, G., "Audience Tracking Becomes High-Tech," *Los Angeles Times*, May 6, 2002.

Gilmore, J., and B. J. Pine (eds.), *Markets of One: Creating Customer-Unique Value through Mass Customization*. Boston: Harvard Business School Press, 2000.

Goldman Sachs Group. Special Report, *gs.com*, February 15, 2001.

Goodhue, D. L. et al. "Realizing Business Benefits through CRM: Hitting the Right Target in the Right Way," *MIS Quarterly Executive*, 1(2), June 2002, available at *misqe.org/V0102–03.pdf*. Accessed June 2003.

Gorton, I., *Enterprise TPS: Putting the CORBA OTS, ENGINA, and OrbixOTM to Work*. Reading, MA: Addison Wesley, 2000.

Greenberg, P., *CRM at the Speed of Light: Capturing and Keeping Customers in Internet Real Time*, 2nd ed. New York: McGraw-Hill, 2002.

Grimes, S., "Declaration Support: The B.P.M. Drumbeat," *Intelligent Enterprise*, April 23, 2003.

Harrington, A., "Can Anyone Build a Better Monster?" *Fortune*, May 13, 2002.

Holweg, M., and F. K. Pil, "Sucessful Build-to-Order Strategies Start with the Customer," *MIS Sloan Management Review*, Fall 2001.

InternetWeek, July 2000.

jaguar.com. Accessed October 13, 2000 and February 8, 2003.

Jandt, E. F., and Nemnich, M. B. (eds.), *Using the Internet and the Web in Your Job Search*, 2nd ed. Indianapolis, IN: Jistwork, 1999.

Jareb, E., and V. Rajkovic, "Use of an Expert System in Personnel Selection," *Information Management*, July–Dec. 2001.

Kahn, R. H., and M. Sloan, "Twenty-First Century Training," *Sales and Marketing Management*, June 1997.

Kalakota, R., and M. Robinson, *e-Business: Roadmap for Success*. Reading, MA: Addison-Wesley, 2000, Chapter 5.

Kannan, P. K. et al., "Marketing Information on the I-Way," *Communications of the ACM*, March 1999.

Keen, P., "The E-Commerce Imperative," in G. W. Dickson and G. DeSanctis (eds.), *Information Technology and the Future Enterprise: New Models for Management*. Upper Saddle River, NJ: Prentice Hall, 2001.

Kroll, K. M., "Video-Based Systems Seek Cleaner Focus on Store Traffic," *Stores*, April 2002.

Lawson.com, 2002.

Lee, Y. M., and E. J. Chen, "BASF Uses a Framework for Developing Web-Based Production-Planning Optimization Tools," *Interfaces*, November–December 2002.

Liao, Z., "Real Time Tax: Dispatching Using GPS," *Communications of the ACM*, May 2003.

Maxemchuk, N. F., and D. H. Shur, "An Internet Multicast System for the Stock Market," *ACM Transactions on Computer Systems*, August 2001.

McClenahen, J. S., "The Book on the One-Day Close," *Industry Week*, April 2002.

McCullough, D. C., *Oracle 9i*. New York: Hungry Minds, 2002.

Meredith, J. R., and S. M. Shafer, *Operations Management*. New York: John Wiley & Sons, 2002.

Palaniswamy, R., and T. Frank, "Enhancing Manufacturing Performance with ERP Systems," *Information Management Journal*, Summer 2000.

Patricia Seybold Group, *An Executive's Guide to CRM*. Boston, MA: Patricia Seybold Group, 2002, *psgroup.com/freereport/imedia/resport/asp*. Accessed April 15, 2003.

Peppers, D., and M. Rogers, *Enterprise One to One: Tools for Competing in the Interactive Age*. New York: Doubleday, 1999.

Petersen, G. S., *Customer Relationship Management Systems: ROI and Results Measurement*. New York: Strategic Sales Performance, 1999.

pg.com. Accessed February–December 2002.

Pittaras, A., "Automated Modeling," *PC AI*, January–February 1996.

qvc.com. Accessed June 2003.

Raskin, A., "A Faster Ride to Market," *Business* 2.0, October 2002.

Reda, S., "Word-of Mouth Marketing Enjoys New Life as Potent Online Advertising Strategy," *Stores*, October 2002.

Reed, C. et al., *eCFO: Sustaining Value in New Corporations*. Chichester, U.K.: Wiley, 2001.

Romano, N. C., Jr., and J. Fjermestad (eds.), "Introduction to the Special Section: Electronic Commerce Customer Relationship Management (ECCRM)," *International Journal of Electronic Commerce*, Winter 2001–2002.

Sadeh, N. M., *M-Commerce: Technologies, Services, and Business Models*. New York: John Wiley & Sons, 2002.

Salodof-MacNeil, J., "The Factoring Factor," *Inc. Magazine*, February 1, 2002.

Schafer, S., "Super Charged Sell," *Inc. Technology*, No. 2, 1997.

Seidman, T., "Retail Fast-Food Marketing Targets Workers on the Job," *Stores*, February 2002.

Society of Manufacturing Engineers, "CASA/SME Manufacturing Enterprise," Dearborn, Michigan, 1999.

Subrahmanyam, A., "Nuts and Bolts of Transaction Processing: A Comprehensive Tutorial," *subrahmanyam.com…articles/transactions/NutsAndBoltsOfTP.html*. Accessed March 2, 2002.

Strauss, J. et al., *E-Marketing*, 3rd ed. Upper Saddle River, NJ: Prentice Hall, 2003.

Sung, N. H., and J. K. Lee, "Knowledge Assisted Dynamic Pricing for Large-Scale Retailers," *Decision Support Systems*, June 2000.

Sweeney, T., "Web Kiosks Spur Spending in Stores," *Information Week.com*, March 12, 2001, *informationweek.com/828/kiosk.htm*. Accessed June 2003.

Tan, X. et al., "Internet Integrated Customer Relationship Management," *Journal of Computer Information Systems*, Spring 2002.

Thomas, S. L., and K. Ray, "Recruiting and the Web: High-Tech Hiring," *Business Horizons*, May–June 2000.

Thompson, B., "What Is CRM?," *CRMguru.com*, *crmguru.com*.

Totty, P., "MCIF Systems Are Gaining Broader Acceptance," *Credit Union Magazine*, May 2000.

Training and Development, February 1997.

Turban, E. et al., *Electronic Commerce: A Managerial Perspective*, 3rd ed. Upper Saddle River, NJ: Prentice Hall, 2004.

Varney, S. E., "Arm Your Salesforce with the Web," *Datamation*, October 1996.

Vijayakumar, S., "Improving Software Cost Estimation," *Project Management Today*, May 2002.

Voss, C., "Developing an eService Strategy," *Business Strategy Review*, 11(11), 2000.

"Web Breathes Life into Medical Firm's Training Program," *Internet Week*, July 27, 1988, *internetwk.com/search/results.jhtml?queryText=Omnitech&site_id=3*. Accessed October 2002.

"What EMA Systems Now Offer Accounting Departments?" *Acct. Dept. Mgt. & Administration Report*, February 2002.

Wind, Y., "The Challenge of Customization in Financial Services," *Communications of the ACM*, July 2001.

Yakhou, M., and B. Rahali, "Integration of Business Functions: Roles of Cross-Functional Information Systems," *APICS*, December 1992.

Zakaria, Z., "Many Currencies, One FMIS System," *MIS Asia*, April 2002.

Zaremba, M. B., and G. Morel, "Integration and Control of Intelligence in Distributed Manufacturing," *Journal of Intelligent Manufacturing*, February 2003.

Zdnetindia.com/news, September 29, 2000.

Zipkin, P., "The Limits of Mass Customization," *MIT Sloan Management Review*, Spring 2001.

PART III
Organizational Applications

7. Transaction Processing, Functional Applications, CRM, and Integration
▶ 8. Supply Chain Management and Enterprise Resource Planning
9. IT Planning and Business Process Redesign

CHAPTER

8

Supply Chain Management and Enterprise Resource Planning

8.1
Essentials of the Supply and Value Chains

8.2
Supply Chain Problems and Solutions

8.3
Computerized Systems: MRP, MRPII, SCM, and Integration

8.4
Enterprise Resource Planning (ERP)

8.5
E-Commerce and Supply Chains

8.6
Partner Relationship Management

8.7
Global Supply Chains

LEARNING OBJECTIVES

After studying this chapter, you will be able to:

❶ Understand the concept of the supply chain, its importance, and its management.

❷ Describe the problems of managing the supply chain and some innovative solutions.

❸ Trace the evolution of software that supports activities along the supply chain and describe the need for software integration.

❹ Describe ERP and understand the relationships between ERP and SCM software.

❺ Describe order fulfillment problems and solutions in e-commerce and how EC solves other supply chain problems.

❻ Describe the process and activities of partner relationship management.

❼ Understand the process and issues of global supply chain management.

CHEVRONTEXACO'S MODERNIZED SUPPLY CHAIN

⟹ THE PROBLEM

ChevronTexaco (*chevrontexaco.com*) is the largest U.S. oil company and is multinational in nature. Its main business is drilling, refining, transporting, and selling petroleum products (oil and gasoline). In this competitive business a saving of even a quarter of a penny for each gallon totals up to millions of dollars. Two problems have plagued the industry: running out of gasoline when needed at each pump, and a delivery that is aborted because a tank at the gas station is too full (called "retain"). Run-outs and retains, known as the industry's "twin evils," have been a target for improvements for years, with little success.

The causes of the twin evils have to do with the supply chain: Gasoline flows in the supply chain start with the upstream part of the chain (Chapter 2), which includes oil hunting, drilling, and extracting. Then the oil is processed, and finally it goes to the downstream, customer-facing part of the supply chain. The difficulty is to match the three parts of the chain. ChevronTexaco owns oil fields and refineries, but it also buys both crude and refined oil to meet demand. Purchases are of two types: those that have long-term contracts and those that are purchased "as needed," in the spot market, at prevailing prices (which usually are higher than contract prices).

In the past ChevronTexaco acted like a mass-production manufacturing company, just trying to make products and sell them (a supply-driven strategy). The problem with this strategy is that each time you make too much or too little, you are introducing extra cost into the supply chain.

⟹ THE SOLUTION

The company decided to change its supply chain business model from *supply-driven* to *demand-driven*. Namely, instead of worrying about how much oil it would process and "push," it started worrying about how much oil its customers wanted. This change necessitated a major transformation in the business and extensive support by information technologies.

To implement the IT support, the company is investing $15 million (each year, in the U.S. alone), in proprietary supply chain software that can capture data in real time. Each tank in each gas station is equipped with an electronic monitor that conveys real-time information about the oil level, through a cable, to the station's IT-based management system, and then via a satellite, to the main inventory system at the company's main office. There, an advanced DSS-based planning system processes the data to help refining, marketing, and logistics decisions. This DSS also includes information collected at trucking and airline companies. Using an enterprise resource planning (ERP) and the business planning system, ChevronTexaco determines how much to refine, how much to buy in spot markets, and when and how much to ship to each of its retail stations.

The system uses demand forecasting to determine how much oil it would refine on a monthly basis, with weekly and daily checks. This way production is matched to customer demand. It is necessary to integrate the supply and demand information systems, and this is where the ERP software is useful. Planners at various points across the supply chain (e.g., refineries, terminals, stations, transportation, and production) have to share data constantly.

Recent corporate IT projects that support the ChevronTexaco supply chain and extend it to a global reach are NetReady (which enables 150 e-business initiatives), Global Information Link (GIL2), which enables connectivity throughout the company), e-Guest (which enables sharing of information with business partners), and the Human Resources information system.

➡ THE RESULTS

The integrated system, which allows data to be shared across the company, has improved decision making at every point in the customer-facing and processing parts of the supply chain. Better decision making increased the company's profit by more than $300 million in 1999 and by more than an additional $100 million in 2000. Managers attribute the increase to various company initiatives, but mostly to the change in the supply chain.

According to Worthen (2002), studies indicate that companies that belong to the top 20 percent in their industries operate their supply chains twice as efficiently as median companies. The successful companies carry half as much inventory, can respond to a significant rise in demand (20% or higher) twice as fast, and know how to minimize the number of deliveries they must make to any retail outlets. ChevronTexaco belongs to this category.

Sources: Compiled from Worthen (2002) and from *chevrontexaco.com* (see "Information Technology"; site accessed May 2003).

➡ LESSONS LEARNED FROM THIS CASE

The ChevronTexaco case illustrates the importance of supply chain management for the modern enterprise. It demonstrates the need to significantly improve the management of the supply chain (in this case from supply-driven to demand-driven). Such a drastic change was feasible only with the support of IT tools. In this case, IT is used to enable real-time communication between each tank at each gas station (many thousands) and the corporate management center, where DSS analysis can be done on a continuous basis. Also, knowing demand in real-time helps a company's acquisition of raw materials (in this case, oil) and drives its production (refinery) operations. Finally, all decision makers along the supply chain share information and collaborate.

Supply chain management is not a simple task, as will be seen in this chapter, but IT solutions enable even a large multinational company like ChevronTexaco to tame the supply chain, increasing both its profits and customer satisfaction. Finally, we see that the company is extending its supply chain improvement to its business partners. We also cover a related topic, order fulfillment in EC.

8.1 ESSENTIALS OF THE SUPPLY AND VALUE CHAINS

Initially, the concept of a *supply chain* referred only to the flow of materials from their sources (suppliers) to the company, and then inside the company to places where they were needed. There was also recognition of a *demand chain,* which described the process of taking orders and delivering finished goods to customers. Soon it was realized that these two concepts are interrelated, so they were combined under the single concept named the *extended supply chain*, or just *supply chain.*

Concepts and Definitions

The following concepts and definitions are helpful for the study of this chapter.

SUPPLY CHAIN. As defined in Chapter 2, **supply chain** refers to the flow of materials, information, payments, and services from raw material suppliers, through factories and warehouses, to the end customers. A supply chain also includes the *organizations* and *processes* that create and deliver products, information, and services to the end customers. It includes many tasks such as purchasing, payment flow, materials handling, production planning and control, logistics and warehousing, inventory control, and distribution and delivery.

SUPPLY CHAIN MANAGEMENT. The function of **supply chain management (SCM)** is to plan, organize, and coordinate all the supply chain's activities. Today the concept of SCM refers to a total systems approach to managing the entire supply chain. SCM is usually supported by IT (see Kumar, 2001; Hugos, 2002; and Vakharia, 2002). The topic of supply chain management was found to be the number 1 priority of chief information officers (CIOs) in 2001, and their number 3 priority in 2002 (see Morgan Stanley, 2001, 2002).

SCM SOFTWARE. *SCM software* refers to software intended to support specific segments of the supply chain, especially in manufacturing, inventory control, scheduling, and transportation. This software concentrates on improving decision making, optimization, and analysis.

E-SUPPLY CHAIN. When a supply chain is managed electronically, usually with Web-based software, it is referred to as an **e-supply chain.** As will be shown in this chapter, improvements in supply chains frequently involve an attempt to convert an organization's supply chain to an e-supply chain—that is, to automate the information flow in the chain (see Poirier and Bauer, 2000).

SUPPLY CHAIN FLOWS. There are three flows in the supply chain: materials, information, and financial flows.

- *Materials flows.* These are all physical products, new materials, and supplies that flow along the chain. Included in the materials flows are returned products, recycled products, and materials or products for disposal.
- *Information flows.* All data related to demand, shipments, orders, returns, schedules, and changes in the above are information flows.
- *Financial flows.* Financial flows include all transfers of money, payments, credit card information and authorization, payment schedules, e-payments (Chapter 5), and credit-related data.

In service industries there may be no physical flow of materials, but frequently there is flow of documents (hard and/or soft copies). Service industries, according to the above definition, fit the definition of a supply chain, since the information flow and financial flow still exist. As a matter of fact the digitization of products (software, music, etc.) results in a supply chain without physical flow. Notice however that in such a case, there are two types of information flows: one that replaces material flow (e.g., digitized software), and one that is the supporting information (orders, billing, etc).

In managing the supply chain it is necessary to coordinate all the above flows among all the parties involved in the supply chain (see Viswanadham, 2002).

BENEFITS. The goals of modern SCM are to reduce uncertainty and risks in the supply chain, thereby positively affecting inventory levels, cycle time, business processes, and customer service. All these benefits contribute to increased profitability and competitiveness, as demonstrated in the opening case. The benefits of supply chain management have long been recognized both in business and in the military.

In today's competitive business environment, the efficiency and effectiveness of supply chains in most organizations are critical for their survival and are greatly dependent upon the supporting information systems.

The Components of Supply Chains

The term *supply chain* comes from a picture of how the partnering organizations in a specific supply chain are linked together. A typical supply chain, which links a company with its suppliers and its distributors and customers was shown in Figure 2.6 (page 63). The supply chain involves three segments: (1) *upstream*, where sourcing or procurement from external suppliers occurs, (2) *internal*, where packaging, assembly, or manufacturing takes place, and (3) *downstream*, where distribution or dispersal takes place, frequently by external distributors.

A supply chain also involves a *product life cycle* approach from "dirt to dust." However, a supply chain is more than just the movement of tangible inputs, since it also includes the movement of information and money and the procedures that support the movement of a product or a service. Finally, the organizations and individuals involved are part of the chain as well. As a matter of fact, the supply chain of a service or of a digitizable product may not include *any* physical materials.

Supply chains come in all shapes and sizes and may be fairly complex, as shown in Figure 8.1. As can be seen in the figure, the supply chain for a car manufacturer includes hundreds of suppliers, dozens of manufacturing plants (for parts) and assembly plants (for cars), dealers, direct business customers (fleets), wholesalers (some of which are virtual), customers, and support functions such as product engineering and purchasing. For the sake of simplicity we do not show here the flow of information and payments.

Notice that in this case the chain is not strictly linear as it was in Figure 2.6. Here we see some loops in the process. In addition, sometimes the flow of information and even goods can be bidirectional. For example, not shown in this figure is **reverse logistics,** which is the *return* of products. For the automaker, that would be cars returned to the dealers in cases of defects or recalls by the manufacturer.

Types of Supply Chains

The supply chains shown in Figures 2.6 and 8.1 are those of manufacturing companies. Such companies may have warehouses in different locations, making the chain even more complex. As a matter of fact there are several major types of supply chain. These types can be classified into four categories: integrated

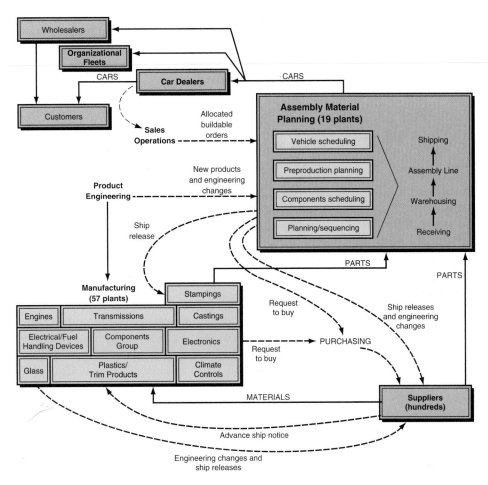

FIGURE 8.1 An automotive supply chain. (*Source:* Modified from *Introduction to Supply Chain Management* by Handfield and Nichols, 1999. Reprinted by permission of Pearson Education, Inc., Upper Saddle River, N.J.)

make-to-stock, continuous replenishment, build-to-order, and channel assembly. Details are provided in Online File W8.1.

The flow of goods, services, information, and financial resources is usually designed not only to effectively transform raw items to finished products and services, but also to do so in an efficient manner. Specifically, the flow must be followed with an increase in value, which can be analyzed by the *value chain.*

The Supply Chain and the Value Chain

In Chapter 3 we introduced the concepts of the *value chain* and the *value system.* A close examination of these two concepts shows that they are closely related to the supply chain. The *primary activities* of the value chain, corresponding to the internal part of the model, are shown in Figure 2.6. Some of the *support activities* of the value chains (such as moving materials, purchasing, and shipping) can be identified in Figure 8.1.

Porter's value chain (1985) emphasized that value is added as one moves along the chain. One of the major goals of SCM is to maximize this value, and this is where IT in general and e-commerce in particular enter the picture, as will be shown in Sections 8.3 and 8.4. But let us first see why it is difficult to optimize the value and supply chains.

8.2 SUPPLY CHAIN PROBLEMS AND SOLUTIONS

Adding value along the supply chain is essential for competitiveness or even survival. Unfortunately, the addition of value is limited by many potential problems along the chain.

Background

Supply chain problems have been recognized both in the military and in business operations for generations. Some even caused armies to lose wars and companies to go out of business. The problems are most evident in complex or long supply chains and in cases where many business partners are involved. For example, a well-known military case is the difficulties the German army in World War II encountered in the long supply chain to its troops in remote Russian territories, especially during the winter months. These difficulties resulted in a major turning point in the war and the beginning of the Germans' defeat. Note that during the 1991 and the 2003 wars in Iraq, the allied armies had superb supply chains that were managed by the latest computerized technologies (including DSS and intelligent applications). These chains were a major contributor to the swift victories.

In the business world there are numerous examples of companies that were unable to meet demand, had too large and expensive inventories, and so on. Some of these companies paid substantial penalties; others went out of business. On the other hand, some world-class companies such as Wal-Mart, Federal Express, and Dell have superb supply chains with innovative IT-enhanced applications (see *IT at Work 3.4*, page 108, on how Dell does it).

Problems Along the Supply Chain

An example of a supply chain problem was the difficulty of fulfilling orders received electronically for toys during the 1999 holiday season. During the last months of 1999, online toy retailers, including eToys (now kbkids.com), Amazon.com, and ToysRUs, conducted massive advertising campaigns to encourage Internet ordering. These campaigns included $20 to $30 discount vouchers for shopping online. Customer response was overwhelming, and the retailers that underestimated it were unable to get the necessary toys from the manufacturing plants and warehouses and deliver them to the customers' doors by Christmas Eve. The delivery problems cost the toy retailers dearly, in terms of both money and goodwill. ToysRUs, for example, ended up offering each of its unhappy customers a $100 store coupon as compensation. Despite its generous gift, over 40 percent of the unhappy ToysRUs customers said they would not shop online at ToysRUs again (Conlin, 2000).

These and similar problems create the need for innovative solutions. For example, during the oil crises in the 1970s, Ryder Systems, a large trucking company, purchased a refinery to control the upstream supply chain and ensure availability of gasoline for its trucks. Such vertical integration is effective in some cases but ineffective in others. (Ryder later sold the refinery.) In the remaining portion of this section we will look closely at some of the major problems in managing supply chains and at some possible solutions, many of which are supported by IT.

SOURCES AND SYMPTOMS OF SUPPLY CHAIN PROBLEMS. Problems along the supply chain stem mainly from two sources: (1) from uncertainties, and (2) from the need to coordinate several activities, internal units, and business partners.

A major source of supply chain uncertainties is the *demand forecast*, as demonstrated by the 1999 toy season. The demand forecast may be influenced by several factors such as competition, prices, weather conditions, technological development, and customers' general confidence. Other supply chain uncertainties exist in *delivery times*, which depend on many factors, ranging from machine failures to road conditions and traffic jams that may interfere with shipments. *Quality problems* of materials and parts may also create production delays.

A major symptom of ineffective SCM is poor customer service, which hinders people or businesses from getting products or services when and where needed, or gives them poor-quality products. Other symptoms are high inventory costs, loss of revenues, extra cost of expediting shipments, and more. One of the most persistent SCM problems related to uncertainty is known as the *bullwhip effect.*

THE BULLWHIP EFFECT. The **bullwhip effect** refers to erratic shifts in orders up and down the supply chain (see Donovan, 2002/2003). This effect was initially observed by Procter & Gamble (P&G) with its disposable diapers product, Pampers. While actual sales in retail stores were fairly stable and predictable, orders from distributors to P&G (the manufacturer) had wild swings, creating production and inventory problems. An investigation revealed that distributors' orders were fluctuating because of poor demand forecasting, price fluctuation, order batching, and rationing within the supply chain. All of this resulted in unnecessary and costly inventories in various areas along the supply chain, fluctuations of P&G orders to their suppliers, and flow of inaccurate information. Distorted information can lead to tremendous inefficiencies, excessive inventories, poor customer service, lost revenues, ineffective shipments, and missed production schedules (Donovan, 2002/2003).

The bullwhip effect is not unique to P&G. Firms ranging from Hewlett-Packard in the computer industry to Bristol-Myers Squibb in the pharmaceutical field have experienced a similar phenomenon (see Shain and Robinson, 2002). Basically, even slight demand uncertainties and variabilities become magnified when viewed through the eyes of managers at each link in the supply chain. If each distinct entity makes ordering and inventory decisions with an eye to its own interest above those of the chain, stockpiling may be simultaneously occurring at as many as seven or eight places along the supply chain, leading in some cases to as many as 100 days of inventory—which is waiting, "just in case" (versus 10–20 days' inventory in the normal case).

A 1998 industry study projected that $30 billion in savings could materialize in the grocery industry supply chains alone through sharing information and collaborating. Thus, companies are trying to avoid the "sting of the bullwhip," as well as to solve other SCM problems.

Solutions to Supply Chain Problems

SOLVING THE BULLWHIP PROBLEM. A common way to solve the bullwhip problem is by sharing information along the supply chain (e.g., see Reddy, 2001). Such sharing can be facilitated by EDI, extranets, and groupware technologies. Information sharing among supply chain partners is part of interorganizational EC or *c-commerce* (Chapters 4 and 5), and is sometimes referred to as the *collaboration supply chain* (see Simatupang and Sridharan, 2002).

One of the most notable examples of information sharing is between Procter & Gamble and Wal-Mart. Wal-Mart provides P&G access to sales information for every item P&G supplies to Wal-Mart, every day in every store. With that information, P&G is able to manage the inventory replenishment for Wal-Mart. By monitoring inventory levels, P&G knows when inventories fall below the threshold for each product at any Wal-Mart store. This automatically triggers an immediate shipment. All this is part of a **vendor-managed inventory (VMI) strategy.** The benefit of the strategy for P&G is accurate and timely demand information. P&G has similar agreements with other major retailers. Thus, P&G can plan production more accurately, minimizing the "bullwhip effect." P&G deployed in 2000 a Web-based "Ultimate-Supply System," which replaced 4,000 different EDI links to suppliers and retailers in a more cost-effective way. Later on we will show how Warner-Lambert and other manufacturers are doing similar information sharing with wholesalers and retailers in order to solve the bullwhip effect and other supply problems.

OPTIMIZING INVENTORY LEVELS.   Over the years organizations have developed many solutions to the supply chain problems. Undoubtedly, the most common solution used by companies is *building inventories* as an "insurance" against supply chain uncertainties. This way products and parts flow smoothly through the production process.

The main problem with this approach is that it is very difficult to correctly determine inventory levels for each product and part. If inventory levels are set too high, the cost of keeping the inventory will be very large. If the inventory is too low, there is no insurance against high demand or slow delivery times, and revenues (and customers) may be lost. In either event the total cost, including cost of keeping inventories, cost of lost sales opportunities, and bad reputation, can be very high. Thus, companies make major attempts to control and optimize inventory levels, as shown in *IT at Work 8.1.*

SUPPLY CHAIN COORDINATION AND COLLABORATION.   Proper supply chain and inventory management requires coordination of all different activities and links of the supply chain. Successful coordination enables goods to move smoothly and on time from suppliers to manufacturers to customers, which enables a firm to keep inventories low and costs down. Such coordination is needed since companies depend on each other but do not always work together toward the same goal.

As part of the coordination effort, business partners must learn to *trust* each other. The lack of trust is a major inhibitor of collaboration. Gibbons-Paul (2003) reports that 75 percent of senior IT managers cited the lack of trust as the number one barrier to electronic collaboration. To overcome this problem Gibbons-Paul offers six strategies. One strategy, for example, is that both suppliers and buyers must participate together in the design or redesign of the supply chain to achieve their shared goals.

To properly control the uncertainties mentioned earlier, it is necessary to identify and understand their causes, determine how uncertainties in some activities will affect other activities up and down the supply chain, and then formulate specific ways to reduce or eliminate the uncertainties. Combined with this is the need for effective and efficient communication and collaboration environments among all business partners (see Chapter 4). A rapid flow of information along the supply chains makes them very efficient. For example, computerized point-of-sale (POS) information can be transmitted once a day, or even in real time, to distribution centers, suppliers, and shippers. (Recall the Dell case, in Chapter 2.)

IT at Work 8.1

HOW LITTLEWOODS STORES IMPROVED ITS SCM

Littlewoods Stores (*littlewoods.co.uk*) is one of Britain's largest retailers of high-quality clothing. It has about 140 stores around the U.K. and Northern Ireland. The retail clothing business is very competitive, and every problem can be expensive. A serious supply chain problem for the company was *overstocking*. So in the late 1990s the company embarked on an IT-supported initiative to improve its supply chain efficiency.

In order to better manage the supply chain, the company introduced a Web-based performance reporting system, using SCM software. The new system analyzes, on a daily basis, inventory, marketing and finance data, space allocation, merchandising, and sales data. For example, merchandising personnel can now perform sophisticated sales, stock, and supplier analyses to make key operational decisions on pricing and inventory. Using the Web, analysts can view sales and stock data in virtually any grouping of levels and categories. Furthermore, users can easily drill down to detailed sales and other data.

The system also uses a data warehouse–based decision support system and other end-user–oriented software, to make better decisions. The savings have been dramatic: The cost of buying and holding backup inventory was cut by about $4 million a year. For example, due to quicker replenishment, stock went down by 80 percent. In addition, reducing the need for stock liquidations that resulted from too high inventories saved Littlewoods $1.4 million each year. The ability to strategically price merchandise differently in different stores and improved communication and delivery abilities among stores saved another $1.2 million each year. Marketing distribution expenses were cut by $7 million a year, due to collaboration among sales, warehouses, suppliers, and deliveries. And, finally, the company was able to reduce inventory and logistics-related staff from 84 to 49 people, a saving of about $1 million annually.

Within a year the number of Web-based users of the system grew to 600, and the size of the data warehouse grew to over 1 gigabyte. In November 1999 the company launched its Online Home Shopping Channel (*shop-i.co.uk*) and other e-commerce projects. Further improvements in SCM were recorded as of fall 2000.

Sources: Compiled from *microstrategy.com* (site accessed January 2000, Customers' Success Stories), and from *littlewoods.co.uk* (site accessed March 25, 2003).

For Further Exploration: Explain how integrated software solved the excess inventory problem. Also, review the role of data warehouse decision support in this case.

SUPPLY CHAIN TEAMS. The change of the linear supply chain to a hub (Chapters 1 and 5) shows the need for the creation of **supply chain teams** at times. According to Epner (1999), a supply chain team is a group of tightly integrated businesses that work together to serve the customer. Each task is done by the member of the team who is best positioned, trained, and capable of doing that specific task. For example, the team member that deals with the delivery will handle a delivery problem even if he or she works for a delivery company rather than for the retailer whose product is being delivered. This way, redundancies will be minimized. If the customer contacts the delivery company about a delivery problem, that specific employee will deal with the problem, rather than passing it along to the retailer, and the retailer will not have to spend valuable resources following up on the delivery. The task assignment to team members as well as the team's control is facilitated by IT tools such as workflow software and groupware (see Chapter 4).

PERFORMANCE MEASUREMENT AND METRICS. Measuring the supply chain performance is necessary for making decisions about supply chain improvements. IT provides for the data collection needed for such measurement. Some potential metrics for supply chain operations are: on-time delivery (%), quality at unloading area (number of defects), cost performance, lead time for procurement, inventory levels (or days of "turning" an inventory), shrinkage (%), obsolescence (% of inventory), cost of maintaining inventory, speed of finding needed items in the storeroom, availability of items when needed (%), the percentage of rush orders, percentage of goods returned, and a customers' complaints rate.

Establishing such metrics and tracking them with business partners is critical to the success of one's business. Companies that use such measures have the needed data to minimize supply chain problems. For a comprehensive discussion of metrics see Sterne (2002) and Bayles (2001).

OTHER IT-ASSISTED SOLUTIONS TO SCM PROBLEMS. Here are some other generic IT-assisted solutions to solve SCM problems:

- Use wireless technology to expedite certain tasks in the supply chain (e.g., vehicle location and sales force automation; see Chapter 6).
- Configure optimal shipping plans. Use quantitative analysis, DSS, and intelligent systems for the configuration. (See Keskinocak and Tayur, 2001.)
- Create strategic partnerships with suppliers. Use DSS to determine which partnerships and which suppliers to use.
- Use the just-in-time approach, in which suppliers deliver small quantities whenever supplies, materials, and parts are needed.
- Use outsourcing rather than do-it-yourself, especially during demand peaks. Use DSS models to decide what and when to outsource.
- Similarly, buy rather than make production inputs whenever appropriate. Use DSS to make appropriate decisions.
- By proper planning, reduce the lead time for buying and selling. Use business intelligence models.
- Use fewer suppliers. Use business intelligence models to decide on how many and which suppliers.
- Improve supplier–buyer relationships by using CRM and PRM software solutions.
- Manufacture only after orders are in, as Dell does with its custom-made computers and servers.
- Achieve accurate demand by working closely with suppliers, using online collaboration tools (Chapter 4).
- Automate materials flow, information flow, and partner relationships (Viswanadham, 2002).

For more specific IT solutions, see Table 8.1 and Kumar (2001).

Large companies, such as Dell Computer, employ several methods to achieve supply-chain superiority (see *IT at Work 3.4* and Online Minicase W8.1). Wal-Mart is another company that is well-known for its ability to combine information from companies across its supply chain with demand inventory data from its stores, to minimize operating cost and reduce prices. This requires lots of collaboration with business partners. Nestlé USA, for example, created a vice-president-level position exclusively to manage business with Wal-Mart (Worthen, 2002). For a comprehensive example of global

TABLE 8.1 IT Solutions to Supply Chain Problems

Supply Chain Problem	IT Solution
Linear sequence of processing is too slow.	Parallel processing, using workflow software.
Waiting times between chain segments are excessive.	Identify reason (DSS software) and expedite communication and collaboration (intranets, groupware).
Existence of non-value-added activities.	Value analysis (SCM software), simulation software.
Slow delivery of paper documents.	Electronic documents and communication system (e.g., EDI, e-mail).
Repeat process activities due to wrong shipments, poor quality, etc.	Electronic verifications (software agents), automation; eliminating human errors, electronic control systems.
Batching; accumulate work orders between supply chain processes to get economies of scale (e.g., save on delivery).	SCM software analysis, digitize documents for online delivery.
Learn about delays after they occur, or learn too late.	Tracking systems, anticipate delays, trend analysis, early detection (intelligent systems).
Excessive administrative controls such as approvals (signatures). Approvers are in different locations.	Parallel approvals (workflow), electronic approval system. Analysis of need.
Lack of information, or too-slow flow.	Internet/intranet, software agents for monitoring and alert. Barcodes, direct flow from POS terminals.
Lack of synchronization of moving materials.	Workflow and tracking systems. Synchronization by software agents.
Poor coordination, cooperation, and communication.	Groupware products, constant monitoring, alerts, collaboration tools.
Delays in shipments from warehouses.	Use robots in warehouses, use warehouse management software.
Redundancies in the supply chain. Too many purchasing orders, too much handling and packaging.	Information sharing via the Web, creating teams of collaborative partners supported by IT (see Epner, 1999).
Obsolescence of parts and components that stay too long in storage.	Reducing inventory levels by information sharing internally and externally, using intranets and groupware.
Scheduling problems, manufacturing lack of control.	Intelligent agents for B2B modeling (see *gensym.com*).

supply chain improvements at another large company, John Deere, see Nelson (2002).

8.3 COMPUTERIZED SYSTEMS: MRP, MRPII, SCM, AND INTEGRATION

The concept of the supply chain is interrelated with the computerization of its activities, which has evolved over 50 years.

The Evolution of Computerized Supply Chain Aids

Historically, many of the supply chain activities were managed with paper transactions, which can be very inefficient. Therefore, since the time when computers first began to be used for business, people have wanted to automate the processes along the supply chain.

The first software programs, which appeared in the 1950s and early 1960s, supported short segments along the supply chain. Typical examples are inventory management systems, scheduling, and billing. The supporting software was called *supply chain management (SCM) software*. The major objectives were to reduce cost, expedite processing, and reduce errors. Such applications were developed in the functional areas, independent of each other, and they became more and more sophisticated with the passage of time (as was shown in Chapter 7). Of special interest were transaction processing systems and decision support procedures such as management science optimization and financial decision-making formulas (e.g., for loan amortization).

In a short time it became clear that interdependencies exist among some of the supply chain activities. One early realization was that production scheduling is related to inventory management and purchasing plans. As early as the 1960s, the **material requirements planning (MRP)** model was devised. This model essentially integrates production, purchasing, and inventory management of interrelated products (see Chapter 7). It became clear that computer support could greatly enhance use of this model, which may require daily updating. This resulted in commercial MRP software packages coming on the market.

While MRP packages were and still are useful in many cases, helping to drive inventory levels down and streamlining portions of the supply chain, they failed in as many (or even more) cases. One of the major reasons for the failure was the realization that schedule-inventory-purchasing operations are closely related to both financial and labor resources, which were not represented in MRP packages. This realization resulted in an enhanced MRP methodology (and software) called **manufacturing resource planning (MRP II),** which adds labor requirements and financial planning to MRP (see Sheikh, 2002).

During this evolution there was more and more *integration* of functional information systems. This evolution continued, leading to the *enterprise resource planning (ERP)* concept, which integrates the transaction processing and other routine activities of all functional areas in the entire enterprise. ERP initially covered all routine transactions within a company, including internal suppliers and customers, but later it was expanded to incorporate external suppliers and customers in what is known as *extended ERP software.* A typical ERP includes dozens of integrated modules, in all functional areas; a listing of typical modules can be viewed in Online File W8.2 at our Web site. We'll look at ERP, which is also known as an *enterprise software,* again in a bit more detail later in this section.

The next step in this evolution, which started in the late 1990s, is the inclusion of business intelligence and other application software (such as CRM software). At the beginning of the twenty-first century, the integration expanded to include entire industries and the general business community. (See *mySAP.com* for details.) This evolution of integrated systems is shown in Figure 8.2.

Notice that throughout this evolution there have been more and more integrations along several dimensions (more functional areas, combining transaction processing and decision support, inclusion of business partners). Therefore, before we describe the essentials of ERP and SCM software it may be beneficial to analyze the reasons for software and activities integration.

Systems Integration   Creating the twenty-first-century enterprise cannot be done effectively with twentieth-century computer technology, which is *functionally* oriented. Functional systems may not let different departments communicate with each other in the same language. Worse yet, crucial sales, inventory, and production data

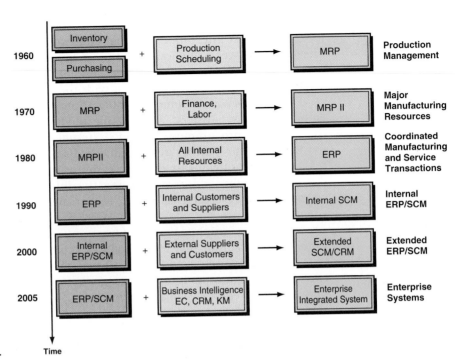

FIGURE 8.2 The evolution of integrated systems.

often have to be painstakingly entered manually into separate computer systems every time a person who is not a member of a specific department needs ad hoc information related to the specific department. In many cases employees simply do not get the information they need, or they get it too late.

Sandoe et al. (2001) list the following major benefits of systems integration (in declining order of importance):

- *Tangible benefits:* inventory reduction, personnel reduction, productivity improvement, order management improvement, financial-close cycle improvement, IT cost reduction, procurement cost reduction, cash management improvement, revenue/profit increases, transportation logistics cost reduction, maintenance reduction, and on-time delivery improvement.

- *Intangible benefits:* information visibility, new/improved processes, customer responsiveness, standardization, flexibility, globalization, and business performance.

Notice that many of both the tangible and intangible benefits cited above are directly related to improved supply chain management.

Integration of the links in the supply chain has been facilitated by the need to streamline operations in order to meet customer demands in the areas of product and service cost, quality, delivery, technology, and cycle time brought by increased global competition. Furthermore, new forms of organizational relationships and the information revolution, especially the Internet and e-commerce, have brought SCM to the forefront of management attention. Upper-level management has therefore been willing to invest money in hardware and software that are needed for seamless integration.

For further discussion of the improvements that integration provides to SCM, see Novell.com (look for Novell Nterprise).

TYPES OF INTEGRATION: FROM SUPPLY TO VALUE CHAIN. There are two basic types of systems integration: internal and external. *Internal integration* refers to integration between applications, and/or between applications and databases, inside a company. For example, one may integrate the inventory control with an ordering system, or a CRM suite with the database of customers.

External integration refers to integration of applications and/or databases among business partners. An example of this is the suppliers' catalogs with the buyers' e-procurement system. External integration is especially needed for B2B and for partner relationship management (PRM) systems (Section 8.6). The most obvious external integration is that of linking the segments of the supply chain, and/or connecting the information that flows among the segments. We discussed this topic earlier and will discuss it further in this chapter.

But there is another type of integration, and this is the integration of the value chain. Traditionally, we thought of supply chain in terms of purchasing, transportation, warehousing, and logistics. The *integrated value chain* is a more encompassing concept. It is the process by which *multiple enterprises* within a shared market channel collaboratively plan, implement, and (electronically as well as physically) manage the flow of goods, services, and information along the entire chain in a manner that increases customer-perceived value. This process optimizes the efficiency of the chain, creating competitive advantage for all stakeholders in the value chain. Whereas the supply chain is basically a description of flows and activities, the value chain expresses the *contributions* made by various segments and activities both to the profit and to customers' satisfaction. (For a survey see Drickhamer, 2002.)

Another way of defining value chain integration is as a *process of collaboration* that optimizes all internal and external activities involved in delivering greater perceived value to the ultimate customer. A supply chain transforms into an integrated value chain when it does the following:

- Extends the chain all the way from subsuppliers (tier 2, 3, etc.) to customers
- Integrates back-office operations with those of the front office (see Figure 8.3)
- Becomes highly customer-centric, focusing on demand generation and customer service as well as demand fulfillment and logistics
- Seeks to optimize the value added by information and utility-enhancing services

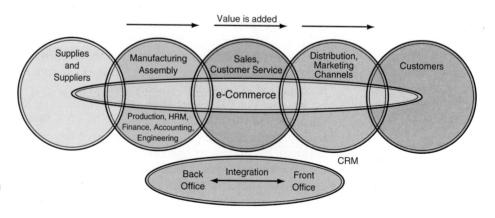

FIGURE 8.3 Back office and front office integration in a value chain.

● Is proactively designed by chain members to compete as an "extended enterprise," creating and enhancing customer-perceived value by means of cross-enterprise collaboration

Collaboration Along the Supply Chain

Presently only a few large companies are successfully involved in a comprehensive collaboration to restructure the supply and value chains. One such effort is described in *IT at Work 8.2* (pages 370–371).

For a special report on supply chain collaboration, see ASCET (2000), where such collaboration is called **collaborative commerce networks** or simply **collaborative commerce** (see Chapter 4 and 5).

Another example of supply chain collaboration that requires system integration is product-development systems that allow suppliers to dial into a client's intranet, pull product specifications, and view illustrations and videos of a manufacturing process. (For further discussion, see Selland, 1999a and 1999b; and Hagel, 2002.)

A popular solution to the integration problems in large companies is to use an integrated application, in what is known as enterprise resource planning.

8.4 ENTERPRISE RESOURCE PLANNING (ERP)

One of the most successful tools for managing supply chains is enterprise resource planning (ERP). ERP systems are in use in thousands of large and medium companies worldwide. As this section will show, some ERP systems are producing dramatic results (see *erpassist.com*).

What Is ERP?

With the advance of enterprisewide client/server computing comes a new challenge: how to control all major business processes with a single software architecture in real time. Such an integrated software solution, known as **enterprise resource planning (ERP)** or just **enterprise systems,** is a process of planning and managing all resources and their use in the entire enterprise. It is a software comprised of a set of applications that automate routine back-end operations, such as financial, inventory management, and scheduling, to help enterprises handle jobs such as order fulfillment (see O'Leary, 2000). For example, in an ERP system there is a module for cost control, for accounts payable and receivable, and for fixed assets and treasury management. ERP promises benefits ranging from increased efficiency to improved quality, productivity, and profitability. (See Ragowsky and Somers, 2002, for details.)

The term *enterprise resource planning* is misleading because the software does not concentrate on either planning or resources. ERP's major objective is to *integrate all departments and functions across a company* onto a single computer system that can serve all of the enterprise's needs (see Stratman and Roth, 2002). For example, improved order entry allows immediate access to inventory, product data, customer credit history, and prior-order information. This availability of information raises productivity and increases customer satisfaction. ERP, for example, helped Master Product Company increase customers' satisfaction and, consequently, sales by 20 percent and decrease inventory by 30 percent, thus increasing productivity (Caldwell, 1997).

For businesses that want to use ERP, one option is to self-develop an integrated system by using existing functional packages or by programming one's own systems. The other option is to use commercially available integrated ERP

IT at Work 8.2
HOW WARNER-LAMBERT APPLIES AN INTEGRATED SUPPLY CHAIN

Warner-Lambert is a major U.S. pharmaceutical company that is now owned by Pfizer (*pfizer.com*). One of its major products is Listerine antiseptic mouthwash. The materials for making Listerine come mainly from eucalyptus trees in Australia and are shipped to the Warner-Lambert (WL) manufacturing plant in New Jersey. The major problem there is to *forecast* the *overall demand* in order to determine how much Listerine to produce. Then one can figure how much raw materials are needed and when. A wrong forecast will result either in high inventories of raw materials and/or of finished products, or in shortages. Inventories are expensive to keep; shortages may result in loss of business.

Warner-Lambert forecasts demand with the help of Manugistic Inc.'s Demand Planning Information System (an SCM product). Used with other software in Manugistics' Supply Chain Planning suite, the system analyzes manufacturing, distribution, and sales data against expected demand and business climate information. Its goal is to help WL decide how much Listerine (and other products) to make and how much of each raw ingredient is needed, and when. For example, the model can anticipate the impact of seasonal promotion or of a production line being down.

The sales and marketing group of WL also meets monthly with WL employees in finance, procurement, and other departments. The group enters the expected demand

for Listerine into the Prism Capacity Planning system (now Invensys plc), which schedules the production of Listerine in the amounts needed and generates electronic purchase orders for WL's suppliers.

WL's supply chain excellence stems from the Collaborative Planning, Forecasting, and Replenishment (CPFR) program. This is a retailing industry project for which piloting was done at WL. In the pilot project, WL shared strategic plans, performance data, and market insight with Wal-Mart over private networks. The company realized that it could benefit from Wal-Mart's market knowledge, just as Wal-Mart could benefit from WL's product knowledge. In CPFR, trading partners collaborate on the demand forecast using *collaborative e-commerce* (see figure, next page). The project includes major SCM and ERP vendors such as SAP and Manugistics.

During the CPFR pilot, WL increased its products' shelf-fill rate—the extent to which a store's shelves are fully stocked—from 87 percent to 98 percent, earning the company about $8 million a year in additional sales. This was the equivalent of a new product launch, but for much less investment. WL is now using the Internet to expand the CPFR program to all its major suppliers and retail partners.

Warner-Lambert is involved in another collaborative retail industry project, the Supply-Chain Operations Reference (SCOR), an initiative of the Supply-Chain Council in

(continues on page 371)

software. The leading ERP software is **SAP R/3.** Oracle, J.D. Edwards, Computer Associates, and PeopleSoft also make similar products. These products include Web modules.

Another alternative is to lease systems from *application service providers (ASPs).* This option is described later in this chapter and at length in Chapters 13 and 14. A major advantage of this approach is that even a small company can enjoy ERP since users can lease only the modules they need, rather than buying the entire package. Some ERP vendors are willing now (2003) to sell only relevant modules.

First-Generation ERP

An ERP suite provides a single interface for managing all the routine activities performed in manufacturing—from entering sales orders, to coordinating shipping, to after-sales customer service. As of the late 1990s, ERP systems were extended along the supply chain to suppliers and customers. They can incorporate functionality for customer interaction and for managing relationships with suppliers and vendors, making the system less inward-looking.

Large companies have been successful in integrating several hundred applications using ERP software, saving millions of dollars and significantly increasing

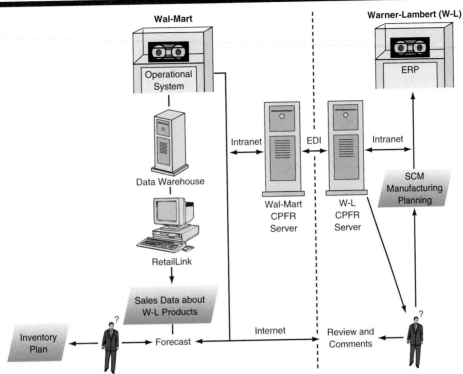

the United States. SCOR divides supply chain operations into parts, giving manufacturers, suppliers, distributors, and retailers a framework within which to evaluate the effectiveness of their processes along the same supply chains.

For Further Exploration: Why would Listerine have been a target for the pilot CPFR collaboration? For what industries, besides retailing, would such collaboration be beneficial?

Sources: Compiled from Bresnahan (1998) and *Logistics Management and Distribution Report* (1998, 1999).

customer satisfaction. For example, ExxonMobil consolidated 300 different information systems by implementing SAP R/3 in its U.S. petrochemical operations alone. ERP forces discipline and organization around business processes, making the alignment of IT and business goals more likely. Such change is related to business process redesign (BPR) (Chapter 9). Also, by implementing ERP a company can discover all the "dusty corners" of its business.

However, ERP software can be extremely complex to implement: Companies often need to change existing business processes to fit ERP's format, and some companies require only some of the ERP's software modules yet must purchase the entire package. For these reasons, ERP software may not be attractive to everyone. For example, Caldwell and Stein (1998) report that Inland Steel Industries, Inc., opted to write its own ERP system (containing 7 million lines of code), which supports 27 integrated applications, rather than use commercial ERP. Also, some companies, such as Starbucks, decided to use a *best-of-breed* approach, building their ERP with ready-made components from several vendors. As indicated earlier, the option of leasing individual modules from ASPs may lessen this problem.

In whatever form it is implemented, ERP has played a critical role in getting manufacturers to focus on business processes, thus facilitating business process changes across the enterprise. By tying together multiple plants and distribution facilities, ERP solutions have also facilitated a change in thinking that has its ultimate expression in an enterprise that is better able to expand operations and in better supply chain management. (For a comprehensive treatment of ERP, its cost, implementation problems, and payback, see Koch et al., 1999; James and Wolfe, 2000; Jacobs and Whybark, 2000; and Lucas and Bishop, 2001.) Palaniswamy and Frank, 2002, describe positive results of Oracle ERP and discuss its implementation process.

But ERP originally was never meant to fully support supply chains. ERP solutions are centered on *business transactions*. As such, they do not provide the computerized models needed to respond rapidly to real-time changes in supply, demand, labor, or capacity, nor to be effectively integrated with e-commerce. This deficiency has been overcome by the second generation of ERP.

Post-ERP (Second-Generation ERP)

First-generation ERP aimed at automating routine business transactions. And indeed ERP projects do save companies millions of dollars. A report by Merrill Lynch noted that nearly 40 percent of all U.S. companies with more than $1 billion in annual revenues have implemented ERP systems. However, by the late 1990s the major benefits of ERP had been fully exploited. It became clear that with the completion of the Y2K projects that were an integral part of many ERP implementations, the first generation of ERP was nearing the end of its useful life.

But the ERP movement was far from over. A second, more powerful generation of ERP development started. Its objective is to leverage existing systems in order to increase efficiency in handling transactions, improve decision making, and further transform ways of doing business into e-commerce. (See James and Wolf, 2000.) Let's explain:

The first generation of ERP has traditionally excelled in its ability to manage administrative activities like payroll, inventory, and order processing. For example, an ERP system has the functionality of electronic ordering or the best way to bill the customer—but all it does is automate the transactions. Palaniswamy and Frank (2000) cite five case studies indicating that ERP significantly enhances the performance of manufacturing organizations *as a result of automating transactions*.

The reports generated by first-generation ERP systems gave planners statistics about company transactions and activities, costs, and financial performance. However, the planning systems with ERP were rudimentary. Reports from first-generation ERP systems provided a snapshot of the business at a point in time. But they did not support the *continuous* planning that is central to supply chain planning, which continues to refine and enhance the plan as changes and events occur, up to the very last minute before executing the plan. Attempting to come up with an optimal plan using first-generation ERP-based systems has been compared to steering a car by looking in the rear-view mirror. Therefore, the need existed for planning systems oriented toward *decision making*. As discussed in *A Closer Look 8.1*, SCM software vendors set out to meet this need.

From the list of the solutions in *A Closer Look 8.1*, it is clear that SCM differs from ERP, and companies need both of them, as illustrated next.

COMBINING ERP WITH SCM SOFTWARE. To illustrate how ERP and SCM may work together, despite their fundamentally different approaches, let's look at the

A CLOSER LOOK
8.1 SCM SOFTWARE VERSUS ERP SOFTWARE

SCM software refers to software specifically designed to improve decision making along the supply chain, such as what is the best way to ship to your customer, or what is the optimal production plan inside your own manufacturing system. This decision-making focus is in contrast with ERP software, which streamlines the flow of routine information along the supply chain (such as order taking, inventory levels reporting, or sales data). Data collected by ERP system are frequently used as input data for analysis done with ERP software (Latamore, 2000).

To better understand the differences between SCM software and ERP software, let's look at the functionalities of products offered by two SCM vendors, i2 and Manugistics.

i2'S OPTIMIZATION SOLUTIONS. The i2 Corporation (i2.com) offers a set of five integrated optimization solutions, which are shown in the upper part of the nearby figure (shown between "Suppliers" and "Customers"). Notice that all are SCM optimization tools, to help with decision making: For example, logistics optimization enables companies to procure, plan, execute, and monitor freight movements across multiple modes, borders, and enterprises. Optimization is usually built on DSS models, such as linear programming and simulation, as well on other analytical tools (see Chapter 12).

The optimization tools (each of which includes several applications; see *i2.com/solutionareas/index.cfm*) are supported by content subscription and supply chain services modules. The entire set of solutions can be connected to both ERP and legacy systems which provide the data for the analysis and optimization done by the optimization modules.

MANUGISTICS SUPPLY CHAIN MANAGEMENT SOLUTIONS. Manugistics offers the following integrated solution suites:

Network design and optimization

Manufacturing planning and scheduling

Sales and operations planning

Order fulfillment management

Collaborative VMI and CPFR

Private Trading Intelligent Hub (for external integration)

Service and parts management

Logistics management

Profitable Order Management

Profitable Demand Management

Enterprise Profit Optimization

Each suite has several applications (see *manugistics.com*).

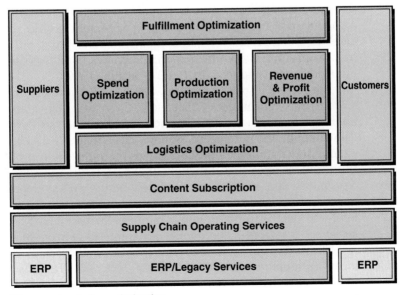

i2's supply chain optimization.

task of order processing: The ERP approach is, "How can I best take or fulfill your order?" In contrast, the question for SCM software is, "Should I take your order?" The SCM and ERP software are actually information systems and will be referred to as such.

Thus, the analytical SCM systems have emerged as a *complement* to ERP systems, to provide intelligent decision support or business intelligence capabilities (e.g., see Keskinocak and Tayur, 2001). An SCM system is designed to overlay existing systems and to pull data from every step of the supply chain. Thus it is able to provide a clear, global picture of where the enterprise is heading.

An example of a successful SCM effort is that of IBM. IBM has restructured its global supply chain in order to achieve quick responsiveness to customers and to do so with minimal inventory. To support this effort, IBM developed an extended-enterprise supply-chain analysis tool, called the Asset Management Tool (AMT). AMT integrates graphical process modeling, analytical performance optimization, simulation, activity-based costing, and enterprise database connectivity into a system that allows quantitative analysis of inter-enterprise supply chains. IBM has used AMT to analyze and improve such issues as inventory budgets, turnover objectives, customer-service targets, and new-product introductions. The system was implemented at a number of IBM business units and their channel partners. AMT benefits include savings of over $750 million in materials costs and price-protection expenses each year. (For details, see Yao et al., 2000.) The system was also a prerequisite to a major e-procurement initiative at IBM.

Creating an ERP/SCM integration model allows companies to quickly assess the impact of their actions on the entire supply chain, including customer demand. Therefore, it makes sense to integrate ERP and SCM.

ALTERNATIVE WAYS TO INTEGRATE ERP WITH SCM. How is integration of ERP with SCM done? One approach is to work with different software products from different vendors. For example, a business might use SAP as an ERP and add to it Manugistics' manufacturing-oriented SCM software, as shown in the Warner-Lambert (Pfizer) case. Such an approach requires fitting different software, which may be a complex task unless special interfaces known as "adapters" and provided by middleware vendors exist (see Linthicum, 1999).

The second integration approach is for ERP vendors to add decision support and analysis capabilities. Collectively, these capabilities are known as business intelligence. **Business intelligence** refers to analysis performed by DSS, ESS, data mining, and intelligent systems (see Chapters 2, 11, and 12). Using one vendor and a combined product solves the integration problem. However, most ERP vendors offer such functionalities for another reason: It is cheaper for the customers. The added functionalities, which create the *second-generation ERP,* include not only decision support but also CRM, electronic commerce (Section 8.5), and data warehousing and mining (Chapter 11). Some systems include a *knowledge management* component (Chapter 10) as well. In 2003, vendors started to add product life cycle management (PLM, Chapter 7) in an attempt to optimize the supply chain (Hill, 2003)

An example of an ERP application that includes an SCM module is provided in *IT at Work 8.3.*

Supply Chain Intelligence   The inclusion of business intelligence in supply chain software solutions is called by some **supply chain intelligence (SCI).** SCI applications enable

IT at Work 8.3
COLGATE-PALMOLIVE USES ERP TO SMOOTH ITS SUPPLY CHAIN

Colgate-Palmolive is the world leader in oral-care products (toothpaste, toothbrushes, and mouthwashes) and a major supplier of personal-care products (baby care, deodorants, shampoos, and soaps). In addition, the company's Hill's Health Science Diet is a leading pet-food brand worldwide. Foreign sales account for about 70 percent of Colgate's total revenues.

To stay competitive, Colgate continuously seeks to streamline its supply chain, where thousands of suppliers and customers interact with the company. At the same time, Colgate faces the challenges of new-product acceleration, which has been a factor in driving faster sales growth and improved market share. Also, Colgate is devising ways to offer consumers a greater choice of better products at a lower cost to the company, which creates complexities in the manufacturing and the supply chains. To better manage and coordinate its business, Colgate embarked on an ERP implementation to allow the company to access more timely and accurate data and to reduce costs. The structure of the ERP is shown in the figure below.

An important factor for Colgate was whether it could use the ERP software across the entire spectrum of the business. Colgate needed the ability to coordinate globally but to act locally. Colgate's U.S. division installed SAP R/3 for this purpose.

Source: Compiled from Kalakota and Robinson (2001).

For Further Exploration: What is the role of the ERP for Colgate-Palmolive? Who are the major beneficiaries?

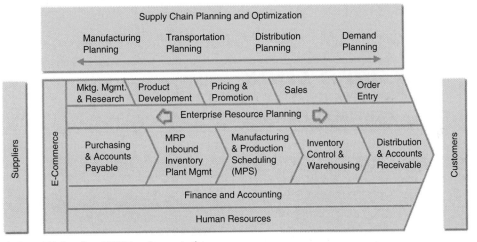

Colgate-Palmolive ERP implementation.

strategic decision making by analyzing data along the entire supply chain. This so-called intelligence is provided by the tools and capabilities discussed in Chapters 11 and 12. A comparison of SCI with SCM is provided in Online File W8.3.

HOW ARE SCI CAPABILITIES PROVIDED? The following are common ways to provide SCI capabilities:

- Use an enhanced ERP package that includes business intelligence capabilities. For example, see Oracle and SAP products of 2001 or later.
- Integrate the ERP with business intelligence software from a specialized vendor, such as Brio, Cognus, Information Builders, or Business Objects.

- Use Web services (see Chapter 14).
- Create a best-of-breed system by using *components* from several vendors that will provide the required capabilities. (For component-based application development, see Chapter 14.)

ERP Failures and Justification

Despite improvements such as second-generation ERP and supply chain intelligence, ERP projects, especially large ones, may fail (see the Nike case, page 24). *A Closer Look 8.2* discusses some additional examples of ERP failures.

In order to avoid failures and ensure success, according to *thespot4sap.com*, it is necessary for the partners involved in ERP implementation to hold open and honest dialogue at the start of each project, and to nail down the critical success factors of the implementation. Included in this initial dialogue should be consideration of the following factors: the customer's expectations; the ERP product capabilities and limitations; the level of change the customer has to go through to make the system fit; the level of commitment within the customer's organization to see the project through to completion; the risks presented by politics within the organization, and (if applicable) the implementing consultant's capabilities, responsibilities, and role.

Various other considerations can affect the success or failure of an ERP project. For example, failures can be minimized if appropriate cost-benefit and cost justification is done in advance (Oliver and Romm, 2002; O'Brien, 2002; and

A CLOSER LOOK

8.2 EVEN THE BEST-PLANNED ERP SOMETIMES FAILS

The complexity of ERP projects causes some of them to fail. Here are several examples:

EXAMPLE 1. Hershey's chocolate bars and its other products were not selling well in late 1999. Hershey Foods Corporation (*hersheys.com*) reported a 19 percent drop in third-quarter net earnings, due to computer problems. The problems continued for several months, causing Hershey to lose market share and several hundred million dollars. The major problem, according to the company, was its new order and distribution system, which uses software from both SAP (the ERP) and Siebel Systems (the CRM). Since the integrated system went live in July 1999, Hershey had been unable to fill all orders and get products onto shelves on time. It took many months to fix the problem.

EXAMPLE 2. In November 1999, Whirlpool Corp. (*whirlpool.com*) reported major delays in shipment of appliances due to "bugs" in its new ERP. Orders for quantities smaller than one truckload met with snags in the areas of order processing, tracking, and invoicing. According to Collett (1999), SAP gave Whirlpool a red light twice prior to the date on which the project would go live, saying the supply chain was not ready, but Whirlpool ignored the signals.

EXAMPLE 3. FoxMeyer, a major distributor of prescription drugs to hospitals and pharmacies, filed for bankruptcy in 1996. In August 2001, FoxMeyer sued both SAP and Accenture Consulting for $500 million each, claiming that the ERP system they constructed led to its demise. Many customers sued FoxMeyer as well. All cases are still pending (May 2003). For the complete case, see Online File W8.4 at the book's Web site.

EXAMPLE 4. W.L. Gore and Associates (*gore.com*), a multinational manufacturer of industrial products, filed a lawsuit against PeopleSoft and Deloitte & Touche, because the ERP project that the two companies developed for the company cost twice the original estimate.

Note: In both the FoxMeyer and the W.L. Gore cases, the ERP vendors and consultants blamed their clients' poor management teams for the ERP problems. Both cases were in court at the time this was written.

Sources: Compiled from Davenport (2000); *cnet.com*; *cio.com*; and *Business Courier* (miscellaneous dates).

Murphy and Simon, 2002). Another way to avoid failures, or at least minimize their cost, is to use ASPs to lease rather than buy or build ERPs. ERP implementation may also be affected by cultural and global factors. For an analysis of some Asian experiences with ERPs, see Soh et al. (2000). Finally, Willcocks and Sykes (2000) tie the successful implementation of ERP to the need to identify and build key in-house IT capabilities before embarking on ERP.

Application Service Providers and ERP Outsourcing

As noted above, a popular option today for businesses that need ERP functions is to lease applications rather than to build systems. An *application service provider (ASP)* is a software vendor that offers to lease applications to businesses. In leasing applications, the vendor takes care of the functionalities and the internal integration problems. This approach is known as the "ASP alternative." ASP is considered a risk-management strategy, and it best fits small- to midsize companies. (See Chapters 13 and 14 for further details.) The delivery of the software is usually done effectively via the Internet.

ASPs offer ERP systems as well as ERP-added functions such as electronic commerce, CRM, desktop productivity, human resources information systems (HRISs), and other supply-chain-related applications.

The ASP concept is useful in ERP projects, which are expensive to install, take a long time to implement, and require additional staffing. Flexibility to the renter is a major benefit: You pay only for the ERP models used, and for a specific time period.

The use of an ASP has its downside. First, ASP vendors typically want a five-year commitment. Some companies may not want to lock themselves in for that long, reasoning that within five years ERP may be simplified and easier to implement in house. Second, organizations lose some flexibility with the use of an ASP. Rented systems are fairly standard and may not fit the organization's specific needs. (For other benefits and limitations of ASPs, see Chapters 13 and 14 and Segev and Gebauer, 2001.)

8.5 E-COMMERCE AND SUPPLY CHAINS

E-commerce is emerging as a superb tool for providing solutions to problems along the supply chain. As seen earlier in this chapter and in Chapter 5, many supply chain activities, from taking customers' orders to procurement, can be conducted as part of an EC initiative. In general, EC can make the following contributions to supply chain management:

1. EC can digitize some products, such as software, which expedites the flow of materials in the chain. It is also much cheaper to create and move electronic digits than physical products.

2. EC can replace all paper documents that move physically with electronic documents. This change improves speed and accuracy, and the cost of document transmission is much cheaper.

3. A single business transaction could involve many messages, totaling thousands of messages per week or even per day for a company. E-commerce can replace related faxes, telephone calls, and telegrams with an electronic messaging system at a minimal cost.

4. EC can change the nature and structure of the supply chain from linear to a hub (see the Orbis case, page 8). Such restructuring enables faster, cheaper, and better communication, collaboration, and discovery of information.

5. EC enhances several of the activities discussed in the previous sections, such as collaboration and information sharing among the partners in the supply chain. These enhancements can improve cooperation, coordination, and demand forecasts.

6. EC typically shortens the supply chain and minimizes inventories. Production changes from mass production to build-to-order as a result of the "pull" nature of EC. The auto industry, for example, is expected to save billions of dollars annually in inventory reduction alone by moving to e-commerce–supported build-to-order strategy.

7. EC facilitates customer service. Of special interest is the reduced customer-service staffing needs due to innovations such as FAQs and self-services such as self-tracking of shipments.

8. EC introduces efficiencies into buying and selling through the creation of e-marketplaces and e-procurement, as we saw in Chapter 5.

Let's look now at some specific buying and selling activities along the supply chain.

Buying and Selling Electronically Along the Supply Chain

A major role of EC is to facilitate buying and selling along all segments of the supply chain. The major activities are: upstream, internal supply chain activities, downstream, and combined upstream/downstream activities.

UPSTREAM ACTIVITIES. There are many innovative EC models that improve the upstream supply chain activities. These models are generally described as *e-procurement.* Several were presented in Chapter 5: reverse auctions, aggregation of vendors' catalogs at the buyer's site, procurement via consortia, and group purchasing. (For others, see Mitchell, 2000; Adamson, 2001; and Varley, 2000.)

INTERNAL SUPPLY ACTIVITIES. Internal SCM activities include several *intrabusiness EC* activities. These activities, from entering orders of materials, to recording sales, to tracking shipments, are usually conducted over a corporate intranet. The ChevronTexaco case illustrates several EC internal applications. Details and examples are provided in Chapters 5 and 7.

DOWNSTREAM ACTIVITIES. Typical EC models of downstream supply chain activities are provided in Chapters 5 and 7. Some examples follow.

Selling on Your Own Web Site. Large companies such as Intel, Dell, Cisco, and IBM use this model. At the selling company's Web site, buyers review electronic catalogs from which they buy. Large buyers get their own pages and customized catalogs. Companies sell their standard products from their corporate site, and many (e.g., Cisco, National Semiconductor Corp.) allow customers to configure customized products.

Auctions. As discussed in Chapter 5, large companies such as Dell conduct auctions of products or obsolete equipment on their Web sites. Electronic auctions can shorten cycle time and sometimes save on logistics expenses.

For example, in the United States more than 2.5 million "pre-owned" cars are sold in auctions. Many of these auctions are offered online, supplied by car rental companies, government agencies, banks, and some large organizations that replace their fleets frequently. One pure online B2B auctioneer, for example, is *manheimauctions.com.* The buyers are car dealers who then resell the cars

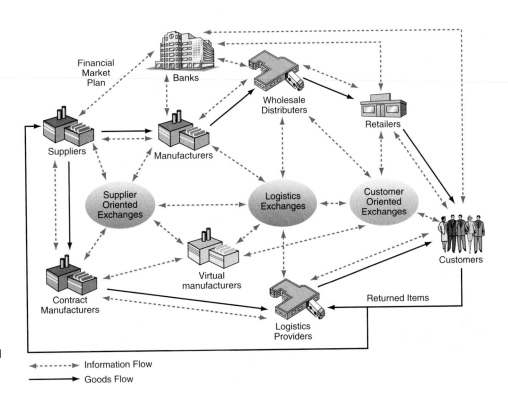

FIGURE 8.4 Web-based supply chain, involving trading exchanges.

to individuals. Traditional car auctions are done on large lots, where the cars are displayed and physically auctioned. In the electronic auction, the autos do not need to be transported to a physical auction site, nor do buyers have to travel to an auction site. Savings of up to $500 per car are realized as a result.

Exchanges.   Considerable support to B2B supply chains can be provided by electronic exchanges (Chapter 5). Such exchanges are shown in Figure 8.4. Notice that in this example there are three separate exchanges. In other cases there may be only one exchange for the entire industry.

UPSTREAM AND DOWNSTREAM ACTIVITIES COMBINED.   It is sometimes advisable to combine upstream and downstream EC supply chain activities. These can be done in *B2B exchanges,* where many buyers and sellers meet, as discussed in Chapter 5. Most of these exchanges are centered one in each industry, so they are referred to as **vertical exchanges.** A typical vertical portal is the one organized by ChemConnect. Similar markets exist for metals, electricity (which is sold among electricity-generating companies), and many commodities. Some vertical exchanges use auctions and reverse auctions, as described in Chapter 5.

Supply Chains in E-Commerce: Characteristics, Problems, and Solutions

In previous sections of this chapter we described how e-commerce can solve some problems of non-EC companies that are selling and buying in a traditional way along the supply chain. However, some applications of EC, especially B2C and sometimes B2B, may have problems with their own supply chains. These problems usually occur in order fulfillment. Examining the characteristics of EC supply chains will help us understand the problems and the potential solutions.

THE CHARACTERISTICS OF EC SUPPLY CHAINS.   EC supply chains need to deliver small quantities to a very large number of customers. Also, it is very difficult to forecast demand due to lack of experience and to the fact that many vendors sell some or mostly customized products. New dot-com companies do not have any existing supply chain operations; they are "starting from scratch." (Click-and-mortar companies, in contrast, have existing supply chains and so have a bit of a head start.)

When a company sells online direct to customers it must take care of the following activities: quickly find the products to be shipped, and pack them; arrange for the packages to be delivered quickly to the customer's door; collect the money from every customer, either in advance, COD (collect on delivery), or by billing the individual; and handle the return of unwanted or defective products. It may be difficult to fulfill these activities both effectively and efficiently. For this reason, both online companies and click-and-mortar companies have difficulties in their online-related supply chains. Let's begin by looking at order fulfillment.

ORDER FULFILLMENT.   **Order fulfillment** refers not only to providing what customers ordered and doing it on time, but also to providing all related customer service. For example, the customer must receive assembly and operating instructions for the appliance he or she just purchased. This can be done by including a paper document with the product or by providing the instructions on the Web. (A nice example is available at *livemanuals.com*.) In addition, if the customer is not happy with a product, an exchange or return must be arranged. Thus, while order fulfillment is basically a part of the *back-office* operations, it is strongly related to *front-office* operations as well.

When dot-com operations were still quite new, e-tailers faced continuous problems with order fulfillment, especially during the holiday season. The problems included inability to deliver on time, delivering wrong items, paying too much for deliveries, and heavily compensating unhappy customers. As a matter of fact, many e-tailers have experienced fulfillment problems since they started EC. Amazon.com, for example, which initially operated as a totally online company, added physical warehouses in order to expedite deliveries and reduce its order fulfillment costs. Woolworths of Australia, a large supermarket that added online services, had serious difficulties with order fulfillment and delivery of fresh foods, and had to completely restructure its delivery system. Taking orders over the Internet for some e-tailers proved to be the easy part of B2C e-commerce. Fulfillment to customers' doors was the harder part. The e-tailers who have survived have proved that they have learned from past mistakes and are learning how to solve their order fulfillment problems.

Several factors can be responsible for delays in deliveries. They range from inability to accurately forecast demand, to ineffective supply chains of the e-tailers. Similar problems exist also in off-line businesses. However, EC is more typically based on the concept of "pull" operations, which begin with an order, frequently a customized one. (This is in contrast with traditional retailing that begins with a production to inventory, which is then "pushed" to customers.) In the pull case, it is more difficult to forecast demand, due to unique demands of customized orders and lack of sufficient years of experience (see Appendix 2A).

Another order fulfillment problem in e-commerce is that the goods need be delivered to the customer's door, with small quantities to each customer, whereas in brick-and-mortar retailing, the customers come to the stores to get the products. The costs of shipping merchandise can quickly add up, and many customers do not like to pay them.

INNOVATIVE SOLUTIONS TO THE ORDER FULFILLMENT PROBLEM. In the last few years companies have developed interesting solutions to both B2C and B2B order fulfillment (e.g., see Robb, 2003). Here are two examples:

- Garden.com, a retailer of plants and flowers, developed proprietary software that allowed it to collaborate with its 70 suppliers efficiently and effectively. Orders were batched and organized in such a way that pullers were able to find, pack, and deliver the plants and flowers efficiently. Customers were able to track the status of their orders in real time (Kaplan, 2002). However, despite its efficient supply chain, the company went out of business in December 2000 due to an insufficient number of customers.

- SkyMall.com (now a subsidiary of Gem-Star TV Guide International) is a retailer selling from catalogs on board airplanes, over the Internet, and by mail order. It relies on catalog partners to fill the orders. For small vendors that do not handle their own shipments, and for international shipments, SkyMall contracts distribution centers owned by fulfillment outsourcer Sykes Enterprise. To coordinate the logistics of sending orders to thousands of customers, SkyMall uses an EC order management integrator called Order Trust. As orders come in, SkyMall conveys the data to Order Trust, which disseminates it to the appropriate vendor, or to a Sykes distribution center. A report is then sent to SkyMall, and SkyMall pays Order Trust the transaction fees. This arrangement has allowed SkyMall to increase its online business by 3 percent annually (*skymall.com*).

Despite these and many other innovative solutions (e.g., see Bayles, 2001; Johnston et al., 2000; Rigney, 2000), most e-tailers are choosing to outsource order fulfillment to avoid problems.

OUTSOURCING ORDER FULFILLMENT. A most common solution in B2C is to outsource the delivery and possibly other logistics activities to companies such as FedEx and UPS. Especially if customers pay directly for the delivery, this is a viable solution to the selling company, as described in *IT at Work 8.4* (page 382).

SAME-DAY, EVEN SAME-HOUR DELIVERY. In the digital age, next-morning delivery may not be fast enough. Today we talk about same-day delivery, and even delivery within an hour. Quick delivery of pizza has been practiced for a long time (e.g., by Domino's Pizza). Today, pizza orders in many places are accepted online. Delivering groceries is another area where speed is important. An example is *groceryworks* (now part of *shop.safeway.com*).

Many restaurants also accept orders online, an approach known as "dine online." Some companies (e.g., *dialadinner.com.hk* in Hong Kong) offer aggregating services, which process orders for several restaurants and also make the deliveries.

Here is how dine online works: Customers click on the online menu to indicate dishes they want (which sometimes can be mixed and matched from two or more restaurants), and they then submit their request electronically. Order processors at the aggregating company receive the order and forward the orders electronically to the participating restaurants (or fax orders to those that do not use computers). A staff member phones first-time customers to check delivery details,

IT at Work 8.4
HOW BIKEWORLD FULFILLS ORDERS

Bikeworld (San Antonio, Texas) is a small company (16 employees) known for its high-quality bicycles and components, expert advice, and personalized service. The company opened its Web site (*bikeworld.com*) in February 1996, using it as a way to keep customers from using out-of-state mail-order houses.

Bikeworld encountered one of the Internet retailing's biggest problems: fulfillment. Sales of its high-value bike accessories over the Internet steadily increased, including global markets, but the time spent processing orders, manually shipping packages, and responding to customers' order status inquiries was overwhelming for the company.

In order to focus on its core competency, Bikeworld decided to outsource its order fulfillment to FedEx. FedEx offered reasonably priced quality express delivery, exceeding customer expectations while automating the fulfillment process. "To go from a complete unknown to a reputable worldwide retailer was going to require more than a fair

price. We set out to absolutely amaze our customers with unprecedented customer service. FedEx gave us the blinding speed we needed," says Whit Snell, Bikeworld's founder.

The nearby figure shows the five steps in the process. Explanations are provided in the figure.

Four years after venturing online, Bikeworld's sales volume more than quadrupled, and the company was on track to surpass $8 million in 2003. The company is consistently profitable; has a fully automated and scalable fulfillment system; has access to real-time order status, enhancing customer service and leading to greater customer retention; and has the global capacity to service customers.

Source: Compiled from FedEx (2000).

For Further Exploration: Is outsourcing the only alternative for a small business like Bikeworld? Why or why not? Why is logistics a critical success factor?

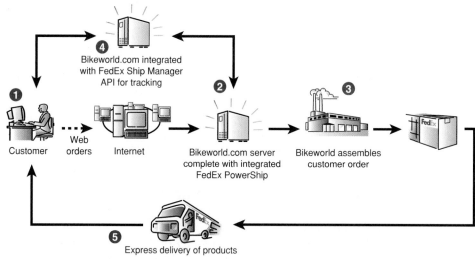

How orders are fulfilled at Bikeworld.

discuss payment method, and confirm that the order is genuine. Delivery staff receive a copy of the order by SMS e-mail on their mobile phones, telling them which restaurant to go to. There they are handed the food and delivery details, and they make the delivery in small cars or on bicycles. Customers receive their meals and pay cash on delivery if needed. The average time from order to delivery is 30 to 40 minutes. (For another example of quick delivery, see *sameday.com*.)

AUTOMATED WAREHOUSES. Traditional warehouses are built to deliver *large quantities* to a *small number* of stores and plants. In B2C EC, companies need to send *small quantities* to a *large number* of individuals. The picking and packing process therefore is different, and usually more labor-intensive.

Large-volume EC fulfillment requires special warehouses. Automated warehouses, for example, may include robots and other devices that expedite the pickup of products. Several e-tailers, such as Amazon.com, operate their own warehouses. Most B2C is probably shipped via outsourcers, mainly UPS, FedEx, and the U.S. Post Office. One of the largest EC warehouses in the United States was operated by a mail-order company, Fingerhut (*fingerhut.com*). This company handled the logistics of all types of mail orders (including online orders) for Wal-Mart, Macy's, and many others. The company (now owned by Pettess Group LLC) temporarily suspended warehousing operation but is now back in operation; the process they use is described in Online File W8.5. A similar warehouse is operated by L.L. Bean, which ships up to 150,000 packages a day (El Sawy, 2001).

Other companies (e.g., *submitorder.com*) provide similar services. The key for all such services is *speed* and *efficiency*. Plumbing wholesaler Davis & Warshow uses several IT tools to enhance their newly constructed central warehouse, as shown in Online File W8.6.

DEALING WITH RETURNS. Returning unwanted merchandise and providing for product exchanges or refunds are necessary activities for maintaining customers' trust and loyalty. The Boston Consulting Group found that the "absence of good return mechanism" was the second-biggest reason shoppers cited for refusing to buy on the Web frequently.

For their part, merchants face the major problem of how to deal with returns. Several options exist (e.g., see Trager, 2000):

- *Return an item to the place where it was purchased.* This is easy to do in a brick-and-mortar store, but not in a virtual one. To return an item to a virtual store, you need to get authorization, pack everything up, pay to ship it back, insure it, and wait up to two billing cycles for a credit to show up on your statement. The buyer is not happy, and neither is the seller, who must unpack the item, check the paperwork, and try to resell the item, usually at a loss. This solution is good only if the number of returns is small.

- *Separate the logistics of returns from the logistics of delivery.* Returns are shipped to an independent unit and handled there. This solution may be more efficient from the seller's point of view, but is no better for the buyer.

- *Allow the customer to physically drop the returned items at collection stations* (such as convenience stores or physical stores of the same company if they exist; e.g, ToyRUs or Staples), from which the returns can be picked up in bulk. This method is used at 7-Eleven stores in some countries, at BP Australia Ltd. (gasoline service stations), which teamed up with *wishlist.com.au*, and at Caltex Australia in their convenience stores. This solution requires good collaboration among retailers and the collection stations.

- *Completely outsource returns.* Several outsourcers, including FedEx and the United Postal Service (UPS), provide such services. The services they offer deal not only with shipments, but also with the entire logistics process of returns. This can be efficient and the customer may be happier, but the cost may be high.

Integration of EC with ERP

Since many middle-sized and large companies already have an ERP system, or are installing one, and since EC needs to *interface* with ERP, it makes sense to tightly integrate the two. Such interface is needed mainly for order fulfillment and for collaboration with business partners, as in the case of inventory managed by suppliers (the P&G-WalMart situation, cited earlier).

Efforts to integrate EC with ERP are still in their infancy in many organizations. ERP vendors started to integrate EC with ERP only since 1997 on a small scale and only since 2000 as a major initiative (see Siau and Messersmith, 2002). For example, SAP started building some EC interfaces in 1997, and in 1999 introduced *mySAP.com* as a major initiative. The mySAP initiative is a multifaceted Internet product that includes EC, online trading sites, an information portal, application hosting, and more user-friendly graphical interfaces (see Online File W8.7).

An example of EC/ERP integration is presented in *IT at Work 8.5*.

IT at Work 8.5
INTEGRATING EC WITH ERP AT CYBEX

Cybex International (*cybex.com*), a global maker of fitness machines, was unable to meet the demand for its popular fitness machines, which increased dramatically in the late 1990s. To maintain its market share, the company had to work with rush orders from its close to 1,000 suppliers, at an extremely high cost. This was a result of a poor demand forecast for the machine's components. This forecast was done by using three different legacy systems that Cybex inherited from merger partners.

After examining the existing supply chain software, Cybex decided to install an ERP system (from People-Soft Inc.) for its supply chain planning and manufacturing applications. In conjunction with the software installation, Cybex analyzed its business processes and made some needed improvements. It also reduced the number of suppliers from 1,000 to 550.

Here is how Cybex's new system works: Customer orders are accepted at the corporate Web site and are instantly forwarded to the appropriate manufacturing plant (the company has two specialized plants). The ERP uses its *planning module* to calculate which parts are needed for each model. Then, the ERP's *product configurator* constructs, in just a few seconds, a component list and a bill-of-materials needed for each specific order.

The ERP system helps with other processes as well. For example: Cybex can e-mail a vendor detailed purchase orders with engineering changes clearly outlined. These changes are visible to everyone, so if one engineer is not at work, or has left the company, his or her knowledge is in the system and is easy to find. Furthermore, dealers now know that they will get deliveries in less than two weeks instead of the previous one to four weeks. They can also track the status of each order.

The system also helps Cybex to better manage its 550 suppliers. For example, the planning engine looks at price variations across product lines, detecting opportunities to negotiate price reductions by showing suppliers that their competitors offer the same products at lower prices. Also, by giving their suppliers projected long- and short-term production schedules, Cybex is making sure that all parts and materials are available when needed; it is also reducing the inventory level it must hold at Cybex. Furthermore, suppliers that cannot meet the required dates are replaced after quarterly reviews.

Despite intense industry price-cutting over the last year, Cybex remained very profitable, mainly due to its e-supply chain. Some of the most impressive results were: Cybex cut its bill-of-materials count (the number of items that might be included on a bill of materials) from 15,200 items to 200; reduced the number of vendors from 1,000 to 550; cut paperwork by two-thirds; and reduced build-to-order time from four to two weeks.

Introducing the system cost money of course. In addition to the cost of the software, the technology staff has increased from three to twelve. Yet, the company feels that the investment was more than justified, especially because it provided for much greater harmony between Cybex and its suppliers and customers.

Sources: Compiled from Sullivan et al. (2002); Paulson (2000); and *peoplesoft.com* (2003).

For Further Exploration: What are the relationships between Cybex's EC applications and ERP? What is the role of the planning module? What are the critical success factors for implementation?

The logic behind integrating EC and ERP is that by extending the existing ERP system to support e-commerce, organizations not only leverage their investment in the ERP solution, but also speed up the development of EC applications.

The problem with this approach is that the ERP software is very complex and inflexible (difficult to change), so it is difficult to achieve easy, smooth, and effective integration. One other potential problem is that ERP systems deal more with back-office (e.g., accounting, inventory) applications, whereas EC deals with front-office applications such as sales and order taking, customer service, and other customer relationship management (CRM) activities. This problem may be solved by using Web services.

8.6 PARTNER RELATIONSHIP MANAGEMENT

Every company that has business partners has to manage the relationships with them. Partners need to be identified, recruited, and maintained. Communication needs to flow between the organizations. Information needs to be updated and shared. All of the efforts made to apply CRM to all types of business partners can be categorized as **partner relationship management (PRM).**

Before the spread of Internet technology, there were few automated processes to support partnerships. Organizations were limited to manual methods of phone, fax, and mail. EDI was used by large corporations, but usually only with their largest partners. Also, there were no systematic ways of conducting PRM. Internet technology changed the situation by offering a way to connect different organizations easily, quickly, and affordably.

PRM solutions connect vendors with their business partners (suppliers, customers, services) using Web technology to securely distribute and manage information. At its core, a PRM application facilitates partner relationships. According to *Business Wire* (2003), a Gartner Group survey conducted in late 2002 showed that of all sales-related applications, PRM programs had the highest return on investment.

Specific PRM functions include: partner profiles, partner communications, lead management (of clients), targeted information distribution, connecting the extended enterprise, partner planning, centralized forecasting, group planning, e-mail and Web-based alerts, messaging, price lists, and community bulletin boards. As described in Chapter 4, many large companies offer suppliers or partners customized portals for improved communication and collaboration. (For more on PRM, see *channelwave.com*, and *it-telecomsolutions.com*.)

One of the major categories of PRM is *supplier relationship management* (SRM). For many companies, such as retailers and manufacturers, working properly with suppliers is a major critical success factor.

PeopleSoft's SRM Model

PeopleSoft.Inc. (*peoplesoft.com*) developed a model for managing supplier relationships in real time. The model is generic and could be considered by any large company. It includes 13 steps, which are illustrated in Figure 8.5 (page 386). The details of the steps are shown in Online File W8.8.

The core idea of this SRM model is that an e-supply chain is based on integration and collaboration (Sections 8.3–8.5). In this model, the supply chain process is connected, decisions are made collectively, performance metrics are based on common understanding of the partners, and information flows in real

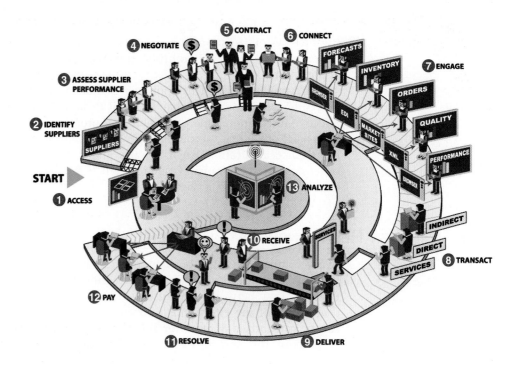

FIGURE 8.5 Managing supplier relationships in real time. (*Source:* Shecterle, 2003.)

time (whenever possible). The only thing a new partner needs in order to join an SRM system is just a Web browser.

8.7 GLOBAL SUPPLY CHAINS

Supply chains that involve suppliers and/or customers or other business partners who are located in more than one country are referred to as *global supply chains.*

Characteristics and Problems along Global Supply Chains

Companies go global for a variety of reasons. The major reasons are: lower costs (of materials, products, services and labor); availability of products that are unavailable domestically; the firm's global strategy; technology available in other countries; high quality of products; intensification of global competition, which drives companies to cut costs; the need to develop a foreign presence to increase sales; and fulfillment of counter trade.

Supply chains that involve suppliers and/or customers in other countries are referred to as **global supply chains** (e.g., see Harrison, 2001, and Handfield and Nichols, 1999) E-commerce has made it much easier to find suppliers in other countries (e.g., by using electronic bidding) as well as to find customers in other countries (see Handfield et al., 2002, and Turban et al., 2004).

Global supply chains are usually longer than domestic ones, and they may be complex. Therefore, additional uncertainties are likely. Some of the issues that may create difficulties in global supply chains are legal issues, customs fees and taxes, language and cultural differences, fast changes in currency exchange rates, and political instabilities. An example of difficulties in a global supply chain can be seen in *IT at Work 8.6.*

Information technologies are found to be extremely useful in supporting global supply chains (Harrison, 2001). For example, TradeNet in Singapore

IT at Work 8.6
LEGO STRUGGLES WITH GLOBAL ISSUES

Lego Company of Denmark (*lego.com*) is a major producer of toys, including electronic ones. It is the world's best-known toy manufacturer (voted as the "toy of the century") and has thousands of Web sites created by fans all over the world.

In 1999 the company decided to market its Lego Mindstorms on the Internet. This product is a unique innovation. Its users can build a Lego robot using more than 700 traditional Lego elements, program it on a PC, and transfer the program to the robot. Lego sells its products in many countries using several regional distribution centers. When the decision to do global e-commerce was made, the company had to face the following concerns and issues:

● It did not make sense to go to all countries, since the company's sales are very low in some countries and some countries offer no logistical support services. Lego had to choose where to market Mindstorms.

● A supportive distribution and service system would be needed, including software support and returns from around the globe.

● There was an issue of merging the off-line and online operations versus creating a new centralized unit, which seemed to be a complex undertaking.

● Existing warehouses had been optimized to handle distribution to commercial buyers, not to individual customers.

● Lego products were selling in different countries in different currencies and at different prices. Should the product be sold on the Net at a single price? In which currency? How would this price be related to the off-line prices?

● How should the company handle the direct mail and track individual shipments?

● Invoicing had to comply with the regulations of many countries.

● Should Lego create a separate Web site for Mindstorms? What languages should be used there?

● Some countries have strict regulations regarding advertising and sales to children. Also laws on consumer protection vary among countries.

● How to handle restrictions on electronic transfer of individuals' personal data.

● How to handle the tax and import duty payments in different countries.

In the rush to get its innovative product to market, Lego did not solve all of these issues before the direct marketing was introduced. The resulting problems forced Lego to close the Web site for business in 1998. It took about a year to solve all global trade-related issues and eventually reopen the site.

By 2001 Lego was selling online many of its products, priced in U.S. dollars, but the online service was available in only 15 countries. By 2003 Lego.com was operating as an independent unit. It offers many Web-only deals and allows online design of many products (e.g., see "Train Configurator"). The site is visited by over 4 million visitors each day.

Sources: Compiled from *lego.com*, from Damsguard and Horluck (2000), and from Stoll (2003).

For Further Exploration: Visit Lego's Web site (*lego.com*) and see the latest EC activities. Also, investigate what the competitors are doing. Do you think that the Web was a good way for Lego to go global?

connects sellers, buyers, and government agencies via electronic data interchange (EDI). (TradeNet is described in detail in Online File W5.11 at the book's Web site.) A similar network, TradeLink, operates in Hong Kong, using both EDI and EDI/Internet attempting to connect about 70,000 trading partners. Promising as global supply chains are, one needs to design them carefully to optimize their functioning.

IT provides not only EDI and other communication options, but also online expertise in sometimes difficult and fast-changing regulations. IT also can be instrumental in helping businesses find trade partners (via electronic directories and search engines, as in the case of *alibaba.com* and *chemconnect.com*). IT also allows for automatic Web page translation to many languages. Finally, IT facilitates outsourcing of products and services, especially computer programming, to countries with a plentiful supply of labor, at low cost.

➡ **MANAGERIAL ISSUES**

1. *Ethical issues.* Conducting a supply chain management project may result in the need to lay off, retrain, or transfer employees. Should management notify the employees in advance regarding such possibilities? And what about those older employees who are difficult to retrain? Other ethical issues may involve sharing of personnel information, which may be required for a collaborative organizational culture.

2. *How much to integrate?* While companies should consider extreme integration projects, including ERP, SCM, and e-commerce, they should recognize that integrating long and complex supply chain segments may result in failure. Therefore, many times companies tightly integrate the upstream, inside-company, and downstream activities, each part by itself, and loosely connect the three.

3. *Role of IT.* Almost all major SCM projects use IT. However, it is important to remember that in most cases the technology plays a supportive role, and the primary role is organizational and managerial in nature. On the other hand, without IT, most SCM efforts do not succeed.

4. *Organizational adaptability.* To adopt ERP, organization processes must, unfortunately, conform to the software, not the other way around. When the software is changed, in a later version for example, the organizational processes must change also. Some organizations are able and willing to do so; others are not.

5. *Going global.* EC provides an opportunity to expand markets globally. However, it may create long and complex supply chains. Therefore, it is necessary to first check the logistics along the supply chain as well as regulations and payment issues.

ON THE WEB SITE... Additional resources, including quizzes; online files of additional text, tables, figures, and cases; and frequently updated Web links to current articles and information can be found on the book's Web site (*wiley.com/college/turban*).

KEY TERMS

Bullwhip effect *361*

Business intelligence *374*

Collaborative commerce *369*

Collaborative commerce networks *369*

E-supply chain *357*

Enterprise resource planning (ERP) *369*

Enterprise systems *369*

Global supply chain *386*

Manufacturing resource planning (MRP II) *366*

Material requirements planning (MRP) *366*

Order fulfillment *380*

Partner relationship management (PRM) *385*

Reverse logistics (returns) *358*

SAP R/3 *370*

Supply chain *357*

Supply chain intelligence (SCI) *374*

Supply chain management (SCM) *357*

Supply chain teams *363*

Vendor-managed inventory (VMI) strategy *362*

Vertical exchanges *379*

CHAPTER HIGHLIGHTS (Numbers Refer to Learning Objectives)

① It is necessary to properly manage the supply chain to ensure superb customer service, low cost, and short cycle time.

① The supply chain must be completely managed, from the raw materials to the end customers.

② It is difficult to manage the supply chain due to the uncertainties in demand and supply and the need to coordinate several business partners' activities. A major inventory problem along the chain is known as the bullwhip effect.

② Innovative approaches to SCM require cooperation and coordination of the business partners, facilitated by IT innovations such as inventory optimization and VMI over extranets, which allow suppliers to view companies' inventories in real time and manage them for their customers.

③ Software support for supply chain management has increased both in coverage and scope, from MRP to MRP II, to ERP, to enhanced ERP (with business partners), and to an ERP/SCM software integration.

④ ERP is an integrated software (known also as an enterprise software) that manages all transformation-type information processing in the enterprise.

④ Today, ERP software, which is designed to improve standard business transactions, is enhanced with business intelligence and decision-support capabilities as well as Web interfaces.

⑤ Electronic commerce is able to provide new solutions to problems along the supply chain by integrating the company's major business activities with both upstream and downstream entities via an electronic infrastructure.

⑤ E-commerce tools, such as e-procurement and collaborative commerce, are used to solve supply chain problems.

⑤ Order fulfillment in EC is difficult due to the need to ship many small packages to customers' doors. Outsourcing the logistics and delivery jobs is common, but it can be expensive.

⑤ Special large and automated warehouses help in improving the EC order fulfillment, but they can be expensive to build and operate.

⑥ PRM should be approached as a comprehensive topic, like the life cycle approach of PeopleSoft (see Figure 8.5). While supply chain interactions are a major part of PRM, collaboration and joint venture should be nourished as well.

⑦ Global supply chains are usually long and can be complex. Therefore they must be carefully analyzed before a decision to go global is finalized.

QUESTIONS FOR REVIEW

1. Define supply chain and supply chain management (SCM).
2. Describe the components of a supply chain.
3. What is an e-supply chain?
4. Describe the bullwhip effect.
5. Describe some solutions to supply chain problems.
6. Define MRP and MRP II.
7. Describe SCM software
8. Define ERP and describe its major characteristics.
9. How can integration solve supply chain problems?
10. Define order fulfillment in EC.
11. List the major difficulties of order fulfillment in EC.
12. Define reverse logistics.
13. Describe some solutions to the order fulfillment problem.
14. Define PRM and SRM.
15. Describe the major SRM activities according to the PeopleSoft model.
16. Describe a global supply chain and some difficulties in going global.

QUESTIONS FOR DISCUSSION

1. Identify the supply chain(s) and the flow of information described in the opening case.
2. Relate the concepts of supply chain and its management to Porter's value chain and value system model.
3. Discuss the Warner-Lambert (Pfizer) Listerine case, and prepare a chart of the product's supply chain.
4. Distinguish between ERP and SCM software. In what ways do they complement each other?

5. It is said that SCM software created more changes in logistics than 100 years of continuous improvement did. Discuss.

6. Discuss what it would be like if the registration process and class scheduling process at your college or university were restructured on an online, real-time, seamless basis with good connectivity and good empowerment in the organization. (If your registration is already online, find another manual process that can be automated.) Explain the supply chain in this situation.

7. Relate ERP to software integration.

8. Compare MRP to MRP II to ERP.

9. Discuss how cooperation between a company that you are familiar with and its suppliers can reduce inventory cost.

10. Find examples of how organizations improve their supply chains in two of the following: manufacturing, hospitals, retailing, education, construction, agribusiness, shipping.

11. The normal way to collect fees from travelers on expressways is to use tollbooths. Automatic coin-collecting baskets can expedite the process, but do not eliminate the long waiting lines during rush hours. About 80 percent of the travelers are frequent users of the expressways near their homes. The money collection process on some highways has been reengineered by using smart cards that can be scanned. Lately, further improvement has been made. The smart ID cards can be read wirelessly from 30–40 feet, so cars do not have to stop. Fees are charged to travelers' accounts, which reduces travelers' waiting time by 90 percent and money processing cost by 80 percent. (See details in Chapter 6, page 268.)
    a. Identify the supply chain.
    b. Several new information technologies including smart cards are used in the process. Find information on how this is accomplished.

12. Discuss the problem of reverse logistics in EC. What kind of companies may suffer the most? (View some solutions offered by FedEx.)

13. Explain why UPS defines itself as a "technology company with trucks" rather than a "trucking company with technology."

14. Discuss the meaning of the word *intelligence* in the term *supply chain intelligence.*

15. It is said that supply chains are essentially "a series of linked suppliers and customers; every customer is in turn a supplier to the next downstream organization, until the ultimate end-user." Explain. Use a diagram to make your point.

16. Explain the bullwhip effect. In which type of business is it most likely to occur? How can the effect be controlled?

EXERCISES

1. Draw the supply chain of the Davis & Warshow plumbing parts business (Online File W8.6). Show the use of IT in various places of the chain.

2. Draw the supply chains of Warner-Lambert (Pfizer) and Dell Computer (see Online Minicase 8.1). What are the similarities? The differences?

3. Draw the supply chain of Lego (see additional description at *lego.com*). Include at least two countries.

4. Enter *supplychain.aberdeen.com* and observe its "online supply chain community." Most of the information there is free. Prepare an outline of the major resources available in the site.

5. Automated warehouses play a major role in B2C and mail order fulfillment. Find material on how they operate. (Use *google.com* and *findarticles.com* for more information.) Try to find information about Lands' End's warehouse.

6. Examine the functionalities of ERP software from SAP or other vendors.

7. *Kozmo.com* was a company that rented videos and delivered them to customers within 30 to 60 minutes. Find out what you can about why it failed. Was there a problem with the company's order-fulfillment promises? Were there any drawbacks in Kozmo's alliances with Starbucks and Amazon.com? Explain.

8. Read the opening case and answer the following:
    a. The company business is not to make the product, but "to sell the product." Explain this statement,
    b. Why was it necessary to use IT to support the change?
    c. Identify all the segments of the supply chain.
    d. Identity all supporting information systems in this case.

GROUP ASSIGNMENTS

1. Each group in the class will be assigned to a major ERP/SCM vendor such as SAP, PeopleSoft, Oracle, J.D. Edwards, etc. Members of the groups will investigate topics such as: (a) Web connections, (b) use of business intelligence tools, (c) relationship to CRM and to EC, (d) major capabilities, and (e) availability of ASP services by the specific vendor.

Each group will prepare a presentation for the class, trying to convince the class why the group's software is best for a local company known to the students (e.g., a supermarket chain).

2. Each team should investigate the order fulfillment process of an e-tailer, such as *amazon.com*, *staples.com*, or *landsend.com*. Contact the company, if necessary, and examine related business partnerships if they exist. Based on the content of this chapter, prepare a report with suggestions for how the company can improve its order ful-

fillment process. All the groups' findings will be discussed in class. Based on the class's findings, draw some conclusions about how order fulfillment can be improved.

3. FedEx, UPS, the U.S. Postal Service, and others are competing in the EC logistics market. Each team should examine one such company and investigate the services it provides. Contact the company, if necessary, and aggregate the findings into a report that will convince classmates or readers that the company in question is the best. (What are its best features?)

INTERNET EXERCISES

1. Enter *ups.com*. Examine some of the IT-supported customer services and tools provided by the company. Write a report on how UPS contributes to supply chain improvements.

2. Enter *supply-chain.org, cio.com, findarticles.com,* and *google.com* and search for recent information on supply chain management integration.

3. Enter *logic-tools.com*. Find information on the bullwhip effect and on the strategies and tools used to lessen the effect.

4. Enter *coca-colastore.com*. Examine the delivery and the return options available there.

5. The U.S. Post Office provides EC logistics. Examine its services and tracking systems at *uspsprioritymail.com*. What are the potential advantages for EC shippers?

6. Enter *brio.com* and identify Brio's solution to SCM integration as it relates to decision making for EC. View the demo.

7. Enter *rawmart.com* and find what information they provide that supports logistics. Also find what shipment services they provide online.

8. Visit *ups.com* and find its recent EC initiatives. Compare them with those of *fedex.com*. Then go to *onlinestore.ups.com* and simulate a purchase. Report your experiences.

9. Enter *efulfillmentservice.com*. Review the products you find there. How does the company organize the network? How is it related to companies such as FedEx? How does this company make money?

10. Enter *submitorder.com* and find out what they offer. Comment on the uniqueness of the services.

Minicase 1
Quantum Corporation Streamlined Its Supply Chain

Quantum Corporation (*quantum.com*) is a major U.S. manufacturer of hard-disk drives and other high-technology storage components. Quantum faced two key challenges in its manufacturing process.

The first challenge was streamlining its component supply process in order to reduce on-hand inventory. Quantum's traditional ordering process was labor-intensive, involving numerous phone calls and manual inventory checks. To ensure that production would not be interrupted, the process required high levels of inventory. Quantum needed a solution that would automate the ordering process to increase accuracy and efficiency, reduce needed inventory to 3 days' supply, and provide the company's purchasing agents with more time for non-transactional tasks.

Quantum's second challenge was to improve the quality of the components' data in its material requirements planning (MRP) system. Incomplete and inaccurate data caused delays in production. Quantum's solution of manually reviewing reports to identify errors was labor intensive and occurred too late; problems in production were experienced before the reports were even reviewed. Quantum needed a technology solution that would enable it to operate *proactively* to catch problems before they caused production delays.

The solution that Quantum chose to automate its component supply process was an interenterprise system that automatically e-mails reorders to suppliers. Initiated in 1999, the system uses an innovative event detection and notification solution from Categoric Software (*categoric.com*). It scans Quantum's databases twice daily, assessing material requirements from one application module against inventory levels tracked in another. Orders are automatically initiated and sent to suppliers as needed, allowing suppliers to make regular deliveries that match Quantum's production schedule. The system not only notifies suppliers of the quantity of components required in the immediate orders, but also gives the supplier a valuable window into the amount of inventory on hand and future weekly requirements.

The system also provided other improvements. It enabled Quantum to tap into multiple data sources to identify critical business events. To elevate data quality, Quantum implemented Categoric Alerts to proactively catch any data errors or omissions in its MRP database. The systems' notifications are now sent whenever any critical MRP data fall outside the existing operational parameters.

The system has produced the desired results. For example, the estimated value of the improved ordering process using the new system is millions of dollars in inventory reductions each year. The buyers have reduced transaction tasks and costs, and both Quantum and its buyers get a lot more information with a lot less work. Before the implementation of Categoric Alerts, Quantum's analysts would search massive reports for MRP data errors. Now that the new system is implemented, exceptions are identified as they occur. This new process has freed the analysts from the drudgery of scanning reports and has greatly increased employee satisfaction.

Data integrity of the MRP increased from 10 percent to almost 100 percent, and Quantum is now able to quickly respond to changing customer demand. The system paid for itself in the first year.

Sources: Compiled from an advertising supplement in *CIO Magazine* (November 1, 1999), from information at *categoric.com* (accessed May 28, 2000), and from *quantum.com* (accessed June 10, 2003).

Questions for Minicase 1

1. Identify the internal and external parts of the supply chain that were enhanced with the system.
2. Enter *categoric.com* and find information about Categoric Alerts. Describe the capability of the product.
3. Explain how purchasing was improved.
4. Describe how Quantum's customers are being better served now.
5. Identify the EC solutions used in this case.

Minicase 2
Green Mountain Coffee Roasters Integrates Electronic Commerce and Supply Chain Management

Green Mountain Coffee Roasters (GMCR) (*gmcr.com*), a medium-sized distributor of quality coffee in the United States, experienced a high growth rate in recent years (from $34 million in 1996 to about $100 million in 2002). Sales are made through over 5,000 wholesalers and re-sellers, including supermarkets, restaurants, and airlines. In addition, mail-order shipments are made to over 40,000 loyal individual customers.

The rapid expansion of the business made it necessary to provide all employees access to the latest data so they could make better decisions regarding demand forecast, inventory management, and profitability analysis. To meet this need the company decided to install an ERP software.

In 1997, GMCR replaced its custom legacy information system with an ERP from PeopleSoft. The ERP includes functional modules such as production and inventory control, financial management, and human resources management. GMCR decided in 1998 to hook the ERP to the Internet for the following reasons:

- The company expected to double its online sales to individual customers. This was going to be done by displaying the culture and image of the company, allowing customers to learn more about coffee, and creating a "GMCR coffee community."
- The existing coffee tours and coffee club were well adapted to the Internet.
- The company estimated that at least 30 percent of its 5,000 business partners prefer to do business online.
- The company needed a better mechanism for CRM and PRM. The company wanted to get quick feedback, be able to solve customer and partners' problems quickly, and provide an efficient and easy order-taking facility.

The integration of the Web with ERP provided the following capabilities:

- Many of the business customers are small proprietor-managed shops. They are busy during the day, so they prefer to place orders in the evenings when GMCR's call center is closed.
- The customers like to know, immediately, if a product is in stock and when it will be shipped.

- Customers want to see their order histories, including summaries such as a most-frequently ordered product list.
- Customers want to track the status of their orders.

All of the above capabilities can be done by customers themselves, any time and from anywhere. In addition, the system can support the requests of GMCR's sales force for instant information about customers, inventory levels, prices, competition, overnight delivery services, and so forth.

PeopleSoft's eStore, an Internet storefront that is tightly integrated with the ERP suite (from order fulfillment to the rest of the supply chain management), was implemented in 1999. GMCR benefited not only from improved customer service and efficient online marketing, but also from providing access to the latest data to all employees. Some of the results so far: Forecasts have improved, inventory is minimized (using the just-in-time concept), and profitability analysis by product and/or customer is done in minutes.

Sources: Condensed from customer success stories at *peoplesoft.com* (January 2000); from *gmcr.com* (December 2000); from *Business Wire* (August 22, 2002, March 20, 2003, and May 6, 2003).

Questions for Minicase 2

1. Enter *gmcr.com* and identify the major customer-related activities. How are such activities supported by information technology?
2. Coffee club members make up about 90 percent of all the company's direct mail business. Why? (Check the Web site.)
3. How can the ERP system improve GMCR's inventory system?
4. It is said that "Internet sales data must be taken into account by enterprise planning, forecast demand, and profitability studies." Explain why.
5. It is said that "Because the customer's account and pricing information are linked to the order, accurate invoicing will flow automatically from the Internet transaction." Explain, and relate to the concept of the supply chain.

Virtual Company Assignment
Integrated Restaurant Software

You've reached the halfway point in your internship at The Wireless Cafe (TWC), and you feel pretty confident you understand the processes at the front of the house and the back of the house.

You had just read about ERP systems when Jeremy mentioned to you the problems he has getting information from the point-of-sale (POS) systems to his inventory, financial, and kitchen management systems. You are excited about the possibility of applying some ERP principles to TWC, and so you suggest to Jeremy an investigation of integrated restaurant applications.

Instructions

1. Review the capabilities of restaurant management software such as RestaurantPlus (*restaurantplus.com/*), Micros (*micros.com/*), NextPOS (*nextpos.com/*), Aloha (*alohapos.com*), or others you can find on the Web.

2. Describe some similarities and differences between the systems you reviewed in Question 1 and the ERP systems you read about in this chapter.

3. Many restaurants establish a relationship with a single restaurant purveyor (Sysco, for example) to provide nearly everything the restaurant needs for daily operations. What are the issues in this type of relationship in light of SCM?

REFERENCES

Adamson, J., "E-Procurement Comes of Age," *Proceedings, E-Commerce for Transition Economy*, Geneva, June 2001.

ASCET, "From Supply Chain to Collaborative Network: Case Studies in the Food Industry," white paper, April 15, 2000, *ascet.com/documents.asp?grID=134&d_ID=266#* (accessed June 2003).

Bayles, D. L., *E-Commerce Logistics and Fulfillment*. Upper Saddle River, NJ: Prentice Hall, 2001.

Bresnahan, J., "The Incredible Journey," CIO.com, August 15, 1998, *cio.com/archive/enterprise/081598_jour.html* (accessed June 2003).

Business Wire, August 22, 2002.

Business Wire, March 20, 2003.

Business Wire, May 6, 2003.

Caldwell, B., "Taming the Beast," *Information Week*, March 10, 1997.

Caldwell, B., and T. Stein, "Beyond ERP: New IT Agenda," *Information Week*, November 30, 1998, *ChevronTexaco.com* (accessed May 2003).

CIO.com, "Supply Chain Integration: The Name of the Game Is Collaboration," Special Advertising Supplement, *CIO Magazine*, November 1, 1999, *cio.com/sponsors/110199_supplychain_1.html* (accessed June 2003).

Collett, S., "SAP: Whirlpool's Rush to Go Live Led to Shipping Snafus," *Computer World*, November 4, 1999, *computerworld.com/cwi/story/0,1199,NAV47_STO29365,00.html* (accessed June 2003).

Conlin, R., "Toysrus.com Slapped with Class Action Lawsuit," *E-Commerce Times*, January 12, 2000, available at *crmdaily.com/perl/story/2190.html* (accessed June 2003).

Damsguard, L., and J. Horluck, "Designing www.LEGO.com/shop: Business Issues and Concerns," case 500–0061, *European Case Clearing House*, 2000.

Davenport, T. H., *Mission Critical: Realizing the Promise of Enterprise Systems*. Cambridge, MA: Harvard Business School Press, 2000.

Donovan, R. M., "Supply Chain Management: Cracking the Bull-whip Effect," *Material Handling Management*, Director Issue, 2002/2003.

Drickhamer, D., "Value-Chain Management Moves from Dream to Reality," *Industry Week*, April 1, 2002, *iwvaluechain.com/Features/articles.asp?ArticleId=1217* (accessed June 2003).

El Sawy, D. A., *Redesigning Enterprise Processes for e-Business*. New York: McGraw-Hill, 2001.

Epner, S., "The Search for a Supply Team," *Industrial Distribution*, December 1999.

FedEx, "BikeWorld Goes Global Using FedEx Technologies and Shipping," *FedEx Case Study*, August 2000, *fedex.com/us/ebusiness/ecommerce/bikeworld.pdf?link=4* (accessed June 2003).

Gibbons-Paul, L., "Suspicious Minds," *CIO.com*, January 15, 2003, *cio.com/archive/011503/minds.html* (accessed June 2003).

Hagel, J., III, *Out of the Box*. Boston: Harvard Business School Press, 2002.

Handfield, R. B., and E. L. Nichols, Jr., *Introduction to Supply Chain Management*. Upper Saddle River, NJ: Prentice-Hall, 1999.

Handfield, R. B., et al., *Supply Chain Redesign: Transforming Supply Chains into Integrated Value Systems*, Upper Saddle River, NJ: Financial Times/ Prentice Hall, 2002.

Harrison, T. P., "Global Supply Chain Design," *Information Systems Frontiers*, Oct.–Dec., 2001.

Hill, K., "Next Big Thing for ERP Vendors?" *CRM Daily*, February 19, 2003.

Hugos, M. H., *Essentials of Supply Chain Management*. New York: John Wiley & Sons, 2002.

Jacobs, F. R., and D. C. Whybark, *Why ERP?* Boston: McGraw-Hill, 2000.

James, D., and M. L. Wolf, "A Second Wind for ERP," *McKinsey Quarterly*, No. 2, 2000.

Johnston, R. B., et al., "An Emerging Vision of the Internet-Enabled Supply Chain Electronic Commerce," *International Journal of E-Commerce*, Summer 2000.

Kalakota, R., and M. Robinson, *eBusiness 2.2.* Boston, MA: Addison-Wesley, 2001.

Kaplan, P. J., *F'd Companies: Spectacular Dot-com Flameouts*. New York: Simon & Schuster, 2002.

Keskinocak, P., and S. Tayur, "Quantitative Analysis for Internet-Enabled Supply Chains," *Interfaces*, March–April 2001.

Koch, C. et al., "The ABCs of ERP," *CIO Magazine* (cio.com), December 22, 1999.

Kumar K., ed., "Technology for Supply Chain Management," special issue, *Communications of the ACM*, June 2001.

Latamore, G. B., "Using ERP Data to Get Closer to Customers," *APICS*, Sept. 2000.

Linthicum, D. S., *Enterprise Application Integration*. Boston: Addison-Wesley, 1999.

littlewoods.co.uk (accessed March 2003).

Logistics Management and Distribution Report, October 1998 and November 1999.

Lucas, M. E., and R. Bishop, *ERP for Dummies*. Greensboro, NC: Resource Publication, October 2001.

microstrategy.com, "Customers' Success Stories" (accessed January 2000).

Miodonski, B., "Davis & Warshow Hit 75 Running," *Supply House Times*, July 2000.

Mitchell, P., "E-Procurement Systems: Beyond Indirect Procurement," *Proceedings, E-Commerce for Transition Economy*, Geneva, June 2000.

Morgan Stanley, CIO Survey Series: Release 2.7, October 2, 2001, *ksg.harvard.edu/iip/seminars/PhillipsCIOSurvey.pdf* (accessed June 2003).

Morgan Stanley, CIO Survey Series: Release 3.0, February 11, 2002, *saugatech.com/STPerspectives/Morgan%20Stanley%20CIO%20Survey%20-%20Release%203.0.pdf* (accessed June 2003).

Murphy, K. E., and S. J. Simon, "Intangible Benefits Valuation in ERP Projects," *Information Systems Journal*, Vol. 12, October 2002.

Nelson, D., "John Deere Optimizes Operations with Supply Chain Efforts," *Journal of Organizational Excellence*, Spring 2002.

O'Brien, K., "Value-Chain Report—Error Proofing Improves Supply Chain Reliability, *Industryweek.com*, January 7, 2002, *iwvaluechain.com/Columns/columns.asp?ColumnId=846* (accessed June 2003).

O'Leary, D. E., *Enterprise Resource Planning Systems*. London: Cambridge University Press, 2000.

Oliver, D., and C. Romm, "Justifying Enterprise Resource Planning Adoption," *Journal of Information Technology*, December 2002.

Palaniswamy, R., and T. G. Frank, "Enhancing Manufacturing Performance with ERP Systems: Five Case Studies," *Information System Management*, Summer 2000.

Palaniswamy, R., and T. G. Frank, "Oracle ERP and Network Computing Architecture," *Information Systems Management*, Spring 2002.

Paulson, L. D., "Cybex International Sees ERP as a Huge Investment with Returns to Match," *Computer.org*, 2000, *computer.org/itpro/Sept_Oct/trends/cybex.htm* (accessed June 2003).

Peoplesoft.com, "Cybex Brings Fitness to the Web with PeopleSoft eStore," *peoplesoft.com/corp/en/products/mid/case_studies/cybex.jsp* (accessed June 2003).

Poirier, C. C., and M. J. Bauer, *E-supply Chain: Using the Internet to Revolutionize Your Business*. San-Francisco, CA: Berrett-Koehler, 2000.

Porter, M. E., *Competitive Advantage: Creating and Sustaining Superior Performance*. New York: Free Press, 1985.

Ragowsky, A., and T. M. Somers, eds., "Enterprise Resource Planning," a special issue, *Journal of Management Information Systems*, Summer 2002.

Reddy, R., "Taming the Bullwhip Effect," *Intelligent Enterprise*, June 13, 2001.

Rigney, P., "Eliminate Fulfillment Problems," *e-Business Advisor*, March 2000.

Robb, D., "The Virtual Enterprise: How Companies Use Technology to Stay in Control of A Virtual Supply Chain," *Information Strategy*, Summer 2003.

Russom, P., "Increasing Manufacturing Performance Through Supply Chain Intelligence," *DM Review*, September 2000.

Sandoe, K. et al., *Enterprise Integration*. New York: Wiley, 2001.

Segev, A., and J. Gebauer, "B2B Procurement and Marketplace Transformation," *Information Technology and Management*, April–June 2001.

Selland, C., "Extending E-Business to ERP," *E-Business Advisor*, January 1999a.

Selland, C., "The Key to E-Business: Integrating the Enterprise," *E-Business Advisor*, October 1999b.

Shain, F., and P. Robinson, "Flow Coordination and the Information Sharing in Supply Chains," *Decision Sciences*, Fall 2002.

Shecterle, B., "Managing and Extending Supplier Relationships," *People Talk*, April–June 2003, *peoplesoft.com.au/corp/en/peopletalkonline/april_2003/sidebar2.jsp* (accessed June 2003).

Sheikh, K., *Manufacturing Resource Planning (MRP II)*. New York: McGraw Hill, 2002.

Siau, K., and J. Messersmith, "Enabling Technologies for E-commerce and ERP Integration," *Quarterly Journal of Electronic Commerce*, January–March 2002.

Simatupang, T. M., and R. Sridharan, "The Collaborative Supply Chain, *International Journal of Logistics Management*, 13(1), 2002.

Soh, C. et al., "Is ERP a Universal Solution?" *Communications of the ACM*, April 2000.

Sterne, J., *Web Metrics: Proven Methods for Measuring Web Site Success*. New York: Wiley, 2002.

Stratman, J. K., and A. V. Roth, "ERP Competence Constructs," *Decision Sciences*, Fall 2002.

Stoll, R., "How We Built LEGO.com," *Practical Internet*, March. 2003.

Sullivan, M. et al., "Case Studies: Digital D-Overs," *Forbes.com*, October 7, 2002, *forbes.com/best/2002/1007/002.html* (accessed June 2003).

Trager, L., "Not So Many Happy Returns," *Interactive Week*, March 20, 2000.

Turban, E. et al., *Electronic Commerce. A Managerial Perspective*, 3/e. Upper Saddle River, NJ: Prentice-Hall, 2004.

Vakharia, J., ed., "E-business and Supply Chain Management," special issue, *Decision Sciences*, Fall 2002.

Varley, S., "E-Procurement—Beyond the First Wave" (*wmrc.com*), *Proceedings, E-Commerce for Transition Economy*, Geneva, June 2000.

Viswanadham, N., "The Past, Present and Future of Supply Chain Automation," *IEEE Robotics and Automation Magazine*, June 2002.

Willcocks, L. P., and R. Sykes, "The Role of the CIO and IT Function in ERP," *Communications of the ACM*, April 2000.

Worthen, B., "Drilling for Every Drop of Value," *CIO Management*, June 1, 2002.

Yao, D. D. et al., "Extended Enterprise Supply–Chain Management at IBM," *Interfaces*, January–February 2000.

PART III
Organizational Applications

7. Transaction Processing, Functional Applications, CRM, and Integration
8. Supply Chain Management and Enterprise Resource Planning
▶ 9. IT Planning and Business Process Redesign

CHAPTER

9

IT Planning and Business Process Redesign

9.1
IT Planning—A Critical Issue for Organizations

9.2
Strategic IT Planning

9.3
Information Requirements Analysis, Resource Allocation, Project Planning

9.4
Planning IT Architectures

9.5
Some Issues in IT Planning

9.6
Planning for Web-based Systems and E-Commerce

9.7
Business Process Redesign

9.8
The Role of IT in Business Process Redesign

9.9
Restructuring Processes and Organizations

9.10
Organization Transformation and Change Management

LEARNING OBJECTIVES

After studying this chapter, you will be able to:

1. Discuss the importance, evaluation, and approaches to IT planning.

2. Explain the four-stage model of information systems planning, and discuss the importance of aligning information systems plans with business plans.

3. Describe several different methodologies for conducting strategic information systems planning.

4. Describe information requirement analysis, project payoff and portfolios, resource allocation, and project planning.

5. Identify the different types of information technology architectures and outline the processes necessary to establish an information architecture.

6. Discuss the major issues addressed by information systems planning.

7. Distinguish the major Web-related IT planning issues and understand application portfolio selection.

8. Describe the need for business process redesign and the methodologies for doing it.

9. Explain the IT support for processes redesign and BPR, and describe redesign efforts, successes, and failures.

10. Describe organizational transformation and change management related to business process redesign.

HOW TRUSERV PLANNED ITS INFORMATION TECHNOLOGY

 THE PROBLEM

TruServ Corp. (*truserv.com*) was created in 1997 by the merger of Cotter & Co. and Servistar Corp. TruServ, one of the largest hardware suppliers in the United States, has annual wholesale sales of about $5 billion, which supports sales of some $15 billion retail. A major challenge was to merge the information systems of the two companies. The two systems were completely different, so their integration was a major problem for TruServ.

 THE SOLUTION

To do the integration, Paul Lemerise, CIO of TruServ, relied on a *strategic IT plan*. Lemerise turned first to Ernst & Young, a major CPA/IT consultant with which he had worked before on external auditing. He created a planning team that included the consultants and executives from the two merging companies. Lemerise did not include IT executives because he wanted strong input from the business side. He felt that he and the consultants knew enough about IT to represent the interest of the IT managers.

The team decided to include both a short-term tactical plan and a long-term strategic plan. The short-term plan was aimed at supporting the immediate needs of TruServ. It ensured that projects such as the corporate intranet would be on track. It also established a help desk. The long-term plan examined such issues as e-procurement and other e-commerce applications.

The team examined the merger plans and the business plan of the new corporation. It conducted interviews with 30 top executives regarding business goals and technology wish lists. Of special importance were long meetings with the CEO, who got very excited about the possibilities the new system could offer, in particular, e-business.

Once the interviews were completed, Lemerise met with all the executives together, in an attempt to reach a consensus about the priorities of IT projects and the entire strategic plan. The formal IT strategic plan was completed in July 1997. It included all major initiatives for three years, such as the move to one common retail system, and delineated how the company would use the intranet and e-commerce. The topics ranged from the use of wireless technologies in the warehouses to collaboration with business partners.

 THE RESULTS

The plan has remained fluid. It has been reevaluated and updated with new business goals every six months since its inception. This flexibility has enabled TruServ to introduce new initiatives as needed. For example, in 2000 and 2001 the company embarked on several Web-based projects, including a Web-centric collaborative technology to streamline its supply chain and transportation networks. An e-commerce linkage with midmarket suppliers was announced in December 2000. TruServ decided not to plan for more than three years in the future ("anything beyond planning for three years often doesn't happen"), but every year the planning horizon is extended one year. The plan includes a return on investment (ROI) section, which takes into account such intangible items as improving communication with customers.

Sources: Condensed from Blodgett (1998) and from *truserv.com* (2001).

 LESSONS LEARNED FROM THIS CASE

The case of TruServ demonstrates the benefits of a formal IT plan, especially for large corporations. It also demonstrates that there are different types of plans (e.g., tactical and strategic), and that end users as well as the CEO must be involved in the planning.

One of the major concerns of organizations today is how to transform yesterday's organization into a successful one in the digital economy. Many times, before e-commerce is undertaken, processes such as procurement must be redesigned or reengineered. Therefore IT planning frequently involves planning to redesign business processes as well (see El Sawy, 2001).

This chapter first describes the evolution and issues of IT systems planning. Then it presents a four-stage model of information systems planning: strategic planning, requirements analysis, resource allocation, and project planning. Next, it discusses methodologies for operationalizing the model, with primary emphasis on the stages of strategic planning and requirements analysis. (Planning for developing individual applications is discussed in Chapter 14.) Moving to business process redesign and to organizational transformation, the chapter describes the value and method of redesign and BPR and how IT supports them. Finally, the chapter deals with transforming organizations into e-businesses and managing change.

9.1 IT PLANNING—A CRITICAL ISSUE FOR ORGANIZATIONS

IT planning is the organized planning of IT infrastructure and applications portfolios done at various levels of the organization. The topic of IT planning is very important for both planners and end users: End-users often do IT planning for their own units, and they also frequently participate in the corporate IT planning. Therefore end-users must understand the planning process. Corporate IT planning determines how the IT infrastructure will look. This in turn determines what applications end users can deploy. Thus the future of every unit in the organization could be impacted by the IT infrastructure.

Business Importance and Content

A survey of more than 500 IT executives, conducted in 2003 by *cio.com.*, revealed that *strategic thinking and planning* was the number-one concern for CIOs (*cio.com*, 2003). It was also among the top issues in 2000 and 2001. Why does strategic planning continuously rank high as an issue of concern among IT executives? Simply put, because IT has to work closely with an organization's business side to make sure the company stays competitive. Aligning the goals of the organization and the ability of IT to contribute to those goals can deliver great gains in productivity to the organization. According to Blodgett (1998), as the demands of an increasingly competitive workplace call for closer integration of IT goals and the business mission, strategic plans for the whole enterprise become more important. In addition, with advances in Web-based supply chain collaborations and integration of e-marketplaces with buyers, sellers, and service providers, a good business strategy involves an IT strategy that keeps in mind the internal customers as well as the external customers and vendors. Aligning IT with the business is a process rather than an event, and IT strategy should be based on adding value to the organization's activities.

The Evolution of IT Planning

During the early years of information technology, in the late 1950s and 1960s, developing new applications and then revising existing systems were the focal points for the first planning and control systems. Organizations adopted methodologies for developing systems, and they installed project management systems to assist with implementing new applications. These initial mechanisms addressed *operational* planning. As organizations became more sophisticated in their use of information systems, emphasis shifted to *managerial* planning, or resource-allocation control. In the 1990s, the role of IT evolved to helping organizations to reach their business goals and to create competitive advantage. Currently the particular focus of IT strategy is on how IT creates business value.

Typically, annual planning cycles are established to identify potentially beneficial IT services, to perform cost-benefit analyses, and to subject the list of potential projects to resource-allocation analysis. Often the entire process is conducted by an IT *steering committee* (see Chapter 15). The steering committee reviews the list of potential projects, approves the ones considered to be beneficial, and assigns them relative priorities. The approved projects are then mapped onto a development schedule, usually encompassing a one- to three-year time frame. This schedule becomes the basis for determining IT resources requirements such as long-range hardware, software, personnel, facilities, and financial requirements.

Some organizations extend this planning process by developing additional plans for longer time horizons. They have a *long-range IT plan,* sometimes referred to as the *strategic IT plan* (see Ward and Peppard, 2002, and Boar, 2000). This plan typically does not refer to specific projects; instead it sets the overall directions in terms of infrastructure and resource requirements for IT activities for five to ten years in the future.

The next level down is a *medium-term IT plan.* It identifies the **applications portfolio,** a list of major, approved IS projects that are consistent with the long-range plan. Since some of these projects will take more than a year to complete, and others will not start in the current year, this plan extends over several years.

The third level is a *tactical plan,* which has budgets and schedules for current-year projects and activities. In reality, because of the rapid pace of change in technology and the environment, short-term plans may include major items not anticipated in the other plans.

The planning process just described is currently practiced by many organizations. Specifics of the IT planning process, of course, vary among organizations. For example, not all organizations have a high-level IT steering committee. Project priorities may be determined by the IT director, by his or her superior, by company politics, or even on a first-come, first-served basis.

Executing IT Planning

IT planning is a lengthy and complex process, and it can be done by several alternative approaches.

IT PLANNING APPROACHES. In the IT planning process, organizations need to first determine whether the use of IT is to achieve a competitive advantage or to support an operational role. Earl (1989) identified five types of planning approaches in response to the changing focus and increasing maturity of the IT strategy process. The five different approaches, which are still valid, are:

- *Business-led approach.* The IT investment plan is defined on the basis of the current business strategy. This approach emphasizes that business strategy should lead IT strategy.
- *Method-driven approach.* The IS needs are identifed with the use of techniques and tools (often used or prescribed by consultants).
- *Technological approach.* Analytical modeling (e.g., computer-aided software engineering, CASE) and other tools are used to execute the IT plans.
- *Administrative approach.* The IT plan is established by the steering committee or management to implement an approved IS initiative.
- *Organizational approach.* The IT investment plan is derived from a business-consensus view of all stakeholders in the organization (management and end users) of how IT/IS fits the organization's overall business objectives.

Organizations may use one or more of these approaches, or some combination or variant of them. They may also use some formal model of planning.

A FOUR-STAGE MODEL OF IT PLANNING. Several models have been developed to facilitate IT planning (e.g., see Ward and Peppard, 2002; Cassidy, 1998; and Papp, 2001). Of special interest is Wetherbe's (1993) **four-stage model of planning.** The model (depicted in Figure 9.1) consists of four major activities—*strategic planning, requirements analysis, resource allocation,* and *project planning*—and it is valid today. The stages involve the following activities:

- *Strategic IT planning:* establishes the relationship between the overall organizational plan and the IT plan
- *Information requirements analysis:* identifies broad, organizational information requirements to establish a strategic information architecture that can be used to direct specific application development
- *Resource allocation:* allocates both IT application development resources and operational resources
- *Project planning:* develops a plan that outlines schedules and resource requirements for specific information systems projects

Most organizations engage in all four stages, but their involvement in the specific stages tends to be sporadic and prompted by problems as they occur, instead of reflecting a systematic, stage-by-stage process. The four-stage model can be expanded to include major activities and outputs of the four stages. The model moves from a high level of abstraction to a more concrete formulation

FIGURE 9.1 Basic four-stage model of IS planning.

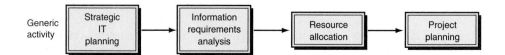

Generic activity → Strategic IT planning → Information requirements analysis → Resource allocation → Project planning

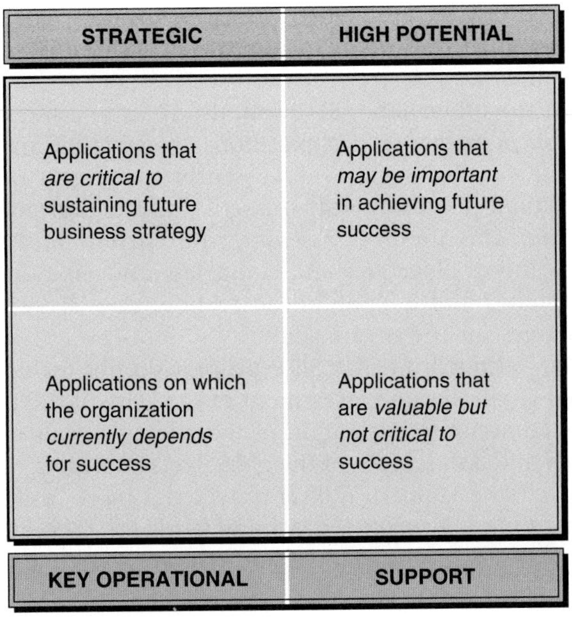

STRATEGIC	HIGH POTENTIAL
Applications that *are critical to* sustaining future business strategy	Applications that *may be important* in achieving future success
Applications on which the organization *currently depends* for success	Applications that are *valuable but not critical to* success
KEY OPERATIONAL	SUPPORT

FIGURE 9.2 Applications portfolio matrix. (*Sources:* Ward and Peppard, 2002, Figure 1.7, p. 42.)

of IT planning activities. Some useful methodologies for conducting each planning stage are discussed later in this chapter.

The four-stage planning model is the foundation for the development of a portfolio of applications that is both highly aligned with the corporate goals and has the ability to create an advantage over competitors. There is also a relationship between the four-stage planning model and the various versions of the system development life cycle (SDLC) described in Chapter 14. The four-stage planning model identifies projects and general resource requirements necessary to achieve organizational objectives. In Sections 9.2 and 9.3, we describe the four stages in more detail.

A major issue in IT planning is to determine what specific applications an organization needs to have during the period covered by the plan. For this purpose, organizations use an applications portfolio.

 APPLICATIONS PORTFOLIO.   An **applications portfolio** is the mix of computer applications that the information system department has installed or is developing on behalf of the company. Building upon the "McFarlan grid" (see Online File W3.2), the applications portfolio categorizes existing, planned, and potential information systems based on their business contributions. This 2 × 2 matrix (as shown in Figure 9.2), is a powerful IT planning tool which is very easy to grasp and understand.

Let's now begin at Stage 1 in the four-stage model of IT planning.

9.2 STAGE 1: STRATEGIC INFORMATION TECHNOLOGY PLANNING

The first stage of the IT planning model is **strategic information technology planning (SITP).** It includes several somewhat different types of activities. On the one hand, it refers to identifying the *applications portfolio* through which an organization will conduct its business. These applications make it possible for an organization to implement its business strategies in a competitive environment.

On the other hand, SITP can also refer to a process of searching for *strategic information systems (SIS)* applications that enable an organization to develop a competitive advantage, as discussed in Chapter 3, rather than just maintaining its position. To accomplish this goal, the organization must do some creative thinking: This involves assessing the current business environment and the organization's objectives and strategies, understanding the capabilities of existing systems, and looking ahead to how new IT systems could produce future advantages for the organization.

The output from the SITP process should include the following: a new or revised IT charter and assessment of the state of the information systems department; an accurate evaluation of the strategic goals and directions of the organization; and a statement of the objectives, strategies, and policies for the IT effort.

Ward and Peppard (2002) provided a more in-depth analysis on the strategic planning and proposed a framework for IT strategy formulation and planning. Details are found in Online File W9.1.

IT Alignment with Organizational Plans

Improving the planning process for information systems has long been one of the top concerns of information systems department management. The Society for Information Management (SIM) (*simnet.org,* 2002) found this to be the number-one issue in surveys of senior IT executives in 1997/1998. A survey of 420 organizations, conducted by NCC in 2003 (*ncc.co.uk,* 2003), found that keeping IT strategy aligned with business strategy was their number-one strategic concern.

Strategic information technology planning (SITP) must be aligned with overall organizational planning, whenever relevant, so that the IT unit and other organizational personnel are working toward the same goals, using their respective competencies (Chan, 2002; Pickering, 2000; Ward and Peppard, 2002). The primary task of IT planning is therefore to identify information systems applications that fit the objectives and priorities established by the organization. Figure 9.3 graphically illustrates the alignment of IS strategy, business strategy, and IT strategy and deployment. *IT at Work 9.1* demonstrates how alignment was done at Hewlett-Packard. For another example of alignment of business strategy and IT strategy, see Cale and Kanter (1998).

CHALLENGES FOR IT ALIGNMENT. Despite the theoretical importance of IT alignment, organizations continue to demonstrate limited actual alignment. People 3 Inc. (2003) reported that about 65 percent of companies have either a negative or neutral view of the ability of IT and business managers to work together in supporting corporate goals and objectives. Alignment is a complex management activity (Hackney et al., 2000), and its complexity increases in accordance with the increasing complexity of organizations. (For the IS complexity framework, see Hackney et al., 1999, and Hackney et al., 2000.) A study conducted by Chan (2002) also found that informal organizational structure results in better IT alignment and performance. (For a listing of the fundamentals assumptions upon which the SITP process is grounded, and the challenges to those assumptions, see Online File W9.2 and Hackney et al., 2000.)

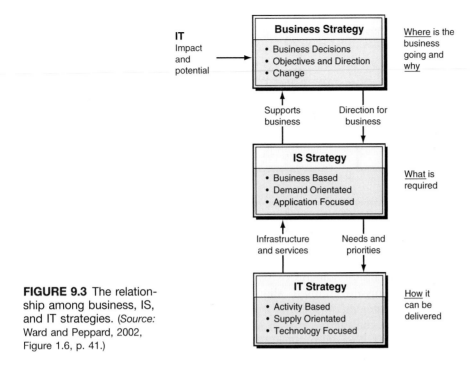

FIGURE 9.3 The relationship among business, IS, and IT strategies. (*Source:* Ward and Peppard, 2002, Figure 1.6, p. 41.)

IT at Work 9.1
HEWLETT-PACKARD ALIGNS BUSINESS AND IT STRATEGIES

Hewlett-Packard (*hp.com*) developed a planning methodology in which business process strategies and technologies are defined and aligned concurrently. This methodology was designed to allow the company to make process changes regardless of the limitations of the existing technology, and it gives visibility to the impacts that new technologies and processes have on each other.

In the past, Hewlett-Packard had used a sequential process. First, it defined the business strategy and the operations and supporting strategies, including technologies. Then, all these functions were aligned and replanned, taking into consideration the technologies available. In the new methodology, the planning is performed for all areas *concurrently*. Furthermore, the entire approach is complemented by a strong focus on teamwork, specialized and objective-driven functional areas and business units, and a commitment to quality and customer satisfaction. The approach links strategy and action. The business alignment framework takes into account the necessary process changes resulting from changes in the business environment, as well as potential technological developments. But, because major changes may result in a change in value systems as well as culture and team structures of the organization, H-P includes these factors within the planning methodology.

Target processes, technologies, and standards drive the selection of potential solutions. The participative management approach ensures effective implementation. According to the framework, business processes and information requirements are defined in parallel with technology enablers and models, which are then linked throughout the alignment process. Adjustments and refinements are made continuously.

Sources: Compiled from Feurer et al. (2000) and from *hp.com* (2001).

For Further Exploration: Why is concurrent planning superior? What communication and collaboration support is needed?

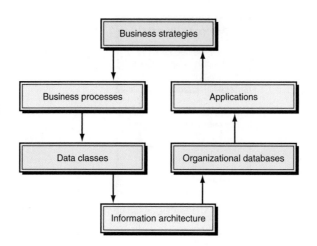

FIGURE 9.4 Business
systems planning (BSP)
approach. (*Source:* Derived
from *Business Systems
Planning—Information
Systems Planning Guide,*
Application Manual GE20-
0527-3, 3rd ed., IBM
Corporation, July 1981.
Courtesy of the International
Business Machines
Corporation.)

Tools and Methodologies of IT Planning

Several tools and methodologies exist to facilitate IT planning. These methods are used to help organizations to align their business IT/IS strategies with the organizational strategies, to identify opportunities to utilize IT for competitive advantage, and to analyze internal processes. Most of these methodologies start with some investigation of strategy that checks the industry, competition, and competitiveness, and relates them to technology (*alignment*). Others help create and justify new uses of IT (*impact*). Ward and Peppard (2002) further categorized these methods with respect to their nature (see Online File W9.3). In the next section, we look briefly at some of these methodologies.

THE BUSINESS SYSTEMS PLANNING (BSP) MODEL. The **business systems planning (BSP) model** was developed by IBM, and it has influenced other planning efforts such as Andersen Consulting's (now Accenture's) *method/1* and Martin and Finkelstein's *information engineering* (Martin and Finkelstein, 1981). BSP is a top-down approach that starts with business strategies. It deals with two main building blocks—*business processes* and *data classes*—which become the basis of an information architecture. From this architecture, planners can define organizational databases and identify applications that support business strategies, as illustrated in Figure 9.4. BSP relies heavily on the use of metrics in the analysis of processes and data, with the ultimate goal of developing the information architecture. (For details see Business Systems Planning, 1981, and Online File W9.4.)

THE STAGES OF IT GROWTH MODEL. Nolan (1979) indicated that organizations go through six **stages of IT growth** (called "IS growth" at that time). *A Closer Look 9.1* describes these six stages. In each stage, four processes are active to varying degrees. These are the applications portfolio, users' role and awareness, IT resources, and management planning and control techniques. The *y* axis in the figure in *A Closer Look 9.1* refers to IT expenditures. Note that the growth *rate* of IT expenses is low during data administration, medium during initiation and maturity, and high during expansion (contagion) and integration. In addition to serving as a guide for expenditure, the model helps in determining the seriousness of problems. (For more on Nolan's stages of IT growth, see Online File W9.5.)

A CLOSER LOOK
9.1 NOLAN'S SIX STAGES OF IT GROWTH MODEL

The six stages of IT growth (see the figure below) are:

1. *Initiation.* When computers are initially introduced to the organization, batch processing is used to automate clerical operations in order to achieve cost reduction. There is an operational systems focus, general lack of management interest, and a centralized information systems department (ISD).

2. *Expansion (Contagion).* Centralized rapid growth takes place as users demand more applications based on high expectations of benefits. There is a move to online systems as ISD tries to satisfy all user demands and little, if any, control. IT expenses increase rapidly.

3. *Control.* In response to management concern about cost versus benefits, systems projects are expected to show a return, plans are produced, and methodologies/ standards are enforced. The control stage often produces a backlog of applications and dissatisfied users. Planning and controls are introduced.

4. *Integration.* There is considerable expenditure on integrating (via telecommunications and databases)

existing systems. User accountability for systems is established, and ISD provides a service to users, not just solutions to problems. At this time there is a transition in computer use and an approach from data processing to information and knowledge processing (transition between the two curves).

5. *Data administration.* Information requirements rather than processing drive the applications portfolio, and information is shared within the organization. Database capability is exploited as users understand the value of the information and are willing to share it.

6. *Maturity.* The planning and development of IT in the organization are closely coordinated with business development. Corporatewide systems are in place. The ISD and the users share accountability regarding the allocation of computing resources. IT has truly become a strategic partner.

Source: Compiled from R. L. Nolan, "Managing the Crises in Data Processing," *Harvard Business Review,* March–April 1979. Reprinted with permission of the *Harvard Business Review.*

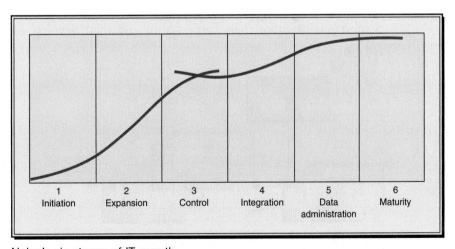

Nolan's six stages of IT growth.

CRITICAL SUCCESS FACTORS. Critical success factors (CSFs) are those few things that must go right in order to ensure the organization's survival and success. The *CSF approach* to IT planning was developed to help identify the information needs of managers. The fundamental assumption is that in every organization there are three to six key factors that, if done well, will result in the organization's success. Therefore organizations should continuously measure performance in these areas, taking corrective action whenever necessary. CSFs also exist in business units, departments, and other organizational units.

Critical success factors vary by broad industry categories—manufacturing, service, or government—and by specific industries within these categories. For organizations in the same industry, CSFs will vary depending on whether the firms are market leaders or weaker competitors, where they are located, and what competitive strategies they follow. Environmental issues, such as the degree of regulation or amount of technology used, influence CSFs. In addition, CSFs change over time based on temporary conditions, such as high interest rates or long-term trends.

IT planners identify CSFs by interviewing managers in an initial session, and then refine these CSFs in one or two additional sessions. Sample questions asked in the CSF approach are:

● What objectives are central to your organization?
● What are the critical factors that are essential to meeting these objectives?
● What decisions or actions are key to these critical factors?
● What variables underlie these decisions, and how are they measured?
● What information systems can supply these measures?

The first step following the interviews is to determine the organizational objectives for which the manager is responsible, and then the factors that are critical to attaining these objectives. The second step is to select a small number of CSFs. Then, one needs to determine the information requirements for those CSFs and measure to see whether the CSFs are met. If they are not met it is necessary to build appropriate applications (see Figure 9.5).

The critical success factors approach encourages managers to identify what is most important to their performance and then develop good indicators of

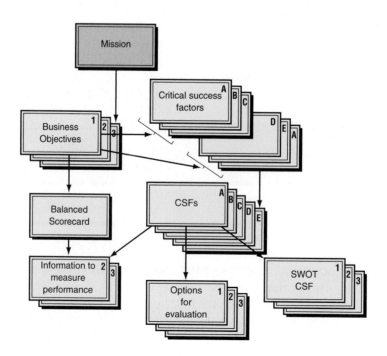

FIGURE 9.5 Critical success factors—basic processes. (*Source:* Ward and Peppard, 2002, Figure 4.7, p. 211.)

performance in these areas. Conducting interviews with all key people makes it less likely that key items will be overlooked. On the other hand, the emphasis on critical factors avoids the problem of collecting too much data, or including some data just because they are easy to collect.

SCENARIO PLANNING. **Scenario planning** is a methodology in which planners first create several scenarios, then a team compiles as many as possible future events that may influence the outcome of each scenario. This approach is used in planning situations that involve much uncertainty, like that of IT in general and e-commerce in particular. With the rapid changes of technologies and business environment, Stauffer (2002) emphasized the need for scenario planning. Five reasons to do scenario planning are: (1) to ensure that you are not focusing on catastrophe to the exclusion of opportunity, (2) to help you allocate resources more prudently, (3) to preserve your options, (4) to ensure that you are not still "fighting the last war," and (5) to give you the opportunity to rehearse testing and training of people to go through the process. Scenario planning follows a rigorous process; the essential steps are summarized in Table 9.1.

Scenario planning has been widely used by major corporations to facilitate IT planning (e.g., *ncri.com* and *gbn.com*). It also has been particularly important to e-commerce planning. For instance, creating customer scenarios helps the company better fit the products and services into the real lives of the customers, resulting in sales expansion and customer loyalty. Seybold (2001) described three cases (National Semiconductor, Tesco, Buzzsaw.com) that used customer scenarios to strengthen customer relationships, to guide business strategy, and to deliver business value.

Although EC proliferation would certainly allow any combination or variation of business scenarios, each company has to select the most appropriate model for its needs. The use of this model can help EC planners to determine the EC initiatives that best fit their organization. (See Minicase 2 for an example of implementation.)

TABLE 9.1 Essential Steps of Scenario Planning

- Determine the scope and time frame of the scenario you are fleshing out.
- Identify the current assumptions and mental models of individuals who influence these decisions.
- Create a manageable number of divergent, yet plausible, scenarios. Spell out the underlying assumptions of how each of these imagined futures might evolve.
- Test the impact of key variables in each scenario.
- Develop action plans based on either (a) the solutions that play most robustly across scenarios, or (b) the most desirable outcome toward which a company can direct its efforts.
- Monitor events as they unfold to test the corporate direction; be prepared to modify it as required.

The educational experience that results from this process includes:

- Stretching your mind beyond the groupthink that can slowly and imperceptibly produce a sameness of minds among top team members in any organization.
- Learning the ways in which seemingly remote potential developments may have repercussions that hit close to home.
- Learning how you and your colleagues might respond under both adverse and favorable circumstances.

Source: Compiled from Stauffer (2002).

9.3 STAGES 2–4: INFORMATION REQUIREMENTS ANALYSIS, RESOURCE ALLOCATION, AND PROJECT PLANNING

The next three stages of the four-stage planning model are interrelated; they start with information requirements.

Information Requirements Analysis: Stage 2 of the 4-Stage Model

The second stage of the model is the **information requirements analysis,** which is an analysis of the information needs of users and how that information relates to their work. The goal of this second stage is to ensure that the various information systems, databases, and networks can be integrated to support the requirements identified in stage 1 to enable decision making.

In the first step of information requirements analysis, IT planners assess what information is needed to support current and projected decision making and operations in the organization. This is different from the detailed information requirements analysis associated with developing *individual* application systems (i.e., identifying required outputs and the inputs necessary to generate them, which we describe in Chapter 14). Rather, the stage 2 information requirements analysis is at a more comprehensive level of analysis. It encompasses infrastructures such as the data needed in a large number of applications (e.g., in a data warehouse or a data center) for the whole organization. Similarly, requirements for the intranet, extranet, and corporate part are established.

There are several alternative approaches for conducting the requirements analysis. One of them is presented as a five-step model in Table 9.2. Also, some of the methods described in Chapter 14, such as JAD, can be used here.

The results of the requirements analysis exercise are threefold: It identifies high-payoff information categories, it provides a basis for the architecture of IT, and it guides in resource allocation.

IDENTIFYING HIGH PAYOFFS. To determine which IT projects will produce the highest organizational payoff, the organization can identify categories with high

---

TABLE 9.2 The Five-Step Requirements-Analysis Model

Step 1: Define underlying organizational subsystems. The first step is to identify the underlying organizational processes, such as order fulfillment or product analysis.

Step 2: Develop a subsystem matrix. The next phase is to relate specific managers to organizational processes. This relationship can be represented by a matrix. The matrix is developed by reviewing the major decision responsibilities of each middle-to-top manager and relating them to specific processes.

Step 3: Define and evaluate information requirements for organizational subsystems. In this phase, managers with major decision-making responsibility for each process are interviewed in groups by information analysts in order to obtain the information requirements of each organizational process.

Step 4: Define major information categories and map interview results into them. The process of defining information categories is similar to the process of defining data items for individual application into entities and attributes.

Step 5: Develop an information/subsystem matrix. Mapping information categories against organizational subsystems creates an information-categories-by-organizational-process matrix. Information categories can be, for example, accounts receivable, customers' demographics, or products' warranties. In each cell of the matrix an important information category value is inserted.

importance-value scores, and should consider them first for feasibility. In order to identify high payoff, planners use a matrix that relates information categories to organizational processes. But this matrix does not indicate whether it is technically, economically, or operationally feasible to develop systems for each information category. The matrix merely indicates the relative importance of information. Feasibility studies and other project-related tasks must still be performed, as described in Chapter 14. This step requires substantial creativity (e.g., see Ruohonen and Higgins, 1998). In Section 9.6, we demonstrate how this is done for Web-based systems. An example of identifying high-payoff projects is provided at *IT at Work 9.2* (page 410).

PROVIDING AN ARCHITECTURE.   Clearly defining the intersection of information and processes helps an organization avoid separate, redundant information systems for different organizational processes. When an organization decides to improve information for one process, other processes that need such information can be taken into consideration. By completing the conceptual work first, an organization can identify information systems projects that offer the most benefit and lead to cohesive, integrated systems. The resulting systems are far better than the fragmented, piecemeal systems that must continually be reworked or abandoned because they do not mesh with the organization's general requirements. To develop such integrated systems requires systematic planning from the top down, rather than randomly from the bottom up, and this is done in the architecture phase. In Chapter 13, we describe how this has been done in the State of Iowa (see the opening case there).

GUIDANCE IN RESOURCE ALLOCATION.   Once high-payoff areas of IT have been identified it is reasonable to give those areas high priority when the organization allocates resources. Such an allocation is described next.

Resource Allocation: Stage 3 of the 4-Stage Model

Resource allocation, the third stage of the IT planning model, consists of developing the hardware, software, data communications and networks, facilities, personnel, and financial plans needed to execute the master development plan as defined in the requirements analysis. This stage provides the framework for technology and labor procurement, and it identifies the financial resources needed to provide appropriate service levels to users. The financial aspect will be discussed briefly here (with a more in-depth discussion in Chapter 13).

Resource allocation is a contentious process in most organizations because opportunities and requests for spending far exceed the available funds. (See the opening case in Chapter 13.) This can lead to intense, highly political competition among organizational units, which makes it difficult to objectively identify the most desirable investments.

Requests for funding approval from the steering committee fall into two categories. Some projects and infrastructure are necessary in order for the organization to stay in business. For example, it may be imperative to purchase or upgrade hardware if the network, or disk drives, or the processor on the main computer are approaching capacity limits. Obtaining approval for this type of spending is largely a matter of communicating the gravity of the problems to decision makers.

On the other hand, the IT planning process identifies an information architecture that usually requires additional funding for less critical items: new projects,

IT at Work 9.2
IDENTIFYING HIGH PAYOFF PROJECTS

Wing Fat Foods (WFF) is a wholesaler, delivering perishable and nonperishable foodstuffs, as well as hardware, kitchenware, and household goods, to restaurants, groceries, and similar businesses along the Atlantic Coast of the United States. WFF is famous for its quality and service, which is accomplished with a relatively low level of IT investment. WFF hopes that its additional IT investment will help it to sustain its edge over competitors.

In response to the need of identifying potential new IT projects, Peffers and Gengler (2003) proposed to WFF a new method, the *critical success chain (CSC) method,* for IT planning. The CSC method includes four steps:

Step 1: Pre-study preparation: Determine scope and participants and collect project idea stimuli. The analyst invited 25 IT users (6 senior managers, 11 middle managers, 5 journeyman employees, and 3 WFF customers) to participate in an in-depth interview. At the same time, she collected project ideas to serve as stimuli. For example, she asked each participant to describe the functionality of a system that would benefit WFF.

Step 2: Participant interviews: Elicit personal constructs from organization members. The analyst then conducted 25–50 minute interviews with each participant, showing the participant three system descriptions and asking them to rank the system attributes and explain their importance to the organization. A line of questions was asked until the participants suggested a concrete feature or attribute that would become part of the project idea. This line of questions was designed to produce specific ideas for features of the system, expected performance, and related organizational values or objectives. In this study, the analyst collected about 8 chains of suggestions per participant.

Step 3: Analysis: Aggregate personal constructs into CSC models. The analyst first clustered the interview statements into constructs and mapped the constructs into a matrix. She then clustered the chains using the Ward and Peppard strategic planning framework (found in *Online File W9.1*). Mapping each cluster into a CSC map, she represented the constructs as nodes and the links in the chains as lines connecting the nodes. The figure on page 411 depicts an organization-specific CSC model consisting of, from left to right, descriptions of desired system attributes, resulting expected performance outcomes (CSF), and associated organizational goals.

Step 4: Idea workshops: Elicit feasible strategic IT from technical and business experts and customers. The CSC maps were used by both IT professionals from within WFF and non-IT customers as a starting point for developing a portfolio of IT proposals. Provid-

(continues on page 411)

---

maintenance or upgrades of existing systems, and infrastructure to support these systems and future needs. Approval for projects in this category may become more difficult to obtain because the ISD is already receiving funding for mandatory projects.

After setting aside funds for the first category, the organization can use the remainder of the IT budget for projects related mainly to the improved information architecture. The organization can prioritize spending among items in the architecture developed by using information requirements analysis. In addition to formally allocating resources through budgeting decisions, an organization can use chargeback mechanisms to fund corporate-level projects. In a *chargeback system,* some or all of a system's cost is charged to users. In addition, management may encourage individual units to make their own decisions about IT expenses. Chapter 13 discusses chargeback, cost-benefit analysis, and other, more sophisticated analyses that can also be used to assess investments in individual IT projects as well as infrastructure.

Another major factor in resource allocation is the *outsourcing strategy* (Chapter 13). The more that is outsourced, the less capital investment and internal resources are needed.

ing the technical and business experts at WFF with the CSC maps, the workshop finally yielded 14 project ideas, including a decision support system for scheduling, routing, and loading trucks for delivery, as well as the support activities for existing systems, including training and updated equipment and maintenance support.

Sources: Compiled from Peffers and Gengler (2003).

For Further Exploration: Why is the method called the CS chain? Why is such a lengthy process, with so many participants, needed?

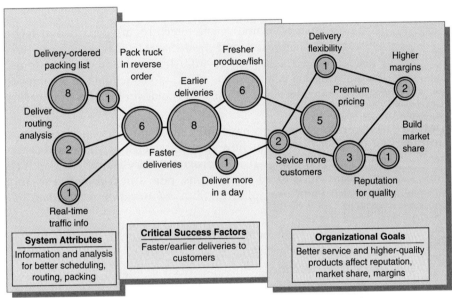

Critical success chain network map. (*Source:* Peffers and Gengler (2003).)

Project Planning: Stage 4 of the 4-Stage Model

The fourth and final stage of the model for IT planning is **project planning.** It provides an overall framework within which specific applications can be planned, scheduled, and controlled. Since this stage is associated with systems development, it will be covered in Chapter 14. Also, this stage depends on the outsourcing strategy. The more an organization outsources, the more vendor management and control will need to be included in project planning.

9.4 PLANNING INFORMATION TECHNOLOGY ARCHITECTURES

The term **information technology architecture** refers to the overall (high-level) structure of all information systems in an organization. This structure consists of applications for various managerial levels (operational control, management planning and control, and strategic planning) and applications oriented to various functional-operational activities (such as marketing, R&D, production, and distribution). The information architecture also includes infrastructure (e.g., the databases, supporting software, and networks needed to connect applications together). In the simplest view, an IT architecture consists of a description of the combination of hardware, software, data, personnel, and telecommunications elements within an organization, along with procedures to employ them. An information architecture for an organization should guide the long-range development as well as allow for responsiveness to diverse, short-range information systems demands. (The configuration of these architectures is discussed in Technology Guide 4.)

An **information architecture** is a high-level, logical plan of the information requirements and the structures or integration of information resources needed to meet those requirements. An information technology architecture specifies the technological and organizational infrastructure that physically implements an information architecture.

Three types of technology architectures are described in Technology Guide 4: *centralized, noncentralized,* and *client/server.* In this section we discuss the general considerations relating to IT infrastructure and provide some guidelines for choosing among achitecture options. We conclude the section with a look at the issue of reengineering *legacy systems* (holdover systems from earlier architectures).

IT Infrastructure Considerations

Different organizations have different IT infrastructure requirements. Broadbent et al. (1996) looked at how the characteristics and environments of organizations influenced their IT infrastructure. They identified several core *infrastructure services* provided in all of the firms, plus others provided by some of the firms. They also found the following four *infrastructure relationships* in a sample of 26 large firms:

1. *Industry.* Manufacturing firms use fewer IT infrastructure services than retail or financial firms.
2. *Market volatility.* Firms that need to change products quickly use more IT infrastructure services.
3. *Business unit synergy.* Firms that emphasize synergies (e.g., cross-selling) use more IT infrastructure services.
4. *Strategy and planning.* Firms that integrate IT and organizational planning, and track or monitor the achievement of strategic goals, use more IT infrastructure services.

Based on analysis of their data, Broadbent et al. developed a model of the relationship between firm context and IT infrastructure (shown in Online File W9.6). This model indicates that two general factors influence infrastructure levels: The first factor is *information intensity,* the extent to which products or processes incorporate information. The second factor is *strategic focus,* the level of emphasis on strategy and planning. Firms with higher levels of these two factors use more IT infrastructure services, and they have greater reach and range in their use of these services.

Choosing Among Architecture Options

A poorly organized IT architecture can disrupt a business by hindering or misdirecting information flows. Each organization—even within the same industry—has its own particular needs and preferences for information. Therefore each organization requires an IT architecture specifically designed and deployed for its use.

In today's computing environment, IT architectures are becoming increasingly complex, yet they still must be responsive to changing business needs. Actually, today's IT architecture is designed around *business processes* rather than around the traditional application hierarchy of the functional departments. These requirements call for tough decisions about a number of architectural issues. The choices among *centralized computing, distributed computing,* and *blended computing* architectures are discussed below.

IN FAVOR OF CENTRALIZED COMPUTING. Centralized computing has been the foundation of corporate computing for over 30 years. **Centralized computing** puts all processing and control authority within one (mainframe) computer to which all other computing devices respond.

There are a number of benefits of centralized computing: Centralized computing can exploit the economies of scale that arise whenever there are a large number of IT applications and users in an organization. It may be more cost-effective to have one large-scale computing resource that is used by many than it is to have many small-scale computing resources. The cost of a centralized facility can be divided among many users, usually reducing duplication of effort and more efficiently managing an operation (housing the computer, providing support services, etc.). Centralized approaches can also offer easier control from an enterprise perspective. If important corporate data are stored on a centralized computing platform, a company is able to impose strict physical access controls to protect the data. When data are spread throughout an organization, securing and preserving data becomes much more difficult (see Chapter 15).

However, with increasing use of *client/server* systems, the role of the mainframe computer has shifted toward a more collaborative relationship with other computing resources within an organization. A few proponents of PCs go so far as to claim that the mainframe is dead. Many experts, though, agree that the mainframe is likely to exist for many years, particularly as a repository for data that can be centrally maintained for enterprisewide use (the data center; see Technology Guide 3). Providing access to and analyzing very large quantities of data are uses for which mainframes are still very appropriate. This is especially important in banking, insurance, airlines, and large retailing. The Internet and intranets can be extremely useful in distributing information stored on mainframe (and smaller) computers.

IN FAVOR OF DISTRIBUTED COMPUTING. **Distributed computing** gives users direct control over their own computing. This approach argues that choices for computing are best handled at the point of the computing need—that individual needs are best met with individualized computing. The rise in popularity of PCs, with their decreasing costs and increasing performance, has led many organizations to embrace distributed computing. Applications data can be entered, verified, and maintained closer to their source.

Distributed computing can also offer a high degree of flexibility and desirable system redundancy. When an organization expands, it may be much easier and less expensive to add another local, distributed processor than to replace a centralized mainframe with an even larger mainframe. Also, a computer in a decentralized environment may be noticeably faster than a centralized computer very far away from a user.

Moreover, a malfunctioning distributed computer ordinarily does not prevent other distributed computers from working, especially if data are partially or fully duplicated around the system, such as in the case of Lotus Notes/Domino or some intranets. (In contrast, a centralized approach has a single point of failure—the central computer. When it goes down, no one computes.) Consider an organization that sells online; if its order processing system goes down for a day in the holiday season, it could lose hundreds of thousands of dollars in sales.

IN FAVOR OF BLENDING CENTRALIZED AND DISTRIBUTED COMPUTING. As noted earlier, computing does not have to be entirely centralized or entirely distributed—it can be a blending of the two models. Many distributed systems are based on client/server architecture. In some circumstances, the mainframe (centralized resource) is viewed as a kind of peripheral device for other (distributed) computing resources. The mainframe can be a large file server that offers the economies of scale and data control that are desirable in most organizations, and yet still allows processing and handling of local needs via distributed computing resources. *What* to distribute *where* (and what *not* to distribute) then become key issues.

INFORMATION ARCHITECTURES AND END-USER COMPUTING. Like an automobile, a personal computer gives its user great flexibility, power, and freedom. But just as the user of an automobile needs access to an infrastructure of highways, the user of a personal computer needs access to an infrastructure of databases and communication networks, including the Internet, a corporate portal, and intranets. Creating such an architecture for end-users invariably involves PC linkage issues.

There are five basic configurations of PCs for end users:

1. Centralized computing with the PC functioning as a "dumb terminal" (or sometimes "not-so-dumb," yet not smart)—the thin PCs.
2. A single-user PC that is not connected to any other device.
3. A single-user PC that is connected to other PCs or systems, using ad hoc telecommunications (such as dial-up telephone connections).
4. Workgroup PCs connected to each other in a small *peer-to-peer network* (see Technology Guide 4).
5. Distributed computing with many PCs fully connected by LANs via wireline or Wi-Fi.

End-user computing with interconnected desktop PCs or network computers appears inevitable. Given this inevitability, it is important that organizations maximize corporate business benefits and, at the same time, minimize risks and undue constraints on user initiative, business knowledge, and organizational unity. (For more on the development of end-user computing, see Chapter 14.)

THE IMPACT OF OUTSOURCING AND UTILITY COMPUTING. As the amount of IT that is outsourced increases, and with the development of utility computing (the purchase of computing services, much as one today purchases electricity and water services; see Chapters 2 and 14), the amount of infrastructure needed by organizations will decline. Theoretically, there will be no need even for a data center. The architecture then will be comprised of LANs and PCs, intranets, corporate portals, and extranets. While outsourcing is spreading rapidly, it is mostly *selected outsourcing* (Chapter 13), namely, only some of the IT operations are outsourced. However, within about 5 to 10 years the impact of both outsourcing and utility computing are expected to be significant.

Reengineering Legacy Systems

Holdovers of earlier architectures that are still in use after an organization migrates to a new architecture are described as **legacy systems.** These systems may continue in use even after an organization switches to an architecture that is different from, and possibly incompatible with, the architectures on which they are based. They may still be capable of meeting business needs, and so might not require any immediate changes. Or they may be in need of reengineering to meet some current business needs, requiring significant changes.

Each legacy system has to be examined on its own merits, and a judgment made regarding the current and future value of the system to the organization. This type of decision—to keep, improve, or replace—can present management with agonizing alternatives. On one hand, keeping a legacy system active offers stability and return on previous investments ("If it ain't broke, don't fix it"). On the other hand, increasing processing demands and high operational costs make replacement attractive if not imperative. Newer systems, however, may be more risky and less robust.

Reverse engineering is the process of examining systems to determine their present status, and to identify what changes are necessary to allow the system to meet current and future business needs. The results of this process can then guide the redesign and redevelopment of the system. Some reverse engineering tools, when applied to legacy systems, automatically generate up-to-date documentation. Other tools in this category help programmers convert code in older programs into a more efficient form.

Legacy systems are not just mainframe systems. A legacy system might consist of PC programs that need to be reengineered and "ported" to a mainframe, a process that is called *upsizing* the system. Or a legacy system might be a mainframe application that needs to reengineered and "rehosted" onto PCs, an example of *downsizing* a system. In each instance, a business is trying to effectively "rightsize" a legacy system to meet evolving business requirements. An important area is in the *integration* of legacy systems with enterprise systems (such as ERP, CRM, and KM) and with e-commerce systems.

Finally, organizations should reengineer legacy systems in concert with business process redesign (refer to the "retooling" discussion in Section 9.8). Changes to the computerized or automated side of a business should synchronize with changes in other business processes. While reengineering legacy systems might be justified solely on a cost or efficiency basis, significant business gains can also be made when this effort is a coordinated part of restructuring business processes to improve efficiency and effectiveness.

9.5 SOME ISSUES IN IT PLANNING

IT planning is a complex process. Of the many special topics in this category, we have elected to focus on IT planning in interorganizational and international systems. Information technology planning may get more complicated when several organizations are involved, as well as when we deal with multinational corporations. In this section, we also address the problems and challenges for IT planning.

Planning for Interorganizational Systems

Internal information systems of business partners must "talk" with each other effectively and do it efficiently. In Chapters 4 and 5, we introduced IT technologies such as EDI, e-mail, and extranets that facilitate communication and collaboration between companies. IT planning that involves several organizations may be complex. The problem is that some information systems may involve hundreds or even thousands of business partners. IT planners in such a case could use focus groups of customers, suppliers, and other business partners, especially during the strategic information planning as well as during the information requirements analysis.

Planning for project management of interorganization systems (IOSs) can be fairly complex. IT planners may create virtual planning teams that will work together on projects such as extranets or EDI. Such collaboration is especially important in strategic planning that involves infrastructure. Questions such as who is going to pay for what can become critical factors in cost/benefit analysis and justification of information systems applications.

A comprehensive study of global IT strategic planning was conducted by Curry and Ferguson (2000). In order to increase the success of such planning, they suggest that organizations reduce the planning horizon to two to three years (from three to five years) and that they increase the collaboration between the IT planners and end users.

Examples of joint planning for interorganizational systems can include using an extended supply chain approach and adopting the same enterprise software. If company A will use software from SAP and company B will use Oracle software, there could be additional expenses for connecting these softwares to each other. Web services (Chapters 2 and 15) may provide the solution for such an integration.

IT Planning for Multinational Corporations

Multinational corporations face a complex legal, political, and social environment, which complicates corporate IT planning. Therefore, many multinational companies prefer to decentralize their IT planning and operations, empowering their local IT managers. An illustrative example is shown in *IT at Work 9.3*. However, such a policy may be self-defeating since communication, coordination, and collaboration among decentralized business units may require large expenses. ExxonMobil Corporation, for example, was forced to centralize its IT operations because of such high expenditures (see Online File W9.7).

Problems for IT Planning

IT planning can be an expensive and time-consuming process. A study of five large-scale planning projects found that such projects may involve ten or more employees, on a half-time or full-time basis, for periods lasting from ten weeks to a year. The estimated costs of these projects ranged from $450,000 to $1.9 million. In addition, a survey reported by King (2000) disclosed that more than 50 percent of the companies surveyed were conducting IS planning using obsolete methodologies.

Teo and Ang (2001) emphasized the importance of understanding IT planning problems. They argued that these problems may result in wasted resources, lost opportunities, duplicated efforts, and incompatiable systems. They studied 138 companies and identified IT planning problems at the three phases of IS planning: the launching phase, the plan development phase, and the implementation phase. In all three phases, failing to get top management support for the IS planning was the most serious problem. Other major IS planning problems included: not having free communication flow and not being able to obtain sufficiently qualified personnel in the planning phase; ignoring business goals and failing to translate goals and strategies into action plans in the plan development phase;

IT at Work 9.3

IT PLANNING AT AN INTERNATIONAL LAW FIRM

Rouse & Co. International is a U.K.-based law firm with 15 offices worldwide. Kamran Hussain joined the firm in 1998 as the global head of IT operations and development. His first task was to look closely at office locations, in particular, those located in Asia, including Jakarta, Beijing, Hong Kong, Bangkok, and Vietnam.

At that time, Hussain's biggest challenge was to convince the company about good technology. Each office had its own culture that he had to adapt to. For example, the Chinese in the Beijing office are loyal to their local people; they had their own way of developing the regional office's strategy and did not want to integrate globally. The Jarkarta office, on the other hand, was more confident about integrating new technologies.

The law firm employs a wide range of professionals, including lawyers, patent and trademark attorneys, investigators, linguists, and researchers. With so many employees sharing information, it was important to get all offices connected. Since not all offices had the same level of IT sophistication, Hussain chose a Windows 2000 network running on TCP/IP, with a Watchguard firebox (a security appliance designed to provide mid-sized organizations with firewall and virtual private network functions). This network lets the company maintain the IT systems remotely, but allows Hussain to hire IT staff in each office locally, as local staff tend to have better insight into the local information. The networking project now helps the firm manage its knowledge management strategy, allows the company to save resources, and enables it to group the database by countries, as the criteria set by the client tend to be country-specific.

Source: Condensed from Zakaria (2002).

For Further Exploration: Why was it important to integrate the systems from different countries? Apart from cultural differences, what are other challenges for IT planning in an international firm?

neglecting to adjust the IS plan to reflect major environmental changes; and ignoring the IS plan once it has been developed in the implementation phase. (Details of these planning problems are shown in Online File W9.8.)

In response to the rapid change of technology and the business environment, IT strategies have to be more flexible and more responsive in order to take advantage of opportunities quickly and in the most cost-effective way. Details in planning for Web-based system and e-commerce are described in the following section.

9.6 PLANNING FOR WEB-BASED SYSTEMS AND E-COMMERCE (E-PLANNING)

Strategic planning for Web-based systems can be viewed as a subset of IT strategic planning. However, in many cases it is done independently of IT planning. Here, we will refer to this specialized process as *e-planning* and will examine some of its features.

E-Planning   IT planning in this chapter refers mostly to corporate planning of IT infrastructure rather than to applications planning. In contrast, **e-planning** is electronically supported IT planning that touches on EC infrastructure and mostly deals with uncovering business opportunities and deciding on an applications portfolio that will exploit those opportunities (see *IT at Work 9.2,* pages 410–411).

Some of the infrastructure needed for e-commerce and Web-based systems may be already in place, as part of the organization's overall IT infrastructure.

Nevertheless, e-planning may be conducted as a separate planning exercise. In such a case, ISD people will participate in the steering committee together with end users. Of course, alignment between the two processes is needed. One reason for such separation is that technology is an enabler of e-commerce, but the major objective of e-commerce is to rejuvenate organizations. If the process is controlled by IT people, the success of e-commerce may be constrained. Another reason for the separation is that e-planning is usually less formal, and it must be done quickly. Furthermore, due to rapid changes the e-planning must be more flexible.

Planning for Web-based individual applications is very similar to the planning of any IT application. However, at the macro level of planning, the emphasis is different. The areas where more attention is given in e-planning are the applications portfolio, risk analysis, and strategic planning issues such as the use of metrics. Let's elaborate.

APPLICATIONS PORTFOLIO FOR E-COMMERCE.   The importance of the applications portfolio in regular IT planning may be declining. Most organizations have their mission-critical systems already in place, and IT activities are fairly distributed. In e-commerce, however, most organizations are starting from scratch. The cost of building systems is high, and so is the risk. Therefore, it is advisable to conduct centralized EC planning and to select appropriate applications and prioritize them, as was shown in *IT at Work 9.2*. Another methodology for planning an applications portfolio was proposed by Tjan (2001).

Tjan's Portfolio Strategy.   Tjan (2001) adopted a business project portfolio applications approach to create an Internet portfolio planning matrix. (Also see Boar, 2000.) However, instead of trading off industry growth and market position, here the strategy is based on *company fit,* which can be either low or high, and the *project's viability,* which can also be low or high. Together these create an *Internet portfolio map (matrix).*

A project's viability can be assessed by four criteria: market-value potential, time to positive cash flow, personnel requirements, and funding requirements. EC initiatives such as a B2B procurement site, a B2C store, or a portal for kids, for example, can be evaluated on a scale of 1 to 100, for each of the four metrics. Then, an average score (simple average) for each metric is computed. For *fit,* the following criteria are used: alignment with core capabilities, alignment with other company initiatives, fit with organizational structure, fit with company's culture and values, and ease of technical implementation. Again, each EC initiative is assessed on a scale of 1 to 100 (or on a qualitative scale of high, medium, low), and an average is computed.

The various applications initiatives are then mapped on the *Internet portfolio matrix,* based on the average scores for viability and fit. The Internet matrix is divided into four cells, as shown in Figure 9.6. If both *viability* and *fit* are low, the project is killed. If both are high, then the project is adopted. If *fit* is high, but *viability* is low, the project is sent to redesign. Finally, if the *fit* is low but the *viability* is high, the project may be sold or spun off. The figure shows how several applications were rated for an e-marketplace company for a toy company in Hong Kong.

Tjan's portfolio strategy introduces a systematic approach to EC project selection. The assessment of the points per criterion can be done by several experts to ensure quality. Cases where there is more agreement can be considered with more confidence. Organizations can add their own criteria to the methodology.

Viability Metric

EC Application	Market-Value Potential	Time to Positive Cash Flow	Personnel Requirement	Funding Requirement	Average
E-Marketplace	85	70	20	20	49
Sell-side	70	70	60	50	63
MRO Procurement	80	60	80	90	80

(on 1–100 scale)

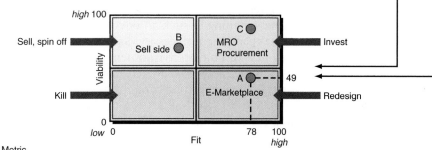

FIGURE 9.6 Application portfolio analysis for a toy distributor. Potential applications: (A) create e-marketplace; (B) direct sale (sell-side); and (C) MRO procurement. The average results determine the location on the grid. Results (at center): invest in project C; redesign project A so it will become viable; and sell the idea (B) to someone else since it does not pay to reengineer the company. (*Source:* Drawn by E. Turban.)

Fit Metric

EC Application	Alignment with Core Capabilities	Alignment with Other Company's Initiatives	Fit with Organizational Structure	Fit with Company's Culture and Values	Ease of Technical Implement-ation	Average, Overall Fit
E-Marketplace	90	60	90	70	80	78
Sell-side	10	30	30	40	60	35
MRO Procurement	90	60	90	80	80	84

(on 1–100 scale)

RISK ANALYSIS. The degree of risk of some Web-based systems is very high, and such risk often leads to failure. For example, Disney Inc. aborted two major EC initiatives in 2000: First, Disney closed its e-toy company (*smartkid.com*), and second, it closed its company (*go.com*) that was managing all of Disney's EC initiatives. The loss was many millions of dollars. Failures of IT applications do not usually cost so much money, especially if they are not enterprisewide in nature. Conducting an appropriate risk analysis could reduce the chance of failures. However, this was difficult to do at that time due to lack of historical data.

STRATEGIC PLANNING ISSUES. Several strategic planning issues are unique to the Web environment. Each of these may involve IT infrastructure, but the market and organizational implications may be more important. Here are some examples:

● *Who and where?* Should the EC initiatives be conducted in a completely independent division or even a separate company?
● *Use of metrics.* EC planning is difficult because the field is evolving, the history is brief, and few planners have experience. Therefore it is desirable to use industry standards, also known as **metrics,** for executing various steps of the planning process (see Plant, 2000). (Metrics are discussed in Chapters 5 and 13.)

- *Learn from failures.* During 2000/2001 there were many EC failures, both major initiatives and whole companies. Planners should study such failures, to learn what went wrong in the hope of avoiding such problems in the future. (For lessons for planners, see Useem, 2000; Agrawal et al., 2001; and Chapter 5 of this book.)
- *Use a different planning process.* The Web environment requires a different planning process, as illustrated by Turban et al. (2004).
- *Integration.* Information systems strategic planning must integrate, in many cases, e-business and knowledge management (see Galliers, 1999, for details).

Planning in a Turbulent Web Environment

The Web environment is very turbulent. Some people question the validity of formal planning in such an environment. Others insist that the turbulence makes formal planning a necessity. Samela et al. (2000) investigated the issue of planning in a turbulent environment in two organizations and concluded that a formal comprehensive approach may be more beneficial than not having a formal plan. Of course, generalizing from only two organizations may not tell the whole story. Samela and Spil (2002) recently suggested a continuous e-business planning process, with four basic planning cycles: (1) agreeing on planning objectives, (2) aligning business objectives and information objectives, (3) analyzing IS resources and IT infrastructure, and (4) authorizing actions. The four cycles are repeated each period in order to ensure continuous review and improvement of the strategies. (Details are shown in Online File W9.9.)

Whether an organization uses formal planning for the Web environment or not, the planning of Web systems frequently requires redesign of business processes, our next topic.

9.7 BUSINESS PROCESS REDESIGN

Of the major environmental pressures described in Chapter 1, three are considered most important by Hammer and Champy (1993)—customers, competition, and change, known as the *three C's. Customers* today know what they want, what they are willing to pay, and how to get products and services on their own terms. Their considerable influence puts pressure on organizations to meet their terms, or lose their business. In addition, *competition* is generally increasing with respect to price, quality, selection, service, and promptness of delivery. The introduction of e-commerce has caused competition to intensify through removal of trade barriers, increased international cooperation, and the creation of technological innovations. Finally, *change* continues to occur. Markets, products, services, technology, the business environment, and people keep changing, frequently in an unpredictable and significant manner.

These pressures can be very strong in certain industries or countries, and they tend to be even stronger as time passes. Some of the conventional methods of organizational responses do not always work in this environment. Therefore, a more comprehensive response—called *business process redesign*—is sometimes called for. Of the organizational responses to environmental pressures, business process redesign and its variants have received lots of management attention (e.g., see Evangelista and Burke, 2003, and Rajaram and Corbett, 2002). (One variant, and predecessor, of business process redesign is *business process reengineering,* or BPR.) These approaches encompass several of the responses described in Chapter 1. In this section we will explore the topic of business process redesign. Let's begin by looking at some of the drivers of process redesign.

The Drivers of Process Redesign

A **business process** is a collection of activities that take one or more kinds of inputs and create an output. As indicated earlier, business processes may need to be redesigned in response to business pressures and/or to enable transformation to e-businesses. Here are some representative drivers behind the need for business process redesign:

- *Fitting commercial software.* It is frequently more economic to *buy* or *lease* software than to develop custom software. However, to reap the best benefit of buying or leasing software, it is best to use the software as it is. (Remember the Nike disaster discussed in Chapter 1.) But what if the software does not fit your business processes, and it is not possible or advisable to change the software? The best solution sometimes is to redesign the affected business processes. Typical software in this category are the functional information systems, ERP, business intelligence (Chapter 11), and profitability software.

- *Streamlining the supply chain.* As seen in Chapter 8, it is frequently necessary to change segments in the supply chain to streamline its operations and to better collaborate with business partners. Redesign is frequently done on small segments of the chain, but sometimes the entire chain is redesigned (e.g., the Orbis case of Chapter 1, where a linear chain was changed to a hub).

- *Participating in private or public e-marketplaces.* With the increased trend to use e-marketplaces (Chapter 5) comes the need to get connected to them, as well as to the organization's back-end processes. To enable such integration it is frequently necessary to redesign internal as well as external processes. The same is true with participation in auction sites. Not changing the processes results in manual operations (e.g., data entry) which may be expensive, slow, and error-prone.

- *Improving customer service.* To properly introduce CRM, it is often necessary to change business processes. As will be seen later in this chapter, centralizing 800 numbers and empowering frontline employees involve process restructuring.

- *Conducting e-procurement.* Introduction of e-procurement methods (Chapter 5) frequently requires complete redesign of the purchasing process (requisition, approval, control, and payment for purchases).

- *Enabling direct online marketing.* Many manufacturers as well as wholesalers are using direct marketing to consumers, mostly via the Internet. Moving to such a business model requires design or redesign of order taking and order fulfillment.

- *Reducing cost and improving productivity.* For generations companies have sought to reduce costs and increase productivity. An example is industrial engineering methods. Many of these are part of continuous small improvements, while others require radical changes in business processes (e.g., see Barua et al., 2001, and Selladurai, 2002).

- *Automating old processes.* Many organizations believe that the solution to their problem is to automate business processes. While in some cases it make sense to do it, in many others it does not. Automating ineffective processes can result in only small savings, whereas restructuring can result in a much larger savings.

Several other drivers may contribute to the need for redesign. In the following sections we will describe some of them: reducing cycle time, need for customization, and empowering employees. Another of these drivers, the problem of the stovepipe, is described in *A Closer Look 9.2* (page 422).

A CLOSER LOOK
9.2 THE PROBLEM OF THE STOVEPIPE

All organizations have both horizontal and vertical dimensions. The organization's layers—usually top, middle, and low (supervisory) management—define the *horizontal* dimensions; the organization's functional departments define the *vertical* dimensions.

The vertical dimension of the organization, primarily focused on functional specialization, has caused many problems in organizations as they have tried to move into the information-based economy. One recurring problem is sometimes referred to as "stovepipes," in recognition of its vertical nature. Because of the vertical structure of organizations, there is a lack of effective collaboration between functional areas. Interaction among vertical functions—that is, across the "stovepipes"—turns out to be crucial in order for organizations to operate efficiently and effectively.

Often, the difference between duties of functional units and business processes in an organization is confused. The figure below illustrates how an organization can have vertical functions (the stovepipes) but also have processes, sometimes referred to as **cross-functional activities,** that transcend departmental boundaries. Product development, order processing, planning, sourcing,

quality control, and customer service are processes that can transcend the functional boundaries of several departments such as distribution, purchasing, research and development, manufacturing, and sales.

Here is an example of a stovepipe problem: A customer places an order with Sales. After a few days, she calls Sales to find out the status of the order. Sales calls various departments. Frequently, it is difficult to trace the order. People push the order from place to place and feel only a small sense of responsibility and accountability, so Sales may not be able to give the customer an answer in time, or may even give an incorrect answer. The problem of the stovepipe can intensify if the supporting information systems are improperly structured.

Focusing on vertical functions and their corresponding information systems to support the business has resulted in fragmented, piecemeal information systems that operate in a way in which the "left hand doesn't know what the right hand is doing." Integration of information is required for good decision making (see Chapter 7). Achieving it is one of the goals of business process redesign.

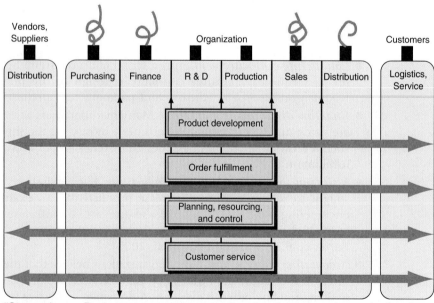

"Stove-pipes—Business processes across functional areas and organizational boundaries.

Methodologies for Restructuring

As indicated earlier, business process redesign was preceded by **business process reengineering (BPR),** a methodology in which an organization *fundamentally* and *radically* changes its business processes to achieve *dramatic improvement.* Initially, attention in BPR was given to *complete restructuring* of organizations (Hammer and Champy, 1993). Later on, the concept was changed to include only one of a few processes (rather than an entire organization) due to numerous failures of BPR projects (e.g., Sarker and Lee, 1999) and the emergence of Web-based applications that solved many of the problems that BPR was supposed to solve.

Today, the concept of BPR has been modified to *business process redesign,* which can focus on anything from the redesign of an individual process, to redesign of a group of processes (e.g., all the processes involved in e-procurement), to redesign of the entire enterprise (see El Sawy, 2001). The redesign of several processes became a necessity for many companies aspiring to transform themselves to e-businesses. For El Sawy's principles of redesign, see Online File W9.10. For a table showing how BPR has changed with time and with technology development, see Online File W9.11.

BUSINESS PROCESS MANAGEMENT. **Business process management (BPM)** is a new method for restructuring that combines workflow systems (Chapter 4) and redesign methods. This emerging methodology covers three process categories—people-to-people, systems-to-systems, and systems-to-people interactions—all from a process-centered perspective. In other words, BPM is a blending of workflow, process management, and applications integration. Le Blond (2003) describes the use of BPM in McDonald's Singapore operations. One area of redesign there was the scheduling of crews at McDonald's restaurants; several other successful applications related to performance improvements. (Staffware Inc., a BPM software vendor and consultant, provides a free online demo as well as case studies at *staffware.com.* For comprehensive coverage see also Smith and Fingar, 2002.)

The conduct of a comprehensive business process redesign, or even of the redesign of only one process, is almost always enabled by IT, which we address in the next section.

9.8 THE ROLE OF IT IN BUSINESS PROCESS REDESIGN

IT has been used for several decades to improve productivity and quality by automating existing processes. However, when it comes to restructuring or redesign, the traditional process of looking at problems first and then seeking technology solutions for them may need to be reversed. A new approach is first to recognize powerful redesign solutions that redesign and BPR make possible, and then to seek the processes that can be helped by such solutions. This approach requires *inductive* rather than *deductive* thinking. It also requires innovation, since a company may be looking for problems it does not even know exist.

IT can break old rules that limit the manner in which work is performed. Some typical rules are given in Table 9.3 (page 424). IT-supported redesign and BPR examples can be found in any industry, private or public (e.g., MacIntosh,

TABLE 9.3 Changes in Business Processes Brought by IT

Old Rule	Intervening Technology	New Rule
Information appears in only one place at one time.	Shared databases, client/server architecture, Internet, intranets	Information appears simultaneously wherever needed.
Only an expert can perform complex work.	Expert systems, neural computing	Novices can perform complex work.
Business must be either centralized or distributed.	Telecommunications and networks: client/server, intranet	Business can be both centralized and distributed.
Only managers make decisions.	Decision support systems, enterprise support systems, expert systems	Decision making is part of everyone's job.
Field personnel need offices to receive, send, store, and process information.	Wireless communication and portable computers, the Web, electronic mail	Field personnel can manage information from any location.
The best contact with potential buyers is a personal contact.	Interactive videodisk, desktop teleconferencing, electronic mail	The best contact is the one that is most cost-effective.
You have to locate items manually.	Tracking technology, groupware, workflow software, search engines	Items are located automatically.
Plans get revised periodically.	High-performance computing systems, intelligent agents	Plans get revised instantaneously whenever needed.
People must come to one place to work together.	Groupware and group support systems, telecommunications, electronic mail, client/server	People can work together while at different locations.
Customized products and services are expensive and take a long time to develop.	CAD/CAM, CASE tools, online systems for JIT decision making, expert systems	Customized products can be made quickly and inexpensively (mass customization).
A long period of time is spanned between the inception of an idea and its implementation (time-to-market).	CAD/CAM, electronic data interchange, groupware, imaging (document) processing	Time-to-market can be reduced by 90 percent.
Organizations and processes are information-based.	Artificial intelligence, expert systems	Organizations and processes are knowledge-based.
Move labor to countries where labor is inexpensive (off-shore production).	Robots, imaging technologies, object-oriented programming, expert systems, geographical information systems (GIS)	Work can be done in countries with high wages and salaries.

Source: Compiled from M. Hammer and J. Champy, *Re-engineering the Corporation* (New York: Harper Business, 1993).

2003 and Khan, 2000). The role of IT in redesigning business processes can be very critical and is increasing due to the Internet and intranets. For example, Geoffrey (1996) provides several examples of how intranets have *rescued* BPR projects (Salladurai, 2002).

Need for Information Integration

One objective of redesign is to overcome problems such as that of the stovepipe by *integrating* the fragmented information systems. (Some integration solutions were described in Chapters 4, 7, and 8.) Besides creating inefficient redundancies, information systems developed along departmental or functional boundaries cause difficulties in generating the information that is required for effective decision making. For instance, consider a case where the management of a bank wants to offer more mortgage loans to better utilize large savings deposits. Management decides to send letters encouraging specific customers to consider buying homes, using

IT at Work 9.4
VW OF MEXICO SHIFTED TO E-PROCUREMENT

Facing strong competition and the North American Free Trade Agreement (NAFTA) environment, Volkswagen of Mexico (*vw.com.mex*) turned to IT. In 1996, VW implemented an ERP system, using SAP R/3 software. By 1998, the company integrated its enterprise system, which was used to cut inventory and production costs, with an extranet, which streamlined spare-parts ordering by its dealers in Mexico. The major reason for the project was the increased demand that resulted from NAFTA and from VW's decision to market the Beetle (called the "New Beetle") in the United States and Canada. These cars are manufactured in Mexico, where labor and services are cheaper.

The integrated system allows people at every level of the company, from manufacturing to car servicing at the dealership, to take advantage of the SAP system. The SAP system integrates the manufacturing, finance, marketing, and other departments among themselves and, thanks to the extranet, now also links these departments with the dealers and business partners. In order to implement SAP, VW had to redesign many of its production, accounting, and sales processes. This was done using some of the methods we describe later in this chapter.

The R/3 system orchestrates all the different areas of the manufacturing and parts-ordering tasks, such as supplier orders, receiving, warehousing, client orders, packing, and billing. By tapping into R/3 modules, the dealers can cut the turnaround time for ordering spare parts from 10 days to fewer than 5—a very important competitive advantage. The dealers can check the status of their orders on the computer.

One problem with the integrated system is that some of the dealers in Mexico were not ready to buy, install, and use computers. However, the fact that the new system means a low inventory level, which can save the dealers considerable money, motivated them to join in. The company projected that the application will result in $50 million in cost savings over three years for the dealers.

Sources: Compiled from *PC Week* (1998), and from press releases of *vw.com.mex* (1999–2002).

For Further Exploration: Can VW's suppliers be added to the system? What competitive advantage could be realized with such an addition?

---

convenient financing available through the bank. Management also decides that the best customers to whom to send such letters are: customers who do not currently have mortgage loans or who have loans for a very small percentage of the value of their homes; customers who have good checking account records (e.g., few or no overdrafts); customers with sufficient funds in their savings accounts to make a down payment on a home; and customers with good payment records on installment loans with the bank.

Because the data necessary to identify such customers may be available in different files of different information systems, there may be no convenient or economical way to integrate them. Using innovations such as *data warehouses* and special integrated software can be helpful, but expensive. Therefore, extensive programming and clerical work are required to satisfy such an information request. The scenario of the bank can be translated into other organizational settings.

Integration should cross not only departmental boundaries but also organizational ones, reaching suppliers and customers. Namely, it should work along the *extended supply chain*. This is especially important in company-centric B2B e-marketplaces and in B2B exchanges (see Chapter 5). An example of an internal integration followed by integration with dealers is provided in *IT at Work 9.4.*

The integration of an organization's information systems enables redesign innovations such as the introduction of a single point of contact for customers, called a *case manager* or a *deal structurer.* We can see how this single point of contact works by looking at a credit-approval process at IBM. The old process took seven days and eight steps. It involved creation of a paper folder that was routed, sequentially, through four departments (sales, credit check, business practices, finance, and back to sales). In the redesigned process, one person, the deal structurer, conducts all the necessary tasks. This one generalist replaces four specialists. To enable one person to execute the above steps, an intelligent DSS (Chapter 12) provides the deal structurer with the guidance needed. The program guides the generalist in finding information in the databases, plugging numbers into an evaluation model, and pulling standardized clauses—"boilerplates"—from a file. For difficult situations, the generalist can get help from a specialist. As a result, the turnaround time has been slashed from seven days to four hours.

Retooling of IT for Business Process Redesign

Redesign of business processes often means a need to change some or all of the organizational information systems. The reason for this is that information systems designed along hierarchical lines may be ineffective in supporting the redesigned organization. Therefore, it is often necessary to redesign the information systems. This process is referred to as *retooling.*

Retooling focuses on making sure the information systems are responsive to the process-redesign effort and to the use of e-business. Many organizations found that once they realized they had a business problem and wanted to do something about it, their information systems function could not accommodate the desired changes. For example, a government agency in Singapore decided to defer a badly needed BPR project when it discovered that it would cost over $15 million just to rewrite the applicable computer programs.

To retool for redesign, a key issue is getting a good understanding of the current installed base of IT applications and databases. It is also important to understand the existing infrastructure in terms of computing devices, networks, and the like, and their relationships to the current available software, procedures, and data. Another key issue is an assessment of what the ideal IT architecture would be for the organization in terms of hardware and software, as well as an appropriate information architecture.

In planning a retooling, it is very important to *benchmark* the technology being used in the organization against what the best competitors are using. It is also imperative to find out what the latest technologies are and to determine in what direction the organization needs to go. For an example of a massive IT retooling in a public agency, in which the technology enabled the company to restructure all its major business processes, see Tung and Turban (1996).

IT INFRASTRUCTURE AND DEVELOPMENT SOFTWARE FOR BUSINESS PROCESS REDESIGN. Information technology can either enable or constrain successful redesign and BPR. The links between enterprise IT infrastructure and business-process change were explored by Broadbent et al. (1999). Exploratory case analysis of four firms was used to understand the ways IT infrastructure contributes to success in implementing redesign and BPR. The researchers found that all firms needed a basic level of IT infrastructure capability in order to implement process redesign and especially BPR. The firms that had developed a higher level of IT infrastructure capabilities, before or concurrent with undertaking business process redesign, were able to implement extensive changes to their business processes over relatively short time frames.

IT TOOLS FOR BUSINESS PROCESS REDESIGN AND BPR. A large variety of IT tools can be used to support redesign and BPR. Some of these tools are generic and can be used for other purposes, while others are specifically designed for redesign and BPR. Let's elaborate.

Special BPR and Process Redesign Software. According to El Sawy (2001), special BPR software enables the capture of the key elements of a business process in a visual representation made up of interconnected objects on a time line. The elements of this visual representation usually include activities, sequencing, resources, times, and rules. BPR software is much more than drawing or flowcharting software in that the objects on the screen are intelligent and have process and organizational data and rules associated with them. The software is also interactive, in real time. BPR software may incorporate some aspects of project management in terms of allocating resources and costs to work activities and their time sequencing. BPR software also has "what-if" capabilities in that it enables process simulation and performance comparison of alternative process designs. The better BPR software packages are quite intuitive and relatively easy to learn. The 10 major reasons why special BPR software is of value for business process redesign are summarized in Online File W9.12.

The most comprehensive special BPR suite, which includes many functionalities, was BPR Workflow from Holosofx (now a part of IBM's WebSphere). For a detailed description of this package and usable software, see El Sawy (2001). In addition to BPR Workflow one can find integrated BPR tool kits in some ERP software (e.g., see Oracle 9i and SAP R/3).

Some people believe that BPR can be done with CASE tools (Chapter 14). This is not the case, since CASE tools can be used to execute only a few BPR activities, and they are difficult to use. Other believe that workflow tools can be used. Again, this is true only for some redesign activities. Furthermore, the workflow capabilities in custom-designed BPR software are usually superior to those of generic tools. However, for many projects there is no need for a comprehensive suite; in those situations, generic tools or special tools designed to be used for only one or two BPR activities are both efficient and effective. For a listing of some generic and single-activity tools that may be of use in business process redesign, see Online File W9.13.

9.9 RESTRUCTURING PROCESSES AND ORGANIZATIONS

Redesign, restructuring, and reengineering efforts involve many activities, four of which are described in this section: redesign of processes, mass customization, cycle time reduction, and restructuring the entire organization. In this section we also look at some BPR failures.

Redesign of One or a Few Processes

Redesign efforts frequently involve only one or a few processes. One of the most publicized examples of process redesign is the accounts payable process at Ford Motor Company, described in *IT at Work 9.5* (page 428). The Ford example demonstrates changes in a simple process. Khan (2000) describes the restructure of an air cargo process that was much more complicated and involved several IT tools.

Mass Customization

One of the most successful models of e-commerce is build-to-order, which is implemented via mass customization. (See Appendix 2A.) The concept of *mass*

IT at Work 9.5
REENGINEERING PROCESSES AT FORD MOTOR COMPANY

As part of its productivity improvement efforts, the management of Ford Motor Company (*ford.com*) put its North American Accounts Payable Department under the microscope in search of ways to cut costs. Management thought that by streamlining processes and installing new computer systems, it could reduce the head count by some 20 percent, to 400 people.

But after visiting Mazda's accounts payable department (Ford is part owner of Mazda), Ford managers increased their goal: perform accounts payable with only 100 clerks. Analysis of Ford's old system revealed that when the purchasing department wrote a purchase order, it sent a copy to accounts payable. Later, when material control received the goods, it sent a copy of the receiving document to accounts payable. Meanwhile, the vendor also sent an invoice to accounts payable. If the purchase order, receiving document, and invoice all matched, then accounts payable issued a payment. Unfortunately, the department spent most of its time on many mismatches. To prevent them, Ford instituted "invoiceless processing." Now, when the purchasing department initiates an order, it enters the information into an online database. It does not send a copy of the purchase order to anyone. The vendor receives notification through an EDI.

When the goods arrive at the receiving dock, the receiving clerk checks the database to see whether the goods correspond to an outstanding purchase order. If so, he or she accepts them and enters the transaction into the computer system. (If there is no database entry for the received goods, or if there is a mismatch, the clerk returns the goods.)

Under the old procedures, the accounting department had to match 14 data items among the receipt record, the purchase order, and the invoice before it could issue payment to the vendor. The new approach requires matching only four items—part number, amount, unit of measure, and supplier code—between the purchase order and the receipt record. The matching is done automatically, and the computer prepares the check, which accounts payable sends to the vendor (or an electronic transfer is made). There are no invoices to worry about since Ford has asked its vendors not to send them. The restructured system as compared to the old one is shown in the figure below.

Ford did not settle for the modest increases it first envisioned. Instead it opted for a radical change, and it achieved dramatic improvement: a 75 percent reduction in head count, not the 20 percent it would have achieved with a conventional improvement program. And since there are no discrepancies between the financial record and physical record, material control is simpler, receipts are more likely to be correct, and financial information is more accurate.

Source: Condensed from Hammer and Champy (1993).

For Further Exploration: How did the EDI help attain the reduction? What other support was provided by IT?

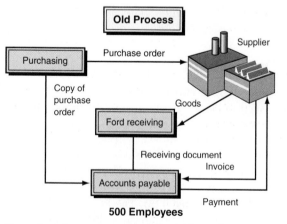

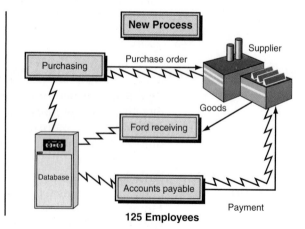

Reengineering processes at Ford Motor Company.

customization involves production of large quantities of customized items, as Dell is doing with personal computers (e.g., see Pine and Davis, 1999, and Gilmore and Pine, 2000). Mass customization enables a company to provide flexible and quick responsiveness to a customer's needs, as expressed in their self-configured orders, at a low cost and with high quality. A build-to-order strategy is made possible by allowing fast and inexpensive production changes, by reducing the ordering and sales cycle time using e-commerce, and by shortening the production time (e.g., by using prefabricated parts and sub-assemblies). Often, such a mass customization strategy must be preceded and/or supported by a business process redesign.

Cycle Time Reduction

Cycle time refers to the time it takes to complete a process from beginning to end. As discussed earlier, competition today focuses not only on cost and quality, but also on speed. Time is recognized as a major element that provides competitive advantage, and therefore **cycle time reduction** is a major business objective.

The success of Federal Express, for example, is clearly attributable to its ability to reduce the delivery time of packages. It does this by using complex computer-supported systems that allow flexible planning, organization, and control (see Wetherbe, 1996). The comeback of Chrysler Corporation and its success in the 1990s can be attributed largely to its "technology center," which brought about a more than 30 percent reduction in its time to market (the time from beginning the design of a new model to the delivery of the car). General Motors achieved even larger reduction of delivery times in recent years (see case in Chapter 8). Boeing Corporation reengineered its design of airplanes by moving to total computerization. In a fundamental change to Boeing's processes, a physical prototype was never built. In addition to reducing the cycle time, Boeing was able to improve quality and reduce costs. Because of these changes, Boeing was able to compete better with Airbus Industries.

Notice that in Boeing's, GM's, and Chrysler's cases the change was *fundamental* and *dramatic*. First, the role of the computer was changed from a tool to a platform for the total design. Second, it was not just a process change, but a *cultural change* relative to the role of the computer and the design engineers. According to Callon (1996), the engineers are now a part of a computer-based design system. Computing also played a major communications role during the entire design process. As was shown in the Ford case (*IT at Work 9.5*), IT makes a major contribution in shortening cycle times by allowing the combination or elimination of steps and the expediting of various activities in the process. In Chapter 2 we demonstrated a significant reduction in cycle time achieved by Dell due to introduction of Web services and redesigning the communication processes between the manufacturing plants and the suppliers.

There is an old saying that "time is money," so saving time saves money. But cycle time reduction does more than save money. If you beat your competitors with a new product, a product improvement, or a new service, you can gain a substantial market share. Pharmaceutical companies, for example, are desperately trying to reduce the cycle time of new drugs. If successful, they will be the first on the market, they may receive a patent on the innovation, and revenues will begin flowing sooner to repay their huge investments.

Additionally, the Internet, extranets, and intranets provide a means of economically reducing cycle time by cutting communications time through the use of e-mail and EDI (also Internet/EDI) and by allowing collaboration in design and operations of products and services.

Restructuring the Whole Organization

We've seen that one problem in many current organizations is vertical structures. How should a contemporary organization be organized? There are several alternatives. Let's look at how it can be done with business process redesign.

The fundamental problem with the hierarchical organizational structure is that any time a decision needs to be made, it must climb up and down the hierarchy. If one person says "no" to a pending decision, everything comes to a screeching halt. Also, if information is required from several "functional sources," getting all the right information coordinated can be a time-consuming and frustrating process for employees and customers alike.

So, how is organizational redesign done? It varies, depending on the organization and the circumstances. For example, providing each customer with a single point of contact can solve the stovepipe problem described earlier. In the traditional bank, for example, each department views the same customer as a separate customer. Figure 9.7 depicts a redesigned bank in which the customer deals with a single point of contact, the account manager. The account manager is responsible for all bank services and provides all services to the customer, who receives a single statement for all of his or her accounts and can access all accounts on the same Web page. Notice that the role of IT is to back up the account manager by providing her with expert advice on specialized topics, such as loans. Also, by having easy access to the different databases, the account manager can answer queries, plan, and organize the work with customers.

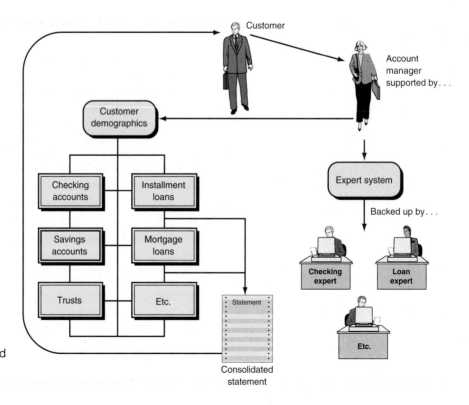

FIGURE 9.7 Reengineered bank with integrated system.

An alternative to the single-point contact is a networked structure, usually supported by a call center. In this structure, regardless of where and when a client contacts the company, the networked agents would have access to all customer data, so that *any* employee can provide excellent customer service. Companies such as USAA, Otis Elevator, and others have all agents located in one city and give customers all over the country the same toll-free number and a centralized Web address. In this model, the company also can install a computer-based call-center technology, which brings up complete customer information (or information about a customer's elevator in the case of Otis) on the computer screen, whenever a customer calls. This means that anyone who answers the call would know all the information necessary to make a quick, frontline decision (see Chapter 12). There is no need to ask questions of the customer, and any agent can give personalized and customized service. This is especially important in services such as reservation systems for hotels or airlines, as well as for utility companies, financial services, universities, and health care services.

Reengineering and restructuring is not limited to a specific type of organization. Studies indicate that 70 percent of all large U.S. corporations are reengineering or considering some major redesign projects. In addition, the public sector, including the U.S. federal government, is continuously implementing restructuring projects. See *IT at Work 9.6*, which describes one such project by the U.S. federal government.

IT at Work 9.6
INFORMATION TECHNOLOGY IN RESTRUCTURING THE FEDERAL GOVERNMENT

The U.S. federal government is using IT to streamline its bureaucracy and improve public services. The plan is to create an "electronic government," moving from the Industrial Age into the Information Age. It is also part of e-government, where processes are being redesigned to enable e-purchasing and other EC activities. For details of the plan see E-Government Strategy (2003).

Information technology is playing a key role in such restructuring of government operations and services. The document cited above describes the new e-government systems as a "virtual agency" in which information is shared throughout the government. The U.S. Department of Agriculture already distributes food stamps electronically. Medicare payments may be integrated into that system (expected in 2004). Other e-government services being proposed include a national network serving law enforcement and public safety agencies; electronic linkage of tax files at federal, state, and local agencies; an interna-

tional trade data system; a national environmental data index; government-wide electronic mail; and an integrated information infrastructure, including consolidated data centers. Various IT teams are also looking at client/server networks and intranets to eliminate the need for large mainframe data centers. Tens of millions of U.S. citizens receive Social Security and other payments periodically. The distribution of these services is also moving to the Internet for greater savings and shorter cycle times. Smaller countries such as Hong Kong and Singapore have already restructured many of their services to go online (e.g., see *ecitizen .gov.sg* and *cnfo.gov.hk*).

Sources: Compiled from *npa.gov* (1998), *fcw.com, govexec.com,* and e-Government Strategy (2003).

For Further Exploration: Why are these systems referred to as a virtual agency? Is so much computerization of the government beneficial? Why or why not?

Virtual Organizations

One of the most interesting organizational structures is the *virtual organization,* also referred to as a *virtual corporation (VC).* The creation, operation, and management of a virtual organization is heavily dependent on IT and is especially facilitated by the Internet and e-commerce (see Venkatraman and Henderson, 1998).

DEFINITION AND CHARACTERISTICS. A **virtual organization (virtual corporation, VC)** is an organization composed of several business partners sharing costs and resources for the purpose of producing a product or service. In a virtual organization the resources of the business partners remain in their original locations but are integrated. The virtual organization can be temporary, with a onetime mission such as launching a satellite, or it can be permanent. According to Goldman et al. (1995), permanent virtual corporations are designed to: (1) create or assemble productive resources rapidly, (2) create or assemble productive resources frequently and concurrently, and (3) create or assemble a broad range of productive resources. They are considered permanent in that they expect to continue their activities indefinitely.

The virtual organization is usually composed of several business units, each in a different location. Each partner contributes complementary resources that reflect its strengths and determine its role in the virtual enterprise. VCs are not necessarily organized directly along the supply chain. For example, a virtual business partnership may include several partners, each creating a portion of a product or service, in an area in which each has special advantage, such as expertise or low cost.

The concept of virtual organizations is not new, but recent developments in IT allow new implementations that exploit its capabilities (see Suhas, 2000). The modern virtual organization can be viewed as a *network* of creative people, resources, and ideas connected via online services and/or the Internet, who band together to produce products or services. The major attributes of virtual organizations are:

- *Excellence.* Each partner brings its core competency, so an all-star winning team is created. No single company can match what the virtual corporation can achieve.
- *Utilization.* Resources of the business partners are frequently underutilized, or utilized in a merely satisfactory manner. In the virtual corporation, resources can be put to use more profitably, thus providing a competitive advantage.
- *Opportunism.* The partnership is opportunistic. A virtual organization is organized to meet a market opportunity.
- *Lack of borders.* It is difficult to identify the boundaries of a virtual corporation; it redefines traditional boundaries. For example, more cooperation among competitors, suppliers, and customers makes it difficult to determine where one company ends and another begins in the virtual corporation partnership.
- *Trust.* Business partners in a VC must be far more reliant on each other and require more trust than ever before. They share a sense of destiny.
- *Adaptability to change.* The virtual corporation can adapt quickly to the environmental changes discussed in Chapter 1 because its structure is relatively simple or fluid.

● *Technology.* Information technology makes the virtual organization possible. A networked information architecture is a must.

For an analysis of why virtual organizations work, see Markus et al. (2000). For strategies used by virtual organizations, see Venkatraman and Henderson (1998).

HOW IT SUPPORTS VIRTUAL ORGANIZATIONS. There are several ways for IT to support virtual organizations. The most obvious are those that allow communication and collaboration among the dispersed business partners. For example, e-mail, desktop videoconferencing, screen sharing, and several other groupware technologies described in Chapter 4 are frequently used to support virtual corporations.

Since the partners in a virtual organization are in different locations, they need information systems for supporting communication and collaboration. Such systems are a special case of interorganizational information systems (IOSs)—information systems that cross organizational lines to one or more business partners (see Chapter 8). Standard transactions in the interorganizational information systems are supported by extranets, Internet/EDI, and EFT (see Chapter 5).

The Internet is the infrastructure for these and other technologies used by VCs. Virtual office systems, for example, can be supported by intelligent agents. Modern database technologies and networking permit business partners to access each other's databases. Lotus Notes and similar integrated groupware tools permit diversified interorganizational collaboration. Turban et al. (2004) provide numerous examples of collaborative applications. ERP software is extensively used to support standard transactions among business partners. In general, most virtual organizations cannot exist without IT. (For a survey of other tools see Boudreau et al., 1999; for the effect of IT on VCs, see Peng and Chang, 2000.)

9.10 ORGANIZATION TRANSFORMATION AND CHANGE MANAGEMENT

The examples in the previous sections demonstrated restructuring and BPR approaches that can be helpful in solving problems and exploiting opportunities created by the changing business environment. Such approaches need to be introduced into an organization and accepted by its members. Major organizational changes such as transformation to e-business are referred to as *organization transformation*; such major transformation usually requires *change management*. In this section we also address the topics of empowerment and BPR failures and successes.

Organization Transformation

Introducing a corporate-wide e-business or other major business process redesign is likely to result in transforming an old organization to a new one. Generally speaking, **organization transformation** refers to an organization with a "new face," whose business processes, structure, strategy, and procedures are completely different from the old one. Taking an organization through a radical transformation can be a lengthy, expensive, and complex process, which may involve organizational learning, changes in management and personnel, creation of a new structure, and employee retraining.

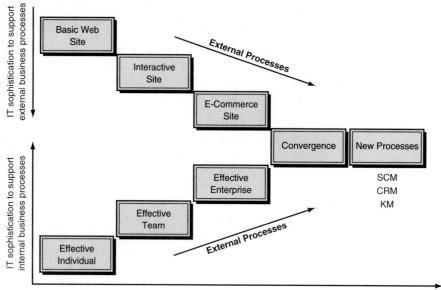

FIGURE 9.8 Roadmap to becoming e-business. (*Source:* Ginige et al., (2001), Figure 2, p. 43.)

A major organization transformation, which many companies have had to face recently, is transformation to an e-business.

TRANSFORMATION TO AN E-BUSINESS. Transforming an organization into an e-business, especially for a large company, can be a very complex endeavor. (Recall the Siemans case in Chapter 1.) To do so, the organization needs to transform several major processes, such as procurement, sales, CRM, and manufacturing.

Such a transformation involves several strategic issues. Lasry (2002) raises several of these issues when investigating the rate at which "brick-and-mortar" retail firms adopt the Web as an additional sales channel. He examined organizational strategies such as internal restructuring, forming a joint venture, or outsourcing. He concluded that implementing EC requires a disruptive and potentially hazardous change in core features, and therefore he suggested that companies spin off the EC activities as part of the transformation process.

Ginige et al. (2001) provide a comprehensive description of the transformation to e-business, describing both the internal and external processes supported by IT, as shown in Figure 9.8. They then show the support of IT at each stage, as seen in Online File W9.14. Finally they describe the necessary change management activities.

Several other studies are dedicated to the transformation to e-business. For example, Chen and Ching (2002) explored the relationship of BPR and e-business and investigated the change process both for individuals and organizations. They propose a process of redesigning an organization for e-business, providing several research propositions. Bosilj-Vuksic et al. (2002) explored the use of simulation modeling for enabling transformation to e-business. They examined the process of BPR and suggest how to use simulation and process maps to support the process. Lee (2003) describes the use of business intelligence (Chapter 11) and intelligent systems (Chapter 12) to facilitate the transformation of process and data to e-business. An organization transformation process is facilitated by change management.

Change Management

Changing business processes, organizational structure, operating procedures, and so forth are interrelated, as shown by the classic Scott-Morton framework (see Online File W1.4). Major changes in business processes and/or in technology move organizations out of equilibrium, creating changes in structure, strategy, and in people and their roles. When the magnitude of the changes is significant, the changes may be resisted by employees. Therefore, change is a learning process that needs to be properly managed. Management scholars have developed guidelines for how to introduce change into organizations (e.g., see Mintzberg and Westley, 1992, and Anderson, 2001) and how to diffuse innovations into organizations (e.g., see Rogers, 1983). These guidelines for managing organizational change or redesign are called **change management.**

The faster the speed of change, the more difficult and stressful it is to manage it. Moving to e-business is very rapid, and so are many redesign projects. The classic change management approaches, such as use of benchmarking (Clarke and Manton, 1997), were adapted for IT changes. For example, Burn and Ash (2001) developed a model for introducing e-business changes in an ERP environment.

Of the many topics related to organization transformation and change management, we will deal here with only two: changing organizational structures, and empowerment of employees. The related topics are also important but are outside the scope of this textbook.

Changing Organizational Structure

A major issue in organization transformation, including transformation to e-business, is the change in organizational structure. One common potential change is to a networked organization.

Many experts have advocated the concept of networked organizations (e.g., see Majcharzak and Wang, 1996). The term **networked organizations** refers to organizational structures that resemble computer networks and are supported by information systems. This structure is promising, but it is difficult to implement. (See Online File W9.15.)

The tendency in recent years has been for organizations to become somewhat "flatter" in terms of management layers, and managerial roles and organizational processes have been changing to follow this trend. Although the basic hierarchical structure is still most common, many organizations use temporary and/or permanent teams that are assigned to specific processes. For the use of teams as they related to business process and work redesign, see Choudrie et al. (2002) and Launonen and Kess (2002). Team-based structure requires empowerment of employees.

Empowerment Using IT

Empowerment is the vesting of decision-making or approval authority in employees in situations in which such authority was traditionally a managerial prerogative. Empowered employees are allowed to make operational and managerial decisions. Empowerment frequently accompanies redesign efforts. As a philosophy and set of behavioral practices, empowerment means allowing self-managing autonomous teams (e.g., see Hinks, 2002) or individuals to be in charge of their own career destinies, as they work toward company and personal goals through a shared company vision (see Murrell and Meredith, 2000).

EMPOWERMENT'S RELATIONSHIP TO INFORMATION TECHNOLOGY. Empowerment can be enhanced through IT. Perhaps IT's most important contribution is the provision of the right information, at the right time, of the right quality, and at the right cost. Information is necessary, but it may not be sufficient. To be fully empowered means to be *able to make decisions,* and these require *knowledge.* Knowledge is scarce in organizations, and specialists usually hold it. To empower employees means to increase the availability of such knowledge. Expert systems and other intelligent systems can play a major role in knowledge sharing, as can the Internet and intranets.

Empowered employees are expected to perform better, and to do so they may need new tools. Information technology can provide, for example, tools that will enhance the creativity and productivity of employees, as well as the quality of their work. These tools can be special applications for increasing creativity (Chapter 12), spreadsheets for increasing productivity, and hand-held computers to improve communication. Examples are provided in Chapters 4 and 7.

Finally, empowerment may require training. Self-directed teams, for example, may need more skills and higher levels of skills. Once organized, teams will require training, which can be provided by IT. For example, many companies provide online training, use multimedia, and even apply intelligent computer-aided instruction.

EMPOWERMENT OF CUSTOMERS, SUPPLIERS, AND BUSINESS PARTNERS. In addition to empowering employees, companies are empowering their customers, suppliers, and other business partners. For example, Levi Strauss & Company allows its textile suppliers to access its database, so they know exactly what Levi Strauss is producing and selling and can ship supplies just in time. The company is using a similar approach with all its suppliers. Federal Express is using the Internet to empower its customers to check prices, prepare shipping labels, find the location of the nearest drop box, and trace the status of packages. Finally, Dell empowers its customers to configure and track orders and troubleshoot problems.

The topics we have considered in this section—organization transformation, change management, and empowerment—can have a significant impact in determining success or failure in business process redesign.

BPR Failures and Successes

During the 1990s, there were many success stories of BPR (Grant, 2002, El Sawy, 2001) and just as many cases of failures.

FAILURES. The PROSCI organization conducted a survey of several hundred companies to learn the best BPR practices and the reasons for BPR failures, which can be found at the organization's Web site (*prosci.com*). Another summary of research into business process redesign failure is available at *managingchange.com/bpr/bprcult/4bprcult.htm.* The summary indicates a failure rate of 50 to 80 percent. According to Grant (2002) at least 70 percent of all BPR projects fail. Some of the reasons cited for failure are high risk, inappropriate change management, failure to plan, internal politics, high cost of retooling, lack of participation and leadership, inflexible software, lack of motivation, and lack of top management support. A highly detailed case study on BPR failures is provided by Sarker and Lee (1999). For more on BPR failures and suggestions on how to avoid them, see El Sawy (2001).

BPR SUCCESSES. Despite the high failure rate of business process redesign, there are many cases of success, especially when less than the entire organization is restructured. While BPR failures tend to get more widespread publicity, success stories are published mostly by vendors and in academic and trade journals. For example, there is evidence of the success of BPR in the public sector (MacIntosh, 2003). Khong and Richardson (2003) report on extensive BPR activities and successes in banking and finance companies in Malaysia, and Mohanty and Deshmukh (2001) found successful BPR initiatives in a large cement manufacturing plant in India. (For details, see Online File W9.16.)

Organizations should consider restructuring their business processes or sometimes the entire business (see opening case, Chapter 1). When successful, redesign has great potential to improve an organization's competitive position.

➡ MANAGERIAL ISSUES

1. **Importance.** Getting IT ready for the future—that is, planning—is one of the most challenging and difficult tasks facing all of management, including IS management. Each of the four steps of the IT strategic planning process—strategic planning, information requirements analysis, resource allocation, and project planning—presents its own unique problems. Yet, without planning, or with poor planning, the organization may be doomed.

2. **Organizing for planning.** Many issues are involved in planning: What should be the role of the ISD? How should IT be organized? Staffed? Funded? How should human resources issues, such as training, benefits, and career paths for IS personnel, be handled? What about the environment? The competition? The economy? Governmental regulations? Emerging technologies? What is the strategic direction of the host organization? What are its key objectives? Are they agreed upon and clearly stated? Finally, with these strategies and objectives and the larger environment, what strategies and objectives should IS pursue? What policies should it establish? What type of information architecture should the organization have: centralized or not centralized? How should investments in IT be justified? The answer to each of these questions must be tailored to the particular circumstances of the ISD and the larger organization of which it is a part.

3. **Fitting the IT architecture to the organization.** Management of an organization may become concerned that its IT architecture is not suited to the needs of the organization. In such a case, there has likely been a failure on the part of the IT technicians to determine properly the requirements of the organization. Perhaps there has also been a failure on the part of management to understand the type and manner of IT architecture that they have allowed to develop or that they need.

4. **IT architecture planning.** IT specialists versed in the technology of IT must meet with business users and jointly determine the present and future needs for the IT architecture. In some cases, IT should lead (e.g., when business

users do not understand the technical implications of a new technology). In other cases, users should lead (e.g., when technology is to be applied to a new business opportunity). Plans should be written and published as part of the organizational strategic plan and as part of the IT strategic plan. Plans should also deal with training, career implications, and other secondary infrastructure issues.

5. *IT policy.* IT architectures should be based on corporate guidelines or principles laid out in policies. These policies should include the roles and responsibilities of IT personnel and users, security issues, cost-benefit analyses for evaluating IT, and IT architectural goals. Policies should be communicated to all personnel who are managing or directly affected by IT.

6. *Ethical and legal issues.* Conducting interviews for finding managers' needs and requirements must be done with full cooperation. Measures to protect privacy must be taken.

   In designing systems one should consider the people in the system. Reengineering IT means that some employees will have to completely reengineer themselves. Some may feel too old to do so. Conducting a supply chain or business process reorganization may result in the need to lay off, retrain, or transfer employees. Should management notify the employees in advance regarding such possibilities? And what about those older employees who may be difficult to retrain?

   Other ethical issues may involve sharing of computing resources (in a client/server environment, for example) or of personal information, which may be part of the new organizational culture. Finally, individuals may have to share computer programs that they designed for their departmental use, and may resist doing so because they consider such programs their intellectual property. Appropriate planning must take these and other issues into consideration.

   Implementing organizational transformation by the use of IT may tempt some to take unethical or even illegal actions. Companies may need to use IT to monitor the activities of their employees and customers, and in so doing may invade the privacy of individuals. When using business intelligence to find out what competitors are doing, companies may be engaged in unethical tactics such as pressuring competitors' employees to reveal information, or using software that is the intellectual property of other companies (frequently without the knowledge of these other companies).

7. *IT strategy.* In planning IT it is necessary to examine three basic strategies: (1) *Be a leader in technology.* Companies such as FedEx, Dell, and Wal-Mart are known for their leading strategy. The advantages of being a leader are the ability to attract customers, to provide unique services and products, and to be a cost leader. However, there is a high development cost of new technologies and high probability of failures. (2) *Be a follower.* This is a risky strategy because you may be left behind. However, you do not risk failures, and so you usually are able to implement new technologies at a fraction of the cost. (3) *Be an experimenter, on a small scale.* This way you minimize your research and development investment and the cost of failure. When new technologies prove to be successful you can move fairly quickly for full implementation.

8. *Integration: The role of IT in redesign and BPR.* Almost all major supply chain management (SCM) and/or BPR projects use IT. However, it is important to remember that in most cases the technology plays a *supportive* role. The primary role is organizational and managerial in nature. On the other hand, without IT, most SCM and BPR efforts do not succeed.

9. *Failures.* A word of caution: One of the lessons from the history of IT is that very big projects have a tendency to fail when expectations exceed real capabilities. For example, many of the early material requirements planning (MRP) systems, artificial intelligence, and complex transaction processing systems never worked. BPR and some ERP projects also have failed, for many reasons. One of the reasons for failure is a miscalculation of the required amount of IT. It simply may be too expensive to rebuild and retool the IT infrastructure and adjust applications that are necessary for BPR. The solution may be instead to defer the BPR and use incremental improvements, or to reengineer only the most critical processes.

ON THE WEB SITE... Additional resources, including quizzes; online files of additional text, tables, figures, and cases; and frequently updated Web links to current articles and information can be found on the book's Web site (*wiley.com/college/turban*).

KEY TERMS

Applications portfolio *399*

Business process *421*

Business process management (BPM) *423*

Business process reengineering (BPR) *423*

Business systems planning (BSP) model *404*

Centralized computing *413*

Change management *435*

Critical success factors (CSFs) *405*

Cross-functional activities *422*

Cycle time reduction *429*

Distributed computing *413*

E-planning *417*

Empowerment *435*

Four-stage model of planning *400*

Information architecture *412*

Information requirements analysis *408*

Information technology architecture *411*

IT planning *398*

Legacy systems *415*

Metrics *419*

Networked organizations *435*

Organization transformation *433*

Project planning *411*

Resource allocation *409*

Reverse engineering *415*

Scenario planning *407*

Stages of IT growth *404*

Strategic information technology planning (SITP) *401*

Virtual organization (virtual corporation, VC) *432*

CHAPTER HIGHLIGHTS (Numbers Refer to Learning Objectives)

1 Information technology planning can help organizations meet the challenges of a rapidly changing business and competitive environment. There are several approaches to IT planning (e.g., method driven, technological approach).

1 IT planning methods have evolved over time. Today they are centered around e-planning.

2 Aligning IT plans with business plans makes it possible to prioritize IS projects on the basis of contribution to organizational goals and strategies.

❷ The four-stage IT planning model includes strategic planning, requirements analysis, resource allocation, and project planning.

❸ Strategic information systems planning involves methodologies such as business systems planning (BSP), stages of IT growth, and critical success factors (CSFs).

❹ IS planning requires analysis of the information needed by the organization. Several methods exist for doing it. Also, implementing the planning requires planning—including resource allocation, cost-benefit analysis, and project management (using software).

❺ Information technology architecture can be centralized or distributed. When it is distributed, it often follows the client/server architecture model.

❺ Organizations can use enterprise architecture principles to develop an information technology architecture.

❻ The major information systems planning issues are strategic alignment, architecture, resource allocation, and time and budget considerations.

❼ To prioritize an e-commerce applications portfolio, IT planners can use the validity of the application and its fit with the organization, plotting it on a grid that indicates company fit and project viability and suggests one of four strategies.

❽ BPR is the fundamental rethinking and radical redesign of business processes to achieve dramatic improvements.

❾ IT helps not only to automate existing processes, but also to introduce innovations that change structure (e.g., create case managers and interdisciplinary teams), reduce the number of processes, combine tasks, enable economical customization, and reduce cycle time.

❾ Mass customization, which is facilitated by IT, enables production of customized goods by methods of mass production at a low cost.

❾ Cycle time reduction is an essential part of many BPR projects and is usually attainable only by IT support.

❿ One of the most innovative BPR strategies is the creation of business alliances and virtual corporations.

❿ Process redesign and/or BPR result in transforming organizations to new structures and operations, such as e-business.

❿ Transforming organizations means change that may be resisted or poorly done. Therefore, change management is needed.

QUESTIONS FOR REVIEW

1. Briefly discuss the evolution of IT planning.
2. What are some of the problems associated with IT planning?
3. Define and discuss the four-stage model of IT planning.
4. Identify the methods used for strategic planning and review their characteristics.
5. What is information technology architecture and why is it important? List the major types.
6. What are the advantages and disadvantages of centralized computing architectures?
7. What is a legacy system? Why do companies have legacy systems?
8. Define scenario planning.
9. What is an applications portfolio?
10. Define business process and BPR.
11. List the drivers of process redesign.
12. Describe the stovepipe problem.
13. Define BPM.
14. Describe the enabling role of IT in BPR.
15. What is meant by mass customization? Give examples.
16. Define cycle time reduction.
17. Define a virtual corporation.
18. Describe the major characteristics of empowerment and describe its benefits.
19. Define organization transformation and change management.

QUESTIONS FOR DISCUSSION

1. Discuss how strategic planning, as described in this chapter, could help an electric utility plan its future.

2. How might an organization with a good strategic idea be limited in its ability to implement that idea if it has

an inferior or inappropriate information architecture? Provide an example.

3. What type of problems might an organization encounter if it focuses only on resource allocation planning and project planning?

4. Why is it so important to align the IT plan with organizational strategies? What could happen if the plan is not aligned with these strategies?

5. Discuss the advantages of using Tjan's approach to an applications portfolio.

6. Some organizations feel that IT planning is a waste of time, because the competitive environment and technologies are changing so rapidly. They argue that their plans will be obsolete before they are completed. Discuss.

7. Should there be a correlation between a firm's architecture structure (and chart) and its IT architecture (e.g., centralized IT for a centralized structure)?

8. Review the opening case. What approach was used to develop an information systems plan?

9. Relate the concepts of supply chain and its management to BPR and IT.

10. Explain why IT is an important BPR enabler.

11. Some people say that BPR is a special case of a strategic information system, whereas others say that the opposite is true. Comment.

12. Relate virtual corporations to networked organizations. Why is a VC considered to be a BPR activity?

13. What are some of the reasons for maintaining a functional structure of an organization?

14. Explain the role intranets can play in lessening the stovepipe problem.

EXERCISES

1. Using the CSF method of strategic planning, identify new strategic initiatives that a university might take using information technology.

2. Examine *IT at Work 9.2* and Tjan's applications portfolio method. Compare the two, showing the advantages and limitations of each.

3. What kind of IT planning is done in your university or place of work to ensure that the Internet demand in the future will be met? Does the university have a CIO? Why or why not?

4. Examine some business processes in your university, city, or company. Identify two processes that need to be redesigned. Employ some of El-Sawy's 10 principles (see Online File W9.10) to plan the redesign. Be innovative.

GROUP ASSIGNMENTS

1. Divide the class into groups of six people or less. Each group will be entrepreneurs attempting to start some kind of nationwide company. Each group should describe the IT architecture it would build, as well as the expected benefits from, and potential problems with, the IT architecture it has chosen.

2. Have teams from the class visit IT project development efforts at local companies. The team members should interview members of the project team to ascertain the following information.

   a. How does the project contribute to the goals and objectives of the company?

   b. Is there an information architecture in place? If so, how does this project fit into that architecture?

   c. How was the project justified?

   d. What planning approach, if any, was used?

   e. How is the project being managed?

3. Assign groups to the following industries: banking, airlines, health care, insurance, and large retailing. Each group will investigate the use of the mainframe in one industry and prepare a report on the future of the mainframe. Also, include information on how client/server architecture is used in the industry.

4. Each group in the class will be assigned to a major ERP/SCM vendor such as SAP, PeopleSoft, Oracle, etc. Members of the groups will investigate topics such as:

   a. Web connections.

   b. Use of business intelligence tools.

   c. Relationship to BPR.

   d. Major capabilities.

   e. Use of ASPs.

   f. Low cost approaches.

   Each group will prepare a presentation for the class.

INTERNET EXERCISES

1. Go to *dwinc.com/strat.htm* and read the content. Compare and contrast the approach on this page to other approaches to strategic information systems planning.

2. Enter *cio.com*. Review the latest IT planning surveys and reviews reported. Start with the October 1997 survey conducted by CIO Communications Inc.

3. Find 10 to 15 examples of mass customization not cited in this book. Look for shoes, clothing, industrial products, etc.

4. There is an increased use of the Internet/intranets to enable employees to make their own travel arrangements. Several Internet travel companies provide opportunities for companies to reengineer their travel processes. Surf the Internet to find some vendors that provide such services. Prepare a report that summarizes all the various activities. Also discuss the potential impact on the travel agency industry.

5. Enter *truserv.com* and find "news" in the media relations section. Identify all IT-related plans announced by the company in the last six months. Comment on your findings.

6. Surf the Internet to find some recent material on the role IT plays in supporting BPR. Search for products and vendors and download an available demo.

7. Identify some newsgroups that are interested in BPR. Initiate a discussion on the role of IT in BPR.

8. Enter *gensym.com* and find their modeling products. Explain how they support BPR and redesign.

9. Enter *xelus.com/index.asp* and find how Xelus Corporation software can facilitate planning (e.g., see the Cisco case).

Minicase 1
Oregon Geographic Information System Plan

Geographic information systems (GISs) are becoming increasingly important to governmental agencies in conducting their business and serving the public. Such systems use spatial data such as digitized maps and can combine these data with other text, graphics, icons, and symbols (see Chapter 11). The state government in Oregon (*sscgis.state.or.us*) recognized the increasing importance of GISs as a tool to support decisions that are related to data represented by maps. GISs also offer the potential benefit of coordination among agencies to avoid duplicated efforts and incompatible data.

The state therefore created a Geographic Information Council, consisting of 22 people from agencies at the federal, state, and local levels, to develop a strategic plan to promote the effective use of GISs in Oregon. The planning process commenced in 1995 and produced a comprehensive plan dated March 1996. The plan identified and prioritized goals and strategies, including leadership responsibilities and time frames for each major item. The Council circulated the draft plan to GIS personnel in different organizations, to obtain a peer review before finalizing the document.

The plan starts with a "vision for GIS," a scenario for potential types and levels of usage. This vision incorporates potential advances in technology such as multimedia,

organizational structures including a statewide centralized GIS data administration function, a high-bandwidth telecommunications infrastructure, and adequate funding for GIS activities.

Benchmarks for Success

The plan identified criteria for evaluating its own validity:

- GIS integrated into governmental processes ("as common as word processing")
- Geographic data gathered and managed cooperatively and made available to the public
- Statewide standards for spatial data
- A centralized catalog of statewide GIS data
- GIS as an integral part of curriculum for K–12 and higher education throughout the state

Goals and Strategies

The plan also established specific goals, strategies for achieving them, agencies with lead responsibilities, and target dates. The goals include data requirements such as:

(1) currency and completeness; (2) security; (3) ease of use and accessibility; (4) incorporation of metadata indicating applicability; (5) coordination of collection and maintenance; and (6) standardization.

For technology, the goals include: (1) network access for agencies and public; (2) compatible data exchange formats; (3) real-time update capability; (4) master contracts for hardware/software/training; (5) integration with global positioning system (GPS) technology; and (6) a centralized data repository.

For people and organizations, the goals include: (1) stable funding and resources; (2) recruitment and retention of GIS employees; (3) definition of a model GIS organizational structure; (4) development of an educational program; (5) effective marketing of Oregon's GIS program.

Follow-Up

The planning group recognized that this plan would lose its value if not maintained, or if there were no follow-up on its recommendations. Therefore the plan included the following ongoing strategies: (1) monthly meetings of the planning group; (2) workgroups to address specific recommendations; (3) development of GIS plans at other state agencies; (4) distribution of supplements and updates four times a year; and (5) measurement against benchmarks and revision of the plan for the next two-year period.

Source: Compiled from *sscgis.state.or.us/coord/orisplan.htm.* Adapted and reprinted with permission from Oregon Department of Administration and PlanGraphics, Inc.

Questions for Minicase 1

1. Which stage(s) and activities of the four-stage planning model is/are included in the Oregon GIS planning effort?

2. Based on material presented in this chapter and your own personal evaluation, identify things that the planners did well in this project.

3. Can you see any problems or weaknesses with this planning effort?

4. Discuss possible differences in IT planning for governmental agencies, as discussed in this minicase, versus planning in business organizations.

5. Identify businesses and other private organizations that might want to use GIS data created and maintained by public agencies in Oregon. Discuss how (and whether) public agencies should charge private organizations for such data.

Minicase 2
Scenario Planning at National City Bank Aligns IT with Business Planning

The Problem. The banking industry is very competitive. National City Corp. of Cleveland (*national-city.com*) was confronting three challenges: (1) it needed new ways to generate earnings; (2) it faced increasing competition for market share; and (3) the bank was losing customers who wanted to do banking using the Internet.

National City saw the customer information system it was developing with IBM as a solution to these problems. The bank hoped to use this system to develop new, high-revenue products, tailor programs for customers, and cross-sell products to appropriate customers. But to design it, the bank had to know what kind of information the system would be aggregating. Would it track information about the products the bank offered or the people who bought them? If it was product-focused, it would have to include detailed descriptions of each financial service, whether credit cards or mortgages. If the system was customer-focused, it would track whether they used ATMs, branch offices, or call centers, and would indicate demographics in order to build customer profiles. Furthermore, the bank would need to set up business rules to determine customer profitability.

Management quickly realized that they simply could not answer these questions because the answers were linked to a larger issue: Management didn't have a clear sense of the bank's strategic direction. The required investment in technology was $40 million, so planning to invest it properly was critical.

The Solution. To clarify the business direction, the bank hired a consulting company, *ncri.com*, to employ scenario planning. The planning process involved six phases used by an implementation team:

Phase I: Alternative Visions (Scenarios)

In this phase, a few possible visions of the future are selected. In the case of National City, the scenarios were:

- *Utilize a CRM-based strategy.* This was a major industry trend in which everything would be geared to individual customer need. This business model is complex and expensive to pursue.
- *Specialize solely in certain financial services.* This is a low-cost option, but may not bring new customers and may even result in losing existing customers.
- *Create a separate online bank.*

Phase II: Events Generation

Next, a list of 150 internal and external events that might influence any of the outcomes was generated by the team. Events included new regulations and technological developments (e.g., wireless). These events were simulated as newspaper headlines (e.g., "Demand for real-time banking information via cell phones is skyrocketing"). These events were used later to create scenarios.

Phase III: The Workshop

A three-day workshop with the 24 top executives was conducted. The participants were divided into three groups. The first task was to rank all 150 events by the *chance that they will occur.* Once done, all participants met to discuss the rankings and, after appropriate discussion, reach a consensus. This process can be lengthy, but it is essential.

Then, each team was assigned one of the bank's three scenarios and was asked to analyze the impact of the most-likely-to-occur events on that scenario, within a five-year planning horizon.

Phase IV: Presentation

Each group made an oral presentation, in which their goal was to convince the other groups that their vision was the most feasible. This was a difficult task since some team members, who had to play the role of supporters, actually did not like the scenario they were suppose to "sell."

Phase V: Deliberation and Attempt to Reach a Consensus

The entire group of participants needed to agree on which alternative was the best for the bank. After long deliberation, the group decided to support alternative #1, the CRM-based strategy.

Phase VI: IT Support

To facilitate the IT planning, an IS plan was devised in which a data warehouse was planned, so that customers' profiles could be built. Data mining was planned for identifying the bank's most profitable customers, and a Web-based call center was designed to provide personalized services.

All in all, the scenario planning process was an exercise in contingency thinking that resulted in prosperity when the system was eventually deployed.

Sources: Condensed from Levinson (2000), *ncri.com*, and *national-city.com*.

Questions for Minicase 2

1. One critique of this approach is that some members who are asked to "sell" a specific scenario may not be enthusiastic to do so. Find information in the scenario planning literature on this issue, or e-mail a scenario consultant (*ncri.com* or *gbn.com*). Write a report on your findings.

2. Can group decision support systems (Chapter 10) be used in this case? Why and what for, or why not?

3. How can the end users learn about technology in scenario planning?

4. What can IT tools be used to facilitate this scenario planning process, which was done manually?

5. How did the scenario planning help the IT people to better understand the business?

6. Why is scenario planning considered a risk-management tool?

Virtual Company Assignment
IT Planning at The Wireless Café

During your internship at The Wireless Café, you've uncovered many opportunities for IT to offer more effective management, better information, and improved customer care. You've got everybody's heads spinning with the possibilities, but you realize that it takes careful planning, alignment, and integration to make the best use of information technologies at the diner. While you and Jeremy were recently talking about the potential of wireless wait-staff software, you realized he's quite excited about it and may just go out and buy the system. You decide you really need to talk with Barbara and Jeremy about the importance of IT planning, so you start to set out your "plan to plan."

Instructions

1. Discuss the long-range planning approach you'd recommend that TWC undertake. Include issues such as the planning approach, who you would include (and how you would get the staff together in a 24/7 operation),

the planning activities you would use to get started, and the proposed results of the IT strategic planning effort.

2. As the senior cook, Marie-Christine works closely with Barbara and Jeremy in menu planning, meal costing, and food ordering. At the French Culinary Institute where she was trained, Marie-Christine learned how to cost meals manually. Many automated menu costing programs are now available, such as RestaurantPlus (*restaurantplus.com/*), Micros (*micros.com/*) NextPos (*nextpos.com/*), and Aloha (*alohapos.com*). You sense that Marie-Christine is very proud of her background and training and has a strong reluctance to use the computer. What steps would you take to overcome this reluctance?

3. It is beginning to look like IT may drive the business decisions at TWC. After reviewing TWC's mission and considering the myriad possibilities for reengineering many front-of-the-house and back-of-the-house processes, what advice do you have for Barbara and Jeremy, who seem very enthusiastic about adopting many new technologies?

REFERENCES

Agrawal, V. et al., "E-Performance: The Path to Rational Exuberance," *McKinsey Quarterly,* First Quarter, 2001.

Anderson, L. A., *The Change Leader's Roadmap: How to Navigate Organizations' Transformation.* New York: Wiley, 2001.

Barua, A. et al., "Driving E-business Excellence," *MIT Sloan Management Review,* 43(1), 2001.

Blodgett, M., "Game Plans (Strategic Plans)," *CIO Magazine,* January 1998.

Boar, B. H., *The Art of Strategic Planning for Information Technology,* 2nd ed. New York: Wiley, 2000.

Bosilj-Vuksic, V. et al., "Assessment of E-Business Transformation Using Simulation Modeling," *Simulation,* December 2002.

"Bottom-Up GIS," *Journal of the American Planning Association,* Summer 2000.

Boudreau, M. C. et al., "Going Global: Using IT to Advance the Competitiveness of the Virtual Transactional Organization," *Academy of Management Executives,* 12(4), 1998.

Broadbent, M. et al., "Firm Context and Patterns of IT Infrastructure Capability," *Proceedings of the 17th International Conference on Information Systems,* Cleveland, December 16–18, 1996.

Broadbent, M. et al., "The Implications of IT Infrastructure for Business Process Redesign," *MIS Quarterly,* June 1999.

Burn, J. M., and C. G. Ash, "Managing Change for E-Business Success," *Proceedings, 14th Bled E-Commerce Conference,* Bled, Slovenia, June 25–26, 2001.

Business Systems Planning—Information Systems Planning Guide, Application Manual GE20-0527-3, 3rd ed., IBM Corporation, July 1981.

Cale, E. G., and J. Kanter, "Aligning Information Systems and Business Strategy: A Case Study," *Journal of Information Technology Management,* 9(1), 1998.

Callon, J. D., *Competitive Advantage Through Information Technology.* New York: McGraw-Hill, 1996.

Cassidy, A., *A Practical Guide to IT Strategic Planning.* Boca Raton, FL: CRC Press, 1998.

Chan, Y. E., "Why Haven't We Mastered Alignment? The Importance of the Informal Organizational Structure," *MIS Quarterly Executive,* 1(2), 2002.

Chen, J. S., and R. K. H. Ching, "A Proposed Framework for Transition to an e-Business Model," *Quarterly Journal of E-Commerce,* Oct.–Dec. 2002.

CIO.com, *cio.com/archive(040103)strategy.html.* Accessed July 2003.

Clarke, A., and S. Manton, "A Benchmarking Tool for Change Management," *BPMJ,* 3(3), 1977.

Computer Sciences Corporation (CSC), *CSC's 14th Annual Critical Issues of Information Systems Management Survey,* 2001.

Choudrie, J. et al., "Teams and Their Motivation for Business Process Reengineering: A Research Note," *International Journal of Flexible Manufacturing Systems,* 14(1), 2002.

Curry, J., and J. Ferguson, "Increasing the Success of IT Strategic Planning Process," *Proceedings, 33rd Hawaiian International Conference on Systems Sciences (HICSS),* Hawaii, January 2000.

Earl, M. J., *Management Strategies for Information Technology,* Englewood Cliffs, NJ: Prentice Hall, 1989.

E-Government Strategy: Special Report, *whitehouse.gov/omb/egov/2003egov_strat.pdf,* April 2003.

El Sawy, O., *Redesigning Enterprise Processes for E-Business.* New York: McGraw-Hill, 2001.

Evangelista, A. S., and L. A. Burke, "Work Redesign and Performance Management in Times of Downsizing," *Business Horizons,* 46(2), 2003.

Feurer, R. et al., "Aligning Strategies, Processes, and IT: A Case Study," *Information Systems Management,* Winter 2000.

Galliers, B., "Towards the Integration of E-Business, KM, and Policy Considerations Within an Information Systems Strategy Framework," *Strategic Information Systems,* Vol. 8, 1999.

Geoffrey, J., "Intranets Rescue Reengineering," *Datamation,* December 1996.

Gilmore, J. H., and B. J. Pine (eds)., *Market of One: Creating Customer-Unique Value Through Mass Customization.* Boston: Harvard Business School Press, 2000.

Ginige, A. et al., "A Road Map for Successfully Transforming SMEs into E-Business," *Cutter IT Journal,* May 2001.

Goldman, S. L. et al., *Agile Competitors and Virtual Organizations.* New York: Van Nostrand Reinhold, 1995.

Grant, D., "A Wilder View of Business Process Reengineering," *Association for Computing Machinery,* 45(2), 2002.

Hackney, J. Burn, and G. Dhillon, "Challenging Assumptions for Strategic Information Systems Planning," *Communications of AIS,* 3(9), 2000.

Hackney, R. A., G. Griffiths, and J. Burn, "Strategic Information Systems Planning: A Resource and Capabilities-Based View for Sustainability of Competitiveness," *Proceedings of British Academy of Management (BAM99),* Manchester Metropolitan University (UK), September 1999.

Hammer, M., and J. Champy, *Re-engineering the Corporation.* New York: Harper Business, 1993.

Hinks, J., "The Transition to Virtual: The Impact of Changes in Business Operations on Facilities Management," *Journal of Facilities Management,* 1(3), 2002.

Khan, M. R. R., "BPR of an Air Cargo Handling Process," *International Journal of Production Economics,* January 2000.

Khong, K. W., and S. Richardson, "BPR in Malaysian Banks and Finance Companies," *Managing Service Quality,* January 2003.

King, W. R., "Assessing the Efficiency of IS Strategic Planning," *Information Systems Management,* Winter 2000.

Kwahk, K. Y., and Y. G. Kim, "Supporting Business Process Redesign Using Cognitive Maps," *Decision Support Systems,* March 1999.

Lasry, E. M., "Inertia.com: Rates and Processes of Organizational Transformation in the Retail Industry," *Quarterly Journal of E-Commerce,* July–Sept. 2002.

Launonen, M., and P. Kess, "Team Roles in Business Process Reengineering," *International Journal of Production Economics,* 77(3), 2002.

Le Blond, R., "BPM: Look Under the Hood," *CIO Asia,* March 2003 (*cio-asia.com*).

Lee, J., Smart Products and Services for E-Business Transformation," *Int. J. Technology Management,* Jan.–March 2003.

Levinson, M., "Don't Stop Thinking About Tomorrow," *CIO Magazine,* January 1, 2000.

MacIntosh, R., "BPR: Alive and Well in the Public Sector," *International Journal of Operations & Production Management,* 23(¾), 2003.

Majcharzak, A., and Q. Wang, "Breaking the Functional Mind-Set in Process Organizations," *Harvard Business Review,* September–October 1996.

Markus, M. L. et al., "What Makes a Virtual Organization Work: Lessons from the Open-Source World," *Sloan Management Review*, Fall 2000.

Martin, J., and C. Finkelstein, "Information Engineering," Technical Report, two volumes, November 1981. Lancs, U.K.: Savant Institute, Carnforth.

Mintzberg, H., and Westley F., "Cycles of Organizational Change," *Strategic Management Journal*, Vol. 14, 1992.

Mohanty, R. P., and S. G. Deshmukh, "Reengineering of Materials Management System: A Case Study," *International Journal of Production Economics*, 70(3), 2001.

Murrell, K. L., and M. Meredith, *Empowering Employees*. New York: McGraw-Hill, 2000.

ncc.co.uk, Report on IT Strategy. Accessed July 20, 2003.

Nolan, R. L., "Managing the Crises in Data Processing," *Harvard Business Review*, March–April 1979.

Papp, R. (ed.), *Strategic Information Technology: Opportunities for Competitive Advantage*. Hershey, PA: Idea Group, 2001.

Peffers, K., and C. E. Gengler, "How to Identify New High-Payoff Information Systems for the Organization," *Communications of the ACM*, 46(1), January 2003.

Peng, K. L., and C. Y. Chang, "An Exploratory Study of the Virtual Organization from the Viewpoint of Information Science and Technology," *Proceedings, Western DSI*, Hawaii, 2000.

People 3 Inc., "Achieving IT and Business Alignment: A Human Capital Management View," 2003.

Pickering, C., *E-Business Success Strategies: Achieving Business and IT Alignment*. Charleston, SC: 2000 Computer Technology Research, 2000.

Pine, B. J., and S. Davis, *Mass Customization: The New Frontier in Business Competition*. Boston: Harvard Business School Press, 1999.

Plant, T., *E-Commerce: Formulation of Strategy*. Upper Saddle River, NJ: Prentice Hall, 2000.

Rajaram, K., and C. J. Corbett, "Achieving Environmental and Productivity Improvements Through Model-Based Process Redesign," *Operations Research*, 50(5), 2002.

Rogers, E. M., *Diffusion of Innovation*. New York: Free Press, 1983.

Ruohonen, M., and L. F. Higgins, "Application of Creativity Principles to IS Planning," *Proceedings HICSS*, Hawaii, January 1998.

Salladurai, R., "An Organizational Profitability, Productivity, Performance (PPP) Model: Going Beyond TQM and BPR," *Total Quality Management*, 13(5), 2002.

Samela, H. et al., "Information Systems Planning in a Turbulent Environment," *European Journal of Information Systems*, 9(1), 2000.

Samela, H., and T. A. M. Spil, "Dynamic and Emergent Information Systems Strategy Formulation and Implementation," *International Journal of Information Management*, December 2002.

Sarker, S., and A. S. Lee, "IT-Enabled Organizational Transformation: A Case Study of BPR Failure at TELECO," *Journal of Strategic Information Systems*, Vol. 8, 1999.

Seybold, P. B., "Get Inside the Lives of Your Customers," *Harvard Business Review*, May 2001.

Simnet.org, Surveys of Senior IT Executives. Accessed June 6, 2002.

Smith, H., and P. Fingar, *Business Process Management (BPM): The Third Wave*. Tampa, FL: Meghan-Kiffar, 2002.

Stauffer, D., "Five Reasons Why You Still Need Scenario Planning," *Harvard Business Review*, June 2002.

Suhas, H. K., *From Quality to Virtual Corporation: An Integrated Approach*. Boca Raton, FL: CRC Press, 2000.

Teo, T. S. H., and J. S. K. Ang, "An Examination of Major IS Planning Problems," *International Journal of Information Management*, December 2001.

Tjan, A. K., "Finally, A Way to Put Your Internet Portfolio in Order," *Harvard Business Review*, February 2001.

Tung, L. L., and E. Turban, "The Reengineering of the ISD of the Housing Development Board in Singapore," in B. S. Neo (ed.), *Exploring Information Technology for Business Competitiveness*. Reading, MA: Addison Wesley, 1996.

Turban, E. et al., *Electronic Commerce: A Managerial Perspective*, 3rd ed. Upper Saddle River, NJ: Prentice-Hall, 2004.

Useem, J., "Dot-coms: What Have We Learned?" *Fortune*, October 30, 2000.

Venkatraman, N., and J. Henderson, "Real Strategies for Virtual Organizing," *Sloan Management Review*, Fall 1998.

Ward, J., and J. Peppard, *Strategic Planning for Information Systems*, 3rd ed. New York: John Wiley & Sons, 2002.

Wetherbe, J. C., "Four-Stage Model of MIS Planning Concepts, Techniques, and Implementation," in R. Banker, R. Kaufman, and M. Mahmood (eds.), *Strategic Information Technology Management: Perspectives on Organizational Growth and Competitive Advantage*. Harrisburg, PA: Idea Group, 1993.

Wetherbe, J. C., *The World on Time*. Santa Monica, CA: Knowledge Exchange, 1996.

Zakaria, Z., "Legal Action," *MIS Asia*, April 2002.

PART IV
Managerial and Decision Support Systems

▶ 10. Knowledge Management
11. Data Management: Warehousing, Analyzing, Mining, and Visualization
12. Management Decision Support and Intelligent Systems

CHAPTER

10

Knowledge Management

10.1
Introduction to Knowledge Management

10.2
Knowledge Management Initiatives

10.3
Approaches to Knowledge Management

10.4
Information Technology in Knowledge Management

10.5
Knowledge Management Systems Implementation

10.6
Roles of People in Knowledge Management

10.7
Ensuring Success of KM Efforts

LEARNING OBJECTIVES

After studying this chapter, you will be able to:

❶ Define knowledge and describe the different types of knowledge.

❷ Describe the activities involved in knowledge management.

❸ Describe different approaches to knowledge management.

❹ Describe the technologies that can be utilized in a knowledge management system.

❺ Describe the issues associated with implementing knowledge management in organizations.

❻ Describe the activities of the chief knowledge officer and others involved in knowledge management.

❼ Describe benefits as well as drawbacks to knowledge management initiatives.

SIEMENS LEARNS WHAT IT KNOWS THROUGH KNOWLEDGE MANAGEMENT

 THE PROBLEM

Siemens AG, a $73 billion electronics and electrical-engineering conglomerate, produces everything from lightbulbs to X-Ray machines, from power generation equipment to high-speed trains. During its 156-year history, Siemens (*siemens.com*) developed into one of the world's largest and most successful corporations. Siemens is well known for the technical brilliance of its engineers; however, much of their knowledge was locked and unavailable to other employees. Facing competitive pressure (see opening case, Chapter 1), Siemens is trying to maximize the contributions of each business unit. One way to do it was to learn to leverage the knowledge and expertise of its 460,000 employees worldwide.

 THE SOLUTION

The roots of knowledge management (KM) at Siemens go back to 1996 when a number of people within the corporation with an interest in KM formed a "community of interest." They researched the subject, learned what was being done by other companies, and looked for ways that knowledge management could benefit Siemens. Without any suggestion or encouragement from senior executives, mid-level employees in Siemens business units began creating knowledge repositories, communities of practice, and informal techniques of sharing knowledge. By 1999, the senior management of Siemens AG confirmed the importance of knowledge management to the entire company by creating an organizational unit that would be responsible for the worldwide deployment of KM.

At the heart of Siemens' technical solution to knowledge management is a Web site called ShareNet, which combines elements of a database repository, a chat room, and a search engine. Online entry forms allow employees to store information they think might be useful to colleagues. Other Siemens employees are able to search the repository or browse by topic, and then contact the authors for more information using one of the available communication channels. In addition, the system lets employees post an alert when they have an urgent question.

Although KM implementation at Siemens involved establishing a network to collect, categorize, and share information using databases and intranets, Siemens realized that IT was only the tool that enabled knowledge management. Randall Sellers, Director of Knowledge Management for the Americas Region of Siemens stated, "In my opinion, the technology or IT role is a small one. I think it's 20 percent IT and 80 percent change management—dealing with cultural change and human interfaces."

The movement toward knowledge management by Siemens has presented several challenges to the company, some of which are cultural. Siemens used a three-pronged effort to convince employees that it is important to participate in the exchange of ideas and experiences and to share what they know. It has assigned 100 internal KM "evangelists" throughout the world who are responsible for training, answering questions, and monitoring the system. Siemens' top management has shown its full support for the knowledge management projects. And the company is providing incentives to overcome employees' resistance to change.

In exchange for employees posting documents to the system and for using the knowledge, Siemens rewards its employees with "shares," much like frequent-flyer miles. Once collected and accumulated, these shares can be exchanged for things like consumer electronics or discounted trips to other countries.

However, the real incentive of the system is much more basic. Commission-driven salespeople have already learned that knowledge and expertise of their colleagues available through ShareNet can be indispensable in winning lucrative contracts. Employees in marketing, service, R&D, and other departments are also willing to participate and contribute as long as they realize that the system provides them with useful information in a convenient way.

The ShareNet has undergone tremendous growth, which resulted in several challenges for Siemens. The company strives to maintain balance between global and local knowledge initiatives as well as between knowledge management efforts that support the entire company or individual business units. Furthermore, Siemens works to prevent ShareNet from becoming so overloaded with information that it becomes useless. It employs a group of people who monitor the system and remove trivial and irrelevant content.

 THE RESULTS

The ShareNet has evolved into a state-of-the-art Web-based knowledge management system that stores and catalogues volumes of valuable knowledge, makes it available to every employee, and enhances global collaboration. Numerous companies, including Intel and Volkswagen, studied ShareNet before setting up their own knowledge management systems. Furthermore, Teleos, an independent knowledge management research company, acknowledged Siemens as being one of the Most Admired Knowledge Enterprises worldwide for five years in a row.

Siemens also has realized a variety of quantifiable benefits afforded by knowledge management. For example, in April 1999, the company developed a portion of ShareNet to support its Information & Communications Networks Group at the cost of $7.8 million. Within 2 years, the tool had helped to generate $122 million in additional sales.

Ultimately, knowledge management may be one of the major tools that will help Siemens prove that large diversified conglomerates can work and that being big might even be an advantage in the Information Age.

Sources: Adapted from Vasilash (2002), *The Economist* (2001), and Williams (2001).

 LESSONS LEARNED FROM THIS CASE

This case illustrates the importance and value of identifying an organization's knowledge and sharing it throughout the organization. In a major initiative, Siemens AG developed ShareNet and other knowledge management systems to capture the valuable knowledge of the employees. Siemens transformed its culture as the knowledge management system was deployed, leading to significantly lower operating costs and more collaboration throughout the global enterprise. Organizations recognize the value of their intellectual assets, though they may be hard to measure. Fierce global competition drives companies to better utilize their intellectual assets by transforming themselves into organizations that foster the development and sharing of knowledge.

In this chapter we describe the characteristics and concepts of knowledge management. In addition, we will explain how firms are using information technology to implement knowledge management systems and how these systems are transforming modern organizations.

10.1 INTRODUCTION TO KNOWLEDGE MANAGEMENT

Concepts and Definitions

With roots in expert systems, organizational learning, and innovation, the idea of knowledge management is itself not new (e.g., see Cahill, 1996). Successful managers have always used intellectual assets and recognized their value. But these efforts were not systematic, nor did they ensure that knowledge gained was shared and dispersed appropriately for maximum organizational benefit. Moreover, sources such as Forrester Research, IBM, and Merrill Lynch estimate that 85 percent of a company's knowledge assets are not housed in relational databases, but are dispersed in e-mail, Word documents, spreadsheets, and presentations on individual computers (Ziff Davis, 2002). The application of information technology tools to facilitate the creation, storage, transfer, and application of previously uncodifiable organizational knowledge is a new and major initiative in organizations.

Knowledge management (KM) is a process that helps organizations identify, select, organize, disseminate, and transfer important information and expertise that are part of the organization's memory and that typically reside within the organization in an unstructured manner. This structuring of knowledge enables effective and efficient problem solving, dynamic learning, strategic planning, and decision making. Knowledge management initiatives focus on identifying knowledge, explicating it in such a way that it can be shared in a formal manner, and leveraging its value through reuse.

Through a supportive organizational climate and modern information technology, an organization can bring its entire organizational memory and knowledge to bear upon any problem anywhere in the world and at any time. For organizational success, *knowledge, as a form of capital, must be exchangeable among persons, and it must be able to grow.* Knowledge about how problems are solved can be captured, so that knowledge management can promote organizational learning, leading to further knowledge creation.

KNOWLEDGE. In the information technology context, knowledge is very distinct from data and information (see Figure 10.1). Whereas *data* are a collection of facts, measurements, and statistics, *information* is organized or processed data that are timely (i.e., inferences from the data are drawn within the time frame

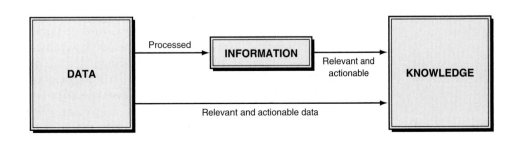

FIGURE 10.1 Data, information, and knowledge.

of applicability) and accurate (i.e., with regard to the original data) (Holsapple, 2003). **Knowledge** is information that is *contextual, relevant,* and *actionable.*

For example, a map giving detailed driving directions from one location to another could be considered data. An up-to-the-minute traffic bulletin along the freeway that indicates a traffic slowdown due to construction several miles ahead could be considered information. Awareness of an alternative, back-roads route could be considered knowledge. In this case, the map is considered data because it does not contain current relevant information that affects the driving time and conditions from one location to the other. However, having the current conditions as information is useful only if the individual has knowledge that will enable him or her to avert the construction zone. The implication is that knowledge has strong experiential and reflective elements that distinguish it from information in a given context. Having knowledge implies that it can be exercised to solve a problem, whereas having information does not carry the same connotation.

An *ability to act* is an integral part of being knowledgeable. For example, two people in the same context with the same information may not have the same ability to use the information to the same degree of success. Hence there is a difference in the human capability to add value. The differences in ability may be due to different experiences, different training, different perspectives, and so on. While data, information, and knowledge may all be viewed as assets of an organization, knowledge provides a higher level of meaning about data and information. It conveys *meaning,* and hence tends to be much more valuable, yet more ephemeral.

Knowledge has the following characteristics that differentiates it from an organization's other assets (Gray, 1999; Holsapple, 2003):

- *Extraordinary leverage and increasing returns.* Knowledge is not subject to diminishing returns. When it is used, it is not consumed. Its consumers can add to it, thus increasing its value.
- *Fragmentation, leakage, and the need to refresh.* As knowledge grows, it branches and fragments. Knowledge is dynamic; it is information in action. Thus, an organization must continually refresh its knowledge base to maintain it as a source of competitive advantage.
- *Uncertain value.* It is difficult to estimate the impact of an investment in knowledge. There are too many intangible aspects.
- *Uncertain value of sharing.* Similarly, it is difficult to estimate the value of sharing the knowledge, or even who will benefit most.
- *Rooted in time.* The utility and validity of knowledge may vary with time; hence, the immediacy, age, perishability, and volatility of knowledge are important attributes.

There is a vast amount of literature about what knowledge and knowing means in epistemology (study of the nature of knowledge), the social sciences, philosophy, and psychology (Polanyi, 1958, 1966). Though there is no single definition of what knowledge and knowledge management specifically mean, the business perspective on them is fairly pragmatic. Information as a resource is not always valuable (i.e., information overload can distract from the important); knowledge is a resource when it is clear, relevant, and important to an individual processing the knowledge (Holsapple, 2003). Knowledge implies an implicit understanding and experience that can discriminate between its use and misuse. Over time, information accumulates and decays, while knowledge evolves. The word *knowledge* tends to carry positive connotations (Schultze and Leidner, 2002). However, because *knowledge is dynamic in nature,* today's knowledge may well become tomorrow's ignorance if an individual or organization fails to update knowledge as environmental conditions change. For more on the potential drawbacks of managing and reusing knowledge, see Section 10.7.

Intellectual capital (or **intellectual assets**) is another term often used for knowledge, and it implies that there is a financial value to knowledge (Edvinsson, 2003). Though intellectual capital is difficult to measure, some industries have tried. For example, the value of the intellectual capital of the property-casualty insurance industry has been estimated to be between $270 billion to $330 billion (Mooney, 2000). The Organization for Economic Co-operation and Development (OCED) has scored its 30 member nations according to their investments in intellectual capital such as R&D, education, and patents. According to OCED, those countries with the most intellectual capital activities will be the winners of future wealth (Edvinsson, 2003).

Knowledge evolves over time with experience, which puts connections among new situations and events in context. Given the breadth of the types and applications of knowledge, we adopt the simple and elegant definition that knowledge is *information in action* (O'Dell et al., 1998).

TACIT AND EXPLICIT KNOWLEDGE. Polanyi (1958) first conceptualized and distinguished between an organization's tacit and explicit knowledge. **Explicit knowledge** deals with more objective, rational, and technical knowledge (data, policies, procedures, software, documents, etc.). **Tacit knowledge** is usually in the domain of subjective, cognitive, and experiential learning; it is highly personal and difficult to formalize (Nonaka and Takeuchi, 1995).

Explicit knowledge is the policies, procedural guides, white papers, reports, designs, products, strategies, goals, mission, and core competencies of the enterprise and the information technology infrastructure. It is the knowledge that has been codified (documented) in a form that can be distributed to others or transformed into a process or strategy without requiring interpersonal interaction. For example, a description of how to process a job application would be documented in a firm's human resources policy manual. Moreover, there is a simple relationship between the codification of knowledge and the costs of its transfer: the more that knowledge is made explicit, the more economically it can be transferred (Teece, 2003). Explicit knowledge has also been called **leaky knowledge** because of the ease with which it can leave an individual, document, or the organization, after it has been documented (Alavi, 2000).

Tacit knowledge is the cumulative store of the experiences, mental maps, insights, acumen, expertise, know-how, trade secrets, skill sets, understanding, and learning that an organization has, as well as the organizational culture that has embedded in it the past and present experiences of the organization's people, processes, and values. Tacit knowledge, also referred to as *embedded knowledge* (Madhaven and Grover, 1998), is usually either localized within the brain of an individual or embedded in the group interactions within a department or a branch office. Tacit knowledge typically involves expertise or high skill levels. It is generally slow and costly to transfer and can be plagued by ambiguity (Teece, 2003).

Sometimes tacit knowledge is easily documentable but has remained tacit simply because the individual housing the knowledge does not recognize its potential value to other individuals. Other times, tacit knowledge is unstructured, without tangible form, and therefore difficult to codify. Polanyi (1966) suggests that it is difficult to put some tacit knowledge into words. For example, an explanation of how to ride a bicycle would be difficult to document explicitly, and thus is tacit. Tacit knowledge has been called **sticky knowledge** because it may be relatively difficult to pull it away from its source.

Successful transfer or sharing of tacit knowledge usually takes place through associations, internships, apprenticeship, conversations, other means of social and interpersonal interactions, or even through simulations (e.g., see Robin, 2000). Nonaka and Takeuchi (1995) claim that intangibles like insights, intuitions, hunches, gut feelings, values, images, metaphors, and analogies are the often-overlooked assets of organizations. Harvesting this intangible asset can be critical to a firm's bottom line and its ability to meet its goals.

The Need for Knowledge Management Systems

The goal of knowledge management is for an organization to be aware of individual and collective knowledge so that it may make the most effective use of the knowledge it has (Bennet and Bennet, 2003). Historically, MIS has focused on capturing, storing, managing, and reporting explicit knowledge. Organizations now recognize the need to integrate both explicit and tacit knowledge in formal information systems. **Knowledge management systems (KMSs)** refers to the use of modern information technologies (e.g. the Internet, intranets, extranets, Lotus-Notes, software filters, agents, data warehouses) to systematize, enhance, and expedite intra- and interfirm knowledge management (Alavi and Leidner, 1999). KMSs are intended to help an organization cope with turnover, rapid change, and downsizing by making the expertise of the organization's human capital widely accessible. They are being built in part from increased pressure to maintain a well-informed, productive workforce. Moreover, they are built to help large organizations provide a consistent level of customer service, as illustrated in *IT at Work 10.1.*

Knowledge Management System Cycle

A functioning knowledge management system follows six steps in a cycle (see Figure 10.2, page 456). The reason the system is cyclical is that knowledge is dynamically refined over time. The knowledge in a good KM system is never finished because, over time, the environment changes, and the knowledge must be updated to reflect the changes. The cycle works as follows:

1. *Create knowledge.* Knowledge is created as people determine new ways of doing things or develop know-how. Sometimes external knowledge is brought in.
2. *Capture knowledge.* New knowledge must be identified as valuable and be represented in a reasonable way.
3. *Refine knowledge.* New knowledge must be placed in context so that it is actionable. This is where human insights (tacit qualities) must be captured along with explicit facts.
4. *Store knowledge.* Useful knowledge must then be stored in a reasonable format in a knowledge repository so that others in the organization can access it.
5. *Manage knowledge.* Like a library, the knowledge must be kept current. It must be reviewed to verify that it is relevant and accurate.
6. *Disseminate knowledge.* Knowledge must be made available in a useful format to anyone in the organization who needs it, anywhere and any time.

IT at Work 10.1
CINGULAR CALLS ON KNOWLEDGE

How do you make sure that each of your customer service agents at 22 call centers nationwide can answer virtually any question asked by one of your 22 million clients? That was the challenge faced by Cingular Wireless (*cingular.com*), a major mobile communications provider based in Atlanta, Georgia.

To accomplish this Herculean task, Cingular Wireless turned to knowledge management. Cingular benchmarked knowledge management solutions of technology-oriented companies, such as Dell and Microsoft. Steve Mullins, vice president of customer experience for Cingular Wireless, and Monica Browning, Cingular's director of knowledge management, met with several knowledge management software vendors to learn how their tools operate. Following a review of knowledge management solutions used by other companies, Cingular chose eService Suite by ServiceWare of Edison, New Jersey.

To ensure successful implementation of the system, Cingular embarked on a campaign to obtain support of everyone involved, from senior executives to each call center agent who would use the system. A pilot program was initiated at technical support departments at three call centers. In addition, to help manage organizational changes that accompany a shift to knowledge management, Cingular enlisted the help of leading consulting firms Cap Gemini, Ernst and Young, and Innovative Management Solutions.

A major issue in developing the knowledge management system involved capturing the knowledge and storing it in the system. Cingular accomplished it by combining the efforts of its employees and an external authoring group from Innovative Management Solutions. Cingular divided the process into phases, which allowed the company to populate the knowledge base with technical support information, common topics, information on rate plans, and so on. It took about four months before the knowledge base was ready for the first group of users.

The knowledge management system uses complex algorithms to process natural language queries and provide customer service agents with lists of most likely answers to their questions. Furthermore the software determines the relevance of possible answers by ranking them partly on exact text and phrase matching. In addition, the system can match synonyms and assign additional weight to certain things. The system attempts to provide even more focused solutions by retrieving answers from the pool of knowledge that is relevant to a particular user and his or her profile.

Understanding that knowledge must grow and evolve, Cingular encourages users to contribute their expertise to the system. The software can automatically record a sequence of steps that an agent took to find a correct solution to a certain problem and give the agent an option to provide additional feedback.

Cingular realized that ensuring validity and integrity of the knowledge stored and distributed by the knowledge management system is one of the key factors of the system's success. To that end, the company employs a knowledge management team that is responsible for monitoring, maintaining, and expanding the knowledge management system. The team consists of about 25 full-time employees based in Cingular's Atlanta headquarters. The KM team works closely with various departments of the company and subject matter experts to ensure that the knowledge base has the right answers in a user-friendly format at the right time. In addition, the team reviews contributions to the knowledge base made by the agents and makes appropriate changes or additions to the knowledge base.

Cingular's clients are often the ultimate beneficiaries of the company's knowledge. That is why Cingular plans to bring its knowledge closer to its customers by extending the knowledge management system online and to retail stores. Customers will be able to access instructions on using wireless services and features, handsets, and other devices that Cingular carries, as well as troubleshooting tips.

Source: Adapted from O'Herron (2003).

For Further Exploration: Explain the advantages and disadvantages of a professional knowledge management team administering the content of an organization's knowledge base.

As knowledge is disseminated, individuals develop, create, and identify new knowledge or update old knowledge, which they replenish into the system. Knowledge is a resource that is not consumed when used, though it can age. (For example, driving a car in 1900 was different from driving one now, but many of the basic principles still apply.) Knowledge must be updated. Thus, the amount of knowledge grows over time.

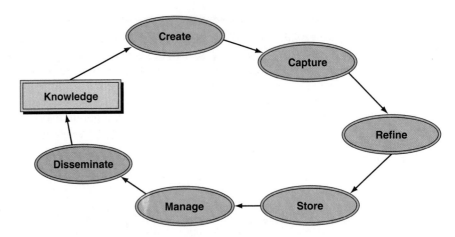

FIGURE 10.2 The knowledge management cycle.

10.2 KNOWLEDGE MANAGEMENT INITIATIVES

When asked why the organization was building a worldwide knowledge management system, the Chief Knowledge Officer (CKO) of a large multinational consulting firm replied, "We have 80,000 people scattered around the world that need information to do their jobs effectively. The information they needed was too difficult to find and, even if they did find it, often inaccurate. Our intranet is meant to solve this problem." (Leidner, 2003). A survey of European firms by KPMG Peat Marwick in 1998 found that almost half of the companies reported having suffered a significant setback from losing key staff (KPMG, 1998). Similarly, a survey conducted in the same year by Cranfield University found that the majority of responding firms believed that much of the knowledge they needed existed inside the organization, but that finding and leveraging it were ongoing challenges. It is precisely these types of difficulties that have led to the systematic attempt to manage knowledge.

Most knowledge management initiatives have one of three aims: (1) to make knowledge visible mainly through maps, yellow pages, and hypertext, (2) to develop a knowledge-intensive culture, or to (3) build a knowledge infrastructure (Davenport and Prusak, 1998). These aims are not mutually exclusive, and indeed, firms may attempt all three as part of a knowledge management initiative.

There are several activities or processes that surround the management of knowledge. These include the creation of knowledge, the sharing of knowledge, and the seeking and use of knowledge. Various terms have been used to describe these processes. What is important is an understanding of how knowledge flows through an organization, rather than any particular label assigned to a knowledge activity.

Knowledge Creation

Knowledge creation is the generation of new insights, ideas, or routines. It may also be referred to as *knowledge acquisition* (Holsapple and Joshi, 2003). It is helpful to distinguish between the creation of fundamentally new knowledge versus the acquisition of existing knowledge (Ford, 2003). Nonaka (1994) describes knowledge creation as interplay between tacit and explicit knowledge and as a growing spiral as knowledge moves among the individual, group, and organizational levels.

There are four modes of knowledge creation: socialization, externalization, internalization, and combination. The *socialization* mode refers to the conversion of tacit knowledge to new tacit knowledge through social interactions and shared experience among organizational members (e.g., mentoring). The *combination* mode refers to the creation of new explicit knowledge by merging, categorizing, reclassifying, and synthesizing existing explicit knowledge (e.g., statistical analyses of market data). The other two modes involve interactions and conversion between tacit and explicit knowledge. *Externalization* refers to converting tacit knowledge to new explicit knowledge (e.g., producing a written document describing the procedures used in solving a particular client's problem). *Internalization* refers to the creation of new tacit knowledge from explicit knowledge (e.g., obtaining a novel insight through reading a document). These final two modes of knowledge creation deal less with the creation of new knowledge than with the conversion of existing knowledge to a new mode.

Holsapple and Joshi (2003) suggest that there are two important dimensions to the acquisition of knowledge: one is the identification of existing knowledge from external sources and the other, the selection of needed knowledge from an organization's existing knowledge resources. These two activities require different skills, levels of effort, and costs.

Knowledge Sharing

Knowledge sharing is the willful explication of one's ideas, insights, solutions, experiences (i.e., knowledge) to another individual either via an intermediary, such as a computer-based system, or directly. However, in many organizations, information and knowledge are not considered organizational resources to be shared, but individual competitive weapons to be kept private (Davenport et al., 1998). Organizational members may share personal knowledge with a certain trepidation—the perceived threat that they are of less value if their knowledge is part of the organizational public domain. Also, a primary constraint on individual's knowledge sharing behaviors might simply be time. Moreover, sharing knowledge is a risky proposition since one does not know how that knowledge might be reused (Ford, 2003).

Research in organizational learning and knowledge management suggests that some facilitating conditions include trust, interest, and shared language (Hanssen-Bauer and Snow, 1996), fostering access to knowledgeable members (Brown and Duguid, 2000), and a culture marked by autonomy, redundancy, requisite variety, intention, and fluctuation (Nonaka, 1994). Several organizations have made knowledge sharing a guiding principal for the organization (Liebowitz and Chen, 2003). Johnson & Johnson has knowledge fairs designed to promote new relationships among colleagues in order to facilitate knowledge transfer. The World Bank includes such factors as openness to new ideas, continual learning, and sharing of knowledge as part of their annual performance evaluation of employees (Liebowitz and Chen, 2003).

Knowledge Seeking

Knowledge seeking, also referred to as *knowledge sourcing* (Gray and Meister, 2003), is the search for and use of internal organizational knowledge. While the lack of time or the lack of reward may hinder the sharing of knowledge, the same can be said of knowledge seeking. Individuals may sometimes feel compelled to come up with new ideas, rather than use tried-and-true knowledge, if they feel that their own performance review is based on the originality or creativity of their ideas. Such was the case for marketing employees in a global consumer goods organization described in Alavi et al. (2003).

Individuals may engage in knowledge creation, sharing, and seeking with or without the use of information technology tools. We next describe two common approaches to knowledge management.

10.3 APPROACHES TO KNOWLEDGE MANAGEMENT

There are two fundamental approaches to knowledge management: the process and the practice approaches.

The Process Approach

The **process approach** attempts to codify organizational knowledge through formalized controls, processes, and technologies (Hansen et al., 1999). Organizations adopting the process approach may implement explicit policies governing how knowledge is to be collected, stored, and disseminated throughout the organization. The process approach frequently involves the use of information technologies to enhance the quality and speed of knowledge creation and distribution in the organizations. These technologies may include intranets, data warehousing, knowledge repositories, decision support tools, and groupware (Ruggles, 1998).

There are several different levels of the process approach (van der Spek et al., 2003). At the most rudimentary, knowledge may be codified in project descriptions, stories, or other forms of documentation, but limited filtering has been done. At the next level, knowledge may be codified into structured concepts, frameworks, and theories. At the highest level, knowledge is embedded into work practices that give direction to employees (van der Spek et al., 2003).

The main criticisms of the process approach are that it fails to capture much of the tacit knowledge embedded in firms and that it forces individuals into fixed patterns of thinking (DeLong and Fahey, 2000; Brown and Duguid, 2000; Von Krogh, 2000; Hargadon, 1998). The process approach is favored by firms that sell relatively standardized products that fill common needs. Most of the valuable knowledge in these firms is fairly explicit because of the standardized nature of the products and services. For example, a kazoo manufacturer has minimal product changes or service needs over the years, and yet there is steady demand and a need to produce the item. In these cases, the knowledge is typically static in nature.

Even large firms that utilize tacit knowledge, such as Ernst & Young, have invested heavily to ensure that the process approach works efficiently. The 250 people at Ernst & Young's Center for Business Knowledge manage an electronic repository and help consultants find and use information. Specialists write reports and analyses that many teams can use. And each of Ernst & Young's more than 40 practice areas has a staff member who helps codify and store documents. The resulting area databases are linked through a network (Hansen et al., 1999). Naturally, people-to-documents is not the only way consultants in firms like Ernst & Young and Accenture share knowledge; they talk with one another as well. But they do place a high degree of emphasis on the codification strategy (Hansen et al., 1999).

The Practice Approach

In contrast, the **practice approach** to knowledge management assumes that a great deal of organizational knowledge is tacit in nature and that formal controls, processes, and technologies are not suitable for transmitting this type of understanding. Rather than building formal systems to manage knowledge, the focus of this approach is to build the social environments or communities of practice necessary to facilitate the sharing of tacit understanding (Brown and Duguid, 2000; DeLong and Fahey, 2000; Gupta and Govindarajan, 2000; Wenger and Snyder, 2000; Hansen et al., 1999). Communities of practice are groups of individuals with a common interest who work together informally. Within such a community, individuals collaborate directly, teach each other, and share experiences (Smith and McKeen, 2003).

The practice approach is typically adopted by companies that provide highly customized solutions to unique problems. The valuable knowledge for these firms is tacit in nature, which is difficult to express, capture, and manage. In this case, the environment and the nature of the problems being encountered are extremely dynamic. For these firms, knowledge is shared mostly through person-to-person contacts. Collaborative computing methods (for example, Lotus Notes/Domino Server or e-mail) help people communicate. Because tacit knowledge is difficult to extract, store, and manage, the explicit knowledge that points to *how* to find the appropriate tacit knowledge (people contacts, consulting reports) is made available to an appropriate set of individuals who might need it.

To make their practice approach work, firms like Bain invest heavily in building networks of people and communications technology such as telephone, e-mail, and videoconferencing. Also they commonly have face-to-face meetings (Hansen et al., 1999).

Table 10.1 summarizes the process and practice approaches.

TABLE 10.1 Process and Practice Approaches to Knowledge Management

	Process Approach	Practice Approach
Type of knowledge supported	Explicit knowledge—codified in rules, tools, and processes (DeLong and Fahey, 2000)	Mostly tacit knowledge—unarticulated knowledge not easily captured or codified (Leonard and Sensiper, 1998)
Means of transmission	Formal controls, procedures, and standard operating procedures with heavy emphasis on information technologies to support knowledge creation, codification, and transfer of knowledge (Ruggles, 1998).	Informal social groups that engage in story telling and improvisation (Wenger and Snyder, 2000).
Benefits	Provides structure to harness generated ideas and knowledge (Brown and Duguid, 2000). Achieves scale in knowledge reuse (Hansen et al., 1999).	Provides an environment to generate and transfer high-value tacit knowledge (Brown and Duguid, 2000; Wenger & Snyder, 2000). Provides spark for fresh ideas and responsiveness to changing environment (Brown and Duguid, 2000).
Disadvantages	Fails to tap into tacit knowledge. May limit innovation and forces participants into fixed patterns of thinking.	Can result in inefficiency. Abundance of ideas with no structure to implement them.
Role of information technology	Heavy investment in IT to connect people with reusable codified knowledge (Hansen et al., 1999).	Moderate investment in IT to facilitate conversations and transfer of tacit knowledge (Hansen et al., 1999).

Source: Alavi et al. (2003), p. 3.

IT at Work 10.2
TEXACO DRILLS FOR KNOWLEDGE

Texaco (now ChevronTexaco, *texaco.com*), a company that pumps over a million barrels of oil a day, has discovered a new source of power—the collective knowledge and expertise of its 18,000 employees in 150 countries around the world. Texaco believes that connecting people who have questions with people who have answers gives it the power to work faster and more efficiently.

At Texaco, managing knowledge is a critical business challenge. John Old, Texaco's knowledge guru, approaches this challenge with a strategy that leverages human connections. He states that knowledge by its nature is contextual; thus, systems that simply allow people to record what they know are ineffective. He strongly believes that a successful knowledge management solution must recognize the importance of human connections.

Texaco uses technology to help people build personal relationships and share knowledge. One of the systems at work at Texaco is PeopleNet, a search engine for employees on the company's intranet. Employees who have questions can use PeopleNet to review profiles of their colleagues who might have the right answers. Texaco discovered that having biographies and pictures of its employees online makes it possible to establish credibility and trust between people who have not met each other. And it is trust that makes effective knowledge transfer possible.

Another tool that Texaco uses to connect its employees is a software system called Knowledge Mail (from Tacit Knowledge Systems). This software analyzes e-mail sent and received by employees to help them make good contacts with colleagues who work on the same issues.

John Old speaks of several important lessons that Texaco learned while managing knowledge. He points out that people are more eager to share knowledge when they are united by a clear, specific, and measurable business purpose. Knowledge sharing becomes even more successful when they trust each other and see direct benefits that can be derived from the knowledge exchange. In addition, it is important to give people enough time to reflect on what they know and what they need to learn.

Texaco's approach to knowledge management has provided many positive results. The knowledge management efforts help Texaco's employees successfully resolve numerous issues that range from adjusting oil well pumps to deciding whether or not to enter into new lines of business.

Source: Adapted from Warner (2001).

For Further Exploration: Texaco relies primarily on the practice approach to knowledge management. Why was this approach effective for Texaco? Would this approach be optimal for your college or place of work?

In reality, a knowledge management initiative can, and probably will, involve both process and practice approaches. The two are not mutually exclusive. Alavi et al. (2003) describe the case of an organization that began its KM effort with a large repository but evolved the knowledge management initiative into a community-of-practice approach that existed side-by-side with the repository. In fact, community members would pass information from the community forum to the organizational repository when they felt that the knowledge was valuable outside their community. *IT at Work 10.2* illustrates how Texaco successfully manages its knowledge using the practice approach.

10.4 INFORMATION TECHNOLOGY IN KNOWLEDGE MANAGEMENT

Knowledge management is more a methodology applied to business practices than a technology or product. Nevertheless, information technology is *crucial* to the success of every knowledge management system. Information technology enables KM by providing the enterprise architecture upon which it is built.

Components of Knowledge Management Systems

Knowledge management systems are developed using three sets of technologies: *communication, collaboration,* and *storage and retrieval.*

Communication technologies allow users to access needed knowledge, and to communicate with each other—especially with experts. E-mail, the Internet, corporate intranets, and other Web-based tools provide communication capabilities. Even fax machines and the telephone are used for communication, especially when the practice approach to knowledge management is adopted.

Collaboration technologies provide the means to perform group work. Groups can work together on common documents at the same time (synchronous) or at different times (asynchronous), in the same place, or in different places. This is especially important for members of a community of practice working on knowledge contributions. Collaborative computing capabilities such as electronic brainstorming enhance group work, especially for knowledge contribution. Additional forms of group work involve experts working with individuals trying to apply their knowledge. This requires collaboration at a fairly high level. Other collaborative computing systems allow an organization to create a virtual space so that individuals can work online anywhere and at any time.

Storage and retrieval technologies originally meant using a database management system to store and manage knowledge. This worked reasonably well in the early days for storing and managing most explicit knowledge, and even explicit knowledge about tacit knowledge. However, capturing, storing, and managing tacit knowledge usually requires a different set of tools. Electronic document management systems and specialized storage systems that are part of collaborative computing systems fill this void.

Technologies Supporting Knowledge Management

Several technologies have contributed to significant advances in knowledge management tools. Artificial intelligence, intelligent agents, knowledge discovery in databases, and Extensible Markup Language (XML) are examples of technologies that enable advanced functionality of modern knowledge management systems and form the base for future innovations in the KM field.

ARTIFICIAL INTELLIGENCE. In the definition of knowledge management, *artificial intelligence* (Chapter 11) is rarely mentioned. However, practically speaking, AI methods and tools are embedded in a number of knowledge management systems, either by vendors or by system developers.

AI methods can assist in identifying expertise, eliciting knowledge automatically and semiautomatically, in interfacing through natural language processing, and in intelligent search through intelligent agents. AI methods, notably expert systems, neural networks, fuzzy logic, and intelligent agents, are used in knowledge management systems to perform various functions: They assist in and enhance searching knowledge (e.g., intelligent agents in Web searches), including scanning e-mail, documents, and databases and helping establish knowledge profiles of individuals and groups. They forecast future results using existing knowledge. AI methods help determine the relative importance of knowledge, when knowledge is both contributed to and accessed from the knowledge repository, and help determine meaningful relationships in the knowledge. They identify patterns in data (usually through neural networks), induce rules for expert systems, and provide advice directly from knowledge by using neural networks or expert systems. Finally, they provide a natural language or voice command–driven user interface for a knowledge management system.

INTELLIGENT AGENTS. *Intelligent agents* are software systems that learn how users work and provide assistance in their daily tasks. For example, when these software programs are told what the user wants to retrieve, passive agents can monitor incoming information for matches with user interests, and active agents can seek out information relevant to user preferences (Gray and Tehrani, 2003). Intelligent agents of various kinds are discussed in Chapter 12.

There are a number of ways that intelligent agents can help in knowledge management systems. Typically they are used to elicit and identify knowledge. Examples are:

- IBM (*ibm.com*) offers an intelligent data mining family, including Intelligent Decision Server (IDS), for finding and analyzing massive amounts of enterprise data.
- Gentia (Planning Sciences International, *gentia.com*) uses intelligent agents to facilitate data mining with Web access and data warehouse facilities.
- Convectis (HNC Software Inc.) uses neural networks to search text data and images, to discern the meaning of documents for an intelligent agent. This tool is used by InfoSeek, an Internet search engine, to speed up the creation of hierarchical directories of Web topics.

Combining intelligent agents with enterprise knowledge portals is a powerful technique that can deliver to a user exactly what he or she needs to perform his or her tasks. The intelligent agent learns what the user prefers to see, and how he or she organizes it. Then, the intelligent agent takes over to provide it at the desktop like a good administrative assistant would (King and Jones, 1995).

KNOWLEDGE DISCOVERY IN DATABASES. **Knowledge discovery in databases (KDD)** is a process used to search for and extract useful information from volumes of documents and data. It includes tasks known as knowledge extraction, data archaeology, data exploration, data pattern processing, data dredging, and information harvesting. All of these activities are conducted automatically and allow quick discovery, even by nonprogrammers. Data are often buried deep within very large databases, data warehouses, text documents, or knowledge repositories, all of which may contain data, information, and knowledge gathered over many years. **Data mining,** the process of searching for previously unknown information or relationships in large databases, is ideal for eliciting knowledge from databases, documents, e-mail, and so on. (For more on data mining, see Chapter 12.)

AI methods are useful data mining tools that include automated knowledge elicitation from other sources. Intelligent data mining discovers information within databases and other repositories that queries and reports cannot effectively reveal. Data mining tools find patterns in data and may even (automatically) infer rules from them. Patterns and rules can be used to guide decision making and forecast the effect of these decisions. KDD can also be used to identify the meaning of data or text, using KM tools that scan documents and e-mail to build an expertise profile of a firm's employees. Data mining can speed up analysis by providing needed knowledge.

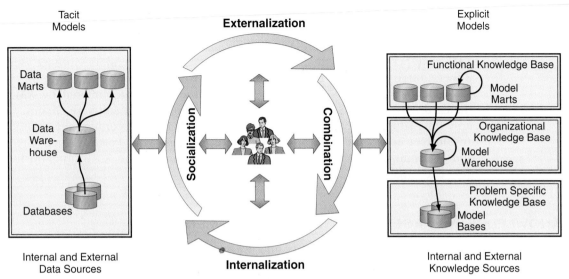

FIGURE 10.3 Framework for integrating decision support and knowledge management systems. (*Source:* Bolloju et al., 2001.)

Extending the role of data mining and knowledge discovery techniques for knowledge externalization, Bolloju et al. (2002) propose a framework for integrating knowledge management into enterprise environments for next-generation decision support systems. Their framework, shown in Figure 10.3, includes **model marts** and **model warehouses.** Both of these act as repositories of knowledge created by employing knowledge-discovery techniques on past decision instances stored in data repositories. (Model marts are small versions of model warehouses.) The model marts and model warehouses capture operational and historical decision models. For example, a model mart can store decision rules corresponding to problem-solving knowledge of different decision makers in a particular domain, such as loan approvals in a banking environment. (As you will discover in Chapter 12, model marts and model warehouses are analogous for models to data marts and data warehouses for data.)

This integrated decision support–knowledge management framework accommodates different types of knowledge transformations proposed by Nonaka and Takeuchi (1995). Systems built around this framework are expected to enhance the quality of support provided to decision makers; to support knowledge management functions such as acquisition, creation, exploitation, and accumulation; to facilitate discovery of trends and patterns in the accumulated knowledge; and to provide means for building up organizational memory.

EXTENSIBLE MARKUP LANGUAGE (XML). Extensible Markup Language (XML) enables standardized representations of data structures, so that data can be processed appropriately by heterogeneous systems without case-by-case programming. This method suits e-commerce applications and supply chain management systems that operate across enterprise boundaries. XML not only can automate processes and reduce paperwork, but also can unite business partners and supply chains for better collaboration and knowledge transfer. XML-based messages can be taken from back-end repositories and fed out through the portal interface and back again. A portal that uses XML allows the company to communicate better with its customers, linking them in a virtual demand chain, where changes in customer requirements are immediately reflected in production plans. Due to its potential to tremendously simplify systems integration, XML may become the universal language that all portal vendors embrace (see Ruber, 2001). (For more technical detail on XML, see Technology Guide 2.)

Vendors are quickly moving to integrate the advantages offered by XML standards. For example, Interwoven's content management software, Teamsite, now fully supports XML, enabling organizations to provide content available in any format across the enterprise. Sequoia Software's XML Portal Server (XPS) and Hummingbird's Enterprise Portal Suite also support the XML standard for data exchange.

10.5 KNOWLEDGE MANAGEMENT SYSTEMS IMPLEMENTATION

The KMS challenge is to identify and integrate the three essential components—communication technologies, collaboration technologies, and storage and retrieval technologies—to meet the knowledge management needs of an organization. The earliest knowledge management systems were developed with networked technology (intranets), collaborative computing tools (groupware), and databases (for the knowledge repository). They were constructed from a variety of off-the-shelf IT components (e.g., see Ruggles, 1998). Many organizations, especially large management consulting firms like Accenture and J.D. Edwards, developed their knowledge architecture with a set of tools that provided the three technology types. Collaborative computing suites such as Lotus Notes/Domino Server provide many KMS capabilities. Other systems were developed by integrating a set of tools from a single or multiple vendors. For example, J.D. Edwards used a set of loosely integrated Microsoft tools and products to implement its Knowledge Garden KMS, as did KPMG. In the early 2000s, KMS technology has evolved to integrate the three components into a single package. These include enterprise knowledge portals and knowledge management suites.

Knowledge Management Products and Vendors

Technology tools that support knowledge management are called **knowware.** Most knowledge management software packages include one or more of the following seven tools: collaborative computing tools, knowledge servers, enterprise knowledge portals, electronic document management systems, knowledge harvesting tools, search engines, and knowledge management suites. Many packages provide several tools because several are necessary in an effective knowledge management system. For example, most electronic document management systems also include collaborative computing capabilities.

Knowledge management systems can be purchased in whole or in part from one of numerous software development companies and enterprise information systems vendors, they can be acquired through major consulting firms, or they can be outsourced to the application service providers (ASPs). All three alternatives will be discussed in the latter part of this chapter.

SOFTWARE DEVELOPMENT COMPANIES AND ENTERPRISE INFORMATION SYSTEMS VENDORS. Software development companies and enterprise information systems vendors offer numerous knowledge management packages, from individual tools to comprehensive knowledge management suites. The variety of knowware that is readily available on the market allows companies to find the tools that will meet their unique knowledge management needs. Following is a review of some software packages and their vendors in each of the seven knowware categories cited earlier.

Collaborative Computing Tools. Collaboration tools, or groupware, were the first used to enhance tacit knowledge transfer within an organization. One of the earliest collaborative computing systems, GroupSystems, provides many of the tools that support group work, including electronic brainstorming and idea categorization. Lotus Notes/Domino Server provides an enterprisewide collaborative environment. Other collaboration tools include MeetingPlace (Latitude), QuickPlace (Lotus Development Corp.), eRoom Documentum (Documentum), and PlaceWare (PlaceWare Inc.). For a discussion, details, and examples of collaborative computing, see Chapter 4.

Knowledge Servers. A knowledge server contains the main knowledge management software, including the knowledge repository, and provides access to other knowledge, information, and data. Examples of knowledge servers include the Hummingbird Knowledge Server, the Intraspect Software Knowledge Server, the Hyperwave Information Server, the Sequoia Software XML Portal Server, and Autonomy's Intelligent Data Operating Layer (IDOL) Server. Autonomy's IDOL Server connects people to content, content to content, and people to people through modules that enable organizations to integrate various personalization, collaboration, and retrieval features. The server provides a **knowledge repository,** a central location for searching and accessing information from many sources, such as the Internet, corporate intranets, databases, and file systems, thereby enabling the efficient distribution of time-sensitive information. The server seamlessly extends and integrates with the company's e-business suite, allowing rapid deployment applications that span the enterprise and leverage AI-assisted technology to harvest knowledge assets.

Enterprise Knowledge Portals. Enterprise knowledge portals (EKPs) are the doorways into many knowledge management systems. They have evolved from the concepts underlying executive information systems, group support systems, Web-browsers, and database management systems. According to an IDC report, individuals may spend as much as 30 percent of their time looking for information (Ziff Davis, 2002). An enterprise knowledge portal presents a single access point for a vast body of explicit information, such as project plans, functional requirements, technical specifications, white papers, training materials, and customer feedback survey data (Kesner, 2003).

Enterprise knowledge portals are a means of organizing the many sources of unstructured information in an organization. Most combine data integration, reporting mechanisms, and collaboration, while document and knowledge management is handled by a server. The portal aggregates each user's total information needs: data and documents, e-mail, Web links and queries, dynamic feeds from the network, and shared calendars and task lists. The personal information portal has evolved into an enterprise knowledge portal (Silver, 2000).

One highly successful portal is Cisco's Employee Connection. The portal provides any time, anywhere access to the company's intranet; it has been credited with helping save the company $551 million, thanks primarily to improved self-service (Anderson, 2002). The intent of the system is to connect as many systems and applications as possible so that the user has a single entree into all of Cisco's information systems (Anderson, 2002).

When enterprise information portals first entered the market, they did not contain knowledge management features. Now, most do. Leading portal vendors include Autonomy, Brio, Corechange, Dataware, Intraspect, Hummingbird, InXight, IBM/Lotus, Knowmadic, OpenText, Plumtree, Verity, Viador, and Vignette. Database vendors such as Microsoft, Oracle, and Sybase are also selling knowledge portals. Portals can range in cost from less than $500,000 to $8 million (Steinberg, 2002).

The Knowledge Center (from KnowledgeTrack) offers integrated business-to-business (B2B) functions and can scale from dot-coms to large enterprises. Knowledge Center can be built into the enterprise architecture instead of simply sitting on top, the way most intranet portals do. The Knowledge Center integrates with external data sources including ERP, online analytical processing (OLAP) (see Chapter 11), and CRM systems (see Chapter 7). Knowledge Center supports communities of practice and enables them for large project management, allowing information to be shared among all of the extended enterprise value chains.

Hyperwave's Hyperwave Information Portal (HIP) aggregates information from disparate sources and features dynamic link management, which verifies the quality of the link and hides links to unauthorized content. HIP manages connections between information sources and makes structured and unstructured corporate information searchable via a standard browser. See *IT at Work 10.3* about how the Canadian law firm Smith Lyons developed a successful enterprise knowledge portal. For more on such portals, see Collins (2001), Liautaud and Hammond (2000), and *InfoWorld* (2000).

Electronic Document Management. Electronic document management (EDM) systems focus on the document in electronic form as the collaborative focus of work. EDM systems allow users to access needed documents, generally via a Web-browser over a corporate intranet. EDM systems enable organizations to better manage documents and workflow for smoother operations. They also allow collaboration on document creation and revision.

Many knowledge management systems use an EDM system as the knowledge repository (see Minicase 2). There is a natural fit in terms of the purpose and benefits of the two. For example, Pfizer uses a large-scale document management system to handle the equivalent of truckloads of paper documents of drug approval applications passed between Pfizer and the FDA, its regulating agency. This EDM system dramatically cut the time required for FDA submission and review, making Pfizer more competitive in getting new and effective drugs to market (Blodgett, 2000).

Systems like DocuShare (Xerox Corporation) and Lotus Notes (Lotus Development Corporation) allow direct collaboration on a common document. Some other EDM systems include Documentum (Documentum Inc.), ViewStar (eiStream), FYI (Identitech), FileNet Content Manager (FileNet Corporation), Livelink (Open Text Corporation), PaperPort (ScanSoft Inc.), and CaseCentral.com (Document Repository Inc.).

Knowledge Harvesting Tools. Tools for capturing knowledge unobtrusively are helpful since they allow a knowledge contributor to be minimally (or not at all) involved in the knowledge-harvesting efforts. Embedding this type of tool in a KMS is an ideal approach to knowledge capture.

For example, Tacit Knowledge Systems' KnowledgeMail is an expertise-location software package that analyzes users' outgoing e-mail to parse subject

IT at Work 10.3
PORTAL OPENS THE DOOR TO LEGAL KNOWLEDGE

Richard Van Dyk, CIO of Smith Lyons, a Toronto-based international law firm, knew exactly what kind of system he was looking for to manage the firm's documents and knowledge. He had spent a year defining his requirements and had composed a complex flowchart on his whiteboard. Smith Lyons (*smithlyons.com*) wanted to take thousands of pieces of information, give people different views into that information, and have a high level of link management. Van Dyk considered document management tools to be too inflexible for the way lawyers practice law. "We needed a flexible environment that we could massage and manipulate and that would allow people to continue working as they have," says Van Dyk.

"Lawyers are basically document generators," he says. "Due to time constraints, they spend more time collecting documents than organizing them." Because the firm's 550 attorneys and support specialists each had a distinct working methodology, often reflecting the requirements of a specific area of practice, Van Dyk knew they would resent having a rigid system they could not easily personalize.

The profusion of document management, knowledge management, and portal systems makes finding the right product difficult. Each has its strengths and weaknesses. Organizations coming from a document-centric perspective, like Smith Lyons, need to organize and manage content at the back end while developing highly customized individual user interfaces at the front end.

The solution that best met Van Dyk's criteria was the Hyperwave Information Portal from Hyperwave Information Management of Westford, Massachusetts. "What I liked about Hyperwave's portal environment was that as soon as we installed it, we had a framework to begin knowledge mapping—tagging and indexing documents by subject and key words and phrases—and for building the database structures in our repositories," says Van Dyk. The firm had definite ideas on how to structure templates and specific pieces of information that are unique to a legal practice. These issues included myriad legal forms and documents generated by the proprietary software applications used for different practice areas.

Once the portal was set up, Smith Lyons' developers began to customize the views for each desktop PC by creating wizards that connect users to their own secure information areas and to intranet pages containing company activity information. In development, too, is an extranet on which lawyers will be able to post status reports to clients and deliver confidential documents and contracts.

"That flexibility in building our DM portal allows our lawyers and specialists to be incredibly specific in their searches," says Van Dyk. Lawyers also can share their accumulated knowledge more easily with colleagues in the same practice areas, by referencing legal citations, court decisions, and winning strategies that have worked in the past.

Source: Adapted from Ruber (2000).

For Further Exploration: How is the practice of law different from the operations of other businesses? How can enterprise knowledge portals benefit the entire legal system (courts, and so on)?

---

expertise. It maintains a directory of expertise and offers ways to contact experts, while maintaining privacy controls for those experts. Autonomy's Active-Knowledge performs a similar analysis on e-mail and other standard document types. Intraspect Software's Intraspect platform monitors an organization's group memory, captures the context of its use (such as who used it, when, for what, how it was combined with other information, and what people said about it), and then makes the information available for sharing and reuse.

Search Engines. Search engines perform one of the essential functions of knowledge management—locating and retrieving necessary documents from vast collections accumulated in corporate repositories. Companies like Google, Verity, and Inktomi are offering a wide selection of search engines that are capable of indexing and cataloging files in various formats as well as retrieving and prioritizing relevant documents in response to user queries.

Knowledge Management Suites. Knowledge management suites are complete knowledge management solutions out-of-the-box. They integrate the communications, collaboration, and storage technologies into a single convenient package. A knowledge management suite must still access internal databases and other external knowledge sources, so some integration is required to make the software truly functional. Knowledge management suites are powerful approaches to developing a KMS because they offer one user interface, one data repository, and one vendor.

IBM/Lotus offers an extensive range of knowledge management products: the Domino platform, QuickPlace and Sametime, Discovery Server, and Learning Space, as well as the WebSphere portal. See *IT at Work 10.4* to learn how Commerce Bank implemented a knowledge management system based on the IBM/Lotus platform.

Several vendors also provide fairly comprehensive sets of tools for KM initiatives, which include Dataware Knowledge Management Suite, KnowledgeX by KnowledgeX, Inc., and many others. Autonomy Knowledge Management Suite offers document categorization and workflow integration. Microsoft provides central components of knowledge management solutions, and is working on developing an encompassing KM framework. Some enterprise information systems vendors, such as SAP, PeopleSoft, and Oracle, are developing knowledge-management-related technologies as a platform for business applications. Siebel Systems is repositioning itself as a business-to-employee knowledge management platform.

CONSULTING FIRMS. All of the major consulting firms (Accenture, Ernst & Young, and so on) have massive internal knowledge management initiatives. Usually these become products after they succeed internally and provide assistance in establishing knowledge management systems and measuring their effectiveness. Consulting firms also provide some direct, out-of-the-box proprietary systems for vertical markets. Most of the major consulting firms define their knowledge management offerings as a *service.* For more on consulting firm activities and products, see McDonald and Shand (2000).

KNOWLEDGE MANAGEMENT APPLICATION SERVICE PROVIDERS. Application service providers (ASPs) have evolved as a form of KMS outsourcing on the Web. There are many ASPs for e-commerce on the market.

For example, Communispace is a high-level ASP collaboration system that focuses on connecting people to people (not just people to documents) to achieve specific objectives, regardless of geographic, time, and organizational barriers. As a hosted ASP solution, it is easy to rapidly deploy within organizations. Unlike conventional KM systems that organize data and documents, or chat rooms where people simply swap information, Communispace contains a rich assortment of interactions, activities, and tools that connect people to the colleagues who can best help them make decisions, solve problems, and learn quickly. Communispace is designed to build trust online. It attempts to make a community self-conscious about taking responsibility for its actions and knowledge. Its Climate component helps participants to measure and understand how people are feeling about the community. The Virtual Café gives dispersed employees a way to meet and learn about each other through pictures and profiles.

IT at Work 10.4

FINDING THE RIGHT ANSWERS WITH KNOWLEDGE MANAGEMENT

Commerce Bank (*commerceonline.com*) is a $15.4 billion financial institution that is quickly growing to become a dominant player in the financial services market of Philadelphia and southern New Jersey. During 30 years of its existence, it has developed a network of 214 branches and made ambitious plans for continuous growth. Commerce Bank names itself "America's Most Convenient Bank." It lives up to that name by maintaining a strong banking network and by empowering each branch to make business decisions in an effort to better meet the needs of its customers.

While undergoing explosive growth, Commerce Bank encouraged its associates to learn all about the customers and the right ways to service them. However, the company realized that its most important asset, knowledge, was locked away in file cabinets and in the heads of its associates. In order to support this initiative, Commerce Bank needed to tap into that knowledge and find a way to train employees consistently and conveniently across the entire branch network.

The first step for new employees is Commerce University, a boot camp where they are instilled with the fundamentals of customer service. But the program covers only a few of the range of issues that an associate might encounter.

The need for knowledge management at Commerce Bank was apparent. Jack Allison, VP of Systems Development, said, "We had folks in administration who could spend 70 percent of their time answering calls and clarifying answers for branches. At times, we could wait weeks or months for the right answer to certain questions. Knowing that training may not give answers for every scenario, we needed to give associates a tool that could help them find any answer to any topic at any time."

Commerce Bank envisioned a solution—a workflow-based knowledge management system that could provide instant answers to questions for the bank's employees and online customers. To make this vision a reality, Commerce chose to develop a system based on IBM's Lotus Notes, which the bank had been using since 1995. Using IBM's Domino server, the Lotus Notes client, and an application development toolkit, Commerce Bank created a full-fledged knowledge management system, called Wow Answer Guide.

Introduced in 2000, Wow Answer Guide provides a central repository of knowledge about all bank transactions, helps employees learn a process and respond to customer inquiries, and stores information electronically. In addition, the system allows employees to register for the bank's continuing education courses.

The complete Wow Answer Guide contains more than 400 applications, and Commerce plans to add even more, such as a customer relationship management system. The flexibility of the platform simplifies application development and allows adding new features and expanding functionality with minimal investments of time and effort. By drawing on the power of the Domino platform, Commerce Bank created workflow-based applications that streamline internal knowledge sharing and that route data and information to the appropriate employees within the organization. This dramatically reduces the completion time for approval-intensive transactions, improves the bank's capacity, and minimizes labor costs.

"[Wow Answer Guide] is especially good for the green associate, or the veteran, who is still learning how to process a new product," says Allison. "We don't want our associates on a scavenger hunt to get the correct information."

Commerce Bank realized that knowledge management would be beneficial not only to the bank's employees, but also to the bank's clients. "We wanted to put information in our customers' hands so they could conduct [online] transactions with confidence," said Allison. In the summer of 2000, Commerce Bank deployed a new version of Wow Answer Guide that empowered the bank's online customers.

Knowledge management at Commerce Bank proved to be an effective investment. According to Allison, the application has saved the bank $20,000 per week, or approximately $1 million a year. In fact, the bank achieved a return on its investment within a month of launching Wow Answer Guide.

Source: Adapted from Amato-McCoy (2003).

For Further Exploration: How do knowledge requirements of bank employees differ from those of bank customers? How would these differences influence the functionality of knowledge management systems designed to serve these two groups of users?

A recent trend among application service providers is to offer a complete knowledge management solution, including a KM suite and the consulting to set it up.

Integration of KM Systems with Other Business Information Systems

Since a knowledge management system is an enterprise system, it must be integrated with other enterprise and other information systems in an organization. Obviously, when it is designed and developed, it cannot be perceived as an add-on application. It must be truly integrated into other systems. Through the structure of the organizational culture (changed if necessary), a knowledge management system and its activities can be directly integrated into a firm's business processes. For example, a group involved in customer support can capture its knowledge to provide help on customers' difficult problems. In this case, help-desk software would be one type of package to integrate into a KMS, especially into the knowledge repository.

Since a KMS can be developed on a knowledge platform consisting of communication, collaboration, and storage technologies, and most firms already have many such tools and technologies in place, it is often possible to develop a KMS in the organization's existing tools (e.g., Lotus Notes/Domino Server). Or, an enterprise knowledge portal can provide universal access and an interface into all of an individual's relevant corporate information and knowledge. In this case, the KMS effort would provide the linkage for everyone into the entire enterprise information system.

In the remainder of this section, we look at how KM systems can be integrated with other types of business information systems.

INTEGRATION WITH DECISION SUPPORT SYSTEMS. Knowledge management systems typically do not involve running models to solve problems, which is an activity typically done in decision support systems (DSSs). However, since a knowledge management system provides help in solving problems by applying knowledge, part of the solution may involve running models. A KMS could integrate into an appropriate set of models and data and activate them, when a specific problem may call for it.

INTEGRATION WITH ARTIFICIAL INTELLIGENCE. Knowledge management has a natural relationship with artificial intelligence (AI) methods and software, though knowledge management, strictly speaking, is not an artificial intelligence method. There are a number of ways in which knowledge management and artificial intelligence can integrate. For example, if the knowledge stored in a KMS is to be represented and used as a sequence of if-then-else rules, then an expert system becomes part of the KMS (see Rasmus, 2000). An expert system could also assist a user in identifying how to apply a chunk of knowledge in the KMS.

Much work is being done in the field of artificial intelligence relating to knowledge engineering, tacit-to-explicit knowledge transfer, knowledge identification, understanding, dissemination, and so on. Companies are attempting to realign these technologies and resultant products with knowledge management. The AI technologies most often integrated with knowledge management are intelligent agents, expert systems, neural networks, and fuzzy logic. Several specific methods and tools were described earlier.

INTEGRATION WITH DATABASES AND INFORMATION SYSTEMS. Since a KMS utilizes a knowledge repository, sometimes constructed out of a database system or an electronic document management system, it can automatically integrate to this part of the firm's information system. As data and information updates are made, the KMS can utilize them. Knowledge management systems also attempt to glean knowledge from documents and databases (knowledge discovery in databases) through artificial intelligence methods, as was described earlier.

INTEGRATION WITH CUSTOMER RELATIONSHIP MANAGEMENT SYSTEMS. Customer relationship management (CRM) systems help users in dealing with customers. One aspect is the help-desk notion described earlier. But CRM goes much deeper. It can develop usable profiles of customers and predict their needs, so that an organization can increase sales and better serve its clients. A KMS can certainly provide tacit knowledge to people who use CRM directly in working with customers.

INTEGRATION WITH SUPPLY CHAIN MANAGEMENT SYSTEMS. The supply chain is often considered to be the logistics end of the business. If products do not move through the organization and go out the door, the firm will fail. So it is important to optimize the supply chain and manage it properly. As discussed in Chapter 8, supply chain management (SCM) systems attempt to do so. SCM can benefit through integration with KMS because there are many issues and problems in the supply chain that require the company to combine both tacit and explicit knowledge. Accessing such knowledge will directly improve supply chain performance.

INTEGRATION WITH CORPORATE INTRANETS AND EXTRANETS. Communication and collaboration tools and technologies are necessary for KMS to function. KMS is not simply integrated with the technology of intranets and extranets, but is typically developed on them as the communications platform. Extranets are specifically designed to enhance the collaboration of a firm with its suppliers and sometimes with customers. If a firm can integrate its KMS into its intranets and extranets, knowledge will flow more freely, both from a contributor and to a user (either directly or through a knowledge repository), and the firm also can capture knowledge directly with little user involvement and can deliver it when the system "thinks" that a user needs knowledge.

10.6 ROLES OF PEOPLE IN KNOWLEDGE MANAGEMENT

Managing a knowledge management system requires great effort. Like any other information technology, getting it started, implemented, and deployed requires a champion's effort. Many issues of management, people, and culture must be considered to make a knowledge management system a success. In this section, we address those issues.

Managing the knowledge repository typically requires a full-time staff, similar to a reference-library staff. This staff examines, structures, filters, catalogues, and stores knowledge so that it is meaningful and can be accessed by the people who need it. The staff assists individuals in searching for knowledge, and performs "environmental scanning": If they identify specific knowledge that an employee or client might need, they send it directly to them, thus adding value to the organization. (This is standard procedure for Accenture knowledge management personnel.) Finally, the knowledge repository staff may create communities of practice (see Minicase 1) to gather individuals with common knowledge areas to identify, filter, extract, and contribute knowledge to a knowledge repository.

Most of the issues concerning the success, implementation, and effective use of a knowledge management system are people issues. And since a knowledge management system is an enterprisewide effort, many people need to be involved in it (Robb, 2003). They include the chief knowledge officer (CKO), the CEO, the other officers and managers of the organization, members and leaders of communities of practice, KMS developers, and KMS staff. Each person or group has an important role in either the development, management, or use of a KMS. By far, the CKO has the most visible role in a KMS effort, but the system cannot succeed unless the roles of all the players are established and understood. Ensuring that a KM team is properly constituted is therefore an essential factor in the success of any KM initiative (Robb, 2003).

The Chief Knowledge Officer

Knowledge management projects that involve establishing a knowledge environment conducive to the transfer, creation, or use of knowledge attempt to build *cultural receptivity*. These attempts are centered on changing the behavior of the firm to embrace the use of knowledge management. Behavioral-centric projects require a high degree of support and participation from the senior management of the organization to facilitate their implementation. Most firms developing knowledge management systems have created a knowledge management officer, a **chief knowledge officer (CKO),** at the senior level. The objectives of the CKO's role are to maximize the firm's knowledge assets, design and implement knowledge management strategies, effectively exchange knowledge assets internally and externally, and promote system use.

A chief knowledge officer must do the following (adapted from Duffy, 1998):

- Set strategic priorities for knowledge management.
- Establish a knowledge repository of best practices.
- Gain a commitment from senior executives to support a learning environment.
- Teach information seekers how to ask better and smarter questions.
- Establish a process for managing intellectual assets.
- Obtain customer satisfaction information in near real time.
- Globalize knowledge management.

The CKO is responsible for defining the area of knowledge within the firm that will be the focal point, based on the mission and objectives of the firm (Davis, 1998). The CKO is responsible for standardizing the enterprisewide vocabulary and for controlling the knowledge directory. This is critical in areas that must share knowledge across departments, to ensure uniformity. CKOs must get a handle on the company's repositories of research, resources, and expertise, including where they are stored and who manages and accesses them. (That is, the CKO must perform a *knowledge audit.*) Then the CKO must encourage "pollination" (sharing of knowledge) among disparate workgroups with complementary resources.

The CKO is responsible for creating an infrastructure and cultural environment for knowledge sharing. He or she must assign or identify the *knowledge champions* within the business units. The CKO's job is to manage the content their group produces (e.g., the Chrysler Tech Clubs in Minicase 1), continually add to the knowledge base, and encourage their colleagues to do the same. Successful CKOs should have the full and enthusiastic support of their managers and of top management. Ultimately, the CKO is responsible for the entire knowledge management project while it is under development, and then for management of the system and the knowledge once it is deployed.

CEO, Officers, and Managers of the Organization

Briefly, vis-à-vis knowledge management, the CEO is responsible for championing the KM effort. He or she must ensure that a competent and capable CKO is found and that the CKO can obtain all the resources (including access to people with knowledge sources) needed to make the project a success. The CEO must also gain organization-wide support for the contribution to and use of the KMS. The CEO must also prepare the organization for the cultural changes that are expected to occur when the KMS is implemented. Support for the KMS and the CKO is the critical responsibility of the CEO.

The various other officers in the organization generally must make resources available to the CKO so that he or she can get the job done. The chief financial officer (CFO) must ensure that the financial resources are available. The chief operating officer (COO) must ensure that people begin to embed knowledge management practices into their daily work processes. There is a special relationship between the CKO and chief information officer (CIO). Usually the CIO is responsible for the IT vision of the organization and for the IT architecture, including databases and other potential knowledge sources. The CIO must cooperate with the CKO in making these resources available. KMSs are expensive propositions, and it is wise to use existing systems if they are available and capable.

Managers must also support the KM effort and provide access to sources of knowledge. In many KMSs, managers are an integral part of the communities of practice.

Communities of Practice

The success of many KM systems has been attributed to the active involvement of the people who contribute to and benefit from using the knowledge. Consequently, communities of practice have appeared within organizations that are serious about their knowledge management efforts. As discussed earlier, a **community of practice (COP)** is a group of people in an organization with a common professional interest. Ideally, all the KMS users should each be in at least one COP. Creating and nurturing COPs properly is one key to KMS success.

In a sense, a community of practice "owns" the knowledge that it contributes, because it manages the knowledge on its way into the system, and as owner, must approve modifications to it. The community is responsible for the accuracy and timeliness of the knowledge it contributes and for identifying its potential use.

A number of researchers have investigated how successful COPs form and function. One study, by Storck and Hill (2000), investigated one of the earliest communities of practice, at Xerox. When established at Xerox, the COP was a new organizational form. The word *community* captured the sense of responsible, independent action that characterized the group, which continued to function within the standard boundaries of the large organization. Management sponsored the community, but did not mandate it. Community members were volunteers. For more on communities of practice, see Barth (2000a), Cothrel and Williams (1999a, 1999b), Eisenhart (2000), and Smith and McKeen (2003).

KMS Developers   KMS developers are the team members who actually develop the system. They work for the CKO. Some are organizational experts who develop strategies to promote and manage the organizational culture shift. Others are involved in system software and hardware selection, programming, testing, deploying, and maintaining the system. Still others initially are involved in training users. Eventually the training function moves to the KMS staff.

KMS Staff   Enterprisewide KM systems require a full-time staff to catalogue and manage the knowledge. This staff is either located at the firm's headquarters or dispersed throughout the organization in the knowledge centers. Most large consulting firms have more than one knowledge center.

Earlier we described the function of the staff to be similar to that of reference librarians. They actually do much more. Some members are functional-area experts who are now cataloguing and approving knowledge contributions, and pushing the knowledge out to clients and employees who they believe can use the knowledge. These functional experts may also work in a liaison role with the functional areas of the communities of practice. Others work with users to train them on the system or help them with their searches. Still others work on improving the system's performance by identifying better methods with which to manage knowledge. For example, Ernst & Young has 250 people managing the knowledge repository and assisting people in finding knowledge at its Center for Business Knowledge. Some staff members disseminate knowledge, while others are liaisons with the forty practice areas. They codify and store documents in their areas of expertise (see Hansen et al., 1999).

10.7   ENSURING SUCCESS OF KM EFFORTS

Organizations can gain several benefits from implementing a knowledge management strategy. Tactically, they can accomplish some or all of the following: reduce loss of intellectual capital due to people leaving the company; reduce costs by decreasing the number of times the company must repeatedly solve the same problem, and by achieving economies of scale in obtaining information from external providers; reduce redundancy of knowledge-based activities; increase productivity by making knowledge available more quickly and easily; and increase employee satisfaction by enabling greater personal development and empowerment. The best reason of all may be a strategic need to gain a *competitive advantage* in the marketplace (Knapp, 1998).

Knowledge Management Valuation   In general, companies take either an asset-based approach to knowledge management valuation or one that links knowledge to its applications and business benefits (Skyrme and Amidon, 1998). The former approach starts with the identification of intellectual assets and then focuses management's attention on increasing their value. The second uses variants of a *balanced scorecard*, where financial measures are balanced against customer, process, and innovation measures. Among the best-developed financial measurement methods in use are the balanced-scorecard approach, Skandia's Navigator, Stern Stewart's economic value added (EVA), M'Pherson's inclusive valuation methodology, the return on management ratio, and Levin's knowledge capital measure. See Skyrme and Amidon (1998) for details on how these measures work in practice.

Another method of measuring the value of knowledge is to estimate its price if it was offered for sale. Most firms are reluctant to sell knowledge, unless they are expressly in the business of doing so. Generally a firm's knowledge is an asset that has competitive value, and if it leaves the organization, the firm loses its competitive advantage. However, it is possible to price the knowledge and the access to the knowledge in order to make it worth a firm's while to sell it. For example, American Airlines' Decision Technologies Corp. grew from a small internal analysis team in the 1970s. Initially the team was created to solve problems and provide decision support to American Airlines only. As it grew, it became an independent corporation within AMR Corp., and it began to provide consulting and systems to other airlines, including American's competitors. AMR evidently had decided that the revenue it could obtain by selling some knowledge overrode any competitive advantage it would lose by doing so. The major consulting firms are in the business of selling expertise. Their knowledge management efforts, which often began as internal systems, evolved into quite valuable systems that their clients use on a regular basis.

Success indicators with respect to knowledge management are similar to those for assessing the effectiveness of other business-change projects. They include growth in the resources attached to the project, growth in the volume of knowledge content and usage, the likelihood that the project will survive without the support of a particular individual or individuals, and some evidence of financial return either for the knowledge management activity itself or for the entire organization (Davenport et al., 1998).

There are in general two types of measures that can be used to assess the effectiveness of a KM initiative: results-oriented and activity-oriented (O'Dell et al., 2003). The results-oriented measures are financial in nature and might include such things as increase in goods sold. The activities-based measures consider how frequently users are accessing knowledge or contributing to knowledge (O'Dell et al., 2003).

FINANCIAL METRICS. Even though traditional accounting measures are incomplete for measuring KM, they are often used as a quick justification for a knowledge management initiative. Returns on investment (ROIs) are reported to range from 20:1 for chemical firms to 4:1 for transportation firms, with an average of 12:1, based on the knowledge management projects assisted on by one consulting firm (Abramson, 1998). In order to measure the impact of knowledge management, experts recommend focusing KM projects on specific business problems that can be easily quantified. When the problems are solved, the value and benefits of the system become apparent and often can be measured (MacSweeney, 2002).

At Royal Dutch/Shell group, the return on investment was explicitly documented: The company had invested $6 million in a knowledge management system in 1999 and within two years obtained $235 million in reduced costs and new revenues (King, 2001). Hewlett-Packard offers another example of documented financial returns: Within six months of launching its @HP companywide portal in October 2000, Hewlett-Packard realized a $50 million return on its initial investment of $20 million. This was largely due to a reduction in volume of calls to internal call centers and to the new paperless processes (Roberts-Witt, 2002).

The financial benefit might be perceptual, rather than absolute, but it need not be documented in order for the KM system to be considered a success.

NONFINANCIAL METRICS. Traditional ways of financial measurement may fall short when measuring the value of a KMS, because *they do not consider intellectual capital an asset.* Therefore there is a need to develop procedures for valuing the *intangible* assets of an organization, as well as to incorporate models of intellectual capital that in some way quantify innovation and the development and implementation of core competencies.

When evaluating intangibles, there are a number of new ways to view capital. In the past, only customer goodwill was valued as an asset. Now the following are also included (adapted from Allee, 1999):

- *External relationship capital:* how an organization links with its partners, suppliers, customers, regulators, and so on
- *Structural capital:* systems and work processes that leverage competitiveness, such as information systems, and so on
- *Human capital:* the individual capabilities, knowledge, skills, and so on, that people have
- *Social capital:* the quality and value of relationships with the larger society
- *Environmental capital:* the value of relationships with the environment

For example, a knowledge management initiative undertaken by Partners HealthCare System, Inc. has not resulted in quantifiable financial benefits, but has greatly increased the social capital of the company. The knowledge management system for physicians implemented by Partners reduced the number of serious medication errors by 55 percent at some of Boston's most prestigious teaching hospitals. Calculating return on investment for such a system turns out to be an extremely difficult proposition, which is why only a small fraction of hospitals use similar systems. While the company is unable to determine how the system affects its bottom line, it is willing to justify the costs based on the system's benefits to the society (Melymuka, 2002).

Causes of KM Failure

No system is infallible. There are many cases of knowledge management failing. Estimates of KM failure rates range from 50 percent to 70 percent, where a failure is interpreted to mean that *all* of the major objectives were not met by the effort (Ambrosio, 2000).

Some reasons for failure include having too much information that is not easily searchable (Steinberg, 2002) and having inadequate or incomplete information in the system so that identifying the real expertise in an organization becomes foggy (Desouza, 2003). Failure may also result from an inability to capture and categorize knowledge as well as from the overmanagement of the KM process such that creativity and communities of practice are stifled (Desouza, 2003). Other issues include lack of commitment (this occurred at a large Washington, D.C., constituent lobbying organization), not providing incentive for people to use the system (as occurred at Pillsbury Co.; see Barth, 2000b, and Silver, 2000), and an

IT at Work 10.5
ESCAPING A KNOWLEDGE MANAGEMENT FAILURE

In the late 1990s, Frito-Lay Inc., a Plano, Texas-based snack foods division of PepsiCo, Inc., realized that its sales teams had difficulties collaborating and finding pertinent information. These difficulties led to frustration, declining performance, and rising turnover rates. To alleviate these problems and boost performance, Frito-Lay (*fritolay.com*) envisioned a Web-based portal that would combine tools for knowledge management and collaboration. The company engaged Dallas-based consulting firm Navigator Systems Inc. to develop the portal.

Frito-Lay selected a pilot sales team to describe the kinds of knowledge they needed. The requests ranged from simple information, such as why Frito-Lay merchandises Lays and Ruffles products in one part of a store and Doritos in another, to more complex questions on what motivates shoppers as they move through a store. To collect the required knowledge, developers searched Frito-Lay's databases in departments such as marketing, sales, and operations. They also referenced external sources such as trade publications and industry organizations, and identified in-house subject matter experts.

In October 1999, a working prototype of the system was presented to the pilot sales team. Only then did Frito-Lay discover that in the quest for speed, a classic and crippling mistake had been made: The development team had failed to obtain sufficient input from the sales team and did not involve users in the design process. The prototype had the potential to be marginally useful to any sales team, but it was not specific enough to offer fundamental benefits for the pilot team. Therefore, the pilot team was reluctant to accept the system. "Conceptually, it was a great idea," said Frito-Lay sales team leader Joe Ackerman. "But when folks are not on the front line, their view of what is valuable is different from those running 100 miles an hour in the field."

Frito-Lay learned valuable lessons from that mistake and chose to redesign the system. However, at this stage, it not only needed to add the missing features, but also had to win back the sales force and convince them that the redesigned system would indeed streamline their work by facilitating knowledge exchange. The team of developers spent the following four months working with salespeople to transform the prototype into a system they would embrace.

The redesigned portal has been a big success. Better collaboration has helped to significantly reduce turnover, while improved access to knowledge-base resources has enabled salespeople to present themselves as consultants with important knowledge to share. Today, the knowledge management portal is used for daily communication, call reporting, weekly cross-country meetings, training, document sharing, and access to data and industry news. The pilot team exceeded its sales plan for 2000 and grew its business at a rate almost twice that of Frito-Lay's other customer teams. The KMS concept is now being tailored to three other Frito-Lay sales teams and departments, and other divisions of PepsiCo have expressed interest in it as well.

Source: Adapted from Melymuka (2001).

For Further Exploration: Why did Frito-Lay find it difficult to correct the mistake identified in a late stage of the development cycle? If you were responsible for the development of a knowledge management system, what specific actions would you take to ensure that it satisfies the needs of end users?

---

over-emphasis on technology at the expense of larger knowledge and people issues (Hislop, 2002).

IT at Work 10.5 illustrates how Frito-Lay narrowly avoided failure of its KMS.

Factors Leading to KM Success　To increase the probability of success of knowledge management projects, companies must assess whether there is a strategic need for knowledge management in the first place. The next step is to determine whether the current process of dealing with organizational knowledge is adequate and whether the organization's culture is ready for procedural changes. Only when these issues are resolved should the company consider technology infrastructure and decide if a new system is needed. When the right technological solution is chosen, it

TABLE 10.2 Major Factors that Lead to KM Project Success

- A link to a firm's economic value, to demonstrate financial viability and maintain executive sponsorship.
- A technical and organizational infrastructure on which to build.
- A standard, flexible knowledge structure to match the way the organization performs work and uses knowledge. Usually, the organizational culture must change to effectively create a knowledge-sharing environment.
- A knowledge-friendly culture leading directly to user support.
- A clear purpose and language, to encourage users to buy into the system. Sometimes simple, useful knowledge applications need to be implemented first.
- A change in motivational practices, to create a culture of sharing.
- Multiple channels for knowledge transfer—because individuals have different ways of working and expressing themselves. The multiple channels should reinforce one another. Knowledge transfer should be easily accomplished and be as unobtrusive as possible.
- A level of process orientation to make a knowledge management effort worthwhile. In other words, new, improved work methods can be developed.
- Nontrivial motivational methods, such as rewards and recognition, to encourage users to contribute and use knowledge.
- Senior management support. This is critical to initiate the project, to provide resources, to help identify important knowledge on which the success of the organization relies, and to market the project.

Source: Adapted from Davenport et al. (1998).

becomes necessary to properly introduce the system to the entire organization and to gain participation of every employee (Kaplan, 2002).

A case study of Nortel Network's KM initiative indicated that there were three major issues that influenced the success of KM: (1) having effective managerial influence in terms of coordination, control and measurement, project management, and leadership; (2) having key resources such as financial resources and cross-functional expertise, and (3) taking advantage of technological opportunities. Together, these enabled a well-defined process, the understanding of people issues, and the successful incorporation of technology (Massay et al., 2002). Other factors that may lead to knowledge management project success are shown in Table 10.2.

Effective knowledge sharing and learning requires cultural change within the organization, new management practices, senior management commitment, and technological support. We recognize that organizational culture must shift to a culture of sharing. This should be handled through strong leadership at the top, and by providing knowledge management tools that truly make people's jobs better. As far as encouraging system use and knowledge sharing goes, people must be *properly* motivated to contribute knowledge. The mechanism for doing so should be part of their jobs, and their salaries should reflect this. People must also be motivated to utilize the knowledge that is in the KMS. Again, this should be part of their jobs and their reward structures.

As more companies develop their knowledge management capabilities, some of the ground rules are becoming apparent. Success depends on a clear strategic logic for knowledge sharing, the choice of appropriate infrastructure (technical or non-technical), and an implementation approach that addresses the typical barriers: motivation to share knowledge, resources to capture and synthesize organizational learning, and ability to navigate the knowledge network to find the right people and data.

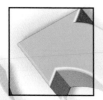

A CLOSER LOOK
10.1 ADAPTABILITY—A MISSING INGREDIENT

Mrs. Fields Cookies, a national chain of cookie stores, grew remarkably fast and successfully during the early 1980s. A key aspect of the company's strategy was to provide expertise directly from the headquarters to every store. As the number of stores increased, the only feasible way to achieve such direct control was through the use of information systems that were designed to mimic the decision making of Mrs. Fields herself. Decision-making systems were placed in each store. The system would take input (such as the temperature, the day of the week, the date, and so forth), would process the data, and would provide, as output, information to each store manager about how many cookies of each type to bake each hour. In essence, the software provided each store manager with explicit directions for planning each day's production, sales, and labor scheduling, along with inventory control and ordering. Because of the well-functioning computer systems, which in principle were systems designed to make Mrs. Fields' tacit knowledge available to all stores, the company was able to successfully function with few managerial levels.

However, as the market began to change and consumers became more health conscious, Mrs. Fields was very slow to respond. In a sense, by embedding so much knowledge into systems that were incapable of adaptation, the organization tied itself to a certain way of doing things and failed to engage in knowledge creation. That is, it failed to pick up the signals in the environment, which might have suggested a change in strategy or product focus. By the early 1990s, the company had fallen into bankruptcy.

Source: Adapted from Henfridsson and Söderholm (2000).

Potential Drawbacks to Knowledge Management Systems

While there are many positive outcomes of managing knowledge, as discussed in examples throughout this chapter, it would be short-sighted not to consider the potential negative outcomes associated with reusing knowledge. As an example, Henfridsson and Söderholm (2000) analyzed the situation that faced Mrs. Fields cookies, as described in *A Closer Look 10.1.*

The case of Mrs. Fields illustrates that while organizations might achieve significant short-term gains through knowledge management systems, they must not neglect to allow for the creative process of new knowledge creation, lest they eventually find themselves applying yesterday's solutions to tomorrow's problems.

Closing Remarks

For millennia we have known about the effective use of knowledge and how to store and reuse it. Intelligent organizations recognize that knowledge is an intellectual asset, perhaps the only one that grows over time, and when harnessed effectively can sustain competition and innovation. Organizations can use information technology to perform true knowledge management. Leveraging an entire organization's intellectual resources can have tremendous financial impact.

With knowledge management, the definition is clear, the concepts are clear, the methodology is clear, the challenges are clear and surmountable, the benefits are clear and can be substantial, and the tools and technology—though incomplete and somewhat expensive—are viable. Key issues are executive sponsorship and measuring success. Technological issues are minimal compared to these. Knowledge management is not just another expensive management fad. Knowledge management is a new paradigm for how organizations work.

MANAGERIAL ISSUES

1. *Organizational culture change.* This issue is how we can change organizational culture so that people are willing both to contribute knowledge to and use knowledge from a KMS. There must be strong executive leadership, clearly expressed goals, user involvement in the system, and deployment of an easy-to-use system that provides real value to employees. A viable reward structure for contributing and using knowledge must also be developed.

2. *How to store tacit knowledge.* This is extremely difficult. Most KMSs (based on the network storage model) store explicit knowledge about the tacit knowledge that people possess. When the knowledgeable people leave an organization, they take their knowledge with them. Since knowledge requires active use by the recipient, it is important for the person generating knowledge to articulate it in a way that another, appropriately educated person can understand it.

3. *How to measure the tangible and intangible benefits of KMS.* There are a number of ways to measure the value of intellectual assets and of providing them to the organization, as discussed in Section 10.7.

4. *Determining the roles of the various personnel in a KM effort.* This issue is described in Section 10.6.

5. *The lasting importance of knowledge management.* Knowledge management is extremely important. It is not another management fad. If it is correctly done, it can have massive impact by leveraging know-how throughout the organization. If it is not done, or is not correctly done, the company will not be able to effectively compete against another major player in the industry that does KM correctly.

6. *Implementation in the face of quickly changing technology.* This is an important issue to address regarding the development of many IT systems. Technology has to be carefully examined, and experiments done, to determine what makes sense. By starting now, an organization can get past the managerial and behavioral issues, which have greater impact on the eventual success (or not) of a KMS. As better and cheaper technology is developed, the KMS can be migrated over to it, just as legacy systems have migrated to the PC.

 ON THE WEB SITE... Additional resources, including quizzes; online files of additional text, tables, figures, and cases; and frequently updated Web links to current articles and information can be found on the book's Web site (*wiley.com/college/turban*).

KEY TERMS

Chief knowledge officer
  (CKO) *472*
Community of practice (COP) *473*
Data mining *462*

Explicit knowledge *453*
Intellectual capital (intellectual
  assets) *453*
Knowledge *452*

Knowledge discovery in databases
  (KDD) *462*
Knowledge management
  (KM) *451*

Knowledge management system (KMS) *454*

Knowledge repository *465*

Knowware *464*

Leaky knowledge *453*

Model marts *463*

Model warehouses *463*

Practice approach *458*

Process approach *458*

Sticky knowledge *453*

Tacit knowledge *453*

CHAPTER HIGHLIGHTS (Numbers Refer to Learning Objectives)

❶ Knowledge is different from information and data. Knowledge is information that is contextual, relevant, and actionable. It is dynamic in nature.

❶ Explicit (structured, leaky) knowledge deals with more objective, rational, and technical knowledge. Tacit (unstructured, sticky) knowledge is usually in the domain of subjective, cognitive, and experiential learning. Tacit knowledge is highly personal and hard to formalize.

❷ Knowledge management is a process that helps organizations identify, select, organize, disseminate, and transfer important information and expertise that typically reside within the organization in an unstructured manner.

❷ Knowledge management requires a major transformation in organizational culture to create a desire to share (give and receive) knowledge, plus a commitment to KM at all levels of a firm.

❷ The knowledge management model involves the following cyclical steps: create, capture, refine, store, manage, and disseminate knowledge.

❷ Standard knowledge management initiatives involve the creation of knowledge bases, active process management, knowledge centers, and collaborative technologies.

❷ Knowledge management is an effective way for an organization to leverage its intellectual assets.

❸ The two strategies used for KM initiatives are the process approach and the practice approach.

❹ A knowledge management system is generally developed using three sets of technologies: communication, collaboration, and storage.

❹ A variety of technologies can make up a knowledge management system: the Internet, intranets, data warehousing, decision-support tools, groupware, and so on. Intranets are the primary means of displaying and distributing knowledge in organizations.

❹ Knowledge management systems can be purchased in whole or in part from one of numerous software development companies and enterprise information systems vendors, they can be acquired through major consulting firms, or can be outsourced to the application service providers (ASPs).

❺ Knowledge portals can be used to provide a central location from which various KM applications are searched.

❻ The chief knowledge office (CKO) is primarily responsible for changing the behavior of the firm to embrace the use of knowledge management and then managing the development operation of a knowledge management system.

❻ Knowledge management typically involves the cooperation of managers, developers, KM staff, and users.

❻ Communities of practice (COPs) provide pressure to break down the cultural barriers that hinder knowledge management efforts.

❼ It is difficult to measure the success of a KMS. Traditional methods of financial measurement fall short, as they do not consider intellectual capital an asset. Nonfinancial metrics are typically used to measure the success of a KM, yet some firms have been able to determine financial payoffs.

QUESTIONS FOR REVIEW

1. Discuss what is meant by an intellectual asset.
2. Define knowledge and knowledge management.
3. Define explicit knowledge. Why is it also called leaky?
4. Define tacit knowledge. Why is it also called sticky?
5. How can tacit knowledge be transferred or shared?
6. List some ways in which organizational culture can impact a knowledge management effort.

7. What is the primary goal of knowledge management?
8. Describe the process approach to knowledge management.
9. Describe the practice approach to knowledge management.
10. Describe the roles and responsibilities of the people involved in a knowledge management system, especially the CKO.

11. What is a community of practice?

12. List the steps in the cyclical model of knowledge management. Why is it a cycle?

13. List the major knowledge management success factors.

14. Describe the role of IT in knowledge management.

QUESTIONS FOR DISCUSSION

1. Why is the term knowledge so hard to define?

2. Describe and relate the different characteristics of knowledge.

3. Explain why it is important to capture and manage knowledge.

4. Compare and contrast tacit knowledge and explicit knowledge.

5. Explain why organizational culture must sometimes change before knowledge management is introduced.

6. How does knowledge management attain its primary objective?

7. How can employees be motivated to contribute to and use knowledge management systems?

8. What is the role of a knowledge repository in knowledge management?

9. Explain the importance of communication and collaboration technologies to the processes of knowledge management.

10. Explain why firms adopt knowledge management initiatives.

11. Explain the role of the CKO in developing a knowledge management system. What major responsibilities does he or she have?

12. Discuss some knowledge management success factors.

13. Why is it hard to evaluate the impacts of knowledge management?

14. Explain how the Internet and its related technologies (Web browsers, intranets, and so on) enable knowledge management.

15. Explain the roles of a community of practice.

16. Describe an enterprise knowledge portal and explain its significance.

EXERCISES

1. Make a list of all the knowledge management methods you use during your day (work and personal). Which are the most effective? Which are the least effective? What kinds of work or activities does each knowledge management method enable?

2. Investigate the literature for information on the position of CKO. Find out what percentage of firms with KM initiatives have CKOs and what their responsibilities are.

3. Investigate the literature for new measures of success (metrics) for knowledge management and intellectual capital. Write a report on your findings.

4. Describe how each of the key elements of a knowledge management infrastructure can contribute to its success.

5. Based on your own experience or on the vendor's information, list the major capabilities of a particular knowledge management product, and explain how it can be used in practice.

6. Describe how to ride a bicycle, drive a car, or make a peanut butter and jelly sandwich. Now, have someone else try to do it based solely on your explanation. How can you best convert this knowledge from tacit to explicit (or can't you)?

7. Consider why knowledge management systems would be so important to a modern organization that firms would initiate such systems.

GROUP ASSIGNMENTS

1. Compare and contrast the capabilities and features of electronic document management with those of collaborative computing and those of knowledge management systems. Each team represents one type of system. Present the ways in which these capabilities and features can create improvements for an organization.

2. Search the Internet for knowledge management products and systems and create categories for them. Assign one vendor to each team. Describe the categories you created and justify them.

3. If you are working on a decision-making project in industry for this course (or if not, use one from another

class or from work), examine some typical decisions in the related project. How would you extract the knowledge you need? Can you use that knowledge in practice? Why or why not?

4. Read the article by A. Genusa titled "Rx for Learning," available at *cio.com* (February 1, 2001), which describes Tufts University Medical School's experience with knowledge management. Determine how these concepts and such a system could be implemented and used at your college or university. Explain how each aspect would work, or if not, explain why not.

INTERNET EXERCISES

1. How does knowledge management support decision making? Identify products or systems on the Web that help organizations accomplish knowledge management. Start with *brint.com, decisionsupport.net,* and *knowledge management.ittoolbox.com.* Try one out and report your findings to the class.

2. Try the KPMG Knowledge Management Framework Assessment Exercise at *kmsurvey.londonweb.net* and assess how well your organization (company or university) is doing with knowledge management. Are the results accurate? Why or why not?

3. Search the Internet to identify sites dealing with knowledge management. Start with *google.com, kmworld.com,* and *km-forum.org.* How many did you find? Categorize the sites based on whether they are academic, consulting firms, vendors, and so on. Sample one of each and describe the main focus of the site.

4. Identify five real-world knowledge management success stories by searching vendor Web sites (use at least three different vendors). Describe them. How did knowledge management systems and methods contribute to their success? What features do they share? What different features do individual successes have?

5. Search the Internet for vendors of knowledge management suites, enterprise knowledge portals, and out-of-the-box knowledge management solutions. Identify the major features of each product (use three from each), and compare and contrast their capabilities.

6. J.D. Edwards (*jdedwards.com*) developed a knowledge management intranet initiative called the Knowledge Garden. Access both the J.D. Edwards and Microsoft Web sites and investigate its current capabilities.

Minicase 1
DaimlerChrysler EBOKs with Knowledge Management

In 1980 Chrysler Corporation came back from near bankruptcy with innovative designs and a view of a shared culture in design, development, and manufacturing. The company began new ways of looking at its business, its suppliers, and its workers. After the acquisition of American Motors Corporation (AMC) in 1987, executives developed and deployed advanced, dedicated platform design and production methods, which showed enormous potential. Jack Thompson, the technology center development director, worked closely with Chairman Lee Iacocca on the development of a new, modern engineering and design facility. Thompson designed the center around knowledge-sharing and productivity principles: open air, natural light, and escalators (people don't talk on elevators).

In 1994 the tech center opened, providing a home for a transformed engineering culture. Two years later, the corporate headquarters was moved next to the tech center so executives could be nearby. By 2000, over 11,000 people were working at the Auburn Hills, Michigan, center. In November 1998, Daimler-Benz became the majority owner of Chrysler Corporation, renaming the company Daimler-Chrysler (*daimlerchrysler.com*). Chrysler's fast, efficient, and innovative nature, as a result of the extremely successful platform approach to design and engineering, led to the buy-in—the largest merger in manufacturing history.

Platform production at DaimlerChrysler has teams of engineers focused on a single type of car platform (small car, minivan, and so on), working on new models as a system from concept to production. Cars are designed by a single team considering customer needs and preferences, as opposed to the standard practice of organizing the new designs by organizational functions (silos). Platform teams of employees work and learn together, focused on the product, with a payoff in market responsiveness, reduced cost, and increased quality. The Chrysler LH, the first model developed with the platform approach, took 39 months to produce; typically the time to market exceeds 50 months.

While the benefits were clear, Chrysler executives noticed that unexplained errors were popping up in the new platforms (like leaving a moisture barrier out of car doors). *There was an organizational memory problem:* Mentoring and peer support had become limited. Informal and formal professional collaboration had stopped. The same mistakes were being made, corrected, and repeated. People were not learning about new developments in their core areas. The typical collaboration found among groups doing similar work was sharply reduced, and so problems and solutions were not being documented or shared.

Collaboration and communication needed to be reestablished within groups that have common training, interests, and responsibilities (design, engineering, body, engine, manufacturing, and so on). The goal was to reestablish these links while becoming more competitive with even faster product-cycle times. Chrysler needed to institutionalize knowledge sharing and collaboration. In 1996 Chrysler Corporation made *knowledge management* a vital condition for design and engineering, leading to dramatic improvements in productivity.

First, engineers mapped out where the knowledge was within the organization (a knowledge audit). There were many categories, or "buckets of knowledge," ranging from product databases to CAD/CAM systems to manufacturing, procurement, and supply vehicle test data. Within each category, details were identified and codified. Sharing knowledge meant integrating these knowledge buckets, while resolving cultural issues that impeded sharing across platform boundaries. Chrysler created informal cross-platform *Tech Clubs,* functionally organized communities of practice to reunite designers and engineers with peers from other platform groups. Each community would then codify its knowledge and provide mentoring and apprenticing opportunities for learning.

The *Engineering Book of Knowledge (EBOK)* is Chrysler's intranet supporting a knowledge repository of process *best practices* and technical know-how to be shared and maintained. It was initially developed by two engineering managers but continues through encouraged employee participation in grassroots (i.e., supported at the lower levels of the organization) Tech Clubs. EBOK is written in GrapeVine (GrapeVine Technologies), running as a Lotus Notes application, and is accessed with the Netscape browser and NewsEdge.

Knowledge is explored and entered into the EBOK through an iterative team approach: the Tech Clubs. Best practices are identified, refined, confirmed, and finally entered into the EBOK in a secure interactive electronic repository. When an author proposes a best practice, users in the Tech Club responsible for that area of knowledge react by commenting on the knowledge through a discussion list. One manager, the *Book Owner,* is ultimately responsible for approving new entries and changes to the book. The Book Owner joins the conversation. The author can respond to the comments by either building a better case or going along with the discussion. Ultimately the Tech Club decides, and the Book Owner enters the new knowledge. The Book Owner is the individual who is ultimately responsible for the accuracy of the book, and therefore approves entries to, modifications to, and deletions from the book.

The EBOK is DaimlerChrysler's official design review process. The EBOK even contains best practices information about DaimlerChrysler's competitors. DaimlerChrysler has determined that EBOK is both a best practices tool (the process approach) and a collaboration tool (the practice approach). DaimlerChrysler officials recognize that because the environment changes and new methods are being continually developed, the EBOK will never be fully complete. The EBOK is a *living book*. The EBOK *leverages* technology knowledge.

The EBOK is central to DaimlerChrysler's new way of working. The plan is to have more than 5,000 users with access to 3,800 chapters, of which just over half were completed by early 1999. Through the EBOK, DaimlerChrysler reconciled its platform problems and developed a technical memory while tracking competitive information, quality information, and outside standards. Even though there is no central budget for books of knowledge and associated processes, DaimlerChrysler is deploying knowledge in other departments such as manufacturing, finance, and sales and marketing.

The EBOK is only one of several initiatives that promote and facilitate knowledge sharing at DaimlerChrysler. In early 1999, soon after the merger, the company began an information-sharing project called ProBench. The objective of ProBench was to help Chrysler and Mercedes determine how to best use each other's manufacturing expertise. Extensive collaboration enabled Chrysler to benefit from the engineering strengths of Mercedes, while Mercedes was able to learn from Chrysler's know-how in launching new vehicle models. One of the biggest accomplishments of ProBench was Chrysler's decision to use Mercedes' superior rear-wheel-drive automatic transmission on future vehicles. "We are able to save [$600 million in] investment money, get variable costs down, and gain many other advantages by not inventing the wheel twice," says Dieter Zetsche, DaimlerChrysler's Chief Executive Officer. Zetsche concludes: "[Collaboration] has been a real value to us, and it is a very positive result of the merger."

Sources: Adapted from Karlenzig (1999), Maynard (2001), and *daimlerchrysler.com*.

Questions for Minicase 1

1. Platform design at DaimlerChrysler led directly to a reduction in the time to market and in costs for new vehicles. Explain how it caused new problems.

2. What is meant by a community of practice? How did DaimlerChrysler leverage the knowledge within such a community?

3. Describe the Engineering Book of Knowledge (EBOK). Explain how it is updated by adding new knowledge of practice.

4. It has been said that "the proper role for all knowledge management tools is to leverage technology in service to human thinking." Explain this statement.

5. How successful was the knowledge management initiative at DaimlerChrysler?

6. Consider how a book of knowledge could impact another organization, ideally one with which you are affiliated (e.g., your university, job, part-time job, family business). Describe the potential impacts, and list the benefits. Would there be any organizational culture issues to deal with? Why or why not?

Minicase 2
Chevron's Knowledge Management Initiatives
Cook with Gas

Chevron (now ChevronTexaco, *chevron.com*) wanted to explore, develop, adapt, and adopt knowledge management methods to leverage its expertise throughout the enterprise to maintain a competitive position in the marketplace. The improvements gained from identifying, sharing, and managing intellectual assets can impact positively on drilling, office work, safety, and refineries. Improvements were generated by focusing on process, culture, best practices, and technology, including Internet technology.

Chevron uses knowledge management in drilling, refinery maintenance and safety management, capital project management, and other areas. The electronic document-management system impacts on several different areas at Chevron.

Drilling

Chevron adopted an *organizational learning system (OLS)* that improves drilling performance by sharing information globally. The system uses a simple software tool to capture lessons from the first wells in a new area, and then uses that knowledge to drill the rest of the wells faster and cheaper. Well costs have dropped by 12 to 20 percent and cycle time has been reduced as much as 40 percent in some cases (offshore drilling vessels can cost up to $250,000 a day). Oil & Gas Consultants International developed the OLS for Amoco. Chevron found it through a best-practices survey.

Refineries

The company uses knowledge management IS to maintain six refineries. Sam Preckett, reliability-focused maintenance system manager, is developing a process to improve information and knowledge sharing. Preckett and others realized that they were not effectively using the data and information already stored in Chevron's enterprise information systems. Preckett has been developing an informal best-practices methodology for maintenance by "trying to learn how we do things." Getting knowledge to users is only part of the system; another part captures the tacit knowledge and experiences of workers. Chevron is trying to motivate workers to participate. Preckett said that at Chevron creative thinking is promoted from the executive level, which "allows him to do interesting things" to achieve efficiency gains through knowledge sharing.

Electronic Document Management

Another specific need under the knowledge management umbrella was addressed by the DocMan system, initiated in December 1994 to improve the timeliness of document access, management, and integration, and sharing of information among individual divisions to meet regulatory compliances. A long-standing application, DocMan is used by the Warren Petroleum Limited Partnership Mont Belvieu complex in Texas (of which Chevron is a joint owner).

To handle cultural resistance to change, management emphasized the benefits of the DocMan system: faster access to documents, elimination of wasted effort searching for documents, and assets protection. DocMan delivered a 95 percent return on investment over its 5-year project life. The investment payout period was 1.1 years based on an annual savings of $480,000.

Capital Project Management

Through knowledge management, Chevron implemented a new standard methodology for capital project management. In one case, 60 companies shared data and practices, and so it was possible to compare performance to determine which companies were best and why.

These remarkable achievements did not take place overnight, but were a part of a continuous process that started in 1985 with a focus on Total Quality Management training and benchmarking. By 2000, knowledge management was established as a corporate value, virtual collaboration among groups was practiced worldwide, and knowledge management became an important part of performance appraisals.

What have been the overall results? Improved management of knowledge was instrumental in reducing operating costs from $9.4 billion to $7.4 billion from 1992 to 1998 and in reducing energy costs by $200 million a year. During the 1990s, efforts like this were essential in reducing costs, achieving productivity gains of over 50 percent (in barrels of output per employee), and improving employee safety performance more than 50 percent. Chevron now calls itself a *learning organization* (an organization capable of learning from its past experiences). Some gains from knowledge management at Chevron are qualitative: Employees' work is more interesting and challenging when it involves finding and applying new knowledge. Jobs are potentially more fulfilling and more personally rewarding.

Sources: Adapted from Velker (1999), *CIO.com* (1999), and Silverman et al. (2000).

Questions for Minicase 2

1. What is meant by a learning organization?
2. Describe the gains that Chevron experienced through its knowledge management programs.

3. To what different areas did Chevron apply knowledge management, and how successful were they?
4. Why is it important to document cost savings of knowledge management systems?
5. If dramatic payoffs can be achieved through knowledge management (as with the DocMan system), why don't more companies do so?

Virtual Company Assignment
Knowledge Management at The Wireless Café

You've noticed that Barbara and Jeremy spend quite a bit of time interviewing potential employees, and some quick Web research reveals that average turnover of restaurant employees for the past few years has been running over 100 percent. This news is alarming to you, as you think of all of the new information systems and technologies that could help The Wireless Café run more efficiently. How will the staff ever develop system expertise if they stay less than a year?

Instructions

1. What kinds of knowledge is The Wireless Café losing with such a high turnover? Consider both tacit and explicit knowledge accumulated by employees in the different positions. How important is this knowledge to the well-being and long-term success of The Wireless Café? What can Barbara and Jeremy do about capturing it?

2. Using The Wireless Café's Web site (*wiley.com/college/ turban*), match the jobs with information systems that The Wireless Café might adopt. Try to rank the level of training or expertise you think an employee needs to have before using the system on the job, and determine whether online training would be beneficial.

3. Discuss the problems of retaining organizational knowledge in an industry with high turnover. Is a knowledge management effort cost-effective for The Wireless Café? What are some guidelines to help management decide on the level of knowledge capture and management they should practice?

REFERENCES

Abramson, G., "Measuring Up," *CIO,* June 15, 1998.

Alavi, M., "Managing Organizational Knowledge," Chapter 2 in Zmud, W. R. (ed.), *Framing the Domains of IT Management: Projecting the Future.* Cincinnati, OH: Pinnaflex Educational Resources, 2000.

Alavi, M., and D. Leidner, "Knowledge Management Systems: Emerging Views and Practices from the Field," *Proceedings of 32nd Annual HICSS,* Maui, HI, January 1999, available at *computer .org/proceedings/hicss/0001/00017/00017009.pdf?SMSESSION=NO* (accessed July 2003).

Alavi, M. T. et al., "An Empirical Examination of the Influence of Knowledge Management on Organizational Culture," working paper, Baylor University, 2003.

Allee, V., "Are You Getting Big Value from Knowledge?" *KMWorld,* September 1999, pp. 16–17.

Amato-McCoy, D., "Commerce Bank Manages Knowledge Profitably," *Bank Systems and Technology,* January 2003.

Ambrosio, J., "Knowledge Management Mistakes," *Computerworld,* 34(27), July 3, 2000.

Anderson, L., "Cisco Employee Connection: Saving Money, Keeping Employees," Smartbusinessmag.com, June 2002, p. 49.

Barth, S., "KM Horror Stories," *Knowledge Management,* October 2000b.

Barth, S., "Knowledge as a Function of X," *Knowledge Management,* February 2000a.

Bennet, A., and D. Bennet, "The Partnership between Organizational Learning and Knowledge Management," in *Handbook on Knowledge Management,* Volume 1k (ed. C. W. Holsapple). New York: Springer-Verlag, 2003, pp. 439–460.

Blodgett, M., "Prescription Strength," *CIO,* February 1, 2000.

Bolloju, N. et al., "Integrating Knowledge Management into Enterprise Environments for the Next Generation of Decision Support," *Decision Support Systems,* 33(2), June 2002, pp. 163–176.

Brown, S. J., and Duguid, P., "Balancing Act: How to Capture Knowledge Without Killing It," *Harvard Business Review,* May–June 2000, 73–80.

Cahill, T., *How the Irish Saved Civilization.* New York: Anchor, 1996.

CIO.com, "The Means to an Edge: Knowledge Management—Key to Innovation," *CIO* white paper, September 15, 1999.

Collins, H., *Corporate Portals: Revolutionizing Information Access to Increase Productivity and Drive the Bottom Line,* AMACOM, 2001.

Cothrel, J., and R. L. Williams, "On-line Communities: Getting the Most Out of On-line Discussion and Collaboration," *Knowledge Management Review,* No. 6, January–February 1999b.

Cothrel, J., and R. L. Williams, "On-line Communities: Helping Them Form and Grow," *Journal of Knowledge Management,* 3(1), 1999a.

Cranfield University, "The Cranfield/Information Strategy Knowledge Survey: Europe's State of the Art in Knowledge Management," *The Economist Group,* 1998.

Davenport, T. H., and L. Prusak, *Working Knowledge: How Organizations Manage What They Know.* Boston: Harvard Business School Press, 1998.

Davenport, T. et al., "Successful Knowledge Management Projects," *Sloan Management Review,* 39(2), Winter 1998.

Davis, M., "Knowledge Management," *Information Strategy: The Executive's Journal,* Fall 1998.

DeLong, D. W., and Fahey, L., "Diagnosing Cultural Barriers to Knowledge Management, *Academy of Management Executive,* 14(4), November 2000, pp. 113–127.

Desouza, K.C., "Knowledge Management Barriers: Why the Technology Imperative Seldom Works," *Business Horizons,* January/February 2003, pp. 25–29.

Duffy, D., "Knowledge Champions," *CIO* (Enterprise-Section 2), November 1998.

Economist, "Business: Electronic Glue," *The Economist,* May 31, 2001, *economist.com/displaystory.cfm?story_id=638605* (accessed July 2003).

Edvinsson, L., "The Intellectual Capital of Nations" in *Handbook on Knowledge Management,* Volume 1k (ed. C. W. Holsapple), New York: Springer-Verlag, 2003, pp. 153–163.

Eisenhart, M., "Around the Virtual Water Cooler: Sustaining Communities of Practice Takes Plenty of Persistence," *Knowledge Management,* October 2000.

Ford, D. P., "Trust and Knowledge Management: The Seeds of Success," in *Handbook on Knowledge Management,* Volume 1k (ed. C. W. Holsapple). New York: Springer-Verlag, 2003, pp. 553–576.

Genusa, A., "Rx for Learning," *cio.com,* February 1, 2001, *cio.com/archive/020101/tufts.html* (accessed July 2003).

Gray, P., "Tutorial on Knowledge Management," *Proceedings of the Americas Conference of the Association for Information Systems,* Milwaukee, WI, August 1999.

Gray, P., and Meister, D., "Knowledge Sourcing Effectiveness," working paper, University of Pittsburgh, 2003.

Gray, P., and S. Tehrani, "Technologies for Disseminating Knowledge," in *Handbook on Knowledge Management,* Volume 1k (ed. C. W. Holsapple). New York: Springer-Verlag, 2003, pp. 109–128.

Gupta, A. K., and Govindarajan, V., "Knowledge Management's Social Dimension: Lessons from Nucor Steel," *Sloan Management Review,* 42(1), Fall 2000, pp. 71–80.

Hansen, M. et al., "What's Your Strategy for Managing Knowledge?" *Harvard Business Review,* 77(2), March–April 1999.

Hanssen-Bauer, J., and C. C. Snow, "Responding to Hypercompetition: The Structure and Processes of a Regional Learning Network Organization," *Organization Science,* 7(4), 1996, pp. 413–427.

Hargadon, A. B., "Firms as Knowledge Brokers: Lessons in Pursuing Continuous Innovation," *California Management Review,* 40(3), Spring 1998, pp. 209–227.

Henfridsson, O., and A.Söderholm, "Barriers to Learning: On Organizational Defenses and Vicious Circles in Technological Adoption," *Accounting, Management and Information Technologies,* 10(1), 2000, pp. 33–51.

Hislop, D., "Mission Impossible? Communicating and Sharing Knowledge via Information Technology," *Journal of Information Technology,* September 2002, pp. 165–177.

Holsapple, C. W., "Knowledge and its Attributes," in *Handbook on Knowledge Management,* Volume 1k (ed. C. W. Holsapple). New York: Springer-Verlag, 2003, pp. 165–188.

Holsapple, C. W. and K. D. Joshi, "A Knowledge Management Ontology," in *Handbook on Knowledge Management,* Volume 1k (ed. C. W. Holsapple). New York: Springer-Verlag, 2003, pp. 89–128.

InfoWorld, "Enterprise Knowledge Portals Wise Up Your Business," *InfoWorld,* 22(49), December 4, 2000, *archive .infoworld.com/gui/infographics/00/12/04/001204tcvit.gif* (accessed July 2003).

Kaplan, S., "KM the Right Way," *CIO,* July 15, 2002.

Karlenzig, W., "Chrysler's New Know-Mobiles," *Knowledge Management,* May 1999, pp. 58–66.

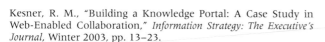

Kesner, R. M., "Building a Knowledge Portal: A Case Study in Web-Enabled Collaboration," *Information Strategy: The Executive's Journal*, Winter 2003, pp. 13–23.

King, D., and K. Jones, "Competitive Intelligence, Software Robots, and the Internet: The NewsAlert Prototype," *Proceedings, 28th HICSS*, Wailea, Maui, Hawaii, January 1995.

King, J., "Shell Strikes Knowledge Gold," *Computerworld*, July/August 2001.p

Knapp, E. M., "Knowledge Management," *Business and Economic Review*, 44(4), July–September 1998.

KPMG Management Consulting, *Knowledge Management: Research Report*, 1998.

KPMG Consulting (*kpmgconsulting.com/kpmgsite/service/km/publications.htm*), press release 2000.

Leidner, D. E., "Understanding Information Culture: Integrating Knowledge Management Systems into Organizations," in *Strategic Information Management* (eds. R. D. Galliers and D. E. Leidner). Oxford: Butterworth Heinemann, 2003, pp. 497–525.

Leonard, D., and S. Sensiper, "The Role of Tacit Knowledge in Group Innovations," *California Management Review*, 40(3), Spring 1998.

Liautaud, B., and M. Hammond, *E-Business Intelligence: Turning Information into Knowledge into Profit*. New York: McGraw-Hill, 2000.

Liebowitz, J., and Y. Chen, "Knowledge Sharing Proficiencies: The Key to Knowledge Management," in *Handbook on Knowledge Management*, Volume 1k (ed. C. W. Holsapple). New York: Springer-Verlag, 2003, pp. 409–438.

MacSweeney, G., "The Knowledge Management Payback," *Insurance & Technology*, June 2002.

Madhaven, R., and R. Grover, "From Embedded Knowledge to Embodied Knowledge: New Product Development as Knowledge Management," *Journal of Marketing*, 62(4), October 1998.

Massay, A. P. et al., "Knowledge Management in Pursuit of Performance: Insights from Nortel Networks," MIS *Quarterly*, 26(3), September 2002, pp. 269–289.

Maynard, M., "Amid the Turmoil, a Rare Success at Daimler-Chrysler," *Fortune*, January 2001.

McDonald, M., and D. Shand, "Request for Proposal: A Guide to KM Professional Services," *Knowledge Management*, March 2000.

Melymuka, K., "Profiting from Mistakes," *Computerworld*, April 2001.

Melymuka, K., "Knowledge Management Helps Cut Errors by Half," *Computerworld*, July 8, 2002, *computerworld.com/databasetopics/data/story/0,10801,72513,00.html* (accessed July 2003).

Mooney, S. F., "P-C 'Knowledge Capital' Can be Measured," *National Underwriter*, 104(51–52), December 25, 2000.

Nonaka, I., "A Dynamic Theory of Organizational Knowledge Creation," *Organization Science*, 5(1), Feb. 1994, pp. 14–37.

Nonaka, I., and H. Takeuchi, *The Knowledge-Creating Company: How Japanese Companies Create the Dynamics of Innovation*. New York: Oxford University Press, 1995.

O'Dell, C. et al., *If Only We Knew What We Know: The Transfer of Internal Knowledge and Best Practice*. New York: Free Press, 1998.

O'Dell, C. S. et al., "Achieving Knowledge Management Outcomes," in *Handbook on Knowledge Management*, Volume 1k (ed. C. W. Holsapple). New York: Springer-Verlag, 2003, pp. 253–288.

O'Herron, J., "Building the Bases of Knowledge," *Call Center Magazine*, January 2003.

Polanyi, M., *Personal Knowledge*. Chicago: University of Chicago Press, 1958.

Polanyi, M., *The Tacit Dimension*. London: Routledge & Kegan Paul, 1966.

Rasmus, D. W., "Knowledge Management: More than AI But Less Without It," *PC AI*, 14(2), March–April 2000.

Robb, D., "Assembling Knowledge Management Teams," *Information Strategy Executive Journal*, Winter 2003, pp. 37–48.

Roberts-Witt, S. L., "The @HP Way," *Portals Magazine*, November, 2002.

Robin, M., "Learning by Doing," *Knowledge Management*, March 2000.

Ruber, P., "Finding the Right Balance: A Canadian Law Firm Interrogated Its Requirements Before Selecting a Portal Solution," *Knowledge Management*, September 2000.

Ruber, P., "Build a Dynamic Business Portal with XML," *Knowledge Management*, January 11, 2001.

Ruggles, R., "The State of the Notion: Knowledge Management in Practice," *California Management Review*, 40(3), 1998.

Schultze, U., and D. E. Leidner, "Studying Knowledge Management in Information Systems Research: Discourses and Theoretical Assumptions," *MIS Quarterly*, 26(3), September, 2002, pp. 213–242.

Silver, C. A., "Where Technology and Knowledge Meet," *Journal of Business Strategy*, 21(6), November–December 2000.

Silverman, S. et al., "Reaping the Rewards," *Oil & Gas Investor*, 2000.

Skyrme, D. J., and D. Amidon, "New Measures of Success," *Journal of Business Strategy*, January–February 1998.

Smith, H. A., and J. D. McKeen, "Creating and Facilitating Communities of Practice," in *Handbook on Knowledge Management*, Vol. 1 (ed. C. W. Holsapple). New York: Springer-Verlag, 2003, pp. 393–408.

Steinberg, D., "Bringing Order to the Information Explosion," Smartbusinessmag.com, June 2002, pp. 48–53.

Storck, J., and P. A. Hill, "Knowledge Diffusion Through Strategic Communities," *Sloan Management Review*, 41(2), Winter 2000.

Teece, D. J., "Knowledge and Competence as Strategic Assets," in *Handbook on Knowledge Management*, Volume 1k (ed. C. W. Holsapple). New York: Springer-Verlag, 2003, pp. 129–152.

Van der Spek,) et al., "The Knowledge Strategy Process," in *Handbook on Knowledge Management*, Volume 1k (ed. C. W. Holsapple). New York: Springer-Verlag, 2003, pp. 443–466.

Vasilash, G. S., "447,000 Heads Are Better than One," *Automotive Design & Production*, June 2002.

Velker, L., "Knowledge the Chevron Way," *KMWorld*, 8(2), February 1, 1999, pp. 20–21.

Von Krogh, G. et al., eds., *Knowledge Creation: A Source of Value*. New York: St. Martin's Press, 2000.

Warner, F., "He Drills for Knowledge," *Fast Company*, September 2001.

Wenger, E. C., and Snyder, W. M., "Communities of Practice: The Organizational Frontier," *Harvard Business Review*, January–February 2000, pp. 139–145.

Williams, S., "The Intranet Content Management Strategy Conference," *Management Services*, September 2001.

Ziff Davis Smart Business, "Inside Information," *Smartbusinessmag.com*, June 2002, pp. 46–54.

PART IV
Managerial and Decision Support Systems

10. Knowledge Management
▶ 11. Data Management: Warehousing, Analyzing, Mining, and Visualization
12. Management Decision Support and Intelligent Systems

CHAPTER

11

Data Management: Warehousing, Analyzing, Mining, and Visualization

11.1
Data Management: A Critical Success Factor

11.2
Data Warehousing

11.3
Information and Knowledge Discovery with Business Intelligence

11.4
Data Mining Concepts and Applications

11.5
Data Visualization Technologies

11.6
Marketing Databases in Action

11.7
Web-based Data Management Systems

LEARNING OBJECTIVES

After studying this chapter, you will be able to:

❶ Recognize the importance of data, their managerial issues, and their life cycle.

❷ Describe the sources of data, their collection, and quality issues.

❸ Describe document management systems.

❹ Explain the operation of data warehousing and its role in decision support.

❺ Describe information and knowledge discovery and business intelligence.

❻ Understand the power and benefits of data mining.

❼ Describe data presentation methods and explain geographical information systems, visual simulations, and virtual reality as decision support tools.

❽ Discuss the role of marketing databases and provide examples.

❾ Recognize the role of the Web in data management.

FINDING DIAMONDS BY DATA MINING AT HARRAH'S

 THE PROBLEM

Harrah's Entertainment (*harrahs.com*) is a very profitable casino chain. With 26 casinos in 13 states, it had $4 billion sales in 2002 and net income of $235 million. One of Harrah's casinos, located on the Las Vegas strip, typifies the marketing issues that casino owners face. The problem is very simple: how to attract visitors to come and spend money in your casino, and to do it again and again. There is no other place like the Las Vegas strip, where dozens of mega casinos and hundreds of small ones lure visitors by operating attractions ranging from fiery volcanoes to pirate ships.

Most casino operators use intuition to plan inducements for customers. Almost all have loyalty cards, provide free rooms to customers who visit frequently, give you free shows, and more. The problem is that there is only little differentiation among the casinos. Casinos believe they must give those incentives to survive, but do they help casinos to excel? Harrah's is doing better than most competing casinos by using management and marketing theories facilitated by information technology, under the leadership of Gary Loveman, a former Harvard Business School professor.

 THE SOLUTION

Harrah's strategy is based on technology-based CRM and the use of customer database marketing to test promotions. This combination enables the company to fine-tune marketing efforts and service-delivery strategies that keep customers coming back. Noting that 82.7 percent of its revenue comes from slot machines, Harrah's started by giving each player a loyalty smart card. A smart-card reader on each slot machine in all 26 of its casinos records each customer's activities. (Readers are also available in Harrah's restaurants, gift shops, etc., to record any spending.)

Logging your activities, you earn credit, as in other loyalty programs, for which you get free hotel rooms, dinners, etc. Such programs are run by most competitors, but Harrah's goes a step further: It uses a 300-gigabyte transactional database, known as a data warehouse, to analyze the data recorded by the card readers. By tracking millions of individual transactions, the IT systems assemble a vast amount of data on customer habits and preferences. These data are fed into the enterprise data warehouse, which contains not only millions of transactional data points about customers (such as names, adddresses, ages, genders) but also details about their gambling, spending, and preferences. This database has become a very rich repository of customer information, and it is mined for decision support.

The information found in Harrah's database indicated that a loyalty strategy based on same-store (same casino, in this case) sales growth could be very beneficial. The goal is to get a customer to visit your establishment regularly. For example, analysis discovered that the company's best customers were middle-aged and senior adults with discretionary time and income, who enjoyed playing slot machines. These customers did not typically stay in a hotel, but visited a casino on the way home from work or on a weekend night out. These customers responded better to an offer of $60 of casino chips than to a free room, two steak meals, and $30 worth of chips, because they enjoyed the anticipation and excitement of gambling itself (rather than seeing the trip as a vacation get-away).

This strategy offered a way to differentiate Harrah's brand. Understanding the lifetime value of the customers became critical to the company's marketing strategy. Instead of focusing on how much people spend in the casinos during a single visit, the company began to focus on their total spending over a long time. And, by gathering more and more specific information about customer preferences, running experiments and analyses on the newly collected data, and determining ways of appealing to players' interests, the company was able to increase the amount of money customers spent there by appealing to their individual preferences.

As in other casinos with loyalty programs, players are segregated into three tiers, and the biggest spenders get priorities in waiting lines and in awards. There is a visible differentiation in customer service based on the three-tier hierarchy, and every experience in Harrah's casinos was redesigned to drive customers to want to earn a higher-level card. Customers have responded by doing what they can to earn the higher-tiered cards.

However, Harrah's transactional database is doing much more than just calculating gambling spending. For example, the casino knows which specific customers were playing at particular slot machines and at what time. Using data mining techniques, Harrah's can discover what specific machines appealed to specific customers. This knowledge enabled Harrah's to configure the casino floor with a mix of slot machines that benefited both the customers and the company.

In addition, by measuring all employee performance on the matrices of speed and friendliness and analyzing these results with data mining, the company is able to provide its customers with better experiences as well as earn more money for the employees. Harrah's implemented a bonus plan to reward hourly workers with extra cash for achieving improved customer satisfaction scores. (Bonuses totaling $43 million were paid over three years.) The bonus program worked because the reward depends on everyone's performance. The general manager of a lower-scoring property might visit a colleague at a higher-scoring casino to find out what he could do to improve his casino's scores.

➡ THE RESULTS

Harrah's experience has shown that the better the experience a guest has and the more attentive you are to him or her, the more money will be made. For Harrah's, good customer service is not a matter of an isolated incident or two but of daily routine. So, while somewhere along the Las Vegas strip a "Vesuvian" volcano erupts loudly every 15 minutes, a fake British frigate battles a pirate ship at regular intervals, and sparkling fountains dance in a lake, Harrah's continues to enhance benefits to its Total Rewards program, improves customer loyalty through customer service supported by the data mining, and of course makes lots of money.

Sources: Compiled from Loveman (2003) and from Levinson (2001).

LESSONS LEARNED FROM THIS CASE

The opening case about Harrah's illustrates the importance of data to a large entertainment company. It shows that it is necessary to collect vast amount of data, organize and store them properly in one place, and then analyze the data and use the results to make better marketing and other corporate decisions. The case shows us that new data go through a process and stages: Data are collected, processed, and stored in a data warehouse. Then, data are processed by analytical tools such as data mining and decision modeling. The findings of the data analysis direct promotional and other decisions. Finally, continuous collection and analysis of fresh data provide management with feedback regarding the success of management strategies.

In this chapter we explain how this process is executed with the help of IT. We will also deal with some additional topics that typically supplement the data management process.

11.1 DATA MANAGEMENT: A CRITICAL SUCCESS FACTOR

As illustrated throughout this textbook, IT applications cannot be done without using some kind of data. In other words, without data you cannot have most IT applications, nor can you make good decisions. Data, as we have seen in the opening case, are at the core of management and marketing operations. However, there are increasing difficulties in acquiring, keeping, and managing data.

The Difficulties of Managing Data, and Some Potential Solutions

Since data are processed in several stages and possibly places, they may be subject to some problems and difficulties.

DATA PROBLEMS AND DIFFICULTIES. Managing data in organizations is difficult for various reasons:

● The amount of data increases exponentially with time. Much past data must be kept for a long time, and new data are added rapidly. However, only small portions of an organization's data are relevant for any specific application, and that relevant data must be identified and found in order to be useful.

● Data are scattered throughout organizations and are collected by many individuals using several methods and devices. Data are frequently stored in several servers and locations, and in different computing systems, databases, formats, and human and computer languages.

● An ever-increasing amount of external data needs to be considered in making organizational decisions.

● Data security, quality, and integrity are critical, yet are easily jeopardized. In addition, legal requirements relating to data differ among countries and change frequently.

● Selecting data management tools can be a major problem because of the huge number of products available.

These difficulties, and the critical need for timely and accurate information, have prompted organizations to search for effective and efficient data management solutions.

SOLUTIONS TO MANAGING DATA. Historically, data management has been geared to supporting transaction processing by organizing the data in a *hierarchical format* in one location. This format supports secured and efficient high-volume processing; however, it may be inefficient for queries and other ad-hoc applications. Therefore, *relational databases,* based on organization of data in rows and columns, were added to facilitate end-user computing and decision support. (Data organization is described further in Technology Guide 3.)

With the introduction of client/server environments and Web technologies, databases became distributed throughout organizations, creating problems in finding data quickly and easily. This was the major reason that Harrah's sought the creation of a *data warehouse.* As we will see later, the intranet, extranets, and Web technologies can also be used to improve data management.

It is now well recognized that data are an asset, although they can be a burden to maintain. The purpose of appropriate data management is to ease the burden of maintaining data and to enhance the power from their use. To see how this is done, let's begin by examining how data are processed during their life cycle.

Data Life Cycle Process

Businesses do not run on raw data. They run on data that have been processed to information and knowledge, which managers apply to business problems and opportunities. As seen in the Harrah's case, *knowledge* fuels solutions. Everything from innovative product designs to brilliant competitive moves relies on knowledge (see Markus et al., 2002). However, because of the difficulties of managing data, cited earlier, deriving knowledge from accumulated data may not be simple or easy.

Transformation of data into knowledge and solutions is accomplished in several ways. In general, it resembles the process shown in Figure 11.1. It starts with new data collection from various sources. These data are stored in a database(s). Then the data are preprocessed to fit the format of a data warehouse or data marts, where they are stored. Users then access the warehouse or data mart and take a copy of the needed data for analysis. The analysis is done with data analysis and mining tools (see Chopoorian et al., 2001) which look for patterns, and with intelligent systems, which support data interpretation.

Note that not all data processing follows this process. Small and medium companies do not need data warehouses, and even many large companies do not need them. (We will see later who needs them.) In such cases data go directly from data sources or databases to an analysis. An example of direct processing is an application that uses real-time data. These can be processed as they are collected and immediately analyzed. Many Web data are of this type. In such a case, as we will see later, we use Web mining instead of data mining.

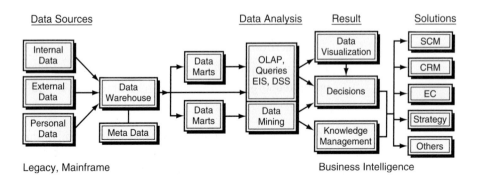

FIGURE 11.1 Data life cycle.

The result of these activities is the generating of decision support and knowledge. Both the data (at various times during the process) and the knowledge (derived at the end of the process) may need to be presented to users. The presentation can be accomplished by using different visualization tools. The created knowledge may be stored in an organizational knowledge base (as shown in Chapter 10) and used, together with decision support tools, to provide solutions to organizational problems. The elements and the process shown in Figure 11.1 are discussed in the remaining sections of this chapter and in Chapter 12.

Data Sources   The data life cycle begins with the acquisition of data from data sources. Data sources can be classified as internal, personal, and external.

INTERNAL DATA SOURCES.   An organization's internal data are about people, products, services, and processes. Such data may be found in one or more places. For example, data about employees and their pay are usually stored in the corporate database. Data about equipment and machinery may be stored in the maintenance department database. Sales data can be stored in several places—aggregate sales data in the corporate database, and details at each regional database. Internal data are usually accessible via an organization's intranet.

PERSONAL DATA.   IS users or other corporate employees may document their own expertise by creating personal data. These data are not necessarily just facts, but may include concepts, thoughts, and opinions. They include, for example, subjective estimates of sales, opinions about what competitors are likely to do, and certain rules and formulas developed by the users. These data can reside on the user's PC or be placed on departmental or business units' databases or on the corporate knowledge bases.

EXTERNAL DATA SOURCES.   There are many sources for external data, ranging from commercial databases to sensors and satellites. Government reports constitute a major source for external data. Data are available on CD-ROMs and memory chips, on Internet servers, as films, and as sound or voices. Pictures, diagrams, atlases, and television are other sources of external data. Hundreds of thousands of organizations worldwide place publicly accessible data on their Web servers, flooding us with data. Most external data are irrelevant to any single application. Yet, much external data must be monitored and captured to ensure that important data are not overlooked. Large amounts of external data are available on the Internet.

The Internet and Commercial Database Services.   Many thousands of databases all over the world are accessible through the Internet. Much of the database access is free. A user can access Web pages of vendors, clients, and competitors. He or she can view and download information while conducting research. Some external data flow to an organization on a regular basis through EDI or through other company-to-company channels. Much external data are free; other data are available from commercial database services.

A commercial *online database publisher* sells access to specialized databases, newspapers, magazines, bibliographies, and reports. Such a service can provide external data to users in a timely manner and at a reasonable cost. Many commercial database publishers will customize the data for each user. Several thousand services are currently available, most of which are accessible via the Internet. Many consulting companies (e.g., *aberdeen.com*) sell reports online.

Methods for Collecting Raw Data

The diversity of data and the multiplicity of sources make the task of data collection fairly complex. Sometimes it is necessary to collect raw data in the field. In other cases it is necessary to elicit data from people.

Raw data can be collected manually or by instruments and sensors. Some examples of manual data collection methods are time studies, surveys, observations, and contributions from experts. Data can also be scanned or transferred electronically. Although a wide variety of hardware and software exists for data storage, communication, and presentation, much less effort has gone into developing software tools for data capture in environments where complex and unstable data exist. Insufficient methods for dealing with such situations may limit the effectiveness of IT development and use. One exception is the Web. **Clickstream data** are those that can be collected automatically, using special software, from a company's Web site or from what visitors are doing on the site (see Chapter 5, and Turban et al., 2004). In addition, the use of online polls and questionnaires is becoming very popular (see Baumer, 2003, and Ray and Tabor, 2003).

The collection of data from multiple external sources may be an even more complicated task. One way to improve it is to use a *data flow manager* (DFM), which takes information from external sources and puts it where it is needed, when it is needed, in a usable form (e.g., see *smartdraw.com*). A DFM consists of (1) a decision support system, (2) a central data request processor, (3) a data integrity component, (4) links to external data suppliers, and (5) the processes used by the external data suppliers.

The complexity of data collection can create data-quality problems. Therefore, regardless of how they are collected, data need to be validated. A classic expression that sums up the situation is "garbage in, garbage out" (GIGO). Safeguards for data quality are designed to prevent data problems.

Data Quality and Integrity

Data quality (DQ) is an extremely important issue since quality determines the data's usefulness as well as the quality of the decisions based on the data (Creese and Veytsel, 2003). Data are frequently found to be inaccurate, incomplete, or ambiguous, particularly in large, centralized databases. The economical and social damage from poor-quality data has actually been calculated to have cost organizations billions of dollars (see Redman, 1998). According to Brauer (2001), data quality is the cornerstone of effective business intelligence.

Interest in data quality has been known for generations. For example, according to Hasan (2002), treatment of numerical data for quality can be traced to the year 1881. An example of typical data problems, their causes, and possible solutions is provided in Table 11.1. For a discussion of data auditing and controls, see Chapter 15.

Strong et al. (1997) conducted extensive research on data quality problems. Some of the problems are technical ones such as capacity, while others relate to potential computer crimes. The researchers divided these problems into the following four categories and dimensions.

- *Intrinsic DQ:* Accuracy, objectivity, believability, and reputation.
- *Accessibility DQ:* Accessibility and access security.
- *Contextual DQ:* Relevancy, value added, timeliness, completeness, amount of data.
- *Representation DQ:* Interpretability, ease of understanding, concise representation, consistent representation.

TABLE 11.1 Data Problems and Possible Solutions

Problem	Typical Cause	Possible Solutions (in Some Cases)
Data are not correct.	Raw data were entered inaccurately.	Develop a systematic way to ensure the accuracy of raw data. Automate (use scanners or sensors).
	Data derived by an individual were generated carelessly.	Carefully monitor both the data values and the manner in which the data have been generated. Check for compliance with collection rules.
Data are not timely.	The method for generating the data was not rapid enough to meet the need for the data.	Modify the system for generating the data. Move to a client/server system. Automate.
Data are not measured or indexed properly.	Raw data were gathered according to a logic or periodicity that was not consistent with the purposes of the analysis.	Develop a system for rescaling or recombining the improperly indexed data. Use intelligent search agents.
Needed data simply do not exist.	No one ever stored the data needed now.	Whether or not it is useful now, store data for future use. Use the Internet to search for similar data. Use experts.
	Required data never existed.	Make an effort to generate the data or to estimate them (use experts). Use neural computing for pattern recognition.

Source: Compiled and modified from Alter (1980).

Different categories of data quality are proposed by Brauer (2001). They are: *standardization* (for consistency), *matching* (of data if stored in different places), *verification* (against the source), and *enhancement* (adding of data to increase its usefulness). Whichever system is used, once the major variables and relationships in each category are identified, an attempt can be made to find out how to better manage the data.

An area of increasing importance is data quality that is done very fast in *real time.* Many decisions are being made today in such an environment. For how to handle data in such a case, see Creese and Veytsel (2003) and Bates (2003).

Another major data quality issue is **data integrity.** This concept means that data must be accurate, accessible, and up-to-date. Older filing systems may lack integrity. That is, a change made in the file in one place may not be made in a related file in another place. This results in *conflicting* data.

DATA QUALITY IN WEB-BASED SYSTEMS. Data are collected from the Internet on a routine basis or for a special application. In either case, it is necessary to organize and store the data before they can be used. This may be a difficult task especially when media-rich Web sites are involved. For a comprehensive approach on how to ensure quality of Internet-generated data, see Creese and Veytsel (2003). For discussion of object-oriented and multi-media databases, widely used for Web applications, see Online File W11.1.

Document Management

There are several major problems with paper documents. For example, in maintaining paper documents, we can pose the following questions: (1) Does everyone have the current version? (2) How often does it need to be updated? (3) How secure are the documents? and (4) How can the distribution of documents to the appropriate individuals be managed in a timely manner? The answers to these and similar questions may be difficult.

Electronic data processing overcomes some of these problems. One of the earliest IT-enabled tools of data management is called *document management*. When documents are provided in electronic form from a single repository (typically a Web server), only the current version is provided. For example, many firms maintain their telephone directories in electronic form on an intranet to eliminate the need to copy and distribute hard copies of a directory that requires constant corrections. Also, with data stored in electronic form, access to various documents can be restricted as required (see Becker, 2003).

WHAT IS DOCUMENT MANAGEMENT?   **Document management** is the automated control of electronic documents, page images, spreadsheets, word processing documents, and other complex documents through their entire life cycle within an organization, from initial creation to final archiving. Document management offers various benefits: It allows organizations to exert greater control over production, storage, and distribution of documents, yielding greater efficiency in the reuse of information, the control of a document through a workflow process, and the reduction of product cycle times.

Electronic delivery of documents has been around since 1999, with UPS and the U.S. Post Office playing a major role in such service. They deliver documents electronically over a secured system (e-mail is not secured), and they are able to deliver complex "documents" such as large files and multimedia videos (which can be difficult to send via e-mail). (See *exchange.ups.com*, and take the test drive there.) The need for greater efficiency in handling business documents to gain an edge on the competition has fueled the increased availability of document management systems, also known as electronic document management. Essentially, **document management systems (DMSs)** provide information in an electronic format to decision makers. The full range of functions that a document management system may perform includes document identification, storage, and retrieval; tracking; version control; workflow management; and presentation. The Thomas Cook Company, for example, uses a document management system to handle travel-refund applications. The system works on the PC desktop and has automated the workflow process, helping the firm double its volume of business while adding only about 33 percent more employees (see Cole, 1996). Another example is the Massachusetts Department of Revenue, which uses imaging systems to increase productivity of tax return processing by about 80 percent (see *civic.com/pubs*, 2001).

Document management deals with knowledge in addition to data and information. See Asprev and Middleton (2003) for an overview and for the relationship of document management with knowledge management.

The major tools of document management are workflow software, authoring tools, scanners, and databases (known as object-relational database management systems; see Technology Guide 3). Document management systems usually include computerized imaging systems that can result in substantial savings, as shown in Online File W11.2.

One of the major vendors of document management is Lotus Development Corporation. Its document databases and their replication property provide

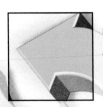

A CLOSER LOOK
11.1 HOW COMPANIES USE DOCUMENT MANAGEMENT SYSTEMS

Here are some examples of how companies use document management systems to manage data and documents:

The Surgery Center of Baltimore stores all of its medical records electronically, providing instant patient information to doctors and nurses anywhere and any time. The system also routes charts to the billing department, whose employees can scan and e-mail any related information to insurance providers and patients. The DMS also helps maintain an audit trail, including providing records for legal purposes or action. Business processes have been expedited by more than 50 percent, the cost of such processes is significantly lower, and morale of office employees in the center is up (see *laserfiche.com/newsroom/baltimore.html*).

American Express is using a DMS to collect and process over one million customer satisfaction surveys each year. The data are collected in templates of over 600 different survey forms, in 12 languages, in 11 countries. The system (TELEform from Alchemy and Cardiff Software) is integrated with AMEX's legacy system and is capable of distributing processed results to many managers. Staff who process these forms have been reduced from 17 to 1, saving AMEX over $500,000 each year (see *imrgold.com/en/case-studies/fin_AMEX_Cardiff.asp*).

LifeStar, an ambulance service in Tulare, California, is keeping all historical paper documents on optical disks. Hundreds of boxes with documents were digitized, and so are all new documents. Furthermore, all optical disks are backed up and are kept in different locations for security purposes (see *laserfiche.com/newsroom/tulare.html*).

Toronto, Canada, Works and Emergency Services Department uses a Web-based record document-retrieval solution. With it, employees have immediate access to drawings and the documents related to roads, buildings, utility lines, and more. Quick access to these documents enables emergency crews to solve problems, and even save lives, much faster. Laptop computers are installed in each departmental vehicle, loaded with maps, drawings, and historical repair data (see *laserfiche.com/newsroom/torantoworks.html*).

The University of Cincinnati, a state university in Ohio, is required to provide authorized access to the personnel files of 12,000 active employees and tens of thousands of retirees. There are over 75,000 queries about the personnel records every year, and answers need to be found among 2.5 million records. Using an antiquated microfilm system to find answers took days. The solution was a DMS that digitized all paper and microfilm documents, making them available via the Internet and the intranet. An authorized employee can now use a browser and access a document in seconds (see *imrgold.com/en/case_studies/edu_Univ_of_Cin.asp*).

The European Court of Human Rights (44 countries in Europe) created a Web-based document and KM system which was originally stored on an intranet and now is stored in a separate organizational knowledge base. The DMS has had over 20 million hits in 2002 (Canada NewsWire, 2003). Millions of euros are saved each year just on printing and mailing documents.

McDonnell-Douglas (now part of the Boeing Company) distributed aircraft service bulletins to its customers around the world using the Internet. The company used to distribute a staggering volume of bulletins to over 200 airlines, using over 4 million pages of documentation every year. Now it is all on the Web, saving money and time both for the company and for its customers.

Motorola uses a DMS not only for document storage and retrieval, but also for small-group collaboration and companywide knowledge sharing. It develops virtual communities where people can discuss and publish information, all with the Web-enabled DMS.

---

many advantages for group work and information sharing (see *lotus.com*). For further discussion see *imrgold.com* and *docuvantage.com*.

WEB-BASED DMS. In many organizations, documents are now viewed as multimedia objects with hyperlinks. The Web provides easy access to pages of information. DMSs excel in this area (see examples in *A Closer Look 11.1*). Web-enabled DMSs also make it easy to put information on intranets, since many of them provide instantaneous conversion of documents to HTML. BellSouth, for example, saves an estimated $17.5 million each year through its intranet-enabled forms-management system. For another example of Web-enabled document management systems see Delcambre et al. (2003).

In all of the examples cited in the text and in *A Closer Look 11.1*, time and money are saved. Also, documents are not lost or mixed up. An issue related to document management systems is how to provide the privacy and security of personal data. We address that issue in Chapters 15 and 16.

11.2 DATA WAREHOUSING

Many large and even medium-size companies are using data warehousing to make it easier and faster to process, analyze, and query data.

Transactional versus Analytical Processing

Data processing in organizations can be viewed either as *transactional* or *analytical*. The data in transactions processing systems (TPSs) are organized mainly in a *hierarchical structure* (Technology Guide 3) and are centrally processed. The databases and the processing systems involved are known as *operational systems*, and the results are mainly transaction reports. This is done primarily for fast and efficient processing of routine, repetitive data.

Today, however, the most successful companies are those that can respond quickly and flexibly to market changes and opportunities, and the key to this response is the effective and efficient use of data and information, as shown in the Harrah's case. This is done not only via transaction processing, but also through a supplementary activity, called **analytical processing,** which involves analysis of accumulated data, frequently by end users. Analytical processing, also refered to as *business intelligence*, includes data mining, decision support systems (DSSs), enterprise information systems (EISs), Web applications, querying, and other end-user activities. Placing strategic information in the hands of decision makers aids productivity and empowers users to make better decisions, leading to greater competitive advantage. A good data delivery system should be able to support easy data access by the end users themselves, as well as quick, accurate, flexible and effective decision making.

There are basically two options for conducting analytical processing. One is to work directly with the operational systems (the "let's use what we have" approach), using software tools and components known as front-end tools and *middleware* (see Technology Guide 3). The other is to use a data warehouse.

The first option can be optimal for companies that do not have a large number of end users running queries and conducting analyses against the operating systems. It is also an option for departments that consist mainly of users who have the necessary technical skills for an extensive use of tools such as spreadsheets (see BIXL, 2002) and graphics. (See Technology Guide 2.) Although it is possible for those with fewer technical skills to use query and reporting tools, they may not be effective, flexible, or easy enough to use in many cases.

Since the mid-1990s, there has been a wave of *front-end tools* that allow end users to solve these problems by directly conducting queries and reporting on data stored in operational databases. The problem with this approach, however, is that the tools are only effective with end users who have a medium to high degree of knowledge about databases. This situation improved drastically with the use of Web-based tools. Yet, when data are in several sources and in several formats, it is difficult to bring them together to conduct an analysis.

The second option, a data warehouse, overcomes these limitations and provides for improved analytical processing. It involves three concepts:

1. A business representation of data for end users
2. A Web-based environment that gives the users query and reporting capabilities
3. A server-based repository (the data warehouse) that allows centralized security and control over the data

The Data Warehouse The Harrah's case illustrates some major benefits of a **data warehouse,** which is a repository of subject-oriented historical data that are organized to be accessible in a form readily acceptable for analytical processing activities (such as data mining, decision support, querying, and other applications). The major benefits of a data warehouse are (1) the ability to reach data quickly, since they are located in one place, and (2) the ability to reach data easily and frequently by end users with Web browsers. To aid the accessibility of data, detail-level operational data must be transformed into a relational form, which makes them more amenable to analytical processing. Thus, data warehousing is not a concept by itself, but is interrelated with data access, retrieval, analysis, and visualization. (See Gray and Watson, 1998, and Inmon, 2002.)

The process of building and using a data warehouse is shown in Figure 11.2. The organization's data are stored in operational systems (left side of the figure). Using special software called ETL (extraction, transformation, load), data

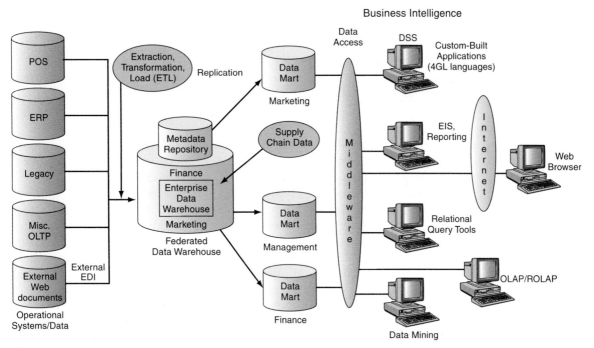

FIGURE 11.2 Data warehouse framework and views. (*Source:* Drawn by E. Turban.)

are processed and then stored in a data warehouse. Not all data are necessarily transferred to the data warehouse. Frequently only a summary of the data is transferred. The data that are transferred are organized within the warehouse in a form that is easy for end users to access. The data are also standardized. Then, the data are organized by subject, such as by functional area, vendor, or product. In contrast, operational data are organized according to a business process, such as shipping, purchasing, or inventory control and/or functional department. (Note that ERP data can be input to a data warehouse, and ERP and SCM decisions use the output from data warehouse. See Grant, 2003.)

Data warehouses provide for the storage of **metadata,** meaning data about data. Metadata include software programs about data, rules for organizing data, and data summaries that are easier to index and search, especially with Web tools. Finally, middleware tools enable access to the data warehouse (see Technology Guide 3, and Rundensteiner et al., 2000).

CHARACTERISTICS OF A DATA WAREHOUSE.   The major characteristics of data warehousing are:

1. *Organization.* Data are organized by subject (e.g., by customer, vendor, product, price level, and region), and contain information relevant for decision support only.
2. *Consistency.* Data in different operational databases may be encoded differently. For example, gender data may be encoded 0 and 1 in one operational system and "m" and "f" in another. In the warehouse they will be coded in a consistent manner.
3. *Time variant.* The data are kept for many years so they can be used for trends, forecasting, and comparisons over time.
4. *Nonvolatile.* Once entered into the warehouse, data are not updated.
5. *Relational.* Typically the data warehouse uses a relational structure.
6. *Client/server.* The data warehouse uses the client/server architecture mainly to provide the end user an easy access to its data.
7. *Web-based.* Today's data warehouses are designed to provide an efficient computing environment for Web-based applications (Rundensteiner et. al., 2000).

BENEFITS.   Moving information off the mainframe presents a company with the unique opportunity to restructure its IT strategy. Companies can reinvent the way in which they shape and form their application data, empowering end users to conduct extensive analysis with these data in ways that may not have been possible before (e.g., see Minicase 1, about Sears). Another immediate benefit is providing a consolidated view of corporate data, which is better than providing many smaller (and differently formatted) views. For example, separate applications may track sales and coupon mailings. Combining data from these different applications may yield insights into the cost-efficiency of coupon sales promotions that would not be immediately evident from the output data of either application alone. Integrated within a data warehouse, however, such information can be easily extracted and analyzed.

Another benefit is that data warehousing allows information processing to be offloaded from expensive operational systems onto low-cost servers. Once this is done, the end-user tools can handle a significant number of end-user information requests. Furthermore, some operational system reporting requirements can be moved to decision support systems, thus freeing up production processing.

These benefits can improve business knowledge, provide competitive advantage (see Watson et. al., 2002), enhance customer service and satisfaction (see Online File W11.3), facilitate decision making, and help in streamlining business processes.

COST. The cost of a data warehouse can be very high, both to build and to maintain. Furthermore, it may be difficult and expensive to incorporate data from obsolete legacy systems. Finally, there may be a lack of incentive to share data. Therefore, a careful feasibility study must be undertaken before a commitment is made to data warehousing.

ARCHITECTURE AND TOOLS. There are several basic architectures for data warehousing. Two common ones are two-tier and three-tier architectures. (See Gray and Watson, 1998.) In three-tier architecture, data from the warehouse are processed twice and deposited in an additional *multidimensional database*, organized for easy multidimensional analysis and presentation, or replicated in data marts. For a Web-based architecture see Rundensteiner et al. (2000). The architecture of the data warehouse determines the tools needed for its construction (see Kimball and Ross, 2002).

PUTTING THE WAREHOUSE ON THE INTRANET. Delivery of data warehouse content to decision makers throughout the enterprise can be done via an intranet. Users can view, query, and analyze the data and produce reports using Web browsers. This is an extremely economical and effective method of delivering data (see Kimball and Ross, 2002, and Inmon, 2002).

SUITABILITY. Data warehousing is most appropriate for organizations in which some of the following apply: Large amounts of data need to be accessed by end users (see the Harrah's and Sears cases); the operational data are stored in different systems; an information-based approach to management is in use; there is a large, diverse customer base (such as in a utility company or a bank); the same data are represented differently in different systems; data are stored in highly technical formats that are difficult to decipher; and extensive end-user computing is performed (many end users performing many activities; for example, Sears has 5,000 users).

Some of the successful applications are summarized in Table 11.2 (page 504). Hundreds of other successful applications are reported (e.g., see client success stories and case studies at Web sites of vendors such as Brio Technology Inc., Business Objects, Cognos Corp., Information Builders, NCR Corp., Oracle, Platinum Technology, Software A&G, and Pilot Software). For further discussion see Gray and Watson (1998) and Inmon (2002). Also visit the Data Warehouse Institute (*dw-institute.org*).

Data Marts, Operational Data Stores, and Multidimensional Databases

Data warehouses are frequently supplemented with or substituted by the following: data marts, operational data stores, and multidimensional databases.

DATA MARTS. The high cost of data warehouses confines their use to large companies. An alternative used by many other firms is creation of a lower cost,

TABLE 11.2 Summary of Strategic Uses of Data Warehousing

Industry	Functional Areas of Use	Strategic Use
Airline	Operations and Marketing	Crew assignment, aircraft deployment, mix of fares, analysis of route profitability, frequent flyer program promotions
Apparel	Distribution and Marketing	Merchandising, and inventory replenishment
Banking	Product Development, Operations, and Marketing	Customer service, trend analysis, product and service promotions, reduction of IS expenses
Credit Card	Product Development and Marketing	Customer service, new information service for a fee, fraud detection
Health Care	Operations	Reduction of operational expenses
Investment and Insurance	Product Development, Operations, and Marketing	Risk management, market movements analysis, customer tendencies analysis, portfolio management
Personal Care Products	Distribution and Marketing	Distribution decisions, product promotions, sales decisions, pricing policy
Public Sector	Operations	Intelligence gathering
Retail Chain	Distribution and Marketing	Trend analysis, buying pattern analysis, pricing policy, inventory control, sales promotions, optimal distribution channel decisions
Steel	Manufacturing	Pattern analysis (quality control)
Telecommunications	Product Development, Operations, and Marketing	New product and service promotions, reduction of IS budget, profitability analysis

Source: Park (1997), p. 19, Table 2.

scaled-down version of a data warehouse called a data mart. A **data mart** is a small warehouse designed for a strategic business unit (SBU) or a department.

The advantages of data marts include: low cost (prices under $100,000 versus $1 million or more for data warehouses); significantly shorter lead time for implementation, often less than 90 days; local rather than central control, conferring power on the using group. They also contain less information than the data warehouse. Hence, they have more rapid response and are more easily understood and navigated than an enterprisewide data warehouse. Finally, they allow a business unit to build its own decision support systems without relying on a centralized IS department.

There are two major types of data marts:

1. *Replicated (dependent) data marts.* Sometimes it is easier to work with a small subset of the data warehouse. In such cases one can replicate some subsets of the data warehouse in smaller data marts, each of which is dedicated to a certain area, as was shown in Figure 11.2 (page 501). In such a case the data mart is an *addition* to the data warehouse.

2. *Standalone data marts.* A company can have one or more independent data marts without having a data warehouse. Typical data marts are for marketing, finance, and engineering applications.

OPERATIONAL DATA STORES. An **operational data store** is a database for transaction processing systems that uses data warehouse concepts to provide clean data. That is, it brings the concepts and benefits of the data warehouse to the operational portions of the business, at a lower cost. It is used for short-term decisions involving mission-critical applications rather than for the medium- and long-term decisions associated with the regular data warehouse. These decisions depend on much more current information. For example, a bank needs to know about all the accounts for a given customer who is calling on the phone. The operational data store can be viewed as situated between the operational data (in legacy systems) and the data warehouse. A comparison between the two is provided by Gray and Watson (1998).

MULTIDIMENSIONAL DATABASES. **Multidimensional databases** are specialized data stores that organize facts by dimensions, such as geographical region, product line, salesperson, or time. The data in multidimensional databases are usually preprocessed and stored in what is called a (multi-dimensional) *data cube*. Facts, such as quantities sold, are placed at the intersection of the dimensions. One such intersection might be the quantities of widgets sold by Ms. Smith in the Morristown, New Jersey, branch of XYZ Company in July 2003. Dimensions often have a hierarchy. Sales figures, for example, might be presented by day, by month, or by year. They might also roll up an organizational dimension from store to region to company. Multidimensional databases can be incorporated in a data warehouse, sometimes as its core, or they can be used as an additional layer.

11.3 INFORMATION AND KNOWLEDGE DISCOVERY WITH BUSINESS INTELLIGENCE

Business Intelligence

Once the data are in the data warehouse and/or data marts they can be accessed by managers, analysts, and other end users. Users can then conduct several activities. These activities are frequently referred to as analytical processing or more commonly as *business intelligence*. (Note: For a glossary of these and other terms, see *Dimensional Insight*, 2003.) **Business intellignce (BI)** is a broad category of applications and techniques for gathering, storing, analyzing and providing access to data to help enterprise users make better business and strategic decisions (see Oguz, 2003, and Moss and Atre, 2003). The process of BI usually, but not necessarily, involves the use of a data warehouse, as seen in Figure 11.3 (page 506).

HOW BUSINESS INTELLIGENCE WORKS. Operational raw data are usually kept in corporate databases. For example, a national retail chain that sells everything from grills and patio furniture to plastic utensils, has data about inventory, customer information, data about past promotions, and sales numbers in various databases. Though all this information may be scattered across multiple systems—and may seem unrelated—a data warehouse–building software can bring it together to the data warehouse. In the data warehouse (or mart), tables can be linked, and *data cubes* (another term for multidimensional databases) are formed. For instance, inventory information is linked to sales numbers and customer databases, allowing for extensive analysis of information. Some data warehouses have a dynamic link to the databases; others are static.

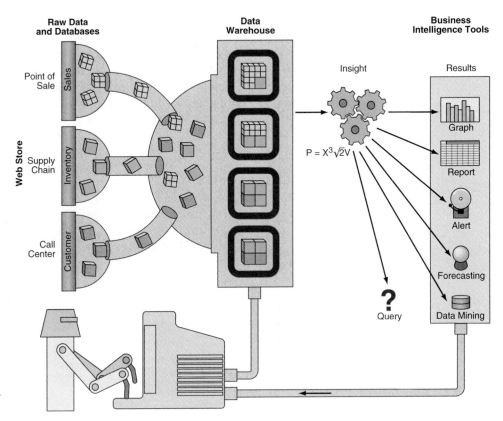

FIGURE 11.3 How business intelligence works.

Using business intelligence software, the user can ask queries, request ad-hoc reports, or conduct any other analyses. For example, analysis can be carried out by performing multilayer queries. Because all the databases are linked, you can search for what products a store has too much of. You can then determine which of these products commonly sell with popular items, based on previous sales. After planning a promotion to move the excess stock along with the popular products (by bundling them together, for example), you can dig deeper to see where this promotion would be most popular (and most profitable). The results of your request can be reports, predictions, alerts, and/or graphical presentations. These can be disseminated to decision-makers.

More advanced applications of business intelligence include outputs such as financial modeling, budgeting, resource allocation, and competitive intelligence. Advanced business intelligence systems include components such as decision models, business performance analysis, metrics, data profiling and reengineering tools, and much more. (For details see *dmreview.com*.)

THE TOOLS AND TECHNIQUES OF BUSINESS INTELLIGENCE. BI employs large numbers of tools and techniques. The major applications include the activities of query and reporting, online analytical processing (OLAP), DSS, data mining, forecasting, and statistical analysis. A major BI vendor is SAS (*sas.com*). Other vendors include Microstrategy, Cognos, SPSS, and Business Objects. We have divided the BI tools into two major categories: (1) *information and knowledge discovery* and (2) *decision support and intelligent analysis*. In each category there are

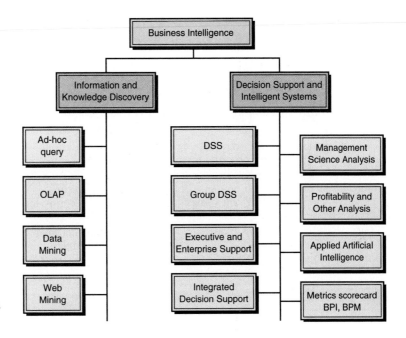

FIGURE 11.4 Categories of business intelligence.

several tools and techniques, as shown in Figure 11.4. In this chapter we will describe the information and knowledge discovery category, while Chapter 12 is dedicated to decision support and intelligent systems.

The Tools and Techniques of Information and Knowledge Discovery

Information and knowledge discovery differs from decision support in its main objective: discovery. Once discovery is done the results can be used for decision support. Let's distinguish first between information and knowledge discovery.

THE EVOLUTION OF INFORMATION AND KNOWLEDGE DISCOVERY. *Information discovery* started in the late 1960s and early 1970s with data collection techniques. It was basically simple data collection and answered queries that involved one set of historical data. This analysis was extended to answer questions that involved several sets of data with tools such as SQL and relational database management systems (see Table 11.3, page 508, for the evolution). During the 1990s, a recognition of the need for better tools to deal with the ever increasing amount of data was initiated. This resulted in the creation of the data warehouse and the appearance of OLAP and multidimensional databases and presentation. When the amount of data to be analyzed exploded in the mid-1990s, *knowledge discovery* emerged as an important analytical tool.

The process of extracting useful knowledge from volumes of data is known as **knowledge discovery in databases (KDD),** or just **knowledge discovery,** and it is the subject of extensive research (see Fayyad et al., 1996). KDD's major objective is to identify valid, novel, potentially useful, and ultimately understandable patterns in data. KDD is useful because it is supported by three technologies that are now sufficiently mature: massive data collection, powerful multiprocessor computers, and data mining and other algorithms. KDD processes have appeared under various names and have shown different characteristics. As time has passed, KDD has become able to answer more complex

TABLE 11.3 Stages in the Evolution of Knowledge Discovery

Evolutionary Stage	Business Quesstion	Enabling Technologies	Characteristics
Data collection (1960s)	What was my total revenue in the last five years?	Computers, tapes, disks	Retrospective, static data delivery
Data access (1980s)	What were unit sales in New England last March?	Relational databases (RDBMS), structured query language (SQL)	Retrospective, dynamic data delivery at record level
Data warehousing and decision support (early 1990s)	What were the sales in region A, by product, by salesperson?	OLAP, multidimensional databases, data warehouses	Retrospective, dynamic data delivery at multiple levels
Intelligent data mining (late 1990s)	What's likely to happen to the Boston unit's sales next month? Why?	Advanced algorithms, multiprocessor computers, massive databases	Prospective, proactive information delivery
Advanced intelligent system	What is the best plan to follow?	Neural computing, advanced AI models, complex optimization, Web services	Proactive, integrative; multiple business partners
Complete integration (2000–2004)	How did we perform compared to metrics?		

Source: Based on material from *accure.com* (Accure Software).

business questions. In this section we will describe two tools of information discovery: ad-hoc queries, and OLAP. Data mining as a KDD tool is described in Section 11.4. We discuss multidimensionality in Section 11.5, and Web-based query tools are described in Section 11.7.

AD-HOC QUERIES AND REPORTING. Ad-hoc queries allow users to request, in real time, information from the computer that is not available in periodic reports. Such answers are needed to expedite decision making. The system must be intelligent enough to understand what the user wants. Simple ad-hoc query systems are often based on menus. More intelligent systems use structured query language (SQL) and query-by-example approaches, which are described in Technology Guide 3. The most intelligent systems are based on natural language understanding (Chapter 12), and some can communicate with users using voice recognition. Later on we will describe the use of Web tools to facilitate queries.

 Querying systems are frequently combined with reporting systems that generate routine reports. For an example of such a combination in a radio rental store see Amato-McCoy (2003). For Web-based information discovery tools see Online File W11.4.

ONLINE ANALYTICAL PROCESSING. The term **online analytical processing (OLAP)** was introduced in 1993 by E. F. Codd, to describe a set of tools that can analyze data to reflect actual business needs. These tools were based on a set of 12 rules: (1) multidimensional view, (2) transparency to the user, (3) easy accessibility, (4) consistent reporting, (5) client/server architecture, (6) generic dimensionality, (7) dynamic sparse matrix handling, (8) multiuser support, (9) cross-dimensional operations, (10) intuitive data manipulation, (11) flexible reporting, and (12) unlimited levels of dimension and aggregation. (For details see Codd et al., 1993.) Let's see how these rules may work:

Assume that a business might organize its sales force by regions, say the Eastern and Western. These two regions might then be broken down into states. In an OLAP database, this organization would be used to structure the sales data so that the VP of sales could see the sales figures for each region. The VP might then want to see the Eastern region broken down by state so that the performance of individual state sales managers could be evaluated. Thus OLAP reflects the business in the data structure.

The power of OLAP is in its ability to create these business structures (sales regions, product categories, fiscal calendar, partner channels, etc.) and combine them in such a way as to allow users to quickly answer business questions. "How many blue sweaters were sold via mail-order in New York so far this year?" is the kind of question that OLAP is very good at answering. Users can interactively slice the data and drill down to the details they are interested in.

In terms of the technology, an OLAP database can be implemented on top of an existing relational database (this is called ROLAP, for relational OLAP) or it can be implemented via a specialized multidimensional data store (this is called MOLAP, for multidimensional OLAP). In ROLAP, the data request is translated into SQL and the relational database is queried for the answer. In MOLAP, the specialized data store is preloaded with the answers to (all) possible queries so that any request for data can be returned quickly. Obviously there are performance and storage tradeoffs between these two approaches. (Another technology called HOLAP attempts to combine these two approaches.)

Unlike online transaction processing (OLTP) applications, OLAP involves examining many data items (frequently many thousands or even millions) in complex relationships. In addition to answering users' queries, OLAP may analyze these relationships and look for patterns, trends, and exceptions.

A typical OLAP query might access a multigigabyte, multiyear sales database in order to find all product sales in each region for each product type. (See the Harrah's case.) After reviewing the results, an analyst might further refine the query to find sales volume for each sales channel within region or product classifications. As a last step, the analyst might want to perform year-to-year or quarter-to-quarter comparisons, for each sales channel. This whole process must be carried out *online* with rapid response time so that the analysis process is undisturbed.

The 12 original rules of Codd are reflected in today's software. For example, today's software permits access (usually with a browser) to very large amounts of data, such as several years of sales data, and analysis of the relationships between many types of business elements, such as sales, products, regions, and channels. It enables users to process aggregated data, such as sales volumes, budgeted dollars, and dollars spent, to compare aggregated data over time and to present data in different perspectives, such as sales by region versus sales by product or by product within each region. Today's software also enables complex calculations between data elements, such as expected profit as calculated as a function of sales revenue for each type of sales channel in a particular region, and it responds quickly to user requests so that users can pursue an analytical thought process without being stymied by the system.

OLAP can be combined with data mining to conduct a very sophisticated multidimensional-based decision support as illustrated by Fong et al. (2002). By attaching a rule-based component to the OLAP, one can make this type of integrated system an intelligent data mining system (see Lau et al., 2001). For more information, products, and vendors, visit *olapreport.com* and *olap.com*.

Although OLAP and ad-hoc queries are very useful in many cases, they are retrospective in nature and cannot provide the automated and prospective knowledge discovery that is done by advanced data mining techniques.

11.4 DATA MINING CONCEPTS AND APPLICATIONS

Data mining is becoming a major tool for analyzing large amounts of data, usually in a data warehouse (Nemati and Barko, 2002) as well for analyzing Web data. **Data mining** derives its name from the similarities between searching for valuable business information in a large database, and mining a mountain for a vein of valuable ore. Both processes require either sifting through an immense amount of material or intelligently probing it to find exactly where the value resides (see the Harrah's case at the start of the chapter). In some cases the data are consolidated in a data warehouse and data marts (e.g., see Chopoorian et al., 2001). In others they are kept on the Internet and intranet servers.

Capabilities of Data Mining

Given databases of sufficient size and quality, data mining technology can generate new business opportunities by providing these capabilities:

- *Automated prediction of trends and behaviors.* Data mining automates the process of finding predictive information in large databases. Questions that traditionally required extensive hands-on analysis can now be answered directly and quickly from the data. A typical example of a predictive problem is *targeted marketing*. Data mining can use data from past promotional mailings to identify the targets most likely to respond favorably to future mailings. Other predictive examples include forecasting bankruptcy and other forms of default, and identifying segments of a population likely to respond similarly to given events.

- *Automated discovery of previously unknown patterns.* Data mining tools identify previously hidden patterns in one step. An example of pattern discovery is the analysis of retail sales data to identify seemingly unrelated products that are often purchased together, such as baby diapers and beer. Other pattern discovery problems include detecting fraudulent credit card transactions and identifying invalid (anomalous) data that may represent data entry keying errors.

When data mining tools are implemented on high-performance parallel-processing systems, they can analyze massive databases in minutes. Often, these databases will contain data stored for several years. Faster processing means that users can experiment with more models to understand complex data. High speed makes it practical for users to analyze huge quantities of data. Larger databases, in turn, yield improved predictions (see Winter, 2001, and Hirji, 2001).

Data mining also can be conducted by nonprogrammers. The "miner" is often an end user, empowered by "data drills" and other power query tools to ask ad-hoc questions and get answers quickly, with little or no programming skill. Data mining tools can be combined with spreadsheets and other end-user software development tools, making it relatively easy to analyze and process the mined data. Data mining appears under different names, such as knowledge extraction, data dipping, data archaeology, data exploration, data pattern processing, data dredging, and information harvesting. "Striking it rich" in data mining often involves finding unexpected, valuable results.

The Tools of Data Mining

Data mining consists of two steps, building a data cube and using the cube to extract data for the mining functions that the mining tool supports. A data cube is multidimensional, as shown in Online File W11.5. Data miners can use several tools and techniques; see a list and definitions in *A Closer Look 11.2*.

Data Mining Applications

Large numbers of applications exist in data mining both in business (see Apte et al., 2002) and other fields. According to a GartnerGroup report (*gartnergroup.com*), more than half of all the Fortune 1000 companies worldwide are using data mining technology.

A CLOSER LOOK

11.2 DATA MINING TECHNIQUES AND INFORMATION TYPES

The most commonly used techniques for data mining are the following.

- *Case-based reasoning.* The case-based reasoning approach uses historical cases to recognize patterns (see Chapter 12). For example, customers of Cognitive Systems, Inc., utilize such an approach for helpdesk applications. One company has a 50,000-query case library. New cases are matched quickly against the 50,000 samples in the library, providing more than 90 percent accurate and automatic answers to queries.

- *Neural computing.* Neural computing is a machine learning approach by which historical data can be examined for pattern recognition. These patterns can then be used for making predictions and for decision support (details are given in Chapter 12). Users equipped with neural computing tools can go through huge databases and, for example, identify potential customers of a new product or companies whose profiles suggest that they are heading for bankruptcy. Most practical applications are in financial services, in marketing, and in manufacturing.

- *Intelligent agents.* One of the most promising approaches to retrieving information from the Internet or from intranet-based databases is the use of intelligent agents. As vast amounts of information become available through the Internet, finding the right information is more difficult. This topic is further discussed in Chapters 5 and 12.

- *Association analysis.* Association analysis is a relatively new approach that uses a specialized set of

algorithms that sort through large data sets and express statistical rules among items. (See Moad, 1998, for details.)

- *Other tools.* Several other tools can be used. These include decision trees, genetic algorithms, nearest-neighbor method, and rule induction. (For details, see Inmon, 2002.)

The most common information types are:

- *Classification.* Implies the defining characteristics of a certain group (e.g., customers who have been lost to competitors).

- *Clustering.* Identifies groups of items that share a particular characteristic. Clustering differs from classification in that no predefining characteristic is given.

- *Association.* Identifies relationships between events that occur at one time (e.g., the contents of a shopping basket). (For an application in law enforcement see Brown and Hagen, 2003.)

- *Sequencing.* Similar to association, except that the relationship exists over a period of time (e.g., repeat visits to a supermarket or use of a financial planning product).

- *Forecasting.* Estimates future values based on patterns within large sets of data (e.g., demand forecasting).

There are a large number of commerical products available for conducting data mining (e.g., *dbminer.com*, *data miner.com*, and *spss.com*). For a directory see *kdnuggets.com/software*.

A SAMPLER OF DATA MINING APPLICATIONS. Data mining is used extensively today for many business applications (see Apte et al., 2002), as illustrated by the 12 representative examples that follow. Note that the intent of most of these examples is to identify a business opportunity in order to create a sustainable competitive advantage.

1. *Retailing and sales.* Predicting sales; determining correct inventory levels and distribution schedules among outlets and loss prevention. For example, retailers such as AAFES (store in military bases) use data mining to combat fraud done by employees in their 1,400 stores, using the Fraud Watch solution from a Canadian company, Triversity (see Amato-McCoy, 2003b). Eddie Bauer (see Online File W11.6) uses data mining for serveral applications.

2. *Banking.* Forecasting levels of bad loans and fraudulent credit card use, credit card spending by new customers, and which kinds of customers will best respond to (and qualify for) new loan offers.

3. *Manufacturing and production.* Predicting machinery failures; finding key factors that control optimization of manufacturing capacity.

4. *Brokerage and securities trading.* Predicting when bond prices will change; forecasting the range of stock fluctuations for particular issues and the over-all market; determining when to buy or sell stocks.

5. *Insurance.* Forecasting claim amounts and medical coverage costs; classifying the most important elements that affect medical coverage; predicting which customers will buy new insurance policies.

6. *Computer hardware and software.* Predicting disk-drive failures; forecasting how long it will take to create new chips; predicting potential security violations.

7. *Policework.* Tracking crime patterns, locations, and criminal behavior; identifying attributes to assist in solving criminal cases.

8. *Government and defense.* Forecasting the cost of moving military equipment; testing strategies for potential military engagements; predicting resource consumption.

9. *Airlines.* Capturing data on where customers are flying and the ultimate destination of passengers who change carriers in hub cities; thus, airlines can identify popular locations that they do not service and can check the feasibility of adding routes to capture lost business.

10. *Health care.* Correlating demographics of patients with critical illnesses; developing better insights on symptoms and their causes and how to provide proper treatments.

11. *Broadcasting.* Predicting what is best to air during prime time and how to maximize returns by interjecting advertisements.

12. *Marketing.* Classifying customer demographics that can be used to predict which customers will respond to a mailing or buy a particular product (as illustrated in Section 11.6).

Text Mining and Web Mining

TEXT MINING. **Text mining** is the application of data mining to nonstructured or less-structured text files (see Berry, 2002). Data mining takes advantage of the infrastructure of stored data to extract predictive information. For example, by mining a customer database, an analyst might discover that everyone who buys product A also buys products B and C, but does so six months later. Text mining, however, operates with less structured information. Documents rarely have strong internal infrastructure, and when they do, it is frequently focused on document format rather than document content. Text mining helps organizations to do the following: (1) find the "hidden" content of documents, including additional useful relationship and (2) group documents by common themes (e.g., identify all the customers of an insurance firm who have similar complaints).

WEB MINING. **Web mining** is the application of data mining techniques to discover actionable and meaningful patterns, profiles, and trends from Web resources (see Linoff and Berry, 2002). The term Web mining is used to refer to both Web-content mining and Web-usage mining. *Web-content mining* is the process of mining Web sites for information. Web-usage mining involves analyzing Web access logs and other information connected to user browsing and access patterns on one or more Web localities.

Web mining is used in the following areas: information filtering (e-mails, magazimes, and newspaper); surveillance (of competitors, patents, technological development); mining of Web-access logs for analyzing usage (clickstream analysis); assisted browsing, and services that fight crime on the Internet.

In e-commerce, Web content mining is especially critical, due to the large number of visitors to e-commerce sites. For example, when you look for a certain book on Amazon.com, the site will use mining tools to also provide you with a list of books purchased by the customers who have bought the specific book you are looking for. By providing such mined information, the Amazon.com site minimizes the need for additional search and provides customers with a valuable service.

According to Etzioni (1996), Web mining can perform the following functions:

- *Resource discovery:* locating unfamiliar documents and services on the Web.
- *Information extraction:* automatically extracting specific information from newly discovered Web resources.
- *Generalization:* uncovering general patterns at individual Web sites and across multiple sites. Miner3D (*miner3d.com*) is a suite of visual data analysis tools including a Web-mining tool that displays hundreds and even thousands of search hits on a single screen. The actual search for Web pages is performed through any major search engine, and this add-on tool presents the resulting search in the form of a 3-D graphic instead of displaying links to the first few pages. For details on a number of Web-mining products see *Kdnuggets.com/software/web.html*. Also see *spss.com* and *bayesia.com* (free downloads).

Failures of Data Warehouses and Data Mining

Since their early inceptions, data warehouses and mining have produced many success stories. However, there have also been many failures. Carbone (1999) defined levels of data warehouse failures as follows: (1) Warehouse does not meet the expectations of those involved; (2) warehouse was completed, but went severely over budget in relation to time, money, or both; (3) warehouse failed one or more times but eventually was completed; and (4) warehouse failed with no effort to revive it.

Carbone provided examples and identified a number of reasons for failures (which are typical for many other large information systems): These are summarized in Table 11.4 (page 514). Suggestions on how to avoid data warehouse failure

TABLE 11.4 The Reasons Data Warehouses and Mining Fail

- Unrealistic expectations—overly optimistic time schedule or underestimation of cost.
- Inappropriate architecture.
- Vendors overselling capabilities of products.
- Lack of training and support for users.
- Omitted information.
- Lack of coordination (or requires too much coordination).
- Cultural issues were ignored.
- Use of the warehouse only for operational, not informational, purposes.
- Not enough summarization of data.
- Poor upkeep of technology.
- Improper management of multiple users with various needs.
- Failure to align data marts and data warehouses.

- Unclear business objectives; not knowing the information requirements.
- Lack of effective project sponsorship.
- Lack of data quality.
- Lack of user input.
- Use of data marts instead of data warehouses (and vice versa).
- Inexperienced/untrained/inadequate number of personnel.
- Interfering corporate politics.
- Insecure access to data manipulation (users should not have the ability to change any data).
- Inappropriate format of information—not a single, standard format.
- Poor upkeep of information (e.g., failure to keep information current).

Source: Compiled from Carbone (1999).

are provided at *datawarehouse.com*, at *bitpipe.com*, and at *teradatauniversotynetwork .com*. Suggestions on how to properly implement data mining are provided by Hirji (2001).

11.5 DATA VISUALIZATION TECHNOLOGIES

Once data have been processed, they can be presented to users as text, graphics, tables, and so on, via several data visualization technologies. A variety of methods and software packages are available to do visualization for supporting decision making (e.g., see I/S Analyzer, 2002 and Li, 2001).

Data Visualization Visual technologies make pictures worth a thousand numbers and make IT applications more attractive and understandable to users. **Data visualization** refers to presentation of data by technologies such as digital images, geographical information systems, graphical user interfaces, multidimensional tables and graphs, virtual reality, three-dimensional presentations, vedios and animation. Visualization is becoming more and more popular on the Web not only for entertainment, but also for decision support (see *spss.com*, *microstrategy.com*). Visualization software packages offer users capabilities for self-guided exploration and visual analysis of large amounts of data. By using visual analysis technologies, people may spot problems that have existed for years, undetected by standard analysis methods. Data visualization can be supported in a dynamic way (e.g., by video clips). It can also be done in real time (e.g., Bates, 2003). Visualization technologies can also be integrated among themselves to create a variety of presentations, as demonstrated by *IT at Work 11.1.*

Data visualization is easier to implement when the necessary data are in a data warehouse. Our discussion here will focus mainly on the data visualization techniques of multidimensionality, geographical information systems, visual interactive modeling, and virtual reality. Related topics, such as multimedia (see *informatica.com*) and hypermedia, are presented in Technology Guide 2.

IT at Work 11.1
DATA VISUALIZATION HELPS HAWORTH TO COMPETE

Manufacturing office furniture is an extremely competitive business. Haworth Corporation (*haworth.com*) operates in this environment and has been able to survive and even excel with the help of IT. To compete, Haworth allows its customers to customize what they want to buy (see demo at *haworth.com*). It may surprise you to learn that an office chair can be assembled in 200 different ways. The customization of all Haworth's products resulted in 21 million potential product combinations, confusing customers who were not able to visualize, until the item was delivered, how the customized furniture would look.

The solution was computer visualization software that allowed sales representatives with laptop computers to show customers exactly what they were ordering. Thus, the huge parts catalogs became more easily understood, and sales representatives were able to configure different options by entering the corporate database, showing what a product would look like, and computing its price. The customers can now make changes until the furniture design meets their needs. The salesperson can do all this from the customer's office by connecting to the corporate

intranet via the Internet and using Web tools to allow customers to make the desired changes. As of 2000 the company operates, on the Web, a design studio in which customers can interact with the designers.

These programs allow the company to reduce cycle time. After the last computer-assisted design (CAD) mockup of an order has been approved, the CAD software is used to create a bill of materials that goes to Haworth's factory for manufacturing. This reduces the time spent between sales reps and CAD operators, increasing the time available for sales reps to make more sales calls and increasing customer satisfaction with quicker delivery. By using this visualization program, Haworth has increased its competitive advantage.

Sources: Compiled from *Infoworld* (1997), p. 92 and from *haworth.com* (2003).

For Further Exploration: How can the intranet be used to improve the process? How does this topic relate to car customization at *jaguar.com?* How can this case be related to wireless?

Multidimensionality Visualization

Modern data and information may have several dimensions. For example, management may be interested in examining sales figures in a certain city by product, by time period, by salesperson, and by store (i.e., in five dimensions). The common tool for such sitations is OLAP, and it often includes a visual presentation. The more dimensions involved, the more difficult it is to present multidimensional information in one table or in one graph. Therefore, it is important to provide the user with a technology that allows him or her to add, replace, or change dimensions quickly and easily in a table and/or graphical presentation. Such changes are known as "slicing and dicing" of data. The technology of slicing, dicing, and similar manipulations is called *OLAP multidimensionality*, and it is available in most business intelligence packages (e.g., *brio.com*)

Figure 11.5 (page 516) shows three views of the same data, organized in different ways, using multidimensional software, usually available with spreadsheets. Part (a) shows travel hours of a company's employees by means of transportation and by country. The "next year" column gives projections automatically generated by an embedded formula. In part (b) the data are reorganized, and in part (c) they are reorganized again and manipulated as well. All this is easily done by the end user with one or two clicks of the mouse.

The major advantage of multidimensionality is that data can be organized the way managers like to see them rather than the way that the system analysts do. Furthermore, different presentations of the same data can be arranged and rearranged easily and quickly.

Travel Hours	Planes		Trains		Automobiles	
	This Year	Next Year	This Year	Next Year	This Year	Next Year
Canada	740	888	140	168	640	768
Japan	430	516	290	348	150	180
France	320	384	460	552	210	252
Germany	425	510	430	516	325	390

Country

(a)

Hours		This Year	Next Year
Planes	Canada	740	888
	Japan	430	516
	France	320	384
	Germany	425	510
Trains	Canada	140	168
	Japan	290	348
	France	460	552
	Germany	430	516
Automobiles	Canada	640	768
	Japan	150	180
	France	210	252
	Germany	325	390

Travel | Country

(b)

Worksheet1-View1-TUTORIAL

Hours			This Year	Next Year
Planes	Canada		740	888
	Japan		430	516
		France	320	384
		Germany	425	510
	Europe	Total	745	894
Trains	Canada		140	168
	Japan		290	348
		France	460	552
		Germany	430	516
	Europe	Total	890	1068
Automobiles	Canada		640	768
	Japan		150	180
		France	210	252
		Germany	325	390
	Europe	Total	535	642

Travel | Country

Next Year = (This Year)*1.2

- The software adds a *Total* Item

- The software adds formula 2 and calculates *Total*

- Auto-making shades the formulas using two shades of gray

Shows how formula 1 calculates cells (in this case, the cells *Total:Next Year*)

Shows that formula 2 calculates all Total cells.

(c)

FIGURE 11.5 Multidimensionality views.

Three factors are considered in **multidimensionality:** dimensions, measures, and time.

1. *Examples of dimensions:* products, salespeople, market segments, business units, geographical locations, distribution channels, countries, industries
2. *Examples of measures:* money, sales volume, head count, inventory profit, actual versus forecasted results
3. *Examples of time:* daily, weekly, monthly, quarterly, yearly

For example, a manager may want to know the sales of product M in a certain geographical area, by a specific salesperson, during a specified month, in terms of units. Although the answer can be provided regardless of the database structure, it can be provided much faster, and by the user himself or herself, if the data are organized in multidimensional databases (or data marts), or if the query tools are designed for multidimensionality (e.g., via OLAP). In either case, users can navigate through the many dimensions and levels of data via tables or graphs and then conduct a quick analysis to find significant deviations or important trends.

Multidimensionality is available with different degrees of sophistication and is especially popular in business intelligence software (e.g., see Campbell, 2001). There are several types of software from which multidimensional systems can be constructed, and they often work in conjunction with OLAP tools.

Geographical Information Systems

A **geographical information system (GIS)** is a computer-based system for capturing, storing, checking, integrating, manipulating, and displaying data using digitized maps. Its most distinguishing characteristic is that every record or digital object has an identified geographical location. By integrating maps with spatially oriented databases and other databases (called *geocoding*), users can generate information for planning, problem solving, and decision making, increasing their productivity and the quality of their decisions.

The field of GIS can be divided into two major categories: *functions* and *applications.* There are four major functions: design and planning, decising modeling, database management, and spatial imaging. These functions support six areas of applications as shown in Figure 11.6 (page 518). Note that the functions (shown as pillars) can support all the applications. The applications they support the most are shown closest to each pillar.

GIS SOFTWARE. GIS software varies in its capabilities, from simple computerized mapping systems to enterprisewide tools for decision support data analysis (see Minicase 2). Because a high-quality graphics display and high computation and search speeds are necessary, most early GIS implementations were developed for mainframes. Initially, the high cost of GISs prevented their use outside experimental facilities and government agencies. Since the 1990s, however, the cost of GIS software and its required hardware has dropped dramatically. Now relatively inexpensive, fully functional PC-based packages are readily available. Representative GIS software vendors are ESRI, Intergraph, and Mapinfo.

GIS DATA. GIS data are available from a wide variety of sources. Government sources (via the Internet and CD-ROM) provide some data, while vendors provide diversified commercial data as well. Some are free (see CD-ROMs from MapInfo, and downloadable material from *esri.com* and *gisdatadepot.com*.)

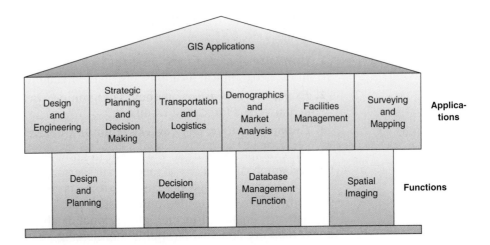

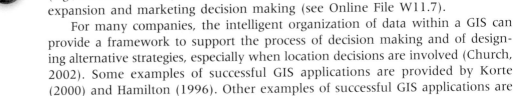

FIGURE 11.6 GIS functions and applications.

GIS AND DECISION MAKING. GISs provide a large amount of extremely useful information that can be analyzed and utilized in decision making. Its graphical format makes it easy for managers to visualize the data. For example, as Janet M. Hamilton, market research administrator for Dow Elanco, a $2 billion maker of agricultural chemicals based in Indianapolis, Indiana, explains, "I can put 80-page spreadsheets with thousands of rows into a single map. It would take a couple of weeks to comprehend all of the information from the spreadsheet, but in a map, the story can be told in seconds" (Hamilton, 1996, p. 21).

There are countless applications of GISs to improve decision making in the public or private sector (see Nasirin and Birks, 2003). They include the dispatch of emergency vehicles, transit management (see Minicase 2), facility site selection, and wildlife management. GISs are extremely popular in local governments, where the tools are used not only for mapping but for many decision-making applications (see O'Looney, 2000). States, cities and counties are using a GIS application related to property assessment, mapping, and flood control (e.g., Hardester, 2002). Banks have been using GIS for over a decade to support expansion and marketing decision making (see Online File W11.7).

For many companies, the intelligent organization of data within a GIS can provide a framework to support the process of decision making and of designing alternative strategies, especially when location decisions are involved (Church, 2002). Some examples of successful GIS applications are provided by Korte (2000) and Hamilton (1996). Other examples of successful GIS applications are summarized in *A Closer Look 11.3*.

GIS AND THE INTERNET OR INTRANETS. Most major GIS software vendors are providing Web access, such as embedded browsers or a Web/Internet/intranet server that hooks directly into their software. Thus, users can access dynamic maps and data via the Internet or a corporate intranet.

A number of firms are deploying GISs on the Internet for internal use or for use by their customers. For example, Visa Plus, which operates a network of automated teller machines, has developed a GIS application that lets Internet users call up a locator map for any of the company's 300,000 ATM machines worldwide. A common application on the Internet is a store locator. Not only do you get an address near you, but you are also told how to get there in the

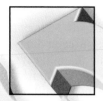

A CLOSER LOOK
11.3 GIS SAMPLE APPLICATIONS

COMPANY/INDUSTRY	APPLICATION OF GIS FOR DECISION SUPPORT
Pepsi Cola Inc., Super Value, Acordia Inc.	Used in site selection for new Taco Bell and Pizza Hut restaurants; combining demographic data and traffic patterns used in deciding on new facilities and on marketing strategy decision
CIGNA (health insurance)	Uses GIS to answer such questions as "How many CIGNA-affiliated physicians are available within an 8-mile radius of a business?"
Western Auto (a subsidiary of Sears)	Integrates data with GIS to create a detailed demographic profile of a store's neighborhood to determine the best product mix to offer at the store (Narisin and Birks, 2003).
Sears, Roebuck & Co.	Uses GIS to support planning of truck routes.
U.S. Department of Agriculture	Using GISs to support drought risk management (Goddard et al., 2003).
Health maintenance organizations	Tracks cancer rate and other diseases to determine expansion strategy and allocation of expensive equipment in their facilities.
Wood Personnel Services (employment agencies)	Maps neighborhoods where temporary workers live; for locating marketing and recruiting cities.
Orange County, Florida	Map real estate for tax assessments, property appraisals, flood control, land surveys, and related applications (see Hardester, 2002).
Wilkening & Co. (consulting services)	Designs optimal sales territories and routes for their clients, reducing travel costs by 15 percent.
CellularOne Corp.	Maps its entire cellular network to identify clusters of call disconnects and to dispatch technicians accordingly.
Civil engineering, environmental science, land-use planning	Make decisions regarding location of facilities (Church, 2002).
Sun Microsystems	Manages leased property in dozens of places worldwide.
Consolidated Rail Corp.	Monitors the condition of 20,000 miles of railroad track and thousands of parcels of adjoining land.
Federal Emergency Management Agency	Assesses the damage of hurricanes, floods, and other natural disasters by relating videotapes of the damage to digitized maps of properties.
Toyota and other car manufacturers	Combine GIS and GPS as a navigation tool. Drivers are directed to destinations via the shortest route.

shortest way (e.g., try *frys.com*). As GIS Web server software is deployed by vendors, more applications will be developed. Maps, GIS data, and information about GISs are available over the Web through a number of vendors and public agencies. (For design issues see Sikder and Gangopadhyay, 2002.)

EMERGING GIS APPLICATIONS. The integration of GISs and global positioning systems (GPSs) has the potential to help restructure and redesign the aviation, transportation, and shipping industries. It enables vehicles or aircraft equipped with a GPS receiver to pinpoint their location as they move (Steede-Terry, 2000). Emerging applications of GPSs include personal automobile mapping systems, vehicle tracking (Terry and Kolb, 2003), and earth-moving equipment tracking. The price of these applications is dropping with improvements in hardware, increased demand, and the availability of more competing vendors. (A simple GPS cost less than $50 in 2003.) GPSs have also become a major source of new GIS data (see Group Assignment 1). Some researchers have developed intelligent GISs that link a GIS to an expert system or to intelligent agents (Tang et al., 2001).

L-Commerce. In Chapter 6 we introduced the concept of location-based commerce (l-commerce), a major part of mobile-commerce (m-commerce). In l-commerce, advertising is targeted to an individual whose location is known (via a GPS and GIS combination). Similarly, emergency medical systems identify the location of a car accident in a second, and the attached GIS helps in directing ambulances to the scene. For other interesting applications, see Sadeh (2002).

CONCLUSIONS. Improvements in the GIS user interface have substantially altered the GIS "look" and "feel." Advanced visualization (three-dimensional graphics) is increasingly integrated with GIS capabilities, especially in animated and interactive maps. GISs can provide information for virtual reality engines, and they can display complex information to decision makers. Multimedia and hypermedia play a growing role in GISs, especially in help and training systems. Object linking and embedding is allowing users to import maps into any document. More GISs will be deployed to provide data and access data over the Web and organizational intranets as "Web-ready" GIS software becomes more affordable. See Korte (2000) for an overview of GISs, their many capabilities, and potential advances.

Visual Interactive Models and Simulation

Visual interactive modeling (VIM) uses computer graphic displays to represent the impact of different management or operational decisions on goals such as profit or market share. VIM differs from regular simulation in that the user can intervene in the decision-making process and see the results of the intervention. A visual model is much more than a communication device; it is an integral part of decision making and problem solving.

A VIM can be used both for supporting decisions and for training. It can represent a static or a dynamic system. Static models display a visual image of the result of one decision alternative at a time. (With computer windows, several results can be compared on one screen.) Dynamic models use animation or video clips to show systems that evolve over time. These are also used in real-time simulations.

VIM has been used with DSSs in several operations management decision processes (see Beroggi, 2001). The method loads the current status of a plant (or a business process) into a virtual interactive model. The model is then run rapidly on a computer, allowing management to observe how a plant is likely to operate in the future.

One of the most developed areas in VIM is **visual interactive simulation (VIS),** a method in which the end user watches the progress of the simulation

IT at Work 11.2
COMPUTER TRAINING IN COMPLEX LOGGING MACHINES AT PARTEK FOREST

The foresting industry is extremely competitive, and countries with high labor costs must automate tasks such as moving, cutting, delimbing, and piling logs. A new machine, called the "Harvester," can replace 25 lumberjacks.

The Harvester is a highly complex machine that takes six months to learn how to operate. The trainee destroys a sizeable amount of forest in the process, and terrain suitable to practice on is decreasing. In unskilled hands, this expensive machine can also be damaged. Therefore, extensive and expensive training is needed. Sisu Logging of Finland (a subsidiary of Partek Forest) found a solution to the training problem by using a real-time simulation (*partekforest.com*).

In this simulation, the chassis, suspension, and wheels of the vehicles have to be modeled, together with the forces acting on them (inertia and friction), and the movement equations linked with them have to be solved in real time. This type of simulation is mathematically complex, and until recently it required equipment investment running into millions of dollars. However, with the help of a visual simulations program, simulation training can now be carried out for only 1 percent of the cost of the traditional method.

Inside the simulator are the Harvester's actual controls, which are used to control a virtual model of a Harvester plowing its way through a virtual forest. The machine sways back and forth on uneven terrain, and the grapple of the Harvester grips the trunk of a tree, fells it, delimbs it, and cuts it into pieces very realistically in real time.

The simulated picture is very sharp: even the structures of the bark and annual growth rings are clearly visible where the tree has been cut. In traditional simulators, the traveling path is quite limited beforehand, but in this Harvester simulator, you are free to move in a stretch of forest covering two hectares (25,000 square yards).

In addition, the system can be used to simulate different kinds of forest in different parts of the world, together with the different tree species and climatic conditions. An additional advantage of this simulator is that the operations can be videotaped so that training sessions can be studied afterward. Moreover, it is possible to practice certain dangerous situations that cannot be done using a real machine.

Source: Condensed from *Finnish Business Report,* April 1997.

For Further Exploration: Why is the simulated training time shorter? Why is visualization beneficial?

---

model in an animated form using graphics terminals. The user may interact with the simulation and try different decision strategies. (See Pritsker and O'Reilly, 1999.) VIS is an approach that has, at its core, the ability to allow decision makers to learn about their own subjective values and about their mistakes. Therefore, VIS can be used for training, as in the case of flight simulators and as shown in *IT at Work 11.2.*

Animation systems that produce realistic graphics are available from many simulation software vendors (e.g., see SAS.com and Vissim.com). The latest visual simulation technology is tied in with the concept of virtual reality, where an artificial world is created for a number of purposes—from training to entertainment to viewing data in an artificial landscape.

Virtual Reality   There is no standard definition of virtual reality. The most common definitions usually imply that **virtual reality (VR)** is interactive, computer-generated, three-dimensional graphics delivered to the user through a head-mounted display. Defined technically, virtual reality is an environment and/or technology that provides artificially generated sensory cues sufficient to engender in the user some willing suspension of disbelief. So in VR, a person "believes" that what he or she is doing is real even though it is artificially created.

More than one person and even a large group can share and interact in the same artificial environment. VR thus can be a powerful medium for communication, entertainment, and learning. Instead of looking at a flat computer screen, the VR user interacts with a three-dimensional computer-generated environment. To see and hear the environment, the user wears stereo goggles and a headset. To interact with the environment, control objects in it, or move around within it, the user wears a computerized display and hand position sensors (gloves). Virtual reality displays achieve the illusion of a surrounding medium by updating the display in real time. The user can grasp and move virtual objects.

VIRTUAL REALITY AND DECISION MAKING. Most VR applications to date have been used to support decision making indirectly. For example, Boeing has developed a virtual aircraft mockup to test designs. Several other VR applications for assisting in manufacturing and for converting military technology to civilian technology are being utilized at Boeing. At Volvo, VR is used to test virtual cars in virtual accidents; Volvo also uses VR in its new model-designing process. British Airways offers the pleasure of experiencing first-class flying to its Web site visitors. For a comprehensive discussion of virtual reality in manufacturing, see Banerjee and Zetu (2001).

Another VR application area is data visualization. VR helps financial decision makers make better sense of data by using visual, spatial, and aural immersion virtual systems. For example, some stock brokerages have a VR application in which users surf over a landscape of stock futures, with color, hue, and intensity indicating deviations from current share prices. Sound is used to convey other information, such as current trends or the debt/equity ratio. VR allows side-by-side comparsions with a large assortment of financial data. It is easier to make intuitive connections with three-dimensional support. Morgan Stanley & Co. uses VR to display the results of risk analyses.

VIRTUAL REALITY AND THE WEB. A platform-independent standard for VR called **virtual reality markup language (VRML)** (*vrmlsite.com*, and Kerlow, 2000) makes navigation through online supermarkets, museums, and stores as easy as interacting with textual information. VRML allows objects to be rendered as an Internet user "walks" through a virtual room. At the moment, users can utilize regular browsers, but VRML browsers will soon be in wide circulation.

Extensive use is expected in e-commerce marketing (see Dalgleish, 2000). For example, Tower Records offers a virtual music store on the Internet where customers can "meet" each other in front of the store, go inside, and preview CDs and videos. They select and purchase their choices electronically and interactively from a sales associate. Applications of virtual reality in other areas are shown in Table 11.5.

Virtual supermarkets could spark greater interest in home grocery shopping. In the future, shoppers will enter a virtual supermarket, walk through the virtual aisles, select virtual products, and put them in their virtual carts. This could help remove some of the resistance to virtual shopping. Virtual malls, which can be delivered even on a PC (*synthonics.com*), are designed to give the user a feeling of walking into a shopping mall.

Virtual reality is just beginning to move into many business applications. An interactive, three-dimensional world on the Internet should prove popular because it is a metaphor to which everyone can relate.

TABLE 11.5 Examples of Virtual Reality Applications	
Applications in Manufacturing	**Applications in Business**

Training
Design testing and interpretation of
  results
Safety analysis
Virtual prototyping
Engineering analysis
Ergonomic analysis
Virtual simulation of assembly,
  production, and maintenance
	Real estate presentation and evaluation
	Advertising
	Presentation in e-commerce
	Presentation of financial data

Applications in Medicine	**Applications in Research and Education**
Training surgeons (with simulators) Interpretation of medical data Planning surgeries Physical therapy	Virtual physics lab Representation of complex mathematics Galaxy configurations
Amusement Applications	**Applications in Architecture**
Virtual museums Three-dimensional race car games (on PCs) Air combat simulation (on PCs) Virtual reality arcades and parks Ski simulator	Design of buildings and other structures

11.6 MARKETING DATABASES IN ACTION

Data warehouses and data marts serve end users in all functional areas. However, the most dramatic applications of data warehousing and mining are in marketing, as seen in the Harrah's case, in what is referred to as *marketing databases* (also referred to as *database marketing*).

In this section we examine how data warehouses, their extensions, and data mining are used, and what role they play in new marketing strategies, such as the use of Web-based marketing transaction databases in interactive marketing.

The Marketing Transaction Database

Most current databases are static: They simply gather and store information about customers. They appear in the following categories: operations databases, data warehouses, and marketing databases. Success in marketing today requires a new kind of database, oriented toward targeting the personalizing marketing messages in real time. Such a database provides the most effective means of capturing information on customer preferences and needs. In turn, enterprises can use this knowledge to create new and/or personalized products and services. Such a database is called a **marketing transaction database (MTD).** The MTD combines many of the characteristics of the current databases and marketing data sources into a new database that allows marketers to engage in real-time personalization and target every interaction with customers.

MTD'S CAPABILITIES. The MTD provides dynamic, or interactive, functions not available with traditional types of marketing databases. In marketing terms, a transaction occurs with the exchange of information. With interactive media, each exposure to the customer becomes an opportunity to conduct a marketing "transaction." Exchanging information (whether gathered actively through registration or user requests, or passively by monitoring customer behavior) allows marketers to refine their understanding of each customer continuously and to use that information to target him or her specifically with personalized marketing messages. This is done most frequently on the Web.

Comparing various characteristics of MTDs with other marketing-related databases shows the advantages of MTDs. For example, marketing databases focus on understanding customers' behavior, but do not target the individual customer nor personalize the marketing approach, as do MTDs. Additionally, data in MTDs can be updated in real time, as opposed to the periodic (weekly, monthly, or quarterly) updates that are characteristic of data warehouses and marketing databases. Also, the data quality in an MTD is focused, and is verified by the individual customers. It thus is of much higher quality than data in many operations databases, where legacy systems may offer only poor assurance of data quality. Further, MTDs can combine various types of data—behavioral, descriptive, and derivative; other types of marketing databases may offer only one or two of these types. Note that MTDs do not eliminate the need for traditional databases. They complement them by providing additional capabilities.

THE ROLE OF THE INTERNET.   Data mining, data warehousing, and MTDs are delivered on the Internet and intranets. The Internet does not simply represent another advertising venue or a different medium for catalog sales. Rather, it contains new attributes that smart marketers can exploit to their fullest degree. Indeed, the Internet promises to revolutionize sales and marketing. Dell Computer (see Minicase W11.1) offers an example of how marketing professionals can use the Internet's electronic sales and marketing channels for market research, advertising, information dissemination, product management, and product delivery. For an overview of marketing databases and the Web, see Grossnickle and Raskin (2000).

Implementation Examples

Fewer and fewer companies can afford traditional marketing approaches, which include big-picture strategies and expensive marketing campaigns. Marketing departments are being scaled down (and so are the traditional marketing approaches), and new approaches such as one-to-one marketing, speed marketing, interactive marketing, and relationship marketing are being employed (see Strauss et al., 2003).

The following examples illustrate how companies use data mining and warehousing to support the new marketing approaches. For other examples, see Online File W11.8.

- Through its online registry for expectant parents, Burlington Coat Factory tracks families as they grow. The company then matches direct-mail material to the different stages of a family's development over time. Burlington also identifies, on a daily basis, top-selling styles and brands. By digging into reams of demographic data, historical buying patterns, and sales trends in existing stores, Burlington determines where to open its next store and what to stock in each store.

- Au Bon Pain Company, Inc., a Boston-based chain of cafés, discovered that the company was not selling as much cream cheese as planned. When it analyzed point-of-sale data, the firm found that customers preferred small, one-serving packaging (like butter). As soon as the package size of the cream cheese was changed, sales shot up.

● Bank of America gets more than 100,000 telephone calls from customers every day. Analyzing customers' banking activities, the bank determines what may be of interest to them. So when a customer calls to check on a balance, the bank tries to sell the customer something in which he or she might be interested.

● Supermarket chains regularly analyze reams of cash register data to discover what items customers are typically buying at the same time. These shopping patterns are used for issuing coupons, designing floor layouts and products' location, and creating shelf displays.

● In its data warehouse, the *Chicago Tribune* stores information about customer behavior as customers move through the various newspaper Web sites. Data mining helps to analyze volumes of data ranging from what browsers are used to what hyperlinks are clicked on most frequently.

The data warehouses in some companies include several terabytes or more of data (e.g., at Sears; see Minicase 1). They need to use supercomputing to sift quickly through the data. Wal-Mart, the world's largest discount retailer, has a gigantic database, as described in *IT at Work 11.3*.

IT at Work 11.3
DATA MINING POWERS WAL-MART

With more than 50 terabytes of data (in 2003) on two NCR (National Cash Register) systems, Wal-Mart (*walmart.com*) manages one of the world's largest data warehouses. Besides the two NCR Teradata databases, which handle most decision-support applications, Wal-Mart has another 6 terabytes of transaction processing data on IBM and Hitachi mainframes.

Wal-Mart's formula for success—getting the right product on the appropriate shelf at the lowest price—owes much to the company's multimillion-dollar investment in data warehousing. "Wal-Mart can be more detailed than most of its competitors on what's going on by product, by store, by day—and act on it," says Richard Winter, a database consultant in Boston. "That's a tremendously powerful thing."

The systems house data on point of sale, inventory, products in transit, market statistics, customer demographics, finance, product returns, and supplier performance. The data are used for three broad areas of information discovery and decision support: analyzing trends, managing inventory, and understanding customers. What emerges are "personality traits" for each of Wal-Mart's 3,500 or so outlets, which Wal-Mart managers can use to determine product mix and inventory levels for each store.

Wal-Mart is using a data mining–based demand-forecasting application that employs neural-networking software and runs on a 4,000-processor parallel computer. The application looks at individual items for individual stores to decide the seasonal sales profile of each item. The system keeps a year's worth of data on the sales of 100,000 products and predicts which items will be needed in each store and when.

Wal-Mart is expanding its use of market-basket analysis. Data are collected on items that comprise a shopper's total purchase so that the company can analyze relationships and patterns in customer purchases. The data warehouse is available over an extranet to store managers and suppliers. In 2003, 6,000 users made over 40,000 database queries each day.

"What Wal-Mart is doing is letting an army of people use the database to make tactical decisions," says consultant Winter. "The cumulative impact is immense."

Sources: This information is courtesy of NCR Corp. (2000) and *walmart.com*.

For Further Exploration: Since small retailers cannot afford data warehouses and data mining, will they be able to compete?

11.7 WEB-BASED DATA MANAGEMENT SYSTEMS

Data management and business intelligence activities—from data acquisition (e.g., Atzeni et al., 2002), through warehousing, to mining—are often performed with Web tools, or are interrelated with Web technologies and e-business (see Liautaud, 2001). Users with browsers can log onto a system, make inquiries, and get reports in a real-time setting. This is done through intranets and for outsiders, via extranets (see *remedy.com*).

E-commerce software vendors are providing Web tools that connect the data warehouse with EC ordering and cataloging systems. Hitachi's EC tool suite, Tradelink (at *hitachi.com*), combines EC activities such as catalog management, payment applications, mass customization, and order management with data warehouses and marts and ERP systems. Oracle (see Winter, 2001) and SAP offer similar products.

Data warehousing and decision support vendors are connecting their products with Web technologies and EC. Examples include Brio's Brio One, Web Intelligence from Business Objects, and Cognos's DataMerchant. Hyperion's Appsource "wired for OLAP" product connects OLAP with Web tools. IBM's Decision Edge makes OLAP capabilities available on the intranet from anywhere in the corporation using browsers, search engines, and other Web technologies. MicroStrategy offers DSS Agent and DSS Web for help in drilling down for detailed information, providing graphical views, and pushing information to users' desktops. Oracle's Financial Analyzer and Sales Analyzer, Hummingbird's Bi/Web and Bi/Broker, and several of the products cited above bring interactive querying, reporting, and other OLAP tasks to many users (both company employees and business partners) via the Web. Also, for a comprehensive discussion of business intelligence on the Web, see the white paper at *businessobjects.com*.

The systems described in the previous sections of this chapter can be integrated on Web-based platforms, such as the one shown in Figure 11.7. The Web-based system is accessed via a portal, and it connects these parts: the

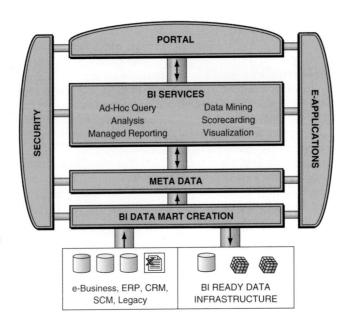

FIGURE 11.7 Web-based data management system. (*Source:* Cognos.com. Platform for Enterprise Business Intelligence. © Cognos Inc. 2001.)

business intelligence (BI) services, the data warehouse and marts, the corporate applications, and the data infrastructure. A security system protects the corporate proprietary data. Let's examine how all of these components work together via the corporate portal.

Enterprise BI Suites and Corporate Portals

Enterprise BI suites (EBISs) integrate query, reporting, OLAP, and other tools. They are scalable, and offered by many vendors (e.g., IBM, Oracle, Microsoft, Hyperion Solution, Sagent Technology, AlphaBlox, MicroStrategy and Crystal Decisions). EBISs are offered usually via enterprise portals.

In Chapter 4 we introduced the concept of corporate portals as a Web-based gateway to data, information, and knowledge. As seen in Figure 11.8, the portal integrates data from many sources. It provides end users with a single Web-based point of personalized access to BI and other applications. Likewise, it provides IT with a single point of delivery and management of this content. Users are empowered to access, create, and share valuable information.

Intelligent Data Warehouse Web-Based Systems

The amount of data in the data warehouse can be very large. While the organization of data is done in a way that permits easy search, it still may be useful to have a search engine for specific applications. Liu (1998) describes how

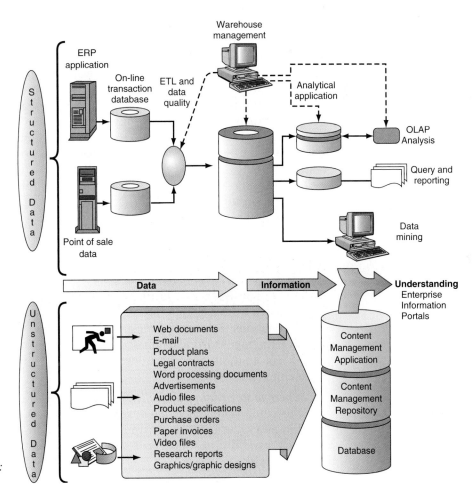

FIGURE 11.8 Sources of content for an enterprise information portal. (*Source:* Merrill Lynch, 1998.)

an intelligent agent can improve the operation of a data warehouse in the pulp and paper industry. This application supplements the monitoring and scanning of external strategic data. The intelligent agent application can serve both managers' ad-hoc query/reporting information needs and the external data needs of a strategic management support system for forest companies in Finland.

Clickstream Data Warehouse

Large and ever-increasing amounts of B2C data about consumers, products, etc. can be collected. Such data come from several sources: internal data (e.g., sales data, payroll data etc.), external data (e.g., government and industry reports), and clickstream data. Clickstream data occur inside the Web environment, when customers visit a Web site. They provide a trail of the users' activities in the Web site, including user behavior and browsing patterns. By looking at clickstream data, an e-tailer can find out such things as which promotions are effective and which population segments are interested in specific products.

According to Inmon (2001), clickstream data can reveal information to answer questions such as the following: What goods has the customer looked at or purchased? What items did the customer buy in conjunction with other items? What ads and promotions were effective? Which were ineffective? Are certain products too hard to find? Are certain products too expensive? Is there a substitute product that the customer finds first?

The Web is an incredibly rich source of business intelligence, and many enterprises are scrambling to build data warehouses that capture the knowledge contained in the clickstream data from their Web sites. By analyzing the user behavior patterns contained in these clickstream data warehouses, savvy business can expand their markets, improve customer relationships, reduce costs, streamline operations, strengthen their Web sites, and hone their business strategies. One has two options: incorporate Web-based data into preexisting data warehouses, or build new **clickstream data warehouses** that are capable of showing both e-business activities and the non-Web aspects of the business in an integrated fashion (see Sweiger at el., 2002).

➡ MANAGERIAL ISSUES

1. *Cost-benefit issues and justification.* Some of the data management solutions discussed in this chapter are very expensive and are justifiable only in large corporations. Smaller organizations can make the solutions cost effective if they leverage existing databases rather than create new ones. A careful cost-benefit analysis must be undertaken before any commitment to the new technologies is made.

2. *Where to store data physically.* Should data be distributed close to their users? This could potentially speed up data entry and updating, but adds replication and security risks. Or should data be centralized for easier control, security, and disaster recovery? This has communications and single point of failure risks.

3. *Legal issues.* Data mining may suggest that a company send catalogs or promotions to only one age group or one gender. A man sued Victoria's Secret Corp. because his female neighbor received a mail order catalog with deeply discounted items and he received only the regular catalog (the discount was actually given for volume purchasing). Settling discrimination charges can be very expensive.

4. *Internal or external?* Should a firm invest in internally collecting, storing, maintaining, and purging its own databases of information? Or should it subscribe to external databases, where providers are responsible for all data management and data access?

5. *Disaster recovery.* Can an organization's business processes, which have become dependent on databases, recover and sustain operations after a natural or other type of information systems disaster? (See Chapter 15.) How can a data warehouse be protected? At what cost?

6. *Data security and ethics.* Are the company's competitive data safe from external snooping or sabotage? Are confidential data, such as personnel details, safe from improper or illegal access and alteration? A related question is, Who owns such personal data? (See Smith, 1997.)

7. *Ethics: Paying for use of data.* Compilers of public-domain information, such as Lexis-Nexis, face a problem of people lifting large sections of their work without first paying royalties. The Collection of Information Antipiracy Act (Bill HR 2652 in the U.S. Congress) will provide greater protection from online piracy. This, and other intellectual property issues, are being debated in Congress and adjudicated in the courts.

8. *Privacy.* Collecting data in a warehouse and conducting data mining may result in the invasion of individual privacy. What will companies do to protect individuals? What can individuals do to protect their privacy? (See online Chapter 16.)

9. *The legacy data problem.* One very real issue, often known as the legacy data acquisition problem, is what to do with the mass of information already stored in a variety of systems and formats. Data in older, perhaps obsolete, databases still need to be available to newer database management systems. Many of the legacy application programs used to access the older data simply cannot be converted into new computing environments without considerable expense. Basically, there are three approaches to solving this problem. One is to create a database front end that can act as a translator from the old system to the new. The second is to cause applications to be integrated with the new system, so that data can be seamlessly accessed in the original format. The third is to cause the data to migrate into the new system by reformatting it. A new promising approach is the use of Web services (see Chapter 14).

10. *Data delivery.* Moving data efficiently around an enterprise is often a major problem. The inability to communicate effectively and efficiently among different groups, in different geographical locations, is a serious roadblock to implementing distributed applications properly, especially given the many remote sites and mobility of today's workers. Mobile and wireless computing (Chapter 6) are addressing some of these difficulties.

ON THE WEB SITE... Additional resources, including quizzes; online files of additional text, tables, figures, and cases; and frequently updated Web links to current articles and information can be found on the book's Web site (*wiley.com/college/turban*).

KEY TERMS

Analytical processing *500*

Business intelligence (BI) *505*

Clickstream data *496*

Clickstream data warehouses *528*

Data integrity *497*

Data mart *504*

Data mining *510*

Data quality (DQ) *496*

Data visualization *514*

Data warehouse *501*

Document management *498*

Document management system (DMS) *498*

Geographical information system (GIS) *517*

Knowledge discovery *507*

Knowledge discovery in databases (KDD) *507*

Marketing transaction database (MTD) *523*

Metadata *502*

Multidimensional database *505*

Multidimensionality *517*

Online analytical processing (OLAP) *508*

Operational data store *504*

Text mining *512*

Virtual reality (VR) *521*

Virtual reality markup language (VRML) *522*

Visual interactive modeling (VIM) *520*

Visual interactive simulation (VIS) *520*

Web mining *513*

CHAPTER HIGHLIGHTS (Numbers Refer to Learning Objectives)

❶ Data are the foundation of any information system and need to be managed throughout their useful life cycle, which converts data to useful information, knowledge, and a basis for decision support.

❷ Data exist in internal and external sources. Personal data and knowledge are often stored in people's minds.

❷ The Internet is a major source of data and knowledge. Other sources are databases, paper documents, videos, maps, pictures, and more.

❷ Many factors that impact the quality of data must be recognized and controlled.

❸ Today data and documents are managed electronically. They are digitized, stored, and used in electronic management systems.

❸ Electronic document management, the automated control of documents, is a key to greater efficiency in handling documents in order to gain an edge on the competition.

❸ Multidimensional presentation enables quick and easy multiple viewing of information in accordance with people's needs.

❹ Data warehouses and data marts are necessary to support effective information discovery and decision making. Relevant data are indexed and organized for easy access by end users.

❺ Online analytical processing is a data discovery method that uses analytical approaches.

❺ Business intelligence is an umbrella name for a large number of methods and tools used to conduct data analysis.

❻ Data mining for knowledge discovery is an attempt to use intelligent systems to scan volumes of data to locate necessary information and knowledge.

❼ Visualization is important for better understanding of data relationships and compression of information. Several computer-based methods exist.

❼ A geographical information system captures, stores, manipulates, and displays data using digitized maps.

❼ Virtual reality is 3-D, interactive, computer-generated graphics that provides users with a feeling that they are inside a certain environment.

❽ Marketing databases provide the technological support for new marketing approaches such as interactive marketing.

❽ Marketing transaction databases provide dynamic interactive functions that facilitate customized advertising and services to customers.

❾ Web-based systems are used extensively in supporting data access and data analysis. Also, Web-based systems are an important source of data. Finally, data visualization is frequently combined with Web systems.

QUESTIONS FOR REVIEW

1. List the major sources of data.
2. List some of the major data problems.
3. What is a terabyte? (Write the number.)
4. Review the steps of the data life cycle and explain them.
5. List some of the categories of data available on the Internet.
6. Define data quality.
7. Define document management.
8. Describe a data warehouse.
9. Describe a data mart.
10. Define business intelligence.
11. Define online analytical processing (OLAP).
12. Define data mining and describe its major characteristics.
13. Define data visualization.
14. Explain the properties of multidimensionality and its vizualization.
15. Describe GIS and its major capabilities.
16. Define visual interactive modeling and simulation.
17. Define a marketing transaction database.
18. Define virtual reality.

QUESTIONS FOR DISCUSSION

1. Compare data quality to data integrity. How are they related?
2. Discuss the relationship between OLAP and multidimensionality.
3. Discuss business intelligence and distinguish between decision support and information and knowledge discovery.
4. Discuss the factors that make document management so valuable. What capabilities are particularly valuable?
5. Relate document management to imaging systems.
6. Describe the process of information and knowledge discovery, and discuss the roles of the data warehouse, data mining, and OLAP in this process.
7. Discuss the major drivers and benefits of data warehousing to end users.
8. Discuss how a data warehouse can lessen the stovepipe problem. (See Chapter 9.)
9. A data mart can substitute for a data warehouse or supplement it. Compare and discuss these options.
10. Why is the combination of GIS and GPS becoming so popular? Examine some applications related to data management.
11. Discuss the advantages of terabyte marketing databases to a large corporation. Does a small company need a marketing database? Under what circumstances will it make sense to have one?
12. Discuss the benefits managers can derive from visual interactive simulation in a manufacturing company.
13. What is the logic of targeted marketing, and how can data management be used in such marketing?
14. Distinguish between operational databases, data warehouses, and marketing data marts.
15. Relate the Sears minicase to the phases of the data life cycle.
16. Discuss the potential contribution of virtual reality to e-commerce.
17. Discuss the interaction between marketing and management theories and IT support at Harrah's case.

EXERCISES

1. Review the list of data management difficulties in Section 11.1. Explain how a combination of data warehousing and data mining can solve or reduce these difficulties. Be specific.
2. Interview a knowledge worker in a company you work for or to which you have access. Find the data problems they have encountered and the measures they have taken to solve them. Relate the problems to Strong's four categories.
3. Ocean Spray Cranberries is a large cooperative of fruit growers and processors. Ocean Spray needed data to determine the effectiveness of its promotions and its advertising and to make itself able to respond strategically to its competitors' promotions. The company also wanted to identify trends in consumer preferences for new products and to pinpoint marketing factors that might be causing changes in the selling levels of certain brands and markets.

Ocean Spray buys marketing data from InfoScan (*infores.com*), a company that collects data using barcode scanners in a sample of 2,500 stores nationwide and from A.C. Nielsen. The data for each product include sales volume, market share, distribution, price information, and information about promotions (sales, advertisements).

The amount of data provided to Ocean Spray on a daily basis is overwhelming (about 100 to 1,000 times more data items than Ocean Spray used to collect on its own). All the data are deposited in the corporate marketing data mart. To analyze this vast amount of data, the company developed a DSS. To give end users easy access to the data, the company uses an expert system–based data-mining process called CoverStory, which summarizes information in accordance with user preferences. CoverStory interprets data processed by the DSS, identifies trends, discovers cause-and-effect relationships, presents hundreds of displays, and provides any information required by the decision makers. This system alerts managers to key problems and opportunities.

a. Find information about Ocean Spray by entering Ocean Spray's Web site (*oceanspray.com*).
b. Ocean Spray has said that it cannot run the business without the system. Why?
c. What data from the data mart are used by the DSS?
d. Enter *infores.com* or *scanmar.nl* and review the marketing decision support information. How is the company related to a data warehouse?
e. How does Infoscan collect data? (Check the Data Wrench product.)

GROUP ASSIGNMENTS

1. Several applications now combine GIS and GPS.
  a. Survey such applications by conducting literature and Internet searches and query GIS vendors.
  b. Prepare a list of five applications, including at least two in e-commerce (see Chapter 5).
  c. Describe the benefit of such integration.

2. Prepare a report on the topic of "data management and the intranet." Specifically, pay attention to the role of the data warehouse, the use of browsers for query, and data mining. Also explore the issue of GIS and the Internet. Finally, describe the role of extranets in support of business partner collaboration. Each group will visit one or two vendors' sites, read the white papers, and examine products (Oracle, Red Bricks, Brio, Siemens Mixdorf IS, NCR, SAS, and Information Advantage). Also, visit the Web site of the Data Warehouse Institute (*dw-institute.org*).

3. Companies invest billions of dollars to support database marketing. The information systems departments'

(ISD) activities that have supported accounting and finance in the past are shifting to marketing. According to Tucker (1997), some people think that the ISD should report to marketing. Do you agree or disagree? Debate this issue.

4. Using data mining, it is possible not only to capture information that has been buried in distant courthouses, but also to manipulate and cross-index it. This can benefit law enforcement but invade privacy. In 1996, Lexis-Nexis, the online information service, was accused of permitting access to sensitive information on individuals. The company argued that the firm was targeted unfairly, since it provided only basic residential data for lawyers and law enforcement personnel. Should Lexis-Nexis be prohibited from allowing access to such information or not? Debate the issue.

INTERNET EXERCISES

1. Conduct a survey on document management tools and applications by visiting *dataware.com*, *documentum.com*, and *aiim.org/aim/publications*.

2. Access the Web sites of one or two of the major data management vendors, such as Oracle, Informix, and Sybase, and trace the capabilities of their latest products, including Web connections.

3. Access the Web sites of one or two of the major data warehouse vendors, such as NCR or SAS; find how their products are related to the Web.

4. Access the Web site of the GartnerGroup (*gartnergroup .com*). Examine some of their research notes pertaining to marketing databases, data warehousing, and data management. Prepare a report regarding the state of the art.

5. Explore a Web site for multimedia database applications. Visit such sites as *leisureplan.com*, *illustra.com*, or *adb.fr*. Review some of the demonstrations, and prepare a concluding report.

6. Enter *microsoft.com/solutions/BI/customer/biwithinreach_ demo.asp* and see how BI is supported by Microsoft's tools. Write a report.

7. Enter *teradatauniversitynetwork.com*. Prepare a summary on resources available there. Is it valuable to a student?

8. Enter *visualmining.com* and review the support they provide to business intelligence. Prepare a report.

9. Survey some GIS resources such as *geo.ed.ac.uk/home/hiswww.html*, and *prenhall.com/stratgis/sites.html*. Identify GIS resources related to your industry, and prepare a report on some recent developments or applications. See *http://nsdi.usgs.gov/nsdi/pages/what_is_ gis.html*.

10. Visit the sites of some GIS vendors (such as *mapinfo.com, esri.com, autodesk.com,* or *bently.com*). Join a newsgroup and discuss new applications in marketing, banking, and transportation. Download a demo. What are some of the most important capabilities and new applications?

11. Enter *websurvey.com, clearlearning.com,* and *tucows.com/webforms*, and prepare a report about data collection via the Web.

12. Enter *infoscan.com*. Find all the services related to dynamic warehouse and explain what it does.

13. Enter *ibm.com/software* and find their data mining products, such as DB2 Intelligent Miner. Prepare a list of products and their capabilities.

14. Enter *megapuker.com*, Read "Data Mining 101," "Text Analyst," and "WebAnalyst." Compare the two products. (Look at case studies.)

Minicase 1
Precision Buying, Merchandising, and Marketing at Sears

The Problem

Sears, Roebuck and Company, the largest department store chain and the third-largest retailer in the United States, was caught by surprise in the 1980s as shoppers defected to specialty stores and discount mass merchandisers, causing the firm to lose market share rapidly. In an attempt to change the situation, Sears used several response strategies, ranging from introducing its own specialty stores (such as Sears Hardware) to restructuring its mall-based stores. Recently, Sears has moved to selling on the Web. It discontinued its paper catalog. Accomplishing the transformation and restructuring required the retooling of its information systems.

Sears had 18 data centers, one in each of 10 geographical regions as well as one each for marketing, finance, and other departments. The first problem was created when the reorganization effort produced only seven geographical regions. Frequent mismatches between accounting and sales figures and information scattered among numerous databases forced users to query multiple systems, even when they needed an answer to a simple query. Furthermore, users found that data that were already summarized made it difficult to conduct analysis at the desired level of detail. Finally, errors were virtually inevitable when calculations were based on data from several sources.

The Solution

To solve these problems, Sears constructed a single sales information data warehouse. This replaced the 18 old databases which were packed with redundant, conflicting, and sometimes obsolete data. The new data warehouse is a simple repository of relevant decision-making data such as authoritative data for key performance indicators, sales inventories, and profit margins. Sears, known for embracing IT on a dramatic scale, completed the data warehouse and its IT reengineering efforts in under one year—a perfect IT turnaround story.

Using an NCR enterprise server, the initial 1.7 terabyte (1.7 trillion bytes) data warehouse is part of a project dubbed the Strategic Performance Reporting System (SPRS). By 2003, the data warehouse had grown to over 70 terabytes. SPRS includes comprehensive sales data; information on inventory in stores, in transit, and at distribution centers; and cost per item. This has enabled Sears to track sales by individual items(skus) in each of its 1,950 stores (including 810 mall-based stores) in the United States and 1,600 international stores and catalog outlets. Thus, daily margin by item per store can be easily computed, for example. Furthermore, Sears now fine-tunes its buying, merchandising, and marketing strategies with previously unattainable precision.

SPRS is open to all authorized employees, who now can view each day's sales from a multidimensional perspective (by region, district, store, product line, and individual item). Users can specify any starting and ending dates for special sales reports, and all data can be accessed via a highly user-friendly graphical interface. Sears managers can now monitor the precise impact of advertising, weather, and other factors on sales of specific items. This means that buyers and other specialists can examine and adjust if needed, inventory quantities, merchandising, and order placement, along with myriad other variables, almost immediately, so they can respond quickly to environmental changes. SPRS users can also group together widely divergent kinds of products, for example, tracking sales of items marked as "gifts under $25." Advertising staffers can follow so-called "great items," drawn from vastly different departments, that are splashed on the covers of promotional circulars. SPRS enables extensive data mining, but only on sku- and location-related analysis.

In 1998 Sears created a large customer database, dubbed LCI (Leveraging Customer Information) which contained customer-related sale information (which was not available on SPRS). The LCI enables hourly records of transactions, for example, guiding hourly promotion (such as 15% discounts for early-bird shoppers).

In the holiday season of 2001 Sears decided to replace its regular 10% discount promotion by offering deep discount during early shopping hours. This new promotion, which was based on SPRS, failed, and only when LCI was used the problem was corrected. This motivated Sears to combine LCI and SPRS in a single platform, which enables sophisticated analysis (in 2002).

By 2001 Sears also had the following Web initiatives: an e-commerce home improvement center, a B2B supply exchange for the retail industry, a toy catalog (*wishbook .com*), an e-procurement system, and much more. All of these Web-marketing initiatives feed data into the data warehouse, and their planning and control are based on accessing the data in the data warehouse.

The Results

The ability to monitor sales by item per store enables Sears to create a sharp local market focus. For example, Sears keeps different shades of paint colors in different cities to meet local demands. Therefore, sales and market share have improved. Also, Web-based data monitoring of sales at LCI helps Sears to plan marketing and Web advertising.

At its inception, the data warehouse had been used daily by over 3,000 buyers, replenishers, marketers, strategic planners, logistics and finance analysts, and store managers. By 2003, there were over 5,000 users, since users found the system very beneficial. Response time to queries has dropped from days to minutes for typical requests. Overall, the strategic impact of the SPRS-LCI data warehouse is that it offers Sears employees a tool for making better decisions, and Sears retailing profits have climbed more than 20 percent annually since SPRS was implemented.

Sources: Compiled from Amato-McCoy (2002), Beitler and Leary (1997); and press releases of Sears (2001–2003).

Questions for Minicase 1

1. What were the drivers of SPRS?
2. How did the data wareshouse solve Sears's problems?
3. Why was it beneficial to integrate the customers' database with SPRS?

Minicase 2
GIS at Dallas Area Rapid Transit

Public transportation in Dallas and its neighboring communities is provided by Dallas Area Rapid Transit (DART), which operates buses, vans, and a train system. The service area has grown very fast. By the mid-1980s, the agency was no longer able to respond properly to customer requests, make rapid changes in scheduling, plan properly, or manage security.

The solution to these problems was discovered using GISs. A GIS digitizes maps and maplike information, integrates it with other database information, and uses the combined information for planning, problem solving, and decision making. DART (*dart.org*) maintains a centralized graphical database of every object for which it is responsible.

The GIS presentation makes it possible for DART's managers, consultants, and customers to view and analyze data on digitized maps. Previously, DART created service maps on paper showing bus routes and schedules. The maps were updated and redistributed several times a year, at a high cost. Working with paper maps made it difficult to respond quickly and accurately to the nearly 6,000 customer inquiries each day. For example, to answer a question concerning one of the more than 200 bus routes or a specific schedule, it was often necessary to look at several maps and routes. Planning a change was also a time-consuming task. Analysis of the viability of bus route alternatives made it necessary to photocopy maps from map books, overlay tape to show proposed routes, and spend considerable time gathering information on the demographics of the corridors surrounding the proposed routes.

The GIS includes attractive and accurate maps that interface with a database containing information about bus schedules, routes, bus stops (in excess of 15,000), traffic surveys, demographics, and addresses on each street in the database. The system allows DART employees to:

- Respond rapidly to customer inquiries (reducing response time by at least 33 percent).

- Perform the environmental impact studies required by the city.
- Track where the buses are at any time using a global positioning system.
- Improve security on buses.
- Monitor subcontractors quickly and accurately.
- Analyze the productivity and use of existing routes.

For instance, a customer wants to know the closest bus stop and the schedule of a certain bus to take her to a certain destination. The GIS automatically generates the answer when the caller says where she is by giving an address, a name of an intersection, or a landmark. The computer can calculate the travel time to the desired destination as well.

Analyses that previously took days to complete are now executed in less than an hour. Special maps, which previously took up to a week to produce at a cost of $13,000 to $15,000 each, are produced in 5 minutes at the cost of 3 feet of plotter paper.

In the late 1990s, the GIS was combined with a GPS. The GPS tracks the location of the buses and computes the expected arrival time at each bus stop. Many maps are on display at the Web site, including transportation lines and stops superimposed on maps.

Sources: Condensed from *GIS World* (July 1993); updated with information compiled from *dart.org* (2003).

Questions for Minicase 2

1. Describe the role of data in the DART system.
2. What are the advantages of computerized maps?
3. Comment on the following statement: "Using GIS, users can improve not only the inputting of data but also their use."
4. Speculate on the type of information provided by the GPS.

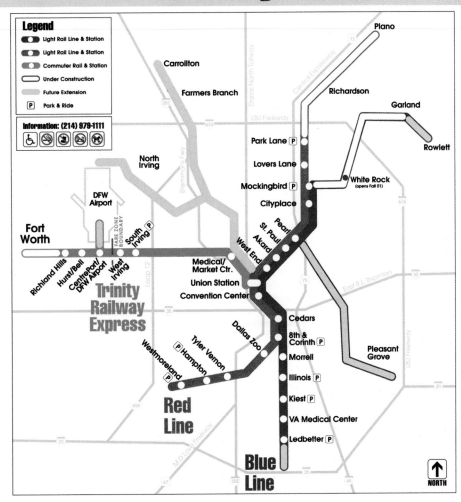

Virtual Company Assignment
Data Management at The Wireless Café

You were intrigued by the opening story of Harrah's use of CRM data to improve the customer experience, and it seems to you that there are many parallels between satisfying Harrah's customers and The Wireless Café's customers (aside from the slot machines, of course). You have noticed that Jeremy likes to review The Wireless Café's financial and customer data using Excel charts and graphs, so you think he might be interested in discussing ways to exploit existing The Wireless Café data for improving the customer experience in the diner.

Instructions

1. As you've grown quite fond of Marie-Christine's cooking, you would like to help her develop even more popular menu hits. The idea of using business intelligence and data mining to better predict customer ordering trends and behaviors strikes you as something that would help. For example, do customers buy more desserts on Friday and Saturday than during the week? Do some research on business intelligence software and prepare a brief report for Jeremy and Marie-Christine to describe the kinds of business intelligence that could be used to prepare smash-hit menus.

2. The Wireless Café does not have a significant marketing budget; however, some inexpensive Web-based marketing strategies can be effective. Earlier, Barbara expressed interest in creating a CRM system to better know and serve The Wireless Café's customers. Describe a strategy whereby you could combine CRM data and Web-based marketing to increase the business at The Wireless Café.

3. Business intelligence, data warehousing, data mining, and visualization are activities that could benefit The Wireless Café's bottom line. Many CIOs these days expect an IT project to pay for itself within 12 months or less. How would you measure the benefits of introducing new data management software to determine which competing projects to implement and whether you could expect a 12-month payback on the software?

REFERENCES

Adjeroh, D. A., and K. C. Nwosu, "Multimedia Database Management—Requirements and Issues," *IEEE Multimedia*, July—September 1997.

Alter, S. L., *Decision Support Systems*, Reading, MA: Addison Wesley, 1980.

Amato-McCoy, D. M., "Sears Combines Retail Reporting And Customer Databases on a Single Platform," *Stores*, November 2002.

Amato-McCoy, D. M., "Movie Gallery Mines Data to Monitor Associate Activities," *Stores*, May 2003a.

Amato-McCoy, D. M., "AAFES Combats Fraud with Exception Reporting Solution," *Stores*, May 2003b.

Apte, C., et al., "Business Application of Data Mining," *Communications of the ACM*, August 2002.

Asprev, L., and M. Middleton, (eds.), *Integrative Document and Content Management*, Hershey, PA: The Idea Group, 2003.

Atzeni, P., et al., "Managing Web-Based Data," *IEEE Internet Computing*, July–August, 2002.

Banerjee, P., and D. Zetu, *Virtual Manufacturing: Virtual Reality and Computer Vision Techniques*. New York: Wiley, 2001.

Bates, J., "Business in Real Time–Realizing the Vision," *DM Review*, May 2003.

Baumer, D., "Innovative Web Use to Learn about Consumer Behavior and Online Privacy," *Communications of the ACM*, April, 2003.

Becker, S. A., (Ed.) *Effective Database for Text and Document Management*, Hershey, PA: IRM Press, 2003.

Beitler, S. S., and R. Leary, "Sears' Epic Transformation: Converting from Mainframe Legacy Systems to OLAP," *Journal of Data Warehousing*, April 1997.

Beroggi, G.E., "Visual Interactive Decision Modeling in Policy Management," *Eurpoean Journal of Operational Research*, January 2001.

Berry, M., *Survey of Text Mining: Clustering, Classification and Retrieval.* Berlin: Springer–Verlag, 2002.

Best's Review Magazine, May 1993.

BIXL, *Business Intelligence for Excel*, a white paper, Business Intelligence Technologies, Inc. 2002 (*BIXL.com*).

Brauer, J. R., "Data Quality Is the Cornerstone of Effective Business Intelligence," *DM Review*, October 5, 2001.

Brown, D. E., and S. Hagen, "Data Association Methods with Applications to Law Enforcement," *Decision Support Systems*, March 2003.

Campbell, D., "Visualization for the Real World," *DM Review*, September 7, 2001.

Canada NewsWire, "European Court of Human Rights Saves Time and Money for a News Wire," April 29, 2003 NAICS#922110.

Carbone, P. L., "Data Warehousing: Many of the Common Failures," Presentation, *mitre.org/support/papers/tech...9_00/d-warehoulse_presentation.htm* (May 3, 1999).

Church, R. L., "Geographical Information Systems and Location Science," *Computers and Operations Research*, May 2002.

Chopoorian, J. A., et al., "Mind Your Business by Mining Your Data," *SAM Advanced Management Journal*, spring 2001.

Civic.com/pubs (accessed March 2001).

Codd, E. F., et al., "Beyond Decision Support," *Computerworld*, July 1993.

Cognos.com. "Platform for Enterprise Business Intelligence," Cognos Inc., 2001.

Cohen, J. B., "'Virtual Newsstand' Debuts Online," *Editor and Publisher*, Vol. 129, No. 24, June 15, 1996, pp. 86–87.

Cole, B., "Document Management on a Budget," *Network World*, Vol. 13, No. 8, September 16, 1996.

Creese, G., and A. Veytsel, "Data Quality at a Real-Time Tempo," *InSight*, An Aberdeen Group publication, January 9, 2003, *aberdeen.com/2001/research/01030003.asp*.

Dalgleish, J., *Customer-Effective Web Sites*. Upper Saddle River, NJ: Pearson Technology Group, 2000.

Datamation, May 15, 1990.

Delcambre, L., et al., "Harvesting Information to Sustain Forests," *Communications of the ACM*, January 2003.

Dimensional Insight, *Business Intelligenc and OLAP Terms: An Online Glossary, dimins.com/Glossary1.html* (accessed June 15, 2003).

Etzioni, O., "The WWW: Quagmire or Gold Mine," *Communications of the ACM*, November 1996.

Fayyad, U. M., et al., "The KDD Process for Extracting Useful Knowledge from Volumes of Data," *Communications of the ACM*, November 1996.

Finnish Business Report, April 1997.

Fong, A. C. M., et al., "Data Mining for Decision Support," *IT Pro*, March/April, 2002.

Fortune, "1994 Information Technology Guide," August 1993.

GIS World, July 1993.

Goddard, S., et al., "Geospatial Decision Support for Drought Risk Management," *Communications of the ACM*, January 2003.

Grant, G., ed., *ERP and Datawarehousing in Organizations: Issues and Challenges*, Hershey, PA: IRM Press, 2003.

Gray, P., and H. J. Watson, *Decision Support in the Data Warehouse*. Upper Saddle River, NJ, Prentice-Hall, 1998.

Grossnickle, J., and O. Raskin, *The Handbook of Marketing Research*. New York: McGraw-Hill, 2000.

Hamilton, J. M., "A Mapping Feast," *CIO*, March 15, 1996.

Hardester, K. P., "Au Enterprise GIS Solution for Integrating GIS and CAMA," *Assessment Journal*, November/December, 2002.

Hasan, B., "Assesing Data Authenticity with Benford's Law," *Information Systems Control Journal*, July 2002.

Hirji, K. K., "Exploring Data Mining Implementation," *Communications of the ACM*, July 2001.

IBM Systems Journal, Vol. 29, No. 3, 1990.

Information Week (May 14, 2001).

Infoworld, January 27, 1997.

Inmon, W. H., *Building The Data Warehouse*, 3rd ed. New York: Wiley, 2002.

Inmon, W. H., "Why Clickstream Data Counts," *e-Business Advisor*, April 2001.

I/S Analyzer, "Visualization Software Aids in Decision Making," *I/S Analyzer*, July 2002.

Kimball, R., and M. Ross, *The Data Warehouse Tool Kit*, 2nd ed. New York: Wiley, 2002.

Kerlow, I. V., *The Art of 3D*, 2nd ed. New York: Wiley, 2000.

Korte, G. B., *The GIS Book*, 5th ed. Albany, NY: Onward Press, 2000.

Lau, H. C. W., et al., "Development of an Intelligent Data-Mining System for a Dispered Manufacturing Network," *Expert Systems*, September 2001.

Levinson, M., "Jackpot! Harrah's Entertainment," *CIO Magazine*, February 1, 2001.

Li, T., et al., "Information Visualization for Intelligent DSS," *Knowledge Based Systems*, August 2001.

Liautaud, B., *E-Business Intelligence*, New York: McGraw-Hill, 2001.

Linoff, G. S., and J. A. Berry, *Mining the Web: Transforming Customer Data*. New York: Wiley, 2002.

Liu, S., "Data Warehousing Agent: To Make the Creation and Maintenance of Data Warehouse Easier," *Journal of Data Warehousing*, Spring 1998.

Loveman, G., "Diamonds in the Data," *Harvard Business Review*, May 2003.

Markus, M. L., et al., "A Design Theory for Systems that Support Emergent Knowledge Processes," *MIS Quarterly*, September 2002.

Mattison, R., *Winning Telco Customers Using Marketing Databases*. Norwood, MA: Artech House, 1999.

Merrill Lynch, 1998.

MIS Quarterly, December 1991.

Moad, J., "Mining a New Vein," *PC Week*, January 5, 1998.

Moss, L. R., and S. Atre, *Business Intelligence Road Map*, Boston: Addison Weeky, 2003.

Nasirin, S., and D. F. Birks, "DSS Implementation in the UK Retail Organizations: A GIS Perspective," *Information and Management*, March, 2003.

NCR Corp., 2000.

Nemati, H. R., and C. D. Barko, "Enhancing Enterprise Decision through Organizational Data Mining," *Journal of Computer Information Systems*, Summer, 2002.

Nwosu, K. C., et al., "Multimedia Database Systems: A New Frontier," *IEEE Multimedia*, July–September 1997.

O'Looney, J. A., *Beyond Maps: GIS Decision Making in Local Governments*. Redlands, CA: ESRI Press, 2000.

Oguz, M. T., "Strategic Intelligence: Business Intelligence in Competitive Strategy," *DM Review*, May 31, 2003.

Park, Y. T., "Strategic Uses of Data Warehouses," *Journal of Data Warehousing*, April 1997.

Pritsker, A. A. B., and J. J. O'Reilly, *Simulation with Visual SLAM and Awesim*, 2nd ed. New York: Wiley, 1999.

Radding, A., "Going with GIS," *Bank Management*, December 1991; updated February 2003.

Ray, N., and S.W. Tabor, "Cyber-Surveys Come of Age," *Marketing Research*, Spring 2003.

Redman, T. C., "The Impact of Poor Data Quality on the Typical Enterprise," *Communications of the ACM*, February 1998.

Rudnensteiner, E. A., et al., "Maintaining Data Warehousing over Changing Information Sources," *Communications of the ACM*, June 2000.

Sadeh, N., *M-Commerce*. New York: Wiley, 2002.

Sears (2001–2003).

Sikder, I., and A. Gangopadhyay, "Design and Implementation of a Web-Based Collaborative Spatial Decision Support System: Organizational and Managerial Implications," *Information Resources Management Journal*, October–December 2002.

Smith, H. J., "Who Owns Personal Data?" *Beyond Computing*, November–December 1997.

Southam.com, "Southam on the Web," 2001.

Steede-Terry, K., *Integrating GIS and GPS*. Redlands, CA: Environmental Systems Research (*eSRI.com*), 2000.

Strauss, J., et al., *E-Marketing*. Upper Saddle River, NJ: Prentice Hall, 2003.

Strong, D. M., et al., "Data Quality in Context," *Communications of the ACM*, May 1997.

Sweiger, M., et al., *Clickstream Data Warehousing*, New York: John Wiley and Sons, 2002.

Tang C., et al., "An Agent-Based Geographical Information System," *Knowledge-Based Systems*, Vol. 14, 2001.

Terry, K., and D. Kolb, "Integrated Vehicle Routing and Tracking Using GIS-Based Technology," *Logistics*, March/April, 2003.

Tucker, M. J., "Poppin' Fresh Dough," (Database Marketing), *Datamation*, May 1997.

Turban, E., et al., *Electronic Commerce: A Managerial Perspective*. 3rd ed., Upper Saddle River, NJ: Prentice-Hall, 2004.

usaa.com (2001).

Watson, H. J., et al., "The Effects of Technology-Enabled Business Strategy At First American Corporation," *Organizational Dynamics*, Winter, 2002.

Weiss, T. R., "Online Retail Sales On the Rise," *PC World*, January 2003.

Winter, R., *Large Scale Data Warehousing with Oracle 9i Database*, Special Report, Waltham MA: Winter Corp., 2001.

PART IV
Managerial and Decision Support Systems

10. Knowledge Management
11. Data Management: Warehousing, Analyzing, Mining, and Visualization
▶ 12. Management Decision Support and Intelligent Systems

CHAPTER

12

Management Decision Support and Intelligent Systems

12.1
Managers and Decision Making

12.2
Decision Support Systems

12.3
Group Decision Support Systems

12.4
Enterprise and Executive Decision Support Systems

12.5
Intelligent Support Systems: The Basics

12.6
Expert Systems

12.7
Other Intelligent Systems

12.8
Web-Based Support Management Systems

12.9
Advanced and Special Decision Support Topics

Online Appendix W12.1
Intelligent Software Agents

LEARNING OBJECTIVES

After studying this chapter, you will be able to:

❶ Describe the concepts of managerial, decision making and computerized support for decision making.

❷ Justify the role of modeling in decision making.

❸ Describe decision support systems (DSSs) and their benefits, and describe the DSS structure.

❹ Describe the support to group (including virtual) decision making.

❺ Describe organizational DSS and executive support systems, and analyze their role in management support.

❻ Describe artificial intelligence (AI) and list its benefits and characteristics.

❼ List the major commercial AI technologies.

❽ Define an expert system and its components, and describe its benefits and limitations.

❾ Describe natural language processing and compare it to speech understanding.

❿ Describe artificial neural networks (ANNs), their characteristics and major applications; compare them to fuzzy logic and describe its role in hybrid intelligent systems.

⓫ Describe the relationships between the Web, DSS, and intelligent systems.

⓬ Describe special decision support applications including the support of frontline employees.

541

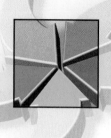

SINGAPORE AND MALAYSIA AIRLINES EXPERT SYSTEMS

➡️ THE PROBLEM

Airlines fly around the globe, mostly with their native crew. Singapore Airlines and Malaysia Airlines are relatively small airlines, but they serve dozens of different countries. If a crewmember is ill on route, there is a problem of quickly finding a replacement. This is just one example why crew scheduling may be complex, especially when it is subject to regulatory constraints, contract agreements, and crew preferences. Disturbances such as weather conditions, maintenance problems, etc. also make crew management difficult.

➡️ THE SOLUTION

Singapore airlines uses Web-based intelligent systems such as expert systems and neural computing to manage the company's flight crew scheduling and handle disruptions to the crew rosters. The Integrated Crew Management System (ICMS) project, implemented in Singapore in 1997, consists of three modules: one roster assignment module for cockpit crew, one for the cabin crew, and a crew tracking module. The first two modules automate the tracking and scheduling of the flight crew's timetable. The second module tracks the positions of the crew and includes an *intelligent system* that handles crew pattern disruptions.

For example, crews are rearranged if one member falls ill while in a foreign port; the system will find a backup in order to prevent understaffing on the scheduled flight. The intelligent system then determines the best way to reschedule the different crew members' rosters to accommodate the sick person. When a potentially disruptive situation occurs, the intelligent system automatically draws upon the knowledge stored in the database and advises the best course of action. This might mean repositioning the crew or calling in backup staff. The crew tracking system includes a crew disruption handling module which provides decision-support capabilities in real time.

A similar Web-based system is used by Malaysia Airlines, as of summer 2003, to optimize flight crew utilization. Also called ICMS, it leverages optimization software from *ilog.com*. Its Crew Pairing Optimization (CPO) module utilizes Ilog Cplex and Ilog Solver optimization components to ensure compliance with airline regulations, trade union agreements, and company policies, to minimize the costs associated with crew accommodations and transportation, and to efficiently plan and optimize staff utilization and activities associated with long-term planning and daily operations. The Crew Duty Assignment (CDA) module provides automatic assignment of duties to all flight crews. The system considers work rules, regulatory requirements, and crew requests to produce an optimal monthly crew roster.

➡️ THE RESULTS

Despite the difficult economic times, both airlines are competing successfully in the region, and their balance sheets are better than most other airlines.

Sources: Compiled from news item at *Computerworld Singapore* (April 10, 2003), and from *ilog.com* (accessed June 9, 2003).

LESSONS LEARNED FROM THIS CASE

The opening case illustrates that a solution to complex scheduling and other problems can be enhanced with the use of an intelligent decision support system (DSS). As a matter of fact, the DSS software supported several important decisions. We also learned that decisions are supported both in operational and HRM areas. Furthermore, much of the case illustrates the concepts of optimization and quantitative analysis. Finally, the Web is playing an increasing role in facilitating the use of such systems.

This chapter is dedicated to describing computer and Web support to *managerial decision makers*. We begin by reviewing the manager's job and the nature of today's decisions, which helps explain why computerized support is needed. Then we present the concepts and methodology of the computerized decision support system for supporting individuals, groups, and whole organizations. Next, we introduce several types of intelligent systems and their role in decision support. Finally, the topic of decision support in the Web environment is addressed. A discussion of intelligent agents and their role in decision support appears in an online appendix to the chapter.

12.1 MANAGERS AND DECISION MAKING

Decisions are being made by all of us, every day. However, most major organizational decisions are made by managers. We begin with a brief description of the manager's job, of which making decisions is a major activity.

The Manager's Job
Management is a process by which organizational goals are achieved through the use of resources (people, money, energy, materials, space, time). These resources are considered to be *inputs*, and the attainment of the goals is viewed as the *output* of the process. Managers oversee this process in an attempt to optimize it.

To understand how computers support managers, it is necessary first to describe what managers do. They do many things, depending on their position in the organization, the type and size of the organization, organizational policies and culture, and the personalities of the managers themselves. Mintzberg (1973) divided the manager's roles into three categories: *interpersonal* (figurehead, leader, liaison), *informational* (monitor, disseminator, spokesperson), and *decisional* (entrepreneur, problem solver, resource allocator, and negotiator). Mintzberg and Westley (2001) also analyzed the role of decision makers in the information age.

Early information systems mainly supported informational roles. In recent years, however, information systems have grown to support all three roles. In this chapter, we are mainly interested in the support that IT can provide to *decisional* roles. We divide the manager's work, as it relates to decisional roles, into two phases. Phase I is the identification of problems and/or opportunities. Phase II is the decision of what to do about them. Online File W12.1 provides a flowchart of this process and the flow of information in it.

DECISION MAKING AND PROBLEM SOLVING. A *decision* refers to a choice made between two or more alternatives. Decisions are of diverse nature and are made continuously by both individuals and groups. The purposes of decision making in organizations can be classified into two broad categories: *problem solving* and *opportunity exploiting*. In either case managers must make decisions.

The ability to make crisp decisions was rated first in importance in a study conducted by the Harbridge House in Boston, Massachusetts. About 6,500 managers in more than 100 companies, including many large, blue-chip corporations, were asked how important it was that managers employ certain management practices. They also were asked how well, in their estimation, managers performed these practices. From a statistical distillation of these answers, Harbridge ranked "making clear-cut decisions when needed" as the *most important* of ten management practices. Ranked second in importance was "getting to the heart of the problems rather than dealing with less important issues." Most of the remaining eight management practices were related directly or indirectly to decision making. The researchers also found that only 10 percent of the managers thought management performed "very well" on any given practice, mainly due to the difficult decision-making environment. It seems that the trial-and-error method, which might have been a practical approach to decision making in the past, is too expensive or ineffective today in many instances.

Therefore, managers must learn how to use the new tools and techniques that can help them make better decisions. Many such techniques use a quantitative analysis (see the opening case) approach, and they are supported by computers. Several of the computerized decision aids are described in this chapter.

Computerized Decision Aids

The discussion on computerized decision aids here deals with four basic questions: (1) Why do managers need the support of information technology in making decisions? (2) Can the manager's job be fully automated? (3) What IT aids are available to support managers? (4): How are the information needs of managers determined? We answer the first three here; for answers to the fourth, see Online File W12.2.

WHY MANAGERS NEED THE SUPPORT OF INFORMATION TECHNOLOGY. It is very difficult to make good decisions without valid and relevant information. Information is needed for each phase and activity in the decision-making process.

Making decisions while processing information manually is growing increasingly difficult due to the following trends:

- The *number of alternatives* to be considered is ever *increasing*, due to innovations in technology, improved communication, the development of global markets, and the use of the Internet and e-business. A key to good decision making is to explore and compare many relevant alternatives. The more alternatives there are the more computer-assisted search and comparisons are needed.

- Many decisions must be made *under time pressure*. Frequently, it is not possible to manually process the needed information fast enough to be effective.

- Due to increased fluctuations and uncertainty in the decision environment, it is frequently necessary to *conduct a sophisticated analysis* to make a good decision. Such analysis usually requires the use of mathematical modeling. Processing models manually can take a very long time.

- It is often necessary to rapidly access remote information, consult with experts, or have a group decision-making session, all without large expenses. Decision makers can be in different locations and so is the information. Bringing them all together quickly and inexpensively may be a difficult task.

These trends cause difficulties in making decisions, but a computerized analysis can be of enormous help. For example, a DSS can examine numerous alternatives very quickly, provide a systematic risk analysis, can be integrated with communication systems and databases, and can be used to support group work. And, all this can be done with relatively low cost. *How* all this is accomplished will be shown later. According to Bonabeau (2003), intuition plays an important role in decision making, but it can be dangerously unreliable. Therefore one should use analytical tools such as those presented in this chapter and in Chapter 11.

 Complexity of Decisions. Decisions range from simple to very complex. Complex decisions are composed of a sequence of interrelated sub-decisions. As an example, see the decision process pursued by a pharmaceutical company, Bayer Corp., regarding developing a new drug, as shown in Online File W12.3.

CAN THE MANAGER'S JOB BE FULLY AUTOMATED?   The generic decision-making process involves specific tasks (such as forecasting consequences and evaluating alternatives). This process can be fairly lengthy, which is bothersome for a busy manager. Automation of certain tasks can save time, increase consistency, and enable better decisions to be made. Thus, the more tasks we can automate in the process, the better. A logical question that follows is this: Is it possible to completely automate the manager's job?

In general, it has been found that the job of middle managers is the most likely job to be automated. Mid-level managers make fairly routine decisions, and these can be fully automated. Managers at lower levels do not spend much time on decision making. Instead, they supervise, train, and motivate non-managers. Some of their routine decisions, such as scheduling, can be automated; other decisions that involve behavioral aspects cannot. But, even if we completely automate their decisional role, we cannot automate their jobs. Note: The Web also provides an opportunity to automate certain tasks done by *front-line* employees. (This topic is discussed in Section 12.9.) The job of top managers is the least routine and therefore the most difficult to automate.

WHAT INFORMATION TECHNOLOGIES ARE AVAILABLE TO SUPPORT MANAGERS?
In addition to discovery, communication, and collaboration tools (Chapters 4 and 11) that provide indirect support to decision making, several other information technologies have been successfully used to support managers. The Web can facilitate them all. Collectively, they are referred to as **management support systems (MSSs)** (see Aronson et al., 2004). The first of these technologies are *decision support systems*, which have been in use since the mid-1970s. They provide support primarily to analytical, quantitative types of decisions. Second, *executive (enterprise) support systems* represent a technology developed initially in the mid-1980s, mainly to support the informational roles of executives. A third technology, *group decision support systems*, supports managers and staff working in groups. A fourth technology is *intelligent systems*. These four technologies and their variants can be used independently, or they can be combined, each providing a different capability. They are frequently related to data warehousing.

A simplified presentation of such support is shown in Figure 12.1 (page 546). As Figure 12.1 shows, managers need to find, filter, and interpret information to determine potential problems or opportunities and then decide what to do about them. The figure shows the support of the various MSS tools (circled) as well as the role of a data warehouse, which was described in Chapter 11.

Several other technologies, either by themselves or when integrated with other management support technologies, can be used to support managers. One

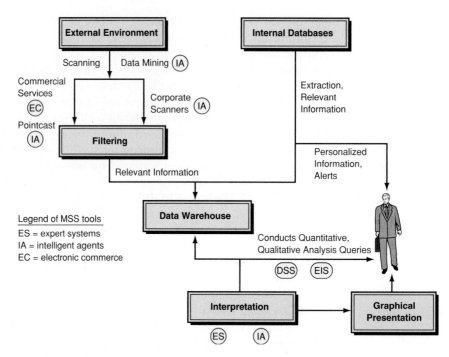

FIGURE 12.1
Computerized support for decision making.

example is the **personal information manager (PIM).** A set of tools labeled PIM is intended to help managers be more organized. A PIM can play an extremely important role in supporting several managerial tasks. Lately, the use of mobile PDA tools, such as personal Palm computers, is greatly facilitating the work of managers. Several other analytical tools are being used. For example, McGuire (2001) describes the use of such tools in the retail industry, and Bonabeau (2003) describes them in complex decision situations.

The Process of Computer-Based Decision Making

When making a decision, either organizational or personal, the decision maker goes through a fairly systematic process. Simon (1977) described the process as composed of three major phases: *intelligence, design,* and *choice.* A fourth phase, *implementation,* was added later. Simon claimed that the process is general enough so that it can be supported by *decision aids* and modeling. A conceptual presentation of the four-stage modeling process is shown in Figure 12.2, which illustrates what tasks are included in each phase. Note that there is a continuous flow of information from intelligence to design to choice (bold lines), but at any phase there may be a return to a previous phase (broken lines). For details see Stonebraker (2002).

The decision-making process starts with the *intelligence phase,* in which managers examine a situation and identify and define the problem. In the *design phase,* decision makers construct a model that simplifies the problem. This is done by making assumptions that simplify reality and by expressing the relationships among all variables. The model is then validated, and decision makers set criteria for the evaluation of alternative potential solutions that are identified. The process is repeated for each subdecision in complex situations. The output of each subdecision is an input for the main decision. The *choice phase* involves selecting a solution, which is tested "on paper." Once this proposed solution seems to be feasible, we are ready for the last phase—*implementation.* Successful

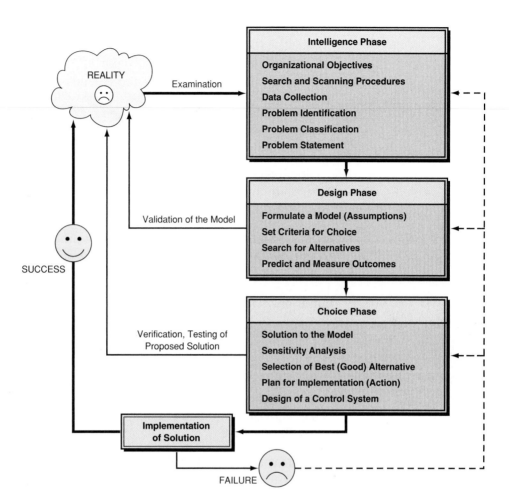

FIGURE 12.2 The process and phases in decision making/modeling.

implementation results in resolving the original problem or opportunity. Failure leads to a return to the previous phases. A computer-based decision support attempts to automate several tasks in this process, in which *modeling* is the core.

MODELING AND MODELS. A **model** (in decision making) is a *simplified representation*, or abstraction of reality. It is usually simplified because reality is too complex to copy exactly, and because much of its complexity is actually irrelevant to a specific problem. With modeling, one can perform virtual experiments and an analysis on a model of reality, rather than on reality itself. The benefits of modeling in decision making are:

1. The cost of virtual experimentation is much lower than the cost of experimentation conducted with a real system.
2. Models allow for the simulated compression of time. Years of operation can be simulated in seconds of computer time.
3. Manipulating the model (by changing variables) is much easier than manipulating the real system. Experimentation is therefore easier to conduct, and it does not interfere with the daily operation of the organization.
4. The cost of making mistakes during a real trial-and-error experiment is much lower than when models are used in virtual experimentation.

5. Today's environment holds considerable uncertainty. Modeling allows a manager to better deal with the uncertainty by introducing many "what-ifs" and calculating the risks involved in specific actions.

6. Mathematical models allow the analysis and comparison of a very large, sometimes near-infinite number of possible alternative solutions. With today's advanced technology and communications, managers frequently have a large number of alternatives from which to choose.

7. Models enhance and reinforce learning and support training.

Representation by models can be done at various degrees of abstraction. Models are thus classified into four groups according to their degree of abstraction: iconic, analog, mathematical, and mental. Brief descriptions follow.

ICONIC (SCALE) MODELS. An *iconic model*—the least abstract model—is a physical replica of a system, usually based on a *smaller scale* from the original. Iconic models may appear to scale in three dimensions, such as models of an airplane, car, bridge, or production line. Photographs are another type of iconic model, but in only two dimensions.

ANALOG MODELS. An *analog model*, in contrast to an iconic model, does not look like the real system but behaves like it. An analog model could be a physical model, but the *shape* of the model differs from that of the actual system. Some examples include organizational charts that depict structure, authority, and responsibility relationships; maps where different colors represent water or mountains; stock charts; blueprints of a machine or a house; and a thermometer.

MATHEMATICAL (QUANTITATIVE) MODELS. The complexity of relationships in many systems cannot conveniently be represented iconically or analogically, or such representations and the required experimentations may be cumbersome. A more abstract model is possible with the aid of mathematics. Most DSS analysis is executed numerically using mathematical or other quantitative models.

Mathematical models are composed of three types of variables (decision, uncontrollable, and result) and the relationships among them. These are shown in Online File W12.4. With recent advances in computer graphics, there is an increased tendency to use iconic and analog models to complement mathematical modeling in decision support systems.

MENTAL MODELS. In addition to the three explicit models described above, people frequently use a behavioral mental model. A *mental model* provides a subjective description of how a person thinks about a situation. The model includes beliefs, assumptions, relationships, and flows of work as perceived by an individual. For example, a manager's mental model might say that it is better to promote older workers than younger ones and that such a policy would be preferred by most employees. Mental models are extremely useful in situations where it is necessary to determine which information is important.

Developing a mental model is usually the first step in modeling. Once people perceive a situation, they may then model it more precisely using another type of model. Mental models may frequently change, so it is difficult to document them. They are important not only for decision making, but also for human–computer interaction (see Saxby et al., 2000).

A Framework for Computerized Decision Analysis

Gorry and Scott-Morton (1971) proposed a framework for decision support, based on the combined work of Simon (1977) and Anthony (1965). The first half of the framework is based on Simon's idea that decision-making processes fall along a continuum that ranges from highly structured (sometimes referred to as *programmed*) to highly unstructured (*nonprogrammed*) decisions. *Structured* processes refer to routine and repetitive problems for which standard solutions exist. *Unstructured* processes are "fuzzy," complex problems for which there are no cut-and-dried solutions.

In a structured problem, the intelligence, design, and choice are all structured, and the procedures for obtaining the best solution are known. Whether the solution means finding an appropriate inventory level or deciding on an optimal investment strategy, the solution's criteria are clearly defined. They are frequently cost minimization or profit maximization.

In an unstructured problem, *none* of the three phases is structured, and human intuition is frequently the basis for decision making. Typical unstructured problems include planning new services to be offered, hiring an executive, or choosing a set of research and development projects for next year.

Semistructured problems, in which only some of the phases are structured, require a combination of standard solution procedures and individual judgment. Examples of semistructured problems include trading bonds, setting marketing budgets for consumer products, and performing capital acquisition analysis. Here, a DSS is most suitable. It can improve the quality of the information on which the decision is based (and consequently the quality of the decision) by providing not only a single solution but also a range of what-if scenarios.

The second half of the decision support framework is based upon Anthony's taxonomy (1965). It defines three broad categories that encompass managerial activities: (1) *strategic planning*—the long-range goals and policies for resource allocation; (2) *management control*—the acquisition and efficient utilization of resources in the accomplishment of organizational goals; and (3) *operational control*—the efficient and effective execution of specific tasks. Anthony's and Simon's taxonomies can be combined in a nine-cell decision support framework (see Online File W12.5).

COMPUTER SUPPORT FOR STRUCTURED DECISIONS. Structured and some semistructured decisions, especially of the operational and managerial control type, have been supported by computers since the 1950s. Decisions of this type are made in all functional areas, especially in finance and operations management.

Problems that are encountered fairly often have a high level of structure. It is therefore possible to abstract, analyze, and classify them into standard classes. For example, a "make-or-buy" decision belongs to this category. Other examples are capital budgeting (e.g., replacement of equipment), allocation of resources, distribution of merchandise, and some inventory control decisions. For each standard class, a prescribed solution was developed through the use of mathematical formulas. This approach is called *management science* or *operations research*, and it is also executed with the aid of computers.

Management Science. The *management science* approach takes the view that managers can follow a fairly systematic process for solving problems. Therefore, it is possible to use a scientific approach to managerial decision making. This approach, which also centers on modeling, is presented in Online File W12.6. For a list of management science problems and tools see Online File W12.7. Management science frequently attempts to find the best possible solution, an approach known as **optimization**.

12.2 DECISION SUPPORT SYSTEMS

DSS Concepts   Broadly defined, a **decision support system (DSS)** is a computer-based information system that combines models and data in an attempt to solve semi-structured and some unstructured problems with extensive user involvement. But the term decision support system (DSS), like the terms MIS and MSS, means different things to different people. DSSs can be viewed as an *approach* or a *philosophy* rather than a precise methodology. However, a DSS does have certain recognized characteristics, which we will present later. First, let us look at a classical case of a successfully implemented DSS, which occurred long ago, yet the scenario is typical, as shown in *IT at Work 12.1*.

The case demonstrates some of the major characteristics of a DSS. The risk analysis performed first was based on the decision maker's initial definition of the situation, using a management science approach. Then, the executive vice president, using his experience, judgment, and intuition, felt that the model should be modified. The initial model, although mathematically correct, was incomplete. With a regular simulation system, a modification of the computer program would have taken a long time, but the DSS provided a very quick analysis. Furthermore, the DSS was flexible and responsive enough to allow managerial intuition and judgment to be incorporated into the analysis.

Many companies are turning to DSSs to improve decision making. Reasons cited by managers for the increasing use of DSSs include the following: New and accurate information was needed; information was needed fast; and tracking the company's numerous business operations was increasingly difficult. Or, the company was operating in an unstable economy; it faced increasing foreign and domestic competition; the company's existing computer system did not properly support the objectives of increasing efficiency, profitability, and entry

IT at Work 12.1
USING A DSS TO DETERMINE RISK

An oil and minerals corporation in Houston, Texas was evaluating a proposed joint venture with a petro-chemicals company to develop a chemical plant. Houston's executive vice president responsible for the decision wanted analysis of the risks involved in areas of supplies, demand, and prices. Bob Sampson, manager of planning and administration, and his staff built a DSS in a few days by means of a specialized planning language. The results strongly suggested that the project should be accepted.

Then came the real test. Although the executive vice president accepted the validity and value of the results, he was worried about the potential downside risk of the project, the chance of a catastrophic outcome. Sampson explains that the executive vice president said something like this: "I realize the amount of work you have already done,

and I am 99 percent confident of it. But I would like to see this in a different light. I know we are short of time and we have to get back to our partners with our yes or no decision."

Sampson replied that the executive could have the risk analysis he needed in less than one hour. As Sampson explained, "Within 20 minutes, there in the executive board-room, we were reviewing the results of his what-if questions. Those results led to the eventual dismissal of the project, which we otherwise would probably have accepted."

Source: Information provided to author by Comshare Corporation (now Geac Computer Corp.).

For Further Exploration: What were the benefits of the DSS? Why might it have reversed the initial decision?

into profitable markets. Other reasons include: the IS department was unable to address the diversity of the company's needs or management's ad-hoc inquiries, and business analysis functions were not inherent within the existing systems. For a brief history of DSS, see Power (2002).

In many organizations that have adopted a DSS, the conventional information systems, which were built for the purpose of supporting transaction processing, were *not sufficient* to support several of the company's critical response activities, described in Chapter 1, especially those that require fast and/or complex decision making. A DSS, on the other hand, can do just that. (See Carlsson and Turban, 2002.)

Another reason for the development of DSS is the *end-user computing movement*. With the exception of large-scale DSSs, end users can build systems themselves, using DSS development tools such as Excel.

Characteristics and Capabilities of DSSs

Because there is no consensus on exactly what constitutes a DSS, there obviously is no agreement on the characteristics and capabilities of DSSs. However, most DSSs at least have some of the attributes shown in Table 12.1. DSSs also employ mathematical models and have a related, special capability, known as sensitivity analysis.

SENSITIVITY ANALYSIS: "WHAT-IF" AND GOAL SEEKING.   Sensitivity analysis is the study of the impact that changes in one (or more) parts of a model have on other parts. Usually, we check the impact that changes in input variables have on result variables.

Sensitivity analysis is extremely valuable in DSSs because it makes the system flexible and adaptable to changing conditions and to the varying requirements of different decision-making situations. It allows users to enter their own data, including the most pessimistic data (worst scenario) and to view how systems will behave under varying circumstances. It provides a better understanding of the model and the problem it purports to describe. It may increase the users' confidence in the model, especially when the model is not so sensitive to changes. A *sensitive model* means that small changes in conditions dictate a

---

TABLE 12.1 Capabilities of a DSS

A DSS provides support for decision makers at all management levels, whether individuals or groups, mainly in semistructured and unstructured situations, by bringing together human judgment and objective information.

A DSS supports several interdependent and/or sequential decisions.

A DSS supports all phases of the decision-making process—intelligence, design, choice, and implementation—as well as a variety of decision-making processes and styles.

A DSS is adaptable by the user over time to deal with changing conditions.

A DSS is easy to construct and use in many cases.

A DSS promotes learning, which leads to new demands and refinement of the current application, which leads to additional learning, and so forth.

A DSS usually utilizes quantitative models (standard and/or custom made).

Advanced DSSs are equipped with a knowledge management component that allows the efficient and effective solution of very complex problems.

A DSS can be disseminated for use via the Web.

A DSS allows the easy execution of *sensitivity analyses*.

different solution. In a *nonsensitive model,* changes in conditions do not significantly change the recommended solution. This means that the chances for a solution to succeed are very high. Two popular types of sensitivity analyses are *what-if* and *goal seeking* (see Online File W12.8).

Structure and Components of DSS

Every DSS consists of at least data management, model management components, user interface, and end users. A few advanced DSSs also contain a knowledge management component. What does each component (subsystem) consist of?

DATA MANAGEMENT SUBSYSTEM.   A DSS data management subsystem is similar to any other data management system. It contains all the data that flow from several sources and that usually are *extracted* prior to their entry into a DSS database or a data warehouse. In some DSSs, there is no separate database, and data are entered into the DSS model as needed (i.e., as soon as they are collected by sensors, as in the ChevronTexaco case in Chapter 7).

MODEL MANAGEMENT SUBSYSTEM.   A model management subsystem contains completed models and the building blocks necessary to develop DSS applications. This includes standard software with financial, statistical, management science, or other quantitative models. An example is Excel, with its many mathematical and statistical functions. A model management subsystem also contains all the custom models written for the specific DSS. These models provide the system's analytical capabilities. Also included is a **model-based management system (MBMS)** whose role is analogous to that of a DBMS. (See Technology Guide 3.) The major functions (capabilities) of an MBMS are shown in Online File W12.9.

The model base may contain standard models (such as financial or management science) and/or customized models as illustrated in *IT at Work 12.2.*

THE USER INTERFACE.   The term *user interface* covers all aspects of the communications between a user and the DSS. Some DSS experts feel that the user interface is the most important DSS component because much of the power, flexibility, and ease of use of the DSS are derived from this component. For example, the ease of use of the interface in the Guinness DSS enables, and encourages, managers and salespeople to use the system. Most interfaces today are Web-based and some are supplemented by voice.

The user interface subsystem may be managed by software called *user interface management system (UIMS),* which is functionally analogous to the DBMS.

THE USERS.   The person faced with the problem or decision that the DSS is designed to support is referred to as the *user,* the *manager,* or the *decision maker.*

The user is considered to be a part of the system. Researchers assert that some of the unique contributions of DSSs are derived from the extensive interaction between the computer and the decision maker. A DSS has two broad classes of users: managers, and staff specialists (such as financial analysts, production planners, and market researchers).

DSS Intermediaries.   When managers utilize a DSS, they may use it via an intermediary person who performs the analysis and reports the results. However, with Web-based systems, the use of DSSs becomes easier. Managers can use the Web-based system by themselves, especially when supported by an intelligent knowledge component.

IT at Work 12.2

WEB-BASED DECISION SUPPORT SYSTEM
HELPS A BREWERY TO COMPETE

Guinness Import Co., a U.S. subsidiary of U.K.'s Guinness Ltd. (*guinness.com*), needed a decision support system for (1) executives, (2) salespeople, and (3) analysts. The company did not want three separate systems. Using InfoAdvisor (from Platinum Technology Inc., now part of Computer Associates, *cai.com*), a client/server DSS was constructed. In the past, if manager Diane Goldman wanted to look at sales trends, it was necessary to ask an analyst to download data from the mainframe and then use a spreadsheet to compute the trend. This took up to a day and was error-prone. Now, when Diane Goldman needs such information she queries the DSS herself and gets an answer in a few minutes. Furthermore, she can quickly analyze the data in different ways. Over 100 salespeople keep track of sales and can do similar analyses, from anywhere, using a remote Internet access.

To expedite the implementation of the system, highly skilled users in each department taught others how to use the DSS. The DSS helped to increase productivity of the employees. This improved productivity enables the company to compete against large companies such as Anheuser-Busch, as well as against microbrewers. The system reduced the salespeople's paperwork load by about one day each month. For 100 salespeople, this means 1,200 extra days a year to sell. Corporate financial and marketing analysts are also using the system to make better decisions. As a result, sales increased by 20 percent every year since the system was installed.

Sources: Compiled from *Computerworld* (July 7, 1997); *platinum.com* (2000); and *dmreview.com* (2001).

For Further Exploration: What can a DSS do that other computer programs cannot do for this company?

KNOWLEDGE-BASED SUBSYSTEMS. Many unstructured and semistructured problems are so complex that they require expertise for their solutions. Such expertise can be provided by a knowledge-based system, such as an expert system. Therefore, the more advanced DSSs are equipped with a component called a *knowledge-based* (or *an intelligent*) *subsystem.* Such a component can provide the required expertise for solving some aspects of the problem, or provide knowledge that can enhance the operation of the other DSS components.

The knowledge component consists of one or more expert (or other intelligent) systems, or it draws expertise from the *organizational knowledge base* (see Chapter 10).

A DSS that includes such a component is referred to as an *intelligent DSS*, a *DSS/ES*, or a *knowledge-based DSS (KBDSS).* An example of a KBDSS is in the area of estimation and pricing in construction. It is a complex process that requires the use of models as well as judgmental factors. The KBDSS includes a knowledge management subsystem with 200 rules incorporated with the computational models. (For details, see Kingsman and deSouza, 1997.)

How DSS Works   The DSS components (see Figure 12.3, page 554) are all software. They are housed in a computer and can be facilitated by additional software (such as multimedia). Tools like Excel include some of the components and therefore can be used for DSS construction by end users.

The figure also illustrates how the DSS works. As you recall from Chapter 11, the DSS users gets their data from the data warehouse, databases, and other data sources. When a user has a problem, it is evaluated by the processes described in Figures 12.1 and 12.2. A DSS system is then constructed. Data are entered from the sources on the left side and the models on the right side in Figure 12.3. Knowledge can be also tapped from the corporate knowledge base. As more

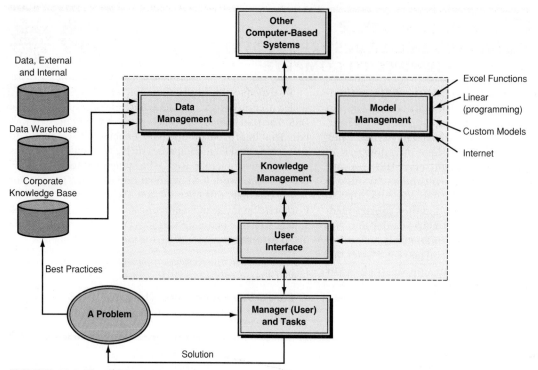

FIGURE 12.3 The DSS and its computing environment. Conceptual model of a DSS shows four main software components and their relationships with other systems.

problems are solved, more knowledge is accumulated in the organizational knowledge base. For an application of DSS, see Online Minicase W12.1.

The DSS methodology just described was designed initially to support individual decision makers. However, most organizational decisions are made by groups, such as an executive committee. Next we see how IT can support such situations.

12.3 GROUP DECISION SUPPORT SYSTEMS

Decision making is frequently a shared process. For example, meetings among groups of managers from different areas are an essential element for reaching consensus. The group may be involved in making a decision or in a decision-related task, like creating a short list of acceptable alternatives or deciding on criteria for accepting an alternative. When a decision-making group is supported electronically, the support is referred to as *group decision support.* Two types of groups are considered: a one-room group whose members are in one place (e.g., a meeting room), and a **virtual group,** whose members are in different locations.

A **group decision support system (GDSS)** is an interactive computer-based system that facilitates the solution of semistructured and unstructured problems when made by a group of decision makers. The objective of a GDSS is to support the *process* of arriving at a decision. Important characteristics of a GDSS, according to DeSanctis and Gallupe (1987), are shown in Online File W12.10. These characteristics can negate some of the dysfunctions of group processes described in Chapter 4, Table 4.2 (page 145).

IT *at Work* 12.3
VIRTUAL MEETINGS AT THE WORLD ECONOMIC FORUM

The World Economic Forum (WEF, at *weforum.org*) is a consortium of top business, government, academic, and media leaders from virtually every country in the world. WEF's mission is to foster international understanding. Until 1998, the members conferred privately or debated global issues only at the forum's annual meeting in Davos, Switzerland, and at regional summits. Follow-up was difficult because of the members' geographic dispersion and conflicting schedules.

A WEF online strategy and operations task force developed a collaborative computing system to allow secure communication among members, making the nonprofit group more effective in its mission. Now WEF is making faster progress toward solutions for the global problems it studies. Called the World Electronic Community (WELCOM), the GDSS and its complementary videoconferencing system give members a secure channel through which to send e-mail, read reports available in a WEF library, and communicate in point-to-point or multipoint videoconferences. Forum members now hold real-time discussions and briefings on pressing issues and milestones, such as, for example, when the 2003 Iraqi War ended.

The WELCOM system was designed with a graphical user interface (GUI) to make it easily accessible to inexpe-
rienced computer users, because many WEF members might not be computer-literate or proficient typists. The forum also set up "concierge services," based in Boston, Singapore, and Geneva, for technical support and to arrange videoconferences and virtual meetings. To handle any time/any place meetings, members can access recorded forum events and discussions that they may have missed, as well as an extensive library, which is one of the most heavily used features of the system. The site also operates a knowledge base ("knowledge navigator") and media center.

As of 2001 the system has been completely on the Web. With *Webcasting*, all sessions of the annual meetings can be viewed in real time. The virtual meetings are done in a secured environment, and private chat rooms are also available.

Sources: Compiled from *weforum.org* (accessed June 29, 2003) and *PC Week* (August 17, 1998).

For Further Exploration: Check the Netmeeting and Netshow products of Microsoft, and see how their capabilities facilitate the WEF virtual meetings. How does an environment such as *eroom* at *documentum.com* support the process of group decision making, if at all?

The first generation of GDSSs was designed to support face-to-face meetings in what is called a **decision room.** Such a GDSS is described in Online File W12.11.

Some Applications of GDSSs

An increasing number of companies are using GDSSs, especially when virtual groups are involved. One example is the Internal Revenue Service, which used a one-room GDSS to implement its quality-improvement programs based on the participation of a number of its quality teams. The GDSS was helpful in identifying problems, generating and evaluating ideas, and developing and implementing solutions. Another example is the European automobile industry, which used a one-room GDSS to examine the competitive automotive business environment and make ten-year forecasts, needed for strategic planning. Atkins et al. (2003) report on successful application at the U.S. Air Force. A virtual GDSS application is described in *IT at Work 12.3.*

12.4 ENTERPRISE AND EXECUTIVE DECISION SUPPORT SYSTEMS

Two types of enterprise decision support systems are described here: systems that support whole organizational tasks and systems that support decisions made by top-level managers and executives.

Organizational Decision Support System

The term **organizational decision support system (ODSS)** was first defined by Hackathorn and Keen (1981), who discussed three levels of decision support: individual, group, and organization. They maintained that computer-based systems can be developed to provide decision support for *each* of these levels. They defined an ODSS as one that focuses on an organizational task or activity involving a *sequence* of operations and decision makers, such as developing a divisional marketing plan or doing capital budgeting. Each individual's activities must mesh closely with other people's work. The computer support was primarily seen as a vehicle for improving communication and coordination, in addition to problem solving.

Some decision support systems provide support throughout large and complex organizations (see Carter et al., 1992). A major benefit of such systems is that many DSS users become familiar with computers, analytical techniques, and decision supports, as illustrated in Online File W12.12.

The major characteristics of an ODSS are: (1) it affects several organizational units or corporate problems, (2) it cuts across organizational functions or hierarchical layers, and (3) it involves computer-based technologies and usually also communications technologies. Also, an ODSS often interacts or integrates with enterprisewide information systems such as executive support systems.

For further information on a very-large-scale ODSS, see El Sharif and El Sawy (1988) and Carter et al. (1992).

Executive Information (Support) Systems

The majority of personal DSSs support the work of professionals and middle-level managers. Organizational DSSs provide support primarily to planners, analysts, researchers, or to some managers. For a DSS to be used by top managers it must meet the executives' needs. An executive information system (EIS), also known as an executive support system (ESS), is a technology designed in response to the specific needs of executives, as shown in the *IT at Work 12.4.*

The terms *executive information system* and *executive support system* mean different things to different people, though they are sometimes used interchangeably. The following definitions, based on Rockart and DeLong (1988), distinguish between EIS and ESS:

● **Executive information system (EIS).** An EIS is a computer-based system that serves the information needs of top executives. It provides rapid access to timely information and direct access to management reports. An EIS is very user friendly, is supported by graphics, and provides the capabilities of *exception reporting* (reporting of only the results that deviate from a set standard) and *drill down* (investigating information in increasing detail). It is also easily connected with online information services and electronic mail.

● **Executive support system (ESS).** An ESS is a comprehensive support system that goes beyond EIS to include analysis support, communications, office automation, and intelligence support.

Capabilities and Characteristics of ESSs

Executive support systems vary in their capabilities and benefits (e.g., see Singh et al., 2002). Capabilities common to many ESSs are summarized in Table 12.2. One of these capabilities, the CSF, is measured by key performance indicators (KPIs), as shown in Online File W12.14.

IT at Work 12.4
AN EXECUTIVE SUPPORT SYSTEM AT HERTZ CORPORATION

Hertz (*hertz.com*), the world's largest car rental company (a subsidiary of Ford Motor Company), competes against dozens of companies in hundreds of locations worldwide. Several marketing decisions must be made almost instantaneously (such as whether to follow a competitor's price discount). Marketing decisions are decentralized and are based on information about cities, climates, holidays, business cycles, tourist activities, past promotions, competitors' actions, and customer behavior. The amount of such information is huge, and the only way to process it in a timely manner is to use a computer. The problem faced by Hertz was how to make such information accessible to employees at each branch and how to help them use it properly.

To address its decision-making needs, Hertz developed a mainframe DSS to allow fast routine analysis by executives and branch managers. But if a manager had a question, or or a non-routine analysis was needed, he she had to go through a staff assistant to get an answer, which made the process lengthy and cumbersome. The need for a better system was obvious.

Therefore, the following year Hertz decided to add an ESS, a PC-based system used as a companion to the DSS. The combined system gave executives the tools to analyze the mountains of stored information and make real-time decisions without the help of assistants. The system is extremely user-friendly and is maintained by the marketing staff. Since its assimilation into the corporate culture conformed to the manner in which Hertz executives were used to working, implementation was easy.

With the ESS, executives can manipulate and refine data to be more meaningful and strategically significant to them. The ESS allows executives to draw information from the mainframe, store the needed data on their own PCs, and perform a DSS-type analysis without tying up valuable mainframe time. Hertz managers feel that the ESS creates synergy in decision making. It triggers questions, a greater influx of creative ideas, and more cost-effective marketing decisions.

In the late 1990s, the system was integrated with a data warehouse and connected to the corporate intranets and the Internet. Today local managers use the Web to find competitors' prices, in real time, and by using supply-demand model, they can assess the impact of price changes on the demand for cars. (This model is similar to the price setting model described in *A Closer Look 2.2*, in Chapter 2.)

Sources: Compiled from O'Leary, (1990) and from *hertz.com* (1998).

For Further Exploration: Why was the DSS insufficient by itself, and how did the addition of the ESS make it effective?

TABLE 12.2 Capabilities of an ESS

Capability	Description
Drill down	Ability to go to details at several levels; can be done by a series of menus or by direct queries (using intelligent agents and natural language processing).
Critical success factors (CSFs)	The factors most critical for the success of business. These can be organizational, industry, departmental, etc.
Key performance indicators (KPIs)	The specific measures of CSFs. (Examples are provided in *Online File W12.13*).
Status access	The latest data available on KPIs or some other metric, ideally in real time.
Trend analysis	Short-, medium-, and long-term trend of KPIs or metrics are projected using forecasting methods.
Ad-hoc analysis	Make analysis any time, and with any desired factors and relationships.
Exception reporting	Based on the concept of management by exception, reports highlight deviations larger than certain thresholds. Reports may include only deviations.

ESS TYPES. ESSs can be enhanced with multidimensional analysis and presentation, friendly data access, user-friendly graphical interface, imaging capabilities, intranet and Internet access, e-mail, and modeling. These can be helpful to many executives. There are two types of ESSs: (1) those designed especially to support top executives and (2) those intended to serve a wider community of users. The latter type of ESS applications support professional decision makers throughout the enterprise. For this reason, some people define the acronym ESS to mean *enterprise support systems*, or *everybody's support systems*. Most Web-based system and enterprise portals are of this nature. Only a few companies have a top executive–only ESS. However, in the enterprise system, some data can be accessed by executives only.

Some of the capabilities discussed in this section are now part of a business intelligence product, as shown in Figure 12.4.

INTELLIGENT ESS. In order to save the executive's time in conducting a drill down, finding exceptions, or identifying trends, an *intelligent ESS* has been

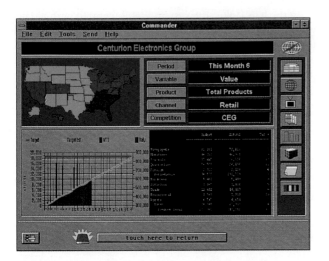

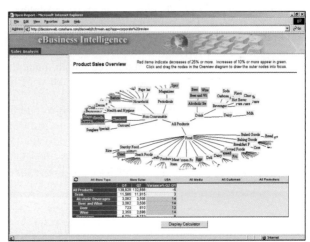

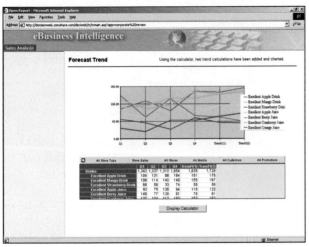

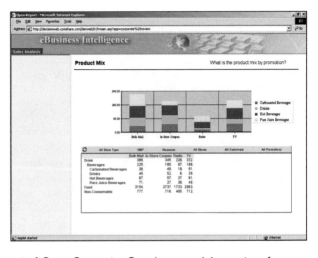

FIGURE 12.4 Sample screens from Comshare Decision (now part of Geac Computer Corp.)—a modular system for generating a business intelligence report.

developed. Automating these activities not only saves time but also ensures that the executive will not miss any important indications in a large amount of data. Intelligent ESSs may include an intelligent agent for alerting management to exceptions. For further details, see King and O'Leary (1996) and Liu et al. (2000).

INTEGRATION WITH DSS. Executive support systems are especially useful in identifying problems and opportunities. Such identification can be facilitated by an intelligent component. In addition, it is necessary to do something if a problem or an opportunity is discovered. Therefore, many software vendors provide ESS/DSS integrated tools that are sold as part of a business intelligence suite.

Enterprise Decision Simulator

An interesting example of enterprise decision support is the corporate war room. This concept has been used by the military for a long time, and it has now been transformed by SAP for use in industry, as described in *A Closer Look* 12.1 (page 560).

DSS Failures

Over the years there have been many cases of failures of all types of decision support systems. There are multiple reasons for such failures, ranging from human factors to software glitches. Here are two examples:

1. The ill-fated Challeger Shuttle mission was partially attributed to a flawed GDSS (see *http://frontpage/hypermall.com/jforrest/challenger/challenger_sts.htm*). NASA used a mismanaged GDSS session in which anonymity was not allowed and other procedures were violated.

2. In an international congress on airports, failures in Denver, Hong Kong, and Malaysia airports were analyzed (*onera.fr/congress/jso2000airport*). Several DSS applications did not work as intended for reasons such as poor planning and inappropriate models.

Brezillon and Pomerol (1997) describe some failures of intelligent DSSs. Also, Briggs and Arnoff (2002) conducted a comprehensive evaluation of a DSS failure and identified areas that could create system failures. Most DSS failures can be eliminated by using appropriate planning, collaboration, and management procedures. Also, attaching an intelligent system makes DSSs more useful and less likely to fail.

12.5 INTELLIGENT SUPPORT SYSTEMS: THE BASICS

Intelligent systems is a term that describes the various commercial applications of artificial intelligence (AI).

Artificial Intelligence and Intelligent Behavior

Most experts (see Cawsey, 1998, and Russell and Norvig, 2002) agree that **artificial intelligence (AI)** is concerned with two basic ideas. First, it involves studying the thought processes of humans; second, it deals with representing those processes via machines (computers, robots, and so on). Following 9/11, AI has been getting lots of attention, due to its capability to assist in fighting terrorism (Kahn, 2002). Another development that helps AI to get attention is the large number of intelligent devices in the marketplace (Rivlin, 2002).

One well-publicized definition of AI is "behavior by a machine that, if performed by a human being, would be considered *intelligent*." Let us explore the

A CLOSER LOOK
12.1 THE MANAGEMENT COCKPIT

The Management Cockpit (*management-cockpit.com*) is a strategic management room that enables managers to pilot their businesses better. The aim is to create an environment that encourages more efficient management meetings and boosts team performance via effective communication. To help achieve this, key performance indicators and information relating to critical success factors are displayed graphically on the walls of a meeting room (see photo).

performance; the Blue Wall, the performance of internal processes and employees; and the White Wall, the status of strategic projects. The Flight Deck, a six-screen high-end PC, enables executives to drill down to detailed information.

Board members and other executives can hold meetings in this room. Typically, managers will also meet there with their comptrollers to discuss current business issues. For this purpose, the Management Cockpit can implement

The Management Cockpit supports top-level decision-makers by letting them concentrate on the essentials and conduct "what-if" scenarios. The cockpit-like arrangement of instrument panels and displays enables top managers to recognize whether corporate structures need changing and to grasp how all the different factors interrelate.

Executives can call up this information on their laptops, of course, but a key element of the concept is the Management Cockpit Room. There, on the four walls—Black, Red, Blue, and White—ergonomically designed graphics depict performance as reflected in mission-critical factors. The Black Wall shows the principal success factors and financial indicators; the Red Wall, market

various scenarios. A major advantage of the Management Cockpit is that it provides a common basis for information and communication. At the same time, it supports efforts to translate a corporate strategy into concrete activities by identifying performance indicators, in addition to permitting appropriate monitoring.

The Cockpit environment is integrated with SAP's ERP products and reporting systems. External information can be easily imported to the room to allow competitive analysis.

Sources: Compiled from *management-cockpit.com, sap.com,* and from *origin-it.com.*

meaning of the term *intelligent behavior*. The following capabilities are considered to be signs of intelligence: learning or understanding from experience, making sense of ambiguous or contradictory messages, and responding quickly and successfully to a new situation. Using reasoning to solve problems and direct actions effectively is another indicator of intelligence. Some other indicators include dealing with complex situations, and understanding and inferring in ordinary, rational ways. Applying knowledge to manipulate the environment and recognizing the relative importance of different elements in a situation complete our list.

AI's ultimate goal is to build machines that will mimic human intelligence. So far, current intelligent systems, exemplified in commercial AI products, are far from exhibiting any significant intelligence. Nevertheless, they are getting better with the passage of time, and are currently useful in making faster, more efficient, and cheaper many cumbersome tasks that require some human intelligence.

An interesting test to determine whether a computer exhibits intelligent behavior was designed by Alan Turing, a British AI pioneer. According to the **Turing test,** a computer could be considered "smart" only when a human interviewer, conversing with both an unseen human being and an unseen computer, cannot determine which is which.

So far we have concentrated on the concept of *intelligence*. According to another definition, artificial intelligence is the branch of computer science that deals with ways of representing *knowledge*. It uses symbols rather than numbers, and *heuristics*, or rules of thumb, rather than algorithms for processing information.

KNOWLEDGE AND AI. Although a computer cannot have experiences or study and learn as a human can, it can use knowledge given to it by human experts. Such knowledge consists of facts, concepts, theories, heuristic methods, procedures, and relationships. Knowledge is also information organized and analyzed to make it *understandable* and *applicable* to problem solving or decision making. The collection of knowledge related to a specific problem (or an opportunity) to be used in an intelligent system is organized and stored in a **knowledge base.** The collection of knowledge related to the operation of an organization is called an **organizational knowledge base** (see Chapter 10).

Comparing Artificial and Natural Intelligence

The potential value of AI can be better understood by contrasting it with natural (human) intelligence. AI has several important commercial advantages over natural intelligence, but also some limitations, as shown in Table 12.3 (page 562).

Benefits of AI

Despite their limitations, AI applications can be extremely valuable. They can make computers easier to use and can make knowledge more widely available. One major potential benefit of AI is that it significantly increases the speed and consistency of some problem-solving procedures, including those problems that are difficult to solve by conventional computing and those that have incomplete or unclear data. Another benefit of AI is that it significantly increases the productivity of performing many tasks; it helps in handling information overload by summarizing or interpreting information and by assisting in searching through large amounts of data.

TABLE 12.3 Comparison of the Capabilities of Natural vs. Artificial Intelligence

Capabilities	Natural Intelligence	Artificial Intelligence
Preservation of knowledge	Perishable from an organizational point of view	Permanent
Duplication and dissemination of knowledge	Difficult, expensive, takes time	Easy, fast, and inexpensive once knowledge is in a computer
Total cost of knowledge	Can be erratic and inconsistent Incomplete at times	Consistent and thorough
Documentability of process and knowledge	Difficult, expensive	Fairly easy, inexpensive
Creativity	Can be very high	Low; uninspired
Use of sensory experiences	Direct and rich in possibilities	Must be interpreted first; limited
Recognizing patterns and relationships	Fast, easy to explain	Machine learning still not as good as people in most cases, but in some cases can do better than people
Reasoning	Making use of wide context of experiences	Good only in narrow, focused, and stable domains

Conventional versus AI Computing

Conventional computer programs are based on algorithms. An *algorithm* is a mathematical formula or sequential procedure that leads to a solution. It is converted into a computer program that tells the computer exactly what operations to carry out. The algorithm then uses data such as numbers, letters, or words to solve problems. AI software is using knowledge and heuristics instead of, or along with, algorithms.

In addition, AI software is based on **symbolic processing** of knowledge. In AI, a symbol is a letter, word, or number that represents objects, processes, and their relationships. Objects can be people, things, ideas, concepts, events, or statements of fact. Using symbols, it is possible to create a knowledge base that contains facts, concepts, and the relationships that exist among them. Then various processes can be used to manipulate the symbols in order to generate advice or a recommendation for solving problems.

The major differences between AI computing and conventional computing are shown in Online File W12.14.

DOES A COMPUTER REALLY THINK? Knowledge bases and search techniques certainly make computers more useful, but can they really make computers more intelligent? The fact that most AI programs are implemented by search and pattern-matching techniques leads to the conclusion that *computers are not really intelligent.* You give the computer a lot of information and some guidelines about how to use this information, and the computer can then come up with a solution. But all it does is test the various alternatives and attempt to find some combination that meets the designated criteria. The computer appears to be "thinking" and often gives a satisfactory solution. But Dreyfus and Dreyfus (1988) feel that the public is being misled about AI, whose usefulness is overblown and whose goals are unrealistic. They claim, and we agree, that the human mind is just too complex to duplicate. *Computers certainly cannot think,* but they can be very useful for increasing our productivity. This is done by several commercial AI technologies.

TABLE 12.4 Commercial AI Techniques	
Name	**Short Description**
Expert system (ES)	Computerized advisory systems usually based on rules. (See Section 12.6.)
Natural language processing (NLP)	Enables computers to recognize and even understand human languages. (See Section 12.7.)
Speech understanding	Enables computers to recognize words and understand short voice sentences. (See Section 12.7.)
Robotic and sensory systems	Programmable combination of mechanical and computer programs. Recognize their environments via sensors.
Computer vision and scene recognition	Enable computers to interpret the content of pictures captured by cameras.
Machine learning	Enables computers to interpret the content of pictures captured by sensors (see next three techniques).
Handwriting recognition	Enables computers to recognize characters (letters, digits) written by hand.
Neural computing (networks)	Using massive parallel processing, able to recognize patterns in large amount of data. (See Section 12.7.)
Fuzzy logic	Enables computers to reason with partial information. (See Section 12.7.)
Intelligent agents	Software programs that perform tasks for a human or machine master. (See Online Appendix W12.1.)
Semantic Web	An intelligent software program that "understands" content of Web pages. (See Section 12.7.)

Commercial AI Technologies

The development of machines that exhibit intelligent characteristics draws upon several sciences and technologies, ranging from linguistics to mathematics (see the roots of the tree in Online File W12.15.) Artificial intelligence itself is not a commercial field; it is a collection of concepts and ideas that are appropriate for research but cannot be marketed. However, AI provides the scientific foundation for several commercial technologies.

The major intelligent systems are: expert systems, natural language processing, speech understanding, robotics and sensory systems, fuzzy logic, neural computing, computer vision and scene recognition, and intelligent computer-aided instruction. In addition, a combination of two or more of the above is considered a *hybrid* intelligent system. The major intelligent systems are listed in Table 12.4 and are discussed further in Online File W12.16.

SOFTWARE AND INTELLIGENT AGENTS. As described in Chapters 4 and 5, software and intelligent agents play a major role in supporting work on computers (such as search, alerts, monitor Web activities, suggestions to users) and work in general (e.g., configure complex products diagnose malfunctions in networks). Fuller coverage of the topic is provided in Online Appendix W12.1.

12.6 EXPERT SYSTEMS

When an organization has a complex decision to make or a problem to solve, it often turns to experts for advice. These experts have specific knowledge and experience in the problem area. They are aware of alternative solutions, chances of success, and costs that the organization may incur if the problem is not solved. Companies engage experts for advice on such matters as equipment purchase, mergers and acquisitions, and advertising strategy. The more unstructured the situation, the more specialized and expensive is the advice. **Expert systems (ESs)** are an attempt to mimic human experts. Expert systems can either *support* decision makers or completely *replace* them (see Edwards et al., 2000). Expert systems are the most widely applied and commercially successful AI technology.

Typically, an ES is decision-making software that can reach a level of performance comparable to a human expert in some specialized and usually narrow problem area. The basic idea behind an ES is simple: *Expertise* is transferred from an expert (or other source of expertise) to the computer. This knowledge is then stored in the computer. Users can call on the computer for specific advice as needed. The computer can make inferences and arrive at a conclusion. Then, like a human expert, it advises the nonexperts and explains, if necessary, the logic behind the advice. ESs can sometimes perform better than any single expert can.

Expertise and Knowledge

Expertise is the extensive, task-specific knowledge acquired from training, reading, and experience. It enables experts to make better and faster decisions than nonexperts in solving complex problems. Expertise takes a long time (possibly years) to acquire, and it is distributed in organizations in an uneven manner. A senior expert possesses about 30 times more expertise than a junior (novice) staff member.

The transfer of expertise from an expert to a computer and then to the user involves four activities: *knowledge acquisition* (from experts or other sources), *knowledge representation* (in the computer), *knowledge inferencing*, and *knowledge transfer* to the user.

Knowledge is acquired from experts or from documented sources. Through the activity of knowledge representation, acquired knowledge is organized as rules or frames (object-oriented) and stored electronically in a knowledge base. Given the necessary expertise stored in the knowledge base, the computer is programmed so that it can make inferences. The inferencing is performed in a component called the **inference engine,** which is the "brain" of the ES, and results in a recommendation for novices. Thus, the expert's knowledge has been *transferred* to users.

A unique feature of an ES is its ability to explain its recommendations. The explanation and justification is done in a subsystem called the *justifier* or the *explanation subsystem* (e.g., presents the sequence of rules used by the inference engine to generate a recommendation).

The Benefits and Limitations of Expert Systems

THE BENEFITS OF EXPERT SYSTEMS. Expert systems have considerable benefits, but their use is constrained. During the past few years, the technology of expert systems has been successfully applied in thousands of organizations worldwide to problems ranging from AIDS research to the analysis of dust in mines. Why have ESs become so popular? It is because of the large number of capabilities and benefits they provide. The major ones are listed in Table 12.5. For examples of ES applications, see Online File W12.17.

THE LIMITATIONS OF EXPERT SYSTEMS. Despite their many benefits, available ES methodologies are not always straightforward and effective. Some factors that have slowed the commercial spread of ES are listed in Online File W12.18.

In addition, expert systems may not be able to arrive at any conclusions. For example, even some fully developed complex expert systems are unable to

TABLE 12.5 Benefits of Expert Systems	
Benefit	**Description/Example**
Increased output and productivity	At Digital Equipment Corp. (now part of Hewlett-Packard), an ES plans configuration of components for each custom order, increasing preparation production fourfold.
Increased quality	ESs can provide consistent advice and reduce error rates.
Capture and dissemination of scarce expertise	Physicians in Egypt and Algeria use an eye-care ES developed at Rutgers University to diagnose ailments and to recommend treatment.
Operation in hazardous environments	ESs that interpret information collected by sensors enable human workers to avoid hot, humid, or toxic environments.
Accessibility to knowledge and help desks	ESs can increase the productivity of help-desk employees (there are over 30 million in the U.S. alone), or even automate this function.
Reliability	ESs do not become tired or bored, call in sick, or go on strike. They consistently pay attention to details and do not overlook relevant information.
Increased capabilities of other systems	Integration of an ES with other systems makes the other systems more effective.
Ability to work with incomplete or uncertain information	Even with an answer of "don't know" or "not sure," an ES can still produce an answer, though it may not be a certain one.
Provision of training	Novices who work with an ES become more experienced thanks to the explanation facility, which serves as a teaching device and knowledge base.
Enhancement of decision-making and problem-solving capabilities	ESs allow the integration of expert judgment into analysis. Successful applications are diagnosis of machine malfunction and even medical diagnosis.
Decreased decision-making time	ESs usually can make faster decisions than humans working alone. American Express authorizers can make charge authorization decisions in 3 minutes without an ES and in 30 seconds with one.
Reduced downtime	ESs can quickly diagnose machine malfunctions and prescribe repairs. An ES called Drilling Advisor detects malfunctions in oil rigs, saving the cost of downtime (as much as $250,000/day).

fulfill about 2 percent of the orders presented to it. Finally, expert systems, like human experts, sometimes produce incorrect recommendations.

Failing Expert Systems. Various organizational, personal, and economic factors can slow the spread of expert systems, or even cause them to fail, as shown in *IT at Work 12.5* (page 566).

The Components of Expert Systems

The following components exist in an expert system: knowledge base, inference engine, blackboard (workplace), user interface, and explanation subsystem (justifier). In the future, systems will include a knowledge-refining component. The relationships among components are shown in Figure 12.5 (page 567).

DESCRIPTION OF THE COMPONENTS. The major components of expert systems are described below.

The *knowledge base* contains knowledge necessary for understanding, formulating, and solving problems. It includes two basic elements: (1) *facts*, such as the problem situation and theory of the problem area, and (2) *rules* that direct the use of knowledge to solve specific problems in a particular domain.

IT at Work 12.5
EVEN AN INTELLIGENT SYSTEM CAN FAIL

Mary Kay (*marykay.com*), the multinational cosmetics company, uses teams of managers and analysts to plan its products. This process attempted to iron out potential weaknesses before production. However, the company still faced costly errors resulting from such problems as product-container incompatibility, interaction of chemical compositions, and marketing requirements with regard to packaging and distribution.

An eclectic group of Mary Kay managers, representing various functional areas, used to meet every six weeks to make product decisions. The group's decision-making process was loosely structured: The marketing team would give its requirements to the product formulator and the package engineer at the same time. Marketing's design requests often proved to be beyond the allocated budget or technical possibilities, and other problems arose as a result of not knowing the ultimate product formulation. The result was more meetings and redesign.

Mary Kay decided to implement an expert system to help. In an effort to keep costs to a minimum, it engaged the services of a research university that developed a system that consisted of a DSS computational tool plus two ES components. The decision support tool was able to select compatible packages for a given cosmetic product and to test product and package suitability. The ES component used this information to guide users through design and to determine associated production costs.

At first the system was a tremendous success. There was a clear match between the abilities of the system technology and the nature of the problem. The director of package design enthusiastically embraced the system solution. The entire decision process could have been accomplished in two weeks with no inherent redesign. By formulating what previously was largely intuitive, the ES improved understanding of the decision process itself, increasing the team's confidence. By reducing the time required for new product development, executives were freed for other tasks, and the team met only rarely to ratify the recommendations of the ES.

However, without support staff to *maintain* the ES, no one knew how to add or modify decision rules. Even the firm's IT unit was unable to help, and so the system fell into disuse. More importantly, when the director of package design left the firm, so did the enthusiasm for the ES. No one else was willing to make the effort necessary to maintain the system or sustain the project. Without managerial direction about the importance of the system to the firm's success, the whole project floundered.

Source: Condensed from Vedder et al. (1999).

For Further Exploration: What can a company do to prevent such failures? Can you speculate on why this was not done at Mary Kay?

The "brain" of the ES is the *inference engine*. This component is essentially a computer program that provides a methodology for reasoning and formulating conclusions.

The *user interface* in ESs allows for user–computer dialogue, which can be best carried out in a natural language, usually presented in a questions-and-answers format and sometimes supplemented by graphics. The dialogue triggers the inference engine to match the problem symptoms with the knowledge in the knowledge base and then generate advice.

The *blackboard* is an area of working memory set aside for the description of a current problem, as specified by the input data; it is also used for recording intermediate results. It is a kind of database.

The *explanation subsystem* can trace responsibility for arriving at a conclusion and explain the ES's behavior by interactively answering questions such as the following: *Why* was a certain question asked by the expert system? *How* was a certain conclusion reached? *What* is the plan to reach the solution? (See the discussion by Gregor and Benbasat, 1999.)

Human experts have a *knowledge-refining* system; that is, they can analyze their own performance, learn from it, and improve it for future consultations.

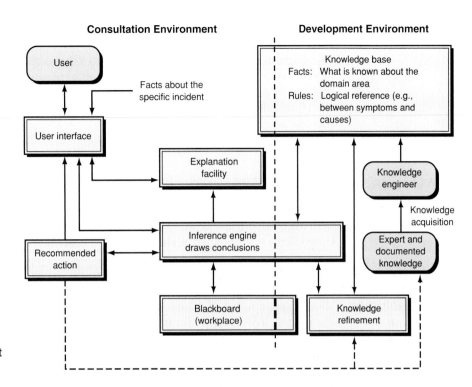

Consultation Environment

Development Environment

FIGURE 12.5 Structure and process of an expert system.

Similarly, such evaluation is necessary in computerized learning so that the program will be able to improve by analyzing the reasons for its success or failure. Such a component is not available in commercial expert systems at the moment, but it is being developed in experimental systems.

The process of building and using expert systems is described in Online File W12.19, which includes an example of how an ES consultation is done.

Applications of Expert Systems

Expert systems are in use today in all types of organizations. For many examples, by industry, see *exsys.com* (in the case studies) and Jackson (1999). Expert systems are especially useful in ten generic categories, displayed in Table 12.6. For other examples see Jareb and Rajkovic (2001) and Pontz and Power (2003).

TABLE 12.6 Generic Categories of Expert Systems

Category	Problem Addressed
1. Interpretation	Inferring situation descriptions from observations.
2. Prediction	Inferring likely consequences of given situations.
3. Diagnosis	Inferring system malfunctions from observations.
4. Design	Configuring objects under constraints.
5. Planning	Developing plans to achieve goal(s).
6. Monitoring	Comparing observations to plans, flagging exceptions.
7. Debugging	Prescribing remedies for malfunctions.
8. Repair	Executing a plan to administer a prescribed remedy.
9. Instruction	Diagnosing, debugging, and correcting student performance.
10. Control	Interpreting, predicting, repairing, and monitoring systems behavior.

EMBEDDED EXPERT SYSTEMS. One of the most useful applications of expert systems is as an embedded component in other systems, including robots. The ES components are so integrated that they have turned into transparent parts of processes or systems. Actually, many software and hardware products include embedded ESs or other intelligent systems, which the users may not be aware of. IT systems are sold based on their functionalities, not on whether they include an intelligent component.

12.7 OTHER INTELLIGENT SYSTEMS

An expert system's major objective is to provide expert advice. Other intelligent systems can be used to solve problems or provide capabilities on areas in which they excel. Several such technologies are described next.

Natural Language Processing and Voice Technologies

Today, when you tell a computer what to do, you type commands on the keyboard. In responding to a user, the computer outputs message symbols or other short, cryptic notes of information. Many problems could be minimized or even eliminated if we could communicate with the computer in our own language. We would simply type in directions, instructions, or information. Better yet, we would converse with the computer using voice. The computer would be smart enough to interpret the input, regardless of its format. **Natural language processing (NLP)** refers to communicating with a computer in English or whatever language you may speak.

To understand a natural language inquiry, a computer must have the knowledge to analyze and then interpret the input. This may include linguistic knowledge about words, domain knowledge, common-sense knowledge, and even knowledge about the users and their goals. Once the computer understands the input, it can take the desired action. For details see Reiter and Dale (2000).

In this section we briefly discuss two types of NLP:

1. Natural language *understanding*, which investigates methods of allowing a computer to comprehend instructions given in ordinary English, via the keyboard or by voice (speech understanding), so that computers are able to understand people

2. Natural language *generation*, which strives to allow computers to produce ordinary English language, on the screen or by voice (known as voice synthesis), so people can understand computers more easily

APPLICATIONS OF NATURAL LANGUAGE PROCESSING. Natural language processing programs have been applied in several areas. The most important are human-to-computer interfaces, which include abstracting and summarizing text, analyzing grammar, understanding speech, and even composing letters by machines. These programs translate one natural language to another, or one computer language to another, and they even translate Web pages (see Chapter 4).

By far the most dominant use of NLP is "front-ends" for other software packages, especially databases that allow the user to operate the applications programs with everyday language.

SPEECH (VOICE) RECOGNITION AND UNDERSTANDING. Speech recognition is a process that allows us to communicate with a computer by speaking to it. The term **speech recognition** is sometimes applied only to the first part of the communication process, in which the computer recognizes words that have been spoken without necessarily interpreting their meanings. The other part of the process, wherein the meaning of speech is ascertained, is called **speech understanding.** It may be possible to understand the meaning of a spoken sentence without actually recognizing every word, and vice versa. When a speech recognition system is combined with a natural language processing system, the result is an overall system that not only recognizes voice input but also understands it. For multiple applications in stores and warehouses, see Amato-McCoy (2003). Speech recognition is deployed today in wireless PDAs as well (see Kumagai, 2002 and Alesso and Smith, 2002).

Advantages of Speech Recognition and Understanding. The ultimate goal of speech recognition is to allow a computer to understand the natural speech of any human speaker at least as well as a human listener could understand it. Speech recognition offers several other advantages:

- *Ease of access.* Many more people can speak than can type. As long as communication with a computer depends on typing skills, many people may not be able to use computers effectively.

- *Speed.* Even the most competent typists can speak more quickly than they can type. It is estimated that the average person can speak twice as quickly as a proficient typist can type.

- *Manual freedom.* Obviously, communicating with a computer through typing occupies your hands. There are many situations in which computers might be useful to people whose hands are otherwise engaged, such as product assemblers, pilots of aircraft, and busy executives. Speech recognition also enables people with hand-related physical disabilities to use computers (see online Chapter 16).

- *Remote access.* Many computers can be accessed remotely by telephones. If a remote database includes speech recognition capabilities, you could retrieve information by issuing oral commands into a telephone.

- *Accuracy.* People tend to make mistakes when typing, especially in spelling. These could be reduced with voice input.

American Express Travel Related Services (AETRS) is using interactive voice recognition (IVR) (Chapter 6) that allows its customers to check and book domestic flights by talking to a computer over the phone. The system asks customers questions such as: Where do you want to travel? When do you want to go? The system can handle 400 city and airport names, and lets callers use more than 10,000 different ways to identify a location. The reservation transaction costs were reduced about 50 percent compared to operator-handled costs. The average transaction time was reduced from 7 to 2 minutes. AETRS offers a similar service on the Web.

Limitations of Speech Recognition and Understanding. The major limitation of speech understanding is its inability to recognize long sentences, or the long time needed to accomplish it. The better the system is at speech recognition, the higher is its cost. Also, in voice recognition systems, you cannot manipulate icons and windows, so speech may need to be combined with a keyboard entry, which slows communication.

VOICE SYNTHESIS. The technology by which computers speak is known as **voice synthesis.** The synthesis of voice by computer differs from the simple playback of a prerecorded voice by either analog or digital means. As the term *synthesis* implies, sounds that make up words and phrases are electronically constructed from basic sound components and can be made to form any desired voice pattern.

The current quality of synthesized voice is very good, but the technology remains somewhat expensive. Anticipated lower cost and improved performance of synthetic voice should encourage more widespread commercial voice applications, especially those in the Web. Opportunities for its use will encompass almost all applications that can provide an automated response to a user, such as inquiries by employees pertaining to payroll and benefits. A number of banks already offer a voice service to their customers, informing them about their balance, which checks were cashed, and so on. Many credit card companies provide similar services, telling customers about current account balances, recent charges, and payments received. For a list of other voice synthesis and voice recognition applications, see Table 12.7.

TABLE 12.7 Examples of Voice Technology Applications

Company	Applications
Scandinavian Airlines, other airlines	Answering inquiries about reservations, schedules, lost baggage, etc.[a]
Citibank, many other banks	Informing credit card holders about balances and credits, providing bank account balances and other information to customers[a]
Delta Dental Plan (CA)	Verifying coverage information[a]
Federal Express	Requesting pickups, ordering supplies[b]
Illinois Bell, other telephone companies	Giving information about services,[a] receiving orders[b]
Domino's Pizza	Enabling stores to order supplies, providing price information[a,b]
General Electric, Rockwell International, Austin Rover, Westpoint Pepperell, Eastman Kodak	Allowing inspectors to report results of quality assurance tests[b]
Cara Donna Provisions	Allowing receivers of shipments to report weights and inventory levels of various meats and cheeses[b]
Weidner Insurance, AT&T	Conducting market research and telemarketing[b]
U.S. Department of Energy, Idaho National Engineering Laboratory, Honeywell	Notifying people of emergencies detected by sensors[a]
New Jersey Department of Education	Notifying parents when students are absent and about cancellation of classes[a]
Kaiser-Permanente Health Foundation (HMO)	Calling patients to remind them of appointments, summarizing and reporting results[a]
Car manufacturers	Activating radios, heaters, and so on, by voice[b]
Taxoma Medical Center	Logging in and out by voice to payroll department[b]
St. Elizabeth's Hospital	Prompting doctors in the emergency room to conduct all necessary tests, reporting of results by doctors[a,b]
Hospital Corporation of America	Sending and receiving patient data by voice, searching for doctors, preparing schedules and medical records[a,b]

[a]Output device.
[b]Input device.

Artificial Neural Networks

Artificial neural networks (ANNs) are biologically inspired. Specifically, they borrow ideas from the manner in which the human brain works. The human brain is composed of special cells called *neurons*. Estimates of the number of neurons in a human brain cover a wide range (up to 150 billion), and there are more than a hundred different kinds of neurons, separated into groups called *networks*. Each network contains several thousand neurons that are highly interconnected. Thus, the brain can be viewed as a collection of neural networks.

Today's ANNs, whose application is referred to as **neural computing,** use a very limited set of concepts from biological neural systems. The goal is to simulate massive parallel processes that involve processing elements interconnected in a network architecture. The artificial neuron receives inputs analogous to the electrochemical impulses biological neurons receive from other neurons. The output of the artificial neuron corresponds to signals sent out from a biological neuron. These artificial signals can be changed, like the signals from the human brain. Neurons in an ANN receive information from other neurons or from external sources, transform or process the information, and pass it on to other neurons or as external outputs.

The manner in which an ANN processes information depends on its structure and on the algorithm used to process the information, as explained in Online File W12.20.

BENEFITS AND APPLICATIONS OF NEURAL NETWORKS. The value of neural network technology includes its usefulness for pattern recognition, learning, and the interpretation of incomplete and "noisy" inputs.

Neural networks have the potential to provide some of the human characteristics of problem solving that are difficult to simulate using the logical, analytical techniques of DSS or even expert systems. One of these characteristics is **pattern recognition.** Neural networks can analyze large quantities of data to establish patterns and characteristics in situations where the logic or rules are not known. An example would be loan applications. By reviewing many historical cases of applicants' questionnaires and the "yes or no" decisions made, the ANN can create "patterns" or "profiles" of applications that should be approved or denied. A new application can then matched by the computer against the pattern. If it comes close enough, the computer classifies it as a "yes" or "no"; otherwise it goes to a human for a decision. Neural networks are especially useful for financial applications such as determining when to buy or sell stock (see Shadbolt, 2002, for examples), predicting bankruptcy (Gentry et al., 2002), and predicting exchange rates (Davis et al., 2001).

Neural networks have several other benefits, which are discussed in Online File W12.21, together with typical applications. For a comprehensive coverage see Smith and Gupta (2002).

Beyond its role as an alternative computing mechanism, and in data mining, neural computing can be combined with other computer-based information systems to produce powerful hybrid systems, as illustrated in *IT at Work 12.6* (page 572).

Neural computing is emerging as an effective technology in pattern recognition. This capability is being translated to many applications (e.g., see Haykin

IT at Work 12.6
BANKS ARE CRACKING DOWN ON CREDIT CARD FRAUD

Only 0.2 percent of Visa International's turnover in 1995 was lost to fraud, but at $655 million it is a loss well worth addressing. Visa (*visa.com*) is now concentrating its efforts on reversing the number of fraudulent transactions by using neural network technology.

Most people stick to a well-established pattern of credit card use and only rarely splurge on expensive nonessentials. Neural networks are designed to notice when a card that is usually used to buy gasoline once a week is suddenly used to buy a number of tickets to the latest theater premiere on Broadway.

Visa's participating banks believe the neural network technology has been successful in combating fraud. Bank of America uses a cardholder risk identification system (CRIS) and has cut fraudulent card use by up to two-thirds. Toronto Dominion Bank found that losses were reduced, and overall customer service improved, with the introduction of neural computing. Another bank recorded savings of $5.5 million in six months. In its first year of use, Visa member banks lost 16% to counterfeiters; considering such numbers, the $2 million Visa spent to implement CRIS certainly seems worth the investment. In fact, Visa says, CRIS paid for itself in one year.

In 1995, CRIS conducted over 16 billion transactions. By 2003, VisaNet (Visa's data warehouse and e-mail operations)

and CRIS were handling more than 8,000 transactions per second or about 320 billions a year. By fall 2003, CRIS was able to notify banks of fraud within a few seconds of a transaction. The only downside to CRIS is that occasionally the system prompts a call to a cardholder's spouse when an out-of-the-ordinary item is charged, such as a surprise vacation trip or a diamond ring. After all, no one wants to spoil surprises for loved ones.

Sumitomo Credit Service Co., a credit card issuer in Japan, is using Falcon, a neural network-based system from HNC Corp (hnc.com). The product works well reading Japanese characters, protecting 18 million cardholders in Japan. The system is used by many other banks worldwide.

Sources: Condensed from "Visa Stamps Out Fraud" (1995), p. viii; "Visa Cracks Down on Fraud" (1996); customer success stories at *hnc.com* (July 6, 2003) and *visa.com* (press releases, accessed June 19, 2003).

For Further Exploration: What is the advantage of CRIS over an automatic check against the balance in the account? What is the advantage of CRIS against a set of rules such as "Call a human authorizer when the purchase price is more than 200 percent of the average previous bill"?

1998, Chen 1996, and Giesen 2002) and is sometimes integrated with fuzzy logic.

Fuzzy Logic   **Fuzzy logic** deals with uncertainties by simulating the process of human reasoning, allowing the computer to behave less precisely and logically than conventional computers do. Fuzzy logic is a technique developed by Zadeh (1994), and its use is gaining momentum (Nguyen and Walker, 1999). The rationale behind this approach is that decision making is not always a matter of black and white, true or false. It often involves gray areas where the term *maybe* is more appropriate. In fact, creative decision-making processes are often unstructured, playful, contentious, or rambling.

According to experts, productivity of decision makers can improve many times using fuzzy logic (see Nguyen and Walker, 1999). At the present time, there are only a few examples of pure fuzzy logic applications in business, mainly in prediction-system behavior (see Peray, 1999, for investment, and Flanagan, 2000, for project evaluation). An interesting application is available at *yatra.net/solutions*, where fuzzy logic is used to support services for corporate travelers (see *Information Week*, May 15, 2000). More often, fuzzy logic is used together with other intelligent systems.

Semantic Web   One of the major problems of the Web is the information overload, which is growing rapidly with time. Software and search agents are helpful, but they cannot (yet) understand words that have multiple meanings. Meaning depends on content, context, graphics and even positioning on a Web page. The proposed solution is known as **semantic Web.** It is an extension of the current Web, in which information is given a well-defined meaning, better enabling computers and people to work in cooperation. The technology behind semantic Web is based in part on NLP, on XML presentation, and new technologies such as resource description framework (RDF).

Semantic Web is expected to facilitate search, interoperability, and the composition of complex applications. It is an attempt to make the Web more homogenous, more data-like, and more amenable to computer understanding. If Web pages contained their own semantics, then software agents could conduct smarter searches. Semantic Web will enable software agents to understand Web forms and databases.

According to Cherry (2002), semantic Web, if become successful, could provide "personal assistants" to people in term of software agents that will be able to conduct many useful tasks such as completely booking your business trip.

Hybrid Intelligent   Intelligent systems are frequently integrated with other intelligent systems or
Systems   with conventional systems, such as DSSs. The following examples illustrate such *hybrid* systems.

DEVELOPING MARKETING STRATEGY.   Developing marketing strategy is a complex process performed by several people working as a team. The process involves many tasks that must be performed sequentially, with contributions from corporate experts. Numerous marketing strategy models were developed over the years to support the process. Unfortunately, most of the models support only one IT goal (e.g., to perform forecasting). A proposal to integrate expert systems, fuzzy logic, and ANN was made by Li (2000). The process of developing marketing strategy and the support of the three technologies in that process is shown in Figure 12.6 (page 574). This hybrid system is powerful enough to incorporate strategic models, such as Porter's five forces, and the directional policy matrices model. The integrated technologies and their roles are:

- *Neural networks.* These are used to predict future market share and growth.
- *Expert systems.* These provide intelligent advice on developing market strategy to individuals and to the planning team.
- *Fuzzy logic.* This helps managers to handle uncertainties and fuzziness of data and information.

The integration of the technologies helps in sharing information, coordination, and evaluation. The system is designed to support both individuals and groups. It allows for inclusion of users' judgment in implementing the model.

OPTIMIZING THE DESIGN PROCESS.   Lam et al. (2000) applied an integrated fuzzy logic, ANN, and algorithmic optimization to the design of a complex design process for ceramic casting manufacturing. The ANN estimates the inputs

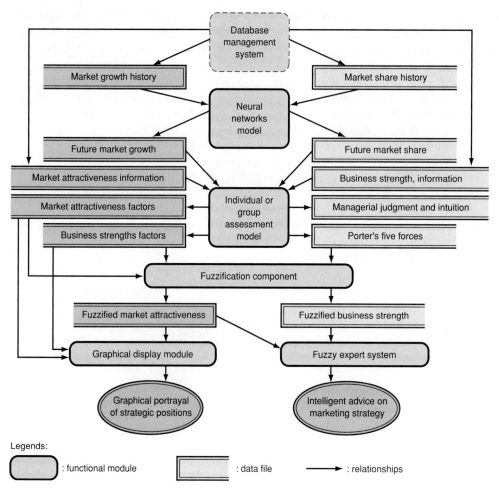

FIGURE 12.6 The architecture of a hybrid intelligent system. (*Source*: Reprinted from *Decision Support Systems,* January 2000, S. Li, "The Development of a Hybrid Intelligent System for Developing Market Strategy," p. 399. © 2000, with permission from Elsevier Science.)

needed by the fuzzy-rule base and also provides evaluation of the objective function of the optimization model. The system was successfully used, enabling fast and consistent production decision making.

12.8 WEB-BASED MANAGEMENT SUPPORT SYSTEMS

The Web is a perfect medium for deploying decision support capabilities on a global basis (see Power and Kaparthi, 2002 and Simic and Devedzic, 2003). Let's look at **Web-based management support systems (MSSs)** that can benefit both users and developers. These systems include decision support systems of all types, including intelligent and hybrid ones. Web-based MSSs are especially suitable for enterprise systems. An example is provided in *IT at Work 12.7.* For more, see Online File W12.22.

The major beneficial features of Web-based MSSs are provided in Table 12.8. For examples of applications see Cohen et al. (2001).

IT at Work 12.7
WEB-BASED MSS AT A LUXEMBOURG BANK

SEB Private Bank is the Luxembourg subsidiary of Swedish Bank SEB, an elite international bank that is quickly moving to take advantage of big growth opportunities in Europe with Internet banking. SEB is finding that customers on the Internet conduct more transactions than others, a trend that could deliver high profitability. The bank sees its greatest and most attractive opportunity in Europe, where SEB participates in a growing investment market and distinguishes itself with high-performance financial tools that empower managers to offer superior customer service. The bank has set an ambitious goal of having 5 million Internet customers by the end of 2004 with the help of a pan-European Internet partner.

To move into real-time 24/7 operations, SEB Private Bank decided to investigate an MSS software called WebFOCUS (from Information Builders.) The software allows users to quickly build self-service production reporting and business analysis systems. Everything from standard to customized reports can be developed quickly and delivered immediately, internally or externally, by intranets, extranets, and over the Internet. As a result, the entire *decision-making process* is shifted onto a real-time transaction platform. The bank developed over 600 reports, of which more than 150 are used by the bank's managers on a day-to-day basis.

Two core elements of SEB Private Bank's information system are the IBM AS/400 hardware platform and Olympic, a Swiss-developed financial application. The combination of WebFOCUS and Information Builders' EDA (integration middleware that offers access to virtually any database) has improved information access for account managers.

Olympic software generates messages to leading stock exchanges, which in turn deliver a return message to the application, giving current financial updates. This streamlines the bank's reaction times with the outside world, giving up-to-the-minute information.

But having this intelligent information source is one thing; making full use of it is another. SEB Private Bank sees the increasing use of its intranet, with its Web-based, thin-client architecture, as a move toward fewer paper reports. For example: Through this system, the bank's managers can easily check the inventory value of a client's assets; when the DSS is asked to evaluate a dossier, it can quickly produce a result.

With reliable security and high value-added services, SEB Private Bank feels well positioned to expand its markets with new expatriate investor business.

Source: Compiled from *informationbuilders.com/applications/seb.html* (2001).

For Further Exploration: What other applications can be developed with such an MSS?

TABLE 12.8 Benefits of Web-Based MSSs

Benefit	Description
Reach rich data sources	The Web can have many resources with multimedia presentation, all accessible with a browser.
Easy data retrieval	Data can be accessed any time, from anywhere. Salespeople for example, can run proposals, using DSS models at a client's place of business.
Ease of use and learning	Use of browser, search engine, hypertext, etc., makes DSSs easy to learn and use. Even top executives are using them directly.
Reduce paperwork and processing efforts for raw data	All data are visible on the Web. If a data warehouse exists, data are organized for view.
Better decisions	With accessibility to more and current information, as well as to DSS models and technology, users of DSSs can make better decisions.
Expanding the use of ready-made DSSs	ASPs are using the Internet to lease DSS models as needed. Soon utility computing will make such distribution a common scenario. Also, more and cheaper applications are available.
Reduced development cost	Building one's own DSS can be cheaper when one uses components (Chapter 14) available on the Web. Also customizing vendors' products is faster and cheaper when done in the Internet environment.

12.9 ADVANCED AND SPECIAL DECISION SUPPORT TOPICS

Several topics are involved in implementing DSSs. The major ones are presented in this section. (For others and more details, see Aronson et al., 2004.)

Simulation for Decision Making

Simulation has many meanings. In general, to *simulate* means to assume the appearance of characteristics of reality. In DSSs, **simulation** generally refers to a technique for conducting experiments (such as "what-if") with a computer on a model of a management system.

Because a DSS deals with semistructured or unstructured situations, it involves complex reality, which may not be easily represented by optimization or other standard models but often can be handled by simulation. Therefore, simulation is one of the most frequently used tools of DSSs. (See Law and Kelton, 1999.)

MAJOR CHARACTERISTICS. To begin, simulation is not a regular type of model. Models in general *represent* reality, whereas simulation usually *imitates* it closely. In practical terms, this means that there are fewer simplifications of reality in simulation models than in other models.

Second, simulation is a technique for *conducting experiments* especially "what if" ones. As such it can describe or predict the characteristics of a given system under different circumstances. Once the characteristics' values are computed, the best among several alternatives can be selected. The simulation process often consists of the repetition of an experiment many, many times to obtain an estimate of the overall effect of certain actions. It can be executed manually in some cases, but a computer is usually needed. Simulation can be used for complex decision making, as illustrated in an application of an automated underground freight transport system (Heijden 2002) and in Online File W12.23.

Advantages of Simulation. Simulation is used for decision support because it:

- *Allows for inclusion of the real-life complexities of problems.* Only a few simplifications are necessary. For example, simulation may utilize the real-life probability distributions rather than approximate theoretical distributions.

- *Is descriptive.* This allows the manager to ask what-if type questions. Thus, managers who employ a trial-and-error approach to problem solving can do it faster and cheaper, with less risk, using a simulated problem instead of a real one.

- *Can handle an extremely wide variation in problem types,* such as inventory and staffing, *as well as higher managerial-level tasks* like long-range planning. Further, the manager can experiment with different variables to determine which are important, and with different alternatives to determine which is best.

- *Can show the effect of compressing time,* giving the manager in a matter of minutes some feel as to the long-term effects of various policies.

- *Can be conducted from anywhere* using Web tools on the corporate portal or extranet.

Of the various types of simulation, the most comprehensive is *visual interactive simulation* (see Chapter 11).

Specialized Ready-Made Decisions Support

Initially, DSSs were custom-built. This resulted in two categories of DSS: The first type was small, end-user DSSs which were built by inexpensive tools such as Excel. The second type was large scale, expensive DSSs built by IT staff and/or vendors with special tools. For most applications, however, building a custom system was not justified. As a result, vendors started to offer DSSs in specialized areas such as financial services, banking, hospitals, or profitability measurements (or combinations of these areas). The popularity of these DSSs has increased since 1999 when vendors started to offer them online as ASP services. Examples of ready-made DSS applications are provided in Online File W12.24.

These tools and many more can be customized, at additional cost. However, even when customized, the total cost to users can be usually much lower than that of developing DSSs from scratch.

Decision support in ready-made expert systems is also provided on the Web. For examples see Online File W12.25.

Frontline Decision Support Systems

Decisions at all levels in the organization contribute to the success of a business. But decisions that maximize a sales opportunity or minimize the cost of customer service requests are made on the front lines by those closest to situations that arise during the course of daily business. Whether it is an order exception, an upselling opportunity, resolving a customer complaint, or a contract that hangs on a decision, the decision maker on the frontline must be able to make effective decisions rapidly, sometimes in seconds, based on context and according to strategies and guidelines set forth by senior management.

FRONTLINE SYSTEMS. **Frontline decision making** is the process by which companies automate decision processes and push them down into the organization and sometimes out to partners. It includes *empowering employees* by letting them devise strategies, evaluate metrics, analyze impacts, and make operational changes.

Frontline decision making automates simple decisions—like freezing the account of a customer who has failed to make payments—by predefining business rules and events that trigger them. At more complex decision points, such as inventory allocation, frontline decision making gives managers the necessary context—available alternatives, business impacts, and success measurements—to make the right decision.

Frontline decision making serves business users such as line managers, sales representatives, and call-center staff by incorporating decision making into their daily work. These workers need applications to help them make good operational decisions that meet overall corporate objectives. Frontline decision making provides users with the right questions to ask, the location of needed data, and metrics that translate data into corporate objectives and suggest actions that can improve performance. Analytical application products are now emerging to support these actions.

Frontline software that started to appear on the market in late 1999 can solve standard problems (such as what to do if a specific bank customer withdraws 100 percent more than the average withdrawal) by packaging in a single browser a self-service solution that requires some business logic (including rules, algorithms, intelligent systems, and so on). Also provided are metrics such as life-cycle expectancy, decision workflow, and so on. Finally, to be successful, such systems must work hand in hand with transactional systems.

According to Forrester Research Inc., such systems are essential for the survival of many companies, but it is expected to take five years for the technology to mature. The major current vendors are Hyperion Solutions Corporation, NCR Corporation, SAS Institute Inc., and i2 Technology. However, almost all the SCM, ERP, and business intelligence vendors mentioned in this and the previous chapter may be involved in such systems. For further details see McCullough (1999) and Sheth and Sisodia (1999).

Real-Time Decision Support

Business decisions today must be made at the right time, and frequently under time pressure. To do so, managers need to know what is going on in the business at any moment and be able to quickly select the best decision alternatives. In recent years, special decision support software has been developed for this purpose. These tools appear under different names such as *business activity monitoring* (BAM) and *extreme analytic frameworks* (EAF). For details and examples see Bates (2003). Variants of these methods are *business performance intelligence* (BPI) (Sorensen, 2003) and *business performance management* (BPM) (Choy, 2003). Also related are *business performance measurement* (BPM) programs such as benchmarking and balanced scorecard (Chapter 9).

Creativity in Decision Support

In order to solve problems or assess opportunities it is often necessary to generate alternative solutions and/or ideas. Creativity is an extremely important topic in decision support, but it is outside the scope of this IT book. However, there is one topic that clearly belongs to IT and this is the use of computers to support the process of idea generation (some of which we discussed in Section 12.3) as well as the use of computers to generate ideas and solutions by themselves. Actually, expert systems can be considered contributors to creativity since they can generate proposed solutions that will help people generate new ideas (e.g., via association, a kind of a "brainstorming"). Interested readers are referred to Yiman-Seid and Kobsa (2003) and Online File W12.26.

➡ MANAGERIAL ISSUES

1. ***Cost justification; intangible benefits.*** While some of the benefits of management support systems are tangible, it is difficult to put a dollar value on the intangible benefits of many such systems. While the cost of small systems is fairly low and justification is not a critical issue, the cost of medium-to-large systems can be very high, and the benefits they provide must be economically justified.

2. ***Documenting personal DSS.*** Many employees develop their own DSSs to increase their productivity and the quality of their work. It is advisable to have an inventory of these DSSs and make certain that appropriate documentation and security measures exist, so that if the employee leaves the organization, the productivity tool remains.

3. ***Security.*** Decision support systems may contain extremely important information for the livelihood of organizations. Taking appropriate security measures, especially in Web-based distributed applications, is a must. End users who build a DSS are not professional systems builders. For this reason, there could be problems with data integrity and the security of the systems developed.

4. ***Ready-made commercial DSSs.*** With the increased use of Web-based systems and ASPs, it is possible to find more DSS applications sold off the shelf, frequently online. The benefits of a purchased or leased DSS application sometimes make it advisable to change business processes to fit a commercially available DSS. Some vendors are willing to modify their standard software to fit the customer's needs. Commercial DSSs are available both for certain industries (hospitals, banking) and for specific tasks (profitability analysis).

5. ***Intelligent DSS.*** Introducing intelligent agents into a DSS application can greatly increase its functionality. The intelligent component of a system can be less than 3 percent of the entire system (the rest is models, a database, and telecommunications), yet the contribution of the intelligent component can be incredible.

6. ***Organizational culture.*** The more people recognize the benefits of a DSS and the more support is given to it by top management, the more the DSS will be used. If the organization's culture is supportive, dozens of applications can be developed.

7. ***Embedded technologies.*** Intelligent systems are expected to be embedded in at least 20 percent of all IT applications in about 10 years. It is critical for any prudent management to closely examine the technologies and their business applicability.

8. ***Ethical issues.*** Corporations with management support systems may need to address some serious ethical issues such as privacy and accountability. For example, a company developed a DSS to help people compute the financial implications of early retirement. However, the DSS developer did not include the tax implications, which resulted in incorrect retirement decisions.

   Another important ethical issue is human judgment, which is frequently used in DSSs. Human judgment is subjective, and therefore, it may lead to unethical decision making. Companies should provide an ethical code for DSS builders. Also, the possibility of automating managers' jobs may lead to massive layoffs.

   There can be ethical issues related to the implementation of expert systems and other intelligent systems. The actions performed by an expert system can be unethical, or even illegal. For example, the expert system may advise you to do something that will hurt someone or will invade the privacy of certain individuals. An example is the behavior of robots, and the possibility that the robots will not behave the way that they were programmed to. There have been many industrial accidents, caused by robots, that resulted in injuries and even deaths. The issue is, Should an organization employ productivity-saving devices that are not 100 percent safe?

   Another ethical issue is the use of knowledge extracted from people. The issue here is, Should a company compensate an employee when knowledge that he or she contributed is used by others? This issue is related to the motivation issue. It is also related to privacy. Should people be informed as to who contributed certain knowledge?

   A final ethical issue that needs to be addressed is that of dehumanization and the feeling that a machine can be "smarter" than some people (see online Chapter 16). People may have different attitudes toward smart machines, which may be reflected in the manner in which they will work together.

ON THE WEB SITE... Additional resources, including quizzes; online files of additional text, tables, figures, and cases; and frequently updated Web links to current articles and information can be found on the book's Web site (*wiley.com/college/turban*).

KEY TERMS

Artificial intelligence (AI) 559

Artificial neural network (ANN) 571

Decision room 555

Decision support system (DSS) 550

Executive information system (EIS) 556

Executive support system (ESS) 556

Expert system (ES) 564

Frontline decision making 577

Fuzzy logic 572

Group decision support system (GDSS) 554

Inference engine 564

Knowledge base 561

Management support system (MSS) 545

Model (in decision making) 547

Model-based management system (MBMS) 552

Natural language processing (NLP) 568

Neural computing 571

Optimization 549

Organizational decision support system (ODSS) 556

Organizational knowledge base 561

Pattern recognition 571

Personal information manager (PIM) 546

Semantic Web 573

Sensitivity analysis 551

Simulation 576

Speech recognition 569

Speech understanding 569

Symbolic processing 562

Turing test 561

Virtual groups 554

Voice synthesis 570

Web-based MSS 574

CHAPTER HIGHLIGHTS (Numbers Refer to Learning Objectives)

1 Managerial decision making is synonymous with management.

1 In today's business environment it is difficult or impossible to conduct analysis of complex problems without computerized support.

1 Decision making is becoming more and more difficult due to the trends discussed in Chapter 1. Information technology enables managers to make better and faster decisions.

1 Decision making involves four major phases: intelligence, design, choice, and implementation; they can be modeled as such.

2 Models allow fast and inexpensive virtual experimentations with systems. Models can be iconic, analog, or mathematical.

3 A DSS is an approach that can improve the effectiveness of decision making, decrease the need for training, improve management control, facilitate communication, reduce costs, and allow for more objective decision making. DSSs deal mostly with unstructured problems.

3 The major components of a DSS are a database and its management, the model base and its management, and the user friendly interface. An intelligent (knowledge) component can be added.

4 Computer support to groups is designed to improve the process of making decisions in groups, which can meet face-to-face or online. The support increases the effectiveness of decisions and reduces the wasted time and other negative effects of face-to-face meetings.

5 Organizational DSSs are systems with many users throughout the enterprise. This is in contrast with systems that support one person or one functional area.

5 Executive support systems are intended to support top executives. Initially these were standalone systems, but today they are part of enterprise systems delivered on intranets.

6 The primary objective of AI is to build computers that will perform tasks that can be characterized as intelligent.

6 The major characteristics of AI are symbolic processing, use of heuristics instead of algorithms, and application of inference techniques.

6 AI has several major advantages: It is permanent; it can be easily duplicated and disseminated; it can be less expensive than human intelligence; it is consistent and thorough; and it can be documented.

7 The major application areas of AI are expert systems, natural language processing, speech understanding, intelligent robotics, computer vision, neural networks, fuzzy logic, and intelligent computer-aided instruction.

8 Expert system technology attempts to transfer knowledge from experts and documented sources to the computer, in order to make that knowledge available to nonexperts for the purpose of solving difficult problems.

8 The major components of an ES are a knowledge base, inference engine, user interface, blackboard, and explanation subsystem.

8 Expert systems can provide many benefits. The most important are improvement in productivity and/or quality, preservation of scarce expertise, enhancing other systems, coping with incomplete information, and providing training.

9 Natural language processing (NLP) provides an opportunity for a user to communicate with a computer in day-to-day spoken language.

9 Speech understanding enables people to communicate with computers by voice. There are many benefits to this emerging technology, such as speed of data entry and having free hands.

10 Neural systems are composed of processing elements called artificial neurons. They are interconnected, and they receive, process, and deliver information. A group of connected neurons forms an artificial neural network (ANN). ANNs are used to discover patterns of relationships among data, make difficult forecasts, and fight fraud. They can process incomplete input information.

10 Fuzzy logic is a technology that helps analyze situations under uncertainty. The technology can also be combined with an ES and an ANN to conduct complex predictions and interpretations. ANNs, fuzzy logic, and ESs complement each other.

11 The Web can facilitate decision making by giving managers easy access to information and to modeling tools to process this information. Furthermore, Web tools such as browsers and search engines increase the speed of gathering and interpreting data. Finally, the Web facilitates collaboration and group decision making.

11 The Web helps in building decision support and intelligent systems, providing easy access to them from anywhere, reducing their per item cost, and improving information discovery and customer service.

12 Special applications of decision support include complex simulations, ready-made systems, and empowerment of frontline employees.

QUESTIONS FOR REVIEW

1. Describe the manager's major roles.
2. Define models and list the major types used in DSSs.
3. Explain the phases of intelligence, design, and choice.
4. What are structured (programmed) and unstructured problems? Give one example of each in the following three areas: finance, marketing, and personnel administration.
5. Give two definitions of DSSs. Compare DSS to management science.
6. Explain sensitivity analysis.
7. List and briefly describe the major components of a DSS.
8. What is the major purpose of the model-based component in a DSS?
9. Define GDSS. Explain how it supports the group decision-making process.
10. What is an organizational DSS?
11. What is the difference between an EIS and an ESS?

12. What are the major benefits of an ESS?
13. What is an enterprise decision simulator?
14. What cause different decision support systems to fail?
15. Define artificial intelligence and list its major characteristics.
16. What is the Turing test?
17. List the major advantages and disadvantages of artificial intelligence as compared with natural intelligence.
18. List the commercial AI technology.
19. List three major capabilities and benefits of an ES.
20. Define the major components of an ES.
21. Which component of an ES is mostly responsible for the reasoning capability?
22. List the ten generic categories of ESs.
23. Describe some of the limitations of ESs.
24. Describe a natural language and natural language processing; list their characteristics.

25. List the major advantages of voice recognition and voice understanding.
26. What is an artificial neural network?
27. What are the major benefits and limitations of neural computing?
28. Define fuzzy logic, and describe its major features and benefits.

29. Describe simulation as a decision support tools.
30. Define software and intelligent agents and describe their capabilities.
31. How can frontline employees be supported for decision making?

QUESTIONS FOR DISCUSSION

1. What could be the biggest advantages of a mathematical model that supports a major investment decision?
2. Your company is considering opening a branch in China. List several typical activities in each phase of the decision (intelligence, design, choice, and implementation).
2. How is the term *model* used in this chapter? What are the strengths and weaknesses of modeling?
4. American Can Company announced that it was interested in acquiring a company in the health maintenance organization (HMO) field. Two decisions were involved in this act: (1) the decision to acquire an HMO, and (2) the decision of which one to acquire. How can a DSS, ES, or ESS be used in such situation?
5. Relate the concept of a knowledge subsystem to frontline decision support. What is the role of Web tools in such support?

6. Discuss how GDSSs can negate the dysfunctions of face-to-face meetings (Chapter 4).
7. Discuss the advantages of Internet-based DSSs.
8. A major difference between a conventional decision support system and an ES is that the former can explain a "how" question whereas the latter can also explain a "why" question. Discuss.
9. What is the difference between voice recognition and voice understanding?
10. Compare and contrast neural computing and conventional computing.
11. Fuzzy logic is frequently combined with expert systems and/or neural computing. Explain the logic of such integration.
12. Explain why even an intelligent system can fail.

EXERCISES

1. Sofmic (fictitious name) is a large software vendor. About twice a year, Sofmic acquires a small specialized software company. Recently, a decision was made to look for a software company in the area of data mining. Currently, there are about 15 companies that would gladly cooperate as candidates for such acquisitions.

    Bill Gomez, the corporate CEO, asked that a recommendation for a candidate for acquisition be submitted to him within one week. "Make sure to use some computerized support for justification, preferably from the area of AI," he said. As a manager responsible for submitting the recommendation to Gomez, you need to select a computerized tool for conducting the analysis. Respond to the following points:

    a. Prepare a list of all the tools that you would consider.
    b. Prepare a list of the major advantages and disadvantages of each tool, as it relates to this specific case.
    c. Select a computerized tool.

    d. Mr. Gomez does not assign grades to your work. You make a poor recommendation and you are out. Therefore, carefully justify your recommendation.

2. Table 12.6 provides a list of ten categories of ES. Compile a list of ten examples from the various functional areas in an organization (accounting, finance, production, marketing, human resources, and so on) that will show functional applications as they are related to the 10 categories.

3. Review the opening case and answer these questions:

    a. Why do airlines need optimization systems for crew scheduling?
    b. What role can experts' knowledge play in this case?
    c. What are the similarities between the systems in Singapore and Malaysia?

4. *Debate:* Prepare a table showing all the arguments you can think of that justify the position that computers cannot think. Then, prepare arguments that show the opposite.

GROUP ASSIGNMENTS

1. Development of an organizational DSS is proposed for your university. As a group, identify the management structure of the university and the major existing information systems. Then, identify and interview several potential users of the system. In the interview, you should check the need for such a system and convince the potential users of the benefits of the system.

2. Prepare a report regarding DSSs and the Web. As a start go to *dssresources.com*. (Take the DSS tour.) Each group represents one vendor such as *microstrategy.com, sas.com,* and *cai.com*. Each group should prepare a report that aims to convince a company why its DSS Web tools are the best.

3. Find recent application(s) of intelligent systems in an organization. Assign each group member to a major functional area. Then, using a literature search, material from vendors, or industry contacts, each member should find two or three recent applications (within the last six months) of intelligent systems in this area. (*Primenet.pcai.com* is a good place to search. Also try the journals *Expert Systems* and *IEEE Intelligent Systems*.)

   a. The group will make a presentation in which it will try to convince the class via examples that intelligent systems are most useful in its assigned functional area.

   b. The entire class will conduct an analysis of the similarities and differences among the applications across the functional areas.

   c. The class will vote on which functional area is benefiting the most from intelligent systems.

4. Each group member composes a list of mundane tasks he or she would like an intelligent software agent to prepare. The group will then meet and compare and draw some conclusions.

5. Investigate the use of NLP and voice recognition techniques that enable consumers to get information from the Web, conduct transactions, and interact with others, all by voice, through regular and cell telephones. Investigate articles and vendors of voice portals and find the state of the art. Write a report.

INTERNET EXERCISES

1. Enter the site of *microstrategy.com* and identify its major DSS products. Find success stories of customers using these products.

2. Find DSS-related newsgroups. Post a message regarding a DSS issue that is of concern to you. Gather several replies and prepare a report.

3. Several DSS vendors provide free demos on the Internet. Identify a demo, view it, and report on its major capabilities. (Try *microstrategy.com, sas.com, brio.com,* and *crystaldecision.com*. You may need to register at some sites.)

4. Search the Internet for the major DSSs and business intelligence vendors. How many of them market a Web-based system? (Try *businessobjects.com, brio.com, cognos.com*.)

5. Enter *asymetrix.com*. Learn about their decision support and performance management tool suite (Toolbook Assistant). Explain how the software can increase competitive advantage.

6. Find ten case studies about DSSs. (Try *microstrategy.com, sas.com,* and *findarticles.com*.) Analyze for DSS characteristics.

7. Enter *solver.com, ncr.com, hyperion.com,* and *ptc.com*. Identify their frontline system initiatives.

8. Prepare a report on the use of ESs in help desks. Collect information from *ginesys.com, exsys.com, ilog.com,* and *pcai.com/pcai*.

9. Enter the Web site of Carnegie Mellon University (*cs.cmu.edu*) and identify current activities on the Land Vehicle. Send an e-mail to ascertain when the vehicle will be on the market.

10. At MIT (*media.mit.edu*) there is a considerable amount of interest in intelligent agents. Find the latest activities regarding IA. (Look at research and projects.)

11. Visit *sas.com/pub/neural/FAZ.html/*. Identify links to real-world applications of neural computing in finance, manufacturing, health care, and transportation. Then visit *hnc.com*. Prepare a report on current applications.

12. Visit *spss.com* and *accure.com* and identify their Internet analytic solutions. Compare and comment. Relate your findings to business performance measurement.

13. Enter *del.gov/eLaws/* and *exsps.com* and identify public systems–oriented advisory systems. Summarize in a report.

Minicase 1
A DSS Reshapes the Railway in the Netherlands

More than 5,000 trains pass through 2,800 railway kilometers and 400 stations each day in the Netherlands. As of the mid-1990s, the railway infrastructure was hardly sufficient to handle the passenger flow. The problem worsened during rush hours, and trains were delayed. Passengers complained and tended to use cars, whose variable cost is lower than that of using the train. This increased the congestion on the roads, adding pollution and traffic accidents. Several other problems plagued the system. The largest railway company, Nederlandse Spoorweges (NS), was losing money in rural areas and agreed to continue services there only if the government would integrate the railways with bus and taxi systems, so that commuters would have more incentives to use the trains. Government help was needed.

Rail 21 is the name of the government's attempt to bring the system into the twenty-first century. It is a complex, multibillion-dollar project. The government wanted to reduce road traffic among the large cities, stimulate regional economies by providing a better public transportation system, stimulate rail cargo, and reduce the number of short-distance passenger flights in Europe. NS wanted to improve service and profitability. A company called Railned is managing the project, which is scheduled for completion in 2010.

Railned developed several alternative infrastructures (called "cocktails"), and put them to analysis. The analysis involved four steps: (1) use experts to list possible alternative projects, (2) estimate passenger flows in each, using an econometric model, (3) determine optimization of rail lines, and (4) test feasibility. The last two steps were complex enough that the following computerized DSSs were developed for their execution:

- **PROLOP:** This DSS was designed to do the lines optimization. It involves a database and three quantitative models. It supports several decisions regarding rails, and it can be used to simulate the scenarios of the "cocktails." It incorporates a management science model, called integer linear programming. PROLOP also compares line systems based on different criteria. Once the appropriate line system is completed, an analysis of the required infrastructure is done, using the second DSS, called DONS.

- **DONS:** This system contains a DSS database, graphical user interface, and two algorithmic modules. The first algorithm computes the arrival and departure times for each train at each station where it stops, based on "hard" constraints (must be met), and "soft" constraints (can be delayed). It represents both safety and

customer-service requirements. The objective is to create a feasible timetable for the trains. If a feasible solution is not possible, planners relax some of the "soft" constraints. If this does not help, modifications in the lines system are explored.

- **STATIONS:** Routing the trains through the railway stations is an extremely difficult problem that cannot be solved simultaneously with the timetable. Thus, STATIONS, another DSS, is used. Again, feasible optimal solutions are searched for. If these do not exist, system modifications are made.

This DSS solution is fairly complex due to conflicting objectives of the government and the railway company (NS), so negotiations on the final choices are needed. To do so, Railned developed a special DSS model for conducting cost-benefit evaluations. It is based on a multiple-criteria approach with conflicting objectives. This tool can rank alternative "cocktails" based on certain requirements and assumptions. For example, one set of assumptions emphasizes NS long-term profitability, while the other one tries to meet the government requirements.

The DSSs were found to be extremely useful. They reduced the planning time and the cost of the analysis and increased the quality of the decisions. An example was an overpass that required an investment of $15 million. DONS came up with a timetable that required an investment of only $7.5 million by using an alternative safety arrangement. The DSS solution is used during the operation of the system as well for monitoring and making adjustments and improvements in the system.

Source: Compiled from Hooghiemstra et al. (1999).

Questions for Minicase 1

1. Why were management science optimizations by themselves not sufficient in this case?

2. What kinds of DSSs were used?

3. Enter *NS.nl* and find information about NS's business partners and the system. (English information is available on some pages.)

4. Given the environment described in the case, which of the DSS generic characteristics described in this chapter are likely to be useful, and how?

5. In what steps of the process can simulation be used, and for what?

6. Identify sensitivity analysis in this case.

Minicase 2
Gate Assignment Display Systems

Gate assignment, the responsibility of gate controllers and their assistants, is a complex and demanding task at any airport. At O'Hare Airport in Chicago, for example, two gate controllers typically plan berthing for about 500 flights a day at about 50 gates. Flights arrive in clusters for the convenience of customers who must transfer to connecting flights, and so controllers must sometimes accommodate a cluster of 30 or 40 planes in 20 to 30 minutes. To complicate the matter, each flight is scheduled to remain at its gate a different length of time, depending on the schedules of connecting flights and the amount of servicing needed. Mix these problems with the need to juggle gates constantly because of flight delays caused by weather and other factors, and you get some idea of the challenges. The problem is even more complex because of its interrelationship with remote parking of planes and constraints related to ground equipment availability and customer requirements.

To solve these problems, many airports are introducing expert systems. The pioneering work was done at Chicago O'Hare in 1987 and 1988. The Korean Air system at Kimpo Airport, Korea, won the 1999 innovative application award from the American Association of Artificial Intelligence (*aaai.org*). The two systems have several common features and similar architectures.

An intelligent gate assignment system can be set up and quickly rescheduled and contains far more information than a manual system. Its superb graphical display shows times and gate numbers. The aircraft are represented as colored bars; each bar's position indicates the gate assigned, and its length indicates the length of time the plane is expected to occupy the gate. Bars with pointed ends identify arrival-departure flights; square ends are used for originator-terminator flights. The system also shows, in words and numbers near each bar, the flight number, arrival and departure times, plane number, present fuel load, flight status, ground status, and more.

Each arriving aircraft carries a small radio transmitter that automatically reports to the mainframe system when the nose wheel touches down. The system immediately changes that plane's bar from "off," meaning off the field, to "on," meaning on the field. When the plane is parked at its gate, the code changes to "in." So gate controllers have access to an up-to-the-second ground status for every flight in their display.

The system also has a number of built-in reminders. For instance, it won't permit an aircraft to be assigned to the wrong kind of gate and explains why it can't. The controller can manually override such a decision to meet an unusual situation. The system also keeps its eye on the clock—when an incoming plane is on the field and its gate hasn't been assigned yet, flashing red lines bracket the time to alert the controller.

Three major benefits of the system have been identified. First, the assistant gate controller can start scheduling the next day's operations 4 or 5 hours earlier than was possible before. The Korean system, for example, produces a schedule in 20 seconds instead of in 5 manually worked hours. Second, the ES is also used by zone controllers and other ground operations (towing, cleaning, resupply). At O'Hare, for example, each of the ten zone controllers is responsible for all activities at a number of gates (baggage handling, catering service, crew assignment, and the rest). Third, superreliability is built into these systems.

Sources: Compiled from press releases from the American Association of Artificial Intelligence (1999) and Texas Instruments Data System Group (1988).

Questions for Minicase 2

1. Why is the gate assignment task so complex?
2. Why is the system considered a real-time ES?
3. What are the major benefits of the ES compared to the manual system? (Prepare a detailed list.)
4. Can a system be replicated for similar use in a non-airport environment? Give an example and discuss.

Virtual Company Assignment
Management Decision Support at The Wireless Cafè

Everyday, you see Jeremy and Barbara make dozens of decisions, from deciding how much lettuce to buy, to accommodating a schedule request from an employee, to creating a bid on a large dinner party. Given the timing, information, and complexity of these decisions, their responses impress you, but still you wonder if they could make even better decisions if they had the right automated tools.

Instructions

1. Describe the interpersonal, informational, and decisional roles of the three shift managers at The Wireless Cafè (Jeremy, Larry, and Arun). How can decision support systems help them in each of these roles?

2. Since the employees of The Wireless Café are quite mobile within the diner, without desks or workstations, they need to have mobile (and possibly wireless) PDAs. What would you recommend Jeremy and Barbara buy for their managers to help them in their on-the-job decision making?

3. DSS implementation failures can be costly, both in terms of money invested and bad implementations that lead to bad decisions. What are some critical success factors for successful implementation of decision support systems for small as well as large organizations? In your recommendation, consider the kinds of users and the types of interfaces and information.

REFERENCES

Alesso, P., and C. F. Smith, *Intelligent Wireless Web*. Boston: Addison Wesley, 2002.

Amato-McCoy, D. M., "Speech Recognition System Picks Up the Pace in Kwik Trip DC," *Stores*, May 2003.

American Association of Artificial Intelligence 1999.

Anthony, R. N., *Planning and Control Systems: A Framework for Analytics*. Cambridge, MA: Harvard University Press, 1965.

Aronson, J., et al., *Decision Support Systems and Intelligent Systems*, 7th ed. Upper Saddle River, NJ: Prentice Hall, 2004.

Atkins, M., et al., "Using GSS for Strategic Planning with the U.S. Air Force,"*Decisions Support Systems*, February 2003.

Ba, S. et al., "Enterprise Decision Support Using Intranet Technology," *Decision Support Systems*, Vol. 20, 1997.

Bates, J., "Business in Real Time-Realizing the Vision," *DM Review*. May 2003.

Bonabeau, E., "Don't Trust Your Gut," *Harvard Business Review*, May 2003.

Brezillon, P., and Pomerol, J. C., "User Acceptance of Interactive Systems: Lessons from Knowledge-Based DSS," *Failure and Lessons Learned in IT Management*, 1(1), 1997.

Briggs, D., and D. Arnoff, "DSSs Failures: An Evolutionary Perspective," *Proceedings DSI AGE 2002, Cork, Ireland*, July 2002.

Carlsson, C., and E. Turban, "DSS: Directions for the Next Decade," *Decision Support Systems*, June 2002.

Carter, G. M., et al., *Building Organizational Decision Support Systems*. Cambridge, MA: Academic Press, 1992.

Cawsey, A., *The Essence of Artificial Intelligence*. Upper Saddle River, NJ: Prentice Hall PTR, 1998.

Chen, C. H., *Fuzzy Logic and Neural Network Handbook*. New York, McGraw Hill, 1996.

Cherry, S. M., "Weaving a Web of Ideas," *IEEE Spectrum*. September 2002.

Choy, J., "Growing Interest in Business Performance Management," *Asia Computer Weekly. Singapore*. April 28, 2003.

Cohen, H. D., et al., "Decision Support with Web-Enabled Software," *Interfaces*, March–April 2001.

Computerworld, July 7, 1997.

Computerworld Singapore, April 10, 2003.

Davis, J. T., et al., "Predicting Direction Shifts on Canadian-US Exchange Rates with Artificial Neural Networks," *International Journal of Intelligent Systems in Accounting, Finance & Management*, Vol. 10. 2001.

DeSanctis, G., and B. Gallupe, "A Foundation for the Study of Group Decision Support Systems," *Management Science*, 33(5), 1987.

dmreview.com, 2001.

Dreyfus, H., and S. Dreyfus, *Mind Over Machine*. New York: Free Press, 1988.

Edwards, J. S. et al., "An Analysis of Expert Systems for Decision Making," *European Journal of Information Systems*, March 2000.

El Sharif, H., and O. A. El Sawy, "Issue-based DSS for the Egyptian Cabinet," *MIS Quarterly*, December 1988.

Flanagan, R., "A Fuzzy Stochastic Technique for Project Selection," *Construction Management and Economics*, January 2000.

Gentry, J. A. et al., "Using Inductive Learning to Predict Bankruptcy," *Journal of Organizational Computing and Electronic Commerce*. Vol. 12, 2002.

Giesen, L., "Artificial-Intelligence System Separates Good Check Writers from Bad," *Store*. March 2002.

Gorry, G. A., and M. S. Scott-Morton, "A Framework for Management Information Systems," *Sloan Management Review*, 13(1), Fall 1971.

Gregor, S., and I. Benbasat, "Explanations from Intelligent Systems," *MIS Quarterly*, December 1999.

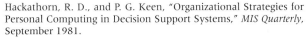

Hackathorn, R. D., and P. G. Keen, "Organizational Strategies for Personal Computing in Decision Support Systems," *MIS Quarterly*, September 1981.

Haykin, S., *Neural Networks: A Comprehensive Foundation*. Upper Saddle River, NJ: Prentice Hall, 1998.

Heijden, M. C. et al., "Using Simulation to Design an Automated Underground System for Transporting Freight Around Schiphol Airport," *Interfaces, July–August 2002.

hertz.com 1998.

hnc.com, customer success stories (accessed July 2003).

Hooghiemstra, J. S. et al., "Decision Support Systems Support the Search for Win–Win Solutions in Railway Network," *Interfaces*, March–April 1999.

ilog.com (accessed June 9, 2003).

informationbuilders.com/applications/seb.html 2001.

Information Week, May 15, 2000.

Jareb, E. and Rajkovic, V., "Use of an Expert System in Personnel Selection," *Information Management*. Vol. 14, 2001.

Kahn. J., "It's Alive," *Wired*, March 2002.

King, D., and D. O'Leary, "Intelligent Executive Information Systems," *IEEE Expert*, December 1996.

Kingsman, B. G., and A. A. deSouza, "A KBDSS for Cost Estimation and Pricing Descision," *International Journal of Production Economics*, November 1997.

Kumagai, J., "Talk to the Machine," *IEEE Spectrum*. September 2002.

Jackson, P., *Introduction to Expert Systems*, 3rd ed. Reading, MA: Addison Wesley, 1999.

Law, A. M., and D. W. Kelton, *Simulation Modeling and Analysis*. New York: McGraw-Hill, 1999.

Lam, S. S. Y., et al., "Prediction and Optimization of a Ceramic Casting Process Using a Hierarchical Hybrid System of Neural Network and Fuzzy Logic," *IIE Transactions*, January 2000.

Li, S., "The Development of a Hybrid Intelligent System for Developing Marketing Strategy," *Decision Support Systems*, January 2000.

Liu, S., et al., "Software Agents for Environmental Scanning in Electronic Commerce," *Information Systems Frontier*, Vol. 2, No. 1, 2000.

McCullough, S., "On the Front Lines," *CIO Magazine*, October 15, 1999.

McGuire, P. A., "The Analytics Divide," *Store*, October 2001.

Mintzberg, H., *The Nature of the Managerial Work*. New York: Harper & Row, 1973.

Mintzberg, H. and Westley, F., "Decision Making: It's Not What You Think," *MIT Sloan Management Review*. Spring 2001.

Nguyen, H. T., and E. A. Walker, *A First Course in Fuzzy Logic*. Boca Raton, FL: CRC Press, 1999.

O'Leary, D. E., "AI and Navigation on the Internet and Intranet," *IEEE Expert*, April 1996.

O'Leary, D. E., "Internet-based Information and Retrieval Systems," *Decision Support Systems*, December 1999.

O'Leary, M., "Putting Hertz Executives in the Driver's Seat," *CIO Magazine*, February 1990.

PC Week, August 17, 1998.

Peray, K., *Investing in Mutual Funds Using Fuzzy Logic*. Boca Raton, FL: CRC Press, 1999.

platinum.com, 2000.

Pontz, C., and Power, D. J., "Building an Expert Assistance System for Examiners (EASE) at the Pennsylvania Department of Labor and Industry," *dssresources.com/cases/Penndeptlabor.html*, 2003 (accessed July 2003).

Power, D. J., *Decision Support Systems: Concepts and Resources for Managers*. Westport, CT: Quorum Books, 2002.

Power, D. J., and S. Kaparthi, "Building Web-based DSSs," *Studies in Informatics and Control*, December 2002.

Reiter, E., and R. Dale, *Building Natural Language Generation Systems*. Cambridge U.K.: Cambridge University Press, 2000.

Rivlin, G., "The Things They Carry," *Fortune*. Winter, 2002, *fortune.cnet.com/fortune/0,10000,0-5937473-7-7707001,00.html?tag=txt* (accessed July 2003).

Rivlin, G., "They Carry (Intelligent Devices)," *Fortune.Cnet.com*, winter 2002.

Rockart, J. F., and D. DeLong, *Executive Support Systems*. Homewood, IL: Dow Jones-Irwin, 1988.

Russell, S. J., and P. Norvig, *Artificial Intelligence*, 2nd ed. Upper Saddle River, NJ: Prentice Hall, 2002.

Saxby, C. L. et al., "Managers' Mental Categorizations of Competitors," *Competitive Intelligence Review*, 2nd Quarter, 2000.

Shadbolt, J., et al., *Neural Networks and the Financial Markets: Predicting, Combining, and Portfolio Optimisation (Perspectives in Neural Computing).*, New York: Springer-Verlag, 2002.

Sheth, J. N., and R. S. Sisodia, "Are Your IT Priorities Upside Down?" *CIO Magazine*, November 15, 1999.

Simic, G., and V. Devedzic, "Building an Intelligent System Using Modern Internet Technologies," *Expert System With Applications*, August 2003.

Simon, H., *The New Science of Management Decisions*, rev. ed. Englewood Cliffs, NJ: Prentice-Hall, 1977.

Singh, S. K., et al., "EIS Support of Strategic Management Process," *Decision Support Systems*, May 2002.

Smith, K., and J. Gupta (eds.), *Neural Networks in Business: Techniques and Applications*, Hershey PA: The India Group, 2002.

Sorensen, D., "Emerging Technology Innovation and Products in the Vanguard," *CIO Magazine*, February 2003.

Texas Instruments Data System Group (1988).

Vedder, R. G., et al., "An Expert System That Was," *Proceedings, DSI International*, Athens, Greece, July 1999.

"Visa Cracks Down on Fraud," *Information Week*, August 26, 1996.

visa.com, press releases. Accessed June 19, 2003.

"Visa Stamps Out Fraud," *International Journal of Retail and Distribution Management*, 23(11), Winter 1995, p. viii.

weforum.org (accessed June 29, 2003).

Yiman-Seid, D., and Kobsa, A., "Expert-Finding Systems for Organizations: Problem and Domain Analysis and the DEMOIR Approach," *Journal of Organizational Computing and Electronic Commerce*, Vol. 13, 2003.

Zadeh, L., "Fuzzy Logic, Neural Networks, and Self Computing," *Communications of the ACM*, March 1994.

PART V
Implementing and Managing IT

▶ 13. Information Technology Economics
14. Building Information Systems
15. Managing Information Resources and Security
16. Impacts of IT on Organizations, Individuals, and Society (online)

CHAPTER

13

Information Technology Economics

13.1
Financial and Economic Trends

13.2
Evaluating IT Investment: Benefits, Costs, and Issues

13.3
Methods for Evaluating and Justifying IT Investment

13.4
IT Economics Strategies: Chargeback and Outsourcing

13.5
Economics of Web-Based Systems and E-Commerce

13.6
Other Economic Aspects of Information Technology

LEARNING OBJECTIVES

After studying this chapter, you will be able to:

① Identify the major aspects of the economics of information technology.

② Explain and evaluate the productivity paradox.

③ Describe approaches for evaluating IT investment and explain why is it difficult to do it.

④ Explain the nature of intangible benefits and the approaches to deal with such benefits.

⑤ List and briefly describe the traditional and modern methods of justifying IT investment.

⑥ Identify the advantages and disadvantages of approaches to charging end users for IT services (chargeback).

⑦ Identify the advantages and disadvantages of outsourcing.

⑧ Describe the economic impact of EC.

⑨ Describe economic issues related to Web-based technologies including e-commerce.

⑩ Describe causes of systems development failures, the theory of increasing returns, and market transformation through new technologies.

JUSTIFYING IT INVESTMENT IN THE STATE OF IOWA

 THE PROBLEM

For years there was little planning or justification for IT projects developed by agencies of the state of Iowa. State agencies requested many projects, knowing that they would get only a few. Bargaining, political favors, and pressures brought to bear by individuals, groups, and state employees determined who would get what. As a result some important projects were not funded, some unimportant ones were funded, and there was very little incentive to save money.

This situation existed in Iowa until 1999, and it exists even today in most other states, countries, cities, and other public institutions. Any agency that needed money in Iowa for an IT project slipped it into its budget request. A good sales pitch would have resulted in approval. But, this situation, which cost taxpayers lots of money, changed in 1999 when a request for $22.5 million to fix the Y2K problem was made. This request triggered work that led Iowans to realize that the state government needed a better approach to planning and justifying IT investment.

 THE SOLUTION

The solution that Iowa chose is an *IT value model*. The basic idea was to promote *performance-based government,* an approach that measures the results of government programs. Using the principles deployed to justify the investment in the Y2K fix, a methodology was developed to measure the value an IT project would create. The system is based on the return on investment (ROI) financial model, and is known as R.O. Iowa (a play on words). Its principles are described below.

First, new IT investments are paid for primarily from a pot of money called the Pooled Technology Account, which is appropriated by the legislature and is controlled by the state's IT department. Pooling the funds makes budget oversight easier and helps avoid duplication of systems. Second, the IT department reimburses agencies for expenses from this fund only after verifying that they are necessary. If an agency's expenditures are not in line with the project schedule, it's a red flag for auditors that the project could be in trouble.

To support spending decisions, agency managers have to document the expected costs and benefits according to a standard set of factors. The score for each factor ranges from 5 to 15 points, for a maximum total score of 100 points. In addition they must specify metrics related to those factors to justify requests and later to determine the project's success. The scores are based on ten criteria that are used to determine values. Besides asking for standard financial data, the ROI program also requires agencies to detail their technology requirements and functional needs. This level of detail enforces standards, but it also helps officials identify duplicative expenditures. For example, in 2001 several agencies were proposing to build pieces of an ERP system, such as electronic procurement and human resources management. The IS department suggested that, for less money, the state could deploy a single ERP system that agencies could share. The project, which had an estimated cost of $9.6 million, could easily have cost many times that amount, if agencies were allowed to go it alone.

As noted earlier, once a project is funded, the state scrutinizes agencies' expenses. Agencies have to submit their purchase orders and invoices to the Enterprise Quality Assurance Office for approval before they can be reimbursed.

 THE RESULTS

The R.O. Iowa system became, by 2002, a national model for documenting value and prioritizing IT investments in the U.S. public sector. In 2002 the program was named the "Best State IT Management Initiative" by the National Association of State CIOs. It saved Iowa taxpayers more than $5 million in less than 4 years (about 16 percent of the spending on new IT projects).

The process has changed users' behavior as well. For example, during the fiscal-year 2003 budget approval process, agencies asked for 17 IT projects, and were granted only six. For the year 2004 they asked for only four projects, all of which were granted. Also, there is considerable collaboration among agencies and use of cross-functional teams to write applications, so the need to "play games" to get project funding is largely gone. Another improvement is elimination of duplicated systems. Finally, the methodology minimizes politics and political pressures.

The success of R.O. Iowa led to the Iowa Accounting Government Act, which requires establishing similar methodology in all state investments, not just for IT projects.

Source: Compiled form Varon (2003).

 LESSONS LEARNED FROM THIS CASE

Justifying the cost of IT is a major financial decision that organizations must make today. The unique aspects of IT make its justification and economics different in many respects from the economics of other aspects of business. This chapter explores the issues related to IT economics.

In order to understand the factors that determine the IT investment justification, we need to understand the technological trends of increasing investment in technology and the changes that IT makes to productivity. These are the first topics we address in the chapter.

A major problem in making IT-related economic decisions is the measurement and comparison of performance under alternative methods. This is done with approaches such as scoring (used in R.O. Iowa), benchmarking, and metrics. Other important issues are assessing intangible variables and dealing with costs, including chargeback and outsourcing, which are viable strategies that are explored in this chapter. We also deal with e-commerce, whose economic foundations are also explained here. Finally, we discuss some failure issues which, as pointed out throughout the book, are common in IT and can cost dearly.

13.1 FINANCIAL AND ECONOMIC TRENDS

Technological and Financial Trends

Information technology capabilities are advancing at a rapid rate, and this trend is likely to continue for the foreseeable future. Expanding power and declining costs enable new and more extensive applications of information technology,

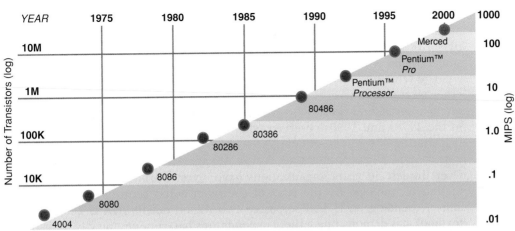

FIGURE 13.1 Moore's Law as it relates to Intel microprocessors. (*Source:* Intel Corporation, *intel.com.research/silicon/mooreslaw.htm*. Reprinted by permission of Intel Corporation, ©Intel Corporation.)

which makes it possible for organizations to improve their efficiency and effectiveness.

On the hardware side, capabilities are growing at an exponential rate. As discussed in Chapter 1, **Moore's Law,** named for one of the founders of Intel Corp., posited that the number of transistors, and thus the power, of an integrated circuit (now, computer chip) would double every year, while the cost remained the same. Moore later revised this estimate to a slightly less rapid pace: doubling every 18 months. Figure 13.1 illustrates Moore's Law as it relates to the power of Intel microprocessors, measured in MIPS, or millions of (computer) instructions per second. Moore has also applied the law to the Web, electronic commerce, and supply chain management (see Moore, 1997). Others applied it, with slight modifications, to storage capability.

Assuming the current rate of growth in computing power, organizations will have the opportunity to buy, for the same price, twice the processing power in $1\frac{1}{2}$ years, four times the power in 3 years, eight times the power in $4\frac{1}{2}$ years, and so forth. Another way of saying this is that the **price-to-performance ratio** will continue to decline exponentially. Limitations associated with current technologies could end this trend for silicon-based chips in 10 or 20 years (or possibly earlier; see Pountain, 1998), but new technologies will probably allow this phenomenal growth to continue. Advances in network technology, as compared to those in chip technology, are even more profound, as shown in Chapter 1.

What does this growth in computing power mean in economic terms? First, most organizations will perform existing functions at decreasing costs over time and thus become more efficient. Second, creative organizations will find new uses for information technology—based on the improving price-to-performance ratio—and thus become more effective. They will also apply technology to activities that are technically feasible at current power levels but will not be economically feasible until costs are reduced. Information technology will become an even more significant factor in the production and distribution of almost every product and service.

These new and enhanced products and services will provide competitive advantage to organizations that have the creativity to exploit the increasing power of information technology. They will also provide major benefits to consumers, who will benefit from the greater functionality and lower costs.

The remainder of this chapter focuses on evaluating the costs, benefits, and other economic aspects of information technology. Productivity is a major focus of economists, and those who studied the payoff from massive IT investments in the 1970s and 1980s observed what has been called the *productivity paradox.* It is that topic we address next.

What Is the Productivity Paradox?

Over the last 50 years, organizations have invested trillions of dollars in information technology. By the start of the twenty-first century, total worldwide *annual* spending on IT had surpassed two trillion dollars (ITAA, 2000). As this textbook has demonstrated, these expenditures have unquestionably transformed organizations: The technologies have become an integral aspect of almost every business process. The business and technology presses publish many "success stories" about major benefits from information technology projects at individual organizations. It seems self-evident that these investments must have increased productivity, not just in individual organizations, but throughout the economy.

On the other hand, it is very hard to demonstrate, at the level of a national economy, that the IT investments really have increased outputs or wages. Most of the investment went into the service sector of the economy which, during the 1970s and 1980s, was showing much lower productivity gains than manufacturing. Fisher (2001) reports on a study that showed that only 8 percent of total IT spending actually delivers value. Nobel prize winner in economics Robert Solow quipped, "We see computers everywhere except in the productivity statistics." The discrepancy between measures of investment in information technology and measures of output at the national level has been called the **productivity paradox.**

To understand this paradox, we first need to understand the concept of productivity. Economists define *productivity* as outputs divided by inputs. Outputs are calculated by multiplying units produced (for example, number of automobiles) by their average value. The resulting figure needs to be adjusted for price inflation and also for any changes in quality (such as increased safety or better gas mileage). If inputs are measured simply as hours of work, the resulting ratio of outputs to inputs is *labor productivity.* If other inputs—investments and materials—are included, the ratio is known as *multifactor productivity.* A *Closer Look 13.1* shows an example of a simple productivity calculation.

Explaining the Productivity Paradox

Economists have studied the productivity issue extensively in recent years and have developed a variety of possible explanations of the apparent paradox (e.g., see Olazabal, 2002). These explanations can be grouped into several categories: (1) Problems with data or analyses hide productivity gains from IT, (2) gains from IT are offset by losses in other areas, and (3) IT productivity gains are offset by IT costs or losses. We discuss these explanations in more detail next.

DATA AND ANALYSIS PROBLEMS HIDE PRODUCTIVITY GAINS. Productivity numbers are only as good as the data used in their calculations. Therefore, one possible explanation for the productivity paradox is that the data or the analysis of the data is actually hiding productivity gains.

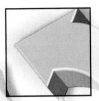

A CLOSER LOOK
13.1 CALCULATING LABOR PRODUCTIVITY AT THE DRISCOLL COMPANY

Assume that The Driscoll Company uses 10 employees who manually process 1,000 customer service inquiries per day. Unit sales are increasing at 5 percent per year, and the number of customer inquiries is increasing at about the same rate. Turnover among customer service representatives is 20 percent: On the average, two of these employees leave the company every year.

The company purchased an automated call-answering and customer-service system, which should make it possible to increase output per employee by 50 percent. That increase will make it possible to answer the calls using fewer customer-service reps. However, rather than having a layoff to achieve the 50 percent productivity gain right away, the company will rely on attrition; it will wait until employees leave on their own and then just not replace them. The following calculations compare productivity with the previous system and new systems.

PRODUCTIVITY WITH THE MANUAL SYSTEM:

1,000 inquiries/10 employees = 100 inquiries handled
per employee per day

PRODUCTIVITY WITH THE AUTOMATED SYSTEM (ONE YEAR LATER):

1,050 inquiries/8 employees = 131 inquiries handled
per employee per day

The productivity increase is 31 percent (131 − 100 = 31 ÷ 100 calls = 31%). Productivity will increase further as additional employees leave, up to the 50 percent increase determined by the technology.

For manufacturing, it is fairly easy to measure outputs and inputs. General Motors, Ford, and DaimlerChrysler, for example, produce motor vehicles, relatively well-defined products whose quality changes gradually over time. It is not difficult to identify, with reasonable accuracy, the inputs used to produce these vehicles. However, the trend in the United States and other developed countries is away from manufacturing and toward services.

In service industries, such as finance or health care delivery, it is more difficult to define what the products are, how they change in quality, and how to allocate to them the corresponding costs. For example, banks now use IT to handle a large proportion of deposit and withdrawal transactions through automated teller machines (ATMs). The ability to withdraw cash from ATMs 24 hours per day, 7 days per week is a substantial quality increase in comparison to the traditional 9 A.M. to 4 P.M. hours for live tellers. But what is the value of this quality increase in comparison with the associated costs? If the incremental value exceeds the incremental costs, then it represents a productivity gain; otherwise the productivity impact is negative.

Similarly, the productivity gains may not be apparent in all processes supported by information systems. Mukhopadhyay et al. (1997), in an assessment of productivity impacts of IT on a toll-collection system, found that IT had a significant impact on the processing of complex transactions, but not on simple transactions. Based on an investigation of IT performance in 60 construction-industry firms in Hong Kong, Li et al. (2000) found productivity improvements in architecture and quantity-surveying firms (which perform a wide range of functions involved in the estimation and control of construction project costs) and no evidence of productivity improvement in engineering firms.

Another important consideration is the amount of time it takes to achieve the full benefits of new technologies. Economists point out that it took many decades to start achieving the full productivity impacts of the Industrial Revolution. Productivity actually may decrease during the initial learning period of new software and then increase over a period of a year or longer.

Hitt and Brynjolfsson (1996) point out that answers to questions about the value of IT investments depend on how the issue is defined. They emphasize that productivity is not the same thing as profitability. Their research indicates that IT increases productivity and value to consumers but does not increase organizational profitability. Brynjolfsson and Hitt (1998) suggest using alternate measures, other than traditional productivity measures, to measure productivity.

IT PRODUCTIVITY GAINS ARE OFFSET BY LOSSES IN OTHER AREAS. Another possible explanation of the productivity paradox is that IT produces gains in certain areas of the economy, but that these gains are offset by losses in other areas. One company's IT usage could increase its share of market at the expense of the market share of other companies. Total output in the industry, and thus productivity, remains constant even though the competitive situation may change.

Offsetting losses can also occur within organizations. Consider the situation where an organization installs a new computer system that makes it possible to increase output per employee. If the organization reduces its production staff but increases employment in unproductive overhead functions, the productivity gains from information technology will be dispersed.

IT PRODUCTIVITY GAINS ARE OFFSET BY IT COSTS OR LOSSES. The third possibility is that IT in itself really does not increase productivity. This idea seems contrary to common sense: Why would organizations invest tremendous amounts of money in something that really does not improve performance? On the other hand, there are considerations that support this possibility. Strassmann (1997) compared relative IT spending at a sample of corporations and found little or no relationship between IT spending and corporate profitability. (See Online File W13.1.)

To determine whether IT increases productivity, it is not enough simply to measure changes in outputs for a new system. If outputs increase 40 percent but inputs increase 50 percent, the result is a decline in productivity rather than a gain. Or consider a situation where a new system is developed and implemented but then, because of some major problems, is replaced by another system. Even though the second system has acceptable performance, an analysis that includes the costs of the unsuccessful system could indicate that IT did not increase productivity, at least in the short run.

Therefore, productivity evaluations must include changes in inputs, especially labor, over the total life cycle, including projects that are not implemented. These inputs need to include not just the direct labor required to develop and operate the system, but also indirect labor and other costs required to maintain the system. Examples of factors that, under this broader perspective, reduce productivity include:

- *Support costs.* The GartnerGroup estimates the total cost of a networked PC can be as high as $13,000 per year (Munk, 1996). Technical support accounts

FIGURE 13.2 Dilbert analyzes the productivity paradox. (*Source:* Dilbert; reprinted by permission of United Feature Syndicate, Inc.)

for 27 percent of this cost, and administration for another 9 percent. The additional employees required for these support activities could offset a significant portion of the productivity benefits from the hardware and software.

- *Wasted time.* Personal computers make it possible to work more productively on some tasks but also result in nonproductive activities. A survey of 6,000 workers indicated the average PC user loses 5 hours per week waiting—for programs to run, reports to print, tech support to answer the phone, and so on—or "futzing" with the hardware or software (Munk, 1996). The GartnerGroup estimates that businesses lose 26 million hours of employee time per year to these nonproductive activities, and that these activities account for 43 percent of the total cost of a personal computer on a network. The cartoon in Figure 13.2 highlights the issue of wasted time. Employees also use the Internet and e-mail for private purposes, wasting even more time.

- *Software development problems.* Some information systems projects fail and are not completed. Others are abandoned—completed but never used. Others are **runaway projects,** systems that are eventually completed but require much more time and money than originally planned. Software development problems are not uncommon: One survey (King, 1997) found that 73 percent of software projects at 360 U.S. corporations were canceled, over budget, or were late. Labor hours associated with these projects can offset productivity gains from more successful projects.

- *Software maintenance.* The expense of software maintenance, which includes fixing bugs and modifying or enhancing system functionality, now accounts for up to 80 percent of IS budgets (see Murphy, 2003). Many of the modifications—for example, updates to payroll systems to reflect tax law changes—do not increase outputs. They are necessary just to keep the system at the same level of performance, so productivity declines because labor increases while output volumes do not. The "Year 2K Problem" is a notable example of software maintenance that did not add to productivity. (For more on this aspect of the Y2K problem, see Online File W13.2.)

  Most global organizations are also required to incur additional costs for acquiring and maintaining domain name registrations. GartnerGroup (2000) estimated that the average global organization has to register a total of at least 300 name variants, which may amount to $75,000. Many additional names are required because companies want to avoid cyberbashing.

- *Incompatible systems and workarounds.* Although individual systems produce productivity gains, the increased labor required to get them to work together (or at all) could offset these benefits.

Other possible explanations of the productivity paradox have been noted. A number of researchers have pointed out, for example, that time lags may throw off the productivity measurements (Reichheld and Scheffer, 2000; Qing and Plant, 2001). Many IT investments, especially those in CRM, for example, take five or six years to show results, but many studies do not wait that long to measure productivity changes. For a list of other explanations of the paradox proposed by Devaraj and Kohli (2002), see Online File W13.3.

Conclusion: Does the Productivity Paradox Matter?

The productivity-offsetting factors described earlier largely reflect problems with the administration of IT, rather than with the technologies themselves. In many cases these problems in administration are controllable through better planning or more effective management techniques. For organizations, the critical issue is not whether and how IT increases productivity *in the economy as a whole*, but how it improves their own productivity. Lin and Shao (2000) find a robust and consistent relationship between IT investment and efficiency, and they support evaluating IT investments in terms of organizational efficiency rather than productivity. For the results of a comprehensive study on the economic value of IT in Europe see Legrenzi (2003).

Some of the difficulties in finding the relationship between IT investment and organizational performance can be seen in Figure 13.3. The relationships are basically indirect, via IT assets and IT impacts. The figure shows that the relationships between IT investment and performance are not direct; other factors exist in between. This is exactly why the productivity paradox exists, since these intermediary factors (in the middle of the figure) can moderate and influence the relationship.

The inconclusiveness of studies about the value of IT investment and inaccuracies in measurements have prompted many companies to skip formal evaluations (see Seddon et al., 2002, and Sawhney, 2002). However, as became apparent during the dot-com bubble, when many dot-coms were started and almost as many quickly failed, this can be a very risky approach. Therefore, before deciding to skip evaluation, an organization should examine some of the new methods that may result in more accurate evaluation (see Section 13.3).

Many believe that the productivity paradox as it relates to IT is no longer valid, since we are able to explain what caused it. Others believe that the issue is still very relevant, especially on the level of the economy as a whole. They claim that the paradox still matters because IT has failed to lift productivity growth throughout the economy, although it may have improved productivity

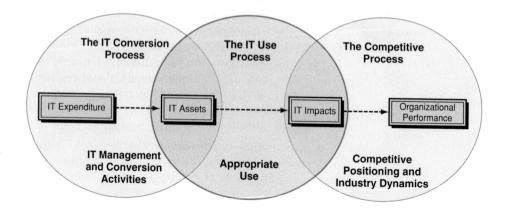

FIGURE 13.3 Process approach to IT organizational investment and impact. (*Source:* Soh and Markus, 1995.)

at the level of firms or of industries. We may not at this point be able to provide a final answer to the question about whether the paradox still matters. The important conclusion that we can draw is that we need to be careful in measuring the economic contributions of information technology on all three levels—firms, industries, and economies. Because almost 50 percent of all capital investment in the United States is in IT and it is growing with time, it is even more important to properly assess its benefits and costs, and that is what this chapter is attempting to do.

The next three sections cover ways organizations can evaluate IT benefits and costs and target their IT development and acquisition toward systems that will best contribute to the achievement of organizational goals.

13.2 EVALUATING IT INVESTMENT: BENEFITS, COSTS, AND ISSUES

Evaluating IT investment covers many topics. Let's begin by categorizing types of IT investment.

IT Investment Categories

One basic way to segregate IT investment is to distinguish between investment in infrastructure and investment in specific applications.

IT infrastructure, as defined in Chapter 2, provides the foundations for IT applications in the enterprise. Examples are a data center, networks, data warehouse, and knowledge base. Infrastructure investments are made for a long time, and the infrastructure is shared by many applications throughout the enterprise. For the nature and types of IT infrastructure, see Broadbent and Weill (1997). *IT applications,* as defined in Chapter 2, are specific systems and programs for achieving certain objectives—for example, providing a payroll or taking a customer order. The number of IT applications is large. Applications can be in one functional department, as shown in Chapter 7, or they can be shared by several departments, which makes evaluation of their costs and benefits more complex.

Another way to look at IT investment categories is proposed by Ross and Beath (2002). As shown in Table 13.1 (page 598), their categories are based on the purpose of the investment (called drivers in the table). They also suggest a cost justification (funding approach) as well as the probable owner. Still other investment categories are offered by Devaraj and Kohli (2002), who divide IT investments into operational, managerial, and strategic types, and by Lucas (1999), whose types of investment are shown in Online File W13.4. The variety of IT investment categories demonstrates the complex nature of IT investment.

The Value of Information in Decision Making

People in organizations use information to help them make decisions that are better than they would have been if they did not have the information. Senior executives make decisions that influence the profitability of an organization for years to come; operational employees make decisions that affect production on a day-to-day basis. In either case, the value of information is the difference between the *net benefits* (benefits adjusted for costs) of decisions made using information and the net benefits of decisions made without information. The value of the net benefits with information obviously needs to reflect the additional costs of obtaining the information. The value of information can be expressed as follows:

Value of information = Net benefits with information
                          − Net benefits without information

TABLE 13.1 Categories of IT Investments

Investment Type	Drivers	Funding Approach	Probable Owner	Sample Initiatives
Transformation	A core infrastructure that is inadequate for desired business model	Executive-level allocation	Entire company or all affected business units	ERP implementations Transforming network to TCP/IP Standardizing desktop technologies Building data warehouses Implementing middleware layer to manage Web environment
Renewal	Opportunity to reduce cost or raise quality of IT services A vendor's decision to stop supporting existing technology	Business case Annual allocation under CIO	Technology owner or service provider (usually IT for shared components)	Purchasing additional capacity Enabling purchase discounts Facilitating access to existing data Upgrading technology standards Retiring outdated systems and technologies
Process improvement	Opportunity to improve operational performance	Business case	Strategic business unit (SBU), process owner, or functional area that will realize the benefits	Shifting customer services to lower-cost channel Allowing employees to self-serve for benefits, HR services Shifting data capture to customers Eliminating costs of printing and mailing paper reports of bills Streamlining cycle times for processes Capturing new data automatically
Experiments	New technologies, new ideas for products or processes, new business models	Business or executive-level allocation	IT unit, SBU, or functional area needing to learn	Testing demand for new products Testing cannibalization of channels Learning if customers can self-serve Testing new pricing strategy Assessing customer interest in new channels, new technologies Assessing costs of new channels

Source: Ross and Beath (2000), p. 54.

It is generally assumed that systems that provide relevant information to support decision making will result in better decisions, and therefore they will contribute toward the return on investment. But, this is not always the case. For example, Dekker and de Hoog (2000) found that the return on most knowledge assets created for loan evaluation decisions in a large bank was negative. However, as technology gets cheaper and applications get more sophisticated, this situation is changing, making it more attractive to use technology not only to improve service but also to increase profit. Careful evaluation of investment in information systems is needed.

A popular alternative is to have the decision maker subjectively estimate the value of the information. This person is most familiar with the problem and has the most to lose from a bad decision. However, to make sure the estimates are not inflated in order to get an approval, the organization needs to hold the decision maker accountable for the cost of the information. Before we deal with such accountability we will examine the methodologies of evaluating automation of business processes with IT.

Evaluating IT Investment by Traditional Cost-Benefit Analysis

Automation of business processes is an area where it is necessary to define and measure IT benefits and costs. For example, automation was implemented in the organization's business offices when word processing replaced typing and spreadsheet programs replaced column-ruled accounting pads and 10-key calculators. In the factory, robots weld and paint automobiles on assembly lines. In the warehouse, incoming items are recorded by barcode scanners. The decision of whether to automate is an example of a *capital investment* decision. Another example is replacement of an old system by a new or improved one. Traditional tools used to evaluate capital investment decisions are net present value and return on investment.

USING NPV IN COST-BENEFIT ANALYSIS. Capital investment decisions can be analyzed by **cost-benefit analyses,** which compare the total value of the benefits with the associated costs. Organizations often use net present value (NPV) calculations for cost-benefit analyses. In an NPV analysis, analysts convert future values of benefits to their present-value equivalent by discounting them at the organization's cost of funds. They then can compare the present value of the future benefits to the cost required to achieve those benefits, in order to determine whether the benefits exceed the costs. (For more specific guidelines and decision criteria on how NPV analysis works, consult financial management textbooks.)

The NPV analysis works well in situations where the costs and benefits are well defined or "tangible," so that it is not difficult to convert them into monetary values. For example, if human welders are replaced by robots that produce work of comparable quality, the benefits are the labor cost savings over the usable life of the robots. Costs include the capital investment to purchase and install the robots, plus the operating and maintenance costs.

RETURN ON INVESTMENT. Another traditional tool for evalating capital investments is *return on investment* (ROI), which measures the effectiveness of management in generating profits with its available assets. The ROI measure is a percentage, and the higher this percentage return, the better. It is calculated essentially by dividing net income attributable to a project by the average assets invested in the project. An example of a detailed study of the ROI of a portal, commissioned by Plumtree Software and executed by META group, can be found at *plumtree.com* (also white papers at *metagroup.com*). Davamanirajan et al. (2002) found an average 10 percent rate of return on investment in IT projects in the financial services sector. For a comprehensive study see Kudyba and Vitaliano (2003).

Costing IT Investment

Placing a dollar value on the cost of IT investments may not be as simple as it may sound. One of the major issues is to allocate fixed costs among different IT projects. *Fixed costs* are those costs that remain the same in total regardless of change in the activity level. For IT, fixed costs include infrastructure cost, cost of IT services (Gerlach et al., 2002), and IT management cost. For example, the salary of the IT director is fixed, and adding one more application will not change it.

Another area of concern is the fact that the cost of a system does not end when the system is installed. Costs for keeping it running, dealing with bugs, and for improving and changing the system may continue for some time. Such costs can accumulate over many years, and sometimes they are not even anticipated when the investment is made. An example is the cost of the Y2K reprogramming projects that cost billions of dollars to organizations worldwide. (For a discussion see Read et al., 2001.)

The fact that organizations use IT for different purposes further complicates the costing process (see DiNunno, 2002, for discussion). There are multiple kinds of values (e.g., improved efficiency, improved customer or partner relations); the return of a capital investment measured in numeric terms (e.g., dollar or percentage) is only one of these values. In addition, the probability of obtaining a return from an IT investment also depends on the probability of implementation success. These probabilities reflect the fact that many systems are not implemented on time, within budget, and/or with all the features orginally envisioned for them. Finally, the expected value of the return on IT investment in most cases will be less than that originally anticipated. For this reason, Gray and Watson (1998) point out that managers often make substantial investments in projects like data warehousing by relying on intuition when evaluating investment proposals rather than on concrete evaluation.

After the dot-com problems of 2000–2002 it become almost mandatory to justify IT projects with a solid business case, including ROI. However, according to Sawhney (2002), and others, this may have little value due to the difficulties in dealing with intangible benefits. These are real and important, but it is not easy to accurately estimate their value. (For further guidelines on cost-benefit analysis, see Clermont, 2002.)

The Problem of Intangible Benefits

As indicated above, in many cases IT projects generate **intangible benefits** such as increased quality, faster product development, greater design flexibility, better customer service, or improved working conditions for employees. These are very desirable benefits, but it is difficult to place an accurate monetary value on them. For example, many people would agree that e-mail improves communications, but it is not at all clear how to measure the value of this improvement. Managers are very conscious of the bottom line, but no manager can prove that e-mail is responsible for so many cents per share of the organization's total profits.

Intangible benefits can be very complex and substantial. For example, according to Arno Penzias, a Nobel Laureate in physics, the New York Metropolitan Transit Authority (MTA) had not found the need to open another airport for almost two decades, even when traffic had tripled. This, according to his study, was due to productivity gains derived from improved IT systems (quoted by Devaraj and Kohli, 2002). IT systems added by the MTA played critical roles in ticket reservations, passenger and luggage check-in, crew assignment and scheduling, runway maintenance and management, and gate assignments. These improvements enabled MTA to cope with increased traffic without adding new facilities, saving hundreds of millions of dollars. Many similar examples of increased capacity exist.

An analyst could ignore such intangible benefits, but doing so implies that their value is zero and may lead the organization to reject IT investments that could substantially increase revenues and profitability. Therefore, financial analyses need to consider not just tangible benefits but also intangible benefits in such a way that the decision reflects their potential impact. The question is how to do it.

HANDLING INTANGIBLE BENEFITS. The most straightforward solution to the problem of evaluating intangible benefits in cost-benefit analysis is to make *rough estimates* of monetary values for all intangible benefits, and then conduct a NVP or similar financial analysis. The simplicity of this approach is attractive, but in many cases the assumptions used in these estimates are debatable. If the technology is acquired because decision makers assigned too high a value to intangible benefits, the organization could find that it has wasted some valuable resources. On the other hand, if the valuation of intangible benefits is too low, the organization might reject the investment and then find that it is losing market share to competitors who did implement the technology. (See Plumtree Corp., 2001, for a study on translating intangible benefits to dollar amounts.)

There are many approaches to handling intangibles (e.g., see Read et al., 2001). Sawhney (2002) suggests the following solutions:

- *Think broadly and softly.* Supplement hard financial metrics with soft ones that may be more strategic in nature and may be important leading indicators of financial outcomes. Measures such as customer and partner satisfaction, customer loyalty, response time to competitive actions, and improved responsiveness are examples of soft measures. Subjective measures can be objective if used consistently over time. For instance, customer satisfaction measured consistently on a five-point scale can be an objective basis for measuring the performance of customer-facing initiatives.

- *Pay your freight first.* Think carefully about short-term benefits that can "pay the freight" for the initial investment in the project. For example, a telecom company found that it could justify its investment in data warehousing based on the cost savings from data mart consolidation, even though the real payoffs from the project would come later from increased cross-selling opportunities.

- *Follow the unanticipated.* Keep an open mind about where the payoff from IT and e-business projects may come from, and follow opportunities that present themselves. Eli Lilly & Co. created a Web site called InnoCentive (*innocentive.com*) to attract scientists to solve problems in return for financial rewards ("bounties"). In the process, Lilly established contact with 8,000 exceptional scientists, and Lilly's HR department has used this list of contacts for recruiting.

The Business Case Approach

One method used to justify investments in projects, or even in entire new companies, is referred to as the *business case approach*. The concept of a business case received lots of attention in the mid-1990s when it was used to justify funding for investment in dot-coms. In 2002–2003, it has become clear that one of the reasons for the collapse of the dot-com bubble was improper business cases submitted to investors. Nevertheless, if done correctly, business cases can be a useful tool.

A **business case** is a written document that is used by managers to garner funding for one or more specific applications or projects. Its major emphasis is the justification for a specific required investment, but it also provides the bridge between the initial plan and its execution. Its purpose is not only to get approval

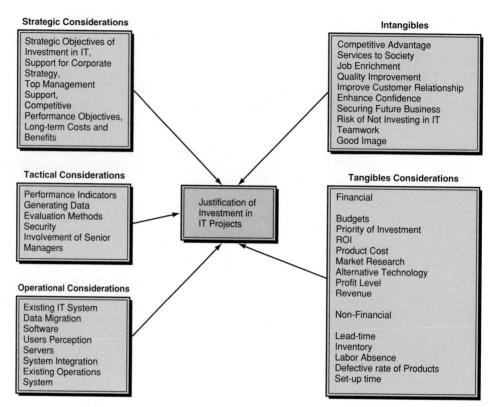

FIGURE 13.4 A model
for investment justification
in IT projects. (*Source:*
Gunagekaran et al., 2001,
p. 354.)

and funding, but also to provide the foundation for tactical decision making and technology risk management. A business case is usually conducted in existing organizations that want to embark on new IT projects (for example, an e-procurement project). The business case helps to clarify how the organization will use its resources in the best way to accomplish the IT strategy. It helps the organization concentrate on justifying the investment, on risk management, and on fit of an IT project with the organization's mission. Software for preparing a business case for IT (and for EC in particular) is commercially available (e.g., from *paloalto.com* and from *bplans.com*).

A business case for IT investment can be very complex. Gunasekaran et al. (2001) divided such justification into five parts as shown in Figure 13.4.

Sometimes an IT project is necessary in order for the organization to stay in business, and in those instances, the business case is very simple: "We must do it, we have no choice." For example, the U.S. Internal Revenue Service is requiring businesses to switch to electronic systems for filing their tax returns. Similarly, sometimes an organization must invest because its competitors have done so and if it does not follow, it will lose customers. Examples are e-banking and some CRM services. These types of investments do not require firms to do a lot of analysis.

For a description of business cases in e-commerce, see Turban et al. (2004). For a tool for building a business case, see *sap.com/solutions/case builder*. For a discussion of how to conduct a business case for global expansion, see DePalma (2001). An example of a business case for wireless networks, prepared by Intel Corp. (2002), is presented in Online File W13.5.

TABLE 13.2 Traditional Methods of Evaluating Investments

Method	Advantages	Disadvantages
Internal rate of return (IRR)	Brings all projects to common footing. Conceptually familiar.	Assumes reinvestment at same rate. Can have multiple roots. No assumed discount rate.
Net present value or net worth (NPV or NW)	Very common. Maximizes value for unconstrained project selection.	Difficult to compare projects of unequal lives or sizes.
Equivalent annuity (EA)	Brings all project NPVs to common footing. Convenient annual figure.	Assumes projects repeat to least common multiple of lives, or imputes salvage value.
Payback period	May be discounted or nondiscounted. Measure of exposure.	Ignores flows after payback is reached. Assumes standard project cash flow profile.
Benefit-to-cost ratio	Conceptually familiar. Brings all projects to common footing.	May be difficult to classify outlays between expense and investment.

Source: Compiled from *Capital Budgeting and Long-Term Financing Decisions,* 2nd ed., by N. E. Seitz © 1995. Reprinted with permission of South-Western College Publishing, a division of Thomson Learning.

Evaluating IT Investment: Conclusions

This section has showed that several traditional methods can be used to assess the value of IT information and IT investment. Table 13.2 lists some of the traditional financial evaluation methods with their advantages and disadvantages. Different organizations use different methods, which often are chosen by management and may change over time as an organization's finance personnel come and go. For example, many companies have automated programs that use company-specific inputs and hurdles for making ROI calculations.

However, traditional methods may not be useful for assessing some of the newest technologies (e.g., see Violino, 1997). (An example of such a case—acquiring expert systems—is shown in Online File W13.6). Because traditional methods may not be useful for evaluating new technologies, there are special methodologies (some of them incorporated in computerized models) for dealing with investment in IT. We will address some of these methods next.

13.3 METHODS FOR EVALUATING AND JUSTIFYING IT INVESTMENT

As indicated earlier, evaluating and justifying IT investment can pose problems different from traditional capital investment decisions such as whether to buy a new delivery truck. However, even though the relationship between intangible IT benefits and performance is not clear, some investments should be better than others. How can organizations increase the probability that their IT investments will improve their performance?

A comprehensive list of over 60 different appraisal methods for IT investments can be found in Renkema (2000). The appraisal methods are categorized into the following four types.

- *Financial approach.* These appraisal methods consider only impacts that can be monetary-valued. They focus on incoming and outgoing cash flows as a result of the investment made. Net present value and return on investment are examples of financial-approach methods.

● *Multicriteria approach.* These appraisal methods consider both financial impacts and nonfinancial impacts that cannot be (or cannot easily be) expressed in monetary terms. These methods employ quantitative and qualitative decision-making techniques. Information economics and value analysis are examples.

● *Ratio approach.* These methods use several ratios (e.g., IT expenditures vs. total turnover) to assist in IT investment evaluation.

● *Portfolio approach.* These methods apply portfolios (or grids) to plot several investment proposals against decision-making criteria. The portfolio methods are more informative compared to multicriteria methods and generally use fewer evaluation criteria.

The following specific evaluation methods that are particularly useful in evaluating IT investment are discussed in this section: total cost of ownership, value analysis, information economics, use of benchmarks, management by maxim, and real-option valuation. Other methods are cited briefly at the end of the section.

Total Cost of Ownership

As mentioned earlier, the costs of an IT system can sometimes accumulate over many years. An interesting approach for IT cost evaluation is the **total cost of ownership (TCO).** TCO is a formula for calculating the cost of owning, operating, and controlling an IT system, even one as simple as a PC. The cost includes *acquisition cost* (hardware and software), *operations cost* (maintenance, training, operations, evaluation, technical support, installation, downtime, auditing, virus damage, and power consumption), and *control cost* (standardization, security, central services). The TCO can be a hundred percent higher that just the cost of the hardware, especially for PCs (David et al., 2002). By identifying these various costs, organizations can make more accurate cost-benefit analyses. A methodology for calculating TCO is offered by David et al. (2002). They also provide a detailed example of the items to be included in the TCO calculations (see Online File W13.7). For further discussion, see Vijayan (2001) and Blum (2001), and for a comprehensive study, see Ferrin and Plank (2002).

A concept similar to TCO is **total benefits of ownership (TBO).** These benefits cover both tangible and the intangible benefits. By calculating and comparing both TCO and TBO, one can compute the payoff of an IT investment [Payoff = TBO − TCO]. For details on the calculations, see Devaraj and Kohli (2002) and also Online File W13.7.

Value Analysis

The **value analysis** method evaluates intangible benefits on a low-cost, trial basis before deciding whether to commit to a larger investment in a complete system. Keen (1981) developed the value analysis method to assist organizations considering investments in decision support systems (DSSs). The major problem with justifying a DSS is that most of the benefits are intangible and not readily convertible into monetary values. Some—such as better decisions, better understanding of business situations, and improved communication—are difficult to measure even in nonmonetary terms. These problems in evaluating DSSs are similar to the problems in evaluating intangible benefits for other types of systems. Therefore, value analysis could be applicable to other types of IT

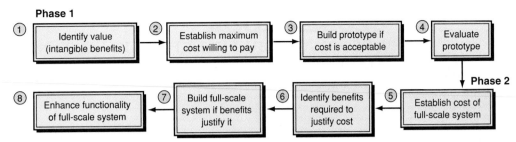

FIGURE 13.5 Steps in the value analysis approach.

investments in which a large proportion of the added value derives from intangible benefits.

The value analysis approach includes eight steps, grouped into two phases. As illustrated in Figure 13.5, the first phase (first four steps) works with a low-cost prototype. Depending on the initial results, this prototype is followed by a full-scale system in the second phase.

In the first phase the decision maker identifies the desired capabilities and the (generally intangible) potential benefits. The developers estimate the cost of providing the capabilities; if the decision maker feels the benefits are worth this cost, a small-scale prototype of the DSS is constructed. The prototype then is evaluated.

The results of the first phase provide information that helps with the decision about the second phase. After using the prototype, the user has a better understanding of the value of the benefits, and of the additional features the full-scale system needs to include. In addition, the developers can make a better estimate of the cost of the final product. The question at this point is: What benefits are necessary to justify this cost? If the decision maker feels that the system can provide these benefits, development proceeds on the full-scale system.

Though it was designed for DSSs, the value analysis approach is applicable to any information technology that can be tested on a low-cost basis before deciding whether to make a full investment. The current trend of buying rather than developing software, along with the increasingly common practice of offering software on a free-trial basis for 30 to 90 days, provide ample opportunities for the use of this approach. Organizations may also have opportunities to pilot the use of new systems in specific operating units, and then to implement them on a full-scale basis if the initial results are favorable. For further discussion see Fine et al. (2002).

Information Economics

The **information economics** approach is similar to the concept of critical success factors in that it focuses on key organizational objectives, including intangible benefits. Information economics incorporates the familiar technique of *scoring* methodologies, which are used in many evaluation situations.

A **scoring methodology** evaluates alternatives by assigning weights and scores to various aspects and then calculating the weighted totals. The analyst first identifies all the key performance issues and assigns a weight to each one. Each alternative in the evaluation receives a score on each factor, usually between zero and 100 points, or between zero and 10. These scores are multiplied by the weighting factors and then totaled. The alternative with the highest score is judged the best (or projects can be ranked, as in the R.O. Iowa case at the beginning of the chapter). *A Closer Look 13.2* (page 606) shows an example of using a scoring methodology to evaluate two different alternatives.

A CLOSER LOOK
13.2 SCORING WORKSHEET FOR EVALUATION OF ALTERNATIVES A VERSUS B

Decision Participant Most Interested in Criteria	Criteria	Weight	Alternative A Grade	Alternative A Score	Alternative B Grade	Alternative B Score
	Intangibles (Benefits and Risks)					
CEO	Improve revenues, profits, and market share.	4	2	8	2	8
CEO	Integrate global operations.	4	3	12	5	20
CFO	Have flexibility for business changes and growth.	4	4	16	2	8
CFO	Have more end-user self-sufficiency.	4	3	12	3	12
VP, Human Resources (HR)	Improve employee morale.	2	2	4	1	2
CIO	Manage risk of organizational resistance to change.	2	−1	−2	−3	−6
CIO	Manage risk of project failure.	2	−1	−2	−2	−4
	Total Senior Management	**22**		**48**		**40**
CFO	Increase earnings per share.	2	2	4	2	4
CFO	Improve cash flow.	2	2	4	3	6
Dir. Acctg.	Close books faster.	2	3	6	2	4
Director, Fincl. Reporting	Expand profitability by better product line reporting.	2	3	6	3	6
	Total Finance	**8**		**20**		**20**
VP-HR	Improve employee productivity.	2	3	6	3	6
VP-HR	Attract, retain high-quality employees.	2	3	6	2	4
Dir. Employee Relations (ER)	Strengthen labor relations.	2	3	6	2	4
VP-HR	Enhance "employee service" image of HR.	2	3	6	2	4
Dir.-ER	Manage risk of insufficient communications with employees.	2	−2	−4	−3	−6
	Total Human Resources	**10**		**20**		**12**
CIO	Rapid implementation.	2	4	8	2	4
Director, Systems	Openness and portability.	2	4	8	3	6
Dir.-Sys	Easier software customization.	2	4	8	3	6
Dir.-Sys	Less software modification over time.	2	4	8	4	8
CIO	Global processing and support.	2	2	4	4	8
	Total Information Systems	**10**		**36**		**32**
	Total Intangibles	**50**		**124**		**104**
	Tangible Benefits					
CEO	Return on investment.	20	3	60	3	60
CEO	Payback period	20	3	60	2	40
	Total Tangibles	**40**		**120**		**100**
	Grand Total	**90**		**244**		**204**

The results favor option A (total of 244 vs. 204).

Source: Compiled from "Peoplesoft Strategic Investment Model," *Peoplesoft.com* (accessed August 1997).

The information economics approach uses *organizational objectives* to determine which factors to include, and what weights to assign, in the scoring methodology. The approach is flexible enough to include factors in the analysis such as impacts on customers and suppliers (the value chain). Executives in an organization determine the relevant objectives and weights at a given point in time, subject to revision if there are changes in the environment. These factors and weights are then used to evaluate IT alternatives; the highest scores go to the items that have the greatest potential to improve organizational performance.

Note that this approach can incorporate both tangible and intangible benefits. If there is a strong connection between a benefit of IT investment (such as quicker decision making) and an organizational objective (such as faster product development), the benefit will influence the final score even if it does not have a monetary value. Thus the information economics model helps solve the problem of assessing intangible benefits by linking the evaluation of these benefits to the factors that are most important to organizational performance.

Approaches like this are very flexible. The analyst can vary the weights over time; for example, tangible benefits might receive heavier weights at times when earnings are weak. The approach can also take risk into account, by using negative weights for factors that reduce the probability of obtaining the benefits. Information economics studies appear in various shapes depending on the circumstances. An example in banking is provided by Peffers and Sarrinan (2002). Note that in this study, as in many others, special attention is paid to the issue of *risk assessment*. (See also Gaulke, 2002.) Online File W13.8 shows an analysis of a decision of whether to develop a system in-house or buy it. Information economics can be implemented by software packages such as Expert Choice (*expertchoice.com*).

Assessing Investments in IT Infrastructure

Information systems projects are usually not standalone applications. In most cases they depend for support on enabling infrastructures already installed in the organization. These infrastructure technologies include mainframe computers, operating systems, networks, database management systems, utility programs, development tools, and more. Since many of the infrastructure benefits are intangible and are spread over many different present and future applications, it is hard to estimate their value or to evaluate the desirability of enhancements or upgrades. In other words, it is much more difficult to evaluate infrastructure investment decisions than investments in specific information systems application projects. Two methods are recommended: use of benchmarks and management by maxim.

USING BENCHMARKS TO ASSESS INFRASTRUCTURE INVESTMENTS. One approach to evaluating infrastructure is to focus on *objective* measures of performance known as **benchmarks.** These measures are often available from trade associations within an industry or from consulting firms. A comparison of measures of performance or a comparison of an organization's expenditures with averages for the industry or with values for the more efficient performers in the industry indicates how well the organization is using its infrastructure. If performance is below standard, corrective action is indicated. The benchmark approach implicitly assumes that IT infrastructure investments are justified if they are managed efficiently.

Benchmarks come in two very different forms: *Metrics* and *best-practice benchmarks*. **Metric benchmarks** provide numeric measures of performance; for example: (1) IT expenses as percent of total revenues, (2) percent of downtime (time when the computer is unavailable), (3) central processing unit (CPU) usage as a percentage of total capacity, and (4) percentage of IS projects completed on time and within budget. These types of measures are very useful to managers, even though sometimes they lead to the wrong conclusions. For example, a ratio of IT expenses to revenues that is lower than the industry average might indicate that a firm is operating more efficiently than its competitors. Or it might indicate that the company is investing less in IT than it should and will become less competitive as a result. An illustration of typical support expected from benchmarking tools in complex IT environments is described in Online File W13.9.

Metric benchmarks can help diagnose problems, but they do not necessarily show how to solve them. Therefore, many organizations also use **best-practice benchmarks.** Here the emphasis is on how information system activities are actually performed rather than on numeric measures of performance. For example, an organization might feel that its IT infrastructure management is very important to its performance. It then could obtain information about best practices about how to operate and manage IT infrastructure. These best practices might be from other organizations in the same industry, from a more efficient division of its own organization, or from another industry entirely. The organization would then implement these best practices for all of its own IT infrastructure, to bring performance up to the level of the leaders.

MANAGEMENT BY MAXIM FOR IT INFRASTRUCTURE. Organizations that are composed of multiple business units, including large, multidivisional ones, frequently need to make decisions about the appropriate level and types of infrastructure that will support and be shared among their individual operating units. These decisions are important because infrastructure can amount to over 50 percent of the total IT budget, and because it can increase effectiveness through synergies across the organization. However, because of substantial differences among organizations in their culture, structure, and environment, what is appropriate for one will not necessarily be suitable for others. The fact that many of the benefits of infrastructure are intangible further complicates this issue.

Broadbent and Weill (1997) suggest a method called **management by maxim** to deal with this problem. This method brings together corporate executives, business-unit managers, and IT executives in planning sessions to determine appropriate infrastructure investments through five steps that are diagrammed in Figure 13.6. In the process, managers articulate *business maxims*—short well-defined statements of organizational strategies or goals—and develop corresponding *IT maxims* that explain how IT could be used to support the business maxims. The five steps are further discussed in Online File W13.10.

Notice that Figure 13.6 also shows a line at the bottom flowing through an item labeled "Deals." This represents a theoretical alternative approach in the absence of appropriate maxims, where the IT manager negotiates with individual business units to obtain adequate funding for *shared infrastructure*. This approach can work where there is no shared infrastructure, or where the infrastructure category is a utility. However, Broadbent and Weill have not found any cases of firms that developed an enabling infrastructure via deals.

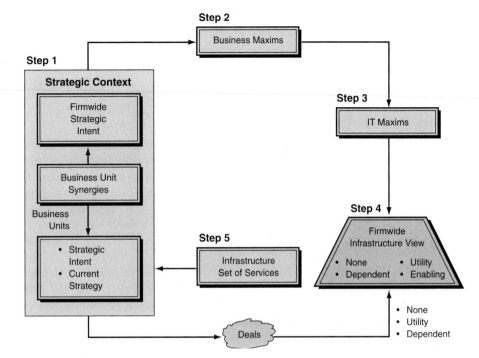

FIGURE 13.6
Management by maxim: Linking strategy and infrastructure. (*Source:* M. Broadbent and P. Weill, "Management by Maxim," *Sloan Management Review,* Spring 1997, p. 79, by permission of publisher. ©2001 by Massachusetts Institute of Technology. All rights reserved.)

Real-Option Valuation of IT Investment

A promising new approach for evaluating IT investments is to recognize that they can increase an organization's performance in the future. The concept of real options comes from the field of finance, where financial managers have in recent years developed a strategic approach to capital budgeting decisions. Instead of using only traditional measures like NPV to make capital decisions, financial managers are looking for opportunities that may be *embedded in* capital projects. These opportunities, if taken, will enable the organization to alter future cash flows in a way that will increase profitability. These opportunities are called **real options** (to distinguish them from *financial options* that give investors the right to buy or sell a financial asset at a stated price on or before a set date). Common types of real options include the option to expand a project (so as to capture additional cash flows from such growth), the option to terminate a project that is doing poorly (in order to minimize loss on the project), and the option to accelerate or delay a project. Current IT investments, especially for infrastructure, can be viewed as another type of real option. Such capital budgeting investments make it possible to respond quickly to unexpected and unforeseeable challenges and opportunities in later years. If the organization waits in its investment decisions until the benefits have been established, it may be very difficult to catch up with competitors that have already invested in the infrastructure and have become familiar with the technology.

Applying just the NPV concept (or other purely financial) measure to an investment in IT infrastructure, an organization may decide that the costs of a proposed investment exceed the tangible benefits. However, if the project creates opportunities for additional projects in the future—that is, if it creates opportunities for real options—the investment also has an options value that should be added to its other benefits (see Benaroch, 2002 and Devaraj and Kohli, 2002).

The mathematics of real-option valuation are well established but unfortunately are too complex for many managers. (See Dixit and Pindyck, 1995, for details.) For a discussion on using real-option pricing analysis to evaluate a real-world IT project investment in four different settings, see Benaroch and Kauffman (1999). Li and Johnson (2002) use a similar approach. For an example of DSS evaluation using real-option theory, see Kumar (1999). Rayport and Jaworski (2001) applied the method for evaluating EC initiatives (see Online File W13.11).

Other Methods and Tools

Several other methods exist for evaluating IT investment. For example, most large vendors provide proprietary calculators for ROI. However, according to King (2002), those may be biased (and may lead to a sometimes-unjustified decision to adopt a project). To make the decision less biased, some companies use a third-party evaluator, such as IDC (*idc.co*m) or META Group (*metagroup.com*) to conduct ROI studies. An example of such a calculator is SAP Business Case Builder. (For details see *sap.com/solutions/casebuilder*.) Several independent vendors offer ROI calculators (e.g., CIO View Corporation).

In addition, there are other popular methods (e.g., see Irani and Love, 2000–2001), a few of which we describe briefly before ending this section.

THE BALANCED SCORECARD METHOD. The **balanced scorecard method** evaluates the overall health of organizations and projects. Initiated by Kaplan and Norton (1996), the method advocates that managers focus not only on short-term financial results, but also on four other areas for which metrics are available. These areas are: (1) finance, including both short- and long-term measures; (2) customers (how customers view the organization); (3) internal business processes (finding areas in which to excel); and (4) learning and growth (the ability to change and expand). The key idea is that an organization should consider all four strategic areas when considering IT investments.

Swany (2002) attempted to use the balanced scorecard to measure the performance of EC systems, including intangible benefits. He examined the EC systems from two perspectives: that of the e-business and that of the user. Rayport and Jawarski (2001) developed a variant of the balanced scorecard called *performance dashboard,* which they advocate for evaluation of EC strategy. Several other attempts to fit the balanced scorecard approach to IT project assessment have been made (e.g., see *balancedscorecard.org*). The methodology actually is embedded in several vendors' products (e.g., *sas.com/solutions/bsc/*). For demos see *corvu.com*.

THE EXPLORATION, INVOLVEMENT, ANALYSIS, AND COMMUNICATIONS (EIAC) MODEL. Devaraj and Kohli (2002) propose a methology for implementing IT payoff initiatives. The method is composed of nine phases, divided into four categories: exploration (E), involvement (I), analysis (A), and communication (C). These are shown in Online File W13.12 at the book's Web site. For details see Devaraj and Kohli (2002).

ACTIVITY-BASED COSTING. A more recent approach for assessing IT investment is proposed by Gerlach et al. (2002), who suggest use of the *activity-based costing* (ABC) approach to assist in IT investment analysis. (For details on how ABC works, see a management or managerial accounting textbook.) Using a case study, Gerlach et al. showed that the company that utilized ABC derived significant benefits from a better understanding of IT delivery costs and a rationale for explaining IT costs to department managers. Mutual understanding of IT costs is a necessary condition for shared responsibility of IT, which in turn leads to effective economic decision making that optimizes resource utilization and the alignment of IT with business strategy. In addition, the use of ABC helps in reducing operational costs.

EXPECTED VALUE ANALYSIS. It is relatively easy to estimate **expected value (EV)** of possible future benefits by multiplying the size of the benefit by the probability of its occurrence. For example, an organization might consider investing in a corporate portal only if there is a 50 percent probability that this would result in new business worth $10 million in additional profits and the cost will be less than $5 million. The value of this specific benefit would be 50 percent times $10 million, or $5 million. This method is simple but like any EV approach, it can be used only for repetitive investments.

Unfortunately, none of the above methods is perfect, and it is not simple for organizations to decide which method to use in which case.

13.4 IT ECONOMICS STRATEGIES: CHARGEBACK AND OUTSOURCING

In addition to identifying and evaluating the benefits of IT, organizations also need to account for its costs. Ideally, the organization's accounting systems will effectively deal with two issues: First, they should provide an accurate measure of total IT costs for management control purposes. Second, they should charge users for shared (usually infrastructure) IT investments and services in a manner that contributes to the achievement of organization goals. These are two very challenging goals for any accounting system, and the complexities and rapid pace of change make them even more difficult to achieve in the context of IT.

In the early days of computing it was much easier to identify costs than it is today. Computers and other hardware were very expensive and were managed by centralized organizational units with their own personnel. Most application software was developed internally rather than purchased. IT was used only for a few well-defined applications, such as payroll, inventory management, and accounts payable/receivable. In contrast, nowadays computers are cheap, and software is increasingly purchased or leased. The overwhelming majority of the total processing power is located on the collective desktops of the organization rather than in centralized computer centers, and it is managed by individual organizational units rather than a centralized IS department. A large proportion of the costs are in "hidden," indirect costs that are often overlooked (e.g., see Barthelmy, 2001.)

These trends make it very difficult just to identify, let alone effectively control, the total costs of IT. As a practical matter, many organizations track costs associated with centralized IS and leave management accounting for desktop IT to the user organizations. However, the trend toward attaching personal computers to networks, and the availability of network management software, make it easier to track and manage costs related to desktop IT. Some organizations indicate "six-digits" savings by using network management software to identify which computers use what software, and then reducing the site licenses to correspond to the actual usage (see Coopee, 2000, for details).

In this section we look at two strategies for costing of IT services: chargeback and outsourcing.

Chargeback

Although it is hard to accurately measure total IT costs, organizations can nevertheless use accounting systems to influence organizational IT usage in desirable directions. Large organizations typically require individual operating and support units to develop annual budgets and to justify variances. Services from the central IS department represent a significant budget item for most of these units, so the way users are charged for these services will influence how much they use them.

In some organizations, the ISD functions as an unallocated cost center: All expenses go into an overhead account. The problem with this approach is that IT is then a "free good" that has no explicit cost, so there are no incentives to control usage or avoid waste.

A second alternative is called **chargeback** (also known as chargeout or cost recovery). In this approach, all costs of IT are allocated to users as accurately as possible, based on actual costs and usage levels. Accurate allocation sounds desirable in principle, but it can create problems in practice. The most accurate measures of use may reflect technological factors that are totally incomprehensible to the user. If fixed costs are allocated on the basis of total usage throughout the organization, which varies from month to month, charges will fluctuate for an individual unit even though its own usage does not change. These considerations can reduce the credibility of the chargeback system.

BEHAVIOR-ORIENTED CHARGEBACK. A third approach is to employ a **behavior-oriented chargeback** system. Such a system sets IT service costs in a way that meets organizational objectives, even though the charges may not correspond to actual costs. The primary objective of this type of system is influencing users' behavior. For example, it is possible to encourage (or discourage) usage of certain IT resources by assigning lower (or higher) costs. For example, the organization may wish to encourage use in off-peak hours and so might decide to charge business units less for processing from 1 to 4 A.M. than from 9 A.M. to noon. Or, the organization may encourage use of wireline over wireless technologies, or encourage the use of a central printer rather than a departmental one.

Although more difficult to develop, a behavior-oriented chargeback system recognizes the importance of IT—and its effective management—to the success of the organization. It not only avoids the unallocated cost center's problem of overuse of "free" resources; it can also reduce the use of scarce resources where demand exceeds supply, even with fully allocated costs. For more on behavior-oriented chargeback see Online File W13.13.

There are other methods of chargeback in addition to the regular and behavior-oriented methods. The reason for the variety of methods is that it is very difficult to approximate costs, especially in companies where multiple independent operating units are sharing a centralized system. Therefore, organizations have developed chargeback methods that make sense to their managers and their particular needs. For a review of methods, see McAdam (1996).

The difficulties in applying chargeback systems may be one of the drivers of IT outsourcing.

Outsourcing as an Economic Strategy

Information technology is now a vital part of almost every organization and plays an important supporting role in most functions. However, IT is not the primary business of many organizations. Their core competencies—the things they do best and that represent their competitive strengths—are in manufacturing, or retailing, or services, or some other function. IT is an enabler only, and it is complex, expensive, and constantly changing. IT is difficult to manage, even for organizations with above-average management skills. For such organizations, the most effective strategy for obtaining the economic benefits of IT and controlling its costs may be **outsourcing,** which is obtaining IT services from outside vendors rather than from internal IS units within the organization. According to a survey reported by Corbett (2001), the major reasons cited by large U.S. companies for use of outsourcing are: focus on core competency (36%), cost reduction (36%), improved quality (13%), increased speed to market (10%), and faster innovation (4%).

Companies typically outsource many of their activities, from contract manufacturing to physical security. But most of all they outsource IT activities (see Minicases 1 and 2 at the end of the chapter, and Online Minicase W13.1). Outsourcing is more than just purchasing hardware and software. It is a long-term result-oriented relationship for whole business activities, over which the provider has a large amount of control and managerial direction. For an overview of the past, present, and future of outsourcing, see Lee et al. (2003).

Outsourcing IT functions, such as payroll services, has been around since the early days of data processing. Contract programmers and computer time-sharing services are longstanding examples. What is new is that, since the late 1980s, many organizations are outsourcing the majority of their IT functions rather than just incidental parts. The trend became very visible in 1989 when Eastman Kodak announced it was transferring its data centers to IBM under a 10-year, $500 million contract. This example, at a prominent multibillion-dollar company, gave a clear signal that outsourcing was a legitimate approach to managing IT. Since then, many mega outsourcing deals were announced, some for several billion dollars. (For a list of some recent outsourcing deals and the story of a 10-year, $3 billion contract between Procter & Gamble and Hewlett-Packard, see Cushing, 2003. For the case of outsourcing at Pilkington, see Online File W13.14.)

In a typical situation, the outsourcing firm hires the IS employees of the customer and buys the computer hardware. The cash from this sale is an important incentive for outsourcing by firms with financial problems. The outsourcer provides IT services under a five- to ten-year contract that specifies a baseline level of services, with additional charges for higher volumes or services not identified in the baseline. Many smaller firms provide limited-scale outsourcing of individual services, but only the largest outsourcing firms can take over large proportions of the IT functions of major organizations. In the mid-1990s, IBM, EDS, and Computer Sciences Corp. were winning approximately two-thirds of the largest outsourcing contracts. Today other vendors (e.g., HP and Oracle) also provide such services.

Offshore outsourcing of software development has become a common practice in recent years. About one-third of Fortune 500 companies have started to outsource software development to software companies in India (Carmel and Agarwal, 2002). This trend of offshore outsourcing is largely due to the emphasis of Indian companies on process quality by adhering to models such as Software Engineering Institute's Software Capability Maturity Model (SW-CMM) and through ISO 9001 certification. India has fifteen of the twenty-three organizations worldwide that have achieved Level 5, the highest in SW-CMM ratings. For further details on offshore outsourcing, see Cusumano (2000), Gillin (2003), and Carmel and Agarwal (2002).

In addition to the traditionally outsourced services, Brown and Young (2000) identify two more scenarios for future outsourcing: creation of shared environments (e.g., exchanges, portals, e-commerce backbones), and providing access to shared environments (e.g., application service providers, Internet data centers). For example, Flooz.com, an online gift-currency store, outsourced its storage requirements to StorageNetworks, a storage service provider (Wilkinson, 2000). See *outsourcing-center.com* for details on practices in outsourcing of various types of services.

Finally, a relatively new approach is *strategic outsourcing* (Garner, 1998), whereby you can generate new business, retain skilled employees, and effectively manage emerging technologies. Strategic outsourcing facilitates the leveraging of knowledge capabilities and investments of others by exploiting intellectual outsourcing in addition to outsourcing of traditional functions and services (Quinn, 1999).

ASPs AND UTILITY COMPUTING.   The concept behind an **application service provider (ASP)** is simple: From a central, off-site data center, a vendor manages and distributes software-based services and solutions, via the Internet. Your data seem to be run locally, whereas they are actually coming from the off-site data center. The user company pays subscription and/or usage fees, getting IT services on demand (utility computing). In other words, ASPs are a form of outsourcing.

ASP services are becoming very popular, but they do have potential pitfalls. A comprehensive comparison of the advantages and pitfalls of ASPs is provided by Segev and Gebauer (2001). According to Lee et al. (2003), the ASP approach is the future of outsourcing. The authors provide a list of ASPs in different areas and suggest a collaborative strategy with the users. For further discussion see Chapter 14 and Trudy (2002).

MANAGEMENT SERVICE PROVIDERS.   A **management service provider (MSP)** is a vendor that remotely manages and monitors enterprise applications—ERP, CRM, firewalls, proprietary e-business applications, network infrastructure, etc. Like ASPs, MSPs charge subscription fees. But they claim to be an improvement over the ASP model because they permit companies to outsource the *maintenance* of their applications. MSPs make sure that applications are up and running, thus providing a relatively cheap, easy, and unobtrusive way for an organization to prevent outages and malfunctions. Meanwhile, because MSPs provide 24/7 monitoring, companies do not have to worry about staffing up to handle that nonrevenue-producing task. And if the MSP suddenly shuts its doors, as has happened all too often in the ASP world (and recently in the MSP world too), the organization can continue with minimal disruption because it still has its applications.

OUTSOURCING AND E-COMMERCE.   Consider the following story, described by Palvia (2002): In the spring of 1996 the competitors of Canadian Imperial Bank of Commerce (CIBC) were ahead in implementing Internet banking, and CIBC was starting to lose market share. The bank needed to move quickly to implement its own Internet capabilities. But, being a bank and not an IT expert, this was a challenge. So the bank decided to outsource the job to IBM's Global Services. Together, CIBC and IBM were able to implement home banking in six months. By 1998 the bank regained market share, having 200,000 online clients.

CIBC's dilemma is becoming a familiar story in just about every industry. Time constraints brought on by competitive challenges, security issues, and a shortage of skilled system developers in the Internet/intranet field contribute to a boom in the outsourcing business. Some organizations may decide to outsource because they need to sell off IT assets to generate funds. In addition, implementing EC applications forces companies to outsource mission-critical applications on a scale never before seen. According to the GartnerGroup, this need for EC applications will result in the tripling of IT outsourcing in three years. Forrester Research found that 90 percent of the companies they polled use or plan to use Internet-related outsourcing (Palvia, 2002).

A special EC outsourcing consideration is the implementation of extranets. Implementing an extranet is very difficult due to security issues and the need to have the system be rapidly expandable. (Some companies report 1,000 percent growth for EC activities in a year; e.g., see *hotmail.com*.) General Electric Information Services (*geis.com*), an extranet outsourcer, charges between $100,000 and $150,000 to set up an extranet, plus a $5,000/month service fee. However, users of these services report an ROI of 100 to 1,000 percent. For details see Duvall (1998).

OUTSOURCING ADVANTAGES AND DISADVANTAGES. The use of IT outsourcing is still very controversial (e.g., see Hirschheim and Lacity, 2000). Outsourcing advocates describe IT as a commodity, a generic item like electricity or janitorial services. They note the potential benefits of outsourcing, in general, as listed in Table 13.3 (page 616).

In contrast, others see many limitations of outsourcing (e.g., see Cramm, 2001). One reason for the contradicting opinions is that many of the benefits of outsourcing are intangible or have long-term payoffs. Clemons (2000) identifies the following risks associated with outsourcing:

- *Shirking* occurs when a vendor deliberately underperforms while claiming full payment (e.g., billing for more hours than were worked, providing excellent staff at first and later replacing them with less qualified ones).
- *Poaching* occurs when a vendor develops a strategic application for a client and then uses it for other clients (e.g., vendor redevelops similar systems for other clients at much lower cost, or vendor enters into client's business, competing against it).
- *Opportunistic repricing* ("*holdup*") occurs when a client enters into a long-term contract with a vendor and the vendor changes financial terms at some point or overcharges for unanticipated enhancements and contract extensions.

Another possible risk of outsourcing is failure to consider all the costs. Some costs are hidden. Barthelmy (2001) discusses the following hidden costs: (1) vendor search and contracting, (2) transitioning from in-house IT to a vendor, (3) cost of managing the effort, and (4) transition back to in-house IT after outsourcing. These costs can be controlled to some extent, however.

Despite the risks and limitations, the extent of IT outsourcing is increasing rapidly together with the use of ASPs. We will return to these topics in Chapter 14.

TABLE 13.3 Potential Outsourcing Benefits

FINANCIAL
- Avoidance of heavy capital investment, thereby releasing funds for other uses.
- Improved cash flow and cost accountability.
- Cost benefits from economies of scale and from sharing computer housing, hardware, software, and personnel.
- Less need for expensive office space.

TECHNICAL
- Greater freedom to choose software due to a wider range of hardware.
- Ability to achieve technological improvements more easily.
- Greater access to technical skills.

MANAGEMENT
- Concentration on developing and running core business activity.
- Delegation of IT development (design, production, and acquisition) and operational responsibility to supplier.
- Elimination of need to recruit and retain competent IT staff.

HUMAN RESOURCES
- Opportunity to draw on specialist skills, available from a pool of expertise, when needed.
- Enriched career development and opportunities for staff.

QUALITY
- Clearly defined service levels.
- Improved performance accountability.
- Quality accreditation.

FLEXIBILITY
- Quick response to business demands.
- Ability to handle IT peaks and valleys more effectively.

STRATEGIES FOR OUTSOURCING.   Organizations should consider the following strategies in managing the risks associated with outsourcing contracts.

1. *Understand the project.* Clients must have a high degree of understanding of the project, including its requirements, the method of its implementation, and the source of expected economic benefits. A common characteristic of successful outsourcing contracts is that the client was generally capable of developing the application but chose to outsource simply because of constraints on time or staff availability (Clemons, 2000).

2. *Divide and conquer.* Dividing a large project into smaller and more manageable pieces will greatly reduce programmatic risk and provides clients with an exit strategy if any part of the project fails (Clemons, 2000).

3. *Align incentives.* Designing contractual incentives based on activities that can be measured accurately can result in achieving desired performance (Clemons, 2000).

4. *Write short-period contracts.* Outsourcing contracts are often written for five- to ten-year terms. Because IT and the competitive environment change so rapidly, it is very possible that some of the terms will not be in the customer's best interests after five years. If a long-term contract is used, it needs to include adequate mechanisms for negotiating revisions where necessary (Marcolin and McLellan, 1998).

5. *Control subcontracting.* Vendors may subcontract some of the services to other vendors. The contract should give the customer some control over the circumstances, including choice of vendors, and any subcontract arrangements (Marcolin and McLellan, 1998).

6. *Do selective outsourcing.* This is a strategy used by many corporations who prefer not to outsource the majority of their IT, but rather to outsource certain areas (such as system integration or network security) (Marcolin and McLellan, 1998). Cramm (2001) suggests that an organization *insource* important work, such as strategic applications, investments, and HRM.

At this point of time, the phenomenon of large-scale IT outsourcing is approximately 20 years old. The number of organizations that have used it for at least several years is growing. Business and IT-oriented periodicals have published numerous stories about their experiences. Outsourcing is also popular on a global basis, as is demonstrated in Minicase 2 and as described by Zviran et al. (2001). The general consensus of the various sources of anecdotal information is that the cost savings of outsourcing are not large (perhaps around 10 percent) and that not all organizations experience savings. This still leaves the question of whether outsourcing IT can improve organizational performance by making it possible to focus more intensely on core competencies. Further research is necessary to answer this question.

13.5 ECONOMICS OF WEB-BASED SYSTEMS AND E-COMMERCE

As indicated throughout this text, Web-based systems can considerably increase productivity and profitability. In order to understand the economic logic of this, let us first examine the cost curves of digital products versus nondigital products, as shown in Figure 13.7. As the figure shows, for regular physical products (a), the average cost declines up to a certain quantity, but then, due to increased production (e.g., adding a manager) and marketing costs, the cost will start to increase. For digital products (b), the cost will continue to decline with increased quantity. The variable cost in the case of digital products is very little, so increases in quantity produce little or no change in average cost.

However, even for nondigital products, e-commerce can shift economic curves, as shown in Figure 13.8 (page 618). The production function will decline (from L1 to L2 in part a) since you can get the same quantity with less labor and IT cost. The *transaction cost* for the same quantity (size) will be lower due to computerization (part b). And finally, the administrative cost for the same quantity will be lower (part c).

FIGURE 13.7 Cost curves of regular and digital products.

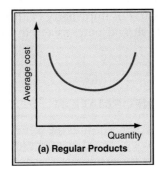

(a) Regular Products

(b) Digital Products

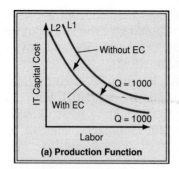

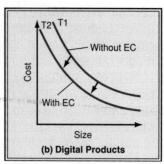

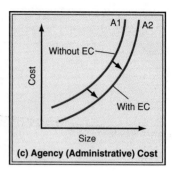

FIGURE 13.8
Economic effects
of e-commerce.

The justification of EC applications can be difficult. Usually one needs to prepare a business case, as described earlier in the chapter. A proper business case develops the baseline of desired results against which actual performance can and should be measured. The business case should cover both the financial and nonfinancial performance metrics against which to measure the e-business implementation. For further details on use of metrics to justify e-commerce, see Straub et al. (2000a and 2000b), Sterne (2002), Tjan (2001 and in Chapter 9 of this book), and Turban et al. (2004).

The benefits and costs of EC depend on its definitions. The complexity of the EC payoff can be seen in Online File W13.15. (For a discussion see Devaraj and Kohli, 2002). But even when the applications are well defined, we still have measurement complexities. It is difficult even to conduct risk analysis, not to mention cost-benefit analysis. (See insights from Thomas Mesenbourg, of the Economic Programs of the U.S. Bureau of the Census, at *census.gov/epdc/ www/ebusins.htm.*)

Web-based systems are being implemented by many organizations. However, hardly any efforts are being made to perform cost-benefit analysis or measure return on investment (ROI) on Web-based systems. Instead, most decisions to invest in Web-based systems are based on the assumption that the investments are needed for strategic reasons and that the expected returns cannot be measured in monetary values. Raskin (1999) advocates determining a

return on investment (ROI) for extranet projects, though it is a difficult task, and suggests strategies for calculating ROI. Online File W13.16 illustrates that some organizations calculate ROIs for their intranets and extranets and others do not.

As indicated earlier, many vendors provide ROI examples, proprietary methodologies, and calculators for IT projects, including EC, such as for portals (e.g., *plumtree.com*). Although use of third-party evaluators, such as IDC, is common, the reported high ROIs should be considered with care. As noted earlier, bias is possible.

13.6 OTHER ECONOMIC ASPECTS OF INFORMATION TECHNOLOGY

In this final section of the chapter, we look at some other associated economic aspects of information technology. The first of these is IT failures and runaway projects, many of which occur for economic reasons.

IT Failures and "Runaway" Projects

Information technology is difficult to manage and can be costly when things do not go as planned. Indeed, a high proportion of IS development projects either fail completely or fail to meet some of the original targets for features, development time, or cost. Many of these are related to economic issues, such as an incorrect cost-benefit analysis.

Many failures occur in smaller systems that handle internal processes within an organization, and they usually remain corporate secrets. The total investment is not large, the failure does not have a major economic impact, and the effects are generally not visible to outsiders so we do not know about them. On the other hand, some IS failures result in losses in excess of 10 million dollars and may severely damage the organization, as well as generate a lot of negative publicity, as in the Nike case in Chapter 1 or the ERP cases cited in Chapter 8. Failures in large public organizations such as the IRS and Social Security Administration have also been well advertised. Another large-scale, very public failure is described in *IT at Work 13.1.*

Because of the complexity and associated risks of developing computer systems, some IT managers refuse to develop systems in-house beyond a certain size. The "one, one, ten rule" says not to develop a system if it will take longer than one year, has a budget over one million dollars, and will require more than ten people. Following this strategy, an organization will need to buy rather than develop large systems, or do without them.

The economics of software production suggest that, for relatively standardized systems, purchasing or leasing can result in both cost savings and increased functionality. Purchasing or leasing can also be the safest strategy for very large and complex systems, especially those that involve multiple units within an

IT at Work 13.1
A LARGE-SCALE FAILURE AT DENVER INTERNATIONAL AIRPORT

The Denver International Airport (DIA), at 53 square miles, was designed to be the largest U.S. airport. By 1992, it was recognized that baggage handling would be critically important and that this issue could not be off-loaded to the airlines that would be operating out of DIA. Consequently, an airportwide, IT-based baggage handling system was planned to dramatically improve the efficiency of airport luggage delivery. BAE Automated Systems, Inc., a world leader in the design and implementation of material handling systems, was commissioned by the City of Denver to develop the system. The system was composed of 55 networked computers, 5,000 electric sensors, 400 radio frequency receivers, and 56 barcode scanners. It was to orchestrate the safe and timely arrival of every suitcase and ski bag at DIA.

Problems with the baggage system, however, kept the new airport from opening as originally scheduled in

October 1993. Soon the national and international media began to pick up the story, and the DIA came under investigation by various federal agencies. By the time the airport opened in late February 1995, it was 16 months behind schedule and close to $2 billion over budget. DIA eventually opened with two concourses served by a manual baggage system and one concourse served by a scaled-down semi-automated system. It took more than 2 additional years to put all the information systems into place. Major reasons were inappropriate ROI analysis, underestimation of costs, and lack of a contingency plan for unforeseen delays.

Source: Compiled from Monealegre and Keil (2000).

For Further Exploration: Why do organizations keep investing money in large IT-enabled projects in spite of clear evidence that they are failing? What are the issues in a decision to terminate a failing project?

organization. For example, the SAP AG software firm offers a family of integrated, enterprise-level, large-scale information systems (see Chapter 8). These systems are available in versions tailored for specific industries, including aerospace, banking, utilities, retail, and so forth, as well as for SMEs. Many organizations feel that buying from a good vendor reduces their risk of failure, even if they have to change their business processes to be compatible with the new system.

The Economics of the Web

In the preceding sections, our focus has been on the economics of *the use of IT* in organizations as an enabler. In this section, we turn to the economics of IT *as a product in itself*, rather than in a supporting role.

In 1916, David Sarnoff attempted to persuade his manager that the American Marconi Company should produce inexpensive radio receivers to sell to the consumer market. Others in the company (which subsequently became RCA) opposed the idea because it depended on the development of a radio broadcasting industry. They did not expect such an industry to develop because they could not see how broadcasters could generate revenues by providing a service without any charges to the listeners. The subsequent commercial development of radio, and the even greater success of television, proved that Sarnoff was right. If it is possible to provide a popular service to a large audience at a low cost per person, there will be ways of generating revenues. The only question is, How?

The World Wide Web on the Internet resembles commercial broadcasting in its early days. Fixed costs—initial investments and production costs—can be high in themselves, but they are low in terms of average cost per potential customer. The incremental or variable costs of delivering content to individual customers or of processing transactions are very low (see Choi and Whinston, 2000).

The market for the Web is large. About 60 percent of the U.S. population, plus foreign markets, now have access to the Internet. Many people who do not have computers at home can access the Internet through computers at work, schools, libraries, or via mobile devices. The arrival in 1995 of Web TV adapters for TV sets made it possible for homes without computers to get on the Internet for as little as $400. By 2003, the cost of the Simputer and other thin computers has come down to about $200. These trends could lead to a situation of "universal connectivity," in which almost every citizen in the industrialized countries has access to the Net. Using wireless, nearly universal connectivity can be achieved in developing countries as well.

The Web is different from broadcasting in ways that increase its economic potential. For example, Chapter 5 provides detailed information on specific applications of e-commerce. These applications demonstrate how favorable economic factors are leading to a wide variety of approaches to generating income using the Web or other aspects of the Internet. In 1996–2001, in the rush to introduce Web systems in general and e-commerce in particular, basic economic principles often were neglected, resulting in failures of many projects as well as entire companies. For further discussion see Kohli et al. (2003) and Choi and Whinston (2000).

Increasing Returns

Stanford University economist Brian Arthur (1996) is the leading proponent of the economic theory of *increasing returns,* which applies to the Web and to other forms of information technology. He starts with the familiar concept that the

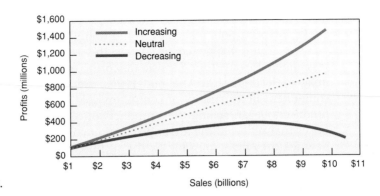

FIGURE 13.9 Increasing versus decreasing returns.

economy is divided into different sectors, one that produces physical products and another that focuses on information. Producers of physical products (e.g., foodstuffs, petroleum, automobiles) are subject to what are called diminishing returns: Although they may have initial increasing economies of scale, they eventually reach a point where costs go up and additional production becomes less profitable.

Arthur notes that in the information economy the situation is very different. For example, initial costs to develop new software are very high, but the cost of producing additional copies is very low. The result is **increasing returns,** where profitability rises more rapidly than production increases. A firm with a high market share can use these higher profits to improve the product or to enhance the marketing in order to strengthen its leading position. Figure 13.9 illustrates the difference between increasing and decreasing returns.

In addition to higher profitability, two other factors favor firms with higher market share. The first is **network effects.** The leading products in an industry attract a base of users, and this base leads to development of complementary products, further strengthening the position of the dominant product. For example, the open architecture of the IBM PC made it possible to develop add-on hardware and to create clones that run the same software. The market for PCs became much larger than the market for Apple computers, which have a closed architecture. Software companies shifted production to PC versions of their products, which further enhanced the dominance of the PC. All this happened in spite of a substantial amount of evidence that Apple's computers really were better products.

The second factor is the **lock-in effect.** Most new software is hard to learn, so users typically will not switch to a different product unless it is much more powerful or they are forced into making the change. The end result of these factors is that when a firm establishes a clear lead over its competitors, it tends to become stronger and stronger in its market.

The potential for increasing returns requires management strategies that are very different from those in other industries. Arthur (1996) suggests strategies for producing increasing returns which are shown in Online File W13.17.

Market Transformation through New Technologies

In some cases, IT has the potential to completely transform the economics of an industry. For example, until recently the encyclopedia business consisted of low-volume sales, primarily to schools and libraries. The physically very bulky product resulted in relatively high manufacturing and shipping costs, which made the price even higher. The high price, and the space required to store the books, reduced potential sales to the home market.

Two things happened to change this situation. First, CD-ROM technology was adapted from storing music to storing other digital data, including text and images. Second, since the mid-1990s use of CD-ROMs has been a standard component of a majority of computers sold for the home market. Encyclopedia producers began selling their products on CD-ROMs, in some cases at reduced prices that reflected the lower production costs. These CD-ROM versions include new features made possible by the technology, most notably sound and hyperlink cross-references to related material in other sections. Lower prices and additional features have the potential to substantially increase the size of the total market. The hypothetical example in *A Closer Look 13.3* shows how the economics of this business could change.

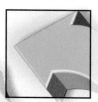

A CLOSER LOOK
13.3 THE ENCYCLOPEDIA ATLANTICA

The attached table shows a financial analysis for an aggressive scenario in which the (hypothetical) *Encyclopedia Atlantica* immediately shifts all its production from the traditional hardbound book format to a CD-ROM version. Note that manufacturing and shipping costs drop from $150 to $10 per unit. The cost of the contents increases by $2 million, reflecting the addition of sound, greater use of graphics, and the effort required to set up hyperlinks between different sections. The price per unit is reduced by 50 percent, from $700 to $350, while unit sales more than double and marketing expenses increase in proportion to unit sales. Despite the lower price and higher costs for content and marketing, the profit margin on the CD-ROM version is projected at 19.6 percent versus 16.7 percent on the hardbound version.

In practice, some customers in *Atlantica*'s traditional markets (e.g., libraries and schools) will continue buying the hardbound version for many years to come. Additional scenarios are necessary to show a more gradual transition to a market dominated by CD-ROM versions.

The scenarios also need to include additional revenues from customers after the initial sale. Customers can receive annual updates for $25 per year, as well as the opportunity to buy new editions at a 50 percent discount every five years.

Some interesting questions may be raised regarding this situation:

● Should *Atlantica* cut the price of the CD-ROM version to reflect economies of production and shipping and to dramatically increase the size of the total market? Or should it set the price at the same level as the hardbound version, and try to market the CD-ROM version as a low-volume, high-margin, premium product?

● What will happen if *Atlantica* starts to publish on the Web? Should it do so?

To answer these questions you may want to see what happened to *Encyclopedia Britannica* (*britannica.com*).

	Hardbound	CD-ROM
Unit sales	30,000	70,000
Price per unit	$700	$350
Gross revenue	$21,000,000	$24,500,000
−Cost of content	−10,000,000	−12,000,000
−Manufacturing & shipping costs	−4,500,000	−700,000
−Marketing costs	−3,000,000	−7,000,000
=Profit before taxes	$3,500,000	$4,800,000
Profit margin	16.7%	19.6%

➡ **MANAGERIAL ISSUES**

Information technology has certain characteristics that differentiate it, and its economics, from other aspects of the organizational world. Therefore IT requires management practices that are more effective than, and in some cases different from, those that are adequate for non-IT activities. For example, organizational resistance on many fronts can turn the most promising system into a failure (Watson and Haley, 1998). Managers need to be aware of and responsive to the following issues.

1. ***Constant growth and change.*** The power of the microprocessor chip doubles every two years, while the cost remains constant. This ever-increasing power creates both major opportunities and large threats as its impacts ripple across almost every aspect of the organization and its environment. Managers need to continuously monitor developments in this area to identify new technologies relevant to their organizations and to keep themselves up-to-date on their potential impacts.

2. ***Shift from tangible to intangible benefits.*** Few opportunities remain for automation projects that simply replace manual labor with IT on a one-for-one basis. The economic justification of IT applications will increasingly depend on intangible benefits, such as increased quality or better customer service. In contrast to calculating cost savings, it is much more difficult to accurately estimate the value of intangible benefits prior to the actual implementation. Managers need to understand and use tools that bring intangible benefits into the decision-making processes for IT investments.

3. ***Not a sure thing.*** Although IT offers opportunities for significant improvements in organizational performance, these benefits are not automatic. Managers need to very actively plan and control implementations to increase the return on their IT investments.

4. ***Chargeback.*** Users have little incentive to control IT costs if they do not have to pay for them at all. On the other hand, an accounting system may allocate costs fairly accurately to users but discourage exploration of promising new technologies. The solution is to have a chargeback system that has the primary objective of encouraging user behaviors that correspond to organizational objectives.

5. ***Risk.*** Investments in IT are inherently more risky than investments in other areas. Managers need to evaluate the level of risk before committing to IT projects. The general level of management involvement as well as specific management techniques and tools need to be appropriate for the risk of individual projects.

6. ***Outsourcing.*** The complexities of managing IT, and the inherent risks, may require more management skills than some organizations possess. If this is the case, the organization may want to outsource some or all of its IT functions. However, if it does outsource, the organization needs to make sure that the terms of the outsourcing contract are in its best interests both immediately and throughout the duration of the agreement.

7. ***Increasing returns.*** Industries whose primary focus is IT, or that include large amounts of IT in their products, often operate under a paradigm of increasing returns. In contrast, industries that primarily produce physical outputs

are subject to diminishing returns. Managers need to understand which paradigm applies to the products for which they are responsible and apply management strategies that are most appropriate.

 ON THE WEB SITE... Additional resources, including quizzes; online files of additional text, tables, figures, and cases; and frequently updated Web links to current articles and information can be found on the book's Web site (*wiley.com/college/turban*).

KEY TERMS

Application service provider (ASP) *614*
Balanced-scorecard method *610*
Behavior-oriented chargeback *612*
Benchmarks *607*
Best-practice benchmarks *608*
Business case *601*
Chargeback *612*
Cost-benefit analysis *599*
Expected value (EV) *611*
Increasing returns *621*

Information economics *605*
Intangible benefits *600*
Lock-in effect *621*
Management by maxim *608*
Management service provider (MSP) *614*
Metric benchmarks *608*
Moore's Law *591*
Network effects *621*
Offshore outsourcing *613*
Outsourcing *613*

Price-to-performance ratio *591*
Productivity paradox *592*
Real options *609*
Runaway project *595*
Scoring methodology *605*
Total benefits of ownership (TBO) *604*
Total cost of ownership (TCO) *604*
Value analysis *604*

CHAPTER HIGHLIGHTS (Numbers Refer to Learning Objectives)

① The power of computer hardware should continue increasing at an exponential rate for at least 10 years, doubling every 18 months, while costs remain at the same levels as before. Also the performance/cost ratio of storage and networks behaves in a similar way.

② Although organizations have spent tremendous amounts of money on IT, it is difficult to prove that this spending has increased national or industry productivity. The discrepancy between measures of IT investment and measures of output is described as the productivity paradox.

③ Evaluating IT investment requires finding the total costs of ownership and the total benefits of ownership and subtracting the costs from the benefits. The value of information to an organization should be part of that calculation.

③ The major difficulty in evaluating IT investment is assessing the intangible benefits. Also, some costs are difficult to relate to specific projects.

③ Traditional financial approaches can be used to evaluate IT investment, but in many cases methods such as value analysis, benchmarking, or real option analysis fit better, especially for investment in infrastructures.

④ Intangible benefits cover many areas ranging from customer satisfaction to deferring IT investments. To include intangible benefits in IT justification, one may attempt to quantify them, to list them as arguments for justification, or to ignore them. Specific methodologies may be useful.

⑤ The NPV and ROI methods work well with tangible benefits. When intangible benefits are involved one may try one of the following: value analysis, information economics, benchmarks, management by maxim, real option valuation, balanced scorecard, and activity-based costing.

⑥ Behavior-oriented chargeback systems, if properly designed, encourage efficient and effective usage of IT resources.

7 Outsourcing may reduce IT costs and can make it possible for organizations to concentrate their management efforts on issues related to their core competencies. However, outsourcing may reduce the company's flexibility to find the best IT fit for the business, and it may also pose a security risk.

8 EC enables electronic delivery of digital products at very low cost. Also, many nondigital products can be produced and delivered with lower overhead and with less administrative cost.

9 Web-based technologies may be approached differently for conducting cost-benefit analysis due to their different economic curves, lack of baseline data, frequent changes, etc. Modifying existing concepts, such as is done in portfolio selection, is advisable.

10 Several topics are related to the economics of IT. IT failures are frequently the result of poor cost-benefit analysis, and IT projects sometimes linger because of poor planning of economic resources.

QUESTIONS FOR REVIEW

1. Describe Moore's Law.
2. Define productivity.
3. Define the productivity paradox. Why is it important?
4. List three major explanations of the productivity paradox.
5. Define information infrastructure and list some of its costs.
6. Define cost-benefit analysis.
7. What is TCO? What is TBO?
8. List some tangible and intangible benefits of IT.
9. Describe the value analysis method.
10. Define information economics.
11. Define IT benchmarks.
12. Describe best-practice benchmarks.
13. What is management by maxim?
14. What is real-option valuation in IT?
15. Describe IT chargeback.
16. Define behavior-oriented chargeback.
17. Define IT outsourcing.
18. List five benefits of outsourcing.
19. List five drawbacks or limitations of outsourcing.
20. Describe increasing returns in IT.

QUESTIONS FOR DISCUSSION

1. What are the general implications for managers, organizations, and consumers of constantly increasing computer capabilities and declining costs?
2. What are the impacts of exponentially increasing computer hardware power and declining price-to-performance ratios on business production activities and new-product development?
3. Discuss what is necessary to achieve productivity gains from IT investments.
4. Why is it more difficult to measure productivity in service industries?
5. Compare and contrast metrics and best practices. Give an example of each in an IT in a university.
6. Discuss what may happen when an organization does not charge users for IT services.
7. Identify circumstances that could lead a firm to outsource its IT functions rather than continue with an internal IS unit.
8. Identify arguments for including estimated values for intangible benefits in net present value (NPV) analyses of IT investments, and contrast them with the arguments for excluding such estimates.
9. What is IT infrastructure, and why is it difficult to justify its cost?
10. Discuss the economic advantages of digital products compared to nondigital ones.
11. Explain how a behavior-oriented chargeback system can be superior to an accounting system that charges users fairly accurate estimates of the costs of services they use.
12. Discuss the pros and cons of outsourcing IT, including alternatives to outsourcing.
13. Discuss how giving products away can be a profitable strategy in industries with increasing returns.

EXERCISES

1. Conduct research on how long exponential growth in computer hardware capabilities (Moore's Law) will continue.

2. Create a scoring methodology that reflects your personal requirements, and use it to evaluate two competing software products in the same category (for example, two Web browsers or two corporate portal development environments).

3. If you have access to a large organization, conduct research on the methods it uses to charge users for IT services and how the users feel about these charges.

4. Enter *ibm.com* and find information about how IBM measures the ROI on WebSphere. Then examine ROI from CIOView Corporation (*CIOview.com*). Identify the variables included in the analysis (at both *ibm.com* and *CIOview.com*). Prepare a report about the fairness of such a tool.

5. A small business invests $50,000 in robotic equipment. This amount is shown as a negative value in Year 0. Projected cash flows of $20,000 per year in Year 1 through Year 5 result from labor savings, reduced material costs, and tax benefits. The business plans to replace the robots with more modern ones after 5 years and does not expect them to have any scrap value. The equipment generates a total of $100,000 in savings over 5 years, or $50,000 more than the original investment. However, a dollar saved in the future is worth less than a dollar invested in the present. If the business estimates its return on investment as 15 percent, then $1.00 should be worth $1.15 in one year, $1.32 after 2 years with compound interest, and so on. Cash flows are divided by these "discount factors" to estimate what they are worth at present. Calculate the total cash flow after this discounting, and discuss whether the investment can be justified.

GROUP ASSIGNMENTS

1. Considerable discussions and disagreements occur among IS professionals regarding outsourcing. Divide the group into two parts: One will defend the strategy of large-scale outsourcing. One will oppose it. Start by collecting recent material at *google.com* and *cio.com*.

2. Each group is assigned to an ROI calculator (e.g., from PeopleSoft, Oracle, IBM, etc.). Each group should prepare a list of the functionalities included and the variables. Make a report that shows the features and limitations of each tool.

INTERNET EXERCISES

1. Enter *google.com* and search for material on the use of the balanced scorecard method for evaluating IT investments. Prepare a report on your findings.

2. Read the *Information Week* article at *techweb.com/se/directlink.cgi?IWK19970630S0038*. Compare and contrast the approaches to evaluating intangible benefits in the article to those suggested in this textbook.

3. Enter the Web sites of the GartnerGroup (*gartnergroup.com*), The Yankee Group (*yankeegroup.com*), and *CIO* (*cio.com*). Search for recent material about outsourcing, and prepare a report on your findings.

4. Enter the Web site of IDC (*idc.com*) and find how they evaluate ROI on intranets, supply chain, and other IT projects.

5. Visit the Web site of Resource Management Systems (*rms.net*) and take the IT investment Management Approach Assessment Self-Test (*rms.net/self_test.htm*) to compare your organization's IT decision-making process with those of best-practices organizations.

6. Enter *compaq.com/tco* and *cosn.org/tco*. Find information about the total cost of ownership model. Write a report on the state of the art.

7. Enter *plumtree.com* and see how they conduct ROI on portals. List major elements of the analysis. Is it biased?

8. Enter *sap.com* and use the casebuilder calculator for a hypothetical (or real) IT project. Write a report on your experience.

Minicase 1
Intranets: Invest First, Analyze Later?

The traditional approach to information systems projects is to analyze potential costs and benefits before deciding whether to develop the system. However, for moderate investments in promising new technologies that could offer major benefits, organizations may decide to do the financial analyses after the project is over. A number of companies took this latter approach in regard to intranet projects initiated prior to 1997.

Judd's

Located in Strasburg, Virginia, Judd's is a conservative, family-owned printing company that prints *Time* magazine, among other publications. Richard Warren, VP for IS, pointed out that Judd's "usually waits for technology to prove itself . . . but with the Internet the benefits seemed so great that our decision proved to be a no-brainer." Judd's first implemented Internet technology for communications to meet needs expressed by customers. After this it started building intranet applications to facilitate internal business activities. One indication of the significance of these applications to the company is the bandwidth that supports them. Judd's increased the bandwidth by a magnitude of about 900 percent in the 1990s without formal cost-benefit analysis.

Eli Lilly & Company

A very large pharmaceutical company with headquarters in Indianapolis, Eli Lilly has a proactive attitude toward new technologies. It began exploring the potential of the Internet in 1993. Managers soon realized that, by using intranets, they could reduce many of the problems associated with developing applications on a wide variety of hardware platforms and network configurations. Because the benefits were so obvious, the regular financial justification process was waived for intranet application development projects. The IS group that helps user departments develop and maintain intranet applications increased its staff from three to ten employees in 15 months.

Needham Interactive

Needham, a Dallas advertising agency, has offices in various parts of the country. Needham discovered that, in developing presentations for bids on new accounts, employees found it helpful to use materials from other employees' presentations on similar projects. Unfortunately, it was very difficult to locate and then transfer relevant material in different locations and different formats. After doing research on alternatives, the company identified intranet technology as the best potential solution.

Needham hired EDS to help develop the system. It started with one office in 1996 as a pilot site. Now part of DDB Needham, the company has a sophisticated corporate-wide intranet and extranet in place. Although the investment was "substantial," Needham did not do a detailed financial analysis before starting the project. David King, a managing partner explained, "The system will start paying for itself the first time an employee wins a new account because he had easy access to a co-worker's information."

Cadence Design Systems

Cadence is a consulting firm located in San Jose, California. It wanted to increase the productivity of its sales personnel by improving internal communications and sales training. It considered Lotus Notes but decided against it because of the costs. With the help of a consultant, it developed an intranet system. Because the company reengineered its sales training process to work with the new system, the project took somewhat longer than usual.

International Data Corp., an IT research firm, helped Cadence do an after-the-fact financial analysis. Initially the analysis calculated benefits based on employees meeting their full sales quotas. However, IDC later found that a more appropriate indicator was having new sales representatives meet half their quota. Startup costs were $280,000, average annual expenses were estimated at less than $400,000, and annual savings were projected at over $2.5 million. Barry Demak, director of sales, remarked, "We knew the economic justification . . . would be strong, but we were surprised the actual numbers were as high as they were."

Sources: Compiled from Korzenioski (1997) and the cited companies' Web sites.

Questions for Minicase 1

1. Where and under what circumstances is the "invest first, analyze later" approach appropriate? Where and when is it inappropriate? Give specific examples of technologies and other circumstances.

2. How long do you think the "invest first, analyze later" approach will be appropriate for intranet projects? When (and why) will the emphasis shift to traditional project justification approaches? (Or has the shift already occurred?)

3. What are the risks of going into projects that have not received a thorough financial analysis? How can organizations reduce these risks?

4. Based on the numbers provided for Cadence Design System's intranet project, use a spreadsheet to calculate the net present value of the project. Assume a 5-year life for the system.

5. Do you see any relationship between the "invest first, analyze later" approach to financial analysis and the use of behavior-oriented chargeback systems?

6. Relate the Needham case to the concept of a repository knowledge base.

Minicase 2
Outsourcing Its IT, Kone Is Focusing on Its Core Competencies

The Problem

Kone Inc. is a multinational corporation, based in Finland. Kone makes over 20,000 new escalators and elevators each year, installing and servicing them in more than 40 countries, with about 30 percent of Kone's business in the United States. The company embarked on a globalization strategy several years ago, and soon discovered that the internal IT processes were insufficient to support the expansion. The same was true with the IT for the company's value-added private communication networks. IT costs were growing rapidly, yet their contribution to reducing the administrative cost of global sales was minimal. Kone was managing different IT platforms around the world with a variety of home-grown and nonstandard applications. None of the regional IT infrastructures was integrated, nor were they connected or compatible. Kone's global strategy was in danger.

The Solution

Kone Inc. realized that it must implement and manage a global-standard IT environment. But the company also realized that its business is about escalators and elevators, not IT, so it decided to pursue IT outsourcing. Kone had had an experience with IT outsourcing before, when it outsourced its mainframe operations to Computer Science Corp. But this time the scope of outsourcing was much larger, so the company solicited proposals and finally decided to partner with two global IT providers, SAP AG from Germany and Hewlett-Packard (HP) from the United States.

As described in Chapter 8, SAP is the world's largest ERP provider, and almost all of the 72 modules of SAP R/3 software (including a data warehouse) were deployed at Kone. The SAP environment is deployed in 16 countries, with 4,300 users, in all functional areas.

HP was hired to provide and manage the hardware on which SAP is run. The decision to use two vendors was not easy. IBM and Oracle each could have provided both the software and hardware, but using two separate vendors promised the best-of-breed approach.

HP manages 20 Kone Unix Servers in three data centers (one in Atlanta for North America, one in Singapore for Asia, and one in Brussels for Europe). HP uses its latest technology. HP's OpenView network and system management and security software are also deployed with the system to ensure high availability environment. The system is linked with EMC storage and backup. The annual cost of this global outsourcing is $5 million.

The entire global IT infrastructure is connected and integrated, and it supports identical business processes and practices in all countries. The system provides management with real-time data on product sales, profitability, and backlogs—on a country, regional, or global basis.

Kone maintains some IT competencies to allow it to actively manage its outsourcing partners. The internal team meets online regularly, and SAP and HP collaborate and work closely together.

The Results

The outsouring arrangement allows Kone to concentrate on its core competencies. The cost is only 0.02 percent of sales. Large fixed costs in infrastructure and people have been eliminated. The company has better cost control, as well as flexible opportunity for business process redesign, thus speeding up restructuring. The outsourcing vendors guarantee to have the system available 99.5 percent of the time. Actual uptime has been very close to 100 percent.

Sources: Compiled from "The Elevation of IT Outsourcing Partnership" (2002), and *rsleads.com/208cn-254* (accessed February 13, 2003).

Questions for Minicase 2

1. What were the major drivers of the outsourcing at Kone?

2. Why did Kone elect to work with several vendors?

3. What are some of the risks of this outsourcing?

4. How can Kone control its vendors?

Virtual Company Assignment
Information Technology Economics at The Wireless Café

This chapter has brought you back to reality. Over the course of your internship, you've recommended many useful and innovative technologies that would help make everybody's job at The Wireless Café more productive and interesting, including CRM, SCM, DSS, and wireless networks and applications, to name a few. However, The Wireless Café's budget definitely won't support all of your recommendations in one year. Barbara is concerned that Jeremy may overextend The Wireless Café's finances, because he sees benefits in all of the technologies, so she has asked you to help with a more reasoned analysis of the IT economics for The Wireless Café.

Instructions

1. What is the *business case* for implementing the following systems at The Wireless Café?

   a. CRM

   b. SCM

   c. Wireless networks and applications

2. Consider the costs of acquiring and implementing the Wireless Waitress software package. What are the components of TCO and TBO that should be analyzed in an acquisition decision?

3. This chapter presents a number of ways to evaluate the economic viability of a technology investment. Which method would you choose for a small business such as The Wireless Café and why?

REFERENCES

Arthur, W. B., "Increasing Returns and the New World of Business," *Harvard Business Review*, July–August 1996.

Barthelemy, J., "The Hidden Costs of IT Outsourcing," *MIT Sloan Management Review*, spring 2001.

Benaroch, M., "Management Information Technology Investment Risk: A Real Options Perspective," *Journal of Management Information Systems*, Fall 2002.

Benaroch, M., and R. J. Kauffman, "A Case for Using Real Options Pricing Analysis to Evaluate Information Technology Project Investments," *Information Systems Research*, 10(1), March 1999.

Bennett, R. F., and C. J. Dodd, "Y2K Aftermath—Crisis Averted, Final Committee Report," *The United States Special Committee on the Year 2000 Technology Problem*. Washington, D.C.: Government Printing Office, February 29, 2000.

Blum, R., *Network and System Management TCO*. Murry Hill, NJ: Lucent Technologies, 2001.

Broadbent, M., and P. Weill, "Management by Maxim: How Business and IT Managers Can Create IT Infrastrucures," *Sloan Management Review*, spring 1997.

Brown, R. H., and A. Young, "Scenarios for the Future of Outsourcing," GartnerGroup, December 12, 2000.

Brynjolfsson, E., and L. M. Hitt, "Beyond the Productivity Paradox," *Communications of the ACM*, August 1998.

Carmel, E., and R. Agrawal, "The Maturation of Offshore Sourcing of Information Technology Work," *MIS Querterty Executive*, June 2002.

Choi, S. Y., and A. B. Whinston, *The Internet Economy: Technology and Practice*. Austin TX: SmartEcon, 2000.

Clemons, E. K., "The Build/Buy Battle," *CIO Magazine*, Dec. 1, 2000.

Clermout, P., Cost-Benefit Analysis: IT's Back in Fashion, Now Let's Make It Work. *Information Strategy: The Executive's Journal*, winter 2002.

Cline, M. K., and S.C. Guynes, "A Study of the Impact of Information Technology Investment on Firm Performance," *Journal of Computer Information Systems*, spring 2001.

Colgan D., and E. Mazzawi, "Transactional Outsourcing," *NOA News, noa.co.uk/news021212trans.htm*, 2002.

Coopee, T., "Building a Strong Foundation," *Network World*, January 31, 2000.

Corbett, M. F., "Taking the Pulse of Outsourcing," *Firmbuilder.com* (Data and Analysis from the 2001 Outsourcing World Summit), December 6, 2001.

Cramm, S. H., "The Dark Side of Outsourcing," *CIO Magazine*, Nov. 15, 2001.

Cule, P. et al., "Strategies for Heading Off IS Project Failures," *Information Systems Management*, spring 2000.

Cushing, K., "Procter & Gamble's 3bn HP Deal Shows Mega IT Outsourcing Is Still Tempting Some," *Computer Weekly*, April 22, 2003.

Cusumano, M., "'Made in India'—A New Sign of Software Quality," *Computerworld*, February 28, 2000.

Davamanirajan, P. et al., "Assessing the Business Value of Information Technology in Global Wholesale Banking: Case of Trade Service," *Journal of Organizational Computing and Electronic Commerce*, Jan–March 2002.

David, J. S. et al., "Managing Your IT Total Cost of Ownership," *Communications of the ACM*, January 2002.

Dekker, R., and R. de Hoog, "The Monetary Value of Knowledge Assets: A Micro Approach," *Expert Systems with Applications*, Vol. 18, 2000.

Deoalma, D., "Make the Business Case for Global Expansion," *e-Business Advisor*, April 1, 2001.

Devaraj, S., and R. Kohli, *The IT Payoff*. New York: Financial Times/Prentice Hall, 2002.

Devaraj, S., and R. Kohli, "Information Technology Payoff Paradox and System Use: Is Actual Usage the Missing Link?" *Management Science*, 49(3), 2003.

DiNunno, D., "Measuring Return of IT Projects," *CIO* Magazine, Sept. 25, 2002.

Dixit, A. K., and Pindyck, R. S., "The Options Approach to Capital Investment," *Harvard Business Review*, May–June 1995.

Duvall, M., "Companies Size Up Outsourcing," *Interactive Week*, January 12, 1998.

"The Elevation of IT Outsourcing Partnership: With HP/SAP Trained Staff, Kone's Global Strategy In Top Level," *Communication News*, August 2002.

Ferrin, B. G., and R. E. Plank, "Total Cost of Ownership Models: An Exploratory Study," *Journal of Supply Chain Management*, Summer 2002.

Fine, C. H. et al., "Rapid-Response Capability in Value-Chain Design," *MIT Sloan Management Review*, winter 2002.

Fisher, A., "A Waste of Money?" *Financial Times*, October 25, 2001.

Gerlach, J. et al., "Determining the Cost of IT Services," *Communications of the ACM*, September 2002.

Garner, R., "Strategic Outsourcing: It's Your Move," *Datamation*, February 1998.

Gartner Group, *gartnerweb.com/public/static/aboutgg/pressrel/pr20000 1120b.html*, November 20, 2000.

Gaulke, M., "Risk Management in TI Projects, *Information Systems Control Journal*, Nov.–Dec. 2002.

Gillin, P., "Offshore Outsourcing Becoming 'In' Thing for CIOs," *CIO News & Analysis*, June 24, 2003.

Gray, P., and H. Watson, "Present and Future Directions in Data Warehousing," *Database*, summer 1998.

Gunasekaran, et al., "A Model for Investment Justification in Information Technology Projects," *International Journal of Information Management*, March 2001.

Hirscheim, R., and M. Lacity, "Information Technology Insourcing: Myths and Realities," *Communications of the ACM*, February 2000.

Hitt, L. M., and E. Brynjolfsson, "Productivity, Business Profitability, and Consumer Surplus: Three Different Measures of Information Technology Value," *MIS Quarterly*, June 1996.

Irani, Z., and P. E. D. Love, "The Propagation of Technology Management Taxonomies for Evaluating Investments in Information Systems," *Journal of Management Information Systems*, winter 2000–2001.

Intel Corp., "Building the Foundation for Anytime, Anywhere Computing," white paper #251290–002, *Intel Information Technology Publication*, June 13, 2002.

ITAA (Information Technology Association of America), "Skills Study 2000—Bridging the Gap: Information Technology Skills for a New Millennium," *uen.org/techday/html/technology.html*, April 2000.

Kaplan, R. S., and D. Norton, *The Balanced Scorecard*. Boston. MA: Harvard Business School Press, 1996.

Keen, P. G. W., "Value Analysis: Justifying DSS," *Management Information Systems Quarterly*, March 1981.

King, J., "IS Reins in Runaway Projects," *Computerworld*, February 24, 1997.

King, J., "User Beware," *Computerworld*, March 18, 2002.

Korzenioski, P., "Intranet Bets Pay Off," *InfoWorld*, January 13, 1997.

Kudyba, S., and D.Vitaliano, "Information Technology and Corporate Profitability: A Focus on Operating Efficiency." *Information Resources Management Journal*, January–March 2003.

Kumar, R. L., "Understanding DSS Value: An Options Perspective," *Omega*, June 1999.

Lee, J. N. et al., "IT Outsourcing Evaluation—Past, Present and Future," *Communications of the ACM*, May 2003.

Legrenzi, C., "The 2nd Edition of the European Survey on the Economic Value of IT," *Information Systems Control Journal*, May–June 2003.

Li, H. et al., "The IT Performance Evaluation in the Construction Industry," *Proceedings, 33rd Hawaiian International Conference on Systems Sciences (HICSS)*, Maui, HI, January 2000.

Li, X., and J. D. Johnson, "Evaluate IT Investment Opportunities Using Real Options Theory." *Information Resources Management Journal*, July–September 2002, pp. 32–47.

Liebowitz, J., "Information Systems: Success or Failure?" *Journal of Computer Information Systems*, Fall 1999.

Lin, W. T., and B. M. Shao, "Relative Sizes of Information Technology Investments and Productivity Efficiency: Their Linkage and Empirical Evidence," *Journal of AIS*, September 2000.

Lucas, H. C., *Information Technology and the Productivity Paradox: Assessing the Value of Investing in IT*. New York: Oxford University Press, 1999.

Marcolin, B. L., and K. L. McLellan, "Effective IT Outsourcing Arrangements," *Proceedings, 31st HICSS*, January 1998.

McAdam, J. P., "Slicing the Pie: Information Technology Cost Recovery Models," *CPA Journal*, February 1996.

Montealegre, R., and M. Keil, "De-escalating Information Technology Projects: Lessons from the Denver International Airport," *MIS Quarterly*, September 2000.

Moore, G. E., "Moore's Law," *CIO*, January 1, 1997.

Mukhopadhyay, T. et al., "Assessing the Impact of Information Technology on Labor," *Decision Support Systems*, Vol. 19, 1997.

Murphy, V., "The Exterminator (of Computer Bugs)," *Forbes Global*, May 16, 2003.

Munk, N., "Technology for Technology's Sake," *Forbes*, October 21, 1996.

Olazabal, N. G., "Banking: the IT Paradox," *The McKinsey Quarterly*, January–March 2002.

Palvia, S., "Is E-Commerce Driving Outsourcing to Its Limits?" *Journal of IT Cases & Applications*, January 2002.

Peffers, K., and T. Saarinen, "Measuring the Business Value of IT Investments: Inferences from a Study of a Senior Bank Executive." *Journal of Organizational Computing and Electronic, Commerce* January–March 2002.

Plant, R. T., *E-Commerce: Formulation of Strategy*, Upper Saddle River, NJ: Prentice Hall, 2000.

Plumtree Corp., "MyAPlus.com: A Return-on-Investment Study of Portals," *A Meta Group White Paper*, Nov. 12, 2001.

PricewaterhouseCoopers, "European Private Banking Survey," *pwcglobal.com/ch/eng/inssol/publ/bank/privatbanking.html*, 1999 (Accessed November 16, 2000.)

Pountain, D., "Amending Moore's Law," *Byte*, March 1998.

Qing, H. U., and R. Plant, "An Empirical Study of the Casual Relationship Between IT Investment and Firm Performance," *Information Resources Management Journal*, July–September 2001.

Quinn, J. B., "Strategic Outsourcing: Leveraging Knowledge Capabilities," *Sloan Management Review*, summer 1999.

Raskin, A., "The ROIght Stuff," *CIO Web Business Magazine*, February 1, 1999.

Rayport, J., and B. J. Jaworski, *E-Commerce*. New York: McGraw-Hill, 2001.

Read, C. et al., *eCFO: Sustaining Value in the New Corporation*. Chichester, U.K.: Wiley, 2001.

Reichheld, F., and P. Schefter, "E-loyalty—Your Secret Weapon on the Web," *Harvard Business Review*, July–August 2000.

Renkema, T. J. W., *The IT Value Quest: How to Capture the Business Value of IT-Based Infrastructure*. Chichester, England: Wiley, 2000.

Ross, J. W., and C. M. Beath, "Beyond the Business Case: New Approaches to IT Investment," *MIT Sloan Management Review*, winter 2002.

Ryan, S. D. et al., "Information-Technology Investment Decisions: When Do Costs and Benefits in the Social Subsystem Matter? *Journal of Management Information Systems*, fall 2002.

sap.com. (Accessed June 27, 2003.)

Sawhney, M., "Damn the ROI, Full Speed Ahead," *CIO Magazine*, July 15, 2002.

Seddon, P. et al., "Measuring Organizational IS Effectiveness: An Overview and Update of Senior Management Perspectives," *The Data BASE for Advances in Information Systems*, Spring 2002.

Segev, A., and J. Gebauer, "B2B Procurement and Marketplace Transformation," *Information Technology and Mangement*, July 2001.

Soh, C., and L. M. Markus, "How IT Creates Business Value: A Process Theory Synthesis," *Proceedings of the 16th International Conference on Information Systems*, December 1995.

Standish Group, "Chaos," Standish Research Paper, *standish-group.com/visitor/chaos.htm*, 1995.

Sterne, J, *Web Metrics*. New York: John Wiley & Sons, 2002.

Strassmann, P. A., *The Squandered Computer*. New Canaan, CT: Information Economics Press, 1997.

Straub, D. W. et al., "Measuring e-Commerce in Net-Enabled Organizations, *Information Systems Research*, June 2002a.

Straub, D. W. et al., "Toward New Metrics for Net-Enhanced Organizations," *Information Systems Research*, September 2002b.

Swamy, Remash, "Strategic Performance Measurement in the New Millennium," *CMA Management*, May 2002.

Tjan, A. K., "Put Your Internet Portfolio in Order," *Harvard Business Review*, February 2001.

Truby, K. C., "Finding the Value Proposition in the ASP Business Model," *CPA Journal*, 72(3), March 2002, pp. 73–74.

Varon, E., "R. O. Iowa," *CIO Magazine*, June 1, 2003.

Vijavan, J., "The New TCO Metric," *Computerworld*, June 18, 2001.

Violino, B., "Return on Investment Profiles: The Intangible Benefits of Technology Are Emerging as the Most Important of All," *Information Week*, June 30, 1997.

Vistica, G. L. et al., "The Day the World Shuts Down," *Newsweek*, June 2, 1997.

Waltner, C., "Intranet ROI: Leap of Faith," *Information Week*, May 24, 1999.

Watson, H. J., and B. J. Haley, "Managerial Considerations," *Communications of ACM*, September 1998.

Wilkinson, S., "Phone Bill, Electricity Bill . . . Storage Bill? Storage Utilities Attract New Economy Companies with Pay-as-you-go Service," *Earthweb.com*, October 24, 2000.

Zviran, M. et al., "Building Outsourcing Relationships Across the Global Community: The UPS-Motorola Experience," *Journal of Strategic Information Systems*, December 2001.

PART V
Implementing and Managing IT

13. Information Technology Economics
▶ 14. Building Information Systems
15. Managing Information Resources and IT Security
16. Impacts of IT on Organizations, Individuals, and Society (online)

CHAPTER

14

Building Information Systems

14.1
The Concept of a Systems Development Life Cycle

14.2
Methods for Complex or Quickly Needed Systems

14.3
Component-Based Development and Web Services

14.4
Systems Developed Outside the IS Department

14.5
Building E-Business Applications

14.6
Some Important Systems Development Issues

LEARNING OBJECTIVES

After studying this chapter, you will be able to:

❶ Explain the concept of a systems development life cycle (SDLC).

❷ Compare and contrast prototyping, rapid application development (RAD), joint application design (JAD), object-oriented (OO) development, extreme programming (XP), and traditional SDLC approaches to systems development.

❸ Describe the contributions of component-based development and Web services to building information systems.

❹ Evaluate alternatives (including the adoption of utility computing) to in-house systems development.

❺ Discuss the major strategies, methods, and tools for building e-commerce applications.

❻ Identify advantages and disadvantages of CASE tools, and describe alternative approaches to software process quality improvement.

UTILITY COMPUTING: "THE NEXT BIG THING"

THE PROBLEM

Imagine this scene. It's noon on Friday and you just found out that your relatives are coming to spend the weekend. It's time to contact the electric company to let them know that you will need extra electricity for the weekend. You're told you have to fill out a purchase order and it will be five to seven days before you can get extra electricity. Of course, life is not like this, because basic utilities have extra capacity built into their delivery systems. But this would be a likely scenario if you were to find out at noon on Friday that you were expecting a major spike in usage on your servers. You'd have to call your provider, do a bunch of paperwork, and maybe in a few days you could get the extra capacity you need. That's the kind of problem that utility computing aims to solve.

THE SOLUTION

Utility computing vendors are looking toward a future in which computing capacity is as easy to acquire as electricity. Rather than having a fixed amount of computing resources, you would have access to computing resources on an as-needed basis—just like with electricity. Many IT market leaders are now starting to catch on to the concept of utility computing as a bullet-proof utility service that we can virtually take for granted. IBM announced it is spending $10 billion on its on-demand computing initiatives. HP also announced its Utility Data Center architecture, and Sun has its own N1 data virtualization center plans. Sun, HP, and IBM are duking it out over how best to meet utility computing requirements and command a leadership position.

THE RESULTS

Already present in a variety of capacity-based pricing models, utility computing is poised to expand throughout the enterprise as various key technologies—such as Web services, grid computing, and provisioning—intersect. Growth of utility computing in the enterprise will deliver to the industry not only equal access to supercomputing resources, but also new revenue streams for commercial data centers, new application pricing models based on metered use, and an open computing infrastructure for companies with little or no standing IT maintenance budget. Utility computing is on track to be the "next big thing" for IT vendors and services companies that sell to large enterprises.

Sources: Compiled from Zimmerman (2003) and from Neel (2002).

LESSONS LEARNED FROM THIS CASE

Utility computing (also called "on-demand computing") has become one of the hot topics in the IT analyst community and, increasingly, in larger enterprises that are looking for ways to reduce the fixed costs and complexity of IT. Utility computing tools provide total flexibility in information systems development, from in-house and self-managed to fully outsourced, with everything in between—including a hybrid deployment model in which in-house capacity can be supplemented by third-party resources to handle peak needs.

In this chapter we will look at the topic of building information systems. Since organizational environments and general technologies change over time, organizations need new systems, or major revisions to existing systems, to continue to meet their objectives. Therefore, systems development is an ongoing process in all organizations that use IT.

In this chapter we discuss various approaches to development that can increase the probability of favorable outcomes. We initially present the concept of a systems development life cycle. We then discuss various systems development alternatives (prototyping, rapid application development, joint application design, object-oriented development, and extreme programming). Then we provide a comprehensive discussion of the contributions of component-based development and Web services to building information systems. The subsequent section covers end-user development, acquiring systems from outside sources, utility computing, and deciding between development approaches. Next is a section on the approaches, methods, and techniques used in developing Web-based information systems. The final section looks at the use of CASE tools, discusses quality improvement, and presents project-planning techniques used to improve outcomes of the development process.

14.1 THE CONCEPT OF A SYSTEMS DEVELOPMENT LIFE CYCLE

In the early years of data processing, many software developers did not use any kind of formal approach. They would simply ask users a few questions about what the system was supposed to do and then start programming. Sometimes this approach resulted in desirable outcomes, but often it failed. The failures were frequent enough to indicate that a more formal approach was necessary. **Systems development** refers to the set of activities that create systems for the effective and efficient processing of information. One approach to systems development is the **systems development life cycle (SDLC).** It provides a comprehensive framework for formal design and development activities.

To understand the idea of a systems development life cycle, consider this analogy. A business firm moves from one city to another. The moving project requires a very detailed plan. Someone has to acquire property in the new city. Someone has to arrange for telephone and utility services at the new location. People need to pack, ship, unpack, and install furniture and equipment at the new location. The list goes on and on. The plan should identify every significant task and assign it to an individual or groups within or outside the organization. Every task needs a start date and a completion date, and some tasks cannot start until after the completion of others. Also, the plan needs to coordinate the start and completion dates of the individual tasks within the limitation of the target completion date for the whole project.

Looking at the plans for several such moving projects, we could find many similar tasks. With a little more effort, we could group the tasks into logically related categories and then arrange the categories in a sequence corresponding to the different phases of a moving project over time. These general categories would apply to most moving projects, even though the individual tasks could vary from project to project.

Substitute the words "information systems development" for the word "moving" in the above paragraphs and you get an idea of what a systems development life cycle is like. An SDLC shows the major steps, over time, of an

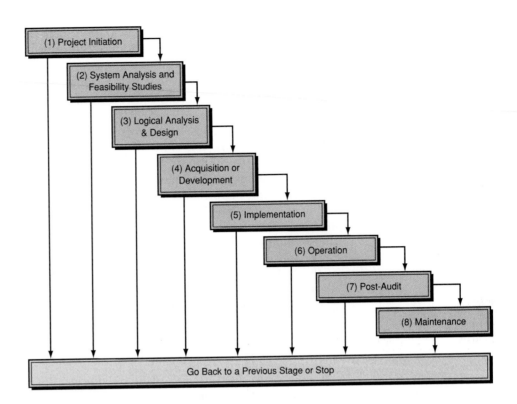

FIGURE 14.1 An eight-stage SDLC.

information systems development project. Within these general categories are individual tasks. Some of these tasks are present in most projects, while others would apply only to certain types of projects. For example, smaller projects may not require as many tasks as larger ones.

Note that there is no universal, standardized version of the SDLC. Consulting firms, as well as IS groups within organizations, develop individualized versions appropriate to their own operations. They give their versions unique names. For example, Accenture calls its version Method/1. The Microsoft certification programs include training in its Solution Development Discipline (SDD) methodology. This chapter's version of an SDLC is relevant to most other SDLCs.

An Eight-Stage SDLC

Figure 14.1 provides a graphic model of an SDLC that has eight stages, or groups of major tasks. Note also that the stages overlap: One stage may start before the previous stage ends. This is in contrast to the traditional **waterfall method,** in which the work flows through all the tasks in one stage before going on to the next stage. Also note that this process can go backward more than one stage, if necessary. These overlapping stages provide flexibility for adapting quickly to the volatile demands of the current business environment. The method also allows for the implementation of ideas or correction of defects that are discovered in later stages. The following discussion outlines the individual stages and their major tasks.

STAGE 1: PROJECT INITIATION.   Projects often start when a manager has a problem or sees an opportunity related to the area where he or she works. The manager calls IS and requests that a formal planning process be initiated to

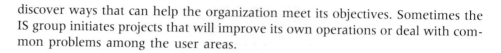

discover ways that can help the organization meet its objectives. Sometimes the IS group initiates projects that will improve its own operations or deal with common problems among the user areas.

STAGE 2: SYSTEMS ANALYSIS AND FEASIBILITY STUDIES. Stage 2 consists of two phases of analysis: systems analysis and feasibility studies.

Systems Analysis. After a project is initiated, the systems analysis phase begins. **Systems analysis** is the phase that develops a thorough understanding of the existing organization, its operation, and the situation that is causing a problem. Systems analysis methods include observation, review of documents, interviews, and performance measurement. Several methods exist for the execution of systems analysis, and some of them are supported by software. Systems analysis also examines the proposed system and its anticipated contribution to the solution of the problem.

Feasibility Studies. **Feasibility studies** calculate the probability of success of the proposed solution; they may be run several times throughout the systems development life cycle. They determine whether the solution is achievable, given the organization's resources and constraints. The feasibility study often includes an impact analysis that examines the effect of the system on other processes and its impact on the surrounding environment. The major areas of study are:

- *Technology.* Are the performance requirements achievable utilizing current information technologies?
- *Economics.* Are the expected benefits greater than the costs?
- *Organizational factors.* Are the skill levels needed to use the new system consistent with the employees who will operate it?
- *Legal, ethical, and other constraints.* Does the system meet all regulatory requirements?

If the proposed project is feasible (and the sponsors are still interested), planning can go on to the next stage.

STAGE 3: LOGICAL ANALYSIS AND DESIGN. The emphasis at the third stage is on **logical design,** the design of a system from the (business) user's point of view. The analyst identifies *information requirements* and specifies processes and generic IS functions such as input, output, and storage, rather than writing programs or identifying hardware. The analysts often use modeling tools such as *data flow diagrams* (DFDs, see Figure 14.2) and *entity-relationship diagrams* (ERDs, see Figure 14.3) to represent logical processes and data relationships.

Logical design is followed by a *physical design,* which translates the abstract logical model into the specific technical design (the "blueprints") for the new system.

The trend toward purchasing software, instead of developing it, is changing both the general emphasis and the specific tasks in the logical analysis and design phase. Analysts still need to identify user requirements. However, they now spend more time *comparing* requirements to features of available software, and less time on *designing* systems. They need to prepare detailed specifications only when the functionality that users need is not available in software in the marketplace. They also have to identify configuration requirements for commercial

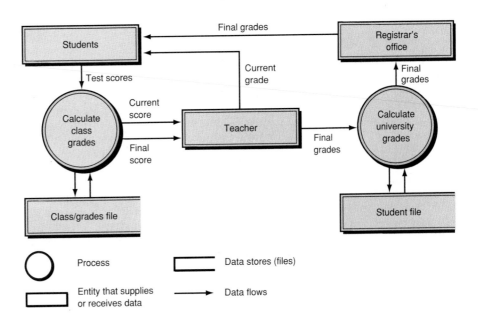

FIGURE 14.2 Data flow diagram for student grades example.

packages that offer a wide range of customization options. *IT at Work 14.1* (page 638) shows how an information system fails due to poor choice of software.

STAGE 4: DEVELOPMENT OR ACTUAL ACQUISITION. The logical design of the new system guides the actual development or acquisition, just as blueprints guide the construction of a new building. IS personnel use the specifications to purchase the hardware and software required for the system and then to configure it as needed. Programmers write code for parts of the system when commercial sources are not available or appropriate. Technical writers develop documentation and training materials. IS personnel test the system, and users do some testing prior to the actual implementation. The testing identifies bugs and also compares system performance to the specifications in the design.

STAGE 5: IMPLEMENTATION. Implementation is obviously an important stage; the system can fail here even if it has all the specified functionality. The project team should plan the implementation very carefully, to avoid problems that could lead to failure or user resistance. The users need training in the mechanics of the system to reduce frustration and to minimize productivity losses in the transition period. In addition to developing technical skills, the training should also attempt to motivate users, for example, by stressing the benefits the system brings to the organization.

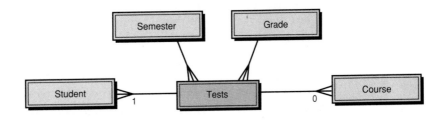

FIGURE 14.3 Entity-relationship diagram of students, courses, and grades.

IT at Work 14.1
HOW DO TECHNOLOGY INITIATIVES FAIL?

Mail Boxes Etc. (MBE) spent $25 million to position itself as the real-world shipping partner to the virtual e-tail space. It was indisputably a great idea. Only one problem: the technology doesn't appear to work. Many franchisees revolted against the system, calling it "a pipe dream." Headquarters insists everything is just fine. But key customers are disenchanted. What follows is a cautionary saga of frustration, stubbornness, poor communication, arrogance, raw power, and wasted opportunity.

The iShip system is part of a massive technology overhaul MBE embarked on two years ago. The brainchild of MBE President and CEO Jim H. Amos Jr., the project was meant to position San Diego-based MBE as the premier shipping partner for e-tailers. "Because of our bricks-and-mortar on the ground, I thought we might have an opportunity that no one else had," said Amos.

By building a satellite network to connect the 3,500 domestic franchises with corporate systems, an Internet-enabled point-of-sale (POS) system, and the iShip manifest system, shipping at MBE would become enticingly simple. The idea was that a returning customer would need to give only his phone number to the MBE clerk for service. Up would pop his entire order history and recipient address information. Customers would no longer need to carry their address books into the store. They would feel instantly at home, as if they were part of a special group. At least, that was the plan.

"It's a great idea, all right. It just doesn't work," said Sousa. Besides using the DOS manifest as the default shipping system, Sousa ditched the satellite network in favor of a local digital subscriber line (DSL) provider for Internet service. He relies on paper forms in duplicate to do the bulk of his business. To Sousa, the new systems have been a big disappointment. "None of it connects. This is all a pipe dream."

Although MBE executives insist that the technology works fine, an internal MBE memo obtained by *Darwin* Magazine seems to suggest that the company is indeed rethinking its technology strategy, which would mean "deep-sixing" (discarding) a lot of time and money. All told, MBE spent in the neighborhood of $25 million on its technology program, including equity investments in a host of dot-coms such as iShip, in which MBE invested $4 million. That's a significant chunk of change for a company with only $81 million in revenues (sales for the global MBE network were approximately $1.4 billion in fiscal 2000). The system is only part of the problem with Amos' e-business strategy. Its high-profile agreement to be the exclusive shipper for online auction giant eBay has stalled, and iShip is faltering financially. As *Darwin* went to press in May 2001, MBE announced that it had been acquired by shipping giant United Parcel Service of America (UPS).

The MBE story is shaping up as one giant case study for how not to do a strategic technology initiative. While the UPS deal will likely add an infusion of capital to help mend MBE's technology woes, it's still worth asking why such a well-intentioned idea failed so signally. After all, the plan to connect the franchises and to Internet-enable their operations was not fundamentally flawed. The answer seems to lie in a tangle of poor technology decisions, bad market timing, and a disconnect between the services MBE offers and what many of the e-tailers want.

Sources: Condensed from Paul (2001) and from *mbe.com* (2003).

For Further Exploration: What are the problems with MBE's "jump into new technology"? Discuss the possible impacts on MBE of its poor technology decision.

In most cases, implementing a new system requires a *conversion* from a previous system. Approaches to conversion include:

- **Parallel conversion:** The old and new systems operate concurrently for a test period, and then the old system is discontinued.
- **Direct cutover:** The old system is turned off, and the new system is turned on.
- **Pilot conversion:** The new system is implemented in a subset of locations (for example, some of the branches in a large banking chain) and is extended to remaining locations over time.

● **Phased conversion:** Large systems often are built from distinct modules. If the modules were originally designed to be relatively independent, it may be possible to replace the modules one at a time.

STAGE 6: OPERATION. After a successful conversion, the system will operate for an indefinite period of time, until the system is no longer adequate or necessary, or cost effective.

STAGE 7: POST-AUDIT EVALUATION. An organization should perform a **post-audit** to evaluate all its larger systems projects after their completion. Post-audits introduce an additional element of discipline into the development process. If the implementation was successful, an audit should occur after the system's operations have stabilized. If the project failed, the audit should be done as soon as possible after the failure.

STAGE 8: MAINTENANCE. Every system needs two regular kinds of maintenance: fixing of bugs and regular system updating. Maintenance is expensive, accounting for up to 80 percent of organizational IS budgets. Therefore it is important that the design and development stages produce systems that are easy to maintain and are flexible enough to handle future expansion, upgrading, and capacity increases.

Traditional versus Modern SDLCs

There are two major problems with systems development life cycle methodologies. First, many systems projects fail, even though the project management incorporates a formal SDLC approach. Second, the environment is very different from what it was 30 years ago. Information technology is much more powerful and includes features such as graphical user interfaces and client/server architectures that are very different from earlier forms of programming.

Do these problems mean that project managers should abandon the SDLC concept? Not really. All the stages in Figure 14.1 are still either absolutely necessary or highly desirable for larger projects. The benefits described above are still important. The increasing complexity of systems development means that some form of structure is even more necessary now than 30 years ago. However, the general organization of the SDLC needs to adjust to the realities of the current environment. IS groups considering the implementation of a formal SDLC methodology and associated tools for managing projects should look for the characteristics listed at Online File W14.1 at the book's Web site. Yourdon (1989, 2002) proposes a modern structured project life cycle.

A Light SDLC Methodology for Web-Based System Development

The SDLC (both traditional and modern) is a formal and disciplined approach to systems development. The time pressures for e-business development projects in the twenty-first century have tempted many project teams to simply abandon whatever degree of disciplined and formal process methodology they may have used in the 1980s and 1990s and simply proceed with an anarchical approach.

That "winging it" may have succeeded in first-generation e-business projects, but the risk of building a mission-critical system that's unstable, buggy, non-scalable, and vulnerable to hacker attacks is forcing more and more companies to look for a methodology that strikes a balance between rigor and speed (Yourdon,

2000, 2002). Such a so-called **light methodology** imposes discipline upon the most critical project activities, without wasting precious time on bureaucratic processes associated with old mainframe-era projects. It is less structured than the traditional SDLC and serves more as a framework or reference guide for skilled people than as a foolproof recipe for success.

14.2 METHODS FOR COMPLEX OR QUICKLY NEEDED SYSTEMS

The traditional systems development life cycle approach works best on projects in which users have a clear idea about what they want. The typical automation project is a good example because, in this type of project, computer systems replace manual labor with only minimal changes in processes. Unfortunately, simple automation projects are becoming less common. Nowadays projects tend to require major changes in existing processes, through reengineering or through development of processes that are new to the organization. Furthermore, the need to build inter-organizational and international systems using Web technologies such as extranets, and the need to build or modify systems quickly (see Minicases 1 and 2), created a major shift in the nature of information systems.

This shift in emphasis, along with the high failure rate in traditional systems development, indicates a need for alternatives to conventional SDLC methodologies. Prototyping, rapid application development, joint application design, object-oriented development, and component-based development are five possible alternatives.

Prototyping

The **prototyping** approach to systems development is, in many ways, the very opposite of an old-style SDLC. Instead of spending a lot of time producing very detailed specifications, the developers find out only generally what the users want. The developers do not develop the complete system all at once. Instead they *quickly* create a prototype, which either contains portions of the system of most interest to the users, or is a small-scale working model of the entire system. After reviewing the prototype with the users, the developers refine and extend it. This process continues through several iterations until either the users approve the design or it becomes apparent that the proposed system cannot meet their needs. If the system is viable, the developers create a full-scale version that includes additional features.

In this approach, which is also known as *evolutionary development*, the emphasis is on producing something quickly for the users to review. To speed up the process, programmers may use a fourth-generation language (4GL) and other tools such as screen generators or spreadsheet software for parts of the prototype. Figure 14.4 shows a flowchart of the prototyping process, using a relational database for the initial versions of the system.

Prototyping is particularly useful for situations in which user interaction is especially important. Examples of such situations would be decision support (DSS), e-commerce "sell-sides," or executive information systems. Prototyping is also good for IS projects that substantially change business processes. For users of these types of systems, prototyping allows opportunities to work with the model, and to identify necessary changes and enhancements, before making a

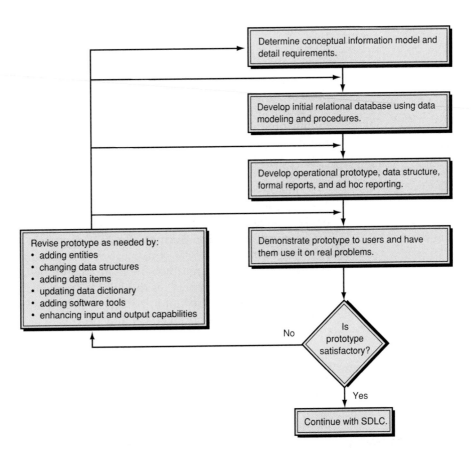

FIGURE 14.4 Model of prototyping process.

major commitment to development. Users should also consider prototyping if it is necessary to start using the system as soon as possible, even before it is complete.

Prototyping does have some disadvantages. It largely replaces the formal analysis and design stage of a conventional SDLC. As a result, the systems analysts may not need to produce much formal documentation for the programmers during the project. If managers do not follow up on this, the documentation may be inadequate years later when the system needs maintenance. Another problem is that users, after working with the final prototype, may not understand why additional work and associated changes are necessary to bring the system up to organizational standards.

Joint Application Design

Joint application design (JAD) is a group-based method for collecting user requirements and creating system designs. JAD is most often used within the systems analysis and systems design stages of the SDLC.

In the traditional SDLC, systems analysts interview or directly observe potential users of the new information system individually to understand each user's needs. The analysts will obtain many similar requests from users, but also many conflicting requests. The analysts must then consolidate all requests and go back to the users to resolve the conflicts, a process that usually requires a great deal of time.

In contrast to the SDLC requirements analysis, JAD has a meeting in which all users meet simultaneously with analysts. During the meeting, all users jointly define and agree upon systems requirements. This process saves a tremendous amount of time.

The JAD approach to systems development has several advantages. First, the group process involves more users in the development process while still saving time. This involvement leads to greater support for and acceptance of the new system and can produce a system of higher quality. This involvement also may lead to easier implementation of the new system and lower training costs.

The JAD approach also has disadvantages. First, it is very difficult to get all users to the JAD meeting. For example, large organizations may have users literally all over the world; to have all of them attend a JAD meeting would be prohibitively expensive. Second, the JAD approach has all the problems caused by any group process (e.g., one person can dominate the meeting, some participants may be shy and not contribute in a group setting, or some participants may sit back and let others do the work). To alleviate these problems, JAD sessions usually have a facilitator, who is skilled in systems analysis and design as well in managing group meetings and processes.

JOINT APPLICATION DESIGN AND WEB SITE DESIGN. The emphasis now for e-business Web sites is to improve customer satisfaction and to make the users' experience at the site simple, intuitive, and efficient. Companies that invest in designing solutions that make Web site navigation easy for their users are more likely to achieve customer retention—the key to the success or failure of any business on the Web.

Critical design features are those requirements that a Web site must support to allow a user to complete a task in an enjoyable and efficient way. For users to accept and adopt the interface of a Web site, it is useful to have them involved in its design. An electronic JAD session can be conducted offsite/online with technology support. This brings the key representatives of users (customers), managers, systems designers, and other stakeholders together for requirements determination. The initial set of requirements can serve as the basis for the development of a larger survey to determine user (customer) preferences and priorities. JAD is thus of particular interest to Web site designers (see Kendall and Kendall, 2002).

Rapid Application Development

Rapid application development (RAD) methodologies and tools make it possible to develop systems faster, especially systems where the user interface is an important component. RAD can also improve the process of rewriting legacy applications. An example of how quickly experienced developers can create applications with RAD tools is provided in *IT at Work 14.2.*

What are the components or tools and capabilities of a RAD system? Typical packages include the following.

- *GUI development environment:* the ability to create many aspects of an application by "drag-and-drop" operations. For example, the user can create a report by clicking on file names, and then clicking and dragging fields from these files to the appropriate locations in the report.

IT at Work 14.2

BLUE CROSS & BLUE SHIELD DEVELOPS AN
AWARD-WINNING APPLICATION USING RAD

A Y2K problem without a solution led to the development of an innovative customer-service application in less than a year at Blue Cross & Blue Shield of Rhode Island (BCBSRI). The new system is based on an internally developed architecture that the Application Development Trends' 2000 Innovator Awards judges lauded as modular and flexible enough to easily allow for system upgrades and the incorporation of new technology.

BCBSRI decided in mid-1998 to build a new customer-service system, a mission-critical application that monitors and records communications with policyholders. The internal work on the project began in January 1999 after the development plan and blueprint were validated by outside consultants.

The development team adhered to a phased-rollout approach and rapid application development (RAD) methodology. Developers used several productivity tools (including the Sybase EAServer, Sybase PowerBuilder, and Riverton HOW), as well as performance monitoring techniques and heavy user involvement to ensure the quality of the system throughout its life cycle. By September 1, 1999, the application was available to more than a hundred Windows 98-based clients. Since then, the customer-service unit has averaged about 1,800 daily calls and more than 20,000 transactions a day over the system.

By early 2000, the new customer-service system had already realized an ROI of $500,000, boosts in user productivity, significant strides in system performance, and increased data accuracy. The integration, power, and scalability of the BCBSRI solution are truly exemplary.

Sources: Condensed from Bucken (2000) and from a paper published at *adtmag.com* (April 2000).

For Further Exploration: To what extent do you think the adoption of the RAD methodology contributed to the success of the BCBSRI project?

- ***Reusable components:*** a library of common, standard "objects" such as buttons and dialog boxes. The developer drags-and-drops these items into the application.
- ***Code generator.*** After the developer drags-and-drops the standard objects into the design, the package automatically writes computer programs to implement the reports, input screens, buttons, dialog boxes, and so forth.
- ***Programming language:*** such as BASIC (in Visual Basic), Object Pascal (in Delphi), or C++. This component includes an integrated development environment (IDE) for creating, testing, and debugging code. It may be possible to use drag-and-drop operations to create up to 80 percent of the code for a system.

As Figure 14.5 (page 644) shows, the same phases followed in the traditional SDLC are also followed in RAD, but the phases in RAD are combined to produce a more streamlined development technique. The emphasis in RAD is generally less on the sequence and structure of processes in the life cycle and more on doing different tasks in parallel with each other and on using prototyping extensively.

In addition to the benefits of speed and portability, RAD is used to create applications that are easier to maintain and to modify. However, RAD packages also have some disadvantages. Like prototyping, the iterative development process can continue indefinitely if there is no unambiguous criterion for ending it. RAD packages may have capabilities to document the system, but having these features does not guarantee that developers will produce appropriate documentation.

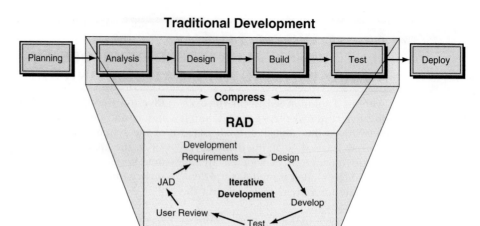

FIGURE 14.5 A rapid application development SDLC. (*Source: datawarehouse-training.com/Methodologies/rapid-application-development.*)

RAPID APPLICATION DEVELOPMENT IN THE AGE OF THE INTERNET. RAD has been a key component of client/server systems development. According to Yourdon (2000), WWW applications are likely to accelerate the RAD process to the point where it becomes "FAD," or frantic application development. The technology-driven nature of the Internet is forcing developers to deliver applications that use these new technologies, such as streaming video and audio, in shorter and shorter time spans. This is spurred further by the development efforts of vendors, including Netscape and Microsoft, who continually release new versions of their Web browser software. Pressure arising from the constant introduction of new technology has introduced a FAD approach into organizations that are developing Web-based solutions. It appears that the FAD approach will become more prevalent as organizations become increasingly aware of the strategic value of an Internet presence.

Object-Oriented Development

Object-oriented development (see Technology Guide 2) is based on a fundamentally different view of computer systems than that found in traditional SDLC approaches. Traditional approaches provide specific step-by-step instructions in the form of computer programs, in which programmers must specify every procedural detail. They usually result in a system that performs the original task but may not be suited for handling other tasks, even when the other tasks involve the same real-world entities.

An object-oriented (OO) system begins not with the task to be performed, but with the aspects of the real world that must be modeled to perform that task. Therefore, if a firm has a good model of its customers and its interactions with them, this model can be used equally well for billings, mailings, and sales leads. Object technology enables the development of purchasable, sharable, and reusable information assets (objects) existing in a worldwide network of interoperable interorganizational information systems.

BENEFITS AND LIMITATIONS OF THE OBJECT-ORIENTED APPROACH. The OO approach to software development can lead to many benefits. First, it reduces the complexity of systems development and leads to systems that are easier and quicker to build and maintain, because each object is relatively small, self-contained, and manageable. Second, the OO approach improves programmers' productivity and quality. Once an object has been defined, implemented, and tested, it can be reused in other systems. Third, systems developed with the OO approach are more flexible. These systems can be modified and enhanced easily, by changing some types of objects or by adding new types. A fourth benefit is that the OO approach allows the systems analyst to think at the level of the real-world system (as users do) and not at the level of the programming language.

On the other hand, there are some disadvantages to the OO approach. OO systems (especially those written in Java) generally run more slowly than those developed in other programming languages. By all appearances, object-oriented systems development (OOSD) is in the throes of a dilemma. Dozens of well-known experts claim the advantages of OOSD make it vastly superior to conventional systems development. But some of them also point to OOSD's disadvantages and question whether it will ever be a dominant approach to systems development. Online Files W14.2 and W14.3 show some of the advantages and disadvantages of OOSD. For a more detailed discussion of the ups and downs of the object-oriented approach, see Johnson (2000).

UNIFIED MODELING LANGUAGE. The techniques and notations that are incorporated into a standard object-oriented language are called *unified modeling language* (UML). The UML allows a developer to specify, visualize, and construct the artifacts of software systems, as well as business models. Figure 14.6 provides an example of two UML artifacts, class and object diagrams.

Figure 14.6a shows two object classes: Student and Course, along with their attributes and operations. Objects belonging to the same class may also participate in similar relationships with other objects. For example, all students register

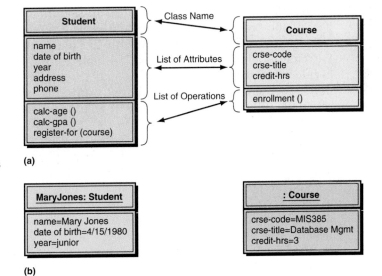

FIGURE 14.6 UML class and object diagrams. (*Source:* Valacich et al., *Essentials of Systems Analysis and Design*, Prentice-Hall, 2001, p. 375. Reprinted by permission of Pearson Education, Inc., Upper Saddle River, NJ.)

for courses, and therefore the Student class can participate in a relationship called "register-for" with another class called Course. Figure 14.6b shows two object instances (think examples), one for each of the classes that appears in Figure 14.6a. The object instance's attributes and their values are shown in the second compartment. An operation such as "calc-gpa" in the Student class (see Figure 14.6a) is a function or a service that is provided for all the instances of a class. It is only through such operations that other objects can access or manipulate the information stored in an object.

OBJECT TECHNOLOGY AND WEB-BASED SYSTEMS DEVELOPMENT. The object-oriented approach is ideal for developing Web applications. First, the data and code of object-oriented systems are encapsulated into reusable components, each of which can be developed and enhanced independently. This increases development speed and flexibility, as well as reducing system maintenance. Object technology allows companies to share business applications on the Internet.

A second reason why the object-oriented approach is ideal for developing Web applications is that as the Web evolves from static data to active data, it is moving toward object-based software systems. Objects become useful in this context because, by definition, they join software code and data. Objects provide a modular way of organizing, configuring, and reusing code instead of "reinventing the wheel" each time a new routine is written. When users click on a Web page, for example, they are downloading objects into their client machines. This combination of data and code can be configured in new ways, manipulated, and operated actively.

Extreme Programming

Extreme programming (XP) is a discipline of software development based on values of simplicity, communication, feedback, and courage. It works by bringing the whole team together in the presence of simple practices, with enough feedback to enable the team to see where they are and to tune the practices to their unique situation.

In extreme programming, every contributor to the project is an integral part of the "whole team." The team forms around a business representative called "the customer," who sits with the team and works with them daily. Extreme programming teams use a simple form of planning and tracking to decide what should be done next and to predict when the project will be done. Focused on business value, the team produces the software in a series of small, fully integrated releases that pass all the tests the customer has defined.

Extreme programmers work together in pairs and as a group, with simple design and obsessively tested code, improving the design continually to keep it always just right for the current needs. The extreme programming team keeps the system integrated and running all the time. The programmers write all production code in pairs, and all work together all the time. They code in a consistent style so that everyone can understand and improve all the code as needed. The extreme programming team shares a common and simple picture of what the system looks like. Everyone works at a pace that can be sustained indefinitely. Figure 14.7 shows the practices and the main "cycles" of extreme programming.

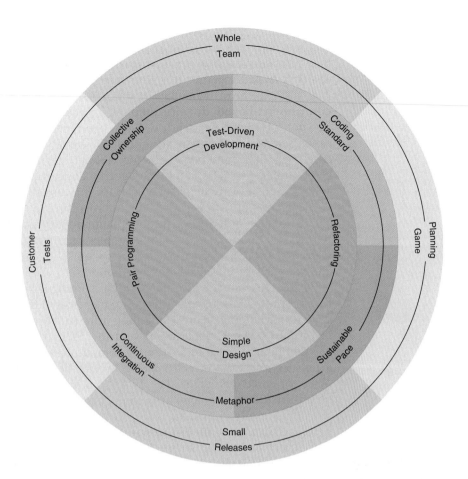

FIGURE 14.7 Extreme programming practices.

14.3 COMPONENT-BASED DEVELOPMENT AND WEB SERVICES

The efficient development of software reuse, as discussed in Section 14.2, has become a critical aspect in the overall IS strategies of many organizations. An increasing number of companies have reported reuse successes. While the traditional reuse paradigm *allows changes* to the code that is to be reused (white-box reuse), component-based software development advocates that components are reused *as is* (black-box reuse). Currently emerging Web services are also aiming at improving application development by leveraging existing software; however, they go an entirely different route. Instead of requiring the Web service user to own the component, Web services reside on the provider's host. Program-to-program communication between the existing application and the Web service is enabled through a set of standardized interfaces, thus taking the black-box reuse concepts one step further. The importance of these trends is reflected by the growing interest of the IS community in the component-based software development and Web services research areas.

Component-Based Development

Object technology, as discussed in Section 14.2, however, does have its downside, including a steep learning curve. Business objects, though they represent things in the real world, become unwieldy when they are combined and recombined in large-scale commercial applications. What is needed are suites of business objects that provide major chunks of application functionality (e.g., pre-programmed workflow, transaction processing, and user event notification) that can be snapped together to create complete business applications.

This approach is embodied in the next step in the evolution beyond objects, **component-based development.** *Components* are self-contained packages of functionality that have clearly defined, open interfaces that offer high-level application services. Components can be distributed dynamically for reuse across multiple applications and heterogeneous computing platforms. Components take the best features of objects to a higher level of abstraction, thus enabling mainstream commercial software developers to learn and use the technology more easily.

User interface icons (small), word processing (a complete software product), a GUI, online ordering (a business component), and inventory reordering (a business component) are a few examples of components. Search engines, fire-walls, Web servers, browsers, page displays, and telecommunications protocols are examples of intranet-based components.

Code reusability, which makes programming faster and more accurate, is the first of several reasons for using component-based development. Others include: support for heterogeneous computing infrastructure and platforms; rapid assembly of new business applications; and the ability of an application to scale.

Components used in distributed computing need to possess several key characteristics to work correctly, and they can be viewed as an extension of the object-oriented paradigm. The two main traits borrowed from the world of object-oriented technology are *encapsulation* and *data hiding.*

Components *encapsulate* the routines or programs that perform discrete functions. In a component-based program, one can define components with various published interfaces. One of these interfaces might be, for example, a date-comparison function. If this function is passed to two date objects to compare, it returns the results. All manipulations of dates are required to use the interfaces defined by the date object, so the complete function is encapsulated in this object, which has a distinct interface to other systems. Now, if the function has to be changed, only the program code that defines the object must be changed, and the behavior of the date comparison routine is updated immediately, a feature known as *encapsulation.*

Data hiding addresses a different problem. It places data needed by a component object's functions within the component, where it can be accessed only by specially designated functions in the component itself. Data hiding is a critical trait of distributed components. The fact that only designated functions can access certain data items, and outside "requestors" have to query the component, simplifies maintenance of component-oriented programs.

A component-based application architecture provides the business benefits of rapid application development for quick time to market, enterprise-wide consistency of business rules, and quick response to changing business requirements. And because major software vendors are committed to a component architecture, applications can mix and match best-of-breed solutions. Components hide the complexity of the underlying systems technology. Plug-and-play business application components can be assembled or "glued together" rapidly to develop complex distributed applications needed for e-commerce. The execution of component-based development, however, requires special training and skill. For a methodology of evaluating component-based systems see Dahanayake et al. (2003).

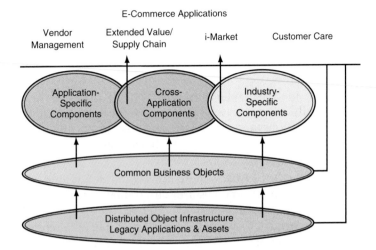

FIGURE 14.8
E-commerce applications and component logical architecture. (*Source:* Drawn by E. Turban.)

COMPONENT-BASED DEVELOPMENT OF E-COMMERCE APPLICATIONS. Component-based EC development is gaining momentum. It is supported by Microsoft and the Object Management Group (OMG), which have put in place many of the standards needed to make component-based development a reality. A logical architecture for component-based development of e-commerce applications can be described in layers as shown in Figure 14.8.

Component-based development for e-commerce applications is a process of assembly and refinement. The process begins with *cross-application components* that provide functionality common to most types of e-commerce applications. Typical of such core components are user-profile management, authentication, authorization, data management, and so on. These cross-application components can be customized and extended to form *application-specific components*. For example, in a procurement application, a profiling component will contain attributes for identifying a user's role and buying power.

When applied to an I-market (Internet market) application, the profiling component will be extended to hold information that can be used to track customer buying patterns. In addition to the tailored cross-application components, application-specific components will include best-of-breed search engines, shopping carts, catalogs, or other elements required for the application. These may be built in-house or purchased. Cross-application components also can be extended to develop *industry-specific components*. For example, in a manufacturing industry a workflow component can be extended to handle work-in-progress and integrate workflows across enterprises to make "just-in-time" a reality.

The final step in the component-based development process is the configuration of the components to incorporate the organization's unique business rules and user presentation and navigation. It is in this step that a company's competitive advantage is built. Components come in many shapes and can be purchased from special vendors. For ways to combine them into meaningful applications, see Arsanjani (2002).

There are several methods that developers can use for integrating components (e.g., see Linthicum, 2001). These methods can have limitations. For example, they can be vendor or platform dependent, expensive, complex to learn, and inflexible. A potential solution is Web services.

Web Services in System Development

As described in Chapter 2, the major application of Web services is system integration. System integration is one of the major activities done in system development. For example, the whole concept of components is based on the idea of gluing them together. Applications need to be integrated with databases and with other applications. Users need to interface with the data warehouse to conduct analysis, and almost any new system needs to be integrated with old ones. Finally, the increase of B2B and e-business activities requires the integration of applications and databases of business partners (external integration). Let us examine the essentials of Web services.

BASIC CONCEPTS. There are several definitions of Web services. Here is a typical one: **Web services** are self-contained, self-describing business and consumer modular applications, delivered over the Internet, that users can select and combine through almost any device from personal computers to mobile phones. By using a set of shared protocols and standards, these applications permit disparate systems to "talk" with one another—that is, to share data and services—without requiring human beings to translate the conversations.

The following definition provides a preview of some of the functionalities of Web services: "Web service is a URL-addressable software resource that performs functions and provides answers. A Web service is made by taking a set of software functionalities and wrapping it up so that the services it performs are visible and accessible to other software applications. Web services can request services from other Web services, and they can expect to receive the results or responses from those requests. Web services may interoperate in a loosely-coupled manner; they can request services across the Net and wait for a response. Web services may be combined to create new services. And they may be recombined, swapped or substituted, or replaced at runtime" (Seybold, 2002).

Specifically, a Web service fits the following three criteria: (1) It is able to expose and describe itself to other applications, allowing those applications to understand what the service does. (2) It can be located by other applications via an online directory, if the service has been registered in a proper directory. (3) It can be invoked by the originating application by using standard protocols.

The Key Protocols: The Building Blocks of the Web Services Platforms. Web services are based on a family of key protocols (standards). The major protocols are:

- *The XML Language. Extensible Markup Language (XML)* is an open standard, a universal language for defining data schemes. XML makes it easier to exchange data among a variety of applications as well as to validate and interpret such data. An XML document describes a Web service and includes information detailing exactly how the Web service can be run.

- *SOAP. Simple Object Access Protocol (SOAP)* is a set of rules that facilitate XML exchange between network applications. SOAP defines a common standard that allows different Web services to interoperate (i.e., it enables communications, such as allowing Visual Basic clients to access a JAVA server). It is a platform-independent specification that defines how messages can be sent between two software systems through the use of XML. These messages typically follow a Request/Response pattern (computer-to-computer).

- *WSDL.* The *Web Services Description Language (WSDL)* is a protocol used to create the XML document that describes tasks performed by a Web service. It actually defines the programmatic interface of the Web services. Tools such as VisualStudio.Net automate the process of accessing the WSDL, read it, and code the application to reference the specific Web service.

- *UDDI.* *Universal Description, Discovery, and Integration (UDDL)* is a protocol that allows for the creation of public or private searchable directories of Web services. It is the registry of Web services descriptions.
- *Security protocols.* Several security standards are in development such as *Security Assertion Markup Language (SAML)*, which is a standard for authentication and authorization. Other security standards are XML signature, XML encryption, XKMS, and XACML.

See Cerami (2002) for a list of other protocols that are under development.

THE NOTION OF SERVICES AS COMPONENTS. Traditionally, people view information systems and IT, including the Web, as dealing with information (or data) processing. Web services enable the Web to become a platform for applying *business services*. By services we mean components in IT applications that are well defined and perform a useful task. For example, user authentication, currency conversion, and shipping arrangements are building blocks of broad business processes or applications, such as e-commerce ordering or e-procurement systems. For discussion see Stal (2002).

The idea of taking elementary services and gluing them together to create new applications is not new. As a matter of fact, the approach of using components for system development has become very popular in recent years due to savings that can be gained from usability (e.g., see Allen and Frost, 1998). The problem is that earlier approaches were cumbersome and expensive. According to Tabor (2002) existing technologies used for component integration exhibit problems with data format, data transmission, interoperability, inflexibility (they are platform specific), and security. Web services offer a fresh approach to integration. Furthermore, business processes that are comprised of Web services are much easier to adapt to changing customer needs and business climates than are today's home-grown or purchased applications (Seybold, 2002). For further understanding of how this approach works, see the description of a Web services building process in Online File W14.4.

WHAT WEB SERVICES CAN DO. The major functionalities of Web services are as follows: (1) They provide for faster and cheaper integration. (2) Web services communicate with other programs automatically without human intervention. (3) They can be deployed for use over the Internet or on an intranet inside a corporate firewall. (4) They can run in a protected environment set up by business partners. (5) They can be written using a wide variety of development tools. These development tools can perform a wide variety of tasks including: automating business processes, integrating disparate components of an enterprise-wide system, delivering alerts to individuals about stock prices and the weather, and streamlining online buying and selling.

Key to the promise of Web services is that, in theory, they can be used by anyone, anywhere, any time, using any hardware and any software, as long as the modular software components of the services are built using the set of standards described earlier (see Fremantle et al., 2002 and Patton, 2002). The generic types of Web services are described in Online File W14.5.

A Web Service Example. As a simple example of how Web services operate, consider an airline Web site that provides consumers with the opportunity

TABLE 14.1 Web Services: Advantages and Limitations

Advantages	Limitations
Web services rely on universal, open, text-based standards that greatly simplify the problems posed by interoperability and lower the IT costs of collaborating with external partners, vendors, or clients.	Web services are not a silver bullet. The standards underlying Web services are still being defined, so interoperability is not automatic. Even in those instances where the standards are relatively stable, it still requires programming skill and effort to implement and deploy Web services.
Web services enable software running on different platforms to communicate, reducing the cost and headaches of multiple platforms running on everything from mainframes to servers to desktops to PDAs.	One area where the Web services standards are not well-defined is security. The good news is that Web services enable distributed applications to communicate with ease. The bad news is that Web services also enable applications to bypass security barriers (such as firewalls) with ease. Standards such as XML, SOAP, WSDL, and UDDI say nothing about privacy, authentication, integrity, or non-repudiation. In an effort to bridge the gap between these standards and existing security standards (such as public key encryption), several vendors and organizations have proposed and are currently debating a number of Web services security standards. One of these is WS-Security, proposed by Microsoft, IBM, and Verisign.
Web services promote modular programming which enables reuse by multiple organizations.	While Web services rely on XML as the mechanism for encoding data, higher-level standards are still required, especially in B2B applications. For example, if two banks want to communicate, they still need standards to define the specific content being communicated. Standards such as OFX (Open Financial Exchange), which defines the content of transactions between financial institutions, come into play. The lack of coordination among all interested parties for high-level standards is why Web services will first be adopted within organizations and later across organizations.
Web services are easy and inexpensive to implement because they operate on the existing Internet infrastructure. They also offer a way to maintain and integrate legacy IT systems at a lower cost than typical Enterprise Application Integration (EAI) efforts.	
Web services can be implemented incrementally, rather than all at once.	

Sources: Dietel et al. (2003); Shirky (2003).

to purchase tickets online. The airline recognizes that customers also might want to rent a car and reserve a hotel as part of their travel plans. The consumer would like the convenience of logging onto only one system rather than three, saving time and effort. Also, the same consumer would like to input personal information only once.

The airline does not have car rental or hotel reservation systems in place. Instead, the airline relies on car rental and hotel partners to provide Web service access to their systems. The specific services the partners provide are defined by a series of WSDL documents. When a customer makes a reservation for a car or hotel on the airline's Web site, SOAP messages are sent back and forth in the background between the airline's and the partners' servers. In setting up their systems, there is no need for the partners to worry about the hardware or operating systems each is running. Web services overcome the barriers imposed by these differences. An additional advantage for the hotel and car reservation systems is that their Web services can be published in UDDI so that other businesses can take advantage of their services.

ADVANTAGES AND LIMITATIONS OF WEB SERVICES. Over the years, there have been a number of programming initiatives aimed at solving the problem of interoperability (i.e., getting software and applications from different vendors running on different hardware and operating systems to communicate with one another in a transparent fashion). Web services is the latest of these initiatives. Why is this initiative different from its predecessors? Table 14.1 (previous page) cites advantages (Dietel et al., 2003; Shirky, 2003) and limitations of Web services.

14.4 SYSTEMS DEVELOPED OUTSIDE THE IS DEPARTMENT

The methodologies presented earlier are usually used by the information systems department (ISD). Their execution requires highly skilled employees, and the methodologies are fairly complex. The result is a backlog in application development, and a high failure rate. Therefore, many organizations are using approaches that shift the construction task from the ISD to others. Of the various ways of doing this, three are most common: Let users build their own systems; outsource the entire systems development process; or let end users use packages. These options and models are described next.

End-User Development

In the early days of computing, an organization housed its computer in a climate-controlled room, with locked doors and restricted access. The only people who interacted with the computer (most organizations had only one computer) were specialists: programmers, computer operators, and data entry personnel. Over the years, computers became cheaper, smaller, and more widely dispersed throughout the organization. Now almost everybody who works at a desk has a computer.

Along with this proliferation of hardware, many computer-related activities shifted out into the work area. Users now handle most of their own data entry. They create many of their own reports and print them locally, instead of waiting for them to arrive in the interoffice mail after a computer operator has run them at a remote data center. They provide unofficial training and support to other workers in their area. Users also design and develop an increasing proportion of their own applications, sometimes even relatively large and complex systems. Online Files W14.6 and W14.7 on the Web site provide a detailed discussion of the reasons favoring end-user development and types of end-user computing.

END-USER COMPUTING AND WEB-BASED SYSTEMS DEVELOPMENT. The development of client/server applications in the 1980s and 1990s was characterized by user-driven systems development. End users have been directly or indirectly making decisions for systems designers and developers on how the programs should operate. Web-based systems development in the twenty-first century, however, is application driven rather than user driven. The end user can still determine what the requirements will be and has some input into the design of the applications. But because of the nature of the technologies used

IT at Work 14.3
ANSETT AUSTRALIA AND IBM SIGN
END-USER COMPUTING DEAL

Ansett Australia, one of Australia's leading airlines, announced on January 4, 1999, that it had appointed IBM Global Services Australia to manage its end-user computing support functions. Ansett (*ansett.com.au*), based in Melbourne, Australia, operates an extensive range of domestic airline services and also flies to Japan, Hong Kong, Taiwan, Bali, and Fiji.

Ansett Australia General Manager for IT Infrastructure and Operations, Hal Pringle, said, "IBM Global Services Australia's appointment would significantly improve desktop services to the airline's end users while at the same time delivering substantial cost savings." Such service was previously delivered by a mixture of external contractors and in-house staff.

Mr. Pringle said the decision to hire an external provider of end-user computing (EUC) support arose from a benchmarking study conducted by Ansett earlier that year. The study showed that a move to a single external provider of the caliber of IBM Global Services Australia would: achieve a more consistent end-to-end delivery of applications; assist the implementation of best-practice EUC support at the best cost; deliver substantial cost savings; allow Ansett to

better manage EUC supply and demand; and deliver a more consistent and better quality support service to end users.

"The study highlighted the fact that Ansett had in effect 'outgrown' the level of end-user service provided at that time, and that a quantum leap in service was required to ensure a full return on our end-user computing investment," Pringle said.

"Improving delivery of services to end users and enhancing end-user productivity are becoming key focus areas for many Australian corporations. I am very pleased that we have been chosen to deliver these additional services to Ansett," said Mr. Bligh, General Manager of IBM Global Services Australia, Travel and Transportation Services.

Sources: Sachdeva (2000) and *ansett.com.au* (2003).

For Further Exploration: What strategic advantages can Ansett Australia gain by ensuring consistent and reliable support to its end-user computing? Is it worth it for a company to invest in end-user computing?

---

in Web-based application design, the function, not the user, determines what the application will look like and how it will perform. An innovative way of managing end-user computing is shown in *IT at Work 14.3.*

Outsourcing

Outsourcing, in its broadest sense, is the purchase of any product or service from another company (see Chapter 13). In general, companies outsource the products and services they are unable or unwilling to produce themselves. IS departments have outsourced computer hardware, telecommunications services, and systems software (such as operating systems) for some time. They also purchase end-user software (e.g., Microsoft Office) because there is no reason to reinvent tools that a software company specializing in these products can provide more cheaply.

Recently, information technology has hired outside organizations to perform functions that in the past have been performed internally by IS departments. Common areas for outsourcing have included maintaining computer centers and telecommunications networks. Some companies, however, outsource most of the IT functions, including systems and applications development, leaving only a very small internal information systems department. This department develops IS plans and negotiates with the vendors performing the outsourced functions.

Typically, the outsourcing firm hires the IS employees for the customer and buys the computer hardware. The outsourcer provides IT services under a contract that specifies a baseline level of services, with additional charges for higher volumes or services not identified in the baseline contract. Many smaller firms provide limited-scale outsourcing of individual services, but only the largest outsourcing firms can take over large parts of the IT functions of major organizations. The benefits and problems of outsourcing are listed in Online File W14.8 at the Web site of this chapter.

TRENDS TO OUTSOURCE WEB-BASED SYSTEMS DEVELOPMENT. There is a growing trend to outsource Web-based systems development. This includes planning, Web site design and development, installation of the hardware and software, and more. A principal reason for outsourcing all or part of a Web project is that few companies are fully equipped to do everything themselves, and many demand proof that their online presence will pay off before hiring additional staff. There are many skills needed to develop a Web site and get it up and running. You need people who know graphic design, marketing, networking, HTML, programming, copywriting, public relations, database design, account management, and sales. In addition, issues dealing with the back-end job of running a real business require office managers, accountants, lawyers, and so forth. Outsourcing provides a one-stop shopping alternative to customers who do not have the expertise or time to develop and maintain a commercial site. Consulting providers are broadening their skill sets and geographic reach to try to fill their clients' needs.

Outsourcing Web work means establishing a new, long-term relationship with a stranger. Careful questioning can minimize the risk of making a mistake. Look at the vendor's home page and the home pages it has created for others. Then ask questions:

ABOUT CAPABILITIES

- What portion of the work did you do? What was outsourced to subcontractors?
- What services can you provide?
- Who are your graphic designers, and what are their backgrounds?
- What can you do to publicize my Web site?

ABOUT TECHNICAL MATTERS

- What computer resources do you provide?
- Are your systems backed up?
- Do you have an alternative site in case of hardware failure?
- If you do the programming, how much of the code will be proprietary?
- What provisions do you make for security?

ABOUT PERFORMANCE

- What bandwidth do you provide? How much is dedicated to my home page?
- How much experience do you have managing high-traffic Web sites?
- How high is the volume at your most active site?

ABOUT THE BUSINESS RELATIONSHIP

- What statistical reports do you provide?
- What provisions do you make for handling complaints and problems?

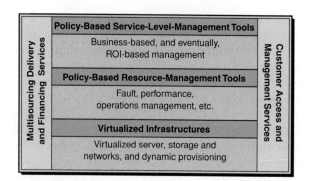

FIGURE 14.9 The five elements of a successful utility-computing value proposition.

Utility Computing

Tapping into computer resources with a simplicity equal to plugging a lamp into an outlet has been a goal of pervasive computing efforts from the start. Known as **utility computing,** the idea is to provide unlimited computing power and storage capacity that can be used and reallocated for any application—and billed on a pay-per-use basis.

Utility computing consists of a virtualized pool of "self-managing" IT resources that can be dynamically provisioned via policy-based tools that ensure these resources are easily and continually reallocated in a way that addresses the organization's changing business and service needs. These resources can be located anywhere and managed by anyone (an organization's IT staff or a third-party service provider), and the usage of these resources can be tracked and billed down to the level of an individual user or group.

As shown in Figure 14.9, the utility-computing value proposition consists of three layers of tools and two types of value-added services. Each tool must be seamlessly integrated to create a comprehensive solution, but will usually be implemented separately and tactically—often with little advance planning for the ultimate solution. These tools are:

- *Virtualization tools* that allow server, storage, and network resources to be deployed and managed as giant pools, and to be seamlessly and dynamically reprovisioned as needs change.
- *Policy-based resource-management tools* that automate and standardize all types of IT management best practices, from initial configuration to ongoing fault management and asset tracking.
- *Policy-based service-level-management tools* that coordinate, monitor, and report on the ways in which multiple infrastructure components come together to deliver a business service.

Utility computing still faces daunting obstacles. These include the immaturity of the tools, the difficult economy, and the fact that each of the vendors prefers to tout its own unique variation on the vision with different, often confusing, names and terminology—not to mention cloudy value propositions. However, utility computing will, as discussed in the opening case, inevitably prompt considerable consolidation, as industry giants seek to acquire myriad technologies that they cannot develop themselves. It will also accelerate acceptance of the long-simmering service-provider value proposition, as all providers offer choices of utility-computing implementation models and migration paths among those models.

External Acquisition of Software

The choice between developing proprietary software in-house and purchasing existing software is called the *make-or-buy decision*. Developing (building) proprietary application software gives the organization exactly what it needs and wants, as well as a high level of control in the development process. In addition, the organization has more flexibility in modifying the software during the development process to meet new requirements. On the other hand, developing proprietary software requires a large amount of resources (time, money, personnel) that the in-house staff may have trouble providing. The large quantity of resources needed for this software increases the risk of the decision to "make" the software in-house.

The initial cost of off-the-shelf software is often lower because a software development firm can spread the cost over a number of customers. There is lower risk that the software will fail to meet the firm's business needs, because the software can be examined prior to purchase. The software should be of high quality, because many customers have used and helped debug it. However, buying off-the-shelf software may mean that an organization has to pay for features and functions that are not needed. Also, the software may lack necessary features, causing the buyer to have to make expensive modifications to customize the package. Finally, the buyer's particular IT infrastructure may differ from what the software was designed for, and may require some additional modification to run properly.

SELECTING VENDORS AND COMMERCIAL SOFTWARE PACKAGES. Externally acquired systems should be evaluated to ensure that they provide the organization with the following advantages. If they do not provide most of these advantages, then the organizations may be better off developing proprietary systems. The most prominent considerations are:

- *On-time.* Completion and implementation of the system on or before the scheduled target date.
- *On-budget.* The system cost is equal to or less than the budget.
- *Full functionality.* The system has all the features in the original specifications.

These outcomes are very desirable, especially because fewer than half of all systems projects achieve all three. However, it is possible to succeed on each of these criteria but still have a system that does not increase the effectiveness of the organization. Other important considerations for selecting vendors and commercial software packages are listed in Online File W14.9 at the book's Web site.

Criteria that may be used to select an application package to purchase include those listed in Table 14.2 (page 657). Several independent organizations and magazines conduct software package comparisons from time to time. For smaller packages, you can use "trialware" from the Internet before purchase is made. Most vendors will give you the software for a limited testing time. Also, they will come and demonstrate the software. (Be sure to let them use your data in the demo.)

ENTERPRISE SOFTWARE. A recent trend in the software business is **enterprise software,** integrated software that supports enterprise computing. These systems include accounting and finance, human resources, sales and procurement,

> ## Table 14.2 Criteria for Selecting an Application Package
>
> - Cost and financial terms
> - Upgrade policy and cost
> - Vendor's reputation and availability for help
> - Vendor's success stories (visit their Web site, contact clients)
> - System flexibility
> - Ease of Internet interface
> - Availability and quality of documentation
> - Necessary hardware and networking resources
> - Required training (check if provided by vendor)
> - Security
> - Learning (speed of) for developers and users
> - Graphical presentation
> - Data handling
> - Environment and hardware

inventory management, production planning and control, and so on. One of the major attractions of enterprise packages is that they incorporate many of the best practices in the various functional areas. Organizations thus have the opportunity to upgrade their processes at the same time they install the new software. Major suppliers in this category include SAP/AG, Oracle, Baan, and PeopleSoft. Since these companies sell their products to a large number of customers, they can hire more specialized personnel and spend more on development than an individual organization would spend to develop its own systems.

The implementation and integration of enterprise software represents the single largest information system project ever undertaken by an organization. It can cost tens of millions of dollars and require an army of managers, users, analysts, technical specialists, programmers, and consultants. Most enterprise software vendors provide their methodology and consulting partners to help their customers implement such a massive software solution. For discussion on enterprise resource planning (ERP) systems development, see Ahituv et al. (2002).

E-COMMERCE SOFTWARE. E-commerce software is a powerful yet affordable e-commerce solution that is geared toward Web entrepreneurs of varying skill levels and can greatly reduce the development time needed to launch an effective site. It can provide a comprehensive fix for the rapid construction and deployment of database-driven applications. Its back-end integration capabilities, combined with wizards and templates, make it both powerful and easy to integrate. E-commerce software also facilitates sales by sending orders to the warehouse, adjusting inventory tracking, and even e-mailing stock replenishment alerts to the merchant. Real-time credit card verification and processing is also a great advantage and can also be optimized for use with CyberCash from *Verisign.com*. The software will also provide comprehensive detailed statistics on sales, users, product categories, and browser types.

With all these options and capabilities provided with just one software package, many companies opt to go with e-commerce software instead of developing their own system. Most e-commerce software is fully customizable for your particular company and is easily integrated into your business processes. This

IT at Work 14.4
BILL BROADBENT, THE T-SHIRT KING

Bill Broadbent has been involved in the T-shirt business for over twenty years. Less than six months after he opened his online store, T-Shirt King (*www.t-shirtking.com*) had already achieved startling results. In this interview Bill explains why he decided to take his bricks-and-mortar store online and how he went about it.

INTERVIEWER: What made you decide to take your business online?

BROADBENT: In discussing the advantages of cybersales we realized that we could show thousands of designs to anyone with Internet access. Also the Internet gave us the world as a market and the ability to bring any design we wanted into a huge online catalogue. Finally, the cost of overhead in a bricks-and-mortar store is sinful. The advantages of selling online are truly unfair. Bricks-and-mortar retailers are not prepared for the inevitable growth of online sales.

INTERVIEWER: What server and shopping-cart software are you using and why?

BROADBENT: We began T-Shirt King as a Yahoo Store while we were still in the experimental mind. Launching the store cost less than $1,000, maintenance less than $500. Now that we are serious, our new site will be about $50,000 and our marketing and maintenance (hard to separate these on the Internet) will be in the six figures per month. We have still to choose an e-commerce software solution for this second phase.

INTERVIEWER: What are your top tips for anyone considering opening his or her own Web store?

BROADBENT: Start with Icat or Yahoo to test the waters. Plan on growing, and go for it. This is the new frontier of retailing, and it is going to grow a lot over the next decade. New fortunes are being made right now. Cost of entry is minimal, and the opportunity to support growth through revenue created is a dream.

Source: Condensed from Paul (1999) and *tshirtking.com* (2003).

For Further Exploration: What are the advantages and disadvantages of buying instant e-commerce solutions from software vendors?

---

trend of using commercially available software will rapidly increase as more merchants go online. As illustrated in *IT at Work 14.4*, an organization can set up its online store on the Web instantly and at minimal cost.

Management Considerations

Because organizations and their systems requirements vary along many dimensions, it is not possible to neatly match all types of systems projects with the acquisition approaches identified in this chapter. Therefore, in many cases it might be advisable to use a combination of approaches.

In this section we provide general considerations related to the different approaches. These considerations should be reviewed in the context of the desirable outcomes discussed earlier. If coupled with good judgment, these considerations may help managers make better decisions regarding new systems' acquisition.

TRADITIONAL SDLC METHODOLOGY. The SDLC approach often works well for large projects with well-defined requirements, where there is *not* a lot of pressure to finish the project quickly. Use of this approach requires appropriate and effective management, possibly including an end user as the leader if the project is not highly technical.

PROTOTYPING. Prototyping is especially useful in situations where the requirements (and therefore the costs) are poorly defined or when speed is needed. However, it requires effective management to make sure that the iterations of prototyping do not continue indefinitely. It is important to have tools such as 4GLs and screen generators when using this approach. If the project is large, it is probably better to establish the information requirements through prototyping and then use a more formal SDLC to complete the system.

RAPID APPLICATION DEVELOPMENT (RAD). This is an obvious candidate when new systems are needed very quickly. RAD tools can work well for developing client/server systems or front-ends for mainframe systems. RAD may be less appropriate than conventional programming languages for larger projects, or for developing systems with a lot of calculations or real-time processing.

JOINT APPLICATION DESIGN (JAD). JAD is easy for senior management to understand. The methodology also provides the needed structure to the process of collecting user requirements. However, it is difficult and expensive to get all people to the same place at the same time. Another disadvantage of JAD is its potential to have dysfunctional groups.

OBJECT-ORIENTED DEVELOPMENT. OO development is becoming increasingly popular, but usage is limited by a shortage of personnel with OO skills. Java is an OO language that is especially suitable for developing network applications. However, OO languages in general, and Java in particular, tend to run slowly. Reusability of code is a potential advantage of OO development, but reuse will not occur without appropriate cataloging, search engines, and experienced and motivated employees.

END-USER DEVELOPMENT. Although most appropriate for small projects, end-user development is also a possibility for larger projects whose priorities are not high enough to lead to a timely response from the central IS unit. Managers should beware of end-user development in situations where problems with the system can lead to significant risks for the organization, such as system failures, inaccurate results, disclosure of confidential data, inefficiency, incompatibility with other systems, and inability to maintain the system if the developer leaves.

PURCHASING OR OUTSOURCING. For large and complex systems with a significant risk of failure, organizations should *always* consider using an outside vendor (e.g., see Lee et al., 2003). The exception to this rule is that in-house development may be necessary if the system is highly strategic or incorporates critical proprietary information. If scalability is important to the organization, it may be advisable to buy systems rather than make them, even for smaller systems. However, managers need to be aware of relatively high additional implementation costs when purchasing enterprise software packages.

EXTREME PROGRAMMING. The fundamental idea of extreme programming is to start simply. Build something real that works in its limited way. Then fit it into a design structure that is built as a convenience for further code building rather than as an ultimate and exhaustive structure.

UTILITY COMPUTING. Although not a development methodology, utility computing promises a way to cut technology management expenses while consolidating resources. However, it is believed that technology has a lot of catching up to do before utility computing will become a reality for a company with many computing needs.

14.5 BUILDING E-BUSINESS APPLICATIONS

The diversity of e-business models and applications, which vary in size from a small store to a global exchange, requires a variety of development methodologies and approaches. Small storefronts can be developed with HTML, Java, or other programming languages. They can also be quickly implemented with commercial packages or leased from application service providers (ASPs) for a small monthly fee. Some packages are available for a free trial period ranging from 30 to 90 days. Larger applications can be outsourced or developed in-house. Building medium to large applications requires extensive integration with existing information systems such as corporate databases, intranets, enterprise resource planning (ERP), and other application programs.

The development process of e-business applications consists of five major steps, which are discussed in detail in Online File W14.10 at the Web site of this chapter. The five steps of the development process can be fairly complex, and therefore they must be managed properly. A project team is usually created to manage the progress of the development and the vendors. Collaboration with business partners is critical. Some e-business failures are the results of delays and lack of cooperation by business partners. For instance, you can install a superb e-procurement system, but if your vendors will not use it, the system will collapse.

Development Strategies for E-Business Applications

There are several options for developing e-business (e-biz) applications: buy, lease, or develop in-house.

BUY THE E-BIZ APPLICATIONS. Standard features required by e-business applications can be found in commercial packages. Buying an existing package can be cost-effective and timesaving in comparison to in-house application development. The *buy* option should be carefully considered and planned for, to ensure that all critical features for current and future needs are included in the selected package. Otherwise such packages may quickly become obsolete.

In addition, business needs can rarely be fully satisfied by buying a single package. It is sometimes necessary to acquire multiple packages to fulfill different needs. Integration may then be required amongst these packages as well as with existing software. Major criteria for consideration in buying e-business applications are listed in Online File 14.11. The buy option may not be attractive in cases of high obsolescence rate or high software cost. In such a case, one should consider leasing.

LEASE THE E-BIZ APPLICATIONS. As compared to the buy option and to an in-house development, the *lease* option can result in substantial savings of both cost and time. Though the packages for lease may not always exactly fit with the application requirements (the same is true with the buy option), many common features that are needed by most organizations are often included.

Leasing is advantageous over buying in those cases where extensive maintenance is required, or where the cost of buying is very high. Leasing can be especially attractive to SMEs (small to medium enterprises) that cannot afford major investments in e-biz. Large companies may also prefer to lease packages in order to test potential e-commerce solutions before committing to heavy IT investments. Also, since there is a shortage of IT personnel with appropriate skills for developing novel e-commerce applications, several companies lease instead of develop. Even those companies that have in-house expertise may decide they cannot afford to wait for strategic applications to be developed in-house. Hence they may buy or lease applications from external resources in order to establish a quicker presence in the market.

Types of Leasing Vendors. Leasing can be done in two major ways. One is to lease the application from an outsourcer and install it on the company's premises. The vendor can help with the installation, and frequently will offer to contract for the operation and maintenance of the system. Many conventional applications are leased this way. Vendors that lease e-biz applications are sometimes referred to as *commerce system providers* (CSPs). However, in e-business a second leasing option is becoming popular: leasing from an application service provider, which provides both the software and hardware at its site.

DEVELOP E-BIZ APPLICATIONS IN-HOUSE: INSOURCING. The third option to developing an e-business application is to *build it in-house*. Although this approach is usually more time-consuming and may be more costly than buying or leasing, it often leads to better satisfaction of the specific organizational requirements. Companies that have the resources to develop their e-business application in-house may follow this approach in order to differentiate themselves from the competition, which may be using standard applications that can be bought or leased. The in-house development of e-biz applications, however, is a challenging task, as most applications are novel, have users from outside of the organization, and involve multiple organizations.

Development Options. Three major options exist: program from scratch, use components, or use enterprise application integration.

- ***Build from scratch.*** This is a rarely used option that should be considered only for specialized applications for which components are not available. It is expensive and slow, but it can provide the best fit.

- ***Build from components.*** Those companies with experienced IT staff can use standard components (e.g., a secure Web server), some software languages (e.g., C++, Visual Basic, or Perl), and third-party APIs (application program interfaces) and subroutines to create and maintain an electronic storefront solely on their own.

  Alternatively, companies can outsource the entire development process using components. From a software standpoint, this alternative offers the greatest flexibility and is the least expensive. However, it can also result in a number of false starts and wasted experimentation. For this reason, even those companies with experienced staff are probably better off customizing one of the packaged solutions. (For details about using components, see Section 14.3.)

- ***Enterprise application integration.*** The **enterprise application integration (EAI)** option is similar to the previous one, but instead of components, one uses an entire application. This is an especially attractive option when applications from several business partners need to be integrated.

OTHER DEVELOPMENT STRATEGIES. Besides the three major options for developing e-biz applications (buy, lease, and develop in-house), several others are in use and are appropriate under certain circumstances. See Online File W14.12 on the book's Web site for a detailed discussion of these options.

Application Service Providers

In developing e-business systems, outsourcing is a most valuable option since these systems need to be built quickly and special expertise is needed. EC software delivery from ASPs is another very popular option.

An **application service provider (ASP)** is an agent or vendor who assembles functionality needed by enterprises, and packages it with outsourced development, operation, maintenance, and other services. Although several variations of ASPs exist, in general, monthly fees are paid by the client company. ASP fees for services include the application software, hardware, service and support, maintenance, and upgrades. The fees can be fixed, or based on utilization.

The essential difference between an ASP and an outsourcer is that an ASP will manage application servers in a centrally controlled location, rather than on a customer's site. Applications are accessed via the Internet or WANs through a standard Web browser interface. In such an arrangement, applications can be scaled, upgrades and maintenance can be centralized, physical security over the applications and servers can be guaranteed, and the necessary critical mass of human resources can be efficiently utilized.

ASPs are especially active in enterprise computing and e-commerce. These areas are often too complex to build and too cumbersome to modify and maintain on one's own (e.g., see Ward, 2000). Therefore, the major providers of ERP software, such as SAP and Oracle, are offering ASP options. Microsoft, and Computer Associates, Ariba, and other major vendors of e-business also offer such services.

BENEFITS OF LEASING FROM ASPs. Leasing from ASPs is a particularly desirable option for SMEs, for which in-house development and operation of e-business applications can be time-consuming and expensive. Leasing from ASPs not only saves various expenses (such as labor costs) in the initial development stage, but also helps to reduce software maintenance and upgrading and user training costs in the long run. A company can always select another software package from the ASP to meet its changing needs and does not have to further invest in upgrading the existing one. In this way, overall business competitiveness can be strengthened through reducing the time-to-market and enhancing the ability to adapt to changing market conditions. This is particularly true of e-commerce applications for which timing and flexibility are crucial. A detailed list of the benefits and potential risks of leasing from ASPs is provided in Online File W14.13 at the book's Web site.

Leasing from ASPs is not without disadvantages. Many companies are particularly concerned with the adequacy of protection offered by the ASP against hackers, theft of confidential information, and virus attacks. Also, leased software may not provide a perfect fit for the desired application.

It is important to ensure that the speed of Internet connection is compatible with that of the application in order to avoid distortions to the performance of the application. For example, it is not advisable to run heavy-duty applications on a modem link below a T1 line or a high-speed DSL. Some criteria for selecting an ASP vendor are listed in Online File W14.14 at the book's Web site.

IT at Work 14.5
SNAP-ON'S APPROACH TO SETTING UP
AN E-BUSINESS SITE

Snap-On, a tool and equipment maker in Washington state, wanted to set up an e-commerce site, and do so quickly. The problem the company faced was whether to build the site in-house, or buy the services of an outside contractor to set up the site.

Brad Lewis, e-commerce manager for Snap-On, decided to hire application service provider (ASP) OnLink Technologies to implement a catalog for the company's e-commerce site. Lewis wanted his industrial customers to navigate easily through the 17,000 products listed in Snap-On's paper catalog, and he wanted to integrate the site with Snap-On's ERP system. "If we developed this application in-house, we would have spent six to nine months just designing and implementing it," he said. By using an ASP, Snap-On was able to get the entire catalog up and running in four months.

What was unusual is that Lewis integrated his staff with OnLink's to help transfer those catalog-building skills. Lewis himself spent several days a week during the four-month development period at OnLink's headquarters, where he had his own office. He concentrated on developing application features and integration with back-end systems. "By spending so much time at OnLink, I became a member of their engineering group, and other members of my staff became temporary members of their professional services catalog group," Lewis says.

The result was that Lewis created an in-house ASP consulting service for Snap-On, providing guidance to other departments and subsidiaries that want to put up catalogs

on their own Web sites. "One of the first questions we pondered before we outsourced was whether we could later bring that expertise in-house," Lewis says. "We didn't want to do it any other way." The desire to have expertise in-house was fostered by Snap-On's desire for control of their Web site. "When e-commerce solutions become a mission-critical application, companies can become uncomfortable outsourcing them. If the outsourcer's site goes down, the company's business goes down," says Leah Knight, an analyst for the Gartner Group. Snap-On found a way to both buy and build its e-commerce applications.

Snap-On.com is an example of what end users and analysts say is the newest trend in constructing e-commerce sites. With this approach, the site would already be in a host environment, and components are already there, so you can quickly add to the site. Most companies, feeling the "Internet-speed" pressure to get their sites up fast, need the experience and resources of outside vendors. At the same time, however, these end users are taking charge of those sites as soon as possible. Local control enables them to make improvements faster and save money on expensive hourly fees each time they need to make a small change to the site.

Sources: Compiled from Mullich (2000) and *snap-on.com* (2003.)

For Further Exploration: As Web sites evolve, e-businesses find that moving programming talent in-house is the way to go. Do you agree?

IT at Work 14.5 provides a successful story of a using an ASP as a contracted partner to develop an e-biz application. For a study about satisfaction with ASP services, see Susarla et al. (2003).

Java,
a Promising Tool

Internet and intranet Web pages are coded primarily in *HTML* (hypertext markup language), a simple language that is most useful for displaying static content to viewers. HTML has very limited capabilities for interacting with viewers or for providing information that is continually being updated. It is not suitable for collecting information, such as names and addresses, or for providing animation or changing information such as stock quotes. To do these types of things it is necessary to add programs (written in some form of programming language) to the HTML for a Web site.

Java (see Technology Guide 2) is relatively new, but it has already established itself as the most important programming language for putting extra features into Web pages. It has many similarities to C and C++, but omits some of the more complex and error-prone features of the programming languages. Java was specifically designed to work over networks: Java programs can be sent from a Web server over the Internet and then run on the computer that is viewing the Web page. It has numerous security features to prevent these downloaded programs from damaging files or creating other problems on the receiving computer.

Java is an object-oriented language, so the concepts of object-oriented development are relevant to its use. However, the Java Web-page programs, called **applets,** need to be relatively small to avoid delays in transmitting them over the Internet. (Java programs run more slowly than programs in other languages, which is another reason to keep them small.) Therefore it is not necessary that Java developers use the very formal development methodologies appropriate for large system projects. Prototyping is probably the most suitable approach for developing Java applets, because it provides for a high level of interaction between the developers and users in regard to the critical issues of the appearance and ease-of-use of the Web page.

Managerial Issues in E-Business Applications

Several managerial issues apply specifically to building e-business applications:

- *It is the business issues that count.* When one thinks of the Web, one immediately thinks of the technology. Some of the most successful sites on the Web rely on basic technologies—freeware Web servers, simple Web-page design, and few bells and whistles. What makes them successful is not the technology but their understanding of how to meet the needs of their online customers.

- *Build in-house or outsource.* Many large-scale enterprises are capable of running their own publicly accessible Web sites for advertising purposes. However, Web sites for online selling may involve complex integration, security, and performance issues. For those companies venturing into such Web-based selling, a key issue is whether the site should be built in-house, thus providing more direct control, or outsourced to a more experienced provider. Outsourcing services, which allow companies to start small and evolve to full-featured functions, are available through many ISPs, telecommunications companies, Internet malls, and software vendors who offer merchant server and e-biz applications.

- *Consider an ASP.* The use of ASPs is a must for SMEs and should be considered by any company. However, due to the newness of the concept, care must be used in selecting a vendor (see Chapter 13).

14.6   SOME IMPORTANT SYSTEMS DEVELOPMENT ISSUES

Building information systems, either by the ISD or by end users, involves many issues not discussed in the preceding sections. Some additional issues that may be of interest to managers and end users are discussed here.

CASE Tools

For a long time, computer programmers resembled the cobbler in the old story: He was so busy mending his customers' shoes that he didn't have time to repair the holes in his own children's shoes. Similarly, programmers were so busy developing systems to increase the productivity of other functions, such as accounting and marketing, that they didn't have time to develop tools to enhance their own productivity. However, this situation has changed with the emergence of **computer-aided software engineering (CASE)** tools. These are marketed as individual items or in a set (toolkit) that automates various aspects of the development process. For example, a systems analyst could use a CASE tool to create data-flow diagrams on a computer, rather than drawing them manually (see Technology Guide 2).

MANAGERIAL ISSUES REGARDING CASE. Individual system personnel or IS groups may use a variety of specific CASE tools to automate certain SDLC activities on a piecemeal basis. Or the IS group may acquire an integrated (I-CASE) package, whose components are tightly integrated and which often embodies a specific systems development methodology. (See Technology Guide 2.) These two approaches are quite different in terms of their implications for the organization.

Using tools independently can provide some significant productivity benefits. Because the tools are acquired on an individual basis, the organization has many options and can select the ones that offer the best performance for the cost and are best suited to the organization's needs. The tools can be used independently as needed, so developers have the option of learning, at their own pace, the tools that are most helpful to them.

On the other hand, the components in integrated packages are specifically designed to work together, and therefore they offer the potential for higher productivity gains. However, the learning pace for these packages is much slower than for individual tools. This means that after adoption, productivity may decline in the short term, which may be unacceptable for an organization with a large backlog of high-priority IS projects. In addition to productivity issues, some components of an I-CASE package may not be as good as corresponding tools that can be purchased separately.

The relatively high turnover rate among systems personnel also creates problems for use of I-CASE systems. New employees will need time to learn the integrated package. Existing employees may resist using the package, because they feel it will reduce their opportunities to move to other organizations that use either traditional development methods or some other I-CASE package that is incompatible with the one at the present organization.

In addition to the costs of training and productivity losses, organizations need to purchase the actual I-CASE systems. In the past, this often required purchasing workstations in addition to software. Now, with the availability of much more powerful PCs and servers in client/server systems, many organizations may not find it necessary to buy any additional hardware (except possibly a plotter for printing large diagrams). Even without additional hardware costs, buying an I-CASE system may still cost more than buying a few of the most helpful individual tools.

Software Quality Improvement and ISO-9000

The success of quality management in manufacturing suggests that quality management could also be helpful in dealing with the problems of IS development. To implement this concept for systems development, the Software Engineering Institute at Carnegie Mellon University developed the *Capability Maturity Model (CMM)*. The original purpose of this model was to provide guidelines for the U.S. Department of Defense in selecting contractors for software development. The CMM identifies five levels of maturity in the software development process, as summarized in Table 14.3.

TABLE 14.3 Levels of the Capability Maturity Model

Level	Characteristics
1. Initial	Processes are ad hoc, undefined, possibly chaotic. Success depends on individual efforts and heroics.
2. Repeatable	Basic project management tracks cost, schedule, and functionality. On similar applications, organization is able to repeat earlier successes.
3. Defined	Project management and software engineering activities are documented, standardized, and integrated into development through an organization-specific process (i.e., an SDLC).
4. Managed	Both software process activities and quality are measured in detail and are quantitatively understood and controlled.
5. Optimizing	Processes are improved continuously based on feedback from quantitative measures, and from pilot projects with new ideas and technologies.

Source: Compiled from J. Herbsleb et al., "Software Quality and the Capability Maturity Model," *Communications of the ACM,* June 1997, p. 32. ©1997 Association for Computing Machinery, Inc. Reprinted by permission.

As an organization moves to higher maturity levels of the CMM, both the productivity and the quality of its software development efforts will improve. Results of a case study, summarized in Table 14.4, verified substantial gains in both areas through software process improvement (SPI) programs based on the capability maturity model. Organizations need to understand, however, that software process improvement requires significant spending and organizational effort.

ISO 9000 STANDARDS. Another approach to software quality is to implement the *ISO 9000* software development standards. The International Organization for Standardization (ISO) first published its quality standards in 1987, revised them in 1994, and then republished an updated version in 2000. The new standards are referred to as the "ISO 9001:2000 Standards." These international standards are very extensive: They identify a large number of actions that must be performed to obtain certification. In addition, they define software developer responsibilities, as well as the responsibilities of the purchaser or client, in developing quality software. The purchaser needs to clearly identify the requirements and have an established process for requesting changes in these requirements. However, the specifications do offer a substantial amount of leeway in many areas. (For an example of ISO 9000 Standards, see Online File W14.15 at the book's Web site.)

TABLE 14.4 Improvements from Capability Maturity Model Implementations

Category	Range	Median	# of Cases
Productivity gain	9–67%	35%	4
Faster time to market	15–23%	NA	2
Reduction in defects	10–94%	39%	5

Source: Compiled from J. Herbsleb et al., "Software Quality and the Capability Maturity Model," *Communications of the ACM,* June 1997, pp. 30–40. ©1997 Association for Computing Machinery, Inc. Reprinted by permission.

An ISO 9001:2000 Quality Management System is made up of many processes that are glued together by means of many input-output relationships. This turns a simple list of processes into an integrated system. Under ISO standards, the supplier needs to have documented processes for developing software. The supplier's senior management is responsible for developing the *quality policy* document, a short statement that requires employees to use generally accepted quality practices in all areas of the organization. This quality policy is implemented through a *quality system,* the development and quality-control processes that implement the quality policy. The quality system requires preparation of *quality plans* for types of products and processes. An internal auditing process is required to ensure compliance with the plans. ISO 9000 requires appropriate funding for quality activities, and appointment of personnel and assignment of responsibilities necessary to implement the program.

Reverse Engineering for Legacy Systems

Legacy systems are older, large software systems that are still in use and are being maintained. They were developed using traditional methods, such as structured analysis and design, or even individual programming techniques and styles. Over time, maintenance may have changed the original program structure and specifications. Often, the specifications are not maintained, and the current design and program understanding cannot be determined. Maintenance of these systems becomes so costly that they become candidates for reverse engineering.

Reverse engineering aims at discovering design and specifications of existing software programs. The technology reads the program code for an existing database, application program, and user interface, and automatically generates an equivalent system model. The resulting model can then be edited and improved by systems analysts and users to provide a blueprint for a new and improved system. The goal of reverse engineering is to achieve a sufficient understanding of the whats, hows and whys of the legacy system as a whole so that its code can be reengineered to meet new user requirements. For additional information see Martin (2003).

Project Planning

Project planning can mitigate the risk of failure and provide a structure for managing development risk. Chapter 9 provided a four-stage model for information systems planning for IT infrastructure projects. The final stage of this process, **project planning,** is also used in development of individual applications. Project planning provides an overall framework in which the systems development life cycle can be planned, scheduled, and controlled. Milestones are one of the more effective project management tools used by managers in the project planning process.

MILESTONES.   Milestone planning techniques allow projects to evolve as they are developed. Rather than try to predict all project requirements and problems in advance, management allows the project to progress at its own pace. **Milestones,** or checkpoints, are established to allow periodic review of progress so that management can determine whether a project merits further commitment of resources, requires adjustments, or should be discontinued.

Milestones can be based on time, budget, or deliverables. For example, a project's progress might be evaluated weekly, monthly, or quarterly. It might be evaluated after a certain amount of resources are used, such as $50,000.

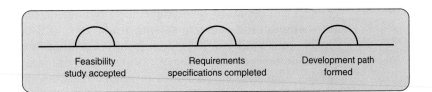

FIGURE 14.10
Milestones.

However, milestones are most effective when they identify that specific events have occurred, such as the completion of a feasibility study. Figure 14.10 illustrates the simplicity of a milestone chart.

PROJECT PROPERTIES AND PRIORITIES. Setting budget and time frames *prior* to defining the system design constraints is perhaps the greatest mistake made in project planning. For example, management may decide to install a new order entry system in nine months, for which it is willing to spend $1 million. This leaves one important issue undefined: What will the new system do? By setting a budgetary constraint, management has, de facto, limited the functionality of the new system.

The proper sequence for managing a project is first to get a good functional definition of what the system is designed to do, and then to have people with experience and expertise in information systems and in project management develop a budget and schedule. If management cannot accept the schedule or budget, then the capabilities of the new system can be scaled down to meet the schedule and/or budget constraints.

In developing a budget, schedule, and specifications for a system, managers need to consider and understand several properties of projects and their management. The following five properties most significantly influence the overall nature of an IT project.

1. *Predefined structure.* The more predefined the structure of a project is, the more easily it can be planned and controlled.
2. *Stability of technology.* The greater the experience with a given technology to be used for a new system, the more predictable the development process.
3. *Size.* The larger the project, the more difficult it is to estimate the resources (time and costs) required to complete it.
4. *User proficiency.* The more knowledgeable and experienced users and managers are in their functional areas and in developing systems, the more proficient they will be relative to information technology and the easier it will be to develop systems for them.
5. *Developer proficiency.* The more knowledge and experience the systems analyst assigned to a project has, the easier the project will go, and vice versa.

Projects can possess variations of each of the preceding properties. For example, a project can have predefined structure but use unstable technology, or it can be a massive undertaking and have low user and developer proficiencies (e.g., most initial online airline reservations systems could be described this way).

WEB-BASED PROJECT MANAGEMENT. Web-based project management provides a central Web site, or project portal, where everyone involved in a project can get up-to-date project information, share documents, and participate in planning and problem-solving using such collaboration features as shared notebooks, threaded discussion groups, and chat forums. By making it easy for team members and managers to exchange information and ideas, Web-based project management promises to reduce mistakes caused by poor communication. It also can minimize or eliminate delays due to the time it takes to move documents and people around for approvals and meetings. Examples of Web-based project management packages include: TeamCenter (from Invoie Software), TeamPlay (from Primavera Systems), and WebProject (from WebProject).

MANAGERIAL ISSUES

1. *Importance.* Some general and functional managers believe that system development is a technical topic that should be of interest only to technical people. This is certainly not the case. Appropriate construction of systems is necessary for their success. Functional managers must participate in the development process and should understand all the phases. They must also participate in the make-or-buy decisions and software selection decisions. Inappropriate development methodologies can result in the system's failure.

2. *Building interorganizational and international information systems.* Building systems that connect two or more organizations, or one organization that operates in different countries, can be very complicated. (See Tractinsky and Jarvenpaa, 1995.) As seen in Chapter 9, you need to carefully plan for such systems, considering different requirements and cultures. In addition to planning, the analysis, design, and other phases of system development must take into account the information needs of the various parties. (See Minicase 2.) One of the major problems with international systems is that what is ethical or legal in one country may be unethical or illegal in another.

3. *Ethical and legal issues.* Developing systems across organizations and countries could result in problems in any phase of system development. For example, in developing the Nagano Olympics system in 1998, IBM found at the last minute that pro-North-Korea groups in Japan took offense at a reference to the Korean War written on the Web site. Although the material was taken from the *World Book Encyclopedia,* it offended some people. IBM had to delete the reference and provide an apology. IBM commented, "Next time we're going to do a ton of research first versus just do it and find out the hard way." A special difficulty exists with Internet-related projects, where legislation is still evolving.

4. *User involvement.* The direct and indirect users of a system are likely to be the most knowledgeable individuals concerning requirements and which alternatives will be the most effective. Users are also the most affected by a new information system. IS analysts and designers, on the other hand, are likely to be the most knowledgeable individuals concerning technical and data-management issues as well as the most experienced in arriving at viable systems solutions. The right mixture of user involvement and information systems expertise is crucial.

5. *Traditional approaches vs. prototyping.* The traditional development approach stresses detailed, lockstep development with established decision points. Prototyping stresses flexible development based on actual use of partially functional systems. Experience has shown that the traditional approach can be better for low-risk, environmentally stable, and technology-simple situations; prototyping is often better under the opposite conditions.

6. *Tool use by developers.* Development tools and techniques can ensure that developers consider all necessary factors and standardize development, documentation, and testing. Forcing their use, on the other hand, may unnecessarily constrain innovation, development efficiency, and personnel productivity.

7. *Quality assurance vs. schedules.* Quality counts in the short term and the long term, but it can lengthen development and increase developmental costs. Trying to meet tight development schedules can induce poor quality with even worse schedule, cost, and morale problems.

8. *Behavior problems.* People use information systems and often become quite used to how existing systems work. They may react to new systems in unexpected ways, making even the best technically designed systems useless. Changes brought about by information systems need to be managed effectively. Of special interest is the issue of motivating programmers to increase their productivity by learning new tools and reusing preprogrammed modules.

9. *Perpetual development.* Information systems are designed to meet organizational needs. When they don't accurately meet these needs, or these needs change, information systems need to be redeveloped. Developing a system can be a major expense, but perpetually developing a system to maintain its usefulness is usually much more expensive.

10. *Risk level.* Building information systems involves risk. Systems may not be completed, completed too late, or require more resources than planned. The risk is large in enterprise systems. For how to manage such risk, see Scott and Vessey (2002).

ON THE WEB SITE... Additional resources, including quizzes; online files of additional text, tables, figures, and cases; and frequently updated Web links to current articles and information can be found on the book's Web site (*wiley.com/college/turban*).

KEY TERMS

Applets (Java) *665*

Application service provider (ASP) *663*

Component-based development *648*

Computer-aided software engineering (CASE) *666*

Direct cutover *638*

Enterprise application integration (EAI) *662*

Enterprise software *657*

Extreme programming (XP) *646*

Feasibility study *636*

Java *664*

Joint application design (JAD) *641*

Light methodology *640*

Logical design *636*

Milestones *668*

Object-oriented development *644*

Outsourcing *654*

Parallel conversion *638*

Phased conversion *639*

Pilot conversion *638*

Post-audit *639*

Project planning *668*

Prototyping *640*

Rapid application development (RAD) *642*

Reverse engineering *668*

Systems analysis *636*

Systems development *634*

Systems development life cycle (SDLC) *634*

Utility computing *656*

Waterfall method *635*

Web services *650*

CHAPTER HIGHLIGHTS (Numbers Refer to Learning Objectives)

1 A systems development life cycle (SDLC) identifies the major steps, or stages, in the development or acquisition of an information system. Organizations may use a proprietary SDLC methodology to help manage systems projects. Traditional SDLCs try to complete much of their analysis and design activities before starting development and are more appropriate where requirements are easier to identify.

2 Various methods can be used to develop complex or quickly needed systems. The prototyping approach is an iterative process that creates simple versions of a system to help users identify their requirements. Rapid application development (RAD) packages can speed development. Joint application design (JAD) is a structured process in which users, managers, and analysts work together to specify or review systems requirements. Object-oriented development makes it easier to develop very complex systems rapidly and with relatively few errors.

2 Extreme programming (XP) is a pragmatic approach to program development that emphasizes business results first and takes an incremental approach to building the product.

3 Many e-business applications are assembled from a set of components, rather than being constructed from scratch. Components have evolved from the objects of object-oriented methodology. However, they are much larger, providing a kind of plug-and-play building blocks that help in developing large complex systems, such as ERP or e-commerce.

3 Web services are URL-addressable software resources that perform functions and provide answers to users. A Web service is made by taking a set of software functionality and wrapping it up so that the services it performs are visible and accessible to other software applications.

4 End-user developed systems, on a whole, can be completed more rapidly than those developed through the conventional systems life cycle.

4 Outsourcing custom development or purchasing generic systems are alternatives to in-house development. Utility computing vendors are looking toward a future in which as-needed computing capacity is as easy to acquire as electricity.

5 Web-based applications are easy to develop and implement. However, organizations need to establish consistent policies and practices to make sure that Web-page development activities support organizational goals.

5 There are several options for developing e-business applications. The major applications are buy, lease, and develop in-house. Application service providers manage e-business application services for customers from a central location.

6 CASE tools can substantially increase programmer productivity. However, the more integrated packages are difficult to learn, which initially reduces productivity and can lead to resistance to implementation within IS groups.

6 Software quality can be improved by implementing the capability maturity model (CMM) or ISO 9001:2000 standards.

6 Reverse engineering can help discover design specifications of legacy systems. Milestone planning allows projects to evolve as they are developed.

QUESTIONS FOR REVIEW

1. Describe the major stages of the SDLC.

2. Explain why it is important to understand the concept of SDLC.

3. List four different approaches to converting from one system to another. Which is most risky? Least risky?

4. Describe the tools that are commonly included in rapid application development (RAD) packages. What capabilities can they provide?

5. Why do many companies use the prototyping approach to develop their e-business applications? What are the limitations of the prototyping approach?

6. Describe object-oriented development and its increasing importance.

7. Describe the architecture of component-based development of e-commerce applications.

8. Define Web services.

9. List the major areas of Web services applications.
10. List five major advantages and three major disadvantages of Web services.
11. List the advantages and disadvantages of purchasing generic software versus using in-house staff or outsourcers to develop customized applications.
12. Identify the major reasons why utility computing tools will become the next big thing.
13. List the e-business application options.
14. Describe an application service provider (ASP).
15. Describe Java and its role in Internet development.
16. Identify and explain the five levels of the capability maturity model (CMM).
17. List the issues in controlling the quality of systems development. What is the role of IS-9000?

QUESTIONS FOR DISCUSSION

1. Why is it advisable in some systems development projects to use prototyping to find information needs? Why can't the analyst just ask the users what they want and use the SDLC?
2. What types of incentives could an IS group provide to its programmers to encourage reuse of objects and other software they develop?
3. What type of development approaches would be most appropriate for developing small systems? For developing very large systems? Why? What other factors need to be considered?
4. Is extreme programming (XP) really "extreme"?
5. Discuss the use of Web services for systems development. What kind of systems are especially amenable to Web services?
6. End-user systems developers usually work for managers whose IT knowledge is limited. Discuss the types of problems to which this situation could lead, and suggest possible ways of dealing with these problems.
7. Do you think technology has a lot of catching up to do before utility computing will become a reality for companies with many computing needs?
8. Although the CASE concept—automated tools to increase programmer productivity—seems valid, many IS organizations do not use integrated (I-CASE) packages. Discuss the barriers to the increasing use of I-CASE.
9. Some programmers feel that implementing the capability maturity model (CMM) will make the development process too rigid and bureaucratic, thus stifling their creativity. Discuss the pros and cons of this issue.
10. Building Web-based systems such as intranets can be a fast and fairly easy process. Based on Chapters 4 and 5, can you explain why? What are the long-term implications of this for IS professionals? For end-user systems developers? For outsourcing firms?
11. Discuss the advantages of a lease option over a buy option in e-business applications development.
12. Compare component-based development to enterprise application integration.
13. A large company with a number of products wants to start selling on the Web. Should it use a merchant server or an electronic suite? Assuming the company elects to establish an electronic storefront, how would you determine whether it should outsource the site or run it itself?

EXERCISES

1. Contact a major information systems consulting firm and ask for literature on its systems development life cycle methodology (or search for it on the Internet). Compare and contrast the proprietary methodology to the eight-stage SDLC described in this chapter.
2. Identify and interview some end users who develop systems at their organizations. Ask them whether their organization has any standards for documenting and testing systems developed by end users. If it has such policies, are they enforced? If not, what do the end users do to ensure the accuracy and maintainability of the systems they develop?
3. Contact an administrator at your university or workplace and find out what purchased systems, especially larger ones, are in use. Do these systems meet the organization's needs, or are some important features missing that should be included in these packages?
4. Contact IS managers at some large organizations and find out whether their IS developers use any CASE tools. If the IS units use an integrated (I-CASE) tool, what things do they like and dislike about it? If the units do not use I-CASE tools, what are the reasons for not using them?

GROUP ASSIGNMENTS

1. Divide the class into two teams. Have both teams collect information on SAP's integrated enterprise management software, and on Oracle's comparable software packages. After the teams analyze the data, stage a debate with one team arguing that the SAP products are the more desirable and with the other team supporting Oracle (or other vendor).

2. Several vendors offer products for creating online stores. The Web sites of each vendor usually list those online stores using their software. Assign one or more vendors to each team member. Visit the online stores using each vendor's software. Prepare a report comparing the similarities and differences among the sites. Do the sites take advantage of the functionality provided by the various products?

INTERNET EXERCISES

1. Explore the General Electric site at *ge.com,* and then compare it to the Kodak site at *kodak.com.* Try to identify the organizational objectives for these two different types of sites. In the context of these objectives, discuss the advantages and disadvantages of having either: (1) a relatively simple site with limited graphics, or (2) a site that contains extensive graphics.

2. Go to the site at *geocities.com/~rfinney/case.htm.* Follow the links on the page to look at the features of several CASE tool packages. Prepare a report on the capabilities of one or two packages with multiple features.

3. Look at the Netron Corporation site (*netron.com*). Examine the tools they have for working with legacy systems (gap analysis) and for rapid application development.

Write a report. Prepare a report on Netron's approach to and tools for renovating and maintaining legacy systems.

4. StoreFront (*storefront.net*) is the leading vendor of e-biz software. At their site they provide demonstrations illustrating the types of storefronts that they can create for shoppers. They also provide demonstrations of how their software is used to create a store.

   a. Run either the StoreFront 5.0 or StoreFront 6.0 demonstration to see how this is done.
   b. What sorts of features are provided by StoreFront 5.0?
   c. Does StoreFront 5.0 support larger or smaller stores?
   d. What other products does StoreFront offer for creating online stores? What types of stores do these products support?

Minicase 1
Do or Die

A direct cutover from an existing system to a new one is risky. If the system is critical to the operations of the organization, the risks are magnified to an even higher level. Yet Quantum Corp. (*quantum.com*), a Milpitas, California, disk-drive manufacturer, did just that—and lived to tell about it. The vendors and consultants on the project claim that this was one of the largest-ever direct cutovers of a distributed business system.

Quantum realized that it had to take action. The limitations of its existing systems were making it difficult for the company to compete in the disk-drive market. Sales representatives needed to determine how much of a specific item—in inventory or in production—had not yet been committed to other customers. However, because databases did not share information, it was very difficult for them to get this information.

Quantum was especially interested in a piece of information known as available-to-promise (ATP). This indicates how many units of a given item could be delivered, by what date, to specific locations throughout the world. Calculating these values requires coordination and real-time processing of sales, inventory, and shipping data. If Quantum implemented its new system by phasing in the modules one at a time, the conversion would take much longer. Furthermore, the system would not be able to provide this key information until the end of the transition.

Quantum felt that the business risks of this kind of delay were greater than the technical risks of a direct cutover. The company was also concerned about possible resistance in some departments if the full implementation took a long time. The departments had enough autonomy to implement other systems if they lost confidence in the new system and, if they did, Quantum would lose the benefits of having an integrated system.

Although the actual cutover took eight days, the planning and preparation required over three years. The initial analysis was in October 1992, and Quantum sent out requests for proposals in April 1993. In March 1994, the company chose Oracle, Hewlett-Packard, and Price Waterhouse as its business partners on the project.

Quantum created a project team of 100 people, composed of key employees from each business unit and the IS department, and moved them into a separate building. The purchase of the disk-drive business of Digital Equipment Corp. in October 1994, which brought in another set of legacy applications and assorted hardware platforms, set the project back by about four months.

In February 1995, Quantum started a public relations campaign with a three-day conference for the users. The following month, "project evangelists" made presentations at all organizational locations.

In August 1995, the team conducted a systems validation test. It failed. The team worked intensely to solve the problems and then tested the system again for four weeks starting in December 1995. This time, it was successful.

In March 1996, Quantum provided a very extensive and absolutely mandatory user-training program. In April, it conducted final briefings, tested the system at all locations throughout the world, and set up a "mission control" center.

At 5 P.M. on April 26, Quantum shut down the old system. Hank Delavati, the CIO, said, "Business as we know it stopped . . . we could not place an order, we could not receive material, we could not ship products. We could not even post cash." Data records from the old system were loaded into the new system. At 4 P.M. on May 5, the new system started up successfully.

Mark Jackson, an executive vice president at Quantum, noted afterward that the relatively large project budget was not the company's primary concern. He said, "We could have figured out how to save 10 percent of the project's cost . . . but that would have raised the risk to an unacceptable level. To succeed, you have to spend the money and take care of the details."

Source: Condensed from Radosevich (1997) and *quantum.com* (2003).

Questions for Minicase 1

1. Estimate Quantum Corporation's chances of survival if this project failed. Provide some reasons to support your estimate.

2. What did Quantum do to minimize the risks of this direct cutover?

3. Evaluate the claim that, because of business and organizational issues, this direct cutover was less risky than a phased conversion.

4. Under what, if any, circumstances would you recommend this kind of direct cutover for critical operational systems?

5. Discuss the impact of this project on the internal power relationships between the IS department and the other departments in the organization.

6. It appears that Quantum spent a substantial amount of money on this project and was willing to increase spending when it seemed necessary for the success of the project. Discuss the risks of a "whatever it takes" approach.

Minicase 2
Implementing SAP R/3 at the University of Nebraska

On a Monday morning in August 1998, Jim Buckler, project manager of the University of Nebraska's Administrative System Project (ASP), was preparing for his weekly meeting with the project's steering committee, the Financial System Task Force (FSTF). The ASP is an effort charged with implementing SAP's R/3 client/server enterprise resource planning (ERP) product for the University of Nebraska's multicampus system.

As a result of mapping the University's future business processes to the SAP R/3 system, a number of gaps were identified between these processes and those offered by the SAP R/3 system. These critical gaps were tracked as one of

the project's critical success factors. Project management and the FSTF had to consider all factors that could potentially be impacted by the critical gaps. Such factors include the scope of the project, resources (human and budgetary), the timeline, and the previous configuration of the system, to name a few.

Four options were developed as possible solutions to resolve the 14 critical gaps. Table 14.5 summarizes the options presented to the FSTF by project management.

With a number of constraints and issues in mind, Buckler contemplated which one or combination of the four options was the best course of action. Should SAP and IBM be

TABLE 14.5 Possible Solutions to Critical Gaps

Option	Description	Gaps Affected	Risk	Costs
SAP provides on-site developer(s)	SAP provides on-site developers to edit the R/3 system's core program code and incorporate the changes in future R/3 system releases.	This option would resolve all gaps.	Moderate risk, as solutions will be incorporated in future R/3 system releases; however, developers must begin immediately.	Expected low cost to the University as SAP would be asked to absorb most of the costs.
IBM provides developers to create workarounds	IBM creates temporary workaround solutions that are "bolted on" to the system and are not part of the core SAP R/3 system code.	This option would resolve most gaps as attempts to develop workarounds for some gaps would not be feasible.	High risk, as solutions are not guaranteed to be in future R/3 system releases.	High cost to the University for the consulting resources needed to complete the workarounds.
Extend project timeline until July 1, 1999, to implement the next version of SAP R/3	Push project timeline back three months, resulting in some implementation activities being conducted simultaneously to meet the July 1 "Go live" date	SAP validates that all critical gaps are resolved in the next R/3 system release.	High risk, as new version must be delivered on time and resolution of critical gaps must be supported.	Moderate cost for some additional resources; potential for high cost if gaps are not resolved in new version.
University delays payroll until the next phase of implementing functionality	"Go live" with non-HR modules as outlined in the project scope and interface the R/3 system with the University's current human resource management system.	This option addresses only those gaps related to the human resources (HR) application module.	Low risk, as current payroll system is functional.	Moderate cost for some additional resources and to address change management issues; potential for high cost if payroll system has to be updated for Y2K compliance.

677

working concurrently on resolving the gaps (i.e., options 1 and 2)? This seemed to be the safest course of action, but it would be very costly. Should the project timeline be extended until July 1, 1999? What if SAP could not resolve all the gaps by that time? Would that deter the University from transitioning smoothly into the new millennium? Should the implementation of the HR/Payroll module be delayed? These options would have to be carefully considered and a recommendation made at Buckler's meeting with the FSTF in a few hours' time.

Sources: Condensed from Sieber et al. (1999) and *sap.com* (2003).

Questions for Minicase 2

1. Which of the four options or combination of options would you recommend to project management and the steering committee? What are the risks involved in your recommendation? How would you manage the risks?

2. Discuss the advantages and disadvantages of a purchased system that forces different organizational units to change their business processes and policies to conform to the new system. Identify situations where this standardization would be desirable, and other situations where it would be undesirable.

3. Can you think of circumstances where a company might want to install an enterprise management system, such as SAP R/3, even though it appears that this would be significantly more expensive than developing a comparable system in-house? Discuss.

4. Go to the site at *sap.com*. Follow the links on the page to look at the features of some cross-industry solutions. Prepare a report on the capabilities of the SAP solutions.

Virtual Company Assignment
Building Information Systems at The Wireless Café

Barbara and Jeremy have done some serious economic justification of the myriad technologies that could benefit their business, and they have chosen CRM as the top priority. They feel that they have grown to a point where they will need a full-time project manager to oversee the acquisition and implementation of the CRM, and they have asked you to describe how you would proceed on this project. At the start of your internship, you were hopeful it might lead to a full-time job offer after graduation, so you see this as your opportunity to impress Barbara and Jeremy with your business education and your systems expertise.

Instructions

1. Propose a systems development life cycle for implementing a CRM at The Wireless Café (TWC). Consider methodologies that are well-suited to rapid development of Web-based applications.

2. Once a CRM system is identified, should its implementation be outsourced? Assuming you do decide to outsource the entire implementation of the selected CRM, how would you manage the outsourcer to make sure the implementation is successful?

3. As TWC expands its utilization of IT, the concept of an application service provider becomes increasingly attractive. What are some risks and benefits to a small business of using an ASP for major applications?

REFERENCES

Ahituv, N. et al., "A System Development for ERP Systems," *Journal of Computer Information Systems*, Spring 2002.

Allen, P., and S. Frost, *Component-Based Development for Enterprise Systems*. England: Cambridge University Press, 1998.

ansett.com.au (accessed July 2003).

Arsanjani, A. (ed.), "Developing and Integrating Enterprise Components and Services," *Communications of the ACM*, October 2002.

bcbsri.com (accessed July 2003).

Bucken, M. W., "2000 Innovator Awards: Blue Cross & Blue Shield," *Application Development Trends Magazine*, April 2000, *adtmag.com/article.asp=2692* (accessed July 2003).

Cerami, E., *Web Services Essentials*. Cambridge, MA: O'Reilly and Associates, 2002.

Cule, P. et al., "Strategies for Heading Off IS Project Failures," *Information Systems Management*, Spring 2000.

Dahanayake, A. et al., "Methodology Evaluation Framework for Component-Based System Development," *Journal of Database Management,* March 2003.

Dietel, E. M. et al., *Web Services Technical Introduction.* Upper-Saddle River, NJ: Prentice-Hall, 2003.

Fremantle, P. et al., "Enterprise Services," *Communications of the ACM,* October 2002.

Herbsleb, J. et al., "Software Quality and the Capability Maturity Model," *Communications of the ACM,* June 1997.

Johnson, R. A., "The Ups and Downs of Object-Oriented Systems Development," *Communications of the ACM,* October 2000.

Kendall, K. E., and J. E. Kendall, *Systems Analysis and Design,* 5th ed. Upper Saddle River, NJ: Prentice-Hall, 2002.

Kern, T., and J. Kreijger, "An Exploration of the ASP Outsourcing Option," *Proceedings, 34th HICSS,* Maui, HI, January 3–6, 2001.

Lee, J. N. et al., "IT Outsourcing Evolution: Past, Present, and Future," *Communications of the ACM,* May 2003.

Liebowitz, J., "Information Systems: Success or Failure?" *Journal of Computer Information Systems,* fall 1999.

Linthicum, D. S., *B2B appliation Integration: e-Business-Enable Your Enterprise.* Boston: Addison Wesley, 2001.

Martin, C. F., "Legacy Value Engineering: the Foundation of Youth to Maximize the Value of Existing Technology Investments," *The Executive's Journal,* winter 2003.

mbe.com (accessed July 2003).

Montealegre, R., and M. Keil, "De-escalating Information Technology Projects: Lessons from the Denver International Airport," *MIS Quarterly,* September 2000.

Mullich, J., "Web Site Development: Back Home," *InternetWeek,* January 2000, *internetweek.com/indepth/indepth011000.htm* (accessed July 2003).

Neel, D., "The Utility Computing Promise," *InfoWorld,* April 2002.

Patton, S., "Web Services in the Real World," *CIO,* April 2002.

Paul, L., "T-Shirt King," *The Internet Marketing Center,* February 1999, *sellitontheweb.com/ezine.mystore008.shtml* (accessed July 2003).

Paul, L. G., "How Do Technology Initiatives Fail?" *Darwin Magazine,* May 2001, *darwinmagazine.com/read/050101/po.html* (accessed July 2003).

quantum.com (accessed July 2003).

Radosevich, L., "Quantum's Leap," *CIO,* February 15, 1997.

Rooney, J. T., Newtrade Technologies, *Web Services Before Their Time,* October 2001, *dcb.sun.com/practices/casestudies/newtrade.jsp* (accessed July 2003).

Sachdeva, S., "Outsourcing Strategy Helps Ansett Australia Streamline Its Business," *IBM Success Story, 2000 ibm.com/services/ successess/ansett.html* (accessed July 2003).

sap.com (accessed July 2003).

Scott, J. E., and I. Vessey, "Managing Risks in Enterprise Systems Implementations," *Communications of the ACM,* April 2002.

Seybold, P., *An Executive Guide to Web Services.* Boston, MA: Patricia Seybold Group *(psgroup.com),* 2002.

Sieber, T. et al., "Implementing SAP R/3 at the University of Nebraska," *Proceedings of the 20th ICIS Conference,* December 12–15, 1999.

Shirky, C., *Planning for Web Services.* Cambridge, MA: O'Reilly and Associates, 2002.

Shohoud, Y., *Real World XML Web Services.* Boston: Addison Wesley Professionals, 2002.

snap-on.com (accessed July 2003).

Stal, M., "Web Services; Beyond Component-Based Computer," *Communications of the ACM,* October 2002.

Standish Group, "Chaos," Standish Research Paper, *standishgroup. com/visitor/chaos.htm,* 1995.

Susarla, A., Barua, A., and Whinston, A. B., "Understanding the Service Component of Application Service Provision: An Empirical Analysis of Satisfaction with ASP Services," *MIS Quarterly,* March 2003.

Tabor R., *Microsoft.Net XML Web Services.* Indianapolis, IN: SAMS, 2002.

Tractinsky, M., and S. L. Jarvenpaa, "Information Systems Design Decisions in a Global vs. Domestic Context," *MIS Quarterly,* December 1995.

Valacich, J. et al., *Essentials of Systems Analysis and Design.* Upper Saddle River, NJ: Prentice-Hall, 2001.

Ward, L., "How ASPs Can Accelerate Your E-Business," *e-Business Advisor,* March 2000.

Yourdon, E., "What's So Different About Managing E-Projects?" *Computerworld,* August 2000.

Yourdon, E., *Managing High-Intensity Internet Projects.* Upper Saddle River, NJ: Prentice-Hall, 2002.

Yourdon, E., *Modern Structured Analysis.* Englewood Cliffs, NJ: Prentice-Hall, 1989.

Zimmerman, J., "Utility Computing Is the Next Big Thing," *ZDNetUK: Tech Update,* March 2003, *techupdate.zdnet.co.uk/story/ 0,,t481-s2131446,00.html* (accessed July 2003).

PART V
Implementing and Managing IT

13. Information Technology Economics
14. Building Information Systems
▶ 15. Managing Information Resources and Security
16. Impacts of IT on Organizations, Individuals, and Society (online)

CHAPTER

15

Managing Information Resources and Security

15.1
The IS Department and End Users

15.2
The CIO in Managing the IS Department

15.3
IS Vulnerability and Computer Crimes

15.4
Protecting Information Resources: From National to Organizational Efforts

15.5
Securing the Web, Intranets, and Wireless Networks

15.6
Business Continuity and Disaster Recovery Planning

15.7
Implementing Security: Auditing and Risk Analysis

LEARNING OBJECTIVES

After studying this chapter, you will be able to:

1. Recognize the difficulties in managing information resources.

2. Understand the role of the IS department and its relationships with end users.

3. Discuss the role of the chief information officer.

4. Recognize information systems' vulnerability, attack methods, and the possible damage from malfunctions.

5. Describe the major methods of defending information systems.

6. Describe the security issues of the Web and electronic commerce.

7. Describe business continuity and disaster recovery planning.

8. Understand the economics of security and risk management.

CYBERCRIME IN THE NEW MILLENNIUM

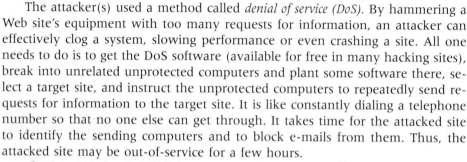

On January 1, 2000, the world was relieved to know that the damage to information systems due to the YK2 problem was minimal. However, only about six weeks into the new millennium, computer systems around the world were attacked by criminals.

On February 6, 2000, the biggest e-commerce sites were falling like dominos. First was Yahoo, which was forced to close down for three hours. Next were eBay, Amazon.com, E*Trade, and several other major EC and Internet sites that had gone dark.

The attacker(s) used a method called *denial of service (DoS)*. By hammering a Web site's equipment with too many requests for information, an attacker can effectively clog a system, slowing performance or even crashing a site. All one needs to do is to get the DoS software (available for free in many hacking sites), break into unrelated unprotected computers and plant some software there, select a target site, and instruct the unprotected computers to repeatedly send requests for information to the target site. It is like constantly dialing a telephone number so that no one else can get through. It takes time for the attacked site to identify the sending computers and to block e-mails from them. Thus, the attacked site may be out-of-service for a few hours.

The magnitude of the damage was so large that on February 9, the U.S. Attorney General pledged to track down the criminals and ensure that the Internet remains secure. This assurance did not last too long, as can be seen from the following story told by Professor Turban:

> When I opened my e-mail on May 4, 2000, I noticed immediately that the number of messages was larger than usual. A closer observation revealed that about 20 messages were titled I LOVE YOU, and most of them came from faculty, secretaries, and administrators at City University of Hong Kong. It was not my birthday and there was no reason to believe that so many people would send me love messages the same day. My initial thought was to open one message to find out what's going on. But, on second thought I remembered the "Melissa" virus and the instructions not to open any attachment of a strange e-mail. I picked up the telephone and called one of the senders, who told me not to open the attachment since it contained a deadly virus.

Although Professor Turban's system escaped the virus, thousands of users worldwide opened the "love" attachment and released the bug. It is interesting to note that the alleged attacker, from the Philippines, was not prosecuted because he did not break any law in the Philippines. The damage, according to Zetter and Miastkowski (2000), was estimated at $8.7 billion worldwide.

Sources: Compiled from news items during May 3–11, 2000, and from Zetter and Miastkowski (2000).

 LESSONS LEARNED FROM THIS CASE

Since May 2000 there have been more than a dozen major virus attacks, and hundreds of small ones, causing damage to organizations and individuals (see Richardson, 2003).

Clearly, information resources, including computers, networks, programs, and data, are vulnerable to unforeseen attacks. Attackers can zero in on a single company, or can attack many companies and individuals without discrimination, using various attack methods. Although variations of the attack methods are known, the defense against them is difficult and/or expensive. As the story of the "love" virus demonstrated, many countries do not have sufficient laws to deal with computer criminals. For all of these reasons, protection of networked systems can be a complex issue.

The actions of people or of nature can cause an information system to function in a way different from what was planned. It is important, therefore, to know how to ensure the continued operation of an IS and to know what to do if the system breaks down. These and similar issues are of concern to the management of information resources, the subject of this chapter.

In this chapter we look at how the IS department and end users work together; the role of the chief information officer; and the issue of information security and control in general and of Web systems in particular. Finally, we deal with plans of business continuity after a disaster, and the costs of preventing computer hazards.

15.1   THE IS DEPARTMENT AND END USERS

Throughout this book, we have seen that information systems are used to increase productivity and help achieve quality, timeliness, and satisfaction for both employees and customers. Most large, many medium, and even some small organizations around the world are strongly dependent on IT. Their information systems have considerable strategic importance.

The IS Department in the Organization

IT resources are very diversified; they include personnel assets, technology assets, and IT relationship assets. The management of information resources is divided between the information services department (ISD) and the end users. **Information resources management (IRM)** encompasses all activities related to the planning, organizing, acquiring, maintaining, securing, and controlling of IT resources. The division of responsibility depends on many factors, beginning with the amount of IT assets and nature of duties involved in IRM, and ending with outsourcing policies. Decisions about the roles of each party are made during the IS planning (Chapter 9). (For some insights, see Sambamurthy et al., 2001.)

A major decision that must be made by senior management is where the ISD is to report in the organizational hierarchy. Partly for historical reasons, a common place to find the ISD is in the accounting or finance department. In such situations, the ISD normally reports to the controller or the chief financial officer. The ISD might also report to one of the following: (1) a vice president of technology, (2) an executive vice president (e.g., for administration), or (3) the CEO.

THE IS DIRECTOR AS A "CHIEF."   To show the importance of the IS area, some organizations call the director of IS a **chief information officer (CIO),** a title similar to chief financial officer (CFO) and chief operating officer (COO). Typically, only important or senior vice presidents receive this title. Other common titles are *vice president for IS, vice president for information technology,* or *director of information systems.* Unfortunately, as Becker (2003) reports, some companies provide the title CIO, but do not accord the position the importance other "chiefs" are getting. The *title* of CIO and the position to whom this person reports reflect, in many cases, the degree of support being shown by top management to the ISD. The *reporting relationship* of the ISD is important in that it reflects the focus of the department. If the ISD reports to the accounting or finance areas, there is often a tendency to emphasize accounting or finance applications at the expense of those in the marketing, production, and logistics areas. In some organizations the IS functions are distributed, depending on their nature (see Minicase 1). To be most effective, the ISD needs to take as broad a view as possible.

THE NAME AND POSITION OF THE IS DEPARTMENT.   The *name* of the ISD is also important. Originally it was called the Data Processing (DP) Department. Then the name was changed to the Management Information Systems (MIS) Department and then to the Information Systems Department (ISD). In addition, one can find names such as Information Technology Department, Corporate Technology Center, and so on. In very large organizations the ISD can be a division, or even an independent corporation (such as at Bank of America and at Boeing Corp.).

Some companies separate their e-commerce activities, creating a special online division. This is the approach taken by Qantas Airways, for example. In others, e-commerce may be combined with ISD in a technology department or division. Becker (2003) reports on a study that shows that companies get the largest return from IT when they treat the ISD like any other important part of their business.

The status of the ISD also depends on its mission and internal structure. Agarwal and Sambamurthy (2002) found in a survey that companies usually organize their IT functions in one of the following ways: making IT an active partner in business innovation, providing IT resources for innovation and global reach, or seeking flexibility via a considerable amount of outsourcing.

The increased role and importance of IT and its management, both by a centralized unit and by end users, require careful understanding of the manner in which ISD is organized as well as of the relationship between the ISD and end users. These topics are discussed next. Also, for more on the connection between the ISD and the organization, see the IRM feedback model in Online File W15.1 at the book's Web site.

The IS Department and End Users

It is extremely important to have a good relationship between the ISD and end users. Unfortunately, though, this relationship is not always optimal. The development of end-user computing and outsourcing was motivated in part by the poor service that end users felt they received from the ISD. (For the issue of how to measure the quality of IS services, see Jiang et al., 2002). Conflicts occur for several reasons, ranging from the fact that priorities of the ISD may differ from those of the end users to lack of communication. Also, there are some fundamental differences between the personalities, cognitive styles, educational backgrounds, and gender proportion of the end users versus the ISD staff (generally more males in the ISD) that could contribute to conflicts. An example of such conflict is illustrated in *IT at Work 15.1*.

The situation described in *IT at Work 15.1* is fairly common. One of this book's authors, when acting as a consultant to an aerospace company in Los Angeles, found that end users frequently bought nonstandard equipment by making several smaller purchases instead of one large, because the smaller purchases did

IT at Work 15.1
MINNESOTA'S DEPARTMENT OF TRANSPORTATION VIOLATES PROCEDURES

The Department of Transportation in Minnesota (*dot.state.mn.us*) had come across a hybrid PC system that would allow road surveys to be accomplished with less time and effort, and greater accuracy. The system would require two people to conduct a survey instead of the usual three, and because of the precision of the computer-based system, the survey could be done in half the time.

The department ran into a problem because the ISD for the State of Minnesota had instituted standards for all PCs that could be purchased by any state agency. Specifically, a particular brand of IBM PC was the only PC purchase allowed, without going through a special procedure. The red tape, as well as the unwillingness of the ISD to allow any deviation from the standard, caused a great deal of frustration.

As a last resort, the Department of Transportation procured the hybrid PC and camouflaged the transaction as engineering equipment for conducting surveys. From that point on, its staff decided they would do what they needed to do to get their jobs done, and the less the ISD knew about what they were doing, the better. When asked why they behaved this way, the administrator of the Department of Transportation simply said, "We have to do it this way because the ISD will either try to stop or hold up for a long period of time any decision we want to make, because they just are not familiar enough with the issues that we are facing in our department."

For Further Exploration: What are the organizational risks when the Transportation Department takes this attitude? How can the conflict be resolved?

---

not require authorization by the ISD. When asked if the ISD knew about this circumventing of the rules, a violating manager answered, "Of course they know, but what can they do—fire me?"

Generally, the ISD can take one of the following four approaches toward end-user computing:

1. ***Let them sink or swim.*** Don't do anything; let the end user beware.
2. ***Use the stick.*** Establish policies and procedures to control end-user computing so that corporate risks are minimized, and try to enforce them.
3. ***Use the carrot.*** Create incentives to encourage certain end-user practices that reduce organizational risks.
4. ***Offer support.*** Develop services to aid end users in their computing activities.

Each of these responses presents the IS executive with different opportunities for facilitation and coordination, and each has its advantages and disadvantages.

Fostering the ISD/End-User Relationships

The ISD is a *service organization* that manages the IT infrastructure needed to carry on end-user IT applications. Therefore, a partnership between the ISD and the end user is a must. This is not an easy task since the ISD is basically a technical organization that may not understand the business and the users. The users, on the other hand, may not understand information technologies. Also, there could be differences between the ISD (the provider) and the end users in terms of agreement on how to measure the IT services provided (quality, quantity) (see Jiang et al., 2002). Another major reason for tense relationships in many organizations is the difficulties discussed in Chapter 13 regarding the evaluation of IT investment (Seddon et al., 2002).

To improve collaboration, the ISD and end users may employ three common arrangements: the steering committee, service-level agreements, and the information center. (For other strategies, see Online File W15.2.)

THE STEERING COMMITTEE. The corporate **steering committee** is a group of managers and staff representing various organizational units that is set up to establish IT priorities and to ensure that the ISD is meeting the needs of the enterprise (see Minicase 1). The committee's major tasks are:

- *Direction setting.* In linking the corporate strategy with the IT strategy, planning is the key activity (see Chapter 9 and Willcocks and Sykes, 2000).
- *Rationing.* The committee approves the allocation of resources for and within the information systems organization. This includes outsourcing policy.
- *Structuring.* The committee deals with how the ISD is positioned in the organization. The issue of centralization–decentralization of IT resources is resolved by the committee.
- *Staffing.* Key IT personnel decisions involve a consultation-and-approval process made by the committee. Notable is the selection of the CIO and major IT outsourcing decisions.
- *Communication.* It is important that information regarding IT activities flows freely.
- *Evaluating.* The committee should establish performance measures for the ISD and see that they are met. This includes the initiation of *service-level agreements.*

The success of steering committees largely depends on the establishment of **IT goverance,** a formally established set of statements that should direct the policies regarding IT alignment with organizational goals, risk determination, and allocation of resources (Cilli, 2003).

SERVICE-LEVEL AGREEMENTS. **Service-level agreements (SLAs)** are formal agreements regarding the division of computing responsibility between end users and the ISD and the expected services to be rendered by the ISD. A service-level agreement can be viewed as a *contract* between each end-user unit and the ISD. If a chargeback system exists, it is usually spelled out in the SLA. The process of establishing and implementing SLAs may be applied to each of the *major* computing resources: hardware, software, people, data, networks, and procedures.

The divisions of responsibility in SLAs are based on critical computing decisions that are made by *end-user managers,* who agree to accept certain computing responsibilities and to turn over others to the ISD. Since end-user managers make these decisions, they are free to choose the amount and kind of support they feel they need. This freedom to choose provides a check on the ISD and encourages it to develop and deliver support services to meet end-user needs.

An approach based on SLAs offers several advantages. First, it reduces "finger pointing" by clearly specifying responsibilities. When a PC malfunctions, everyone knows who is responsible for fixing it. Second, it provides a structure for the design and delivery of end-user services by the ISD. Third, it creates incentives for end users to improve their computing practices, thereby reducing computing risks to the firm.

Establishing SLAs requires the following steps: (1) Define service levels. (2) Divide computing responsibility at each level. (3) Design the details of the service levels, including measurement of quality (see Jiang et al., 2002). (4) Implement service levels. Kesner (2002) adds to these: (5) Assign SLA owner (the person or department that gets the SLA), (6) monitor SLA compliance, (7) analyze performance, (8) refine SLAs as needed, and (9) improve service to the department or company.

Due to the introduction of Web-based tools for simplifying the task of monitoring enterprise networks, more attention has recently been given to service-level agreement, (Adams, 2000). (For an overview of SLAs, see Pantry and Griffiths, 2002; for suggestions of how to control SLAs, see Diao et al., 2002.)

THE INFORMATION CENTER. The concept of **information center (IC)** (also known as the user's service center, technical support center, or IS help center) was conceived by IBM Canada in the 1970s as a response to the increased number of end-user requests for new computer applications. This demand created a huge backlog in the IS department, and users had to wait several *years* to get their systems built. Today, ICs concentrate on end-user support with PCs, client/server applications, and the Internet/intranet, helping with installation, training, problem resolution, and other technical support.

The IC is set up to help users get certain systems built quickly and to provide tools that can be employed by users to build their own systems. The concept of the IC, furthermore, suggests that the people in the center should be especially oriented toward the users in their outlook. This attitude should be shown in the training provided by the staff at the center and in the way the staff helps users with any problems they might have. There can be one or several ICs in an organization, and they report to the ISD and/or the end-user departments.

Further information on the purpose and activities of the IC is provided in Online File W15.3.

The New IT Organization

To carry out its mission in the digital economy, the ISD needs to adapt. Rockart et al. (1996) proposed eight imperatives for ISDs, which are still valid today. These imperatives are summarized in Table 15.1.

Information technology, as shown throughout this book, is playing a critical role in the livelihood of many organizations, small and large, private and

TABLE 15.1 The Eight Imperatives for ISDs in the Digital Age

Imperative	Description
Achieve two-way strategic alignment	You must align IT and the organization's strategies (Chapter 9).
Develop effective relations with line manangement	An efficient partnership must be cultivated between the end users and the ISD.
Develop and deploy new systems quickly	When companies compete on time, the speed of installing new applications and having them run properly are critical needs (Chapter 14).
Build and manage infrastructure	Infrastructure is a shared resource. Therefore its planning, architecture, and policy of use must be done properly (Chapter 9).
Manage vendor relationships	As more vendors are used in IT projects, their management becomes critical. Vendor relations must be not only contractual, but also strategic and collaborative (Chapter 13).
Reskill the IT organization	The skills of IT managers, staff, and technical people must be constantly updated. Using the Web, e-training is popular (Chapters 5, 7).
Build high performance	With shrinking IT budgets and need for new equipment, systems must be very reliable and of high performance, as well as justifiable in terms of cost (Chapter 13). Using a six-sigma approach is recommended.
Redesign and manage the centralized IT organization	The ISD, its role, power sharing with end users, and outsourcing strategies must be carefully crafted.

Source: Compiled from Rockart et al. (1996).

public, throughout the world. Furthermore, the trend is for even more IT involvement. Effective ISDs will help their firms apply IT to transform themselves to e-businesses, redesign processes, and access needed information on a tight budget. For more on managing IT in the digital era, see Sambamurthy et al. (2001).

15.2 THE CIO IN MANAGING THE IS DEPARTMENT

Managing the ISD is similar to managing any other organizational unit. The unique aspect of the ISD is that it operates as a service department in a rapidly changing environment, thus making the department's projections and planning difficult. The equipment purchased and maintained by the ISD is scattered all over the enterprise, adding to the complexity of ISD management. Here we will discuss only one issue: the CIO and his or her relationship with other managers and executives.

The Role of the Chief Information Officer

The changing role of the ISD highlights the fact that the CIO is becoming an important member of the organization's top management team (Ross and Feeny, 2000). Also, the experience of 9/11 changed the role of the CIO, placing him or her in a more important organizational position (see Ball, 2002) because of the organization's realization of the need for IT-related disaster planning and the importance of IT to the organization's activities.

The prime role of the CIO is to align IT with the business strategy. Secondary roles are to implement state-of-the-art solutions and to provide and improve information access. These roles are supplemented today by several strategic roles because IT has become a strategic resource for many organizations. Coordinating this resource requires strong IT leadership and ISD/end-user collaboration within the organization. In addition, CIO–CEO relationships are crucial for effective, successful utilization of IT, especially in organizations that greatly depend on IT, where the CIO joins the top management "chiefs" group.

The CIO in some cases is a member of the corporate *executive committee,* the most important committee in any organization, which has responsibility for strategic business planning. Its members include the chief executive officer and the senior vice presidents. The executive committee provides the top-level oversight for the organization's information resources. It guides the IS steering committee that is usually chaired by the CIO. Related to the CIO is the emergence of the chief knowledge officer (CKO, see Chapter 10). A CIO may report to the CKO, or the same person may assume both roles, especially in smaller companies.

Major responsibilities that are part of the CIO's evolving role are listed in Online File W15.4.

The CIO in the Web-Based Era

According to Ross and Feeny (2000) and Earl (1999–2000), the CIO's role in the Web-based era is influenced by the following three factors:

● *Technology and its management are changing.* Companies are using new Web-based business models. Conventional applications are being transformed to Web-based. There is increasing use of B2B e-commerce, supply chain management, CRM, ERP (see Willcocks and Sykes, 2000), and knowledge management applications. The application portfolio includes more and more Web-based applications.

- *Executives' attitudes are changing.* Greater attention is given to opportunities and risks. At the very least, CIOs are the individuals to whom the more computer literate executives look for guidance, especially as it relates to e-business. Also, executives are more willing to invest in IT, since the cost-benefit ratio of IT is improving with time.

- *Interactions with vendors are increasing.* Suppliers of IT, especially the major ones (HP, Cisco, IBM, Microsoft, Sun, Intel, and Oracle), are influencing the strategic thinking of their corporate customers.

The above factors shape the roles and responsibilities of the CIO in the following seven ways: (1) The CIO is taking increasing responsibility for defining the strategic future. (2) The CIO needs to understand (with others in the organization) that the Web-based era is more about fundamental business change than about technology. (3) The CIO is responsible for protecting the ever-increasing IT assets, including the Web infrastructure, against ever-increasing hazards, including terrorists' attacks. (4) The CIO is becoming a *business visionary* who drives business strategy, develops new business models on the Web, and introduces management processes that leverage the Internet, intranets, and extranets. (5) The CIO needs to argue for a greater measure of central control. For example, placing inappropriate content on the Internet or intranets can be harmful and needs to be monitored and coordinated. (6) The IT asset-acquisition process must be improved. The CIO and end users must work more closely than ever before. (7) The increased networked environment may lead to disillusionment with IT—an undesirable situation that the CIO should help to avoid. These seven challenges place lots of pressure on CIOs, especially in times of economic decline (see Leidner et al., 2003).

As a result of the considerable pressures they face, CIOs may earn very high salaries (up to $1,000,000/year in large corporations), but there is high turnover at this position (see Earl, 1999/2000 and Sitonis and Goldberg, 1997). As technology becomes increasingly central to business, the CIO becomes a key mover in the ranks of upper management. For example, in a large financial institution's executive committee meeting, attended by one of the authors, modest requests for additional budgets by the senior vice presidents for finance and for marketing were turned down after long debate. But, at the same meeting the CIO's request for a tenfold addition was approved in only a few minutes.

It is interesting to note that CEOs are acquiring IT skills. According to Duffy (1999), a company's best investment is a CEO who knows technology. If both the CIO and the CEO have the necessary skills for the information age, their company has the potential to flourish. For this reason some companies promote their CIOs to CEOs.

According to *eMarketer Daily* (May 12, 2003), CEOs see security as the second most important area for IT over the next two to three years. We will now turn our attention to one area where the CIO is expected to lead—the security of information systems in the enterprise.

15.3 IS VULNERABILITY AND COMPUTER CRIMES

Information resources are scattered throughout the organization. Furthermore, employees travel with and take home corporate computers and data. Information is transmitted to and from the organization and among the organization's

TABLE 15.2 IT Security Terms

Term	Definition
Backup	An extra copy of the data and/or programs, kept in a secured location(s).
Decryption	Transformation of scrambled code into readable data after transmission.
Encryption	Transformation of data into scrambled code prior to its transmission.
Exposure	The harm, loss, or damage that can result if something has gone wrong in an information system.
Fault tolerance	The ability of an information system to continue to operate (usually for a limited time and/or at a reduced level) when a failure occurs.
Information system controls	The procedures, devices, or software that attempt to ensure that the system performs as planned.
Integrity (of data)	A guarantee of the accuracy, completeness, and reliability of data. System integrity is provided by the integrity of its components and their integration.
Risk	The likelihood that a threat will materialize.
Threats (or hazards)	The various dangers to which a system may be exposed.
Vulnerability	Given that a threat exists, the susceptibility of the system to harm caused by the threat.

components. IS physical resources, data, software, procedures, and any other information resources may therefore be vulnerable, in many places at any time.

Before we describe the specific problems with information security and some proposed solutions, it is necessary to know the key terminology in the field. Table 15.2 provides an overview of that terminology.

Information Systems Breakdowns

Most people are aware of some of the dangers faced by businesses that are dependent on computers. Information systems, however, can be damaged for many other reasons. The following incidents illustrate representative cases of breakdowns in information systems.

INCIDENT 1. On September 12, 2002, Spitfire Novelties fell victim to what is called a "brute force" credit card attack. On a normal day, the Los Angeles–based company generates between 5 and 30 transactions. That Thursday, Spitfire's credit card transaction processor, Online Data Corporation, processed 140,000 fake credit card charges, worth $5.07 each. Of these, 62,000 were approved. The total value of the approved charges was around $300,000. Spitfire found out about the transactions only when they were called by one of the credit card owners who had been checking his statement online and had noticed the $5.07 charge.

Brute force credit card attacks require minimal skill. Hackers simply run thousands of small charges through merchant accounts, picking numbers at random. (For details on a larger credit card scam see *money.cnn.com/2003/02/18/technology/creditcards/index.htm.*)

INCIDENT 2. In January 2003 a hacker stole from the database of Moscow's MTS (mobile phone company) the personal details (passport number, age, home address, tax ID number, and more) of 6 million customers, including Russia's president V. V. Putin, and sold them on CD-ROMs for about $15 each. The database can be searched by name, phone number, or address. The information can be used for crimes such as **identity theft,** where someone uses the personal information of others to create a false identify and then uses it for some fraud (e.g., to get a fake credit card). However, in Russia neither the theft of such information nor its sale was illegal (see Walsh, 2003).

INCIDENT 3. Destructive software (viruses, worms, and their variants, which are defined and discussed more fully later in the chapter) is flooding the Internet. Here are some examples of the 2003 vintage: SQL Slammer is a worm that carries a self-regenerating mechanism that enables it to multiply quickly across the Internet. It is so good at replicating that it quickly generates a massive amount of data, which slowed Internet traffic mainly in South Korea, Japan, Hong Kong, and some European countries in January 2003. It is a variation of Code Red, that slowed traffic on the Internet in July 2001. On May 18, 2003, a new virus that masqueraded as an e-mail from Microsoft technical support attacked computers in 89 countries. In June 2003, a high-risk virus w32/ Bugbear started to steal VISA account information (see "Bugbear worm steals...," 2003).

INCIDENT 4. On March 15, 2003, a student hacked into the University of Houston computer system and stole Social Security numbers of 55,000 students, faculty, and staff. The student was charged with unauthorized access to protected computers using someone else's ID, with intent to commit a federal crime. The case is still in the courts, and prison time is a possibility.

INCIDENT 5. On February 29, 2000, hundreds of automated teller machines (ATMs) in Japan were shut down, a computer system at a nuclear plant seized up, weather-monitoring devices malfunctioned, display screens for interest rates at the post offices failed, seismographs provided wrong information, and there were many other problems related to programming for "leap year." The problem was that years that end in "00" do not get the extra day, added every four years, unless they are divisible by 400 (2000 is such a leap year, but not 1900, or 2100). This rule was not programmed properly in some old programs in Japan, thus creating the problems. In May 2001, a glitch in Japan's air-traffic systems grounded 1,600 domestic flights for 30 minutes while the system was operated manually.

INCIDENT 6. For almost two weeks, a seemingly legitimate ATM operating in a shopping mall near Hartford, Connecticut, gave customers apologetic notes that said, "Sorry, no transactions are possible." Meanwhile, the machine recorded the card numbers and the personal identification numbers that hundreds of customers entered in their vain attempts to make the machine dispense cash. On May 8, 1993, while the dysfunctional machine was still running in the shopping mall, thieves started tapping into the 24-hour automated teller network in New York City. Using counterfeit bank cards encoded with the numbers stolen from the Hartford customers, the thieves removed about $100,000 from the accounts of innocent customers. The criminals were successful in making an ATM machine do what it was supposedly designed not to do: breach its own security by recording bank card numbers together with personal security codes.

INCIDENT 7.   Netscape security is aimed at scrambling sensitive financial data such as credit card numbers and sales transactions so they would be safe from break-ins, by using a powerful 128-bit program. However, using 120 powerful workstations and two supercomputers, in 1996 a French student breached the encryption program in eight days, demonstrating that no program is 100 percent secure.

INCIDENT 8.   In 1994 a Russian hacker (who did not know much English) broke into a Citibank electronic funds transfer system and stole more than $10 million by wiring it to accounts around the world. Since then, Citibank, a giant bank that moves about a trillion dollars a day, increased its security measures, requiring customers to use electronic devices that create new passwords very frequently.

INCIDENT 9.   On April 30, 2000, the London Stock Exchange was paralyzed by its worst computer system failure, before finally opening nearly eight hours late. A spokesman for the exchange said the problem, which crippled the supply of prices and firm information, was caused by corrupt data. He gave no further details. Dealers were outraged by the fault, which came on the last day of the tax year and just hours after violent price swings in the U.S. stock markets. The British Financial Services Authority said it viewed the failure seriously, adding it would insist any necessary changes to systems be made immediately and that lessons be "learned rapidly" to ensure the breakdown would not be repeated.

These incidents and the two in the opening case illustrate the vulnerability of information systems, the diversity of causes of computer security problems, and the substantial damage that can be done to organizations anywhere in the world as a result. The fact is that computing is far from secure (e.g., see Austin and Darby, 2003, and the 2003 FBI report in Richardson, 2003).

System Vulnerability

Information systems are made up of many components that may be housed in several locations. Thus, each information system is vulnerable to many potential *hazards* or *threats*. Figure 15.1 presents a summary of the major threats to the security of an information system. Attacks on information systems can be either on internal systems (suffered by about 30% of the responding organizations in the CSI/FBI survey, as reported in Richardson, 2003), or via remote dial-ins (18%), or on Internet-based systems (78%). (See also *sons.org/top20*, for the most critical Internet security vulnerabilites.)

According to CVE (Common Vulnerabilities and Exposure, an organization based at Mitre Corp. that provides information, educations, and advice regarding IT vulnerabilities and exposure)(*cve.mitre.org/about/terminology.html*), there is a distinction between vulnerability and exposure:

> A universal **vulnerability** is a state in a computing system (or set of systems) which either: allows an attacker to execute commands as another user; allows an attacker to access data that is contrary to the specified access restrictions for that data; allows an attacker to pose as another entity; or allows an attacker to conduct a denial of service.

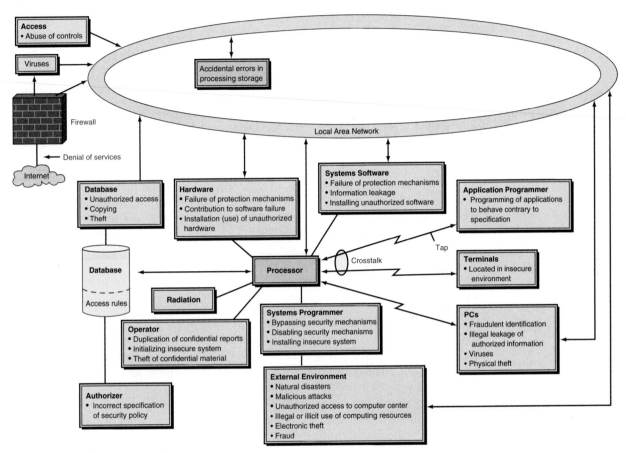

FIGURE 15.1 Security threats.

An **exposure** is a state in a computing system (or set of systems) which is not a universal vulnerability, but either: allows an attacker to conduct information gathering activities; allows an attacker to hide activities; includes a capability that behaves as expected, but can be easily compromised; is a primary point of entry that an attacker may attempt to use to gain access to the system or data; and is considered a problem according to some reasonable security policy.

We will use the term vulnerability here to *include* exposure as well (including unintentional threats). Incidentally, by 2002 CVE identified more than 5,000 different security issues and problems (see Mitre, 2002).

The vulnerability of information systems is increasing as we move to a world of networked and especially wireless computing. Theoretically, there are hundreds of points in a corporate information system that can be subject to some threats. And actually, there are thousands of different ways that information systems can be attacked or damaged. These threats can be classified as *unintentional* or *intentional.*

UNINTENTIONAL THREATS.   Unintentional threats can be divided into three major categories: human errors, environmental hazards, and computer system failures.

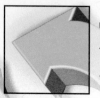

A CLOSER LOOK
15.1 COMPUTER GLITCHES DELAY AIRPORT OPENINGS

When the multibillion-dollar airport was opened in Hong Kong on July 6, 1999, a combination of computer glitches and unprepared personnel turned the airport into chaos. Both travelers and cargo were affected. For example, one software bug erased all inventory records, leaving no clue as to who owned what. Another software bug erased flight information from monitors, preventing passengers from finding flights. Computer problems in the baggage system resulted in 10,000 lost bags. Fresh food and seafood being shipped to restaurants and hotels got spoiled, and considerable business was lost. In the United States, Denver's airport, which opened in 1995, had been plagued by computer glitches as well (see Chapter 14). Similarly, in Malaysia, when a new facility opened on July 1, 1999, a computerized total airport management system collapsed on the first day.

In all these airport cases, the problem was not external hackers' attacks or internal intentional acts. The bugs resulted from poor IS planning, lack of coordination, and insufficient testing.

Many computer problems result from *human errors*. Errors can occur in the design of the hardware and/or information system. They can also occur in the programming, testing, data collection, data entry, authorization, and instructions. Human errors contribute to the *vast majority* (about 55 percent) of control- and security-related problems in many organizations.

Environmental hazards include earthquakes, severe storms (e.g., hurricanes, snow, sand, lightning, and tornadoes), floods, power failures or strong fluctuations, fires (the most common hazard), defective air conditioning, explosions, radioactive fallout, and water-cooling-system failures. In addition to damage from combustion, computer resources can incur damage from other elements that accompany fire, such as smoke, heat, and water. Such hazards may disrupt normal computer operations and result in long waiting periods and exorbitant costs while computer programs and data files are recreated.

Computer systems failures can occur as the result of poor manufacturing or defective materials. Unintentional malfunctions can also happen for other reasons, ranging from lack of experience to inappropriate testing. See *A Closer Look 15.1* for the story about some systems failures at airports.

INTENTIONAL THREATS. As headlines about computer crime indicate, computer systems can be damaged as a result of intentional actions as well. These account for about 30 percent of all computer problems, according to the Computer Security Institute (*gocsi.com*), but the monetary damage from such actions can be extremely large. Examples of intentional threats include: theft of data; inappropriate use of data (e.g., manipulating inputs); theft of mainframe computer time; theft of equipment and/or programs; deliberate manipulation in handling, entering, processing, transferring, or programming data; labor strikes, riots, or sabotage; malicious damage to computer resources; destruction from viruses and similar attacks; and miscellaneous computer abuses and Internet fraud. In addition, while terrorists' attacks do not usually directly target computers, the computers and information systems can be destroyed in such cases, as happened in the 9/11 disaster in New York and Washington, D.C. Intentional threats can even be against whole countries. Many fear the possibility of *cyber-attacks* by some countries against others.

Computer Crimes
According to the Computer Security Institute (*gocsi.com*), 64 percent of all corporations experienced computer crimes in 1997. The figures in the years 1998 through 2003 were even higher—about 96 percent in 2003 (per Richardson, 2003). The number, magnitude, and diversity of computer crimes are increasing. Lately, increased fraud related to the Internet and e-commerce is in evidence. For an overview of computer crime, see Loundy (2003); for FBI statistics for 2002/2003, see Richardson (2003).

TYPES OF COMPUTER CRIMES AND CRIMINALS. In many ways, computer crimes resemble conventional crimes. They can occur in various ways. First, the computer can be the *target* of the crime. For example, a computer may be stolen or destroyed, or a virus may destroy data. The computer can be the *medium* or *tool* of the attack, by creating an environment in which a crime or fraud can occur. For example, false data are entered into a computer system to mislead individuals examining the financial condition of a company. Finally, the computer can be used to *intimidate* or *deceive*. For instance, a stockbroker stole $50 million by convincing his clients that he had a computer program with which he could increase their return on investment by 60 percent per month. Crimes done on the Internet, called cybercrimes (discussed later), can fall into any of these categories.

Crimes can be performed by *outsiders* who penetrate a computer system (frequently via communication lines) or by *insiders* who are authorized to use the computer system but are misusing their authorization. **Hacker** is the term often used to describe an outside person who penetrates a computer system. For an overview of hacking and the protection against it, see Fadia (2002). A **cracker** is a *malicious hacker*, who may represent a serious problem for a corporation.

Hackers and crackers may involve unsuspecting insiders in their crimes. In a strategy called **social engineering,** computer criminals or corporate spies build an inappropriate trust relationship with insiders for the purpose of gaining sensitive information or unauthorized access privileges. For description of social engineering and some tips for prevention, see Damle (2002) and Online File W15.5.

Computer criminals, whether insiders or outsiders, tend to have a distinct profile and are driven by several motives (see Online File W15.6). Ironically, many employees fit this profile, but only a few of them are criminals. Therefore, it is difficult to predict who is or will be a computer criminal.

A large proportion of computer crimes are performed by insiders. According to Richardson (2003) the likely sources of attacks on U.S. companies are: independent hackers (82%), disgruntled employees (78%), U.S. competitors (40%), foreign governments (28%), foreign corporations (25%).

In addition to computer crimes against organizations there is an alarming increase of fraud committed against individuals, on the Internet. These are a part of cybercrimes.

CYBERCRIMES. The Internet environment provides an extremly easy landscape for conducting illegal activities. These are known as **cybercrimes,** meaning they are executed on the Internet. Hundreds of different methods and "tricks" are used by innovative criminals to get money from innocent people, to buy without paying, to sell without delivering, to abuse people or hurt them, and much more.

According to Sullivan (2003), between January 1 and April 30, 2003, agencies of the U.S. government uncovered 89,000 victims from whom Internet criminals bilked over $176 million. As a result, on May 16, 2003, the U.S. Attorney General announced that 135 people were arrested nationwide and charged with cybercrime. The most common crimes were investment swindles and identity theft. The Internet with its global reach has also resulted in a growing amount of cross-border fraud (see *A Closer Look 15.2*).

Identity Theft. A growing cybercrime problem is *identity theft,* in which a criminal (the *identity thief*) poses as someone else. The thief steals Social Security numbers and credit card numbers, usually obtained from the Internet, to commit fraud (e.g., to buy products or consume services) that the victim is required to pay for later. The biggest damage to the person whose identity was stolen is to restore the damaged credit rating. For details and commercial solutions see *idthief.com*.

CYBERWAR. There is an increasing interest in the threat of **cyberwar,** in which a country's information systems could be paralyzed by a massive attack of destructive software. The target systems can range from the ISs of business, industry, government services, and the media to military command systems.

One aspect of cyberwar is *cyberterrorism*, which refers to Internet terrorist attacks. These attacks, like cyberwar, can risk the national information infrastructure. The U.S. presidential Critical Infrastructure Protection Board (CIPB) is preparing protection plans, policies, and strategies to deal with cyberterrorism. The CIPS is recommending investment in cybersecurity programs. Some of the areas of the CIPB report are: a general policy on information security; asset protection requirements, including controls to ensure the return or destruction of information; technology insurance requirements; intellectual property rights; the right to monitor, and revoke, user activity; specification of physical and technical security standards; and communication procedures in time of emergency. (For more details and debates, see *cdt.org/security/critinfra* and *ciao.gov*. For more details on cyberterrorism, see Verton and Brownlow, 2003.)

Methods of Attack on Computing Facilities

There are many methods of attack, and new ones appear regularly. Of the many methods of attack on computing facilities, the CSI/FBI reports (per Richardson, 2003) the following as most frequent (percentage of responding companies): virus (82%), insider abuse of Internet access (80%), unauthorized access by insiders (45%), theft of laptop (59%), denial of service (DoS) attack (42%), system penetration (36%), sabotage (21%), and theft of proprietary information (21%). In this section we look at some of these methods. Two basic approaches are used in deliberate attacks on computer systems: data tampering and programming attack.

Data tampering, the most common means of attack, refers to entering false, fabricated, or fraudulent data into the computer or changing or deleting existing data. This is the method often used by insiders. For example, to pay for his wife's drug purchases, a savings and loan programmer transferred $5,000 into his personal account and tried to cover up the transfer with phony debit and credit transactions.

A CLOSER LOOK
15.2 CROSS-BORDER CYBERCRIMES

As the Internet grows, so do cross-border scams. According to the U.S. Federal Trade Commission (FTC), there was an increase in the complaints filed by U.S. consumers about cross-border scams, of 74 percent in 2002 (to 24,213) (Davidson, 2003). Most complaints involved advance-fee loans, foreign cash offers, and sweepstakes. Scammers based in one country elude authorities by victimizing residents of others, using the Internet.

For example, David Lee, a 41-year-old Hong Kong resident, replied to an advertisement in a respected business magazine that offered him free investment advice. After he replied, he received professional-looking brochures and a telephone sales speech. Then he was directed to the Web site of Equity Mutual Trust (Equity) where he was able to track the impressive daily performance of a fund that listed offices in London, Switzerland, and Belize. From that Web site he was linked to sister funds and business partners. Lee also was linked to what he believed was the well-known investment-fund evaluator company Morningstar (*morningstar.com*). Actually, the site was an imitation that replicated the original site. The imitation site provided a very high, but false, rating on the Equity Mutual Trust funds. Finally, Lee was directed to read about Equity and its funds in the respected *International Herald Tribune*'s Internet edition; the article appeared to be news but was actually an advertisement.

Convinced that he would receive super short-term gains, he mailed US$16,000, instructing Equity to invest in the Grand Financial Fund. Soon he grew suspicious when letters from Equity came from different countries, telephone calls and e-mails were not answered on time, and the daily Internet listings dried up.

When Lee wanted to sell, he was advised to increase his investment and shift to a Canadian company, Mit-Tec, allegedly a Y2K-bug troubleshooter. The Web site he was directed to looked fantastic. But this time Lee was careful. He contacted the financial authorities in the Turks and Caicos Islands—where Equity was based at that time—and was referred to the British police.

Soon he learned that chances were slim that he would ever see his money again. Furthermore, he learned that several thousand victims had paid a total of about $4 billion to Equity. Most of the victims live in Hong Kong, Singapore, and other Asian countries. Several said that the most convincing information came from the Web sites, including the "independent" Web site that rated Equity and its funds as safe, five-star funds.

According to Davidson (2003), the FTC admitted that the laws in the United States and other countries are set up based on an old-economy view and are not effective enough in cross-border cases involving new-economy realities. To solve the problem, some countries (e.g., Germany, Netherlands) rely on self-regulatory business groups that can merely urge an offending company to change its practice. Some countries try to bar rogue marketers from conducting unethical or even illegal marketing activities, but cannot even impose financial sanctions. Offending companies are simply looking for jurisdictions of convenience. (Incidentally, the same situation exists with companies that support free *file sharing*, such as Kazaa; they are operating from outside the United States and so are not subject to U.S. laws, however outdated the laws may be.)

What can be done? In June 2003, 29 nations belonging to the Organization for Economic Cooperation and Development (OECD) announced an agreement on unified guidelines for far greater cooperation in prosecuting online scammers and in enforcing existing laws. There will be information sharing and collaboration among investigators from different countries (e.g., relaxing privacy rules that in most nations, including the United States, now strictly limit the information that can be shared). Participating countries will try to pass laws adopting the guidelines. For example, in the United States, which has the most victims of cross-border fraud, a pending bill in Congress would give the FTC new authority to prosecute cross-border fraud.

Sources: Compiled from Davidson (2003), from *ftc.org*, and a news item in *South China Morning Post* (Hong Kong, May 21, 1999).

Programming attack is popular with computer criminals who use *programming techniques* to modify a computer program, either directly or indirectly. For this crime, programming skills and knowledge of the targeted systems are essential. *Programming attacks* appear under many names, as shown in

TABLE 15.3 Methods of Programming Attack on Computer Systems

Method	Definition
Virus	Secret instructions inserted into programs (or data) that are innocently run during ordinary tasks. The secret instructions may destroy or alter data, as well as spread within or between computer systems.
Worm	A program that replicates itself and penetrates a valid computer system. It may spread within a network, penetrating all connected computers.
Trojan horse	An illegal program, contained within another program, that "sleeps" until some specific event occurs, then triggers the illegal program to be activated and cause damage.
Salami slicing	A program designed to siphon off small amounts of money from a number of larger transactions, so the quantity taken is not readily apparent.
Superzapping	A method of using a utility "zap" program that can bypass controls to modify programs or data.
Trap door	A technique that allows for breaking into a program code, making it possible to insert additional instructions.
Logic bomb	An instruction that triggers a delayed malicious act.
Denial of service	Too many requests for service, which crashes a Web site.
Sniffer	A program that searches for passwords or content in a packet of data as they pass through the Internet.
Spoofing	Faking an e-mail address or Web page to trick users to provide information or send money.
Password cracker	A password that tries to guess passwords (can be very successful).
War dialing	Programs that automatically dial thousands of telephone numbers in an attempt to identify one authorized to make a connection with a modem; then someone can use that connection to break into databases and systems.
Back doors	Invaders to a system create several entry points; even if you discover and close one, they can still get in through others.
Malicious applets	Small Java programs that misuse your computer resources, modify your file, send fake e-mail, etc.

Table 15.3. Several of the methods were designed for Web-based systems. Viruses merit special discussion here, due to their frequency, as do denial of service attacks, due to the effects they have had on computer networks.

VIRUSES. The most publicized and most common attack method is the **virus.** It receives its name from the program's ability to attach itself to ("infect") other computer programs, without the owner of the program being aware of the infection (see Figure 15.2). When the software is used, the virus spreads, causing damage to that program and possibly to others.

According to Bruno (2002), 93 percent of all companies experienced virus attacks in 2001, with an average loss of $243,845 per company. A virus can spread throughout a computer system very quickly. Due to the availability of public-domain software, widely used telecommunications networks, and the Internet, viruses can also spread to many organizations around the world, as shown in the incidents listed earlier. Some of the most notorious viruses are "international," such as Michelangelo, Pakistani Brain, Chernobyl, and Jerusalem. (For the history of viruses and how to fight them, see Zetter and Miastkowski, 2000.)

When a virus is attached to a legitimate software program, the legitimate software is acting as a **Trojan horse,** a program that contains a hidden function that presents a security risk. The name is derived from the Trojan horse in

Just as a biological virus disrupts living cells to cause disease, a computer virus—introduced maliciously—invades the inner workings of computers and disrupts normal operations of the machines.

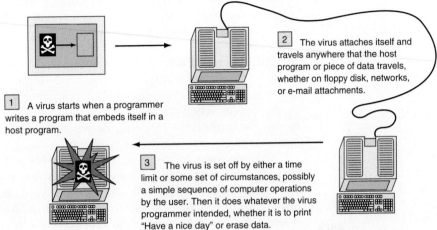

2 The virus attaches itself and travels anywhere that the host program or piece of data travels, whether on floppy disk, networks, or e-mail attachments.

1 A virus starts when a programmer writes a program that embeds itself in a host program.

3 The virus is set off by either a time limit or some set of circumstances, possibly a simple sequence of computer operations by the user. Then it does whatever the virus programmer intended, whether it is to print "Have a nice day" or erase data.

FIGURE 15.2 How a computer virus can spread.

Greek legend. The Trojan horse programs that present the greatest danger are those that make it possible for someone else to access and control a person's computer over the Internet.

We'll look at viruses and how to fight them later in the chapter, when we describe security on networks.

DENIAL OF SERVICE.   The opening case of this chapter described a denial of service incident. In a **denial-of-service (DoS)** attack, an attacker uses specialized software to send a flood of data packets to the target computer, with the aim of overloading its resources. Many attackers rely on software that has been created by other hackers and made available free over the Internet.

With a **distributed denial of service (DDoS)** attack, the attacker gains illegal administrative access to computers on the Internet. With access to a large number of computers, the attacker loads the specialized DDoS software onto these computers. The software lies in wait for a command to begin the attack. When the command is given, the distributed network of computers begins sending out requests to one or more target computers. The requests can be legitimate queries for information or can be very specialized computer commands designed to overwhelm specific computer resources.

The machines on which DDoS software is loaded are known as **zombies** (Karagiannis, 2003). Zombies are often located at university and government sites. Increasingly, with the rise of cable modems and DSL modems, home computers that are connected to the Internet and left on all the time have become good zombie candidates.

DoS attacks are not new. In 1996, a New York Internet service provider had service disrupted for over a week by a DoS attack, denying service to over 6,000 users and 1,000 companies. A recent example of a DoS attack is the one on RIAA (Recording Industry Association of America) whose site (*riaa.org*) was rendered largely unavailable for a week starting January 24, 2003. The attack was done mainly by those who did not like the RIAA's attempts to fight pirated music done by file sharing. Due to the widespread availability of free intrusion tools and scripts and the overall interconnectivity on the Internet, the intruder population now consists of virtually anyone with minimal computer experience (often a teenager with time on his hands). Unfortunately, a successful DoS attack can literally threaten the survival of an EC site, especially for SMEs.

ATTACKS VIA MODEMS. In many companies employees who are on the road use modems for dial-in access to the company intranet. Two types of modems exist: authorized and not authorized (known as *rogue modems*). The latter are installed by employees when there are no authorized modems, when it is inconvenient to use the authorized modems, or when the authorized modems provide only limited access.

Modems are very risky. It is quite easy for attackers to penetrate them, and it is easy for employees to leak secret corporate information to external networks via rogue modems. In addition, software problems may develop, such as downloading programs with viruses or with a "back door" to the system. Back doors are created by hackers to repenetrate a system, once a successful penetration is made. For ways to protect systems that use modems, see White (1999).

15.4 PROTECTING INFORMATION RESOURCES: FROM NATIONAL TO ORGANIZATIONAL EFFORTS

Organizations and individuals can protect their systems in many ways. Let's look first at what protections the national efforts can provide. Then we will look at what organizations can do to protect information resources.

Representative Federal Laws Dealing with Computer Crime and Security

A "crime" means breaching the law. In addition to breaking regular law related to physically stealing computers or conducting fraud, computer criminals may break the specially legislated computer crime laws. According to the FBI, an average robbery involves about $3,000; an average white-collar crime involves $23,000; but an average computer crime involves about $600,000. Table 15.4 lists some key U.S. federal statutes dealing with computer crime. (For more on these laws, see *epic.org/security.*)

Legislation can be helpful but not sufficient. Therefore, the FBI has formed the *National Infrastructure Protection Center (NIPC)*. This joint partnership between government and private industry is designed to protect the nation's infrastructure—its telecommunications, energy, transportation, banking and finance, emergency, and governmental operations. The FBI has also established *Regional Computer Intrusion Squads,* which are charged with the task of investigating violations of the Computer Fraud and Abuse Act. The squads' activities are focused on intrusions to public switched networks, major computer network intrusions, privacy violations, industrial espionage, pirated computer software, and other cybercrimes.

Another national organization is the *Computer Emergency Response Team (CERT)* at Carnegie Mellon University (*cert.org*). The CERT Coordination Center (CC) consists of three teams: the Incident Handling Team, the Vulnerability Handling Team, and the Artifact Analysis Team. The Incident Handling Team receives incident reports of cyberattacks from Internet sites and provides information and

TABLE 15.4 Key U.S. Federal Statutes Dealing with Computer Crime

Federal Statute	Key Provisions
Privacy Act of 1974	Prohibits the government from collecting information secretly. Information must be used only for a specific purpose.
Counterfeit Access Device and Computer Crime Control Act (passed in October 1984)	Prohibits fraud in online transactions.
Computer Fraud and Abuse Act (1986), 18 USC, section 1030	Prohibits unauthorized access to computer systems.
Electronic Communications Privacy Act of 1986	Prohibits interception of private e-mail without a court order.
Computer Security Act of 1987	Requires security of information of individuals.
Video Privacy Protection Act of 1988	Protects privacy in transmission of pictures.
Computer Abuse Amendment Act of 1994	Prohibits knowing transmission of computer viruses.
National Information Infrastructure Protection Act of 1996	Protects proprietary economic information.
Gramm-Leach-Bliley Act of 1999	Specific when a financial institution must give notice to a customer that their personal information has been accessed.

guidance to the Internet community on combating reported incidents. The Vulnerability Handling Team receives reports on suspected computer and network vulnerabilities, verifies and analyzes the reports, and works with the Internet community to understand and develop countermeasures to those vulnerabilities. The Artifacts Analysis Team focuses on the code used to carry out cyberattacks (e.g., computer viruses), analyzing the code and finding ways to combat it.

Organizing for Information Security

Information security problems are increasing rapidly, causing damages to many organizations. Protection is expensive and complex. Therefore, companies must not only use controls to prevent or detect security problems, they must do so in an organized way, assigning responsibilities and authority throughout the organization (e.g., see Talleur, 2001 and Atlas and Young, 2002). Any program that is adopted must be supported by three organizational components: people, technology, and process (see Doughty, 2003).

One way to approach the problem of organizing for security is similar to the familiar total quality management approach—namely, recognizing the importance of a corporatewide security program, which will deal with all kinds of security issues, including protecting the information assets. Doll et al. (2003) present this approach as having six major characteristics:

- *Aligned.* The program must be aligned with the organizational goals.
- *Enterprisewide.* Everyone in the organization must be included in the security program.

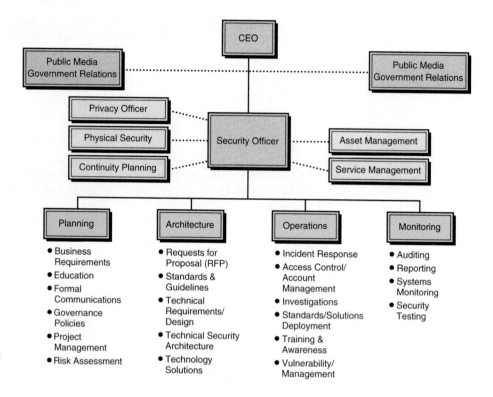

FIGURE 15.3 Corporate security plan. (*Source:* Doll et al., 2003.)

- *Continuous.* The program must be operational all the time.
- *Proactive.* Do not wait for trouble; be aware and ready; use innovative, preventive, and protective measures.
- *Validated.* The program must be tested and validated to ensure it works.
- *Formal.* It must be a formal program with authority, responsibility, and accountability.

A corporate security model proposed by Doll et al. (2003) is illustrated in Figure 15.3. Obviously, only very large organizations can afford such a comprehensive security structure. We will present several of the components and concepts in the figure in the remaining portions of this chapter. A case study for implementing enterprise security is provided by Doughty (2003). A major issue is the role the person responsible for security (the chief security officer) is going to assume (see Robinson, 2003).

Controls and Awareness

Knowing about major potential threats to information systems is necessary, but understanding ways to defend against these threats is equally critical (see *cert.org* and *sans.com*). Defending information resources is not a simple or inexpensive task. The major difficulties of protecting information are listed in Table 15.5. Because of its importance to the entire enterprise, organizing an appropriate defense system is one of the major activities of any prudent CIO and of the functional managers who control information resources. As a matter of fact, IT security is the business of *everyone* in an organization (see Pooley, 2002).

Protection of information resources is accomplished mostly by inserting *controls* (defense mechanisms) intended to prevent accidental hazards, deter

TABLE 15.5 The Difficulties in Protecting Information Resources

- Hundreds of potential threats exist.
- Computing resources may be situated in many locations.
- Many individuals control information assets.
- Computer networks can be outside the organization and difficult to protect.
- Rapid technological changes make some controls obsolete as soon as they are installed.
- Many computer crimes are undetected for a long period of time, so it is difficult to learn from experience.
- People tend to violate security procedures because the procedures are inconvenient.
- Many computer criminals who are caught go unpunished, so there is no deterrent effect.
- The amount of computer knowledge necessary to commit computer crimes is usually minimal. As a matter of fact, one can learn hacking, for free, on the Internet.
- The cost of preventing hazards can be very high. Therefore, most organizations simply cannot afford to protect against all possible hazards.
- It is difficult to conduct a cost-benefit justification for controls before an attack occurs since it is difficult to assess the value of a hypothetical attack.

intentional acts, detect problems as early as possible, enhance damage recovery, and correct problems. Controls can be integrated into hardware and software during the system development phase (the most efficient approach). They can also be added on once the system is in operation, or during its maintenance. The important point is that defense should stress *prevention*; defense does no good *after the crime*.

In addition to controls a good defense system must include security *awareness*. All organizational members must be aware of security threats and watch for potential problems and crimes constantly. Suggestions of how to develop such programs are offered by security consultants (e.g., see Wiederkehr, 2003). Awareness training is recommended by Talleur (2001).

Since there are many security threats, there are also many defense mechanisms. Controls are designed to protect all the components of an information system, specifically data, software, hardware, and networks. In the next section, we describe the major defense strategies.

Defense Strategy: How Do We Protect?

The selection of a specific defense strategy depends on the objective of the defense and on the perceived cost-benefit. The following are the major objectives of *defense strategies:*

1. *Prevention and deterrence.* Properly designed controls may prevent errors from occurring, deter criminals from attacking the system, and better yet, deny access to unauthorized people. Prevention and deterrence are especially important where the potential damage is very high (see Scalet, 2003).

2. *Detection.* It may not be economically feasible to prevent all hazards, and deterrence measures may not work. Therefore, unprotected systems are vulnerable to attack. Like a fire, the earlier an attack is detected, the easier it is to combat, and the less damage is done. Detection can be performed in many cases by using special diagnostic software.

3. *Limitation of damage.* This strategy is to minimize (limit) losses once a malfunction has occurred. This can be accomplished by including a *fault-tolerant system* that permits operation in a degraded mode until full recovery is made. If a fault-tolerant system does not exist, a quick (and possibly expensive) recovery must take place. Users want their systems back in operation as fast as possible.

4. *Recovery.* A recovery plan explains how to fix a damaged information system as quickly as possible. Replacing rather than repairing components is one route to fast recovery.

5. *Correction.* Correcting the causes of damaged systems can prevent the problem from occurring again.

6. *Awareness and compliance.* All organization members must be educated about the hazards and must comply with the security rules and regulations.

Any defense strategy that aims to attain one or more of these objectives may involve the use of several controls. The defense controls are divided in our discussion into two major categories: *general controls* and *application controls.* Each has several subcategories, as shown in Figure 15.4. **General controls** are established to protect the system regardless of the specific application. For example, protecting hardware and controlling access to the data center are independent of the specific application. **Application controls** are safeguards that are intended to protect specific applications. In the next two sections, we discuss the major types of these two groups of information systems controls.

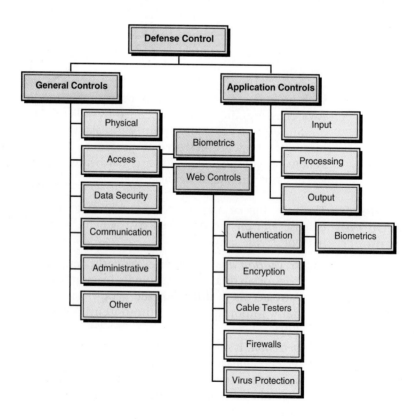

FIGURE 15.4 Major defense controls.

General Controls   The major categories of general controls are physical controls, access controls, data security controls, communications (networks) controls, and administrative controls.

PHYSICAL CONTROLS.   Physical security refers to the protection of computer facilities and resources. This includes protecting physical property such as computers, data centers, software, manuals, and networks. Physical security is the first line of defense and usually the easiest to construct. It provides protection against most natural hazards as well as against some human hazards. Appropriate physical security may include several controls such as the following:

- Appropriate design of the data center. For example, the site should be noncombustible and waterproof.
- Shielding against electromagnetic fields.
- Good fire prevention, detection, and extinguishing systems, including sprinkler system, water pumps, and adequate drainage facilities. A better solution is fire-enveloping Halon gas systems.
- Emergency power shutoff and backup batteries, which must be maintained in operational condition.
- Properly designed, maintained, and operated air-conditioning systems.
- Motion detector alarms that detect physical intrusion.

Another example of physical controls is the need to protect against theft of mobile computers. Such protection is important not only because of the loss of the computer but also because of loss of data. Several interesting protection devices are offered by *targus.com*.

ACCESS CONTROL.   Access control is the restriction of unauthorized user access to a portion of a computer system or to the entire system. It is the major defence line against unauthorized insiders as well as outsiders. To gain access, a user must first be *authorized*. Then, when the user attempts to gain access, he or she must be *authenticated*.

Access to a computer system basically consists of three steps: (1) physical access to a terminal, (2) access to the system, and (3) access to specific commands, transactions, privileges, programs, and data within the system. Access control software is commercially available for large mainframes, personal computers, local area networks, mobile devices, and dial-in communications networks. Access control to *networks* is executed through firewalls and will be discussed later.

Access procedures match every valid user with a *unique user-identifier (UID)*. They also provide an authentication method to verify that users requesting access to the computer system are really who they claim to be. User identification can be accomplished when the following identifies each user:

- Something only the user *knows*, such as a password.
- Something only the user *has*, for example, a smart card or a token.
- Something only the user *is*, such as a signature, voice, fingerprint, or retinal (eye) scan. It is implemented via *biometric controls*, which can be physiological or behavioral (see Alga, 2002) and whose cost is relativly very small.

Biometric Controls. A **biometric control** is an automated method of verifying the identity of a person, based on physiological or behavioral characteristics. The most common biometrics are the following:

- *Photo of face.* The computer takes a picture of your face and matches it with a prestored picture. In 2002, this method was successful in correctly identifying users except in cases of identical twins.

- *Fingerprints.* Each time a user wants access, a fingerprint (finger scan) is matched against a template containing the authorized person's fingerprint to identify him or her. Note that in 2001 Microsoft introduced a software program, now a part of Windows, that allows users to use Sony's fingerprint recognition device. Computer manufacturers will start shipping laptops secured by fingerprint-scanning touchpads in 2004. These devices will reject unauthorized access (see *synaptics.com*).

- *Hand geometry.* This biometric is similar to fingerprints except that the verifier uses a television-like camera to take a picture of the user's hand. Certain characteristics of the hand (e.g., finger length and thickness) are electronically compared against the information stored in the computer.

- *Iris scan.* This technology uses the colored portion of the eye to identify individuals (see *iriscan.com*). It is a noninvasive system that takes a photo of the eye and analyzes it and is a very accurate method.

- *Retinal scan.* A match is attempted between the pattern of the blood vessels in the back-of-the-eye retina that is being scanned and a prestored picture of the retina.

- *Voice scan.* A match is attempted between the user's voice and the voice pattern stored on templates.

- *Signature.* Signatures are matched against the prestored authentic signature. This method can supplement a photo-card ID system.

- *Keystroke dynamics.* A match of the person's keyboard pressure and speed is made against prestored information.

Several other methods, such as *facial thermography,* exist.

Biometric controls are now integrated into many e-commerce hardware and software products (e.g., see *keywaretechnologies.com*). For an overview and comparison of technologies, see Jain et al. (1999 and 2000) and Alga (2002). Biometric controls do have some limitations: they are not accurate in certain cases, and some people see them as an invasion of privacy (see Caulfield, 2002).

DATA SECURITY CONTROLS. Data security is concerned with protecting data from accidental or intentional disclosure to unauthorized persons, or from unauthorized modification or destruction. Data security functions are implemented through operating systems, security access control programs, database/data communications products, recommended backup/recovery procedures, application programs, and external control procedures. Data security must address the following issues: confidentiality of data, access control, critical nature of data, and integrity of data.

Two basic principles should be reflected in data security.

- *Minimal privilege.* Only the information a user needs to carry out an assigned task should be made available to him or her.

> **TABLE 15.6** Representative Administrative Controls
>
> - Appropriately selecting, training, and supervising employees, especially in accounting and information systems
> - Fostering company loyalty
> - Immediately revoking access privileges of dismissed, resigned, or transferred employees
> - Requiring periodic modification of access controls (such as passwords)
> - Developing programming and documentation standards (to make auditing easier and to use the standards as guides for employees)
> - Insisting on security bonds or malfeasance insurance for key employees
> - Instituting separation of duties, namely dividing sensitive computer duties among as many employees as economically feasible in order to decrease the chance of intentional or unintentional damage
> - Holding periodic random audits of the system

- *Minimal exposure.* Once a user gains access to sensitive information, he or she has the responsibility of protecting it by making sure only people whose duties require it obtain knowledge of this information while it is processed, stored, or in transit.

Data integrity is the condition that exists as long as accidental or intentional destruction, alteration, or loss of data *does not* occur. It is the preservation of data for their intended use.

COMMUNICATIONS AND NETWORK CONTROLS. Network protection is becoming extremely important as the use of the Internet, intranets, and electronic commerce increases. We will discuss this topic in more detail in Section 15.5.

ADMINISTRATIVE CONTROLS. While the previously discussed general controls were technical in nature, administrative controls deal with issuing guidelines and monitoring compliance with the guidelines. Representative examples of such controls are shown in Table 15.6.

OTHER GENERAL CONTROLS. Several other types of controls are considered general. Representative examples include the following:

Programming Controls. Errors in programming may result in costly problems. Causes include the use of incorrect algorithms or programming instructions, carelessness, inadequate testing and configuration management, or lax security. Controls include training, establishing standards for testing and configuration management, and enforcing documentation standards.

Documentation Controls. Manuals are often a source of problems because they are difficult to interpret or may be out of date. Accurate writing, standardization updating, and testing are examples of appropriate documentation controls. Intelligent agents can be used to prevent documentation problems.

System Development Controls. System development controls ensure that a system is developed according to established policies and procedures. Conformity with budget, timing, security measures, and quality and documentation requirements must be maintained.

Application Controls

General controls are intended to protect the computing facilities and provide security for hardware, software, data, and networks regardless of the specific application. However, general controls do not protect the *content* of each specific application. Therefore, controls are frequently built into the applications (that is, they are part of the software) and are usually written as validation rules. They can be classified into three major categories: *input controls, processing controls,* and *output controls.* Multiple types of application controls can be used, and management should decide on the appropriate mix of controls.

INPUT CONTROLS. Input controls are designed to prevent data alteration or loss. Data are checked for accuracy, completeness, and consistency. Input controls are very important; they prevent the GIGO (garbage-in, garbage-out) situation.

Four examples of input controls are:

1. *Completeness.* Items should be of a specific length (e.g., nine digits for a Social Security number). Addresses should include a street, city, state, and Zip code.
2. *Format.* Formats should be in standard form. For example, sequences must be preserved (e.g., Zip code comes after an address).
3. *Range.* Only data within a specified range are acceptable. For example, Zip code ranges between 00000 to 99999; the age of a person cannot be larger than say, 120; and hourly wages at the firm do not exceed $50.
4. *Consistency.* Data collected from two or more sources need to be matched. For example, in medical history data, males cannot be pregnant.

PROCESSING CONTROLS. Processing controls ensure that data are complete, valid, and accurate when being processed and that programs have been properly executed. These programs allow only authorized users to access certain programs or facilities and monitor the computer's use by individuals.

OUTPUT CONTROLS. Output controls ensure that the results of computer processing are accurate, valid, complete, and consistent. By studying the nature of common output errors and the causes of such errors, security and audit staff can evaluate possible controls to deal with problems. Also, output controls ensure that outputs are sent only to authorized personnel.

15.5 SECURING THE WEB, INTRANETS, AND WIRELESS NETWORKS

Some of the incidents described in Section 15.3 point to the vulnerability of the Internet and Web sites (see Sivasailam et al., 2002). As a matter of fact, the more networked the world becomes, the more security problems we may have. Security is a race between "lock makers" and "lock pickers." Unless the lock makers have the upper hand, the future of the Internet's credibility and of e-business is in danger.

Over the Internet, messages are sent from one computer to another (rather than from one network to the other). This makes the network difficult to protect, since at many points people can tap into the network and the users may never know that a breach had occurred. For a list of techniques attackers can

TABLE 15.7 Attacking Web Applications

Category	Description
SQL injection	Passing SQL code into an application that was not intended to receive it
Parameter tampering	Manipulating URL strings to retrieve information
Cookie poisoning	Altering the content of a cookie
Hidden manipulation	Changing hidden field values
Backdoor and debug options	Executing debug syntax on URLs
Buffer overflow	Sending large numbers of characters to a Web site form/field
Stealth commanding	Attempting to inject Trojan horses in form submissions and run malicious or unauthorized code on the Web server
Third-party misconfiguration	Attempting to find programming errors and exploit them to attack system vulnerabilities
Known vulnerability	Exploiting all publicly known vulnerabilities
Cross-site scripting	Entering executable commands into Web site buffers
Forceful browsing	Attempting to browse know/default directories that can be used in constructing an attack

Source: Modified from Stasiak (2002), Table 2.

use to compromise Web applications, in addition to what was described in Section 15.3, see Table 15.7. The table covers the major security measures of the Internet. Security issues regarding e-business are discussed in Chapters 5 and 6.

McConnell (2002) divides Internet security measures into three layers: *border security* (access), *authentication,* and *authorization.* Details of these layers are shown in Figure 15.5. Several of these are discussed in some detail in the remainder of this chapter. Some commercial products include security measures for all three levels—all in one product (e.g., WebShield from McAfee, and Firewall/VPN Appliance from Symantec).

Many security methods and products are available to protect the Web. We briefly describe the major ones in the following sections.

Border Security   The major objective of border security is access control, as seen in Figure 15.5. Several tools are available. First we consider firewalls.

FIREWALLS.   Hacking is a growing phenomenon. Even the Pentagon's system, considered a very secure system, experiences more than 250,000 hacker infiltrations per year, many of which are undetected (*Los Angeles Times,* 1998). It is

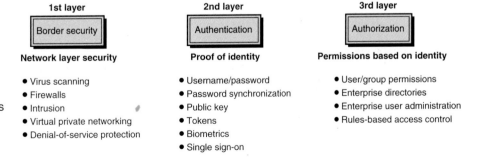

FIGURE 15.5 Three layers of Internet security measures. (*Source:* McConnell, 2002.)

believed that hacking costs U.S. industry several billion dollars each year. Hacking is such a popular activity that over 80,000 Web sites are dedicated to it. Firewalls provide the most cost-effective solution against hacking (see Fadia, 2002).

A **firewall** is a system, or group of systems, that enforces an access-control policy between two networks. It is commonly used as a barrier between a secure corporate intranet or other internal networks and the Internet, which is assumed to be unsecured.

Firewalls are used to implement control-access policies. The firewall follows strict guidelines that either permit or block traffic; therefore, a successful firewall is designed with clear and specific rules about what can pass through. Several firewalls may exist in one information system.

Firewalls are also used as a place to store public information. While visitors may be blocked from entering the company networks, they can obtain information about products and services, download files and bug-fixes, and so forth. Useful as they are, firewalls do not stop viruses that may be lurking in networks. Viruses can pass through the firewalls, usually hidden in an e-mail attachment.

VIRUS CONTROLS. Many viruses exist (about 100,000 known in 2003) and the number is growing by 30 percent a year according to the International Computer Security Association (reported by *statonline*, 2003). So the question is, What can organizations do to protect themselves against viruses? Some solutions against virus penetrations are provided in Zenkin (2001) and in Table 15.8. The most common solution is to use antivirus software (e.g., from *symantec.com*). However, antivirus software provides protection against viruses only after they have attacked someone and their properties are known. New viruses are difficult to detect in their first attack.

The best protection against viruses is to have a comprehensive plan such as shown in *A Closer Look 15.3*.

INTRUSION DETECTING. Because protection against denial of service (see the opening vignette) is difficult, the sooner one can detect an usual activity, the better. Therefore, it is worthwhile to place an *intrusion detecting* device near the

---

TABLE 15.8 Protecting Against Viruses

Possible Mode of Entrance	Countermeasure
• Viruses pass through firewalls undetected (from the Internet).	• User must screen all downloaded programs and documents before use.
• Virus may be resident on networked server; all users are at risk.	• Run virus scan daily; do comprehensive backup to restore data; maintain audit trail.
• Infected floppy; local server system at risk; files shared or put on server can spread virus.	• Use virus checker to screen floppies locally.
• Mobile or remote users exchange or update large amounts of data; risk of infection is greater.	• Scan files before upload or after download; make frequent backups.
• Virus already detected.	• Use a clean starter disk or recovery disk.

Source: Compiled from Nance (1996, updated 2003), p. 171.

A CLOSER LOOK
15.3 HOW TO MINIMIZE THE DAMAGE FROM VIRUSES

To minimize the damage from viruses, take the following preventive actions:

1. Install a good antivirus program. These are also known as *gateway virus scanners* (e.g., Norton AntiVirus, McAfee VirusScan).
2. Scan the hard drive for viruses at least weekly.
3. Write-protect your floppy disks and scan them before using them.
4. Write-protect your program disks.
5. Back up data fully and frequently.
6. Don't trust outside PCs.
7. Virus scan before "laplinking" or synchronizing files.
8. Develop an antivirus policy.
9. Identify the areas of risk in case of virus attack. These are:
    a. Direct losses (e.g., time spent to restore systems)
    b. Losses your customers and suppliers suffer when your system is down
    c. Losses to a third party to which your company had passed on a virus, possibly due to your employees' negligence
10. Minimize losses by the following measures:
    a. Install strict employee guidelines dealing with e-mail viruses.
    b. Use a service provider to handle virus detection and control. This way you get the latest technology, make it more difficult for insiders to perform crimes, and may transfer the risk to the service provider.
    c. Have contracts that will protect you from a legal action by your customers/suppliers who suffer damage when your systems are damaged (called a "force majeure" clause).
    d. Instruct your employees on how to scan all outgoing e-mails to your business partners.
11. The SANS Institute (*sans.org*) is an IT cooperative research and education organization for system administrators and security professionals; it has more than 96,000 members. SANS recommends the following guidelines for action during virus attacks:
    a. *Preparation.* Establish policy, design a form to be filed when a virus is suspected (or known), and develop outside relationships.
    b. *Identification.* Collect evidence of attack, analyze it, notify officals (e.g., at *cert.org*).
    c. *Containment.* Back up the system to capture evidence, change passwords, determine the risk of continuing operations.
    d. *Eradication.* Determine and remove the cause, and improve the defense.
    e. *Recovery.* Restore and validate the system.
    f. *Follow up.* Write a follow-up report detailing lessons learned.
12. Get information and sometimes free software at the following sites:

antivirus.com	*cert.org*	*pgp.com*
symantec.com	*ncsa.com*	*rsa.com*
mcafee.com	*iss.net*	*tis.com*

entrance point of the Internet to the intranet (close to a firewall). The objective is early detection, and this can be done by several devices (e.g., BladeRunner from Raytheon, Praesidium from HP, Caddx from Caddx Controls, and IDS from Cisco). Intrusion detecting is done by different tools, such as statistical analysis or neural networks. Biermann et al. (2001) provide a comparison of 10 different methods and discuss which methods are better at detecting different types of intrusions.

PROTECTING AGAINST DENIAL OF SERVICE ATTACKS. After the February 6, 2000, DoS attack, the industry started to find solutions. A special task force of experts was formed at the Internet Engineering Task Force (IETF); it included vendors and companies that were attacked. The IETF group developed procedures on what to do in the event of such attack. One approach suggested was tracking the attacker in real time (e.g., by tracking the flow of data packets through the Net).

Automated Attack Traceback. Investigation to find attackers can be done manually or can be automated. **Attack traceback** refers to a system that would identify the person responsible for a virus, DoS, or other attacks. For example, it would identify the computer host that is the source of the attack. Attackers usually try to hide their identity. The automatic traceback attempts to circumvent the methods used by attackers (such as zombies, discussed earlier). According to Lee and Shields (2002), however, the use of automatic attack traceback programs may raise legal issues (e.g., what data you can legally track).

VIRTUAL PRIVATE NETWORKING (VPN). The last major method of border security is a virtual private network (VPN). A VPN uses the Internet to carry information within a company that has multiple sites and among known business partners, but it increases the security of the Internet by using a combination of encryption, authentication, and access control. It replaces the traditional private leased line and/or remote access server (RAS) that provide direct communication to a company's LAN (see Technology Guide 4). According to Prometheum Technologies (2003), costs can be reduced by up to 50 percent by using the VPN, which can also be used by remote workers (here the savings can reach 60–80 percent). Confidentiality and integrity are assured by the use of protocol tunneling for the encryption (McKinley 2003). For further details on VPNs, see Garfinkel (2002), Fadia (2002), and McKinley (2003).

Authentication

As applied to the Internet, an authentication system guards against unauthorized dial-in attempts. Many companies use an access protection strategy that requires authorized users to dial in with a preassigned personal identification number (PIN). This strategy is usually enhanced by a unique and frequently changing password. A communications access control system authenticates the user's PIN and password. Some security systems proceed one step further, accepting calls only from designated telephone numbers. Access controls also include biometrics.

HOW AUTHENTICATION WORKS. The major objective of authentication is the proof of identity (see Figure 15.5). The attempt here is to identify the legitimate user and determine the action he or she is allowed to perform, and also to find those posing as others. Such programs also can be combined with authorization, to limit the actions of people to what they are authorized to do with the computer once their identification has been authenticated.

Authentication systems have five key elements (Smith, 2002): (1) a person (or a group) to be authenticated; (2) a distinguishing characteristic that differentiates the person (group) from others; (3) a proprietor responsible for the system being used; (4) an authentication mechanism; and (5) an access control mechanism for limiting the actions that can be performed by the authenticated person (group).

A stronger system is *two-factor-authentication,* which combines something one knows (password, answer to a query) with something one has (tokens, biometrics). An access card is an example of a passive token, carried to enter into certain rooms or to gain access to a network. *Active tokens* are electronic devices that can generate a one-time password after being activated with a PIN. Note that public key systems (PKI, see Chapter 5) include an authentication feature.

Authorization

Authorization refers to permission issued to individuals or groups to do certain activities with a computer, usually based on verified identity. The security system, once it authenticates the user, must make sure that the user operates within his or her authorized activities. This is usually done by monitoring user activities and comparing them to the list of authorized ones.

Other Methods of Protection

Other methods of protecting the Web and intranets include the following.

ENCRYPTION.   As discussed in Chapter 5, **encryption** encodes regular digitized text into unreadable scrambled text or numbers, which are decoded upon receipt. Encryption accomplishes three purposes: (1) identification (helps identify legitimate senders and receivers), (2) control (prevents changing a transaction or message), and (3) privacy (impedes eavesdropping). Encryption is used extensively in e-commerce for protecting payments and for privacy.

A widely accepted encryption algorithm is the Data Encryption Standard (DES), produced by the U.S. National Bureau of Standards. Many software products also are available for encryption. *Traffic padding* can further enhance encryption. Here a computer generates random data that are intermingled with real data, making it virtually impossible for an intruder to identify the true data.

To ensure secure transactions on the Internet, VeriSign and VISA developed encrypted digital certification systems for credit cards. These systems allow customers to make purchases on the Internet without giving their credit card number. Cardholders create a digital version of their credit card, called *virtual credit card* (see Chapter 5), VeriSign confirms validity of the buyer's credit card, and then it issues a certificate to that effect. Even the merchants do not see the credit card number. For further discussion of encryption, see *sra.co* and *verisign.com*.

TROUBLESHOOTING.   A popular defense of local area networks (LANs) is troubleshooting. For example, a *cable tester* can find almost any fault that can occur with LAN cabling. Another protection can be provided by *protocol analyzers*, which allow the user to inspect the contents of information packets as they travel through the network. Recent analyzers use *expert systems*, which interpret the volume of data collected by the analyzers. Some companies offer integrated LAN troubleshooting (a tester and an intelligent analyzer).

PAYLOAD SECURITY.   *Payload security* involves encryption or other manipulation of data being sent over networks. *Payload* refers to the contents of messages and communication services among dispersed users. An example of payload security is Pretty Good Privacy (PGP), which permits users to inexpensively create and encrypt a message. (See *pgp.com* for free software.)

HONEYNETS. Companies can trap hackers by watching what the hackers are doing. These traps are referred to as **honeypots;** they are traps designed to work like real systems but to attract hackers. A network of honeypots is called a **honeynet.** For details, see Piazza (2001) and *honeynet.org.*

Securing Your PC

Your PC at home is connected to the Internet and needs to be protected (Luhn and Spanbauer, 2002). Therefore, solutions such as antivirus software (e.g., Norton Antivirus 2002) and a personal firewall are essential. (You can get a free Internet connection firewall with Microsoft Windows or pay $30–$50 for products such as McAfee Firewall.)

If you use a gateway or router at home, you need to protect it as well, if it does not have built-in protection. You need protection against stealthware as well. **Stealthware** refers to hidden programs that come with free software you download. These programs track your surfing activities, reporting them to a marketing server. Programs such as Pest Control and Spy Blocker can help. Finally you need an antispam tool (e.g., SpamKiller).

All of the tools just mentioned can be combined in suites (e.g., Internet Security from McAFee or Symantec).

Securing Wireless Networks

Wireless networks are more difficult to protect than wireline ones. While many of the risks of desktop Internet-based commerce will pervade m-commerce, m-commerce itself presents new risks. This topic was discussed in Chapter 6. In addition, lately there is recognition that malicious code may penetrate wireless networks. Such a code has the ability to undermine controls such as authentication and encryption (Ghosh and Swaminatha, 2001 and Biery and Hager, 2001). For a comprehensive commercial suite to protect wireless networks, see MebiusGuard at *symbal.com.*

Summary

It should be clear from this chapter how important it is for organizations to secure networks. What protective measures actually employ? What security technologies are used the most? According to the CSI/FBI report (Richardson, 2003), 99 percent of all companies use anti-virus software, 92 percent use access control, 98 percent use firewalls, 91 percent use physical security, 73 percent use intrusion detection, 69 percent use encrypted files, 58 percent use encrypted login, 47 percent use reusable passwords, and only 11 percent use biometrics. While some measures are commonly used, others, especially new ones such as biometrics, are not yet in regular use.

15.6 BUSINESS CONTINUITY AND DISASTER RECOVERY PLANNING

Disasters may occur without warning. According to Strassman (1997), the best defense is to be prepared. Therefore, an important element in any security system is the **business continuity plan,** also known as the **disaster recovery plan.** Such a plan outlines the process by which businesses should recover from a major disaster. Destruction of all (or most) of the computing facilities can cause significant damage. Therefore, it is difficult for many organizations to obtain insurance for their computers and information systems without showing a satisfactory disaster prevention and recovery plan. It is a simple

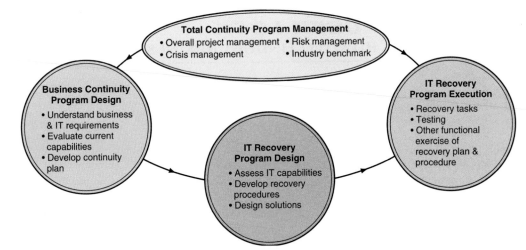

FIGURE 15.6
Business continuity services managed by IBM. (*Source:* IBM, Business Continuity and Recovery Services, January 2000, produced in Hong Kong. Courtesy of IBM.)

concept that advance crisis planning can help minimize losses (Gerber and Feldman, 2002). The comprehensiveness of a business recovery plan is shown in Figure 15.6.

Business Continuity Planning

Disaster recovery is the chain of events linking the business continuity plan to protection and to recovery. The following are some key thoughts about the process:

- The purpose of a business continuity plan is to keep the business running after a disaster occurs. Both the ISD and line management should be involved in preparation of the plan. Each function in the business should have a valid recovery capability plan.
- Recovery planning is part of *asset protection*. Every organization should assign responsibility to management to identify and protect assets within their spheres of functional control.
- Planning should focus first on recovery from a total loss of all capabilities.
- Proof of capability usually involves some kind of what-if analysis that shows that the recovery plan is current (see Lam, 2002).
- All critical applications must be identified and their recovery procedures addressed in the plan.
- The plan should be written so that it will be effective in case of disaster, not just in order to satisfy the auditors.
- The plan should be kept in a safe place; copies should be given to all key managers, or it should be available on the intranet. The plan should be audited periodically.

For a methodology of how to conduct business continuity planning, see *A Closer Look 15.4* (page 714). Other methodologies can be found in Devargas (1999) and Rothstein (2002).

Disaster recovery planning can be very complex, and it may take several months to complete (see Devargas, 1999). Using special software, the planning job can be expedited.

A CLOSER LOOK
15.4 HOW TO CONDUCT BUSINESS CONTINUITY PLANNING

There are many suggestions of how to conduct business continuity planning (BCP). Lam (2002) suggests an 8-step cyclical process shown in the figure below.

In conducting BCP one should devise a policy which is central to all steps in the process. One also must test the plan on a worst-case scenario, for each potential disaster (e.g., system failure, information hacking, terrorist attack). Disruptions are analyzed for their impact on technology, information, and people.

Finally, it is important to recognize the potential pitfalls of BCP. These include:

- An incomplete BCP (may not cover all aspects).
- An inadequate or ineffective BCP (unable to provide remedy).
- An impractical BCP (e.g., does not have enough time and money).

- Overkill BCP (usually time consuming and costly).
- Uncommunicated BCP (people do not know where to find it, or its details).
- Lacking defined process (not clearly defined, chain of needed events not clear).
- Untested (may looks good on paper, but no one knows, since it was never tested).
- Uncoordinated (it is not a team's work, or the team is not coordinated).
- Out of date (it was good long ago, but what about today?).
- Lacking in recovery thinking (no one thinks from A to Z about how to do it).

For details see Lam (2002).

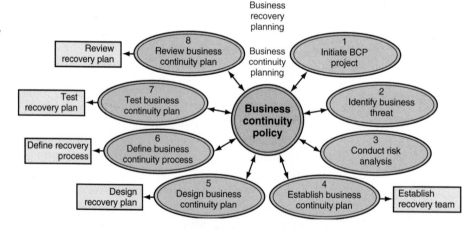

Business continuity plan. [*Source:* Lam (2001), Fig. 1.]

Backup Arrangements

One of the most logical ways to deal with loss of data is to *back them up*. A business continuity plan includes backup arrangements. Organizations should make copies of all important files and keep them separately. In addition to backing up data, organizations should be interested in quick recovery. Also, as part of business continuity one can back up an entire computer or data center. Let's look at these two arrangements.

BACKING UP DATA FILES. While everyone knows how important it is to back up data files, many neglect to do so because the process is cumbersome and time consuming. Several programs make this process easier, and some restore data as well (e.g., Ontrack.com provides EasyRecovery and File repair, 10mega.com provides QuickSync, and Officerecovery.com provides for office recovery). For tips how to avoid data loss by backing up data files, see Spector (2002). Backup arrangements may also include the use of network attached storage (NAS) and storage area networks (NAS) (see Technology Guide 4 and Hunton, 2002).

BACKING UP COMPUTER CENTERS. As preparation for a major disaster, such as in the 9/11 case, it is often necessary for an organization to have a *backup location*. External *hot-site* vendors provide access to a fully configured backup data center.

To appreciate the usefulness of a hot-site arrangement, consider the following example: On the evening of October 17, 1989, when a major earthquake hit San Francisco, Charles Schwab and Company was ready. Within a few minutes, the company's disaster plan was activated. Programmers, engineers, and backup computer tapes of October 17 transactions were flown on a chartered jet to Carlstadt, New Jersey. There, Comdisco Disaster Recovery Service provided a hot site. The next morning, the company resumed normal operations. Montgomery Securities, on the other hand, had no backup recovery arrangement. On October 18, the day after the quake, the traders had to use telephones rather than computers to execute trades. Montgomery lost revenues of $250,000 to $500,000 in one day.

A less costly alternative arrangement is external *cold-site* vendors that provide empty office space with special flooring, ventilation, and wiring. In an emergency, the stricken company moves its own (or leased) computers to the site.

One company that did its disaster planning right is Empire Blue Cross and Blue Shield, as explained in *IT at Work 15.2* (page 716).

Physical computer security is an integral part of a total security system. Cray Research, a leading manufacturer of supercomputers (now a subsidiary of Silicone Graphics, Inc.), has incorporated a corporate security plan, under which the corporate computers are automatically monitored and centrally controlled. *Graphic displays* show both normal status and disturbances. All the controlled devices are represented as icons on floor-plan graphics. These icons can change colors (e.g., green means normal, red signifies a problem). The icons can flash as well. Corrective-action messages are displayed whenever appropriate. The alarm system includes over 1,000 alarms. Operators can be alerted, even at remote locations, in less than one second.

Of special interest is disaster planning for Web-based systems, as shown in an example in Online File W15.7. For some interesting methods of recovery, see the special issue of *Computers and Security* (2000). Finally, according to Brassil (2003), mobile computing and other innovations are changing the business continuity industry by quickly reaching a large number of people, wherever they are, and by the ability of mobile devices to help in quick restoration of service.

DISASTER AVOIDANCE. **Disaster avoidance** is an approach oriented toward *prevention*. The idea is to minimize the chance of avoidable disasters (such as fire or other human-caused threats). For example, many companies use a device called *uninterrupted power supply (UPS)*, which provides power in case of a power outage.

IT at Work 15.2
9/11 DISASTER RECOVERY AT EMPIRE BLUE CROSS/BLUE SHIELD

Empire Blue Cross and Blue Shield provides health insurance coverage for 4.7 million people in the northeastern United States. It is a regional arm of the Blue Cross/Blue Shield Association (*bcbs.com*). On September 11, 2001, the company occupied an entire floor of the World Trade Center (WTC). Information assets there included the e-business development center as well as the enterprise network of 250 servers and a major Web-enabled call center. Unfortunately, nine employees and two consultants lost their lives in the terrorist attack. But, the company's operations were not interrupted. Let's see why.

The company had built redundancy into all its applications and moved much of its business to Internet technology for connecting workforce, clients, and partners. Forty applications are available on its corporate intranet; Web-enabled call centers handle 50,000 calls each day; and Web-based applications connect the huge system of hospitals and health-care providers. Michael Galvin, chief infrastructure officer of the company, evacuated his 100 employees from the thirtieth floor and tried to contact staff at other locations to initiate the disaster recovery plan. It was well over an hour later when he was finally able to get through jammed communication lines to find out that a quick decision made by a senior server specialist in Albany, NY, had already switched the employee profiles to the Albany location. This action saved the company days of downtime and the need to rebuild the

profiles by hand. As employees moved to temporary offices, they were able to log on as if they were sitting at their desks in the WTC.

The disaster recovery protocol, which is shown in the figure on page 717, worked without a glitch. Calls to the customer support center in the WTC were rerouted to centers in Albany and on Long Island; customers accessing the Web site experienced no interruptions; and 150 servers, 500 laptops, and 500 workstations were ordered within an hour of the attack. In off-facility sites, the main data center was not affected; the backup tapes allowed full restoration of data; the network restructured automatically when the private enterprise network was destroyed; and all necessary information needed at the main off-site data center was rerouted, bypassing the WTC.

Besides building in the redundancy in the system, the company had also been testing different disaster scenarios frequently, making sure everything worked. As a result, the company and the technoloy were prepared to deal with the disaster. Everything was backed up, so once the servers were rebuilt, all information was available, and all applications were functioning within days thanks to a 300-member IT team working around the clock. Three days after the attack, a new VPN was running, enabling employees to work at home.

Since that experience, Empire has made even more use of Internet technology to connect the staff that is dispersed among five temporary offices in Manhattan, and it does

(continues on page 717)

15.7 IMPLEMENTING SECURITY: AUDITING AND RISK ANALYSIS

Implementing controls in an organization can be a very complicated task, particularly in large, decentralized companies where administrative controls may be difficult to enforce. Of the many issues involved in implementing controls, three are described here: auditing information systems, risk analysis, and IT security trends, including use of advanced intelligent systems.

Controls are established to ensure that information systems work properly. Controls can be installed in the original system, or they can be added once a system is in operation. Installing controls is necessary but not sufficient. It is also necessary to answer questions such as the following: Are controls installed as intended? Are they effective? Did any breach of security occur? If so, what actions are required to prevent reoccurrence? These questions need to be answered by independent and unbiased observers. Such observers perform the information system *auditing* task.

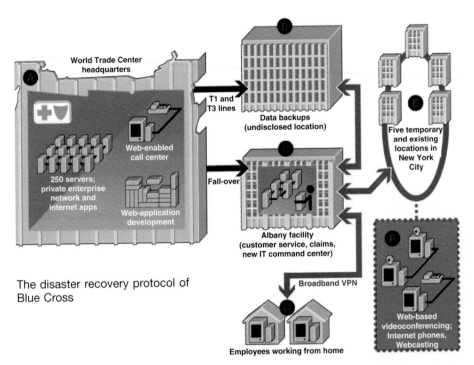

The disaster recovery protocol of Blue Cross

more business by Internet-based videoconferencing, Webcasting, and IP-based phones. The new corporate headquarters was opened in May 2003 in Brooklyn, NY.

Galvin emphasized that the most important part of this or any disaster is the people who act within minutes to get things done without direct guidance of senior management.

Source: Compiled from Levin (2002).

For Further Exploration: Explore the usefulness of Internet technology for disaster planning. What is its advantage over older technology? Why are people the most important part when a disaster strikes?

Auding Information Systems

An **audit** is an important part of any control system. In an organizational setting, it is usually referred to as a periodical *examination and check* of financial and accounting records and procedures. Specially trained professionals execute an audit. In the information system environment, auditing can be viewed as an additional layer of controls or safeguards. Auditing is considered as a deterrent to criminal actions (Wells, 2002), especially for insiders.

TYPES OF AUDITORS AND AUDITS. There are two types of auditors (and audits): internal and external. An *internal auditor* is usually a corporate employee who is not a member of the ISD.

An *external auditor* is a corporate outsider. This type of auditor reviews the findings of the internal audit and the inputs, processing, and outputs of information systems. The external audit of information systems is frequently a part of the overall external auditing performed by a certified public accounting (CPA) firm.

IT auditing can be very broad, so only its essentials are presented here. Auditing looks at all potential hazards and controls in information systems. It focuses attention on topics such as new systems development, operations and maintenance, data integrity, software application, security and privacy, disaster planning and recovery, purchasing, budgets and expenditures, chargebacks, vendor management, documentation, insurance and bonding, training, cost control, and productivity. Several guidelines are available to assist auditors in their jobs. *SAS No. 55* is a comprehensive guide provided by the American Institute of Certified Public Accountants. Also, guidelines are available from the Institute of Internal Auditors, Orlando, Florida. (See Frownfelter-Lohrke and Hunton, 2002 for a discussion of new directions in IT auditing.)

Auditors attempt to answer questions such as these:

Are there sufficient controls in the system? Which areas are not covered by controls?

Which controls are not necessary?

Are the controls implemented properly?

Are the controls effective? That is, do they check the output of the system?

Is there a clear separation of duties of employees?

Are there procedures to ensure compliance with the controls?

Are there procedures to ensure reporting and corrective actions in case of violations of controls?

Other items that IT auditors may check include: the data security policies and plans, the business continuity plan (Von-Roessing, 2002), the availability of a strategic information plan, what the company is doing to ensure compliance with security rules, the responsibilities of IT security, the measurement of success of the organization's IT security scheme, the existence of a security awareness program, and the security incidents reporting system.

Two types of audits are used to answer these questions. The *operational audit* determines whether the ISD is working properly. The *compliance audit* determines whether controls have been implemented properly and are adequate. In addition, auditing is geared specifically to general controls and to application controls (see Sayana, 2002). For details on how auditing is executed, see Online File W15.8.

AUDITING WEB SYSTEMS AND E-COMMERCE. According to Morgan and Wong (1999), auditing a Web site is a good preventive measure to manage the legal risk. Legal risk is important in any IT system, but in Web systems it is even more important due to the content of the site, which may offend people or be in violation of copyright laws or other regulations (e.g., privacy protection). Auditing EC is also more complex since in addition to the Web site one needs to audit order taking, order fulfillment, and all support systems (see Blanco, 2002). For more about IT auditing see Woda (2002).

Risk Management and Cost-Benefit Analysis

It is usually not economical to prepare protection against every possible threat. Therefore, an IT security program must provide a process for assessing threats and deciding which ones to prepare for and which ones to ignore or provide reduced protection against. Installation of control measures is based on a balance

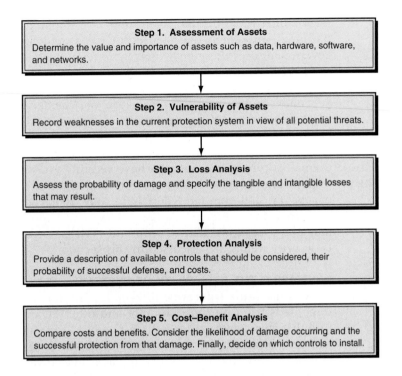

> **Step 1. Assessment of Assets**
> Determine the value and importance of assets such as data, hardware, software, and networks.

> **Step 2. Vulnerability of Assets**
> Record weaknesses in the current protection system in view of all potential threats.

> **Step 3. Loss Analysis**
> Assess the probability of damage and specify the tangible and intangible losses that may result.

> **Step 4. Protection Analysis**
> Provide a description of available controls that should be considered, their probability of successful defense, and costs.

> **Step 5. Cost–Benefit Analysis**
> Compare costs and benefits. Consider the likelihood of damage occurring and the successful protection from that damage. Finally, decide on which controls to install.

FIGURE 15.7 The risk management process.

between the cost of controls and the need to reduce or eliminate threats. Such analysis is basically a **risk-management** approach, which helps identify threats and selects cost-effective security measures (see Hiles, 2002).

Major activities in the risk-management process can be applied to existing systems as well as to systems under development. These are summarized in Figure 15.7. A more detailed structure for a strategic risk management plan suggested by Doughty (2002) is provided in Online File W15.9.

RISK-MANAGEMENT ANALYSIS.   Risk-management analysis can be enhanced by the use of DSS software packages. A simplified computation is shown here:

$$\boxed{\text{Expected loss} = P_1 \times P_2 \times L}$$

where:

P_1 = probability of attack (estimate, based on judgment)
P_2 = probability of attack being successful (estimate, based on judgment)
L = loss occurring if attack is successful

Example:

$$P_1 = .02, \; P_2 = .10, \; L = \$1,000,000$$

Then, expected loss from this particular attack is:

$$P_1 \times P_2 \times L = 0.02 \times 0.1 \times 1,000,000 = \$2,000$$

The expected loss can then be compared with the cost of preventing it. The value of software programs lies not only in their ability to execute complex computations, but also in their ability to provide a structured, systematic framework for ranking both threats and controls.

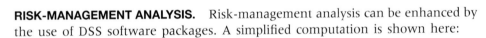

HOW MUCH TO SECURE? The National Computer Security Center (NCSC) of the U.S. Department of Defense published guidelines for security levels. The government uses these guidelines in its requests for bids on jobs where vendors must meet specified levels. The seven levels are shown in Online File W15.10 at the book's Web site. Vendors are required to maintain a certain security level depending on the security needs of the job. The decision of how much to secure can be treated as an insurance issue (see Kolodzinski, 2002, and Gordon et al., 2003).

IT Security in the Twenty-first Century

Computer control and security have recently received increased attention. For example, the story of the "I Love You" bug captured the headlines of most newspapers, TV, and computer portals in May 2000, and other wide-scale viruses since then have received similar media play. Almost 97 percent of the world's major corporations battled computer viruses in 2002. Several important IT-security trends are discussed in this section.

INCREASING THE RELIABILITY OF SYSTEMS. The objective relating to reliability is to use **fault tolerance** to keep the information systems working, even if some parts fail. Compaq Computer and other PC manufacturers provide a feature that stores data on more than one disk drive at the same time; if one disk fails or is attacked, the data are still available. Several brands of PCs include a built-in battery that is automatically activated in case of power failure.

Some systems today have 10,000 to 20,000 components, each of which can go a million hours without failure, but a combined system may go only 100 hours until it fails. With future systems of 100,000 components, the mathematical odds are that systems will fail every few minutes—clearly, an unacceptable situation. Therefore, it is necessary to improve system reliability.

SELF-HEALING COMPUTERS. As computing systems become more complex, they require higher amounts of human intervention to keep operating. Since the level of complexity is accelerating (e.g., see Grid Computing in Chapter 2), there is an increasing need for **self-healing computers.** Ideally, recovery can be done instantly if computers can find their problems and correct them themselves, before a system crashes.

According to Van (2003), IBM is engaged in a project known as *automatic computing*, which aims at making computers more self-sufficient and less fragile. The basic idea is borrowed from the human body and its immune system. IBM's first known self-healing computer is called eLiza; it is attached to a huge supercomputer, called Blue Sky, at the National Center for Atmospheric Research in the United States. For further discussion see Pescovitz (2002).

INTELLIGENT SYSTEMS FOR EARLY INTRUSION DETECTION. Detecting intrusion at its beginning is extremely important, especially for classified information and financial data. Expert systems and neural networks are used for this purpose. For example, *intrusion-detecting systems* are especially suitable for local area networks and client/server architectures. This approach compares users' activities on a workstation network against historical profiles and analyzes the significance of any discrepancies. The purpose is to detect security violations.

The intrusion-detecting approach is used by several government agencies (e.g., Department of Energy and the U.S. Navy) and large corporations (e.g.,

Citicorp, Rockwell International, and Tracor). It detects other things as well, for example, compliance with security procedures. People tend to ignore security measures (20,000–40,000 violations were reported each month in a large aerospace company in California). The system detects such violations so that improvements can be made.

INTELLIGENT SYSTEMS IN AUDITING AND FRAUD DETECTION. Intelligent systems are used to enhance the task of IS auditing. For example, expert systems evaluate controls and analyze basic computer systems, while neural networks and data mining are used to detect fraud (e.g., see Sheridan, 2002).

ARTIFICIAL INTELLIGENCE IN BIOMETRICS. Expert systems, neural computing, voice recognition, and fuzzy logic can be used to enhance the capabilities of several biometric systems. For example, Fuijitsu of Japan developed a computer mouse that can identify users by the veins of their palms, detecting unauthorized users.

EXPERT SYSTEMS FOR DIAGNOSIS, PROGNOSIS, AND DISASTER PLANNING. Expert systems can be used to diagnose troubles in computer systems and to suggest solutions. The user provides the expert systems with answers to questions about symptoms. The expert system uses its knowledge base to diagnose the source(s) of the trouble. Once a proper diagnosis is made, the computer provides a restoration suggestion. For example, Exec Express (*e-exec.co.uk*) sells intranet-based business recovery planning expert systems that are part of a bigger program called Self-Assessment. The program is used to evaluate a corporation's environment for security, procedures, and other risk factors.

SMART CARDS. Smart card technology can be used to protect PCs on LANs. An example is Excel MAR 10 (from MacroArt Technology, Singapore), which offers six safety levels: identification of authorized user, execution of predetermined programs, authentication, encryption of programs and files, encryption of communication, and generation of historical files. This product can also be integrated with a fingerprint facility. The user's smart card is authenticated by the system, using signatures identified with a secret key and the encryption algorithm. Smart cards containing embedded microchips can generate unique passwords (used only once) that confirm a person's identity.

FIGHTING HACKERS. Several products are available for fighting hackers. Secure Networks (*snc-net.com*) developed a product that is essentially a honeynet, a decoy network within network. The idea is to lure the hackers into the decoy to find what tools they use and detect them as early as possible.

ETHICAL ISSUES. Implementing security programs raises many ethical issues (see Azari, 2003). First, some people are against any monitoring of individual activities. Imposing certain controls is seen by some as a violation of freedom of speech or other civil rights. Reda (2002) cited a Gartner Group study that showed that even after the terrorist attacks of 9/11/2001, only 26 percent of Americans approved a national ID database. Using biometrics is considered by many a violation of privacy. Finally, using automated traceback programs, described earlier, may be unethical in some cases or even illegal (Lee and Shields, 2002).

➡ **MANAGERIAL ISSUES**

1. *To whom should the IS department report?* This issue is related to the degree of IS decentralization and to the role of the CIO. Having the IS department reporting to a functional area may introduce biases in providing IT priorities to that functional area, which may not be justifiable. Having the IS report to the CEO is very desirable.

2. *Who needs a CIO?* This is a critical question that is related to the role of the CIO as a senior executive in the organization. Giving a title without authority can damage the ISD and its operation. Asking the IS director to assume a CIO's responsibility, but not giving the authority and title, can be just as damaging. Any organization that is heavily dependent on IT should have a CIO.

3. *End users are friends, not enemies, of the IS department.* The relationship between end users and the ISD can be very delicate. In the past, many ISDs were known to be insensitive to end-user needs. This created a strong desire for end-user independence, which can be both expensive and ineffective. Successful companies develop a climate of cooperation and friendship between the two parties.

4. *Ethical issues.* The reporting relationship of the ISD can result in some unethical behavior. For example, if the ISD reports to the finance department, the finance department will have access to information about individuals or other departments that could be misused.

5. *Responsibilities for security should be assigned in all areas.* The more organizations use the Internet, extranets, and intranets, the greater are the security issues. It is important to make sure that employees know who is responsible and accountable for what information and that they understand the need for security control. The vast majority of information resources is in the hands of end users. Therefore, functional managers must understand and practice IT security management and other proper asset management tasks.

6. *Security awareness programs are important for any organization, especially if it is heavily dependent on IT.* Such programs should be corporatewide and supported by senior executives. In addition, monitoring security measures and ensuring compliance with administrative controls are essential to the success of any security plan. For many people, following administrative controls means additional work, which they prefer not to do.

7. *Auditing information systems should be institutionalized into the organizational culture.* Organizations should audit IS not because the insurance company may ask for it, but because it can save considerable amounts of money. On the other hand, overauditing is not cost-effective.

8. *Multinational corporations.* Organizing the ISD in a multinational corporation is a complex issue. Some organizations prefer a complete decentralization, having an ISD in each country or even several ISDs in one country. Others keep a minimum of centralized staff. Some companies prefer a highly centralized structure. Legal issues, government constraints, and the size of the IS staff are some factors that determine the degree of decentralization.

ON THE WEB SITE... Additional resources, including quizzes; online files of additional text, tables, figures, and cases; and frequently updated Web links to current articles and information can be found on the book's Web site (*wiley.com/college/turban*).

KEY TERMS

Application controls 702

Attack traceback 710

Audit 717

Authorization 711

Biometric control 704

Business continuity plan 712

Chief information officer (CIO) 681

Cracker 693

Cybercrime 693

Cyberwar 694

Data integrity 705

Data tampering 694

Denial of service (DoS) 697

Disaster avoidance 715

Disaster recovery plan 712

Distributed denial of service (DDoS) 697

Encryption 711

Exposure 691

Fault tolerance 720

Firewall 708

General controls 702

Hacker 693

Honeynets 712

Honeypots 712

Identity theft 689

Information center (IC) 685

Information resources management (IRM) 681

IT governance 684

Programming attack 695

Risk management 719

Self-healing computers 720

Service-level agreement (SLA) 684

Social engineering 693

Stealthware 712

Steering committee 684

Trojan horse 696

Virus 696

Vulnerability 690

Zombies 697

CHAPTER HIGHLIGHTS (Numbers Refer to Learning Objectives)

1 Information resources scattered throughout the organization are vulnerable to attacks, and therefore are difficult to manage.

2 The responsibility for IRM is divided between the ISD and end users. They must work together.

2 Steering committees, information centers, and service-level agreements can reduce conflicts between the ISD and end users.

2 ISD reporting locations can vary, but a preferred location is to report directly to senior management.

3 The chief information officer (CIO) is a corporate-level position demonstrating the importance and changing role of IT in organizations.

4 Data, software, hardware, and networks can be threatened by many internal and external hazards.

4 The attack to an information system can be caused either accidentally or intentionally.

4 There are many potential computer crimes; some resemble conventional crimes (embezzlement, vandalism, fraud, theft, trespassing, and joyriding).

4 Computer criminals are driven by economic, ideological, egocentric, or psychological factors. Most of the

criminals are insiders, but outsiders (such as hackers, crackers, and spies) can cause major damage as well.

4 A virus is a computer program hidden within a regular program that instructs the regular program to change or destroy data and/or programs. Viruses spread very quickly along networks worldwide.

5 Information systems are protected with controls such as security procedures, physical guards, or detecting software. These are used for *prevention, deterrence, detection, recovery,* and *correction* of information systems.

5 General controls include physical security, access controls, data security controls, communications (network) controls, and administrative controls.

5 Biometric controls are used to identify users by checking physical characteristics of the user (e.g., fingerprints and retinal prints).

5 Application controls are usually built into the software. They protect the data during input, processing, or output.

6 Encrypting information is a useful method for protecting transmitted data.

6 The Internet is not protected; therefore anything that comes from the Internet can be hazardous.

6 Firewalls protect intranets and internal systems from hackers, but not from viruses.

6 Access control, authentication, and authorization are the backbone of network security.

7 Disaster recovery planning is an integral part of effective control and security management.

7 Business continuity planning includes backup of data and computers and a plan for what to do when disaster strikes.

8 It is extremely difficult and expensive to protect against all possible threats to IT systems. Therefore, it is necessary to use cost-benefit analysis to decide how many and which controls to adopt.

8 A detailed internal and external IT audit may involve hundreds of issues and can be supported by both software and checklists.

QUESTIONS FOR REVIEW

1. What are possible reporting locations for the ISD?
2. Why has the ISD historically reported to finance or accounting departments?
3. List the mechanisms for ISD–end users cooperation.
4. Summarize the new role of the CIO.
5. List Rockart's eight imperatives.
6. What is a steering committee?
7. Define SLAs and discuss the roles they play.
8. What are the services to end users that are usually provided by an information (help) center?
9. Define controls, threats, vulnerability, and backup.
10. What is a computer crime?
11. List the four major categories of computer crimes.
12. What is a cybercrime?
13. What is the difference between hackers and crackers?
14. Explain a virus and a Trojan horse.
15. Explain a corporatewide security system.
16. Define controls.
17. Describe prevention, deterrence, detection, recovery, and correction.
18. Define biometrics; list five of them.
19. Distinguish between general controls and application controls.
20. What is the difference between authorized and authenticated users?
21. Explain DoS and how to defend against it.
22. How do you protect against viruses?
23. Define firewall. What is it used for?
24. Explain encryption.
25. Define a business continuity plan.
26. Define and describe a disaster recovery plan.
27. What are "hot" and "cold" recovery sites?
28. Describe auditing of information systems.
29. List and briefly describe the steps involved in risk analysis of controls.

QUESTIONS FOR DISCUSSION

1. What is a desirable location for the ISD to report to, and why?
2. What information resources are usually controlled by the ISD, and why?
3. Discuss the new role of the CIO and the implications of this role to management.
4. Why should information control and security be of prime concern to management?
5. Compare the computer security situation with that of insuring a house.
6. Explain what firewalls protect and what they do not protect. Why?
7. What is the purpose of biometrics? Why they are popular?
8. Describe how IS auditing works and how it is related to traditional accounting and financial auditing.
9. Why are authentication and authorization important in e-commerce?
10. Some insurance companies will not insure a business unless the firm has a computer disaster recovery plan. Explain why.
11. Explain why risk management should involve the following elements: threats, exposure associated with each threat, risk of each threat occurring, cost of controls, and assessment of their effectiveness.
12. Some people have recently suggested using viruses and similar programs in wars between countries. What is the logic of such a proposal? How could it be implemented?

13. How important is it for a CIO to have an extensive knowledge of the business?

14. Why is it necessary to use SLAs with vendors? What are some of the potential problems in such situations?

15. Compare TQM to a corporatewide security plan. What is similar? What is different?

16. Why do intelligent systems play an increasing role in securing IT?

17. Why is cross-border cybercrime expanding rapidly? Discuss some possible solutions.

18. Discuss the relationships between grid computing and self-healing computers.

EXERCISES

1. Examine Online File W15.4. Read some new material on the CIO and add any new roles you find in your reading. Which of the roles in the list seem to have gained importance and which seem to have lost importance?

2. Assume that the daily probability of a major earthquake in Los Angeles is .07%. The chance of your computer center being damaged during such a quake is 5%. If the center is damaged, the average estimated damage will be $1.6 million.
   a. Calculate the expected loss (in dollars).
   b. An insurance agent is willing to insure your facility for an annual fee of $15,000. Analyze the offer, and discuss whether to accept it.

3. The theft of laptop computers at conventions, hotels, and airports is becoming a major problem. These categories of protection exist: physical devices (e.g., *targus.com*), encryption (e.g., *networkassociates.com*), and security policies (e.g., at *ebay.com*). Find more information on the problem and on the solutions. Summarize the advantages and limitations of each method.

4. Expert systems can be used to analyze the profiles of computer users. Such analysis may enable better intrusion detection. Should an employer notify employees that their usage of computers is being monitored by an expert system? Why or why not?

5. Ms. M. Hsieh worked as a customer support representative for the Wollongong Group, a small software company (Palo Alto, California). She was fired in late 1987. In early 1988, Wollongong discovered that someone was logging onto its computers at night via a modem and had altered and copied files. During investigation, the police traced the calls to Ms. Hsieh's home and found copies there of proprietary information valued at several million dollars. It is interesting to note that Ms. Hsieh's access code was canceled the day she was termi-

nated. However, the company suspects that Ms. Hsieh obtained the access code of another employee. (*Source:* Based on *BusinessWeek,* August 1, 1988, p. 67.)
   a. How was the crime committed? Why were the controls ineffective? (State any relevant assumptions.)
   b. What can Wollongong, or any company, do in order to prevent similar incidents in the future?

6. Guarding against a distributed denial of service attack is not simple. Examine the major tools and approaches available. Start by downloading software from *nipc.gov.* Also visit *cert.org, sans.org,* and *ciac.llnl.gov.* Write a report summarizing your findings.

7. Twenty-five thousand messages arrive at an organization each year. Currently there are no firewalls. On the average there are 1.2 successful hackings each year. Each successful hacking results in loss to the company of about $130,000.

A major firewall is proposed at a cost of $66,000 and a maintenance cost of $5,000. The estimated useful life is 3 years. The chance that an intruder will break through the firewall is 0.0002. In such a case, the damage will be $100,000 (30%) or $200,000 (50%), or no damage. There is annual maintenance cost of $20,000 for the firewall.
   a. Should management buy the firewall?
   b. An improved firewall that is 99.9988 percent effective costs $84,000, with a life of 3 years and annual maintenance cost of $16,000, is available. Should this one be purchased instead of the first one?

8. In spring 2000 the U.S. government developed an internal intrusion detection network (*fidnet.gov*) to protect itself from hackers. The Center for Democracy and Technology (*cdt.org*) objected, claiming invasion of privacy. Research the status of the project (FIDNet) and discuss the claims of the center.

GROUP ASSIGNMENTS

1. With the class divided into groups, have each group visit an IS department. Then present the following in class: an organizational chart of the department; a discussion on the department's CIO (director) and her or his re-

porting status; information on a steering committee (composition, duties); information on any SLAs the department has; and a report on the extent of IT decentralization in the company.

2. Each group is to be divided into two parts. The first part will interview students and businesspeople and record the experiences they have had with computer security problems. The second part of each group will visit a computer store (and/or read the literature or use the Internet) to find out what software is available to fight different computer security problems. Then, each group will prepare a presentation in which they describe the problems and identify which of the problems could have been prevented with the use of commercially available software.

3. Create groups to investigate the latest development in IT and e-commerce security. Check journals such as *CIO.com* (available free online), vendors, and search engines such as *techdata.com.* and *google.com*.

4. Research the Melissa attack in 1999. Explain how the virus works and what damage it causes. Examine Microsoft's attempts to prevent similar future attacks. Investigate similarities between the 2003 viruses (Slammer, Bugbear, etc.) and earlier ones (e.g., "I Love You" and Melissa). What preventive methods are offered by security vendors?

INTERNET EXERCISES

1. Explore some job-searching Web sites (such as *brassring.com,* and *headhunter.com*), and identify job openings for CIOs. Examine the job requirements and the salary range. Also visit *google.com* and *cio.com*, and find some information regarding CIOs, their roles, salaries, and so forth. Report your findings.

2. Enter *scambusters.org*. Find out what the organization does. Learn about e-mail scams and Web site scams. Report your findings.

3. Access the site of *comdisco.com*. Locate and describe the latest disaster recovery services.

4. Enter *epic.org/privacy/tools.html,* and examine the following groups of tools: Web encryption, disk encryption, and PC firewalls. Explain how these tools can be used to facilitate the security of your PC.

5. Access the Web sites of the major antivirus vendors (*symantec.com, mcafee.com,* and *antivirus.com*). Find out what the vendors' research centers are doing. Also download VirusScan from McAfee and scan your hard drive with it.

6. Many newsgroups are related to computer security (*groups.google.com; alt.comp.virus; comp.virus; maous.comp. virus*). Access any of these sites to find information on the most recently discovered viruses.

7. Check the status of biometric controls. See the demo at *sensar.com*. Check what Microsoft is doing with biometric controls.

8. Enter *v:l.nai.com/vil/default.asp*. Find information about viruses. What tips does McAfee (*mcafee b2b.com*) give for avoiding or minimizing the impact of viruses?

9. You have installed a DSL line in your home. You read in this chapter that you need a personal firewall. Enter *securitydogs.com, macafee.com*, or *symantec.com*. Find three possible products. Which one do you like best? Why?

10. Access a good search engine (e.g., *google.com* or *findart icles.com*). Find recent articles on disaster planning. Prepare a short report on recent developments in disaster recovery planning.

11. The use of smart cards for electronic storage of user identification, user authentication, changing passwords, and so forth is on the rise. Surf the Internet and report on recent developments. (For example, try the Web sites *microsoft.com/windows/smartcards, litronic.com, gemplus.com*, or *scia.org*.)

12. Access the Web site *2600.com* and read the *2600 Magazine*. Also try *waregone.com* and *skynamic.com*. Prepare a report that shows how easy it is to hack successfully.

13. Enter *ncsa.com* and find information about "why hackers do the things they do." Write a report.

14. Enter *biopay.com* and other vendors of biometrics and find the devices they make that can be used to access control into information systems. Prepare a list of major capabilities.

Minicase 1
Putting IT to Work at Home Depot

Home Depot is the world's largest home-improvement retailer, a global company that is expanding rapidly (about 200 new stores every year). With over 1,500 stores (mostly in the United States and Canada, and now expanding to other countries) and about 50,000 kinds of products in each store, the company is heavily dependent on IT, especially since it started to sell online.

To align its business and IT operations, Home Depot created a business and information service model, known as the Special Projects Support Team (SPST). This team collaborates both with the ISD and business colleagues on new projects, addressing a wide range of strategic and tactical needs. These projects typically occur at the intersection of business processes. The team is composed of highly skilled employees. Actually, there are several teams, each with a director and a mix of employees, depending on the project. For example, system developers, system administrators, security experts, and project managers can be on a team. The teams exist until the completion of a project; then they are dissolved and the members are assigned to new teams. All teams report to the SPST director, who reports to a VP of Technology.

To ensure collaboration among end users, the ISD and the SPST created structured (formal) relationships. The basic idea is to combine organizational structure and process flow, which is designed to do the following:

- Achieve consensus across departmental boundaries with regard to strategic initiatives.
- Prioritize strategic initiatives.
- Bridge the gap between business concept and detailed specifications.
- Result in the lowest possible operational costs.
- Achieve consistently high acceptance levels by the end-user community.
- Comply with evolving legal guidelines.
- Define key financial elements (cost-benefit analysis, ROI, etc.).
- Identify and render key feedback points for project metrics.
- Support very high rates of change.
- Support the creation of multiple, simultaneous threads of work across disparate time lines.
- Promote known, predictable, and manageable workflow events, event sequences, and change management processes.

- Accommodate the highest possible levels of operational stability.
- Leverage the extensive code base, and leverage function and component reuse.
- Leverage Home Depot's extensive infrastructure and IS resource base.

Online File W15.11 shows how this kind of organization works for Home Depot's e-commerce activities. There is a special EC steering committee which is connected to the CIO (who is a senior VP), to the VP for marketing and advertising, and to the VP for merchandising (merchandising deals with procurement). The SPST is closely tied to the ISD, to marketing, and to merchandising. The data center is shared with non-EC activities.

The SPST migrated to an e-commerce team in August 2000 in order to construct a Web site supporting a national catalog of products, which was completed in April 2001. (This catalog contains over 400,000 products from 11,000 vendors.) This project required the collaboration of virtually every department in Home Depot (e.g., see finance/ accounting, legal, loss prevention, etc., in the figure). Also contracted services were involved. (The figure in Online File W15.11 shows the workflow process.)

Since 2001, SPST has been continually busy with EC initiatives, including improving the growing Home Depot online store. The cross-departmental nature of the SPST explains why it is an ideal structure to support the dynamic, ever-changing work of the EC-related projects. The structure also considers the skills, strengths, and weaknesses of the IT employees. The company offers both online and offline training aimed at improving those skills. Home Depot is consistently ranked among the best places to work for IT employees.

Sources: Compiled from Alberts (2001) and from *homedepot.com* (2003).

Questions for Minicase 1

1. Read Chapter 9 (Sections 9.9 and 9.10) regarding team-based organizations. Explain why the team-based structure at Home Depot is so successful.
2. The structure means that the SPST reports to both marketing and technology. This is known as a matrix structure. What are the potential advantages and problems?
3. How is collaboration facilitated by IT in this case?
4. Why is the process flow important in this case?

Minicase 2
Managing Security

The Internet Security Alliance (*isalliance.org*) was formed in April 2001. The alliance is a collaborative endeavor of Carnegie Mellon University's Software Engineering Institute (SEI); its CERT Coordination Center (CERT/CC); the Electronics Industries Alliance (EIA), a federation of trade groups; and other private and pubic member organizations and corporations. Their goal is to provide information sharing and leadership on information security and to represent its members and regulators.

On September 9, 2002, the alliance released results from a recent security survey conducted jointly with the National Association of Manufacturers (NAM) and Red-Siren Technologies Inc. (Durkovich, 2002). The survey asked 227 information security specialists worldwide to compare their current attitudes toward information security with their attitudes prior to the 9/11 terrorist attacks. Overall, the results showed that the security specialists view information security as more of an issue now and that they see it as crucial to the survival of their organization or business. However, most answered that they still feel inadequately prepared to meet their current security challenges, and just as importantly, that most lacked senior management commitment to address these challenges.

The following are some of the specific survey findings:

- 91 percent recognize the importance of information security.

- Most of the organizations reported at least one attack in the past year, with approximately 30 percent reporting more than six attacks.

- 48 percent said that the 9/11 attacks made them more concerned about information security, while 48 percent said there had been no change in their attitudes.

- 47 percent said that their organization had increased spending on information security since the attacks.

- 40 percent said that they had improved their physical security, electronic security, network security, and security policies since the attacks.

- 30 percent indicated that their companies are still inadequately prepared to deal with security attacks.

The Internet Security Alliance has identified 10 of the highest priority and most frequently recommended practices necessary for implementation of a successful security process. The practices encompass policy, process, people, and technology. They include (IS Alliance, 2002):

1. *General management.* Information security is a normal part of everyone's responsibilities—managers and employees alike. Managers must ensure that there are adequate resources, that security policies are well defined, and that the policies are reviewed regularly.

2. *Policy.* Security policies must address key areas such as security risk management, identification of critical assets, physical security, network security, authentication, vulnerability and incident management, privacy, and the like. Policies need to be embedded in standard procedures, practices, training, and architectures.

3. *Risk management.* The impacts of various risks need to be identified and quantified. A management plan needs to be developed to mitigate those risks with the greatest impact. The plan needs to be reviewed on a regular basis.

4. *Security architecture and design.* An enterprise-wide security architecture is required to protect critical information assets. High-risk areas (e.g., power supplies) should employ diverse and redundant solutions.

5. *User issues.* The user community includes general employees, IT staff, partners, suppliers, vendors, and other parties who have access to critical information systems.

6. *System and network management.* The key lines of defense include access control for all network devices and data, encrypted communications and VPNs where required, and perimeter protection (e.g., firewalls) based on security policies. Any software, files, and directories on the network should be verified on a regular basis. Procedures and mechanisms must be put in place that ensure that software patches are applied to correct existing problems; adequate levels of system logging are deployed; systems changes are analyzed from a security perspective; and vulnerability assessments are performed on a periodic basis. Software and data must also be backed up on a regular schedule.

7. *Authentication and authorization.* Strict policies must be formulated and implemented for authenticating and authorizing network access. Special attention must be given to those employees accessing the network from home and on the road and to partners, contractors, and services who are accessing the network remotely.

8. *Monitor and audit.* Security-breaching events and changing conditions must be monitored, and the network must be inspected on a regular basis. Standards should be in place for responding to suspicious or unusual behavior.

9. *Physical security.* Physical access to key information assets, IT services, and resources should be controlled by two-factor authentication.

10. *Continuity planning and disaster recovery.* Business continuity and recovery plans need to be implemented and periodically tested to ensure that they are effective.

Sources: Compiled from Durkovich (2002) and ISAlliance (2002).

Questions for Minicase 2

1. Why does the Internet Security Alliance include both private and public members?
2. What is the mission of the Alliance?
3. Why is it beneficial to prioritize issues?
4. How would you justify the existence of the Alliance? Who should pay its costs?

Virtual Company Assignment
Managing Information Resources and IT Security at The Wireless Café

Recently, you went into Jeremy's office to chat with him about the new wireless network standards and their implications for The Wireless Café. Jeremy wasn't there, but you were surprised to see that the office was open, his computer was on, and an application displayed employee information on the screen. You've been reading about privacy and security laws and data vulnerabilities, and so you shut off Jeremy's monitor before leaving his office.

Instructions

1. What particular exposures and vulnerabilities can you identify for information technologies at The Wireless Café? As the restaurant's information systems become automated, what are some intentional and unintentional threats the information is exposed to?

2. You'd like to suggest that Barbara and Jeremy institute a formal set of security controls covering all of their computerized information. What physical and application controls would be appropriate in a restaurant? What employees would you include in a privacy and security orientation program? Take a look at TWC's Web site for an overview of the various positions in the restaurant.

3. Use the risk management and cost benefit analysis framework in the chapter to provide a rough estimate of an information security budget for TWC. Since a small business like TWC cannot afford to cover many threats, rank the systems and data by importance of protection. Consider disasters (especially fire, in a restaurant), security, and administrative errors as part of your risk analysis in ranking systems.

REFERENCES

Adams, S., "Effective SLAs Define Partnership Roles," *Communications News*, June 2000, comnews.com (accessed August 2003).

Agarwal R., and V. Sambamurthy, "Principles and Models for Organizing the IT function," *MIS Querterly Executive*, March 2002.

Alberts, B., "Home Depot's Special Projects Support Team Powers Information Management for Business Needs," *Journal of Organization Excellence*, winter 2001.

Alga, N., "Increasing Security Levels," *Information Systems Control Journal*, March–April 2002.

Austin R.D., and C. A. R. Darby, "The Myth of Secure Computing," *Harvard Business Review*, June 2003.

Atlas, R. I., and S. A. Young, "Planting and Shaping Security Success," *Security Management*, August 2002.

Azari, R. (ed.), *Current Security Managemnt and Ethical Issues of Information*, Hershey PA: IRM Press, 2003.

Ball, L. D., "CIO on Center Stage: 9/11 Changes Everything," *Information Systems Management*, spring 2002.

Becker, D., "Equal Rights for CIOs," *CNET News.Com*, June 16, 2003.

Biery K., and D. Hager, "The Risks of Mobile Communication," *Security Management*, December 2001.

Biermann E. et al., "A Comparison of Intrusion Detection Systems," *Computers and Security*, Vol. 20, 2001.

Brassil, R. A., "The Changing Realities of Recovery: How Onsite and Mobile Options Have Revolutionalize the Business Continuity Industry," *Information Systems Control Journal*, March–April 2003.

Blanco L., "Audit Trail in an E-Commerce Environment," *Information Systems Control Journal*, September–October 2002.

Bruno L., "Out, Out Damned Hacker!" *Red Herring*, January 2002.

"Bugbear Worm Steals Credit Card and Password Details," *Information Management and Computer Security*, June 2003.

Caulfield, B., "The Trouble with Biometrics," *Business 2.0*, September 2002.

Cilli, C., "IT Governance: Why a Guideline?" *Information Systems Control Journal*, May–June 2003.

Computers and Security, special issue, 19(1), 2000.

Davidson, P., "29 Nations Team Up vs. Cross-Border Scams," *USA Today* (International issue), June 17, 2003.

Davis, J. L., "Using Authentication to Help Prevent Online Fraud," *Direct Marketing,* October 2001.

Damle, P., "Social Engineering: A Tip of the Iceberg," *Information Systems Control Journal,* March–April 2002.

Devargas, M., "Survival Is Not Compulsory: An Introduction to Business Continuity Planning," *Computers and Security,* 18(1), 1999.

Diao Y. et al., "Using Fuzzy Control to Mazimize Profits in Service Level Agreement, *IBM Systems Journal,* XYZ, 2002.

Doll, M. W. et al., *Defending the Digital Frontier.* New York: Wiley, 2003.

Doughty, K., "Business Continuity: A Business Survival Strategy, *Information Systems Control Journal,* January–February 2002.

Doughty, K.,"Implementing Enterprise Security," *Information Systems Control Journal,* May–June 2003.

Duffy, D., "Chief Executives Who Get IT," *CIO Magazine,* July 15, 1999.

Durkovich, C. et al. "Global Computer Security Survey–Results Analysis," September 9, 2002, *redsiren,com/survey.html* (accessed July 18, 2003).

Earl, M. J., "Blue Survivors (the CIO's)," CIO Magazine, December 15, 1999–January 1, 2000.

Fadia, A., *Network Security: A Hacker's Perspective.* Boston, MA: Premier Press, 2002.

Frownfelter–Lohrke, C., and J. E. Hunton, "New Opportunities for Information Systems Auditors," *Information Systems Control Journal,* May–June, 2002.

Garfinkel, S., *Web Security, Privacy and Commerce.* Sebastopal, CA: O'Reilly and Associates, 2002.

Gerber, J. A., and E. R. Feldman, "Is Your Business Prepared for the Worst?" *Journal of Accountancy,* April 2002.

Ghosh, A. K., and T. M. Swaminatha, "Software Security and Privacy Risks in Mobile E-Commerce," *Communications of the ACM,* February 2001.

Granger, S., "Social Engineering Fundamentals. Part I: Hacker Tactics, " December 18, 2001, *online.securityfocus.com* (accessed July 20, 2003).

Hiles, A., *Enterprise Risk Assessment and Business Impact Analysis.* Rothstein Assoc., 2002.

Hinde, S., "The Law, Cybercrime, Risk Assessment and Cyber Protection," *Computers and Security,* February 2003.

Hunton, J. E., "Back Up Your Data to Survive a Disaster," *Journal of Accountancy,* April 2002.

ISAlliance, "Common Sense Guide for Senior Managers." Internet Security Alliance, July 2002, *www.isalliance.org* (accessed July 15, 2003).

Jain, A. et al., "Biometric Identification," *Communications of the ACM,* February 2000.

Jain, A. et al. (eds.), *Biometrics: Personal Identification in Networked Security.* NewYork: Kluwer, 1999.

Jiang, J. J. et al., "Measuring Information Systems Service Quality," *MIS Quarterly,* June 2002.

Karagiannis, K., "DDoS: Are You Next?" *PC Magazine,* January 1, 2003, *pcmag.com/article2/0,4149,768385,00.asp* (accessed August 2003).

Kesner, R. M., "Running Information Services as a Business: Managing IS Commitments within the Enterprise," *Information Strategy: The Executive Journal,* Summer 2002.

Kolodzinski, O., "Aligning Information Security Imperatives with Business Needs," *The CPA Journal,* July 2002, *luca.com/cpajournal/2002/0702/nv/nv10.htm* (accessed August 2003).

Lam, W., "Ensuring Business Continuity," *IT Pro,* June 2002.

Lee, S. C., and C. Shields, "Technical Legal and Societal Challenges to Automated Attack Traceback," *IT Pro,* May–June 2002.

Leidner, D. E. et al., "How CIOs Manage IT During Economic Decline: Surviving and Thriving Amid Uncertainty," *MIS Quarterly Executive,* March 2003.

Levin, C., "The Insurance Plan that Came to the Rescue," *PC Magazine,* January 29, 2002.

Los Angeles Times, April 24, 1998.

Loundy, D. L., *Computer Crime, Information Warefare and Economic Espionage.* Durham, N.C: Carolina Academic Press, 2003.

Luhn, R., and S. Spanbauer, "Protect Your PC," *PC World,* July 2002.

Lux, A. G., and S. Fitiani, "Fighting Internal Crime Before It Happens," *Information Systems Control Journal,* May–June, 2002.

McConnell, M., "Information Assurance in the Twenty-first Century," *Supplement to Computer,* February 2002.

McKinley, E., "VPN Provides Rent-A-Center with a Multitude of Positive Changes," *Stores,* May 2003.

Mitnick, K., and W. Simon, *The Art of Deception.* New York: Wiley, 2002.

Mitre, "CVE List Exceeds 5,000 Security Issues," September 9, 2002, *cve.mitre.org/news/* (accessed July 20, 2003).

Morgan, J. P., and N. A. Wong, "Conduct a Legal Web Audit," *e-Business Advisor,* September 1999.

Nance, B., "Keep Networks Safe from Viruses," *Byte,* November 1996, p. 171. Updated June 2003,

O'Harrow, R., "Financial Database to Screen Accounts," *Washington Post,* May 30, 2002.

Pantry, S., and P. Griffiths, *A Complete Guide for Preparing and Implementing Service Level Agreements,* 2nd Ed. London: Library Association Publishing, 2002.

Pescovitz, D., "Helping Computers Help Themselves," *IEEE Spectrum,* September 2002.

Piazza, P., "Honeynet Attracts Hacker Attack," *Security Management,* November 2001.

Pooley, J., "Blocking Information Passes," *Security Management,* July 2002.

Prometheum Technologies, "How Does a Virtual Private Network (VPN) Work?" April 2003, *prometheum.com/m_vpn.htm* (accessed August 2003).

Reda, S., "Brave New World of Biometrics," *Stores,* May 2002.

Richardson, R., *2003 CSI/FBI Computer Crime and Security Survey.* San Francisco: Computer Security Insitute (*gocsi.com*), 2003.

Robinson, C., "The Role of a Chief Security Officer," *CIO Asia,* April 2003 (*cio-asia.com*).

Rockart, J. F. et al., "Eight Imperatives for the New IS Organization," *Sloan Management Review,* fall 1996.

Ross, J. W. et al., "Develop Long-Term Competitiveness Through IT Assets," *Sloan Management Review,* fall 1996.

Ross, J. W., and D. F. Feeny, "The Evolving Role of the CIO," in R. Zmud (ed.), *Framing the Domain of IT Management.* Cincinnati, OH: Pinnaflex Educational Resources, 2000.

Rothstein, P. J., *Develop a Disaster Recovery/Business Continuity Plan.* Brookfield, CT: Rothstein Assoc., 2002.

Sambamurthy, V. et al., "Managing in the Digital Era," in G. Dickson and G. DeSanctis, *Information Technology and the Future Enterprise.* Upper Saddle River, NJ: Prentice-Hall, 2001.

sans.org, "The Twenty Most Critical Internet Security Vulnerabilities," SANS Institute, *sans.org/top20* (accessed April 2003).

Sayana, S.A., "Auditing General and Application Controls," *Information Systems Control Journal,* September–October 2002.

Scalet, S. D., "Immune Systems," *CIO Magazine,* June 1, 2003.

Seddon, P. B. et al., "Measuring Organizational IS Effectivness," *Data Base,* spring 2002.

Shand, D., "Service Level Agreements," *Computerworld,* January 22, 2001.

Sheridan, R. M., "Working the Data Mines," *Security Management,* April 2002.

Sitonis, J. G., and B. Goldberg, "Changing Role of the CIO," *InformationWeek,* March 24, 1997.

Sivasailam, N. et al., "What Companies Are(n't) Doing about Web Site Assurance," *IT Pro,* May–June 2002.

Smith, R., *Authentication: From Password to Public Keys.* Boston: Addison Wesley, 2002.

South China Morning Post, news item, Hong Kong, May 21, 1999.

Spector, L., "How to Avoid Data Disaster," *PC World,* June 2002.

Stasiak, K., "Web Application Security," *Information Systems Control Journal,* November–December, 2002.

Statonline, "Technology Facts and Links," *statonline.com/technologies/facts.asp* (accessed August 2003).

Strassman, P., "What Is the Best Defense? Being Prepared," *ComputerWorld,* March 31, 1997.

Sullivan A., "U.S. Arrests 135 in Nationwide Cybercrime Sweep," *Yahoo!News,* provided by Reuters, May 16, 2003.

Talleur, T., "Can Your Organization Survive a Cybercrime?" *e-Business Advisor,* September 2001.

Van, J., "Self Healing Computers Seen as Better Fix," *Chicago Tribune,* January 2, 2003.

Verton, E., and J. Brownlow, *Black Ice: The Invisible Threat of Cyberterrorism.* New York: McGraw Hill, 2003.

Von-Roessing, R., *Auditing Business Continuity: Global Best Practices.* Brookfield, CT: Rothstein Assoc., 2002.

Walsh, N. P., "Stolen Details of 6 Million Phone Users Hawked on Moscow Streets," *The Guardian,* January 27, 2003.

Wells, J. T., "Occupational Fraud: The Audit as a Deterrent," *Journal of Accountancy,* April 2002.

White, G. B., "Protecting the Real Corporate Networks," *Computer Security Journal,* 1(4), 1999.

Whitemone, J. J., "A Method for Designing Secure Solutions, *IBM Systems Journal,* 40(3), 2001.

Wiederkehr, B., "IT Securiy Awareness Programme,"*Information Systems Control Journal,* May–June 2003.

Willcocks, L. P., and R. Sykes, "The Role of the CIO and IT Function in ERP," *Communications. of the ACM,* April 2000.

Williams, D., "Are You IT-Dependent?" *CA Magazine,* August 2002.

Woda, A., "The Role of the Auditor in IT Governance," *Information Systems Control Journal,* Vol. 2, 2002.

Zenkin, D., "Guidelines for Protecting the Corporate Against Viruses," *Computers and Security,* August 2001.

Zetter, K., and S. Miastkowski, "Viruses: The Next Generation," *PC World,* December 2000.

Glossary

Access point A wireless hardware device that attaches to a wired network and sends data to and receives data from your wireless network adaptors.

Ad-hoc analysis The analysis of ad-hoc reports.

Ad-hoc reports Management reports that are issued in reply to a special request, in contrast with *periodic* reports.

Advocacy marketing See *Viral marketing*.

Affiliate marketing (programs) Programs in which companies pay a very small commission to other sites for "driving traffic" to their sites online. The target site uses its affiliate program to help acquire customers; the members of the program earn a commission every time a customer "clicks through" their site to the target site or makes a purchase.

Affinity portals Gateways to the Web that support an entire community of affiliated interests.

Alliance strategy Competitive strategy in which a company works with business partners in partnerships, alliances, joint ventures, or virtual companies.

Analytical processing Analysis of accumulated data, frequently by end users, through data mining, decision support systems (DSS), enterprise information systems (EIS), and Web applications; also referred to as *business intelligence*.

Applets (of Java) Small programs written in Java for executing simple tasks such as developing a Web page or selecting a product that matches buyer's preferences.

Application controls Controls designed to protect specific applications.

Application portfolio The collection of corporate IT applications, sometimes including those under development.

Application program A set of computer instructions written in a programming language, the purpose of which is to provide functionality to a user.

Application service provider (ASP) Company that provides business applications (standard or customized) over the Internet for a per-use or fixed monthly fee. It is a form of outsourcing.

Artificial intelligence (AI) A subfield of computer science concerned with symbolic reasoning and problem solving.

Artificial neural network (ANN) A computer technology attempting to build computers that will operate like a human brain; ANN programs can work with ambiguous information.

Asynchronous communication The sending and receiving of messages in which there is a time delay between the sending and receiving; as opposed to *synchronous communication*.

Key terms from the Technology Guides are not included here, but can be found at the book's Web site (*wiley.com/college/turban*).

Attack traceback A system that would trace and identify the person or computer responsible for a virus, DOS, or other attack.

Audit A regular examination or check of systems, their inputs, outputs, and processing.

Audit trail List of all changes made to a file, for checking or control purposes.

Authorization Permission issued to individuals or groups to do certain activities with a computer, usually based on verified identity.

Auto Identification Center (Auto-ID) Joint partnership among global companies and research universities to create an Internet of Things.

Automatic crash notification (ACN) Still-experimental device that would automatically notify police of the location of an ACN-equipped car involved in an accident.

Backbone The long-distance, high-capacity, and high-speed network that links the major Internet computer nodes. Also may connect networks for an organization.

Backup A copy of software or data.

Balanced-scorecard method Method that evaluates the overall health of organizations and projects by looking at metrics in finance, customers' view the organization, internal business processes, and ability to change and expand.

Banners Electronic billboards, which typically contain a short text or graphical message to promote a product or a vendor.

Batch processing Processing system that processes inputs at fixed intervals as a file and operates on it all at once; in contrast, *online* (or *interactive*) processing operates on a transaction as soon as it occurs.

Behavior-oriented chargeback Accounting system that sets IS service costs in a way that encourages usage consistent with organizational objectives, even though the charges may not correspond to actual costs.

Best-practice benchmarks Activities and methods that the most effective organizations use to operate and manage various IS functions.

Best practices The best methods for solving problems; these are often stored in the knowledge repository.

Biometric controls Security controls that involve physically or behaviorally unique characteristics of people, such as fingerprints or voice.

Blog A personal Web site, open to the public, in which the owner expresses his or her feelings or opinions.

Blogging (Weblogging) A technology that offers an opportunity for individuals to do personal publishing on the Internet.

Bluetooth Chip technology that enables voice and data communications between many wireless devices through low-power, short-range, digital two-way radio frequency.

Brick-and-mortar (organizations) Organizations that do business in old-economy style, basically offline.

Bullwhip effect Large fluctuations in inventories along the uncoordinated supply chain that result from small fluctuations in the demand for the finished products.

Business architecture Organizational plans, visions, objectives and problems, and the information required to support them.

Business case A written document that is used by managers to justify funding for a specific investment and also to provide the bridge between the initial plan and its execution.

Business continuity plan A comprehensive plan for how the business and IT systems will operate in case a disaster strikes.

Business intelligence Computer-based decision analysis usually done online by managers and staff. It includes forecasting, analyzing alternatives, and evaluating risk and performance.

Business model A method by which a company generates revenue to sustain itself.

Business pressures Forces, such as global competition, in the organization's environment that create pressures on the organization's operations.

Business process A collection of activities that take one or more kinds of inputs and create an output.

Business process reengineering (BPR) A methodology for introducing a fundamental change in specific business processes, usually supported by an information system.

Business systems planning (BSP) Planning that concentrates on identifying problems and related decisions, based on business processes and data classes. (An IBM methodology.)

Business-to-business EC (B2B) E-commerce where both the buyers and the sellers are organizations.

Business-to-consumer EC (B2C) E-commerce in which a business is selling online to individual consumers.

Business-to-employees (B2E) Special type of intrabusiness e-commerce in which an organization deliver products or services to its employees.

Business process management (BPM) Method for business restructuring that combines workflow systems and redesign methods and covers three process categories—people-to-people, systems-to-systems, and systems-to-people interactions.

Buy-side model (marketplace) A marketplace where one buyer buys from many sellers, frequently by using reverse auctions.

Byte A number of bits (usually eight) used to represent one alphanumeric character.

CD-ROM (compact disc read-only memory) A secondary digital storage medium that uses laser-made pits in plastic to represent bits.

Central processing unit (CPU) The "brain" of a computer — controlling all computational, input, output, and storage activities.

Centralized computing IS architecture that puts all processing and control authority at a single computer site to which all other computing devices respond.

Change management Management of significant organizational change and business process redesign.

Channel conflict The conflict between the existing distribution channels and the new channel of selling directly to customers, caused by bypassing traditional distribution partners.

Channel systems A network of the materials and product distribution system within an organization, and between the organization and its suppliers and customers.

Chargeback Systems that treat the MIS function as a service bureau or utility, charging organizational subunits for MIS services with the objective of recovering MIS expenditures.

Chargeout See *Chargeback*.

Chat room A Web page where people can interact ("chat") in real time; a virtual meeting place.

Chief information officer (CIO) The director of the IS department in a large organization, analogous to a CEO, COO, or CFO.

Chief knowledge officer (CKO) The title given to the director assigned to manage an organization's knowledge management program.

Chief network officer (CNO) The title given to the director of telecommunications; reflects the importance of the role in the organization.

Click-and-mortar (organizations) Organizations that employ both offline and online strategy, basically adapting the old economy to the new one rather than going 100 percent online; the most common e-commerce model.

Clickstream data The data collected on users' activities on a Web site, captured by various methods, including *cookies*, and mined by advertisers.

Client A computer such as a PC attached to a network, which is used to access shared network resources.

Client/server architecture A type of distributed architecture where end-user PCs (clients) request services or data from designated processors or peripherals (servers).

Code Division Multiple Access (CDMA) Wireless communication protocol, used with most 2.5G and 3G systems, that separates different users by assigning different codes to the segments of each user's communications.

Code of ethics A set of ethical-behavior rules developed by organizations or by professional societies.

Codification strategy The knowledge management approach that attempts to identify tacit knowledge in best practices and so on, and store the tacit knowledge in a knowledge repository. The opposite is the *personalization strategy*.

Collaboration The mutual efforts by two or more individuals who perform activities in order to accomplish certain tasks.

Collaborative commerce (c-commerce) Collaboration among business partners.

Collaborative commerce networks Physical networks such as extranets or EDI, and the procedures of collaboration among them.

Collaborative filtering agents Software agents that use customer data to *infer* customer interest in other products or services.

Commercial (public) portals Gateways to the Web that offer content for broad and diverse audiences; these are the most popular portals on the Internet, such as *yahoo.com* and *msn.com*.

Community of practice (COP) A group of people in an organization with a common professional interest.

Company-centric EC (for B2B) E-commerce conducted on a company's server where either there is one seller and many corporate buyers (sell side), or one corporate buyer and many corporate sellers (sell side).

Competitive advantage An advantage over a competitor, such as lower cost or quicker deliveries.

Competitive forces model A business framework devised by Porter, depicting five forces in a market (e.g., bargaining power of customers).

Competitive intelligence The activities conducted by companies, frequently with the aid of IT and the Internet, to spy on their competitors and to collect marketing information.

Component-based development A strategy for developing applications from a preprogrammed component. A component can be a shopping cart in e-commerce or a statistical routine in a DSS.

Computer-aided design (CAD) software Software that allows designers to design and "build" production prototypes, "test" them as a computer object under given parameters, compile parts and quantity lists, outline production and assembly procedures, and then transmit the final design directly to milling and rolling machines.

Computer-aided engineering (CAE) Software that enables engineers to execute complex engineering analysis on a computer.

Computer-aided manufacturing (CAM) software Software that uses a digital design such as that from a CAD system to directly control production machinery.

Computer-aided software engineering (CASE) An integrated set of systems development tools.

Computer-based information systems (CBIS) Information systems that include a computer for their operation.

Computer-integrated manufacturing (CIM) Integrates several computerized systems, such as CAD, CAM, MRP, and JIT into a whole, in a factory.

Conflict resolution team A team that resolves conflicts between end users and the IS department.

Consumer-to-business (C2B) E-commerce in which consumers make known a particular need for a product or service, and suppliers compete to provide the product or service to consumers; an example is Priceline.com.

Consumer-to-consumer (C2C) E-commerce in which an individual sells products or services to other individuals.

Context awareness Capturing a broad range of contextual attributes to better understand what the consumer needs, and what products or services he or she might possibly be interested in.

Contextual computing Active adaptation of the computational environment for each user, at each point of computing.

Cookie A text string stored on the user's hard drive file to record the history of the user's computer visits to particular Web sites.

Cooperative processing Teams two or more geographically dispersed computers to execute a specific task.

Corporate portal The gateway for entering the corporate Web site. It is usually a home page, which allows for communication, collaboration, and access to diversified information. Companies may have separate portals for outsiders and for employees.

Cost-benefit analysis Study that helps in decisions on IT investments by determining if the benefits (possibly including intangible ones) exceed the costs.

Cost leadership The ability of a company to produce quality products at the lowest cost in its industry group.

Courseware Software support for distance learning; it includes collaboration tools and content.

Cracker A malicious hacker.

Critical response activities The major activities used by organizations to counter *business pressures.*

Critical success factors (CSFs) Those few things that must go right in order to ensure the organization's survival and success.

Cross-functional activities Activities that are performed in several functional areas along the same business processes.

Customer-orientation strategy Competitive strategy in which a company concentrates on making customers happy.

Customer relationship management (CRM) The entire process of maximizing the value proposition to the customer through all interactions, both online and traditional. Effective CRM advocates one-to-one relationships and participation of customers in related business decisions.

Cyberbanking Banking conducted over the Internet or private networks, enabling people to bank from home or on the road.

Cybercafé A public place such as a coffee house or restaurant in which Internet terminals are available to users, usually for a small fee.

Cybercrime Illegal activities executed on the Internet.

Cybermall An electronic shopping center on the Internet (may include thousands of stores).

Cybersquatting The practice of registering domain names in order to sell them later at a higher price.

Cyberwar War in which a country's information systems would be paralyzed by a massive attack of destructive software.

Cycle time reduction The reduction of the time required to execute a task or produce a product. It is usually done by using information technologies.

Data Raw facts that can be processed into accurate and relevant information.

Data conferencing Data sent along with voice and/or video, enabling real-time communication.

Data integrity The accuracy of and accessibility to data.

Data item An elementary description of things, events, activities, and transactions that are recorded, classified, and stored, but not organized to convey any specific meeting; can be numeric, alphanumeric, figures, sounds, or images.

Data mart A subset of the data warehouse, usually originated for a specific purpose or major data subject.

Data mining The process of searching for unknown information or relationships in large databases using tools such as neural computing or case-based reasoning.

Data quality (DQ) A measure of the accuracy, objectivity, accessibility, relevance, timeliness, completeness, and other characteristics that describe useful data.

Data tampering Deliberately entering false data, or changing and deleting true data.

Data visualization Visual presentation of data and information by graphics, animation, or any other multimedia.

Data warehouse A repository of historical data, subject-oriented and organized, summarized, and integrated from various sources so as to be easily accessed and manipulated for decision support.

Data workers Clerical workers who use, manipulate, or disseminate information, typically using document management, workflow, e-mail, and coordination software to do so.

Database A collection of files serving as a data resource for computer-based information systems.

Database management system (DBMS) A software program (or group of programs) that manages and provides access to a database.

Decision metrics See *Metric benchmarks.*

Decision room A face-to-face arrangement for a group DSS in which terminals are available to the participants.

Decision support system (DSS) A computer-based information system that combines models and data in an attempt to solve semistructured problems with extensive user involvement.

Decryption The restoration (uncoding) of scrambled data into the original format using some key.

Dehumanization A condition that makes people lose their personalities and sense of identity when working with computers and information systems.

Delphi method A qualitative forecasting methodology using anonymous questionnaires done in several iterations, to find consensus.

Denial of service (DoS) Cyber attack in which an attacker uses specialized software to send a flood of data packets to the target computer, with the aim of overloading its resources.

Desktop publishing systems Computer systems that produce professional quality documents, combining text, photos, and graphics.

Desktop purchasing E-procurement method in which suppliers' catalogs are aggregated into an internal master catalog on the buyer's server for use by the company's purchasing agents.

Differentiation strategy Competitive strategy in which a company offers different products, services, or product features than those offered by competitors.

Differentiation (of product or service) A strategy of gaining competitive advantage by providing a product (or service) of the same cost and quality as a competitor, but with some additional attribute(s) that makes it different from the competition.

Digital divide The gap within a country, or between countries, between those that have information technology, particularly access to the Internet, and those that do not.

Digital economy Another name for today's Web-based, or Internet, economy.

Digital signature Authorizing signature added to electronic messages or electronic checks, usually encrypted in the sender public key for authentication purposes.

Direct cutover The option of converting to a new system by shutting off the old system and starting the new one at the same time.

Directories An Internet search facility that is a hierarchically organized collection of links to Web pages.

Disaster avoidance plan A comprehensive plan to avoid a controllable catastrophe in the corporate information systems.

Disaster recovery plan A plan to operate an IS area after a disaster (such as an earthquake) and to restore the functioning of the systems.

Disintermediation The elimination of intermediaries; removing the layers of intermediaries between sellers and buyers.

Distance learning A learning approach in which teachers and students are in different locations.

Distributed computing Computing architecture that breaks centralized computing into many semiautonomous computers that may not be (and usually aren't) functionally equal.

Distributed denial of service (DDoS) A denial of service attack in which the attacker gains illegal access to many computers and uses these computers to send a flood of data packets to the target computers.

Distributed processing See *Distributed computing.*

Document management The automated management and control of digitized documents throughout their life cycle.

Document management system (DMS) The system that provides document management.

Domain name The major (upper-level) category in an Internet name (URL).

Drill down The ability to investigate information in increasing detail; e.g., find not only total sales, but also sales by region, by product, or by salesperson.

Dynamic pricing The determination of prices based on supply and demand relationships at any given time, such as in auctions or stock markets; results in constantly changing prices.

E-business The broadest definition of e-commerce, including intrabusiness, IOS, and c-commerce; many use the term interchangeably with e-commerce.

E-commerce application An e-commerce program for a defined end-user activity such as e-procurement, e-auction, or ordering a product online.

eCRM The use of Web browsers, the Internet, and other electronic touch points in customer relationship management.

802.11b Standard, developed by the IEEE, on which most of today's WLANs run.

E-government The use of e-commerce to improve the internal operation of the government as well as its communication and collaboration with citizens and businesses.

E-learning Learning supported by the Web, in a variety of settings (either in physical classrooms or in virtual classrooms from home).

Electronic auctions Market mechanism by which sellers place offers and buyers make sequential bids, online; prices are determined dynamically by competitive bidding.

Electronic banking See *Cyberbanking.*

Electronic bartering The online exchange of commodities and/or services between business partners.

Electronic benefits transfer (EBT) Transfer of direct payments made by the government or other organization to recipients' bank accounts or smart cards.

Electronic cash (e-cash) A computerized stored value that can be used as cash; it is stored on a smart card or on a computer's hard drive.

Electronic certificates Verification, provided by a trusted third party, that a specific public encryption key belongs to a specific individual.

Electronic checks (e-checks) Payment mechanism made with electronic rather than paper checks.

Electronic commerce (e-commerce) The exchange of products, services, information, or money with the support of computers and networks; business conducted online.

Electronic communities Groups of people with similar interests who use the Internet to communicate or collaborate.

Electronic credit cards Payment mechanism that enables online payments with the characteristics of regular credit cards (e.g., pay within 30 days).

Electronic data interchange (EDI) Computer-to-computer direct communication of standard business transactions between or among business partners.

Electronic document management (EDM) See *Document management system.*

Electronic exchange See *Exchanges.*

Electronic funds transfer (EFT) The transmission of funds, debits and credits, and charges and payments electronically among banks and between banks and their customers.

Electronic mail (e-mail) Computer-based messages that can be electronically manipulated, stored, combined with other information, and exchanged with other computers.

Electronic mall An online shopping center with many (sometimes thousands) of stores in one Web site.

Electronic markets The networks of interactions and relationships where products, services, information, and payments are exchanged.

Electronic product code (EPC) Universal standard for product identification, stored on an RFID tag.

Electronic retailing Online selling of products or services to individuals, similar to regular retailing. Also known as *e-tailing.*

Electronic storefront A Web site of a single company in which orders can be placed. It includes a catalog, shopping cart, payment, search engine, shipment arrangements, etc.

Electronic surveillance The tracking of people's activities, online or offline. It is often done with the aid of computers (e.g., monitoring e-mail).

Electronic wallet (or purse) The storage and distribution of buying information, including credit card numbers, so buyers do not have to reenter information each time they buy.

E-mail agent Agent that manages users' e-mail by routing, deleting, prioritizing, or blocking e-mail.

E-marketplace (electronic markets) A place where buyers and sellers negotiate, submit bids, agree on orders, and if appropriate, finish the transactions electronically.

Employee relationship management (ERM) The use of Web-based applications to streamline the Human Resources process and to better manage employees.

Empowerment The vesting of decision-making or approval authority in employees in situations in which such authority was traditionally a managerial prerogative.

Encryption Scrambling of data so that they cannot be recognized by unauthorized readers.

Ends/means analysis (E/M analysis) Study that determines information requirements based on desired ends (effectiveness) and available means (efficiency) to achieve the ends.

End-user computing The use or development of information systems by the principal users of the systems' outputs or by their staffs.

Enhanced messaging service (EMS) An extension of SMS capable of simple animation, tiny pictures, and short tunes.

Enhanced product realization (EPR) system System that allows manufacturers to make fast modifications by using collaborative tools over the Internet.

Enterprise application integration (EAI) The process that helps to integrate applications inside an organization (e.g., an ordering system with an inventory on hand), or applications of different organizations in a seamless fashion. It is done by EAI vendors with special software tools.

Enterprise computing (enterprisewide computing) The information system architecture that connects data that are used throughout the enterprise.

Enterprise information system See *Enterprise computing.*

Enterprise knowledge portal (EKP) An electronic doorway into a knowledge management system.

Enterprise resource planning (ERP) An integrated process of planning and managing of all resources and their use in the entire enterprise. It includes contacts with business partners.

Enterprise software An integrated software that supports enterprise computing and ERP. The most notable example is SAP R/3.

Enterprise Web An open environment for managing and delivering Web applications, combining services from different vendors in a technology layer that spans rival platforms and business systems.

Enterprisewide system System that encompasses the entire enterprise, implemented on a companywide network.

Entry-barriers strategy Competitive strategy in which a company creates barriers to entry of new market entrants, e.g., by introducing innovative products or using IT to provide exceptional service.

E-planning Electronically supported IT planning that touches on EC infrastructure and mostly deals with uncovering business opportunities and deciding on an applications portfolio that will exploit those opportunities.

E-procurement Purchasing by using electronic support.

Ergonomics The science of adapting machines and work environments to people.

E-supply chain A supply chain that is managed electronically, usually with Web-based software.

E-tailers Electronic retailers, business-to-consumer (B2C) sellers in online stores; engaging in such activity is termed *e-tailing*.

Ethics A branch of philosophy that deals with what is considered to be right and wrong.

E-wallets (digital wallets) Payment mechanisms that provide security measures to EC purchasing by storing the financial information of the buyer; when buyers want to make a purchase, they click the e-wallet to automatically fill in the information needed to make the purchase.

Exception reporting Management reporting system that calls attention only to results that deviate from a standard by a certain percentage or exceed a threshold.

Exchanges Many-to-many e-marketplaces. Some refer to an exchange only if dynamic pricing (e.g., auctions) is available there.

Executive information systems (EISs) Systems specifically designed to support executive work.

Executive support system (ESS) An executive information system that includes some analytical and communication capabilities.

Expected value A weighted average. It is achieved by multiplying values by their relative importance or frequencies and totaling the results.

Expense Management Automation (EMA) Systems that automate data entry and processing of travel and entertainment expenses.

Expert support system An expert system that supports problem solving and decision making.

Expert system (ES) A computer system that applies reasoning methodologies or knowledge in a specific domain to render advice or recommendations — much like a human expert.

Explicit knowledge The knowledge that deals with objective, rational, and technical knowledge (data, policies, procedures, software, documents, etc.).

Exposure According to the CVE, the state in a computing system which is not a universal vulnerability, but either: allows an attacker to conduct information gathering activities; allows an attacker to hide activities; includes a capability that behaves as expected, but can be easily compromised; is a primary point of entry that an attacker may attempt to use to gain access to the system or data; and is considered a problem according to some reasonable security policy.

Extranet A secured network that allows business partners to access portions of each other's intranets. It is usually Internet-based.

Extreme programming (XP) A software-development discipline based on whole teams of developers using simple practices, with enough feedback to enable the team to see where they are and to tune the practices to their unique situation.

Fault-tolerance The ability to continue operating satisfactorily in the presence of faults.

Feasibility study Investigation that seeks an overview of a problem and a rough assessment of whether feasible solutions exist, prior to committing resources.

File A group of data with some form of commonality.

Financial value chain management (FVCM) The combination of financial analysis with operations analysis, which analyzes all financial functions in order to provide better financial control.

Firewalls Security devices that protect organizations' internal networks from hacking and other unauthorized access coming from the Internet.

Flaming Anonymous insulting or angry messaging on the Internet.

Flattened organizations Organizational structure that has fewer levels of management and a larger span of control than the hierarchical organization.

Forward auction An auction where the bidding price increases with time.

4G The expected next generation of wireless technology.

Four-stage model of planning A generic IS planning model based on four major, generic activities: strategic planning, information requirements analysis, resource allocation, and project planning.

Freeware Software available on the Internet for downloading, without the need to pay or get permission to use.

Frequency Division Multiple Access (FDMA) Wireless communication protocol, used by 1G systems, that gives each user a different frequency to communicate on.

Frontline decision making The decision making of employees who are in direct contact with customers, suppliers, or other outsiders.

Functional MIS An information system for a functional area, such as a marketing information system.

Fuzzy logic A way of reasoning that can cope with uncertain or partial information; a characteristic of human thinking and some expert systems.

General controls Physical, access, communications, administrative, and data security controls aimed at protecting a system in general rather than protecting specific applications.

Geographical information system (GIS) System that integrates GSP data onto digitized map displays.

Global business drivers Entities that benefit from global economies of scale and add value to a global business strategy.

Global positioning system (GPS) A wireless system that uses satellites to enable users to determine their position anywhere on the earth.

Global supply chain A supply chain that involves suppliers and/or customers in other countries.

Goal-seeking (analysis) Study that attempts to find what values certain variables must have in order to attain desired goals.

Graphical user interface (GUI) An interactive, user-friendly interface in which icons and similar graphical devices enable a user to control a computer.

Grid computing The use of networks to harness the unused processing cycles of all computers in a given network to create powerful computing capabilities.

Group decision support system (GDSS) An interactive, computer-based system that facilitates finding solutions to semistructured problems by using a set of decision makers working together as a group.

Group purchasing The aggregation of purchasing orders from many buyers so volume discount (or negotiation, or reverse auction) can be achieved.

Group support systems (GSSs) Information systems that support the working processes of groups (e.g., communication and decision making).

Groupware A generic term for several computerized technologies and tools that aim to support people working in groups.

Growth strategy Competitive strategy in which a company attempts to increase market share, acquire more customers, or sell more products.

Hackers People who illegally or unethically access a computer system.

Hard disk A hard, metal platter coated with a material that can be magnetized in spots to represent bits, primarily for secondary storage.

Hardware The physical equipment, media, and attached devices used in a computer system.

Hierarchical model Data model that rigidly structures data into an inverted "tree" in which records refer to a senior field and any number of subordinate fields (i.e., one "parent" and several "children").

Honeynets A network of *honeypots*.

Honeypots Traps designed to work like real systems and attract hackers.

Hotspot A wireless access point that provides service to a number of users within a small geographical perimeter (up to a couple hundred feet.

Hyperlink The links that connect data notes in hypertext and enable users to automatically move from one Web page to another by clicking on a highlighted word or icon.

Hypertext Markup Language (HTML) A programming language that uses hypertext to establish dynamic links (see *Hyperlink*) to other documents stored in the same or other computers on the Internet or intranets.

Identity theft Crime in which a criminal poses as someone else by stealing Social Security numbers and credit card numbers, usually obtained from the Internet, to commit fraud.

Increase switching costs strategy Competitive strategy in which a company sets up economic hurdles that discourage customers or suppliers from going to competitors.

Increasing returns A concept in economics that expects increased benefits with the volume of operation (the larger, the better).

Inference engine The component of an expert system that performs a reasoning function.

Information Data that are processed or operated on by a computer.

Information anxiety The frustration resulting from some people's inability to cope with the quantity or quality of information.

Information architecture A conceptualization of the manner in which information requirements are met by the information system.

Information centers Facilities that train and support business users with end-user tools, testing, technical support information, and standard certification.

Information economics An approach to cost-benefit analysis that incorporates organizational objectives in a scoring methodology to assess more accurately the value of intangible benefits.

Information infrastructure The physical arrangement of hardware, software, databases, networks, and so forth.

Information intensity The amount of information that measures the actual, or planned, usage of information.

Information portal Generic term for a single point of access through a Web browser to critical business information located inside and outside of an organization; content can vary from narrow to broad, and audience can also vary.

Information requirements analysis An analysis of the information needs of users and how that information relates to their work; stage 2 of the four-stage planning model.

Information resources management All activities related to the planning, organizing, acquiring, maintaining, securing, and controlling of IT resources.

Information superhighway A national information infrastructure to interconnect computer users.

Information system (IS) A physical process that supports an organization by collecting, processing, storing, and analyzing data, and providing information to achieve organizational goals.

Information systems controls The procedures, devices, or software that are used to counter computer hazards (such as crime and human errors).

Information technology (IT) The technology component of an information system (a narrow definition); or the collection of the entire systems in an organization (the broad definition used in this book).

Information technology architecture The field of study and practice devoted to understanding and planning information systems components in the form of an organizational infrastructure.

Innovation strategy Competitive strategy in which a company introduces new products and services, puts new features in existing products and services, or develops new ways to produce them.

Input device A computer system component that accepts data from the user (e.g., a keyboard or mouse).

Input/output (I/O) device A computer system component that transfers data into or out of a computer.

Inputs The resources introduced into a system for transformation into outputs.

Instant messaging Feature that allows users to identify partners and exchange realtime messages.

Intangible benefits Benefits that are hard to place a monetary value on (e.g., greater design flexibility).

Integrated CASE tools Software engineering tools that support prototyping and reusable systems components, including component repositories and automatic computer code generation.

Intellectual assets The valuable knowledge of employees.

Intellectual capital See *Intellectual asset.*

Intelligent agents Expert or knowledge-based software systems embedded in computer-based information systems (or their components).

Intelligent systems Information systems that include a knowledge component, such as an expert system or neural network.

Interactive voice response (IVR) A computer voice system that enables users to request and receive information and to enter and change data through regular telephone lines or through 1G cell phones.

Internet A self-regulated network of computer networks connecting millions of businesses, individuals, government agencies, schools, and other organizations all over the world.

Internet communities See *Electronic communities.*

Internet economy See *Digital economy.*

Internet kiosks Public locations from which people can access the Internet.

Internet of things A network that connects computers to objects in order to be able to track individual items as they move from factories to store shelves to recycling facilities, providing near-perfect supply chain visibility.

Internet2 A U.S. government initiative supporting the creation of a high-speed computer network connecting various research facilities across the country.

Interorganizational information systems (IOSs) Information systems between two or more organizations that support efficient, routine flow of transaction processing data.

Intrabusiness EC An application of EC methods inside one organization, usually on its intranet, creating a paperless environment. Activities range from internal customer service to selling products to employees.

Intranet A corporate network that functions with Internet technologies, such as browsers and search engines, using Internet protocols.

IT planning The organized planning for IT infrastructure and applications portfolios done at various levels of the organization.

Java An object-oriented programming language used extensively for Internet applications. For example, a variation, Java Script, is used with HTML.

Job content The elements of a job as reflected in its description.

Job stress The discomfort experienced by individuals in performing their jobs.

Joint application design (JAD) A structured process for information gathering from a group of key stakeholders, mainly to find the information requirements of users.

Joint application development See *Joint application design.*

Just-in-time (JIT) An inventory scheduling system in which material and parts arrive at a work place when needed, minimizing inventory, waste, and interruptions.

Key (in encryption) The code in which a message is encrypted. Each letter or number of the original message is represented by a series of numbers and letters. It is necessary to know the key in order to decrypt the message.

Keyword banners Messages that appear when a predetermined word is queried from a search engine.

Knowledge The understanding, awareness, or familiarity acquired through education or experience.

Knowledge audit The process of identifying the knowledge an organization has, who has it, and how it flows (or does not flow) through the enterprise.

Knowledge base A collection of facts, rules, and procedures organized in one place.

Knowledge discovery See *Knowledge discovery in databases.*

Knowledge discovery in databases (KDD) The process of extracting knowledge from volumes of data in databases (e.g., in data warehouses); it includes data mining.

Knowledge management (KM) The comprehensive management of the expertise in an organization. It involves collecting, categorizing and disseminating knowledge.

Knowledge management suites Software packages that consist of a comprehensive set of tools.

Knowledge management system (KMS) A system that facilitates knowledge management by ensuring knowledge flow from those who know to those who need to know throughout the organization. KMSs are centered around a corporate knowledge base or depository.

Knowledge network model Model that describes the knowledge transfer process as occurring through person-to-person contacts.

Knowledge repository The software system that is a collection of both internal and external knowledge in a KMS.

Knowledge repository model Model that describes the two-step knowledge transfer procedure of person-to-repository and repository-to-person.

Knowledge workers People who use knowledge as a significant part of their work responsibilities.

Knowledge-based economy The new, global economy that is driven by what people and organizations "know" and not only by capital and labor.

Knowware A name for knowledge management (KM) software.

Labor productivity The ratio of the value of outputs to the quantity of labor required to produce those outputs.

L-commerce See *Location-based commerce.*

Leaky knowledge See *Explicit knowledge.*

Learning organization An organization with the capability of learning from its past experience, implying an organizational memory and a means to save, represent, and share it among its members.

Legacy systems Older systems that have become central to business operations and may be still capable of meeting these business needs; they may not require any immediate changes, or they may be in need of reengineering to meet new business needs.

Light methodology A simplified system development life cycle (SDLC) approach used mainly for Web-based systems. It strikes a balance between rigor and development speed.

Local area network (LAN) A system for interconnecting two or more closely located communicating devices supporting full connectivity so that every user device on the network has the potential to communicate with any other device.

Location-based commerce (l-commerce) M-commerce transactions targeted to individuals in specific locations, at specific times.

Lock in customers or suppliers strategy Competitive strategy in which a company *encourages* customers or suppliers to stay rather than going to competitors.

Lock-in effect The difficulty of switching to a competing product because of the need to learn how to use a different product, or other factors that discourage change.

Logical design The design of information systems from the user's point of view.

Long-range planning A corporate or IT plan usually for five years or longer.

Lotus Notes (now Notes/Domino) An integrated groupware software package that also provides application developers an environment for quickly creating cross-platform client/server applications.

Machine learning A method by which a computer can learn from past experiences (e.g., from historical data).

Mainframe computers Relatively large computers built to handle very large computations and databases, thousands of user terminals with fast response times, and millions of transactions.

Management by maxim Approach that guides investment in IT infrastructure by identifying infrastructure requirements that correspond to organizational strategies and objectives.

Management information systems (MISs) Systems designed to provide past, present, and future routine information appropriate for planning, organizing, and controlling the operations of functional areas in an organization.

Management service provider (MSP) A vendor that, for a subscription fee, remotely manages and monitors enterprise applications (e.g., ERP, CRM, firewalls, proprietary e-business applications).

Management support systems (MSSs) Three major IT technologies designed to support managers: decision support systems, executive support systems, and groupware technologies.

Manufacturing resource planning (MRPII) A planning process that integrates production, inventory, purchasing, financing, and labor in an enterprise.

Marketing databases Large databases that contain marketing-related data and are used for determining advertisement and marketing strategies.

Marketing transaction database (MTD) An interactive marketing database oriented toward targeting messages and marketing in real time.

Mass customization The production of a very large quantity of customized products, such as computers (e.g., by Dell Computers).

Material requirements planning (MRP) A planning process (usually computerized) that integrates production, purchasing, and inventory management of interrelated products.

M-commerce (mobile commerce) E-commerce done with wireless devices including a GPS for location identification.

M-wallet (mobile wallet) A wireless wallet that enables cardholders to make purchases with a single click from their wireless device.

Metadata Data about data, such as indices or summaries.

Metamalls Online supermalls that serve several online malls by providing them with unified services, such as search engines.

Metasearch engines Special indexing agents that integrate the findings of the various search engines to answer queries posted by the users.

Metcalfe's law Maxim that states that the value of a network grows roughly in line with the square of the number of its users.

Metric benchmarks Numeric measures of IS performance relative to other numerical factors such as organizational revenues, CPU capacity, etc.

Metrics See *Metric benchmarks.*

Microbrowser Wireless software, designed with limited bandwidth and limited memory requirements.

Microcomputers Small and relatively inexpensive general-purpose computers; also known as *micros* and *personal computers (PCs).*

Micropayments Electronic payments for small-purchase amounts (generally less than $10).

Milestones Checkpoints established to allow periodic review of progress so that management can determine if a project merits further commitment of resources, if it requires adjustments, or if it should be discontinued.

Minicomputer A relatively smaller, cheaper, and more compact computer that performs the same functions as a larger, mainframe computer, but to a more limited extent.

Mobile agents Software agents that can move from one Internet site to another, access remote systems such as a database, perform tasks there, and send or retrieve data.

Mobile commerce (m-commerce, m-business) Any e-commerce done in a wireless environment, especially via the Internet.

Mobile computing Information system applications in a wireless environment.

Mobile devices Carriable computers such as laptops and PDAs and other handhelds.

Mobile handset A mobile system consisting of two parts—equipment that hosts the applications (e.g., a PDA) and a mobile terminal (e.g., a cell phone) that connects to the mobile network.

Mobile portal A gateway to the Web, accessible from mobile devices, that aggregates content and services for mobile users.

Mobility (of agents) The degree to which the agents themselves travel through the network.

Model (in decision making) A simplified representation or abstraction of reality, which can be used to perform virtual experiments and analysis.

Model base management system (MBMS) A software program to establish, update, and use a model base.

Model marts Small, generally departmental or topical repositories of knowledge created by employing knowledge-discovery techniques on past decision instances. Analogous to *data marts*.

Model warehouses Large, generally enterprisewide repositories of knowledge created by employing knowledge-discovery techniques on past decision instances. Analogous to *data warehouses*.

Modem A device that **mo**dulates and **dem**odulates signals.

Moore's law The expectation that the power of a microprocessor will double every 18 months, while the cost stays at the same level.

Multidimensional database A database organized by dimensions such as geographical region, time, product, or salesperson.

Multidimensionality The need to analyze data by looking at several dimensions. A dimension can be place, time, product, or customer.

Multifactor productivity The ratio of the value of outputs to the value of the inputs — including labor, investments, materials, etc. — used to produce these outputs.

Multimedia The combination of at least two media for input or output of data; these media can be audio (sound), voice, animation, video, text, graphics, and/or images.

Multimedia database A database in which data and procedures are stored as objects containing various multimedia (e.g., video clips).

Multimedia messaging service (MMS) The next generation of wireless messaging, which will be able to deliver rich media.

Natural language processor (NLP) A knowledge-based user interface that allows the user to carry on a conversation with a computer-based system in much the same way as he or she would converse with another human.

Net present value (NPV) Financial analysis that converts future values of benefits to their present-value equivalent by discounting them at the organization's cost of funds.

Netiquette The rules of conduct over the Internet, especially in newsgroups, chat rooms, and bulletin boards.

Network A telecommunications system that permits the sharing of resources such as computing power, software, input/output devices, and data.

Network computer (NC) A network-based terminal, similar to a "dummy" terminal in a mainframe, that allows communication and use of information on the network, but does not have storage capability.

Network effects The support that leading products in an industry receive from their large user base and the complementary products marketed to these users.

Network storage devices Storage devices that are attached to the corporate network (usually intranets) and that can be accessed from network applications throughout the enterprise for data sharing.

Networked computing A corporate information infrastructure that provides the necessary networks for distributed computing. Users can easily contact each other or databases and communicate with external entities.

Networked organization (enterprise) Organizational structure that is a seamless network, extending the corporate contacts to all the entities a company does business with.

Neural computing The technology that attempts to achieve knowledge representations and processing based on massive parallel processing, fast retrieval of large amounts of information, and the ability to recognize patterns based on experiences.

New economy Productive system that is distinguished from the old economy by being Internet based.

Niche strategy Competitive strategy in which a company selects a narrow-scope segment (niche market) and seeks to be the best in quality, speed, or cost in that market.

Nominal group technique (NTG) A group-dynamic procedure to improve the process of people working in a group.

Nonrepudiation The property that the senders of a message cannot deny that they actually sent the message; ability to limit parties from refuting that a legitimate transaction has taken place.

Object Name Service (ONS) Service that points a computer to an address on the Internet where information about a product is stored.

Object technology Technology that includes object-oriented programming, object-oriented databases, and other object-oriented-based components and activities.

Object-oriented database A database that is organized and managed using an object-oriented approach for data presentation and management.

Object-oriented development System development based on interchangeable software components (objects) that model the behavior of persons, places, things, or concepts in the real world.

Object-oriented programming (OOP) Programming that models a system as a set of cooperating objects.

Office automation systems (OASs) Systems used to increase the productivity of office workers and the quality of office work.

Offshore outsourcing Use of vendors in other countries, usually where labor is inexpensive, to do programming or other system development tasks.

1G The first generation of wireless technology, which was analog-based.

One-to-one marketing A new, interactive style of marketing that treats each customer in a unique way to match service with the customer's needs and other characteristics.

Online (electronic) catalogs Presentations of information about products (services) that traditionally were in paper catalogs. Electronic catalogs can include multimedia, such as voice and video clips.

Online analytical processing (OLAP) The processing of data as soon as transactions occur.

Online processing Analysis of databases to determine properties and complex relationships using DSS or other sophisticated software.

Online transaction processing (OLTP) A transaction processing system, created on a client/server architecture, that saves money by allowing suppliers to enter the TPS and look at the firm's inventory level or production schedule.

Operating system software The main system control program, which supervises the overall operation of a computer, including such tasks as monitoring the computer's status, handling executable program interruptions, and scheduling of operations.

Operational data store A database that provides clean data to the operational, mission-critical, short-term-oriented applications.

Operational effectiveness strategy Competitive strategy in which a company improves the manner in which internal business processes are executed so that it performs similar activities better than its rivals do.

Optical character reader (OCR) An input device that scans textual data.

Optical scanners Devices that scan text and graphics forms for input to a computer system.

Optimization An approach used by management science to find the best possible solution.

Option valuation The process of assigning a value to future benefits that could result from a current investment.

Order fulfillment All the activities needed to deliver a product (service) to a customer, after an order has been placed. This is done by the back-office operations.

Organization transformation The change that has taken place when an organization's business processes, structure, strategy, and procedures are completely different from the old ones.

Organizational culture The aggregate attitudes in an organization concerning a certain issue (such as technology, computers, and DSS).

Organizational decision support system (ODSS) A network DSS that serves people at several locations.

Organizational knowledge base The collection of knowledge related to the operation of an organization.

Organizational learning The process of organizations coping with major changes such as BPR. Such learning can be facilitated by knowledge bases.

Organizational memory What an organization "knows" and thus can apply.

Output device The part of a computer system that produces processed data or information.

Outputs The completed products or services of a system.

Outsourcing Acquiring IS services from an external organization rather than through internal employees.

Parallel conversion A process of converting to a new information system by using the old and new systems concurrently until the new system is demonstrably stable and reliable.

Parallel processing Executing several processing instructions at the same time (in parallel) rather than one at a time (serial or sequential processing).

Partner-relationship management (PRM) A strategy that focuses on providing quality service for business partners, facilitating communication and collaboration, and addressing problems quickly and effectively, while monitoring service levels provided by the partners.

Pattern recognition The ability of a computer to classify an item to a predetermined category by matching the item's characteristics with that of a stored category.

Peer-to-peer (P2P) architecture A type of network in which each client computer shares files or computer resources *directly* with others *but not through a central server.*

Peer-to-peer networks Network relationships that stress processing on an equal basis among all processors, sharing devices and data on a mutual basis.

Periodic reports Routine reports executed at predetermined times (in contrast with ad-hoc reports).

Permission marketing Efforts done once customers give their consent to receive advertisement and promotional material.

Personal digital assistant (PDA) A handheld wireless computer.

Personal information manager (PIM) A software package for a manager's personal use, combining the features of project management software and desktop organizers.

Personal portals Gateways to the Web that target specific filtered information for individuals.

Personalization strategy The knowledge management approach that attempts to share knowledge mostly through person-to-person contacts. The opposite is the *codification strategy.*

Person-to-person (P2P) payments Payments between individual customers, made in C2C commerce, such as in e-auctions or e-classified sales. Innovative methods allow such payments to be made without the need for a credit card.

Pervasive computing Invisible, everywhere computing that is embedded in the objects around us.

Phased conversion Switching from an old system to a new system in several phases.

Physical design The process of translating the logical design of a system into the technical design.

Pilot conversion Switching from an old system to a complete, new system in parts of an organization, one part at a time.

Pop-under ad An advertisement that is automatically launched underneath the active browser window.

Pop-up ad An advertisement that is automatically launched in front of the active browser window.

Portals The gateways to Web sites. They can be public (like Yahoo!), or private (corporate portals).

Post-audit The auditing conducted on information systems after their implementation and use.

Practice approach Knowledge management approach that assumes that much organizational knowledge is tacit in nature and so builds communities of practice necessary to facilitate the sharing of tacit understanding.

Price-to-performance ratio The relative cost, usually on a per-mips (millions of instructions per second) basis, of the processing power of a computer.

Primary activities In Porter's value chain model, those activities in which materials are purchased and processed to products, which are then delivered to customers. Secondary activities, such as accounting, support the primary ones.

Primary storage Main memory, which stores data and code for the CPU.

Private exchange E-marketplace owned by a single company; can be either sell-side or buy-side; entry is limited to those the exchange owner allows.

Private key A security encryption/decryption code that is known *only* to its user/owner.

Process approach Knowledge management approach that attempts to codify organizational knowledge through formalized controls, processes, and technologies.

Process-centric integration Integration solutions designed, developed, and managed from a business-process perspective, instead of from a technical or middleware perspective.

Processor A computer device that processes inputs into outputs.

Product lifecycle management (PLM) A business strategy that enables manufacturers and logistics providers to collaborate on product development efforts, typically using Web-based technologies.

Product Markup Language (PML) Proposed new markup language, based on the XML standard, that specifies how a product's name, category, manufacture date, expiration date, and the like will be represented in a computer.

Productivity paradox The seeming contradiction between extremely large IT investments in the economy, in contrast to indications of low productivity growth in the sectors that have received the largest IT investments.

Programming attack Crime popular with computer criminals who use programming techniques to modify a computer program, either directly or indirectly; examples are computer worms, viruses, and denial of service attacks.

Programming fraud A deliberate manipulation of a computer program so that a fraud can be committed.

Project planning The fourth stage of the model for information systems planning, providing an overall framework with which the system development life cycle can be planned, scheduled, and controlled.

Protocol A set of rules that determines how two computers communicate with one another over a network.

Prototyping An approach to systems development that exploits advanced technologies for using trial-and-error problem solving.

Public exchange E-marketplace in which there are many sellers and many buyers, and entry is open to all; frequently owned and operated by a third party.

Public key A security code of a certain individual that is distributed to authorized people so they can encrypt or decrypt messages with it.

Public key infrastructure (PKI) A security schema based on public key encryption that is used to secure e-payments. It also includes a digital signature and certificates.

Publishing portals Gateways to the Web that are intended for communities with specific interests.

Push technology Software that delivers only information that users want, per their preference profile.

Quality of life The measure of how well we achieve a desirable standard of living.

Radio frequency identification (RFID) Generic term for technologies that use radio waves to automatically identify individual items.

Random-access memory (RAM) Digital storage or memory that can be directly written to and read.

Random banners Messages that appear at random, not as a result of the viewer's action.

Rapid application development (RAD) A methodology that enables the rapid construction of information systems applications by using special tools.

Read-only memory (ROM) Digital storage or memory that can be read directly.

Real option valuation Strategic approach to capital budgeting decisions that looks for opportunities ("real options") that may be embedded in capital projects which, if taken, will enable the organization to increase future cash flows.

Reintermediation The process of (1) redefining the role of traditional intermediaries, to provide value-added services that cannot be provided online; or (2) establishing new electronic intermediaries in place of disintermediated traditional intermediaries.

Relationship marketing See *One-to-one marketing.*

Requirements analysis The stage in a system development life cycle in which the goals (outputs) of a system are evaluated against the needs of the users.

Resource allocation   The third stage of the model for information systems planning, consisting of developing the hardware, software, data communications, facilities, personnel, and financial plans needed to execute the master development plan.

Response management   The strategy of responding to competitors or market developments rather than being a leader.

Return on investment (ROI)   The percentage return on an investment in a project, computed as Net return ÷ Required investment.

Reverse auction   An e-procurement mechanism in which sellers are invited to bid on the fulfillment of an order to produce a product or provide a service. During the auction, bid prices will decline, so the lowest bidder wins.

Reverse engineering   The process of converting the code, files, and databases of legacy systems into components that can be used to create new (usually client/server) applications.

Reverse logistics (returns)   The return of products by customers. The items flow in a reverse direction, from the buyer back to the seller.

Risk management   The process of determining the potential risk associated with a project or a problem and considering this risk in cost-benefit analysis.

Robot   An electromechanical device that can be programmed to automate manual tasks.

Runaway project   A systems development project that requires much more spending or time to complete than budgeted or scheduled.

Sales automation software   The software used to automate the work of salespeople.

Sales-force automation   The hardware and software used by salespeople, usually in the field, to automate some of their tasks (e.g., using wireless computers to generate proposals at clients' sites).

SAP R/3   The leading EPR software (from SAP AG Corp.). It is a highly integrated package containing more than 70 modules.

Savant   Software created by the Auto-ID center that gathers information from RFID readers and passes it on to various business applications.

Scenario planning   A methodology of dealing with an uncertain environment by examining different scenarios; a what-if analysis.

Scoring methodology   Methodology that evaluates alternatives by assigning weights and scores to various aspects and then calculating the weighted totals for comparison.

Screen sharing   Technology that enables two or more participants to see the same screen and make changes on it that can be seen by all.

Screenphone   A telephone equipped with a color screen, possibly a keyboard, e-mail, and Internet capabilities.

Search engines   Software agents whose task is to find information by looking at keywords, or by following some guidelines.

Secondary storage   Computer hardware that stores data in a format that is compatible with the data stored in primary storage, but provides space for storing and processing large quantities of software and data for long periods.

Segmentation   Marketing technique of dividing customers into specific segments, like age or gender.

Self-healing computers   Computers that can find their problems and correct them themselves, before a system crashes.

Sell-side models (marketplaces)   Marketplaces with one seller and many buyers (one-to-many).

Semantic Web   An extension of the current Web in which information will be given well-defined meanings, facilitating search, interoperability, and the composition of complex applications.

Sensitivity analysis   Study of the effect of a change in one or more input variables on a proposed solution.

Server   Any system or process that *provides* data, services, or access to other systems for clients.

Service-level agreements (SLAs)   Contracts between the IS department and end users that specify what, when, and how IS services are expected to be rendered.

Shareware   A downloadable software that the user can try without fee, but is expected to pay for if he or she wants to use it.

Short message service (SMS)   The "e-mail" of the wireless environment, consisting of text messages up to 160 characters in length.

Short messaging service (SMS)   Technology that allows for sending of short text messages on some cell phones.

Simputer   A variation of the thin client; short for "simple computer."

Simulation   A process of imitation of reality. It is usually done for computerized experiments with proposed solutions.

Smart appliances   Machines that react to communication over networks (including wireless) and perform tasks such as cooking. They can sense the environment and react like robots.

Smart cards   Storage media the size of a credit card that contain a microprocessor capable of storing and processing information.

Smartphone   Internet-enabled cell phones that can support mobile applications.

Smart terminal   A terminal that contains a keyboard, screen, and disk drive that enables it to perform limited processing tasks, yet whose core processing power is the central mainframe computer to which it is networked.

Social engineering   Getting around security systems by tricking computer users into providing information or carrying out actions that seem innocuous but are not.

Social responsibility   Concern of a corporation for social issues — for example, to improve the air pollution or health level in the community.

Softbot   An abbreviation for **soft**ware ro**bot**s. Another name for *software agents*.

Software   Instructional coding that manipulates the hardware in a computer system.

Software agents Autonomous software programs that execute mundane tasks for the benefit of their users. Also known as *intelligent agents*.

Spamming Indiscriminate distribution of messages (e.g., junk mail) without consideration for their appropriateness.

Span of control A measure of the number of employees who report to one supervisor or manager.

Speech recognition A process that allows people to communicate with a computer by speaking to it.

Speech understanding The ability of computers to understand the meaning of sentences, in contrast with *recognizing* individual words.

Stages of IT growth Six commonly accepted stages, suggested by Nolan, that all organizations seem to experience in implementing and managing an information system from conception to maturity over time.

Stealthware Hidden programs, which come with free software you download, that track your surfing activities, reporting it to a marketing server.

Steering committee Group composed of key managers representing major functional units within the organization to oversee the IS function, to ensure that adequate planning and control processes are present, and to direct IS activities in support of long-range organizational objectives and goals.

Sticky knowledge See *Tacit knowledge*.

Stored-value card A smart card that stores electronic cash that can be used to purchase items or services.

Strategic alliances Business alliances among companies that provide strategic benefits to the partners.

Strategic information planning (SIP) The identification and planning of IT-based strategic applications.

Strategic information systems (SISs) Information systems that provide, or help to provide, strategic advantage.

Strategic management The way an organization maps the strategy of its future long-term operations.

Strategic planning The first stage of the planning model, which aligns IS strategic planning with overall organizational planning by assessing organizational objectives and strategies, setting the IS mission, assessing the environment, and setting IS policies, objectives, and strategies.

Strategic systems Those systems that *significantly* impact the operation of an organization, its success, or even its survival.

Subscriber identification module (SIM) card An extractable storage card used for identification, transaction processing, and the like.

Subscription computing A type of *utility computing* that puts the pieces of a computing platform together as services, rather than as a collection of separately purchased components.

Supercomputers Computers that have the most processing power of computers generally available.

Supply chain All of the activities related to the acceptance of an order from a customer and fulfilling it. In its extended format, it also includes connections with suppliers, customers, and other business partners.

Supply chain intelligence (SCI) Software products that offer analysis of supply chain operations and their improvement.

Supply chain management (SCM) The management of all the activities along the supply chain, from suppliers, to internal logistics within a company, to distribution to customers. This includes ordering, monitoring, and billing.

Supply chain team A group of tightly integrated businesses that work together to serve the customer, with each task done by the member of the team who is best capable of doing that specific task.

Support activities Business activities that do not add value directly to a firm's product or service under consideration but support the primary activities that do add value.

Sustainable strategic advantage A strategic advantage that can be maintained for some length of time.

Symbolic processing The use of symbols, rather than numbers, combined with rules of thumb (or heuristics) to process information and solve problems.

Synchronous (real-time) communication The nearly simultaneous sending and receiving of messages.

System A set of elements that acts as a single, goal-oriented entity.

System development The structuring of hardware and software to achieve the effective and efficient processing of information.

System software A set of instructions that act as the intermediary between the computer hardware and application programs.

Systematic sourcing Purchases made from a supplier with whom a business maintains a long-term relationship and contracts.

Systems analysis In system development, the phase in which cost-benefit and feasibility studies are done.

Systems development life cycle (SDLC) A model for developing a system based on a traditional problem-solving process with sequential steps and options for revisiting steps when problems appear.

Tacit knowledge The knowledge that is usually in the domain of subjective, cognitive, and experiential learning. It is highly personal and hard to formalize.

Telecommunications All types of electronic, high-speed, long-distance voice and data communication, usually through the use of common carriers.

Telecommuting (teleworking) An arrangement whereby employees work at home, at the customer's premises, in special work places, or while traveling, usually using a computer linked to their place of employment.

Teleconferencing The ability to confer with a group of people by telephone or computer systems.

Telematics The integration of computers and wireless communications to improve information flow using the principles of telemetry.

Text mining The application of data mining analysis to nonstructured text files and documents.

3G The third generation of digital wireless technology; supports rich media such as video clips.

Time Division Multiple Access (TDMA) Wireless communication protocol, used with some 2G systems, that assigns different users different time slots on a given communications channel.

Time strategy Competitive strategy in which a company treats time as a resource, then manages it and uses it as a source of competitive advantage.

Total benefits of ownership (TBO) An approach for calculating the payoff of an IT investment by calculating both tangible and the intangible benefits and subtracting the costs of ownership: TBO − TCO = Payoff.

Total cost of ownership (TCO) A formula for calculating the cost of owning and operating a PC.

Total quality management (TQM) An organizationwide effort to improve quality and make it the responsibility of all employees.

Transaction processing system (TPSs) An information system that processes an organization's basic business transactions such as purchasing, billing, and payroll.

Trend analysis The study of performance over time, attempting to show future direction using forecasting methods.

Turing test Named after the English mathematician Alan Turing, test designed to measure if a computer is intelligent or not. A computer is considered intelligent only when a human interviewer, conversing with both an unseen human being and an unseen computer, cannot determine which is which.

2G The second generation of digital wireless technology; accommodates mainly text.

2.5G Interim wireless technology that can accommodate limited graphics.

User interfaces Features that facilitate communications between a user (a person) and an information system and may be tailored uniquely for an individual.

Utility computing Unlimited computing power and storage capacity that, like electricity, water, and telephone services, can be obtained on demand, used and reallocated for any application, and billed on a pay-per-use basis.

Value analysis Study that facilitates decision making in situations where intangible benefits are important, by evaluating benefits and costs through an initial prototype prior to development of a complete system.

Value chain model Model developed by Porter that shows the primary activities that sequentially add value to the profit margin; also shows the support activities.

Value systems In Porter's value chain model, the producers, suppliers, distributors, and buyers (all with their own value chains).

Value-added networks (VANS) Networks that add communications services to existing common carriers.

Vendor-managed inventory (VMI) Strategy used by retailers of allowing suppliers to monitor the inventory levels and replenish inventory when needed, eliminating the need for purchasing orders.

Vertical exchange A B2B exchange that is centered on a specific industry.

Vertical marketplace (vertical exchange) An exchange whose members and activities are in one industry or segment of it (e.g., steel, rubber, or banking).

Vertical portals Electronic exchanges that combine upstream and downstream EC activities of specialized products or services (e.g., chemicals, metals, electricity).

Video mail Application that enables users to transmit photos, pictures, and documents among conversing people, including conferencing.

Video teleconferencing Teleconferencing with the added capability of the participants to see each other as well as documents or other objects.

Viral marketing Word-of-mouth advertisement in which customers promote your product or service without cost to you (or at a minimal cost). The advertising propagates itself the way viruses do.

Virtual banks Banks dedicated solely to Internet transactions.

Virtual close The ability of a company to close its books (accounting records) any time, on short notice.

Virtual collaboration The use of digital technologies to collaboratively plan, design, develop, manage, and research products, services, and innovative IT and EC applications.

Virtual communities See *Electronic communities*.

Virtual corporations Businesses that operate from various locations, usually through telecommunications, without a permanent headquarters.

Virtual group A group whose members are in different locations.

Virtual meetings Electronically supported meetings whose members are in different locations, frequently in different countries.

Virtual organization (virtual corporation, VC) An organization composed of several business partners whose resources are integrated for the purpose of producing a product or service though the partners remain in their original locations.

Virtual reality A pseudo-3-D interactive technology that provides a user with a feeling that he or she is physically present in a computer-generated world.

Virtual Reality Markup Language (VRML) A platform-independent standard for virtual reality.

Virtual society A society in which all the components are based on some functional entities rather than physical ones.

Virtual universities Online universities from which students take classes from home or an off-site location via the Internet.

Virtual work (distributed work) Work done in environments in which the work teams are geographically distributed and sometimes are interorganizational teams.

Virus Software that can damage or destroy data or software in a computer.

Visual interactive modeling (VIM) A method of modeling situations for problem solving where users can interact with the system and the results of their actions are displayed.

Visual interactive simulation (VIS) A VIM where simulation is used as the problem-solving tool.

Visual recognition The computer's ability to interpret scenes. Also known as *computer vision.*

Voice mail Digitized spoken messages that are stored and transferred electronically to receivers.

Voice portal A Web site with audio interface, accessed by making a phone call.

Voice recognition The ability of a computer to understand the meaning of spoken words.

Voice synthesis The technology that transforms computer output to voice or audio output.

Voice XML (VXML) An extension of XML designed to accommodate voice.

Vulnerability (in security) A system's exposure to potential hazards, either intentional or accidental.

Waterfall method The process of system development where work flows down from one stage to the next only after it is completed.

Wearable devices Mobile wireless computing devices for employees who work on buildings and other difficult-to-climb places.

Web conferencing Videoteleconferencing that is conducted solely on the Internet (not on telephone lines) for as few as two and as many as thousands of people.

Web economy See *Digital economy.*

Web mining Finding ("mining") and analyzing data that are collected from the Web, such as clickstream data.

Web services Modular business and consumer applications, delivered over the Internet, that users can select and combine through almost any device, enabling disparate systems to share data and services.

Web-based DSS A DSS that is supported by the Web, either for developing applications and/or disseminating and using them. Both the Internet and intranets can be used.

Web-based system An application delivered on the Internet or intranet using Web tools, such as a search engine.

Webcam A camera whose image information is uploaded to the Web site, sometimes every few seconds, so viewers can see up-to-the-minute showrooms.

Weights (in neural networks) Numbers assigned to express the relative importance of input data.

What-if analysis Study that determines the effect of changing some of the input data on solutions.

Whiteboard (electronic) An area on a computer display screen on which multiple users can write or draw; multiple users can use a single document "pasted" onto the screen.

Wide area networks (WANs) Networks that generally span distances greater than one city and include regional networks such as telephone companies or international networks such as global communications services providers.

Wireless access point An antenna connecting a mobile device (laptop or PDA) to a wired local area network.

Wireless Application Protocol (WAP) A set of communications protocols designed to enable different kinds of wireless devices to talk to a server installed on a mobile network, so users can access the Internet.

Wireless computing Content delivery over wireless devices.

Wireless fidelity (Wi-Fi) The standard on which most of today's WLANs run, developed by the IEEE (Institute of Electrical and Electronic Engineers). Also known as *802.11b.*

Wireless LAN (WLAN) LAN without the cables; used to transmit and receive data over the airwaves.

Wireless Markup Language (WML) Scripting language used for creating content in the wireless Web environment; based on XML, minus unnecessary content to increase speed.

Wireless 911 (e-911) Calls from cellular phones to providers of emergency services.

Wireless Transport Layer Security (WTLS) Communication protocols that enable encrypted communications between a mobile device and the WAP gateway and support the key elements of electronic payment systems.

Wireless Wide Area Networks (WWANs) Wide area networks for mobile computing.

Word processing systems The familiar software (such as Microsoft Word) and supporting hardware that help in creating, editing, combining, formatting, savings, distributing, and printing documents.

Work group Two or more individuals who act together to perform a task.

Work management systems (WMSs) Systems that distribute, route, monitor, and evaluate various types of work by controlling and managing all related information flow.

Workflow systems Systems that use group support software for scheduling, routing, and monitoring specific tasks throughout an organization.

World Wide Web (WWW, the Web) The most widely used application that uses the transport functions of the Internet.

Workflow management Automation of workflows, so that documents, information, or tasks are passed from one participant to another in a way that is governed by the organization's rules or procedures.

WYSIWYG Acronym for "what you see is what you get," indicating that material displayed on a computer screen will look exactly (or almost exactly) as it will look on a printed page.

Zombies The machines on which DDos software is loaded.

Photo Credits

Chapter 1
Page 31: Courtesy of Symbol Technologies

Chapter 2
Page 50: PhotoDisc, Inc./Getty Images

Chapter 6
©Brian Miller Photography

Chapter 7
Page 318: Sonda Dawes/The Image Works

Chapter 11
Page 537: Courtesy of Dallas Area Rapid Transit (DART)

Chapter 12
Page 560: The Management Cockpit ® is a registered trademark of SAP, created by Professor Patrick M. Georges and delivered by N.E.T. Research. Page 453: Courtesy of City University of Hong Kong

Chapter 13
DILBERT reprinted by permission of United Feature Syndicate, Inc.

Name Index

A

Abbott, C., *172*
Abramson, G., 475, *488*
Ackerman, Joe, 477
Adams, S., 685, *729*
Adamson, J., 378, *394*
Adjeroh, D. A., *538*
Afuah, A., 10, *40*, 92, *123*
Agranoff, M. H., 45, *46*
Agrawal, M., 220, 221, *229*
Agrawal, M. T. V., 87, 88, *88*
Agrawal, R., 613, 614, *629*, 729
Agrawal, V., 420, *446*
Agre, P. E., 70, *85*
Ahituv, N., 658, *677*
Ahmad, I., 67, *85*
Alavi, M., 453, 454, 457, 459, 460, *488*
Albalooshi, F., 157, *172*
Alberts, B., 727, *729*
Alesso, P., 569, *586*
Alga, N., 215, *229*, 703, 704, *729*
Allee, V., 476, *488*
Allen, P., 651, *677*
Allison, Jack, 469
Alter, S. L., 497, *538*
Alwang, G., 217, *229*
Amato-McCoy, D., 469, *488*
Amato-McCoy, D. M., 67, *85*, 307, 313, 349, *352*, 508, 512, 535, *538*, 569, *586*
Ambrosio, J., 476, *488*
Amidon, D., 474, 475, *489*
Amit, R., 16, *40*
Amor, D., *292*
Amos, Jim H., Jr., 638
Anderson, C., 249, *292*
Anderson, D., 17, *40*
Anderson, L., 465, *488*
Anderson, L. A., 435, *446*
Aneja, A., 138, *172*
Ang, J. S. K., 416, *447*
Anthony, R. N., 549, *586*
Applegate, L. M., 10, *40*
Apte, C., 511, 512, *538*
Armstrong, C., 95, *123*
Arnoff, D., 559, *586*
Aronson, J., 545, *586*
Arsanjani, A., 649, *677*
Arthur, W. B., 620, 621, *629*
Ash, C. G., 435, *446*
Asprev, L., 498, *538*
Athens, G., *172*
Athitakis, M., 189, 221, 228, *229*
Atkins, M., *586*
Atlas, R. I., 699, *729*
Atre, S., 505, *539*
Atzeni, P., 526, *538*
Austin, R. D., 690, *729*
Azari, R., *729*

B

Ba, S., *586*
Baard, M., 267, *292*
Baker, W., 319, *352*
Ball, L. D., 77, *85*, 686, *729*
Banerjee, P., 522, *538*
Banks, E., 323, *352*
Bantz, D. F., 75, *85*
Barko, C. D., 510, *539*
Barth, S., 474, 476, *488*
Barthelemy, J., 611, 615, *629*
Barua, A., 421, *446*, 678
Barva, A., 24, *40*
Basu, A., 151, *172*
Bates, J., 497, 514, *538*, 578, *586*
Bauer, M. J., 357, *395*
Baumer, D., 496, *538*
Bayers, C., 188, *229*
Bayles, D. L., 215, *229*, 364, 381, *394*
Beath, C. M., 597, 598, *631*
Becker, D., 266, *292*, 681, 682, *729*
Becker, S. A., 498, *538*
Beitler, S. S., 535, *538*
Belanger, F., 159, 160, *172*
Bell, C. R., 96, *123*
Benaroch, M., 609, 610, *629*
Benbasat, I., 566, *586*
Benjaafar, S., 310, *352*
Bennet, A., 454, *488*
Bennet, D., 454, *488*
Bennett, A., *292*
Bennett, R. F., *629*
Berger, N. S., 158, *172*
Berners-Lee, T. J., 134, *172*
Bernstein, P. A., 301, *352*
Beroggi, G. E., 520, *538*
Berry, J. A., 513, *539*
Berry, M., 512, *538*
Bezos, Jeff, 188
Bhise, H., 94, *123*
Bielski, L., 309, *352*
Biermann, E., 709, *729*
Biery, K., 712, *729*
Birks, D. F., 518, 519, *539*
Bishop, R., 372, *395*
Bithos, P., 93, *123*
Blanco, L., 718, *729*
Bligh, Mr., 654
Blodgett, M., 398, *446*, 466, *488*
Blum, R., 604, *629*
Boar, B. H., 399, 418, *446*
Bochenek, G. M., 150, *173*
Bodow, S., 221, *229*
Boisvert, L., 158, *172*, 334, *352*
Boisvert, M., 160, *173*
Bolloju, N., 463, *488*
Bonabeau, E., 545, 546, *586*
Borck, J. R., 330, *352*

Borland, J., *85*, *292*
Bosilj-Vuksic, V., 434, *446*
Boucher-Ferguson, R., 326, *352*
Boudreau, M. C., 433, *446*
Boyett, J. H., 11, *40*
Boyett, J. T., 11, *40*
Bradley, P., 150, *172*
Braiker, B., *229*
Brandeis, L. D., 45, *46*
Brandt, A., *294*
Brassil, R. A., 715, *729*
Brauer, J. R., 496, 497, *538*
Bresnahan, J., 371, *394*
Bretz, E., 279, *292*
Brezillon, P., 559, *586*
Briggs, D., 559, *586*
Broadbent, Bill, 659
Broadbent, M., 65, *85*, 412, 426, *446*, 597, 608, 609, *629*
Broderick, Matthew, 251
Brookman, F., 140, 141, *172*
Brown, D. E., 511, *538*
Brown, R. H., 614, *629*
Brown, S. A., 336, 338, *352*
Brown, S. J., 457–459, *488*
Browning, Monica, 455
Brownlow, J., 694, *731*
Brue, G., 16, *40*
Bruno, L., 696, *729*
Brynjolfsson, E., 594, *629*, 630
Brynolfsson, E., 4, *40*
Bucholz, G. A., 221, *229*
Buchwitz, L., 96, *123*
Bucken, M. W., 643, *677*
Buckler, Jim, 676
Buckley, N., 321, *352*
Bughin, J., 258, *292*
Bunker, E., 156, *172*
Burke, L. A., 420, *446*
Burn, J. M., 435, *446*
Buss, D., 335, *352*
Bussler, L., 329, 332, 334, *352*

C

Cahill, T., 451, *488*
Caldwell, B., 369, 371, *394*
Cale, E. G., 402, *446*
Callaghan, D., 153, *172*
Callon, J. D., 16, *40*, 92–94, 109, 120, *123*, 429, *446*
Campbell, D., 517, *538*
Carbone, P. L., 513, 514, *538*
Carlsson, C., 551, *586*
Carmel, E., 150, *172*, 613, 614, *629*
Carr, N. G., 4, 6, 14, *40*
Carroll, S., 135, *172*

Carter, G. M., 556, *586*
Cassidy, A., 400, *446*
Caulfield, B., 704, *729*
Cawsey, A., 559, *586*
Cerami, E., 677
Chaffee, D., *172*
Champy, J., 17, *40*, 420, 423, 424, 428, *446*
Chan, P. Y. K., 212, *230*
Chan, Y. E., 402, *446*
Chandra, J., 24, 27, *40*
Chang, C. Y., 433, *447*
Chatterjee, A., 272, *292*
Chaudhury, A., 317, *352*
Cheeseman, H. R., 217, *229*
Chen, A., 235, 235, 281, *292*
Chen, C. H., 572, *586*
Chen, E. J., 310, *352*
Chen, H., 206, *229*
Chen, J. S., 434, *446*
Chen, Y., 457, *489*
Cherry, S. M., 573, *586*
Ching, R. K. H., 434, *446*
Choi, S. Y., 5, *40*, 92, *123*, 128, *172*, 177–178, 209, *229*, 620, *629*
Chopoorian, J. A., 494, 510, *538*
Choudrie, J., 435, *446*
Choy, J., 578, *586*
Christenson, E., *229*
Church, R. L., 518, 519, *538*
Cilli, C., 684, *729*
Clark, M., 32, *40*
Clarke, A., 435, *446*
Clemons, E. K., 91, 95, *123*, 615, 616, *629*
Clermout, P., 600, *629*
Cline, M. K., *629*
Cobe, B., 159, *172*
Codd, E. F., 508, 509, *539*
Cohen, A., 239, 246, *292*
Cohen, H. D., 574, *586*
Cohen, J. B., *539*
Cohen, M., 185, *229*
Cole, B., 498, *539*
Colgan, D., *629*
Collett, S., *394*
Collins, H., 466, *488*
Collins, P., 310, *352*
Comcowich, W. J., 96, *123*
Cone, E., 74, *85*
Cone, J. W., 159, *172*
Conley, W. L., 49, *85*
Conlin, R., 360, *394*
Conrad, D., 267, *292*
Coopee, T., 611, *629*
Cope, J., 131, *172*
Corbett, C. J., 420, *447*
Corbett, M. F., 613, *629*
Cortese, A., 57, *85*
Costa, D., 214, *229*
Cothrel, J., 474, *488*
Coursaris, C., 245, 265, *292*
Cramm, S. H., 615, 617, *629*
Creese, G., 496, 497, *539*
Cross, K., 96, *123*
Cule, P., 629, 677
Curry, J., 416, *446*

Cushing, K., 613, *629*
Cusumano, M., 614, *629*

D

Dahanayake, A., 648, *678*
Daisey, M., 188, *229*
Dale, R., 568, *587*
Dalgleish, J., 522, *539*
Dallow, P., 160, *172*
Daly, J., 221, *229*
Damle, P., 693, *729*
Damsguard, L., 387, *394*
Darby, C. A. R., 690, *729*
Davamanirajan, P., 599, *629*
Davenport, T. H., 94, *123*, 376, *394*, 456, 457, 475, 478, *488*
David, J. S., 604, *629*
Davidson, P., 695, *729*
Davies, N., 281, 284, *292*
Davis, B., 13, *40*
Davis, J. L., *729*
Davis, J. T., 571, *586*
Davis, M., *488*
Davis, S., 429, *447*
Davison, R., 149, 150, 160, *172*, *173*
Davison, R. M., 42, 45, *46*
Dawar, N., 95, *124*
Day, M., 311, *352*
DeFazio, D., 339, *352*
Degnan, C., 326, *352*
de Hoog, R., 598, *629*
Deise, M. V., 92, *123*
Deitel, H. M., 185, *229*
Dekker, R., 598, *629*
Delahoussaye, M., 158, 171, *172*
Delavati, Hank, 675
Delcambre, L., 500, *539*
Dell, M., *123*
Dell, Michael, 94
DeLong, D., 556, *587*
DeLong, D. W., 458, 459, *488*
Demak, Barry, 627
DePalma, D., 602, *630*
DeSanctis, G., 4, 11, *40*, 141, *172*, 554, *586*
Deshmukh, S. G., 437, *447*
deSouza, A. A., 553, *587*
Desouza, K. C., 96, *123*, 476, *488*
Devaraj, S., 596, 597, 600, 604, 609, 610, 618, *630*
Devargas, M., 713, *729*
Devedzic, V., 574, *587*
de Vreede, G., 149, 150, *172*
DeYoung, J., *172*
Dhillon, G., *446*
Diao, Y., 685, *729*
DiCarlo, L., 147, *172*
Dick, Philip K., 273
Dickson, G. W., 4, 11, *40*
Dietel, E. M., 652, 653, *678*
DiNunno, D., 600, *630*
DiSanzo, F. J., 160, *174*
Dixit, A. K., 610, *630*
Dodd, C. J., *629*
Dogac, A., 242, 243, *292*

Doll, M. W., 217, *229*, 699, 700, *729*
Dollar, G., 158, *172*
Donofrio, N., 26, *40*
Donovan, R. M., 361, *394*
Doughty, K., 699, 700, 719, *729*
Dreyfus, H., 562, *586*
Dreyfus, S., 562, *586*
Drickhamer, D., 368, *394*
Drucker, D. F., 4, 11, 13, 14, *40*
Drucker, Peter, 18, 221
Drury, J., 143, *172*
Duan, M., 274, *292*
Duffy, D., 472, *488*, 687, *729*
Duguid, P., 457–459, *488*
Dunne, D., 248, *292*
Durkovich, C., 728, *729*, 729
Duvall, M., 615, *630*
Dvaraj, S., *630*

E

Earl, M., 18, *40*
Earl, M. J., *123*, 400, *446*, 686, 687, *729*
Edgington, C., 275, *292*
Edvinsson, L., 453, *488*
Edwards, J. D., 94, 115, 122, *123*
Edwards, J. S., 564, *586*
Eisenhart, M., 474, *488*
Eklund, B., 258, *293*
Eklund, R., 262, *293*
El Sawy, D. A., 383, *394*
El Sawy, O., 398, 423, 427, 436, 437, *446*
El-Sawy, O., 17, *40*
El Sawy, O. A., 556, *586*
El Sharif, H., 556, *586*
Ensher, E. A., 330, 331, *352*
Epner, S., 363, 365, *394*
Erlikh, L., 70, 71, *85*
Estrada, M., 239, 259, *293*
Estrin, D., 275, 277, *293*
Etzioni, O., 513, *539*
Evangelista, A. S., 420, *446*
Evans, P. B., 4, 14, *40*
Evers, J., *293*
"Experts Offer Key Tips on Building, Inegrating Portal Marts," 164, *172*

F

Fahey, L., 458, 459, *488*
Faida, A., 708, 710, *729*
Farhoomand, A., 180, *230*
Farhoomand, Ali F., 49
Favier, J., 220, *230*
Fayad, M., 282, *293*
Fayyad, U. M., 507, *539*
Feeny, D. F., 686, *730*
Feldman, E. R., 713, *729*
Ferguson, J., 416, *446*
Ferguson, M., 138, *172*
Ferrin, B. G., 604, *630*
Feurer, R., 403, *446*
Field, T., 115, *123*

Fikes, B., *293*
Fine, C. H., 605, *630*
Fingar, P., 423, *447*
Finkelstein, C., 404, *447*
Fischer, L., 151, *172*
Fisher, A., 592, *630*
Fisher, K., 160, *172*
Fisher, M. D., 160, *172*
Fitiani, S., *730*
Fjermestad, J., 335, *353*
Flanagan, R., 572, *586*
Fleck, M., 281, *293*
Flohr, U., 164, *172*
Fong, A. C. M., 509, *539*
Ford, D. P., 456, 457, *488*
Fox, B., 94, *123*
Frank, T., 342, *353*
Frank, T. G., 372, *395*
Freeman, C., 11, *40*
Freeman, J., 324, *352*
Fremantle, P., 651, *678*
Frenzel, C. W., 101, 104, *123*
Friar, B., *85*
Frost, S., 651, *677*
Frownfelter-Lohrke, C., 718, *729*

G

Galagan, P. A., 171, *172, 352*
Gallaugher, J. M., 183, *230*
Galliers, B., 420, *446*
Galliers, D. E., 6, *40*
Galliers, R., 92, *123*
Gallupe, B., 141, *172*, 554, *586*
Galvin, Michael, 716, 717
Gangopadhyay, A., 519, *539*
Garfinkel, S., 710, *729*
Garner, R., 614, *630*
Gaskin, J. E., *172*
Gates, B., *123*
Gates, Bill, 74
Gates, H. B., 13, *40*
Gates, R. H., 193, *230*
Gaulke, M., *630*
Gebauer, J., 211, *230*, 377, *395*, 614, *631*
Gellersen, H. W., 284, *292*
Gellman, Bob, 94
Gengler, C. E., 410, 411, *447*
Gentile, G., 317, *352*
Gentry, J. A., 571, *586*
Genusa, A., *488*
Geoffrey, J., 424, *446*
Gerber, J. A., 713, *729*
Gerlach, J., 599, 610, *630*
Gerstner, Louis, 104
Ghaoui, C., *172*
Ghemawat, P., 111, *123*
Ghosh, A. K., 712, *730*
Gibbons-Paul, L., 362, *394*
Gibson-Paul, L., 150, *172*
Giesen, L., 572, *586*
Gilbert, J., 218, *230*
Gillin, P., 614, *630*
Gilmore, J., 88, 338, *352*

Gilmore, J. H., 17, *41*, 429, *446*
Ginige, A., 434, *446*
Ginsburg, M., 121, *123*
Girishankar, S., 68, *85*
Goddard, S., 519, *539*
Goldberg, B., 687, *730*
Goldman, Diane, 553
Goldman, S. L., 432, *446*
Goodhue, D. L., 337, *352*
Gorry, G. A., 549, *586*
Gorton, I., *352*
Gotcher, R., *172*
Govindarajan, V., 459, *488*
Granger, S., *730*
Grant, D., 436, *446*
Grant, G., 502, *539*
Gray, P., 452, 457, 462, *488*, 501, 503, 505, *539*, 600, *630*
Gray, S., *172*
Greenberg, P., 14, *40, 85*, 335, 338, *352*
Gregor, S., 566, *586*
Griffiths, G., *446*
Griffiths, P., 685, *730*
Griffiths, P. M., 92, *123, 124*
Grimes, S., 297, *352*
Grossnickle, J., 524, *539*
Grover, R., 453, *489*
Guimaraes, T., 160, *172*
Guimarares, T., 95, *123*
Gupta, A. K., 459, *488*
Gupta, J., 571, *587*
Guttman, M., *123*
Guynes, S. C., *629*

H

Hackathorn, R. D., 556, *587*
Hackney, R. A., 402, *446*
Hagel, J., III, 369, *394*
Hagen, S., 511, *538*
Hager, D., 712, *729*
Haley, B. J., 623, *631*
Hamblen, M., 284, *293*
Hamilton, Janet M., 518, *539*
Hammer, M., 17, *40*, 420, 423, 424, 428, *446*
Hammerstrom, Paul, 113–114
Hammond, M., 466, *489*
Handfield, R. B., 359, 386, *394*
Hann, I. H., 91, 95, *123*
Hansen, M., 458, 459, 474, *488*
Hanssen-Bauer, J., 457, *488*
Hapgood, F., *85*
Harari, O., 96, *123*
Hardester, K. P., 518, 519, *539*
Hargadon, A. B., 458, *488*
Harmon, P., 99, 100, *123*
Harrington, A., 332, *352*
Harrison, T. P., 386, *394*
Harsh, A., 252, *294*
Hartley, D. E., 159, *172*
Hartman, A., 121, *123*
Hasan, B., 496, *539*
Hassanein, H., 245, 265, *292*

Haykin, S., 571, *587*
Heijden, M. C., 576, *587*
Helmstetter, G., 10, *41*
Henderson, J., 432, 433, *447*
Henfridsson, O., 479, *488*
Henning, T., 264, *293*
Herbsleb, J., 667, *678*
Higa, K., 160, *172*
Higgins, L. F., 409, *447*
Hiles, A., 719, *730*
Hill, K., 262, *293*, 374, *394*
Hill, P. A., 473, *489*
Hinde, S., *730*
Hinks, J., 435, *446*
Hirji, K. K., 510, 514, *539*
Hirscheim, R., 615, *630*
Hislop, D., 477, *488*
Hitt, L. M., 594, 629, *630*
Hoffman, D. L., 10, *41*
Hofmann, D. W., 158, *172*
Holm-Laursen, Chris, 260
Holsapple, C. W., 452, 456, 457, *488*
Holweg, M., 87, 88, *88*, 108, *123*, 316, *352*
Hooghiemstra, J. S., 584, *587*
Horluck, J., 387, *394*
Hornberger, M., 254, *293*
Houck, J., 267, *293*
Hricko, M. F., 158, *172*
Huang, H., 156, *173*
Huff, S., 222, *230*
Huff, S. L., 180, *230*
Hugos, M. H., 357, *394*
Hunter, R., 284, *293*
Hunton, J. E., 715, 718, 729, *730*
Hussain, Kamran, 417

I

Iacocca, Lee, 484
Imhoff, C., 138, *173*
Inmon, W. H., 501, 503, 511, 528, *539*
Irani, Z., 610, *630*
Isenberg, D., 217, *230*
Ishida, T., 281, *293*
Islam, N., 282, *293*
Ives, B., 94, 111, *123*

J

Jackson, Mark, 675
Jackson, P., 567, *587*
Jacobs, F. R., 372, *394*
Jain, A., 704, *730*
James, D., 372, *394*
Jandt, E. F., 330, *352*
Jareb, E., 333, *352*, 567, *587*
Jarvenpaa, S. L., 670, *678*
Jaworski, B. J., 610, *631*
Jiang, J. J., 682–684, *730*
Jiang, X., 284, *293*
Johnson, J. D., 610, *630*
Johnson, R. A., 645, *678*

Johnson, T., 133, 160, *173*
Johnston, R. B., 381, *394*
Jones, K., 462, *489*
Jones, W. D., 279, *293*
Joshi, K. D., 456, 457, *488*

K

Kahin, B., 4, *40*
Kahn, J., 559, *587*
Kahn, R. H., *352*
Kalakota, R., 240, *293*, 335, *352*, 375, *394*
Kambil, A., 121, *123*, 183, *230*
Kannan, P. K., 321, *352*
Kanter, J., 402, *446*
Kaparthi, S., 574, *587*
Kaplan, P. J., 23, *41*, 187, 221, *230*, 381, *395*
Kaplan, R. S., 610, *630*
Kaplan, S., *230*, 478, *488*
Kapp, K., 158, *173*
Karagiannis, K., 697, *730*
Karlenzig, W., 485, *488*
Kauffman, R. J., 610, *629*
Keen, P., 104, *123*, 338, *352*
Keen, P. G., 556, *587*
Keen, P. G. W., 604, *630*
Kehlenbeck, C., 254, *293*
Keil, M., 619, *630*, *678*
Kellner, M., 251, *293*
Kelton, D. W., 576, *587*
Kemerer, C., 93, *123*
Kemp, T., 113, *123*
Kendall, J. E., 642, *678*
Kendall, K. E., 642, *678*
Kerlow, I. V., 522, *539*
Kern, T., *678*
Kerr, Pamela, 184
Keskinocak, P., 364, 374, *395*
Kesner, R. M., 138, *173*, 465, *489*, 684, *730*
Kess, P., 435, *446*
Khalidi, Y., *85*
Khalifa, M., 160, *173*
Khan, B., 18, *40*
Khan, M. R. R., 424, 427, *446*
Khong, K. W., 437, *446*
Kim, Y. G., *446*
Kimball, R., 503, *539*
King, D., *294*, 462, *489*, 559, *587*
King, David, 627
King, J., 475, *489*, 595, 610, *630*
King, P., *123*
King, W. R., 416, *446*
Kingsman, B. G., 553, *587*
Kini, R. B., 70, *85*
Klein, J., *294*
Knapp, E. M., 474, *489*
Knight, Leah, 664
Knopp, Martin, 39
Kobsa, A., 578, *587*
Koch, C., 372, *395*
Kogen, Don, 6, 9
Kohli, R., 596, 597, 600, 604, 609, 610, 618, 620, *630*

Kolb, D., 520, *540*
Kolodzinski, O., 720, *730*
Konicki, S., *173*
Kontzer, T., 262, *293*
Koontz, C., 66, *85*
Koppius, O. R., 53, *85*
Korte, G. B., 518, 520, *539*
Korzenioski, P., 627, *630*
Kounadis, T., 137, 138, *173*
Kreijger, J., *678*
Kridel, T., 246, *293*
Kroll, K. M., 318, *352*
Kudyba, S., 599, *630*
Kumagai, J., 252, 253, *293*, 569, *587*
Kumar, A., 151, *172*
Kumar, K., 357, 364, *395*
Kumar, R. L., 610, *630*
Kumar, V., *173*
Kuo, J., *85*
Kwahk, K. Y., *446*

L

Lacity, M., 615, *630*
Lam, S. S. Y., 573, *587*
Lam, W., 713, 714, *730*
Landay, J. A., 284, *293*
Lasry, E. M., 434, *446*
Latamore, G. B., 373, *395*
Lau, H. C. W., 510, *539*
Launonen, M., 435, *446*
Law, A. M., 576, *587*
Learmouth, G. P., 94, *123*
Leary, R., 535, *538*
Le Blond, R., 423, *446*
Lederer, A. D., 16, *41*
Lederer, A. L., 6, *41*
Lee, A. S., 423, 434, 437, *447*
Lee, David, 695, 710
Lee, J., *446*
Lee, J. K., 319, *353*
Lee, J. N., 613, 614, *630*, 660, *678*
Lee, S. C., 721, *730*
Lee, Y. M., 310, *352*
Le Gal, C., 281, *293*
Legrenzi, C., 596, *630*
Leidner, D., 454, *488*
Leidner, D. E., 453, 456, *489*, 687, *730*
Lemerise, Paul, 397
Leonard, D., 459, *489*
Levin, C., 717, *730*
Levinson, M., 445, *446*, 492, *539*
Lewis, Brad, 664
Lewis, P. V., 42, *46*
Li, H., 593, *630*
Li, S., 573, 574, *587*
Li, T., 514, *539*
Li, X., 610, *630*
Liao, Z., 305, *352*
Liautaud, B., 466, *489*, 526, *539*
Liaw, S., 156, *173*
Lieberman, H., *173*
Liebowitz, J., 457, *489*, *630*, *678*
Liegle, J. O., 159, *173*

Lin, W. T., 596, *630*
Lindstone, H., *173*
Ling, R. R., 131, *173*
Linoff, G. S., 513, *539*
Linthicum, D. S., 374, *395*, 649, *678*
Lipset, V., 254, 255, *293*
Lipson, S., *85*
Lipton, B., 104, *123*
Liu, S., 527, *539*, 559, *587*
Locke, J., *46*
Lohr, S., 75, *85*
Louca, F., 11, *40*
Loundy, D. L., *730*
Love, P. E. D., 610, *630*
Lovelock, P., 180, *230*
Loveman, Gary, 491, 492, *539*
Lucas, H. C., *630*
Lucas, M. E., 372, *395*
Ludorf, C., 261, *293*
Luhn, R., 712, *730*
Lux, A. G., *730*

M

MacIntosh, R., 423, 437, *446*
MacSweeny, G., *489*
Madhaven, R., 453, *489*
Majcharzak, A., 435, *446*
Mankins, M., 281, *293*
Manton, S., 435, *446*
Marcolin, B. L., 616, 617, *630*
Margulius, D., 75, *85*
Markel, M., *173*
Markus, L. M., 596, *631*
Markus, M. L., 433, *447*, 494, *539*
Martin, C. F., 70, *85*, 668, *678*
Martin, D., 198, *230*
Martin, J., 404, *447*
Martin, J. A., 290, *293*
Massay, A. P., 478, *489*
Mathieson, R., 273, *293*
Matthews, D., 156, *173*
Mattison, R., *539*
Maxemchuk, N. F., *352*
Maynard, M., 485, *489*
Mayor, M., 266, *293*
Mazzawi, E., *629*
McAdam, J. P., 612, *630*
McCleanahen, J., 13, *41*
McClenahen, J. S., 326, *352*
McConnell, M., 707, *730*
McCoy, Jack, 291
McCullough, D. C., 343, *352*
McCullough, S., 578, *587*
McDaniel, C., 193, *230*
McDonald, M., 468, *489*
McDougall, P., *293*
McEachern, T., 194, *230*
McGarvey, J., 26, *41*
McGonagle, J. J., 97, *123*
McGuire, P. A., 546, *587*
McHugh, J., 116, *123*
McKeen, J. D., 459, 474, *489*
McKinley, E., 710, *730*

McLellan, K. L., 616, 617, *630*
Meister, D., 457, *488*
Melymuka, K., 476, 477, *489*
Mennecke, B. E., 238, 240, 248, *293*
Meredith, J. R., 306, *352*
Meredith, M., 436, *447*
Mesenbourg, Thomas, 618
Meso, P. N., 159, *173*
Messersmith, J., 384, *395*
Metcalfe, Robert, 27
Metivier, P., 10, *41*
Mevedoth, R., *41*
Miastkowski, S., 680, 696, *731*
Middleton, M., 498, *538*
Millar, V. E., 92, *123*
Mintzberg, H., 435, *447*, 543, *587*
Miodonski, B., *395*
Mitchell, P., 378, *395*
Mitnick, K., *730*
Moad, J., 511, *539*
Mochari, I., *173*
Mohanty, R. P., 437, *447*
Mol, M. J., 53, *85*
Montealegre, R., 619, *630*, 678
Mooney, S. F., 453, *489*
Moore, G. E., 591, *630*
Moore, Gordon, 25
Moore, J. F., 279, *293*
Morel, G., 311, *353*
Morgan, J. P., 718, *730*
Morrison, D. J., 4, *41*
Moss, L. R., 505, *539*
Moss-Kanter, R., 16, *41*
Mottl, J. N., *173*
Mukhopadhyay, T., 593, *630*
Mullich, J., 664, *678*
Mullins, Steve, 455
Munk, N., 594, 595, *630*
Murch, R., 133, *173*
Murphy, K. E., 377, *395*
Murphy, P., 238, *293*
Murphy, V., 24, *41*, 595, *630*
Murrell, K. L., 436, *447*

N

Nance, B., 708, *730*
Nasirin, S., 518, 519, *539*
Needleman, R., 271, *293*
Neel, D., 633, *678*
Nelson, D., 365, *395*
Nelson, M., 264, *293*
Nemati, H. R., 510, *539*
Nemnich, M. B., 330, *352*
Neumann, S., 92, 101, *123*
Ng, Pauline S. P., 49
Nguyen, H. T., 572, *587*
Nichols, E. L., Jr., 359, 386, *394*
Nilles, J. M., 160, *173*
Nolan, R. L., 404, 405, *447*
Nonaka, I., 453, 454, 456, 457, 463, *489*
Norton, D., 610, *630*
Norvig, P., 559, *587*
Novak, T. P., 10, *41*

Nowickow, C., *123*
Nussbaum, G., 233
Nwosu, K. C., *539*

O

O'Brien, K., 376, *395*
O'Connell, Greg, 39
O'Connell, P., 220, *230*
O'Dell, C. S., 453, 475, *489*
O'Donovan, B., 51, *85*
Oguz, M. T., 505, *539*
O'Harrow, R., *730*
O'Herron, J., 455, *489*
Ojala, M., 140, *173*
O'Keefe, R. M., 194, *230*
Olazabal, N. G., 592, *630*
Old, John, 460
O'Leary, D., 557, 559
O'Leary, D. E., 369, *395*, 587
O'Leary, Dennis, 68
O'Leary, M., *587*
Oliver, D., 376, *395*
O'Looney, J. A., 518, *539*
Omidyar, Pierre, 184
O'Reilly, J. J., 521, *539*
Ovans, A., 202, *230*

P

Palaniswamy, R., 342, *353*, 372, *395*
Palvia, S., 614, 615, *630*
Pantry, S., 685, *730*
Paperloop, Inc., 205, *230*
Papp, R., 400, *447*
Parihor, M., *85*
Park, Y. T., 504, *539*
Parlapiano, E. H., 159, *172*
Parsa, I., *173*
Patton, S., 651, *678*
Paul, L., 638, 659, *678*
Paul, L. G., *678*
Paulson, L. D., 384, *395*
Pawar, B. S., 97
Peffers, K., 190, *230*, 410, 411, *447*, 607, *630*
Peng, K. L., 433, *447*
Penzias, Arno, 600
Peppard, J., 92, *124*, 399–404, 406, *447*
Peppers, D., 338, *353*
Peray, K., 572, *587*
Pescovitz, D., 720, *730*
Petersen, G. S., 338, *353*
Phillips, M., 221, *230*
Phillips, S., 144, *173*
Piazza, P., 712, *730*
Picard, R. W., *294*
Piccoli, G., 156, *173*
Pickering, C., 402, *447*
Pil, F., 87, 88, *88*
Pil, F. K., 108, *123*, 316, *352*
Pilato, F., *294*

Pindyck, R. S., 610, *630*
Pine, B. J., 87, *88*, 338, *352*, 429, 446, 447
Pine, J., II, 17, *41*
Pinsonneault, A., 160, *173*
Pinto, J., 278, *294*
Piskurich, G. M., 159, *173*
Pitcher, N., *173*
Pitkow, J., 275, *294*
Pitt, L. F., 13, *41*
Pittaras, A., 327, *353*
Plank, R. E., 604, *630*
Plant, R. T., 596, *630*
Plant, T., 419, *447*
Poirier, C. C., 146, 148, 149, *173*, 357, *395*
Polanyi, M., 452–454, *489*
Pomerol, J. C., 559, *586*
Pontz, C., 567, *587*
Pooley, J., 700, *730*
Poon, S., 212, *230*
Porter, M. E., *395*
Porter, Michael, 92, 98–101, 103, 105–107, 109, 111, 117, *123*
Pountain, D., 591, *630*
Power, B. S., 96, *123*
Power, D. J., 551, 567, 574, *587*
Preckett, Sam, 486
Prince, M., 22, *41*
Princi, M., 148, 149, *174*
Pringle, Hal, 654
Pritsker, A. B., 521, *539*
Procaccino, J. D., 212, *230*
Prusak, L., 456, *488*

Q

Qing, H. U., 596, *630*
Quinn, J. B., 614, *630*

R

Radding, A., *539*
Radosevich, L., 675, *678*
Ragowsky, A., 369, *395*
Ragusa, J. M., 150, *173*
Rahali, B., 342, *353*
Raina, K., 252, *294*
Rajaram, K., 420, *447*
Rajkovic, V., 333, *352*, 567, *587*
Raskin, A., 113, 114, *123*, 271, 281, *294*, 312, *353*, 618, *631*
Raskin, O., 524, *539*
Rasmus, D. W., 470, *489*
Ray, K., 329, 330, *353*
Ray, N., 496, *539*
Rayport, J., 610, *631*
Read, C., 600, 601, *631*
Reda, S., 113, *123*, 210, *230*, 316, *353*, 721, *730*
Reddy, R., 361, *395*
Redman, T. C., 496, *539*
Reed, C., 322, 329, *353*
Reeder, J., 158, *173*

Reichheld, F., 596, *631*
Reid, K. A., *173*
Reiter, E., 568, *587*
Renkema, T. J. W., 603, *631*
Rhey, E., 74, *85*
Richardson, R., 690, 693, 694, *730*
Richardson, S., 437, *446*
Ridell, J., 196, *230*
Rigney, P., 381, *395*
Rihao-Ling, R., 235, *235*
Rivlin, G., 559, *587*
Robb, D., 381, *395*, 472, *489*
Roberts-Witt, S. L., 476, *489*
Robin, M., 454, *489*
Robinson, C., 700, *730*
Robinson, D. G., 159, *172*
Robinson, M., 240, *293*, 335, *352*, 375, *394*
Robinson, P., *395*
Rockart, J. F., 556, *587*, 685, *730*
Rogers, E. M., 435, *447*
Rogers, M., 338, *353*
Romano, N. C., Jr., 335, *353*
Romm, C., 376, *395*
Roode, D., 51, *85*
Rooney, J. T., *678*
Rosen, M., *123*
Rosenbaum, D., 214, *230*
Rosencrance, L., 284, *294*
Ross, J. W., 117, *124*, 597, 598, *631*, 686, *730*
Ross, M., 503, *539*
Roth, A. V., 369, *395*
Rothstein, P. J., 713, *730*
Ruber, P., 464, 467, *489*
Ruggles, R., 458, 459, 464, *489*
Rundensteiner, E. A., 502, 503, *539*
Ruohonen, M., 409, *447*
Ruper, Paul, 160
Rupp, W. T., *294*
Russell, S. J., 559, *587*
Russom, P., *395*
Ryan, M., 198, *230*
Ryan, S. D., *631*

S

Saarinen, T., 607, *630*
Sachdeva, S., 654, *678*
Sadeh, N., *41*, 240, 245, 248, 254–256, 258, 265, 276, *294*, 520, *539*
Sadeh, N. M., 316, *353*
Salladurai, R., 421, 424, *447*
Salodof-MacNeil, J., 326, *353*
Sambamurthy, V., 681, 682, 686, 729, *730*
Samela, H., 420, *447*
Sampson, Bob, 550
Sandoe, K., 367, *395*
Santosus, M., *86*
Sarkar, D., 272, *294*
Sarker, S., 423, 437, *447*
Sarnoff, David, 620
Sarshar, A., 240, *294*
Saunders, Michael, 22
Sawhney, M., *230*, 596, 600, 601, *631*
Saxby, C. L., 548, *587*

Sayana, S. A., 718, *730*
Scalet, S. D., 701, *730*
Scanlon, J., 250, 262, *294*
Schafer, S., 319, *353*
Schefter, P., 596, *631*
Schell, G. P., 158, *173*
Schonfeld, E., *86*
Schram, P., 149, 150, *173*
Schultz, G., *41*
Schultze, U., 453, *489*
Schwartz, E., 95, *124*
Schwartz, Peter, 273
Scott, J. E., 671, *678*
Scott-Morton, M. S., 549, *586*
Seddon, P., 596, *631*
Seddon, P. B., 683, *730*
Segev, A., 211, *230*, 377, *395*, 614, *631*
Seidman, T., 317, *353*
Seitz, N. E., 603
Selland, C., 369, *395*
Sensiper, S., 459, *489*
Seybold, P., 651, *678*
Seybold, P. B., 407, *447*
Shadbolt, J., 571, *587*
Shafer, S. M., 306, *352*
Shain, F., *395*
Shand, D., 468, *489*, *730*
Shao, B. M., 596, *630*
Sharda, R., 96, 97, *123*
Sharke, P., 279, *294*
Shecterle, B., 386, *395*
Sheikh, K., 366, *395*
Shelter, K. M., 212, *230*
Sheridan, R. M., 721, *730*
Sheth, J. N., 578, *587*
Shields, C., 710, 721, *730*
Shin, B., 160, *173*
Shipley, Peter, 251
Shirky, C., 652, 653, *678*
Shohoud, Y., *678*
Shur, D. H., *352*
Siau, K., 244, *294*, 384, *395*
Sieber, T., 677, *678*
Siekert, Vicki, 113
Sifonis, J., 121, *123*
Sikder, I., 519, *539*
Silver, C. A., 465, 476, *489*
Silverman, S., 487, *489*
Simatupang, T. M., 361, *395*
Simic, G., 574, *587*
Simon, H., 549, *587*
Simon, S. J., 377, *395*
Simon, W., *730*
Singh, S. K., 556, *587*
Sisodia, R. S., 578, *587*
Sitonis, J. G., 687, *730*
Sivasailam, N., 706, *730*
Skyrme, D. J., 474, 475, *489*
Slater, D., 119, *124*
Sloan, M., *352*
Slywotzky, A. J., 4, *41*
Smailagic, A., *294*
Smith, A. D., *294*
Smith, C. F., 569, *586*
Smith, Fred, 48
Smith, H., 423, *447*

Smith, H. A., 459, 474, *489*
Smith, H. J., 529, *539*
Smith, K., *41*, 571, *587*
Smith, R., 710, *730*
Snell, Whit, 382
Snow, C. C., 457, *488*
Snyder, W. M., 459, *489*
Söderholm, A., 479, *488*
Soh, C., *395*, 596, *631*
Solomon, M. R., 193, *230*
Solow, Robert, 592
Somers, T. M., 369, *395*
Sorensen, D., 578, *587*
Spanbauer, S., 712, *730*
Spector, L., 715, *730*
Spielberg, Steven, 273
Spil, T. A. M., 420, *447*
Sridharan, R., 361, *395*
Stackpole, B., 114, *124*, 139, *173*
Stafford, A., *294*
Stal, M., 651, *678*
Standford, J., 281, *294*
Stanford, V., 31, *41*, *86*, 282, *294*
Stasiak, K., 707, *730*
Stauffer, D., 407, *447*
Stead, B. A., 218, *230*
Steede-Terry, K., 270, *294*, 520, *540*
Steidlmeier, P., 44, *46*
Stein, T., 371, *394*
Steinberg, D., 466, 476, *489*
Stephenson, W., *173*
Sterlicchi, J., 24, *41*
Sterne, J., 192, 200, *230*, 364, *395*, 618, *631*
Stoll, R., 387, *395*
Storck, J., 473, *489*
Strader, T. J., 238, 240, 248, *293*
Strassman, P., 712, *730*
Strassmann, P. A., 594, *631*
Stratman, J. K., 369, *395*
Straub, D. W., 618, *631*
Strauss, J., 192, 194, 200, *230*, 313, 316, 338, *353*, 524, *540*
Strong, D. M., 496, 497, *540*
Subrahmanyam, A., 301, *353*
Suhas, H. K., 432, *447*
Sullivan, A., 694, *730*
Sullivan, D., 136
Sullivan, J. R., *173*
Sullivan, M., 169, *173*, 384, *395*
Sung, N. H., 319, *353*
Susarla, A., 664, *678*
Swaminatha, T. M., 712, *730*
Swamy, Remash, 610, *631*
Sweeney, T., 317, *353*
Sweiger, M., 195, *230*, 528, *540*
Sykes, R., 377, *395*, 684, 686, *731*
Szuprowicz, B., 235, *235*

T

Tabor, R., *86*, 651, *678*
Tabor, S. W., 496, *539*
Takeuchi, H., 453, 454, 463, *489*
Talarian, Inc., 114, *124*

Talleur, T., 699, 701, *730*
Tan, P. N., *173*
Tan, X., 335, 336, *353*
Tang, C., 520, *540*
Tapscott, D., 4, 11, *41*
Tayur, S., 364, 374, *395*
Tedeschi, B., 137, *173*
Teece, D. J., 453, *489*
Tehrani, S., 462, *488*
Tennehouse, D., *294*
Teo, T. S. H., 96, *124*, 416, *447*
Terry, K., 520, *540*
Thomas, S. L., 329, 330, *353*
Thompson, B., 336, *353*
Thompson, Jack, 484
Timmers, P., *124*
Tjan, A. K., 116, *124*, 418, *447*, 618, *631*
Totty, P., 319, *353*
Tractinsky, M., 670, *678*
Trager, L., 383, *395*
Truby, K. C., 614, *631*
Tucci, C. L., 10, *40*, 92, *123*
Tucker, M. J., 532, *540*
Tumer, A., 242, 243, *292*
Tung, L. L., 115, *124*, 426, *447*
Tunnainen, V. K., 190, *230*
Turban, E., 10, *41*, 64, 72, *86*, 90, 101, 115, *124*, 146, *173*, 177, 187, 189, 201, 208, 215, *230*, *294*, 338, *353*, 386, *395*, 419, 420, 426, 433, *447*, 496, 501, *540*, 551, *586*, 602, 618, 649, 680
Turing, Alan, 561
Turroff, H., *173*

U

Ulph, R., 220, *230*
Urdan, T., 157, *173*
Useem, J., 220, *230*, 420, *447*

V

Vakharia, J., 357, *395*
Valacich, J., 645, *678*
Van, J., 27, *41*, 720, *731*
Vandenbosch, M., 95, *124*
van der Aalst, W. M. P., 150, *174*
Van Dyk, Richard, 467
van-Heck, E., 183, *230*
Van Winkle, Kenneth, 310
Varley, S., 378, *395*
Varney, S. E., 319, *353*
Varon, E., 590, *631*
Varshney, U., 240, *294*

Vasilash, G. S., 450, *489*
Vedder, R. G., 566, *587*
Velker, L., 487, *489*
Vella, C. M., 97, *123*
Venkatraman, N., 101, *124*, 432, 433, *447*
Verton, E., 694, *731*
Vessey, I., 671, *678*
Vetter, R., 240, *294*
Veytsel, A., 496, 497, *539*
Vice, Lowell, 115
Vijavan, J., 604, *631*
Vijayakumar, S., 310, 329, *353*
Vinas, T., 153, *174*
Violino, B., 603, *631*
Vistica, G. L., *631*
Viswanadham, N., 358, 364, *395*
Vitale, M. R., 10, *41*, 65, *86*
Vitaliano, D., 599, *630*
Von Krogh, G., 458, *489*
von Pierer, Heinrich, 3
Von-Roessing, R., 718, *731*
Voss, C., 337, *353*

W

Wainewright, P., 75, *86*
Wales, E., 24, *41*
Walker, C., 9, *41*
Walker, E. A., 572, *587*
Walsh, N. P., 689, *731*
Walstrom, K. A., *173*
Waltner, C., *631*
Walton, B., 148, 149, *174*
Wang, Q., 435, *446*
Ward, J., 92, *124*, 399–404, 406, *447*
Ward, L., 663, *678*
Warkentin, M., 200, *230*
Warner, F., 460, *489*
Warren, Richard, 627
Warren, S. D., 45, *46*
Watad, M. M., 160, *174*
Watson, H., 600, 623, *630*
Watson, H. J., 501, 503, 505, *539*, *540*, *631*
Weaver, P., 158, *174*
Weggen, C., 157, *173*
Weidlich, T., 144, *174*
Weill, P., 10, *41*, 65, 85, *86*, 597, 608, 609, *629*
Weise, E., 281, *294*
Weiser, Mark, 273, 281, *294*
Weiss, G., 133, *174*, *294*
Weiss, T. R., 513, *540*
Wells, J. T., 717, *731*
Wenger, E. C., 459, *489*
Westland, J. C., 189, *230*
Westley, F., 435, *447*, 543, *587*
Wetherbe, J. C., 13, *41*, 400, 429, *447*

Whinston, A. B., 5, *40*, 92, *123*, 128, *172*, 620, *629*, *678*
Whipple, L. C., 66, *86*
White, G. B., 698, *731*
Whitemone, J. J., *731*
Whybark, D. C., 372, *394*
Wiederkehr, B., 701, *731*
Wilkinson, S., 614, *631*
Willcocks, L. P., 377, *395*, 684, 686, *731*
Williams, D., *731*
Williams, J., 219, *230*
Williams, R. L., 474, *488*
Williams, S., 450, *489*
Williams, Seema, 84
Wind, Y., 315, *353*
Winter, R., 510, 526, *540*
Winter, Richard, 525
Wiseman, C., 101, *124*
Woda, A., 718, *731*
Wolf, M. L., 372, *394*
Wong, N. A., 718, *730*
Wong, W. Y., 206, 207, *230*
Worthen, B., 356, 364, *395*
Wreden, N., 4, *41*
Wright, A., *123*
Wurster, T. S., 4, 14, *40*

Y

Yakhou, M., 342, *353*
Yao, D. D., 374, *395*
Yen, D. C., 131, *173*, 235, *235*
Yiman-Seid, D., 578, *587*
Young, A., 614, *629*
Young, S. A., 699, *729*
Youngman, J. A., 111, *123*
Yourdon, E., 639, 644, *678*
Yuan, S. T., 196, *230*

Z

Zadeh, L., 572, *587*
Zakaria, Z., 325, *353*, 417, *447*
Zaremba, M. B., 311, *353*
Zemke, R., 158, 171, *172*
Zenkin, D., 708, *731*
Zetsche, Dieter, 485
Zetter, K., 680, 696, *731*
Zetu, D., 522, *538*
Zhao, Y., 272, *294*
Zimmerman, J., 633, *678*
Zipkin, P., 87, 88, *88*, 315, *353*
Zott, C., 16, *40*
Zviran, M., 617, *631*

Subject Index

1-800-Flowers, 112–113
7-Eleven, 383
802.11b standard, 241, 249
911 calls, 272

A

ABC, *see* Activity-based costing
Accenture Consulting, 376, 458, 635
Access control (security), 703
Accessibility data quality, 496
Accountability (as ethical issue), 45
Accounting and finance systems,
    322–329. *See also* Economics of IT
  control and auditing, 328–329
  financial planning and budgeting,
      322–324
  investment management, 326–328
  transaction management, 324–326
ACN (automatic crash notification), 272
Active badges, 274
ActiveKnowledge, 467
Activity-based costing (ABC), 610–611
Adapters, software, 374
Administrative controls (security), 705
Administrative IT planning approach, 400
Administrative workflow, 151
Advertising, 192, 196–200
  among company employees, 204
  C2C, 207–208
  location-based, 271–272
  payment for exposure to, 258
  targeted, 257–258
  technology and changes in, 316–317
  unsolicited, 162
  wireless, 255
Aeronautica Civil, 122
Affiliate marketing, 10
Affinity portals, 137
After-sales service, 107
Agents, *see* Software agents
AI, *see* Artificial intelligence
AirIQ, 261
Airline industry, value chain for, 109
Alaska Airlines, 267
Alien Technology, 280
Alliance strategy, 102
Alloy.com, 221
ALVs (autonomous land vehicles), 279
"Always-on" cell phones, 273
Amazon.com, 96, 102, 103, 105, 106,
    109–110, 117, 188, 220, 339, 360,
    380, 513
American Airlines, 103, 117, 475
American Express, 499
American Express Travel Related Services,
    569

American Hospital Supply, 103
American Power Conversion Corp., 227
American Telecommuting Association
    (ATA), 160
America Online (AOL), 313
AMEX, 499
Amoco, 486
AMR Corp., 475
AMT (Asset Management Tool), 374
Analog models, 548
Analytical processing, 500
Andersen Consulting, 404
ANNs, *see* Artificial neural networks
Ansett Australia, 654
Anticybersquatting Consumer Protection
    Act of 1999, 218
Antiplagiarism technology, 135
AOL (America Online), 313
Applets, 665
Appliances, smart, 278
Application controls, 702, 706
Application middleware, 247
Application programs (applications), 50,
    657–658. *See also specific topics*
Application server, 246
Application service providers (ASPs), 32,
    74, 341, 377
  defined, 663
  for e-business systems, 663
  for KMS outsourcing, 468, 470
  leasing from, 663, 664
  outsourcing to, 614
Application-specific components, 649
Applications portfolio, 399, 401–402,
    418–419
Arbitron, 317
Architecture:
  blended computing, 414
  business, 65–66
  client-server, 68–69, 413
  information, 412
  information technology, 411–415
  peer-to-peer, 70–71
Artificial intelligence (AI), 461–462,
    559–563
  in biometrics, 721
  commercial technologies for, 563
  conventional vs. AI computing, 562
  integration of KMS and, 470
  and knowledge, 561
  natural intelligence vs., 561, 562
Artificial neural networks (ANNs), 571–574
Asia, 21
AskJeeves, 134
ASP alternative, 377
ASPs, *see* Application service providers
Asset Management Tool (AMT), 374
Association analysis, 511
Association (of information), 511

Asynchronous communication, 141
ATA (American Telecommuting
    Association), 160
Atlanta Summer Olympics, 159
ATMs, *see* Automated teller machines
ATP/CTP (available-to-promise/capacity-
    to-promise) function, 265
AT&T, 249, 266
Attachable keyboards, 245
Attack traceback, 710
Attractions, online, 200
Au Bon Pain Company, Inc., 524–525
Auctions, 183–184
  C2C, 207
  on company Web sites, 378, 379
  reverse, 10
  via cell phone, 241
Audits and auditing:
  audit defined, 717
  financial, 329
  for security, 716–718
Auditors, 717
Augmented computing, *see* Pervasive
    computing
Australia, 111
Authentication, 703, 710–711
Authorization, 703, 711
Auto-by-Tel, 103
Auto Identification (Auto-ID) Center, 280
Automated responses, 339
Automated teller machines (ATMs), 102,
    103, 213, 255, 593, 689–690
Automated warehouses, 383
Automatic computing, 720
Automatic crash notification (ACN), 272
Automatic vehicle identification (AVI), 268
Automation, 421, 545
Automobile industry, 13–14
  GPS navigation systems, 271
  Hertz m-commerce applications, 290
  smart cars, 278–279
  telemetry applications, 272
  used-car auctions, 378, 379
  virtual cars, 316
Automotive Collision Avoidance System, 279
Autonomous land vehicles (ALVs), 279
Autonomy, 465, 467, 468
Available-to-promise/capacity-to-promise
    (ATP/CTP) function, 265
AVI (automatic vehicle identification), 268

B

B2B commerce, *see* Business-to-business
    commerce
B2C commerce, *see* Business-to-consumer
    commerce

B2E commerce, *see* Business to its employees commerce
Back-office operations, 343, 380
Backup arrangements, 714–715
Badges, active, 274
BAE Automated Systems, Inc., 619
Balanced scorecard, 474–475, 610
BAM (business activity monitoring), 578
Bandwidth, 244, 273
Banking, 189–190, 253–255
Bank of America, 525
Banners, 197
Barcodes, 279–280
Bargainfinder, 196
Barnes & Noble, 100, 110, 117
Bartering, 184
Batch processing, 302
Behavior-oriented chargeback system, 612
Bell Canada, 260
BellSouth, 499–500
Benchmarking, 426, 435, 607–608
Benefits administration, 335
Benefit-to-cost ratio, 603
Benetton Group SpA, 283, 284
Best of breed approach, 371
Best-practice benchmarks, 608
BI, *see* Business intelligence
Bible, 42
Bikeworld, 382
Bill presentment/payment, 326
Biometric control, 704
Biometrics, 7, 721
Bizworks, 310
Blackberry handhelds, 245, 246
Blackboard (ES), 566
Blackboard Inc., 157
Blended computing architecture, 414
Blog/blogging/bloggers, 144
BloomLink, 112
Blue Cross & Blue Shield of Rhode Island, 643
Bluetooth, 247, 266. *See also* Multimedia messaging service
Boeing Corporation, 429
Booz-Allen & Hamilton, 95
Borders Books & Music Stores, 250
Border security, 707–710
Bosch, 2
BP Australia Ltd., 383
BPI (business performance intelligence), 578
BPM (business performance management), 578
BPM (business process management), 423
BPR, *see* Business process redesign; Business process reengineering
BPR (business process restructuring), 145
Brick-and-mortar (old-economy) organizations, 100, 178
Bridgeton, 131
Brochures, electronic, 198
"Brute force" credit card attacks, 688
BSP (business systems planning) model, 404

BTO strategy, *see* Build-to-order strategy
Budgetary control, 328–329
Budgeting, 323–324
Build-to-order (BTO) strategy, 17, 108, 427, 429
  production, 87–88
  supply chains, 359
Bullwhip effect, 361–362
Burger King, 87
Burlington Coat Factory, 524
Business, aligning IT with, 398–399
Business activity monitoring (BAM), 578
Business alliances, 17
Business architecture, 65–66
Business case, 601–602
Business continuity planning, 712–716
Business intelligence (BI), 54, 55, 366, 505–507. *See also* Analytical processing
  categories of, 507
  on customer activity, 195
  defined, 505
  information and knowledge discovery with, 505–510
  as integration of decision support and analysis, 374
  portals for, 138
  Web-based systems for, 526–528
Business-led IT planning approach, 400
Business models, 9–10, 179–180
Business Objects, 506
Business partners, 436
Business performance intelligence (BPI), 578
Business performance management (BPM), 578
Business pressures (drivers), 11–15
  global, 111–112
  market, 12–14
  societal, 14–15
  technological, 14
Business process, defined, 421
Business process management (BPM), 423
Business process redesign (BPR), 420–433
  business process reengineering vs., 423
  for cycle time reduction, 429–430
  drivers of, 421
  failures of, 436–437
  for mass customization, 427, 429
  methodologies for, 423
  for one or few processes, 427
  for restructuring entire organization, 430–431
  role of IT in, 423–427
  successes in, 437
  for virtual organizations, 432–433
Business process reengineering (BPR), 16–17, 371, 423
Business process restructuring (BPR), 145
Business systems planning (BSP) model, 404
Business-to-business (B2B) commerce:
  applications for, 200–203
  buy-side marketplaces, 201

distinctions between B2C and, 186–187
  electronic exchanges, 201–203
  mobile applications, 265
  sell-side marketplaces, 200
  transaction types, 178
Business-to-consumer (B2C) commerce, 185–192
  applications for, 185–192
  distinctions between B2B and, 186–187
  electronic retailing, 185–189
  models of, 187
  services online, 189–192
  transaction types, 178
Business to its employees (B2E) commerce, 178, 204
Buyers:
  e-commerce protections for, 216
  organizational, 193
Buy-side marketplaces, 201

C

C2B commerce, 178
C2C commerce, 178
C2C e-commerce, *see* Customer-to-customer e-commerce
CAD, *see* Computer-aided design
CAD/CAM, 54, 55
Cadence Design Systems, 627
CAE (computer-aided engineering), 310
"CAGE distance" framework, 111
California Private Transportation Company, 268
Call centers, 55, 142–143, 339–340
Caltex Australia, 383
Cameras, wearable, 259
Campusfood.com, 22, 221
Canadian Imperial Bank of Commerce (CIBC), 614–615
Cannondale Corp., 113, 312
Capability Maturity Model (CMM), 666–667
Capital budgeting, 324
Carnegie Mellon University (CMU), 275, 698, 699, 728
Case-based reasoning, 54, 511
Case manager, 426
CASE tools, *see* Computer-aided software engineering tools
Cash, electronic, 211–213
Cash Register Express, 318
Catalogs:
  customized, 198
  electronic, 198
Categorical imperative, 42
Caterpillar, Inc., 103, 109, 149–150
CBIS (computer-based information systems), 19
c-commerce, *see* Collaborative commerce
CDMA, *see* Code Division Multiple Access
CDNow, 10, 110
CD-ROM technology, 622
CDSS (Consumer Decision Support System), 194

Cellbucks, 254
Cell phones, 243–246, 252, 254, 255, 272, 273. *See also* Mobile commerce
Centralized computing, 413
Centrino chip, 239
CEO (chief executive officer), 473
CERT, *see* Computer Emergency Response Team
Challenger Shuttle disaster, 559
Champion Chip, 274
Change management, 433, 435
Channels, 187, 312, 317–319
Channel assembly supply chains, 359
Channel conflict, 187
Channel systems, 313, 314
Chargeback, 410, 612
Chargeout, 612
Charles Schwab and Company, 340, 715
Chase Manhattan Bank, 68
Chat rooms, 143, 339
Checkout process (retail), 317–318
Checks, electronic, 210, 326
Check-writers, 318
ChemConnect, 203
Chemdex.com, 220
Chemical Bank, 68
Chevron, 486–487
ChevronTexaco, 355–356
Chicago Tribune, 525
Chief executive officer (CEO), 473
Chief information officer (CIO), 77, 681–682, 686–687
Chief knowledge officer (CKO), 472–473
Choice phase (decision making), 547
Chrysler Corporation, 429, 484–485
CIBC, *see* Canadian Imperial Bank of Commerce
CIM, *see* Computer-integrated manufacturing
Cingular Wireless, 455
CIO, *see* Chief information officer
CIPB (Critical Infrastructure Protection Board), 694
Cisco Connection Online, 120, 465
Cisco Employee Connection, 121
Cisco Systems, 13, 38, 87, 104, 120, 121, 170–171
Citibank, 690
Cities, digital, 281
Citrus Belgium, 110
CKO, *see* Chief knowledge officer
Classification (of information), 511
Classified ad Web sites, 208
Classwave, 266–267
Clerical workers, 62
Click-and-mortar (click-and-brick) organizations, 100, 178, 187
Clickstream data, 195, 496, 528
Clickstream data warehouses, 528
Client (computing), 68
Client/server architecture, 68–69, 413
Clustering (of information), 511
CMM, *see* Capability Maturity Model
CMU, *see* Carnegie Mellon University

Code Division Multiple Access (CDMA), 248, 249
Codes of ethics, 43, 44
Colgate-Palmolive, 321, 375
Collaboration, 55, 130, 144–150
    barriers to e-collaboration/e-commerce, 150
    collaborative networks, 146–149
    conventional approach to, 145
    defined, 144
    groupware technologies for, 151–156
    supply chain, 362–363
    for value chain integration, 368–369
    virtual, 146–150, 155–156
    workflow technologies for, 150–151
Collaboration supply chain, 361
Collaborative commerce (c-commerce), 146, 369
    extranets in, 234
    networks for, 369
    transaction types, 178
Collaborative computing, 459, 465
Collaborative filtering agents, 196
Collaborative Planning, Forecasting, and Replenishment (CPFR) program, 370, 371
Collaborative workflow, 151
Colombia, 122
Combination mode (knowledge creation), 457
Cometa Networks, Inc., 249
Commerce Bank, 469
Commercial database services, 495
Commercial (public) portals, 137
Communication(s), 130, 141–144
    electronic chat rooms, 143
    factors determining use of IT for, 141–142
    generations of technology, 248
    security controls for, 705
    voice, 143–144
    Web-based call centers, 142–143
    Weblogging (blogging), 144
    Web modes of, 163
    WWAN protocols for, 248–249
Communispace, 468
Communities of practice (COPs), 459, 473–474
Compaq Computers, 103, 720
Comparison agents, 196
Competition, global, 13, 111–112
Competitive advantage, 92
Competitive forces model, 98–107
Competitive intelligence, 95–98
Competitive strategy, 92
Compliance audits, 718
Component-based development, 647–649
Compubank, 338
Computer-aided design (CAD), 163, 310
Computer-aided engineering (CAE), 310
Computer-aided software engineering (CASE) tools, 427, 665–666
Computer architecture, 65*n*
Computer-based information systems (CBIS), 19
Computer crimes, 693–695

Computer Emergency Response Team (CERT), 698–699, 728
Computer-integrated manufacturing (CIM), 310–311
Computers:
    early, 53
    increased processing power of, 25, 26
    information systems vs., 20
    network, 30
    self-healing, 27
Computer Sciences Corp., 613
Computing. *See also specific headings*
    end-user, 55
    enterprisewide, 69
    grid, 75
    mobile, 28, 55, 73
    pervasive, 28–31, 75
    quantum, 27
    subscription, 75
    utility, 74–75
    wireless, 73
Comshare, 320
Concurrent audits, 329
Congos, 506
Consortiums, 203
Consulting firms, 468
Consumers:
    behavior models of, 192–193
    decision-making process of, 193–194
    identifying wants of, 195
    individual vs. organizational, 193
    personalized information for, 242
Consumer Decision Support System (CDSS), 194
Consumer protection, 216–217
Consumer-to-business (C2B) commerce, 178
Consumer-to-consumer (C2C) commerce, 178
Contactless cards, 268
Context awareness, 274–275
Contextual computing, 275
Contextual data quality, 496
Continuous improvement, 16
Continuous replenishment supply chains, 359
Control(s):
    application, 702, 706
    financial, 328–329
    general, 702–705
    security, 700–701. *See also* Security issues
Controlled variables, 192
Convectis, 462
Convenience stores, self-service, 317
Conversions, 638–639
Cooperative processing, 67
COPs, *see* Communities of practice
Copyrighted material, 161, 219
Core business, 92
Corporate e-bartering, 184
Corporate portals, 30, 72, 137–140, 527
Corporate training, online, 158–159
Corporations, virtual, 17
Costs. *See also* Economics of IT
    control of, 329

Costs. *See also* Economics of IT (*cont.*)
  as driver of process redesign, 421
  of IT investment, 599–600
  in productivity paradox, 594–595
Cost-benefit analysis, 599
Cost leadership strategy, 101–102
Cost recovery, 612
Covisint, 104
CPFR program, *see* Collaborative Planning,
    Forecasting, and Replenishment
    program
CPM (critical path method), 309
Crackers, 693
Cray Research, 715
Credit card fraud, 572
Credit cards:
  "brute force" attack on, 685
  electronic, 210–211
  virtual, 214
Crimes, computer, 693–695
Critical Infrastructure Protection Board
    (CIPB), 694
Critical path method (CPM), 309
Critical response activities, 11, 15–18, 21–23
Critical success factors (CSFs), 405–407
CRM, *see* Customer relationship
    management
Cross-application components, 649
Cross-functional activities, 422
Cross-selling, 316
Crowne Plaza hotel, 266
CSFs, *see* Critical success factors
Currencies, multiple, 325
Customers:
  bargaining power of, 100
  empowerment of, 436
  increased power of, 13–14
  portals for, 138
Customer care centers, *see* Web-based call
    centers
Customer-centric organizations, 313
Customer-orientation strategy, 104
Customer portals, 342
Customer profiles, 313
Customer relationship management
    (CRM), 14, 55, 335–341
  definitions of, 335–336
  eCRM, 336–337
  evaluation of, 336
  failures of, 340–341
  and functional systems, 298
  integration of KMS and, 471
  interrelationship of SFA and, 204
  IT supports for, 337–340
  market research information for, 196
  mobile computing in, 262–263
  types of, 336
Customer service, 16, 350–351, 421
Customer-to-customer (C2C)
    e-commerce, 207–208
Customization, 13–14, 17, 198, 315, 316,
    338, 427, 429
CVS Corp., 251
Cyberbanking, *see* Electronic banking
Cybercrime, 680–681, 693–695
Cybermalls, 186

Cybersquatting, 218
Cyberterrorism, 694
Cyberwar, 694
Cybex International, 384
Cycle time reduction, 429–430

D

DACODA, 91
Daewoo Securities, 190
Daimler-Benz, 484–485
DaimlerChrysler, 484–485, 593
Dairy Queen, 334
Daiwa Securities, 327
Dallas Rapid Area Transit, 536–537
Dartmouth College, 38
Dartmouth-Hitchcock Medical Center,
    296–298
Dashboards, digital, 163
Data. *See also* Data management
  clickstream, 496, 528
  defined, 451
  life cycle process of, 494–495
  and productivity paradox, 592–594
  sources of, 495
  transformation into knowledge, 494
Database(s), 76. *See also* Data management
  customer, 313, 315
  defined, 19, 51
  integration of KMS and, 471
  marketing, 523–525
  multidimensional, 503, 505
  relational, 494
Database server, 246
Data conferencing, 153
Data cubes, 505, 511
Data drills, 510
Data flow diagrams (DFDs), 636, 637
Data flow manager (DFM), 496
Data hiding, 648
Data integrity, 497, 705
Data items, defined, 51
Data management, 493–529
  for business intelligence, 505–507
  and collection of data, 496
  and data life cycle process, 494–495
  and data mining, 510–514
  and data quality and integrity, 496, 497
  and data sources, 495
  and data visualization, 514–523
  and data warehousing, 500–505
  and document management, 497–500
  geographical information systems,
    517–520
  information and knowledge discovery,
    505–510
  managerial issues with, 528–530
  marketing databases, 523–525
  multidimensionality visualization,
    515–517
  problems with, 493, 497
  solutions to problems with, 493–494, 497
  virtual reality, 521–523
  visual interactive modeling, 520, 521
  Web-based systems for, 526–528

Data management subsystems, 552
Data management systems (DMSs),
    499–500
Data marts, 503, 504
Data mining, 97, 134, 462
  applications of, 511–512
  BI application to, 506
  capabilities of, 510, 511
  combining OLAP with, 509–510
  failures of, 513–514
  text mining, 512–513
  Web mining, 513
Data quality (DQ), 496, 497
Data security controls, 704–705
Data tampering, 694
Data visualization technologies, 514–523
  geographical information systems,
    517–520
  multidimensionality visualization,
    515–517
  virtual reality, 521–523
  visual interactive modeling, 520, 521
Data warehouses, 425, 494, 501–503
  clickstream, 528
  company size and need for, 494
  defined, 501
  failures of, 513–514
  process of building/using, 501–502
  Web-based systems for, 527–528
Data warehousing, 55, 500–505
  characteristics of, 502
  of clickstream data, 195
  transactional vs. analytical processing
    for, 500–501
Data workers, 62
Davis & Warshow, 383
dCRM, 336–337
DDoS (distributed denial of service), 697
Deal structure, 426
Decision making. *See also* Decision Support
  categories of, 543
  computer-based, 546–548
  by e-commerce consumers, 193–194
  frontline, 577–578
  GIS in, 518, 519
  value of information in, 597–599
  virtual reality in, 522
Decision room, 555
Decision support, 543–580
  artificial neural networks, 571, 572
  computer-based, 544–549
  creativity in, 578
  expert systems for, 563–568
  fuzzy logic, 572
  at Hi-Life Corporation, 176–177
  intelligent support systems, 559–563
  managerial issues with, 578–580
  natural language processing, 568
  need for, 543–544
  real-time, 578
  semantic Web, 573
  simulation for, 576
  specialized ready-made, 577
  speech recognition and understanding,
    569
  voice synthesis, 570

Web-based management support systems, 574–575
Decision support systems (DSSs), 54, 55, 545, 550–554
  BI application to, 506
  capabilities of, 551–552
  enterprise/executive, 555–559
  failures of, 559
  frontline, 577–578
  group, 554–555
  hybrid intelligent systems, 573–574
  integration of KMS with, 470
  intelligent, 559–563
  structure/components of, 552–554
  Web-based, 574–575
Decision Technologies Corp., 475
Degree of digitization, 177–178
Dell Computer, 13, 87, 102, 108, 308, 309, 315, 338, 364, 429, 436
Deloitte & Touche, 376
Delphi Automotive Systems, 279
Delphi method, 145
Demand chain, 356–357
Demand forecast, 361
Denial of service (DoS), 680, 697–698, 709–710
Denver International Airport, 559, 619, 692
Departmental information systems, 50, *see* Functional information systems
Dependent data marts, 504
Dependent variables, 192
Design phase (decision making), 546, 547
Design stage (systems development), 636–637
Desktop publishing systems, 54
Desktop purchasing, 201, 211
DFDs, *see* Data flow diagrams
DFM (data flow manager), 496
Differentiation:
  services for, 242
Differentiation strategy, 102
Digital cities, 281
Digital dashboards, 163
Digital economy, 3–10
  and convergence of computing and communication technologies, 5
  defined, 4
  opportunities for entrepreneurs in, 5–10
  representative business models of, 10
Digital Equipment Corp., 565
Digital photography, 7
Digital wallets, 214
Digitization, degree of, 177–178
Dining certificates online, 228
Direct cutover, 638
DirectEmployers.com, 332
Direct online marketing:
  as driver of process redesign, 421
Directories, 133
Direct-response marketing, 196–197
Disaster avoidance, 715
Disaster recovery planning, 712–716
Discovery, 129, 130, 132–141
  corporate portals for, 138–139

industrywide communication networks for, 140–141
information, 507
information portals for, 136–137
Internet software agents for, 133–134
knowledge, 507–508
or foreign language materials, 135
portals for, 136–141
and toolbars, 135
Web mining, 134
Disintermediation, 217, 218
Disney Inc., 419
Distance learning (DL), 156–158
Distributed computing, 413–414, *see* Networked computing
Distributed denial of service (DDoS), 697
Distributed processing (distributed computing), 67–68
Distributed work, 159
Distribution channels, 317–319. *See also* Channels
Division of labor, 87
DL, *see* Distance learning
DMSs, *see* Document management systems
DoCoMo, 258
Dr. Koop, 220
Documentation controls, 705
Document management, 497–500
Document management systems (DMSs), 54, 498
Dollar General, 349
Domain names, 217–218
Donatos Pizzeria, 255
DoS, *see* Denial of service
Dot-coms, 5–6
Downstream supply chain, 64, 378, 379
DPS-Promatic, 254
DQ, *see* Data quality
Dresdner Bank (Germany), 152
Drivers, *see* Business pressures
DSSs, *see* Decision support systems
Dumb terminals, 67
Dun & Bradstreet, 98
Dynamic information, 132–133
DynaQuip Controls Corporation, 275

E

e-911, 272
EA (equivalent annuity), 603
EAF (extreme analytic frameworks), 578
EAI (enterprise application integration), 662
Eastman Kodak, 613
e-auctions, *see* Electronic auctions
eBay, 184–185, 212, 255
EBIS (enterprise BI suites), 527
EBizSearch, 135
e-bonds, 325–326
EBT (electronic benefits transfer), 206
e-business, 177. *See also* Electronic commerce
  defined, 2, 4

transformation to, 434–435
transition to, 78
EC, *see* Electronic commerce
e-cash, *see* Electronic cash
e-checks, *see* Electronic checks
Eckerds, 84
e-collaboration, *see* Virtual collaboration
e-commerce, *see* Electronic commerce
Economics of IT, 590–624
  cost accounting strategies, 611–617
  for e-commerce, 617–618
  evaluating IT investment, 597–603
  failures and "runaway" projects, 619–620
  financial and economic trends, 590–597
  increasing returns theory, 620–621
  investment appraisal methods, 603–611
  and IT as a product in itself, 620
  and managerial issues, 623–624
  and market transformation through new technologies, 621–622
  and productivity paradox, 592–597
  for Web-based systems, 617–618
Economic forecasting, 323
Economic order quantity (EOQ) model, 307
EDCs (electronic data centers), 49
EDGAR database, 98
EDI, *see* Electronic data interchange
EDM (electronic document management), 466
EDS, 163, 613, 627
e-government, 205–207
EIAC (exploration, involvement, analysis, and communications) model, 610
EIS (executive information system), 556
EISs, *see* Enterprisewide information systems
EKPs, *see* Enterprise knowledge portals
Elder care, intelligent, 281, 282
e-learning, 156–159, 170–171
Electronic aggregation, 10
Electronic Art Inc., 103
Electronic auctions (e-auctions), 183–184
Electronic banking, 189–190
Electronic bartering, 184
Electronic benefits transfer (EBT), 206
Electronic brochures, 198
Electronic cash (e-cash), 211–213
Electronic catalogs, 198
Electronic chat rooms, 143
Electronic checks, 210, 326
Electronic commerce (e-commerce, EC), 55, 72–73, 177–235. *See also* Mobile commerce
  advertising online, 192, 196–200
  applications portfolio for, 418–419
  auctions, 183–184
  auditing, 718
  bartering, 184
  benefits of, 180, 182
  B2B applications, 200–203
  B2C applications, 185–192
  business models for, 179–180
  buyer protection with, 216
  component-based development for, 649

Electronic commerce (e-commerce, EC) (*cont.*)
C2C, 207–208
defined, 4, 177
economics of, 617–618
e-government, 205–207
electronic payments, 208–215
electronic retailing, 185–189
ethical issues with, 217
failures in, 219–221
financial transaction applications, 325–326
framework for, 180, 181
fraudulent activities, 216
group work in, 145
history of, 180
integration of ERP and, 384–385
integration of financial transactions and, 326
Internet vs. non-Internet, 178
intrabusiness, 204–205
legal issues with, 217–219
limitations of, 18–182
managerial issues with, 222–223
market research for, 192–196
mechanisms for, 183
order fulfillment, 215
as organizational response, 18
and outsourcing, 614–615
pure vs. partial, 177–178
scope of, 180, 181
seller protection with, 217
service industries online, 189–192
software agents in, 195–196
software for, 658, 659
success in, 221–222
supply chains in, 377–385
support services for, 208, 209
systems development for, 661–665
transaction types, 178–179
Electronic credit cards, 210–211
Electronic data centers (EDCs), 49
Electronic data interchange (EDI), 49, 55, 109, 110, 180, 231–234
Electronic document management (EDM), 466
Electronic exchanges, 73
Electronic malls, 186
Electronic marketplaces, 10, 421
Electronic markets, 72–73
Electronic meeting systems, 153
Electronic networks, 50
Electronic payment systems, 210–215, 254
Electronic retailing (e-tailing), 105, 185–189
Electronic Road Pricing, 280
Electronic storefronts, 72, 186
elibrary, 135
Eli Lilly & Company, 601, 627
Elite Care, 282
eLiza, 720
EMA (expense management automation), 326
e-mail:
advertising via, 198
customer service via, 339
privacy and ethics in, 161
wireless capabilities for, 245–246
e-mail-based chat programs, 143
e-marketplaces, *see* Electronic marketplaces
Embedded computing, *see* Pervasive computing
Embedded expert systems, 568
Embedded knowledge, 453
Emergency cell phone calls, 272
Emergency medical services, 291
Empire Blue Cross and Blue Shield, 715, 716
Employees. *See also* Human resources systems
IT in selection of, 332–333
monitoring e-mail/Internet use of, 160–162
portals for, 138
telecommuting advantages/disadvantages, 159–160
Employee portals, 342
Employee relationship management (ERM), 335
Empowerment, 435–436, 577
EMS (enhanced messaging service), 241
Encryption, 711
Encyclopaedia Britannica, 101
End users:
computing, end-user, 55, 414, 653
relationship between ISD and, 682–685
systems development by, 653–654, 660
Enhanced messaging service (EMS), 241
Enterprise application integration (EAI), 662
Enterprise application server, 246
Enterprise BI suites (EBISs), 527
Enterprise decision simulator, 559
Enterprise information portals, 137
Enterprise information systems vendors, 464–468
Enterprise knowledge portals (EKPs), 465–466
Enterprise portals, 137
Enterprise resource planning (ERP), 53, 64, 114, 116, 369–377
and application service providers, 377
combining SCM software and, 373–374
defined, 369
evolution of, 366
failures of, 376–377
first-generation, 370–372
integration of e-commerce with, 384–385
for integration of information systems, 342, 343
and SCI, 374–376
SCM software vs., 373
second-generation, 372, 374
software for, 369, 370
Enterprise software, 657, 658
Enterprise support systems (ESSs), 558. *See also* Executive support systems
Enterprise Web, 73
Enterprise wheel, 310–311
Enterprisewide computing, 69
Enterprisewide information systems (EISs), 50, 53, 55
Enterprisewide networks, 30
Entertainment, mobile, 266
Entity-relationship diagrams (ERDs), 636, 637
Entrepreneurs, opportunities for, 5–10
Entry-barriers strategy, 104
Environment, defined, 18
Environmental capital, 476
EOQ (economic order quantity) model, 307
e-planning, 417–418
e-procurement, 201, 378, 421
Equity Mutual Trust, 695
Equivalent annuity (EA), 603
ERDs, *see* Entity-relationship diagrams
e-recruitment, 330
Ericsson, 266
ERM (employee relationship management), 335
Ernst & Young, 458
ERP, *see* Enterprise resource planning
Escrow services, 208
Espionage, industrial, 97
ESs, *see* Expert systems
ESSs, *see* Executive support systems
ESSs (enterprise support systems), 558
e-supply chain, 357
e-tailing, *see* Electronic retailing
Ethics, 42–46
and accountability, 45
codes of, 43, 44
and competitive advantage, 118
with decision support systems, 579
defined, 15, 42
dilemmas, ethical, 42–43
with e-commerce, 217
and intellectual property rights, 44–45
and ISD, 79
with IT planning, 437–439
with mobile computing, 283, 284
with network computing, 160–162
and privacy issues, 45–46
with security programs, 721
with systems development, 670
eToys, 220, 360
Europcar, 342
European Court of Human Rights, 499
EV, *see* Expected value
Events, online, 200
EV (expected value), 611
Evolutionary development, 640
e-wallets, 214
Exchanges, 201–203, 253, 379
Exec Express, 721
Executive information system (EIS), 556. *See also* Executive support systems
Executive support systems (ESSs), 54, 55, 545, 556–559
Expected value (EV), 611
Expedia.com, 105
Expense management automation (EMA), 326
Expert systems (ESs), 54, 55, 461, 563–568

applications of, 567, 568
benefits of, 564–565
components of, 565–567
defined, 564
limitations of, 564–565
for security, 721
Explanation subsystems, 566
Explicit knowledge, 453
Exploration, involvement, analysis, and communications (EIAC) model, 610
Exposure (of information systems), 691
Extended ERP software, 366
Extended supply chain, 357, 425
Extensible Markup Language (XML), 463–464, 650
External auditor, 717
External data sources, 495
External integration, 368
Externalization mode (knowledge creation), 457
External relationship capital, 476
Extranets, 4, 28, 72, 131–132, 233–235, 471
Extreme analytic frameworks (EAF), 578
Extreme programming (XP), 646–647, 660
ExxonMobil Corporation, 371, 416

F

Factoring of receivables, 326
Factors, 326
FAD (frantic application development), 644
FAQFinder, 134
FAQs, *see* Frequently asked questions
Fatbrain.com, 96
Fault tolerance, 720
FBI (Federal Bureau of Investigation), 698
FCC (Federal Communication Commission), 272
FDA, *see* Food and Drug Administration
FDMA (Frequency Division Multiple Access), 248
Feasibility studies, 636
Federal Bureau of Investigation (FBI), 698
Federal Communication Commission (FCC), 272
Federal Express, 16, 48–50, 93, 94, 116, 318, 339, 383, 429, 436
Federal government, IT in restructuring, 431
Federal Trade Commission (FTC), 216, 695
Feedback, 18
File management products, 155–156
Finance systems, *see* Accounting and finance systems
Financial auditing, 329
Financial flows, 357
Financial forecasting, 323
Financial metrics, 475–476
Financial planning, 322–324
Financial ratio analysis, 329

Financial trends in IT, 591–592
Financial value chain management (FVCM), 328
Findarticles.com, 135
Fingerhut, 383
Fingerprints, payment using, 214–215
Firewalls, 707, 708
Fitsense Technology, 274
Five-step requirements analysis model, 408
Fixed costs (of IT), 599
Flaming, 162
Flexible-manufacturing systems (FMS), 310
Flooz.com, 614
FMS (flexible-manufacturing systems), 310
Food and Drug Administration (FDA), 219–220, 466
Food.com, 255
Ford Motor Company, 427–429, 593
Forecasting, 323
BI application to, 506
of demand, 361
information for, 511
Foreign language Web pages, 136
Foreign travel, 7
Formal information systems, 19
Forward auctions, 183
Four-stage model of planning, 400–411
information requirements analysis (stage 2), 408–409
project planning (stage 4), 411
resource allocation (stage 3), 409, 410
SITP (stage 1), 401–407
FoxMeyer, 376
Framatome, 2
Frantic application development (FAD), 644
Fraud, Internet, 216
FreeMarkets, 226–227
Freenetworks.org, 251
Free products/services, 338
Free speech, right to, 161
Freeware, 143, 161
Frequency Division Multiple Access (FDMA), 248
Frequently asked questions (FAQs), 134, 339
Frito-Lay Inc., 477
Front-end tools, 500–501
Frontline decision making, 577–578
Front-office operations, 343, 380
FTC, *see* Federal Trade Commission
Fujitsu, 2, 721
Functional areas, 58
Functional (departmental) information systems, 52, 53
Functional departments, 299
Functional exchanges, 202, 203
Functional information systems, 298–300
for accounting and finance, 322–329
characteristics of, 299–300
for customer relationship management, 335–341

for human resources, 329–335
integration of, 341–343
managerial issues with, 343–345
for marketing and sales, 312–321
for production and operations management, 306–312
for transaction processing, 300–306
Functional management information systems, *see* Management information systems
Funk & Wagnalls, 101
Fuzzy logic, 461, 572
FVCM (financial value chain management), 328

G

G2B commerce, *see* Government-to-business commerce
G2C transactions, *see* Government-to-citizens transactions
G2G commerce, *see* Government-to-government commerce
Gambling, mobile, 266
Games, mobile, 266
Garden.com, 220
Gate assignment systems (airports), 585
Gateways, 30
GDSS, *see* Group decision support systems
Gems, 6
General controls, 702
General Electric Corp., 10, 338
General Electric Information Services, 615
General Motors (GM), 117, 169, 272, 279, 429, 593
General Packet Radio Service (GPRS), 242
Generations (of technology), 248
Gentia, 462
Geographical information systems (GISs), 270–271, 517–520
at Dallas Rapid Area Transit, 536–537
integration of GPS and, 519–520
in Oregon, 442–443
Geographic contents, 269
Gillette, 280
GISs, *see* Geographical information systems
Global business drivers, 111–112
Global collaboration, 150
Global competition, 13, 111–112
Globalization, 12–13
Global networked environment, *see* Internet
Global positioning system (GPS), 240, 242, 246, 257, 269–270
in car navigation systems, 271
integration of GIS and, 519–520
tractor guidance from, 262
in vehicle location systems, 305
Global stock exchanges, 325
Global supply chains, 386–387
GM, *see* General Motors
Gnutella, 71
Go2Online, 257
Goals, organizational, 398

Golden Rule, 42
Goodyear, 338
Government regulation/deregulation, 15
Government-to-business (G2B) commerce, 205, 206
Government-to-citizens (G2C) commerce, 179, 205, 206
Government-to-government (G2G) commerce, 205
GPRS (General Packet Radio Service), 242
GPS, see Global positioning system
GPS locator, 246
Green Mountain Coffee Roasters, 393
Grid computing, 75
Grossman's Bargain Centers, 303
Group decision support systems (GDSS), 545, 553, 554
Group dynamics, 153
Group purchasing, 10, 201
Group support systems (GSSs), 54
Group technology (GT), 310
Groupware, 130, 151–156, 433
Groupware suites, 155
Growth strategy, 102
GSM bandwidth, 273
GSSs (group support systems), 54
GTE Laboratories, 134
GT (group technology), 310
Guinness Import Co., 553

H

Hackers, 693, 721
Hacking, 707–708
Handelsbanken (Sweden), 23
Hardware, 19, 76
Harrah's Entertainment, 491–493
Haworth Corporation, 515
HDL, 318
Hershey Foods Corporation, 376
Hertz Corporation, 290, 557
Hewlett-Packard, 403, 475–476, 613, 628, 675
Hierarchical data format, 493–494, 500
High-payoff projects, 408–410
Hi-Life Corporation, 176–177
HIP, see Hyperwave Information Portal
Hitachi, 526
HLT (Home Linking Technology), 278
"Holdup," 615
Holiday Inn, 217–218, 266
Holosofx, 427
Home, shopping from, 9
Home Depot, 100, 727
Home Linking Technology (HLT), 278
Homes, smart, 275, 277–278
Honeynets, 712
Honeypots, 712
Hong Kong, 45–46
Hong Kong Airport, 559, 692
Hong Kong and Shanghai Bank, 289–290
Horizontal consortia, 110–111
Horizontal distributors, 202
Hotels, wireless services at, 266–267

Hotspots, 249, 251
Hotwire.com, 191
Howstuffworks.com, 135
HRISs, see Human resources information systems
HTML (hypertext markup language), 664
Hubs, collaboration, 146, 147
Human capital, 476
Human resources information systems (HRISs), 50, 59, 329–330
Human resources systems, 329–335
    maintenance and development of, 333–334
    planning and management, 334–335
    recruitment, 330, 332–333
    traditional vs. electronic, 331
Hybrid intelligent systems, 573–574
Hypertext markup language (HTML), 664
Hyperwave Information Portal (HIP), 466, 467
Hyundai Investment, 190

I

i2 Technology, 2, 373
IBM, 2, 26, 27, 32, 74, 76, 249, 334, 343, 374, 404, 426, 462, 613, 615, 628, 683, 720
IBM Canada, 685
IBM Global Services Australia, 654
IBM/Lotus, 468
I-CASE systems, 666
ICI Explosives, 95
IC (information center), 685
Iconic (scale) models, 548
Identity theft, 689, 694
IDOL (Intelligent Data Operating Layer) Server, 465
IETF (Internet Engineering Task Force), 709
IIPC, see International Information Products Company LTD
i-mode, 258
Implementation phase (decision making), 547
Implementation stage (systems development), 637–639
Inbound logistics, 107
Incoming funds, planning for, 323
Increase switching costs strategy, 104
Increasing returns, theory of, 620–621
Independent variables, 192
Indexing agents, 134
India, outsourcing to, 613–614
Industrial espionage, 97
Industrial Revolution, 87
Industry-specific components, 649
Industrywide communication portals, 140–141
Inference engine, 566
Infomediation, 218
Informal information systems, 19
Information:
    defined, 51, 451–452
    dynamic, 132–133

static vs. dynamic, 132
    types of, 511
    value of, 597–599
Information architecture, 412
Information center (IC), 685
Information discovery, 507
Information economics, 605, 607
Information engineering, 404
Information ethics, 15
Information flows, 357
Information infrastructure, 62, 65
Information overload, 14
Information portals, 136–137
Information requirements analysis, 400, 408–409
Information resources management (IRM), 76–79, 681–687
    CIO in, 686–687
    IS department, 681–682, 685–686
    managerial issues with, 722
    relationships between ISD and end users, 682–685
    security issues in, see Security of information resources
Information services department (ISD), 681–686
    adaptability of, 685, 686
    imperatives for, 685
    names of, 682
    relationships between end users and, 682–685
Information superhighway, 28, 128
Information systems department (ISD), 76–77
Information systems (ISs), 18–24, 50–52
    capabilities of, 5
    classification of, 52–56
    components of, 50
    computer-based, 19–20
    computers vs., 20
    configurations of, 51–52
    defined, 18, 50
    departmental, 50, 52
    enterprisewide, 50, 52
    examples of, 20–23
    failures of, 23–24
    formal vs. informal, 19
    human resources, 50
    integration of, 341–343
    integration of KMS and, 471
    interorganizational, 50, 52
    and IT, 20
    purpose and social context of, 20
    transaction processing vs. functional, 57–59
Information technology architecture, 411–415
Information technology (IT). See also Information systems; IT planning
    benefits of learning about, 32–33
    capabilities of, 4
    defined, 4
    and distributed computing, 27–32
    and empowerment, 436
    evaluating investment in, 597–603
    factors determining uses of, 141–142

and general technological trends, 25–27
organizational activities supported by, 59–62
as product, 620
and strategic advantage, 92–97
and supply chain, 62–64
time/place framework for, 141–142
Information visualizers, 25
Infrastructure, IT, 412
In-house application development, 662
Initiators of change, organizations as, 61
Innovation, technological, 14
Innovation strategy, 102–103
Inputs, 18, 19, 51
Input controls, 706
Instant messaging, 155
Instant video, 155
Instraspect Software, 467
Intangible benefits, 600–601
Integrated approach (functional systems), 299
Integrated messaging systems, 265
Integrated supply chains, 358
Integrated value chain, 368–369
Integration:
    of e-business and knowledge management, 420
    of ERP and e-commerce, 384–385
    of ERP and SCM, 373–374
    ERP for, 369
    of ESS and DSS, 559
    of front- and back-office operations, 343
    with functional information systems, 341–343
    of information, 424–426
    internal vs. external, 368
    of KMS with other systems, 470
    of legacy and enterprise systems, 415
    with network computing, 162–163
    of supply chain systems, 366–369
Integrity of data, 497
Intel, 221, 239, 249, 334
Intellectual assets, 453
Intellectual capital, 453, 476
Intellectual property rights (IPR), 44–45, 218, 219
Intelligence:
    artificial, 461–462
    business, 54, 55
    competitive, 95–98
Intelligence phase (decision making), 546
Intelligent agents, 97, 133, 195–196, 433, 461–462, 511. See also Artificial intelligence
Intelligent computer-aided instruction (ICAI), 334
Intelligent Data Operating Layer (IDOL) Server, 465
Intelligent DSS, 553, 579
Intelligent elder care, 281, 282
Intelligent ESS, 558, 559
Intelligent indexing agents, 134
Intelligent support systems (ISSs), 55, 559–563
Intelligent systems, 280–281, 545. See also Pervasive computing

for financial and economic forecasting, 323
hybrid, 573–574
for security, 720–721
for troubleshooting, 310
Intentional threats, 692–693
Interactive advertising and marketing, 199
Interactive Internet TPS, 303, 304
Interactive pagers, 245
Interactive voice response (IVR), 14, 82
Interactive whiteboards, 154
Intermediation, 218
Internal auditor, 717
Internal data sources, 495
Internal integration, 368, 425
Internal rate of return (IRR), 603
Internal Revenue Service, 555, 602
Internal supply chain, 63, 64
International banking, 189–190
International Data Corp., 627
International Information Products Company LTD (IIPC), 22–23
Interned-based EDI, 232, 233
Internet, 4, 71, 128–130, 132
    application categories supported by, 129, 130
    data from, 495
    defined, 128
    evolution of commercial applications on, 129
    fraud on, 216
    future versions of, 128
    GIS uses on, 518, 519
    growth of, 28
    manners for using, 162
    in marketing, 524
    market research with, 321
    tracking customer activities on, 195
    value of, 27
    World Wide Web vs., 129
Internet-based wireless intrabusiness applications, 263–264
Internet economy, see Digital economy
Internet-enabled phones, 245
Internet Engineering Task Force (IETF), 709
Internet Home Alliance, 278
Internet of "things," 280
Internet portfolio map (matrix), 418–419
Internet Relay Chat (IRC), 143
Internet Security Alliance, 728
Internet telephony (voiceover IP), 143, 249
Internet2, 128
Interorganizational information systems (IOSs), 50, 53, 110–111
    IT planning for, 415–416
    for virtual organizations, 433
Intrabusiness, 178, 204–205
    mobile, 259–264
    supply chain activities, 378
Intranets, 28, 71–72, 130–132
    data warehouse on, 503
    defined, 4, 130
    financial analysis of, 627
    integration of KMS and, 471
Intranet portals, 138

Intrinsic data quality, 496
Intrusion detection, 708, 709, 720–721
Inventory management, 307–308, 362
Inventories:
    of vacant positions, 330
    vendor replenishment of, 308, 362
Investment management, 326–327
"Invisible" computing, see Pervasive computing
IOSs, see Interorganizational information systems
Iowa, state agencies of, 589–590
iPing.com, 253
IPR, see Intellectual property rights
IRC (Internet Relay Chat), 143
IRM, see Information resources management
IRR (internal rate of return), 603
ISD, see Information services department; Information systems department
ISO 9000 standards, 667, 668
ISs, see Information systems
ISSs, see Intelligent support systems
IT, see Information technology
IT governance, 684
IT planning, 398–420
    alignment with organizational plans, 402–403
    business importance of, 398–399
    defined, 398
    and e-planning, 417–418
    evolution of, 399
    executing, 399–401
    information requirements analysis (stage 2), 408–409
    information technology architectures, 411–415
    for interorganizational systems, 415–416
    managerial issues with, 437–439
    for multinational corporations, 416
    problems for, 416, 417
    project planning (stage 4), 411
    resource allocation (stage 3), 409, 410
    SITP (stage 1), 401–407
    tools and methodologies of, 404–407
iVISION, 91
IVR, see Interactive voice response

J

JAD, see Joint application design
Jaguars, online configuration of, 316
Java, 664–664
JCPenney, 84
J.D. Edwards, 114, 464
JiffyLube, 257
JIT processing, see Just-in-time pr
Job dispatch, mobile devices for, 260–261
Job markets, online, 190–191
John Deere Corp., 117
Johnson Control, 169

Joint application design (JAD), 641–642, 660
J.P. Morgan, 68
J.P. Morgan Chase Company, 68, 97
Judd's, 627
Just-in-time (JIT) processing, 16, 309, 310

K

Kazaa, 71
KBDSS (knowledge-based DSS), 553
KDD, *see* Knowledge discovery in databases
Keiretsu, 17–18
Kelly's Extension of Metcalfe's Law, 27
Kemper Insurance Company, 264
Keyboards:
   attachable, 245
   wearable, 259
Key performance indicators (KPI), 556, 557
Keyword banners, 197
Kinko's, 303
Kitchen Aid, 84
KM, *see* Knowledge management
Kmart, 110
KMSs, *see* Knowledge management systems
Knowbots, 25, 133
Knowledge, 451–454
   and ability to act, 452
   and AI, 561
   characteristics of, 452
   defined, 51, 451, 452
   leaky, 453
   tacit vs. explicit, 453–454
   transformation of data into, 494
Knowledge acquisition, 456, 457
Knowledge base, 2, 561, 565
Knowledge-based DSS (KBDSS), 553
Knowledge Center, 466
Knowledge creation, 456, 457
Knowledge discovery, 507
Knowledge discovery in databases (KDD), 462, 463, 507–508
Knowledge harvesting tools, 466, 467
KnowledgeMail, 466, 467
Knowledge management (KM), 51, 374, 451–480
   tools/processes in, 456–458
   success of, 474–479
   476–477
   other business systems with, 470–471
   468, 470
   480
   –460
   60

cessing

Ss),

cycle in, 454–456
   implementation of, 464–471
   potential drawbacks to, 479
   technologies supporting, 461–464
Knowledge portals, 138
Knowledge repositories, 465
Knowledge seeking, 457
Knowledge servers, 465
Knowledge sharing, 457
Knowledge workers, 61–62
Knowledge work systems (KWSs), 54, 55
Knowware, 464
Kodak Corporation, 60, 82
Kone Inc., 628
Kozmo, 220
KPI, *see* Key performance indicators
KWSs, *see* Knowledge work systems
Kyota, Japan, 281

L

L. L. Bean, 383
Lancaster, U.K., 281
LANs, *see* Local area networks
Lawson Software, 349
l-commerce, *see* Location-based commerce
Leaky knowledge, 453
Learning agents, 195
Leased applications, 661–664
Legacy application software, 247
Legacy systems, 70, 78, 415, 668
Legal issues:
   with computer crime and security, 698–699
   with e-commerce, 217–218
   with IT planning, 437–439
   with mobile computing, 283, 284
   with network computing, 160–162
   with systems development, 670
   with telemedicine, 267
Lego Company, 387
Le Saunda Holding Company, 21
Levi Strauss & Company, 84, 221, 436
LifeStar, 499
Light methodology, 640
Limit Order Application (LORA), 152
Liquidations, auctions for, 183
Littlewoods Stores, 363
Living.com, 220
Local area networks (LANs), 67, 72, 130, 131, 178, 249–251
Localization, 242
Location-based advertising, 271–272
Location-based commerce (l-commerce), 28, 242, 269–273, 520
Location-based technology, 269
Location-specific contents, 269–270
Lock-in effect, 621
Lock-in strategy, 104
Logical design, 636, 637
Logistics:
   with e-tailing, 187
   of returns, 383
   reverse, 358

Logistics management, 307
London Stock Exchange, 690
Long-range IT plan, 399
Longs Drug Stores, 57
LORA (Limit Order Application), 152
Lotus Development Corporation, 498, 499
Lotus Notes, 433
Lotus Notes/Domino, 69, 155, 465
Loyalty cards, 212
Lufthansa, 250

M

Machine-learning capabilities, 55
MacroArt Technology, 721
Macy's, 383
Mail Boxes Etc., 638
Mainframe environment, 66–67
Make-or-buy decision, 657
Make-to-forecast strategy, 108
Make-to-stock supply chains, 359
Malaysia Airlines, 542
Malaysia Airport, 559, 692
Malls:
   electronic, 186
   virtual, 522
Management, defined, 543
Management by maxim, 608–609
The Management Cockpit, 560
Management information systems (MISs), 53, 54, 58–59
Management service providers (MSPs), 614
Management support systems (MSSs), 545, 546, 574–575
Managers, 543–546. *See also* Decision support
Managerial activities, 59–60
Managerial issues:
   with data management, 528–530
   with decision support systems, 578–580
   with e-business applications, 665
   with e-commerce, 222–223
   with economics of IT, 623–624
   with functional information systems, 343–345
   with information resources management, 722
   with IT planning, 437–439
   with knowledge management, 480
   with mobile computing/m-commerce, 285
   with network computing, 163–164
   with security programs, 722
   with supply chain management, 388
   with systems development, 659–661, 670–671
Managerial planning, 398–399
Manufacturing Connection Online (MCO), 120
Manufacturing resource planning (MRP II), 309, 366

Manugistics, 373
Mapinfo.com, 317
Marketing:
    affiliate, 10
    auctions in, 183
    databases for, 523–525
    direct-response, 196–197
    hybrid intelligent systems in, 573
    interactive, 199
    old vs. new models of, 315
    permission, 198–199
    viral, 199, 351
Marketing and sales information systems,
        107, 312–321
    customer information, 313–317
    distribution channels, 317–319
    marketing management decisions,
        319–321
Marketing customer information file
        (MCIF), 319
Marketing management, 319–321
Marketing transaction database (MTD),
        523–524
Marketplaces, 73
Market pressures, 12–14
Market research, 192–196, 321
Marriott International, 149, 266
Mary Kay, 566
MAS 90 and MAS 200, 324
Massachusetts Department of
        Revenue, 498
Mass customization, 17, 315, 316, 427, 429
Mass production, 87
Master Builders, 95, 104
Master files (TPS), 302
MasterTrac, 95
Material requirements planning (MRP),
        308, 310, 366
Materials flows, 357
Materials management, 307
Mathematical (quantitative) models, 548
Maybelline, 82
Mazda, 428
MBMS (model-based management
        system), 552
m-business, see Mobile commerce
McDonald's, 250, 423
McDonnell-Douglas, 499
MCIF (marketing customer information
        file), 319
MCO (Manufacturing Connection
        Online), 120
m-commerce, see Mobile commerce
Mederlandse Spoorweges, 584
Medical emergencies, 267
Medium-term IT plan, 399
MedLink, 267
Meetings, 145, 153–156, 555
Megabeam, 266
Memory buttons, 274
Mental models, 548
Mergers and acquisitions, 221
Merrill-Lynch, 309–310
Metadata, 502
Metasearch engines, 134
Meta searchers, 133

Metcalfe's Law, 27
Method/1, 404, 635
Method-driven IT planning approach, 400
Metrics:
    for knowledge management, 475–476
    for planning process, 419
    for supply chain performance, 363–364
Metric benchmarks, 608
Metropolitan Transit Authority (MTA) of
        New York, 600
MGIF (Mobile Games Interoperability
        Forum), 266
Microbrowser, 247
Micropayments, 209, 254–255
Microsoft, 74, 76, 82, 105, 635, 649, 689
Microsoft Exchange, 69
Microsoft Outlook, 69
Microsoft Passport, 214
Microstrategy, 506
Middleware, 500
Milestones, 668–669
Millstone Coffee, 239
Minneapolis-St. Paul International
        Airport, 250
Minnesota Department of Transportation,
        683
Minority Report (film), 273
MISs, see Management information
        systems
Mrs. Fields Cookies, 479
MIT, 280
MMS (multimedia messaging service), 241
MobileAria, 272
Mobile commerce (m-commerce, m-
        business), 28, 73, 240. See also
        Mobile computing
    attributes of, 241–242
    B2B applications, 265
    banking, 253–255
    contextual computing for, 275
    defined, 179
    drivers of, 242–244
    failures in, 284–285
    inhibitors and barriers of, 282–285
    intrabusiness and enterprise
        applications, 259–264
    micropayments with, 254–255
    mobile (wireless) wallets, 255
    revenue models of, 245
    security issues with, 252
    shopping from wireless devices, 256
    supply chain applications, 265
    targeted advertising, 257–258
    value chain for, 244–245
    voice systems for, 252–253
    wireless payment systems, 254, 255
Mobile computing, 28, 55, 73, 238–240.
        See also Mobile commerce
    attributes of, 241–242
    basic terminology for, 240, 241
    consumer/personal service applications,
        265–268
    defined, 239
    drivers of, 242–244
    ethical and legal issues with, 283, 284
    failures in, 284–285

    hardware for, 245–246
    inhibitors and barriers of, 282–285
    managerial issues with, 285
    mobile portals, 258–259
    security issues with, 252
    in smart cars, 279
    software for, 246, 247
    Wi-Fi standard for, 249–252
    wireless, 239
    wireless local area networks for, 249–250
    wireless personal area networks for,
        249–250
    wireless wide area networks for, 246–249
Mobile computing systems, 54
Mobile devices, 239, 243
    applications for, 262
    for job dispatch, 260–261
    wearable, 259
Mobile entertainment, 266
Mobile gambling, 266
Mobile games, 266
Mobile Games Interoperability Forum
        (MGIF), 266
Mobile networks, 246
Mobile portals, 137, 258–259
Mobile positioning center (MPC), 269
Mobile supply chain management
        (mSCM), 265
Mobile switching centers, 248
Mobile telemetry, 272
Mobile wallets, 255
Mobile workers, 259
Models and modeling, 547–548
    EIAC, 610
    management subsystem for, 552
    for sensitivity analysis, 551, 552
    simulation vs., 576
Model-based management system
        (MBMS), 552
Model marts, 463
Model warehouses, 463
Modems, attacks via, 698
Monster.com, 221
Montogmery Securities, 715
Moore's Law, 25, 26, 591
Morgan Stanley and Company, 328
Moscow MTS, 688–689
Motorola, 255, 266, 334, 499
MP3 Inc., 103
MPC (mobile positioning center), 269
MPR II, see Manufacturing resource
        planning
MRP, see Material requirements planning
mSCM (mobile supply chain
        management), 265
MSPs (management service providers), 614
MSSs, see Management support systems
MTA (Metropolitan Transit Authority) of
        New York, 600
MTD, see Marketing transaction databa[se]
Multidimensional databases, 503, 505
Multidimensionality visualization, 51[5]
Multimedia messaging service (MM[S)]
Multinational corporations, IT plan[ning]
        for, 416
Multiple-currency banking, 190

m-wallet, 255
MyAvantGo.Com, 257

N

Nabisco, 82
Name-your-own-price business model, 10
Nanotechnology, 27
Napster, 71
National Association of Chain Drug
    Stores, 140
National City Corp., 444–445
National Computer Security Center
    (NCSC), 720
National Infrastructure Protection Center
    (NIPC), 698
National Semiconductor Corporation
    (NSC), 126–128, 131
Natural language processing (NLP),
    568–571
NCSC (National Computer Security
    Center), 720
NEC, 82
Needham Interactive, 627
Nestlé USA, 364
Net, *see* Internet
NetCaptor, 133
Netgain, 319
Netiquette, 162
Net present value (NPV), 599, 601,
    603, 609
Netscape Communicator, 69, 690
Nettracker, 195
Network(s), 50, 76
    collaborative, 146–149, 369
    defined, 19
    enterprisewide, 30
    for industrywide communication,
        140–141
    local area, 249–250
    mobile, 246
    neural, 54
    optical, 30
    personal area, 249–250
    protection of, 706–712
    storage, 30, 32
    wide area, 246–249
    wireless, 28, 251, 712. *See also* Mobile
        computing
    wireline vs. wireless, 50
twork-based technologies, 27
    ʹork computers, 30
    ʹk computing, 128–164. *See also*
        llaboration; Communication;
        ʹvery; Internet

ʹing, 156–158
    ʹ–159
    ʹ with, 160–162
ʹ517
ʹ241   ʹs, 151–156
ʹing   ʹ62–163

                164

workflow technologies, 150–151
    and World Wide Web, 129
Network controls (security), 705
Networked organizations, 435
Network effects, 621
Network storage devices, 30, 32
Net worth (NW), 603
Neural computing, 511, 571, 572
Neural networks, 54, 461. *See also*
    Artificial neural networks
New economy, *see* Digital economy
New Line Cinema, 226–227
New product introduction, 320
New York City, 8–9
New York Stock Exchange, 327
NextBus system, 237–238
"Next society," 14
Niche strategy, 102
Nike, 13, 24, 84
Nintendo, 266
NIPC (National Infrastructure Protection
    Center), 698
NLP, *see* Natural language processing
"No free lunch," 42
Nokia, 245, 252, 255, 266, 272
Nominal group technique, 145
Non-Internet mobile applications, 268
Nordea, 255, 258
Nortel Network, 478
Northeast Utilities, 284–285
Northwest Airlines, 320
NPV, *see* Net present value
NSC, *see* National Semiconductor
    Corporation
NTT Docomo, 252
Nucleus firms, 146, 147
NW (net worth), 603
Nygard of Canada, 149

O

OASs, *see* Office automation systems
Object Management Group (OMG), 649
Object-oriented environments, 27
Object-oriented (OO) development,
    644–646, 660
Object-oriented systems development
    (OOSD), 645
Object-oriented transaction processing, 303
Object technology, 27
Obsolescence, 14
ODSS (organizational decision support
    systems), 556
Office automation systems (OASs), 53, 54
Offices, smart, 281
Offshore outsourcing, 613–614
O'Hare Airport, 585
OLAP, *see* Online analytical processing
OLAP multidimensionality, 515
Old-economy organizations, *see* Brick-
    and-mortar organizations
OLS (organizational learning system), 486
OLTP, *see* Online transaction processing
OMG (Object Management Group), 649
Online analytical processing (OLAP), 319,
    506, 508–510, 515, 517

Online corporate training, 158–159
Online database publishers, 495
Online Data Corporation, 685
Online job markets, 190–191
Online processing, 302
Online securities trading, 190
Online transaction processing (OLTP),
    303, 304
OnLink Technologies, 664
OnStar system, 279
OO development, *see* Object-oriented
    development
OOSD (object-oriented systems
    development), 645
Open Market, 220
Operating system (OS), 247
Operations, 107
Operational activities, 59
Operational audits, 329, 718
Operational data sores, 504–505
Operational effectiveness strategy, 103
Operational planning, 398–399
Operational system, 500
Opportunistic repricing, 615
Optical networks, 30
Optimization, 549, 573
Options, real vs. financial, 609
Oracle Corp., 74, 343, 628, 675
Orbis Inc., 8
Order fulfillment, 380–384
    defined, 215, 380
    e-commerce, problems with, 380–381
    as e-commerce support system, 215
    with e-tailing, 187
    outsourcing of, 381
Oregon, 442–443
Organizational activities, 59–62
Organizational buyers, 193
Organizational decision support systems
    (ODSS), 556
Organizational IT planning approach, 400
Organizational knowledge, 51
Organizational knowledge base, 561
Organizational learning system (OLS), 486
Organizational redesign, 430–431
Organizational responses, *see* Critical
    response activities
Organizational structure, changing, 435
Organization transformation, 433–435
OS (operating system), 247
Otis Elevator Company, 304
Outbound logistics, 107
Outputs, 18, 19, 51
Output controls, 706
Outsourcing, 78, 660
    advantages/disadvantages of, 615–616
    and ASPs, 614, 663
    defined, 613
    and e-commerce, 614–615
    as economic strategy, 612–617
    impact of, 414
    of merchandise returns, 383
    to MSPs, 614
    of order fulfillment, 381
    strategic, 614
    strategies for, 410, 616–617
    of systems development, 654–655

P

P2P architecture, *see* Peer-to-peer architecture
Pagers, interactive, 245
Panera Bread Company, 250
PaperX.com, 220
Parallel conversion, 638
Partial electronic commerce, 178
Partner-relationship management (PRM),
    385–386
Partners HealthCare System, Inc., 476
Pattern recognition, 571
PAVECA, 205
Payback period, 603
Payload security, 711
Payments, 208–215
    for C2C transactions, 208
    electronic, 210–215, 326
    for exposure to advertising, 258
    micropayments, 254–255
    security issues for, 213–214
    traditional vs. electronic, 209
    wireless, 254, 255
PayPal, 212, 213
Payroll functions, 334–335
PBXs (private branch exchanges), 253
PC environment, 67
PDA, *see* Personal digital assistant
PDE (position determining equipment), 269
Peachtree.com, 324
Peer-to-peer (P2P) architecture, 70–71
People, defined, 19
PeopleNet, 460
PeopleSoft, Inc., 376, 385–386, 393
Pepsi Bottling Group, 74
Performance dashboard, 610
Performance evaluations, 333
Performance measurement, 363–364
Permission marketing, 198–199, 257
Personal agents, 276
Personal data, 495
Personal digital assistant (PDA), 241, 245,
    246, 252, 255
Personal information manager (PIM), 546
Personalization, 242, 316, 339
Personal portals, 137
Personal services, online purchase of, 208
Personnel planning, 334
Personnel records, 335
Person-to-person payments, 212–213
PERT (program evaluation and review
    technique), 309
Pervasive computing, 28–31, 75, 273–282
    applications of, 275, 277–280
    contextual attributes in, 274–276
    large-scale systems, 280–281
    and need for face-to-face meetings, 156
    smart appliances, 278
    smart cars, 278–279
    smart homes, 275, 277–278
Pfizer, 466
Phased conversion, 639
Philippines, 330
Photography, 6–8
Physical buildings, 76
Physical control (security), 703
Physical design, 626

PictureTel Corporation, 155
Pilot conversion, 638
PIM (personal information manager), 546
Piping technology, 32
Plagiarism, 135
Planning, *see* IT planning
PLC (Power Line Communication), 278
PLM, *see* Product lifecycle management
PLM software, *see* Product lifecycle
    management software
Poaching, 615
PointCast, 220
Policy-based resource-management tools,
    656
Policy-based service-level-management
    tools, 656
POM, *see* Production and operations
    management
Pop-under ads, 197–200
Pop-up ads, 197–200
Portals, 136–141
    corporate, 137–140, 527
    customer, 342
    defined, 136
    employee, 342
    enterprise knowledge, 465–466
    human resources-related, 332
    industrywide communication, 140–141
    information, 136–137
    integration of, 139–140
    mobile, 137, 258–259
    voice, 253, 263
Porter's models, *see* Competitive forces
    model; Value chain model
Position determining equipment (PDE), 269
Position inventory, 330
Post-audit evaluation of systems, 639
Power Line Communication (PLC), 278
Practice approach (knowledge
    management), 458–460
Prada, 274
Preference analysis, 313
Prescriptions, 267
Priceline.com, 10, 103, 104, 117, 191
Price-optimization programs, 57
Price-to-performance ratio, 591
Price Waterhouse, 675
PricewaterhouseCoopers, 221
Pricing decisions, 319, 329
Primary activities (value chain model), 107
Privacy issues, 45–46
    with e-commerce, 217
    with e-government, 207
    with location-based systems, 273
    with network computing, 160–162
    with pervasive computing, 274, 283, 284
Private branch exchanges (PBXs), 253
Private marketplaces, 73
PRM, *see* Partner-relationship
    management
Procedures, 19, 76
Process approach (iknowledge
    management), 458–460
Process-centric integration, 343
Processing controls, 706
Procter & Gamble, 82, 149, 321,
    361–362, 613

Production and operations management
    (POM), 306–312
    computer-integrated manufacturing,
        310–311
    inventory management, 307–308
    just-in-time systems, 309
    logistics management, 307
    manufacturing resource planning, 309
    material requirements planning, 308
    product lifecycle management, 311–312
    project management, 309–310
    quality control, 308
    work management systems, 310
Production workflow, 151
Productivity:
    defined, 592
    as driver of process redesign, 421
    productivity paradox, 592–597
    of salespersons, 319–320
    and telecommuting, 160
Productivity paradox, 592–597
Product life cycle, 358
Product lifecycle management (PLM),
    311–312
Product life-cycle management (PLM)
    software, 113–114
Profitability, 146, 320, 329
Program evaluation and review technique
    (PERT), 309
Programming attacks, 695–696
Programming controls, 705
Project(s):
    defined, 309
    properties/priorities of, 669
Project initiation, 635
Project management, 669–670
Project planning, 400, 411, 668–670
Promotions, online, 199–200
Protocols, 156
Prototyping, 640–641, 659–660
Proximity cards, 268
PSA (company), 115
PSAP (Public Safety Answering Point), 272
Public exchanges, 201–203
Public key infrastructure, 252
Public marketplaces, 73
Public portals, 137
Public Safety Answering Point (PSAP), 272
Public transportation, 9–10, 20
Publishing portals, 137
Pull advertising, 257
Pull systems, 87, 343
Purchasing, group, 10
Purchasing cards, 211
Purchasing-decision model, 194
Pure electronic commerce, 178
Pure-play organizations, *see* Virtual
    organizations
Puritan.xom, 221
Push advertising, 257
Push systems, 87, 343

Q

Quality control, 308, 666–668
Quality system, 668

Quantitative models, 548
Quantum computing, 27
Quantum Corporation, 392, 675
Query-and-reporting tools, 134, 506, 508
QVC, 350–351

R

RAD, *see* Rapid application development
Radio frequency identification (RFID),
    274, 280, 283, 284
RadioShack Online, 94, 104
Random banners, 197
Rapid application development (RAD),
    642–644, 660
Reader's Digest, 155
Real estate, online services for, 191–192
Real options, 609–610
Real-time collaboration (RTC), 154–155
Real-time decision support, 578
Real-time operations, 13, 58
Real-time (synchronous) communication,
    141
Receivables, factoring of, 326
Recording Industry Association of
    America (RIAA), 697–698
Recruitment, online, 191, 330
Red Rocket, 220
Referral malls, 186
Regional Computer Intrusion Squads
    (FBI), 698
Reintermediation, 218
Relational databases, 494
Relational OLAP (ROLAP), 509
RE/MAX, 149
Reorder point, 308
Replicated (dependent) data marts,
    504
Representation data quality, 496
Re-presentment of checks, 326
Requests for quotes (RFQs), 10, 201
Resource allocation, 400, 409, 410
Resource-allocation control, 398–399
Restaurants.com, 228
Restructurings, 17, 430–431. *See also*
    Business process restructuring
Resumix, 332
Retooling, 426
Return on investment (ROI), 599, 603,
    610, 618
    ...urns, merchandise, 383
    ...nue models, 189, 245
    ... auctions, 10, 184
    ...ngineering, 415, 668
    ...istics, 358
    ...io frequency identification
    ...sts for quotes
    ...ng Industry Association
    ...9
    ...–720
    ...s, 719–720

ROLAP, 509
Room 33, 258
Rosenbluth International, 90–91, 93, 95,
    103, 117, 218
Rouse & Co. International, 417
Royal Dutch/Shell, 475
Royal Mile Pub (Silver Spring, MD), 31
RTC, *see* Real-time collaboration
Runaway projects, 595, 619
Ryder systems, 360

S

SABRE system, 53, 103
Salary surveys, 332
Sales analysis, 320
Sales automation software, 320
Sales force automation (SFA), 204, 205, 319
Same-day/same-hour delivery, 381, 382
SAML (Security Assertion Markup
    Language), 651
Samsung Electronics, 334
SAP AG, 74, 221, 343, 376, 384, 425, 559,
    620, 628
SAP R/3, 2, 370, 371, 375, 425, 676–677
SAS, 506
SBS Technologies, 317
SBUs (strategic business units), 204
Scale models, 548
Scenario planning, 407, 444–445
Schlumberger, 202
Schools, smart, 281
SCI, *see* Supply chain intelligence
SCM, *see* Supply chain management
SCM software, *see* Supply chain
    management software
Scoring methodology, 605–606
Scott-Morton framework, 435
Screenphones, 245
Screens, wearable, 259
Screen sharing, 154–155
SDLC, *see* Systems development life cycle
Search agents, 196
Search and comparison (for consumers),
    338
Search engines, 133, 134, 195, 467
Sears, Roebuck and Company, 110,
    534–535
Seattle Mariners, 21
SEB Private Bank (Luxembourg), 575
Secure Networks, 721
Securities trading, online, 190
Security Assertion Markup Language
    (SAML), 651
Security facilities, 76
Security issues, 687–723
    applications controls, 706
    auditing, 717–718
    authentication, 710–711
    authorization, 711
    awareness, 701
    border security, 707–710
    breakdown examples, 688–690
    business continuity planning, 712–716
    for C2C commerce, 208

and computer crimes, 693–695
    controls, 700–701
    defense strategies, 701–702
    with e-government, 207
    with electronic payment systems,
        210–215
    federal laws dealing with, 698–699
    general controls, 703–705
    implementing control, 716
    managerial issues with, 722
    with m-commerce and mobile
        computing, 252
    and methods of attack, 694–698
    with mobile phone payments, 254
    with network computing, 160–162
    network protection, 706–712
    for online banking and securities
        trading, 190
    organizing for security, 699–700
    risk management, 718–720
    terminology related to, 688
    trends in security, 720–721
    vulnerability of systems, 690–693
    with Wi-Fi hotspots, 251
Security protocols, 651
Sega, 266
Segmentation, market, 192
Self-checkout machines, 318
Self-healing computers, 27, 720
Self-service convenience stores, 317
Selling:
    along supply chain, 378–379
    e-commerce protections for, 216
Sell-side marketplaces, 200
Semantic Web, 573
Semistructured problems, 549
Sensitivity analysis, 551, 552
Sequencing (of information), 511
Server, 68–69
Service industries:
    online, 189–192
    productivity in, 593
Service-level agreements (SLAs), 684–685
SETI, 75
SFA, *see* Sales force automation
ShareNet, 449–450
Shareware, 161
Sharing (computing), 69
Shirking, 615
Shopping:
    in digital economy, 10
    online, 360
    reengineering of, 317–318
    and return of merchandise, 383
    virtual, 522
    from wireless devices, 256
Short message service (SMS), 241, 244, 262
Siebel Systems, 376
Siemens AG, 2–4, 266, 449–450
Simple Object Access Protocol (SOAP), 650
Simputers, 30
SIM (subscriber identification module)
    card, 248
Simulation modeling, 434–435, 576
Singapore, 115, 305
Singapore Airlines, 542
Singapore Technologies Engineering, 227

and general technological trends, 25–27
organizational activities supported by, 59–62
as product, 620
and strategic advantage, 92–97
and supply chain, 62–64
time/place framework for, 141–142
Information visualizers, 25
Infrastructure, IT, 412
In-house application development, 662
Initiators of change, organizations as, 61
Innovation, technological, 14
Innovation strategy, 102–103
Inputs, 18, 19, 51
Input controls, 706
Instant messaging, 155
Instant video, 155
Instraspect Software, 467
Intangible benefits, 600–601
Integrated approach (functional systems), 299
Integrated messaging systems, 265
Integrated supply chains, 358
Integrated value chain, 368–369
Integration:
    of e-business and knowledge management, 420
    of ERP and e-commerce, 384–385
    of ERP and SCM, 373–374
    ERP for, 369
    of ESS and DSS, 559
    of front- and back-office operations, 343
    with functional information systems, 341–343
    of information, 424–426
    internal vs. external, 368
    of KMS with other systems, 470
    of legacy and enterprise systems, 415
    with network computing, 162–163
    of supply chain systems, 366–369
Integrity of data, 497
Intel, 221, 239, 249, 334
Intellectual assets, 453
Intellectual capital, 453, 476
Intellectual property rights (IPR), 44–45, 218, 219
Intelligence:
    artificial, 461–462
    business, 54, 55
    competitive, 95–98
Intelligence phase (decision making), 546
Intelligent agents, 97, 133, 195–196, 433, 461–462, 511. *See also* Artificial intelligence
Intelligent computer-aided instruction (ICAI), 334
Intelligent Data Operating Layer (IDOL) Server, 465
Intelligent DSS, 553, 579
Intelligent elder care, 281, 282
Intelligent ESS, 558, 559
Intelligent indexing agents, 134
Intelligent support systems (ISSs), 55, 559–563
Intelligent systems, 280–281, 545. *See also* Pervasive computing

for financial and economic forecasting, 323
hybrid, 573–574
for security, 720–721
for troubleshooting, 310
Intentional threats, 692–693
Interactive advertising and marketing, 199
Interactive Internet TPS, 303, 304
Interactive pagers, 245
Interactive voice response (IVR), 14, 82
Interactive whiteboards, 154
Intermediation, 218
Internal auditor, 717
Internal data sources, 495
Internal integration, 368, 425
Internal rate of return (IRR), 603
Internal Revenue Service, 555, 602
Internal supply chain, 63, 64
International banking, 189–190
International Data Corp., 627
International Information Products Company LTD (IIPC), 22–23
Interned-based EDI, 232, 233
Internet, 4, 71, 128–130, 132
    application categories supported by, 129, 130
    data from, 495
    defined, 128
    evolution of commercial applications on, 129
    fraud on, 216
    future versions of, 128
    GIS uses on, 518, 519
    growth of, 28
    manners for using, 162
    in marketing, 524
    market research with, 321
    tracking customer activities on, 195
    value of, 27
    World Wide Web vs., 129
Internet-based wireless intrabusiness applications, 263–264
Internet economy, *see* Digital economy
Internet-enabled phones, 245
Internet Engineering Task Force (IETF), 709
Internet Home Alliance, 278
Internet of "things," 280
Internet portfolio map (matrix), 418–419
Internet Relay Chat (IRC), 143
Internet Security Alliance, 728
Internet telephony (voiceover IP), 143, 249
Internet2, 128
Interorganizational information systems (IOSs), 50, 53, 110–111
    IT planning for, 415–416
    for virtual organizations, 433
Intrabusiness, 178, 204–205
    mobile, 259–264
    supply chain activities, 378
Intranets, 28, 71–72, 130–132
    data warehouse on, 503
    defined, 4, 130
    financial analysis of, 627
    integration of KMS and, 471
Intranet portals, 138

Intrinsic data quality, 496
Intrusion detection, 708, 709, 720–721
Inventory management, 307–308, 362
Inventories:
    of vacant positions, 330
    vendor replenishment of, 308, 362
Investment management, 326–327
"Invisible" computing, *see* Pervasive computing
IOSs, *see* Interorganizational information systems
Iowa, state agencies of, 589–590
iPing.com, 253
IPR, *see* Intellectual property rights
IRC (Internet Relay Chat), 143
IRM, *see* Information resources management
IRR (internal rate of return), 603
ISD, *see* Information services department; Information systems department
ISO 9000 standards, 667, 668
ISs, *see* Information systems
ISSs, *see* Intelligent support systems
IT, *see* Information technology
IT governance, 684
IT planning, 398–420
    alignment with organizational plans, 402–403
    business importance of, 398–399
    defined, 398
    and e-planning, 417–418
    evolution of, 399
    executing, 399–401
    information requirements analysis (stage 2), 408–409
    information technology architectures, 411–415
    for interorganizational systems, 415–416
    managerial issues with, 437–439
    for multinational corporations, 416
    problems for, 416, 417
    project planning (stage 4), 411
    resource allocation (stage 3), 409, 410
    SITP (stage 1), 401–407
    tools and methodologies of, 404–407
iVISION, 91
IVR, *see* Interactive voice response

J

JAD, *see* Joint application design
Jaguars, online configuration of, 316
Java, 664–664
JCPenney, 84
J.D. Edwards, 114, 464
JiffyLube, 257
JIT processing, *see* Just-in-time processing
Job dispatch, mobile devices for, 260–261
Job markets, online, 190–191
John Deere Corp., 117
Johnson Control, 169

Joint application design (JAD), 641–642, 660
J.P. Morgan, 68
J.P. Morgan Chase Company, 68, 97
Judd's, 627
Just-in-time (JIT) processing, 16, 309, 310

K

Kazaa, 71
KBDSS (knowledge-based DSS), 553
KDD, *see* Knowledge discovery in databases
Keiretsu, 17–18
Kelly's Extension of Metcalfe's Law, 27
Kemper Insurance Company, 264
Keyboards:
    attachable, 245
    wearable, 259
Key performance indicators (KPI), 556, 557
Keyword banners, 197
Kinko's, 303
Kitchen Aid, 84
KM, *see* Knowledge management
Kmart, 110
KMSs, *see* Knowledge management systems
Knowbots, 25, 133
Knowledge, 451–454
    and ability to act, 452
    and AI, 561
    characteristics of, 452
    defined, 51, 451, 452
    leaky, 453
    tacit vs. explicit, 453–454
    transformation of data into, 494
Knowledge acquisition, 456, 457
Knowledge base, 2, 561, 565
Knowledge-based DSS (KBDSS), 553
Knowledge Center, 466
Knowledge creation, 456, 457
Knowledge discovery, 507
Knowledge discovery in databases (KDD), 462, 463, 507–508
Knowledge harvesting tools, 466, 467
KnowledgeMail, 466, 467
Knowledge management (KM), 51, 374, 451–480
    activities/processes in, 456–458
    ensuring success of, 474–479
    failures of, 476–477
    integration of other business information systems with, 470–471
    IT in, 460–464
    knowware for, 464–468, 470
    managerial issues with, 480
    practice approach to, 458–460
    process approach to, 458–460
    roles in, 471–474
    valuation of, 474–476
Knowledge management suites, 468
Knowledge management systems (KMSs), 454, 461–471
    components of, 461

cycle in, 454–456
    implementation of, 464–471
    potential drawbacks to, 479
    technologies supporting, 461–464
Knowledge portals, 138
Knowledge repositories, 465
Knowledge seeking, 457
Knowledge servers, 465
Knowledge sharing, 457
Knowledge workers, 61–62
Knowledge work systems (KWSs), 54, 55
Knowware, 464
Kodak Corporation, 60, 82
Kone Inc., 628
Kozmo, 220
KPI, *see* Key performance indicators
KWSs, *see* Knowledge work systems
Kyota, Japan, 281

L

L. L. Bean, 383
Lancaster, U.K., 281
LANs, *see* Local area networks
Lawson Software, 349
l-commerce, *see* Location-based commerce
Leaky knowledge, 453
Learning agents, 195
Leased applications, 661–664
Legacy application software, 247
Legacy systems, 70, 78, 415, 668
Legal issues:
    with computer crime and security, 698–699
    with e-commerce, 217–218
    with IT planning, 437–439
    with mobile computing, 283, 284
    with network computing, 160–162
    with systems development, 670
    with telemedicine, 267
Lego Company, 387
Le Saunda Holding Company, 21
Levi Strauss & Company, 84, 221, 436
LifeStar, 499
Light methodology, 640
Limit Order Application (LORA), 152
Liquidations, auctions for, 183
Littlewoods Stores, 363
Living.com, 220
Local area networks (LANs), 67, 72, 130, 131, 178, 249–251
Localization, 242
Location-based advertising, 271–272
Location-based commerce (l-commerce), 28, 242, 269–273, 520
Location-based technology, 269
Location-specific contents, 269–270
Lock-in effect, 621
Lock-in strategy, 104
Logical design, 636, 637
Logistics:
    with e-tailing, 187
    of returns, 383
    reverse, 358

Logistics management, 307
London Stock Exchange, 690
Long-range IT plan, 399
Longs Drug Stores, 57
LORA (Limit Order Application), 152
Lotus Development Corporation, 498, 499
Lotus Notes, 433
Lotus Notes/Domino, 69, 155, 465
Loyalty cards, 212
Lufthansa, 250

M

Machine-learning capabilities, 55
MacroArt Technology, 721
Macy's, 383
Mail Boxes Etc., 638
Mainframe environment, 66–67
Make-or-buy decision, 657
Make-to-forecast strategy, 108
Make-to-stock supply chains, 359
Malaysia Airlines, 542
Malaysia Airport, 559, 692
Malls:
    electronic, 186
    virtual, 522
Management, defined, 543
Management by maxim, 608–609
The Management Cockpit, 560
Management information systems (MISs), 53, 54, 58–59
Management service providers (MSPs), 614
Management support systems (MSSs), 545, 546, 574–575
Managers, 543–546. *See also* Decision support
Managerial activities, 59–60
Managerial issues:
    with data management, 528–530
    with decision support systems, 578–580
    with e-business applications, 665
    with e-commerce, 222–223
    with economics of IT, 623–624
    with functional information systems, 343–345
    with information resources management, 722
    with IT planning, 437–439
    with knowledge management, 480
    with mobile computing/m-commerce, 285
    with network computing, 163–164
    with security programs, 722
    with supply chain management, 388
    with systems development, 659–661, 670–671
Managerial planning, 398–399
Manufacturing Connection Online (MCO), 120
Manufacturing resource planning (MRP II), 309, 366

Manugistics, 373
Mapinfo.com, 317
Marketing:
  affiliate, 10
  auctions in, 183
  databases for, 523–525
  direct-response, 196–197
  hybrid intelligent systems in, 573
  interactive, 199
  old vs. new models of, 315
  permission, 198–199
  viral, 199, 351
Marketing and sales information systems, 107, 312–321
  customer information, 313–317
  distribution channels, 317–319
  marketing management decisions, 319–321
Marketing customer information file (MCIF), 319
Marketing management, 319–321
Marketing transaction database (MTD), 523–524
Marketplaces, 73
Market pressures, 12–14
Market research, 192–196, 321
Marriott International, 149, 266
Mary Kay, 566
MAS 90 and MAS 200, 324
Massachusetts Department of Revenue, 498
Mass customization, 17, 315, 316, 427, 429
Mass production, 87
Master Builders, 95, 104
Master files (TPS), 302
MasterTrac, 95
Material requirements planning (MRP), 308, 310, 366
Materials flows, 357
Materials management, 307
Mathematical (quantitative) models, 548
Maybelline, 82
Mazda, 428
MBMS (model-based management system), 552
m-business, see Mobile commerce
McDonald's, 250, 423
McDonnell-Douglas, 499
MCIF (marketing customer information file), 319
MCO (Manufacturing Connection Online), 120
m-commerce, see Mobile commerce
Mederlandse Spoorweges, 584
Medical emergencies, 267
Medium-term IT plan, 399
MedLink, 267
Meetings, 145, 153–156, 555
Megabeam, 266
Memory buttons, 274
Mental models, 548
Mergers and acquisitions, 221
Merrill-Lynch, 309–310
Metadata, 502
Metasearch engines, 134
Meta searchers, 133

Metcalfe's Law, 27
Method/1, 404, 635
Method-driven IT planning approach, 400
Metrics:
  for knowledge management, 475–476
  for planning process, 419
  for supply chain performance, 363–364
Metric benchmarks, 608
Metropolitan Transit Authority (MTA) of New York, 600
MGIF (Mobile Games Interoperability Forum), 266
Microbrowser, 247
Micropayments, 209, 254–255
Microsoft, 74, 76, 82, 105, 635, 649, 689
Microsoft Exchange, 69
Microsoft Outlook, 69
Microsoft Passport, 214
Microstrategy, 506
Middleware, 500
Milestones, 668–669
Millstone Coffee, 239
Minneapolis-St. Paul International Airport, 250
Minnesota Department of Transportation, 683
Minority Report (film), 273
MISs, *see* Management information systems
Mrs. Fields Cookies, 479
MIT, 280
MMS (multimedia messaging service), 241
MobileAria, 272
Mobile commerce (m-commerce, m-business), 28, 73, 240. *See also* Mobile computing
  attributes of, 241–242
  B2B applications, 265
  banking, 253–255
  contextual computing for, 275
  defined, 179
  drivers of, 242–244
  failures in, 284–285
  inhibitors and barriers of, 282–285
  intrabusiness and enterprise applications, 259–264
  micropayments with, 254–255
  mobile (wireless) wallets, 255
  revenue models of, 245
  security issues with, 252
  shopping from wireless devices, 256
  supply chain applications, 265
  targeted advertising, 257–258
  value chain for, 244–245
  voice systems for, 252–253
  wireless payment systems, 254, 255
Mobile computing, 28, 55, 73, 238–240. *See also* Mobile commerce
  attributes of, 241–242
  basic terminology for, 240, 241
  consumer/personal service applications, 265–268
  defined, 239
  drivers of, 242–244
  ethical and legal issues with, 283, 284
  failures in, 284–285

hardware for, 245–246
inhibitors and barriers of, 282–285
managerial issues with, 285
mobile portals, 258–259
security issues with, 252
in smart cars, 279
software for, 246, 247
Wi-Fi standard for, 249–252
wireless, 239
wireless local area networks for, 249–250
wireless personal area networks for, 249–250
wireless wide area networks for, 246–249
Mobile computing systems, 54
Mobile devices, 239, 243
  applications for, 262
  for job dispatch, 260–261
  wearable, 259
Mobile entertainment, 266
Mobile gambling, 266
Mobile games, 266
Mobile Games Interoperability Forum (MGIF), 266
Mobile networks, 246
Mobile portals, 137, 258–259
Mobile positioning center (MPC), 269
Mobile supply chain management (mSCM), 265
Mobile switching centers, 248
Mobile telemetry, 272
Mobile wallets, 255
Mobile workers, 259
Models and modeling, 547–548
  EIAC, 610
  management subsystem for, 552
  for sensitivity analysis, 551, 552
  simulation vs., 576
Model-based management system (MBMS), 552
Model marts, 463
Model warehouses, 463
Modems, attacks via, 698
Monster.com, 221
Montogmery Securities, 715
Moore's Law, 25, 26, 591
Morgan Stanley and Company, 328
Moscow MTS, 688–689
Motorola, 255, 266, 334, 499
MP3 Inc., 103
MPC (mobile positioning center), 269
MPR II, *see* Manufacturing resource planning
MRP, *see* Material requirements planning
mSCM (mobile supply chain management), 265
MSPs (management service providers), 614
MSSs, *see* Management support systems
MTA (Metropolitan Transit Authority) of New York, 600
MTD, *see* Marketing transaction database
Multidimensional databases, 503, 505
Multidimensionality visualization, 515–517
Multimedia messaging service (MMS), 241
Multinational corporations, IT planning for, 416
Multiple-currency banking, 190

m-wallet, 255
MyAvantGo.Com, 257

N

Nabisco, 82
Name-your-own-price business model, 10
Nanotechnology, 27
Napster, 71
National Association of Chain Drug
    Stores, 140
National City Corp., 444–445
National Computer Security Center
    (NCSC), 720
National Infrastructure Protection Center
    (NIPC), 698
National Semiconductor Corporation
    (NSC), 126–128, 131
Natural language processing (NLP),
    568–571
NCSC (National Computer Security
    Center), 720
NEC, 82
Needham Interactive, 627
Nestlé USA, 364
Net, *see* Internet
NetCaptor, 133
Netgain, 319
Netiquette, 162
Net present value (NPV), 599, 601,
    603, 609
Netscape Communicator, 69, 690
Nettracker, 195
Network(s), 50, 76
    collaborative, 146–149, 369
    defined, 19
    enterprisewide, 30
    for industrywide communication,
        140–141
    local area, 249–250
    mobile, 246
    neural, 54
    optical, 30
    personal area, 249–250
    protection of, 706–712
    storage, 30, 32
    wide area, 246–249
    wireless, 28, 251, 712. *See also* Mobile
        computing
    wireline vs. wireless, 50
Network-based technologies, 27
Network computers, 30
Network computing, 128–164. *See also*
        Collaboration; Communication;
        Discovery; Internet
    defined, 4
    distance learning, 156–158
    e-learning, 156–159
    ethical/legal issues with, 160–162
    extranets, 131–132
    groupware technologies, 151–156
    integration issues with, 162–163
    intranets, 130–132
    managerial issues with, 163–164
    telecommuting, 159–160
    virtual work, 159

workflow technologies, 150–151
    and World Wide Web, 129
Network controls (security), 705
Networked organizations, 435
Network effects, 621
Network storage devices, 30, 32
Net worth (NW), 603
Neural computing, 511, 571, 572
Neural networks, 54, 461. *See also*
        Artificial neural networks
New economy, *see* Digital economy
New Line Cinema, 226–227
New product introduction, 320
New York City, 8–9
New York Stock Exchange, 327
NextBus system, 237–238
Niche strategy, 102
Nike, 13, 24, 84
Nintendo, 266
NIPC (National Infrastructure Protection
        Center), 698
NLP, *see* Natural language processing
"No free lunch," 42
Nokia, 245, 252, 255, 266, 272
Nominal group technique, 145
Non-Internet mobile applications, 268
Nordea, 255, 258
Nortel Network, 478
Northeast Utilities, 284–285
Northwest Airlines, 320
NPV, *see* Net present value
NSC, *see* National Semiconductor
        Corporation
NTT Docomo, 252
Nucleus firms, 146, 147
NW (net worth), 603
Nygard of Canada, 149

O

OASs, *see* Office automation systems
Object Management Group (OMG), 649
Object-oriented environments, 27
Object-oriented (OO) development,
        644–646, 660
Object-oriented systems development
        (OOSD), 645
Object-oriented transaction processing, 303
Object technology, 27
Obsolescence, 14
ODSS (organizational decision support
        systems), 556
Office automation systems (OASs), 53, 54
Offices, smart, 281
Offshore outsourcing, 613–614
O'Hare Airport, 585
OLAP, *see* Online analytical processing
OLAP multidimensionality, 515
Old-economy organizations, *see* Brick-
        and-mortar organizations
OLS (organizational learning system), 486
OLTP, *see* Online transaction processing
OMG (Object Management Group), 649
Online analytical processing (OLAP), 319,
        506, 508–510, 515, 517

Online corporate training, 158–159
Online database publishers, 495
Online Data Corporation, 685
Online job markets, 190–191
Online processing, 302
Online securities trading, 190
Online transaction processing (OLTP),
        303, 304
OnLink Technologies, 664
OnStar system, 279
OO development, *see* Object-oriented
        development
OOSD (object-oriented systems
        development), 645
Open Market, 220
Operating system (OS), 247
Operations, 107
Operational activities, 59
Operational audits, 329, 718
Operational data sores, 504–505
Operational effectiveness strategy, 103
Operational planning, 398–399
Operational system, 500
Opportunistic repricing, 615
Optical networks, 30
Optimization, 549, 573
Options, real vs. financial, 609
Oracle Corp., 74, 343, 628, 675
Orbis Inc., 8
Order fulfillment, 380–384
    defined, 215, 380
    e-commerce, problems with, 380–381
    as e-commerce support system, 215
    with e-tailing, 187
    outsourcing of, 381
Oregon, 442–443
Organizational activities, 59–62
Organizational buyers, 193
Organizational decision support systems
        (ODSS), 556
Organizational IT planning approach, 400
Organizational knowledge, 51
Organizational knowledge base, 561
Organizational learning system (OLS), 486
Organizational redesign, 430–431
Organizational responses, *see* Critical
        response activities
Organizational structure, changing, 435
Organization transformation, 433–435
OS (operating system), 247
Otis Elevator Company, 304
Outbound logistics, 107
Outputs, 18, 19, 51
Output controls, 706
Outsourcing, 78, 660
    advantages/disadvantages of, 615–616
    and ASPs, 614, 663
    defined, 613
    and e-commerce, 614–615
    as economic strategy, 612–617
    impact of, 414
    of merchandise returns, 383
    to MSPs, 614
    of order fulfillment, 381
    strategic, 614
    strategies for, 410, 616–617
    of systems development, 654–655

P

P2P architecture, *see* Peer-to-peer architecture
Pagers, interactive, 245
Panera Bread Company, 250
PaperX.com, 220
Parallel conversion, 638
Partial electronic commerce, 178
Partner-relationship management (PRM), 385–386
Partners HealthCare System, Inc., 476
Pattern recognition, 571
PAVECA, 205
Payback period, 603
Payload security, 711
Payments, 208–215
    for C2C transactions, 208
    electronic, 210–215, 326
    for exposure to advertising, 258
    micropayments, 254–255
    security issues for, 213–214
    traditional vs. electronic, 209
    wireless, 254, 255
PayPal, 212, 213
Payroll functions, 334–335
PBXs (private branch exchanges), 253
PC environment, 67
PDA, *see* Personal digital assistant
PDE (position determining equipment), 269
Peachtree.com, 324
Peer-to-peer (P2P) architecture, 70–71
People, defined, 19
PeopleNet, 460
PeopleSoft, Inc., 376, 385–386, 393
Pepsi Bottling Group, 74
Performance dashboard, 610
Performance evaluations, 333
Performance measurement, 363–364
Permission marketing, 198–199, 257
Personal agents, 276
Personal data, 495
Personal digital assistant (PDA), 241, 245, 246, 252, 255
Personal information manager (PIM), 546
Personalization, 242, 316, 339
Personal portals, 137
Personal services, online purchase of, 208
Personnel planning, 334
Personnel records, 335
Person-to-person payments, 212–213
PERT (program evaluation and review technique), 309
Pervasive computing, 28–31, 75, 273–282
    applications of, 275, 277–280
    contextual attributes in, 274–276
    large-scale systems, 280–281
    and need for face-to-face meetings, 156
    smart appliances, 278
    smart cars, 278–279
    smart homes, 275, 277–278
Pfizer, 466
Phased conversion, 639
Philippines, 330
Photography, 6–8
Physical buildings, 76
Physical control (security), 703
Physical design, 626

PictureTel Corporation, 155
Pilot conversion, 638
PIM (personal information manager), 546
Piping technology, 32
Plagiarism, 135
Planning, *see* IT planning
PLC (Power Line Communication), 278
PLM, *see* Product lifecycle management
PLM software, *see* Product lifecycle management software
Poaching, 615
PointCast, 220
Policy-based resource-management tools, 656
Policy-based service-level-management tools, 656
POM, *see* Production and operations management
Pop-under ads, 197–200
Pop-up ads, 197–200
Portals, 136–141
    corporate, 137–140, 527
    customer, 342
    defined, 136
    employee, 342
    enterprise knowledge, 465–466
    human resources-related, 332
    industrywide communication, 140–141
    information, 136–137
    integration of, 139–140
    mobile, 137, 258–259
    voice, 253, 263
Porter's models, *see* Competitive forces model; Value chain model
Position determining equipment (PDE), 269
Position inventory, 330
Post-audit evaluation of systems, 639
Power Line Communication (PLC), 278
Practice approach (knowledge management), 458–460
Prada, 274
Preference analysis, 313
Prescriptions, 267
Priceline.com, 10, 103, 104, 117, 191
Price-optimization programs, 57
Price-to-performance ratio, 591
Price Waterhouse, 675
PricewaterhouseCoopers, 221
Pricing decisions, 319, 329
Primary activities (value chain model), 107
Privacy issues, 45–46
    with e-commerce, 217
    with e-government, 207
    with location-based systems, 273
    with network computing, 160–162
    with pervasive computing, 274, 283, 284
Private branch exchanges (PBXs), 253
Private marketplaces, 73
PRM, *see* Partner-relationship management
Procedures, 19, 76
Process approach (iknowledge management), 458–460
Process-centric integration, 343
Processing controls, 706
Procter & Gamble, 82, 149, 321, 361–362, 613

Production and operations management (POM), 306–312
    computer-integrated manufacturing, 310–311
    inventory management, 307–308
    just-in-time systems, 309
    logistics management, 307
    manufacturing resource planning, 309
    material requirements planning, 308
    product lifecycle management, 311–312
    project management, 309–310
    quality control, 308
    work management systems, 310
Production workflow, 151
Productivity:
    defined, 592
    as driver of process redesign, 421
    productivity paradox, 592–597
    of salespersons, 319–320
    and telecommuting, 160
Productivity paradox, 592–597
Product life cycle, 358
Product lifecycle management (PLM), 311–312
Product life-cycle management (PLM) software, 113–114
Profitability, 146, 320, 329
Program evaluation and review technique (PERT), 309
Programming attacks, 695–696
Programming controls, 705
Project(s):
    defined, 309
    properties/priorities of, 669
Project initiation, 635
Project management, 669–670
Project planning, 400, 411, 668–670
Promotions, online, 199–200
Protocols, 156
Prototyping, 640–641, 659–660
Proximity cards, 268
PSA (company), 115
PSAP (Public Safety Answering Point), 272
Public exchanges, 201–203
Public key infrastructure, 252
Public marketplaces, 73
Public portals, 137
Public Safety Answering Point (PSAP), 272
Public transportation, 9–10, 20
Publishing portals, 137
Pull advertising, 257
Pull systems, 87, 343
Purchasing, group, 10
Purchasing cards, 211
Purchasing-decision model, 194
Pure electronic commerce, 178
Pure-play organizations, *see* Virtual organizations
Puritan.xom, 221
Push advertising, 257
Push systems, 87, 343

Q

Quality control, 308, 666–668
Quality system, 668

Quantitative models, 548
Quantum computing, 27
Quantum Corporation, 392, 675
Query-and-reporting tools, 134, 506, 508
QVC, 350–351

R

RAD, *see* Rapid application development
Radio frequency identification (RFID), 274, 280, 283, 284
RadioShack Online, 94, 104
Random banners, 197
Rapid application development (RAD), 642–644, 660
Reader's Digest, 155
Real estate, online services for, 191–192
Real options, 609–610
Real-time collaboration (RTC), 154–155
Real-time decision support, 578
Real-time operations, 13, 58
Real-time (synchronous) communication, 141
Receivables, factoring of, 326
Recording Industry Association of America (RIAA), 697–698
Recruitment, online, 191, 330
Red Rocket, 220
Referral malls, 186
Regional Computer Intrusion Squads (FBI), 698
Reintermediation, 218
Relational databases, 494
Relational OLAP (ROLAP), 509
RE/MAX, 149
Reorder point, 308
Replicated (dependent) data marts, 504
Representation data quality, 496
Re-presentment of checks, 326
Requests for quotes (RFQs), 10, 201
Resource allocation, 400, 409, 410
Resource-allocation control, 398–399
Restaurants.com, 228
Restructurings, 17, 430–431. *See also* Business process restructuring
Resumix, 332
Retooling, 426
Return on investment (ROI), 599, 603, 610, 618
Returns, merchandise, 383
Revenue models, 189, 245
Reverse auctions, 10, 184
Reverse engineering, 415, 668
Reverse logistics, 358
RFID, *see* Radio frequency identification
RFQs, *see* Requests for quotes
RIAA, *see* Recording Industry Association of America
Risk analysis, 419, 550
Risk management, 718–720
Risk-management analysis, 719–720
Rivalwatch.com, 96
Rogue modems, 698
ROI, *see* Return on investment

ROLAP, 509
Room 33, 258
Rosenbluth International, 90–91, 93, 95, 103, 117, 218
Rouse & Co. International, 417
Royal Dutch/Shell, 475
Royal Mile Pub (Silver Spring, MD), 31
RTC, *see* Real-time collaboration
Runaway projects, 595, 619
Ryder systems, 360

S

SABRE system, 53, 103
Salary surveys, 332
Sales analysis, 320
Sales automation software, 320
Sales force automation (SFA), 204, 205, 319
Same-day/same-hour delivery, 381, 382
SAML (Security Assertion Markup Language), 651
Samsung Electronics, 334
SAP AG, 74, 221, 343, 376, 384, 425, 559, 620, 628
SAP R/3, 2, 370, 371, 375, 425, 676–677
SAS, 506
SBS Technologies, 317
SBUs (strategic business units), 204
Scale models, 548
Scenario planning, 407, 444–445
Schlumberger, 202
Schools, smart, 281
SCI, *see* Supply chain intelligence
SCM, *see* Supply chain management
SCM software, *see* Supply chain management software
Scoring methodology, 605–606
Scott-Morton framework, 435
Screenphones, 245
Screens, wearable, 259
Screen sharing, 154–155
SDLC, *see* Systems development life cycle
Search agents, 196
Search and comparison (for consumers), 338
Search engines, 133, 134, 195, 467
Sears, Roebuck and Company, 110, 534–535
Seattle Mariners, 21
SEB Private Bank (Luxembourg), 575
Secure Networks, 721
Securities trading, online, 190
Security Assertion Markup Language (SAML), 651
Security facilities, 76
Security issues, 687–723
    applications controls, 706
    auditing, 717–718
    authentication, 710–711
    authorization, 711
    awareness, 701
    border security, 707–710
    breakdown examples, 688–690
    business continuity planning, 712–716
    for C2C commerce, 208

and computer crimes, 693–695
controls, 700–701
defense strategies, 701–702
with e-government, 207
with electronic payment systems, 210–215
federal laws dealing with, 698–699
general controls, 703–705
implementing control, 716
managerial issues with, 722
with m-commerce and mobile computing, 252
and methods of attack, 694–698
with mobile phone payments, 254
with network computing, 160–162
network protection, 706–712
for online banking and securities trading, 190
organizing for security, 699–700
risk management, 718–720
terminology related to, 688
trends in security, 720–721
vulnerability of systems, 690–693
with Wi-Fi hotspots, 251
Security protocols, 651
Sega, 266
Segmentation, market, 192
Self-checkout machines, 318
Self-healing computers, 27, 720
Self-service convenience stores, 317
Selling:
    along supply chain, 378–379
    e-commerce protections for, 216
Sell-side marketplaces, 200
Semantic Web, 573
Semistructured problems, 549
Sensitivity analysis, 551, 552
Sequencing (of information), 511
Server, 68–69
Service industries:
    online, 189–192
    productivity in, 593
Service-level agreements (SLAs), 684–685
SETI, 75
SFA, *see* Sales force automation
ShareNet, 449–450
Shareware, 161
Sharing (computing), 69
Shirking, 615
Shopping:
    in digital economy, 10
    online, 360
    reengineering of, 317–318
    and return of merchandise, 383
    virtual, 522
    from wireless devices, 256
Short message service (SMS), 241, 244, 262
Siebel Systems, 376
Siemens AG, 2–4, 266, 449–450
Simple Object Access Protocol (SOAP), 650
Simputers, 30
SIM (subscriber identification module) card, 248
Simulation modeling, 434–435, 576
Singapore, 115, 305
Singapore Airlines, 542
Singapore Technologies Engineering, 227

SingTel Mobile, 258
SISs, *see* Strategic information systems
SITP, *see* Strategic information technology planning
Six Sigma, 16
SLAs, *see* Service-level agreements
Slippery slope rule, 42
Smart appliances, 278
Smart cards, 212, 268, 721
Smart cars, 272, 278–279
Smart homes, 275, 277–278
Smart offices, 281
SmartPad, 246
Smartphones, 73, 241, 243, 245, 271
Smart schools, 281
Smart terminals, 67
Smith Lyons, 466, 467
SMS, *see* Short message service
Snap-On Tools, 664
SOAP (Simple Object Access Protocol), 650
Social capital, 476
Social engineering, 693
Socialization mode (knowledge creation), 457
Social responsibility, 14–15
Societal pressures, 14–15
Society of Manufacturing Engineers, 310
Softbots, 133
Software, 76. *See also* Application programs; *specific topics*
    cost of developing/maintaining, 595
    defined, 19
    as driver of process redesign, 421
    external acquisition of, 657–659
Software agents, 133–134, 195–196. *See also* Intelligent agents
Software development companies, 464–468
Software Engineering Institute, 666–668
Software suites, 155
Sony, 84
Southwest Airlines, 102, 114
Southwest Airlines Online, 221
Spamming, 162, 198
Spam shield, 162
Specialization, 87
Speech translators, wearable, 259
Speech (voice) recognition, 569
Speech (voice) understanding, 569
Spiders, 134, 199
Spitfire Novelties, 688
Spotcast, 258
Spot sourcing, 202
Sprint Inc., 303
SPSS, 506
SQL Slammer, 689
SQL (structured query language), 508
SRM, *see* Supplier relationship management
Staff support, 61
Stages of IT growth model, 404, 405
Standalone data marts, 504
Standards:
    c-commerce and lack of, 150
    Wi-Fi, 249–252
    for WLANs, 241, 249
Starbucks, 250
Starwood Hotels & Resorts, 266–267

Statistical analysis, BI application to, 506
Stealthware, 712
Steering committee, 684
Sticky knowledge, 454
Stock count, 176
Stock exchanges, global, 325
StorageNetworks, 614
Storage networks, 30, 32
Stored-value money cards, 212
Storefronts, electronic, 186, 661
"Stovepipes," 422
Strategic activities, 60–61
Strategic advantage, sustainable, 116–117
Strategic business units (SBUs), 204
Strategic information systems (SISs), 92–93, 402
    examples of, 112–115
    implementation of, 116
    interorganizational, 110–111
    managerial issues related to, 117–118
    and strategic advantage, 116–117
Strategic information technology planning (SITP), 401–407
    alignment of organizational planning and, 402
    tools and methodologies of, 404–407
Strategic IT plan, 399
Strategic management, 93–95
Strategic outsourcing, 614
Strategic planning, 398–399
    e-planning, 417–418
    in four-stage model, 400
    issues in, 419–420
Strategic response activities, 60
Strategic systems, 16
Structural capital, 476
Structured problems, 549
Structured query language (SQL), 508
STSN, 266
Students, monitoring Internet use of, 160–162
Subscriber identification module (SIM) card, 248
Subscription computing, 75
Sunbeam, 278
Sun Microsystems, 74
Supermarket chains, 525
Supervisors, portals for, 138
Suppliers:
    bargaining power of, 100
    empowerment of, 436
    portals for, 138
Supplier relationship management (SRM), 385–386
Supply chains, 62–64
    collaboration, 361
    components of, 358
    coordination/collaboration along, 362–363
    defined, 2, 299, 357
    as driver of process redesign, 421
    in e-commerce, 377–385
    flows in, 357–358
    global, 386–387
    at Nike, 24
    problems along, 360–361

types of, 358–359
    and value chain, 359
Supply chain intelligence (SCI), 374–376
Supply chain management (SCM), 64, 356–385
    collaboration along, 369
    computerized activities along, 365–366
    defined, 357
    ERP for, 369–377
    goals of, 358, 359
    integration of KMS and, 471
    managerial issues with, 388
    mobile applications for, 265
    solving problems, 361–365
    systems integration for, 366–369
    traditional vs. network collaboration in, 146–149
Supply chain management (SCM) software, 357, 366, 373–374
Supply chain teams, 363
Support costs, 594, 595
Surgery, 268
Surgery Center of Baltimore, 499
Sustainable strategic advantage, 116–117
SWIFT, 114
Swiss Federal Institute of Technology, 267
SWOT analysis, 116
Symantec, 159
Symbolic processing, 562
Synchronization, 239
Synchronous (real-time) communication, 141
Synco Software, 343
Systematic sourcing, 202, 203
Systems analysis, 636
Systems development, 634–671
    and CASE tools, 665–666
    component-based, 647–649
    controls for, 705
    defined, 634
    for e-business applications, 661–665
    by end-user, 653–654
    and external acquisition of software, 657–659
    extreme programming, 646–647
    and ISO 9000 standards, 667–668
    joint application design, 641–642
    life cycle approach to, 634–640
    managerial issues with, 659–661, 670–671
    object-oriented development, 644–646
    outside of IS department, 653–661
    outsourcing of, 654–655
    project planning in, 668–670
    prototyping approach to, 640–641
    quality management in, 666–668
    rapid application development, 642–644
Systems development (*cont.*)
    reverse engineering for, 668
    and utility computing, 633–634, 656
    Web services in, 650–653
Systems development life cycle (SDLC), 401, 634–640
    stages in, 635–639
    traditional vs. modern, 639
    for Web-based systems, 639–640

T

Tacit knowledge, 453–454
Tacit Knowledge Systems, 466, 467
Taco Bell, 262
Tactical plan, 399
Taj Group, 266
Target Corporation, 149
Targeted advertising, 257–258
Taxation, 113, 218–219
TBO (total benefits of ownership), 604
TCO (total cost of ownership), 604
TCP/IP protocol, 71
TDMA, see Time Division Multiple Access
Teams:
   supply chain, 363
   virtual, 145
Technical services, 338
Technological innovation, 14
Technological IT planning approach, 400
Technology pressures, 14
Technology trends in IT, 590–591
Telecom Italia Mobile, 264
Telecommuting (teleworking), 159–160
Teleconferencing, 153–154
Telematics, 272
Telemedicine, 267–268
Telemetry, 265, 271–272
Telephony, 249
Telesurgery, 268
TeleVend, Inc., 254
Teleworking, see Telecommuting
Tellme.com, 253
Tellme Networks, Inc., 39
Tendering systems, 10
Terrorism, 15
Texaco, 460
Text mining, 512–513
Thaigem, 6
Thailand, 6
Thinque Corp., 82
Thomas Cook Company, 498
Three C's, 420
Time Division Multiple Access (TDMA), 248, 249
Time/place IT framework, 141–142
Time strategy, 104
Tjan's portfolio strategy, 418–419
T-Mobile, 250
Toolbars (for search engines), 135
Total benefits of ownership (TBO), 604
Total cost of ownership (TCO), 604
Total quality management (TQM), 16, 308
Touch-panel displays, wearable, 259
Tour guides, 133–134
Toyota, 309
ToysRUs, 360
Toysrus.com, 102, 110
TPSs, see Transaction processing systems
TQM, see Total quality management
Tracking, 217
   of consumer behavior, 195, 313
   of personal accounts/orders by
      customers, 339
   of vehicles, 272
Tractors, mobile devices on, 262
TradeCard, 190

TradeLink, 387
TradeNet, 386, 387
Training, online, 158–159, 333–334
Transactional data processing, 500
Transaction costs, 617
Transaction files, 302
Transaction management, 324–326
Transaction manager, 302
Transaction Processing Performance
   Council, 304
Transaction processing systems (TPSs), 53,
   54, 57–58, 300–306
   batch, 302
   data in, 500
   and functional systems, 298
   major characteristics of, 301
   objectives of, 301
   online, 302, 303
   software for, 304
   Web-based interactive, 303, 304
Translations (of Web pages), 136
Transmission media, wireless, 247
Travel services, online, 191
Trends analysis, 320
Trojan horse, 696–697
Troubleshooting, 711
   intelligent systems for, 310
   Web-based, 340
TruServ Corp., 397–398
Trust (in c-commerce), 150
T-Shirt King, 659
Turner Industries, 114–115
Two-factor authentication, 710–711

U

Ubiquitous computing, see Pervasive
   computing
Ubiquity, 239, 242
UCE (unsolicited commercial e-mail), 198
UDDL (Universal Description, Discovery
   and Integration), 651
UIMS (user interface management
   system), 552
Unified modeling language (UML), 645
Unintentional threats, 691, 692
Uninterrupted power supply (UPS), 318,
   383, 715
Universal Description, Discovery and
   Integration (UDDL), 651
Universal e-wallets, 214
Universal Product Code (UPC), 279
Universal Studios, 250
Universities, virtual, 158
University of Adelaide, 280
University of California at Los Angeles,
   281
University of Cambridge, 280
University of Cincinnati, 499
University of Houston, 689
University of Nebraska, 676–677
Unsolicited advertising, 198
Unsolicited commercial e-mail (UCE), 198
Unstructured problems, 549
UPC (Universal Product Code), 279

UPS (company), 638
Up-selling, 316
UPS Stores, 303
Upstream supply chain, 62–64, 79, 378
UPS (uninterrupted power supply), 715
U.S. Fleet Services, 261
U.S. Port Office, 383
U.S. Robotics, 159
Usability (of mobile systems), 283
U-Scan, 318
User interface, 247
   in DSSs, 552
   in ESs, 566
User interface management system
   (UIMS), 552
Utilitarian rule, 42
Utility computing, 74–75, 414, 633–634,
   656, 660–661

V

Value-added networks (VANs), 110
   defined, 178
   EDI on, 232, 233
   integration issues with, 162–163
Value analysis, 604–605
Value chain, 359
   functional areas in, 299
   integration of, 368–369
   for m-commerce, 244–245
Value chain model, 107–110, 359
Value systems, 107, 359
VANs, see Value-added networks
VC, see Virtual organizations
Vendors:
   interactions with, 687
   selection of, 657
Vendor-managed inventory (VMI),
   308, 362
Vertical consortia, 110
Vertical distributors, 201, 202
Vertical exchanges, 202, 379
Vertical marketplaces, 10
Video kiosks, 154
Video teleconferencing (videoconference),
   153
VIM, see Visual interactive modeling
Vindigo.com, 257
Viral marketing, 199, 351
Virtual banks, 189
Virtual cars, 316
Virtual close, 326
Virtual collaboration (e-collaboration),
   146–150
   groupware for, 151–156
   implementation issues with, 155–156
Virtual commissioned sales forces, 10
Virtual corporations, see Virtual
   organizations
Virtual credit cards, 214
Virtual groups (teams), 145, 554
Virtualization tools, 656
Virtual meetings, 145, 153, 555
Virtual organizations (virtual corporations,
   VC), 17, 432–433

Virtual private networks (VPNs), 48, 234, 710
Virtual (pure-play) organizations, 178
Virtual reality markup language (VRML), 522
Virtual reality (VR), 334, 521–523
Virtual universities, 158
Virtual work, 159
Viruses, 689, 696–697
    controls for, 708
    minimizing damage from, 709
VIS, *see* Visual interactive simulation
VISA Cash Card, 212
Visa International, 572
Visual interactive modeling (VIM), 520, 521
Visual interactive simulation (VIS), 520, 521
Visual technologies, 514
    data visualization, 514–523
    information visualizers, 25
VMI, *see* Vendor-managed inventory
Voice communication, 143–144, 252–253
Voice mail, 144
Voiceover IP, *see* Internet telephony
Voice over Wi-Fi, 249
Voice portals, 137, 253, 263
Voice recognition, 569
Voice synthesis, 570
Voice understanding, 569
Voice XML, *see* Wireless Markup Language
Volkswagen of Mexico, 425
VPNs, *see* Virtual private networks
VR, *see* Virtual reality
VRML (virtual reality markup language), 522
Vulnerability (of information systems), 690–693

W

Wallets:
    digital, 214
    wireless, 255
Wal-Mart, 101–102, 106, 110, 149, 280, 308, 361–362, 364, 383, 525
Walt Disney Company, 23
Wanderers, 134
WANs, *see* Wide area networks
WAP, *see* Wireless Application Protocol
War chalking, 251
War dialing, 251
War driving, 251
Warehouses, automated, 383
Warner-Lambert, 370–371
Washington Township Fire Department (Ohio), 291
Wasted time, cost of, 595
Watercop, 275, 277
Waterfall method, 635
Wayport Inc., 266
Wearable devices, 259–260
Web, *see* World Wide Web
Web-based call centers, 55, 142–143, 339–340

Web-based chat programs, 143
Web-based systems, 56, 69, 71–73
    auditing, 718
    customer service, 338–339
    data management, 499–500, 526–528
    data quality in, 497
    development life cycle for, 639–640
    economics of, 617, 618
    interactive transaction processing, 303, 304
    management support, 574–575
    marketing, 320, 321
    object technology and development of, 646
    outsourcing development of, 655
    project management, 669–670
Web-browsing-assisting agents, 133–134
Webchat sites, 143
Web conferencing, 153–154
Webcor Builders, 146, 147
WebCT, 157
WebDAV, 156
Web economy, *see* Digital economy
Weblogging (blogging), 144
Web mining, 513
Webopedia.com, 135
Web pages:
    automatic translation of, 136
    personalization of, 339
Web-purchasing model, 194
Web robots, 134
Web server, 246
Web services, 32, 75–76, 650–653
Web Services Description Language (WSDL), 650–651
WebsiteAlive, 143
Web site design, 199–200, 642
WebSphere Portal, 140
Web tracking, 195, 217
Webvan, 220
WebWatcher, 133
WELCOM (World Electronic Community), 555
WEP, *see* Wireless Encryption Protocol
Western Australian e-government, 206
What Is?, 135
Whirlpool Corp., 376
Whiteboards, 154
Wide area networks (WANs), 68, 246–249
Wi-Fi (wireless fidelity), 38, 241, 249–252
    in digital cities, 281
    for hotel services, 266
    in smart homes, 277–278
Wing Fat Foods, 410–411
Wireless access point, 249, 251
Wireless advertising, 257
Wireless Application Protocol (WAP), 241, 247
Wireless communication media, 239
Wireless computing, 73
Wireless CRM, 340
Wireless electronic payment systems, 254
Wireless Encryption Protocol (WEP), 251, 252
Wireless Internet, 249
Wireless LAN adapter, 246
Wireless local area networks (WLANs), 130, 131, 241, 249–251

Wireless MAN adapter, 246
Wireless Markup Language (WML), 247
Wireless middleware, 247
Wireless mobile computing, 239
Wireless networks, 28, 251, 712
Wireless 911, 272
Wireless wallets, 255
Wireless WAN modem, 246
Wireless wide area networks (WWANs), 74, 246–249
Wireless workstations, 25
Wisconsin, 113
Wizards, 133
W.L. Gore and Associates, 376
WLANs, *see* Wireless local area networks
WML (Wireless Markup Language), 247
WMS (work management systems), 310
Woolworths of Australia, 380
Word processing systems, 54
Workflow, 130
    application categories of, 151
    defined, 150
    wireless intrabusiness applications, 264
Workflow management, 150, 151
Workflow systems, 150–152, 310
Workforce, changes in, 13
Workgroups, 145
Work management systems (WMS), 310
Works and Emergency Services Department (Toronto), 499
World Bank, 325
World Economic Forum, 555
World Electronic Community (WELCOM), 555
World Wide Web (Web):
    current environment of, 420
    economics of, 620
    Enterprise Web, 73
    growth of, 28
    Internet vs., 129
Worms, 689
WSDL, *see* Web Services Description Language
WWANs, *see* Wireless wide area networks

X

Xerox PARC, 273
XML, *see* Extensible Markup Language
XP, *see* Extreme programming
Xybernaut, 260

Y

Yield-management models, 57

Z

Zombies, 697